PRAISE FOR THE

Insider's Guide to Graduate Programs in Clinical and Counseling Psychology

"Your book was the pivotal resource that helped me find my way to my current career. I was one of those first-generation college students who really had no idea what I was doing until I came across your book. The *Insider's Guide* was truly indispensable and is largely responsible for my career today."

—Daniel J. Taylor, Ph.D., Professor of Psychology, University of North Texas

"This book aided me immensely. It was fun to read and contained great suggestions and insights that I would have been clueless about. Thank you for providing this resource for students, which helped me navigate the confusing and overwhelming terrain of applying to graduate school."

—Timothy G. Lock, Ph.D., private practice, Brookfield, Connecticut

"The *Insider's Guide* was an essential tool in helping me find the right doctoral program. When applying to graduate programs in psychology, it can be difficult to navigate between counseling or clinical, and Ph.D. or Psy.D. This book is organized in a way that helps you compare and contrast programs. Seeing the various programs plotted on a continuum from practice-oriented to research-oriented really helps you understand the type of training you will receive. There are so many programs to choose from—use this book to sort out those you are most interested in, and you will end up saving money on applications and finding the best fit."

—Kimia Mansoor, Psy.D. student, The Wright Institute, Berkeley, California

"The *Insider's Guide* was an invaluable resource for me as I tackled the tedious process of applying to graduate school. With so many programs out there, this book provided me with vital information to narrow down which ones would be right for me. The book provides important details on each program—such as types of funding, emphasis areas, and internship statistics—in a clear and organized manner. My application experience was greatly improved by having this guide. I recommend it to all my friends going through the process."

—Mallorie Carroll, M.A., doctoral student in counseling psychology, University of Southern Mississippi

"The advice and insights in this book helped me figure out my career and research interests, and it saved me from a lot of extra effort and heartache that I experienced when I was working on the application process on my own. Highly recommended for anyone considering graduate school!"

—Theresa Trieu, doctoral program applicant

"I highly recommend that all applicants to clinical and counseling psychology graduate programs use this excellent guide to identify programs that match their specific career interests, goals, and strengths. Applicants who start early and follow the step-by-step advice in this manual will be well prepared to submit strong applications to programs that will be interested in offering them admission. As the training director of an APA-accredited counseling psychology program, I appreciate the detailed instructions for preparing a compelling personal statement, creating a flawless CV, forging professional relationships that will lead to strong letters of recommendation, and interviewing successfully. It will be a pleasure to meet prospective graduate students who have put this 'insider' information to good use!"

—Sharon (Sherry) Rostosky, Ph.D., Professor and Director of Training, Counseling Psychology, University of Kentucky

"If you are interested in pursuing psychology in your graduate studies, you should take a deep breath and pick up the *Insider's Guide to Graduate Programs in Clinical and Counseling Psychology*. . . . [The authors] guide the applicant along every step of the application process. They point out the pitfalls, loopholes, benefits, and drawbacks to almost every element of applying to graduate school. They fulfill their purpose to the greatest possible degree and provide a resource that is thorough and articulate. Worry not, potential psychology graduates: the *Insider's Guide to Graduate Programs in Clinical and Counseling Psychology* is your number-one resource and will provide you with all of the information you need."

—PsychCentral.com

"The definitive guide for those who are considering pursuing graduate-level degrees in clinical or counseling psychology. It is the essential, practical reference every student must have when considering graduate study in psychology. As the field continues to evolve, students wishing to pursue further graduate education need this guide to make the right academic decisions. . . . Should be mandatory reading for all undergraduates and others considering graduate psychology education. I have recommended it to all of my undergraduate students who are considering pursuing a career in psychology. *****!"

—Doody's Review Service

"This is a useful resource for public and college libraries. Recommended. Lower-level undergraduates and above; general readers."

—Choice Reviews

"The *Insider's Guide* focuses on the complete application process with sample documents, worksheets, and timelines. Advice, warnings, and an easy-to-read format give this book an edge over resources providing program descriptions only, such as the American Psychological Association's *Graduate Study in Psychology* and *Peterson's Graduate Programs in the Humanities, Arts, and Social Sciences*."

—American Reference Books Annual

INSIDER'S GUIDE TO GRADUATE PROGRAMS IN CLINICAL AND COUNSELING PSYCHOLOGY

INSIDER'S GUIDE to

Graduate Programs in Clinical and Counseling Psychology

2018/2019 Edition

Michael A. Sayette
John C. Norcross

THE GUILFORD PRESS
New York London

A Division of Guilford Publications, Inc.
370 Seventh Avenue, Suite 1200, New York, NY 10001
www.guilford.com

Printed in the United States of America

Last digit is print number: 9 8 7 6 5 4 3 2 1

ISBN 978-1-4625-3211-7 (paperback)
ISBN 978-1-4625-3567-5 (hardcover)

ISSN 1086-2099

CONTENTS

TABLES AND FIGURES

Tables

Figures

ABOUT THE AUTHORS

Michael A. Sayette, Ph.D., received his baccalaureate *cum laude* from Dartmouth College. He earned his master's and doctorate in clinical psychology from Rutgers University and completed his internship at the Brown University School of Medicine. He is Professor of Psychology at the University of Pittsburgh, with a secondary appointment as Professor of Psychiatry at the Western Psychiatric Institute and Clinic, University of Pittsburgh School of Medicine. He also serves on the faculty of the University of Pittsburgh Cancer Institute and the Center for the Neural Bases of Cognition, a joint program of the University of Pittsburgh and Carnegie Mellon University. Dr. Sayette has published primarily in the area of substance abuse. His research, which has been supported by the National Institute on Alcohol Abuse and Alcoholism, the National Institute on Drug Abuse, the National Institute of Mental Health, and the National Cancer Institute, concerns the development of psychological theories of alcohol and tobacco use. Dr. Sayette is a Fellow of the American Psychological Association, the Association for Psychological Science, and the Society for Personality and Social Psychology. He has served on National Institutes of Health grant review study sections and is on the editorial boards of several journals. He also has served as an associate editor of the *Journal of Abnormal Psychology* and of *Psychology of Addictive Behaviors*. Dr. Sayette is Director of Graduate Studies in the Department of Psychology at the University of Pittsburgh and has directed graduate admissions for the clinical psychology program. He has presented seminars on applying to graduate school at several universities in North America and Europe.

John C. Norcross, Ph.D., ABPP, received his baccalaureate *summa cum laude* from Rutgers University, earned his doctorate in clinical psychology from the University of Rhode Island, and completed his internship at the Brown University School of Medicine. He is Distinguished Professor of Psychology at the University of Scranton, Adjunct Professor of Psychiatry at SUNY Upstate Medical University, and a board-certified clinical psychologist. He edited the *Journal of Clinical Psychology: In Session* for 10 years and served on the editorial boards of a dozen journals. Past-president of the American Psychological Association's (APA's) Division of Clinical Psychology and Division of Psychotherapy, he served on the APA's governing Council of Representatives and Board of Educational Affairs. Dr. Norcross has published more than 300 articles and has authored or edited over 20 books, including *Leaving It at the Office: A Guide to Psychotherapist Self-Care*; *Psychotherapy Relationships That Work*; *APA Handbook of Clinical Psychology*; *Self-Help That Works*; and *Systems of Psychotherapy: A Transtheoretical Analysis*, now in its ninth edition. Among his awards are the Pennsylvania Professor of the Year from the Carnegie Foundation, Distinguished Practitioner from the National Academies of Practice, and the Distinguished Career Contribution to Education and Training Award from the APA. Dr. Norcross has conducted workshops and research on graduate study in psychology for many years.

ACKNOWLEDGMENTS

To paraphrase John Donne, no book is an island, entire of itself. This sentiment is particularly true of a collaborative venture such as ours: a coauthored volume in its 15th edition comprising the program reports provided by hundreds of psychology training directors throughout North America. We are grateful to them all.

We are indebted to the many colleagues, students, and workshop participants for their assistance in improving this book over the years. Special thanks to John Dimoff for an outstanding job coordinating the updates on the individual program reports. William Burke, Director of Financial Aid at the University of Scranton, updates our sections on financial aid and loan options every two years. Seymour Weingarten and his associates at The Guilford Press have continued to provide interpersonal support and technical assistance on all aspects of the project. We are grateful to Dr. Tracy Mayne, who coauthored several previous editions of the *Insider's Guide*. Special thanks to our families for their unflagging support and patience with late night work!

Finally, our efforts have been aided immeasurably by our students, undergraduate and graduate alike, who courageously shared their experiences with us about the application and admission process. Thank you for helping others to avoid your miscues and to repeat your successes.

PREFACE

One of the benefits of applying to clinical and counseling psychology programs is that you earn the right to commiserate about it afterwards. A night of anecdotes and complaints led us to review our travails and compare notes on the difficulties we each experienced during the admission process. We emerged from diverse backgrounds but wound up in doctoral programs in clinical psychology.

Although we approached graduate school in different ways, the process was much the same. We each attempted to locate specific information on clinical and counseling psychology admissions, looked to people around us for advice, took what seemed to be sound, and worked with it. Not all the advice was good (one professor persistently recommended law school instead), and it was difficult to decide what was best when advice conflicted.

All in all, there was too little factual information available and too much unnecessary anxiety involved. No clearly defined or organized system was available to guide us through this process. So we decided to write an *Insider's Guide to Graduate Programs in Clinical and Counseling Psychology*. That was 14 editions and 28 years ago.

The last dozen years have seen the entire process of choosing and applying to schools become progressively more complex. Approximately 115,000 bachelor's degrees are awarded every year in psychology (National Center for Education Statistics, 2014), and about 20% of those recipients go on to earn a master's or doctoral degree in psychology. Clinical and counseling psychology programs continue to grow in number and to diversify in mission: APA accredits 240 doctoral programs in clinical psychology, 71 doctoral programs in counseling psychology, and 10 doctoral programs in combined psychology (see Table 1-3). Add in the dozens of non-APA-accredited doctoral programs and the hundreds of master's programs and you get a potential blizzard of graduate programs in diverse subfields of psychology.

How can you develop your qualifications for graduate school in psychology? How should you prepare for admission into these competitive graduate programs? To which should you apply? And which type of program is best for you—master's or doctoral, counseling or clinical, practice-oriented Psy.D. or research-oriented Ph.D.? We'll take you step by step through this confusing morass and help you make informed decisions suited to your needs and goals.

In clear and concise language, we assist *you* through this process, from the initial decision to apply through your final acceptance. In Chapter 1, we describe clinical and counseling psychology and both practice and research alternatives to these subfields. We explain the importance of program accreditation and warn against many online graduate programs that seek to separate you from your money. In Chapter 2, we feature the Boulder model (Ph.D.) and the Vail model (Psy.D.) of training psychologists and highlight their salient differences so that you can make an educated choice between them. In Chapter 3, we discuss the essential preparation for graduate school—the coursework, faculty mentoring, clinical experiences, research skills, entrance examinations, and extracurricular activities.

From there, in Chapter 4, we get you started on the application process and assist you in understanding admission requirements. Special sections for research-oriented, practice-oriented, racial/ethnic minority, LGBT, disabled, and international applicants individualize the admissions advice. In Chapter 5, we show you how to systematically select schools on the basis of multiple considerations, especially research interests, clinical opportunities, theoretical orientations, program outcomes, financial assistance, and quality of life. Then, in Chapter 6, we take you through the application procedure itself—application forms, curricula vitae, personal statements, letters of recommendation, academic transcripts, and the like. In Chapter 7, we review the perils and promises of the interview, required by three-quarters of clinical and counseling psychology programs. Last, in Chapter 8, we walk you through the complexities of the final decisions.

With multiple worksheets and concrete examples, we will help you feel less overwhelmed and better informed. In the end, you will become more aware that *you* are the consumer of a graduate program that best suits *your* needs.

In this new edition, we provide:

- Updates on the required and recommended psychology courses for admission into doctoral programs
- Updates on GRE preparation
- Information on recent changes in graduate student loans (and debt)
- Advice on using APA's new centralized application service, PSYCAS

In addition, throughout the book, we highlight free resources to minimize the cost of applying to graduate school and provide Web addresses to ease the graduate admissions process—locating compatible programs, communicating with potential faculty mentors, submitting application forms, and helping faculty send letters of recommendation electronically. In other words, we remove some of the work and cost of preparing and applying for graduate study in psychology.

We have conducted original studies on graduate psychology programs for this *Insider's Guide* in an effort to inform your decision making. These results provide crucial information on the differences between clinical and counseling psychology (Chapter 1), the distinctions between Ph.D. and Psy.D. programs (Chapter 2), the uniqueness of PCSAS-accredited programs in clinical science (Chapter 2), the importance of various graduate school selection criteria (Chapter 3), the psychology coursework required for graduate admission (Chapter 3), the average acceptance rates into psychology graduate programs (Chapter 4), the probability of financial assistance (Chapter 5), and interview policies (Chapter 7). The results of our studies allow you to search for particular research areas (Appendix E), clinical opportunities (Appendix F), and program concentrations/tracks (Appendix G) as you consider which graduate programs to apply to.

Indeed, we have extensively surveyed all APA-accredited programs in clinical, counseling, and combined psychology for a quarter of a century now and present detailed information on each in the reports on individual programs. This edition features detailed reports on 99% of the APA-accredited doctoral programs in the United States. A detailed time line (Appendix A) and multiple worksheets (Appendices B, C, and D) supply assistance on the heretofore treacherous journey of applying to graduate programs in clinical and counseling psychology.

This volume will assist anyone seeking admission to graduate school in clinical and counseling psychology, both master's and doctoral degrees. Our primary focus is on Ph.D. and Psy.D. applicants, as the doctorate is the entry-level qualification for professional psychology. Just as a master's degree in biology does not make one a physician, a master's in psychology does not, by state licensure and APA policy, typically qualify one as a psychologist. Forty-nine states require the doctorate for licensure as a psychologist; about 20 states grant legal recognition of psychological associates, assistants, or examiners with a master's degree (Association of State and Provincial Psychology Boards, 2016). But the material presented here is relevant for master's (M.A. or M.S.) applicants as well.

With this practical manual, we wish you an application process less hectic and confusing than ours, but equally rewarding in the end result. Welcome and good luck!

CHAPTER 1

INTRODUCING CLINICAL AND COUNSELING PSYCHOLOGY

A warm welcome to the *Insider's Guide*.

If you are reading this book for the first time, we assume you are either considering applying to graduate programs in clinical and counseling psychology or are in the process of doing so. For even the best-prepared applicant, this can precipitate a great deal of stress and confusion. The mythology surrounding this process is foreboding, and you may have heard some "horror" stories similar to these: "It's the hardest graduate program to get into in the country"; "You need a 3.7 grade point average and outrageous GREs or they won't even look at you"; "If you haven't taken time off after your bachelor's degree and worked in a clinic or research lab, you don't have enough experience to apply."

Having endured the application process ourselves, we know how overwhelming and bewildering the task appears at first glance. However, we find that much of the anxiety is unwarranted. It does not take astronomical test scores or years of practical or research experience to get into clinical and counseling psychology programs. Although these qualifications certainly help, they are not sufficient. Equally important are a knowledge of how the admission system works and a willingness to put in extra effort during the application process. In this *Guide*, we will help you to work smarter and harder in getting into graduate school in psychology.

Clinical and Counseling Psychology

Before dealing with the question of "how to apply," we would like to address "why" to apply and what clinical and counseling psychology entail. Reading through the next section may prove useful by making you aware of other programs of study that may better suit your needs.

Let us begin with clinical psychology, the largest specialty and the fastest growing sector in psychology. Two-thirds of the doctoral-level health service providers in the American Psychological Association (APA) identify with the specialty area of clinical psychology. A census of all psychological personnel residing in the United States likewise revealed that the majority reported clinical psychology as their major field (Stapp, Tucker, & VandenBos, 1985).

A definition of clinical psychology was adopted jointly by the APA Division of Clinical Psychology and the Council of University Directors of Clinical Psychology (Resnick, 1991). That definition states that the field of clinical psychology involves research, teaching, and services relevant to understanding, predicting, and alleviating intellectual, emotional, biological, psychological, social, and behavioral maladjustment, applied to a wide range of client populations. The major skill areas essential to clinical psychology are assessment, intervention, consultation, program development and evaluation, supervision, administration, conduct of research, and application of ethical standards. Perhaps the safest observation about clinical psychology is that both the field and its practitioners continue to outgrow the classic definitions.

Indeed, the discipline has exploded since World War II in numbers, activities, and knowledge. Since 1949, the year of the Boulder Conference (see below), there has been a large and significant increase in psychology doctoral graduates. Approximately 3,000 doctoral degrees in clinical psychology are now awarded annually in the United States—about half Ph.D. degrees and about half Psy.D. degrees. All told, doctoral degrees in clinical psychology account for almost half of all psychology doctorates (Norcross et al., 2005). Table 1-1 demonstrates, at 18-year intervals, the continuing popularity of clinical psychology and the growing number of clinical doctorates awarded annually.

These trends should continue well into the future. The percentage of psychology majors among college freshmen has increased nationally to almost 5% (CIRP, 2005). A nationwide survey of almost 2 million high school juniors, reported in the *Occupational Outlook Quarterly*, found that psychology was the sixth most frequent career choice. Indeed, according to data from the U.S. Department of Education, interest in psychology as a major has never been higher. So, if you are seriously considering clinical or counseling psychology for a career, you belong to a large, vibrant, and growing population.

Counseling psychology is the second largest specialty in psychology and another growing sector. As also shown in Table 1-1, counseling psychology has experienced sustained growth over the past four decades. We are referring here to counseling *psychology*, the doctoral-level specialization in psychology, not to the master's-level profession of counseling. This is a critical distinction: our book and research studies pertain specifically and solely to counseling psychology programs, not counseling programs.

As shown in Table 1-2, clinical and counseling psychologists devote similar percentages of their day to the same professional activities. About one-half of their time is dedicated to psychotherapy and assessment and a quarter of their time to research and administration. A stunning finding was that 40% or more of clinical and counseling psychologists are routinely involved in all seven activities—psychotherapy, assessment, teaching, research, supervision, consultation, and administration. Flexible career indeed!

The scope of clinical and counseling psychology is continually widening, as are the employment settings. Many people mistakenly view psychologists solely as practitioners who spend most of their time seeing patients. But in truth, clinical and counseling psychology are wonderfully diverse and pluralistic professions. Consider the full-time employment settings of American clinical psychologists: 41% in private practices, 26% in universities or colleges, 8% in medical schools, 5% in Veterans Administration facilities, 4% in outpatient clinics, 3% in psychiatric hospitals, another 3% in general hospitals, and 10% in "other" placements (Norcross, Karpiak, & Santoro, 2005). This last category includes, just to name a few, child and family services, correctional facilities, rehabilitation centers, school systems, health main-

TABLE 1-1. Number of Doctorates Awarded by Psychology Subfield

	Number of Ph.D.s awarded		
Subfield	1976	1994	2012
Clinical	883	1,329	2,650
Cognitive	—	76	452
Counseling	267	464	420
Developmental	190	158	50
Educational	124	98	470
Experimental	357	143	110
Industrial/organizational	73	124	130
School	143	81	260
Social	271	165	40
Other or general	387	560	1,548
Total	2,883	3,287	6,110

Note. Data from National Research Council, National Science Foundation, and National Center for Education Statistics (selected years).

TABLE 1-2. Professional Activities of Clinical and Counseling Psychologists

	Clinical psychologists		Counseling psychologists	
Activity	% involved in	Average % of time	% involved in	Average % of time
Psychotherapy	64	46	51	37
Diagnosis/assessment	49	24	40	19
Teaching	42	22	60	32
Clinical supervision	40	12	45	14
Research/writing	40	31	51	27
Consultation	32	16	36	12
Administration	39	24	72	24

Note. Data from Norcross & Karpiak (2012), Goodyear et al. (2008), and Lichtenberg, Goodyear, Overland, Hutman, & Norcross (2015).

tenance organizations, psychoanalytic institutes, and the federal government.

Although many psychologists choose careers in private practice, hospitals, and clinics, a large number also pursue careers in research. For some, this translates into an academic position. Continuing uncertainties in the health care system increase the allure of academic positions, where salaries are less tied to client fees and insurance reimbursements. Academic psychologists teach courses and conduct research, usually with a clinical population. They hope to find a "tenure-track" position, which means they start out as an assistant professor. After a specified amount of time (typically 5 or 6 years), a university committee reviews their research, teaching, and service, and decides whether they will be hired as a permanent faculty member and promoted to associate professor. Even though the tenure process can be pressured, the atmosphere surrounding assistant professors is conducive to research activity. They are often given "seed" money to set up research labs and attract graduate students eager to share in the publication process. (For additional information on the career paths of psychology faculty, consult *The Compleat Academic: A Career Guide* [Darley, Zanna, & Roediger, 2009], or *Career Paths in Psychology* [Sternberg, 2016].)

In addition, research-focused industries (like pharmaceutical and biomedical), as well as community-based organizations, are increasingly employing psychologists to design and conduct outcomes research. Evaluation and outcome research combines the use of assessment, testing, program design, and cost-effectiveness analyses. Although lacking the job security of tenure, industry can offer greater monetary compensation and is a viable option for research-oriented Ph.D.s.

But even this range of employment settings does not accurately capture the opportunities in the field. Approximately half of all clinical and counseling psychologists hold more than one professional position (Norcross & Karpiak, 2012; Goodyear et al., 2016). By and large, psychologists incorporate several pursuits into their work, often simultaneously. They combine activities in ways that can change over time to accommodate their evolving interests. Of those licensed psychologists not in full-time private practice, more than half engage in some part-time independent work. Without question, this flexibility is an asset.

As a university professor, for example, you might supervise a research group studying aspects of alcoholism, treat substance abusers and their families in private practice, and teach a course on alcohol abuse. Or, you could work for a company supervising marketing research, do private testing for a school system, and provide monthly seminars on relaxation. The possibilities are almost limitless.

This flexibility is also evident in clinical and counseling psychologists' "self-views." Approximately half characterize themselves primarily as clinical practitioners, 25% as academicians, 7% administrators, 7% researchers, and 2% supervisors.

Also comforting is the consistent finding of relatively high and stable satisfaction with graduate training and career choice. Over two-thirds of graduate students in clinical and counseling psychology express satisfaction with their post-baccalaureate preparation. Moreover, 87 to 91% are satisfied with their career choice (Norcross & Karpiak, 2012; Tibbits-Kleber & Howell, 1987). The conclusion we draw is that clinical and counseling psychologists appreciate the diverse pursuits and revel in their professional flexibility, which figure prominently in their high level of career satisfaction.

According to *Money* magazine and Salary.com, psychologist is one of the 10 best jobs in America. And so, too, is college professor.

Relative Differences

The distinctions between clinical psychology and counseling psychology have steadily faded. Graduates of counseling psychology programs are eligible for the same professional benefits as clinical psychology graduates, such as psychology licensure, independent practice, and insurance reimbursement. The APA ceased distinguishing many years ago between clinical and counseling psychology internships: there is one list of APA-accredited internships for both clinical and counseling psychology students. Both types of programs prepare licensed, doctoral-level psychologists who provide health care services.

At the same time, six robust differences between clinical psychology and counseling psychology are still visible (Morgan & Cohen, 2003; Lichtenberg et al., 2015; Norcross et al., 1998). First, clinical psychology is larger than counseling psychology: in 2017, there were 240 active APA-accredited doctoral programs in clinical psychology and 73 active APA-accredited doctoral programs in counseling psychology (Table 1-3). About half of all doctorates (Ph.D.s and Psy.D.s) awarded each year in psychology are in clinical psychology; about 8% are in counseling psychology. Second, clinical psychology graduate programs are almost exclusively housed in departments or schools of psychology, whereas counseling psychology graduate programs are located in a variety of departments and divisions. Our research (Norcross, Evans, & Ellis, 2010; Turkson & Norcross, 1996) shows that, in rough figures, one-quarter of doctoral programs in counseling psychology are located in psychology departments, one-quarter in departments of counseling psychology, one-quarter in departments or colleges of education, and one-quarter in assorted other departments. The historical placement of counseling psychology programs in education departments explains the occasional awarding of the Ed.D. (doctor of education) by counseling psychology programs.

A third difference is that clinical psychology graduates are more likely trained in projective and intellectual assessment, whereas counseling psychology graduates conduct more career and vocational assessment. Those applicants particularly interested in vocational and career assessment should concentrate on counseling psychology programs. Fourth, counseling psychologists more frequently endorse a humanistic or person-centered/Rogerian approach to psychotherapy, whereas clinical psychologists are more likely to embrace cognitive-behavioral or psychodynamic orientations (Table 5-2, to be discussed later).

A fourth relative difference involves entry into counseling psychology programs. Fully one-third of doctoral counseling psychology programs require a master's degree prior to entry. Essentially no clinical psychology program requires a master's degree before admission (Norcross, Sayette, Stratigis, & Zimmerman, 2014). Thus, counseling psychology programs accept far more master's students (65% vs. 19%) than clinical psychology programs (Norcross, Sayette, Mayne, Karg, & Turkson, 1998; Sayette, Norcross, & Dimoff, 2011).

Fifth, both APA figures (APA Research Office, 1997) and our research (Bechtoldt, Norcross, Wyckoff, Pokrywa, & Campbell, 2001; Norcross & Karpiak, 2012) consistently reveal that 15% more

TABLE 1-3. Number of APA-Accredited Doctoral Programs in Psychology by Area

Program area	Ph.D.	Psy.D.	Total
Clinical	172	68	240
Counseling	66	7	73
School	60	8	68
Combined	6	4	10
Total	304	87	391

Note. As of June 2017. Data from Education Directorate, American Psychological Association (2017).

clinical psychologists are employed in full-time private practice than are counseling psychologists. On the other hand, 10% more counseling psychologists are employed in college counseling centers than are clinical psychologists.

Studies on the functions of clinical and counseling psychologists substantiate these differences, but the similarities are far more numerous (Brems & Johnson, 1997; Goodyear et al., 2016). Thus, as you consider applying to graduate school, be aware of these differences but also remember that the two subfields are similar indeed—which is why we feature both of them in this *Insider's Guide*!

In order to extend the previous research, we conducted several studies on APA-accredited doctoral programs in counseling psychology and clinical psychology regarding their number of applications, characteristics of incoming students, and research areas of the faculty (Norcross, Evans, & Ellis, 2010; Norcross, Sayette, et al., 1998; Sayette et al., 2011). We found:

- The average acceptance rates of Ph.D. clinical (6%) and Ph.D. counseling (8%) psychology programs were quite similar despite the higher number of applications to clinical programs (270 vs. 130).
- The grade point averages (GPAs) and GRE scores for incoming doctoral students were nearly identical in Ph.D. clinical and Ph.D. counseling psychology programs (3.5 for both).
- The counseling psychology faculty were more interested than clinical psychology faculty in research pertaining to minority/multicultural issues (69% vs. 32% of programs) and vocational/career testing (62% vs. 1% of programs).
- The clinical psychology faculty, in turn, were far more interested than the counseling psychology faculty in research pertaining to psychopathological populations (e.g., attention deficit disorders, depression, personality disorders) and activities traditionally associated with medical settings (e.g., neuropsychology, pain management, pediatric psychology).

When interpreting these findings, it is important to realize that Ph.D. programs in clinical psychology encompass an enormously diverse set of schools. Accordingly, comparisons between clinical and counseling Ph.D. programs reflect general trends. For instance, as we describe in more detail in chapter 4, several APA-accredited professional schools offering a Ph.D. in clinical psychology accept more than half of those who applied (Sayette et al., 2011). In contrast, the acceptance rates among Ph.D. clinical scientist programs accredited by PCSAS (see Table 2-1 and below) are vastly different, in the 2% to 8% range. Please rely on the reports on individual doctoral programs at the back of the book, rather than on these generalizations alone.

In addition, please bear in mind that these systematic comparisons reflect broad differences in the APA-accredited Ph.D. programs; they say nothing about Psy.D. programs (which we discuss in the next chapter) or nonaccredited programs. Also bear in mind that these data can be used as a rough guide in matching your interests to clinical or counseling psychology programs. The notion of discovering the best match between you and a graduate program is a recurrent theme of this *Insider's Guide*.

Combined Programs

The American Psychological Association (APA) accredits doctoral programs in five areas: clinical psychology, counseling psychology, school psychology, other developed practice areas, and combined psychology. The last category is for those programs that afford doctoral training in two or more of the specialties of clinical, counseling, and school psychology.

The "combined" doctoral programs represent a relatively new development in graduate psychology training, and thus are small in number, about 4% of APA-accredited programs (Table 1-3). In emphasizing the core research and practice competencies among the specialties, combined programs try to enlist their respective strengths and to capitalize on their overarching competencies. In doing so, the hope is that a combined program will be "greater than the sum of its parts" (Salzinger, 1998). For students undecided about a particular subfield in professional psychology and seeking broad clinical training, these accredited combined programs warrant a close look.

The chief reasons that students select combined doctoral programs are for greater breadth and flexibility of training and for more opportunity of integrative training across subfields. The emphasis on breadth of psychological knowledge ensures that combined training will address the multiplicity of interests that many students have and that many psychologists will need in practice (Beutler & Fisher, 1994). The chief disadvantages of combined programs are, first, their lack of depth and specialization and, second, the fact that other mental health professionals may not understand the combined degree.

Our research on combined training programs (Castle & Norcross, 2002; Cobb, Reeve, Shealy, Norcross, et al., 2004) does, in fact, substantiate the broader training and more varied employment of their graduates. Consult the Reports of Combined Programs at the end of this book for details on these innovative programs. Also consult two special issues of the *Journal of Clinical Psychology* (Shealy, 2004) on the combined-integrative model of doctoral training in professional psychology.

A Word on Accreditation

Accreditation of education in the United States proves confusing, so we apologize in advance for the necessary detour into accreditation matters. But, as you will see, we shall soon apply all of this knowledge to your quest for a graduate degree in clinical, counseling, or combined psychology.

Accreditation comes in many guises, but the two primary types are *institutional accreditation* and *program accreditation*. Institutional applies to an entire institution. Seven regional accreditation bodies, such as the Commission on Higher Education of the Middle States Association of Colleges and Schools, oversee accreditation for the university or college itself. An institution receives accreditation when it has been judged to have met minimum standards of quality for postsecondary education.

Beware of any institution that is not accredited by its regional accreditation body. A degree from this institution will probably not be recognized by licensing boards, certifying organizations, or insurance companies (Dattilio, 1992). Be particularly careful about nontraditional or external degree programs that offer the option of obtaining a degree based on independent study, typically away from the institution itself. Some of these are reputable programs, but many are for-profit "diploma mills" (Angulo, 2016; Stewart & Spille, 1988). Many diploma mills have names similar to legitimate universities, so you must be vigilant. Here are several diploma mills with potentially misleading titles: Columbia State University (Louisiana), La Salle University (Louisiana), American State University (Hawaii), American International University (Alabama). (For additional information about diploma mills, consult the fact sheets at the Council for Higher Education Accreditation (CHEA) at www.CHEA.org and http://collegemouse.com/?s=unaccredited.)

The second type of accreditation pertains to the graduate program (or internship) itself. Specialized accreditation of the discipline is performed by APA and, to a lesser extent, Psychological Clinical Science Accreditation System (PCSAS, as explained below). APA is the only agency approved by both the U.S. Department of Education and the Council for Higher Education Accreditation to accredit all psychology programs and internships. PCSAS is recognized by CHEA (but not the Department of Education) to accredit clinical psychology doctoral programs (but not other psychology programs). See: We told you it can get confusing!

This accreditation is a voluntary procedure for the doctoral program itself, not the entire institution. Most programs capable of meeting the requirements of APA accreditation will choose to apply for accreditation. Accreditation of a clinical, counseling, or combined psychology program by the APA presumes regional accreditation of the entire institution.

As of 2017, APA has accredited 240 active clinical psychology programs (68 of these awarding the Psy.D. degree), 73 active counseling psychology programs (7 of these awarding the Psy.D. degree), and 10 active combined professional–scientific psychology programs (4 of these Psy.D.). Table 1-3 summarizes the number of APA-accredited psychology programs by subfield or area (clinical, counseling, and combined).

The Reports on Individual Programs in this book provide detailed descriptions of these 300+ APA-accredited clinical psychology, counseling psychology, and combined programs, respectively. We do *not* feature in the *Insider's Guide* psychology programs that are unaccredited, inactive, or on probation. Nor do we present information about doctoral school psychology programs, as they blend master's-level certification as a school psychologist by the state department of education with doctoral-level licensure as an independent psychologist by the state board of psychology.

Take note that APA does *not* accredit master's programs. Accordingly, references to "accredited" master's psychology programs are to regional or state, not APA, accreditation.

The Standards of Accreditation for psychology programs can be obtained from the APA Office of Program Consultation and Accreditation (www.apa.org/ed/accreditation). The general areas assessed include institutional support, faculty competence, sensitivity to cultural and individual differences, training models, discipline-specific knowledge, program-specific competencies, evaluation methods, practicum opportunities, internship training, and student outcomes. These standards are designed to insure at least a minimal level of quality assurance and public disclosure of their outcomes.

The APA recognizes several categories of accreditation for doctoral programs. "Full Accreditation" means that the program meets or exceeds the criteria. Accredited programs are scheduled for periodic review every 3 to 10 years. If you complete a program that is recognized as "fully accredited" before your graduation date, then you will have completed an APA-accredited program. "Accredited, on Contingency" means that the program is relatively new and is on its way to meeting all of the required criteria. If you complete a program that is recognized as "accredited, on contingency" effective before your graduation date, you will have also completed an APA-accredited program.

Beware that some doctoral programs advertise their "Intent to Apply" for APA accreditation. Do not be misled. These programs are not accredited by APA. By completing a program that is listed as "intent to apply," you will *not* have completed an APA-accredited program.

"Accredited, Inactive" is the designation for programs that have not accepted students for several successive years. This indicates that the program is phasing out and closing.

"Accredited, on Probation" is the designation for programs that were previously accredited but are not currently in compliance with the criteria. This is considered an adverse action: it serves as notice to the program, its students, and the public that the program is in danger of having its accreditation revoked. We do not feature inactive programs or programs on probation in our Individual Reports at the end of this book.

In the past decades, there has been concern among some clinical psychologists about the proliferation of professional schools unaffiliated with universities offering doctorates in clinical psychology. Some psychologists believe that these professional schools, especially the for-profit chains, have eroded the quality and scientific training of new psychologists. Thus, a new accreditation system—Psychological Clinical Science Accreditation System (PCSAS; pronounced *pee-cee-sass*)—was launched in 2010 to accredit *clinical scientist programs*—clinical psychology training programs that offer high quality science-centered education and training, producing graduates who are successful in generating and applying scientific knowledge (Baker et al., 2008; www.pcsas.org).

This new accreditation system for clinical science Ph.D. programs is steadily growing in numbers and influence. PCSAS is recognized as an accredited body by CHEA, a national gatekeeper of accrediting organizations. While CHEA recognition is not approval from the government, such as that obtained by APA, it is an important step for graduates of PCSAS-accredited clinical science programs to work in settings that require graduation from an accredited program. The nation's single largest employer of clinical psychologists, the Department of Veteran Affairs, accepts students from PCSAS-accredited programs for internships and employment. And regulators in five states have agreed that graduates of PCSAS programs are eligible for licensure in their states.

PCSAS was designed to accredit only clinical Ph.D. programs emphasizing science; not Psy.D. programs, not counseling psychology programs, not internships. Thirty-two Ph.D. clinical programs have gained PCSAS accreditation as of February 2017 (Table 2-1) (with 10 more having submitted letters of intent to apply), and they simultaneously continue their APA accreditation as well. Yes, you read that correctly: all PCSAS-accredited programs thus far have maintained their APA accreditation as well.

What's important for you, as an applicant, to know is that there are two national accrediting organizations for professional psychology: one large and inclusive (APA) and one small and specialized (PCSAS). It's also useful for you to know that there is spirited debate about the quality of for-profit professional schools and the proper role of research training in clinical and counseling psychology.

For more than 30 years, doctoral psychology programs in Canada enjoyed the option of simultaneous accreditation by the Canadian Psychological Association (CPA) and the American Psychological Association (APA). This dual accreditation enabled United States citizens to travel north to attend APA-accredited Canadian programs and facilitated internship placement and licensure in the United States for both American and Canadian students. Graduates of APA-accredited programs, whether located in Canada or the United States, were eligible for the same privileges.

In 2007, APA decided to phase out accrediting Canadian psychology programs over a 7-year period. At the end of 2015, APA accreditation for programs located in Canada came to a full stop. Mutual recognition agreements will continue, but formal APA accreditation of Canadian programs has not. Most jurisdictions in the United States recognize CPA-accredited programs for the purposes of licensure, but a couple do not. Thus, be aware of this transition and the potential consequences on internship and licensure in selected U.S. states.

We do *not* want to discourage anyone from attending excellent Canadian doctoral programs in psychology; we *do* want you to be informed consumers. Toward this end, Table 1-4 provides the names, degrees (Ph.D. or Psy.D.), and locations of all CPA-accredited doctoral programs in clinical, counseling, and combined psychology (for updates, consult www.cpa.ca/accreditation/CPAaccreditedprograms/).

Our Reports on Individual Programs provide crucial descriptive and application information on each APA-accredited doctoral program in clinical, counseling, and combined psychology. The APA Education Directorate updates the listing of accredited programs annually in the December issue of the *American Psychologist* and bimonthly on their website, www.apa.org/ed.

How important is it to attend an APA-accredited program? The consensus ranges from important

TABLE 1-4. CPA-Accredited Doctoral Programs in Clinical, Counseling, and Combined Psychology

Program	Area	Degree	Location
University of Alberta	Clinical	Ph.D.	Edmonton, Alberta
University of Alberta	Counseling	Ph.D.	Edmonton, Alberta
University of British Columbia	Clinical	Ph.D.	Vancouver, British Columbia
University of British Columbia	Counseling	Ph.D.	Vancouver, British Columbia
University of Calgary	Clinical	Ph.D.	Calgary, Alberta
University of Calgary	Counseling	Ph.D.	Calgary, Alberta
Concordia University	Clinical	Ph.D.	Montreal, Quebec
Dalhousie University	Clinical	Ph.D.	Halifax, Nova Scotia
University of Guelph	Clinical	Ph.D.	Guelph, Ontario
Lakehead University	Clinical	Ph.D.	Thunder Bay, Ontario
Université Laval	Clinical	Ph.D.	Ste-Foy, Quebec
Université Laval	Clinical	Psy.D.	Ste-Foy, Quebec
University of Manitoba	Clinical	Ph.D.	Winnipeg, Manitoba
McGill University	Clinical	Ph.D.	Montreal, Quebec
McGill University	Counseling	Ph.D.	Montreal, Quebec
Université de Montréal	Clinical	Psy.D.	Montreal, Quebec
Université de Montréal	Counseling	Ph.D.	Montreal, Quebec
University of New Brunswick	Clinical	Ph.D.	Fredericton, New Brunswick
University of Ottawa	Clinical	Ph.D.	Ottawa, Ontario
Queen's University	Clinical	Ph.D.	Kingston, Ontario
University of Regina	Clinical	Ph.D.	Regina, Saskatchewan
Ryerson University	Clinical	Ph.D.	Toronto, Ontario
University of Saskatchewan	Clinical	Ph.D.	Saskatoon, Saskatchewan
Simon Fraser University	Clinical	Ph.D.	Burnaby, British Columbia
University of Toronto—OISE	Clinical–School	Ph.D.	Toronto, Ontario
University of Toronto—OISE	Counseling–Clinical	Ph.D.	Toronto, Ontario
University of Victoria	Clinical	Ph.D.	Victoria, British Columbia
University of Waterloo	Clinical	Ph.D.	Waterloo, Ontario
University of Western Ontario	Clinical	Ph.D.	London, Ontario
University of Windsor	Clinical	Ph.D.	Windsor, Ontario
York University	Clinical	Ph.D.	North York, Ontario
York University	Clinical Developmental	Ph.D.	North York, Ontario

to essential. APA accreditation ensures a modicum of program stability, quality assurance, and professional accountability. Students in APA-accredited programs have a formal appeals mechanism to the profession and APA, but not so for students attending nonaccredited programs. Graduates of APA-accredited programs are practically guaranteed to meet the educational requirements for state licensure. The federal government, the Veterans Administration, and most universities now insist on a doctorate and internship from APA-accredited programs.

The career outcomes of graduates from APA-accredited programs tend to be better than those hailing from non-APA-accredited programs. Students are in a more advantageous and competitive position coming from an APA-approved program in terms of their internship match rate (Anderson, 2009; Callahan, Collins, & Klonoff, 2010; Graham & Kim, 2011); students enrolled in APA-accredited doctoral programs are three times more likely as those from unaccredited programs to match (Norcross & Karpiak, 2015). In fact, starting in 2018, students from nonaccredited programs will not even be participating in the computerized internship match process until students from APA- and CPA-accredited programs have completed their matches. Graduates of APA programs also score significantly higher, on average, than do students of non-APA-accredited programs on the national licensure exam (Kupfersmid & Fiola, 1991; Schaffer et al., 2012; Templer et al., 2008). The eventual employment outcomes favor psychologists graduating from accredited programs (Graham & Kim, 2011; Walfish & Sumprer, 1984).

Licensure and employment as a psychologist are not precluded by attending a non-APA-accredited program, but the situation is tightening. Only a handful of states now require an APA-accredited doctoral program and internship for licensure, but that number of states will gradually increase. APA has officially requested that state licensure boards revise their regulations to require completion of an APA- or CPA-accredited doctoral program and internship. In fact, psychology is the only health profession that does not currently require graduation from an accredited program to sit for licensure.

All other things being equal, an APA-accredited clinical, counseling, or combined psychology program gives you a definite advantage over a nonaccredited program. As we warn our own students, "Do you want to spend your entire career explaining and defending why you did not attend an APA-accredited program!?"

Online Graduate Programs

Practically every institution of higher education now offers online courses and distance education. The worldwide rate of growth in online courses is staggering; tens of millions of students take them every year. Some institutions have gone further to create graduate programs that are entirely online, with all discussions being conducted electronically on bulletin boards and all assignments being submitted by computer.

Several of these online learning institutions aggressively advertise doctoral programs in clinical psychology, including Walden, Capella, Phoenix, and Fielding. Fielding Graduate University requires several weeks of in-person residency per year, making it the only distance program that has ever been APA accredited. APA does *not* accredit fully online programs in professional psychology.

We are frequently approached by students intrigued with these and other distance-learning doctoral programs and asked whether we think they are credible programs. Our answer is that a couple of programs may prove credible, but definitely not preferred, for several reasons. First, we recommend that students favor APA-accredited programs, and only one of these programs has ever met the minimum educational standards set forth by APA. Second, many psychology licensing boards will not issue licenses to graduates of distance learning programs (Hall, Wexelbaum, & Boucher, 2007). Third, online programs lack quality control over their clinical supervisors, who are scattered around the country. Fourth, much of the learning in clinical and counseling programs occurs in close, interpersonal relationships with faculty on a daily basis. Frequent computer contact is useful, but in our opinion, not equivalent. And fifth, without sounding too stodgy, we believe online programs are still too new and alternative to have developed a track record of producing quality psychologists. Most psychology faculty, internship directors, and potential employers feel likewise (Mandernach, Mason, Forrest, & Hackathorn, 2012); graduates of non–APA-accredited distance programs have experienced difficulty in securing employment as psychologists.

Online education increases accessibility and convenience for students in many areas of study. However, this benefit does not extend as readily to students in graduate psychology programs because, in addition to coursework, they need practical experience, clinical supervision, research mentoring, and residency requirements (Murphy et al., 2007). APA objects to the lack of ongoing, face-to-face interaction and quality control in fully online graduate programs for health service psychologists.

Of course, each online program needs to be evaluated on its own merits, and each doctoral student must be considered for his or her individual abilities. In the end, graduate students will get out of a program what they put in—whether through a traditional, bricks-and-mortar institution or an innovative, online program. The early research on distance and online education indicates that it produces comparable outcomes to traditional education, at least in acquiring knowledge and academic skills. Unfortunately, there is insufficient research on the online preparation of professional psychologists to render any conclusions.

Research demonstrates that many psychology majors—45% or so—are interested in online graduate programs (Bendersky et al., 2008). Given the aforementioned problems with online graduate education in psychology, we repeat our warning to be wary. Students matriculating into these programs often do so under the false belief that these online programs will offer comparable training, licensing, and professional benefits as traditional, accredited programs. They rarely do.

Should you, despite our warnings, decide to apply to online doctoral programs in psychology, we would advise you to:

- complete your master's degree in a conventional program to secure one in-person degree and to meet the admission prerequisites of most online doctoral programs.
- obtain information on the program's track record of producing graduates who secure APA-accredited internships and eventually licensure as psychologists.
- determine the residency requirement (how much time per year is expected on campus).
- expect no financial assistance from the online institution itself (but loans are available).
- become comfortable and savvy with computers, as most of your contact and assignments will be conducted online.
- be an organized, self-motivated individual who can meet deadlines without supervision.
- realize that the vast majority of interaction with fellow students and professors will occur online, not in a conventional classroom.
- be prepared for intensive research and writing on your own.

Practice Alternatives

In addition to doctoral programs in clinical, counseling, and combined psychology, we would like to describe several alternative programs of study that should be considered. We have classified these programs along the practice–research continuum. The practice-oriented programs are outlined first. Additional details on helping professions can be accessed at the trustworthy O*NET OnLine (www.onetonline.org/ and http://teachpsych.org/resources/Documents/otrp/ resources/himelein99.pdf). The latter site, *A Student Guide to Careers in the Helping Professions,* by Melissa Himelein, presents information on job duties, potential earnings, required degrees, and the like.

You are restricted neither to clinical/counseling psychology nor even to psychology in selecting a career in mental health. School psychology, as discussed below, is a viable alternative. Also note that psychology is only one of six nationally recognized mental health disciplines, the others being psychiatry (medicine), clinical social work, psychiatric nursing, marital and family therapy, and counseling.

We do not wish to dissuade you from considering clinical or counseling psychology, of course, but a mature career choice should be predicated on sound information and contemplation of the alternatives. A primary consideration is what you want to do—your desired activities. Conducting psychotherapy is possible in any of the following fields. Prescribing medication is currently restricted to physicians and some nurse practitioners, although psychologists are steadily securing prescription privileges around the country. Psychological testing and empirical research are conducted by psychologists. As discussed previously, psychologists also enjoy a wide range and pleasurable integration of professional activities. Following is a sampling of alternatives to a doctorate in clinical or counseling psychology.

1. School Psychology. Some undergraduates express a particular interest in working with children, adolescents, and their families. Admission into the Boulder-model programs with a child clinical specialty is particularly competitive. A doctorate in school psychology is much more accessible, with two times the acceptance rates of child clinical programs. The APA has accredited 68 of these programs (60 Ph.D., 8 Psy.D.; Table 1-3), which provide doctoral-level training in clinical work with children in school settings.

One disadvantage of pursuing a career as a *master's-level* school psychologist lies in the fact that, unlike the other alternatives, one's professional work is typically limited to the school. If this limitation is not a concern, then training as a school psychologist can be an excellent option for those interested in working with children and families (Halgin, 1986).

At the *doctoral* level, school psychologists are credentialed to function in both school and non-school settings. Research finds substantial overlap in the coursework of child clinical programs and school psychology programs (Minke & Brown, 1996). Some differences remain, of course—such as more courses in consultation and education in school programs and more courses in psychopathology in child clinical programs—but the core curricula are quite similar. School psychology training at the doctoral level is broadening to include experience outside of the school setting and with adolescents and families as well (Tryon, 2000).

In the future, many school psychologist positions will transition to the doctoral degree. The national school psychology organizations and the APA support this evolution, but state credentialing as a school psychologist remains overwhelmingly at the master's level.

For further information, check out the websites of the APA's Division of School Psychology (www.apa.org/about/division/div16.aspx) and the National Association of School Psychologists (www.nasponline.org).

2. *Community Psychology.* This field shares with clinical and counseling psychology a concern with individual well-being and healthy psychological development. However, community psychology places considerably more emphasis on preventing behavioral problems (as opposed to treating existing problems), adopting a broader ecological or community perspective, and changing social policies. Collaborative social action can be taken at neighborhood, organizational, state, national, and international levels to advance social justice and to promote positive behavior.

Graduate training in community psychology occurs within clinical-community psychology programs or within explicit community psychology programs. The former are clinical psychology programs with an emphasis on or a specialization in community; these doctoral programs are listed in Appendix E (Research Areas) under "community psychology." About 10 universities in the United States offer a doctorate in community psychology, and an additional 15 offer a doctorate in clinical-community. If your interests lean toward prevention and community-based interventions, then by all means check out a specialization or a program in community psychology. The lively website of the APA division of community psychology at www.scra27.org/ delivers further information about the field and training programs.

3. *Clinical Social Work.* A master's degree in social work (M.S.W.) is a popular practice alternative these days. One big advantage of this option is a much higher rate of admission to M.S.W. programs, with about 65% of applicants being accepted to any given program, on average (O'Neill, 2001). Other advantages are GREs less often required for admission, fewer research requirements, part-time study and night courses, and completion of the M.S.W. in less than half the time necessary to obtain a psychology Ph.D. With legal regulation in all 50 states and third-party vendor status (insurance reimbursement) in all states, clinical social workers are increasingly achieving autonomy and respect, including more opportunities for independent practice.

The major disadvantages lie in the less comprehensive nature of the training, which is reflected in a lower pay scale as compared to psychologists. Not becoming a "doctor" and not being able to conduct psychological testing also prove troublesome for some.

Students interested in clinical social work as a career should peruse an introductory text on the profession, consult career publications (e.g., Ritter & Vakalahi, 2014), and peruse the website of the National Association of Social Workers (NASW; www.naswdc.org). This organization provides detailed information on the emerging field, student membership, and accredited programs in clinical social work. Two other websites on social work programs also prove handy: www.petersons.com/graduate-schools.aspx and www.socialworksearch.com.

4. *Psychiatry (Medicine).* Students often dismiss the possibility of applying to medical schools, believing that admission is so difficult that it is out of the question (Halgin, 1986). However, the student interested in neuroscience and severe forms of psychopathology may find this to be an attractive choice. Although the application process necessitates more rigorous training in biology, chemistry, and physics than required in psychology programs, the admission rate may also be higher than the most competitive doctoral programs in clinical and counseling psychology. Of the 53,000 people applying to medical school annually, 40% are admitted, and about half of them are women. The average GPA of appli-

cants accepted to medical school is a 3.7 (see aamc.org for details). Wanted in particular are psychiatrists and pediatricians, both attractive specialties to those drawn to mental health and children.

Medical school thus remains an attractive option for many students headed toward a career in mental health. For further information and demystification of this subject, refer to the data-driven *The Official Guide to Medical School Admissions 2016* (by the staff of the Association of American Medical Colleges, 2016) and *The MedEdits Guide to Medical School Admissions: Practical Advice for Applicants and their Parents* (Freedman, 2015). One prime website is www.aamc.org, the official website of the Association of American Medical Colleges.

Several advantages of a medical degree should be recognized. First, an M.D. (allopath) or D.O. (osteopath) allows one to prescribe medication. Second, the average income for psychiatrists is higher than for psychologists. Third, a medical degree permits more work in inpatient (hospital) facilities. Applicants should not dismiss this possibility out of hand, and should explore medicine as a career, especially if their interests lie on biological and neurochemical levels.

5. Psychiatric Nursing. The employment opportunities for nurses are excellent at this time, especially for psychiatric nurses who have the flexibility of working in hospitals, clinics, health centers, or private practice. Of course, psychiatric nurses are nurses first and are required to obtain a bachelor's degree (B.S.N.) and to become registered (R.N.) prior to obtaining their Master of Science in Nursing (M.S.N.). They do not conduct psychological testing and rarely perform research, but psychiatric nurses practice psychotherapy in both inpatient and outpatient settings. Further, certified nurse practitioners now have the authority to write medication prescriptions in virtually all states. Consult a textbook on mental health nursing and visit the website of the American Psychiatric Nurses Association at www.apna.org/ to learn more about psychiatric/mental health nursing and its graduate programs.

6. Counseling. A master's degree in counseling, as distinct from a doctorate in counseling psychology, prepares one for state licensure as a professional counselor. The high acceptance rates of counseling programs, their two-year graduate program, their practical training, and eligibility for state licensure in all 50 states represent definite assets. Master's-level clinicians, such as social workers and counselors, have become the front-line providers of most mental health services in community clinics and public agencies. For those students committed to practice and untroubled by the lack of training in conducting research and psychological testing, the profession of counseling deserves consideration. Their flexible rolling enrollments, part-time study, and night courses—all rarely offered by doctoral programs—may make this a desirable alternative. Visit the Web page of the American Counseling Association (www.counseling.org/) for more information on careers and the Web page of accredited counseling programs (www.cacrep.org/directory/directory.cfm) to locate accredited counseling programs of interest to you.

7. Marital and Family Therapy. Another master's-level mental health profession is devoted to conducting couples and family therapy. The simultaneous strength and weakness of these graduate programs are its specificity—training in couples and family therapy, as opposed to broader and more comprehensive training in multiple professional activities. Securing a master's degree in this field should certainly be considered by students with this definite and focal interest. All states now legally recognize marital and family therapists. Check out the website of the American Association for Marriage and Family Therapy at www.aamft.org.

8. Psychology and the Law. There is a great deal of interest in the burgeoning amalgam of psychology and law, as evidenced by an APA division, two energetic professional societies, and many scholarly journals (Bersoff et al., 1997; Otto & Heilbrun, 2002). Doctoral students must be trained in both fields, of course, increasing the length of graduate training. Several clinical programs now award law degrees and psychology doctorates together—joint J.D. and Ph.D./Psy.D. programs—Arizona State, Drexel, Nebraska, Palo Alto University, and University of California at Irvine (consult www.apadivisions.org/division-41/education/programs/). Graduates pursue both practice and research careers—practicing law in mental health arenas, specializing in forensic psychology, working in public policy, and pursuing scholarship on the interface of law and psychology, for example. This is an exciting career, albeit one requiring extra commitment in terms of effort and knowledge during doctoral studies.

Another three dozen clinical programs offer Ph.D.s or Psy.D.s with specializations in forensic psychology or clinical forensic psychology. (Consult Appendix G and the following websites for a list of the programs.) These clinical psychologists specialize in the practice of forensic psychology. It's a growing and exciting specialization in psychology, but one that rarely involves the criminal profiling featured in television shows and movies! Instead, forensic psychologists are far more likely to conduct child custody evaluations, assess a patient's psychological damage, evaluate a person's competence to stand trial, consult with lawyers on jury selection, and conduct disability evaluations. For tips on undergraduate preparation and graduate training in forensic psychology, consult these Web links:

- http://teachpsych.org/resources/Documents/otrp/resources/helms06.pdf (Undergraduate Preparation for Graduate–Training in Forensic Psychology)
- http://apls.wildapricot.org/resources/Documents/2016_2017GuidetoGraduateProgramsinForensicPsych.pdf (American Law–Psychology Society guide to graduate programs in forensic and legal psychology, 2016–2017)
- www.abfp.com/ (American Board of Forensic Psychology)

9. Other. Art therapy, occupational therapy, human resources, and a plethora of other human service programs present attractive alternatives to clinical and counseling psychology. They are typically less competitive master's-level programs in which admission rates are quite high and in which the training is quite practical. Relative disadvantages of these programs, in addition to lack of a doctorate, include less prestige, lower salaries, diminished probability of an independent practice, and variable licensure status across the United States.

If one or more of these options seem suited to your needs, discuss it with a psychology advisor, interview a professional in that field, and examine the websites for additional information.

Research Alternatives

Some graduate students enter clinical or counseling psychology to become researchers. They are less interested in working with patients than researching clinical phenomena. If you are most interested in research, here are some nonpractice alternatives that might appeal to you.

1. Social Psychology. Social psychology is concerned with the influence of social and environmental factors on behavior. Attitude change, social neuroscience, group processes, interpersonal attraction, personality, goal pursuit, social processes related to health, and self-constructs are some of the research interests. Social psychologists are found in a wide variety of academic settings and, increasingly, in many nonacademic settings. These include positions in advertising agencies, personnel offices, corporations, and other business settings. Check out the official websites of the Society for Personality and Social Psychology (www.spsp.org) and the Social Psychology Network (www.socialpsychology.org) for additional resources.

2. Industrial/Organizational Psychology. This branch of psychology focuses on the individual in the workplace. Industrial/organizational psychologists frequently select and place employees, design jobs, train people, and help groups of workers to function more effectively. Master's programs generally prepare students for jobs in human resources and personnel departments, whereas doctoral programs are geared to preparing students for academic positions and for management and consulting work on larger-scale projects. Industrial/organizational psychologists earn among the highest median salaries compared to other areas of psychology (Finno et al., 2010) and have a bright job outlook (Shoenfelt, Stone, & Kottke, 2015). Academics find positions in both psychology departments and business schools.

The Society for Industrial and Organizational Psychology (2017) produces a useful list of *Graduate Training Programs in Industrial/Organizational Psychology and Related Fields*, which describes 200 plus graduate programs in "I/O" psychology and how to contact each. The list is updated continually and is available free from the society's website (http://www.siop.org/gtp/). Students interested in pursuing a career in I/O should obtain, beyond the I/O psychology or human factors course, offerings in management, business, marketing, and organizational behavior as well as research experience (Shoenfelt et al., 2015).

3. Behavioral Neuroscience. For the student interested in the workings of the brain, the nervous system, and their influence on behavior, programs in neuroscience may constitute a better match than clinical psychology. By employing animal subjects and computer models, researchers can control the conditions of their studies to a rigor often elusive when using human participants. Research areas include psychopharmacology, behavioral genetics, pain mechanisms, and brain functioning. For example, recent investigations on memory have provided valuable insight into the etiology and course of Alzheimer's disease. Go to the Society of Neuroscience website (www.sfn.org/careers-and-training/training-program-directory) for a directory of graduate programs in neuroscience.

Research demonstrates that neuroscience graduate programs expect entering students to possess coursework and lab work beyond the standard psychology curriculum (Boitano, 1999). Essential courses would include biology, chemistry, calculus, and introduction to neuroscience. And desirable courses would sample from cell biology, biochemistry, and anatomy and physiology. These are all possible, with adequate planning, to incorporate into the psychology major, should you decide on this path relatively early in your undergraduate career. The website (www.funfaculty.org/drupal/) of Faculty for Undergraduate Neuroscience (FUN) provides a bounty of useful information on preparing for a career in neuroscience.

4. Developmental Psychology. The developmental psychologist studies human behavior beginning at the prenatal stages and extending through the lifespan—from the cradle to the grave. Areas such as aging, identity, and development of cognitive and social abilities are popular areas within developmental psychology. The characteristics of individuals at different age ranges, such as the work of Piaget on child cognition, are of particular interest here.

Geropsychology, or the psychology of aging, has become a popular specialty as the elderly population in this country presents special needs that are insufficiently addressed. Employment opportunities in geropsychology are sure to grow over the next several decades. Visit the websites of APA's Division of Adult Development and Aging (www.apadivisions.org/division-20/) and the Society of Clinical Geropsychology (www.geropsychology.org) for more.

5. Cognitive Psychology. Cognitive psychology presents an attractive option for students whose interests lie in the exploration of human thought processes. Major areas include language structure, artificial intelligence, learning, memory, cognitive and affective neuroscience, perception, reading, and attention. Research in cognitive psychology has gained insight into what in the past was considered inexplicable behavior. For example, research into how moods affect the interpretation of ambiguous events has implications for the study of depression. Much research on the accuracy of eyewitness testimony has been conducted by cognitive psychologists. You can quickly identify graduate programs in cognitive psychology by searching GradSchools.com (www.gradschools.com/search-programs/cognitive-psychology) and APA's *Graduate Study in Psychology*, available online and in print for a fee.

6. Experimental Psychology. Often a student is interested in research but has not yet defined an area of interest. Or a student is fascinated with a certain psychopathology but does not desire to practice. In both cases, a graduate program in experimental psychology might be the ticket. These programs enable a student to explore several research areas, such as learning, measurement, and memory. Other programs focus on experimental psychopathology, which is geared more specifically for the researcher interested in clinical populations.

Experimental programs offer excellent training in research methods, statistical analysis, and hands-on research experience. In fact, some experimental programs now classify themselves as quantitative or measurement programs. If interested in these programs, consult www.apadivisions.org/division-5/resources/doctoral.aspx for a list of graduate psychology programs with a measurement and quantitative focus.

7. Sport Psychology. This emerging specialization typically entails both research and applied activities. Research focuses on all aspects of sports, whereas application involves individual skills training and group consultation. Research and training encompass stress management, self-confidence, mental rehearsal, competitive strategies, and sensory-kinetic awareness. Consult the *Directory of Graduate Programs in Applied Sport Psychology* (Burke, Sachs, Fry, & Schweighardt, 2015) for information on specific psychology programs. Consult, too, the website of APA's Division of Exercise and Sport Psychology at www.apa.org/about/division/div47.aspx for information on career possibilities in this area.

8. Medicine. A medical degree (M.D., D.O.) earned concurrently or sequentially with a psychology doctorate (Ph.D.) may permit the greatest flexibility of all the aforementioned programs of study. More than 100 M.D.-Ph.D. programs affiliated with medical schools allow one to practice medicine and psychology while also affording advanced training in research and statistics. For an extremely bright and motivated student, this can be a real possibility, but it is certainly the most challenging of all the alternatives. Earning two doctoral degrees will take longer than earning either alone. This choice is for someone interested in the biological aspects of behavior in addition to gaining a rigorous education in the scientific study of human behavior. The Association of American Medical Colleges provides valuable information and a FAQ section on M.D.-Ph.D. programs (https://students-residents.aamc.org/applying-medical-school/article/applying-mdphd-programs-2/).

Once again, if your interest lies in research, there are many options available besides clinical and counseling psychology. Talking to professionals in the relevant discipline and consulting textbooks about the discipline will help you to explore that option more fully. An increasing number of websites also offer valuable career advice. Four of our favorites are:

- www.psychwww.com/careers/index.htm
- www.apa.org/students/
- www.socialpsychology.org/career.htm
- www.gradschools.com

Acceptance Rates

As you have quickly learned, there are dozens of options for practice and research careers, inside and outside of psychology. Our intent in this opening chapter is neither to confuse nor to bedazzle you with these multiple choices. Rather, our intent is to acquaint you with the options so that you become an informed consumer and make the best choices for your career trajectory.

Toward that end, let us summarize here the average acceptance rates in graduate psychology programs. Table 1-5 does just that for the various subfields in psychology, separately for master's and doctoral programs.

The numbers in Table 1-5 represent the average percentage of students who apply and are accepted into a single, particular program (*not* the percentage of students accepted into any graduate program, which will be higher). Take the example of developmental psychology graduate programs: the typical master's program in developmental psychology will accept 44% of its applicants, and the typical doctoral program will accept about 20% of its applicants. The acceptance rates are surprisingly high for master's degrees in all of psychology; about half of the applicants to any master's program are accepted. These numbers should prove comforting to you and reduce some of those pre-application jitters. And remember: you will be applying to several graduate programs, thereby increasing the probability of acceptance even more.

Ph.D. programs are obviously more competitive than master's programs. The applied areas of psychology—clinical, counseling, school, and indus-

TABLE 1-5. Average Acceptance Rates in Graduate Psychology Programs
(% of students who apply and are accepted to a particular program)

Area	Master's	Doctoral
Clinical Psychology	37%	(Table 4-1)
Clinical Neuropsychology	—	26%[a]
Cognitive Psychology	40%	16%
Community Psychology	61%	24%
Counseling Psychology	63%	(Table 4-1)
Developmental Psychology	44%	20%
Educational Psychology	57%[a]	48%
Experimental Psychology	39%	15%
Health Psychology	41%	16%
Industrial/Organizational Psychology	52%	27%
Neuroscience	32%[a]	15%
Quantitative Psychology	78%	36%
School Psychology	34%	31%
Social & Personality Psychology	39%	12%

Source: American Psychological Association Center for Workforce Studies. (2010). *Graduate Applications, Acceptances, Enrollments, and Degrees Awarded to Master's- and Doctoral-Level Students in U.S. and Canadian Graduate Departments of Psychology: 2008-2009.*

[a]Data taken from Norcross, Kohout, & Wicherski (2005).

trial/organizational—tend to be the most selective, if we infer selectivity by the percentage of accepted applicants.

For those interested in doctoral programs in clinical and counseling psychology – approximately one-half of undergrads—the situation is more complex as there is huge variation in acceptance rates. We shall take you step-by-step through the acceptance rates to these programs later in this *Insider's Guide*. For now, we want you to gain a general sense of the odds of getting into graduate school in psychology and to feel confident that there is a place for most serious students in graduate school, even if it is a part-time master's program.

On "Backdoor" Clinicians

The APA ethical code outlines two pathways to becoming a clinical or counseling psychologist. The first is to complete a doctoral program and formal internship in clinical or counseling psychology. The second is to obtain a nonclinical psychology doctorate and then to complete a formal respecialization program in clinical or counseling psychology, which includes the internship. Formal training and supervised experience, not simply the desire to become a clinical or counseling psychologist, are required according to the APA ethical code.

In the past, some psychologists obtained doctorates in developmental, experimental, social, or educational psychology or in a psychology-related discipline and managed to practice as "clinical psychologists" or "counseling psychologists." This was possible because of the paucity of clinical and counseling psychology doctoral programs and because of generic state licensure laws, which recognize only one broad (generic) type of psychologist. However, this educational and licensure process circumvents the established pathway, increases the prospects of inadequate training, and in some cases results in unethical representation. Hence the term *backdoor*—unable to enter through the front door, they sneak in through the back entrance. Major universities, the federal government, the Veterans Administration, and practically all universities now insist on the doctorate (or respecialization) in clinical or counseling psychology for employment as a clinical or counseling psychologist. Although individuals with nonclinical psychology doctorates may be eligible for state licensure, they will be increasingly unable to identify themselves or practice as clinical or counseling psychologists.

Circuitous routes to becoming a healthcare psychologist may still exist, but they have become far less common and ethical. We emphatically recommend against these "backdoor" practices on both clinical and ethical grounds.

To Reiterate Our Purpose

The purpose of this book is to help you navigate the heretofore unknown and frightening process of applying to clinical, counseling, and combined psychology graduate programs. Gaining admission to such competitive programs requires a good deal of time and energy. There are the matters of taking the appropriate undergraduate courses, gaining clinical experience, acquiring research competencies, requesting letters of recommendation, locating compatible schools to which to apply, succeeding on entrance examinations, completing the application, creating personal statements, traveling to interviews, and deciding which program actually to attend. We have known people who have quit jobs or taken months off just to invest all their time to the application process. However, with this *Insider's Guide* and a fair degree of organization, you can make such extreme measures unnecessary.

Emotional strain is an inherent part of the application process. This is unlike many job interviews, where you are marketing yourself merely as a provider of services. Here you are marketing yourself as a human being. This is a personal process. The application forms and interviews require self-exploration and even a certain amount of justification. Why do you like clinical work? What do you enjoy about spending time with people who are disturbed or struggling? Do you really like research? You may end up questioning your answers and may feel compelled to examine the beliefs that have led you to this point in your life.

With the help of our book, you ultimately become the consumer for a program best fitted to you. And 86% of students say that their sense of fit with a program is the single most important factor in choosing a graduate program (Kyle, 2000). By negotiating this process in a systematic manner, you can become an informed, proactive consumer of psychology graduate programs. Most interviewers recommend that applicants complete the final interview in this way. With this approach to the admission process, much of the stress can be allayed.

Although the application process itself can appear intimidating, or the prospect of being rejected upsetting, we urge you *not* to permit fear to cause you to abandon your goal. Do not allow yourself to be one of the students who gets rejected unnecessarily. If you apply to the appropriate programs and present yourself effectively, your chances of getting in are vastly improved. In this book, we will demystify the graduate school application process, help you successfully navigate it, and showcase your credentials.

Our Approach

Having now counseled thousands of clinical and counseling psychology aspirants and conducted scores of workshops on applying to graduate school, the two of us have gravitated toward a particular approach to the topic. It might be called *realistically encouraging*.

It is realistic in that we present the hard facts about the competition for entrance into doctoral psychology programs. We will not resort to the disservice of feeding you illusions ("Anyone can become a clinical/counseling psychologist!"), even though the reality may leave you feeling discouraged at times.

Still, our approach is unabashedly encouraging in that we support people seeking their goals. With knowledge and perseverance, most of our students have made it. Consider the real-life story of Justin, a success story in the quest for a doctorate in clinical psychology.

Justin almost flunked out of college during his first 2 years, before discovering his abiding interest in psychology. He took his GREs late in his senior year without adequate preparation but obtained combined verbal and quantitative scores of 1100 (about 152 on the new GRE scale). His applications to doctoral programs that year were hastily and poorly prepared. Justin was, to complicate matters, grossly unaware of typical admission requirements, acceptance rates, and application guidelines. He had no clinical experience whatsoever and had never engaged in research beyond course requirements. Not surprisingly, letters of recommendation about him were mildly positive but without detail or conviction (the deadly, two-paragraph "He/she's nice, but we haven't had much contact" letters). He received dismal rejections, not even a hint of a possible interview or finalist pool.

Well, as people are apt to do, Justin was about to surrender and throw in the towel. But he then attended one of our workshops and began to understand that he had neglected virtually every guideline for sophisticated application to graduate school. The next year was devoted to preparing himself for the hunt: he took extra courses after receiving his degree to increase his GPA and to improve his GRE psychology score; he volunteered 10 hours a week at two supervised placements; he worked 20 hours a week for a small stipend as a research assistant; and he co-published three articles. Not surprisingly, his letters of recommendation were now enthusiastic and detailed. That year, Justin obtained six acceptances into clinical doctoral programs with full financial support at three of them.

There *are* concrete steps you can take to improve your application. Knowledge of the application process can be as important as your actual credentials. And if you do get rejected once, many steps can enhance the probability of acceptance the next time around, as in Justin's case. Knowledge of the process makes a tremendous difference. Over the past 26 years, this *Insider's Guide* has helped tens of thousands of students reach their goal of a doctorate in clinical or counseling psychology—and we hope you will be among them. In the following chapters, we provide suggestions and strategies that will increase your attractiveness as an applicant. Let's get to it!

CHAPTER 2

CHOOSING THE Ph.D. OR Psy.D.

Clinical psychology has two distinct training models by which students earn their doctorates. In the words of the APA Standards of Accreditation: "In general, PhD programs place relatively greater emphasis upon training related to research, and PsyD programs place relatively greater emphasis on training for engaging in professional practice." Without a firm understanding of the differences in these training models, many applicants will waste valuable time and needlessly experience disappointment.

In this chapter, we explain and distinguish between the two prevalent training models in clinical psychology—the Boulder model (Ph.D.) and the Vail model (Psy.D.). Counseling psychology has parallel differences in training emphases (Norcross, Evans, & Ellis, 2010); however, it offers only a handful of Psy.D. programs (see - 1-3). Thus, we spend most of our time on clinical psychology in this chapter.

The Boulder Model (Ph.D.)

The first national training conference on clinical psychology was held during 1949 in Boulder, Colorado (hence, the "Boulder model"). At this conference, equal weight was accorded to the development of research competencies and practice skills. This dual emphasis resulted in the notion of the clinical psychologist as a *scientist–practitioner.* Clinical psychologists were considered first and foremost as scientific psychologists and were to have a rigorous, broad-based education in psychology. Their training would encompass statistics and research methods, with core courses in development, biopsychology, learning, and the like. The emphasis was on psychology; clinical was the adjective.

The Boulder conference was a milestone for several reasons. First, it established the Ph.D. as the required degree, as in other academic research fields. To this day, all Boulder model, scientist–practitioner programs in clinical psychology award the Ph.D. degree. Second, the conference reinforced the idea that the appropriate location for training was within university departments, not separate schools or institutes as in medicine and law. And third, clinical psychologists were trained for simultaneous existence in two worlds: research/scientific and practice/professional. Boulder-model psychologists are frequently characterized as the practitioners among the scientists *and* the scientists among the practitioners.

The important implication for you, as an applicant, is that Boulder-model programs provide rigorous education as a researcher along with training as a practitioner. Consider this dual thrust carefully before applying to Boulder-model programs. Some first-year graduate students undergo undue misery because they dislike research-oriented courses and the research projects that are part of the degree requirements. These, in turn, lead to the formal dissertation required by Boulder-model programs. Many applicants are specifically seeking this sort of training.

Other applicants are seeking training focused on clinical practice. For these applicants, there is an alternative to the Boulder model: the Vail model of training psychologists.

The Vail Model (Psy.D.)

Some dissension with the recommendations of the Boulder conference emerged at later training meetings; however, there was a strong consensus that the scientist–practitioner model, Ph.D. degree, and university training should be retained. But in the late 1960s and early 1970s, change was in the wind. Training alternatives were entertained, and diversification was encouraged. This sentiment culminated in a 1973 national training conference held in Vail, Colorado (hence, the "Vail model").

The Vail conferees endorsed different principles than the Boulder model, leading to a diversity of training programs (Peterson, 1976, 1982). Psychological knowledge, it was argued, had matured enough to warrant creation of explicitly professional programs along the lines of professional training in medicine, dentistry, and law. These "professional programs" were to be added to, not replace, Boulder-model programs. There was also a clear mandate that students selected for these professional programs be chosen from "a pool of socially responsive, culturally diverse, and professionally sensitive" applicants (Korman, 1974, p. 44) instead of favoring grades and test scores alone.

Further, it was proposed that different degrees should be used to designate the scientist role (Ph.D.—Doctor of Philosophy) from the practitioner role (Psy.D.—Doctor of Psychology). Graduates of Vail-model professional programs would be *scholar–professionals*: the focus would be primarily on practice and less on research.

This revolutionary conference led to the emergence of two distinct training models typically housed in different settings. Boulder-model (Ph.D.) programs are almost universally located in graduate departments of large universities. Vail-model programs are housed in three organizational settings:

- a psychology department (as Ph.D. programs)
- within a university-affiliated psychology school (for instance, Rutgers and Adelphi universities)
- independent, "freestanding" university (for instance, Alliant University, Argosy University)

These last programs are part of independent institutions, some of which are run as for-profit companies. Although they are titled "universities," they are frequently not comprehensive universities offering degrees in dozens of subjects. Rather, they only offer degrees in a handful of subjects and thus are not "universities" in the traditional sense of comprehensive universities.

Clinical psychology boasts two established and complementary training models, each of which graduates about an equal number of psychologists each year. Although Boulder-model (Ph.D.) programs still outnumber Vail-model (Psy.D.) programs more than two to one (Table 1-3), Vail-model programs enroll, as a rule, three to four times the number of incoming doctoral candidates. This creates numerical parity in terms of psychologists produced.

Details on individual PsyD (and PhD) clinical programs may be found in the Reports on Programs in the back of this book. Here we focus on the general patterns of differences between the two training models.

Salient Differences

The primary disparity between Boulder-model and Vail-model programs lies in the relative emphasis on scientific research: Boulder programs aspire to train producers of research; Vail programs train consumers of research. Even Vail programs require research and statistics courses; you simply cannot avoid research sophistication in any APA-accredited psychology program. The practice opportunities are very similar for students in both types of programs.

Several studies have demonstrated that initial worries about employment difficulties, licensure uncertainty, and second-class citizenship for university-based Psy.D.s have *not* materialized (Hershey, Kopplin, & Cornell, 1991; Peterson, Eaton, Levine, & Snepp, 1982). There do not appear to be strong disparities in the pre-internship clinical skills of Ph.D. and Psy.D. students as evaluated by internship supervisors (Snepp & Peterson, 1988). Nor are there discernible differences in employment except, of course, that the research-oriented, Boulder-model graduates are far more likely to be employed in academic positions and medical schools (Gaddy et al., 1995). While Vail-model graduates may be seen as second-class citizens by some Boulder-model traditionalists, this is not the case among health care organizations or individual patients.

Which training model do clinical psychologists themselves prefer? In one of our studies (Norcross, Gallagher, & Prochaska, 1989), we found that 50% favored the Boulder model, 14% the Vail model, and the remaining 36% both models equally. However, preferences varied as a function of the psychologist's own doctoral program: 93% of the psychologists trained in a strong Boulder tradition preferred the Boulder model or both equally. Likewise, 90% of the psychologists trained in a strong Vail tradition preferred the Vail model or both equally. In short, psychologists preferred the training model to which they applied and in which they completed their training.

As we discuss in subsequent chapters, there are important trade-offs between Vail-model and Boulder-model programs. Here are 9 differences to bear in mind as you read through our book and as you become an informed consumer.

1. *Research skills.* Vail-model (Psy.D.) programs provide slightly more clinical experience and courses but less research experience and courses than do Boulder-model programs (Tibbits-Kleber & Howell, 1987). Clinical Ph.D. students will spend approximately half of their time in research (vs. clinical training), whereas Psy.D. students will devote about a quarter of their time to research (Ready & Santorelli, 2014). Psy.D. programs typically require a clinical dissertation, substantially less than an original research dissertation required by Ph.D. programs.

An important caveat: if you desire to teach and conduct research full time at a 4-year college or university, we strongly advise you *not* to seek the Psy.D. degree. The Psy.D. is an explicitly professional or practitioner degree; your training and expertise will be as a practitioner, not as a professor, researcher, or academician.

2. *Length of training.* The additional research training and the large dissertation required in Boulder-model (Ph.D.) programs translate into an additional year of training, on average. Students in Ph.D. programs take significantly longer, 1 to 1.5 years longer, to complete their degrees than do Psy.D. students (Gaddy et al., 1995; Norcross, Castle, Sayette, & Mayne, 2004). Various interpretations are given to this robust difference, from "Psy.D. training is more focused and efficient" on one pole, to "Ph.D. training is more comprehensive and rigorous" on the other.

3. *Class size.* Each year, Boulder-model (Ph.D.) programs in clinical psychology will take in 6 to 10 new students. The rule of thumb is to accept one new student annually for each full-time clinical faculty in that program. Each year, Vail-model (Psy.D.) programs in clinical psychology will take in 20 to 60 new students (Norcross et al., 2011). The natural consequence is that the number of students in graduate courses tends to be much larger in Psy.D. programs than in Ph.D. programs. The amount of individual mentoring by full-time faculty will also be less in Psy.D. programs.

4. *Acceptance rates.* Both Vail and Boulder programs have similar admission criteria, which favor grade point average, entrance examination scores, letters of recommendation, and so on. (All these topics are covered in detail in later chapters.) But Vail-model programs afford easier admission than Boulder-model programs. On average, clinical Ph.D. programs accept 6% to 10% of applicants, whereas clinical Psy.D. programs accept 41 to 50% of applicants (Norcross et al., 2010; see Table 4-1 for details).

5. *Financial assistance.* Admission rates are higher in Psy.D. programs, but financial assistance is lower. These numbers are plainly visible in the Reports on Individual Programs. As a rule, only 1 to 10% of Psy.D. students will receive full financial assistance (tuition waiver plus a paid assistantship), whereas 70 to 100% of clinical Ph.D. students will (Norcross et al., 2010; see Table 5-3 for details).

We will return repeatedly to matters of financial assistance and student debt throughout the *Insider's Guide*, but a few more words here about unequal "pay" in doctoral studies. Students with generous stipends/grants and tuition waivers focus better on learning and career prospects, while the rest frequently spend much of their time preoccupied with making ends meet. Unless born into a wealthy family, those without stipends or fellowships typically have two options: take out loans or work outside the university. Both can prove a gamble and both detract from the educational experience. In this sense, unequal financial assistance frequently leads to unequal education and careers (Patel, 2015). So begin now thinking through the financial consequences of graduate school. No need to become dissuaded or anxious; forewarned is forearmed.

6. *Loan debt.* The paucity of financial assistance to Psy.D. students translates into increased personal debt. If the program does not provide funding, then students are forced to rely on personal funds or loans. The median debt for Psy.D. recipients is now $200,000 (American Psychological Association, 2015). That does not include debt from undergraduate

education, which averages $33,000 to $37,000. The median debt for clinical Ph.D. recipients is $75,000, less than half that of Psy.D.s but still substantial. (For comparison, the median debt for psychology Ph.D.s in nonclinical fields is $35,000; American Psychological Association, 2015.)

7. *Accredited internships.* All doctoral students in clinical and counseling psychology must complete the equivalent of a year-long, full-time internship before receiving their degrees. Students desire an internship accredited by APA or, in lieu of that, an internship belonging to the APPIC (Association of Psychology Postdoctoral and Internship Centers). The competition for an APA-accredited internship can be keen, and in recent years, only 80% of intern applicants matched with an accredited internship (https://appic.org/Match/Match-Statistics). The research consistently demonstrates that students enrolled in large, freestanding Psy.D. programs match at a lower rate than students enrolled in smaller, Ph.D. programs (APPIC, 2006; Norcross & Karpiak, 2015; Parent & Williamson, 2010). Several large, freestanding Psy.D. programs account for over 30% of the unmatched applicants (Parent & Williamson, 2010).

8. *Licensure exam scores.* One disconcerting pattern is that Vail-model (Psy.D.) graduates do not perform as well as Ph.D. graduates on the national licensing examination for psychologists (Graham & Kim, 2011; Templer et al., 2008; Maher, 1999; Schaffer et al., 2012). That is, Psy.D. graduates score lower and pass less frequently, on average, than graduates of traditional Ph.D. clinical programs on the Examination for Professional Practice in Psychology (EPPP), the national licensing test. Higher EPPP scores are reliably associated with the higher GRE scores, lower admission rates, and greater research emphasis of smaller-sized clinical programs (Sharpless & Barber, 2013). EPPP scores correlate .78 with the GRE General Test score, so the selectivity of the doctoral program and the student's ability level may be more predictive than the graduate curriculum per se (Sharpless & Barber, 2013).

9. *Student outcomes.* It should come as no surprise to you that almost all graduates (94%) of Psy.D. programs wind up in practice or in mixed practice and academic positions (Ready & Santorelli, 2014). That's what they sought and were prepared for during their doctoral training. By contrast, clinical Ph.D. graduates wind up employed, in about equal proportions, in academic positions, mixed practice and academic positions, and practice positions. That's the flexibility and double-duty of scientist–practitioner training.

From a student's perspective, these 9 differences between the Boulder (Ph.D.) programs and the Vail (Psy.D.) programs do not reliably favor one training model over the other. As a potential applicant, you will probably prefer the shorter training and higher admission rates among Psy.D. programs, on the one hand. Easier to get in and quicker to finish. You will probably prefer the greater probability of financial assistance, accredited internships, and higher licensure scores among Ph.D. programs, on the other hand. More money and better outcomes.

In the final analysis, the decision comes down to your personal interests and career goals. Certainly if you have primarily academic or research aspirations, then a Boulder model (Ph.D.) program would be wise. Certainly if you adore clinical practice and dislike much of research, then a Vail-model (Psy.D.) program would be your choice. These truly represent choice points for an informed student.

A Bolder Boulder Model (Ph.D.)

The rise of the Vail model and the Psy.D. degree has long concerned many research-oriented academic psychologists, but their simmering concern rose to collective action in the past decades. Some psychologists believe that the professional schools, especially the large multi-campus institutions, have seriously compromised the quality of training and the scientific nature of psychology.

In a provocative monograph, three prominent clinical psychologists argue that the "evidence shows that many clinical psychology doctoral training programs, especially Psy.D. and for-profit programs, do not uphold high standards for graduate admission, have high student–faculty ratios, deemphasize science in their training, and produce students who fail to apply or generate scientific knowledge" (Baker, McFall, & Shoham, 2009; see also Baker & McFall, 2014). As the role of psychotherapist has been increasingly taken up by social workers, counselors, and assorted master's-level clinicians, the distinctive value of a doctorate in clinical psychology lies in a scientific approach to research and evaluation skills. These authors argue for a return to the Boulder model of training and endorse the new accreditation system—Psychological Clinical Science Accreditation System (PCSAS)—which is supported by the Association for Psychological Science.

This movement toward a "bolder" Boulder or *clinical scientist* model was crystallized by the 1995 creation of the Academy of Psychological Clinical Science (APCS) and the initiation of the PCSAS accreditation system. APCS is an alliance of scientifically oriented doctoral and internship training programs. APCS programs are strongly committed to research training and to the integration of such training with clinical practice. They are also committed to raising the standards of graduate education in psychology and upholding a science of psychology, even within professional training. (More information on APCS can be found on their website: acadpsychclinicalscience.org/). Table 2-1 presents the clinical psychology Ph.D. programs that are accredited by PCSAS and those that are members of APCS.

Our studies have determined that APCS and PCSAS-accredited programs are indeed distinct from other APA-accredited clinical psychology programs in that they are more selective and more research-focused. Based on the data from previous editions of our *Insider's Guide*, we found that APCS Ph.D. programs, compared to nonmember Ph.D. programs, admit a lower percentage of applicants (who had higher GRE scores) and were more likely to provide full financial support to their students. APCS programs also subscribe more frequently to a cognitive-behavioral orientation, report a stronger research emphasis, and engage more frequently in research supported by funding agencies than non-APCS programs (Sayette, Norcross, & Dimoff, 2011).

Students interested in the "bolder" Boulder or clinical scientist model will find these APCS-member and PCSAS-accredited Ph.D. programs to be especially attractive. They proudly represent evidence-based, research-focused training in clinical science. And, predictably, 75% plus of their graduates are employed in academic positions (Ready & Santorelli, 2014). That's the avowed mission of clinical scientist programs—to produce academics and researchers, as well as practitioners focused on empirically supported practices.

A Continuum of Training Opportunities

In truth, the doctoral training opportunities in clinical and counseling psychology are more nuanced than the either/or, Ph.D./Psy.D. dichotomy we have presented above. There is considerable variation within the Ph.D. and Psy.D., not only between them.

Think of a training continuum in psychology programs running from practice-oriented on the left side to research-oriented on the right. In the middle are programs equally emphasizing science and practice. Such a practice–research continuum is displayed below.

Practice-Oriented Programs (Practitioners)	**Equal-Emphasis Programs** (Scientist–Practitioners)	**Research-Oriented Programs** (Clinical Scientists)
1 2 3	4 5	6 7
Psy.D. Programs (- - - - -)	Ph.D. Programs (———)	

The practice-oriented Psy.D. programs account for roughly one-third of APA-accredited programs. Psy.D. recipients are typically known as *practitioners*. In the middle of the continuum are the equal-emphasis Ph.D. programs that account for another one-third of the APA-accredited programs. Graduates of these programs are typically called *scientist–practitioners*. On the other end of the continuum are the research-oriented Ph.D. programs that account for the final one-third. These Ph.D. recipients are called either *scientist–practitioners* or increasingly *clinical scientists*, especially if they graduate from a PCSAS-accredited program.

As you will soon discover in the Reports on Individual Programs, training directors rated their programs along this continuum. They assigned themselves a number from 1 to 7 corresponding to their training orientation.

Consider the heterogeneity *within* Psy.D. programs (Norcross, Castle, Sayette, & Mayne, 2004). Yes, all are dedicated to training practitioners (ratings of 1 to 3), but they do so in different settings and in different ways. Some are small, university-based programs accepting 15 students a year, and others are huge, for-profit campuses enrolling 70 to 80 students per year. It's inaccurate to simply lump them all together. For example, the smaller, university-housed Psy.D. programs are more likely to offer financial assistance than the larger, multi-campus Psy.D. programs.

Also look at the diversity of Ph.D. programs in clinical psychology. They range from 4 to 7, from equal-emphasis, scientist–practitioner training to the research-oriented, clinical scientist training. It is mythical to treat clinical psychology Ph.D. programs as homogeneous and unified (McFall, 2002). The differentiation among types of clinical programs—

TABLE 2-1. Clinical Psychology Ph.D. Programs Accredited by PCSAS and Members of APCS

Programs That Are Accredited by PCSAS

- Arizona State University
- Duke University
- Emory University
- Harvard University
- Indiana University
- McGill University
- Northwestern University
- Ohio State University
- Penn State University
- Rutgers University
- Stony Brook University
- Temple University
- University of Arizona
- University of California, Berkeley
- University of California, Los Angeles
- University of Delaware
- University of Georgia
- University of Illinois at Urbana–Champaign
- University of Iowa
- University of Kentucky
- University of Minnesota
- University of Missouri
- University of North Carolina–Chapel Hill
- University of Oregon
- University of Pennsylvania
- University of Pittsburgh
- University of Southern California
- University of South Florida
- University of Virginia
- University of Wisconsin, Madison
- Virginia Tech University
- Washington University in St. Louis

Programs That Are Members of APCS

- Arizona State University
- Binghamton University
- Boston University
- Duke University
- Emory University
- Florida International University
- Florida State University
- George Mason University
- Harvard University
- Indiana University
- Kent State University
- Michigan State University
- Northwestern University
- Ohio State University

Programs That Are Members of APCS *(cont.)*

- Oklahoma State University
- Pennsylvania State University
- Purdue University
- Rutgers University
- San Diego State University
- Stony Brook University
- Temple University
- Texas A&M University
- University of Arizona
- University of Buffalo
- University of California, Berkeley
- University of California, Los Angeles
- University of Delaware
- University of Denver
- University of Georgia
- University of Hawaii
- University of Illinois at Chicago
- University of Illinois at Urbana–Champaign
- University of Iowa
- University of Kansas
- University of Kentucky
- University of Maryland
- University of Massachusetts, Amherst
- University of Memphis
- University of Miami
- University of Michigan
- University of Minnesota
- University of Missouri
- University of Nevada-Reno
- University of New Mexico
- University of North Carolina at Chapel Hill
- University of Oregon
- University of Pennsylvania
- University of Pittsburgh
- University of South Florida
- University of Southern California
- University of Texas
- University of Toronto
- University of Utah
- University of Virginia
- University of Washington
- University of Wisconsin, Madison
- University of Wisconsin, Milwaukee
- Vanderbilt University
- Virginia Commonwealth University
- Virginia Tech University
- Washington University in St. Louis
- West Virginia University
- Yale University

beyond the dichotomy of Ph.D. and Psy.D.—is now abundantly clear and consistently replicated.

Our research substantiates a similar continuum among counseling psychology, except that there are only a handful of Psy.D. programs in counseling psychology. Counseling psychology has historically endorsed scientist–practitioner training and, with a few exceptions, actively resisted the practice-oriented Psy.D. (Neimeyer, Saferstein, & Rice, 2005). Hence, the practice–research continuum in counseling psychology begins with equal-emphasis programs (a rating of 3) and ends with the research-oriented programs (7). As in clinical psychology, the practice-oriented and equal-emphasis Ph.D. programs in counseling psychology accept a higher percentage of applicants but offer less financial assistance than the research-oriented programs (Norcross, Evans, & Ellis, 2010).

In short, you are not simply restricted to the Ph.D. or the Psy.D., but to all the variations and permutations within the practice–research continuum. Most students are, at once, excited and dismayed by this diversity. Excited because they can select doctoral programs that best match their interests and career goals. But also dismayed because the application process becomes more complicated. Do not fret; we shall take you step-by-step through the process of selecting schools and applying to programs.

Can you apply to both Ph.D. and Psy.D. programs? The answer depends on you. Yes, if your interest lies mostly in practice (a rating of 3) or in equal-emphasis (4). Both Psy.D. and Ph.D. programs would fit your career goals. No, if your interests are almost exclusively practice (1 or 2) or research (5, 6, or 7). In those cases, you would be poorly served by applying to a program that trains students for a career in direct conflict to your goal.

Your Informed Choice

In order to become a knowledgeable applicant, know the crucial differences between the Boulder-model (Ph.D.) and the Vail-model (Psy.D.) as well as the diversity within them. Become aware of the recent movement toward a "bolder" Boulder model prizing clinical science. Begin to notice the important tradeoffs; easier to get in but saddled with debt, or difficult to enter but rewarded with full financial assistance, for example. We shall return to these considerations repeatedly throughout the book.

More importantly, know the specific data on programs to which you will apply. The Reports on Individual Programs later in this book present these data—ratings on the practice–research continuum, theoretical orientations, length of training, acceptance rates, financial assistance, internship match rates, practice and research opportunities, and more—for each APA-accredited program.

The key tasks for you as a potential applicant are, first, to recognize the diversity in training emphases and, second, to understand your best fit. The bottom line for applicants to psychology doctoral programs is one of choice, matching, and parity. You have the choice of two training models (and all the programs in between the two extremes). The choice should be matched to your strengths and interests. Parity has been achieved in that half of all doctorates in clinical psychology are now Psy.D.s. The choices are yours, but make informed decisions. The remainder of the *Insider's Guide* is designed to do just that.

CHAPTER 3

PREPARING FOR GRADUATE SCHOOL

People begin the graduate school application process at different stages in their lives. You may be a junior or a senior in college. Maybe you have a bachelor's degree in psychology and have worked for a year or two. Perhaps you are a master's-level counselor or social worker who has decided to return for a doctorate. Or maybe you were not a psychology major but have decided to make a career change. Depending on your situation, your needs will be somewhat different. Therefore, each situation is addressed separately throughout this chapter.

One of the more perplexing decisions in applying to doctoral programs is "When—apply now or later?" A creative study of 1,034 Ph.D. students in clinical psychology determined that, after completing their undergraduate degree, 57% postponed graduate study, 10% went directly to a terminal masters' program, and 33% proceeded directly to a clinical psychology Ph.D. program (Zimak et al., 2011). Many students wait before applying to doctoral programs. The top reasons for postponing graduate school were to gain more research experience, further personal development, secure life experience, take a break from school, obtain a job, and desire to travel. All good reasons to wait until later.

The research data and our experience converge on this central point: There is no preordained "right" or "wrong" time in your life to attend graduate school in psychology. The timing, the now or later decision, obviously depends on your life circumstances, career aspirations, and current credentials.

Whatever your current status, recognize this about becoming a clinical or counseling psychologist: *Do not wait until the year of your application to begin the preparation.* Securing admission into competitive doctoral programs necessitates preparation throughout your undergraduate career and any intervening years. Good grades, adequate test scores, clinical work, and research experience cannot be instantaneously acquired simply because you have made a decision to pursue psychology as your career.

Plan ahead of time using the knowledge and strategies presented in this chapter. Preparing for graduate study is *not* for seniors only (Fretz & Stang, 1980). Timeliness is everything, or, in the vernacular, "you snooze you lose" (Mitchell, 1996).

Much of the "advice" bandied about by fellow students and even some faculty is hopelessly general. Their well-intentioned comments are meant to be universal—one size fits all. However, this advice is akin to the bed of the legendary Greek innkeeper, Procrustes, who insisted on one size bed and who stretched or shortened his unfortunate guests to fit that bed! Do not fall prey to these Procrustean maneuvers; different applicants have different needs. Understanding your particular circumstances and needs will produce an individualized plan for applying to graduate school.

Different Situations, Different Needs

Undergraduates

Some of you are undergraduates, not yet in your senior year. By getting a head start, you can take the prerequisite courses and obtain the optimal clinical and research training possible at your institution. The more time invested in preparation, the better you will meet the requirements of the application process with confidence, which puts you in a very desirable position. This *Insider's Guide* will provide you with information that can guide your undergraduate experiences, academic as well as practical. The "Time Line" presented in Appendix A outlines important steps to be taken during your freshman, sophomore, and junior years.

Seniors

Some of you are seniors, deciding whether to go directly to graduate school. This is a difficult time, and you are likely to be given advice ranging from "everyone *must* take time off" to "if you take off a year, you'll lose the momentum and never go back." Obviously, this decision is based on the needs and experiences of each individual. There are two guidelines, however, that can help you muddle through these decisions.

1. Are you primarily interested in becoming a practitioner and desire only minimal research training? If so, a practice-oriented psychology program will probably best suit your needs. These programs tend to put more emphasis on clinical experience. They favor applicants who have gained clinical experience or a master's degree and who will come into a program with some practice skills already in their repertoire. The average age of students admitted into these programs is slightly older than that in research-oriented programs (McIlvried et al., 2010), reflecting time spent out of school in a work environment. Consequently, if you are interested in a practice-oriented program, you could take time off to acquire experience in clinical work and research.
2. Are you primarily interested in a clinical/counseling psychology program that is research-oriented? If you have a solid grounding in research as an undergraduate, such a program is less likely to emphasize the need for clinical experience. The necessary and sufficient research experience can certainly be obtained during an undergraduate education without taking time off. Adding research experiences and clinical skills to an application, however, can only improve your chances of acceptance into a research-oriented program.

The decision to postpone graduate school for a year or more can be influenced by the time constraints of the application process. Applications for doctoral programs in clinical and counseling psychology are typically due between mid-December and mid-February of the year before you plan to attend school. First-semester seniors just beginning an honors or research project may not be positioned to showcase their talents by application time. The additional preparation for the Graduate Record Examination (GRE; see Entrance Examinations) may lead a potential applicant to wait a year before applying.

For all these reasons, first-semester seniors may not easily meet the requirements of the recommended Time Line presented in Appendix A. This is a frequent predicament, the solution to which is to wait another year to apply or to do what you can in the remaining time available. In either case, do not give up!

Rather, review the Time Line carefully and check off what you have and have not accomplished before making the momentous decision to go for it this year, or to wait until next year. Some shortcuts may well be necessary to apply this year; the ideal time line will need to be modified to fit your reality (Keith-Spiegel, 1991). Some of the items will have to be sacrificed, some accomplished later or more hastily, and others with great energy.

Should you elect to wait a year after receiving your baccalaureate degree, you will begin the application process almost immediately after graduation. In addition to gaining research and clinical experience, the year away from school is spent applying to graduate school. This is not taking a year "off"; rather, it should be an intense year of preparation for graduate admission.

Our research on the admission statistics of APA-accredited clinical psychology programs demonstrates that, on average, 79% of incoming doctoral students held bachelor's degrees only and 21% possessed a master's degree (Norcross et al., 2010; Oliver et al., 2005). However, this generalization is limited by significant differences among the types of programs: research-oriented Ph.D. programs enrolled a significantly higher percentage of baccalaureate-level students (87% on average; 13% master's), while Psy.D. programs enrolled more master's-level students (35% on average).

In summary, the advantages of postponing graduate school depend on the type of psychology training you desire and the strength of your current credentials. If you desire to focus exclusively on clinical practice and a Psy.D. degree, it may be advisable to take time to acquire practical experience and to save some money. If you are more research-oriented and already possess skills in this area, you may be in a position to apply at present. If your current credentials—grades, GRE scores, research—are marginal, then another year may also be required.

In using this book, you will be introduced to the admission criteria for graduate school. By using the worksheets, you can determine how well prepared you are to apply at this point. Following the steps in this book will help you assess how prepared you are to apply to graduate school successfully and whether some time out in the "real world" would be advisable.

Previous College Graduates

Some of you are college graduates and have already taken time off, or you are a member of the working world contemplating a career change. Research suggests that those of you who postponed doctoral studies are actually more satisfied with your decision than your peers who went directly to a terminal master's program (Zimak et al., 2011). A solid work record, life experience, and a mature perspective on psychology are certainly advantageous.

Those of you who have been out of school and in the real world for several years may feel at a disadvantage in terms of taking the GREs, finding academic letters of recommendation, and locating research opportunities. But by faithfully following the strategies in this *Insider's Guide*, you can master these steps—as have thousands of returning students before you. And by reviewing the admissions criteria for graduate programs and using the worksheets provided, you will evaluate the degree of your preparation in order to decide whether it is prudent to begin the application process immediately or to bolster your credentials before beginning. Pay particular attention to the steps listed under "application year" in the Time Line (Appendix A).

Returning Master's-Level Clinicians

Some of you will be master's-level clinicians interested in obtaining the doctorate in clinical or counseling psychology. Although your wealth of clinical experience gives you an immediate edge over undergraduates in the admissions race to Psy.D. programs, you cannot ignore the importance assigned to entrance examinations and research experience.

Psy.D. programs and practice-oriented Ph.D. programs tend to accept proportionally more incoming students with master's degrees than with baccalaureate degrees only. Interestingly, counseling psychology programs also prefer master's-level students: Two-thirds of incoming students in APA-accredited counseling psychology programs already held their master's (Norcross, Evans, & Ellis, 2009). Of course, these are merely averages that mask the huge differences between, for example, the one-third of counseling psychology programs which *only* accept master's recipients and the one-tenth of programs which primarily accept baccalaureate recipients (Turkson & Norcross, 1996).

Hines (1985) conducted a survey of clinical psychology doctoral programs regarding their policies and experiences in accepting students with master's degrees in psychology. Following are several of the salient findings.

The first question was "What effect (if any) will having a master's degree have on an applicant's chances for admission to your program?" Most responses indicated that having a master's per se made little or no difference, with some respondents suggesting that it was the student's performance in the master's program that was more important. However, 10% answered that having a master's degree had a definite positive effect. Only 3% indicated that having a master's would have a definite negative bias.

The second question requested that respondents rate the importance of seven criteria for admission to their programs. Each criterion was rated on a 5-point, Likert-type scale ranging from least important to most important. The three highest ratings were for GRE scores, letters of recommendation, and research experience. The rest, in descending order of importance, were undergraduate grades, graduate grades, quality of the master's program, and practicum experience.

As you can see, GRE scores and research experience definitely count in admissions decisions for master's-level applicants. The lower ratings given to graduate grades and to undergraduate grades reflect concerns about grade inflation and about the difficulty of interpreting grade averages obtained from different institutions of higher education. The standard deviation for graduate grades was particularly high, indicating wide variability in the value accorded to graduate grades. Comments suggested that some schools tended to downplay graduate grades "because they are universally high"; another suggested that "high grades don't help, but poor grades hurt."

Thus, a master's degree *by itself* neither helps

nor hinders your chances in most doctoral admission decisions. It is not possessing the master's degree itself that matters, but the quality of performance in academic courses, clinical practica, and research experiences during master's training and thereafter that give an edge in the admission process.

Master's degree recipients with combined Verbal and Quantitative GRE scores below 290 (or below 1,000 on the old scale) can take hope from a study of similar students admitted to Ph.D. programs (Holmes & Beishline, 1996). Ten such applicants were admitted by virtue of "compensatory virtues," such as research presentations or publications that helped mitigate the effect of low GRE scores. If you find yourself in this position, emphasize the other, positive elements of your application and, again, seriously consider Psy.D. clinical and Ph.D. counseling psychology programs that enroll a higher percentage of master's-level students (Norcross et al., 2010). Assuming other parts of your credentials are acceptable, master's recipients should not be discouraged from applying to doctoral programs on the basis of GRE scores alone.

While clinical experience is valued, for most doctoral programs this factor is a secondary consideration to research. The vast majority of clinical and counseling doctoral programs prefer a research thesis or a journal article over a graduate internship or post-master's clinical experience (Keller, Beam, Maier, & Pietrowski, 1995). All doctoral programs expect evidence of conducting empirical research: Ph.D. programs favor it over clinical experience and Psy.D. programs weigh it equally with clinical experience.

A Master's Degree First?

A common question during our graduate school workshops is whether students should secure a master's degree before seeking the doctorate. Unfortunately, there is no simple answer to such a complex question. Nonetheless, the following are some broad reasons for seeking a master's degree first.

- *Low grade-point average.* The vast majority of APA-accredited doctoral programs will not consider applicants with a GPA below 3.0.
- *Weak GRE scores.* Similarly, most university-based doctoral programs rarely accept bachelor's-level applicants whose combined Verbal and Quantitative scores fall below 290 (or about 1,000 on the old scale).
- *Scarce research or clinical experiences.* Doctoral admission committees understandably desire that you have had some direct experience with those activities you intend to pursue for a lifetime.
- *Uncertain career goal.* Indecision about your subfield in psychology, or outside of psychology, is a strong indicator for a master's program initially.
- *Late application.* Doctoral programs hold to earlier deadlines than do master's programs, so those students waiting too late to apply will be redirected to master's programs.
- *Terse letters of recommendation.* By virtue of late transfer into a university or into the psychology major, some students lack sufficient contact with faculty for them to write positive and detailed letters of recommendation expected by doctoral programs.
- *Inadequate coursework in psychology.* Doctoral programs require a minimum level of education in the discipline prior to acceptance, typically at least 18 credits of psychology coursework.

Completing a rigorous master's program in psychology can correct many of the foregoing impediments to acceptance into a doctoral program. As we describe in Chapter 8, students typically strengthen their grade point average, acquire clinical and research experience, sharpen their career goals, and establish close relationships with faculty during the 2 full-time years of a master's program. For these and other reasons, many students opt for a master's degree at one institution before seeking the doctorate at another.

Doctoral psychology faculty were surveyed in detail regarding the value of a clinical master's degree for gaining admission to their programs (Bonifzi, Crespy, & Rieker, 1997). Assuming a *good* undergraduate GPA and *good* GREs, the effect of having a master's degree on the applicant's chances for admission was negative for 7% of the programs, neutral for 48% of the programs, and positive for the remaining 45%. However, assuming *mediocre* GPA and *mediocre* GREs, the effect of having a master's was more neutral than positive overall. Put another way, it is clearly the applicant's overall credentials—rather than possession of a master's degree per se—that carries the day.

This same study (Bonifzi et al., 1997) and our own research (Mayne et al., 1994; Norcross et al., 2004) consistently demonstrate that Ph.D. clinical programs hold a positive bias toward baccalaureate-level applicants. By contrast, Psy.D. clinical, Ph.D. counseling, and Ph.D. school psychology programs view master's degree recipients more favorably and accept higher proportions of master's-level applicants. Keep these patterns in mind as you consider the selection criteria of graduate schools.

Graduate School Selection Criteria

As an applicant, your perceptions of graduate admissions criteria probably differ from those of the admissions committee. Some of the things you may think are important are actually not so important (Collins, 2001). For two examples, your GRE Psychology Subject score is much less important than your GRE Verbal and Quantitative scores, and your extracurricular accomplishments do not count as much as you might like (Cashin & Landrum, 1991). On the other hand, you probably underestimate the importance of other admissions criteria; two examples are letters of recommendation and research experience, which students routinely undervalue compared to admissions committees (Nauta, 2000).

In this section we acquaint you with the evidence-based practices of graduate admissions committees. Learn what they value in graduate applicants and then tailor your application to those criteria to maximize your success. Remember: Privilege what admissions committees seek, *not* what you personally think they should emphasize.

A number of studies have been conducted to determine the relative importance of selection criteria in psychology graduate programs. The findings of one of our studies (Norcross, Kohout, & Wicherski, 2005) are summarized in Table 3-1. This table presents the average ratings of various criteria for admission into 410 doctoral programs and 179 master's programs in psychology. A rating of 3 denotes high importance; 2, medium importance; and 1, low importance.

The top-rated criteria for doctoral programs were letters of recommendation, personal statements, GPA, interview, research experience, and GRE scores. All received ratings of 2.50 and higher on the 3-point scale, indicative of high importance. Extracurricular activity and work experience were valued substantially less.

The implications for enhancing your application are thus clear and embedded throughout this *Insider's Guide*: secure positive letters of recommendation, write compelling personal statements, maintain your GPA, ace the preadmission interview, obtain research experience, and prepare thoroughly for the GREs. At the same time, being heavily involved in student organizations and campus activities does not carry nearly as much weight as these other criteria. Being a volunteer soccer coach is not a path to graduate school!

Studies of the selection criteria of only APA-accredited doctoral programs reveal time and time again that research experience emerges as a top-rated variable. The authors of one early study (Eddy et al., 1987) pointedly concluded that there is simply no better way to increase one's chances for graduate school acceptance than research. Letters of recommendation, personal statements, interview performance, and clinical experience were also highl[illegible] valued. However, as in previous studies, extr[illegible]ricular activities, such as Psi Chi membersh[illegible] rated relatively unimportant.

TABLE 3-1. Importance of Various Criteria in Psychology Admissions D[illegible]

	Master's programs		Do[illegible]	
Criteria	Mean[a]	*SD*	[illegible]	[illegible]
Letters of recommendation	2.74	.49	[illegible]	[illegible]
Personal statement/goals	2.63	.55	[illegible]	[illegible]
GPA	2.75	.43	[illegible]	[illegible]
Interview	2.30	.7[illegible]	[illegible]	[illegible]
Research experience	2.04	[illegible]	[illegible]	[illegible]
GRE scores	2.36	[illegible]	[illegible]	[illegible]
Clinically related public service	1.94	[illegible]	[illegible]	[illegible]
Work experience	1.91	[illegible]	[illegible]	[illegible]
Extracurricular activity	1.46	[illegible]	[illegible]	[illegible]

Note. Data from Norcross, Kohout, & Wicherski (2005).

[a]Means are calculated on ratings where 1 = low importanc[illegible]

Not all research experiences count equally in graduate admissions. The most important are published articles in referred journals and paper/poster presentations at national conferences. Of course, serving as first author counts more than second or third author. Paper/poster presentations at regional conferences follow in importance, then state conferences. Publishing in nonrefereed or undergraduate journals bring less credit in graduate admissions decisions, but still some credit (Kaiser et al., 2007; Keith-Spiegel et al., 1994).

In sum, the results of these and other studies (e.g., Briihl & Wasielski, 2004; Mayne et al., 1994; Munoz-Dunbar & Stanton, 1999; Purdy, Reinehr, & Swartz, 1989) consistently indicate that the ideal applicant has high GRE scores, strong letters of recommendation, research experience, clinical experience, and high GPA. The results also consistently demonstrate that the admission requirements for doctoral programs are more stringent than for master's programs.

The remainder of this chapter highlights these pivotal criteria used by graduate admissions committees in selecting their students. We consider, in order, coursework, faculty mentoring, clinical experience, research skills, entrance examinations, and extracurricular activities.

Coursework

Although graduate programs in clinical and counseling psychology differ slightly in the courses they prefer you to take prior to admission, there are fortunately several "core" courses that nearly all require (Lawson et al., 2012; Smith, 1985). These include Introduction to Psychology, Statistics, Research Meth-[illegible]ds, Abnormal Psychology, and a smattering of core [illegible]chology courses, such as developmental, person-[illegible] physiological/biopsychology, psychological test-[illegible]nd social psychology.

[illegible]r research on clinical and counseling doctoral [illegible]s reveals that both Vail- and Boulder-model [illegible] hold similar expectations on desirable [illegible]uate courses (Norcross, Sayette, Stratigis, [illegible]an, 2014; Oliver et al., 2005). Approxi-[illegible]f the programs require or recommend [illegible]graduate courses, 20% require an [illegible]sychology major, 7% specify a mini-[illegible]psychology credits (but not specific [illegible]remainder have no set policy on [illegible]ograms, almost all in counseling [illegible]at a master's degree is required [illegible]s et al., 2014).

Table 3-2 presents the percentage of psychology courses required (first column), choose among required (second column), recommended (third column), and any of these (fourth column) for entry into APA-accredited programs. Bear in mind that these figures systematically *underestimate* the actual percentage of programs requiring these courses as they do not include those graduate programs requiring a psychology major as a prerequisite and thus probably requiring most of the courses listed in Table 3-2 (Stoloff et al., 2010). Introduction to Psychology was presumed to be a prerequisite for these advanced psychology courses and was therefore omitted from the table.

Courses you should complete, according to these results, are Statistics, Research Methods, Abnormal Psychology, Developmental Psychology, Personality, Biological/Physiological Psychology, Social Psychology, and Psychological Testing. At least one laboratory course has also emerged as a "must" of late.

Both Psy.D. and Ph.D. programs request similar psychology preparation with a couple of twists. Psy.D. programs desire more clinical courses (e.g., abnormal, personality, and testing), and the Ph.D. programs more frequently desire a research experience and laboratory course (Norcross et al., 2014). The relative emphases along the practice–research continuum often map onto different preferences for undergraduate coursework.

Doctoral programs require more courses on average than do master's programs (Lawson et al., 2012; Smith, 1985). Accordingly, both to meet admissions criteria and to improve your GRE Psychology Subject score, we heartily recommend that you complete Learning and Conditioning, Cognitive Psychology, a clinical or treatment course, and History and Systems. The safest plan, of course, is to complete a rigorous undergraduate major in psychology to satisfy all these courses, but a well-planned minor in psychology may suffice. The rule of thumb: the more competitive the graduate program, the more stringent the required undergraduate coursework.

If you were not a psychology major, it is still important that you take the minimum of core courses mentioned. In addition, you may have to invest additional time studying for the Psychology Subject Test of the Graduate Record Examination (more about this later).

If you have been out of college for several years and feel deficient in this coursework, you might consider taking a few courses as a part-time student at a local university. Such coursework will shore up your record and prepare you more fully for admission

TABLE 3-2. Undergraduate Courses Required or Recommended by APA-Accredited Clinical and Counseling Psychology Programs

	Percentage of programs			
Psychology course	Required	Choose among required	Recommended	All
Statistics	53	6	33	92
Research methods/design	37	9	27	73
Abnormal/psychopathology	32	3	28	63
Developmental/child	12	3	23	38
Personality	14	4	18	36
Physiological/biopsychology	8	5	22	35
Social psychology	7	4	17	28
Psychological testing/assessment	10	2	10	22
Learning and conditioning	4	6	11	21
Cognitive psychology	3	3	7	13
History and systems	2	1	10	13
Clinical/psychotherapy	4	1	3	8
Laboratory course	1	0	4	5
Field experience	3	0	2	5
Sensation and perception	0	1	2	3
Motivation and emotion	0	1	2	3
Multicultural/diversity	1	0	2	3

Note. Adapted from Norcross, Sayette, Stratigis, & Zimmerman (2014).

and the GRE. Those of you who are not psychology majors but have studied extensively for this test and have done well will often be considered favorably by admissions committees.

Graduate selection committees prefer a broad undergraduate background in a variety of arts and sciences (Fretz & Stang, 1980). Exposure to biological sciences, math competency, and verbal skills are generally valued. If you are anxious or phobic regarding oral presentations, then by all means complete a public speaking course. Composition and writing courses also prove vital; you may well face three or four major papers each semester in graduate school.

At this point, you may want to glance at the Reports on Individual Programs following Chapter 8 to get a better idea of which courses particular doctoral programs recommend or require of applicants. You will find the specific courses that each accredited clinical, counseling, and combined psychology program desires its applicants to have taken.

For students who have gotten an early start or who are seniors, we suggest considering advanced coursework. To allay any anxieties, we emphasize that the vast majority of applicants do *not* take these courses as undergraduates. Your application can be very strong without taking the courses we are about to mention. However, those fortunate enough to be in a position to add these to their academic transcripts should seriously consider taking advantage of the opportunity.

Consider an advanced or multivariate statistics course. Statistical acumen is highly regarded, especially in research-oriented programs, and advanced knowledge may pave the way for you receiving funding as a graduate assistant or research assistant. Another suggestion would be to take a course specifically focused on one of the data analysis programs. Learning one of the major statistical packages—Statistical Analysis System (SAS), Statistical Package for the Social Sciences (SPSS), or R—is a definite advantage. Such knowledge increases your employability and may catch the eye of a professor in need of a data analyst.

Lastly, we recommend an advanced course in biopsychology, genetics, or neuroscience. This is certainly helpful in increasing your understanding of the biological aspects of behavior, an increasing focus in psychology today. If you have the time and abilities, these courses can help distinguish a strong application from an outstanding one.

As mentioned earlier, your GPA is an important criterion for admission. Two types of GPA are usually considered by graduate programs: overall GPA and psychology GPA. Most programs focus only on your overall or cumulative GPA. Determine which GPAs programs evaluate and also how much importance they place on them. For example, if you have an overall GPA of 3.2 (on a 4-point scale where $A = 4$, $B = 3$, $C = 2$, and $D = 1$) and a psychology GPA of 3.6, you might concentrate on schools that emphasize the latter.

Our research has shed light on the average GPAs among incoming doctoral and master's students in psychology (Norcross et al., 2005). For doctoral programs, the mean GPA is 3.54 for all undergraduate courses and 3.66 for psychology courses. For master's programs, the mean GPA is 3.37 for all undergraduate courses and 3.48 for psychology courses. Of course, when interpreting these figures, recognize that roughly half of the incoming students will possess GPAs above these scores, and half of the students will possess GPAs below them.

Although we do not want to discourage anyone, a GPA below 3.0 is considered unsatisfactory by most APA-accredited programs. Regardless of the prestige of the institution, admissions committees view a GPA under 3.0 as below the acceptable limits of course performance. If your GPA is below 3.0, then consider the following steps:

- Take additional courses to bolster your GPA.
- Retake courses to improve it.
- Wait another year to apply in order for all of your senior-year grades to be factored into your GPA.
- Complete a master's program to show doctoral admissions committees you can perform academically at a higher level.

Speak with an academic advisor or mentor about how best to improve your standing within the workings of your own institution. Academic performance in your junior and senior psychology courses is particularly vital. Your grades in these courses affect your overall and psychology GPAs.

Your "academic" performance is not limited to exam grades in the classroom. Faculty members—several of whom may submit letters of recommendation on your behalf—also assess your interpersonal skills, verbal ability, and professional commitment in the classroom, outside formal coursework, and in everyday interactions. The direct implication is to avoid undesirable interpersonal behaviors—for instance, silliness, arrogance, and hostility—in any interactions with your professors (Keith-Spiegel, 1991). The wisdom of avoiding such undesirable behaviors should be obvious, but students are frequently unaware of the importance faculty attach to thoughtful questions, genuine attentiveness, respectful disagreements, office visits, mature disposition, interpersonal responsibility, and so forth. These are the characteristics a student heading for graduate studies should manifest in and outside of the classroom.

Finally, there is a corpus of general knowledge regarding clinical and counseling psychology that may not have been covered in your courses. This body of information includes at least a cursory understanding of diagnosis, for example, the *Diagnostic and Statistical Manual*, 5th ed. (DSM-5); various assessment devices, such as the Minnesota Multiphasic Personality Inventory-2 (MMPI-2) and the Wechsler Intelligence Scales (WAIS-IV, WISC-IV); and ordinary therapy practices, such as individual, group, and family therapy. You must have a passing familiarity with theoretical orientations, for example, cognitive-behavioral, psychodynamic, family systems, and integrative, in order to understand program materials. If you are not already familiar with these concepts, it would be wise to review an introductory textbook in clinical or counseling psychology.

You should also be gaining knowledge specifically about psychology as a field and about the current issues within this field. Toward this end, we suggest you begin reading the *Monitor on Psychology*, a publication sent to all APA members and student affiliates, or the *APS Observer*, the publication distributed to all members of the Association for Psychological Science (APS). Both publications feature articles dealing with psychology in general and clinical/counseling psychology in particular. You can become an APA or APS affiliate and receive an online subscription, peruse online abstracts, or ask to borrow a professor's old issues.

Read your textbooks with an eye toward graduate school. If you come across an interesting study, note the author and check in the back of the text for the reference. When you have time, read the original article. If it is recent, note the author's university. You will be surprised at how much you can learn about the field just by completing your typical class work.

Faculty Mentoring

Learning about psychology and achieving good grades represent key components of academic work. But classes are also important in that they provide you with the opportunity to become acquainted and form relationships with faculty. It is natural to feel shy around faculty, especially if you are part of a 300-person lecture class. Courage is required to muster the nerve to ask a question or to stay after class and introduce yourself. Equally anxiety provoking is a visit alone to a professor's office during office hours. In the one case, you expose yourself in front of your peers; in the other, you are individually vulnerable and do not have a crowd of faces to blend into. *But find a way to become comfortable in approaching faculty members.*

The irony of student reticence to approach faculty is that professors generally would like more students to visit them. Many faculty sit alone during office hours wondering why students never come to see them. They love to have students visit after class or during office hours with questions. Ideas for questions can include something mentioned in the lecture, something you encountered in the readings, or something that puzzles you about graduate school. You do not have to be a star pupil or ask brilliant questions to begin a conversation with a professor. If you want to develop a relationship, ask professors about their research or other courses they are teaching. Faculty are passionate about their research, and they will be flattered that you investigated their interests online before visiting them during office hours.

What is the value of meeting faculty? Three compelling reasons spring to mind. First, having a mentor to advise you in your growth as a future psychologist is invaluable. There is no better way to learn about psychology than in a one-on-one, mentoring relationship. When you apply to graduate school (and for employment), having a professor to guide you through the process is a huge advantage. Second, eventually you will need faculty to write letters of recommendation on your behalf. Whether you are applying to graduate school or for employment, everyone wants a few references regarding your performance and responsibility. Occasionally faculty members are asked to write a letter for a pupil who has taken a lecture course with 100 or more students—the professor may not even know the student until he or she requests a letter! It makes a huge difference if you have spent some office hours or time after class with a faculty member, and he or she knows you more personally.

And third, once you get to know professors, you may be able to work with them on a research project or as part of their clinical activities. You will be working closely with your major professor in graduate school, and you might as well begin as soon as possible as a colleague-in-training. Though more will be said about this matter later, we cannot overemphasize the need to cultivate such a relationship and obtain the rewards that can ensue.

To put it bluntly, the single largest contributor to preparedness for graduate school is students' interaction with faculty members at their undergraduate institution. That's what the research concludes and what graduate students report (Huss et al., 2002). Psychology students who had a mentor and who had high-quality interactions with faculty felt more prepared for graduate school. And the second largest contributor to graduate school preparedness is research activity—a point to which we shall return in a few pages.

Odysseus, the hero of Homer's epic poem *The Odyssey*, left for the Trojan War and entrusted his wise friend, Mentor, to oversee the education of his son, Telemachus. The eponym "mentor" now refers to a trusted guide, positive role model, and caring teacher (Wang, 2010). Your task is to be Telemachus (or a mentee) and find at least one Mentor to guide you through the graduate admissions process. This *Insider's Guide* also serves that purpose, but another real-time person is highly recommended.

Clinical Experience

What is clinical experience? In its loosest sense, it involves working in human service or mental health agencies. Graduate programs in clinical and counseling psychology expect that you will have some experience working with emotionally, intellectually, or behaviorally disabled people. Many students volunteer or intern during their undergraduate years, whereas other people get paid as part of a summer job or employment. In all APA-accredited programs, you will be expected to have some clinical experience as a prelude to your graduate training and as an aid to researching clinically relevant problems. Experience of this nature is considered essential.

What kinds of clinical experience count? Largely two types—paid and volunteer—under individual supervision. Paid part-time work in a clinical setting may be available in your community (but your involvement should not be at the expense of your academic performance). Returning master's-level clinicians will obviously have a multitude of employment possibilities, whereas undergraduates will have to search vigilantly for part-time employment.

For college students, a prime opportunity is to complete an undergraduate practicum or field experience for academic credit. This is a great way to "kill two birds with one stone." Ninety percent of colleges and universities provide undergraduate internships or field experiences in psychology (Norcross et al., 2016). Further, students consistently rate fieldwork as one of the most rewarding experiences and relevant courses in their college career. Internships "pay" in multiple ways: clinical experience, academic credit, familiarity with behavioral health agencies, professional supervision, potential sources for letters of recommendation, and a shot at a full-time job.

Check with your undergraduate advisor, faculty mentor, and the college catalogue to determine whether such an opportunity exists for you. To learn more about the specific placements, you should consult the Psychology Department or the faculty member responsible for internship placements.

In selecting a place to work or volunteer, please consider several factors. Although it may be difficult to accomplish, it is ideal to gain clinical experience in a setting that complements a research interest. For example, if your research is in the area of alcohol abuse, you might seek experience in a college counseling center or a substance abuse prevention program. Determine exactly what your responsibilities will entail.

The optimal program is one that will train you in clinical skills (such as crisis counseling on a hot line), will enable you to deal directly with clients (as opposed to solely observing), and will provide regular supervision by an experienced clinician.

Supervision is probably the most important consideration in choosing a clinical setting. Try to receive individual supervision by a licensed professional, one with a master's degree or higher. Determine the qualifications of the person who will be supervising your work. Aside from the valuable insight supervisors can offer, they may also be familiar with faculty at different graduate programs and assist you in selecting schools. In addition, you may eventually decide to request letters of recommendation from them. Letters from a clinical supervisor are particularly valued by practice-oriented graduate programs. In a later section we offer suggestions regarding approaching professors for letters of recommendation. The same strategies apply here.

If you are volunteering, you should insist on receiving supervision. Learn not only who will supervise you, but also how often and for what length of time. Be assertive when searching out and interviewing possible agencies. If this seems challenging for you, try to remember that you are a volunteer—giving your time and energy, without financial compensation, to an agency that is in need of people like yourself. You seek only experience and supervision. You are a valuable commodity; do not sell yourself short!

Numerous settings are available to people seeking clinical experience. Here are several excellent sources of hands-on experience that can be found in most communities:

- *Crisis hot lines.* These typically provide training in counseling skills, suicide prevention, and outreach services. The clientele range from sexual assault victims to suicidal teens to lonely elderly who need to talk with someone. Volunteers usually provide telephone counseling, although opportunities to work with an emergency outreach team may also prove available. This can be a great way to gain exposure to a multitude of psychopathologies and to acquire fundamental helping skills. One word of caution: new members of most crisis hot lines are expected to take a large share of the midnight to 8 A.M. shifts. Be prepared to pay your dues.
- *Centers for homeless or runaway adolescents.* Much of what is done in these settings is similar to case management, in that these teenagers are connected with social service agencies. However, in-house counseling may also be provided to these youths, who frequently come from disadvantaged families. Be particularly careful about specifying the supervision arrangement before starting. The facilities are often understaffed and financially strapped, meaning you may have to be assertive to get the desired training.
- *Schools for emotionally disturbed children and adolescents.* These placements offer exposure to both educational and clinical services. Educational activities might include tutoring, classroom management, and one-on-one homework supervision. Clinical activities typically involve recreational supervision, art therapy, group skills-training, and perhaps individual and family therapy. In recent years, most of these stand-alone schools have transitioned to dedicated classrooms, staffed by counselors and special ed teachers, located in regular schools.
- *Supervised homes for the developmentally disabled or chronically mentally ill.* These are unlocked transitional facilities where clients live and work in a therapeutic milieu (an environment consisting of peers). Depending on your prior experience, you might conduct skills training,

recreational counseling, and work/school supervision. The programs are often behavioral, affording you experience with reinforcement schedules, shaping techniques, and token economies. Often the goal is to graduate clients to the outside world.

- *Summer camps for the physically challenged, developmentally disabled, or emotionally disturbed.* These day and overnight camps expect counselors to supervise recreation and train campers in skills and vocational activities. The positions are usually paid, ideal for college students who want to gain field experience while working for the summer. They also tend to be full-time positions, while they last. They offer short-term but intensive training.
- *Community mental health centers.* These provide experience with patients suffering from serious mental disorders, such as schizophrenia, bipolar disorders, substance abuse, and anxiety disorders. The programs vary but are likely to include an outpatient department, partial (day) hospitalization, and an education/outreach wing. Duties may entail assisting recreational activities, intake interviews, and psycheducational groups. Though supervising recreational activities allows contact with patients, you might not be observing any clinical methods. Do not be shy about asking for greater responsibilities!
- *College peer programs.* These provide students with peer education and assistance on specific disorders, such as bulimia or substance abuse. Less common but still available is peer counseling on more general concerns, for example, "Need to Talk? Call Us." Both peer education and peer counseling programs are typically flexible in the number of hours you work and usually provide training in listening and counseling skills. They may also provide an opportunity to begin learning about a specific clinical problem.
- *Women's resource centers.* These multiservice centers offer or coordinate a plethora of human services for women—rape crisis counseling, domestic violence education, victim advocacy, "safe homes" for victims of abuse, and so on. Possible activities likewise vary, but the training and *esprit de corps* are highly regarded. Students with abiding interest in women's rights and feminist therapy will find these placements particularly satisfying.
- *Drug and alcohol treatment facilities.* These offer a variety of detoxification and rehabilitation interventions designed to help patients cope with the physical and psychological components of addiction. Although not all "D & A" programs will afford undergraduate placements, substance abuse is one of the most popular research areas in clinical and counseling psychology (Dimoff et al., 2017; see also Appendix E). Students can gain exposure to several models of addiction, interact with a multidisciplinary treatment team, and observe clinical services with substance abusers across gender, racial, and socioeconomic lines.
- *Psychiatric hospitals.* These offer comprehensive behavioral care in an inpatient setting and typically feature individual psychotherapy, group treatment, psychoactive medication, psychological assessment, occupational therapy, and recreational therapy. Students are likely to observe patients with severe disorders receiving many treatments provided by multidisciplinary staff. In addition, large state hospitals depend upon the kindness of volunteers to staff social events, community outings, and recreational opportunities for patients.
- *Legal and probation offices.* These offer ideal experiences for students interested in forensic applications. Students frequently volunteer or intern with District Attorney's offices, probation officers, criminal lawyers, state police, and other criminal justice professionals. In these settings, ask to be exposed to the psychological or psychiatric side of criminal justice.

A word of caution about initial clinical encounters. Be careful not to generalize from one experience. One of the authors worked at a crisis center for adolescents in the Times Square area of New York City. The rate of employee turnover at this facility was exceptionally high. The "success" rate for clients was low, and the population was difficult indeed. Although it was a rich experience, some of the volunteers became disillusioned with psychology as a result of working there. An unpleasant experience may only mean that the particular population or setting was not suited to you. Try something else, and you may feel quite differently.

Though clinical work is important (and often rewarding), recall that it is only one of several criteria prized for admission to graduate school. Some Ph.D. applicants make the mistake of accumulating a wealth of clinical experiences at the expense of gaining research training. By doing so, you may be inadvertently presenting yourself as being uninterested in research or perhaps better suited to a Psy.D. than a Ph.D. program. Clinical experience must be balanced with research competencies. This balance will be weighted toward clinical work or research depending on your desire to earn either a Psy.D. or Ph.D. or whether the Ph.D. program is practice or research-oriented.

Research Skills

Research experience, as discussed earlier in this chapter, consistently emerges as a top admission criteria to nearly all Ph.D. programs in clinical and counseling psychology. To a lesser but still significant degree, Psy.D. programs also value your research experience for what it communicates about your intellectual ability and professional commitment. Recall the conclusion of one study on graduate school admission: there is simply no single better way to enhance an application than by obtaining research experience (Eddy et al., 1987). The desired skills—to reason critically, to gather data, to access the research in pursuit of what works, to adapt the research to your professional activities, to write balanced conclusions, among others—are essential. Even though all psychologists need not produce original research, all must intelligently consume and apply research.

The benefits of student research, according to research (Landrum & Nelsen, 2002), boil down to two dimensions. The first might be labeled specific skills and abilities. These skills include developing clear research ideas, conducting literature searches, choosing appropriate measures, analyzing data, using statistical procedures, preparing conference presentations, and improving writing ability. The second dimension might be called interpersonal goals. These tend to be overshadowed by the technical skills listed above, but they are critical benefits in preparing and mentoring psychologists-in-training. These entail influencing decisions about graduate school, meeting other students involved in research, getting to know faculty members better, improving teamwork, forming relationships for the basis of letters of recommendation, developing leadership, and improving interpersonal communication. You seek *both* types of benefits in securing a research experience or assistantship.

Gaining research experience is largely dependent on your own initiative. That can prove intimidating, so in the following sections we highlight the key steps in the process to maximize your research involvement.

Common Paths

Let us begin by outlining 8 common avenues for students engaging in scholarly research. The first is probably the most frequent—volunteering to work with a faculty member on one of his or her research projects. A second avenue is to complete a student research program for a notation on your transcript but not academic credit. Students identify potential professors to work with from a faculty directory of research interests, jointly complete a learning contract, and then devote a minimum number of hours (say, 75) throughout a semester working directly with the faculty sponsor. A third option is to enroll in independent psychology research for academic credit. This entails individual study and research under the supervision of a faculty member and is ordinarily limited to junior and senior psychology majors. These three research paths are generally open to psychology majors attending a particular university as well as to graduated students looking to obtain research skills.

A fourth and increasingly common approach is to work or volunteer for a researcher outside of your university—in a hospital, medical center, research institute, private industry, or community-based organization, for example. Especially in large cities, researchers with major grants depend upon individuals (both pre- and post-baccalaureate) for many elements of study management, data collection, and statistical analyses. Many industries, especially biomedical and pharmaceutical research, offer summer research internships. These positions can provide valuable experience in randomized controlled trials. Conversely, community-based organizations commonly conduct outcomes research around clinical or community interventions and accept interns throughout the year. If you have taken a statistics or research methods course that included SPSS or SAS, you may have sufficient skills for an entry-level position on an active research team outside of a university.

A fifth path is to complete a summer research program, typically at another university for a couple of weeks. These are structured, formal programs for stellar undergraduates interested in pursuing advance training in psychology research. APA, APS, and Psi Chi all offer such summer programs or grants to create your own summer research directed by a psychologist. APA maintains a list of *Undergraduate Research Opportunities & Internships* (at www.apa.org/education/undergrad/research-opps.aspx), which presents dozens of research opportunities lasting for a week up to the entire summer.

A sixth alternative, restricted to matriculated undergraduates, is to complete an honors thesis in either a departmental or a university-wide honors program. As with additional courses and post-college work, an honors thesis is a "feather in your cap." For students desiring to move straight into a Ph.D. program, it is one means of presenting evidence to graduate admissions committees that you are capable of performing graduate-level work. Many schools allow motivated students to complete an honors thesis, an original study that the student conceptualizes, conducts, analyzes, and hopes to present at a regional conference or even publishing. An honors thesis shows a genuine commitment to psychology and is a palpable sign of ability in the applicant.

A seventh path, discussed fully in Chapter 8, is to complete a psychology post-baccalaureate program. These are designed for students with a bachelor's degree in any discipline (including psychology) who seek preparation for graduate training in psychology. "Post-baccs" offer intensive research apprenticeships along with psychology coursework and clinical fieldwork to enhance students' credentials for entry into competitive graduate programs.

An eighth and final avenue toward acquiring research competencies is restricted to master's students. A comprehensive paper or a formal master's thesis, requiring original research, practically guarantees additional experience with research. For this reason, undergraduates denied admission directly into doctoral programs frequently enter master's programs to gain valuable research (and clinical) competencies. And remember: the majority of clinical psychology doctoral programs prefer master's-level applicants to have completed a thesis (Piotrowski & Keller, 1996).

Whichever avenue you eventually pursue, the procedures are quite similar. Following is a step-by-step guide to help you make the most of your research experience.

Determining Your Interests

The initial step is finding a research area that interests you. If you are not interested in the work, it will diminish your energy and enthusiasm and probably your decision to apply to graduate school. A good place to begin is to read through your department brochure or website describing faculty interests and current research. If you are out of school, check with a local university. Visit with the Director of Psychology Advising or the Director of Undergraduate Studies in the psychology department (if a large university) or the department chairperson (if a smaller college) to discuss research possibilities. Speak to other students in the major about potential faculty mentors. Look for professors who have a proven track record of scholarly publications.

Once you have a list of faculty interests, you may find someone interesting but not be sure exactly what the research is all about ("I've heard about autism and think I'd like to study it, but I don't know much about it . . . "). If publications are not provided on the departmental website, or if reprints are not posted in the department, then you can go to *PsycLIT* or *PsycINFO* (found in most university libraries; ask at the reference desk) and read what that professor has published in the area over the last 5 to 7 years. This should make it easier to decide which professors you would like to volunteer to conduct research with. *Do not narrow your choices too quickly!* Find at least two or three professors whose work initially interests you.

Selecting Professors

Next, find out more about that professor as a person. Do you know people who have taken a class with him or her? What did they think? Are there other undergraduate or graduate students working with this professor now? What do they do, and what is it like working under this person? Is the professor easy to get along with? Is the professor helpful to students?

Having narrowed the choice to two or three professors whose research interests you and with whom you think you might get along, consider the rank of the professor. There are tenured faculty (a *full* or *associate* professor) and untenured (an *assistant* professor), both with respective advantages and disadvantages.

Full or associate professors have been in the field longer and will probably have colleagues at other universities. If the professor is well known, it gives your letter of recommendation that much more weight. If your professor's reputation in the discipline is strong, with a long list of publications, you are also likely to learn more and increase your own attractiveness as a candidate. However, once a faculty member becomes tenured, he or she is no longer under the same pressure to produce research as when he or she was pursuing tenure. Certainly if these faculty members are still conducting and publishing research and applying for grants, they are likely to be committed to maintaining their productivity. Regardless, you should establish that tenured faculty are actively engaged in research and are currently publishing their work, probably by reviewing their faculty website, their online CV, or list of recent publications.

Assistant professors are newer to the field, probably 1 to 7 years post doctorate. They often need more undergraduate help and may involve you to your full potential. The possibility of being included on a research presentation or publication as a coauthor may also be increased. New assistant professors, in particular, may not yet have students but may have start-up funds for their research. What they lack in terms of a reputation built on years of publications may be balanced by their energy and their motivation to produce.

Some professors maintain large research facilities and employ vast numbers of undergraduates to help them with their data collection and management. If there are 10 undergraduates working in a lab, the attention given to each individual decreases, as well as the value of the research experience. On the other hand, some large laboratories provide unique research opportunities unavailable elsewhere. The key is to talk to students who have worked there to learn about their experiences and to determine if former students have had success applying to graduate school.

An optimal research context, then, is one in which a faculty member or research mentor has an established reputation in his or her field of inquiry, a record of producing publishable research, similar interests to your own, a history of working successfully with students, a propensity to share authorship credit with students, and the ability to construct discrete research projects. Be guided by these general principles in selecting professors to approach, but do not expect all these qualities to be available to you.

Making Initial Contact

Having chosen a professor or researcher with whom you would like to work, it is now time to make yourself known to him or her. Schedule an appointment or approach the professor during posted office hours. It is natural for you to feel nervous! However, the more familiar with his or her work you are, the more secure you are likely to feel. Once again, read what the professor has written. Additionally, it helps to remember that you are coming to the professor to offer your free services.

A good opening line might be, "Hello, Dr. Jones, my name is Chris Smith. I've been doing some reading on autism and came across several articles you've written. I'm pretty interested and was wondering if I could help with your research projects." As the conversation progresses, let the professor know your long-term goals as well as your immediate desire both to contribute as a member of the research team and to acquire research skills. Let him or her know you are seriously considering graduate study in clinical or counseling psychology—it will increase your appeal.

By way of a summary, here are a dozen steps in asking for a research assistantship (or teaching assistantship)

- Go during office hours
- Bring a CV or resume
- Begin with small talk (schmooze a bit)
- Express interest in the professor's research
- Manifest positive nonverbal behaviors
- Ask explicitly to serve as a research assistant
- Explain why you quality for the position
- Identify the time period or semesters
- Request a decision date
- Thank the professor for his or her time
- Follow-up on or after that decision date
- Have a backup plan (a Plan B)

Negotiating Research Responsibilities

"Well Mr./Ms. Smith, I'd be interested in speaking with you about helping with my research . . . " You have made the contact. If the professor does not need help, you have lost nothing and gained experience in asking. Inquire if he or she knows of someone with similar interests who is looking for help, or simply approach the next person on your list.

After the initial contact, your next move is dictated by your professor's needs and your abilities. Regardless of all your wonderful qualities, be prepared to run some of the grunt work! Photocopying needs to be done, literature searches need to be conducted, and at times you might well be expected to do some lab cleanup. You are "low on the totem pole," so approach this with humility. But if you have experience with test administration or statistical analysis, let the professor know, being aware that ultimately your activities will be dictated by his or her needs. However, if grunt work is the full extent of your duties, your needs are not being addressed properly. Spending a year doing nothing but photocopying or proofreading would constitute a waste of time.

Research experience is, above all, an opportunity to learn. Volunteer to be trained to be of more use. For example, learn the computer skills to input data and conduct statistical analyses. Learn to score and, more importantly, to *understand* a Minnesota Multiphasic Personality Inventory-2 (MMPI-2) or a Beck Depression Inventory (BDI-II). Learn how to calibrate and run psychophysiological equipment. Learn what you can about the various equipment or tests in use. And continuously ask questions about what you do not understand. When it comes time to put your research on your curriculum vitae, these are the responsibilities you will list.

Some researchers have a weekly lab group or research meeting with graduate students, undergraduates, or both. These might entail a discussion of the project at hand, a presentation on another area within psychology, or a training session for new people. In any of these cases, it is an opportunity to learn more about your area of interest. If you have not been invited to these meetings, go ahead and ask about them. Optimize your contact with your professor! Convey your willingness and enthusiasm. Give your professor reason to write an outstanding letter of recommendation.

Finally, there are instances where undergraduates are supervised solely by graduate students and have little contact with the professor in charge of the project. This can happen if faculty members have a large number of students working with them or if they are well known and are continually approached by masses of students. Being supervised exclusively by a graduate student can be an undesirable situation for a potential applicant. Although there is much to be learned from graduate students—and they are fresh from the application process themselves—a letter of recommendation from a graduate student does not carry nearly the same weight as one from a professor. Moreover, a lack of interaction with the professor means that he or she must depend solely on graduate students for feedback on your work, thus detracting from the value of his or her assessment.

This is *not* to say that you must avoid research opportunities that are primarily supervised by graduate students. Again, find out how undergraduates in prior years have fared coming out of this lab. In sum, personal access to the faculty member is one of several factors to be considered in your decision on where to volunteer for research experience.

Arranging Credit and Semesters

Most colleges allow students to complete a certain amount of research experience for academic credit. If the opportunity is available, take advantage of it. Some professors may even demand that you sign up for credit, because it institutes a contract between them and you about the number of hours per week required and how long they can count on you to work with them. Generally speaking, multiply the number of course credits by 3, and this will give you the number of weekly hours that you will spend performing research activities.

Expect to spend two semesters on a project. This demonstrates your commitment and allows ample contact between you and your professor. Thus, work with someone an entire year before you plan to apply to graduate school. For instance, begin research in fall 2018 if you are applying in fall 2019 for a fall 2020 entrance to graduate school.

In consultation with your faculty advisor, consider applying for a university or national grant to fund your research project. These grant monies may be used to purchase equipment, pay postage for surveys, reimburse research participants for their time, and send you to a convention to present your findings. In most colleges and universities, these small grants are called undergraduate research grants, summer research fellowships, or something similar. At the University of Scranton, for example, the President's Fellowships for Summer Research allow undergraduates to live on campus free for the summer, provide a tidy stipend, contribute up to $500 for research materials, and fund travel to a conference to present the research. At the national level, Psi Chi and several publishers provide small awards and grants for research. Go to www.psichi.org/awards to access the list.

In terms of research, there is no such thing as too much for a Ph.D. applicant. The longer you have worked on a project and the greater your responsibilities, the more attractive you are as an applicant. Ideally, you would work with two professors over the course of your undergraduate education. This is not necessary, but when schools expect three letters of recommendation, having two letters summarizing two different research experiences is particularly strong. Although they will allocate less time to research than Ph.D. applicants, Psy.D. applicants are reminded that research is still a valued admission criterion.

One word of caution: do not overextend yourself. Be realistic about the amount of time you can commit. Some students juggle two or three research projects at once and end up performing poorly on them all. Far more important to concentrate your energies and perform solidly on one project than it is to spread yourself too thin. Conduct as much research as your academic studies and other commitments allow.

An ideal time to begin research is during the summer, when you can balance it with a part- or full-time job. Since most undergraduates and some graduate students leave during the summer, professors may be short-staffed during this period. It is a prime opportunity to optimize your usefulness at the outset and increase your chances of picking up desirable skills.

The net result of your research experiences will be skill enhancement and professional identification. Depending on the nature of your project, you will probably have engaged in a literature search, hypothesis generation, experimental design, data collection, statistical analyses, and the write-up.

Presenting and Publishing Research

Presenting or publishing your research is a definite asset. Opportunities for presentation are numerous: a department or university colloquium, a local or regional undergraduate psychology conference, an annual conference of a professional organization, a state or national psychology convention. Participation in research conferences is viewed favorably as an index of your professional identification and scholarly commitment. Check with your advisor or mentor about these and other possibilities for your work to be seen by colleagues.

Publication of your research in a scholarly journal is held in high regard by graduate admissions committees. As we discuss in Chapter 7, research experience leading to a coauthored publication is the most highly rated final selection criterion for Ph.D. (though not necessarily Psy.D.) admission decisions following the interview. The peer-review process by which journals accept papers for publication gives a seal of collegial affirmation that the research contributes to the scientific understanding of behavior. Although not common, undergraduate publication is slowly becoming more frequent.

If your research project is not quite up to the standards of a competitive, peer-reviewed journal, then consider sending the paper to a journal publishing student research in psychology. One such publication is the *Psi Chi Journal of Psychological Research*, which is uniquely dedicated to educating and promoting professional development of undergraduate psychology students. Other publications for student research in psychology include *Modern Psychological Studies*, *Journal of Psychology and Behavioral Sciences*, and *Journal of Psychological Inquiry*. All these journals publish research in psychology conducted and written by students. Look for their instructions to authors on departmental bulletin boards or in *Eye on Psi Chi* (the newsletter of Psi Chi).

Of course, though submission to these journals can be instructive, publishing in them does not carry as much weight as publication in established peer-reviewed journals. In fact, research suggests that a student publication in an undergraduate journal may be judged neutral or even unfavorably by research-oriented professors in a doctoral program (Ferrari & Hemovich, 2004). So, aim to publish your research in peer-reviewed, scholarly journals.

Still impressive is a paper/poster presentation at a state, regional, or national meeting. Only between 10% and 20% of undergraduate psychology majors present their research at a research conference, whether local, regional, or national (Terry, 1996; Titus & Buxman, 1999).

Most regional and national meetings are listed in each issue of the *American Psychologist*, *APS Observer*, and *Eye on Psi Chi*. These meetings are also listed on the Psi Chi website. Psi Chi members who present papers can receive a certificate recognizing their excellence in research. This award should be duly noted on your curriculum vitae and application. Refer to *Eye on Psi Chi*, ask your local Psi Chi moderator or consult their website at www.psichi.org/pdf/postcert.pdf to receive the form entitled "Certificate Recognition Program for Paper Presentations by Psi Chi Members."

Different graduate programs will assess your research experience in different ways, of course. Nonetheless, as an aid to applicants, we reproduce below (with permission) two rating scales employed by one Ph.D. clinical program (University of Rhode Island) over the past dozen years. The first rating scale emphasizes research activity. Examples of relevant activities might include producing honors theses, serving as a research assistant, conducting independent research, coauthoring scientific publications, and developing research skills, such as data analysis and interviewing.

Rating	Criteria
5	Senior author of one or more articles in significant journals in addition to experience that provided a basis for extensive mastery of one or more directly related research skills.
4	Coauthor of one or more articles in significant journals in addition to experiences providing considerable familiarity with one or more directly relevant research skills.
3	Project leadership or significant participation in research activity (beyond activities

connected with coursework) serving to provide for considerable development of mastery of one or more relevant research skills.

2 Experience that provides a basis for some familiarity with relevant research skills.

1 Little if any experience according to these criteria.

The second rating scale, now in use at the University of Rhode Island, favors four criteria in evaluating research experience.

1. *Demonstrated research productivity:* sole or co-authorship of research publications, presentation of papers at scientific meetings, other tangible indications of research achievement.
2. *Breadth and quality of experience:* development of one or more research skills, data collection with different populations, work on more than one project.
3. *Research interest:* the strength of interest in research can be inferred from research activity over a sustained period of time and recommendations from research supervisors documenting skills, motivation, participation, and accomplishments.
4. *Individual autonomy:* responsibility for planning, implementing, and carrying out research tasks as a member of a research team or evidence of independent work.

Rankings are based on the aforementioned criteria and assigned as follows:

Rating	Criteria
5	Satisfies all four criteria
4	Satisfies three criteria
3	Satisfies two criteria
2	Satisfies one criterion
1	Evidence of some prior research involvement or interest

Balance is the key. On the one hand, an absence of research experience is usually seen as a serious drawback to an application to a doctoral psychology program. On the other hand, over committing yourself to multiple projects simultaneously can lead to poor performance and a neglect of clinical experience and GRE preparation. And do not forget: research also provides you with professional networking contacts. The professors or graduate students with whom you collaborate are excellent sources of information about the discipline and about applying to graduate school.

Entrance Examinations

About 90% of doctoral clinical psychology programs, 82% of doctoral counseling psychology programs, and 81% of master's psychology programs require you to complete the Graduate Record Examination (GRE) General Test (Pagano, Wicherski, & Kohout, 2010; Turkson & Norcross, 1996). Fewer will also require the GRE Psychology Subject Test. The two GRE tests are often used to complement each other in admission decisions because the General Test is a measure of broad abilities and the Subject Test is an index of achievement in a specific field of study. The Miller Analogies Test (MAT) is required by fewer programs, about 3% of graduate programs in psychology (Murray & Williams, 1999; Norcross et al., 2005).

Blanket statements about entrance exams remain difficult because not all schools require all tests, and some schools require additional testing (for example, in the past the University of Minnesota required clinical psychology applicants to take the MMPI—a personality and psychopathology inventory!). Moreover, not all schools weight these test scores equally among the admission criteria. Some schools clearly state a minimum score that all applicants must obtain, whereas others state that they have no such criteria.

Interestingly, a study showed that even without an imposed cutoff, applicants admitted into its program had GRE scores of 600 or better, or about 160 on the revised scale (Rem, Oren, & Childrey, 1987). This suggests that, even if a program does not emphasize entrance exams, (1) scores can still play a major role in the selection of candidates, or (2) applicants with high exam scores are also the applicants considered most desirable on the other admissions criteria.

Consequently, the best assistance that we can offer is a brief description of each test, an overview of minimum and actual GRE scores of incoming graduate students, guidelines for deciding how much preparation will be needed, and suggestions as to the study aids for each test.

GRE General Test

Use of GRE scores for admission to clinical and counseling psychology programs continues to be the norm and to be controversial (Dollinger, 1989; Ingram, 1983; Sternberg, 1997). The traditional rationale—buttressed by some evidence—is that the GRE is ordinarily more valid than undergraduate GPA in predicting graduate school success (Goldberg & Alliger, 1992; Kuncel & Hezlett, 2010). Research indicates that, inside the deliberations of graduate admissions committees, GRE scores are accorded priority beyond what most departments would admit or that creators of the test would advise (Posselt, 2016).

Another rationale is that GRE performance is an "equalizer" among the diverse curriculum requirements and grading practices in thousands of undergraduate institutions. As one member of an admissions committee complained, "Grades are increasingly a lousy signal, especially at those elite places that just hand out A's" (Posselt, 2016). The entrance exam is probably the only standardized measure of all applicants that an admissions committee has. Does a 3.7 GPA and stellar letters of recommendation from a small local college reflect more, the same, or less knowledge than a 3.3 GPA and strong letters of recommendation from an Ivy League university? Since all students take the identical GRE test, the playing field is leveled.

Decades of research indicate that the GRE General Test has moderate predictive validity for graduate school performance. A meta-analysis of studies conducted in psychology and counseling departments found that GRE scores predicted about 8% of the variance in graduate school grades (Goldberg & Alliger, 1992). A later meta-analysis of two dozen studies encompassing more than 5,000 test takers similarly reported that 6% of the variance in graduate-level academic achievement was accounted for by GRE scores (Morrison & Morrison, 1995). These and other studies indicate that GRE General Test scores are generalizably valid in a modest way for all sorts of measures of graduate performance, especially when selection/admission ratios are taken into account (Kuncel & Hezlett, 2010).

At the same time, several concerns about relying on GREs also receive support from the research. Socioeconomic status (SES) does relate to test performance, and members of certain ethnic groups tend to score lower than other groups, but GREs predict graduate performance across SES and for all ethnic groups (Sackett et al., 2009). Moreover, Subject Test scores tend to be better predictors of graduate performance than the General Test scores (Kuncel, Hezlett, & Ones, 2001), but programs overwhelmingly look at the General Test scores.

Information about the GRE and registering to take it are all online at www.ets.org/gre/ or www.gre.org. Bookmark that site as you will return to it frequently. At the website you can order (with a credit card) test preparation books and download preparation software.

The test is similar in format to the Scholastic Aptitude Test (SAT) or the American College Test (ACT, minus the science part) that most of you took prior to college. The three GRE scales are Verbal Reasoning (V), Quantitative Reasoning (Q), and Analytical Writing (AW). The Verbal and Quantitative scales are multiple-choice in format, and scores on the test are based on the number of correct answers selected. Most graduate schools rely on the Verbal and Quantitative scores in evaluating candidates.

The Analytical Writing (AW) section is delivered on the computer, and you word-process responses. It is designed to measure your ability to articulate and support complex ideas, examine claims and accompanying evidence, and express the elements of standard written English.

You will write two separate essays. For the "Analyze an Issue" task, you will choose one of two essay topics selected by the computer from a larger pool. For the "Analyze an Argument" task, you do not have a choice of topics; the computer will present you with a single topic for which you provide a critical, logical analysis.

Your essays are read and scored by two trained raters using a holistic 6-point scale (scoring guidelines can be found at www.ets.org/gre/revised_general/scores/?WT.ac). Your Analytical Writing (AW) score is reported on a 0–6 scale in half-point increments. On average, students score 4.2 on the AW, with psychology majors scoring slightly higher at 4.4 (ETS, 2007). Since the AW test is relatively recent, many graduate schools are not placing as much emphasis on it as the Verbal and Quantitative scores in admission decisions.

In August 2011, the GRE General Test was extensively revised and introduced a new score scale. In place of the original 200 to 800 score range in 10-point increments, the Verbal Reasoning and Quantitative Reasoning scores are now presented on a 130 to 170 scale in 1-point increments. (The Analytical Writing scores continue to be reported on the 0–6 scale.) The purpose of compressing the reporting metric is to produce scores that don't exaggerate small performance differences among students.

The scale change caused havoc for both programs and applicants, as some graduate programs continue to report average scores on the old scale and as applicants struggle to compare scores on the new test with scores on the old test. In fact, we report GRE scores in this book as a mix of the old scale and the new scale, as some graduate programs have not yet had sufficient experience with the new scale! The mix of new scores and old scores will fade out in 2018 as GRE scores are valid and reported for five years. At www.gre.org, you will find useful information on understanding the 130–170 scores, using the percentile ranks, and even a video on interpreting them.

Type "GRE concordance" into any Internet search engine to get a copy of the concordance tables showing the equivalence of the old scores (200 to 800) to the new scores (130 to 170). We suggest that you bookmark the site (www.ets.org/s/gre/pdf/concordance_information.pdf) on your computer or smartphone as you will probably be returning to it repeatedly during the application and admission process.

The Quantitative (Q) Reasoning section expects you to know arithmetic, algebra, geometry, probability, and statistics, and it allows you to use an on-screen calculator. Calculus is not needed for, or covered on, the quant section.

The Verbal (V) Reasoning section measures your ability to analyze written material, understand the meaning of words and sentences in context, and comprehend relationships among concepts. The dreaded antonyms and analogies are gone, replaced with additional questions on reasoning skills and reading comprehension. Text completion questions provide a short narrative with certain words omitted from the passage; your task is to select the word that best fits the targeted omission.

The GRE General Test continues to be a computer adaptive test, meaning that correct answers to early questions lead to more difficult subsequent questions. This is not question by question but section by section, so that within a section, you can skip a question and return to it later.

This 3-hour, 45-minute computer-based test begins with the Analytical Writing section. That's followed, in any order, by two Verbal sections, two Quantitative sections, and one unscored section. Within any section, you can skip a question and come back to it later, if you like. Within any section, you can also revise and edit your answers. All told, you will probably spend about 4 to 5 hours at the testing center.

When you complete all sections of the GRE at the testing center, you will be asked on the computer screen three questions: Do you want to cancel your scores? If not, would you like the "Most Recent Option" of sending your scores from only your current test administration or the "All Option" of sending your scores from all General Test administrations in the last five years? And, to which four graduate schools would you like your free score reports sent?

If you do *not* cancel your scores, then your Verbal and Quantitative scores are immediately presented on the computer screen. Your Analytical Writing score will arrive in another 4 weeks or so. If you cancel your scores, then you are not provided with those scores.

The GRE ScoreSelect option lets you decide which GRE scores to send to graduate schools. But now it gets a little complicated. On test day, when viewing your scores at the test center, you can choose to submit your most recent scores or all of them. After test day, when you send additional score reports for a fee, you can opt to submit to graduate schools the scores from the most recent test administration, scores from all test administrations, or from one or as many test administrations as you like from the last five years. That is, after test day and for a fee, you have greater options.

In all cases, you select scores for a particular *test date*. Thus, you cannot pick, say, your Quantitative score from one test administration and your Verbal score from another test date. All scores obtained on a test date are sent.

The folks at GRE advertise the ScoreSelect option as presenting your best to graduate programs. Since it is a relatively new option with the test, it is too early to determine how graduate admission committees will use and interpret receipt of a select subset of your GRE scores. Nonetheless, it is obviously in your best interest to submit only your highest scores.

The testing center consists of multiple cubicles, each containing a computer station. The center may be noisy, so many of our students recommend wearing ear plugs or accepting the offered headphones to minimize the extraneous noise and to enhance your concentration.

Testing centers must maintain test security, so many centers resemble a lockdown and perform airport-level screening. You will probably be asked to empty your pockets and turn them inside out, lift your pants or shirts half-way for inspection, and be subjected to a magnetic wand passing over your body. Some test-takers are unnerved by the presence of cameras in the center (or above the cubicle). But knowing all of these security precautions in advance will probably decrease your anxiety.

The GRE registration booklet and the free tutorial software (POWER PREP II, available off of your new favorite, www.gre.org or www.ets.org/gre/) will familiarize you with the computer-based adaptive format of the Verbal and Quantitative sections. These and other resources will also prepare you for the Analytical Writing section. You should be exquisitely familiar with the test format and computer functions before test day!

In deciding how much and what type of preparation you will need for the Revised General Test, ask yourself several questions:

1. What were my SAT (or ACT) scores? These two tests are highly correlated, so this may be your first clue as to how much preparation is ahead of you.
2. How well have I done on multiple-choice tests in college? There is a certain savvy to taking standardized tests, and this is one way to assess yours.
3. How anxious do I become in a testing situation? A moderate amount of test anxiety is optimal: too little anxiety can breed indifference, but too much begets interference (you may recognize this relationship between arousal and performance as the Yerkes–Dodson Law). If you tend to experience tests with more than moderate discomfort, you might benefit from additional preparation aimed at relaxing yourself and building your confidence.
4. Can I discipline myself to do the necessary studying? Be honest with yourself. If you cannot imagine sitting down regularly and studying independently for the GREs, you might be better off taking a preparatory course offered online or privately in most cities.

Students typically spend an inordinate amount of time worrying about the GREs. The myth exists that clinical applicants need a score of 160 on each of their scales to be considered seriously. This is simply not the case. Some Psy.D. programs do not even require the GREs. On the other hand, many APA-approved Ph.D. programs prefer GREs of 150 or above. The average GRE score (combined Verbal and Quantitative) of first-year graduate students in psychology master's programs is 299; in doctoral psychology programs, 308 (Norcross et al., 2005).

However, even these averages mask considerable variation in preferred minimum GRE scores. In our studies of the admission statistics of APA-accredited clinical programs (Mayne et al., 1994; Turkson & Norcross, 1996), we found that the preferred minimum scores differed consistently according to the type of program. As shown in Table 3-3, research-oriented clinical Ph.D. programs preferred the highest GRE scores—about 150 each for the Quantitative and Verbal scales. Psy.D. programs were willing to accept lower (but still not low) minimum GRE scores—about 145 each on the two scales (Turkson & Norcross, 1996).

Remember that these are the *minimum* scores for admission consideration, not the average scores of accepted students. Those scores are higher than the minimums, of course. Please pay more attention to the average scores of incoming students; the minimum required scores are at the lowest end of acceptable scores to get in the door.

Table 3-4 provides the *average* GRE scores of incoming clinical psychology students across the practice–research continuum. As seen there, the research-oriented Ph.D. programs demand the highest scores: 152 Quantitative, 160 Verbal, and 683 Psychology Subject Test on average. (And if you apply to PCSAS programs, the average scores will probably be even higher (Sayette et al., 2011). Students entering the equal-emphasis programs tend to score a bit lower, followed by students enrolling in university-based Psy.D. programs. Our past research indicates that students entering freestanding Psy.D. programs tend to score lower than students entering the other types of programs; however, of late, those programs have been steadily not requiring or not reporting GRE scores. That's why average scores for students

TABLE 3-3. Minimum GRE Scores Preferred by APA-Accredited Clinical Psychology Programs

	Psy.D. programs	Practice-oriented Ph.D.	Equal-emphasis Ph.D.	Research-oriented Ph.D.	All programs
Preferred minimum score	*M*	*M*	*M*	*M*	*M*
Quantitative scale	145	147	147	148	147
Verbal scale	155	158	158	160	158
Psychology subject test	542	601	581	605	587

Note. Adapted from Mayne, Norcross, & Sayette (1994) and Turkson & Norcross (1996).

TABLE 3-4. Average GRE Scores of Incoming Students in APA-Accredited Clinical Psychology Programs

GRE scores	Freestanding Psy.D. programs *M*	University-based Psy.D. programs *M*	Equal-emphasis Ph.D. *M*	Research-oriented Ph.D. *M*	All programs *M*
Quantitative scale	—	148	151	152	151
Verbal scale	—	156	159	160	159
Analytical writing	—	4.7	4.9	5.1	4.9
Psychology subject test	—	644	669	683	672

Note. Adapted from Norcross, Ellis, & Sayette (2010).

in freestanding Psy.D. programs are not reported in Table 3-4; only 22% of those programs reported such scores (Norcross et al., 2010).

The take-home point here is that the more research-oriented the doctoral program, the more stringent the admission requirements in terms of GREs and GPAs. The payoff for the more stringent admission requirements is far more financial assistance and far less debt, as we detail in Chapter 5.

Even if your scores are lower than 145, you can bolster other areas of your application to overcome low scores. But if your GRE scores are below 140, then most Ph.D. programs will not seriously consider your application. In this case, it will probably be necessary to take them again after completing a preparatory course or after spending time with a study guide. Or you may decide to apply to Psy.D. and master's programs as well.

Overconfidence can be disastrous here. Even if you obtained 700 SATs, aced every multiple-choice exam in college, and are cool-headed in testing situations, you still must familiarize yourself with the test format and complete the practice test offered in the application booklet. It certainly would not hurt to prepare more, but this should be considered the bare minimum.

Many self-study manuals and software packages are sufficient for a disciplined applicant to ready him or herself for the GRE. These resources provide helpful test-taking hints, vocabulary and math reviews, and sample tests that the student can self-administer. Many include actual questions given on past GREs that can provide a real flavor for the material you will see on testing day. Sample questions and downloadable practice software can also be ordered on the official GRE website at www.gre.com.

In addition to the official site, several commercial Internet sites provide valuable tips and full-length practice tests. Some of the material is offered for free; some offered for a price. Visit:

- www.princetonreview.com/gre
- www.kaptest.com/GRE/
- www.mygretutor.com
- www.greguide.com/

We heartily recommend taking an online GRE practice or diagnostic test. A practice GRE test serves as a diagnostic tool to assess your abilities, gauges your competitiveness for admission to graduate programs, and identifies areas that need further improvement (Walfish, 2004). Our favorites are the practice GRE tests at www.kaplan.com and www.princetonreview.com. These are free and confidential; use the practice test as a starting point.

Lastly, give yourself *at least* 6 weeks of study time if you decide to prepare for the GRE on your own and *at least* 8 weeks if you do not have a lot of time to devote solely to studying.

Figure 3-1 provides a worksheet for preparing on your own for the GRE General Test. It has proven a "winner" with our own students in scheduling the administration date and in decreasing their anxiety. The worksheet walks you step-by-step through the process.

Students feeling less confident, more anxious, or "out of the exam business" should contemplate private courses designed to help you prepare for the GRE. They offer a number of benefits beyond those of study guides:

- A structured time each week when the material is taught by an impartial instructor who can assess your strengths and weaknesses
- An abundance of study materials and the possibility of individual tutoring

Today's date: ______________________

When do you plan to take the GRE for the first time? ______________________

Describe how you will prepare for the GRE.

____

____

____

What GRE study resources do you have now?

____

____

____

What GRE study resources do you need to obtain soon?

____

____

____

Have you used the free GRE PowerPrep II? Yes ____ No ____

If no, please go to the ETS website (www.ets.org/gre/revised_general/prepare/powerprep2)

Have you completed a free GRE diagnostic or prognostic test? Yes ____ No ____

If no, please go to Princeton (www.princetonreview.com/grad/free-gre-practice-test#!practice) and/or Kaplan (www.kaptest.com/gre/gre-practice/free-gre-practice-test)

How many hours have you studied *as of the date* you are completing this form? ____ hours

How many total hours do you plan to study? ____ hours

How many weeks are there between now and the date of your scheduled GRE? ____ weeks

Write how many hours you will spend per week on dedicated GRE preparation (use as many weeks as applies to your situation):

Week 1: ____ hours	Week 2: ____ hours	Week 3: ____ hours
Week 4: ____ hours	Week 5: ____ hours	Week 6: ____ hours
Week 7: ____ hours	Week 8: ____ hours	Week 9: ____ hours
Week 10: ____ hours	Week 11: ____ hours	Week 12: ____ hours

Can you realistically dedicate that much time each week? Yes ____ No ____

If yes, congratulations. If no, please rethink your timetable.

FIGURE 3-1. Worksheet for GRE General Test preparation.

- The chance to take the entrance exams under actual test-taking conditions (especially helpful for those with test anxiety)
- Specific work on test-taking skills and the shortcuts that can make problems easier
- Brief introduction to relaxation exercises that can counter test anxiety

The imposed structure on studying and the deliberate use of test-taking skills can prove useful. Although these classes cannot guarantee that they will improve your scores, they are undoubtedly the best course of action for many students. Having advised graduate-school applicants for several decades now, we have repeatedly witnessed the benefits of these formal GRE prep courses.

Many students attempt to strengthen their vocabulary for the GRE Verbal section by preparing flashcards or memorizing a vocabulary word each day. The early research on the word-a-day method suggests it can slightly enrich your vocabulary (Prevoznak & Bubka, 1999), but more importantly, it gets you into the swing of GRE preparation and the admissions process. If you are inclined to try this method, consider receiving a word a day from the app at Dictionary.com or the website www.wordsmith.org, both of which present a word with its pronunciation and examples. Or try the vocabulary builders at www.supervoca.com/gre.php and www.number2.com. They require only a couple of minutes per day.

Scheduling *when* to take your general GRE should be carefully considered. If you do poorly on the test, you can retake it. Consequently, it is prudent to take it at least 6 months before the application deadline, which gives you time to study and prepare for a second administration. For undergraduates planning to apply to doctoral programs during their senior year, this means taking it during the summer following your junior year or early fall of the senior year. For those who have already graduated, this means taking it the late spring or summer before you plan to apply.

We are frequently asked by students in our graduate school workshops if they should retake the GRE General Test if they are dissatisfied with their original scores. Our immediate answer is: it depends. If you studied diligently for the test and performed similarly to the practice tests and your SAT scores, then no—probably do not retake the test.

But if any of the following factors apply to you, then retaking the test seems like a good idea (Keith-Spiegel & Wiederman, 2000):

- You were ill the day you took the GRE
- You were distracted by test anxiety
- You did not prepare sufficiently for the test
- You were unfamiliar with or confused by the computer-based format
- Your SAT scores were much higher than your GRE scores
- Your scores on the GRE practice/diagnostic tests were consistently higher than your actual GRE scores

Should you decide to retake the GRE General Test, please be aware of the probable effects of repeating it. The average score gain for repeaters is about 2 points on both the Verbal scale and the Quantitative scale. Increases of more than 8 points rarely occur, in only 1 or 2% of repeaters (ETS, 2011).

The vast majority of graduate schools take the highest combination of your various GRE scores. Say you scored 154 Verbal and 148 Quantitative the first time, and 157 Verbal and 147 Quantitative the second time. Most graduate programs will calculate your scores for admission purposes as 157 Verbal and 148 Quantitative.

We have not said much about your score on the third GRE scale: the Analytical Writing (AW) test. That's because only about 35% of psychology graduate programs are using it in their admissions process (Briihl & Wasieleski, 2007). Programs using the AW rated it as medium or low in importance in their admissions decisions. Few programs have minimum or cutoff scores for the AW (Briihl & Wasieleski, 2007).

Thus, your GRE scores are still widely calculated as the sum of your Verbal and Quantitative scores—known respectively as the GRE-V and the GRE-Q. Keep in mind, though, that particular professors who are interested in working with you (especially true at research-oriented Ph.D. programs) may decide to weight your various GRE scores differently than what their program suggests. Consequently, all your scores—including the AW—may come into play.

Your GRE General Test scores can partially determine where to apply. Low scores suggest applying only to institutions whose minimum scores you surpass or who do not require the test. In this way, your GREs can help you make realistic decisions as to your chances of being accepted at a given school and ultimately whether to apply there.

GRE Psychology Subject Test

The General Test measures knowledge acquired over a long period of time and not indigenous to any specific field of study. By contrast, the Subject Tests—such as the Psychology Subject Test—assume an undergraduate major or extensive background in the specific subject. Consequently, the test may be relatively difficult if you were not an undergraduate psychology major.

Another difference between the General Test and the Subject Test lies in the mode of administration. The General Test is a computer-based test available year-round at over 850 test centers. The Subject Test, by contrast, continues to be a paper-based test offered three times during the academic year (September, October, and April).

Table 3-5 summarizes the differences between the GRE Revised General Test and the GRE Subject Test. These profound test differences will lead to different preparation and test-taking strategies on your part.

The GRE Psychology Test consists of about 205 multiple-choice questions. Each item has five options, from which you select the correct or best response. The total time allotted for the test is 2 hours and 50 minutes.

The GRE Psychology Test yields a total score and two subscores. The possible scores range from 200 to 990 in 10-point increments. Virtually all graduate programs concentrate on the total score, not on the subscores. The preferred minimum score is 587 for clinical psychology doctoral programs and 541 for counseling psychology doctoral programs (Mayne et al., 1994; Turkson & Norcross, 1996). That is, most programs will expect you to secure a score at or above this number. But here again, as shown in Table 3-3, the preferred minimum ranges from a low of 542 in Psy.D. programs to a high of 605 in research-oriented Ph.D. programs.

The two subscales are an Experimental or natural science orientation (about 40% of the items) and a Social or social science orientation (about 43% of the items). The Experimental subscore covers questions in learning, language, memory, thinking, sensation, perception, and physiological/behavioral neuroscience. The Social subscore includes about an equal number of questions in personality, clinical, abnormal, lifespan developmental, and social psychology. Other areas of psychology—especially measurement and methodology—are tested and included in your total score but not in your two subscores.

Percentages of questions devoted to a subject area will fluctuate from one test administration to another. Nonetheless, the general breakdown of the test content looks like this (ETS, 2011):

TABLE 3-5. Comparison of the GRE Revised General Test and the GRE Psychology Subject Test

	Revised General Test	Psychology Subject Test
Content assessed	Broad knowledge	Specific knowledge in psychology
Test format	Computer	Paper-and-pencil
Administration schedule	Throughout the year	Three times per year (Sep., Oct., & Apr.)
Recommended test date	Summer of junior year Early Fall of senior year	Sep. or Oct. for Ph.D./Psy.D. applicants November for master's applicants
Administration format	Individual	Group
Test cost (2016–2017)	$205	$150
Repeat policy	May repeat test once every 21 days up to 5 times per year	May repeat test as often as it is offered
Testing time	3 hours, 45 minutes	2 hours, 50 minutes
Scoring procedure	Adaptive: your responses determine difficulty level of subsequent questions in that section	Total items answered correctly minus one-fourth the number answered incorrectly
Skipping questions	Permitted within sections; computer administers one question at a time	Permitted
Scores provided	3 scores (Verbal Reasoning, Quantitative Reasoning, Analytical Writing)	1 total score, 2 subscores
Scores range	130–170 for Verbal and Quantitative; 0–6 for Analytical Writing	200–990
Scores mean (SD)	150 (9)	540 (100)
Recommended preparation	Intense	Moderate

Physiological/behavioral neuroscience	13%
Lifespan development	13%
Clinical and abnormal psychology	13%
Social psychology	13%
Measurement and methodology	12%
Memory	8%
Sensation and perception	6%
Thinking and cognition	5%
General (e.g., history, I/O)	5%
Personality	4%
Learning	4%
Language	3%

Scores on the GRE Psychology Test are best predicted by your GRE General Test scores and the number of basic psychology courses completed. The irony is that students can obtain excellent grades in all their psychology courses but still not perform adequately on the Psychology Test if they have not taken the critical courses. A narrow focus on—and many courses in—clinical psychology or counseling will probably detract from your score since this one area only accounts for 13% of the test items. The questions are drawn from courses most commonly offered at the undergraduate level within psychology (ETS, 2011).

A maximum number of "traditional" courses in psychology, as represented in the foregoing list, and a minimum of special topics and "pop" psychology will prepare you best for the GRE Psychology Subject Test. Choose your elective courses for breadth and rigor, not merely your specialized interest.

The GRE Psychology Subject Test is designed to be challenging. Students accustomed to getting 90% correct on in-class exams often worry about the large number of items they miss. The average student answers about half the items correctly, misses about 30%, and omits 20% (Kalat & Matlin, 2000). Because your score is based on the number of questions answered correctly minus one-fourth of the questions answered incorrectly, guessing does *not* lower your score. You are not penalized for guessing; but you are rewarded for eliminating one or two possible answers.

Adequate preparation is essential for this test. We—and others—suggest four steps: (1) obtain online the free *GRE Psychology Test Practice Book* that describes the test structure, content, and instructions and that contains one actual full-length GRE Psychology Test; (2) review a good introductory psychology textbook; (3) volunteer to be a TA (teaching assistant) for the Introduction to Psychology course; and (4) purchase one of the study guides with practice tests. Our favorite study guides are *GRE Psychology Test with CD-ROM* (Kellogg & Pisacreta, 2010, published by Research & Education Association), *Cracking the GRE Psychology Subject Test* (Jay, 2010, published by Princeton Review), *GRE Subject Test: Psychology* (2016, published by Kaplan), and *Barron's GRE Psychology* (Freberg & Palmer, 2015). If these four steps do not suffice, then private courses in preparing for the psychology test are available.

Of late, the number of graduate psychology programs requiring the GRE Psychology Subject Test has dropped. Many doctoral programs request or recommend that applicants complete the test, but not many are requiring it (Morgan, 2015). As a result, we advise you to take the subject test when you are applying to schools that recommend or require it as part of the admissions decision. We also recommend that you take it to demonstrate your knowledge of psychology; virtually all admissions committees will be impressed by a high score even if they do not formally require it. Applicants to master's program, however, may save money and time by skipping the Psychology Subject Test unless one or more of the master's programs insist upon it.

Miller Analogies Test

A few clinical and counseling psychology graduate programs request the MAT, a 50-minute test consisting of 100 word analogies. Your score is the total number correct; the mean for students intending to study psychology in graduate school is 50 to 51 (The Psychological Corporation, 1994). As with the GREs, booklets are available to help improve your scores on the test, and it is useful to take practice tests to familiarize and prepare yourself for the actual event. There are states in which the MAT cannot be administered (e.g., New York) because of test disclosure laws enacted in those states, so be sure to locate the testing center nearest you.

The MATs are rarely required by graduate schools, only 3% of them (Norcross, Kohout, & Wicherski, 2005). Because the test can be scheduled at any time, through a network of over 700 testing centers nationwide, consider taking this test after you have received your GRE scores and after you have selected the program you would like to apply to. You will save time and money if none of the schools that interest you require the test. Or they may be satisfied with your scores on the far more comprehensive GRE General Test.

Finally, low scores on entrance exams do not automatically preclude you from applying to clinical or counseling psychology graduate programs. Rather, low scores mean you will apply to programs that do not emphasize or require GRE scores or that accept scores in your range. You can partially compensate in other areas to help offset weak GRE scores.

Conversely, at highly competitive programs, strong GRE scores do not guarantee acceptance. We have heard from indignant applicants following rejection who did not realize that there were dozens of other applicants with combined Verbal and Quantitative scores above 320 (approximately the 95th percentile). As with each admission criterion, entrance examinations are only one part of the overall picture of a candidate. The best anyone can do is to make his or her application as appealing as possible.

Extracurricular Activities

An applicant's extracurricular pursuits are accorded less weight than GPAs, GRE scores, research competencies, and clinical experiences. The research reviewed earlier in this chapter clearly bears this point out. However, extracurricular activities, such as Psi Chi membership and campus involvement, are still considered in evaluating the "total person" of the applicant.

The admission implications are thus proscriptive and prescriptive. Strictly in terms of enhancing your candidacy (not in terms of other goals, such as life satisfaction), favor good grades and research experience over extracurricular activities. Involvement in a dozen student organizations will not compensate for meager grades and research; doctoral programs will not accept you because you are coaching the junior high's cheerleading squad. When confronted with time conflicts, recall that admissions committees place a premium on variables other than intense campus commitments.

Having stated the obvious but unpleasant facts, we urge you to routinely engage in *some* campus and community pursuits. The reasoning here is that clinical and counseling psychology programs seek well-rounded individuals exhibiting community involvement and diverse interests. The "egghead" or "Mr. Peabody" image is to be avoided in the practice of psychology, where your interpersonal skills are as crucial as your scientific preparation. Moderate involvement can also better acquaint you with faculty members, who may serve as sources of recommendations, and with the discipline of psychology itself. You can create professional opportunities by being involved in departmental activities. "Familiar faces" are frequently given first shots at clinical or research opportunities.

Applicants frequently learn too late that active involvement outside of the classroom is an indispensable education in and of itself. Consider the following student qualities contained in many letter of recommendation forms:

- Academic performance
- Organizational skills
- Interest/enthusiasm
- Interpersonal skills
- Emotional stability
- Communication skills
- Originality/resourcefulness
- Social judgment
- Responsibility/dependability
- Stress tolerance

Most of these dimensions refer to faculty–student interactions *outside* of the classroom, not to your course grades. Many a bright student has sabotaged his or her educational experience, recommendation letters, and career goal by not becoming engaged on campus or in the community.

In your extracurricular activities, try to exhibit the personality traits which, interacting with intelligence, relate most to vocational success—namely, conscientiousness and agreeableness (Jensen, 1998; Sackett & Walmsley, 2014). Be responsible, dependable, friendly, and pleasant. These traits apply to every kind of educational and job success. What's more, you want colleagues and friends to document in their letters of recommendation that you are extraordinarily conscientious and relentlessly cheerful.

Four specific suggestions come to mind regarding the extracurricular activities to pursue. First, join departmental student organizations, such as the Psychology Club, Psi Chi, and the American Psychological Society's Student Caucus. Second, we heartily recommend that you join the American Psychological Association (APA) and/or the Association for Psychological Science (APS) as a student affiliate. Your APA affiliation brings with it monthly issues of the *American Psychologist*, the flagship journal, and the *Monitor on Psychology*, the association's magazine. Similarly, APS membership includes subscriptions to the monthly journal *Psychological Science* and the *APS Observer*. Student membership in professional associations reflects favorably on your commitment to the discipline, and this affiliation should be recorded on your curriculum vitae. Your psychology advisor might have applications for student affiliation in his or her office; if not, go online to www.apa.org/membership/student/index.aspx and www.psychologicalscience.org/join/.

Third, additional campus and community commitments should be guided by your interests. But those associated with human services, social causes, and artistic endeavors seem to be differentially rewarded. These will obviously differ by locale; examples include Hand-in-Hand, campus ministries, course tutoring, peer advising, homeless shelters, women's centers, BACHUSS, environmental causes, SADD, theater productions, creative writing, Amnesty International, and the like.

A fourth and invaluable extracurricular experience is to attend a regional or national psychology convention. The benefits are many: socializing you into the profession; learning about current research; discovering how students and professors present research; meeting and hearing nationally known psychologists; adding to your growing professional network; attending sessions designed for prospective graduate students (e.g., the Psi Chi sessions and workshops); experiencing the intellectual stimulation; and enjoying the interpersonal camaraderie of fellow students and psychologists (Lubin, 1993; Tryon, 1985). For all these reasons, we have never—and we mean *never*—heard a single graduate school applicant express disappointment about attending his or her first psychology convention.

The challenge for most prospective psychologists is to locate and afford one of the regional or national psychology conferences. To locate upcoming conferences in your area, ask your psychology professors, consult the lists regularly published in *Eye on Psi Chi* and *American Psychologist*, and keep an eye open for announcements and posters on departmental bulletin boards. Convention season in psychology is from March to May, when the regional psychological associations hold their annual conventions. These include the Eastern Psychological Association, Midwestern Psychological Association, Rocky Mountain Psychological Association, Western Psychological Association, and Southeastern Psychological Association. The national conventions of APA and APS are annually held in the late spring and summer months. To afford the travel and lodging, consider organizing a convention trip with your fellow students, requesting information on special hotel and registration rates for students, volunteering as a convention assistant, and holding fund-raisers with psychology student organizations to offset your expenses. By hook or crook, definitely plan on expanding your extracurricular horizons by attending a psychology convention.

Extracurricular activities should reflect your active and passionate pursuit of excellence. This is, after all, your chosen profession, your career, your future. Join honor societies, compete for awards, pursue honors, and consider applications for Truman, Rhodes, and Fulbright scholarships. Actively investigated undergraduate grants for your research, such as those administered nationally by Psi Chi or those awarded locally in your university. Passivity doesn't cut it in graduate school (or life).

Finally, as part of your preparation, discuss your graduate plans with those people who will be affected by those plans, such as partner, spouse, parents, children, and close friends. The sooner you start discussing your plans, the better. You may move hundreds of miles away and will probably be working 60 hours a week as a graduate student. Your absence—psychological and physical—will likely impact other people close to you. Begin the discussions now, not after you apply (Megargee, 2001).

In this chapter, we reviewed six admission criteria—coursework, faculty mentoring, clinical experience, research skills, entrance examinations, and extracurricular activities—and recommended ways to improve in these areas. The material covered in this chapter concerns how you as the applicant can enhance your credentials or marketability. But the application process goes both ways. In addition to selling yourself, you are also a consumer, evaluating the programs and deciding which ones are for you.

In the next two chapters, we help you evaluate characteristics of graduate programs.

CHAPTER 4

GETTING STARTED

Up to this point in the *Insider's Guide*, we have focused on what you can do to enhance your credentials before beginning the application process. At some point, you must take realistic stock and evaluate where you stand as an applicant. Maybe you have taken your GREs. Perhaps you have signed up for upper-level psychology courses and have earned a satisfactory GPA. You have been supervised in a clinical setting and have begun research. You have reviewed your credentials and found that you have many strengths but also a few weaknesses. You either shore up the deficient areas or make a decision to go ahead with what you have and hope to sell it well. In other words, you are ready to get started with the application process.

Process is an appropriate word to describe the endeavor that you are about to begin. The way you approach this task will greatly influence your chances of gaining admission. Sure, you can quickly complete an application online and passively wait for an interview. And this may work if your credentials are extremely strong. But for most individuals, an informed approach to the process can make all the difference!

Prospective graduate students frequently become nervous about the application process for several reasons. Perhaps the following remarks sound familiar: "Well, I have good recommendations and a 3.3 GPA, but my GREs are low"; "I have good GREs and spent a year working on a suicide hot line, but I don't have a lot of research experience"; "Although my credentials are excellent, all the schools that I applied to only accept 10 out of 250 applicants." Whichever of these situations applies, simply submitting an application minimizes your chances of acceptance. You can do a great deal to increase your admission probabilities and to decrease your anxiety as you compare yourself to exaggerated standards.

Common Misconceptions

We begin by dispelling three common misconceptions about clinical and counseling psychology programs. The first misconception: there is a strong correlation between a university's undergraduate reputation and the status of its psychology graduate programs. Many of the best undergraduate institutions—Brown, Princeton, and the elite liberal arts colleges, for example—do not even offer graduate studies in clinical or counseling psychology.

A second myth is that you should apply to a graduate psychology program on the basis of that institution's sports performance. We have met a number of students who have used this selection criterion with unfortunate consequences. Please do not allow your application decisions to rest on whether a university has an excellent football team or whether their basketball team made it to the Final Four of the NCAA tournament! Do not scoff at the reality of this practice; careful research has demonstrated that winning a national championship in a visible college sport consistently translates into increased applications to the winning institution (Toma & Cross, 1998).

A third common misconception holds that there

is an authoritative list of the finest graduate programs in clinical psychology. In reality, unlike business or law schools, there is no definitive ranking of the "best" psychology graduate programs. The quality of a program depends on what *you* are looking to get out of it. The best program for someone seeking to become a psychologist conducting psychodynamic psychotherapy in private practice is probably not going to be the program of choice for someone who has set his or her heart on becoming a psychophysiological researcher at a medical school. Each person could attend the "best" school for psychology in his or her interests.

We want to shift the burden from you trying to meet a school's admissions demands to you finding a school that meets *your* needs. Doctoral programs are looking for students with direction and passion. This does not mean you have made an irrevocable commitment to an area of research or type of clinical work. It means that you have an idea of the professional work you would like to do and toward which theoretical orientation(s) you lean.

You are selecting an institution because it will mold you in the direction *you* have chosen. Doctoral programs will look for this attitude in your statement of purpose. During your interviews, you will be asked about which professors you want to work with and what thoughts you have about their research projects. Even more likely, you will be directly asked, "Why are you applying here instead of someplace else?" By identifying your graduate training goals, you will impress interviewers with your direction and passion.

Acceptance Rates

The most pervasive myth about doctoral psychology programs is that "hardly anyone gets in—only 10%." Like most myths, this one does have a grain of truth. The average acceptance rate for *all* APA-accredited Ph.D. programs in clinical and counseling psychology is, in fact, 10% (Norcross et al., 2004; Norcross et al., 2010). But in a very real way, the 10% figure is misleading and inaccurate on many counts.

Let's begin our foray into acceptance rates by defining the term. "Acceptance rate" refers to the percentage of applicants accepted for admission into a single graduate program, *not* the percentage of the entire applicant pool to all programs accepted for admission in a given year. The clinical doctoral program at University X may accept only 15 of 150 applicants (10%), but many of the applicants to University X not accepted there will be admitted elsewhere. Although only 10% of the applicants to a single doctoral program might be accepted into that *particular* program, a far greater percentage of the entire applicant pool will be accepted into *some* clinical or counseling doctoral program.

Note, too, that the 10% figure refers only to acceptance rates of APA-accredited programs in clinical or counseling psychology. The acceptance rates at *non*-APA-accredited doctoral programs are double that for APA-accredited programs: 20% for nonaccredited Ph.D. programs and 60% for nonaccredited Psy.D. programs (Norcross et al., 2005). The acceptance rates for master's programs are also much higher than those for doctoral programs. The average acceptance rates for master's programs are 37% in clinical psychology and 63% in counseling psychology (see Table 1-5).

In reality, that 10% acceptance figure applies only to APA-accredited Ph.D. programs. As we have already emphasized, Psy.D. programs offer higher acceptance rates—40 to 50% of applicants are admitted on average to any single program (Norcross et al., 2010).

Please do not confuse the acceptance rate with the attendance rate, a frequent trick of undergraduate institutions trying to boost their reputations. Academic administrators are fond of asking incoming students to look around at, say, their fellow 1,000 freshmen selected from, say, 10,000 applicants. They imply that 1 in 10 applicants were accepted. In fact, that's the attendance rate or the "yield." The actual acceptance number is probably 5,000 or 6,000 students, of which 1,000 elected to attend. Same lesson in graduate school: Programs typically accept far more students than actually attend.

Acceptance rates vary tremendously from doctoral program to doctoral program as a function of the practice–research dimension. As shown in the Reports on Individual Programs following Chapter 8, acceptance rates at research-oriented clinical Ph.D. programs, such as Harvard and Yale, start as low as 2%. And acceptance rates at freestanding Psy.D. programs go as high as 70%.

Table 4-1 summarizes the results of our studies on acceptance rates to APA-accredited clinical psychology programs as a function of the type of program. All types of programs average between 150 and 250 applications per year. Research-oriented Ph.D. programs accept only 7% of their applicants, on average, whereas the corresponding figures are 14% for equal-emphasis Ph.D. and 16% for practice-oriented Ph.D. programs. University-based Psy.D. programs accept 40% of their applicants on average, and freestanding Psy.D. programs accept 50%. That's quite a range of acceptance rates—7% to 50%—all

TABLE 4-1. Average Acceptance Rates for APA-Accredited Clinical Psychology Programs

	Freestanding Psy.D.	University-based Psy.D.	Practice-oriented Ph.D.	Equal-emphasis Ph.D.	Research-oriented Ph.D.
Number of applications	227	163	155	160	183
Number of acceptances	108	58	18	16	12
Acceptance rate	50%	40%	16%	14%	7%

Note. Data from Norcross, Ellis, & Sayette (2010).

in APA-accredited doctoral programs in clinical psychology. And that's why we urge caution in tossing around the 10% acceptance rate.

Costs of Applying

Applying to graduate school is an expensive proposition—not only in terms of your valuable time but also in terms of hard money. Application fees average $50 per doctoral program and $35 per master's program (Norcross et al., 2004). Only 7% of graduate schools let you apply for free (Norcross et al., 1996). The fee (in 2017) for the GRE General Test is $205, with a $50 rescheduling fee, and the Psychology Subject Test costs another $150. ETS will electronically transmit your GRE scores free of charge to four graduate schools that you designate in advance; however, each additional score report costs $27 per recipient. Throw in the costs of transcripts, postage for letters of recommendation, and the innumerable telephone calls, and the investment can become quite costly. All told, we estimate that applying to 12 doctoral schools will run about $1,000 (and that number can increase depending on the cost of traveling to multiple interviews).

Several students challenged our estimate that the graduate application process would cost them at least $1,000. They protested that our figure was way too high. So, we encouraged them, like good psychologists, to collect data as they proceeded through the process. Here is the breakdown of costs from one applicant who applied to a dozen doctoral programs in 2015:

Taking the GRE General & Subject tests	$340
Sending GRE scores to 12 schools	$216
Forwarding transcripts to 12 schools	$120
Application fees for 12 programs	$610

That's a total of $1,286, before she traveled to three programs for admission interviews. She now realizes that for anyone considering a national search the $1,000 estimate is conservative.

The good news is that graduate schools are sensitive to financial hardship and that, for many students, the burdensome short-term cost is an excellent long-term investment. Schools build into the application process allowances for students who cannot afford the expense. Even the GRE has a fee waiver for students in dire financial circumstances.

Moreover, think of the application cost as an investment in yourself and in your career. If you gain acceptance into a doctoral program with tuition remission and a stipend for 4 years, your $1,250 can be converted into an $80,000 to $120,000 payback over the course of your graduate career.

The bottom line in getting started is this: anticipate the costs of applying to graduate school and plan to have the funds (or waivers) available before you begin completing applications.

Starting Early

Let's discuss timing up front. Applications to doctoral programs are typically due from the middle week in December to the second week in February. The sooner you begin preparing, the more advantage you can take of an aggressive, early start to the admission process. As mentioned in earlier chapters and in the Time Line (Appendix A), for undergraduates, ideally this would take place the summer of your junior year. For others, this would best occur the summer of the year before you plan to attend graduate school. If it is past that point, you are not too late. You can follow the steps we will describe as late as October of your application year.

Applying to graduate school is like planning a political campaign or a military operation. It is impossible to begin too soon or to be too thorough (Megargee, 2001). Recognize this about the application process and *start almost a year before you expect to begin graduate school.* Completing the application materials in the fall semester alone will consume as much time as a 3-credit course!

Virtually all APA-accredited clinical and counseling psychology programs only accept matriculating students for their fall semesters. As mentioned earlier, in order to be accepted for the fall of 2020, most doctoral programs have application deadlines anywhere from mid-December 2019 to February 2020. The typical deadline for doctoral programs in clinical and counseling psychology is January 15 (Norcross et al., 1996). Accordingly, you will need college transcripts, test scores, and letters of recommendation, not to mention time to prepare yourself before the application deadline. You should expect to begin no later than the fall of the year before you intend to attend graduate school. If you are willing to put in the maximum effort to get into a program, expect to begin the spring before that.

The APA has accredited 237 active doctoral programs in clinical psychology, 68 active doctoral programs in counseling psychology, and 10 active doctoral programs in combined psychology throughout the United States and Canada. Toss in nonaccredited doctoral programs and the mass of master's programs in clinical and counseling psychology and you wind up with over a thousand graduate programs. How does one proceed in whittling this list to a manageable number?

To begin the selection process, ask yourself, "What do I want to do as a psychologist? What kind of research or clinical work do I like? Is there some article I've read or presentation I've heard that intrigues me?" There is a certain advantage if you have already conducted research or completed clinical experience as an undergraduate and know something about the discipline. And, if you have completed an honors project or thesis, you may even have a certain degree of expertise. Or you may decide you would like to try something different in the future.

For example, suppose you have an interest in suicidology, but you are not sure that you want to do research in that area or exactly what that research would entail. Or you think you'd like to specialize in suicide prevention, but you're uncertain how psychologists treat the issue clinically. Familiarize yourself with the area. Ask one of your professors for readings. Check out a current textbook devoted to the topic. Go to a suicide prevention or crisis center and read through their literature. Search the Internet. Then decide whether you like the questions being asked and the methods used to answer them. Use as many sources as possible to gain information to narrow down your interests and educate yourself about them.

In addition to the resources in this book, a number of Internet sites will help you at this stage of the process. You can familiarize yourself with psychology graduate programs in the United States and Canada by accessing a large number of websites. Our favorites are:

- www.apa.org/about/students.aspx
  (APA's site for students includes a list of accredited programs, relevant articles, and other useful materials)
- www.socialpsychology.org/clinical.htm
  (features hyperlinks to hundreds of departments in the United States offering a Ph.D. in psychology)
- www.clas.ufl.edu/au/#A
  (links for a plethora of American universities)
- www.petersons.com/graduate-schools.aspx
  (brief descriptions of programs offering graduate training in clinical and counseling psychology)

All these—and other—sites enable you to take a virtual tour of graduate programs in professional psychology. Develop an early feel for various departments and begin to sharpen your interests.

Next is the task of putting this knowledge to use. You have interests, and you now need to learn which graduate programs can provide these research or clinical opportunities. Although knowing how much you enjoy research or clinical work may not take a lot of reflection, deciding whether to select a research-oriented, a practice-oriented, or an equal-emphasis clinical/counseling psychology program is a question with far-reaching ramifications.

This question tends to divide people into three groups: the research-oriented (clinical scientists); the practice-oriented (practitioners); and the dually committed (scientist–practitioners). The following sections are designed to lead each group in its appropriate direction. As explained in Chapter 2, these groups tend to follow three rather distinctive career paths in the profession of clinical and counseling psychology (Bernstein & Kerr, 1993; Conway, 1988; Ready & Santorelli, 2014).

We have repeatedly surveyed the APA-accredited clinical and counseling psychology programs over the past 26 years. Their responses to our questionnaires (e.g., Mayne et al., 1994; Norcross et al., 1998; Norcross et al., 2004; Norcross et al., 2014; Norcross et al., in press; Oliver et al., 2005; Sayette & Mayne, 1990; Sayette et al., 1999; Sayette et al., 2011; Turkson & Norcross, 1996) can serve as the basis for your initial selection of graduate programs. By using their responses, we will lead you through an exercise that will generate a list that ranks schools by how closely they meet your expectations and interests.

As you review the Reports on Individual Programs, bear in mind that the listings are alphabetical, not geographical. We list the programs alphabetically, but sometimes the order is counterintuitive. For example, the University of Arkansas is not listed under "U," but between Arizona State University and Auburn University. Thus, you might need to look under two letters to identify programs of interest.

Please also note that large, multi-campus institutions are listed together in the Reports on Individual Programs. Argosy University, to take the biggest example, offers APA-accredited Psy.D. programs in clinical psychology at a dozen campuses sprinkled around the country. They are all presented under "Argosy" along with their campus location and frequently with their additional name of "American School of Professional Psychology."

For the Research-Oriented and Dually Committed

This section guides those applicants who are centrally focused on research and those with equal interests in practice and research. We group these two sorts of applicants together because their initial selection of schools will place more emphasis on the research available at each program and secondarily on the clinical work available. This will allow people with an equal emphasis to cast their nets as widely and as efficiently as possible.

One question we asked of each graduate program in our studies was "In which areas of research are your faculty presently working? Do they presently have a grant in that area?" Appendix E lists all the research areas provided by the graduate programs along with the number of faculty interested in these areas and an indication of whether they have a grant. This information provides you with an index of how intensively each program is pursuing this area of research. Thus, a program with three faculty members researching autism that has a grant supporting their work indicates serious involvement on the part of that program.

Find your areas of interest in the appendix; underneath them you will see a list of programs doing that type of research. In addition, you will know the number of professors with whom you could potentially work and whether there is grant money supporting this research.

A few words of caution in interpreting this appendix: not all programs were equally comprehensive in completing the survey. Some schools only included core faculty, whereas others included adjunct faculty. This accounts for what seems to be an overrepresentation of some institutions on the list. Also, some programs had research interests combining two different areas—say, Dialectical Behavior Therapy for anxiety disorders – and listed a single grant under both.

Appendix B, entitled "Worksheet for Choosing Programs," is used to select programs to which you will eventually apply. Begin by writing your research interest in the far left-hand column. In the next column, marked "Schools," write the list of schools under that heading in Appendix B. In columns 3 and 4, write down the number of faculty in that area at each school and whether they are grant funded. In addition, some schools merely indicated the presence of grant funding and not the total number of grants. Thus, a "1" in the "Grants" column indicated *at least* one grant. A "0" indicates no grants, and numbers greater than 1 indicate multiple grants.

There are two worksheets provided in Appendix B, allowing you to explore different research areas. If you have more than two main areas of interest, unless they are closely related, you may find the list becoming exceptionally long. In that case, you can either reduce your areas of interest or complete this worksheet with the aid of a trusted professor who can help you pare down the list to a manageable number. If you have more than one area of interest, put stars next to the programs that have faculty doing research in both of them.

If your interests lean toward research, then you want to pick programs highly regarded in the research area you would like to pursue. How do you evaluate the clinical and counseling psychology programs on your list in terms of research?

Refer to Table 4-2, which is adapted from an analysis provided by Calivate Analytics. The data reflect journals indexed in the following Web of Science Core Collection editions: Science Citation Index Expanded, Social Sciences Citation Index, and Arts and Humanities Citation Index. All psychology and psychiatry journals included in the Web of Science collections from 2012 through the end of 2016 were analyzed to determine the institutions with the most citations. The goal was to identify the institutions employing faculty members who authored the most

TABLE 4-2. Institutions with Most Citations, Most Papers, and Greatest Impact in Psychology/Psychiatry

Citation Rank	Institution[a]	Citations	Web of Science Documents	Impact (Citations Per Paper)
1	Harvard University	42538	6288	6.76
3	Yale University	22953	3420	6.71
4	University of California Los Angeles	22700	3321	6.84
6	University of Pittsburgh	17605	2804	6.28
7	University of Michigan	16839	2706	6.22
8	University of Pennsylvania	16606	2428	6.84
9	University of California San Diego[b]	15332	2345	6.54
10	New York University[c]	15088	2392	6.31
11	University of Minnesota Twin Cities	14957	2456	6.09
13	Duke University	14336	2086	6.87
14	University of North Carolina Chapel Hill	13682	2221	6.16
15	University of Washington Seattle	12623	2041	6.18
16	Boston University	11463	1690	6.78
17	Northwestern University	10926	1835	5.95
18	Washington University (WUSTL)	10889	1353	8.05
19	Emory University	9853	1468	6.71
20	Vanderbilt University	9842	1350	7.29
21	Penn State University	9729	2103	4.63
23	University of Wisconsin Madison	9275	1388	6.68
24	Ohio State University	9199	1857	4.95
29	University of California Berkeley	8135	1177	6.91
30	Arizona State University	7963	1591	5.01
31	University of Iowa	7574	1114	6.80
32	Florida State University	7570	1370	5.53
33	University of Maryland College Park	7511	1310	5.73
34	Michigan State University	7476	1318	5.67
35	University of Illinois Urbana-Champaign	7455	1406	5.30
36	University of Southern California	7399	1226	6.04
37	University of Virginia	7345	1022	7.19
38	University of Texas Austin	7017	1401	5.01
39	University of Illinois Chicago	6710	1185	5.66
40	Indiana University Bloomington	6403	1160	5.52
41	University of Rochester	6338	991	6.40
42	University of Connecticut	6164	1185	5.20
43	University of Miami	6156	1289	4.78
44	University of Arizona	6109	869	7.03
45	Rutgers State University	5992	1243	4.82
46	University of Florida	5975	1223	4.89
47	Virginia Commonwealth University	5610	1144	4.90
48	University of South Florida	5484	1264	4.34
49	University of Colorado Boulder	5456	850	6.42
50	University of Missouri Columbia	5452	997	5.47
51	Temple University	5405	1018	5.31
54	University of Georgia	5265	944	5.58
55	State University of New York (SUNY) Stony Brook	4787	791	6.05
56	Purdue University	4728	906	5.22
58	Texas A&M University College Station	4702	877	5.36
59	University of Oregon	4625	750	6.17
61	University of Utah	4411	942	4.68
63	University of Cincinnati	4315	743	5.81
64	University of Kansas	4193	975	4.30
65	Yeshiva University	4116	648	6.35

(cont.)

TABLE 4-2. *(cont.)*

Citation Rank	Institution[a]	Citations	Web of Science Documents	Impact (Citations Per Paper)
67	Indiana University-Purdue University Indianapolis	4046	790	5.12
68	University of California Santa Barbara	3961	582	6.81
69	University of Kentucky	3927	824	4.77
70	University of New Mexico	3795	701	5.41
74	Case Western Reserve University	3622	784	4.62
75	State University of New York (SUNY) Buffalo	3523	797	4.42
77	University of Houston	3450	927	3.72
78	Wayne State University	3340	1022	3.27
79	University of Texas Southwestern Medical Center Dallas	3285	538	6.11
81	San Diego State University[b]	3088	632	4.89
82	Kent State University	3039	558	5.45
83	University of Notre Dame	3010	503	5.98
86	Virginia Polytechnic Institute & State University	2740	548	5.00
87	Georgia State University	2716	715	3.80
88	University of Massachusetts Amherst	2624	553	4.75
89	Florida International University	2615	529	4.94
91	University of Denver	2568	408	6.29
92	University of South Carolina	2556	589	4.34
94	Hofstra University	2523	311	8.11
95	Northeastern University[c]	2462	436	5.65
96	University of North Carolina Greensboro	2456	535	4.59
97	University of Vermont	2453	441	5.56
98	Boston College[c]	2451	478	5.13
99	University of Alabama Tuscaloosa	2384	587	4.06
101	George Mason University	2296	560	4.10
103	George Washington University	2206	618	3.57
104	Brigham Young University	2181	517	4.22
105	University of Delaware	2171	467	4.65
108	University of Alabama Birmingham	2090	513	4.07
109	Washington State University	2071	398	5.20
111	Iowa State University[c]	2014	458	4.40
113	Columbia University Teachers College	1953	369	5.29
115	University of Nebraska Lincoln	1936	516	3.75
118	Colorado State University[c]	1880	378	4.97
119	University of Memphis	1853	455	4.07
120	University of Mississippi	1849	398	4.65
121	Drexel University	1839	467	3.94
122	Auburn University	1675	477	3.51
123	University of Tennessee Knoxville	1675	473	3.54
124	Texas Tech University	1664	518	3.21
125	University of Central Florida	1656	387	4.28
126	University of North Dakota Grand Forks	1646	337	4.88
127	University of North Texas Denton	1642	484	3.39
129	University of Louisville	1586	481	3.30
130	Syracuse University	1584	370	4.28
131	Miami University	1553	363	4.28
135	State University of New York (SUNY) Albany	1448	367	3.95
136	Northern Illinois University	1441	347	4.15
137	University of Massachusetts Boston	1438	346	4.16
138	State University of New York (SUNY) Binghamton	1414	296	4.78
139	Ohio University	1410	368	3.83
140	Uniformed Services University of the Health Sciences	1405	287	4.90

TABLE 4-2. *(cont.)*

Citation Rank	Institution[a]	Citations	Web of Science Documents	Impact (Citations Per Paper)
141	Loyola University Chicago	1369	280	4.89
142	University of Wisconsin Milwaukee	1367	334	4.09
143	University of Colorado Denver	1353	378	3.58
144	Fordham University	1330	347	3.83
146	Southern Methodist University	1303	249	5.23
147	West Virginia University	1292	394	3.28
148	University of Nevada Las Vegas	1287	334	3.85
150	Oklahoma State University–Stillwater	1265	340	3.72
154	Illinois Institute of Technology	1222	164	7.45
156	Saint Louis University	1213	328	3.70
157	DePaul University	1210	299	4.05
163	University of Nevada Reno	1151	248	4.64
164	University of Toledo	1134	234	4.85
165	Bowling Green State University	1124	291	3.86
166	Utah State University	1118	299	3.74
173	Baylor University	993	281	3.53
175	The New School	987	203	4.86
176	University of Wyoming	967	219	4.42
179	University of Southern Mississippi	938	255	3.68
180	University of North Carolina Charlotte	934	265	3.52
181	Alliant International University	927	260	3.57
185	Sam Houston State University	901	211	4.27
187	John Jay College of Criminal Justice (CUNY)	863	203	4.25
188	University of Arkansas Fayetteville	859	269	3.19
190	University of Maryland Baltimore County	821	225	3.65
192	University of Hawaii Manoa	797	233	3.42
195	University of Colorado at Colorado Springs	756	184	4.11
196	East Carolina University	747	267	2.80
197	Queens College NY (CUNY)	737	164	4.49
198	Adelphi University	726	239	3.04
200	University of Missouri Kansas City	704	189	3.72
201	Lehigh University[c]	703	206	3.41
203	American University	654	163	4.01
204	University of South Alabama	651	129	5.05
206	Marquette University	647	170	3.81
207	James Madison University	645	141	4.57
208	University of Missouri Saint Louis	643	180	3.57
210	University of Akron[c]	634	149	4.26
216	Southern Illinois University	617	237	2.60
219	University of Rhode Island	600	182	3.30

Note. The data reflect journals indexed in the following Web of Science Core Collection editions: *Science Citation Index Expanded*, *Social Sciences Citation Index*, and *Arts and Humanities Citation Index*. Data included herein are derived from Clarivate Analytics InCites.

[a]Institutions without APA-accredited programs in clinical or counseling psychology have been omitted from this table.

[b]San Diego State University and the University of California San Diego have a joint clinical psychology Ph.D. program.

[c]This university has an APA-accredited counseling psychology program, but does not have an APA-accredited clinical psychology program.

frequently referenced articles in psychology and psychiatry journals. These two categories of journals publish the bulk of research conducted by clinical and, to a lesser degree, counseling psychologists.

The table lists, in rank order, the frequency with which articles written by members of a particular institution are cited. Only those institutions with an APA-accredited clinical or counseling program are included on this list. It should also be noted that the list only includes those institutions that produced at least 600 papers over the 5-year span; as a result, several smaller institutions with clinical or counseling psychology programs did not make the list. You might examine other rankings, though our sense is that the top programs appear fairly consistently across methods and across lists.

Although it has its critics, another popular ranking of clinical psychology programs appears in the recent *U.S. News and World Report*'s ranking: grad-schools.usnews.rankingsandreviews.com/best-graduate-schools/top-clinical-psychology-schools/rankings. This listing focuses on clinical psychology rather than all of psychology. While *U.S. News* weighs heavily program reputation, you also might review a study that evaluated the scholarly productivity of 166 APA-accredited clinical psychology Ph.D. programs using a number of objective, normative variables (e.g., number of total publications; Stewart, Roberts, & Roy, 2007). These authors also show that rankings based on their analyses reveal a reasonable association with the *U.S. News* rankings. This article also provides a nice summary of prior efforts to rank the productivity of psychology departments.

Using Table 4-2, write the citation ranking for each school in column 5, labeled "Citation Rank." Be advised that this ranking reflects the psychology department in general, not only the clinical or counseling program. In fact, some of the institutions on the original list (e.g., Stanford University, which was ranked #5) were removed from our listing because they do not offer doctoral programs in clinical or counseling psychology. Inclusion of these nonclinical influences will affect the ranking of the schools you have selected. Still, this will provide you with a rough idea of where each school stands in terms of its research productivity. A university that makes it onto this list is probably a strong research-oriented institution. If the school fails to appear on the table, then it may or may not emphasize psychological research.

As mentioned, any APA-accredited program must provide both clinical and research training. Thus, it is important also to evaluate the practice opportunities available. As already mentioned, Psy.D. programs by definition emphasize practice and train students to be practitioners. Although it is possible to obtain research training at a Psy.D. program, this is not the stated intention of such practitioner programs. Consequently, a student with a clear research focus should choose a Ph.D. program. For the research-oriented, this column will be used to cross schools off their application list. Look up each school on your list in the Reports on Individual Programs. If any of these schools offer only Psy.D. programs, you can delete that program.

The first column under the "Clinical" section of Appendix B is marked "Orientation." Under each program listed in our reports on individual programs, you will see a list of five theoretical orientations:

- psychodynamic/psychoanalytic
- radical behavioral/applied behavioral analysis
- systems/family systems
- humanistic/existential
- cognitive/cognitive-behavioral

If you are clearly committed to (or strongly leaning toward) one of these orientations, then some program faculty should share that orientation. Check each program on your list and see if a suitable percentage of the faculty shares your orientation. If so, mark the "Orientation" column with a "+" sign. If not, mark it with a "–" sign.

If you are unsure of an orientation, or see yourself as integrative or eclectic, then gravitate toward programs with a wide variety of faculty orientations. If there is representation among the faculty in three or more of these orientations, that's a good sign. If the total you get when adding up all the percentages in the different orientations is greater than 100%, that also earns a plus. It means several (or most) of the faculty bridge orientations and are integrative themselves. In other words, professors are listed under more than one category. In either case, mark the "Orientation" column with a "+" sign. If the faculty are of one or two orientations and without overlap, then mark this column with a "–" sign.

The second column under "Clinical" is "Res/Clin." Turn to Appendix F, "Specialty Clinics and Practica Sites." This is a list of specialty clinics and practica available at the APA-accredited programs. Specialty clinics focus on a specific clientele, such as depressed, addicted, or eating-disordered clients. Practica are field placements, usually outside the university, where students will conduct clinical work in their second, third, and/or fourth years of study. Some practica also specialize in a certain clientele. If you have a research interest in a particular population, it is important that the population be available for you to study and that you have the chance to work with that population clinically. For this reason, it is a great help for a researcher to have a specialty clinic or practicum in his or her area.

Look up your research area in Appendix F. If any of the programs on your list in Appendix B has a clinic or practicum in that area, mark the "Res/Clin" column with a plus. You can do likewise using Appendix G, "Program Concentrations and Tracks." Programs offering a formal track or concentration in your area of interest deserve a plus as well.

Again, this is only one indicator and must be kept in perspective. Most programs will have their own psychological training clinic, where clients may be seen or made available for research. Additionally, a faculty member may have a research population readily available in the community. And last, a few programs did not include practica placements off campus in the community, thus underrepresenting their practica opportunities. Still, being informed about a clinic or practicum specializing in your population of interest is certainly an advantage in selecting potential graduate programs.

The third column under the "Clinical" section is marked "Rank." Here, we refer to a program's production of students who go on to distinguished careers as clinicians, as measured by becoming ABPP Diplomates. The *ABPP* refers to diplomate status awarded by the American Board of Professional Psychology (www.abpp.org), which certifies excellence in more than a dozen subfields of psychology, including clinical psychology and counseling psychology. ABPP represents board certification for psychologists; the entrance requirements and performance standards are more rigorous than those involved in licensure and represent advanced competence.

Put a "+" in the "Rank" column in the "Clinical" section for programs with multiple faculty with ABPP after their names. Though faculty without ABPP provide fine clinical training, this designation indicates that the faculty have an excellent track record.

Finally, there is a column in Appendix B marked "Self-Rating." The first question we asked each program to answer was, "On a 7-point scale, how research- or practice-oriented would you rate your program?" (1 = practice emphasis; 4 = equal emphasis; and 7 = research emphasis). You will find the school's rating of itself under each individual listing in the reports on individual programs sections. Mark this number under the "Self-Rating" column.

What you now have is a list of programs that offer research in your area of interest. You also have the number of faculty in the area that you might work with and whether they presently have grant funding. Finally, you have an approximate rank of that school's research standing.

In clinical terms, you have some sense of whether that school will conform to your theoretical orientation, whether it has clinical training or a formal track in your area of interest, how it ranks in terms of producing outstanding clinicians, and whether it rates itself as emphasizing practice or research.

Given the information before you, you may already want to begin crossing programs off your list. If you're research-oriented, and the program is a Psy.D. program or rates itself a 1, 2, or 3 (meaning it is practice-oriented), you can probably delete that school. Alternatively, if your interests reflect equal research and clinical emphasis and you lean toward a psychodynamic orientation, you may want to cross off a school that rates itself as a 7 (very research-oriented) or whose faculty is 100% cognitive or behavioral.

Your revised list of schools can probably satisfy your research and clinical interests. In addition, you have the start of a ranking system, which gives a rough idea of how well each school conforms to your interests and needs. Unfortunately, this provides you with only half of the information you need to begin writing to schools. The second part of this process asks, "How close do you come to the standards they specify?" This is covered in a later section entitled "Assessing Program Criteria."

For the Practice-Oriented

This section furnishes guidance to those applicants who are centrally focused on psychological practice. These applicants will begin to choose their graduate programs based on their theoretical orientation and the availability of practice opportunities.

Begin by familiarizing yourself with all the APA-accredited Psy.D. programs listed in the back of this book. With this list, turn to Appendix B, "Worksheet for Choosing Programs." Under the column marked "School," write the names of the programs that interest you. As well, take a look at those comparatively rare Ph.D. programs that emphasize practice over research.

In addition to these Psy.D. and few Ph.D. programs, you may have a specific patient population that you are especially eager to work with. Perhaps you already have a sense that you want to work with patients suffering from, say, anxiety, addictive, or autistic disorders. In this case, turn to Appendix F.

This appendix, "Specialty Clinics and Practica Sites," lists specialty clinics or practica areas available at different programs. Specialty clinics focus on specific clientele, such as depressed or eating-disordered clients. As mentioned in the previous section, practica are placements, typically off campus, where a student will conduct clinical work in his or her second, third, and/or fourth year of study, and some practica also specialize in treating a certain clientele. For a practice-oriented student, it would be especially desirable to be in a program with a specialty clinic in his or her particular area of treatment interest. Therefore, write down the names of programs with specialty clinics or practica in your area of interest on your list in Appendix B.

Do likewise for programs that offer a formal track or concentration in your area of interest. This information can be found in Appendix G, "Program Concentrations and Tracks."

A word of caution is in order. Most programs have their own psychology training clinic where clients may be seen or made available for research. Practica may also be available in a wide range of settings in the community, providing fertile ground for a rich clinical experience. Still, a clinic or practicum specializing in a population of special interest to you is a definite plus and an additional piece of information on which to base your decision. If a program both offers a Psy.D. and has a specialty clinic or concentration in your area, put a star next to it.

The next important column for the practice-oriented applicant is marked "Orientation." In the Reports on Individual Programs, you will find each school listed, along with information pertaining to its program. Among that information, you will see a list of five theoretical orientations, followed by the percentage of the faculty that subscribes to that orientation:

- psychodynamic/psychoanalytic
- radical behavioral/applied behavioral analysis
- systems/family systems
- humanistic/existential
- cognitive/cognitive-behavioral

If you are clearly committed to (or strongly leaning toward) one of these orientations, then it some portion of the faculty should share that orientation. Check each program on your list and determine if a suitable percentage of the faculty shares your orientation. If so, mark the "Orientation" column with a "+" sign; if not, mark it with a "–" sign.

If you are unsure of your orientation or see yourself as integrative or eclectic, then gravitate toward programs offering a wide variety of faculty orientations. If there is representation among the faculty in three or more of these orientations, that's a good sign. If the total you obtain after adding up all the percentages in the different areas is greater than 100%, that also proves advantageous. It means several (or most) of the faculty bridge orientations and are integrative themselves. In either case, mark the "Orientation" column with a "+" sign. If you're integrative and the faculty are of one or two orientations and do not overlap, then mark this column with a "–" sign.

The next column is marked "Res/Clin." As we mentioned previously, even if you are looking for a practice-oriented program, you still will conduct some research: a lengthy professional paper or a clinical dissertation at the very least. Consequently, it is important that someone in your program is conducting research in an area that interests you. With this in mind, look through Appendix E and locate area(s) of research that you find interesting. Under each area, you will find a list of schools that have researchers in that field. If any of the schools on your list in Appendix B is listed here, place a "+" in the column marked "Res/Clin."

The third column under "Clinical" is marked "Rank." Here, we refer to a program's production of students who go on to distinguished careers as clinicians, as imperfectly measured by their becoming ABPP Diplomates. The *ABPP* refers to diplomate status awarded by the American Board of Professional Psychology (www.abpp.org), which certifies excellence in more than a dozen subfields of psychology, including clinical psychology and counseling psychology. ABPP represents board certification for psychologists; the entrance requirements and performance standards are more rigorous than those involved in licensure and represent advanced competence.

As you read through the faculty profiles online, carefully note the doctoral programs with multiple faculty with ABPP after their names. Place a "+" in this column for such programs. Though faculty without ABPP provide fine clinical training, these designations indicate that the faculty have an excellent track record. You also may wish to place a "+" for programs located in densely populated areas, as they may (though not always) offer a wider diversity of clinical training opportunities than would programs in less populated and more homogeneous areas.

Finally, there is a column in Appendix B marked "Self-Rating." In the reports on individual programs you will find each school's rating of itself (1 = practice emphasis; 4 = equal emphasis; and 7 = research emphasis). Mark this number under the "Self-Rating" column. Though Psy.D. programs are practice-oriented by definition, they differ on how much research they expect their students to conduct. Thus, their ratings will allow you to guide your expectations of what each program will expect of you. This self-rating will also help you avoid a Ph.D. program with a specialty clinic in your area that is clearly research-oriented.

What you now have is a list of programs that are practice-oriented and/or that offer a specialty clinic or formal track in your area of interest. You have some sense of whether these schools will conform to your theoretical orientation and whether they have ongoing research in your area of clinical interest. You also have their self-rating of the program's emphasis on practice or research.

Given the information on your worksheet, you may already begin crossing programs off your list. If you're practice-oriented and a Ph.D. program offers a specialty clinic in your area but rates itself with a 6 or 7 (very research-oriented), you may delete that school. Alternatively, if you're very behaviorally oriented, you may want to cross off a school where 100% of the faculty is psychodynamic/psychoanalytic.

Your revised list of schools can provide you with practice-oriented training and possibly specialized clinical training in your population of choice. In addition, you have the start of a ranking system that gives you a rough idea of how well each school conforms to your interests and needs. Unfortunately, this list only provides you with half the information you need to begin writing to schools. The second half of this process is related to how closely you come to the specified standards of these programs. This is covered in the "Assessing Program Criteria" section.

For the Racial/Ethnic Minority Applicant

Before continuing to the assessment of program criteria, it is important to discuss the special case of minority applications. "Minority" in this context refers to racial or ethnic background, although with women comprising 80% of all doctoral students in psychology (IPEDS, 2010), a few graduate student programs are starting to treat men as minority applicants. Black men in particular are woefully under-represented as students in psychology graduate schools, accounting for a mere 2% of psychology Ph.D.s (Gardere, 2015).

Ethnic minority students now account for 21% of master's students in psychology and 27% of doctoral students in psychology (Norcross, Kohout, & Wicherski, 2005). In clinical psychology, that number hovers around 23%. The Reports on Individual Programs in the back of this book show the percentage of ethnic minority students attending each APA-accredited program.

Nearly every APA-accredited program makes special efforts to recruit applicants of color (Munoz-Dunbar & Stanton, 1999; Rogers & Molina, 2006), recognizing the need in our society for well-trained minority professionals. Typical methods for recruiting underrepresented groups to clinical and counseling psychology programs are offers of financial aid, the use of personal contacts, funded visits to programs, use of APA's Minority Undergraduate Students of Excellence (MUSE) program, diversity courses, special events, reimbursements of application fees, and preferential screening (Rogers & Molina, 2006; Steinpreis et al., 1992). Programs often make an extra effort to review minority applications to ensure that qualified candidates are given due consideration.

In fact, a study of Psy.D. programs revealed that 82% of them implemented formal minority admissions policies designed to improve racial representation (Young & VandeCreek, 1996). The study found that:

- 94% of the programs gave extra points on ratings of application materials to minority applicants;
- 69% of the programs waived or lowered GRE scores for minority applicants;
- 41% of the programs waived or lowered GPA cutoffs for minority applicants; and
- 21% of the programs interviewed all minority applicants, regardless of the quality of their application materials.

As a consequence, ethnic minorities in the applicant pool are more likely than whites to receive offers of admission (Munoz-Dunbar & Stanton, 1999). Our guidance and the following worksheets in this *Insider's Guide* may thus not accurately reflect a minority applicant's enhanced chances of acceptance. We recommend that you carefully read program descriptions regarding their minority selection procedures and encourage you to apply to programs that are within reach of your credentials.

Several ethnic/racial minority students have written to us over the years and complained that they were neither actively recruited nor accepted for admission into doctoral psychology programs. So let us be perfectly clear and honest: Most, but not all, doctoral programs have implemented policies (as reviewed above) to recruit and admit underrepresented racial/ethnic minority students. However, that does not mean that all programs will be knocking down your door to interview you. Nor does that mean that most programs will finance your interview. Nor does that mean acceptance is a certainty. Doctoral programs will evaluate all candidates on their GPAs, GREs, letters of recommendation, research experiences, and so on. A modest advantage is just that—an advantage, never a guarantee.

APA is committed to ensuring that the practice of psychology—and the production of psychologists—is in the vanguard of addressing the needs of culturally diverse populations. Several arms of APA have produced free, valuable publications toward this end: the guidebook *For College Students of Color Applying to Graduate & Professional Programs* (www.apa.org/careers/resources/guides/grad-school.aspx) and the *APAGS Resource Guide for Ethnic Minority Graduate Students* (www.apa.org/apags/resources/ethnic-minority-guide.aspx).

Although the special consideration given minority applicants is advantageous, it also represents a special challenge. One well-qualified minority student was advised by a university career counselor that he would have no problem getting into the doctoral program of his choice. He applied to several very competitive programs, and received acceptances and offers of financial aid across the board. Unfortunately, he skipped the process of matching his interests with the strengths of the program. After a single year, he was looking to transfer to another program that had more faculty conducting research and psychotherapy in his areas of interest.

The moral of the story is: Don't let the potential admission advantage of being an ethnic/racial minority candidate become a disadvantage. Just because you can get into a program doesn't mean that it is the program for you. A rigorous, tailored approach to the application process is the best approach for everyone.

If you are a minority student and are not quite ready to pursue a doctoral degree, you may consider enrolling in a post-baccalaurate program to shore up credentials and to become more certain that a doctoral program in psychology is the right path. Some universities offer post-bac experiences targeted to minority students. For instance, at the University of Pittsburgh, the Hot-Metal Bridge program offers a dual-semester post-baccalaurate fellowship program designed to help minority applicants prepare themselves for doctoral training.

For the LGBT Applicant

Lesbian, gay, bisexual, and transgendered (LGBT) applicants to doctoral programs can face the same social and interpersonal hurdles as ethnic/racial minority applicants. There is, however, a key difference: There are limited federal protections for members of the LGBT community. This fact may lead lesbian, gay, bisexual, and transgendered students to question whether to disclose their sexual orientation ("come out") in the application process, or even to inquire about the atmosphere of inclusivity toward sexual minorities within a particular program. In this section, we review the research and advice on LGBT applicants' selection of graduate programs and present potential strategies for those who elect to come out during the application process.

Before turning to the specifics, let us emphasize this general point: The burden should not be placed on the potentially stigmatized applicant to disclose sexual orientation. Such a burden promotes silence and fear. Rather, each applicant should choose his/her own path, and program faculty should create an inclusive, welcoming atmosphere for all students. The APA accreditation guidelines require doctoral programs to embrace diversity in their students.

Qualitative research (e.g., APA, 2006; Lark & Croteau, 1998; Rader, 2000) indicates that LGBT psychology students screen prospective graduate schools for their gay affirming (or at least, nonhomophobic) position. The typical criteria used for screening prospective programs are (Biaggio et al., 2003):

- Reports of other LGBT students
- Presence of faculty who are openly lesbian/gay or heterosexual allies
- Availability of specific training on LGBT issues and opportunity to work with LGBT clients
- Sensitivity to diversity on campus (including the presence of LGBT support and advocacy groups)
- Geographic location of the program (frequently avoiding programs in conservative rural areas)
- Size of the educational institution (larger public institutions being relatively more liberal)

In addition, we recommend that LGBT students look for climate indicators favorable to sexual diversity. Screen prospective programs by:

- searching departmental and university home pages for the presence of an LGBT student union and faculty teaching and researching on sexuality.
- looking for specific housing policies for LGBT couples.
- avoiding institutions that require a religious or doctrinal oath and that prohibit LGBT organizations on campus (more than 50 religious colleges have asked the U.S. Education Department to let

them discriminate on the basis of sexual orientation or gender identity; Jaschik, 2015).

- seeking programs with curricula that explicitly integrate LGBT and other diversity issues.
- reviewing APA's list of graduate faculty in psychology interested in lesbian, gay, and bisexual issues (available at www.apa.org/pi/lgbt/resources/survey/q6-7-table.pdf).
- evaluating the university's mission statement for a formal commitment to diversity of sexual orientation.
- determining if the institution has a coordinator (or office) for lesbian, gay, and bisexual concerns.
- considering the state laws concerning equitable treatment of LGBT.

Homophobia and heterosexism continue to exist in the United States and, unfortunately, also in institutions of higher education. Although the situation has improved considerably in recent decades, some institutions remain "tolerant" as opposed to "affirming" of sexual diversity, whereas other institutions may favor an LGBT student to maintain or expand program diversity.

The question, then, is whether to come out during the application process. On one side, there is the risk of being rejected from a program where some discrimination persists. On the other side, there is the potential advantage of being a member of a minority group in a program that actively pursues diversity. In either case, the alternative to not coming out during the application process is to come out later, or to try to hide your sexual orientation for 4 to 6 years.

If and when to disclose sexual orientation in the admissions process is ultimately a personal decision, and it can occur at different stages in the process: in the application itself, during the interview, upon acceptance to the program, or upon the decision to attend the program. As part of your application, you can indicate your sexual orientation in your research interests (e.g., lesbian health), clinical experiences (e.g., working with gay youth), and/or extracurricular activities (e.g., member of the LGBT alliance on campus). More directly, you can incorporate your sexual identity into the personal statement, especially if it has bearing on your choice of clinical or research work, or your decision to pursue psychology as a career. If you do come out in your personal statement, be sure that this fact is integrated into the overall statement and not simply a dangling fact unconnected to the rest of what you've written.

Some applicants choose to come out during the interview process with a simple but straightforward statement: "As a lesbian (or a gay man), it's important to me to be in a gay-friendly environment. Would being gay be a concern in this program?" Though it would be a mistake to over-generalize, such questions are typically met with positive responses about program diversity and discussions of resources for LGBT students. If such questions are met otherwise, it serves as a key piece of information in your decision process.

Another strategy is to raise sexual orientation at the point at which an offer of admission is tendered. As discussed in subsequent chapters, once an offer is made, an applicant has latitude in negotiating matters around admission, tuition remission, funding, and so on. This can be the time to indicate that having a gay-affirmative environment is one of the factors in your decision of which program to accept and to inquire about the atmosphere in that program. Still other LGBT students elect not to disclose until they actually matriculate in the program and begin coursework.

Whatever path you take, your sexual orientation should not be the defining topic of your application; your composite strengths as a potential doctoral student remain the center of your application. [For additional information, consult the *APAGS Resource Guide for LGBT Students in Psychology* (www.apa.org/apags/resources/lgbt-guide.aspx) and *Graduate Faculty in Psychology Interested in Lesbian, Gay, and Bisexual Issues* (at www.apa.org/pi/lgbt/resources/survey/q6-7-table.pdf).]

For the Disabled Applicant

Organized psychology is increasingly aware that diversity extends beyond gender, ethnicity, and sexual orientation to all individual differences, including disability status. Applicants with disabilities confront many of the same prejudices as other minority populations, including obstacles to graduate applications and interviews. According to the National Science Foundation, psychology and the social sciences are slightly more likely than other disciplines to have graduates with some type of disability—about 2%.

APA's Resource Guide for Psychology Graduate Students with Disabilities (www.apa.org/pi/disability/resources/publications/resource-guide.aspx) presents tips on applying to graduate school, requesting fair accommodations, and preparing for a successful experience. The guide also lists national resources on disability issues; our favorite is Dr. Ken Pope's website on accessibility in psychology graduate education and practice (at kpope.com). APA has also initiated a Disability Mentoring Program to match psychology students with veteran disabled psychologists (www.apa.org/pi/disability/resources/mentoring/ index.aspx).

When and how to disclose a disability is a complex and personal decision, a decision that you must make after sorting through the choices and perhaps discussing them with a knowledgeable mentor. There are eight different occasions during the admissions process when you might choose to disclose (Khubchandani, 2002):

- In your personal statement or application form
- When a prospective graduate school contacts you for an interview
- During the interview
- After the interview but before an offer
- After the offer but before an acceptance
- After you start the graduate program
- After a problem on the job
- Never (disclose)

There are pros and cons for each timing of disclosure, but ultimately your decision will be based on what you know about yourself and what you have learned about the particular graduate program (Khubchandani, 2002). If and when you do disclose a disability, be straightforward and factual about it only as it affects your specific job functions, as defined by the Americans with Disabilities Act (ADA). Specify the type of accommodation that you will require or the work restrictions that are involved. Don't dwell on your disability; instead, be enthusiastic about your skills and resources. Stress that your disability did not interfere with previous performance or attendance.

Your multiple abilities, not select disabilities, are what count in graduate school. As with ethnicity and sexual orientation, your disability status should not occupy center stage in your application. Assertively request fair accommodation and accessibility as provided by law, to be sure. But help the admissions committee avoid the stereotype of equating you with your disability. Your application should focus squarely on your credentials and accomplishments.

For the International Applicant

APA-accredited programs tend to look favorably upon qualified international students. In fact, fully 8% of counseling psychology doctoral students (Norcross et al., 2009) and 7% of clinical psychology doctoral students (Norcross et al., 2010) are international. Graduate psychology education in the United States is definitely going more global.

The unique challenges for international students revolve around demonstrating equivalent academic preparation, mastery of the English language (if not the native tongue), and beginning the entire process earlier than usual. With regard to credentials, the GRE scores will address your knowledge base. But submit your graduate school application well before the deadline and anticipate hearing from the graduate admissions committee about the equivalency of your undergraduate and graduate degrees. With regard to mastery of the English language, most graduate schools will require applicants whose native language is not English to take the Test of English as a Foreign Language (TOEFL; www.toeflgoanywhere.org/). The cost of taking the TOEFL varies by country, but is currently $195 in most U.S. locations.

International students need to start the application process earlier because it takes longer and entails more paperwork. In addition to the TOEFL, international applicants will need to arrange for certified transcripts in English from each university attended and, for those not citizens of the United States, an Affidavit of Support, a document demonstrating they possess adequate funding to meet the costs of at least one full academic year. That Affidavit is required before applying for the student visa (Landi, 2010).

In determining where to apply, the usual criteria pertain to international students, as reviewed in Chapter 5, with a few twists. Search for graduate programs that already enroll some international students (as shown in our Reports on Individual Programs), that feature international faculty, that offer special services for international students, and that conduct cross-cultural research. A multicultural learning environment and greater support from training programs improve international students' psychosocial and academic adjustment (Hasan et al., 2008).

We also heartily recommend two detailed guides: *Studying Psychology in the United States: Expert Guidance for International Students* published by the American Psychological Association (Hasan et al., 2008) and *Succeeding as an International Student in the United States and Canada* published by the University of Chicago Press (Lipson, 2013). In addition, consult with the international student offices at the universities to which you are applying.

Assessing Program Criteria

Assessing the criteria that clinical and counseling psychology programs use to evaluate applicants is a vital step in applying to graduate school. To illuminate this point, we will relate the story of one applicant we knew several years ago. She was a psychology major from an elite university who had conducted research with a prominent psychologist. She had fine letters of recommendation and clinical experience with developmentally disabled children, but her GREs were in the 150s. Thinking that her credentials were superb, she applied to the most competitive research-oriented programs and one practice-oriented program. She was rejected across the board at these top research schools and just barely made it into what she had mistakenly considered her practice-oriented "safety school." Her mistake was to ignore the fact that all the research-oriented programs to which she applied specified minimum GRE scores of 160 or more. Her application was unsuccessful because she ignored one piece of essential information. She was nearly rejected in the more practice-oriented program she had felt was a "sure thing" because she did not possess the clinical experience they were looking for.

The moral of the story is twofold: (1) Attend closely to the admission standards of each program. If a school sets standards you cannot realistically meet, you need to work very, very hard to get them to make an exception. In other words, think thrice about applying there. (2) Apply to programs with a range of admission criteria, and consider a safety school as one that announces admission requirements that you exceed by a wide margin. This does not guarantee acceptance, but does dramatically increase the probability of making it into their finalist pool.

Now, turn your attention to Appendix C, "Worksheet for Assessing Program Criteria." In Appendix C, you will rate yourself on how well you conform to each school's admission requirements. The aim is that you not waste time and money applying to programs that indicate in no uncertain terms that you do not meet their admissions criteria. There is no reason to feel inadequate because you fall short of these specifications. There may be programs on your list with requirements you do meet or exceed. If you are unable to meet the minimum requirements of any programs on your list, you should seriously consider postponing applications to better prepare yourself or applying to less competitive master's programs.

Begin by transferring the name of each school from Appendix B to the "School" column of Appendix C. Simply copy the list from one table to the other. Also copy the number in the "Self-Rating" column from one worksheet to the other. Next, look up the first program on your list in the Reports on Individual Programs. Read through all of the information provided to start familiarizing yourself with that program.

As you begin completing Appendix C and listing each school's admission criteria, remember that these are approximations of your strength as an applicant to that particular program. These scales are not set in stone and do not guarantee that you will be accepted. You may not readily fall into any of the categories listed and may need to make rough estimates. Or you may find that you fall between categories and have to add 0.5 point here or subtract 0.5 point there. If you think it is appropriate to modify the categories or scoring systems, by all means do so. *The most important result is not an absolute number but a relative sense of how well you meet each program's admission criteria.*

You may also discover that a graduate program does not require certain entrance examinations, or gives no mean GRE scores, or doesn't mandate courses for admission. In this case, simply score a "0" in the appropriate column. When it comes time to total each school's score, the 0s will neither detract from nor add to your ability to meet their requirements.

Now, go to the respective Reports on Individual Programs and look at the prerequisite courses. You will see two questions pertaining to course preparation prior to applying: "What courses are required for incoming students to have completed prior to enrolling?" and "Are there courses you recommend that are not mandatory?" Underneath each question you will find a list of courses that the particular school assigned to each category. On your list in Appendix C, under the column marked "Courses," score yourself as follows (in this table, "M" indicates "mandatory" and "R" indicates "recommended"):

+2	You have taken all the M and R courses and earned B+ or better in them all.
+1	You have taken all the M courses and/or several of the R courses and earned B+ or better.
0	You have taken all the M courses, but none of the Rs, or earned B– or lower in some M courses.
–1	You have not taken one or two of the M courses, or have earned B– or lower in several of them.
–2	You have not taken several or any of the M courses or have received C or lower in some of the M or R courses.

The next section on each "Program" page is marked GREs and GPA. This section gives mean scores for the GREs and GPAs for each program listed.

On your list, under the columns marked "GRE-V" (verbal), "GRE-Q" (quantitative), and "GRE-S" (psychology subject test), score yourself as follows:

+2 You exceed the school's mean score by at least 8 points.
+1 You exceed the school's mean score by more than 4 but less than 8 points.
0 You meet the school's mean or exceed it by less than 4 points.
–1 You do not meet the school's mean score, but are less than 8 points below it.
–2 You are below the mean score by 8 points or more.

For GPA, we asked programs for the mean score of their incoming class and asked if that applied to more than one type of GPA. It is not uncommon for programs to look at cumulative or overall GPA (all undergraduate courses taken) and psychology GPA (only psychology courses). Again, it is wise to review the average GPA of incoming students. Under the column marked "GPA," score yourself as follows:

+2 You exceed the school's cumulative GPA by 0.3 points or more.
+1 You exceed the school's cumulative GPA by less than 0.1 point.
0 You meet the school's average GPA.
–1 You do not meet the school's cumulative GPA, but are less than 0.1 below it.
–2 You are below the school's cumulative by more than 0.3 points.

Next, look back to the second column of Appendix C, "Self-Rating." This is how the program rates itself on the practice–research continuum. If a program emphasizes one more than the other, this gives some indication of what it would consider important in an applicant. A program that stresses research will probably desire an applicant to have research experience. Under the "Research" column in Appendix C, rate yourself as follows:

+2 The school rates itself as a 6 or a 7 and you will have completed an honors thesis or will have at least 2 years of experience in psychology research (beyond required coursework).
+1 The school rates itself as a 4, 5, 6, or 7 and you will have at least 1 year of experience in psychology research.
0 The school rates itself as a 1, 2, or 3.
–1 The school rates itself as a 4 or 5, and you have no research experience.
–2 The school rates itself as a 6 or 7, and you have no research experience.

Similarly, a program emphasizing clinical work will prefer that an applicant enter with some practical experience in human services or health care. Under the "Clinical" column, rate yourself as follows:

+2 The school rates itself as a 1 or a 2, and you will have worked in a full-time (35+ hr./week) clinical position for at least 1 year.
+1 The school rates itself as a 1, 2, 3, or 4 and you will have volunteered part-time (8+ hr./week) at a clinical facility for at least 1 year.
0 The school rates itself as a 5, 6, or 7.
–1 The school rates itself as a 3 or 4, and you have no clinical experience.
–2 The school rates itself as a 1 or 2, and you have no clinical experience.

At this point, you should have completed the first nine columns of Appendix C from "School" to "Clinical."

Additional information provided for each program in the Reports on Individual Programs are "How many students applied in 2017?," "How many applicants were offered admission in 2017?," and "How many admitted students are incoming?" These give a rough estimate of the competitiveness of a program.

In applying to programs, be realistic and reasonable. You may have a sterling application, but when Yale and Harvard accept roughly 2 in 100 applicants, you had best be applying to other places as well. Apply to several schools with a range of competitiveness as a precautionary measure.

Bear in mind: Programs accept more applicants than end up attending. This makes programs appear more restrictive than they actually are. This is why we added the third item regarding the number of students who will enter the program—a number invariably smaller than the number of accepted students. For example, an applicant gaining acceptance to five programs will ultimately reject four of them. A Ph.D. program planning on an incoming class of six students may accept ten or twelve students before filling their new class or cohort. A large Psy.D. program may accept 100 students to yield the desired 50 students attending.

In the column marked "Compete" in Appendix C, record the ratio of applications to acceptances. It should be noted that competitiveness is difficult to quantify. Although we have selected the ratio of applicants to acceptances as our measure, other relevant criteria include GRE scores and GPA. Since we have already discussed these criteria, we are using this opportunity to highlight yet another area related to competitiveness.

The last column is marked "Total." Add the numbers under the "Courses," "GRE-V," "GRE-Q," "GRE-S," "GPA," "Research," and "Clinical" columns. This will provide you with a total somewhere between –14 and +14, which is a rough indication of how well you meet each school's admission requirements and expectations.

Now you have a grand list of doctoral programs that are performing research or clinical work in the areas you have specified. In addition, you have several indications of how well each school will address your needs and expectations as a graduate student. Finally, you have a rating of yourself as an applicant to each program.

We recommend that you begin your decision-making process by selecting the programs that have admission requirements within your reach. As you look through the "school requirements" part of your list, note any negative numbers, say, –3 to –14. Unless you can reasonably expect to change these to zeros or better before you complete your applications, you are better off dropping these programs from your list. After that, you will need to decide which are the reasonable places to apply.

Below is a rating system based on your "Total" column for each program. Although this system may help you decide where to apply, it is by no means definitive. *These are approximations*, and ultimately you will have to decide where to apply based on this and any other information to which you are privy. From the "Total" column of Appendix C, evaluate each program as follows:

10 to 14 Your chances are very good. Apply to many of these schools, since your application may be especially strong here.

6 to 9 Your chances are good. These schools are within your reach, as you exceed several of the requirements.

4 to 5 Your chances are moderately good here, but be sure to apply to some schools where you rank more highly.

0 to 3 Your chances are fair here; these schools are within your range of abilities. Your application may not be outstanding, but it is somewhere between "adequate" and "more than adequate." Be sure to apply to several schools in a higher range.

0 to –3 These schools are a stretch for you. Go ahead and apply to a few, but the bulk of your applications should go to schools on which you achieved a higher score.

< –3 These schools are looking for something different from your experience or performance at this time.

Although this worksheet embodies most of the criteria used by admissions committees, it of course cannot integrate all possible criteria. If a professor has expressed interest in conducting research with you, for example, the worksheet total may underestimate your chances for acceptance. Other useful resources when selecting your list of schools include specific professors, undergraduate psychology advisors, and the websites of the respective programs. Graduate students at your local university can also be helpful, and a few large universities have even created notebooks on clinical and counseling psychology graduate programs (Todd & Farinato, 1992). Take advantage of all the available information to augment the data provided in the Reports on Individual Programs.

Using the system in Appendix C, delete some of the schools that list admission criteria outside of your present range. This will enable you to begin the next phase: selecting programs that match your training and career goals.

For the research-oriented applicant, these decisions may be easiest. Look at the schools remaining on your worksheet. Note the number of faculty interested in your research area(s) and whether they are funded. Grant funding is a rough indicator of the intensity of the program's commitment to a particular research area. The premise is that a grant-funded area may offer more opportunities to study the topic and may be more likely to generate research. In addition, grant funding has the potential of making assistantship money available. This by no means suggests that a program that does not have a grant in your area is not conducting current research or will not have money available to you. Additionally, a program with several faculty in an area may simply be "between" grants. Thus, the number of faculty alone also can indicate a school's commitment to this area of research.

Next, check the program's productivity ranking (Table 4-2) and their self-rating as being more practice or research-oriented. Again, if you are research-oriented, you may well find yourself crossing those schools off your list that are low on productivity and that are clearly practice-oriented. You will discover that this shortens your list but that you still have a number of doctoral programs that cover a wide range of desirability. This is exactly where you want to be at this point! What you desire is a list of 15 to 30 programs for which you will secure additional information. Then, you can begin fine-tuning and selecting the 10 to 20 programs to which you will actually apply.

If you are more strongly inclined toward practice, you will find yourself crossing schools off your list that are research-oriented, favor theoretical orientations different from your own, or are too restricted for your needs. The programs highlighting clinical work, and especially those sharing your orientation or providing a track or clinic in your area, will be the most desirable.

The applicant equally emphasizing practice and research training is the most challenged. You want a program that is research-oriented, but not at the expense of clinical work. But you also want a program that will offer high-quality clinical training without sacrificing high standards in research. Using your list, find the programs that are moderate or high in research productivity and that have a number of people interested in your area. Ensure that they rate themselves as a 4 or 5, indicating that they emphasize practice and research nearly equally. Then, determine if their theoretical orientation conforms to yours and whether they offer a specialty clinic or formal tracks in your area. Again, you will find a range of programs, some conforming to your needs better than others. This is exactly what you want at this point in the process.

You are now ready to gather the detailed information necessary to choose among the 15 to 30 programs you will use for your selection pool. If your number of programs does not fall within these parameters, you should consider modifying your list. The website and email address of each program are listed with each entry in the Reports on Individual Programs.

In addition to your direct access to Reports of Individual Programs in the back of this book, you can go online and quickly gather additional information. APA offers a free search feature for all of its accredited doctoral programs at apps.apa.org/accredsearch/. APA's online *Graduate Study in Psychology* provides (for a fee) three-month access to its database, which includes master's programs and doctoral programs outside of the clinical, counseling, and combined areas. Petersons (www.petersons.com/) also provides free searches (albeit with annoying advertising) of graduate programs by degree and state.

At this juncture, all you need is to spend a few hours on the Web. Upwards of 99% of graduate programs post their application forms and instructions online.

Congratulations! You have taken the initial steps in your application process.

CHAPTER 5

SELECTING SCHOOLS

Between late summer and late fall, you will scan websites and download files describing each graduate program. You are ahead of the game if you begin during late summer, because most applicants will not be starting this process for another 2 to 3 months. This presents an opportunity for you to leverage an early start to set yourself apart as an organized and optimal candidate.

When applying for undergraduate study, you probably visited a few colleges to help you decide where to apply. When applying for graduate study, by contrast, visits are rare—at least until you are invited for an interview. The exception may be when you live close to a graduate school of special interest. But otherwise, you will only visit doctoral programs "virtually" through online descriptions until invited for a pre-admission interview.

In order to select programs that best suit your needs and interests, we again return to the foundational questions: What is it I want for myself? What is it I'm interested in doing? And where do I want to do it? A firm commitment to a single practice interest, research area, geographic location, or theoretical orientation is not required at this time; however, the more specific your interests, the more intelligent a choice you are going to make.

In the previous chapter we helped you get started in narrowing your choices of potential graduate programs. We did so by identifying your interests, comparing your credentials to those required by graduate programs of interest, and by searching for potential matches. In this chapter, we will review six critical variables to take into account in tightening your choices: research interests, clinical opportunities, theoretical orientations, financial aid, program outcomes, and quality of life.

A Multitude of Considerations

Each graduate school applicant is undeniably unique in his or her reasons for applying to particular programs in clinical or counseling psychology. As we advise students and conduct workshops on graduate school admission, we hear a litany of restrictions: "I have to stay close to my spouse in Los Angeles," "It must be a Catholic school," "I can only attend if I receive full financial aid," "The program needs to be gay friendly, or have gay faculty mentors," "I am interested solely in cognitive-behavioral programs," "I would really like to be near the mountains," "The program must have lots of women faculty," and so on. There is obviously no single, definitive list of factors to consider in selecting potential schools. Although we will examine the six most common considerations, we will be unable to canvass the almost infinite range of reasons for selecting programs to which to apply.

In an ideal world, graduate student aspirants would have sufficient funds and freedom to consider any psychology program in the country. In the real world, however, you may be limited in your choice by financial, family, and geographic considerations. Although we appreciate these real constraints, we encourage you not to be prematurely limited by your own vision. Try to think broadly and boldly. It is, quite simply, your career at stake.

Geographic location will be a determining factor for some applicants. By this we mean both the area of the country and proximity to significant others in your life, such as parents, spouses/partners, siblings, or lovers. If you do not possess the mobility to relocate to another area of the country, then you might delay applying until your situation changes or apply only to regional schools, even if they are less desirable. Don't spend time, money, and energy on futile missions, in this case applying to programs you will be unable to attend.

At the same time, we heartily encourage you to "get out of town." Far too often students restrict themselves unnecessarily to schools close to their homes or to their undergraduate institution. Yet, graduate programs that better match their needs may be located across the country or four states south. Your future demands that you look around the entire country and Canada.

The gender, ethnicity, or sexual orientation composition of graduate programs may be an influential factor for other applicants. If this is the case for you, obtain updated resource directories from the American Psychological Association and apply accordingly. Three examples are APA's *Graduate Faculty Interested in the Psychology of Women* (forms.apa.org/pi/women/gradsearch/), *Directory of Ethnic Minority Professionals in Psychology* (www.apa.org/pubs/books/4070873.aspx), and *Graduate Faculty Interested in Gay, Lesbian, and Bisexual Issues in Psychology* (www.apa.org/pi/lgbt/resources/survey/q6-7-table.pdf). The Reports on Individual Programs also present the percentage of ethnic minority, international, and women students in each clinical, counseling, and combined psychology program. These can be a useful source of direction in your choice.

Our general point is this: think through your personal reasons for applying to certain programs and then proactively secure information about those considerations. Even if your choice of programs is limited, make it an informed choice. Accept as you must the restrictions in the range of potential graduate schools, but do not leave your future to chance!

The rule of thumb in selecting schools: Applicants to clinical scientist Ph.D. programs match primarily to the research interests of individual faculty, applicants to scientist-practitioner Ph.D. programs match to both the research interests of individual faculty and the offerings of the entire program, and applicants to Psy.D. programs match primarily to the clinical interests and theoretical orientations of the entire program. This general rule will guide how you select graduate schools of potential interest.

Research Interests

The websites for doctoral programs will feature faculty members in that department and their current research. You are looking to learn from the faculty, so our advice is to locate the professors who are experts in your areas of interest. If you are interested in clinical child or pediatric psychology, locate those psychologists active in training and research in that field. If you are interested in clinical health psychology, find the researchers or clinicians tackling that subject. Scan the faculty member's Web page, or the description provided by the department. Read these descriptions carefully. What kind of questions are they asking? Have you asked yourself those same questions? Is this the sort of thing you can envision yourself exploring? Have you read a sample of what they have written?

In selecting professors whose interests parallel your own, you are searching for a good *match*. You are looking for mentors—psychologists who will take you on as an apprentice and teach you about your chosen profession. Indeed, the admission system for virtually all research-oriented Ph.D. programs is explicitly mentor-based: Students are chosen for their interest in working, at least initially, with an individual faculty mentor with a shared research interest.

The more similar your views are, the better the match. For example, if you are practice-oriented, psychodynamically disposed, and interested in private practice, you might choose to cross off your list a program with professors who operate exclusively from behavioral orientations and research perspectives. This does not mean your interest has to be pinpoint focused. Knowing you would rather investigate or treat psychodynamically may be enough to narrow your list of schools down to a sufficient range. But the more focused, the better your fit.

As you review the faculty descriptions and other materials, you will develop a sense of whom you would like to work with, and who is going to have the facilities to allow you to research or treat the populations in which you are interested. Eventually you should have a list of 10 to 20 programs with faculty with whom you would like to work and a general idea of what each of them does.

Having created such a list of programs, we suggest that you review the recent articles or books that these professors have written. Most websites include a sampling of each faculty member's recent publications. So examine their bibliographies online, inspect the program homepage, or search the *Psychological Abstracts* on *PsycInfo* for the last 5 to 7 years to locate some recent publications. Then go online and look them up. What methods do they use? What are the specifics of their treatment or research that hold your attention? If you notice yourself quickly getting bored or saying, "So what? OK, so alcoholics tend to smoke more? Who cares?", then you have a valuable piece of information. If you find these articles interesting, you are on the right track. Get excited about your profession and where you want to attend graduate school!

Here are additional bits of information you can gather to whittle down your number of applications in terms of research interests. Consult:

- the data in the Reports on Individual Programs in this book, especially the section devoted to research areas
- the program's and professor's Web page
- national webpages devoted to research specializations; for example, directories of graduate programs in child clinical (www.clinicalchildpsychology.org) and health psychology (www.healthpsych.org)
- individual faculty via email (discussed in the next section)
- professors and/or graduate students at your own school about the programs in question
- the CUR Registry of Undergraduate Researchers and Graduate Schools (www.cur.org/projects_and_services/registry/students), which links undergraduate students who have research experience with graduate programs interested in recruiting such students.

When it comes to your research interests, discover if there are medical schools, academic health centers, or neuroscience facilities at your disposal. Library facilities should be a prime consideration, but we have found that medical libraries in particular contain journal subscriptions not available elsewhere. More importantly, access to journals online through the university is essential. An associated medical school or hospital may also offer facilities and populations available for your research. Determine if they are present, and then investigate their relationship to the Psychology Department.

In addition, learn more about the research space dedicated to your area. For example, does someone have the equipment you need, lab or research space, funding? If you desire to conduct research in cardiovascular psychophysiology and you have found a professor who has published several articles, determine if he or she has equipment to monitor cardiac responses. If not, there should be equipment available somewhere in the department [or in certain cases (e.g., neuroimaging or genotyping research), there should be resources available somewhere in the university].

We realize that this investigative process requires time and energy. It may also provoke anxiety in an already nerve-wracking application process. This is one reason we advocate an early start. Again, we emphasize that you can get into a graduate program without doing this extra work. This preparation, however, will give you the edge to get into the program of your choice or to overcome weaknesses in your application.

Clinical Opportunities

Having read articles, chapters, or books by the professors with whom you would like to work, you know better which ones you find stimulating. However, if your career interest is primarily practice, it is possible you might determine that the faculty members you're interested in working with do not have recent publications in your area(s) of interest. Or you know a program has a formal track in your area or a substance abuse clinic, but you can't figure out which professors treat clients or supervise students there.

Your first recourse should be to search the university's website to locate this information. If it is not on the psychology program's Web page, it may exist on the individual professor's website or somewhere else within the university's website.

You can also check the Reports on Individual Programs at the back of this book and particularly Appendices F (Specialty Clinics) and G (Programs Concentrations and Tracks). They will immediately inform you of the prominent clinical offerings of the doctoral programs.

Our research indicates 67% of clinical psychology and 27% of counseling psychology programs offer formal tracks or concentrations (Stratigis, Zimmerman, & Norcross, 2014). The most prevalent tracks across all APA-accredited programs are child clinical/pediatric, health psychology, neuropsychology, adult, forensic, family/marriage, and multicultural/cross-cultural.

Certain practice areas are emphasized by clinical programs, others by counseling programs. More than half of the clinical programs offer child clinical/pediatric while none of the counseling programs offer it. More clinical psychology programs also feature neuropsychology, adult, and forensic tracks. By contrast, more counseling psychology programs offer multicultural/cross-cultural, family/marriage, social justice, and vocational tracks (Stratigis et al., 2014). So, in part, your clinical interests may influence whether you are drawn to clinical or counseling psychology.

If all else fails, email the department coordinator and ask this person for materials specific to the track or clinic in which you would like to work. Or ask to speak with the director of that clinic or coordinator of that track to determine which faculty are practicing and supervising there.

Now, we are going to suggest something that can prove useful in making final decisions about where to apply and in increasing your chances of being accepted there. During early fall of the year you apply, contact a *few* of the professors you have been investigating. Email the ones whose interests seem most closely aligned to your own. Practically all program websites include faculty email addresses.

There are many reasons to directly contact a faculty member. First, it gives you an opportunity to gain information you probably could not gather in any other way—information about the program, its facilities, and its faculty. Second, these emails give you a chance to get to know someone you are genuinely interested in working with. It gives you an opportunity to evaluate how happy you would be in a mentorship with this faculty member. Of course, there must be aspects of this person's research or clinical work that attract you. If you do not know his or her interests or the literature well enough to demonstrate a working knowledge of the individual's contributions, do *not* write to him or her. Professors routinely receive letters from people looking to make contact, and unless you can pique their interest and demonstrate familiarity with their work, you are unlikely to receive a response.

Whether your interests are oriented toward research, practice, or both, you are not looking to take this person, or the field, by storm. You seek to make a contribution in this particular area, a contribution made *after* you have taken the time to learn and gain experience under their mentorship. Or, you are looking to gain experience and clinical training with an experienced practitioner.

Take a moment to look at this relationship from the professor's perspective. If she is a researcher, then she is looking for students to help with that research, for students with the knowledge and drive to help design and run studies. If she is a clinician, then she is looking for individuals eager for supervision who will be carry a client load. And that is what you have to offer. You are looking for the best fit between your interests and a program and its faculty.

Contacting a professor is not a necessity. Many students are admitted to excellent programs and then take one or two years to explore, to discern what they want and where they fit in. In fact, some doctoral programs require students to work with several professors during their initial year before selecting an adviser or a major professor. Nonetheless, it is to your advantage to spend sufficient time deciding which professors would best suit you. Locate programs and professors who seem appropriate; then go ahead and contact a few of them to test the waters.

Figures 5-1 and 5-2 show sample email letters of introduction, the former for research-oriented applicants and the latter for practice-oriented. *These are not forms to copy in which you simply insert your own words!* Show a draft of your email to a mentor to preview how well it is likely to be received. When these emails are professional and succinct, they are generally well-received by potential professors. According to our own students, approximately 75% of these emails receive a response, most within three or four days.

But let us forcefully reiterate the caveats about sending letters of introduction. Do *not* send a formulaic letter; it must be tailored to the faculty member. Do *not* send an email inquiring if the faculty member is accepting new students until you have searched his or her website for that information. Do *not* ask about a faculty member's research or clinical interests; those are presented on the website. Do *not* email a request to speak with a professor or a grad student before applying; they will contact you if you rise to their finalist pool. Any of these mistakes will probably place you on the professor's reject list.

Asking a busy professor to stop what she is doing to send you an email describing future research directions at this early stage in the process risks irritating her. Indeed, one of us was told by a prominent faculty member that students who send him a request to elaborate on his research before applying usually are not invited to interview! Keep in mind that even the busiest faculty members are motivated to review the promising graduate applications, and if you are in the mix, there will be ample opportunity to ask your questions as the application process moves along.

Students have asked us whether it is acceptable to send letters to more than one faculty member at the same program. Despite the fact that applicants may have multiple research and clinical interests, most faculty (ourselves included) react negatively to learning that the same person has written to more than one faculty member. Remember, there is a certain

Dear Dr. Morris:

I am a psychology senior at Babylon University, where I have been working with Dr. Frances Murrow, studying the effects of self-esteem on math anxiety. As I was searching the research literature, I read several of your articles concerning the use of mindfulness and acceptance techniques to improve self-esteem and test anxiety.

After reading your article "The Uses of Mindfulness with Children" (December 2016 issue of *School Psychology*), I have a question I hoped you could answer. We used several of the questionnaires that you used in that study. In looking at our data, we have found that participants responded quite differently to the Test Anxiety Questionnaire at various times in the semester. We found that the further into the semester students progressed, the more their anxiety affected their scores. Have you also found this to be the case in your research?

On a related matter, I will soon be applying to clinical psychology doctoral programs that offer research experience in anxiety. I read on your program's website that you are taking on new graduate students. I hope to get the chance to meet with you in the future.

Thank you for your time and consideration. I look forward to hearing from you.

Sincerely yours,

Chris Smith

FIGURE 5-1. Sample email of introduction—research oriented.

amount of self-interest involved: We're looking for bright, motivated students to collaborate in research and practice. It can be awkward when an admissions committee is discussing an applicant, and two faculty express a desire to work with him/her, only to discover that the applicant has been actively expressing detailed interest in *both* of them.

Our advice: Unless a few faculty members share highly overlapping research interests, don't write to more than one faculty member in any doctoral program. If you do write to more than one, be open about it in your emails.

What if the professor does not respond within a few weeks? Absence of a response does not mean that you will not work with that individual if you are accepted. Most likely the professor received too many queries to respond. Indeed, at some schools, professors are receiving dozens of emails during the months leading up to the application deadline. Later, when your application is reviewed, your email may be read.

If the selected professor does write back, then it may be the beginning of a working relationship. Even if you are not accepted to his or her program or ultimately decide not to attend, you are making professional contacts in your field. There is no guideline as to exactly how to behave from here, since each professor is different. But you should begin getting a sense of whether this is the right person (and program) for you.

If the task of introducing yourself to a professor "cold" seems overly daunting, consider alternatives. Local and regional conferences present prime opportunities for meeting potential mentors and gathering information about graduate programs. Numerous societies hold yearly conferences in which research is presented in specialty areas of psychology. For example, if one of your interests lies in health psychology or behavioral medicine, there is the Society for Behavioral Medicine, the American Psychosomatic Society, and the Society for Psychophysiological Research. If, for another example, your interests lie in psychotherapy, there are the annual conferences of the Society for Psychotherapy Research, the Association for Behavioral and Cognitive Therapy, and the Society for the Exploration of Psychotherapy Integration. Your psychology advisor can probably suggest several societies in each area of psychology.

Student membership in a scientific society brings a number of benefits. For beginners, it will probably provide you access to an electronic directory of members (including contact information), which is an easy way of quickly ascertaining who is practicing and researching in your area. Most scientific organizations will invite you to join their electronic listservs. With membership also typically comes a newsletter or a journal, which delivers a sense of the leaders in the field.

Attending a professional conference can provide a great deal more information, as we have already emphasized in Chapter 3. If you are interested in particular professors, you may have a chance to see them in action if they are presenting an address or poster. In this way, you can get acquainted with the person and the research without taking the risk of formally introducing yourself. Alternatively, you may approach the professor directly and express your interest in the research or ask your psychology advisor to make the introduction. Many graduate students first met their mentors in these ways.

Determine if the department's psychological clinic serves the surrounding community or only the college community. College students are fine clients with whom to begin, but you will probably desire a greater diversity of populations and disorders. Learn more about the school's affiliated or specialized departmental clinics. Who can work there and when? Who conducts the clinical supervision? Do you have to be affiliated with a specific professor, or is there a competitive process toward earning that placement? If you're choosing a program in part based on the availability of its clinic, how available will that clinic be to you?

Table 5-1, "Questions to Ask about Psy.D. Programs," contains questions more specific to Psy.D. and practice-oriented Ph.D. applicants. This list was compiled, in part, by surveying the clinical Psy.D. students at the Graduate School of Applied and Professional Psychology at Rutgers University and asking them what questions they had (or wish they had) asked when applying to Psy.D. programs.

Theoretical Orientations

A question related to clinical and research opportunities is whether the graduate program will provide training in your desired theoretical orientations. We are *not* recommending that you prematurely affiliate with a single theoretical camp; rather, we suggest that you identify those orientations you are interested in learning more about and those you are not.

Several programs in the Northeast U.S. are strongly committed to a psychoanalytic approach and offer few training opportunities beyond that. By contrast, the vast majority of research-oriented, PCSAS-accredited programs heavily endorse cognitive and behavioral approaches. The immediate implication is to avoid applying to programs that will

Dear Dr. Morris:

I am a psychology senior at Babylon University, where I recently completed an upper-level course in clinical/counseling psychology. My professor, Dr. Frances Ellis, discussed your social problem-solving program targeted to elementary school children. Dr. Ellis spoke highly about the manner in which you use your clinical findings to derive theoretical models of problem solving and use these models to guide your treatment.

I am interested in learning more about child-based social problem-solving programs. I have been involved in such a project with Dr. Ellis and wish to continue my education in this area. I am preparing applications for Psy.D. programs and would like to learn more about your particular program. I have read the description posted on your website, but have a follow-up question. Specifically, what opportunities exist for clinical Psy.D. students to work on your social problem-solving program? I would like to help train parents, teachers, and clinicians in imparting social problem-solving skills to children.

I would appreciate any materials that you could send me describing your problem-solving program in greater detail. I am especially interested in the role for Psy.D. students. Thank you for your time and consideration.

Sincerely yours,

Chris Smith

FIGURE 5-2. Sample email of introduction—practice oriented.

TABLE 5-1. Questions to Ask about Psy.D. Programs

Is the Psy.D. program freestanding or part of a comprehensive university?
Is the program owned or operated by a for-profit company?
If the program also has a clinical Ph.D. progr-am, are all of the practicum opportunities equally available to Psy.D. students and Ph.D. students? Is it possible to take the Ph.D. courses as well? What is the relationship between the Psy.D. and Ph.D. students?
Will the internship occur in the third or fourth year? Do you complete an internship before or after your clinical dissertation?
What is the annual tuition? Does that amount include summer courses?
What is the typical debt level of graduating students?
Does the university offer housing for Psy.D. students? If not, how much are the monthly rents locally?
Are there opportunities for live supervision? Do the full-time faculty perform the clinical supervision?
Is it possible to gain experience working with . . . ? With families? With groups?
What types of clinical populations are available on campus?
What percentage of the faculty are full-time? What percent are tenured?
How many of my classes here will be taught by full-time faculty members?
Do the faculty have independent practices?
What percentage of first-year students complete the program? What is the attrition rate?
What is the size of the incoming class? How many students are in a typical graduate course?
What percentage of your students obtain an APA-accredited internship?

not offer supervised experience in your theoretical approach(es).

The Reports on Individual Programs provide the approximate percentage of faculty in each program who subscribe to the five most popular theoretical orientations: psychodynamic/psychoanalytic, behavioral analysis/radical behavioral, family systems/systems, existential/phenomenological/humanistic, and cognitive/cognitive-behavioral. Let those figures guide you in ruling out a few programs that fail to address your theoretical predilections or, if you are uncommitted, that neglect exposure to multiple or integrative approaches.

Table 5-2 presents the average percentage of faculty endorsing these five theoretical orientations in APA-accredited clinical and counseling programs. Across those hundreds of programs, the cognitive/cognitive-behavioral tradition predominates, accounting for more than half of the faculty members. Radical behaviorism is relatively infrequent, with psychodynamic, systems, and humanistic theories falling in between these two extremes. Note too that counseling psychology faculty endorse the humanistic/existential orientations much more frequently than do the clinical psychology faculty (22% vs. 9%).

These global figures do not specifically include the integrative/eclectic orientation, which is the most

TABLE 5-2. Theoretical Orientations of Faculty in APA-Accredited Clinical and Counseling Psychology Programs

Orientations	% of clinical faculty	% of counseling faculty
Psychodynamic/Psychoanalytic	16	17
Applied behavioral analysis/Radical behavioral	6	6
Family systems/Systems	16	20
Existential/Phenomenological/Humanistic	9	22
Cognitive/Cognitive-behavioral	65	50

Note. Data from Norcross, Ellis, & Sayette (2010) and Norcross, Sayette, & Pomerantz (2017).

popular approach of mental health professionals (Norcross & Goldfried, 2005). The fact that the percentages add up to more than 100% indicates that faculty practice across orientations.

These averages mask significant differences among doctoral programs as a function of their placement along the practice–research continuum. Research-oriented programs, as a rule, have a higher percentage of cognitive-behavioral faculty, while practice-oriented programs have a higher percentage of psychodynamic faculty (Sayette et al., 2011). These differences are quite large: Fully 84% of faculty members in research-oriented Ph.D. programs are cognitive-behavioral versus 32% in practice-oriented Psy.D. programs. Only 5% of faculty in research-oriented Ph.D. programs are psychodynamic versus 28% in practice-oriented Psy.D. programs (Norcross, Sayette, & Pomerantz, in press).

Our longitudinal data on faculty theoretical orientations reveal that the field has moved from a relative balance of theories to the domination of cognitive-behavioral therapy (CBT; Heatherington et al., 2012; Norcross, Sayette, & Pomerantz, in press; Sayette et al., 2011). This is especially true in clinical psychology Ph.D. programs, as discussed above. The upshot is to investigate thoroughly the area of psychology (clinical, counseling) and the type of program (practice-oriented to research-oriented) that regularly provide training in your preferred theoretical orientation(s). Applicants seeking extensive training in non-CBT will need to be particularly vigilant in investigating and selecting potential graduate programs.

In addition to reviewing the faculty theoretical orientations in the Reports on Individual Programs, those of you with an intense hankering for training in a particular orientation may want to peruse specialty directories. A number of professional societies publish lists of graduate programs that offer training in their theory of choice. The Association for Behavioral and Cognitive Therapies (ABCT), for example, publishes a directory of graduate programs in cognitive-behavior therapy and experimental clinical psychology (www.abct.org). The APA Division of Psychoanalysis, for another example, provides a list of universities in the United States that offer psychoanalytic-friendly graduate programs (www.apadivisions.org/division-39/ leadership/committees/grad-students/graduate-programs.aspx). The Society for the Exploration of Psychotherapy Integration (SEPI), for a final example, has pulled together a list of integrative training programs on its website (www.sepiweb.org/page/training; Norcross, Nolan, et al., 2017). Search the Web and consult your advisors regarding the existence of specialty directories in your field of interest.

The popularity of theories, as with other professional fads, undergoes transformation over time. Extrapolating from historical trends and expert predictions (Norcross et al., 2013), mindfulness, cognitive-behavioral, integrative, multicultural, and exposure therapies will be in the ascendancy in the near future. By contrast, transactional analysis, classical psychoanalysis, Jungian therapy, and existentialism are expected to decline. In an era of managed care, theoretical orientations that emphasize brief problem-focused treatments and document their effectiveness will probably thrive.

Financial Aid

The next question, and it is by no means premature, is the availability of financial aid. Unless you can afford to pay for graduate school on your own or you are prepared to take out substantial loans, you require knowledge about the probability of support directly from the doctoral program. This is not a suggestion to avoid schools with scarce financial aid. It is a suggestion not to apply only to schools with scarce financial aid.

APA's (2017) *Ethical Principles of Psychologists and Code of Conduct* requires truth in advertising about graduate programs. Standard 7.02 (Description of Programs) stipulates that "Psychologists responsible for education and training programs take reasonable steps to ensure that there is a current and accurate description of program content . . . stipends and benefits, and requirements that must be met for satisfactory completion of the program. This information must be made readily available to all interested parties" (www.apa.org/ethics/code/). Not only is it your perfect right to request such information, but it is also the ethical obligation of the graduate psychology program to provide it.

Until recently, only a minority of psychology doctoral programs were fully disclosing all of the information requested by the APA Commission on Accreditation (Burgess, Keeley, & Blashfield, 2008). But the APA now requires accredited doctoral programs to publicly post on their websites their educational outcomes and financial costs to allow for informed decision-making among prospective students. We will discuss where this information is posted and how to access in the next section. For now, please know that a prime objective of this *Insid-*

er's Guide is to present financial aid information in our Reports on Individual Programs.

Calculating the total cost of full-time graduate study must include both academic expenses and living expenses. The academic side includes tuition, fees, supplies, books, and journals. Full-time tuition ranges from a low of $10,000 a year for some in-state Ph.D. students to $35,000 for private, Psy.D. programs. Multiplying the tuition by 4 years gives you some idea of the probable tuition burden. The living side includes rent, transportation, food, clothing, insurance, and entertainment. Health insurance has emerged as a large part of the cost of graduate studies. Some assistantships include health insurance, but others do not. Not surprisingly, most graduate students are relatively poor; at least you will have company in your financial misery (Fretz & Stang, 1980).

Determine the availability of teaching assistantships and research assistantships from the program's home page and the Reports on Individual Programs. In particular, determine the percentage of first-year students who receive assistantships. Is it 100%, 50%, or 0%? Do the assistantships include health insurance? If not, you will either go without insurance or purchase it on your own.

On average, 57% of full-time doctoral students in psychology receive some financial support from the program; the remaining 43% do not. The picture is less encouraging for full-time master's students in psychology: only 23% receive any support (Gehlman, Wicherski, & Kohout, 1995). As you can see, the probability of financial support from the program itself is a very salient consideration in narrowing your choices.

Be wary of online descriptions of doctoral programs that simply declare "all incoming students receive financial aid" unless that same description provides the sources of the aid and the typical monetary stipend. We are aware of several psychology programs that automatically award "fellowships" to every student in the amount of $2,000 but then immediately charge over $30,000 annual tuition! Hence, we use the phrase *full assistantship* in our Reports on Individual Programs.

These reports provide the percentages of incoming doctoral students who receive full tuition waiver only, full assistantship/fellowship only, and both tuition waiver *and* assistantship for each doctoral program.

Table 5-3 summarizes these data across the practice–research continuum for APA-accredited clinical psychology programs. The continuum moves from the freestanding Psy.D. programs on one end, through the equal-emphasis Ph.D. programs in the middle, to the research-oriented Ph.D. programs on the other end. As seen there, the probability of receiving financial assistance in graduate school is a direct function of the type of program (Norcross et al., 2010). Only 1 to 10% of Psy.D. students, on average, will receive both a tuition waiver and a full assistantship, compared to 89% of students in research-oriented Ph.D. programs in clinical psychology. You don't need to perform a *t* test; that is a large, significant difference. Indeed, the gap in funding between freestanding Psy.D. programs and research-oriented Ph.D. programs seems to be expanding. The equal-emphasis Ph.D. programs tend to fall in between; about 54% of their students receive both a tuition waiver and a full assistantship.

Figure 5-3 graphically illustrates the probability of getting in (acceptance rates) and getting money (percentage of students receiving full support) across the various types of APA-accredited clinical psychology programs. The two graphs demonstrate that higher acceptance rates come at a (tuition and living) cost to the incoming student. More rigorous admission standards and acceptance odds translate into increased probability of substantial financial aid. In the most extreme comparison, freestanding Psy.D. students are 7 times more likely to gain admission but 50 times less likely to receive full funding

TABLE 5-3. Percentage of Students Receiving Financial Aid in APA-Accredited Clinical Psychology Programs

	Free-standing Psy.D.	University-based Psy.D.	Equal-emphasis Ph.D.	Research-oriented Ph.D.
Full tuition waiver only	0%	1%	3%	0%
Full assistantship only	13%	21%	20%	8%
Both waiver and assistantship	1%	10%	54%	89%

Note. Data from Norcross, Ellis, & Sayette (2010).

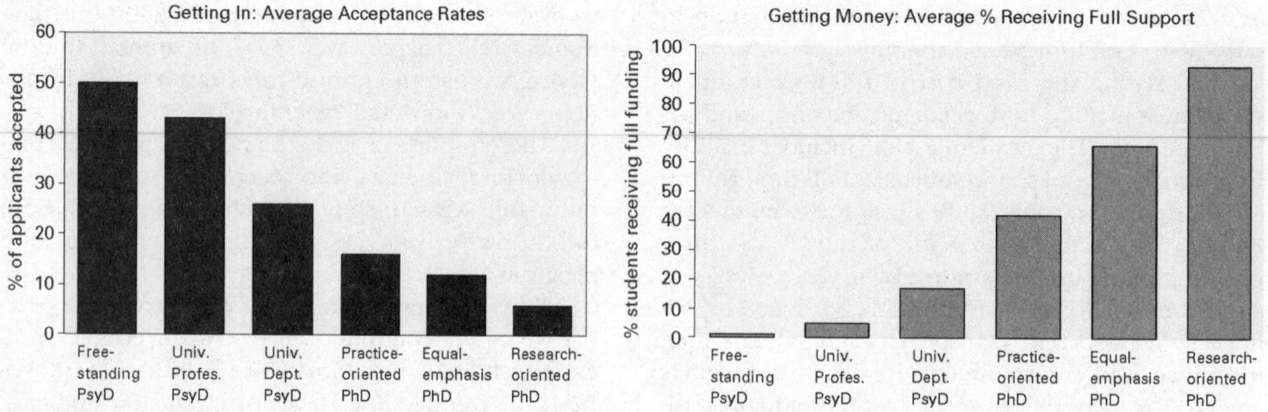

FIGURE 5-3. Getting in and getting money in various types of clinical psychology programs.

(stipend plus tuition waiver) than are students in research-oriented Ph.D. programs (Norcross et al., 2010). An awareness of these trade-offs among the different types of programs will enable you to make informed choices regarding your graduate applications and career trajectories.

There *is* financial aid available from graduate schools to students possessing sterling credentials, and we wish to reaffirm its existence. At the same time, you need to be realistic about the probability of direct financial assistance and pragmatic about the means to obtain funds for what graduate programs do not provide. The increasing number of clinical and counseling psychology doctoral programs during a period of economic downsizing raises difficult questions about internal funding opportunities and federal financial assistance.

Our findings (Norcross et al., 2010; Norcross, Sayette, & Pomerantz, in press) on financial aid portend a "pay as you go" expectation for half of all doctoral candidates in clinical and counseling psychology. This is particularly true, as we have seen, in Psy.D. programs. The explicit expectation, as is true in such other practice disciplines as medicine and law, is that graduates will be able to repay their debt after they are engaged in full-time practice. We should note, however, that uncertainties regarding health care—specifically changes in insurance coverage for mental health—in the United States make this expectation difficult to evaluate at the present time.

The debt may be substantial. Research indicates that 78% of recent graduates in clinical and counseling psychology are saddled with debt related to graduate studies (over and above any debt associated with their undergraduate education; APA Center for Workforce Studies, 2011).

As shown in Figure 5-4, recent graduates of *Psy.D.* programs report a median debt of $200,000 (American Psychological Association, 2015). The median debt for clinical/counseling *Ph.D.* graduates is $75,000, lower but still substantial. These results are adapted from a survey of recent psychology doctoral graduates in late 2014. Of course, attending a doctoral program that remits your tuition and provides a stipend, such as PCSAS-accredited programs, likely leads to less debt than what is depicted in this figure for all Ph.D. programs.

The research is crystal clear: Graduate student debt in psychology has experienced a dramatic increase in the past decade (Doran et al., 2016). This debt is increasing beyond what might be expected on tuition hikes alone. Faculty members need to become more aware of and advocate for financial solutions; potential applicants need to conduct a thoughtful cost/benefit analysis of applying to graduate programs that do not offer substantial financial assistance (Doran et al., 2016).

With a median starting salary of approximately $70,000 for new psychology doctorates, this debt represents a heavy financial burden for many years to come. (Go to the Loan Repayment Calculator at www.finaid.org/calculators/ for a sobering look at repayment schedules.) Estimated monthly payments for the median debt were $2,000 for Psy.D. recipients and $850 for Ph.D. recipients. The rule of thumb is that your debt should not exceed twice your starting salary.

Because of their educational debt, recently minted clinical and counseling psychologists saddled with heavy debt frequently place other life goals on hold. Seventy-three percent of recent graduates report delaying saving for the future, 67% delaying retirement planning, 57% purchasing a home, and 46% having children (American Psychological Asso-

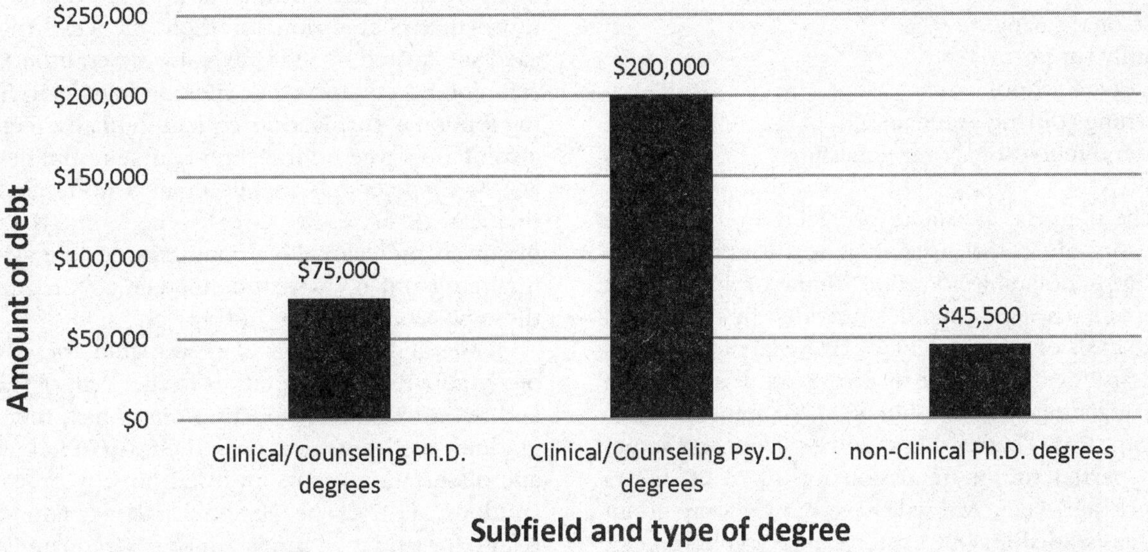

FIGURE 5-4. Median debt by subfield and type of degree for 2013–2014 doctoral graduates. Data from American Psychological Association of Graduate Students (APAGS) survey of recent psychology doctorates in 2014; APA Center for Workforce Studies.

ciation, 2015). These numbers appear scary, but debt is increasingly inevitable for many seeking advanced degrees in health professions. We desire to inform you in the *Insider's Guide*, not to scare or dissuade you from pursuing your vocational dreams.

In large part, the difference in debt between Psy.D.s and Ph.D.s is attributable to the huge differences in financial aid between Vail-model and Boulder-model programs as pictured in Table 5-3. The APA researchers who compile debt data conclude, "It is important to disseminate this information to students who may be considering a career in psychology—so that their decisions can be fully informed" (Kohout & Wicherski, 1999, p. 10). We wholeheartedly agree.

In fact, we conducted a study that looked at the financial assistance offered by various types of Psy.D. programs (Norcross et al., 2004). You may recall from Chapter 2 that Psy.D. programs can be housed in three different settings: (1) in a university's Psychology Department; (2) as a separate school or institute in a university; (3) as a private, freestanding institution without affiliation to a comprehensive university. As you have already learned, Psy.D. programs give proportionally less financial assistance to students than Ph.D. programs. But it gets a bit more complicated because not all Psy.D. programs provide similar amounts of financial assistance. An average of 14% of incoming Psy.D. students to a freestanding program will receive *any* financial support from the program and only 1% of incoming students will receive a full boat (tuition remission plus full assistantship). By contrast, an average of 32% of incoming Psy.D. students to a Psychology Department program will receive some financial support and 10% of incoming students a full boat (see Table 5-3). That's a whopping difference.

Two multicampus universities offering Psy.D. degrees around the country are private, for-profit entities. One is Argosy University, which is 41% owned by Goldman Sachs (Lewin, 2011), and the other is Alliant University. Many applicants are surprised to discover that Argosy and Alliant are for-profit organizations, but APA accredits both private and public, both non-profit and for-profit programs as long as they meet the quality standards. But please be aware that for-profit companies are intent on making that profit, which typically precludes giving many applicants substantial financial assistance.

If you require considerable financial assistance directly from the graduate program, then do not apply to the freestanding Psy.D. programs. Your best bet, financially speaking, will be the university-affiliated Psy.D. programs and, of course, the equal-emphasis and research-oriented Ph.D. programs.

How do students cobble together the necessary funds to pay for doctoral study in clinical and counseling psychology? By a mixture of means:

- university-provided financial assistance
- personal savings
- family support
- graduate school loans
- earnings during graduate school
- federal fellowships or traineeships

The financial assistance provided directly by the university can come in many guises. It may be a fellowship, scholarship, or grant—none of which must be repaid. These are monies provided by the school on the basis of merit, talent, or financial need. Financial assistance may come as a research assistantship (RA), teaching assistantship (TA), or general assistantship (GA). These bring a modest salary and sometimes partial tuition remission for 10 to 20 hours of work per week; we will have more to say about these assistantships in Chapter 8 once you have been admitted to a graduate program. In clinical, counseling, and combined psychology doctoral programs, paid internships and part-time employment are occasionally available as well.

In addition to aid provided by the school itself, financial assistance is available from external private and public organizations. This funding comes under various names—self-sought, external, independent—to distinguish it from financial aid provided internally by the university. External financial aid is provided by foundations, for example, the National Research Council and Fulbright Scholarships, and from the military, such as the Post-9/11 GI Bill. Numerous scholarships and fellowships are offered annually, but you will need to research those that pertain to your circumstances.

Your local Office of Career Services and Office of Financial Assistance can direct you to potential sources of external support for graduate studies. We recommend Princeton Review's (2005) *Paying for Graduate School without Going Broke* and *The Graduate School Funding Handbook* (Hamel & Furlong, 2011). These two books transverse the entire geography of financial aid—grant applications, loan possibilities, training fellowships, federal and state support, and other sources of money for graduate study.

Many universities provide webpages on these sources of funding graduate school. They often list school- or program-specific scholarships and fellowships available to incoming students. It is worth the added effort to examine the financial aid pages at each school to search for scholarship programs for which you may be eligible. As you can anticipate, the Web has exploded with interactive sites devoted to securing financial assistance for graduate school. Many of these are useful, but be wary of and avoid those that charge you for their services. An unbiased site hosted by the University of Scranton (www.scranton.edu/financialaid, click on loans and financing options) furnishes frequent updates. Peterson also offers a free online cram course in financial aid at www.petersons.com/graduate-schools/graduate-financial-aid.aspx. Be sure to check out the loads of advice and searchable databases on line at www.finaid.org and at www.studentaid.ed.gov/. Explore all these possibilities early and actively.

Federal funding is also available for psychology graduate students, either in the form of training and research grants to institutions, which then fund graduate assistantships, or in the form of fellowships and dissertation grants awarded directly to students (Bullock, 1997). The National Science Foundation (NSF), for example, funds Minority Graduate Fellowships. The National Institutes of Health (NIH) fund psychology student awards through the National Institute of Mental Health, the National Institute on Drug Abuse, the National Institute on Alcohol Abuse and Alcoholism, and the Office of AIDS Research. Check out these programs through their webpages: www.nsf.gov and www.nih.gov.

Several funding directories are available free of charge from philanthropic and professional organizations. Among the more prestigious (and therefore, more competitive) are the predoctoral fellowships sponsored by the Danforth Foundation, Ford Foundation, and Armed Forces Health Professions Scholarship. The American Psychological Association publishes a searchable database *Directory of Selected Scholarship, Fellowship, and Other Financial Aid Opportunities for Women and Ethnic Minorities in Psychology*, which we highly recommend (www.apa.org/about/awards/index.aspx). The APA Minority Fellowship Program is online at www.apa.org/pi/mfp. APA offers an online list of resources for financial assistance at www.apa.org/education/grad/applying.aspx.

Federal student loans are available for graduate students, but these are monies that must be repaid with interest. The William D. Ford Federal Direct Loan Program, generally known as Stafford Loans, is available to assist graduate and professional students who may borrow up to $20,500 each academic year (total of $138,500) in Stafford Loans. The interest rates on new federal education loans are tied to the 10-year Treasury rate, plus a fixed margin. The interest rates on new loans are fixed for the life of the loan; however, each year's new loans will have different fixed rates, based on current market rates. In 2016, that interest rate was 5.31%. The in-school interest on these unsubsidized Staffords may be paid semi-annually or deferred and repaid when principal repayments begin.

The government also offers Graduate PLUS Loans, federally sponsored loans for students attending graduate school at least half time. With a Grad PLUS loan, you may borrow up to the full cost of your education, less other financial aid received including Stafford Loans. Graduate students must exhaust their federal Stafford loan eligibility before applying for a Graduate PLUS loan. The bottom line is that every half-time graduate student is eligible for loans to finance his or her education, if necessary.

Speaking of loans reminds us to mention loan repayment options and loan forgiveness programs. We recommend that you visit the U.S. Department of Education website, www.ed.gov, which describes student loan types and loan repayment options. Three options that can trim loan payments for graduate students are the graduated repayment plans, income-sensitive repayment plans, and the loan consolidation plans. See the website for details, but remember that most student loans only permit a single refinancing or consolidation.

About 30 federal agencies offer loan forgiveness or repayment programs, and psychologists are eligible for many of these. Prominent examples are the:

- National Health Services Corps (nhsc.hrsa.gov; for those psychologists pursuing primary care careers)
- Indian Health Service (www.ihs.gov/careeropps/loanrepayment/; for psychologists working in designated underserved areas)
- U.S. Department of Veterans Affairs (for those interested in working with veterans)
- National Institutes of Health (www.lrp.nih.gov/; for those spending at last 50% of professional time conducting research)
- Public Service Loan Forgiveness Program (studentaid.ed.gov/sa/repay-loans/forgiveness-cancellation/public-service)
- Army Reserve Medical Corps (for those in the armed forces)

Regularly visit the APA website (www.apa.org/apags/resources/loan-repayment.pdf) for updates on loan forgiveness. We advise you to thoroughly investigate the options early and often.

Program Outcomes

The success of a doctoral program can be measured in many ways: the knowledge of the graduating students; the quality of the faculty; the careers of the alumni; the public good; and so on. As part of their APA accreditation requirements, doctoral psychology programs must publicly disclose their education and training outcomes to allow for informed decision-making among prospective students. The required information must all be located in one place on the Web and is frequently entitled *Student Admissions, Outcomes, and Other Data*. These data permit you to directly ascertain several key indicators of a program's success—or *program outcomes*, as they are known in research circles—in selecting graduate programs to which to apply.

Table 5-4 summarizes the student admissions and outcomes of the University of Alabama's clinical psychology program for the past seven years in a format prescribed by APA. Similar tables, under the title of *Student Admissions, Outcomes, and Other Data*, must be available on the websites of every APA-accredited program no more than one click away from the home page; these are requirements of APA accreditation in compliance with Implementing Regulation C-20. Use our Reports on Individual Programs to find the Web addresses or search for them online. These tables are loaded with valuable information on acceptance rates, GRE and GPA averages, probability of securing an APA-accredited internship, and time to complete the program.

Of course, we have compiled most of this information for you in this *Insider's Guide*, and will walk you through these considerations throughout the book. For now, we direct your attention to three critical measures of program outcome: internship match, attrition rate, and licensure data.

To receive your doctorate in clinical, counseling, or combined psychology, you must complete the equivalent of a one-year, full-time internship. The best way to do so is to complete an APA-accredited internship, as many universities, states, and government agencies insist on graduation from both an APA-accredited doctoral program and an APA-accredited internship.

In the past, if you were attending an APA-accredited doctoral program, you would rather easily obtain an APA-accredited internship on *match day* (when a computer matches applicants to internship sites in February). But in the present, the proliferating number of doctoral programs, particularly large Psy.D. programs, has dramatically increased the number of doctoral students seeking APA-accredited internships. The number of internship slots has grown steadily, but not quickly enough to keep pace with the number of new students. The result is an imbal-

TABLE 5-4. Representative Summary of Education/Training Outcome Data Found on an APA-Accredited Program's Web Site

The following charts contain information about our most recent cohorts of clinical graduate students at the University of Alabama at Tuscaloosa.

Year of entry	2008	2009	2010	2011	2012	2013	2014
Admissions data							
Number of applicants	204	191	198	223	305	195	261
Number offered admission	23	19	22	23	16	12	16
Size of incoming class	16	10	12	15	11	7	12
Number of incoming students receiving funding[a]	16	10	12	15	11	7	12
GRE and GPA data							
GRE – Verbal mean score	565	620	604	602	681	158	158.5
GRE – Quantitative mean score	680	670	690	676	681	154	155
GRE – Advanced Psy.D. mean score	650	680	695	681	737		
GPA – Average undergraduate	3.6	3.7	3.67	3.71	3.85	3.6	3.81
Internship data							
Number of students applying	12	11	7	11	8	14	10
Obtained Internships	12 (100%)	10 (91%)	7 (100%)	10 (91%)	8 (100%)	14 (100%)	10 (100%)
Obtained APA/CPA-accredited internships	12 (100%)	10 (91%)	7 (100%)	10 (91%)	7 (88%)	14 (100%)	10 (100%)

Graduation data

Number of students who took	Total graduates ($N = 66$)	Cumulative
Less than 5 years to complete degree	1 (1%)	3 (4%)
5 years to complete degree	13 (20%)	19 (26%)
6 years to complete degree	36 (55%)	57 (77%)
7 years to complete degree	13 (20%)	69 (93%)
More than 7 years to complete degree	3 (4%)	74 (100%)

Attrition data

Students admitted to the program between 2001 and 2007 = 81

Students who left the program prior to completion of Ph.D. = 6 (7%)

Licensure data

2004–2012 Ph.D. graduates who are currently licensed = 71 of 81 (88% licensure)

Tuition and fee schedule for graduate students

Full-time rates per semester

Hours	Resident	Nonresident
9–15	$4,913.00	$12,475.00

University fees or costs: $19.50 per credit hour.

Note. Adapted with the kind permission of Dr. Beverly E. Thorne, University of Alabama.

[a]All students admitted to the clinical program are offered a graduate assistantship, which includes a tuition grant for the academic year.

ance between the rapidly growing number of internship applicants and the slowly growing number of internship spots. Psy.D. students tend to match at a lower rate than Ph.D. students, in spite of applying to more internship sites than Ph.D. students (Callahan, Collins, & Klonoff, 2010).

In the past decade, approximately 75% of applicants were matched to an APA-accredited internship position on match day. That leaves one-quarter of doctoral psychology students without an accredited internship. About half of the unmatched students complete an unaccredited internship that year, and about half will need to apply the following year, delaying their graduation by a year. That's why it is important for you to select schools that will maximize the probability of you being in that three-quarters, not in that unfortunate one-quarter.

Attending a selective APA-accredited doctoral program substantially increases the probability of matching to an APA-accredited internship. In 2014, for example, APA-accredited Ph.D. programs placed 81% of their students in accredited internships and APA-accredited Psy.D. programs placed 47%. But the picture is especially bleak for students in unaccredited doctoral programs: only 27% of students from unaccredited Ph.D and 8% from unaccredited Psy.D. programs matched with APA-accredited internships (Norcross & Karpiak, 2015; mitch.web.unc.edu/files/2013/10/MatchRates.pdf). (For student perspectives on the psychology internship crisis, watch a 6-minute video on YouTube at www.youtube.com/watch?v=ooNJdahyXO8r).

APA and the training community have reduced this internship imbalance (Grus et al., 2011) and enrollments in the larger accredited Psy.D. programs have decreased in recent years (Hatcher, 2013, 2015), presaging significant improvement in match outcome during the coming years. However, it is a long-standing and complex problem that will not be fixed soon. The upshot is for you, as an applicant, to critically evaluate the program outcomes—financial assistance, internship match, licensure rates, and so on—before you apply and then again after you have received admission offers.

Another index of program quality is the *attrition* or dropout rate. Doctoral students leave a graduate program prematurely for many reasons, such as pursuing an area other than psychology, health problems, family considerations, financial needs, or program dissatisfaction. But better programs tend to boast higher graduate rates. Be certain that the programs you are considering graduate at least 80% of their students. In other words, avoid any program where 20% or more of its students dropout. That typically spells trouble.

The average attrition rates for APA-accredited clinical and counseling psychology Ph.D. programs hover around 4% (Klonoff, 2016). Attrition tends to be higher for unaccredited and Psy.D. programs, which give less financial assistance and take in far more students. The attrition rates during the past 7 years for individual APA-accredited programs are listed in the respective Reports on Individual Programs.

After years of hard work completing a doctoral program and an internship, you naturally expect to pass the national licensure examination in psychology—the Examination for Professional Practice in Psychology (EPPP). But not everyone passes on the first try or even on subsequent tries. If you attend an APA-accredited program, you stand a 77% chance of passing on any single attempt (www.asppb.net). If you attend a non-APA-accredited program, that chance drops to 65%. The more selective and the smaller the program, the higher the licensure pass rate (Sharpless & Barber, 2013).

Thus, as you select potential programs, seriously consider the licensure pass rates of their graduates. These statistics are helpfully presented on the website of the Association of State and Provincial Psychology Boards at www.asppb.net. Click on the link for Psychology Licensing Exam Scores by Doctoral Program and you will find a table of pass rate for each program. Graduates of the University of Alabama's clinical program, for example, have recently passed at a 94% clip. That's typical of the smaller, more competitive, Ph.D. programs in the scientist-practitioner (Boulder model) tradition. Graduates of the less competitive, huge Psy.D. programs, particularly the for-profit institutions, typically score much lower on the EPPP (Graham & Kim, 2011; Templer et al., 2008; Schaffer et al., 2012). Their average licensure pass rates fall in the 55% to 75% range.

One day, while discussing these figures in class, an undergraduate spontaneously yelled, "Why would anyone even THINK about applying to a program where only half the graduates can pass the licensure exam!?" That memorable event led us to formulate *the three-quarters rule*: Apply only to doctoral programs where three-quarters or more of their students secure an APA-accredited internship, complete their degrees, and pass the licensure examination.

That's our general advice, but you will need to tailor it to your individual situation and goals. On occasion, a couple of our students have entered a doctoral program with an inordinately high attrition rate or a depressingly low licensure pass rate, but they did so with their eyes wide open. That's precisely our intent in helping you select potential graduate programs: well-informed consumers aware of the facts and the tradeoffs about program outcomes.

Quality of Life

A sixth and final consideration in selecting graduate schools concerns the quality of student life. It may be difficult to imagine, but occasionally you will want a break from graduate studies, to relax or engage in some nonpsychological pursuit!

Get a handle on your own needs. Can they be met by the university and surrounding community? Do you want world-class museums, fine dining, and professional theater? Then you probably want to live in or near a city. If not, do you have a car capable of regularly getting you to one? Or do you get away to the mountains, enjoy camping, and find the city distracting? Or do you prefer to work at your office late at night and need a campus that's safe after dark? Then be sure to apply to some rural campuses. Also, consider whether you have friends or family nearby. Having a place to escape to can prove vital, especially if you do not have the funds to *really* escape.

You are not going to base your decisions exclusively on any of these nonacademic factors. But you can increase the probability of having everything you want by applying to schools you know can provide it all.

The Web is an excellent resource for investigating locations, towns, and cities that are far away and that you may not have the time or finances to visit. Large cities have their own Web pages, which include pictures, maps, attractions, and so on, for potential visitors and residents. Take the time to "virtually" explore the cities of programs on your list. You may find that it is far more (or less) desirable than you had imagined.

The weight accorded to the quality of life in application decisions varies considerably among people. At one extreme are those applicants who give little thought to program location and heavily value the research and clinical opportunities. In the words of one colleague, "I'd live in hell for 6 years [the time it ordinarily takes to complete a doctorate] to be trained by the best people in my field." At the other extreme are those who will only apply to programs situated near family, friends, or an attractive community. "Six years," they say, "is too long to be away from what I need as a person." We will not be so presumptuous as to advise which position you should adopt, except to remark that you should carefully weigh personal (location, fit) and professional (reputation, opportunities) considerations.

Putting It All Together

Having seriously reflected on your own interests and having carefully examined the clinical opportunities, research training, theoretical orientations, financial aid, program outcomes, and quality of life of various schools, you are close to completing applications.

Now is the time to put together all the information you have obtained about yourself and graduate programs in the form of a *final list* of schools—anywhere from 10 to 20, depending on the specificity of your interests and the strength of your credentials. As you make a final list of the applications you are about to complete, make one last check to insure that you are applying to the programs that best fit your needs. You may do this informally by mentally reviewing the program information or you may do this systematically by completing Appendix D.

To complete Appendix D, write the name of each graduate program in the first column. In column 2, "School Criteria," write the total you computed for each school in Appendix C. This is an index of your strength as an applicant and should range from about 5 to 15. For each of the next six columns, you can rate your impressions about each program on a 5-point scale. Create these scales in ways that are personally relevant to you. The important thing is to know where each program rates in these areas in terms of your needs and desires. Below are some examples of rating systems you might model your own after.

In the column marked "Research," rate how strongly you feel toward the professors you have singled out as wanting to work with:

- **1** I do not know enough about them, but their research is in my general interests.
- **3** I like the specifics of their research but do not know enough about their lab or their personalities.
- **5** I have been in contact with these professors and am impressed by their facilities and by them personally. I would like to work with them.

In the column marked "Clinical," rate each school according to how its opportunities suit your needs.

1 The school has only a psychological training clinic that treats students, and I want more experience.

3 The school has a fine psychological training clinic, but it has no practica in the community, and getting various populations may be difficult.

5 The school has many excellent clinical opportunities, including a specialty (e.g., eating disorders) clinic or track in my area of interest.

Or, possibly:

1 The program requires students to find their own clinical placements in the community, and I don't like that system.

3 The program has a college counseling center, but I'm not interested in working only with college students.

5 The program maintains an excellent psychological services clinic, and that's all I need.

"Theoretical Orientation" is the following column:

1 The program avers strict adherence to, and training in, a theoretical orientation that contrasts with mine.

3 The program offers some courses and supervision in my preferred theoretical orientation.

5 The program provides considerable training in my preferred theoretical orientation plus other opportunities.

Next, consider "Financial Aid":

1 There is no funding for first-year students and no mention of outside means of support, and I need it.

3 I am likely to get at least tuition remission and have the possibility of working part-time for the university. It is likely that I could be a resident advisor and get free housing.

5 For the last 5 years, all first-year students have gotten full stipends and full tuition remission.

Or, possibly:

1 There is no funding for first-year students and no mention of outside means of support.

3 I am likely to get at least tuition remission, though only for the first 2 years.

5 The school guarantees tuition remission for 4 years, and that's all I need.

Under the column marked "Program Outcomes," rate each program on its record of internship match, attrition rate, and licensure pass-rates. For example:

1 This program matches less than 50% of its students with APA-accredited internships and less than three-quarters of their students pass the licensure exam.

3 This program reports a reasonable attrition rate and about three-quarters of its students match with APA-accredited internships.

5 This program has a consistent track record of high student success in matching to APA-accredited internships and passing the licensure exam.

And last, rate the "Quality of Life":

1 This program is located in an unattractive area and seems bereft of culture.

3 I am indifferent to the location, and there is culture within the college community.

5 The area is ideal for me, and there are museums, concert halls, and theaters nearby.

Or, possibly:

1 This university is located in an unsafe section of a large city where I don't know anyone.

3 This university is located in a small city, and a friend of mine also attends.

5 This university is located in a small college town, and I have several close relatives and friends there.

Look at your list. Are you applying to graduate programs within a realistic range of admission criteria? Are you applying to at least some programs where you like the faculty, where the clinical facilities are suitable, where the theoretical orientation is compatible, where the program outcomes exceed the three-quarters rule, where financial aid is available, and where you will feel comfortable living? If the answer to all of these is "No," then go back a step. Find graduate programs where these qualities are present, possibly in abundance, and add them to your list of applications.

"What," you might reasonably ask, "are acceptable ratings in Appendix D for the program outcomes?" Our threshold of quality is expressed in the three-quarters rule (at least three-quarters of the students complete the program, secure an APA-accredited internship, and pass the licensure exam). But you may need to relax that rule if your credentials are a bit weak or if you are applying to a limited number of schools. However you define quality, we implore you not to apply to any programs below your personal line of acceptability. You owe it to yourself and to your future career.

Before moving on to the next chapter of this *Insider's Guide* and the next step in the application process, take one final moment to celebrate. You deserve it! You have learned much about graduate training in clinical and counseling psychology, investigated potential graduate programs, assessed your match with those programs, and whittled down your final list. You have already mastered challenges more intense than those associated with many college courses. So, after weeks of arduous and sometimes anxious work, you deserve affirmation and reward. Give them to yourself or, at least, allow us to affirm and reward you from afar.

CHAPTER 6

APPLYING TO PROGRAMS

You are ready to complete the graduate applications. You have assessed your interests and have located programs that provide the desired training and mentorship. You have evaluated your credentials and have chosen programs that will consider you seriously. You have downloaded applications and related materials. You have carefully looked at programs' research offerings, clinical opportunities, theoretical orientations, financial aid, student outcomes, quality of life, and other variables of importance to you. Your task now is to actually apply to these graduate programs.

Attack this application process with all the drive and commitment you can muster. The rewards of applying are typically in direct proportion to your exertion. Try to emulate the manic zeal of successful medical school applicants. As they will readily inform you, the application itself reflects directly on your potential as a graduate student. In a real sense, your professional future is at stake.

The *application year*, as it is known, will probably prove intense. We suggest that you take a lighter course load or work schedule during the fall of your application year. Completing applications, securing letters of recommendation, and writing personal statements constitute more work than a typical college course. We also suggest that you inform friends and family members that you will be more preoccupied and distracted than usual. Position yourself for a busy fall.

A completed application will typically consist of the following elements: application form, curriculum vitae, personal statement, letters of recommendation, transcripts, entrance examination scores, and an application fee. In this chapter, we trace the requisite steps of compiling, completing, and transmitting these materials in a coordinated fashion. But before we address the nuts and bolts of doing so, let us touch upon the crucial question of how many programs to apply to.

How Many?

The average number of applications made by students to clinical and counseling psychology programs is about 10. The precise number to which you should apply depends on the strength of your credentials and the competitiveness of the prospective programs; more applications are indicated for weaker credentials and more competitive programs.

Another way to answer the "how many" question is to apply to a sufficient number of programs so that if the worst happens and you are not admitted anywhere, you can reassure yourself that you gave it your best shot. "I did my best" is far better than condemning yourself afterwards for not applying to a few more programs.

Our rule of thumb is to apply to *at least* 10 to 12 programs: five "safe" (you clearly meet or exceed their standards); five "target" or "ambitious" programs (your credentials just make their requirements); and perhaps one or two "reach" or "stretch" programs (where you do not approximate their standards but you have a particular hunch, research compatibility, or personal relationship that has a chance of sweeping you into the finalist pool). We have met industrious students who have applied to over 40 programs and confident students who have applied to just four or five.

But don't pull a Missar, as we say at the University of Scranton. David Missar was an exceptional undergraduate and good-humored fellow (who gave us permission to use his story as a lesson for others to learn). He had a sky-high GPA, impressive GREs, a practicum to his credit, and even a coauthored publication. He was feeling a bit too confident in applying to only four doctoral programs, all located around his home town of Washington, DC, which happens to host some especially competitive programs. Despite his stellar academic credentials, Dave did not receive any acceptances his first year because his research interests and strengths did not match those of the clinical faculty and institutions to which he applied. Had he applied to a greater number or a larger variety of programs, he surely would have been accepted somewhere, as he was easily the next year when he corrected his miscalculations.

Web Self-Audit

For all of its wonders, the Web presents ample opportunities for mischief and an anti-professional impression. Photographs of your high-jinks and drinking games on Facebook may entertain fellow students, but probably not the director of clinical training. Cute email addresses, such as bongmeister@gmail.com or hotchick@aol.com, may delight romantic partners, but certainly not the dean of the graduate school. Almost 70% of Facebook photos among medical students reflect the use or abuse of alcohol, and psychology students are likely to post comparable photos (Linton, 2011).

Before you complete any application is the time to conduct a Web self-audit to assess and probably enhance your Internet and telephone presence so that it conveys a professional demeanor. Nearly one-half of employers research potential job candidates on the Web (National Association of Colleges and Employers, 2013), and that number is growing. We know for a fact that many members of graduate admission committees do likewise.

Here's a self-audit checklist used by several career service offices:

- email address: Is it professional and permanent?
- Google yourself: Are you satisfied with what you found?
- social networking sites (e.g., Facebook, LinkedIn): Would you be comfortable if a potential graduate mentor were to view your profiles, pictures, groups, and friends' comments?
- personal website or blog: Does it follow the rule of "if you wouldn't want to read it in the front page of the newspaper, don't put it on the Web?"
- voice mail: Is your message professional and clear?

Take a few moments before completing applications to evaluate and improve your electronic footprint. What entertains family and friends may alienate academics, who may question your judgment and seriousness.

Application Form

You have a list of 10 to 20 programs in front of you. The deadlines range from mid-December to mid-February. It is now time to start writing.

One of the easiest parts is filling out the application itself. Nearly all graduate programs now request that you submit an application on line. Be careful to scrutinize your materials and catch any errors, including typos, prior to submitting. Proofread the documents several times and try to cut and paste a fully formed personal statement from a word processing file. The completed application reflects on you; keep it professional and neat.

Begin completing the application forms at least one month before the earliest deadline. Some applicants, particularly undergraduates in their senior year, wait until the end of the fall semester on the holiday break. *This is too late*—do not wait, lest you be rushed, unprepared, and working on a tight deadline.

Unlike the medical school process, which uses an identical application form for every school, each graduate program in psychology has its own, unique application. Providing the same information over and over again in slightly different formats can become frustrating and time consuming.

There may be relief from this drudgery in sight. APA offers PSYCAS, a centralized application service for graduate study in psychology. The goal is to streamline the application and review process for both students and graduate programs. PSYCAS is not a common application, but a national online platform to securely submit your application forms, academic transcripts, recommendation letters, and test scores to a single site. In 2017, 20 universities participated in PSYCAS, with more expected to join in the future. Although too early to predict its success, similar centralized application services have become the norm in other health professions as they reduce the workload of all participants.

Until then, each application will request the following information from you in slightly different formats:

- Full name
- Previous and maiden names
- Citizenship status
- Semester of entrance
- Current mailing address
- Permanent home address
- Educational history
- Degree sought
- Field of study
- Relevant courses taken
- Grade point averages
- Academic honors
- Clinical experience
- Special qualifications
- Employment history
- Teaching/research experience
- Career objectives
- Professional references

Submitting applications is worse than filling out income tax returns (Fretz & Stang, 1980). Allow yourself enough uninterrupted time to do it carefully and completely. Incorrect spelling, incomplete answers, and poor grammar will hurt your chances.

Some additional tips:

- Keep the application forms for each school separated. Individual computer files or paper folders for each program might help. Since the application forms are often poorly marked, you may not otherwise know which forms belong to which school.
- Create a spreadsheet to keep track of your multiple applications—the application deadlines, number of recommendations required, what was sent, what was received, and so on. This method helps to organize the blizzard of paperwork, especially if you are applying to more than a few graduate programs.
- Save a hard copy or electronic file of each application. Graduate schools have been known to lose—or misplace—entire forms. A copy and backup file will enable you to quickly resubmit if necessary.

Curriculum Vitae

Curriculum vitae means, literally, "the course of your life." The vitae or CV summarizes your academic and employment history in a structured form.

Both resumes and CVs summarize your credentials, but they differ in several ways. A resume is typically for employment, whereas a CV is for graduate school and academic positions. Resumes are brief, typically on a single page, whereas CVs go on for several pages. Resumes frequently list objectives, such as "To obtain an entry-level position in . . . ", but CVs do not. Resumes often present personal interests and hobbies; CVs rarely do.

Figures 6-1 and 6-2 present two possible formats for a CV; you will need to adapt these samples to your individual needs. Although the samples are single-spaced and occupy only one page, CVs are *double-spaced* between entries (single spaced within an entry) and occupy several pages.

As a general rule, keep the CV honest and positive. Never fabricate, but perhaps "embellish" appropriately. The line to be drawn here is demarcated by whether you can look an interviewer directly in the eye and factually defend an entry that could subsequently be corroborated by a supervisor, professor, or another person. Structured brevity is the key; lengthy expositions of experiences are best left to personal statements or job descriptions.

Your "academic resume" should be positive, upbeat in tone. Avoid any negative features that might red-flag your application. Save confessions and excruciating honesty for the clergy and psychotherapist. Omit sections that do not apply to you, such as "Presentations" or "Publications" if you have none at this point in your career.

Let's proceed through the different sections of a CV and offer additional hints. List your legal name, including any suffixes such as "Jr." Distinguish between a current address and a permanent home address, if this applies to your living circumstances. Note any anticipated changes in your address. Include telephone numbers and email addresses at which program directors or professors can easily reach you. Remember that your email account at your undergraduate institution will eventually expire, so consider putting a second email address on the application. If you share voice mail or an answering machine with other people, insure that they will graciously take a message and reliably transmit that message to you.

Information on your partner/marital status and dependents is definitely optional. Opinions differ on whether you should include this material on your CV: the probable positives are that you are being honest and sharing information about yourself; the likely downsides are that the information may be used against you or lead to illegal considerations in admission decisions. The marital/partner status question

November 2018

CURRICULUM VITAE

Name: Chris Smith
Address: 15 Easy Street
Babylon, NY 12345
Telephone: (516) 555-1212
Email: csmith@babu.edu
Citizenship: United States of America

Education:
H.S. Diploma Cherry Hill High School, City, State, June 2015
B.S. (anticipated) Psychology, Babylon University, May 2019

Honors and Awards:
New York State Regents Scholarship, 2015–2018
Dean's List, Babylon University, 2016–2018
Psi Chi, International Honor Society in Psychology, 2017
Babylon University Honors Program, 2015–present
Who's Who Among Students in American Colleges & Universities, 2017

Clinical Experience:
Mental Health Technician, Friendship House, Jackson, Wyoming, June 2016–August 2017. Duties: recreational counseling and supervision of 20 behaviorally and emotionally disturbed children. Supervisor: Doris Day, M.S. 40 hours weekly.
Telephone Counselor, Mesopotamia County Community Crisis Center, Babylon, New York, 2015–2017. Duties: used a crisis intervention model to counsel a wide range of callers. Supervisor: Randal Kaplan, M.A. 4 hours weekly.

Research Experience:
Research Assistant, Babylon University, Department of Psychology, September 2015–June 2016. Duties: word processing, manuscript preparation, and data analyses for Theodore Demanding, Ph.D. 10 hours weekly.
Honors Research, Babylon University with Rita Murrow, Ph.D., 2014–2016. Duties: proposed and conducted an original project; data input and analysis using SPSS; write-up and oral defense.

Professional and Honor Societies:
Psi Chi, International Honor Society in Psychology
American Psychological Association (student affiliate)
Alpha Gamma Epsilon Omega (National Honor Society in Ergonomics)

Presentations and Publications:
Smith, C., & Murrow, F. A. (2017, April). *Self-esteem and math performance: Another look.* Poster presented at the meeting of the Babylon Psychological Association, New York.
Murrow, F. A., & Smith, C. (2017). The effects of self-esteem on math test performance. *Journal of Psychology, 46,* 113–117.

Campus Activities and Leadership:
Psychology Club, member (2016–2017) and president (2017)
University Singers, Babylon University, 2015–2017
Hand-in-Hand, participant (2014–2016) and campus coordinator (2016)

References:
Frances Murrow, Ph.D., Associate Professor, Department of Psychology, Babylon University, Babylon, NY 12345. Voice: 516-555-1212; email: murrow@babu.edu
Theodore Demanding, Ph.D., Professor and Chair, Department of Psychology, Babylon University, Babylon, NY 12345. Voice: 516-555-1212; email: les@babu.edu
Doris Day, M.S., Senior Therapist, Children's House, 78 Oak Street, Jackson, WY 12345. Voice: 307-555-1212

FIGURE 6-1. One format for curriculum vitae.

Chris Smith

November 2018

Personal History:

Business Address:	Department of Psychology Babylon University Babylon, New York 12345
Phone:	(516) 555-1212
Home Address:	1017 Jefferson Avenue Cherry Hill, NJ 08002
Phone:	(609) 555-1212
Email:	csmith@babu.edu
Citizenship:	United States of America

Educational History:

Babylon University, Babylon, New York
Major: Psychology
Degree: B.S. (anticipated), May 2018
Dean's List, 2015–2018
Who's Who Among Students in American Colleges & Universities, 2017
Honors Thesis: Investigation of the relationship between self-esteem and math performance (Chairperson: Rita Murrow, Ph.D.)

Professional Positions:

1. Telephone Counselor, Mesopotamia County Community Crisis Center, Babylon, New York. Part-time position, 2015–2017. Duties: used a crisis intervention model to counsel a wide range of callers. Supervisor: Randal Kaplan, M.A.
2. Mental Health Technician, Friendship House, Jackson, Wyoming. Full-time summer, 2016. Duties: recreational counseling and supervision of 20 behaviorally and emotionally disturbed children. Supervisor: Doris Day, M.S.
3. Research Assistant, Babylon University. Half-time position, 2016–2017. Duties: word processing, manuscript preparation, and data analysis. Supervisor: Theodore Demanding, Ph.D.

Membership in Professional Associations:

Psi Chi (International Honor Society in Psychology)
American Psychological Association (student affiliate)
Alpha Gamma Epsilon Omega (National Honor Society in Ergonomics)

Professional Activities:

President, Babylon University Chapter of Psi Chi, 2017
Member of Program Committee, Babylon University Psychology Conference, 2017

Papers Presented:

Smith, C. E., & Murrow, F. A. (2016, April). *Self-esteem and math performance: Another look.* Poster presented at the meeting of the Babylon Psychological Association, New York, NY.

Publication:

Murrow, F. A., & Smith, C. (2017). The effects of self-esteem on math test performance. *Journal of Psychology, 46,* 113–117.

Campus Activities:

Psychology Club, member (2014–2017) and president (present)
University Singers, Babylon University, 2015–2017
Hand-in-Hand, participant (2015–2017) and campus coordinator (2017)

References:

Frances Murrow, Ph.D., Associate Professor, Department of Psychology, Babylon University, Babylon, NY 12345. Voice: 516-555-1212; email: murrow@babu.edu

Theodore Demanding, Ph.D., Professor and Chair, Department of Psychology, Babylon University, Babylon, NY 12345. Voice: 516-555-1212; email: les@babu.edu

Doris Day, M.S., Senior Therapist, Children's Hospital, 78 Oak Street, Jackson, WY 12345. Voice: 307-555-1212

Note. Adapted from Hayes & Hayes (1989) with permission of the authors.

FIGURE 6-2. Another format for curriculum vitae.

is now almost moot since approximately half of all graduate students in psychology are married (Pate, 2001).

Regarding education, list degrees as "anticipated" if they have not yet been awarded. Impressive grade point averages may also be listed here. Honors are listed in chronological order, usually excluding those obtained in high school unless they were huge. If you received an award or honor specific to a university (e.g., the Lawrence Lennon Memorial Award), then record what it is for in parentheses following the award. As two examples: Provost's Scholarship, 2015–2019 (one-half tuition scholarship for exceptional academic performance) and Lawrence Lennon Memorial Award, 2016 (awarded for superior performance in psychology). Similarly, specify the disciplines of honor societies; for example, Psi Chi (International Honor Society in Psychology), 2017. Professional memberships listed on your CV should be career relevant, not memberships in fan clubs or on sports teams. Format any presentations or publications in APA style, thereby demonstrating your familiarity with the psychologist's publication manual.

Clinical experiences and research experiences can be listed together or separately, depending on what will strengthen your CV. If you have two or more research experiences and assistantships, then create a separate section to highlight those. In either case, indicate position title, relevant dates, number of hours, duties performed, and the supervisor. Maintain parallelism throughout your listed experiences, using action verbs to describe your duties and responsibilities.

The increasing prevalence of service learning in college has led some students to cite each of their brief service experiences separately under Clinical Experience. We do *not* recommend that you do so. Trying to pass off required, 10 to 20 hour visits as an intensive clinical experience is misleading. Instead, clearly (and honestly) identify them together under a single entry as "Service Learning" and specify the various locations and total number of hours. Exaggerating the required 20 hours of service learning as volunteer experience calls your integrity and judgment into question.

The names of your references should be listed only after you have obtained their permission to do so. *Never list a reference on a CV or application until you have secured that person's agreement to write a letter in support of your application.* Double-check that you accurately list the person's full name, terminal academic degree, professional title, and contact information. Misidentifying a part-time lecturer as a "Professor" or a master's-level clinician as a "Dr." will detract from your application.

Place the date (month and year) in smaller font on the upper right-hand corner of the CV. In this way, you can submit an addendum if your credentials significantly improve by, say, having a paper accepted for publication or receiving your department's student of the year award.

Lay out the information in an attractive and organized manner. Select a plain font, such as Times Roman or Arial, and a large enough font so that readers don't need to squint. Use a consistent format both within each section and between sections. For example, if you opt to list your clinical experiences from the most recent to the past, then maintain that reverse chronological format in all the other sections.

Here is an idea to enhance the CV for students who have developed specific research or computer competencies. List them on your vitae as a separate section. Computer skills might include proficiency with SPSS, SAS, R, Pascal, Harvard Graphics, Chartmaster, SigmaScan, SigmaPlot, CricketGraph, and Aldus Pagemaker. Research skills might include performing computerized library searching on *PsycInfo* or *Medline*, administering the Wisconsin Card Sorting Test (or another psychological test), or operating an electroencephalograph (EEG). Also include here any special skills, such as certification in the Facial Action Coding System, fluency in foreign languages, or proficiency in American Sign Language. A faculty member screening applications may realize that these competencies are exactly what he or she is looking for in a new graduate assistant or research assistant. So use your CV to highlight your abilities! Omit this optional section if you have none or only one specific competency; in the latter case, describe that qualification in your personal statement.

What should *not* be put on the CV? Eliminate listings of religion, hobbies, pets, favorite books, and items of that kind (Hayes & Hayes, 1989). Never include your social security number (someone could steal it), and information about your physical appearance or health isn't appropriate. Nor is a photograph customary.

Padding of all varieties must be avoided. Padding occurs when a reader reacts to the CV as more form than substance ("Who are they trying to fool?!"). Potentially risky is listing professional projects under way—one or two legitimate research projects may pass but any more will probably be considered suspect. Other signs of padding, and therefore sections to exclude, are conventions attended, journals read, and projects you worked on in a nonprofessional capacity.

Pumping up your past on CVs and application forms is common but inadvisable. A survey of 2.6 million job applications discovered that 44% of them contained lies (Kluger, 2002); do not be among the 44%. Once you are caught fibbing on a graduate school application, it is practically impossible to restore your integrity and character at that program. While some of your friends may exhort you to exaggerate your previous positions and to recalculate your GPA, we strongly advise honesty. Inconsistencies between your CV and academic transcripts or letters of recommendation can cost you an admission offer.

Proofread the document carefully; review it with an advisor or mentor before you send it. For the handful of graduate programs requesting hard copies, print your CV on standard-sized white, ivory, or cream stock. Purchase good quality bond paper for these documents. Avoid onionskin paper, goldenrod color, odd-sized papers, memo pads, green or red ink, and other unconventional materials.

Although much of the information contained in the CV is requested on the application form itself, we believe the inclusion of a CV enhances your application—providing it is properly prepared. A CV denotes a scholarly demeanor, highlights your accomplishments, and communicates familiarity with the workings of academia.

Personal Statements

Another bridge you must cross is writing the personal statement or essay. Every program will want to know why you chose psychology and the subfield within it. Admissions committees will also want to know how you came to this decision and what professional goals you have in mind. These essays, required by more than 95% of doctoral programs, go by different names: statement of goals, personal essays, professional objectives, and personal statements.

Each application will ask the questions in a different way because each program has different expectations of students and different approaches to training. *Read the instructions carefully.* You cannot word process one statement and submit it to every program.

Do not misinterpret the meaning of personal in *personal statement*. This essay is not the place to espouse your philosophy of life, to describe your first romance, or to tell the story about your being bitten by the neighbor's dog and subsequently developing an anxiety disorder. Instead, think of the essay as a *professional statement*. Write about your activities and experiences as an aspiring psychologist (Bottoms & Nysse, 1999).

An analysis of 360 essays required as part of the graduate application process demonstrated wide variability in the content requested (Keith-Spiegel & Wiederman, 2000). The most frequent requests were to articulate:

- Career plans
- Clinical experiences
- Interest areas
- Specific faculty of interest
- Research experiences
- Autobiographical statement
- Academic objectives
- Reasons for applying to that particular program
- Educational background

Of late, Psy.D. programs that rarely supply financial assistance have taken to asking applicants to specify how they will finance their graduate studies. We recommend that you respond directly and list a combination of sources—personal savings, family support, summer work, and student loans, for example. No need to be embarrassed or hesitant in responding. In fact, this question prompts you to realistically consider financing your education, if you opt for a Psy.D. program.

Be attentive to what the program requests. If they stress research, highlight your research interests and experience. If they stress clinical work, highlight the development of these interests and your training experiences to date. Show how you started with a question or a clinical observation, how you pursued that question, and how it developed into a greater understanding of the issues at hand and a need to know more. Demonstrate how this program meets your needs and is the ideal place to continue to pursue knowledge. State the goals you wish to attain with this knowledge, the career path you hope to work toward. If you are committed to the Boulder model, indicate how research is useful and how it is clinically applicable. When you make this connection in your personal statement, you will impress on the admission committee the ideal integration for Boulder-model (Ph.D.) programs.

To reiterate: carefully read the question, individualize your response to each program, and respond to all parts of the question posed to you. If the application specifies two pages, then give only two pages, not three. If the application asks for single-spacing and your social security number at the top of the page, then do just that. Follow the instructions in length, content, and format.

A long-time graduate school dean, Dr. Tom Hogan, characterizes applicants who do not adhere to the explicit instructions for writing their personal statements this way. "There are two possibilities: The applicants are either not bright or do not follow instructions. If they are not bright, I do not want them in my graduate school! If they do not follow instructions, then I do not want them in my graduate school!"

Graduate selection committees value clarity, focus, and passion in personal statements (Keith-Spiegel, 1991). Clarity and focus are typically construed as indicators of lucid thought, realistic planning, and self-direction, all valuable assets in a graduate student.

At the same time, try to communicate a heartfelt commitment to your chosen career. "Passion" is not too strong a term—even relentless, obsessed, committed, fascinated; in short, what we call "catching the fever!" Graduate faculty seek students who find it difficult to distinguish between work and pleasure when it comes to academic tasks (Keith-Spiegel & Wiederman, 2000).

Many students ask us if they should begin the personal statement with an inspiring quote or a cute metaphor. Our answer: probably not. Instead, organize your statement around a compelling theme that shows and illustrates your best qualities for entry into a graduate program. Stick to that theme and then return to it at the end of your statement.

The personal statement is a prime opportunity to induce a match with the research and clinical interests of faculty members. Most doctoral programs, as we have said, attempt to match faculty with incoming graduate students on the basis of mutual interest, for example, child therapy, GLBT issues, or neuropsychological assessment. This matching strategy is more often employed by research-oriented than practice-oriented programs, but attempt it in all of your personal statements.

To illustrate, consider the clinical admissions process of the University of Ottawa, a Canadian program with an equal emphasis on research and practice. Like many programs, they create a finalist pool by eliminating applications with low GPAs and GRE scores. Then each of the clinical faculty members reviews all the finalist applications in order to locate several possible matches. These applicants receive interviews. As you can see, and as we have repeated throughout this book, gaining admission into competitive doctoral programs is not limited to one's credentials but also includes a match in research and clinical interests.

Here, then, are a few general guidelines for writing personal statements that increase the probability of a match:

- Depending on the number of faculty members you are interested in working with, you should mention as few as one and perhaps up to four of your interests. If the program is research-oriented and you hope to work with a prominent researcher, you probably do not want to include more than two research interests. You likely will be competing against many other applicants who specifically desire to work with that person and your application might look too diffuse.
- Cast your interests in fairly broad terms—not administering the Wisconsin Card Sorting Test, but neuropsychological assessment; not a mail survey of counseling psychologists, but the characteristics and practices of mental health professionals.
- Nominate at least two professors with whom you would like to work at that graduate program. Some faculty members may go on sabbatical, retire, or not take on new students. This, too, enhances the chance of a successful match.
- In rare instances, you might nominate just one professor; for instance, if the program is research-oriented and there only is one attractive faculty member there with whom you intensely desire to work. In this case, prior to writing your statement, ensure from the faculty member's webpage or from personal communication that he/she is taking a new student that year.
- Integrate the program's training philosophy into your personal statement. For example, "I resonate with Babylon University's goal of producing multiculturally competent psychologists to work directly in the community."

A commonly asked question is, "How personal should I get in my personal statement?" Although there is no universal answer, several suggestions can be offered. A personal detail, such as describing how growing up with a handicapped or disturbed sibling has affected your life and decision to enter psychology, is appropriate. However, depicting the situation in intimate detail without relating it to its contribution to your own growth may lead an admissions committee to question your judgment.

A rule of thumb is to be introspective and self-revealing without sounding exhibitionistic. For example, it is fine for an applicant to state how personal life experiences have contributed to better self-understanding, but it sounds peculiar when the applicant goes into great detail about particular relationships or early life events (Halgin, 1986). Although allusions to applicants' personal psychotherapy in personal statements do not appear to overly stigmatize candidates or lead disproportionately to their rejections (Schaefer, 1995), we recommend against including your personal therapy in written materials sent to virtual strangers.

Many personal statements are ineffective because, first, the student fails to spend time preparing them and, second, the student fails to be "personal" (Osborne, 1996). Therefore, as an applicant you should devote a substantial amount of time thinking, writing, rethinking, and rewriting the personal statement. Expect to prepare four or five drafts. Your statement should include personal details that relate to your ability to be a successful graduate student and that demonstrate maturity, adaptation, and motivation—the very characteristics sought by admissions committees.

Another question we are frequently asked is, "How distinctive or unique should my personal statement be?" Our answer is: as distinctive or unique as you are. Some applicants labor under the delusion that personal statements should resemble creative writing samples that magnify their singular accomplishments or that set the world on fire. Set the bar more realistically and aim for a personal statement that tells your own story clearly and convincingly.

A good idea is to show humility. Even if you have golden research and clinical experiences and 330 GRE scores, you are still entering as a student. You are coming to learn. Mention the areas you hope to develop during your graduate school experience.

Your personal statement should lead the reader to say, "I want to meet and interview this person." It should leave a memorable, positive impression of your accomplishments and potential. You want a ticket to the dance.

Be prepared to back up the claims you make in your personal statements. If you profess a working knowledge of, say, cognitive therapy, then be prepared for questions on the work of Aaron Beck, Albert Ellis, and Marsha Linehan. Similarly, if you claim fluency in Spanish, then expect one of the interviews to be conducted entirely in Spanish (Megargee, 2001).

The "to do's" of personal statements are process suggestions and thus difficult to pinpoint, but the "not to do's" are content-oriented and easier to delineate. We characterize three such "nots" as the three H's: Humor, Hyperbole, and Hard luck stories. Humor rarely works in a formal written statement; so unless you are an unusually gifted satirist, we recommend you avoid jokes, cuteness, and funny stories about your life. Similarly, hyperbole rarely impresses the admissions committee. References to your "overwhelming childhood trauma" and "triumph over undiagnosed learning disabilities" in personal statements cast doubt on the veracity and accuracy of your judgment. Same for over-the-top flattery of graduate programs and faculty members. Avoid the hyperbolic language of *always*, *never*, *worst*, and *every* in your statement.

And hard luck stories typically come off feebly. Many students financed their undergraduate educations, many survived disastrous relationship choices, and many muddled through three academic majors before discovering their niche in psychology. Avoid making adversity the theme of your statement.

Our advice is supported by an interesting study on the "kisses of death" in the graduate school application process (Appleby & Appleby, 2004). Eighty-eight chairs of graduate admissions committees provided examples of application materials that caused the admissions committee to draw negative conclusions about the applicant. These kisses of death in damaging personal statements tended to be (a) overly altruistic, (b) excessively disclosing, (c) nonspecific, or (d) professionally inappropriate.

Examples of the overly altruistic statements were "I want to help all people live happy lives" and "I want to help people because of how very much I have been helped." Examples of excessive self-disclosure were "being a recovering drug addict daughter of a sexually deviant and alcoholic mother" and excruciating details of an applicant's year-long struggle with painful hemorrhoids! The applicant who wrote "I am open to research and practice in any area of psychology" was summarily dismissed from consideration, as such vague, global statements have no place in a graduate application. Our favorite example of professional inappropriateness was the applicant who submitted a statement of purpose titled "Statement of Porpoise" that contained drawings of the sea mammal and a description of the applicant frolicking in the ocean with a porpoise on a visit to Florida. As we said, avoid humor, hyperbole, and hard luck in your personal statement.

To set yourself apart from the pack, avoid the general and the cliché. If we had a dollar for every essay that started with, "I have always wanted to be a psychologist" and "My friends constantly tell me that I am a good listener," then we surely would be independently wealthy! Please say something specific, distinctive, about you and your path.

One way to make your personal statement sparkle is to describe any teaching assistantships or experiences. Talk about how you learned leadership skills and teamwork in this role. Specific examples of how you responsibly handled challenging courses or teaching activities will lead the reader to infer you possess the "right stuff."

Your personal statement should tell a compelling, integrative story of a reflective individual who notes accomplishments without joking or bragging or sobbing. As our colleague Sue Krauss Whitbourne puts it: Don't say it softly or loudly, just say it clearly!

You will be asked in practically every personal statement and personal interview why you chose to apply to *this* particular graduate program in clinical or counseling psychology. Figure 6-3 presents a *portion* of a sample statement, addressing this ubiquitous question, written by one of our undergraduate students in his successful bid for entry into a clinical psychology doctoral program committed to the scientist–practitioner model. His reasons for applying to "State University" are presented only as a single example; your statements will need to be tailored to your interests and credentials as well as the application instructions. Remember that this is just one part of an entire autobiographical statement.

His why-I-applied-to-your-program statement illustrates several important points. First, he advances multiple reasons for applying to that particular program. Five reasons sound much more convincing than one or two (though don't overdo it). Second, his reasons for applying to State U. primarily address his professional match with the program (their reputation, faculty members, clinical opportunities) but nicely concludes with a personal touch (geographic location). Third, he mentions two specific faculty and several potential research interests in an attempt to maximize the chances of a match. Fourth, the statement reflects his careful reading and incorporation of the program's self-description; for example, he cites the opportunity to immerse himself early into research and names the Psychological Services Center. Fifth, the statement is systematically organized and clearly written—indicators of an organized and clear-thinking graduate student!

Some applicants unwittingly insult admissions committees because their personal statements declare that the primary reason for applying is the program's convenient location or inexpensive cost. One of our colleagues, who compares matching with doctoral programs to dating rituals, exclaims that's like saying you are dating someone because he/she is convenient and cheap! Emphasize the quality of the program and academic reasons instead. If cost and location factor in, mention them briefly at the end of your statement, not at the beginning.

Compose your personal statement as carefully as you would a term paper. Write several rough drafts and then set it aside for a few days. Avoid slang words on the one hand, and overly technical or elaborate words on the other. Stick to the information requested; avoid too many "ruffles" and lengthy expositions of your own philosophy (Fretz & Stang,

It is my strong desire to attend a doctoral program in clinical psychology. I am seeking a program committed to the Boulder model, training scientist–practitioners able to serve society in a variety of capacities. The program I attend will stress the importance of understanding and integrating the broad field of psychology, as well as providing the knowledge and training specific to clinical psychology.

After a thorough review of more than 50 Ph.D. programs in clinical psychology, I have chosen to apply to State University for a number of reasons. First, your program is known for producing stellar graduates, and has been repeatedly recommended to me by several psychology faculty. The internship match rate, licensure pass percentage, and employment records of your graduates are impressive indeed. Second, State University allows students to immerse themselves in research early in their graduate careers. Third, I am drawn toward several of your faculty members, including Dr. Sara Ruth for her work in substance abuse and cognitive therapy, and Dr. Mark Cobb for his work in sexual health, stress, and coping. I would be pleased to have either of these faculty members as my mentor. Fourth, the available clinical experiences would allow me to work with a population I find of particular interest, such as adults and families at the Psychological Services Center. And fifth, I am looking to attend school in a scenic area of the country where both my fiancé and I think we would be happy.

FIGURE 6-3. Portion of a sample personal statement.

1980). Write as many drafts as necessary until the statement sounds right to you.

Before you finish a draft of your personal statement, have friends read it for grammar, spelling, and typos. Regardless of the content, technical accuracy really makes a difference.

Once it is error free, have one or more faculty members read it and make suggestions. Do *not* give faculty or mentors a rough draft of your personal statement; give them a formal draft once you have reworked it and your peers have reviewed it. Let them know where the statement is going, and they can guide you on form and content. In fact, some faculty ask that you bring in the exact wording of the questions, along with your formal draft, so that their feedback can be pinpoint targeted.

Then, revise it again. Take the critical feedback seriously and rewrite accordingly. You will understandably protest that you have already devoted hours to your statement. One of our students complained that she had spent 10 hours preparing only 500 words! But remind yourself that the extra hour you put in now may mean the difference between acceptance and rejection by a particular program.

As you examine the final draft, perform a mental checklist: Does the statement have a theme or focus? Does it proceed logically and chronologically? Does it contain proper grammar, spelling, and punctuation? Does it come alive with detail and language? Does it avoid the three H's? Does it begin and end with attention-grabbing sentences? Does it communicate passion? (Keith-Spiegel & Wiederman, 2000).

For further tips on writing your personal statement, skim Donald Asher's (2012) *Graduate Admissions Essays: Write Your Way into the Graduate Program of Your Choice* and visit the following websites:

- www.psywww.com/careers/perstmt.htm
- http://www.apa.org/education/grad/application-video-series.aspx
- www.indiana.edu/~wts/pamphlets/personal_statements.shtml
- depts.washington.edu/psych/files/writing_center/personal.pdf

We hope that our suggestions in this section guide you in writing your personal statement. It is also our hope that they are not too constraining or overly prescriptive. This part of the application permits an admissions committee to see you in a more personal, three-dimensional light, an area where "you can be you."

Letters of Recommendation

An anxiety-provoking step in applying to graduate programs is requesting letters of recommendation. These are unique in that these documents are not prepared by or controlled by you. Here, you must depend on the kindness and support of others.

What do admission committees gain from letters of recommendation? The answer is a personal but objective evaluation of your work from a professional experienced in the field. Admission committees desire a more objective sense of your abilities and experience than what you provide about yourself. Consequently, it is best to have at least two of the people writing your letters be at the doctoral level in psychology or psychology-related disciplines. One fine letter from a master's-level clinician is usually acceptable, but he or she will not be in a position to attest to your ability to complete doctoral studies.

By the same token, bachelor's degree recipients, friends, and relatives should never write letters of recommendation to doctoral programs. They simply do not possess the experience or knowledge of what it takes to earn a doctorate. Letters from politicians, clergy, and your psychotherapists typically are inappropriate as well—they tend to write personal and psychological testimonies instead of academic letters of reference.

Choose people with whom you have worked for a long enough period, preferably for a year or more. That typically excludes a professor with whom you have taken a single class, even if you did get an A. If you wrote a particularly strong paper in the class and the professor knows you a bit better, then he or she could serve as a reference, but this reference is still not the most desirable. At best this person can say, "This student was always on time, participated in discussions, attended office hours, and tested very well. On this basis I consider him/her an intelligent student and a good candidate for graduate school."

By contrast, admissions committees want to hear something more detailed, like: "This student has worked with me for an entire year and completed two of my courses. During that time she scored MMPIs, tested participants using a polygraph, analyzed data, and conducted her own honors thesis. She was dependable and worked beyond what was required by the department. Given this student's intelligence, motivation, and responsibility, I think she would make an outstanding doctoral student." Though the above is a strong example, the point is that you want someone to attest to your ability and responsibility.

Table 6-1 lists some of the self-sabotaging things students do to receive neutral letters of recommendation. Although presented for its humor, it also provides sage warnings about interpersonal behaviors that annoy professors.

Other students receive neutral letters of recommendation through no fault of their own. They experience difficulty in securing detailed letters of recommendation because they:

- Transferred from one college to another college before graduating (which occurs, according to the U.S. Department of Education, to almost one-third of all students);
- Attended a mammoth state university where they took only huge lecture classes and never had the same psychology professor twice;
- Switched majors relatively late in their college career and did not get to know their psychology professors well;
- Completed college part-time for 10 or so years and did not acquire close contacts with full-time faculty members.

We are sympathetic to these plights. If you fall into one of these categories, then you need to double your efforts to get involved in clinical experiences, research activities, and departmental matters—and do so quickly.

Most doctoral programs request three letters of recommendation. Try to secure letters that will furnish the admissions committee the information it needs. At a practice-oriented program, one letter from a clinical supervisor, one letter from a professor, and one from a research advisor would probably prove the ideal mix. At a research-oriented program, two letters from research advisors and one from a clinical supervisor or professor would probably be better. All things being equal, it is preferable to have your "research" letters come from faculty. However, if you believe that a letter from an employer would be substantially more helpful than that of a professor

TABLE 6-1. Professors' Pet Peeves: Avoiding Neutral Letters of Recommendation

Students sometimes are unaware of how the seemingly innocuous things they do and say can annoy their professors. In turn, the professors provide students with less than enthusiastic letters of recommendation. Here are some examples suggested by William W. Nish of Georgia College, reprinted with his kind permission.

Be quick to apply such concise labels as "busy work," "irrelevant," and "boring" to anything you do not like or understand. Not only is this a convenient way of putting the professor down, but also you will not be bothered with the inconvenience of understanding something before you judge it.

Always be ready with reasons why you are an exception to the rules established for the class, such as the dates for submitting written assignments.

Avoid taking examinations at the same time as the rest of the class. Be certain to take it for granted that the professor will give you a make-up exam at your convenience, regardless of your reason for missing the exam.

Be very casual about class attendance. When you see your professor be sure to ask, "Did I miss anything important in class today?" This will do wonders for his or her ego. By all means expect the professor to give a recital of all of the things you missed instead of taking the responsibility for getting the information from another member of the class.

Be consistently late to class and other appointments. This shows other people how much busier you are than they are.

Do not read your assignments in advance of class lecture and discussion. This actually allows you to study more efficiently, for you can take up class time asking about things that are explained in the reading.

Avoid using the professor's office hours or making an appointment. Instead, show up when he or she is frantically trying to finish a lecture before the next class hour and explain that you must see him or her right that minute.

Do not participate in such mundane activities as departmental advising appointments. Instead, wait until the last minute for approval of your schedule, and then expect the professor to be available at your convenience.

with whom you are not well acquainted, then it is probably a good idea to use the employer.

Our general advice was confirmed by an intriguing study (Keith-Spiegel & Wiederman, 2000) that asked members of admissions committees to rank sources of recommendation letters. Raters were asked to assume that the letters from these different sources were equally positive so that rating variations were due solely to the referee's characteristics. The most valuable sources of letters of recommendation were (in descending order): (1) A mentor with whom the applicant has done considerable work; (2) the applicant's professor, who is also a well-known and highly respected psychologist; (3) an employer in a job related to the applicant's professional goals; (4) the chair of the academic department in which the applicant is majoring; (5) a professor from another department from whom the applicant has taken a relevant upper-division course. By contrast, a letter from a graduate teaching assistant was rated, essentially, as no help. And a letter from one's personal therapist was rated negatively!

Applicants are naturally tempted to request a recommendation from, for want of a better term, "nice" professors. As long as those professors have worked extensively with you and are respected, that is a fine plan of action. But asking nice professors instead of credible, respected professors can result in trouble. Even the kindest, student-centered professors cannot comment on what they do not know directly about you. Avoid securing brief, diffuse letters from friendly folks who say nothing of substance or import. Follow the research and seek high-impact letters that yield both gravitas (seriousness) and veritas (the truth).

It's not unusual to seek letters of recommendation from faculty members who have retired or relocated. Ask the department secretary or chairperson to contact the faculty member for you or perhaps they shall give you an email address to do so yourself. Do not worry about asking: academics and researchers understand job changes and expect to contribute recommendations for years after they have left an institution.

Crucial: *First ask the person writing the letters whether he or she can write you a good one.* Ask this direct and specific question: "Would you be comfortable writing a good letter of recommendation for me?" If the person is hesitant or gives any indication of reservations, *ask someone else!* A bad letter of recommendation is deadly. Better to have one brief letter from a professor who gave you an "A" than from someone who might express reservations about your abilities. "I don't know" is better than "I know, and I have reservations."

The way you approach professors for a recommendation is an underappreciated topic. Remember, you will ask, "Are you comfortable writing a good recommendation for me?" If the person responds in the affirmative, we strongly recommend that you provide that person with a letter similar to that shown in Figure 6-4. If you worked in this professor's laboratory and if the lab was fairly large, you might also provide an outline of the various tasks that you conducted while working there. This will help refresh the professor's memory and make for a stronger letter. The person writing a letter of recommendation needs adequate information in order to produce a credible and informative letter. You can be powerful in shaping a professor's letter of recommendation!

Do all of these steps in person. Yes, it is interpersonally anxious to ask someone, "Can you write a good letter of recommendation for me?" And, of course, all of these steps are painstaking and time-consuming. But that is precisely the point: You are demonstrating your interpersonal skills, responsibility, and work ethic to the professor even as you are requesting a letter of recommendation attesting to those very attributes. Thus, ask in person during a formal meeting–not in an email, not by telephone, not in a few minutes before work or class, not by placing a recommendation form in the person's mailbox. Take the initiative and do it directly in real-time (Norcross & Cannon, 2008).

This letter—and the attendant course listing and CV—will promote accuracy and detail. These are essential characteristics of strong letters of recommendation in that the admissions committee looks for positive tone *and* detail. A two-paragraph laudatory letter on the order of "Great student, fine person" simply doesn't make the detailed case for your admission into competitive graduate programs.

What admissions committees also find useless in letters are duplicate and irrelevant information. One set of researchers (Elam et al., 1998) queried members of admissions committees and discovered the five *least* helpful aspects of letters of recommendation:

- Repetition of information from the application (e.g., repeating grades, honors, and scores available elsewhere on the application)
- Unsubstantiated superlatives or vague generalities
- Detailed descriptions of grades in one particular course
- Lack of strong relationship between applicant and letter writer

November 2018

Leslie Jones, Ph.D.
Department of Psychology
East Coast University
1200 Faculty Building
Hausman, MD 43707

Dear Dr. Jones:

Thank you for agreeing to write a letter of recommendation on my behalf. I hereby waive (or do not waive) my right to inspect the letter of recommendation written for me and sent to the designated schools of my choice. I am applying to (master's, doctoral) programs in clinical (counseling, combined) psychology. My earliest deadline is ________________.

Here are the courses I have taken from you.

Fall 2016	Abnormal Psychology	A–
Spring 2016	Clinical Psychology	B+
Fall 2017	Undergraduate Research	

Here are other activities in which I have participated.

2017–2018	Research Assistant
2016–2017	Vice President of Psi Chi

My latest GRE scores were 156 Verbal, 160 Quantitative, and 5.0 Analytical Writing. My Psychology Subject Test score was 610.

(If applicable:)
In your laboratory in Fall 2017, while participating in undergraduate research, I was involved in several different activities. My responsibilities included entering participant data, conducting telephone screening interviews to determine participant eligibility, and coding several indices of social functioning during a key interaction period in the alcohol administration study. I also participated in the weekly journal club meetings.

As we discussed, I would greatly appreciate your addressing my (employment history, clinical experience, department service, lower than expected GPA, etc.) in my letter of recommendation. I will also be discussing the matter in my personal statement, but your perspective would likely prove important to the admissions committee.

Finally, I attach a copy of my current vitae, a list of psychology courses completed, and a summary table of the graduate programs to which I am applying. Please feel free to call me at 555-1212 or to email me at Chris_smith@phonyemail.com for any additional information that you desire. Thanks again.
Sincerely yours,

Chris Smith

Encls.

FIGURE 6-4. Sample letter to request a letter of recommendation.

♦ Inclusion of irrelevant information, such as religious beliefs or hearsay

Put another way, give your referees sufficient data to render informed and positive letters about your personal characteristics, academic strengths, and interpersonal skills so that they do not resort to filling your recommendations with irrelevant content.

Here's how one doctoral program (University of Rhode Island) attempts to translate the content of recommendation letters into numerical ratings.

1 Summary recommendations in all three letters are neutral or negative. Positive and negative assessments are listed. Overall evaluation in all three is neutral.
2 Letters meet criteria between anchor points 1 and 3.
3 Summary recommendations in all three letters are positive and general. Positive statements from all three letters. Statements are general in nature.
4 Letters meet criteria between anchor points 3 and 5.
5 Summary recommendations in all three letters are excellent and detailed. Positive statements from all three letters are very favorable and very detailed in their support.

Note, again, that the emphasis is on positive tone *and* supportive detail. This is the sought-after result of your extra work in providing references with factual information and assertive requests for letters of recommendation. A "liability letter" is one that communicates limited knowledge of the applicant, leading an admissions committee to conclude that the person was only minimally connected to professors in his or her undergraduate or master's department (Halgin, 1986).

Most universities request that recommenders complete a rating form as well as a separate letter. These forms can be handled in two ways, depending upon the graduate school's instructions and the recommender's preferences. One way is to provide your professor with these printed rating forms and stamped envelopes addressed to the schools to which the forms are to be sent. This is a small but crucial precaution—do not take the chance that postage will delay return of the letter. It is also courteous: Your professor is doing you a favor taking considerable time and contemplation to write a strong letter.

The second and more frequent way is that the rating forms are submitted electronically to the graduate program. In this case, you list on your application the names, positions, and email addresses of people writing you letters of recommendation. The graduate schools then directly contact your referees via email and provide them with the URL and a password to electronically submit their letters of recommendation to your application file. Online submission of recommendations streamlines the entire process and has become the rule.

For several years we have been tracking the frequency of graduate programs requesting electronic submission of letters of recommendation. Approximately 90% of Ph.D. programs at large universities have gone electronic. For Psy.D. and master's programs, not so much: we estimate about 65%.

The recommendation forms from graduate schools may appear to be quite different at first glance; however, closer inspection will reveal that they all request essentially the same information. The forms typically ask the recommenders to note the length of time they have known you and in what capacities. Then the referees are asked to rate your research ability, originality, writing skills, organizational ability, maturity, interpersonal skills, persistence, and similar qualities on a structured grid. Typical forms request an appraisal of the applicant in terms of 10 qualities in comparison with others applying for graduate study whom the referees have known in the applicant's proposed field of study. The rating grid offers responses of top 3%, next 10%, next 20%, middle third, lowest third, and unable to judge. On most forms, an open space is then presented for a narrative description of your strengths and weaknesses. The forms usually conclude with a request for a summary rating: a check mark on a continuum from "not recommended" to "highly recommended" or a numerical value representing an overall ranking of this student to others taught in the past.

Researchers have identified the most frequent applicant characteristics that recommenders were requested to rate on these forms (Appleby, Keenan, & Mauer, 1999). The resulting list—based on the analysis of 143 recommendation forms—describes the characteristics that psychology graduate programs value in their applicants. In descending order of frequency, the top dozen are as follows:

♦ Motivated and hardworking
♦ High intellectual/scholarly ability
♦ Research skills
♦ Emotionally stable and mature
♦ Writing skills

- Speaking skills
- Teaching skills/potential
- Works well with others
- Creative and original
- Strong knowledge of area of study
- Character or integrity
- Special skills, such as computer or lab

One vital lesson to be learned is that graduate school aspirants should make a concerted effort to behave in ways that allow them to acquire relevant skills (research, writing, speaking, computer) and to be perceived by at least two of their professors as motivated, bright, emotionally stable, capable of working well with others, and possessing integrity (Appleby et al., 1999).

These forms, by law, will contain a waiver statement asking whether you do or do not waive your right to inspect the completed letter of reference. The Family Education Rights and Privacy Act of 1974 (FERPA or the so-called Buckley Amendment) mandated that students over age 18 be given access to their academic records unless they waive the right. This is a complicated topic, but we invariably advise applicants to waive their right of access *providing*, as previously discussed, the person writing the letter knows the student well and has agreed to provide a strong recommendation. Do not waive access—or better yet, do not request letters—from persons you do not trust or do not know.

A confidential letter carries more weight. By waiving your right to access, you communicate confidence that the letters will be supportive, and you express trust in your reference. In fact, over 90% of health profession schools prefer letters of recommendation that are waived by the student (Chapman & Lane, 1997). Our experiences and naturalistic studies (e.g., Ceci & Peters, 1984; Shaffer & Tomarelli, 1981) indicate that professors' honest evaluations will be compromised when you have access to what they have written. By waiving the right, you are communicating an intent to have the "truth" told. Otherwise, admissions committees may lump the letter with all the other polite and positive testimonials (Halgin, 1986). Worse, admissions committees may suspect that your unwillingness to waive your right means that you are worried that your letters might be weak.

In making your choice of whether to waive or not, be clear about the law. Most students correctly know that if they waive their rights they may never see the letter. However, many students erroneously think that choosing not to waive their rights means that they can see their letter if they do not get accepted or that they have a right to preview the letter before it is sent (Ault, 1993). These are common fallacies, but fallacies nonetheless.

The relevant laws do not dictate that professors must show students the completed letter. One study (Keith-Spiegel, 1991) of college faculty found that 17% never show students their letters of recommendation, 46% usually do not, 8% only to students they know well, 15% only if students ask, and 14% routinely show students their letters. Nor does the law guarantee a student access to letters if the student is rejected from a graduate program; in fact, students may inspect their files at a graduate school only after they have been accepted at and enrolled in that graduate school (Ault, 1993).

Going one step further, contrary to some students' beliefs, faculty do *not* have to write letters of recommendation for students. Letters are a common and voluntary courtesy, not a job requirement.

Why might faculty members decline to write a letter for a student? The single most common reason is that they don't know the student well enough (Keith-Spiegel, 1991). Other frequent reasons given by faculty are that they question the student's motivation level, emotional stability, academic credentials, or professional standards. If faculty defer on your request for a letter, politely inquire about their reasoning and graciously thank them for their candor.

One clever study asked psychologists how they would handle requests for a letter of recommendation from a student exhibiting particular problems (Grote, Robiner, & Haut, 2001). The majority indicated that they would *not* write a letter for a student who was abusing substances or who had shown unethical behavior. For most of the other student problems—interpersonal problems, lack of motivation, paucity of responsibility, marginal clinical skills—psychologists routinely would tell the student about their reservations, then write the letter including the negative information. If faculty members tell you that they have reservations about your behavior, then they will probably include the negative evaluation in their letter. Politely inquire if their reservation will in fact appear in the letter. If so, thank them for their candor and withdraw your request for a letter.

The last impression you make on the recommender concerns your organization and preparation. If your recommendation packet is complete and orderly, then the person feels respected and remembers you as a dedicated student. If, on the other hand, your packet is disorganized and incomplete, you frustrate the person and behaviorally remind him or her of your weaknesses.

TABLE 6-2. Summary Table of a Student's Graduate Program Applications

School	Grad program	Deadline	Letter or form	Submission method
Southwestern University	Ph.D. clinical	December 15	Letter & form	Online link will be emailed
Midwestern University	Ph.D. clinical	January 1	Letter & form	Online link will be emailed
Pacific North University	Ph.D. clinical	January 15	Letter & form	Online link will be emailed
Atlantic University	Ph.D. clinical	February 1	Letter	Online link will be emailed
Northeast University	M.S. clinical	March 15	Form; letter optional	Either mail or online but online preferred
Regional College	M.A. psychology	March 22	Letter	Back to me in sealed envelope; I include it in my application
Southeastern University	M.A. applied psychology	March 22	Letter & form	Mail directly to Psych Dept

We therefore recommend that you create a summary table of your graduate program applications and place it on the top of the materials you deliver to the referee (along with the aforementioned letter, CV, and various forms). A shortened sample of such a table is provided in Table 6.2. The table will assist and impress the recommender while simultaneously helping you remain organized and on-deadline.

Deliver the entire recommendation packet to the recommender at a single time. Do not drib and drab—another form a week later, a forgotten program added later by email, a transcript added two weeks after the packet was delivered. Provide the packet all at once in complete fashion. Get OCD and double-check everything.

Play it safe and provide the reference packet at least 6 weeks before the earliest deadline. Completing your recommendation will not be the top priority of the person you have asked to write it, or he or she may be out of town prior to the deadline. Do not take any chances that a letter will be late. Allow 3 weeks and ask if the letter has been sent. Be politic: do not pester, but do follow up.

If you seek additional information on requesting letters of recommendation, then we suggest the pointers and videos offered by the following websites:

- gradschool.about.com/od/askingforletters/ht/howletter.htm
- www.apa.org/education/grad/application-video-series.aspx
- www.writeexpress.com/recommendation-letters.html
- www.uwm.edu/people/ccp2/work/recletter.html
- www.psychwww.com/careers/lettrec.htm
- www.boxfreeconcepts.com/reco/

Transcripts and GRE Scores

A graduate application will not be complete—and probably not even considered by the admissions committee—unless the required academic transcripts and entrance examination scores have been received. Your task here consists of requesting organizations to transmit official copies of these materials to the graduate schools of your choice and then ensuring that the schools have received them.

With respect to transcripts, you must request that the Registrar's Office of all attended colleges and universities mail an *official* copy of your transcript directly to the graduate school. An official copy is printed on security-sensitive paper and contains the seal, stamp, and authorized signature of the institution. The cost of transcripts varies from place to place, but it averages $5 or $10 per copy. Submit transcript requests at least 1 month before the application deadline. Many universities take two weeks during the semester to process these requests. Most graduate programs continue to require hard copies of transcripts mailed from academic institutions.

Online transcript exchange across the country has been difficult to establish; however, online transcripts are becoming more common. National companies such as Axess and the National Transcript Center provide secure electronic transmissions among institutions (Fauber, 2006).

A reminder: request an unofficial copy of your own transcript in September or October prior to applying. Inspect it closely for errors and omissions. Horror stories abound regarding erroneous transcript entries misleading admissions committees—an initial grade of I (incomplete) becoming an F (failure), honors credits not registered, unpaid term bills delaying transcripts, and so on. Don't leave it to chance; check it out yourself.

One creative researcher (Landrum, 2003) surveyed graduate admissions directors about the impact of transcripts and withdrawals in the admissions process. Results demonstrate that your transcript will get a careful review in practically all programs and will be reviewed by more than one member of the admissions committee in about 87% of the programs. With respect to the effects of course withdrawals (dropping a course after mid-semester) on transcripts, less than 4% of programs indicated that a withdrawal from a single course would hurt an applicant's chance of admission into the graduate program. But more than 20% of the programs indicated that two or more withdrawals hurt a student's entry into their graduate program. Thus, our advice to students contemplating a course withdrawal is that one is probably not hurtful, but that two or more withdrawals, especially from required courses such as statistics and research methods, may well have a negative impact.

With respect to GREs, score reports will automatically be mailed to you and electronically submitted to the four graduate schools you listed when you completed the GRE testing. The mailing date for the score reports is approximately 6 weeks after the test date for paper-based testing (Psychology Subject Test) and 2 weeks for computer-based testing (General Test). Your copy of the score report is intended only for your information; official reports are sent electronically and directly by ETS to the score recipients you designate. This procedure—as with the registrar transmitting an official transcript—is intended to ensure that no questions are raised about the authenticity of a score report.

You will probably be applying to more than the four schools you initially designated for score reports. Toward this end, you will submit online an Additional Score Report After Test Day and remit your payment of $27 for *each* score recipient listed, charged to your credit card. Or, you can use the Phone Service for Additional Score Reports by dialing 1-888-GRE-SCORE. Your scores will be transmitted to you and to the programs within 10 working days. You may have your GRE scores transmitted at any time during the 5-year period after they are initially reported.

Unsolicited Documents

During our workshops, we are frequently asked, "What if a program doesn't ask for something that I'd like to send?" Some examples are the curriculum vitae, a research paper, and job descriptions. If a graduate program does not want additional documents, it will state so clearly on the application. In that case, do as the program requests. But even then, you may make additional documents a part of your application if you have come to know a professor at the school and have shared these documents with him or her.

Send a curriculum vitae and/or job descriptions if they are applicable. One benefit of doing so is that you will spend less time focusing on the details of these work experiences in your personal statement. You can relate how the experiences influenced you without wasting space explaining exactly what you did. For example, prior to graduate school, one of us worked with a psychotherapist conducting a social skills group for preadolescents. In the personal statement he focused on how that experience had affected him. By referring to the "enclosed job description," the personal statement did not get bogged down in the details. As a professional, you will need a CV eventually, and we recommend you begin one even if you do not use it in every application. Start a vitae file and toss notes and memos into it regarding assistantship duties, noteworthy activities, committee assignments, professional associations—in short, everything you need to update your vitae (Hayes & Hayes, 1989).

If you have a large number of work experiences, be careful not to overwhelm admissions committees with paperwork. Choose one or, in a rare case, two experiences that showcase your credentials and that highlight characteristics not likely tapped by those writing your letters of recommendation. If you send more job descriptions than this, you may weaken their impact and increase the chances that the most laudatory ones will not be read (or at least not carefully).

If you have authored an honors thesis, a conference poster, or an original research paper and have received positive faculty feedback on it, then include it with your application materials. If there is someone whose research corresponds with your own, this may open a door for you. However, if there is a question about your paper's quality, do not send it. A questionable paper may do more harm than good.

Application Fees

Last but unfortunately not least, most schools require application fees. These fees range from $0 to $100 per school, and average $50 for doctoral programs and $35 for master's programs (Norcross et al., 2005). Credits cards are typically used when applying electronically. Or, if need be, you can send a personal or a cashier's check (never cash).

If you are in dire financial need or are experiencing trouble meeting application expenses, read the application instructions carefully. There is usually a statement allowing fees to be waived because of financial hardship. Go to the school's application website or call and ask how to have the application fee waived. That some students cannot afford the fees is the reason schools make the allowance in the first place. Graduate schools are sensitive to the impoverished status of many applicants, so feel no compunction about requesting a fee waiver if it applies to you.

Check and Recheck

At this point, you have completed the application forms, requested letters of recommendation (and seen to it they were sent), written your personal statement, asked to have transcripts and GREs transmitted, and prepared the unsolicited documents you plan to include. Once again, before you submit the material, ask your mentor or a professor to check it for accuracy and clarity. Have friends review it for typos and spelling. All material should look neat and professional. It represents you in a real way. Anything sloppy or tattered can convey the message that *you* are careless and unprofessional. Submission of materials should reflect a meticulous attention to detail. *Finally, ensure your personal statement is not among those we see each year that carelessly includes the name of a different university when explaining why it is a perfect match for you!*

After all this effort, make certain your application is sent on time. In most cases, the application is sent electronically. If a couple of programs request that you send the application the old-fashioned way, we suggest (if you can afford the extra expense) that you send your application via FedEx, UPS, Express, or certified mail. Each of these will allow you to track your materials to ensure they have arrived and to document the name of the person to whom they were delivered. However, our suggestion does not imply that you should wait until the last minute to express mail your application, implying procrastination (not a positive quality in a graduate student). Do use express mail, but do it well ahead of the deadline.

One of the most frustrating experiences in the graduate application process is confirming that the respective programs have, in fact, received all of your materials. Your application, transcripts, GREs, letters of recommendation—all need to be received, processed, and filed correctly by the graduate admissions office. Horror stories abound about application materials being lost or misfiled or sent to the wrong department. It happened to one of us!

Recently, one of our students shared a similar story. The ETS claimed that her GRE scores were electronically transmitted to and downloaded at a major midwestern university. The university, which required two official sets of GRE scores, claimed that they never received either set. The student was caught in the middle between two opposing claims. She telephoned ETS again and the university's graduate admissions office repeatedly. The GREs had to be resent, at the student's expense.

We estimate that 50% of graduate programs will send an email apprising you of the application materials they have received on your behalf. Another 20% to 25% of graduate programs will post an application status page on their website where you can check yourself. That leaves 25% of the graduate programs that you can either blindly trust (which we *do not* recommend) or that you can contact (which we *do* recommend).

Call or email the admissions office and verify that the materials have been received. You have invested too much sweat, time, and money to leave the application to chance. Do not rely on graduate schools to keep you apprised; take personal responsibility.

CHAPTER 7

MASTERING THE INTERVIEW

The applications have been electronically submitted or physically mailed and are now out of your hands. Following the short-lived relief of finishing your applications, this period can be a nerve-wracking time. You have sold yourself on paper, and now it is up to the graduate programs to decide which applicants to contact for further consideration and probable interviews.

The doctoral admissions process has been characterized as "multiple hurdles" (King, Beehr, & King, 1986). The initial hurdle in most programs is the minimum GRE or GPA score. The second hurdle is the rating of applications on such criteria as clinical experience, research skills, letters of recommendation, and the like. Being invited for an interview means you have successfully leaped these early hurdles, and this is a great compliment in and of itself. You have been asked to the dance! The final and determining hurdle for most programs is the personal interview.

Let's look at this situation from the perspective of graduate programs. APA-accredited clinical psychology programs receive an average of 150 to 250 applicants (Norcross, Ellis, & Sayette, 2010), and APA-accredited counseling psychology programs receive an average of 60 to 120 applicants (Norcross, Evans, & Ellis, 2010). The admissions committee must narrow the large applicant pool to a smaller number to invite for interviews. Programs ordinarily interview two to three times as many students as they can admit. A research-oriented Ph.D. program will typically invite 20 applicants for interviews, from which 10 to 12 will be tendered an offer to obtain 7 confirmed acceptances. By contrast, a large Psy.D. program may invite 120 applicants for interviews, from which they will accept 90 in order to obtain 50 confirmed acceptances.

A few clinical and counseling psychology programs will not require personal interviews, and they will most likely state so in the application materials. Make a note of this so that you do not become distressed when you are not invited. We wonder which is worse: the disappointment of not being asked to interview or the stress of being asked!

Our research on APA-accredited doctoral psychology programs found that 93% of them expected some type of preadmission interview (Oliver et al.,

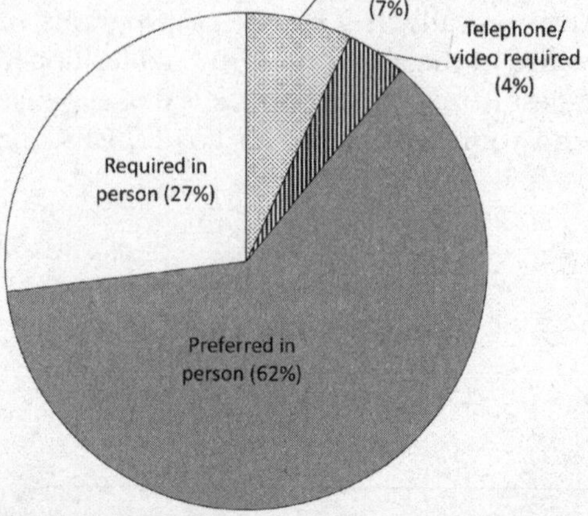

FIGURE 7-1. Preadmission interview policies of APA-accredited programs. Data from Oliver, Norcross, Sayette, Griffin, & Mayne (2005).

2005). As shown in Figure 7-1, 62% of APA-accredited programs strongly preferred an interview in person but were willing to accept a telephone or real-time video interview. Another 27% of the programs absolutely required a face-to-face interview. Four percent required only a telephone or video interview (such as on Skype, Google chat, or ooVoo). All told, only 7% of programs did not require an interview before admission into the program.

Nearly all clinical and counseling psychology programs, then, require a personal interview, be it by phone, video, or in person, prior to acceptance. Since some programs absolutely insist on interviews in person, do *not* apply to distant programs requiring an in-person interview unless you can afford it. Only in rare instances will graduate programs reimburse the applicant for all interview costs, and only 10% of the programs reimburse for some of the costs (Kohout et al., 1991). In other words, more than 80% of the programs expect you to absorb all the interview expenses.

Expect to hear from interested doctoral programs that require interviews from early January through early March. The contact date will depend in part on the practice-research emphasis of the program: the clinical scientist and scientist-practitioner Ph.D. programs contact finalists earlier and typically finish their admission offers in late February or March, whereas practice-oriented Ph.D. and Psy.D. programs contact finalists later. Programs rarely contact students in the finalist pool after March 30 because initial admission offers must go out on April 1, at the latest. It is still possible to be contacted, however, if you are on the alternate or waiting list.

Interview Strategically

Should you receive an invitation for an interview, congratulations! Your odds of eventual acceptance at that graduate program have just skyrocketed.

The simple situation occurs when you are invited on a couple of interviews, the dates of the interviews do not conflict, and you have set aside enough money to travel to all the interviews. If only life were so accommodating! Instead, some applicants will not receive any interview offers, some will be invited to interview on a day they are already scheduled elsewhere for an interview, and still others will have depleted their funds and cannot afford interview travel.

How to handle these complex situations? In a word, *strategically*. Think through your options, discuss them with your mentor, and consider the following strategies.

If you have not received an interview request or a rejection letter by the middle of March, then calmly email or telephone the doctoral program and inquire about the status of your application. If you have been rejected, politely thank the person. You never know: you may apply there again or have professional contact with the people in that program in the future. If your application is still being considered, it is permissible to ask when you might expect a decision. Just be careful not to sound rigid or demanding.

If you are offered a personal interview at two doctoral programs on the same day, not to worry. Should you be so blessed, we recommend that you (1) inquire if the programs have alternative interview days (and schedule one program on the alternative day). If not, then (2) ask if you can complete a video or telephone interview at the less-preferred program. Remember that approximately two-thirds of programs will accept a telephone or video interview. If you value both programs equally, then (3) accept the interview at the least expensive program or the program with the higher likelihood of acceptance.

Many of the best-qualified applicants will wrestle with interview scheduling conflicts. There are only so many weekends available from mid-January to March, and doctoral programs devote a lot of expense and planning on the campus interview day. If you must decline an interview or arrange for a video interview, communicate clearly that it does not reflect your program interest. Be apologetic and sincere.

Likewise, if you have depleted your funds for interview travel, then honestly inform the program and respectfully request a phone interview. Your email might read: "I am very interested in your program and initially planned to attend your interview day on February 15th. Unfortunately, my personal finances do not allow me to travel to State University on that day. I am hopeful that you will permit me to conduct a phone interview on a day that is convenient for you. Thanks very much for understanding; I do wish that I could visit in person." Realize, though, that in some instances, this decision may harm your chances of admission.

Many applicants obtain strategic information on interview invitations and admission offers from online message boards. The last few years have witnessed an increase in the number and popularity of these message boards devoted to doctoral programs in psychology (Fauber, 2006). Three examples spring to mind: PsychGrad.org, the Student Doctor Network (psychology), and Yahoo Message Board. These and other online boards are particularly valuable for notifying everyone the moment interview invitations are extended and admission offers are delivered. They also provide peer support through the taxing application process. However, we have read much online advice that is questionable, even downright wrong. So use the free online boards to secure strategic information and timely support from peers but be wary of the proffered advice.

The Dual Purpose

The interview provides a critical opportunity for information gathering, not only for the graduate program but also for you. That is, the dual purpose of an interview is for the program to check you out and for you to check out the program. Perhaps right now it seems outrageous to contemplate evaluating a doctoral program—you're probably delighted just to be asked! But a few interviews and an acceptance or two will reorient your perspective. If you go on more than one interview, these interactions will give you decisive information in choosing which program to attend. You will find out about clinical training, faculty members, student life, program fit, research facilities, and the like.

Interviewers will look at your social skills, your emotional stability, your professional maturity, your focus, and your goals. The interviewers may want to see the development of your pursuits, the connection between your research and clinical work, or perhaps your adherence to the Boulder or Vail model. You may be asked pointed questions and will be expected to ask probing questions about the program.

The graduate program's emphasis along the practice–research continuum will influence the nature of the interview. Recall our rule of thumb: Applicants to clinical scientist Ph.D. programs match primarily to the research interests of individual faculty, applicants to scientist-practitioner Ph.D. programs match to both the research interests of individual faculty and the offerings of the entire program, and applicants to Psy.D. programs match primarily to the clinical interests and theoretical orientations of the entire program. Expect to spend more time interviewing with your potential research mentor during Ph.D. interviews. You and the program will probably not have even selected a potential mentor or advisor yet in a Psy.D. interview.

Although the interview often generates anxiety for an applicant, it need not. As with anything else in the application process, the more you prepare, the more confident and less nervous you will feel.

The interview is highly charged for the applicants and programs alike. *Both* wish to be evaluated positively and to achieve the best match. You are not alone in trying to put your best foot forward! Interview styles, moreover, vary tremendously—from a conversational tone to grueling questions, from casual to formal, from mundane content to intrusively personal content. Be prepared for all styles, and remember that all count equally in the final analysis. That final analysis is the program's unenviable task of deciding which of the interviewees they will eventually select for admission.

Rehearsal and Mock Interviews

Rehearse the interview beforehand with your mentor, a professor, a career counselor, or a knowledgeable friend. Videotape the "mock" or pretend interview and review it later with an eye toward improvement. Technology has simplified the process, as Big Interview and other online programs allow you to record a practice interview from your computer, to review the video, and then share it with a career counselor or mentor. That will build your comfort and confidence for the real deal.

Although the research-oriented programs are usually less personal and invasive in their interviews, it may behoove you to get accustomed to being asked personal questions without being thrown. Such practice is invaluable, especially for preparing you to think on your feet. Rehearsing also will desensitize you to some degree, take the edge off of your anxiety, and add to your comfort with the process. During the interview you are on stage, selling yourself, and knowing what the interview is all about can only help you.

Leave your mistakes at the mock interview. Rid yourself of the vocal tics that afflict many psychology students: "you know," "like," "really," and "issues." Speak professionally and concisely. Become accustomed to dressing and behaving like the psychologist you aspire to become.

In keeping with the dual purpose of the interview, rehearsing will also afford you practice in the interview style you seek to convey. A respectful and curious tone—"I am wondering about the chances of receiving an assistantship if I am fortunate enough to be accepted?"—is preferable to a blunt and forceful disposition—"How much will you pay me if I come?"

How you phrase a question is important. The interviewer will be more impressed with your eagerness to learn if you ask how many courses in an area are *offered* as opposed to how many are *required* (Megargee, 2001).

Rehearsing will also entail preparation for frequently asked questions of applicants. Table 7-1 presents 25 common interview questions to anticipate and prepare for. *We strongly recommend that you have a concise and thoughtful response ready for each of these.* An "I haven't really given that question much thought" answer hurts. Role-play these questions with a professor or the mock interview. Request that the interviewer ask several of the questions in Table 7-1.

The type of doctoral program will naturally influence the content of interview questions. For those of you interviewing at research-oriented Ph.D. programs, don't be surprised if most of the interview questions focus on your research experiences and how your research interests match with particular faculty members there. The interview also might include discussing past research projects to allow the professor to evaluate how well you think on your feet about research, and how well you can describe the conceptual underpinnings of your past research experiences. For those of you interviewing at Psy.D. programs, most of the questions will center on your clinical experiences and interests and how you match that program's training model.

Beneath the dozens and dozens of possible questions that an interviewer could ask you, career experts say they all boil down to just a few basic questions. The people making the final decisions want to know (Bolles, 2013):

- Why are you *here?* (As opposed to another graduate program; in other words, how well do you fit with us?)
- What can you do for us? (How can your skills, knowledge, and experience enhance our program?)

TABLE 7-1. Common Interview Questions to Anticipate

1. Why do you want to be a psychologist?
2. Why a clinical/counseling psychologist and not, say, a social worker or counselor? Or a quantitative psychologist?
3. What qualifications do you have that will make you a successful psychologist?
4. What specifically attracts you to our program?
5. Will you tell me a little about yourself as a person?
6. Do you think your undergraduate grades (or GRE scores) are valid indicators of your academic abilities?
7. What do you see as your strengths and weaknesses?
8. What do you bring into the program? What are your special attributes?
9. Have you ever had personal therapy? If yes, what sort of issues did you work on? If no, why not?
10. What are your research interests? Tell me about your research project/honors thesis.
11. How do you think you would fit into our research programs and labs?
12. What is your theoretical orientation?
13. How do your theoretical orientation and clinical interests fit with our program?
14. Which of our faculty members do you think you would work with?
15. Where else have you applied or interviewed?
16. Can you tell me about a recent clinical encounter? How did you conceptualize or treat your last client?
17. What are your hobbies, avocations, favorite books, and interests outside of psychology?
18. What are your future plans and goals as a psychologist? Where do you want to be in 10 years?
19. How do you work under stress and pressure? Can you give me examples?
20. How will you finance your graduate education?
21. What specifically attracts you to the Boulder (or Vail) model of training?
22. What is your interest in teaching during graduate school? In your career?
23. What have you read online about our graduate program?
24. How do your career aspirations fit with those of our typical graduates?
25. What questions do you have for me?

- What kind of person are you? (Are you reliable and personable? Can we trust you with our research projects and/or our clinic patients?)
- What distinguishes you from 20 other people who can do the same tasks? (What makes you different from the other qualified applicants? Do you work harder, longer, more thoroughly? Can you better articulate conceptual issues related to past research?)
- Can we get you here? (If we accept you into our program, what is the probability that you will attend? How much will it cost us—in tuition remission or an assistantship, for example?)

Of course, you cannot anticipate all possible questions. Some interviewers pride themselves on avoiding stock questions and instead asking novel questions, thus precluding rehearsed and polished replies. The rationale behind these queries, such as "Who are your heroes?" and "What was the best day in your life?" is that they give a glimpse into your natural response style and tap into spontaneous information processing. One method to handle novel queries is to delay thoughtfully, remark that it is one you have not been asked before, request a moment of contemplation, and then respond forthrightly.

Similar to novel questions are behavior-based interview questions. These increasingly assess an applicant's behavioral repertoire and prior experiences. The behavioral questions rely on the familiar psychological dictum, "Past behavior is the best predictor of future behavior," to glean something about your future behavior in their doctoral program. To answer them effectively, you will prepare several compelling stories that draw on your background to highlight your skills and competences.

Six examples of behavior-based questions are:

- Tell me about an instance when someone asked you to do something that you considered ethically or morally wrong. How did you respond?
- Describe the biggest challenges you faced in the past year and how you handled it.
- Tell me about a work or school situation where you had to do creative problem solving.
- Relate a recent situation in which you had to persuade someone to accept your idea or proposal.
- Present an example when multiple priorities were pulling you in several directions at the same time and how you dealt with it.
- Tell me about an instance when you were unsuccessful in reaching a goal that involved a client, a customer, or a fellow student.

In responding to such questions, follow the *three S's: S*ituation, *S*kills, and *S*uccess. First, describe the situation and your challenge or conflict. For example, "I was working with a group of students for a class project and all of us but one student agreed on the way to proceed." Second, identify your skills that helped you to master the situation. For example, "I tried to understand the dissenter's perspective, communicate that understanding back to him, spoke to the faculty member about her preferences, and asked the dissenter for a compromise." Third, communicate a successful ending, both for you and the other party involved in the situation. "The other person appreciated my listening, instead of arguing, and in the end agreed to go with the group decision. He was happy and the project ended with us all learning a lot and earning an A on the project."

Your answers to behavior-based questions will enable you to concretely demonstrate integrity, resilience, creativity, persuasion, and time management as opposed to simply saying you possess those traits. Apply the three S's to similar questions as those presented above involving conflicted relationships, ethical dilemmas, and complicated decisions. Visit websites on behavioral and situational interviews to get comfortable and competent in answering such questions; two of our favorites are the behavioral interview links off of Quintessential Careers (www.quintcareers.com) and Big Interview (biginterview.com/). Practice the three S's in your mock interview and you will be prepared to tackle the thorniest questions.

Interview Attire

Your interview rehearsal should direct attention to your physical attire, which will be influential in attributions made about you. For women, we recommend a pant suit or a suit with a skirt, dark in color or muted plaid, polished pumps or medium heels in matching color. Wear a simple style blouse, white or soft color. Interview professionals suggest a no-distraction hairstyle, tasteful makeup, and clear or light nail polish. One pair of small earrings should suffice. Nothing too short, tight, or uncomfortable. Avoid wearing spikes or stilettos; others may see them as "club attire" and you may suffer from bruised feet or buckling ankles. Dress for success!

For men, we recommend a conservative two-piece suit or a jacket and slacks, white or light shirt, and contrasting tie. Three-piece suits and "funeral outfits" are out. Wear shined brown or black shoes that are well maintained; as your parents have probably told you, the way you take care of your shoes communicates a lot about you. Dark socks only; save your white socks for work-outs. Hair should be trimmed and neatly groomed.

For men, women, and gender-fluid, plan your interview clothes in advance. Try them on, and lay them out well before the interview to assure that they fit, are clean, and are in good repair. Avoid anything too tight or uncomfortable, especially shoes.

Some applicants prefer to "be themselves" and may still get in without changing their everyday appearance. Nevertheless, we recommend that attire should err on the side of conservative and formal; better to be overdressed and loosen a tie or remove a scarf than to be underdressed for the occasion. Avoid flashy colors and loud fashions. Jewelry should be conservative and understated; go light on the perfume and cologne. Leave the piercings at home. You don't want interviewers remembering you for what you wore, but for who you are and what you will bring to their program. That is, be noticed for your abilities, not your clothing.

Applicants occasionally complain to us that many faculty interviewers are wearing business casual, and thus wonder why they (the applicants) can't wear business casual as well. Our answer is clear: You are an applicant trying to make a stellar impression as a serious, motivated candidate for a competitive graduate program. You are trying to distinguish yourself as one of the premier students, not one of the underdressed herd. We urge you to dress for success in interviews, not in business casual. You can wear casual clothes after you are admitted to the program for most of your graduate life. But during the interview, you never have a second chance to make a first impression.

Questions about the program and other written material should be held in a professional attaché or briefcase. The location and weather will influence your choice of clothing. Reliable answers about expected attire can be provided by graduate students with whom you are staying prior to the interview itself.

Travel Arrangements

While preparing and rehearsing for the interviews, you simultaneously will be making arrangements to travel to the interviews. The costs of travel vary wildly—from a few bucks for driving to and parking at a local university on interview day to more than $1,000 for a 3-day jaunt across the nation involving air travel, rental car, and hotel. Our intent in the following paragraphs is to save you hassle and money in getting to the interviews.

As a general rule, you can save a great deal of money by booking early and paying promptly for air travel, but you will probably incur a stiff penalty for making any changes in your reservation. So begin early to locate those bargains. Start by going online to seek the best fares through airlines' websites. Before booking, take a quick look at kayak.com, expedia.com, travelocity.com, and other commercial sites that promise the lowest possible fares. Compare the schedules and fares from both sources—the airlines' website and commercial websites—and then make a decision.

Remaining flexible in your travel schedule will probably save you money. It may save you money to leave from a different city than the one closest to you. We have saved hundreds of dollars on airfare by simply driving an extra hour to another airport. Or it may save you money to fly to a different city and then drive an hour or two to the interview. Try inserting nearby alternative cities in your computer search and see what fare comes up. One applicant flew out of Washington, DC instead of his home airport of Norfolk, Virginia, and reduced his ticket price from over $1,000 to $278 (Megargee, 2001).

Another way of being flexible is changing when you fly. As most business travelers return home on the weekend, airlines typically offer deep discounts on trips that extend over a Saturday night. The cost of another night at the hotel might save you hundreds in airfare. And consider flying on the "red eye" or "night owl" flights that crisscross the country overnight. To fill otherwise empty seats, airlines frequently offer reduced fares at unpopular (and ungodly) hours.

Booking an airline ticket with multiple destinations (circle trips) can also ease the toll on your credit card. You can fly from Chicago to an interview in Denver and then onto an interview in Dallas before returning to Chicago. This circle ticket often costs less than a separate round trip to each destination.

Build in time for travel delays due to inclement weather. After all, you will be traveling during the months of January, February, and March. Even if your flight is between two uniformly sunny cities in the South, the originating aircraft may be stuck in the snow in the Northeast or grounded because of sleet in the Midwest.

Some doctoral programs coordinate rides from the airport to the university for applicants, but most do not. You are on your own. In advance of your arrival, check out bus and train routes. The university's homepage will typically have public transportation routes and driving directions from the local airport to the campus.

If public transportation is unavailable, you will need to rent a car at the airport. You will discover, again, that the rental costs vary widely. And you will, again, investigate the costs early and aggressively to locate the best fare. Rely on the three traditional sources—the rental company's toll-free number, its website, and the commercial travel websites—for several rental companies.

Renting a car on your own will require at least three things: a valid driver's license; a major credit card in your name; and a chronological age over the minimum, typically 25 years of age. The latter can be a huge hassle if you are still an undergraduate; be aware of the company's age policy in advance. Most companies will charge an extra daily fee for renters age 21 to 24—typically about $25 per day.

Most doctoral programs will extend you an invitation to room with a graduate student in the program the night before the interview. If possible, take advantage of this opportunity. It will allow you to save money, acquire masses of information, and gain a sense of student life and the campus community from people in a position to know. If you reside with a graduate student, request a tour the day or night before the interview. Ask to see the psychology building, the training clinic, the library, and a few labs. If possible, get comfortable with the rooms where the interviews will be held.

Unfortunately, not all programs offer or provide a free place to sleep. In these cases, unless you have a large extended family, you will spend an evening or two in a hotel. Your task here is to secure a safe, convenient location at a reasonable rate. Use the AAA tour book and the Web for preliminary reconnaissance. If you have wheels, you can often save money by staying at one of the less expensive motels on the edge of town or near an Interstate exit. In particular, if you are on a tight budget, be sure to check out places with the code word "Inn" in their names, as in Comfort Inn, Days Inn, Fairfield Inn, Hampton Inn, Hobo Inn, and Red Roof Inn (Megargee, 2001).

Even these inns may have negotiated rates. Ask the person scheduling your interview if the university has negotiated special rates with any local hotels. When booking your room, inquire what discounts are available—for students, AAA members, government employees, and so on.

Whether you spend the night in a hotel or with a graduate student, you may well be invited to dinner. Be sociable and friendly, but do not drink heavily or party hearty the night before (even though you may be invited!). Get a solid night's sleep, arise on time, and eat a sensible breakfast.

Although we discussed attire and appearance in the previous section, it is worth a few more sentences as applied to travel. You may well experience delays or cancellations in your flight itinerary or in your driving time to the interview. As a consequence, you may not have that expected hour or two to clean up and change clothes before the interview. Or you may meet other applicants en route and faculty members at the airport. The moral: take only carry-on luggage and do not travel in cutoffs, warm-up suits, or t-shirts unless you are prepared to interview in that outfit. Dress and travel like a professional.

Interview Style

The objective of your interview style is to present yourself as a confident, knowledgeable, and genuine person—an imperfect human, to be sure, but one without major interpersonal deficits or gross psychopathology. We frequently characterize this as your *best authentic self* – natural, curious, relaxed, and self-assured while on your best behavior, as your parents might say.

Soothe your understandable anxiety with sufficient preparation, relaxation methods, and healthy self-talk. Your best authentic self is most likely to materialize when you moderate your anxiety. Remind yourself that you have been invited for a good reason; you are capable and accomplished. Temper your negative, scary thoughts; by virtue of completing the interview, the odds of your acceptance are much better than before you applied.

The interview is designed for the interviewer to get to know you as a person—your interpersonal skills, career goals, and clinical acumen. One of the few empirical studies on the role of the personal interview in the psychology admission process found that the rating of an applicant's clinical potential was the most highly weighted measure among all the interview data. Ratings of verbal skills and research skills also contributed to the prediction equation, but ratings of clinical potential contributed most to discriminating among groups of accepted applicants, alternates, and rejected applicants (Nevid & Gildea, 1984). In one way or another, you must impress the interviewers as someone they would be comfortable sending a member of their own family to for professional treatment.

The following factors have been found to lead to rejection of an applicant during interviews (Fretz, 1976):

- Poor personal appearance
- Overbearing, overaggressive, know-it-all style
- Inability to express yourself clearly—poor voice, diction, grammar
- Inadequate interest and enthusiasm—passive, indifferent
- Lack of confidence and poise—nervousness, appearing ill at ease
- Making excuses, evasiveness, hedging on unfavorable factors in record
- Lack of tact and maturity
- Condemnation of past professors
- Little sense of humor
- Emphasis on whom (not what) you know
- Inability to take criticism
- Failure to ask questions about the program

The last point is worth emphasizing. Each interviewer will want to get to know you as a person and will expect you to ask questions. Nothing is tougher on an interviewer than the person who does not ask questions or simply responds "Yes" or "No."

So even if it has been a long day, when the fourth interviewer asks you if you have any questions, don't reply, "No, all my questions have already been answered." And respond to the questions of the fourth interviewer with the same enthusiasm as you showed to the first interviewer (Megargee, 2001).

As you respond enthusiastically to the questions, try to headline your answers. If asked, "What attracts you to our program?" respond "Many things" or "I am attracted here for a bunch of reasons" much like a news headline would read. Then detail those particular reasons. "Which faculty would you want to work with here?" can have you gushing, "I match well with several faculty members here, especially . . . " and then rattling off the names of those faculty and the reasons you fit so well with them. Offer the positive, thoughtful big picture before enumerating the details.

At the same time that you are conveying clinical potential and a mature interpersonal presence, you want to acquire the factual program information necessary to make informed decisions. Table 7-2 presents questions you can ask when you interview. You should ask some of these questions during the interview, others before, and others after. Some should be asked of professors, because they are best suited to answer them and asking can make you look prepared and informed. Some questions should be directed toward first-year students because they have recently completed the process and are closest to your situation. Some questions are better asked of advanced graduate students because they are about to leave and may have less investment in hiding the program's shortcomings.

Several research-oriented questions can be directed to potential research advisors or mentors. For example: What is your mentoring style? What are the current projects in your lab? What research projects do you plan to work on in the next three or four years? How do your students select research topics for their theses/dissertations? Present yourself as an inquisitive junior research colleague, ready to work and learn.

The best questions are those that indicate initiative, curiosity, and responsibility (Hersh & Poey, 1984). Try to communicate motivation to learn and eagerness to participate in many activities; avoid questions that promote a speculation that you are demanding, complaining, or single-minded.

A caveat: Never ask for information that is available on the program website or a faculty member's webpage. These questions make you appear unprepared for the interview and uninterested in the program.

Alternatively, link your questions to the information provided on the program's website. Examples might include: "I read that all of your first-year students receive an assistantship and tuition remission. Is this also true of second-year students?" "Your website lists a Couples Therapy course, a special interest of mine, but it does not indicate if clinical supervision in that area is available." "While reading about your impressive Psychological Services Clinic, I wondered how many of the full-time clinical faculty provide supervision there." And so on.

The intent is to get beyond the gloss and formality of the program descriptions to the lived and personal experiences of the program participants. Virtually all portrayals of clinical and counseling psychology programs, for example, will allude to ample opportunities for practical experience in off-campus placements. But when you directly ask students, "What is your clinical placement like?" their answers may diverge substantially from the published information. Their responses may indeed be positive, but it is not uncommon to learn that several of the placements are 50 miles away, do not offer any stipend, and prove competitive to obtain. To be sure, be tactful in your questioning, but also be assertive in securing crucial data.

Recall that the specialty clinics and practica sites listed on the program's website (and in appendices

TABLE 7-2. Interview Questions an Applicant Might Ask

Practice

Is training available in different theoretical orientations? Which orientations are not prominently represented?
Is the supervision individual or group? Is it live supervision?
How much of the clinical supervision is conducted by the full-time faculty?
What type of supervision will I receive?
When do I actually begin clinical work?
How many practica are offered?
What are your off-campus clinical practica like? Where are they located?
What types of patient populations are available?
Are specialty clinics available?
How many of the full-time faculty are licensed?
Do the faculty have active private practices?
Do faculty serve as clinicians or consultants at local mental health facilities?
What has surprised you most about the clinical training here? What did you not expect? (ask of graduate students)

Research

What percentage of students graduate with peer-reviewed publications?
What is the student–faculty ratio?
About how many dissertations and master's theses are chaired by each faculty member?
When and how am I assigned an advisor?
What is the mentoring style of my research advisor/mentor?
Does this person have weekly research meetings?
Could I sit in on a lab meeting?
How many core faculty members regularly publish?
How many research grants finance graduate students?
If I wanted to change my mentor or advisor, is that allowed?
Are there opportunities for summer funding?
How many computers and printers in the department are available to graduate students?
Is SAS, SPSS, or R available?
What is the relationship with the medical or law school?

Finances

What percentage of students receive full financial support (assistantship plus tuition waiver)?
What types of fellowships are available?
What types of research and teaching assistantships are available?
What is the average amount of a 9-month assistantship?
Who gets tuition remission? What are my chances?
How long does it take for grad students to demonstrate residency and get the less expensive, in-state tuition rate?
Do the stipends cover the costs of living in this area? How expensive are the rents?
What percentage of students receive funding during the summer?
Do any of the assistantships include health insurance?
What percentage of doctoral students take out student loans?

Quality of Life

What is it like to live around campus? Is it safe? Fun?
Is it possible to live comfortably and inexpensively in this university town?
What is the surrounding city/town like?
Is graduate housing available through the university? Do most students live on campus?
What is the off-campus housing situation like? The neighborhoods?
Where can I go to get a housing application today?
Are there theaters, movies, decent restaurants nearby?
Is there public transportation, or do I need a car?
What are some of the campus events and clubs?
Is the Graduate Student Association active?
Do the students socialize frequently?
Do students and faculty attend the colloquia?

Department and Politics

What sort of relationships do students and faculty enjoy in this program?
Do graduate students have a role in departmental policy and admission decisions?
In your experience, what are the best and worst features of this program? (ask of graduate students)
What are one or two things you wished you knew before attending this program? (ask of graduate students)
What is the standing of the Psychology Department within the university?
How do the different psychology subfields/programs interact?
What are the professional goals of the current students?
How many fifth-, sixth-, seventh- . . . year students are there?
Is there a sense of competition or cooperation among the students?
How much emphasis is put on coursework and grades?
How common are grades of C?
Do professors tend to collaborate on projects?
Do I get a master's degree along the way? When is this usually done?
What is it like to work with the advisor (Dr. Smith) that I am applying to work with?
When do I take the qualifying exams? What are they like? How many people fail? Can they be retaken?
Could I see a course schedule for next (or last) year?
Are teaching opportunities available for graduate students?
Are you anticipating any major program or faculty changes in the next five years?
For applicants entering with a master's: Once accepted, how are transcripts evaluated regarding credits?

Outcomes (after carefully reading the program materials)

Where do your students complete their internships?
What percentage of your students obtains an APA-accredited internship?
What is the average length of the program (including internship)?
What percentage of your incoming students eventually earn their doctorates here?
Do dissertations usually get published?
In what type of settings do most of your graduates eventually find employment—academic, private practice, clinics?

F and G in this book) are self-reports, may not be controlled by the program itself, and probably evolve over the years. Double-check their existence when you interview. Same for faculty research interests as faculty members retire, relocate, or switch their interests.

Program directors (e.g., Hersh & Poey, 1984) have nominated certain questions to *avoid* asking. These unwittingly annoy interviewers or communicate an undesirable impression: questions regarding the typical length of a graduate-student week, which may indicate fear of hard work or a long week; persistent inquiries regarding an area of interest that the graduate program only minimally provides; questions reflecting resistance to learning the major theoretical orientation offered by that program; and antagonistic questions concentrating on the perceived limitations of the program, be they financial, faculty, or geographical.

Bring your list of questions with you to the interview, but do not constantly have it in plain sight to check off. Your task is to ask the questions of the most appropriate individuals in a respectful manner. On a similar note, many people have PDAs to help organize personal information. Though you might use one to make a note at the *end* of an interview, keep them away during the interview itself.

On that note, cell phones and beepers should be turned off during the interview. Not on vibrate or silent alert; completely off. Having one beep or buzz will be disruptive, and taking a call would be seen as *extremely* unprofessional and rude. Nobody is as important on interview day as the interviewers.

Extreme ideologies—religious, sociopolitical, or clinical—do not bode well in interviews. One interesting study (Gartner, 1986) mailed mock graduate school applications to professors of clinical psychology. The results showed that professors were more likely to admit an applicant who made no mention of religion than they were to admit an otherwise identical applicant who was identified as a fundamentalist Christian. Do not deny your beliefs, of course, but avoid expressions of rigid extremes. Academics favor informed pluralism and critical open-mindedness.

Bernard Lubin (1993), a former national president of Psi Chi and a veteran of conducting admission interviews, enjoins applicants to present themselves as *knowledgeable* and *collaborative* during the interview. Being familiar with the research interests and productivity of the program faculty can go a long way. Carefully reading the program's online material and identifying faculty publications through PsycINFO provide direct evidence of a mature and scholarly attitude. This leads to presenting yourself as a potential collaborator: welcoming opportunities to work with faculty members and fellow students, displaying an affirming and positive attitude toward interdependent activities.

Our final piece of advice on interview style concerns your nonverbal behavior. Applicants can become so preoccupied with asking questions and trying to impress the interviewer that they neglect the way they present themselves nonverbally. But interviewer impressions of candidate personality depend heavily on nonverbal behaviors (Anderson & Shackleton, 1990). Maintaining eye contact, making changes in posture, and varying facial expressions strongly contribute to an image as a mature and enthusiastic person. The research consistently advises interviewees to keep high levels of eye contact with the interviewer and to display frequent positive facial expressions to maximize their chances of success. (Of course, we don't suggest that you fake your smiles, as that likely won't be persuasive and may even be off-putting.) Your mock and actual interviews should strive for an interpersonally engaging style that creates personal liking and that cultivates an impression of interpersonal and intellectual skill.

Literally hundreds of websites offer advice on interviewing skills. Although they are no substitute for live rehearsals and mock interviews, they are a source of considerable information and examples. Some even offer virtual interviews. Our favorite sites are:

- www.quintcareers.com
- www.apa.org/education/grad/application-video-series.aspx
- www.monster.com/career-advice/job-interview
- www.glencoe.com/sec/careers/career_city/
- www.nextsteps.org

Stressful Questions

Let's face together a prominent fear, namely, being placed on the spot with intensely personal questions. You may have heard "war stories" about applicants being asked intimate questions about their families of origin, romantic relationships, and personal history they would prefer not to share. Be prepared to answer personal questions about such relationships and self-perceptions. Answering these questions in a straightforward manner contributes to the interviewer's positive evaluation of an applicant.

The nature of these questions varies with the interviewer's style as well as the program's theoretical orientation. Applying to a research-oriented cognitive-behavioral program, however, is no guarantee that you will not be interviewed by a psychodynamic member of their faculty. Questions pertaining to family conflict or to your personal therapy could arise. Anticipating such questions can help you to determine how to handle them most comfortably and to decide how much information you are willing to disclose. Knowing where to set your boundaries will lead to a smoother interview.

Speaking of boundaries, the APA Ethics Code (APA, 2017) does not require students to disclose sensitive information regarding their "sexual history, history of abuse and neglect, psychological treatment, and relationships with parents, peers, and spouses or significant others" unless the training program has clearly identified this requirement ahead of time. Unless the program notified you of such a requirement for the interview, you are not ethically obliged to reveal such personal information. Our advice is to balance your need for privacy with the program's need for information about your personal history and psychological dynamics.

One stressful but popular question concerns your personal weaknesses. Applicants naturally wonder how honest to be about their deficits and how to balance the need for honesty with the need to leave a favorable impression. We have found three strategies useful in approaching this question. One is to minimize an existing limitation: showing your awareness of it but not articulating the full severity or manifestation. If being taken advantage of frequently is your perceived weakness, for example, you might reply on the order of "Occasionally I find myself being taken advantage of by others in small but consistent ways."

A second strategy is to turn the weakness into a possible strength. Following the same example, you might remark that "I give to a fault on occasion and notice some people will take advantage of my tendency to look for the best in people." A third possible strategy is to express your awareness of the weakness and your efforts to remediate it; this reply demonstrates both introspective and corrective attitudes. "I've been working to become more conscious of how people, especially personality-disordered clients, can take advantage of me. My over-trusting nature is slowly giving way as I attend more closely to this relationship pattern." Whatever strategy—or combination of strategies—you elect, the response must be consistent with who you are. A phony or inauthentic response can immediately strike an applicant from further consideration.

One stressful situation necessitates your careful preparation. A few programs and faculty use what is called a *stress interview*. In this interview, the faculty member intentionally acts inappropriately and tries to intimidate applicants to determine how they handle the stress of the situation. This can come in many forms: long silences after you answer questions; asking overly intimate questions; disagreeing violently with your position or answer; feigning disinterest in you as an applicant; or even giving you coffee in one hand, a powdered donut without a napkin in the other, and then handing you a journal article to browse! In a few programs, the professors place all the applicants in an empty room and suggest they speak with each other while the professors observe the interpersonal process: no other directions, no other structure. This all serves to compound the students' anxiety.

Stress interviews are designed to assess how comfortably you behave under interpersonally challenging conditions. The interviewers deliberately arrange situations or ask questions that you cannot predict, for examples, "How would you redesign a giraffe?" or "Where is Oregon?" The particular answer you give is not as important as the manner in which you answer. Here your interpersonal savvy and presence can triumph. The interviewer is testing your reaction to stress: do you react to stress with humor, anxiety, self-denigration, anger? The stress interview is an ambiguous, semi-projective device.

Our advice is to remain calm and polite, yet assertive. Avoid becoming entangled in a verbal battle or retreat into an apologetic or defensive stance. In the face of an inappropriately personal question, a "I wonder how that question relates to my admission here?" will demonstrate both your personal boundaries and your willingness to broach a difficult topic. In the face of continuing conflict, a polite "we respectfully disagree" can suffice, and leave it at that (Heppner & Downing, 1982). Knowing ahead of time that stress questions occasionally occur will remind you that it is not personal but part of the evaluation process.

Practicing stress interviews with professors or peers may sufficiently desensitize you to keep your head and field the situation without too much ego bruising. Another way to prepare yourself is to stay overnight before the interview and to ask graduate students which professors might conduct such an interview, allowing you to know ahead of time that this person is likely to intentionally try to stress you. Foreknowledge and preparation will prove the best defense.

Interview Formats

Admission interviews in clinical and counseling psychology differ markedly from one program to another. At one extreme, a few programs invite you for a single, multi-hour interview with a senior faculty member. That's it—no tour, no group interview, no program orientation, and no interaction with current graduate students.

At the other extreme, a number of programs invite selected applicants for an entire admissions weekend. At the University of Pittsburgh, for example, invitees to the clinical psychology program's weekend spend a full day (about 7 hours) interviewing with faculty and graduate students. In addition, there are clinical and research information sessions, laboratory tours, evening parties, and a poster session featuring research projects. Most of the applicants arrive on Friday and leave Sunday morning.

In between these two approaches are intensive 1-day interview sessions. For instance, at Fordham University's counseling psychology program (Kopala et al., 1995), the interview process entails a brief orientation to the program, individual interviews with a faculty member and a graduate student, a videotaped group experience, an open session with graduate students, and then a closing session with the director of training.

Here's a typical, 1-day interview itinerary:

8:30 – 9:00 a.m.	Continental Breakfast
9:00 – 9:30 a.m.	Welcome by Director of Clinical Training (DCT)
9:30 – 10:30 a.m.	Tour of Psychological Clinic and Research Labs
10:30 – 11:00 a.m.	Individual Interview with Dr. Smith
11:00 – 11:30 a.m.	Individual Interview with Dr. Jones
11:30 – 12:30 p.m.	Group Interview with Graduate Students
12:30 – 1:00 p.m.	Buffet Lunch
1:00 – 1:30 p.m.	Poster Session (where current students share their work)
1:30 – 2:30 p.m.	Tour of Campus
2:30 – 3:00 p.m.	Individual Interview with Dr. Comas
3:00 – 3:30 p.m.	Closing Remarks

Virtually all programs will arrange for two or more individual interviews with faculty members and for interaction with current doctoral students. A healthy proportion of programs will also include admission interviews featuring multiple candidates in the same room at the same time. This group interview may be conducted in the interest of sheer efficiency, of observing your interpersonal style, or both.

Our advice on your interview style and objectives in these group interviews remains essentially the same as for the individual interviews, but with a couple of twists. First of all, strive to be pleasant and honest with the other interviewees. Share your experiences, never denigrate their credentials, and treat them like future colleagues (which they may well be). A negativistic or superior attitude is likely to be held against you in the deliberations of the admission committee.

Second, since it is a group situation, try to present yourself as an admirable facilitator. Don't be a group psychotherapist or a control maniac, but a respectful co-facilitator of the interview process. If you have already asked a few questions about the program, for instance, you might say that you have additional questions but would first like other people to have an opportunity to have their questions answered. As they say in the social psychology literature, try to manifest both a high task orientation and a high social orientation.

A more recent development is the *multiple mini interview* (MMI) format. The MMI began in the early 2000's in medicine to increase the efficiency and predictive validity of medical school interviews, which until then were not doing well in assessing applicants' interpersonal skills, professionalism, ethical judgment, and other so-called non-cognitive "soft skills." It is widely used in health professions and is gradually being adopted by psychology programs.

The MMI uses many short, independent assessments, typically in a timed circuit of 5 to 10 minutes per station. The format resembles speed dating in which the interviewers stay put and the applicants rotate among the stations at the sound of a bell or buzzer. Each interviewer or station is responsible for objectively assessing one domain, such as ethics, professionalism, communication, or interpersonal skills. The MMI has shown itself as cost-efficient and valid, probably better than unstructured interviews (To, 2013). As it is embraced by psychology programs, the MMI will become one more component of interview day.

Additional Tips

Whether it is an individual interview or a group interview, here are additional tips regarding the interview.

- Arrive at least 15 minutes early on interview day. Find the offices, acclimate to the building, and get settled.
- Be compulsive and double-check your interview schedule. Being late or missing an interview (even when it is not your fault) can reflect poorly on you.
- Greet each interviewer in a friendly, open manner. Your handshake should be firm and your eye contact frequent.
- Demonstrate your active listening skills: wait to answer until the interviewer has completed asking the question and give complete answers to the question posed to you.
- Keep your answers to 1.5 to 2 minutes long. If interested, the interviewer can ask you for details or to expand. If your answer is sufficient, the interviewer can move onto another question or topic.
- Bring extra copies of your CV. Every interviewer may have not received a copy or may have not yet reviewed it, so carry copies to present and leave with people.
- Take cash or a debit card along in case you are invited to lunch or dinner.
- Conclude each interview by thanking the interviewer for her time and information. Wrap it up with a firm hand shake and cordial tone.

Our collective experience in conducting interviews also generates a list of *don'ts:*

- Don't call faculty members by their first names until (or if) they offer. The default option is to call them "Dr." or "Professor."
- Don't whine or complain about the interview arrangements. Accept the free housing with gratitude; be agreeable about the food; act flexibly about interview dates. Nobody, including admissions committees, likes a fussbudget.
- Don't accept offers of coffee or other beverages during the interview itself. It tends to be messy, distracting, and awkward for you as the interviewee. Wait until after the interviews are complete or during breaks to graciously accept the offer.
- Don't say anything negative about other graduate programs or your previous faculty. It comes off as complaining and negative.
- Don't negotiate financial assistance before receiving an offer of admission. The nitty-gritty of finances can wait until later.
- And don't ask questions during the interview that are answered in the materials sent to you or posted on the program website. Yes, we already made this point earlier in the chapter, but it is important enough to reiterate it here.

Follow these tips and you will relax more during the interview. The more relaxed and prepared you are, the more confident and authentic you will feel.

Video and Telephone Interviews

Two situations may dictate a video telephone interview. In the first, you are asked to visit the school for an interview, but you cannot afford to do so. This is no reason to be embarrassed, and the more straightforward you are about it the better. You can request a video or phone interview in advance if you do not have the resources for an actual visit. (As noted earlier, though, at some institutions failure to visit will place you at a competitive disadvantage.) In the second situation, you receive the dreaded, unannounced interview. At least one of your prospective programs may call without prior notice and ask to speak with you on the spot.

Luckily, if you anticipate these surprise interviews, you have no reason to fret. One strategy is to rarely or never take a phone interview "cold." Consider telling the caller, "I'm sorry, but I was just leaving for an appointment. Could you leave a number and arrange for me to call you back at a convenient time for you?" This buys you time to review your information on that program and to prepare for the interview. However, you do not want to communicate disinterest in the program.

Another strategy is to prepare phone cards, smart phone notes, or computer files. You make index cards or short files for each program to which you applied. On it, record a few reasons for your interest in that graduate program and the name(s) of the professor(s) you are interested in working with, a little about their research areas, and questions you may have about clinical training or facilities (many of the questions in Table 7-2). Figure 7-2 presents an example of such a card.

Keep these files with you, on your smart phone, or on a computer and in moments you will find the card for a particular school and not be caught unaware! This extra effort can prevent a serious detraction from your application. If you receive one of these unannounced interviews and cannot remember which professors are at that school, their areas of research, or their facilities, it tells the interviewer that you are not serious about his or her program. Such mistakes can place you lower than an

University of Alexandria

Reasons for my interest: Great reputation in child psychopathology and psychotherapy; specific professors (Smith, Adams); geographic location; has specialty clinic in behavioral medicine.

Key professors:

Dr. Smith: child psychopathology; substance abuse

I read your May [2017] article in the *Journal of Anxiety,* in which you found offspring of alcoholics to be more receptive to the anxiety-reducing effects of alcohol than control subjects. Do you expect to continue this line of research next year? Is an assistantship available?

Dr. Adams: behavioral medicine; psychotherapy

I was impressed that you have a separate clinic in behavioral medicine. What type of clients do you most often treat? What opportunities are there for clinical experience?

Other professors with potential interest:

Dr. Jones: prevention

Dr. Watson: forensic psychology

Program questions: [Refer to Table 7-2 for representative listing]

When do I begin seeing clients in the training clinic?

What percentage of incoming students are financially supported in the second and third years?

What are the research opportunities in child psychopathology?

FIGURE 7-2. Sample telephone card.

applicant who has this information off the top of his or her head.

A handful (4%) of doctoral programs in psychology actually require a video or telephone interview, but these will be scheduled in advance. Thankfully, no surprise calls here. Interviews over Skype, Google Hangouts, FaceTime, Go to Meeting, and other real-time media make these attractive cost-effective alternatives to expensive interview trips.

But that little extra interview preparation can still deliver big dividends. Do not be lulled into thinking that an interview by video is of any less import. Test whatever software you plan to use before the video interview; do a test run with a friend ahead of time. Still dress for success, from head to toe, even if the interviewer can only see you from the waist up. One of us Skype interviewed an applicant who, when getting up from the computer to retrieve a file, revealed that he was wearing underwear and slippers underneath his jacket and tie! Eye contact, careful listening, and other facets of your body language count powerfully, maybe more than during a face-to-face interview. In short, follow the same advice and strategies as any important graduate school interview.

A Note of Thanks

Once you have completed an interview, whether by telephone, video, or in person, a brief emailed note of thanks to the interviewer is in order. This gesture serves multiple purposes: it demonstrates your social skills, communicates your gratitude to the faculty and students involved, reaffirms your interest in the program, and keeps your name alive in the admission process. Seldom will such a brief note do so much for you. (Sending flowers, candies, or gifts is not deemed appropriate in these circumstances.)

The "who" and "what" of these thank-you letters almost entirely depend on your interview experiences. The "who" should certainly include anyone who has shown you special attention, such as a graduate student you roomed with the night before or after the interview, a professor who personally escorted you around a lab or clinic, or a faculty member who offered an unscheduled interview. Letters to several people are often necessary. If the interview was less personal, then at a minimum send the Director of Training a letter of appreciation. A sample email or letter is displayed in Figure 7-3.

February 16, 2018

Patricia Jones, Ph.D.
Director of Clinical Training
Department of Psychology
University of Western States
13 Orangegrove Drive
Wilksville, CA 98765

Dear Dr. Jones:

I want to thank you for interviewing me for a position in your clinical psychology doctoral program. I enjoyed meeting with your faculty and staff and learning more about the program. My enthusiasm for the program was particularly strengthened as a result of my interactions with Drs. Timothy Hogan, Elizabeth Cannon, and Carole Buchanan.

I want to reiterate my strong interest in attending your program; the University of Western States offers a great deal that appeals to me and that fits my career goals. Please feel free to call me at (123) 456-7890 or email me at csmith@university.edu if I can provide you with any additional information.

Again, thank you for the interview and your consideration.

Sincerely yours,

Chris Smith

FIGURE 7-3. Sample letter of appreciation to an interviewer.

The "what" of the letter must be individualized to your particular experiences, but will probably contain at least three components: an expression of gratitude for the interview, an enumeration of your favorable impressions of the program, and a reiteration of your interest in attending that program. Personalize each letter by referring to specific topics or experiences; for instance, recall your discussion of potential research studies or mention the friendliness of the graduate students. There is no definitive list of do's and don'ts, but don't send a generic, impersonal letter and don't promote your candidacy. Do sound appreciative and personal.

As with all written materials, ensure that your letter communicates sincerity and professionalism. Most of the letters should probably be emailed, but a neat, handwritten note is appropriate if an interview was relatively informal and personal.

The Wait

Once you have completed the interviews and emailed the thank-you letters, it becomes a waiting game. But not for the graduate programs, which still have a finalist pool of applicants much larger than they can accept! The interview process has probably weeded out a few, but the faculty are left with too many finalists, all of whom possess acceptable GPAs, GREs, and letters of recommendation.

What, then, are the *final* selection criteria? This pivotal question was addressed in a study by Keith-Spiegel and colleagues (1994), who had 113 faculty members actively involved in selecting psychology Ph.D. students rate criteria used in making the last cuts in admission decisions. (Results of this study should *not* be generalized to Psy.D. programs.) The faculty members were asked to imagine that they were left with a pool of finalists, three times the size of the number they can accept, all of whom had strong undergraduate GPAs, GRE scores, and letters of recommendation. They then rated 31 variables in terms of importance.

Congruent with this book's advice and earlier studies, the top-rated criteria in clinical programs pertained to student match with the program and its faculty, research experience resulting in a journal article or a paper presentation, and the clarity and focus of the applicant's statement of purpose. Considered to be somewhat to very important in assisting selection committees with their final admission decisions were research assistant experience; reputation of the student's referees; relevant clinical experience; membership in an underrepresented ethnic minority group; knowledge and interest in the program; number of statistics, methodology, and hard science courses completed; prestige of the psychology faculty in the student's undergraduate department; reputation of the undergraduate institution itself; and honors bestowed on the student by that undergraduate institution. Rated as *not* important or minimally important were such variables as the student's geographic residence, Psi Chi membership, and a close relationship between the student and former graduates of that program.

Demand always exceeds supply in competitive clinical and counseling psychology programs. The three primary criteria used to evaluate applicants by doctoral selection committees—grade point averages, GREs, and letters of recommendation—typically fail to narrow the applicant pool to the small number of slots available. At that point, research skills, clinical experiences, "good match" factors, and writing skills come to the fore. Bear these considerations in mind as you approach your interview—just as we have in preparing this book.

And now you wait until contacted with the final decision of the admissions committee. During this period, maintain your professional demeanor. Refrain from Twitter posts that track your interviews at various universities and, for heaven's sake, do not over-emote about a particular program on Facebook.

Until mid-March, it is probably not wise to contact a program and ask where you stand. Applicants who make repeated calls or emails may appear overly anxious and irritate the staff (Mitchell, 1996). The one exception is if you have received other admission offers, and the program you would most like to attend has not contacted you—a situation covered in Chapter 8.

This brings us to the last step in the application process and the final chapter of this *Insider's Guide*.

C H A P T E R 8

MAKING FINAL DECISIONS

Before April 1, all APA-accredited clinical, counseling, and combined psychology programs will make their initial round of acceptance offers. This policy pertains only to acceptances; programs need not inform all applicants of their admission status, such as rejection or waiting list, by that date. In fact, many programs will not notify rejected applicants until May. It's frustrating not to hear sooner, but that's how most doctoral programs roll.

Recall that research-oriented Ph.D. programs will almost always tender their first round of admission offers well before April 1st, even as early as February. Practice-oriented Ph.D. and Psy.D. programs tend to run later in the admissions season. Do not be surprised to receive a call or email only a few days after your interview.

At that point you will typically have until April 15th to make your final decision as to where you want to attend graduate school. By APA policy, you have the right to consider offers until mid-April, at which time an offer may be withdrawn. So you must be thoughtful but decisive in these weeks.

To protect applicants from making hasty decisions, all APA-accredited programs and most others have agreed to allow candidates until April 15 for a decision (or the first Monday after April 15, if April 15 falls on a weekend). This accords with a policy adopted by the Council of Graduate Schools in the United States and endorsed by the Council of Graduate Departments of Psychology. The Resolution Regarding Graduate Scholars, Fellows, Trainees and Assistants (www.cgsnet.org/?tabid=201) reads as follows:

> Acceptance of an offer of financial aid (such as graduate scholarship, fellowship, traineeship, or assistantship) for the next academic year by a prospective or enrolled graduate student completes an agreement that both student and graduate school expect to honor. In that context, the conditions affecting such offers and their acceptance must be defined carefully and understood by all parties.
>
> Students are under no obligation to respond to offers of financial support prior to April 15; earlier deadlines for the acceptance of such offers violate the intent of this Resolution. In those instances in which the student accepts the offer before April 15 and subsequently desires to withdraw that acceptance, the student may submit in writing a resignation of the appointment at any time through April 15. However, an acceptance given or left in force after April 15 commits the student not to accept another offer without first obtaining a written release from the institution to which the commitment has been made. Similarly, an offer by an institution after April 15 is conditional on presentation by the student of the written release from any previously accepted offer.

Importantly, this April 15th policy applies only to admission offers *with financial aid*. Thus, Psy.D. and master's programs (and a few Ph.D. programs) not offering financial assistance can and will pressure accepted applicants to confirm their acceptances before April 15th. It happened to a few of our students, and if applying to Psy.D. or master's programs, it can happen to you. If a graduate program is not offering you financial support, the April 15th policy does not apply!

As you wait to hear from programs in February and March, carefully check your emails and missed calls, particularly if you use an account that receives a large volume of incoming messages. Just a couple of years ago, two of our undergraduates missed emailed invitations to interview at doctoral programs because they were lost among a blizzard of unsolicited emails and junk messages. Be vigilant and double check on a daily basis.

Acceptances and Rejections

What do you do when one program makes you an admission offer and you are still waiting to hear from another program you would prefer to accept? To begin with, *don't say yes to any graduate program until you are certain that this is where you want to go!* Once you say "yes," that is it. Saying yes to another program can endanger your acceptance at both places. If you harbor reservations, do not feel pressured to say yes. Thank the person and say that you have received other offers and you need a few days to consider this crucial decision.

Only 50 to 70% of the students accepted at a particular APA-accredited program will accept that offer (Norcross et al., 2009). You need not worry about hurting faculty members' feelings should you decline their offer of admission. Qualified applicants will receive multiple offers. Experienced faculty understand the process. Do not fret about them; focus on what's best for you.

If you have received admission offers but have not heard from the programs that most interest you, email them. Explain that you are considering offers but that you do not want to act on them until you know what your status is there. It's OK to say, "I've been accepted at University X and Y, but I am most interested in your program. Can you give me an indication where my application stands, or at least whether it is still being considered?"

The Guidelines for Graduate School Offers and Acceptances, adopted by the Council of University Directors of Clinical Psychology (1993), encourage directors of training (or admissions) to apprise students of their position on the alternate list. Typically, this entails a placement of high, middle, or low on the alternate list. If such a designation is used, the operational definition of "high on the alternate list" is that, in a normal year, the student would receive an offer of admission (but not necessarily funding) prior to the April 15 decision date.

Earlier, we emphasized the point that you should not accept an offer until you are certain that is the program you want to attend. On the other hand, if you have been accepted at three programs, and one of them is obviously less suited to your needs, be considerate of other applicants and decline that offer. The program can then make their offer to someone else who may very much want to attend that school. *Only keep two offers alive at any one time.* Otherwise, a huge logjam or bottleneck effect will occur across the country, with each program waiting for a few students to decide.

As long as there is a possibility that you may attend a certain program, be careful not to decline prematurely. As other students decline at these schools, you may be offered a better financial package if you have not yet made a formal commitment.

When all is said and done, how will you decide which offer to accept? This is a difficult question to answer because of the multiple factors involved and because the final determinant will be how you, as an individual, weigh those various factors.

One study (McIlvried et al., 2010) had 596 first-year graduate students, some in Boulder-model (Ph.D.) programs and some in Vail-model (Psy.D.) programs, rate the reasons for selecting their doctoral clinical programs. Their average ratings are shown in Table 8-1, where a rating of 1 was "not at all important" and 5 was "very important." As seen there, the most important factors for all students were the sense of fit, curriculum, geographic location, prestige/reputation of the university, reputation of the faculty, gut feeling, discussions with program students, theoretical diversity of the staff, and job placement record. We have emphasized throughout the preceding chapters the prominence of these selection factors.

As you would expect, the reasons differed markedly between those students seeking Boulder-model (Ph.D.) training and those seeking Vail-model (Psy.D.) training. The Ph.D. students prioritized the opportunity to work with specific faculty, scholarship funding, availability of research and teaching assistantships, and other financial incentives much more highly. By contrast, the Psy.D. students placed more weight on the curriculum, geographic location, gut feeling, interdisciplinary training, and availability of minority faculty. These differences reflect several of the fundamental differences between the training models, as reviewed in Chapter 2: the Boulder model emphasizing smaller mentoring programs, research-oriented training, and furnishing generous financial assistance, whereas the Vail model emphasizing larger professional programs, practice-oriented training, and rarely providing direct financial assistance.

TABLE 8-1. Student Reasons for Choosing a Clinical Psychology Program

Reason	Boulder model/Ph.D. Mean rating	Vail model/Psy.D. Mean rating
Sense of fit	4.61	4.50
Curriculum*	3.41	4.17
Geographic location*	3.40	3.85
Prestige/reputation of the university	3.59	3.76
Prestige/reputation of the faculty	3.80	3.53
Gut feeling*	3.20	3.67
Discussions with program students	3.69	3.34
Theoretical diversity of staff	3.08	3.33
Job placement record	3.05	3.21
Other	2.77	3.29
Interdisciplinary training*	2.79	3.23
Projected time to complete degree	2.73	3.02
Opportunity to work with specific faculty*	3.69	2.32
Friends and family living in geographic area	2.60	2.59
Connections for job possibilities in the area	2.31	2.67
Availability of female faculty	2.11	2.45
Safety of geographic area	2.27	2.33
Scholarship*	3.17	2.00
Availability of research assistantships*	3.50	1.87
Availability of teaching assistantships*	3.20	1.93
Other financial incentives*	2.98	1.99
Availability of minority faculty*	1.73	2.12
The only place I received an offer	2.13	1.83
Availability of job opportunity for partner	1.66	1.61
Availability of educational opportunity for partner	1.54	1.38
Other general factor	2.77	3.29

Note. Data adapted from McIlvried et al. (2010). Ratings on a 5-point scale where 1 = *not at all important* to 5 = *very important.*

*indicates statistically significant difference between students selecting Boulder model/Ph.D. programs and students selecting Vail model/Psy.D. programs, $p < .001$.

The emotional and interpersonal ambience of a program should not be underestimated. Seriously consider interactions with faculty and graduate students in your decision. The faculty–student relationship may be the single most significant factor in your intellectual and professional development, and this relationship may be formal or informal, distant or close. Concurrently, the vast majority of graduate student time is spent with other students rather than with faculty members. You are likely to retain these personal contacts and professional relationships over the years. Moreover, fellow students are essential sources of encouragement, companionship, and inspiration. You want a good, lasting fit with the program (Scott & Silka, 1974).

In choosing a graduate program, all students place a premium on general factors such as reputation of the university, the prestige of the faculty, training opportunities, and the emotional atmosphere. At the same time, ethnic minority applicants rate the relevance of multicultural factors higher than do white students (Bernal et al., 1999; Toia et al., 1997). These considerations include minority students in the program, presence of minority faculty, research on minority topics, and opportunity to work with multicultural clients. Be particularly attentive to the program's diversity as it relates to your interests and goals.

The projected length of the doctoral program is a fairly important reason for choosing a particular program, as seen in the middle of Table 8-1. You may recall from Chapter 2 that clinical Ph.D. students take an average of 6 years to complete their doctorates, including the 1-year internship. Psy.D. students take an average of 5 years, a consistent difference of 1 to 1.5 years less. On the one hand, the shorter training period favors the Psy.D. programs. But, on the other hand, the financial aid favors the Ph.D. programs. As you have learned, far more Ph.D. students are receiving tuition waivers and assistantship stipends than Psy.D. students, most of whom are footing the bill for their doctoral education. Also keep in mind your ultimate career goal: it may take longer to gain your degree if you hope to compete for research and faculty positions, where completing multiple publishable studies will be critical to your success. Use the Reports on Individual Programs to consider the expected time to complete the degree in the context of probable financial aid and your career trajectory.

The reasons for choosing a clinical psychology program, as shown in Table 8-1, are largely self-evident, but several reasons *not* listed in that table deserve your consideration. Three of these reasons concern the program's outcomes—attrition rate, internship match, and licensure data—introduced earlier in the book.

Attrition rates, as you will recall, refer to the percentage of students not completing the program. Attrition has been characterized as a "hidden crisis in graduate education" (Lovitts & Nelson, 2000). Between 20 and 24% of full-time psychology students, on average, formally leave programs without completing their doctorates (Fennell & Kohout, 2002). Our data and APA figures demonstrate this number is much smaller—3% to 5%—for APA-accredited clinical and counseling psychology programs (Klonoff, 2016; Norcross, Ellis, & Sayette, 2010; Norcross, Evans, & Ellis, 2010). The median attrition rate for Psy.D. programs is higher and more variable than Ph.D., probably attributable to the larger class size and larger debt load.

Attrition in graduate programs is not solely related to academic ability; life problems, financial difficulties, interpersonal conflicts, and program dissatisfaction enter into the equation. In some cases (e.g., starting a family), the decision is not even related to a "problem." Doctoral programs in which more than 20% of the students fail to graduate should be carefully screened when you make your final decision.

Our Reports on Individual Programs provide the attrition rates for each doctoral program, as reported by that program's director of training. The attrition rate is calculated for the past 7 years as the number of matriculated students who have left the program for any reason divided by the total number of students matriculated in the program. Again, pay close attention to any program in which more than a fifth of students have left the program.

We implored you in Chapter 5 *not* to apply to any doctoral programs below your threshold of quality. In the event one or two questionable programs snuck onto your list, please conduct a final check on the outcomes of that program before accepting an admission offer.

You may recall our three-quarters rule: apply only to doctoral programs where three-quarters or more of their students secure an APA-accredited internship, complete their degrees, and pass the licensure examination if they choose to take it. Carefully inspect the Report on Individual Programs in this book, the required outcomes data on the program's website, and the national licensure site (www.asppb.net) to acquire these numbers. Check out the program's historical success in placing its students in APA-accredited internships (www.appic.org/Portals/0/downloads/APPIC_Match_Rates_2000-10_by_Univ.pdf). If you have questions about the program's accreditation status, examine the final accreditation decision (including number of years of accreditation granted) on the APA's Commission on Accreditation's website (www.apa.org/ed/accreditation/).

In short, determine your own threshold of quality and proceed with your eyes wide open as to the probable consequence of attending that particular graduate program. At the risk of sounding melodramatic, it is literally your career at stake.

Preliminary or qualifying examinations, another consideration in the complexities of your choice, are a series of structured tests that certain programs require at the end of their first or second year. These examinations assume many forms, but they all test a candidate's knowledge of a wide range of areas in psychology—research methodology, learning, development, motivation, history, social, and personality. In some programs, only one attempt may be permitted to pass this examination (Scott & Silka, 1974). You should learn if the program requires "prelims" or "quals," whether multiple attempts are provided, and what percentage of students pass, before you make your final decision. Instead of an exam, many research-oriented clinical programs require submission of a lengthy review paper prior to embarking on a dissertation.

You should now be well acquainted with a program's outcomes and the decision criteria presented in Table 8-1 in your own life and well informed about the program's attractiveness on these criteria. If not, immediately request additional information on any of these for which you lack knowledge prior to making an informed choice of the program to attend.

The Financial Package

Note in Table 8-1 that the finances (scholarship offer, research assistantship, financial incentives) tend to cluster further down the list of selection factors. For many applicants, and particularly for directors of training looking at attracting the best applicants (Dornfeld et al., 2012), the financial aid offered by the school will probably assume a higher priority in making final decisions.

When an offer is made, establish if the program is offering financial assistance. If so, does it cover tuition remission? Is it guaranteed for 4 years? Is it considered taxable at that institution? Does it provide health insurance? If you have a teaching or research assistantship, how many hours per week will it entail? What is the assistantship stipend per year? Are you allowed to earn additional outside income?

On average, private universities are more expensive than public or state universities. Typically, the in-state versus out-of-state cost difference that operates in undergraduate education is not as salient in graduate education. That is because (1) once you begin study, you can establish residency there and pay in-state tuition after the first or second year, and (2) many financial aid packages include a tuition remission.

But graduate training is expensive, and external sources of financial support are slowly drying up. Consider, for instance, the average stipends and accumulated loans for Ph.D. psychology students over the years (Golding, Lang, Eymard, & Shadish, 1988). Back in the 1960s and 1970s the average graduate stipend was higher, and the typical student's accumulated loan lower, than in the 2010s, adjusted for inflation. In fact, the average stipend amount decreased 36% (controlled for inflation) over the past 30 years. About three-quarters of psychology doctoral candidates carry loans. Support is still available but not to the extent it once was—which accounts, in part, for your seasoned professors' fond memories of their "good ol' graduate days."

Federal support for graduate training has been eroding in all fields, including psychology. In the 1970s, for instance, almost 30% of Ph.D. recipients in clinical psychology reported that federal grants and traineeships provided the major support for their graduate training (Coyle & Bae, 1987). Three decades later, federal sources supported less than 4% of full-time graduate students in psychology (Wicherski & Kohout, 2005). Federal sources have slipped as a primary source of support for psychology graduate students and, to compensate for these shrinking resources, students have had to look elsewhere, to personal resources, student loans, and university financial assistance.

Research supports the conclusion that today's graduate students are being asked to shoulder a larger share of their education costs. This is particularly true in Psy.D. programs, which fund proportionally fewer students than Boulder-model (Ph.D.) programs. Refer back to Table 5-3 for the general patterns of financial assistance and to the Reports on Individual Programs for the percentage of a particular program's students who receive funding.

Table 8-2 shows the median tuition costs per year for psychology graduate students in 2010 (APA Center for Workforce Studies, 2010). The numbers demonstrate that tuition is largely a function of three variables: institution type, state residence, and degree level. Private universities uniformly charge higher graduate tuition than public institutions, just as is the case on the undergraduate level. Tuition at private institutions per academic year is typically two or three times higher than state tuition at public institutions. Psy.D. programs routinely charge between $25,000 and $35,000 per year for tuition. Although your state residence does not influence tuition at private universities, it definitely reduces your tuition at public universities—from a median of $18,447 for nonstate residents to $7,789 for state residents per year. Predictably, too, tuition is higher for doctoral programs than for master's programs.

The pattern of tuition costs presented in Table 8-2 comes from the 2010–2011 academic year, the last year that APA systematically collected such data. These patterns still hold true, but the amounts have predictably increased. Graduate tuition in 2016 averages $12,000 for public institutions and $30,000 for private institutions (National Center for Education Statistics, 2016).

So, your annual tuition can range from $0 if you secure tuition remission, to $12,000 if you are a resi-

TABLE 8-2. Median Tuition Costs in Psychology by Institution Type and Degree Level

	Doctoral programs		Master's programs	
	Public	Private	Public	Private
State residents	$7,789	$27,993	$5,892	$16,104
Nonstate residents	$18,447	$28,113	$13,021	$15,988

Note. Data adapted from American Psychological Association Center for Workforce Studies (2010).

dent attending your state university, to $30,000 if you attend a Ph.D. program at a private university with no financial assistance, all the way up to $35,000 if you attend a freestanding Psy.D. program.

Table 8-3 presents the assistantship stipends for psychology graduate students. As seen there, the median 9-month stipends for teaching and research assistantships average about $6,000 for master's students and $13,000 for doctoral students (Mulvey, Wicherski, & Kohout, 2010). Stipends for doctoral students are consistently higher than those for master's students.

The typical hours worked per week for an assistantship are 15 to 16. Practically all graduate programs will expect between 10 and 20 hours a week from their research and teaching assistants (Mulvey et al., 2010).

Financial considerations include the tuition cost, available stipend, and living costs. The latter cannot be ignored: although tuition costs may prove equivalent in New York City and Kansas, the living costs are certainly not.

Once accepted into a doctoral program, you will naturally be eager to learn about the status of your financial assistance, but you will hear from institutions at different times depending on the form of the financial assistance. If it is department-controlled financial assistance, then you will ordinarily hear when you are accepted or shortly thereafter. If it is university financial assistance, not directly controlled by the psychology department, then it may well be weeks after you are accepted. Examples in this category are fellowships from the Graduate School, resident assistantships from Student Affairs, or a Graduate Assistantship in the Admission Office. If it is financial assistance from a government agency, such as the National Science Foundation (NSF) or National Institutes of Health (NIH), then you will hear on or before their published notification dates. Finally, if it is financial assistance in the form of loans, then you will hear from the bank, Sally Mae, or the lending institution on their (painfully slow) schedule.

The Alternate List

Your fervent hope is to receive an email or telephone call in February, March, or early April from the director of admissions offering you acceptance into your top-rated graduate program with generous financial aid. But this glorious dream may not materialize; instead, the sobering reality is that many applicants will be rejected from several programs, will secure offers from programs lower on their list, or will receive offers without financial assistance. Many applicants will also receive calls informing them that they have been wait listed—that is, placed on the alternate list.

As mentioned previously, ask the director of admissions where you stand on the alternate list—high, middle, or low. For your planning purposes, politely assert in probing further: "In typical years, what percentage of students with this position on the alternate list receive an admission offer? What percentage of the students admitted from the alternate list receive funding?" Without answers to these questions, you cannot render an informed decision on your other offers.

The admissions directors will, in all likelihood, arrange for you to be kept abreast of your admissions status until April 15th. They may email you or you may email them on occasion to determine the probability of admission.

When speaking with the representative at the program, try to impress upon him or her three key ideas. First, you are keenly interested in attending that program. Second, express your availability by stating you have not accepted another offer of admission. And third, if you have received another offer, inform the program accordingly; most schools desire people who are attractive to others. Enthusiasm, availability, and attractiveness frequently move students up the alternate list.

The tricky part of this process is how frequently an alternate should contact (by telephone or email) the program representative. Too much contact will appear aggressive or desperate; too little, passive or complacent. Strike a balance by asking the program representative how often you may contact him or her without being irritating.

Decision Making

The choice of which admission offer to accept and which program to attend is a momentous one indeed. You, like 86% of students enrolling in graduate programs, will quickly discover that the decision-making process boils down to your sense of fit with a program (Kyle, 2000). A few fortunate souls may receive an early offer with excellent financial aid from their number one program. But most graduate school applicants will ultimately select the program that makes the best offer—an offer that needs to be seriously weighed on a host of the aforementioned and often conflicting considerations.

The "March and April madness" abounds with such quandaries as: "Should I take Program X with the best training but with no financial aid or Program Y with solid training and half tuition remission for 4 years?"; "Two programs have offered the same money, but the one that I prefer is 600 miles from my partner. What should I do?"; "My top program guaranteed me a teaching assistantship that requires 15 hours a week. My fourth choice is offering tuition remission and a fellowship. Any advice?"

Our advice centers on using systematic decision making. Begin by gathering all the salient data by interviewing program faculty and students, consulting published materials, and speaking with your mentors. Prioritize your primary reasons for selecting one program over another. Then develop a decision-making grid that will assist you in ranking your choices.

Two practical articles describe in detail how to apply decision-making techniques to choosing psychology programs and internships. Jacob's (1987) decision grid asks candidates to evaluate training programs along criteria that are important to them. You weigh those criteria that are more important to you correspondingly higher. You then tally the ratings for each training program to make the final decision. While it may sound a bit over-intellectual, in practice we have found that the decision grid forces applicants to identify the criteria that they value most highly.

Stewart and Stewart (1996) describe a paired-comparison ranking technique, a method originally traced back to psychophysiological methods developed by Gustav Fechner. The first step of this technique is to select the relevant personal, professional, and practical criteria that you will use in comparing programs to one another. Consult the preceding pages to identify these criteria; conduct an honest self-evaluation to determine which of these lie in your heart. The second step involves prioritizing these selection criteria. Do this by writing the name of each criterion on a single index card or piece of paper, and then forcing yourself to rank them in order. The third step entails generating a list of programs that will be compared to one another. We suggest that you use those programs that have accepted you or which have placed you on their waiting list.

The fourth step of the technique involves the actual pairwise comparison of the programs. Write the names of the graduate programs along one side of a large piece of paper and the selection criteria on the other side. Which of the training programs most clearly satisfies your criteria? Make a choice and allow no ties. For each criterion, put a hash mark across from the program that wins. The hash marks will be counted to determine your choice.

Although the final result will generally agree with what you expected, the more productive outcome of these two decision-making techniques may be that they force you to view your selection decision

TABLE 8-3. Median Assistantship Stipends in Psychology by Institution Type and Degree Level

	Doctoral students		Master's students	
	Public	Private	Public	Private
Teaching assistantship	$12,623	$14,000	$6,502	$3,675
Research assistantship	$12,933	$6,425	$6,574	$3,150
Fellowship/scholarship	$15,000	$5,200	$2,000	$2,170
Traineeship	$14,516	$15,000	$6,000	$6,750

Note. Data from Mulvey, Wicherski, & Kohout (2010).

from multiple perspectives and to prioritize numerous criteria. To be sure, this is a complex method for a complex decision, but one that we and our students have repeatedly found effective for making "impossible" choices more thoughtfully and systematically.

Finalizing Arrangements

An offer of admission must eventually be formalized in writing. Verbal offers and verbal acceptances are binding, but your acceptance of the offer should be in writing at the end of the process. Likewise, assistantships, tuition waivers, and stipends should be guaranteed in the written offer; respectfully insist that the financial arrangements be specified so that misunderstandings do not ensue. Should the offer be "contingent on expected funding," determine the odds of the funding coming through. No position is absolutely certain in life, but some are more certain than others.

Weighing offers, negotiating financial aid, and dealing with rejections make this a heady period. Be careful not to get caught up in the experience and forget the most important point: accept one offer and confirm it in writing!

One of our students (the affable Jean Willi) was offered admission to a prestigious doctoral program, with financial assistance. He carefully considered alternative offers, negotiated with other programs, leading to predictable delays. He awoke one morning in a cold sweat, realizing that he had turned down all other offers but had not formally accepted the offer of admission and financial package from his school of choice. He was in graduate school purgatory! Although the school was understanding and everything eventually worked out for Jean, because he missed the deadline, the school had the option of changing the financial aid package, or even revoking the admission offer. The moral of the story: don't pull a Willi! Be clear and decisive and put it in writing.

Figure 8-1 presents a representative letter of acceptance. Note that the letter or email should explicitly mention any conditions of your acceptance, including financial assistance. Most graduate programs will accept an email as your formal confirmation, but a few programs still insist upon a snail-mailed letter.

March 10, 2018

Annika Jones, Ph.D.
Director, Admissions Committee
Department of Psychology
University of Western States
13 Orangegrove Drive
Wilksville, CA 98765

Dear Dr. Jones:

I am pleased to accept your offer of admission to the University of Western States's Ph.D. program in counseling psychology as a full-time matriculated student beginning in the Fall 2019 term. My acceptance is predicated on the conditions outlined in your letter of March 20th (attached), including full tuition remission for three years.

I appreciate your confidence in me and very much look forward to joining the counseling psychology program.

Sincerely yours,

Chris Smith

FIGURE 8-1. Sample letter accepting an admission offer.

Once you have formally accepted an offer of admission in writing, two matters of etiquette remain: (1) informing other programs that have accepted you, and (2) expressing your appreciation to those mentors who wrote letters of recommendation on your behalf and on their own time. Figure 8-2 offers a sample email declining an offer of admission. It should be succinct yet polite. Thereafter, send a brief email or thank-you note to those who have assisted you through your graduate application journey. They will be interested in the outcome of your application process and may well join the ensuing celebration!

Post-Deadline Switches

Well, that is how the admissions process is *supposed* to operate—nice, tidy, finished by the close of April 15th. But reality is not always so obliging and orderly. It turns out that some students will wait vigilantly until the deadline looms, accept the best offer on the table, but then a few days after the deadline suddenly receive a more attractive offer. You have formally committed to one graduate program but would now like to attend another program!

What to do at the crossroads? On the one hand, it seems wildly unprofessional to accept an offer and then renege on your commitment. The graduate program which accepted you before the deadline will have probably completed its admissions work and will not take kindly to an applicant switching his or her mind after the deadline. And, a "jilted" faculty mentor may well remain in your professional universe—seeing you at specialty conferences, belonging to the same professional organizations—for years to come. Yes means yes.

On the other hand, your career and future are at stake. Explore the possibility of a post-deadline switch with the director of admissions at the institution where you were already accepted. Call immediately and respectfully; be apologetic and humble. Ask if the director could release you from your commitment. Explain the last-minute offer and the circumstances, such as more financial assistance or a better fit.

Expect one of three responses from the director of admissions. One: begrudging approval to release you from your commitment. Two: an angry reaction and a flat no. That will particularly prove the case at smaller Ph.D. programs that enroll 6 or 7 students per year (as contrasted to large Psy.D. programs admit-

March 10, 2018

Annika Jones, Ph.D.
Director, Admissions Committee
Department of Psychology
University of Western States
13 Orangegrove Drive
Wilksville, CA 98765

Dear Dr. Jones:

I was pleased to receive your March 9th letter offering me acceptance to the Psy.D. program in clinical psychology at the University of Western States. I thoroughly enjoyed speaking with you and your colleagues and appreciated your generous offer of admission.

Unfortunately, I can only accept one admission offer, and I must regrettably decline your attractive offer. Please extend my genuine thanks and best wishes to the entire Admissions Committee.

Sincerely yours,

Chris Smith

FIGURE 8-2. Sample letter declining an admission offer.

ting 50 or more students per year). Three: a mixed emotional response. That typically goes something like, "We want you to be happy and find a good graduate fit, but we closed our admissions and rejected other qualified candidates because you accepted. Let me check if something can be done."

If you are eventually released from your commitment, count your blessings. If you are not released, then you find yourself on dubious ethical grounds in accepting the other, post-deadline offer. Some students will accept the subsequent offer, but they have committed a breach of ethics and etiquette. A few directors of admissions may even register their complaint with both the applicant and his or her recommenders. Your choice to make but beware the probable consequences.

If Not Accepted

What happens if you are not accepted anywhere? The grim truth is that a substantial percentage of the entire applicant pool to APA-accredited clinical and counseling psychology programs will *not* make it in a given year.

Start by taking time to recover from your disappointment after an emotionally draining process. Relax a few days and break from the graduate school preoccupation. Seek support from your friends and family members. Remind yourself that many psychologists took several tries to enter graduate school. Most importantly, remember that your worth as a person is not dependent on your academic accomplishments. That message will be underscored by online support groups, such as that at https://grieflosssupport.wordpress.com, for applicants not accepted this year.

Then, huddle with your mentors and consider these seven alternatives:

1. *Delay graduation from college.* If you are a college senior and applied to doctoral programs for the first time, consider postponing graduation to enhance your credentials. Take more classes or repeat certain courses that will improve your GPA. Prepare better for the GRE and obtain more research experience, which in turn will probably strengthen your letters of recommendation. Another semester or two of college may prove effective as an investment in your future career.

A word of caution here: such an approach can prove expensive and does not guarantee eventual acceptance into a doctoral program. But it is one alternative that can be thrown into the mix.

2. *Consider a psychology post-baccalaureate program.* Post-baccalaureate programs are designed for students who have a bachelor's degree (in any discipline) and who are seeking additional preparation for psychology-oriented graduate training or careers. They are a recent development in psychology, but have been around for decades in other disciplines, especially for those interested in applying to medical school. More than a dozen such programs exist in psychology, and most of them provide psychology coursework, internship opportunities, and research assistantships (Zinger, 2014). All of these experiences improve a student's credentials and thus the probability of admission into competitive doctoral programs with financial assistance.

We avidly recommend these post-baccalaureate programs to select students with a few essential stipulations. First, most students will require at least a full year of attendance, and sometimes 1.5 or 2 years, in order to remediate their weaknesses or to acquire more clinical or research experience. Second, in addition to the time commitment, there is the cost of another year or two of tuition. Third, doing well in post-bac training will probably not help so much with admission into a research-oriented, PCSAS program. If your academic credentials were not strong enough a year earlier to gain entrance, then post-bac training alone may not move the needle when other top candidates did better the first time in their undergraduate careers. Fourth, beware of the "magical" thought that, "I may have not done well in my undergraduate psychology program but I will now do much better in the post-baccalaureate program." Please possess compelling evidence that your performance will be superior the second time around, lest you spend considerable money and time repeating the same old mistakes.

Enterprising students can complete *informal* post-baccalaureate preparation on their own. That is, they arrange for psychology courses, research assistantships, and clinical experiences at a particular department. These arrangements are more difficult to finalize as most psychology programs are understandably giving priority to their own, full-time undergraduates. But it can and does occur; in fact, we have mentored many such motivated students switching careers or laying the foundation for advanced study.

3. *Consult the APA Education Directorate's Graduate Openings list in late April.* This document contains a list of graduate programs in psychology that still have openings for students in the fall. Although there are typically only a couple of APA-accredited

clinical or counseling Ph.D. programs and only a few nonclinical Ph.D. programs on the list, you may locate a Psy.D. or other program of interest to you. To review the listings, go to the APA website at www.apa.org/education/grad/graduate-openings.aspx.

4. *Apply to master's programs.* Master's degrees represent frequent stepping stones to the doctorate in psychology. Although taking your master's at one institution and transferring to another for the doctorate is not as efficient as being admitted directly into a doctoral program, there are advantages nonetheless. One is that the acceptance odds are more favorable—37% for master's programs in clinical psychology and 63% for master's in counseling psychology on average (Table 1-5). A second advantage is that a few years of graduate training in psychology can improve your grade point average, GRE Psychology Subject Test score, clinical acumen, and research skills. A third plus is an opportunity to confirm that psychology is the career for you. A cruel irony of baccalaureate recipients admitted directly into doctoral programs is that they have little direct contact with the discipline they claim as their lifelong career! A fourth advantage is exposure to twice the number of faculty supervisors and theoretical orientations. A fifth and final advantage is the flexible course offerings—part-time study and, frequently, night courses are available in master's programs (Actkinson, 2000).

Selecting a *quality* master's program in psychology may be a key to eventual admission into a doctoral program. By all means try to avoid master's programs that have come to be pejoratively called "money mills." These programs exhibit most or all of the following features: accepting a very high percentage (80% plus) of applicants; offering courses only in the evening or largely by part-time faculty; providing no funded graduate assistantships; being reluctant or unwilling to state what percentage of their graduates go on to doctoral programs; declaring openly their disinterest in research; requiring little undergraduate preparation in psychology; and communicating greater interest in filling classroom seats than in attracting qualified students.

By contrast, quality terminal master's programs in psychology can be roughly assessed by three criteria: exhibiting few of the aforementioned characteristics of money mills; holding a favorable reputation among the psychological community; and faculty producing published research. Gordon (1990) lists 20 American master's programs ranked highest in productivity in 15 APA journals; interested students are directed to that article.

In addition to the foregoing research-based article, we heartily recommend that you consult an extensive compilation of master's programs in psychology. The classic is APA's (2016) *Graduate Study in Psychology*, which lists hundreds of master's (and doctoral) programs in psychology throughout the United States and Canada. To order, go to APA's website where you can purchase a hard copy or purchase a three-month electronic access.

5. *Apply to doctoral programs that will soon be accredited by APA.* Newer doctoral programs located in credible universities have not been around long enough to gain APA approval. Programs cannot apply for full accreditation until they have graduated doctoral students, which takes several years. Usually these programs will apply for accreditation as soon as they are eligible.

However, there is another category of programs not accredited by APA. These programs (several of them entirely online) do not conform to APA standards and often do not even attempt to gain accreditation. The quality of these programs tends to be considerably lower than APA-accredited programs. Because of their status, non-APA-accredited programs typically provide greater probabilities for acceptance and frequently advertise on the web. We recommend against applying to or attending such programs.

6. *Decide against a doctorate in clinical or counseling psychology.* If your goal is to become a researcher or a practitioner, psychology is not your only option. Reexamine the alternatives listed in Chapter 1 and consult your advisors to see which of these options is suited to your needs.

7. *Apply again in a year or two to APA-accredited programs.* Knowing the criteria used by graduate schools, take a realistic look at the limitations in your application. Many students continue to resubmit the same rejected application year after year to no avail; "doing more of the same" typically results in more of the same misery.

Another year can be an opportunity to remediate your weaknesses. Were your GREs low? Take a professional preparation course and retake the test. Was your GPA a bit low? Then take some additional courses or retake some old courses in which you did not perform your best to improve it. Take some graduate courses in psychology on a nonmatriculating basis to demonstrate your ability. Were you short on research skills? Then take 1 or 2 years and acquire a research position, paid or volunteer, in a psychology or psychiatry department. Did you lack significant clinical experience? Then spend a night or two a week working for a suicide hot line or find a job at a women's shelter. Were your letters of recommendation tepid or brief? Then acquaint yourself better with potential referees so they can write a positive and detailed letter.

Another year can also provide an opportunity to enhance your interview style or to acquire better matches with graduate faculty. Some applicants find themselves in the position of perennial bridesmaids or best men, not because their credentials were inadequate, but because their interview style or matching potential was a tad weak. Spend the extra months improving your interpersonal presentation and investigating programs that promise to be better fits with your interests.

The so-called gap year is not intended as a vacation or a year off. Instead, it is a year dedicated to improving your credentials and working hard at what interests you. When friends or parents ask what you are doing on your purported "year off," we believe the appropriate response is to proudly reply, "Preparing for my career in psychology!"

In summary, reread this text and conduct a rigorous self-assessment of where you are and where you want to be. If you're set on a career in clinical or counseling psychology, be prepared to take the time and energy to make yourself a better applicant. Especially if you are still in college and had planned to go straight on to graduate school, take time to gain some life experiences. As we mentioned in Chapter 2, those clinical psychologists who postponed graduate school after college were significantly more satisfied with their decision than individuals who went directly to a terminal master's degree (Zimak et al., 2011). Age and experience can work in your favor, and they will certainly define your goals better next time through the application process.

Two Final Words

Realism and persistence. Be realistic about your credentials, capacities, and acceptance odds. Some applicants refuse to accept the hard facts of the admission process and tragically resubmit the identically flawed application year after year to no avail. An honest evaluation of your credentials, with the assistance of an experienced professor, will enable you to strengthen your application, select more appropriate programs, or reevaluate your career decisions. This is not to dissuade or discourage you; it is realistic encouragement.

And be persistent! Many successful psychologists have required two or three tries to get into a doctoral program. Thousands of clinical and counseling psychologists have earned a master's degree at one institution before moving on to receive a doctorate at another university. There is no shame in reaching for the stars; the real loss is not to reach at all.

We hope the information and suggestions contained in this *Insider's Guide* have proven helpful to you. We wish you the best success in the application process and in graduate school.

REPORTS ON COMBINED PSYCHOLOGY PROGRAMS

University of Buffalo/State University of New York (Ph.D.)

(counseling/school combined)
Department of Counseling, School, & Educational Psychology
Buffalo, NY 14260
phone#: (716) 645-2484
email: gse-info@buffalo.edu
Web address: www.gse.buffalo.edu/programs/cpsp

1	2	3	**4**	5	6	7
Practice oriented			Equal emphasis			Research oriented

Percentage of faculty subscribing to each of the following orientations:

Psychodynamic/Psychoanalytic	10%
Applied behavioral analysis/Radical behavioral	20%
Family systems/Systems	25%
Existential/Phenomenological/Humanistic	10%
Cognitive/Cognitive-behavioral	50%

Courses required for incoming students to have completed prior to enrolling:
Most students have a B.A. or B.S. in psychology.

Recommended but not mandatory courses: none

GRE mean
Verbal 156 Quantitative 150
Analytical Writing 4.7
Psychology Subject Test not reported

GPA mean
Overall GPA 3.8

Number of applications/admission offers/incoming students in 2017
75 applied/19 offers/9 incoming

% of students receiving:
Full tuition waiver only: 0%
Assistantship/fellowship only: 13%
Both full tuition waiver & assistantship/fellowship: 87%

Approximate percentage of students who are
Women: 75% **Ethnic Minority:** 23% **International:** 2%

Average years to complete the doctoral program (including internship): 5 years

Personal interview
Required in person or via Skype or phone call

Attrition rate in past 7 years: 8%

Percentage of students applying for internship in 2017 accepted into:

APA internships: 100% N=5 **CDSPP internships:** 100% N=5

Formal tracks/concentrations/specializations:
2; as combined doctoral program, students choose either a counseling psychology or school psychology concentration

Research areas	# Faculty	# Grants
assessment	4	1
ADHD	1	1
academic skills interventions	1	0
college student mental health	1	0
eating disorders	2	0
groups	1	0
obesity treatment/family interventions	1	0
interpersonal psychology	1	0
mindfulness/yoga/positive psychology	3	0
multicultural/gender issues	2	0
family/peer relationships	2	1
school violence/bullying prevention	1	2
vocational psychology	2	0

Clinical opportunities
Very diverse, including schools, VA medical centers, community agencies, and hospitals in urban, suburban, rural areas, and college counseling centers.

University of California–Santa Barbara (Ph.D.)

(clinical/counseling/school)
Department of Counseling, Clinical and School Psychology
Santa Barbara, CA 93106
phone#: (805) 893-3375
email: tisrael@ucsb.edu
Web address: www.education.ucsb.edu/Graduate-Studies/CCSP/CCSP-home.html

1	2	3	4	5	**6**	7
Practice oriented			Equal emphasis			Research oriented

Percentage of faculty subscribing to each of the following orientations:

Psychodynamic/Psychoanalytic	30%
Applied behavioral analysis/Radical behavioral	20%
Family systems/Systems	40%
Existential/Phenomenological/Humanistic	30%
Cognitive/Cognitive-behavioral	70%
Developmental	40%
Feminist	30%
Solution focused	20%
Positive psychology	30%

Courses required for incoming students to have completed prior to enrolling: none

Recommended but not mandatory courses: Human development, personality or abnormal psychology, research design or statistics, biopsychology

GRE mean
Verbal 550 Quantitative 625
Analytical Writing not reported
Psychology Subject Test not reported

GPA mean
GPA 3.70

Number of applications/admission offers/incoming students in 2016
230 applied/20 admission offers/10 incoming

% of students receiving:
Full tuition waiver only: 0%
Assistantship/fellowship only: 0%

Both full tuition waiver & assistantship/fellowship: 40%

Approximate percentage of incoming students with a B.A./B.S. only: 80% **Master's:** 20%

Approximate percentage of students who are Women: 83% **Ethnic Minority:** 37% **International:** 0.5%

Average years to complete the doctoral program (including internship): 5.4 years

Personal interview
Preferred in person but telephone acceptable

Attrition rate in past 7 years: 5%

Percentage of students applying for internship last year accepted into APPIC or APA internships: 100%

Formal tracks/concentrations/specializations:
counseling, clinical, school

Research areas

- autism
- career counseling
- child abuse/family violence
- mental health services for high-risk families, children
- multicultural issues
- psychological assessment
- social justice
- substance abuse
- trauma exposure

Clinical opportunities

- autism clinic
- career counseling center
- child abuse community-based agency
- community-based mental health
- family therapy
- LGBT community-based agency
- neuropsychological and personality assessment
- school consultation
- school interventions
- university counseling center

Florida State University (Ph.D.)

(counseling/school)
Psychological and Counseling Services
Department of Educational Psychology and Learning Systems
1114 W. Call Street
Tallahassee, FL 32306-4453
phone#: (850) 644-1789
email: debener@fsu.edu
Web address: http://education.fsu.edu/degrees-and-programs/counseling-psychology-and-school-psychology

1	2	3	4	**5**	6	7
Practice oriented			Equal emphasis			Research oriented

Percentage of faculty subscribing to each of the following orientations:

Psychodynamic/Psychoanalytic	10%
Applied behavioral analysis/Radical behavioral	20%
Family systems/Systems	20%
Existential/Phenomenological/Humanistic	10%
Cognitive/Cognitive-behavioral	100%

Courses required for incoming students to have completed prior to enrolling:
None required; core psychology (e.g., statistics, research) highly recommended

Recommended but not mandatory courses: Core psychology recommended

GRE mean
Verbal 570 Quantitative 610
Analytical Writing 4.5–5.0
Psychology Subject Test not reported

GPA mean
Junior/Senior GPA 3.68

Number of applications/admission offers/incoming students in fall 2017
69 applied/17 admission offers/12 incoming

% of students receiving:
Full tuition waiver only: 0%
Assistantship/fellowship only: 0%
Both full tuition waiver & assistantship/fellowship: 62%

Approximate percentage of incoming students with a B.A./B.S. only: 32% **Master's:** 68%

Approximate percentage of students who are Women: 82% **Ethnic Minority:** 28% **International:** 4%

Average years to complete the doctoral program (including internship): 4.75 years

Personal interview
Very strongly encouraged following invitation to visit campus as finalist

Attrition rate in past 7 years: 10%

Percentage of students applying for internship last year accepted into APPIC or APA internships: 100%

Formal tracks/concentrations/specializations:
Counseling psychology and school psychology

Research areas	**# Faculty**	**# Grants**
career development	2	1
counseling/psychotherapy	3	4
school/community interventions	3	
gifted/talent development	1	

Clinical opportunities
Adult Learning Evaluation Center
Career counseling center
Human services center
University counseling center
Medical and behavioral health care agencies
Private Practices
FSU Multidisciplinary Center
Veteran's Administration outpatient clinic and hospital

James Madison University (Psy.D.)

(clinical/school)
Combined-Integrated Doctoral Program in Clinical and School Psychology
Department of Graduate Psychology
Harrisonburg, VA 22807-7401
phone#: (540) 568-6834
email: critchkl@jmu.edu
Web address: www.psyc.jmu.edu/cipsyd/

1	2	**3**	4	5	6	7
Practice oriented			Equal emphasis			Research oriented

Percentage of faculty subscribing to each of the following orientations:

Psychodynamic/Psychoanalytic	20%
Applied behavioral analysis/Radical behavioral	20%
Family systems/Systems	40%
Existential/Phenomenological/Humanistic	20%
Cognitive/Cognitive-behavioral	20%
Interpersonal	20%
Integrative/Transtheoretical	100%

Note: the program orientation is explicitly integrative, as are all of its faculty members. Percentages here thus exceed 100%; Entries in each specific school reflect primary faculty background and training.

Courses required for incoming students to have completed prior to enrolling:
Students are required to have a Master's degree in a psychology-related field.

Recommended but not mandatory courses: Master's degree and professional experience

GRE mean
Verbal 155 Quantitative 151
Psychology Subject Test 640
Analytical Writing 4.5

GPA mean
Master's GPA 3.9

Number of applications/admission offers/incoming students in 2017
82 applied/6 admission offers/6 incoming

% of students receiving:
Full tuition waiver only: 0%
Assistantship/fellowship only: 0%
Both full tuition waiver & assistantship/fellowship: 100%

Approximate percentage of incoming students with a B.A./B.S. only: 0% **Master's:** 100%

Approximate percentage of students who are Women: 74% **Ethnic Minority:** 22% **International:** 12%

Average years to complete the doctoral program (including internship): 4.1 years

Personal interview
Required

Attrition rate in past 7 years: 4%

Percentage of students applying for internship last year accepted into APPIC or APA internships: 100%

Formal tracks/concentrations/specializations: none

Research areas	**# Faculty**	**# Grants**
attachment theory	2	0
interpersonal theory	2	0
integrative theory	5	0
beliefs and values	3	1
clinical training processes	4	3
depression and suicide	2	0
biofeedback	1	0
family processes	2	0
international/cultural issues	4	1
parent–child interaction	2	0
personality disorder	1	0
social motivation and affect	1	0
social/skill development	4	0
supervision and leadership	1	0
theoretical unification	2	0

Clinical opportunities

adult psychotherapy	multidisciplinary assessment
child/family therapy	neuropsychology
counseling and psychological clinic	outpatient private practice
forensic assessment	school assessment
inpatient/hospital practice	sports psychology
learning disabilities	supervision/leadership

Kean University (Psy.D.)

Department of Advanced Studies in Psychology
1000 Morris Avenue
Union, NJ 07083
phone#: (908) 737-5861
email: jlerner@kean.edu
Web address: http://grad.kean.edu/doctoral-programs/combined-school-and-clinical-psychology

1	2	3	**4**	5	6	7
Practice oriented			Equal emphasis			Research oriented

Percentage of faculty subscribing to each of the following orientations:

Psychodynamic/Psychoanalytic	14%
Applied behavioral analysis/Radical behavioral	29%
Family systems/Systems	29%
Existential/Phenomenological/Humanistic	43%
Cognitive/Cognitive-behavioral	86%

Courses required for incoming students to have completed prior to enrolling: Theories of Personality, Abnormal Psychology, Tests and Measurements, Statistics, and Experimental Psychology

Recommended but not mandatory courses: n/a

GRE mean
Verbal + Quantitative = 154.33 + 153.33
Analytical Writing = 4.4
Psychology Subject Test = 675

GPA mean
Overall GPA = 3.56

Number of applications/admission offers/incoming students in 2017
53 applied/18 admission offers/10 incoming

% of students receiving:
Full tuition waiver only: 0%
Assistantship/fellowship only: 0%
Both full tuition waiver & assistantship/fellowship: 33%

Approximate percentage of incoming students with a B.A./B.S. only: 60% **Master's:** 40%

Approximate percentage of all students who are Women: 76% **Ethnic Minority:** 27% **International:** 2%

Average years to complete the doctoral program (including internship): 5.1 years

Personal interview: Preferred in person but telephone acceptable

Attrition rate since accreditation: 3.4%

Percentage of students applying for internship last year accepted into:

APA internships: 63% **APPIC internships:** 25%

Formal tracks/concentrations: n/a – Combined school and clinical program

Research areas	**# Faculty**	**# Grants**
Autism and developmental disabilities	3	1
Birth to five	2	1
Childhood trauma	3	1
Diversity practices/social justice	4	0
Forensic assessment	1	0
Health psychology	2	0
Higher education/training	2	0
Mindfulness-based interventions	3	1
Older adults	1	0
Pediatric psychology	1	0
Religion/spirituality	2	0
Trauma	5	0
Sport psychology	2	0

Clinical opportunities

anxiety disorders
at-risk college students
autism and other developmental disabilities
depression
geriatric
psycho-oncology
psychoeducational assessment
psychopathology assessment
trauma

Pace University (Psy.D.)

(school/clinical)
Department of Psychology
New York, NY 10038
phone#: (212) 346-1531
email: gradnyc@pace.edu
Web address: appsrv.pace.edu/academics/view-programs/?school=GAS&Cred=DSY&Maj=CSY&Location=nyc+details

1	**2**	3	4	5	6	7
Practice oriented			Equal emphasis			Research oriented

Percentage of faculty subscribing to each of the following orientations:

Psychodynamic/Psychoanalytic	36%
Applied behavioral analysis/Radical behavioral	0%
Family systems/Systems	0%
Existential/Phenomenological/Humanistic	0%
Cognitive/Cognitive-behavioral	27%
Integrative	36%

Courses required for incoming students to have completed prior to enrolling:
General psychology, experimental psychology, statistics, developmental psychology, learning, personality, psychopathology. In addition, students must have courses or show competencies in principles and problems in education and curriculum development or methods of teaching and instruction.

Recommended but not mandatory courses: none

GRE mean
Verbal + Quantitative 156 + 152
Analytical Writing 4.1
Psychology Subject Test suggested

GPA mean
Overall GPA 3.55

Number of applications/admission offers/incoming students in 2016
293 applied/62 admission offers/17 incoming

% of students receiving:
Full tuition waiver only: 25% partial tuition waiver
Assistantship/fellowship only: 75%
Both full tuition waiver & assistantship/fellowship: 0%

Approximate percentage of incoming students with a B.A./B.S. only: 71% **Master's:** 29%

Approximate percentage (varies from year to year) of students who are
Women: 71% **Ethnic Minority:** 24% **International:**

Average years to complete the doctoral program (including internship): 6 years (varies from year to year)

Personal interview
Required in person (on occasion grant telephone interviews)

Attrition rate in past 7 years: 5% approximately

Percentage of students applying for internship last year accepted into APPIC or APA internships: 100%

Formal tracks/concentrations/specializations: None

Research areas	**# Faculty**	**# Grants**
community psychology	2	0
gender	1	0
infant and early childhood	4	0
instructional psychology	0	0
learning disabilities	1	0
learning	1	0
multicultural and diversity	2	0
posttraumatic stress disorder	2	0
psychometric	4	0
technology	1	1
substance abuse	2	0

Clinical opportunities

infant and early childhood psychology
psychotherapy and clinical interventions
neuropsychological assessment
primary prevention
many varied opportunities available in the New York City metropolitan area

University of South Alabama (Ph.D.)

Department of Psychology
UCOMM Building, Suite 1000
Mobile, AL 36688
phone#: (251) 460-6371
email: ccpprogram@southalabama.edu
or jcurrier@southalabama.edu
Web address: http://www.southalabama.edu/ccp/

1	2	3	4	5	6	7
Practice oriented			Equal emphasis			Research oriented

Percentage of faculty subscribing to each of the following orientations:

Psychodynamic/Psychoanalytic	20%
Applied behavioral analysis/Radical behavioral	15%
Family systems/Systems	50%
Existential/Phenomenological/Humanistic	50%
Cognitive/Cognitive-behavioral	100%

Courses required for incoming students to have completed prior to enrolling:
Students entering with a Bachelor's degree must have at least 21 hours of undergraduate psychology, including statistics, research methods, and a lab course. Students entering with a Master's degree in a mental health profession also need at least 21 hours in psychology-related courses.

Recommended but not mandatory courses:
None

GRE mean
Verbal + Quantitative 305
Analytical Writing 4.0
Psychology Subject Test (not reported)

GPA mean
Overall GPA 3.55

Number of applications/admission offers/incoming students in 2017
130 applied/10 admission offers/8 incoming

% of students receiving:
Full tuition waiver only: 0%
Assistantship/fellowship only: 0%
Both full tuition waiver & assistantship/fellowship: 100%

Approximate percentage of incoming students with a B.A./B.S. only: 38% **Master's:** 62%

Approximate percentage of all students who are Women: 68% **Ethnic Minority:** 6% **International:** 0%

Average years to complete the doctoral program (including internship): 5 years

Personal interview
Preferred in person but telephone acceptable in some cases

Attrition rate in past 7 years: 10%

Percentage of students applying for internship last year accepted into:

APA internships: 90% **APPIC internships:** 10%

Formal tracks/concentrations: none

Research areas
clinical health
pediatrics
trauma and resilience
military and veterans
suicide
sports and exercise
autism-spectrum disorder
child psychopathology
youth violence and delinquency
neuropsychology
psychometrics and cognitive assessment
religion and spirituality
mindfulness
minority and LGBTQ

Clinical opportunities
Mitchel Cancer Center
Alabama Institute of Deaf and Blind
The Learning Tree
Veterans Administration
Mobile County school system & private schools
Hospitals and Medical Center

Utah State University (Ph.D.)

(clinical/counseling)
Department of Psychology
Logan, UT 84322-2810
phone#: (435) 797-1460
email: psychology@usu.edu
Web address: https://psychology.usu.edu/academics/grad/clinical-counseling/index

1	2	3	4	5	6	7
Practice oriented			Equal emphasis			Research oriented

Percentage of faculty subscribing to each of the following orientations:

Psychodynamic/Psychoanalytic	10%
Applied behavioral analysis/Radical behavioral	30%
Family systems/Systems	20%
Existential/Phenomenological/Humanistic	40%
Cognitive/Cognitive-behavioral	70%

Courses required for incoming students to have completed prior to enrolling: None

Recommended but not mandatory courses: Highly recommend courses in cognitive, social, biological, developmental, and abnormal psychology as well as elementary statistics.

GRE mean
Verbal 158
Quantitative 153
Analytical Writing 4.36
Psychology Subject Test not reported

GPA mean
Junior/Senior GPA 3.83

Number of applications/admission offers/incoming students in 2017
136 applied/11 admission offers/11 incoming

% of students receiving:
Full tuition waiver only: 0%
Assistantship/fellowship only: 0%
Both full tuition waiver & assistantship/fellowship: 100%

Approximate percentage of incoming students with a B.A./B.S. only: 73% **Master's:** 27%

Approximate percentage of all students who are Women: 72% **Ethnic Minority:** 41% **International:** 8%

Average years to complete the doctoral program (including internship): 6.88 years

Personal interview
Strongly preferred in person but skype acceptable

Attrition rate in past 7 years: 18.75%

Percentage of students applying for internship last year accepted into APPIC or APA internships: 100%

Formal tracks/concentrations/specializations: Child and Adolescent Psychology, Health/Neuropsychology, Rural/Multicultural Psychology, and Contextual Behavioral Science.

Research areas	# Faculty	# Grants
Acceptance and commitment therapy	2	5
Behavioral medicine/health psychology	5	2
Diverse families	2	0
Ethics	2	0
Geriatrics & neuropsychology	1	1
Implementation science	2	1
Multicultural psychology	5	0
Native American mental health	1	1
PTSD	2	2

Clinical opportunities
behavioral medicine
cardiac rehabilitation
neuropsychology
community
disabilities
early intervention
Head Start
minority mental health
pediatric psychology
student counseling center
student wellness center
eating disorders

University of Virginia–Department of Human Services (Ph.D.)

(clinical/school)
Curry School of Education
P.O. Box 400270
Charlottesville, VA 22904-4270
phone#: (434) 924-7472
email: clin-psych@virginia.edu
Web address: curry.virginia.edu/academics/degrees/doctor-of-philosophy/ph.d.-in-clinical-and-school-psychology

1	2	3	**4**	5	6	7
Practice oriented			Equal emphasis			Research oriented

Percentage of faculty subscribing to each of the following orientations:

Psychodynamic/Psychoanalytic	10%
Applied behavioral analysis/Radical behavioral	0%
Family systems/Systems	40%
Existential/Phenomenological/Humanistic	20%
Cognitive/Cognitive-behavioral	50%

Courses required for incoming students to have completed prior to enrolling: none

Recommended but not mandatory courses:
Undergraduate statistics, developmental, cognitive, abnormal, biopsychology, social, affective

GRE mean
Verbal 163 Quantitative 158
Analytical Writing 5.0
Psychology Subject Test n/a

GPA mean
Overall GPA 3.82 Psychology GPA n/a
Junior/Senior GPA n/a

Number of applications/admission offers/incoming students in 2017
180 applied/7 admission offers/7 incoming

% of students receiving:
Full tuition waiver only: 0%
Assistantship/fellowship only: 0%
Both full tuition waiver & assistantship/fellowship: 100%

Approximate percentage of incoming student with a B.A./B.S. only: 100% **Master's:** 0%

Approximate percentage of students who are Women: 93% **Ethnic Minority:** 30% **International:** 0%

Average years to complete the doctoral program (including internship): 5.26 years

Personal interview
Preferred in person but telephone acceptable

Attrition rate in past 7 years: 6%

Percentage of students applying for internship in 2017 accepted into:

APA internships: 100% **APPIC internships:** 100%

Formal tracks/concentrations: school psychology; child clinical

Research areas	# Faculty	# Grants
child clinical	5	2
school interventions	5	5
cognitive/learning disorders	2	0
forensic psychology	1	0
incarcerated populations	1	0
multicultural	1	0
parenting behavior	2	0
youth mentoring	3	2
youth violence	3	1
prevention science	3	3
autism spectrum disorder	1	2

Clinical opportunities
child and family assessment and intervention
school psychology; school interventions
early childhood mental health
medical consultation
neuropsychology
parenting/parent–child interaction
systems consultation

consultation
adult assessment and therapy
crisis intervention
forensic psychology
special education (ld, autism, adhd, mr)
youth and adult correctional facilities
youth and adult inpatient facilities

Yeshiva University (Psy.D.)

(clinical/school)
Ferkauf Graduate School of Psychology
Bronx, NY 10461
phone#: (646) 592-4381
email: abraham.givner@einstein.yu.edu
Web address: http://yu.edu/ferkauf/school-clinical-child-psychology

1	2	3	4	5	6	7
Practice oriented			Equal emphasis			Research oriented

Percentage of faculty subscribing to each of the following orientations:

Psychodynamic/Psychoanalytic	25%
Applied behavioral analysis/Radical behavioral	0%
Family systems/System	0%
Existential/Phenomenological/Humanistic	0%
Cognitive/Cognitive-behavioral	75%

Courses required for incoming students to have completed prior to enrolling:
Statistics, abnormal psychology, child development

Recommended but not mandatory courses: none

GRE mean
Verbal 159 Quantitative 153
Analytical Writing 4.7
Psychology Subject Test not required

GPA mean
Overall GPA 3.61

Number of applications/admission offers/incoming students in 2017
140 applied/42 admission offers/21 incoming

% of students receiving:
Full tuition waiver only: 5%
Assistantship/fellowship only: 60%
Both full tuition waiver & assistantship/fellowship: 0

Approximate percentage of incoming students with a B.A./B.S. only: 80% **Master's:** 20%

Approximate percentage of students who are Women: 85% **Ethnic Minority:** 15% **International:** 5%

Average years to complete the doctoral program (including internship): 5.0 years

Personal interview
Required in person

Attrition rate in past 7 years: 10 students in past 7 years

Percentage of students applying for internship last year accepted into APPIC or APA internships: 100%

Formal tracks/concentrations/specializations: CBT; Psychodynamic

Research areas	# Faculty	# Grants
ADHD	2	0
adolescence	2	0
assessment	2	0
attachment	3	0
behavioral interventions	4	1
early childhood	1	1
fathering	1	0
learning disabilities	2	0
multicultural issues	3	0
nontraditional families	2	0
professional issues	3	0
social-emotional correlates	3	1
symbolic play	1	0

Clinical opportunities
bilingual/multicultural
child/adolescence
early childhood
school consultation
parent training

REPORTS ON CLINICAL PSYCHOLOGY PROGRAMS

Adelphi University (Ph.D.)

Derner Institute of Advanced Psychological Studies
Garden City, NY 11530
phone#: (516) 877-4800
fax#: (516) 877-4805
email: jcmuran@adelphi.edu
Web address: http://derner.adelphi.edu/psychology/doctoral-program/

1	2	3	**4**	5	6	7
Practice oriented			Equal emphasis			Research oriented

Percentage of faculty subscribing to each of the following orientations:

Psychodynamic/Psychoanalytic	70%
Applied behavioral analysis/Radical behavioral	10%
Family systems/Systems	7%
Existential/Phenomenological/Humanistic	7%
Cognitive/Cognitive-behavioral	27%

Courses required for incoming students to have completed prior to enrolling:
General psychology, statistics, experimental methods, developmental, abnormal

Recommended but not mandatory courses: none

GRE mean
Verbal 85% (159.74) Quantitative 51% (153)
Analytical Writing 82% (4.57)
Psychology Subject Test 62% (664)

GPA mean
Overall GPA 3.7 Psychology GPA n/a

Number of applications/admission offers/incoming students in 2017
160 applied/50 admission offers/23 incoming

% of students receiving:
Full tuition waiver only: 0%
Assistantship/fellowship only: 100%
Both full tuition waiver & assistantship/fellowship: 0%

Approximate percentage of incoming students with a B.A./B.S. only: 35% **Master's:** 65%

Approximate percentage of all students who are Women: 77% **Ethnic Minority:** 28% **International:** 8%

Average years to complete the doctoral program (including internship): 6.17

Personal interview
Required in person

Attrition rate in past 7 years: 5.9%

Percentage of students applying for internship in 2017 accepted into:

APA internships: 100% **APPIC internships:** 100%

Formal tracks/concentrations: none

Research areas	# Faculty	# Grants
developmental	4	1
personality	2	2
personal relationships	1	1
couples & group therapy	0	0
suicide risk assessment	1	0
psychoanalysis	5	2
change & psychotherapy process	3	2
therapeutic relationship	3	2
unconscious processes & motivation	1	0
trauma	3	1
cultural competence	1	1
social justice and mental health	1	0
social neuroscience	2	2
addiction	2	1
language development	1	1

Clinical opportunities

psychoanalytic/dynamic psychotherapy	personality assessment
	psychotherapy integration
addiction & eating disorders	short-term psychotherapies
child, adolescent & family therapy	neuropsychological
	couples & group therapy

Adler University (Psy.D.)

17 N. Dearborn
Chicago, IL 60602
phone#: (312) 662-4000
admissions: (312) 662-4100
email: admissions@adler.edu
Web address: http://www.adler.edu/page/areas-of-study/chicago/doctor-of-psychology-in-clinical-psychology/overview

1	2	**3**	4	5	6	7
Practice oriented			Equal emphasis			Research oriented

Percentage of faculty subscribing to each of the following orientations:

Psychodynamic/Psychoanalytic	29%
Applied behavioral analysis/Radical behavioral	0%
Family systems/Systems	12%
Existential/Phenomenological/Humanistic	1%
Cognitive/Cognitive-behavioral	58%

Courses required for incoming students to have completed prior to enrolling:
The equivalent of 18 semester credit hours in psychology with grades of "C" or better, including the following prerequisite courses: general or introductory psychology, abnormal psychology, and research methods or statistics. Equivalent coursework in other social sciences may also be considered.

Recommended but not mandatory courses: none

GRE mean
Verbal 150
Quantitative 146
Analytical Writing 3.9
Psychology Subject Test n/a

GPA mean
Overall GPA 3.32

Number of applications/admission offers/incoming students in 2017–2018:
267 applied/167 admission offers/60 incoming

% of students receiving:
Full tuition waiver only: 0%
Assistantship/fellowship only: 10%
Both full tuition waiver & assistantship/fellowship: 0%

Approximate percentage of incoming students with a BA/BS only: 66% **Master's:** 34%

Approximate percentage of all students who are Women: 83% **Ethnic Minority:** 51% **International:** 8%

Average years to complete the doctoral program (including internship): 5.41 years

Personal interview
Required in person, phone or via skype

Attrition rate in past 7 years: 5.01%

Students applying for internship in 2016-17 accepted into:

APA internships: 88% **APPIC internships:** 11%

Emphases:
Advanced Adlerian Psychotherapy
Child and Adolescent Psychology
Military Clinical Psychology
Primary Care Psychology and Behavioral Medicine
Substance Abuse Treatment
Traumatic Stress Psychology

Research areas	# Faculty	# Grants
adult human development	3	—
community clinical	5	—
primary care	3	—
traumatic stress	5	—
substance abuse	3	—
military psychology	3	—
diversity	7	2
clinical hypnosis in the context of psychotherapy	—	—
clinical supervision and mentorship	—	—
depression	—	—
anxiety	—	—
close relationships	—	—

Clinical opportunities
Doctoral students can complete their clinical training across a range of settings:
Community mental health centers
Hospitals and medical centers
Private clinics
University counseling centers
Correctional facilities
Psychiatric hospitals
Schools
Social service agencies
Residential care facilities
VA medical centers

University of Alabama at Birmingham (Ph.D.)

Department of Psychology
CH 415
1720 2nd Avenue South
Birmingham, AL 35294-1170
phone#: (205) 934-8723
email: ecook@uab.edu
Web address: www.psy.uab.edu/medpsych.htm

1	2	3	**4**	5	6	7
Practice oriented			Equal emphasis			Research oriented

Percentage of faculty subscribing to each of the following orientations:

Psychodynamic/Psychoanalytic	5%
Applied behavioral analysis/Radical behavioral	5%
Family systems/Systems	5%
Existential/Phenomenological/Humanistic	5%
Cognitive/Cognitive-behavioral	80%
Health psychology	50%

Courses required for incoming students to have completed prior to enrolling: We highly recommend at least 24 semester hours of psychology, including abnormal, cognitive/learning, developmental, statistics and research methods.

Recommended but not mandatory courses: at least 12 hours of life sciences including introductory neuroscience and human physiology

GRE mean
Verbal 86th percentile
Quantitative 72nd percentile
Analytical Writing 83rd percentile
Psychology Subject Test not reported

GPA mean
Overall GPA 3.81

Number of applications/admission offers/incoming students in 2017
172 applied/14 admission offers/10 incoming

% of students receiving:
Full tuition waiver only: 0%
Assistantship/fellowship only: 0%
Both full tuition waiver & assistantship/fellowship: 100%

Approximate percentage of incoming students with a B.A./B.S. only: 70% **Master's:** 30%

Approximate percentage of all students who are Women: 84% **Ethnic Minority:** 24% **International:** 2%

Average years to complete the doctoral program (including internship): 6 years

Personal interview
Preferred in person but telephone acceptable

Attrition rate in past 7 years: 2%

Percentage of students applying for internship last year accepted into APPIC or APA internships: 100%

Formal tracks/concentrations: no tracks or concentrations but areas of program emphasis are pediatric psychology; developmental disabilities; child, adolescent and adult mental health; substance abuse; health psychology & pain; neuropsychology & rehabilitation; and geropsychology

Research areas	# Faculty	# Grants
Pediatric psychology	4	7
Child/adolescent mental health	3	1
Neurodevelopmental disabilities	4	8
Adult mental health and substance abuse	4	3
Eating disorders and obesity	4	5
Neuropsychology and rehabilitation	10	7
Geropsychology	4	3

Clinical opportunities
pediatric psychology
child & adolescent mental health
developmental disabilities
adult mental health & substance abuse
eating disorders & obesity
behavioral medicine & pain
neuropsychology
rehabilitation
geropsychology

University of Alabama at Tuscaloosa (Ph.D.)

Department of Psychology
P.O. Box 870348
Tuscaloosa, AL 35487-0348
phone#: (205) 348-1913
email: tabrooksi@as.ua.edu
Web address: psychology.ua.edu/academics/graduate/clinical/clinical.html

1	2	3	4	5	6	7
Practice oriented			Equal emphasis			Research oriented

Percentage of faculty subscribing to each of the following orientations:

Psychodynamic/Psychoanalytic	0%
Applied behavioral analysis/Radical behavioral	10%
Family systems/Systems	10%
Existential/Phenomenological/Humanistic	10%
Cognitive/Cognitive-behavioral	80%

Courses required for incoming students to have completed prior to enrolling:
Undergrad statistics, introduction to psychology, abnormal psychology, research methods/experimental psychology

Recommended but not mandatory courses: none

GRE mean
Verbal 166 Quantitative 154
Analytical Writing 4.5
Psychology Subject Test not reported

GPA mean
Overall GPA 3.6 Psychology GPA 3.8
Junior/Senior GPA 3.7

Number of applications/admission offers/incoming students in 2017
200 applied/14 admission offers/11 incoming

% of students receiving:
Full tuition waiver only: 0%
Assistantship/fellowship only: 0%
Both full tuition waiver & assistantship/fellowship: 98%

Approximate percentage of incoming students with a B.A./B.S. only: 73% **Master's:** 27%

Approximate percentage of students who are Women: 85% **Ethnic Minority:** 17% **International:** 3%

Average years to complete the doctoral program (including internship): 6.25 years

Personal interview
Preferred in person but telephone acceptable

Attrition rate in past 7 years: 11%

Percentage of students applying for internship in 2017 accepted into:

APA internships: 100% **APPIC internships:** 100%

Formal tracks/concentrations: health, child, geropsychology, psychology & law

Research areas	# Faculty	# Grants
adult psychopathology	3	2
affective disorders/depression	1	0
aging	6	5
arthritis	1	2
assessment	2	0
autism	2	2
behavioral medicine	3	2
caregiving	2	2
child clinical	4	4
conduct disorders	2	1
cross-cultural psychology	2	3
diversity in aging	3	3
forensic	3	1
long-term care	3	3
pain management	1	4
professional issues	2	0
psychotherapy process and outcome	3	0
rural mental health	4	2
sleep disorders	2	1
social skills	2	2
violence/abuse	2	2
youth psychopathology	2	1

Clinical opportunities

autism	ADHD
conduct disorder	college student counseling
factitious disorder	family therapy
forensic psychology	state psychiatric hospital
gerontology	youth correctional services
health promotion behavior	state forensic medical center
pain management	
parent–child interaction	PTSD
anxiety	Veterans Medical Center
chronic mental illness	high-risk youth
neuropsychological assessment	elder law
	residential child center
sleep disorders	hospice
rural health	pediatric oncology

University of Alaska, Anchorage-Fairbanks (Ph.D.)

University of Alaska Anchorage
Department of Psychology

3211 Providence Drive, SSB 303
Anchorage, AK 99508
phone#: (907) 786-1640
email: psychphd@uaa.alaska.edu
Web address: https://www.uaa.alaska.edu/academics/college-of-arts-and-sciences/departments/psychology/academic-programs/graduate/phd/index.cshtml
Web address: psyphd.alaska.edu

University of Alaska Fairbanks

Department of Psychology
PO Box 756480
Fairbanks, AK 99775
phone#: (907) 474-7012
Web address: psyphd.alaska.edu

1	2	3	**4**	5	6	7
Practice oriented			Equal emphasis			Research oriented

Percentage of faculty subscribing to each of the following orientations:

Psychodynamic/Psychoanalytic	0%
Applied behavioral analysis/Radical behavioral	0%
Family systems/Systems	0%
Existential/Phenomenological/Humanistic	0%
Cognitive/Cognitive-behavioral	100%

Courses required for incoming students to have completed prior to enrolling:
research methods, abnormal, statistics, and either one of clinical, community, personality, or social

Recommended but not mandatory courses: none

GRE mean
GRE is not required for admission purposes.

GPA mean
Overall GPA 3.81

Number of applications/admission offers/incoming students in 2017
21 applied/5 admission offers/5 incoming

% of students receiving:
Full tuition waiver only: 0%
Assistantship/fellowship only: 0%
Both full tuition waiver & assistantship/fellowship: 47%

Approximate percentage of incoming students with a BA/BS only: 60% **Master's:** 40%

Approximate percentage of all students who are Women: 64% **Ethnic Minority:** 48% **International:** 0%

Average years to complete the doctoral program (including internship): 6 years

Personal interview
In person interview is required.

Attrition rate in past 7 years: 20%

Percentage of students applying for internship in 2017 accepted into:

APA internships: 100% **APPIC internships:** 100%

Formal tracks/concentrations: community psychology

Research areas	**# Faculty**	**# Grants**
Acculturation & wellbeing	1	0
Addictions	1	0
Alcohol misuse & disorders	1	1
Asian American/Pacific Islander psychology	1	0
Comorbid post traumatic stress disorder & substance abuse	1	0
Ethnic minority psychology	2	0
Filipino American psychology	1	0
Health psychology	1	0
Indigenous & postcolonial psychology	1	0
Internalized oppression & mental health	1	—
Motivational processes	1	0
Older adult mental health	1	0
Psychiatric comorbidity	2	0
Risk & resilience among marginalized populations	—	—
Refugee/immigrant health & wellbeing	1	1
Suicidality	1	1
Technology based interventions for substance abuse	2	0

Clinical opportunities
inpatient psychiatric
outpatient substance abuse
adolescent residential
community outpatient clinic
university clinic

University at Albany/State University of New York (Ph.D.)

Department of Psychology
1400 Washington Avenue
Albany, NY 12222
phone#: (518) 442-4820
email: mearleywine@albany.edu
Web address: www.albany.edu/psy/grad_studies.shtml

1	2	3	4	5	**6**	7
Practice oriented			Equal emphasis			Research oriented

Percentage of faculty subscribing to each of the following orientations:

Psychodynamic/Psychoanalytic	0%
Applied behavioral analysis/Radical behavioral	9%
Family systems/Systems	0%
Existential/Phenomenological/Humanistic	0%
Cognitive/Cognitive-behavioral	91%

Courses required for incoming students to have completed prior to enrolling:
18 semester hours in psychology, including classes in statistics and experimental design

Recommended but not mandatory courses: none

GRE mean
Verbal 160 Quantitative 159
Analytical Writing 5
Psychology Subject Test 698

GPA mean
Overall GPA 3.66 Psychology GPA 3.78

Number of applications/admission offers/incoming students in 2017
122 applied/7 admission offers/7 incoming

Financial Assistance: 100%

Approximate percentage of students who are
Women: 85% **Ethnic Minority:** 15% **International:** 3%

Average years to complete the doctoral program (including internship): 6.08 years

Personal interview
Preferred in person, but telephone acceptable

Attrition rate in past 7 years: 7%

Percentage of students applying for internship last year accepted into accepted into APA internships: 100%

Research areas	# Faculty	# Grants
autism/developmental disabilities	1	
behavioral medicine	2	
children & families	4	
eating disorders	1	
emotion regulation/dysregulation	7	
mindfulness-based interventions	3	
minority mental health issues	1	
psychopathology	1	
substance abuse/addiction	2	

Clinical opportunities
acceptance & commitment therapy
addictive disorders
adolescents
anxiety disorders
autism/developmental disabilities
behavioral medicine/health psychology
children & families
cross-cultural issues
eating disorders

Alliant International University—Fresno (Ph.D.)

5130 East Clinton Way
Fresno, CA 93727
phone#: (866) 825-5426
email: admissions@alliant.edu
Web address: www.alliant.edu/cspp

1	2	3	4	5	6	7
Practice oriented			Equal emphasis			Research oriented

Percentage of faculty subscribing to each of the following orientations:

Psychodynamic/Psychoanalytic	25%
Applied behavioral analysis/Radical behavioral	0%
Family systems/Systems	25%
Existential/Phenomenological/Humanistic	25%
Cognitive/Cognitive-behavioral	25%

Courses required for incoming students to have completed prior to enrolling:
If no BA/BS in psychology or score is below the 80th percentile on the GRE Psychology Subject Test, then the following courses are required with a grade of "C" or better:

- Statistics
- Abnormal Psychology or Psychopathology
- Experimental Psychology/Research Methods in Psychology
- Physiological Psychology, Learning/Memory, Cognitive Psychology or Sensation/Perception

Recommended but not mandatory courses: Refer to above.

GRE mean
Verbal not reported Quantitative not used in admissions
Analytical Writing not used in admissions
Psychology Subject Test not reported
(not used in admissions process)

GPA mean for incoming students 2016
Overall GPA 3.10

Number of applications/admission offers/incoming students in 2016
30 applied/14 admission offers/8 incoming

% of students receiving:
Full tuition waiver only: 0%
Assistantship/fellowship only: 0%
Both full tuition waiver & assistantship/fellowship: 0%

Approximate percentage of incoming students with a BA/BS only: 63% **Master's:** 37%

Approximate percentage of all students who are
Women: 70% **Ethnic Minority:** 52% **International:** 5%

Average years to complete the doctoral program (including internship): 5.2 years

Personal interview
Preferred in person but telephone or Skype available (only if necessary)

Attrition rate in past 7 years: 24%

Percentage of students applying for internship in 2015-16 accepted into:

APA internships: 100% **APPIC internships:** 0%
CAPIC internships: 0%

Formal tracks/concentrations: forensic psychology, ecosystemic child, and health psychology

Research areas	# Faculty	# Grants
family/child	1	0
psychotherapy delivery/theory	2	0
multicultural/international	1	0

Clinical opportunities
Clinical practica include our own training clinic, community mental health centers, Veterans hospitals, inpatient mental health facilities, medical settings, rehabilitation programs, residential and day care programs, forensic/correctional facilities, and education programs.

Alliant International University—Fresno (Psy.D.)

5130 East Clinton Way
Fresno, CA 93727

phone#: (866) 825-5426
email: admissions@alliant.edu
Web address: www.alliant.edu/cspp

1	**2**	3	4	5	6	7
Practice oriented			Equal emphasis			Research oriented

Percentage of faculty subscribing to each of the following orientations:

Psychodynamic/Psychoanalytic	33%
Applied behavioral analysis/Radical behavioral	0%
Family systems/Systems	11%
Existential/Phenomenological/Humanistic	11%
Cognitive/Cognitive-behavioral	44%

Courses required for incoming students to have completed prior to enrolling:
If no BA/BS in psychology or score is below the 80th percentile on the GRE Psychology Subject Test, then the following courses are required with a grade of "C" or better:

- Statistics
- Abnormal Psychology or Psychopathology
- Experimental Psychology/Research Methods in Psychology
- Physiological Psychology, Learning/Memory, Cognitive Psychology or Sensation/Perception

Recommended but not mandatory courses:
Refer to above.

GRE mean
GRE scores are not used in the admissions process.

GPA mean for 2016 incoming students
Overall GPA 3.41

Number of applications/admission offers/incoming students in 2016
43 applied/20 admission offers/14 incoming

% of students receiving:
Full tuition waiver only: 0%
Assistantship/fellowship only: 5%
Both full tuition waiver & assistantship/fellowship: 0%

Approximate percentage of incoming students with a BA/BS only: 86% **Master's:** 14%

Approximate percentage of students who are Women: 77% **Ethnic Minority:** 47% **International:** 5%

Average years to complete the doctoral program (including internship): 4.5 years

Personal interview
Preferred in person but telephone or Skype available (only if necessary)

Attrition rate in past 7 years: 25%

Percentage of students applying for internship in 2015–2016 accepted into:

APA internships: 69% **APPIC internships:** 23%
CAPIC internships: 8%

Formal tracks/concentrations: clinical forensic psychology and ecosystemic child

Research areas	# Faculty	# Grants
psychotherapy	1	0
multicultural/international	2	1
health behaviors	2	0
substance abuse	1	0
trauma/PTSD	1	0
gender/psychology of women	1	0
assessment	3	1

Clinical opportunities
Clinical practica include our own training clinic, community mental health centers, medical settings, rehabilitation programs, residential treatment centers, forensic/correctional facilities, university/college health centers, and child/adolescent treatment programs.

Alliant International University—Los Angeles (Ph.D.)

1000 S Fremont Avenue, Unit 5
Alhambra, CA 91803
phone#: (866) 825-5426
email: admissions@alliant.edu
Web address: www.alliant.edu/cspp

1	2	3	**4**	5	6	7
Practice oriented			Equal emphasis			Research oriented

Percentage of faculty subscribing to each of the following orientations:

Psychodynamic/Psychoanalytic	0%
Applied behavioral analysis/Radical behavioral	11%
Family systems/Systems	22%
Existential/Phenomenological/Humanistic	11%
Cognitive/Cognitive-behavioral	67%

Courses required for incoming students to have completed prior to enrolling:
If no BA/BS in psychology or score is below the 80th percentile on the GRE Psychology Subject Test, then the following courses are required with a grade of "C" or better:

- Statistics
- Abnormal Psychology or Psychopathology
- Experimental Psychology/Research Methods in Psychology
- Physiological Psychology, Learning/Memory, Cognitive Psychology or Sensation/Perception

Recommended but not mandatory courses: Refer to above

GRE mean
Verbal not used in admissions
Quantitative not used in admissions
Analytical Writing not used in admissions
Psychology Subject Test not reported
GRE scores are not used as part of the standard admissions process.

GPA mean for 2016 incoming students
Overall GPA 3.30

Number of applications/admission offers/incoming students in 2016
63 applied/32 admission offers/17 incoming

% of students receiving:
Full tuition waiver only: 0%
Assistantship/fellowship only: 5%
Both full tuition waiver & assistantship/fellowship: 0%

Approximate percentage of incoming students with a BA/BS only: 59% **Master's:** 41%

Approximate percentage of all students who are Women: 80% **Ethnic Minority:** 53% **International:** 5%

Average years to complete the doctoral program (including internship): 5.9 years

Personal interview
Preferred in person but telephone or Skype available (only if necessary)

Attrition rate in past 7 years: 11%

Percentage of students applying for internship in 2015–2016 accepted into:

APA internships: 76% **APPIC internships:** 0%
CAPIC internships: 24%

Formal tracks/concentrations: no tracks but emphases in health psychology, family & couple psychology, and multicultural community-clinical psychology

Research areas	# Faculty	# Grants
child/adolescent/pediatric psychology	1	1
psychotherapy delivery/theory	1	0
multicultural/immigrants	7	0
health behaviors/medical interventions	7	1
substance abuse	3	0
trauma/PTSD	2	0
advocacy/social policy	3	0
gender/psychology of women	3	0
community interventions/prevention	3	0
personality/personality disorders	1	0

Clinical opportunities
Practica include community mental health centers, clinics, inpatient mental health facilities, medical settings, specialized service centers, rehabilitation programs, residential programs, forensic/correctional facilities, and education programs.

Alliant International University—Los Angeles (Psy.D.)

1000 S Fremont Avenue, Unit 5
Alhambra, CA 91803
phone#: (866) 825-5426
email: admissions@alliant.edu
Web address: www.alliant.edu/cspp

1	2	3	4	5	6	7
Practice oriented			Equal emphasis			Research oriented

Percentage of faculty subscribing to each of the following orientations:

Biopsychosocial	31%
Psychodynamic/Psychoanalytic	23%
Applied behavioral analysis/Radical behavioral	7%
Family systems/Systems	15%
Existential/Phenomenological/Humanistic	31%
Cognitive/Cognitive-behavioral	66%
Integrative	46%

Courses required for incoming students to have completed prior to enrolling:
If no BA/BS in psychology or score is below the 80th percentile on the GRE Psychology Subject Test, then the following courses are required with a grade of "C" or better:
- Statistics
- Abnormal Psychology or Psychopathology
- Experimental Psychology/Research Methods in Psychology
- Physiological Psychology, Learning/Memory, Cognitive Psychology or Sensation/Perception

Recommended but not mandatory courses: Refer to above.

GRE mean
Verbal not used in admissions
Quantitative not used in admissions
Analytical Writing not used in admissions
Psychology Subject Test not reported
GRE scores are not used as part of the standard admissions process.

GPA mean for 2016 incoming students
Overall GPA: 3.34

Number of applications/admission offers/incoming students in 2016
189 applied/85 admission offers/43 incoming

% of students receiving:
Full tuition waiver only: 0%
Assistantship/fellowship only: 0%
Both full tuition waiver & assistantship/fellowship: 0%

Approximate percentage of incoming students with a BA/BS only: 72% **Master's:** 28%

Approximate percentage of students who are Women: 78% **Ethnic Minority:** 43% **International:** 4%

Average years to complete the doctoral program (including internship): 4.3 years

Personal interview
Preferred in person but telephone or Skype available (only if necessary)

Attrition rate in past 7 years: 11%

Percentage of students applying for internship in 2015-16 accepted into:

APA internships: 63% **APPIC internships:** 5%
CAPIC internships: 27%

Formal tracks/concentrations:
No tracks but emphases in health psychology; family & couple psychology; multicultural community-psychology.

Research areas	# Faculty	# Grants
family/child/adolescent	4	0
psychotherapy services/theory	10	0
multicultural/international	4	0
neuropsychology	2	0
health behaviors/medical interventions	5	0

trauma/PTSD	4	0
personality/personality disorders	2	0
assessment	3	0
LGBT	2	0
professional & training issues	3	0
positive psychology/resilience	2	0

Clinical opportunities
The settings where students complete their clinical practica include community mental health centers, clinics, inpatient mental health facilities, medical settings, specialized service centers, rehabilitation programs, residential or day care programs, forensic/correctional facilities, and education programs. Students are required to train in a different setting each year and gain experience in inpatient and outpatient settings, as well as with child and adult populations.

Alliant International University—Sacramento (Psy.D.)

2030 W El Camino Ave, Suite 200
Sacramento, CA 95833
phone#: (866) 825-5426
email: admissions@alliant.edu
Web address: www.alliant.edu/cspp

1	2	3	4	5	6	7
Practice oriented			Equal emphasis			Research oriented

Percentage of faculty subscribing to each of the following orientations:

Psychodynamic/Psychoanalytic	33%
Behavioral	17%
Family systems/Systems	0%
Existential/Phenomenological/Humanistic	50%
Cognitive/Cognitive-behavioral	50%

Courses required for incoming students to have completed prior to enrolling:
If no BA/BS in psychology or score is below the 80th percentile on the GRE Psychology Subject Test, then the following courses are required with a grade of "C" or better:
- Statistics
- Abnormal Psychology or Psychopathology
- Experimental Psychology/Research Methods in Psychology
- Physiological Psychology, Learning/Memory, Cognitive Psychology or Sensation/Perception

Recommended but not mandatory courses: Refer to above.

GRE mean
GRE scores are not used in the admissions process.

GPA mean for 2016 incoming students
Overall GPA 3.38

Number of applications/admission offers/incoming students in 2016
67 applied/31 admission offers/23 incoming

% of students receiving:
Full tuition waiver only: 0%
Assistantship/fellowship only: 0%
Both full tuition waiver & assistantship/fellowship: 0%

Approximate percentage of incoming students with a BA/BS only: 65% **Master's:** 35%

Approximate percentage of students who are Women: 90% **Ethnic Minority:** 38% **International:** 2%

Average years to complete the doctoral program (including internship): 5.0 years

Personal interview
Preferred in person but telephone or Skype available (only if necessary)

Attrition rate in past 7 years: 17%

Percentage of students applying for internship in 2015–2016 accepted into:

APA internships: 75% **APPIC internships:** 13%
CAPIC internships: 13%

Formal tracks/concentrations: Corrections

Research areas	# Faculty	# Grants
family/child development	1	0
multicultural/international	1	0
assessment/neuropsychology	1	0
health behaviors/psychology	1	0
professional & training issues	1	0
forensic/correction	2	0
organizational psychology	1	0

Clinical opportunities
Clinical practica in a variety of settings, including community mental health centers, inpatient mental health facilities, medical settings, rehabilitation programs, residential and day treatment programs, forensic/correctional facilities, and education programs.

Alliant International University—San Diego (Ph.D.)

10455 Pomerado Road
San Diego, CA 92131
phone#: (866) 825-5426
email: admissions@alliant.edu
Web address: www.alliant.edu/cspp

1	2	3	4	5	6	7
Practice oriented			Equal emphasis			Research oriented

Percentage of faculty subscribing to each of the following orientations:

Psychodynamic/Psychoanalytic	13%
Applied behavioral analysis/Radical behavioral	0%
Family systems/Systems	13%
Existential/Phenomenological/Humanistic	0%
Cognitive/Cognitive-behavioral	61%
Eclectic/Integrative	13%

Courses required for incoming students to have completed prior to enrolling:
If no BA/BS in psychology or score is below the 80th percentile on the GRE Psychology Subject Test, then the following courses are required with a grade of "C" or better:
- Statistics
- Abnormal Psychology or Psychopathology

- Experimental Psychology/Research Methods in Psychology
- Physiological Psychology, Learning/Memory, Cognitive Psychology or Sensation/Perception

Recommended but not mandatory courses: Refer to above.

GRE mean
Verbal not used in admissions
Quantitative not used in admissions
Analytical Writing not used in admissions
Psychology Subject Test not reported
(not used in admissions process)

GPA mean for 2016 incoming students
Overall GPA 3.41

Number of applications/admission offers/incoming students in 2016
83 applied/39 admission offers/16 incoming

% of students receiving:
Full tuition waiver only: 0%
Assistantship/fellowship only: 0%
Both full tuition waiver & assistantship/fellowship: 0%

Approximate percentage of incoming students with a BA/BS only: 75% **Master's:** 25%

Approximate percentage of all students who are Women: 74% **Ethnic Minority:** 38% **International:** 3%

Average years to complete the doctoral program (including internship): 7.1 years

Personal interview
Preferred in person but telephone or Skype available (only if necessary)

Attrition rate in past 7 years: 21%

Percentage of students applying for internship in 2015-16 accepted into:

APA internships: 62% **APPIC internships:** 5%
CAPIC internships: 27%

Formal tracks/concentrations: no tracks but emphases in family & child psychology, forensic psychology, health psychology, and psychodynamic

Research areas	# Faculty	# Grants
family/child/adolescent	4	1
psychotherapy delivery/theory	5	0
multicultural/international	2	0
neuropsychology	2	1
health behaviors/medical interventions	4	0
trauma/PTSD/stress	2	0
gender/psychology of women/male roles	2	0
personality/personality disorders	8	1
assessment	4	0
professional & training issues	2	0

Clinical opportunities
Clinical practica in a variety of settings, including community mental health centers, inpatient mental health facilities, medical settings, rehabilitation programs, residential and day treatment programs, forensic/correctional facilities, and education programs.

Alliant International University—San Diego (Psy.D.)

10455 Pomerado Road
San Diego, CA 92131
phone#: (866) 825-5426
email: admissions@alliant.edu
Web address: www.alliant.edu/cspp

1	2	3	4	5	6	7
Practice oriented			Equal emphasis			Research oriented

Percentage of faculty subscribing to each of the following orientations:

Psychodynamic/Psychoanalytic	30%
Applied behavioral analysis/Radical behavioral	0%
Family systems/Systems	20%
Existential/Phenomenological/Humanistic	20%
Cognitive/Cognitive-behavioral	40%

Courses required for incoming students to have completed prior to enrolling:
If no BA/BS in psychology or score is below the 80th percentile on the GRE Psychology Subject Test, then the following courses are required with a grade of "C" or better:
- Statistics
- Abnormal Psychology or Psychopathology
- Experimental Psychology/Research Methods in Psychology
- Physiological Psychology, Learning/Memory, Cognitive Psychology or Sensation/Perception

Recommended but not mandatory courses: Refer to above.

GRE mean
Verbal not used in admissions
Quantitative not used in admissions
Analytical Writing not used in admissions
Psychology Subject Test not reported
(not used in admissions process)

GPA mean for 2016 incoming class
Overall GPA: 3.22

Number of applications/admission offers/incoming students in 2016
160 applied/79 admission offers/43 incoming

% of students receiving:
Full tuition waiver only: 0%
Assistantship/fellowship only: 0%
Both full tuition waiver & assistantship/fellowship: 0%

Approximate percentage of incoming students with a BA/BS only: 81% **Master's:** 19%

Approximate percentage of all students who are Women: 81% **Ethnic Minority:** 40% **International:** 2%

Average years to complete the doctoral program (including internship): 5.9 years

Personal interview
Preferred in person but telephone or Skype available (only if necessary)

Attrition rate in past 7 years: 16%

Percentage of students applying for internship in 2015–2016 accepted into:

APA internships: 42% **APPIC internships:** 12%
CAPIC internships: 40%

Formal tracks/concentrations: no tracks but emphasis areas in family & child psychology, forensic psychology, health psychology, integrative psychology, multicultural & international, and psychodyamic

Research areas	# Faculty	# Grants
family/couples/child/adolescent	7	1
intervention/therapy/theory	10	0
multicultural/international	5	0
reproductive psychology	1	0
chemical dependency	2	0
trauma/PTSD/stress	2	0
gender/psychology of women	3	0
assessment	2	0
LGBT	1	0
self-injury/suicide	2	0
professional & training issues	2	0

Clinical opportunities
Clinical practica in a variety of settings, including community mental health centers, inpatient mental health facilities, medical settings, rehabilitation programs, residential and day treatment programs, forensic/correctional facilities, and education programs.

Alliant International University—San Francisco (Ph.D.)

One Beach Street, Suite 100
San Francisco, CA 94133
phone#: (866) 825-5426
email: admissions@alliant.edu
Web address: www.alliant.edu/cspp

1	2	3	4	5	6	7
Practice oriented			Equal emphasis			Research oriented

Percentage of faculty subscribing to each of the following orientations:

Psychodynamic/Psychoanalytic	40%
Applied behavioral analysis/Radical behavioral	0%
Family systems/Systems	40%
Existential/Phenomenological/Humanistic	20%
Cognitive/Cognitive-behavioral	80%

Courses required for incoming students to have completed prior to enrolling:
If no BA/BS in psychology or score is below the 80th percentile on the GRE Psychology Subject Test, then the following courses are required with a grade of "C" or better:

- Statistics
- Abnormal Psychology or Psychopathology
- Experimental Psychology/Research Methods in Psychology
- Physiological Psychology, Learning/Memory, Cognitive Psychology or Sensation/Perception

Recommended but not mandatory courses: Refer to above.

GRE mean
Verbal not used in admissions
Quantitative not used in admissions
Analytical Writing not used in admissions
Psychology Subject Test not reported
(not used in admissions process)

GPA mean for 2016 incoming class
Overall GPA: 3.39

Number of applications/admission offers/incoming students in 2016
41 applied/29 admission offers/13 incoming

% of students receiving:
Full tuition waiver only: 0%
Assistantship/fellowship only: 0%
Both full tuition waiver & assistantship/fellowship: 0%

Approximate percentage of incoming students with a BA/BS only: 85% **Master's:** 15%

Approximate percentage of all students who are Women: 73% **Ethnic Minority:** 39% **International:** 2%

Average years to complete the doctoral program (including internship): 6.5 years

Personal interview
Preferred in person but telephone or Skype available (only if necessary)

Attrition rate in past 7 years: 22%

Percentage of students applying for internship in 2015-16 accepted into:

APA internships: 88% **APPIC internships:** 6%
CAPIC internships: 0%

Formal tracks/concentrations: none

Research areas	# Faculty	# Grants
family/couples/child/adolescent	3	0
psychotherapy delivery/theory	3	0
multicultural/international	7	1
health behaviors/medical interventions/ neuropsychology	3	0
substance abuse	2	0
trauma/PTSD/stress/coping	2	0
gender/psychology of women/male roles	3	0
community interventions/prevention	4	0
assessment	1	0
LGBT	2	0
professional & training issues	3	1
violence/forensics	2	0

Clinical opportunities
Clinical practica in a variety of settings, including community mental health centers, inpatient mental health facilities, medical settings, specialized service centers, rehabilitation programs, residential and day treatment programs, forensic/correctional facilities, research programs, and education programs.

Alliant International University—San Francisco (Psy.D.)

One Beach Street, Suite 100
San Francisco, CA 94133
phone#: (866) 825-5426
email: admissions@alliant.edu
Web address: www.alliant.edu/cspp

1	2	3	4	5	6	7
Practice oriented			Equal emphasis			Research oriented

Percentage of faculty subscribing to each of the following orientations:

Psychodynamic/Psychoanalytic	50%
Applied behavioral analysis/Radical behavioral	0%
Family systems/Systems	29%
Existential/Phenomenological/Humanistic	7%
Cognitive/Cognitive-behavioral	71%

Courses required for incoming students to have completed prior to enrolling:
If no BA/BS in psychology or score is below the 80th percentile on the GRE Psychology Subject Test, then the following courses are required with a grade of "C" or better:

- Statistics
- Abnormal Psychology or Psychopathology
- Experimental Psychology/Research Methods in Psychology
- Physiological Psychology, Learning/Memory, Cognitive Psychology or Sensation/Perception

Recommended but not mandatory courses: Refer to above.

GRE mean
Verbal not used in admissions
Quantitative not used in admissions
Analytical Writing not used in admissions
Psychology Subject Test not reported
GRE scores are not used as part of the standard admissions process.

GPA mean for 2016 incoming class
Overall GPA: 3.26

Number of applications/admission offers/incoming students in 2016
102 applied/61 admission offers/30 incoming

% of students receiving:
Full tuition waiver only: 0%
Assistantship/fellowship only: 0%
Both full tuition waiver & assistantship/fellowship: 0%

Approximate percentage of incoming students with a BA/BS only: 77% **Master's:** 23%

Approximate percentage of students who are Women: 77% **Ethnic Minority:** 41% **International:** 8%

Average years to complete the doctoral program (including internship): 5.4 years

Personal interview
Preferred in person but telephone or Skype available (only if necessary)

Attrition rate in past 7 years: 14%

Percentage of students applying for internship in 2015–2016 accepted into:

APA internships: 52% **APPIC internships:** 17%
CAPIC internships: 31%

Formal tracks/concentrations: Child & Family Psychology, Integrate Health, and Social Justice Psychology

Research areas	# Faculty	# Grants
family/child/adolescent	9	0
psychotherapy delivery/theory	14	0
multicultural/international/immigrants	10	0
neuropsychology	1	0
health behaviors/medical interventions	4	0
substance abuse/addictions	3	0
trauma/PTSD	3	0
gender/psychology of women	2	0
community interventions/prevention	5	0
personality/personality disorders	4	0
assessment	3	0
LGBT	1	0
professional & training issues	3	0
forensics	3	0
disability	3	1

Clinical opportunities
Clinical practica in a variety of settings, including community mental health centers, adult outpatient services, hospitals, neuropsychiatric institutes, infant-parent programs, child and adolescent guidance clinics, college counseling centers, family service agencies, residential treatment centers, forensic settings, pediatric psychology programs, school-based settings, and substance abuse treatment centers.

American University (Ph.D.)

Department of Psychology
Washington, DC 20016
phone#: (202) 885-1710
email: gunthert@american.edu
Web address: www.american.edu/cas/psychology/clinical.cfm

1	2	3	4	5	6	7
Practice oriented			Equal emphasis			Research oriented

Percentage of faculty subscribing to each of the following orientations:

Psychodynamic/Psychoanalytic	0%
Applied behavioral analysis/Radical behavioral	0%
Family systems/Systems	0%
Existential/Phenomenological/Humanistic	0%
Cognitive/Cognitive-behavioral	100%

Courses required for incoming students to have completed prior to enrolling: none

Recommended but not mandatory courses: psychology major, including research methods, statistics

GRE mean
Verbal 161 Quantitative 156
Analytical Writing 4.75

Psychology Subject Test 620

GPA mean
Overall GPA 3.65

Number of applications/admission offers/incoming students in 2017
281 applied/10 admission offers/5 incoming

% of students receiving:
Full tuition waiver only: 0%
Assistantship/fellowship only: 0%
Both full tuition waiver & assistantship/fellowship: 100%

Approximate percentage of incoming students with a B.A./B.S. only: 67% **Master's:** 33%

Approximate percentage of all students who are Women: 92% **Ethnic Minority:** 22% **International:** 0%

Average years to complete the doctoral program (including internship): 6 years

Personal interview
Required in person

Attrition rate in past 7 years: 0%

Percentage of students applying for internship last year accepted into

APA internships: 75% **APPIC internships:** 75%

Formal tracks/concentrations: none

Research areas	# Faculty	# Grants
anxiety	3	0
caffeine	1	0
child	1	0
depression	1	0
eating disorders	1	0
gratitude	1	0
human services program evaluation	1	0
mindfulness	1	0
minority mental health	1	0
obsessive compulsive disorder	1	0
personality disorders/DBT	1	0
smoking	2	1
spirituality	1	1
sports psychology	1	0
stress	1	0
treatment outcomes	1	0
trichotillomania	1	1

Clinical opportunities
cognitive-behavior therapy
dialectical behavior therapy
externships – VAs, hospitals, private practice, schools, etc.
neuropsychological testing
person-centered therapy
psychodynamic therapy
psychological testing

American School of Professional Psychology (Psy.D.)

Argosy University–San Francisco Bay Area
1005 Atlantic Avenue
Alameda, CA 94501
phone#: (510) 217-4871
email: ashilling@argosy.edu
Web address: www.asppsanfrancisco.com

1	2	3	4	5	6	7
Practice oriented			Equal emphasis			Research oriented

Percentage of faculty subscribing to each of the following orientations:

Psychodynamic/Psychoanalytic	30%
Applied behavioral analysis/Radical behavioral	0%
Family systems/Systems	20%
Existential/Phenomenological/Humanistic	20%
Cognitive/Cognitive-behavioral	20%
Neuroscience	10%

Courses required for incoming students to have completed prior to enrolling:
Introduction to Psychology/General Psychology (waived for Psychology majors); Statistics and Research Methods; Abnormal Psychology/Psychopathology; and two additional courses in Psychology.

Recommended but not mandatory courses:
Psychology major or related field.

GRE mean
Verbal + Quantitative n/a optional
Analytical Writing n/a optional
Psychology Subject Test n/a optional

GPA mean
3.26 Undergrad GPA, 3.70 Grad GPA

Number of applications/admission offers/incoming students in 2016
49 applied/29 admission offers/11 incoming

% of students receiving:
Full tuition waiver only: 0%
Assistantship/fellowship only: 0%
Both full tuition waiver & assistantship/fellowship: 0%
Scholarships: 20%

Approximate percentage of incoming students with a B.A./B.S. only: 56% **Master's:** 44%

Approximate percentage of all students who are Women: 82% **Ethnic Minority:** 63% **International:** 2%

Average years to complete the doctoral program (including internship): 5.58 years

Personal interview:
Required

Attrition rate in past 7 years: 26.5%

Percentage of students applying for internship last year accepted into:

APA internships: 88% **APPIC internships:** 12%

Formal tracks/concentrations: n/a

Research areas
See website or contact program for more information.

Clinical opportunities
Two on-campus clinics (psychotherapy, assessment, one-way mirror training). Local hospital affiliated practicum program. Access to a wide network of other local BAPIC (www.bapic.info) practicum agencies. Local and national APA and APPIC internships.

Antioch University New England (Psy.D.)

Department of Clinical Psychology
40 Avon Street
Keene, NH 03431
phone#: (603) 283-2191
email: gtremblay@antioch.edu
Web address: https://www.antioch.edu/new-england/degrees-programs/psychology-degree/clinical-psychology-psyd/

1	2	**3**	4	5	6	7
Practice oriented			Equal emphasis			Research oriented

Percentage of faculty subscribing to each of the following orientations:

Psychodynamic/Psychoanalytic	30%
Applied behavioral analysis/Radical behavioral	10%
Family systems/Systems	30%
Existential/Phenomenological/Humanistic	10%
Cognitive/Cognitive-behavioral	30%
Integrative	20%

Courses required for incoming students to have completed prior to enrolling:
Undergraduate or graduate degree in psychology is preferred, at a minimum at least 15 credits of relevant coursework is required.

Recommended but not mandatory courses: none

GRE mean
Verbal 155 Quantitative 151
Analytical Writing not reported
Psychology Subject Test not reported

GPA mean
Overall GPA 3.6

Number of applications/admission offers/incoming students
87 applied/55 admission offers/20 incoming

% of students receiving:
Full tuition waiver only: 0%
Assistantship/fellowship only: 25% (small stipends)
Both full tuition waiver & assistantship/fellowship: 0%

Approximate percentage of incoming students with a B.A./B.S. only: 80% **Master's:** 20%

Approximate percentage of students who are Women: 86% **Ethnic Minority:** 11% **International:** 4%

Average years to complete the doctoral program (including internship): 6.5 years

Personal interview
Required in person

Attrition rate in past 7 years: 8%

Percentage of students applying for internship last year accepted into APPIC or APA internships: 94%

Formal tracks/concentrations: Major Area of Study in Behavioral Health Integration and Population Health, concentrations in child clinical, adult psychotherapy, and heath psychology

Research areas	# Faculty	#Grants
community services	2	4
children	4	3
Behavioral Health Integration	3	4
graduate training	3	1
group	1	0
multicultural psychology	2	0
outcome evaluation	2	0
women's issues	2	0

Clinical opportunities

assessment	group therapy
child clinical psychology	integrated primary care
cognitive/behavioral therapy	neuropsychology/rehabilitation
community services	rural psychology
conduct disorders	school based services
correctional settings	substance abuse
counseling center	supervision
family therapy	women's health
forensic	
GLBTQ	

Argosy University, Atlanta (Psy.D.)

Georgia School of Professional Psychology
980 Hammond Drive, Suite 100
Atlanta, GA 30328
phone#: (770) 671-1200 or (888) 671-4777
email: tcbrown@argosy.edu
Web address: www.gsppatlanta.com

1	**2**	3	4	5	6	7
Practice oriented			Equal emphasis			Research oriented

Percentage of faculty subscribing to each of the following orientations:

Psychodynamic/Psychoanalytic	11%
Applied behavioral analysis/Radical behavioral	0%
Family systems/Systems	22%
Existential/Phenomenological/Humanistic	22%
Cognitive/Cognitive-behavioral	33%
Integrative	44%

Courses required for incoming students to have completed prior to enrolling:
Introductory/General Psychology, Abnormal Psychology, Statistics/Research Methods

Recommended but not mandatory courses: none

GRE mean
GRE not required

GPA mean
Overall GPA 3.34
Psychology GPA not calculated for admission
Junior/Senior GPA not calculated for admission

Number of applications/admission offers/incoming students in 2017–2018
107 applied/45 admission offers/19 incoming

% of students receiving:
Full tuition waiver only: 0%
Assistantship/fellowship only: 10%
Both full tuition waiver & assistantship/fellowship: 0%

Partial tuition waiver only: 30%
Both partial tuition waiver & assistantship/fellowship: 10%

Approximate percentage of incoming students with a B.A./B.S. only: 53% **Master's:** 47%

Approximate percentage of all students who are Women: 83% **Ethnic Minority:** 43% **International:** 1%

Average years to complete the doctoral program (including internship): 6.1 years

Personal interview
Required in-person

Attrition rate in past 7 years: 16%

Percentage of students applying for internship last year accepted into APPIC or APA internships: 100%

Formal tracks/concentrations: General Adult Clinical, Child & Family Psychology, Health Psychology, Neuropsychology

Research areas	# Faculty	# Grants
Neuropsychology	2	0
Psychotherapy process research	1	0
Pediatric psychology	1	0
Trauma/trauma treatment	3	0
Multicultural issues	2	0
Forensic psychology	1	0
Disability/ADA	1	0

Clinical opportunities
Inpatient and outpatient clinical services
Child, adolescent, and adult clinical services
Psychological testing
Individual and group psychotherapy
Pediatric psychology
Trauma/PTSD treatment
Child abuse/maltreatment
Neuropsychology/rehabilitation
Forensic psychology
Eating disorders
College/university counseling centers
School/educational testing

Argosy University, Chicago (Psy.D.)

Illinois School of Professional Psychology
225 N. Michigan, Suite 1300
Chicago, IL 60601
phone#: (312) 777-7612
email: tspears@argosy.edu
Web address: www.isppchicago.com

1	2	3	4	5	6	7
Practice oriented			Equal emphasis			Research oriented

Percentage of faculty subscribing to each of the following orientations:

Psychodynamic/Psychoanalytic	30%
Applied behavioral analysis/Radical behavioral	0%
Family systems/Systems	5%
Existential/Phenomenological/Humanistic	30%
Cognitive/Cognitive-behavioral	35%

Courses required for incoming students to have completed prior to enrolling:
Intro to psychology; Abnormal Psychology; Statistics or Research Methods; two additional psychology courses

Recommended but not mandatory courses: Personality Theory; Tests and Measures

GRE mean
Verbal not reported
Quantitative not reported
Analytical Writing not reported
Psychology Subject Test not reported

GPA mean
Overall GPA 3.4

Number of applications/admission offers/incoming students in 2016
178 applied/67 admission offers/41 incoming

% of students receiving:
Full tuition waiver only: 0%
Assistantship/fellowship only: 20%
Both full tuition waiver & assistantship/fellowship: 0%

Approximate percentage of incoming students with a B.A./B.S. only: 61% **Master's:** 39%

Approximate percentage of all students who are Women: 68% **Ethnic Minority:** 33% **International:** 9%

Average years to complete the doctoral program (including internship): 5.7 years

Personal interview
Required in person
Preferred in person but telephone acceptable (international students only)

Attrition rate in past 7 years: 19%

Percentage of students applying for internship last year accepted into:

APA internships: 50% **APPIC internships:** 50%

Formal tracks/concentrations: child/adolescent psychology, client-centered/experiential psychotherapies, diversity/multicultural psychology, forensic psychology, psychoanalytic psychology, neuropsychology

Research areas	# Faculty	# Grants
adolescence and delinquency	2	0
behavioral medicine	1	1
diverse students' needs	3	1
eating disorders	1	0
gay men adult development	2	0
international psychology	2	0
parenting	1	0
person-centered interventions	1	0
personality disorders	1	0
substance abuse	1	0
therapist development	2	1
severe mental illness	1	0
disaster/trauma	2	0
women's career choices	1	0

Clinical opportunities

behavioral medicine
child and adolescent psychology
chronic mental illness
cognitive-behavioral psychotherapy
community psychology
couples
eating disorders
emergency crisis
multicultural psychology
family psychology
forensic psychology
gay/lesbian/bisexual
gerontology
group therapy
neuropsychology
person-centered and experiential psychotherapy
personality disorders
prevention
psychoanalytic psychotherapy
refugee populations/trauma and torture survivors
rehabilitation
religion/spirituality
school-based programs
victim/abuse/sexual abuse
short-term psychotherapy
sports psychology
substance abuse

Argosy University, Hawaii (Psy.D.)

Hawaii School of Professional Psychology
400 ASB Tower, 1001 Bishop Street
Honolulu, HI 96813
phone#: (808) 536-5555
email: hawaii@argosy.edu
Web address: www.argosy.edu/colleges/programdetail.aspx?ID=627

1	2	3	4	5	6	7
Practice oriented			Equal emphasis			Research oriented

Percentage of faculty subscribing to each of the following orientations:

Psychodynamic/Psychoanalytic	9%
Applied behavioral analysis/Radical behavioral	9%
Family systems/Systems	27%
Existential/Phenomenological/Humanistic	27%
Cognitive/Cognitive-behavioral	27%

Courses required for incoming students to have completed prior to enrolling:
Introduction/General Psychology, Abnormal Psychology, Statistics or Research Methods, & 2 additional psychology courses.

Recommended but not mandatory courses: additional psychology courses, Master's courses

GRE mean
Not required

GPA mean
Overall undergraduate GPA 3.3
Overall graduate GPA 3.8

Number of applications/admission offers/incoming students in 2016
111 applied/44 admission offers/28 incoming

% of students receiving:
Full tuition waiver only: 0%
Assistantship/fellowship only: 10%
Both full tuition waiver & assistantship/fellowship: 10%

Approximate percentage of incoming students with a B.A./B.S. only: 45% **Master's:** 55%

Approximate percentage of all students who are Women: 86% **Ethnic Minority:** 43% **International:** 0%

Average years to complete the doctoral program (including internship): 6

Personal interview
Preferred in person but webcam acceptable

Attrition rate in past 7 years: 3.32%

Percentage of students applying for internship in 2016 accepted into:

APA internships: 53% **APPIC internships:** 29%

Formal tracks/concentrations: none

Research areas	# Faculty	# Grants
diversity education	9	0
gay/lesbian relationships	2	0
health psychology	1	0
neuropsychology	2	0
children	3	1

Clinical opportunities

Psychiatric and medical hospitals
State/federal courts and prisons
Military establishments
Community mental health centers
Public and private schools
Developmental education clinics
Outpatient treatment centers
Substance abuse clinics

Argosy University—Northern Virginia (Psy.D.)

American School of Professional Psychology
1550 Wilson Boulevard, Suite 700
Washington, DC 22209
phone#: 703-526-5800
email: mdlynch@argosy.edu
Web address: https://www.argosy.edu/clinical-psychology/locations/northern-virginia

1	2	3	4	5	6	7
Practice oriented			Equal emphasis			Research oriented

Percentage of faculty subscribing to each of the following orientations:

Psychodynamic/Psychoanalytic	57%
Applied behavioral analysis/Radical behavioral	0%
Family systems/Systems	21%
Existential/Phenomenological/Humanistic	36%
Cognitive/Cognitive-behavioral	64%

Courses required for incoming students to have completed prior to enrolling:
Statistics or research methods, abnormal, plus two other psychology courses (excluding introductory psychology)

Recommended but not mandatory courses: none

GRE mean
Verbal not reported Quantitative not reported
Analytical Writing not reported

Psychology Subject Test not reported

GPA mean
Overall 3.00

Number of applications/admission offers/incoming students in 2016
142 applied/52 admission offers/45 incoming

% of students receiving:
Full tuition waiver only: 0%
Assistantship/fellowship only: 11%
Both full tuition waiver & assistantship/fellowship: 11%

Approximate percentage of incoming students with a B.A./B.S. only: 52% **Master's:** 48%

Approximate percentage of students who are Women: 84% **Ethnic Minority:** 35% **International:** 5%

Average years to complete the doctoral program (including internship): 5 years

Personal interview
Preferred in person but telephone acceptable

Attrition rate in past 7 years: 4% Annual

Percentage of students applying for internship in 2016 accepted into:

APA internships: 89% **APPIC internships:** 11%

Formal tracks/concentrations: forensic, child and family, health, neuropsychology, diversity, integrated health care

Research areas	# Faculty	# Grants
cognitive attributions	1	0
multicultural competence	4	—
psychotherapy integration	2	—
eating disorders	2	—
social psychology	1	—
forensic psychology	4	—
GLBT issues	2	—
child and family	3	—
CBT cognitive schemas	3	—
geopolitical conflict	1	—
neuropsychology	3	—
trauma and PTSD	1	0

Clinical opportunities

anxiety disorders/OCD
child abuse
children's hospitals
community mental health centers
forensic hospitals/prisons
gerontology
integrated behavioral health
neuropsychology
posttraumatic stress disorder
school mental health
sexual orientation
substance abuse
university counseling centers

Argosy University, Orange County (Psy.D.)

American School of Professional Psychology
601 South Lewis Street
Orange, CA 92868
phone#: (714) 620-3700
email: gbruss@argosy.edu
Web address: www.argosy.edu/colleges/programdetail.aspx?ID=679

1	**2**	3	4	5	6	7
Practice oriented			Equal emphasis			Research oriented

Percentage of faculty subscribing to each of the following orientations:

Psychodynamic/Psychoanalytic	30%
Applied /behavioral analysis/Radical behavioral	0%
Family systems/Systems	30%
Existential/Phenomenological/Humanistic	10%
Cognitive/Cognitive-behavioral	30%

Courses required for incoming students to have completed prior to enrolling:
Abnormal Psychology, General or Intro to Psychology, Statistics; any two other undergraduate psychology courses

Recommended but not mandatory courses: none

GRE mean
Verbal not reported Quantitative not reported
Analytical Writing not reported
Psychology Subject Test not reported
GRE scores not required

GPA mean
Bachelor's GPA 3.30 Master's GPA 3.79

Number of applications/admission offers/incoming students in 2017:
136 applied/68 admission offers/36 incoming

% of students receiving:
Full tuition waiver only:
Assistantship/fellowship only:
Both full tuition waiver & assistantship/fellowship:
NOTE: 22% of students granted partial scholarships

Approximate percentage of incoming students with a B.A./B.S. only: 62% **Master's:** 38%

Approximate percentage of all students who are Women: 81% **Ethnic Minority:** 39% **International:** 3%

Average years to complete the doctoral program (including internship): 5.54 years – BA 4.53 years – MA

Personal interview
Preferred in person but telephone acceptable only under extenuating circumstances

Attrition rate in past 7 years: 7%

Percentage of students applying for internship in 2017 accepted into:

APA internships: 80% **APPIC internships:** 15% (95% including APA sites)

Formal tracks/concentrations: child and adolescent psychology, forensic psychology

Research areas
None reported

Clinical opportunities
None reported

Argosy University—Phoenix Campus (Psy.D.)

American School of Professional Psychology
2233 West Dunlap Avenue, Suite 150
Phoenix, AZ 85021
phone#: (602) 216-2600
Web address: https://www.argosy.edu/clinical-psychology/locations/phoenix/programs/doctor-of-psychology

1	**2**	3	4	5	6	7
Practice oriented			Equal emphasis			Research oriented

Percentage of faculty subscribing to each of the following orientations:

Psychodynamic/Psychoanalytic	30%
Applied behavioral analysis/Radical behavioral	0%
Family systems/Systems	10%
Existential/Phenomenological/Humanistic	30%
Cognitive/Cognitive-behavioral	30%

Courses required for incoming students to have completed prior to enrolling: Introduction to psychology (may be waived if applicant has a Bachelors or Masters degree in psychology),abnormal, statistics or research methods, and two other psychology courses.

Recommended but not mandatory courses: none

GRE mean
Verbal not reported Quantitative not reported
Analytical Writing not reported
Psychology Subject Test not reported

GPA mean
Overall 3.61

Number of applications/admission offers/incoming students in 2016-2017
86 applied/ admission offers/33 incoming

% of students receiving:
Full tuition waiver only: 0%
Assistantship/fellowship only: 0%
Both full tuition waiver & assistantship/fellowship: 0%

Approximate percentage of incoming students with a B.A./B.S. only: 65% **Master's:** 35%

Approximate percentage of all students who are Women: 73% **Ethnic Minority:** 35% **International:** 3%

Average years to complete the doctoral program (including internship): 5.5 years

Personal interview
Preferred in person but telephone acceptable

Attrition rate in past 7 years: 5%

Percentage of students applying for internship last year accepted into APPIC or APA internships: 96%

Formal tracks/concentrations: neuropsychology & diversity concentrations

Research areas	# Faculty	# Grants
diversity	5	0
learning disability/ADHD	1	0
neuropsychology	1	0
geropsychology	2	0
health	2	0

Clinical opportunities

forensics	culturally diverse sites
substance abuse	sexual offenders
neuropsychology	pain management
schools/specialty schools	surgical centers
hospital practice/integrated care	inpatient
	community mental health
trauma	HIV/AIDS

Argosy University–Schaumburg Campus (Psy.D.) (2013 Data)

Illinois School of Professional Psychology
999 Plaza Drive, Suite 111
Schaumburg, IL 60173
phone#: (847) 969-4900
email: daanderson@argosy.edu
Web address: www.argosy.edu/clinical-psychology/schaumburg-illinois/psyd-programs-doctorate-degree-79712.aspx

1	2	**3**	4	5	6	7
Practice oriented			Equal emphasis			Research oriented

Percentage of faculty subscribing to each of the following orientations:

Psychodynamic/Psychoanalytic	17%
Applied behavioral analysis/Radical behavioral	0%
Family systems/Systems	17%
Existential/Phenomenological/Humanistic	20%
Cognitive/Cognitive-behavioral	27%
Other or integrative	18%

Courses required for incoming students to have completed prior to enrolling:
abnormal, tests and measurement, personality theory, introductory statistics

Recommended but not mandatory courses: none

GRE mean
Verbal not reported Quantitative not reported
Analytical Writing not reported
Psychology Subject Test not reported

GPA mean
3.52

Number of applications/admission offers/incoming students in 2013
66 applied/26 admission offers/20 incoming

% of students receiving:
Full tuition waiver only: 0%
Assistantship/fellowship only: 25%
Both full tuition waiver & assistantship/fellowship: 0%
Partial tuition waiver: 25%
Partial tuition waiver and assistantship/fellowship: 0%

Approximate percentage of incoming students with a B.A./B.S. only: 55% **Master's:** 45%

Approximate percentage of all students who are Women: 82% **Ethnic Minority:** 18% **International:** 3%

Average years to complete the doctoral program (including internship): 5.2 years

Personal interview
Required in person

Attrition rate in past 7 years: 4.32%

Percentage of students applying for internship last year accepted into APPIC or APA internships: 78%

Formal tracks/concentrations: neuropsychology, forensic psychology; health psychology; child & family psychology

Research areas	# Faculty	# Grants
ADHD and child externalizing	1	0
cultural bias in psychological testing	1	0
effectiveness of EFT	1	1
experiential therapy	3	1
family therapy effectiveness	1	0
men's perception of psychotherapy	1	0
mindfulness and cognition	1	0
multicultural training	2	1
psychotherapy process and outcome	2	1
substance abuse program evaluation	1	1
domestic violence	2	0
eating disorders and trauma	1	1
treating diverse couples	1	1
spirituality	1	1
sleep disorders	1	1
pediatric neuropsychology	1	1

Clinical opportunities
Practica include neuropsychology, child and pediatric psychology, inpatient psychiatric, college counseling center, hospital, adult and community mental health, neuropsychology, correctional psychology, assessment, family and marital counseling, rehabilitation, forensics, severely mentally illness, health and medical psychology, and substance abuse

Argosy University–Tampa (Psy.D.)

Florida School of Professional Psychology
1403 N. Howard Ave
Tampa, FL 33607
phone#: (813) 393-5290
email: snobles@argosy.edu
Web address: www.fspptampa.com

1	2	3	4	5	6	7
Practice oriented			Equal emphasis			Research oriented

Percentage of faculty subscribing to each of the following orientations:

Psychodynamic/Psychoanalytic	0%
Applied behavioral analysis/Radical behavioral	0%
Family systems/Systems	20%
Existential/Phenomenological/Humanistic	10%
Cognitive/Cognitive-behavioral	0%
Integrative	70%
Interpersonal	10%

Courses required for incoming students to have completed prior to enrolling:
The PsyD in Clinical Psychology degree program requires applicants to successfully complete, with a "C" or better, *five* undergraduate courses that serve as a basic foundation for coursework in clinical psychology. Several of these courses serve as direct prerequisites to the PsyD courses. The following three courses are required:
1. Introduction to psychology or general psychology (This course may be waived if the applicant has completed a Bachelors or Masters degree in Psychology)
2. Abnormal, psychopathology, or maladaptive behavior
3. Statistics or research methods
Two additional courses in psychology must also be completed. Students must complete foundation courses *before* they matriculate in the MA/Psy.D. program.

Recommended but not mandatory courses: none

GRE mean
Verbal not reported
Quantitative not reported
Analytical Writing not reported
Psychology Subject Test not reported

GPA mean
3.4

Number of applications/admission offers/incoming students in 2016
120 applied/41 admission offers/15 incoming

% of students receiving:
Full tuition waiver only: 0%
Assistantship/fellowship only: 20%
Both full tuition waiver & assistantship/fellowship: 0%

Approximate percentage of incoming students with a B.A./B.S. only: 33% **Master's:** 67%

Approximate percentage of all students who are Women: 81% **Ethnic Minority:** 44% **International:** 3%

Average years to complete the doctoral program (including internship): 5.85

Personal interview
Not reported

Attrition rate in past 7 years: 18%

Percentage of students applying for internship last year accepted into APPIC or APA internships: 100%

Formal tracks/concentrations: Neuropsychology, Geropsychology, Couple and Family Psychology, Child and Adolescent Psychology

Research areas	# Faculty	# Grants
psychotherapy with diverse populations (underserved; GLBT Ethnic minorities)	4	0
Trauma & stress related disorders; Gender; integrative tx, SPMI	3	0
Biological psychology	1	—
Forensic Psychology	2	0
Child and Adolescent Psychology	3	0
Couples and Family Psychology	4	0
Eating Disorders	2	0
Psychological Assessment	4	0

Clinical opportunities

community centers	psychiatric hospitals
schools	private practice
college counseling centers	residential
court-ordered programs	chemical dependence
behavioral medicine	rehabilitation

Argosy University, Twin Cities (Psy.D.)

Clinical Psychology Program
Graduate Admissions
Minnesota School of Professional Psychology
1515 Central Parkway
Eagan, MN 55121
phone#: (888) 844-2004
email: tcadmissions@argosy.edu
Web address: www.argosy.edu/colleges/programdetail.aspx?ID=186

1	**2**	3	4	5	6	7
Practice oriented			Equal emphasis			Research oriented

Percentage of faculty subscribing to each of the following orientations:

Psychodynamic/Psychoanalytic	33%
Applied behavioral analysis/Radical behavioral	0%
Family systems/Systems	8%
Existential/Phenomenological/Humanistic	8%
Cognitive/Cognitive-behavioral	25%
Other	25%

Courses required for incoming students to have completed prior to enrolling:
at least 15 credits of undergraduate psychology courses, including psychological statistics

Recommended but not mandatory courses: none

GRE mean
Verbal not reported Quantitative not reported
Analytical Writing not reported
Psychology Subject Test not reported

GPA mean
3.47 for students applying with a BA; 3.77 for students applying with an MA

Number of applications/admission offers/incoming students in 2017
55 applied/35 admission offers/19 incoming

% of students receiving:
Full tuition waiver only: 0%
Assistantship/fellowship only: 0%
Both full tuition waiver & assistantship/fellowship: 0%
Scholarship/assistantship/fellowship: 23%

Approximate percentage of incoming students with a BA/BS only: 95% **Master's:** 5%

Approximate percentage of all students who are Women: 72% **Ethnic Minority:** 9% **International:** 3%

Average years to complete the doctoral program (including internship): for all students—6 years

Personal interview
Required in person

Attrition rate in past 7 years: 18%

Percentage of students applying for internship last year accepted into APPIC or APA internships: 100%

Formal tracks/concentrations: forensic psychology, health/neuro psychology, trauma, child and adolescent

Research areas	**# Faculty**	**#Grants**
eating disorders	1	1
grief & loss	1	0
Therapeutic Assessment	1	0
history of psychology	1	0

Clinical opportunities
Over 60 practicum sites in the greater Twin Cities area

University of Arizona (Ph.D.)

Department of Psychology
Psychology Building
Tucson, AZ 85721
phone#: (520) 621-7447
email: psychology@email.arizona.edu
Web address: http://psychology.arizona.edu/clinical

1	2	3	4	5	**6**	7
Practice oriented			Equal emphasis			Research oriented

Percentage of faculty subscribing to each of the following orientations:

Psychodynamic/Psychoanalytic	0%
Applied behavioral analysis/Radical behavioral	10%
Family systems/Systems	10%
Existential/Phenomenological/Humanistic	10%
Cognitive/Cognitive-behavioral	70%

Courses required for incoming students to have completed prior to enrolling:
B.A. or B.S. in psychology; abnormal psychology; statistics and methods.

Recommended but not mandatory courses: Social, biological psychology, cognitive, and developmental

GRE mean
Verbal 161 Quantitative 159
Analytical Writing: 4.6
Psychology Subject Test Not reported

GPA mean
Overall GPA 3.5-3.8

Number of applications/admission offers/incoming students in 2016
162 applied/9 admission offers/7 incoming

% of students receiving:
Full tuition waiver only: 0%
Assistantship/fellowship only: 0%
Both full tuition waiver & assistantship/fellowship: 100%

Approximate percentage of incoming students with a B.A./B.S. only: 90% **Master's:** 10%

Approximate percentage of students who are
Women: 75% **Ethnic Minority:** 22% **International:** 20%

Average years to complete the doctoral program (including internship): 6 years

Personal interview
Preferred in person but Skype is acceptable

Attrition rate in past 7 years: 6%

Percentage of students applying for internship in 2016 accepted into:

APA internships: 66% **APPIC internships:** 83%

Formal tracks/concentrations: none

Research areas	# Faculty	# Grants
clinical neuropsychology	3	5
depression	2	3
family systems	2	4
health psychology	6	6
treatment outcome	3	4

Clinical opportunities
empirically supported treatments
individual and couple therapy
family therapy
depression
community psychology
sleep disorders
neuropsychology/rehabilitation
gerontology
behavioral medicine
neurological disorders

Arizona State University (Ph.D.)

Department of Psychology
Tempe, AZ 85287-1104
phone#: (480) 965-7606
email: psychology@asu.edu
Web address: https://psychology.clas.asu.edu/content/psychology-clinical-phd

1	2	3	4	5	**6**	7
Practice oriented			Equal emphasis			Research oriented

Percentage of faculty subscribing to each of the following orientations:

Psychodynamic/Psychoanalytic	0%
Applied behavioral analysis/Radical behavioral	0%
Family systems/Systems	55%
Existential/Phenomenological/Humanistic	0%
Cognitive/Cognitive-behavioral	100%
3rd Wave (e.g. Mindfulness)	15%
Biopsychosocial	60%

Courses required for incoming students to have completed prior to enrolling:
B.A. in psychology or equivalent

Recommended but not mandatory courses: Social Psychology, Biological Psychology, Developmental Psychology, Cognitive Psychology, History and Systems

GRE mean
Verbal 162 Quantitative 161
Analytical Writing 4.5
Psychology Subject Test not reported

GPA mean
Overall GPA 3.69

Number of applications/admission offers/incoming students in 2017
222 applied/8 admission offers/5 incoming

% of students receiving:
Full tuition waiver only: 0%
Full assistantship/fellowship only: 0%
Both full tuition waiver & assistantship/fellowship: 100%

Approximate percentage of incoming students with a B.A./B.S. only: 85% **Master's:** 15%

Approximate percentage of all students who are
Women: 80% **Ethnic Minority:** 38% **International:** 3%

Average years to complete the doctoral program (including internship): 6.68 years

Personal interview
In person strongly preferred, but telephone acceptable when an in-person visit is not possible

Attrition rate in past 7 years: 9%

Percentage of students applying for internship last year accepted into:

APA internships: 100% **APPIC internships:** 100%

Formal tracks/concentrations: child, community/prevention, health

Research areas	# Faculty	# Grants
behavioral medicine/health psychology	7	6
child clinical	8	6
community psychology	7	5
family interactions	8	5
Hispanic studies	3	1
minority mental health	5	3
personality assessment	1	0
prevention	8	4
substance abuse	5	4

Clinical opportunities
behavioral analysis
behavioral medicine
child clinical psychology
family therapy
forensic psychology
gerontology
individual therapy
intellectual and academic assessment
marital/couples therapy
neuropsychology
parenting
prevention

University of Arkansas (Ph.D.)

Department of Psychological Science
216 Memorial Hall
Fayetteville, AR 72701
phone#: (479) 575-4256
email: ctcgrad@uark.edu
Web address: http://fulbright.uark.edu/departments/psychological-science/graduate-programs/clinical-psychology/index.php

1	2	3	4	5	**6**	7
Practice oriented			Equal emphasis			Research oriented

Percentage of faculty subscribing to each of the following orientations:

Psychodynamic/Psychoanalytic	0%
Applied behavioral analysis/Radical behavioral	25%
Family systems/Systems	50%
Existential/Phenomenological/Humanistic	0%
Cognitive/Cognitive-behavioral	100%

Courses required for incoming students prior to enrolling:
core courses in the science of psychology.

Courses recommended but not mandatory:
18 semester hours in psychology including statistics, abnormal psychology, learning, and experimental psychology

GRE mean
Verbal 157 Quantitative 153
Analytical Writing 4.7
Psychology Subject Test not reported

GPA mean
Overall GPA 3.82

Number of applications/admission offers/incoming students in 2017
155 applied/9 admission offers/7 incoming

% of students receiving:
Full tuition waiver only: 0%
Assistantship/fellowship only: 0%
Both full tuition waiver & assistantship/fellowship: 100%

Approximate percentage of incoming students with a B.A./B.S. only: 60% **Master's:** 40%

Approximate percentage of all students who are Women: 73% **Ethnic Minority:** 27% **International:** 4%

Average years to complete the doctoral program (including internship): 6 years

Personal interview
for invited applicants only

Attrition rate in past 7 years: 7%

Percentage of students applying for internship last year accepted into

APA internships: 100% **APPIC internships:** 100%

Formal tracks/concentrations: none

Research areas	# Faculty	# Grants
aggression & victimization	6	3
school-based prevention	3	2
anxiety disorders	3	1
experimental psychopathology	5	2
family, parent, couples relationships	3	0
multicultural psychology	3	1
substance abuse/addictions	3	2
integrated behavioral health	3	1
adolescent mental health	3	2
implementation science	1	0

Clinical opportunities

integrated primary care	neuropsychology
community mental health	minority mental health
college student mental health	juvenile detention center
school-based mental health	Veteran mental health
addictive behaviors	trauma
domestic violence	correctional center
parenting/family	

Auburn University (Ph.D.)

Department of Psychology
226 Thach
Auburn, AL 36849
phone#: (334) 844-6480
email: correcj@auburn.edu
Web address: www.cla.auburn.edu/psychology/clinical/

1	2	3	**4**	5	6	7
Practice oriented			Equal emphasis			Research oriented

Percentage of faculty subscribing to each of the following orientations:

Psychodynamic/Psychoanalytic	0%
Applied behavioral analysis/Radical behavioral	10%
Family systems/Systems	20%
Existential/Phenomenological/Humanistic	10%
Cognitive/Cognitive-behavioral	100%

Courses required for incoming students to have completed prior to enrolling:
Strong foundation in theoretical or experimental psychology and quantitative methods; evidence of previous research and/or applied experience

GRE mean
Verbal + Quantitative 312
Analytical Writing not reported
Psychology Subject Test not reported

GPA mean
Overall GPA 3.7

Number of applications/admission offers/incoming students in 2017
231 applied/10 admission offers/5 incoming

% of students receiving:
Full tuition waiver only: 0%
Assistantship/fellowship only: 0%
Both full tuition waiver & assistantship/fellowship: 100%

Approximate percentage of incoming students with a B.A./B.S. only: 80% **Master's:** 20%

Approximate percentage of students who are Women: 70% **Ethnic Minority:** 10% **International:** 5%

Average years to complete the doctoral program (including internship): 6.5 years

Personal interview
Required in person

Attrition rate in past 7 years: 7%

Percentage of students applying for internship last year accepted into APPIC or APA internships: 100%

Formal tracks/concentrations: We offer adult and child tracks

Research areas	# Faculty	# Grants
ADHD	1	0
alcohol and substance abuse	1	0
anxiety disorders/PTSD	2	1
bullying and victimization	1	1
child clinical	4	1
eating disorders	1	0
health promotion/prevention	2	1
juvenile sexual offending	1	1
parent-child interaction therapy	1	0
cognitive assessment	1	0
suicidal behavior	1	1

Clinical opportunities
Adolescent residential treatment
Adult and child services (assessment and treatment)
Autism Spectrum Disorders
College counseling services
Community mental health (assessment and treatment)
Developmental disabilities
Forensic psychology
Inpatient psychiatry
Juvenile offenders
Parent-Child Interaction Therapy
Pediatric psychology
Primary Care/Medical Consultation
Substance abuse
Veterans and their family

Azusa Pacific University (Psy.D.)

Department of Clinical Psychology
901 East Alosta Avenue
Azusa, CA 91702-7000
phone#: (626) 815-5008
email: jmdeyo@apu.edu
Web address: http://www.apu.edu/bas/programs/psyd/

1	2	**3**	4	5	6	7
Practice oriented			Equal emphasis			Research oriented

Percentage of faculty subscribing to each of the following orientations:

Psychodynamic/Psychoanalytic	42%
Applied behavioral analysis/Radical behavioral	0%
Family systems/Systems	58%
Existential/Phenomenological/Humanistic	25%
Cognitive/Cognitive-behavioral	33%

Courses required for incoming students to have completed prior to enrolling:
Students with a Bachelor's or Master's in psychology or a closely related field are welcome to apply for entrance into the Psy.D. program without any further prerequisite course fulfillment. Students who have a Bachelor's or Master's unrelated to the field of psychology will be required to take the following undergraduate courses before commencing the Psy.D. program: Introduction to Psychology (general psychology course), Human Growth and Development (developmental psychology course that covers the lifespan), Abnormal Psychology, Introduction to Statistics

Recommended but not mandatory courses: none

GRE mean (since 2011)
Verbal 519, Quantitative 591 (under the new system: Verbal 154, Quantitative 149)
Analytical Writing 4.0
Psychology Subject Test not reported

GPA mean
Overall GPA Master's 3.8 Bachelor's 3.4

Number of applications/admission offers/incoming students for the 2017-2018 academic year
84 applied/51 admission offers/32 incoming

% of students receiving:
Full tuition waiver only: 0%
Assistantship/fellowship only: 15%
Both full tuition waiver & assistantship/fellowship: 0%

Approximate percentage of incoming students with a B.A./B.S. only: 66% **Master's:** 33%

Approximate percentage of all students who are Women: 71% **Ethnic Minority:** 42% **International:** 3%

Average years to complete the doctoral program (including internship): 5 years

Personal interview
Preferred in person but telephone acceptable

Attrition rate in past 7 years: 8.4%

Percentage of students applying for internship last year accepted into APPIC or APA internships: 100%

Formal tracks/concentrations: family (systems) psychology, forensic psychology, consulting psychology

Research areas	# Faculty	# Grants
international/global psychology	3	4
family psychology	2	0
diversity/multiculturalism	2	0
child and adolescent	2	1
counseling skills	2	1
psychological assessment	2	0
forensics	3	1
homelessness/HIV	1	0
moral development	2	1
religion/spirituality	4	1
school-based interventions	2	1
neuropsychology	1	0

Clinical opportunities
behavior medicine
children and family
chronic mental illness
community clinics
forensics
general population
gerontology
HIV/AIDS
inpatient: acute and chronic
school-based
substance abuse
university counseling

Baylor University (Psy.D.)

Department of Psychology and Neuroscience
P.O. Box 97334

Waco, TX 76798-7334
phone#: (254) 710-2961
email: Sara_Dolan@baylor.edu
Web address: www.baylor.edu/psychologyneuroscience/index.php?id=72649

1	2	3	**4**	5	6	7
Practice oriented			Equal emphasis			Research oriented

Percentage of faculty subscribing to each of the following orientations:

Psychodynamic/Psychoanalytic	5%
Applied behavioral analysis/Radical behavioral	0%
Family systems/Systems	5%
Existential/Phenomenological/Humanistic	5%
Cognitive/Cognitive-behavioral	85%

Courses required for incoming students to have completed prior to enrolling: 12 credit hours of unspecified Psychology coursework

Recommended but not mandatory courses:
developmental, psychopathology, theory of counseling and psychotherapy, statistics, biopsychology, personality, social, learning perception/cognitive, human development, research methods

GRE mean
Verbal 163 Quantitative 158
Analytical Writing 5.08
Psychology Subject Test not reported

GPA mean
Overall GPA 3.37 Psychology GPA 3.74
Junior/Senior GPA 3.76

Number of applications/admission offers/incoming students in 2017-2018
274 applied/7 admission offers/6 incoming

% of students receiving:
Full tuition waiver only: 0%
Assistantship/fellowship only: 0%
Both full tuition waiver & assistantship/fellowship: 100%

Approximate percentage of incoming students with a B.A./B.S. only: 75% **Master's:** 25%

Approximate percentage of all students who are Women: 75% **Ethnic Minority:** 15%

Average years to complete the doctoral program (including internship): 5 years

Personal interview
Required in person

Attrition rate in past 7 years: 10%

Percentage of students applying for internship last year accepted into

APA internships: 100% **APPIC internships:** 100%

Formal tracks/concentrations: none

Research areas	**# Faculty**	**# Grants**
behavioral medicine	3	2
child psychopathology	2	0
cognitive/cognitive behavioral therapy	3	1
anxiety	2	2
group therapy	1	0
personality/cognitive assessment	3	2
substance abuse	2	3

Clinical opportunities

alcohol and drug dependence	impulse control
anxiety disorders	mood disorders
behavioral medicine	neuropsychology
child psychotherapy	personality disorder
community psychology	play therapy
crisis intervention	rural psychology
group therapy	schizophrenia/psychoses
family therapy	suicide prevention

Binghamton University/State University of New York (Ph.D.)

Department of Psychology
Vestal Parkway East
Binghamton, NY 13902-6000
phone#: (607) 777-2334
email: clinpsyc@binghamton.edu
Web address: www.binghamton.edu/psychology/graduate/clinical-psychology/

1	2	3	4	**5**	6	7
Practice oriented			Equal emphasis			Research oriented

Percentage of faculty subscribing to each of the following orientations:

Psychodynamic/Psychoanalytic	8%
Applied behavioral analysis/Radical behavioral	16%
Family systems/Systems	0%
Existential/Phenomenological/Humanistic	0%
Cognitive/Cognitive-behavioral	76%

Courses required for incoming students prior to enrolling:
equivalent of a psychology major, with knowledge of experimental psychology and research methods

Courses recommended but not mandatory:
neuroscience, biological, and/or physiological psychology

GRE mean
Verbal 161 Quantitative 158
Analytical Writing 4.5
Psychology Subject Test 630

GPA mean
Overall GPA 3.6

Number of applications/admission offers/incoming students in 2016
151 applied/11 admission offers/6 incoming

% of students receiving:
Full tuition waiver only: 0%
Assistantship/fellowship only: 0%
Both full tuition waiver & assistantship/fellowship: 100%

Approximate percentage of all students who are Women: 73% **Ethnic Minority:** 17% **International:** 2%

Average years to complete the doctoral program (including internship): 6.25 years

Personal interview
Strongly preferred in person but telephone acceptable

Attrition rate in past 7 years: 7%

Percentage of students applying for internship last year accepted into APPIC or APA internships: 100%

Formal tracks/concentrations: none

Research areas	# Faculty	# Grants
adult psychopathology	7	2
anxiety disorders	2	1
autism spectrum disorders	2	3
child clinical	4	3
depression	1	1
developmental disabilities	2	0
hypnosis	1	0
learning disabilities	2	0
marital process and therapy	3	0
obsessive-compulsive disorder	1	0
personality disorders	1	1
posttraumatic stress disorder/trauma	1	0
psychophysiology	1	1
schizophrenia	1	1
social phobia	1	1

Clinical opportunities

adolescent delinquency	disorders of childhood
adult psychopathology	family therapy
anxiety disorders	learning disabilities
autism spectrum disorders	neuropsychology
behavioral medicine	pain management
conduct disorder	supervision
correctional facility	schizophrenia
couples therapy	school consultation
depression	substance abuse

Biola University (Ph.D.)

Rosemead School of Psychology
13800 Biola Avenue
La Mirada, CA 90639
phone#: (562) 903-4752
email: admissions@biola.edu
Web address: www.rosemead.edu/programs/phd/

1	2	3	4	**5**	6	7
Practice oriented			Equal emphasis			Research oriented

Percentage of faculty subscribing to each of the following orientations:

Psychodynamic/Psychoanalytic	50%
Applied behavioral analysis/Radical behavioral	0%
Family systems/Systems	16%
Existential/Phenomenological/Humanistic	6%
Cognitive/Cognitive-behavioral	28%

Courses required for incoming students to have completed prior to enrolling:
General (introductory) psychology, statistics, experimental psychology, abnormal psychology, personality, learning

Recommended but not mandatory courses:
Developmental psychology, measurement theory, history of psychology, biology/zoology,

GRE mean
Verbal + Quantitative 308
Analytical Writing not reported
Psychology Subject Test not reported

GPA mean
Overall GPA 3.7

Number of applications/admission offers/incoming students in 2016-2017
89 applied/16 admission offers/12 incoming

% of students receiving:
Full tuition waiver only: 0%
Assistantship/fellowship only: 84%
Both full tuition waiver & assistantship/fellowship: 0%

Approximate percentage of incoming students with a B.A./B.S. only: 100% **Master's:** 0%

Approximate percentage of students who are Women: 58% **Ethnic Minority:** 33% **International:** 8%

Average years to complete the doctoral program (including internship): 6 years

Personal interview
Required in person

Attrition rate in past 7 years: 6.1%

Percentage of students applying for internship last year accepted into:

APA internships: 71% **APPIC internships:** 15%
Other internships: 14%

Research areas	# Faculty	# Grants
Anxiety	6	1
Cross-cultural adjustment/ issues/experiences	5	0
Developmental/Language acquisition	1	0
Gender issues/work and family balance	3	1
Grief	1	0
Health Psychology	2	2
Marital/Family	1	0
Missions and Mental Health	2	0
Neuropsychology	3	0
Object Relations	2	0
Parenting Behaviors	1	0
Spirituality	10	3

Clinical opportunities

Cultural and Individual Diversity	Outpatient/Inpatient
	Spirituality
Family/Child	Emotion Focused
Individual	Neuropsychology

Biola University (Psy.D.)

Rosemead School of Psychology
13800 Biola Avenue
La Mirada, CA 90639
phone#: (562) 903-4752
email: admissions@biola.edu
Web address: www.rosemead.edu/programs/psyd.cfm/

1	2	3	4	5	6	7
Practice oriented			Equal emphasis			Research oriented

Percentage of faculty subscribing to each of the following orientations:

Psychodynamic/Psychoanalytic%	50%
Applied behavioral analysis/Radical behavioral	0%
Family systems/Systems	16%
Existential/Phenomenological/Humanistic	6%
Cognitive/Cognitive-behavioral	28%

Courses required for incoming students to have completed prior to enrolling:
General (introductory) psychology, statistics, experimental psychology, abnormal psychology, personality, learning

Recommended but not mandatory courses:
Developmental psychology, measurement theory, history of psychology, biology/zoology,

GRE mean
Verbal + Quantitative 302
Analytical Writing not reported
Psychology Subject Test not reported

GPA mean
Overall GPA 3.6

Number of applications/admission offers/incoming students in 2016-2017
94 applied/32 admission offers & 3 waitlist admission offers/20 incoming

% of students receiving:
Full tuition waiver only: 1%
Assistantship/fellowship only: 84%
Both full tuition waiver & assistantship/fellowship: 0%

Approximate percentage of incoming students with a B.A./B.S. only: 75% **Master's:** 25%

Approximate percentage of students who are Women: 75% **Ethnic Minority:** 45% **International:** 15%

Average years to complete the doctoral program (including internship): 5.7 years

Personal interview
Required in person

Attrition rate in past 7 years: 21.5%

Percentage of students applying for internship last year accepted into:

APA internships: 92% **APPIC internships:** 8%

Research areas	# Faculty	# Grants
Anxiety	6	1
Cross-cultural adjustment/issues/experiences	5	0
Developmental/Language acquisition	1	0
Gender issues/work and family balance	3	1
Grief	1	0
Health Psychology	2	2
Marital/Family	1	0
Missions and Mental Health	2	0
Neuropsychology	3	0
Object Relations	2	0
Parenting Behaviors	1	0
Spirituality	10	3

Clinical opportunities

Cultural and Individual Diversity	Outpatient/Inpatient
Family/Child	Spirituality
Individual	Emotion Focused
	Neuropsychology

Boston University (Ph.D.)

Department of Psychological and Brain Sciences
64 Cummington Mall
Boston, MA 02215
phone#: (617) 353-2587
email: nclement@bu.edu
Web address: www.bu.edu/psych/graduate/clinical/

1	2	3	4	5	6	7
Practice oriented			Equal emphasis			Research oriented

Percentage of faculty subscribing to each of the following orientations:

Psychodynamic/Psychoanalytic	0%
Applied behavioral analysis/Radical behavioral	0%
Family systems/Systems	20%
Existential/Phenomenological/Humanistic	0%
Cognitive/Cognitive-behavioral	70%
Neuropsychology	20%
Eclectic	0%

Courses required for incoming students to have completed prior to enrolling:
statistics, abnormal/clinical, experimental

Recommended but not mandatory courses: broad liberal arts and science

GRE mean
Verbal + Quantitative 322
Analytical Writing 5.0
Psychology Subject Test not reported

GPA mean
Overall GPA 3.9

Number of applications/admission offers/incoming students in 2017
641 applied/9 admission offers/8 incoming

% of students receiving:
Full tuition waiver only: 0%
Assistantship/fellowship only: 0%
Both full tuition waiver & assistantship/fellowship: 100%

Approximate percentage of incoming students with a B.A./B.S. only: 75% **Master's:** 25%

Approximate percentage of all students who are Women: 70% **Ethnic Minority:** 30% **International:** 5%

Average years to complete the doctoral program (including internship): 6.5 years

Personal interview
Required in person

Attrition rate in past 7 years: 1%

Percentage of students applying for internship last year accepted into:

APA internships: 100% **APPIC internships:** 100%

Formal tracks/concentrations: adult clinical, child clinical, neuropsychology

Research areas	# Faculty	# Grants
affective disorders	7	0
anxiety disorders	8	8
behavioral genetics	1	1
community psychology	1	0
emotion	2	1
family	3	2
gender	1	0
gerontology	2	2
minority	1	0
neuropsychology	3	2
personality disorders	1	0
schizophrenia	1	0
substance abuse/addiction	3	4
victim/abuse	1	0
women's emotional health	2	1

Clinical opportunities

adolescents	family therapy
affective disorders	gerontology
anxiety disorders	motivational interviewing
behavioral medicine	neuropsychology
cognitive-behavioral therapy	PTSD
community psychology	substance/alcohol use

Bowling Green State University (Ph.D.)

Department of Psychology
Bowling Green, OH 43403
phone#: (419) 372-2306
email: pwatson@bgsu.edu
Web address: http://www.bgsu.edu/arts-and-sciences/psychology/graduate-program/clinical.html

1 2 3 **4** 5 6 7

Practice oriented — Equal emphasis — Research oriented

Percentage of faculty subscribing to each of the following orientations:

Psychodynamic/Psychoanalytic	10%
Applied behavioral analysis/Radical behavioral	0%
Family systems/Systems	30%
Existential/Phenomenological/Humanistic	20%
Cognitive/Cognitive-behavioral/ACT	65%

Courses required for incoming students to have completed prior to enrolling: none

Recommended but not mandatory courses: science, math, statistics, advanced psychology courses, abnormal, psychology lab courses

GRE mean
Verbal 76% Quantitative 65%
Analytical Writing not used for admissions decisions
Psychology Subject Test not reported

GPA mean
Overall GPA 3.68 Psychology GPA 3.8

Number of applications/admission offers/incoming students in 2017
142 applied/13 admission offers/9 incoming

% of students receiving:
Full tuition waiver only: 0%
Assistantship/fellowship only: 0%
Both tuition waiver & assistantship/fellowship: 100%

Approximate percentage of all students who are Women: 83% **Ethnic Minority:** 12% **International:** 6%

Average years to complete the doctoral program (including internship): 6.03 years

Personal interview
Preferred in person but telephone acceptable

Attrition rate in past 7 years: 6%

Percentage of students applying for internship last year accepted into:

APA internships: 100% **APPIC internships:** 100%

Formal tracks/concentrations: health psychology, child clinical psychology, community psychology

Research areas	# Faculty	# Grants
alcohol and substance abuse	1	0
child clinical psychology	3	2
community psychology	1	1
family	2	0
health psychology	2	1
psychology of religion & spirituality	2	1

Clinical opportunities

health psychology	community mental health
child clinical psychology	developmental disabilities
community psychology	family systems

Brigham Young University (Ph.D.)

Department of Psychology
284 TLRB
Provo, UT 84602
phone#: (801) 422-4050
email: patrick_steffen@byu.edu
Web address: https://psychology.byu.edu/Pages/ClinicalPhD.aspx

1 2 3 **4** 5 6 7

Practice oriented — Equal emphasis — Research oriented

Percentage of faculty subscribing to each of the following orientations:

Psychodynamic/Psychoanalytic	10%
Applied behavioral analysis/Radical behavioral	40%
Family systems/Systems	10%
Existential/Phenomenological/Humanistic	30%
Cognitive/Cognitive-behavioral	70%
Interpersonal	40%

Courses required for incoming students prior to enrolling:
psychological statistics, research design, abnormal, personality, learning or cognition, tests and measurements

Courses recommended but not mandatory:
additional coursework in areas of interest may be helpful

GRE mean
Verbal 159 Quantitative 157
Analytical Writing 4.7
Psychology Subject Test not reported

GPA mean
Overall GPA 3.84
Upper-Division Coursework GPA

Number of applications/admission offers/incoming students in 2017
37 applied/8 admission offers/8 incoming

% of students receiving tuition waiver & assistantship/fellowship:
Full tuition waiver only: 0%
Assistantship/fellowship only: 0%
Both full tuition waiver & assistantship/fellowship: 0%
All 1st and 2nd year students receive 15 hours per week in assistantships as well as waivers for part of their tuition. All 2nd-, 3rd-, and 4th-year students are funded in work settings, which are coordinated by the department, and they also receive waivers for part of their tuition.

Approximate percentage of incoming students with a B.A./B.S. only: 80% **Master's:** 20%

Approximate percentage of all students who are Women: 65% **Ethnic Minority:** 16% **International:** 8%

Average years to complete the doctoral program (including internship): 5.4 years

Personal interview
Preferred in person but telephone acceptable

Attrition rate in past 7 years: 5%

Percentage of students applying for internship in 2017 accepted into:

APA internships: 100% **APPIC internships:** 100%

Formal tracks/concentrations: Clinical Neuropsychology; Child, Adolescent, Family; Clinical Research; Clinical Health

Research areas	# Faculty	# Grants
autism: emotional regulation neuroimaging	2	2
child/adolescent development	4	2
child/adolescent psychotherapy	3	2
clinical assessment	4	2
depression/anxiety: neuroimaging	2	1
group psychotherapy: process, outcome	1	1
health psychology/behavioral medicine: stress, weight control	2	2
individual therapy: process, outcome	3	2
marital relationships	1	1
measurement/statistics	3	2
neuropsychology/neuroimaging	4	3
pediatric psych: weight control, etc.	2	1
positive psychology	3	2
religion/spirituality/health	2	1
obsessive compulsive disorder	2	1
traumatic brain injury, seizures	3	2
women's issues	1	1

Clinical opportunities

youth residential centers	community health centers
medical centers	neuropsychology rehab
behavioral medicine	private practices
state hospital	forensic settings
university counseling	VA medical centers

University at Buffalo, The State University of New York (Ph.D.)

Department of Psychology
Park Hall
Buffalo, NY 14260
phone#: (716) 645-3651
email: jpread@buffalo.edu
Web address: www.psychology.buffalo.edu/graduate/phd/clinical

1	2	3	4	5	**6**	7
Practice oriented			Equal emphasis			Research oriented

Percentage of faculty subscribing to each of the following orientations:

Psychodynamic/Psychoanalytic	0%
Applied behavioral analysis/Radical behavioral	25%
Family systems/Systems	0%
Existential/Phenomenological/Humanistic	0%
Cognitive/Cognitive-behavioral	75%

Courses required for incoming students prior to enrolling:
research methods, statistics

Courses recommended but not mandatory:
good science background, abnormal, cognitive, social, developmental

GRE mean
Verbal 156
Quantitative 154
Analytical Writing 4.5
Psychology Subject Test not reported

GPA mean
Overall GPA 3.73

Number of applications/admission offers/incoming students in 2017
147 applied/7 admission offers/4 incoming

% of students receiving:
Full tuition waiver only: 0%
Assistantship/fellowship only: 0%
Both full tuition waiver & assistantship/fellowship: 100%

Approximate percentage of incoming students with a B.A./B.S. only: 100% **Master's:** 0%

Approximate percentage of all students who are Women: 81% **Ethnic Minority:** 11% **International:** 11%

Average years to complete the doctoral program (including internship): 7.0 years

Personal interview
Required

Attrition rate in past 7 years: < 5%

Percentage of students applying for internship last year accepted into APPIC or APA internships: 100%

Formal tracks/concentrations: none

Research areas	# Faculty	# Grants
addictions	4	5
anxiety disorders	3	1
attention-deficit disorder	1	0
behavioral medicine	3	2
child psychopathology	3	1
depression	3	0
personality/psychometrics	1	1

Clinical opportunities
addiction
anxiety disorders
depression
personality disorders
ADHD
child/adolescent externalizing behavior
parent training
psychological services center

University of California–Berkeley (Ph.D.)

Department of Psychology
Berkeley, CA 94720-1650
phone#: (510) 642-2055
email: psychapp@berkeley.edu
Web address: psychology.berkeley.edu/research/clinical-science

1	2	3	4	5	6	7
Practice oriented			Equal emphasis			Research oriented

Percentage of faculty subscribing to each of the following orientations:

Psychodynamic/Psychoanalytic	0%
Applied behavioral analysis/Radical behavioral	0%
Family systems/Systems	20%
Existential/Phenomenological/Humanistic	0%
Cognitive/Cognitive-behavioral	80%

Courses required for incoming students to have completed prior to enrolling: none

Recommended but not mandatory courses: Statistics. Students will receive credit for having taken psychology courses in affective, biological, cognitive, developmental, social, and history and systems.

GRE mean
Verbal 164.12 (92 percentile)
Quantitative 161.37 (81 percentile)
Analytical Writing 5.12 (94 percentile)
Psychology Subject Test not required

GPA mean
Overall GPA 3.82

Number of applications/admission offers/incoming students in 2017
216 applied/6 admission offers/4 incoming

% of students receiving:
Full tuition waiver only: 0%
Assistantship/fellowship only: 0%
Both full tuition waiver & assistantship/fellowship: 100%
All students are guaranteed funding and tuition remission for the first 5 years of graduate school. Some receive University fellowships, others obtain funding through their graduate advisor's grants, and many are provided with teaching fellowships. Our trainees also have a strong record of obtaining NSF and Ford Foundation grants to support their training.

Approximate percentage of incoming students with a B.A./B.S. only: 75% **Master's:** 25%

Approximate percentage of all students who are Women: 80.5% **Ethnic Minority:** 38% **International:** 0%

Average years to complete the doctoral program (including internship): 6.7 years

Personal interview
Greatly preferred in person but skype acceptable

Attrition rate in past 7 years: 0%

Percentage of students applying for internship in 2016 accepted into:

APA internships: 100% **APPIC internships:** 100%

Formal tracks/concentrations: none

Research areas	# Faculty	# Grants
ADHD	1	2
Improving cognitive behavioral therapy	2	2
depression	1	1
emotion and aging	1	1
emotion, cognition, and schizophrenia	1	0
sleep	1	1
bipolar disorder	2	2
stigma and mental illness	1	1
Culture, bilingualism and parenting	1	1
Mental health and entrepreneurship	1	1
Emotion-related impulsivity	1	2
Affective science	4	1
Underrepresented minority outcomes in STEM settings	1	1

Clinical opportunities
In-house clinic provides training in empirically supported individual, couples, and group treatments for a wide range of adult and child conditions. Our in-house clinic also offers assessment training.
Multiple externships in the community, including at the local VAMCs, rotations focused on substance abuse, mood disorders, UCSF memory and aging center, UC Davis MIND Institute for the study of autism, and other child and adolescent assessment and intervention centers.

University of California–Los Angeles (Ph.D.)

Department of Psychology
1285 Franz Hall, Box 951563
Los Angeles, CA 90095-1563
phone#: (310) 825-2617
email: gradadm@psych.ucla.edu
Web address: www.psych.ucla.edu/graduate/areas-of-study/clinical-psychology/clinical-psychology

1	2	3	4	5	6	**7**
Practice oriented			Equal emphasis			Research oriented

Percentage of faculty subscribing to each of the following orientations:

Psychodynamic/Psychoanalytic	0%
Applied behavioral analysis/Radical behavioral	0%
Family systems/Systems	20%
Existential/Phenomenological/Humanistic	0%
Cognitive/Cognitive-behavioral	80%

Courses required for incoming students prior to enrolling:
Psychology major or its equivalent; 1 course in college level math or statistics

Courses recommended but not mandatory:
Research design and methods, psychology research labs, independent research courses; a broad background in the mathematical, biological and social sciences

GRE mean
Verbal 93% Quantitative 85%
Analytical Writing 72%
Psychology Subject Test 89%

GPA mean
Overall GPA 3.8

Number of applications/admission offers/incoming students in 2017
382 applied/14 admission offers/12 incoming

% of students receiving:
Full tuition waiver only: 0%
Assistantship/fellowship only: 0%
Both full tuition waiver & assistantship/fellowship: 100%

Approximate percentage of incoming students with a B.A./B.S. only: 95% **Master's:** 5%

Approximate percentage of students who are Women: 75% **Ethnic Minority:** 42% **International:** 0%

Average years to complete the doctoral program (including internship): 6 years

Personal interview
Preferred in person but telephone acceptable

Attrition rate in past 7 years: 4.5%

Percentage of students applying for internship in 2017 accepted into:

APA internships: 100% **APPIC internships:** 100%

Formal tracks/concentrations: no formal tracks, but there is focused training in severe adult psychopathology, child/adolescent psychopathology, clinical-health psychology, minority mental health, and couples and families

Research areas	# Faculty	# Grants
anxiety disorders and treatment	3	7
child and family issues	3	5
marital and couple relationships and treatments	2	5
medical issues	3	7
minority mental and physical health issues	3	5
mood disorders	3	5
schizophrenia	3	4
school mental health	1	3
substance use disorders	1	3

Clinical opportunities
adoptions, families
child and adult affective disorders
child and adult anxiety disorders
community psychology, community mental health
couples/marital
developmental disabilities/autism
family/child
major mental illness, psychosis
minority populations
psychotherapy supervision
school mental health

California Lutheran University (Psy.D.)

Graduate School of Psychology
60 West Olsen Road, MC 8000
Thousand Oaks, CA 91360
phone#: (805) 493-3675
email: kswavely@callutheran.edu
Web address: http://www.callutheran.edu/academics/graduate/psyd-clinical-psychology/

1	2	**3**	4	5	6	7
Practice oriented			Equal emphasis			Research oriented

Percentage of faculty subscribing to each of the following orientations:

Psychodynamic/Psychoanalytic	45%
Applied behavioral analysis/Radical behavioral	30%
Cognitive/Cognitive-behavioral	30%
Family systems/Systems	15%
Existential/Phenomenological/Humanistic	15%

Courses required for incoming students to have completed prior to enrolling:
Statistics with a grade of B or higher and an additional 12 hours of undergraduate or graduate psychology courses.

Recommended but not mandatory courses:
Abnormal Psychology

GRE mean
Verbal 151 Quantitative 146
Analytical Writing 3.91
Psychology Subject Test: (not reported)

GPA mean
Overall GPA 3.33

Number of applications/admission offers/incoming students in 2016
86 applied/39 admission offers/16 incoming

% of students receiving:
Full tuition waiver only: 0%
Assistantship/fellowship only: 20%
Both full tuition waiver & assistantship/fellowship: 20%

Approximate percentage of incoming students with a B.A./B.S. only: 87% **Master's:** 13%

Approximate percentage of all students who are Women: 83% **Ethnic Minority:** 31% **International:** 6%

Average years to complete the doctoral program (including internship): 5.5 years

Personal interview
Preferred in person but telephone acceptable

Attrition rate in past 7 years: 9%

Percentage of students applying for internship last year accepted into:

APA internships: 64.3% **APPIC internships:** 85.7%

Formal tracks/concentrations: dialectical behavior therapy, forensic psychology, intimate partner violence, acceptance and commitment therapy

Research areas	# Faculty	# Grants
child & family psychology	4	2
parent–child relationships	4	0
intimate partner/domestic violence	3	1
psychological assessment	2	0
multicultural mental health	2	0
attachment	2	0
forensics	1	1
positive psychology	1	1
social interest	1	1
school/youth violence	1	0
health and stress	1	0

Clinical opportunities
Students advance from the internal practicum experience to providing psychological services in the broader community. We have formed partnerships with many agencies, including community mental health centers, county clinics, hospitals or medical centers, residential treatment centers, substance abuse clinics, correctional facilities, and college counseling centers.

Carlos Albizu University, Miami Campus (Psy.D.)

Department of Psychology
2173 NW 99th Avenue
Miami, FL 33172-2209
phone#: (305) 593-1223, ext. 3188
email: gfontan@albizu.edu
Web address: www.albizu.edu

1	2	3	4	5	6	7
Practice oriented			Equal emphasis			Research oriented

Percentage of faculty subscribing to each of the following orientations:

Psychodynamic/Psychoanalytic	20%
Applied behavioral analysis/Radical behavioral	0%
Family systems/Systems	0%
Existential/Phenomenological/Humanistic	10%
Cognitive/Cognitive-behavioral	70%

Courses required for incoming students to have completed prior to enrolling:
Previous academic work should include a concentration in psychology, including courses in statistics, research methods, developmental psychology, physiological psychology, cognitive psychology, abnormal psychology, and personality psychology

Recommended but not mandatory courses:
None

GRE mean
Official scores from the Graduate Record Examination (GRE) general test section, taken in the past five years.
Please note that preference is given to applicants whose GRE scores exceed the following:
GRE Verbal score of 156 (or 550 according to the old GRE score system)
GRE Quantitative score of 146 (or 550 according to the old GRE score system)
GRE Analytic score of 4.5

GPA mean of incoming class:
Not reported

Number of applications/admission offers/incoming students in Fall 2015
96 applied/36 admissions offers/27 incoming

% of students receiving:
Full tuition waiver only: 0%
Assistantship/fellowship only: 0%
Both full tuition waiver & assistantship/fellowship: 0%

Approximate percentage of all students who are
Women: 91% **Ethnic Minority:** 55% **International:** 5%

Average years to complete the doctoral program (including internship): 6 years

Personal interview
Required in person

Percentage of students applying for internship last year accepted into:

APA internships: 63% **APPIC internships:** 30%

Formal tracks/concentrations:
The PsyD program offers five different concentration areas: Clinical Neuropsychology, Child Psychology, Forensic Psychology, Health Psychology and General Psychology

Research areas	# Faculty	# Grants
health psychology	2	0
trauma	4	0
anxiety	2	0
criminal competencies	4	0
substance use	3	0

Clinical opportunities
The program has agreements with approximately 50 practicum sites. Students in clinical practicum work as health service psychologists-in-training at sites approved by the assistant director of clinical training for the Psy.D. program. The program maintains active affiliations with a variety of practicum sites that provide quality clinical experiences for students. Students may choose from over fifty approved sites, including regional and community hospitals, university medical centers, VA medical centers, mental health community centers, community service agencies, correctional centers, and private practice offices. Most practicum sites require a three-semester commitment from students, after which they may apply to different practicum sites to further develop their clinical practice abilities.

Carlos Albizu University, San Juan Campus (Ph.D.)

Department of Psychology
P.O. Box 9023711
San Juan, PR 00902-3711
phone#: (787) 725-6500, ext. 1129
email: cperez@albizu.edu
Web address: http://www.albizu.edu/Academics/Degrees-in-Psychology/Ph-D/Clinical-Psychology-PhD-Program-San-Juan-Campus

1	2	3	4	**5**	6	7
Practice oriented			Equal emphasis			Research oriented

Percentage of faculty subscribing to each of the following orientations:

Psychodynamic/Psychoanalytic	10%
Applied behavioral analysis/Radical behavioral	0%
Family systems/Systems	20%
Existential/Phenomenological/Humanistic	5%
Cognitive/Cognitive-behavioral	65%

Courses required for incoming students to have completed prior to enrolling:
Bachelor's degree in psychology with a minimum of 21 credits in psychology. Applicants with a Bachelor's degree other than psychology will be required to take courses in five areas: experimental, statistics, physiological, personality, and abnormal.

Recommended but not mandatory courses:
Experimental, statistics, physiological, personality, abnormal

GRE mean
Verbal + Quantitative
Analytical Writing

GRE Mean
We do not use GRE; we use a Puerto Rico equivalent exam called the EXAPEP and requires a minimum score of 500

GPA mean
Overall GPA
Minimum GPA of 3.25

Number of applications/admission offers/incoming students in 2016
61 applied/51 admission offers/25 incoming

% of students receiving:
Full tuition waiver only: 0%
Assistantship/fellowship only: 0%
Both full tuition waiver & assistantship/fellowship: 0%
50% of students receive half tuition waiver

Approximate percentage of all students who are
Women: 80% **Ethnic Minority:** 95% Puerto Rican
International: 5%

Average years to complete the doctoral program (including internship): 6.5 years

Personal interview:
Required

Attrition rate in past 7 years: 20%

Percentage of students applying for internship last year accepted into:

APA internships: 64% **APPIC internships:** 36%

Formal tracks/concentrations:
Health psychology, neuropsychology

Research areas:
Anxiety disorders
Attention Deficit Hyperactivity Disorder (ADHD)
Child abuse
Dissociative Disorders
Domestic violence
Gerontology
Human development
Intimate partner violence
Mental health and substance use stigma
Parenting practices
Personality assessment
Personality Disorders
Sexual abuse
Substance Use Disorders (SUD)
Suicide
Trauma
Women's health

Clinical opportunities
We have an in-house primary care clinic serving children and adults. Students are also placed in outside facilities covering a wide range of clinical opportunities.

Carlos Albizu University–San Juan Campus (Psy.D.)

San Juan, PR 00902-3711
phone#: (787) 725-6500, ext. 1508
email: gsifre@albizu.edu
Web address: sju.albizu.edu/code/doctoral_programs/psyd_in_clinical_psychology.asp

1	2	**3**	4	5	6	7
Practice oriented			Equal emphasis			Research oriented

Percentage of faculty subscribing to each of the following orientations:

Psychodynamic/Psychoanalytic	0%
Applied behavioral analysis/Radical behavioral	10%
Family systems/Systems	30%
Existential/Phenomenological/Humanistic	10%
Cognitive/Cognitive-behavioral	50%

Courses required for incoming students to have completed prior to enrolling:
Experimental psychology, physiological psychology, abnormal psychology, introductory statistics, personality theories

Recommended but not mandatory courses: none

GRE mean
Verbal not reported Quantitative not reported
Analytical Writing not reported
Psychology Subject Test not reported
not required for admission

GPA mean
3.25

Number of applications/admission offers/incoming students in 2017
156 applied/43 admission offers/40 incoming

% of students receiving:
Full tuition waiver only: 0%
Assistantship/fellowship only: 10%
Both full tuition waiver & assistantship/fellowship: 10%

Approximate percentage of incoming students with a B.A./B.S. only: not reported **Master's:** not reported

Approximate percentage of students who are Women: 85% **Ethnic Minority:** 100% **International:** not reported

Average years to complete the doctoral program (including internship): 6 years

Personal interview
Required in person

Attrition rate in past 7 years: 19%

Percentage of students applying for internship in 2017 accepted into:

APA internships: 50% **APPIC internships:** 90%

Formal tracks/concentrations: none

Clinical opportunities

assessment	community psychology
consultation	military/veterans
Hispanic studies	private practice
hospitals/medical centers	supervision

Case Western Reserve University (Ph.D.)

Department of Psychological Sciences
Mather Memorial Building
11220 Bellflower Road
Cleveland, OH 44106-7123
phone#: (216) 368-2686 (800) 368-2685
email: cwrupsych@gmail.com
Web address: psychsciences.case.edu/graduate/clinical-psych/

1 2 3 **4** 5 6 7
Practice oriented — Equal emphasis — Research oriented

Percentage of faculty subscribing to each of the following orientations:

Psychodynamic/Psychoanalytic	5%
Applied behavioral analysis/Radical behavioral	0%
Family systems/Systems	5%
Existential/Phenomenological/Humanistic	10%
Cognitive/Cognitive-behavioral	80%

Courses required for incoming students to have completed prior to enrolling:
general undergraduate psychology courses

Recommended but not mandatory courses: psychology major

GRE mean
Verbal 157 Quantitative 155
Analytical Writing not reported
Psychology Subject Test not reported

GPA mean
Overall GPA 3.67

Number of applications/admission offers/incoming students in 2017
214 applications/6 offers/4 incoming students

% of students receiving:
Full tuition waiver only: 0%
Assistantship/fellowship only: 0%
Both full tuition waiver & assistantship/fellowship: 100%

Approximate percentage of incoming students with a B.A./B.S. only: 100% **Master's:** 0%

Approximate percentage of all students who are Women: 90% **Ethnic Minority:** 9% **International:** 1%

Average years to complete the doctoral program (including internship): 6.2 years

Personal interview
Preferred in person but telephone acceptable

Attrition rate in past 7 years: 6%

Percentage of students applying for internship in 2017 accepted into:

APA internships: 100% **APPIC internships:** 100%

Formal tracks/concentrations: child/pediatric psychology, adult psychology

Research areas	# Faculty	# Grants
aging	1	0
anxiety disorders/PTSD	2	1
depression	2	0
developmental disabilities	1	0
learning disabilities	1	0
parent–child interaction	2	0
personality disorders	1	2
religion/spirituality	1	1

Clinical opportunities

ADHD	adjustment disorders
affective disorders	aging/gerontology
anxiety & depression	assessment
child psychology	community mental health
eating disorders	Alzheimer's/dementia
health psychology	schizophrenia/psychosis
student counseling centers	

Catholic University of America (Ph.D.)

Department of Psychology
620 Michigan Avenue, NE
Washington, DC 20064
phone#: 202-319-5750
email: falk@cua.edu
Web address: psychology.cua.edu/graduate/phdclprog.cfm

1 2 3 **4** 5 6 7
Practice oriented — Equal emphasis — Research oriented

Percentage of faculty subscribing to each of the following orientations:

Psychodynamic/Psychoanalytic	20%
Applied behavioral analysis/Radical behavioral	20%
Family systems/Systems	60%
Existential/Phenomenological/Humanistic	50%
Cognitive/Cognitive-behavioral	80%
Integrative	80%

Courses required for incoming students to have completed prior to enrolling:
statistics and research methods; in addition to coursework, research experience is required.

Recommended but not mandatory courses: abnormal, personality, developmental, social

GRE mean
Verbal 162 Quantitative 158
Analytical Writing 4.7
Psychology Subject Test not reported

GPA mean
Overall GPA 3.4

Number of applications/admission offers/incoming students in 2017
132 applied/ admission offers/6 incoming

% of students receiving:
Partial or Full tuition waiver only: 10%
Assistantship/fellowship only: 0%
Both partial or full tuition waiver & assistantship/fellowship: 86%

Approximate percentage of incoming students with a B.A./B.S. only: 100% **Master's:** 0%

Approximate percentage of all students who are Women: 77% **Ethnic Minority:** 10% **International:** 5%

Average years to complete the doctoral program (including internship): Mean 6 years, Median 6 years

Personal interview
Required in person

Attrition rate in past 7 years: 2.8%

Percentage of students applying for internship in 2017 accepted into:

APA internships: 100% **APPIC internships:** 100%

Formal tracks/concentrations: Adult Clinical; Children, Families, and Cultures.

Research areas	# Faculty	# Grants
adolescence	4	1
adult psychopathology	2	0
anxiety	3	0
assessment	2	2
attachment	3	1
child clinical	3	1
cognition	4	0
community context	5	3
couples	1	0
developmental psychopathology	6	2
discrimination	1	0
emotion regulation	8	4
ethics/risk management	1	0
ethnic minorities	3	2
family	5	2
immigration	1	1
interpersonal processes	6	2
language development	1	1
military families	1	1
military mental health	1	2
mindfulness	3	0
mood disorders	8	2
parent-child interactions	5	2
parent training	2	0
psychotherapy process/outcomes	4	2
social anxiety	1	1
stress and coping	4	1
suicide	2	2
veterans' mental health care	1	1
violence	1	1

Clinical opportunities

assessment batteries	bilingual assessment
child, adolescent, and adult	psychotherapy
community mental health	consultation
couple therapy	family therapy
neuropsychology	multicultural mental health
veterans' mental health care	pediatric

University of Central Florida (Ph.D.)

4000 Central Florida Blvd, Psychology Building
Orlando, Florida 32816-1390
phone#: (407) 823-4344
email: psyinfo@ucf.edu
Web address: https://sciences.ucf.edu/psychology/graduate/ph-d-clinical/

1	2	3	4	5	6	**7**
Practice oriented			Equal emphasis			Research oriented

Percentage of faculty subscribing to each of the following orientations:

Psychodynamic/Psychoanalytic	0%
Applied behavioral analysis/Radical behavioral	0%
Family systems/Systems	0%
Existential/Phenomenological/Humanistic	0%
Cognitive/Cognitive-behavioral	0%
Integrative Emphasis	100%

Courses required for incoming students to have completed prior to enrolling:
a minimum of 18 semester hours of undergraduate psychology courses

Recommended but not mandatory courses: research experience is heavily weighted during admissions

GRE mean
Quantitative 154 Verbal 154
Analytical Writing not reported
Psychology Subject Test not reported

GPA mean
Overall GPA 3.8

Number of applications/admission offers/incoming students in 2017
137 applied/11 admission offers/7 incoming

% of students receiving:
Full tuition waiver only: 0%
Assistantship/fellowship only: 0%
Both full tuition waiver & assistantship/fellowship: 100%

Approximate percentage of incoming students with a B.A./B.S. only: 100% **Master's:** 0%

Approximate percentage of all students who are Women: 72% **Ethnic Minority:** 27% **International:** 1%

Average years to complete the doctoral program (including internship): 6 years

Personal interview
Required in person

Attrition rate in past 7 years: 9%

Percentage of students applying for internship in 2017 accepted into:

APA internships: 86% **APPIC internships:**

Formal tracks/concentrations: child, adult

Research areas	**# Faculty**	**# Grants**
acceptance and commitment therapy	1	0
aging	1	0
alcohol and substance abuse	1	0
anxiety disorders	2	0
ADHD/cognition	1	0
health psychology	1	0
schizophrenia	1	0
technology and intervention	1	0
preschool/young child symptoms	1	0

Clinical opportunities

adult	acceptance and commitment therapy
anxiety	ADHD evaluation
child	PTSD
health psychology	schizophrenia
gifted evaluation	
young child	

Central Michigan University (Ph.D.)

Department of Psychology
Mt. Pleasant, MI 48859
phone#: (989) 774-6463
email: Reid.Skeel@cmich.edu
Web address: www.cmich.edu/chsbs/x20739.xml

1	2	3	4	5	6	7
Practice oriented			Equal emphasis			Research oriented

Percentage of faculty subscribing to each of the following orientations:

Psychodynamic/Psychoanalytic	0%
Applied behavioral analysis/Radical behavioral	10%
Family systems/Systems	20%
Existential/Phenomenological/Humanistic	0%
Cognitive/Cognitive-behavioral	70%

Courses required for incoming students to have completed prior to enrolling: none

Recommended but not mandatory courses: statistics, experimental, developmental, abnormal, personality theory, measurement theory

GRE mean
Verbal 158 Quantitative 152
Analytical Writing 4.9
Psychology Subject Test not reported

GPA mean
Overall GPA 3.84

Number of applications/admission offers/incoming students in 2016
102 applied/7 admission offers/4 incoming

% of students receiving:
Full tuition waiver only: 0%
Assistantship/fellowship only: 0%
Both full tuition waiver & assistantship/fellowship: 100%

Approximate percentage of incoming students with a B.A./B.S. only: 90% **Master's:** 10%

Approximate percentage of all students who are Women: 75% **Ethnic Minority:** 0% **International:** 0%

Average years to complete the doctoral program (including internship): 6 years

Personal interview
Interview not required

Attrition rate in past 7 years: 3%

Percentage of students applying for internship in 2016 accepted into:

APA internships: 100% **APPIC internships:**

Formal tracks/concentrations/specializations: none

Research areas	**# Faculty**	**# Grants**
anxiety disorders	1	1
assessment	1	0
children	1	2
diversity and sexual deviance	1	0
health psychology	1	1
neuropsychology	1	1
severe psychopathology	1	1
violence and aggression	1	0

Clinical opportunities

adult clinical	parent–child interaction therapy
behavior therapy	psychodynamic therapy
child clinical	psychological assessment
cognitive-behavioral therapy	rehabilitation
forensic psychology	school-based interventions
neuropsychology	

Chestnut Hill College (Psy.D.)

Department of Professional Psychology
9601 Germantown Avenue
Philadelphia, PA 19118-2693
phone#: (215)-248-7020

email: profpsyc@chc.edu
Web address: www.chc.edu/psyd

1	2	3	4	5	6	7
Practice oriented			Equal emphasis			Research oriented

Percentage of faculty subscribing to each of the following orientations:

Psychodynamic/Psychoanalytic	55%
Applied behavioral analysis/Radical behavioral	0%
Family systems/Systems	33%
Existential/Phenomenological/Humanistic	0%
Cognitive/Cognitive-behavioral	12%

Courses required for incoming students to have completed prior to enrolling:
General Psychology, Abnormal Psychology, Statistics, at least one other psychology class

Recommended but not mandatory courses:
Developmental psychology, Research design

GRE mean
Verbal 155 Quantitative 153
Analytical Writing 4.25
Psychology Subject Test not reported

GPA mean
Overall GPA 3.45

Number of applications/admission offers/incoming students in 2017
152 applied/57 admission offers/24 incoming

% of students receiving:
Full tuition waiver only: 0%
Assistantship/fellowship only: 13%
Both full tuition waiver & assistantship/fellowship: 0%

Approximate percentage of incoming students with a B.A./B.S. only: 65% **Master's:** 35%

Approximate percentage of students who are Women: 77% **Ethnic Minority:** 29% **International:** 2%

Average years to complete the doctoral program (including internship): 5.97 years

Personal interview
Required in person

Attrition rate in past 7 years: 11.6%

Percentage of students applying for internship in 2017 accepted into:

APA internships: 100% **APPIC internships:** 0%

Formal tracks/concentrations: Assessment, Couple & Family Therapy

Clinical opportunities

child clinical	adolescents
adult clinical	family therapy

The Chicago School of Professional Psychology (Psy.D.) – Chicago Campus

325 N. Wells, 3rd Floor
Chicago, IL 60654
phone#: (800) 721-8072
email: admissionsTCSPP-CHI@thechicagoschool.edu
Web address: https://www.thechicagoschool.edu/chicago/programs/clinical-psychology/

1	2	3	4	5	6	7
Practice oriented			Equal emphasis			Research oriented

Percentage of faculty subscribing to each of the following orientations:

Psychodynamic/Psychoanalytic	40%
Applied behavioral analysis/Radical behavioral	5%
Family systems/Systems	40%
Existential/Phenomenological/Humanistic	35%
Cognitive/Cognitive-behavioral	20%
Other : Multicultural	5%

Courses required for incoming students to have completed prior to enrolling:
18 hours in psychology, including statistics, lifespan/human development, abnormal psychology

Recommended but not mandatory courses: none

GRE mean
Verbal 63% Quantitative 41%
Analytical Writing 64%
Psychology Subject Test not required

GPA mean
Overall GPA 3.4

Number of applications/admission offers/incoming students in 2017
392 applications/107 admission offers/56 incoming students

% of students receiving:
Full tuition waiver only: 0%
Assistantship/fellowship only: 7%
Both full tuition waiver & assistantship/fellowship: 0%
HRSA Grant funded scholarship – $30,000. 15 students (8%) each year

Approximate percentage of incoming students with a B.A./B.S. only: 80% **Master's:** 20%

Approximate percentage of all students who are Women: 74% **Ethnic Minority:** 29% **International:** 7%

Average years to complete the doctoral program (including internship): 5 years

Personal interview
Required in person with virtual interview available for hardship

Attrition rate in past 7 years: 14%

Percentage of students applying for internship in 2016 accepted into:

APA internships: 86% **APPIC internships:** 14%

Formal tracks/concentrations: none — many opportunities for research, training, and courses in areas such as Child and Adolescence, Health, and International Psychology are available.(see catalogue for full listing) including Study Abroad opportunities.

Research areas	# Faculty	# Grants
Gender identity/ transgender issues	1	0
Animal assisted therapy	1	0
Professional Issues/Training	2	1
Residential treatment(children)	1	0
Violence prevention	2	1
Models of healthcare	2	0
Human Rights/Refugees	2	0
Latino mental health	2	0
Sexuality	1	0
Child Welfare/Maltreatment	2	1
Minority/Cross-Cultural/Diversity	3	0
Religion/Spirituality	2	1

Clinical opportunities

Adolescent Psychotherapy/At-Risk Adolescents/Delinquency
psychiatric inpatient/outpatient intervention
Assessment
Marriage/Couples
Cognitive/Cognitive-Behavioral Therapy
Family/Family Therapy/Family Systems
Biofeedback/Neurofeedback
Anxiety Disorders/Panic Disorders
Personality assessment
Dialectical Behavior Therapy/Analysis
Child/Pediatric
Psychoanalytic/Psychodynamic Therapy
College counseling center
Day Treatment/partial hospitalization
Eating Disorders/Body Image
Family/Family Therapy/Family Systems
Forensic
Aging/Gerontology
Group Therapy
Community mental health
Mental health administration
Community psychology
Child abuse/neglect
Correctional/forensic settings
Posttraumatic Stress Disorder/Trauma
Medical Center/Hospital Based Services
Private and group practice
Parent-Child Interaction/Parent Training
Creative and expressive arts
Organizational psychology
Neuropsychology
Oncology/Cancer Care
Cross-cultural/international/refugees
Developmental Disabilities/Autism/Assessment
School/Educational
Early education/head start/infants
Religion/Spirituality
Gay/Lesbian/Bisexual/Transgender
Substance Abuse/Addiction
Behavioral medicine/health psychology
Spanish-Speaking Clients
Rehabilitation
Sexual Offenders
Pain management
Affective Disorders/Depression/Mood Disorders
Veterans Hospital/Medical Center
Primary care
Inner city and rural populations
Correctional Psychology/Prisons
Victim/Violence/Sexual Abuse
Weight Management
Presurgical Evaluation

The Chicago School of Professional Psychology, Washington DC (Psy.D.)

Department of Clinical Psychology
901 15th Street NW, 2nd Fl.
Washington, DC 20005
phone#: (202) 706-5000
Web address: www.thechicagoschool.edu/washington-dc/programs/psyd-clinical-psychology/

1	**2**	3	4	5	6	7
Practice oriented			Equal emphasis			Research oriented

Percentage of faculty subscribing to each of the following orientations:

Psychodynamic/Psychoanalytic	40%
Applied behavioral analysis/Radical behavioral	0%
Family systems/Systems	40%
Existential/Phenomenological/Humanistic	20%
Cognitive/Cognitive-behavioral	80%

Courses required for incoming students to have completed prior to enrolling:

18 credits of psychology courses including (all required):

- Statistics
- Abnormal Psychology
- Child/Human Development

Recommended but not mandatory courses:

Multicultural Psychology, Psychological Assessment, Clinical Interview/Counseling Skills, Research Methods

GRE mean

Verbal + Quantitative: 298.9
Analytical Writing: 3.8
Psychology Subject Test:

GPA mean

Overall GPA: 3.2 (undergrad); 3.8 (grad)

Number of applications/admission offers/incoming students in 2017

Applied: 73/Admission offers: 41/Incoming: 23

% of students receiving:

Full tuition waiver only: 0%
Assistantship/fellowship only: 0%
Both full tuition waiver & assistantship/fellowship: 0%

Approximate percentage of incoming students with a B.A./B.S. only: 52% **Master's:** 48%

Approximate percentage of all students who are Women: 79.6% **Ethnic Minority:** 57.4% **International:** 3.7%

Average years to complete the doctoral program (including internship): 5.3 years

Personal interview

Required in person but telephone acceptable

Attrition rate in past 7 years: 29.8%

Percentage of students applying for internship last year accepted into:

APA internships: 12.5% **APPIC internships:** 87.5%

Formal tracks/concentrations: Forensics

Research areas	# Faculty	# Grants
anxiety disorders	1	0
assessment/diagnosis	1	0
attachment	1	0
immigrants and immigration	1	0
infertility	1	0
intergroup relations	1	0
intersectionality	1	0
LGBTQ mental health	2	0
mental health disparities	3	0
mindfulness & acceptance	1	0
multicultural psychology	4	0
research methodology	1	0
trauma	1	0

Clinical opportunities
Assessment
Child/Adolescent
College Counseling Center
Community Psychology
Forensic
Medical Center/Hospital-Based Services
Minority/Multicultural
Severe Mental Illness
Veterans Hospital/Medical Center

University of Cincinnati (Ph.D.)

Department of Psychology
Suite 4130 Edwards One
Cincinnati, OH 45221-0376
phone#: (513) 556-5580
email: Paula.Shear@uc.edu
Web address: http://www.artsci.uc.edu/departments/psychology/grad/phd.html

1 2 3 4 5 **6** 7

Practice oriented — Equal emphasis — Research oriented

Percentage of faculty subscribing to each of the following orientations:

Psychodynamic/Psychoanalytic	0%
Applied behavioral analysis/Radical behavioral	0%
Family systems/Systems	27%
Existential/Phenomenological/Humanistic	0%
Cognitive/Cognitive-behavioral	73%

Courses required for incoming students prior to enrolling:
Research methods in behavioral or social sciences, one course in statistical methods. A minimum of 16 semester credit hours in non-introductory psychology courses.

Courses recommended but not mandatory:
Abnormal Psychology

GRE mean
Verbal 157
Quantitative 154
Analytical Writing 4.35
Psychology Subject Test – test is optional.

GPA mean
Overall GPA 3.735

Number of applications/admission offers/incoming students in 2016
148 applied/8 admission offers/6 incoming

% of students receiving:
Full tuition waiver only: 0%
Assistantship/fellowship only: 0%
Both full tuition waiver & assistantship/fellowship: 100%

Approximate percentage of incoming students with a B.A./B.S. only: 84% **Master's:** 16%

Approximate percentage of all students who are Women: 89% **Ethnic Minority:** 37.14% **International:** .05%

Average years to complete the doctoral program (including internship): 6 years

Personal interview
In-person interview strongly preferred

Attrition rate in past 7 years: 9%

Percentage of students applying for internship in 2016 accepted into:

APA internships: 100% **APPIC internships:** 0%

Formal tracks/concentrations: Neuropsychology, Heath psychology, General clinical

Research areas	# Faculty	# Grants
Addictive behaviors	3	3
Child clinical	5	4
Health psychology	3	4
Neuropsychology	4	3
Serious mental illness	4	3

Clinical opportunities
Addictive behaviors
Child & family
Health psychology
Serious mental illness
Community mental health
Developmental disorders
Clinical neuropsychology

The City College of New York, City University of New York (Ph.D.)

Department of Psychology
New York, NY 10031
phone#: (212) 650-5674
Web address: www.gc.cuny.edu/Page-Elements/Academics-Research-Centers-Initiatives/Doctoral-Programs/Psychology/Training-Areas/Clinical-Psychology-@-City-College

1 2 3 **4** 5 6 7

Practice oriented — Equal emphasis — Research oriented

Percentage of faculty subscribing to each of the following orientations:

Psychodynamic/Psychoanalytic	60%

Applied behavioral analysis/Radical behavioral	0%
Family systems/Systems	10%
Existential/Phenomenological/Humanistic	5%
Cognitive/Cognitive-behavioral	25%

Courses required for incoming students to have completed prior to enrolling:
15 credits in psychology including one semester of statistics and one semester of experimental/laboratory

Recommended but not mandatory courses: none

GRE mean
Verbal 160 Quantitative 154
Analytical Writing 4.1
Psychology Subject Test 697

GPA mean
Overall GPA: 3.6

Number of applications/admission offers/incoming students in 2017
180 applied/15 admission offers/14 incoming

% of students receiving:
Full tuition waiver only: 100%
Assistantship/fellowship only: 0%
Both full tuition waiver & assistantship/fellowship: 20%

Approximate percentage of incoming students with a BA/BS only: 54.5% **Master's:** 45.5%

Approximate percentage of all students who are Women: 70% **Ethnic Minority:** 27.2% **International:** 9.1%

Average years to complete the doctoral program (including internship): 7 years

Personal interview
In person interviews only, with the rare exception of Skype

Attrition rate in past 7 years: 2%

Percentage of students applying for internship in 2017 accepted into:

APA internships: 100% **APPIC internships:** 100%

Formal tracks/concentrations: child or adult

Research areas	**# Faculty**	**# Grants**
affective neuroscience	3	1
adolescent health disparities	1	1
borderline personality disorders	1	1
homeless families and trauma	1	1
health disparities in psychotic disorders	1	1
mentoring racial ethnic minorities	4	1
post-traumatic stress and addictions	2	1

Clinical opportunities
On-site Psychological Center — first four years in Program required

Clark University (Ph.D.)

Frances L. Hiatt School of Psychology
950 Main Street
Worcester, MA 01610
phone#: (508) 793-7276
email: wgrolnick@clarku.edu
Web address: www.clarku.edu/departments/psychology/grad/clinical

1	2	3	4	5	6	7
Practice oriented			Equal emphasis			Research oriented

Percentage of faculty subscribing to each of the following orientations:

Psychodynamic/Psychoanalytic	33%
Applied behavioral analysis/Radical behavioral	50%
Family systems/Systems	17%
Existential/Phenomenological/Humanistic	33%
Cognitive/Cognitive-behavioral	33%

Courses required for incoming students to have completed prior to enrolling: none

Recommended but not mandatory courses: Psychology major, substantial research experience, statistics, research methods, abnormal psychology

GRE mean
Verbal 162 Quantitative 161
Analytical Writing not reported
Psychology Subject Test 753

GPA mean
Overall GPA 3.9

Number of applications/admission offers/incoming students in 2017
152 applied/11 admission offers/3 incoming

% of students receiving:
Tuition waiver only: 0%
Assistantship/fellowship only: 0%
Both tuition waiver & assistantship/fellowship: 100%

Approximate percentage of incoming students with a B.A./B.S. only: 100% **Master's:** 0%

Approximate percentage of students who are Women: 100% **Ethnic Minority:** 33% **International:** 0%

Average years to complete the doctoral program (including internship): 6.5 years

Personal interview
Required in person

Attrition rate in past 7 years: 16.7%

Percentage of students applying for internship in 2017 accepted into:

APA internships: 100% **APPIC internships:** 100%

Formal tracks/concentrations/specializations: Not reported

Research areas	**# Faculty**	**# Grants**
Affective and anxiety disorders	4	0
Child clinical/child psychopathology	2	0
Couples functioning and therapy	3	1
Cultural adaptations	1	0
Depression	3	1
Diverse families	3	2
Gender	3	0
LGBT mental health	2	1

Men and masculinity	1	0
Mental health care disparities	1	0
Mood and anxiety disorders	4	0
Motivation and self-regulation	2	0
Parenting & family	3	1
Prevention	3	0
PTSD/traumatic events	2	0
Substance use disorders	1	0

Clinical opportunities
Adult assessment and therapy
Child assessment and therapy
Couples therapy
Acceptance and Commitment Therapy
Cognitive behavior therapy
Addictive behaviors

University of Colorado Boulder (Ph.D.)

Department of Psychology and Neuroscience
345 UCB
Boulder, CO 80309-0345
phone#: (303) 492-8805
email: info@pysch.colorado.edu
Web address: http://www.colorado.edu/clinicalpsychology/

1	2	3	4	5	**6**	7
Practice oriented			Equal emphasis			Research oriented

Percentage of faculty subscribing to each of the following orientations:

Psychodynamic/Psychoanalytic	0%
Applied behavioral analysis/Radical behavioral	29%
Family systems/Systems	14%
Existential/Phenomenological/Humanistic	14%
Cognitive/Cognitive-behavioral	100%

Courses required for incoming students to have completed prior to enrolling:
None. However, the GRE General Test and GRE Psychology Test are both required.

Recommended but not mandatory courses:
Psychopathology/abnormal, statistics, research methods, neuroscience, psychological assessment, psychotherapy, developmental, social/personality

GRE mean
Verbal 168 Quantitative 160
Psychology Subject Test 793
Analytical Writing 5.5

GPA mean
Overall GPA 3.8

Number of applications/admission offers/incoming students in 2017
127 applied/6 admission offers/3 incoming

% of students receiving:
Full tuition waiver only: 0%
Assistantship/fellowship only: 0%
Both full tuition waiver & assistantship/fellowship: 100%

Approximate percentage of incoming students with a B.A./B.S. only: 100% **Master's:** 0%

Approximate percentage of students who are
Women: 78.5% **Ethnic Minority:** 3.5%
International: 0%

Average years to complete the doctoral program (including internship): 6.7 years

Personal interview
Required

Attrition rate in past 7 years: 10%

Percentage of students applying for internship in 2017 accepted into:

APA internships: 80% **APPIC internships:** 80%

Formal tracks/concentrations: certificate in behavioral genetics; joint PhD in clinical psychology and neuroscience

Research areas	# Faculty	# Grants
adult psychopathology	7	4
affective disorders	4	3
assessment/diagnosis/classification	2	1
child clinical	2	1
developmental	2	2
family research	2	2
genetics	3	3
prevention	1	1
psychotherapy outcome/process	3	3
substance abuse	2	2

Clinical opportunities
acceptance and commitment therapy
behavioral activation
cognitive-behavior therapy
family-focused therapy
marital/couple therapy
neuropsychological assessment
mindfulness interventions

University of Colorado at Colorado Springs (Ph.D.)

Department of Psychology
1420 Austin Bluffs Parkway
Colorado Springs, CO 80918
phone#: 719-255-4500
email: ddubois@uccs.edu
Web address: www.uccs.edu/psych/graduate/phd-program.html

1	2	3	**4**	5	6	7
Practice oriented			Equal emphasis			Research oriented

Percentage of faculty subscribing to each of the following orientations:

Psychodynamic/Psychoanalytic	20%
Applied behavioral analysis/Radical behavioral	20%
Family systems/Systems	20%
Existential/Phenomenological/Humanistic	0%
Cognitive/Cognitive-behavioral	40%

Courses required for incoming students to have completed prior to enrolling:
Recommend equivalent of Psychology major

Recommended but not mandatory courses: statistics, research methods

GRE mean (from 2016–2017 admissions cycle)
PhD Programs combined
Verbal 160
Quantitative 153
Writing 4.6

Psychology Subject Test mean (from 2016–2017 admissions cycle)
Average PY = 740
Average PYSU1 = 67.5
Average PYSU2 = 71.5

GPA mean (from 2016–2017 admissions cycle)
Overall GPA 3.77

Number of applications/admission offers/incoming students in 2017
Geropsychology: 49 applied/8 admission offers/5 incoming
Trauma psychology: 205 applied/5 offers/2 incoming

% of students receiving:
Full tuition waiver only: 0%
Assistantship/fellowship only: 100%
Both full tuition waiver & assistantship/fellowship: 0%

Approximate percentage of incoming students with a B.A./B.S. only: 80% **Master's:** 20%

Approximate percentage of incoming students who are
Women: 86% **Ethnic Minority:** 29% **International:** 0%

Approximate percentage of all students who are
Women: 95% **Ethnic Minority:** 19% **International:** 5%

Average years to complete the doctoral program (including internship): 5.5 years

Personal interview
Required in person

Attrition rate in past 7 years: 10%

Percentage of students applying for internship in 2017 accepted into:

APA internships: 100% **APPIC internships:** 100%

Formal tracks/concentrations: geropsychology and trauma psychology

Research areas	# Faculty	# Grants
geropsychology	5	5
trauma and military psychology	3	3
social psychology	2	2
cognitive psychology	2	1
program evaluation	2	2
biopsychology	1	1
neuropsychology	2	0
behavioral gerontology	1	0
adolescent psychology	1	0
psychology and the law	1	0
child clinical	1	0
lifespan development	1	0
evolutionary psychology	1	1

Clinical opportunities
geropsychology
caregiver programs
neuropsychological
integrated care and specialty mental health
memory and cognition
behavioral medicine
veterans and traumatic brain injury
developmental disabilities
trauma psychology

University of Colorado Denver (Ph.D.)

Department of Psychology
Campus Box 173, PO Box 173364
Denver, CO 80217-3364
Phone#: (303) 315-7050
email: anne.beard@ucdenver.edu
Web address: http://www.ucdenver.edu/academics/colleges/CLAS/Departments/psychology/Programs/PhD/Pages/Overview--FAQs.aspx

1	2	3	4	5	6	7
Practice oriented			Equal emphasis			Research oriented

Percentage of faculty subscribing to each of the following orientations:

Psychodynamic/Psychoanalytic	25%
Applied behavioral analysis/Radical behavioral	0%
Family systems/Systems	25%
Existential/Phenomenological/Humanistic	25%
Cognitive/Cognitive-behavioral	80%

Courses required for incoming students to have completed prior to enrolling: Introduction to Psychology, Abnormal Psychology, Psychological Statistics, and Research Methods

Recommended but not mandatory courses: not reported

GRE mean
Verbal + Quantitative = 85th percentile
Analytical Writing = 80th percentile
Psychology Subject Test = not required

GPA mean
Overall GPA = 3.75

Number of applications/admission offers/incoming students in 2017
200 applied/8 admission offers/6 incoming

% of students receiving:
Full tuition waiver only: 0%
Assistantship/fellowship only: 0%
Both full tuition waiver & assistantship/fellowship: 100%

Approximate percentage of incoming students with a B.A./B.S. only: 83% **Master's:** 17%

Approximate percentage of all students who are
Women: 70% **Ethnic Minority:** 20% **International:** 0%

Average years to complete the doctoral program (including internship): 6 years

Personal interview — Yes

Attrition rate in past 7 years: 15%

Percentage of students applying for internship last year accepted into:

APA internships: 100% **APPIC internships:** 100%

Formal tracks/concentrations: Clinical Health Psychology

Research areas	# Faculty	# Grants
Cardiovascular health psychology	3	2
Religion/spirituality	2	1
PTSD	1	1
Couples/relationships and health	2	1
Pediatric health	2	0
Post-partum depression	2	2
Cancer caregivers	1	1
Neuropsychology	1	2
Addiction	1	0
Pain	2	2

Clinical opportunities

anxiety disorders
depression
psychopathology assessment
integrated primary care
sleep disorders
bone marrow transplantation
community mental health
child assessment
chronic diseases management
child clinical and pediatric psychology
neuropsychology
psychosocial oncology
women's health

University of Connecticut (Ph.D.)

Department of Psychology
406 Babbidge Road, Unit 1020
Storrs, CT 06269-1020
phone#: (860) 486-2057 (Admissions information)
email: psychgrad@uconn.edu
Web address: web.uconn.edu/psychology/academics/graduate/phd_clinical.html

1	2	3	**4**	5	6	7
Practice oriented			Equal emphasis			Research oriented

Percentage of faculty subscribing to each of the following orientations:

Psychodynamic/Psychoanalytic	24%
Applied behavioral analysis/Radical behavioral	8%
Family systems/Systems	16%
Existential/Phenomenological/Humanistic	8%
Cognitive-behavioral	92%

Courses required for incoming students to have completed prior to enrolling: none

Recommended but not mandatory courses: abnormal, research methods

GRE mean
Verbal 161 Quantitative 160
Analytical Writing 4.5
Psychology Subject Test 720

GPA mean
Overall GPA 3.66

Number of applications/admission offers/incoming students in 2016
331 applied/9 admission offers/6 incoming

% of students receiving:
Full tuition waiver only: 0%
Assistantship/fellowship only: 0%
Both full tuition waiver & assistantship/fellowship: 100%

Approximate percentage of incoming students with a B.A./B.S. only: 66% **Master's:** 33%

Approximate percentage of all students who are Women: 78% **Ethnic Minority:** 32% **International:** 4%

Average years to complete the doctoral program (including internship): 6.04 years

Personal interview
Preferred in person but telephone acceptable

Attrition rate in past 7 years: 7%

Percentage of students applying for internship in 2016 accepted into:

APA internships: 100% **APPIC internships:** 100%

Formal tracks/concentrations: child clinical, neuropsychology, health psychology

Research areas	# Faculty	# Grants
adult psychopathology	6	5
anxiety disorders	2	1
autism	3	3
child psychopathology	6	4
domestic violence	1	1
health psychology	3	3
multicultural psychology	2	2
neuropsychology	3	3
trauma	4	3
depression	4	2

Clinical opportunities

Autism Spectrum Disorders
childhood psychopathology
chronic mental illness
health psychology
multicultural psychology
neuroimaging
school/community consultation
traumatic brain injury
traumatic stress disorders
anxiety disorders
psychological assessment
depression
early childhood services
neuropsychology

University of Delaware (Ph.D.)

Department of Psychology
Newark, DE 19716
phone#: (302) 831-0355
email: rbeveridge@psych.udel.edu
Web address: www.psych.udel.edu/graduate/detail/overview_of_clinical_science/

1	2	3	4	5	**6**	7
Practice oriented			Equal emphasis			Research oriented

Percentage of faculty subscribing to each of the following orientations:

Psychodynamic/Psychoanalytic	0%
Applied behavioral analysis/Radical behavioral	0%
Family systems/Systems	0%
Existential/Phenomenological/Humanistic	0%
Cognitive/Cognitive-behavioral	100%

(A more accurate description would be that our faculty have a clinical science orientation)

Courses required for incoming students to have completed prior to enrolling: none

Recommended but not mandatory courses: Statistics, biopsychology, abnormal, history and systems, cognitive, developmental, research design

GRE mean
Verbal 165 Quantitative 160
Analytical Writing 4.7
Psychology Subject Test not reported

GPA mean
Overall GPA 3.88

Number of applications/admission offers/incoming students in 2017
169 applied/8 admission offers/5 incoming

% of students receiving:
Full tuition waiver only: 0%
Assistantship/fellowship only: 0%
Both full tuition waiver & assistantship/fellowship: 100%

Approximate percentage of incoming students with a B.A./B.S. only: 80% **Master's:** 20%

Approximate percentage of all students who are Women: 84% **Ethnic Minority:** 20% **International:** 0%

Average years to complete the doctoral program (including internship): 6 years

Personal interview
Required in person

Attrition rate in past 7 years: 6%

Percentage of students applying for internship in 2017 accepted into:

APA internships: 100% **APPIC internships:** 100%

Formal tracks/concentrations: none

Research areas	# Faculty	# Grants
anxiety, stress, and coping	2	1
attachment theory	2	2
child clinical	—	4
developmental risk	5	3
foster care	1	2
psychophysiology	3	1
psychotherapy research	2	0
couples research	1	1

Clinical opportunities
child (internalizing and externalizing disorders)
behavioral medicine
depression
anxiety

University of Denver (Ph.D.)

Department of Psychology
2155 S. Race Street
Denver, CO
phone#: (303)871-2478
email:
Web address: http://www.du.edu/ahss/psychology/

1	2	3	4	5	**6**	7
Practice oriented			Equal emphasis			Research oriented

Percentage of faculty subscribing to each of the following orientations:

Psychodynamic/Psychoanalytic	0%
Applied behavioral analysis/Radical behavioral	0%
Family systems/Systems	10%
Existential/Phenomenological/Humanistic	0%
Cognitive/Cognitive-behavioral	90%

Courses required for incoming students to have completed prior to enrolling: not reported

Recommended but not mandatory courses: Statistics, Reearch Methods, Psychopathology

GRE mean
Verbal + Quantitative 161
Analytical Writing n/a
Psychology Subject Test n/a

GPA mean
Overall GPA 3.83

Number of applications/admission offers/incoming students in 2015
293 applied/8 admission offers/5 incoming

% of students receiving:
Full tuition waiver only: 0%
Assistantship/fellowship only: 0%
Both full tuition waiver & assistantship/fellowship: 100%

Approximate percentage of incoming students with a B.A./B.S. only: 100% **Master's:**

Approximate percentage of all students who are Women: 80% **Ethnic Minority:** 20% **International:** 0%

Average years to complete the doctoral program (including internship): 6 years

Personal interview not reported

Attrition rate in past 7 years: 14%

Percentage of students applying for internship last year accepted into:

APA internships: 100% **APPIC internships:**

Formal tracks/concentrations: not reported

Research areas	# Faculty	# Grants
attention-deficit disorder	1	1
behavioral genetics	1	1
child abuse	2	0
child psychopathology	5	2
community engaged research	2	0
depression	1	0
developmental neuropsychology	1	0
dissemination of treatments	1	0
eating disorders	1	0
learning disorders	1	0
marriage and marital therapy	3	0
multiculturalism	2	0
parenting	2	0
PTSD	1	0
relationship education	3	9

romantic relationships	2	1
resiliency	2	0
intimate partner violence	3	1
trauma	2	0

Clinical opportunities
Children
Adolescents
Young Adults
Assessment and Intervention with Diverse Populations
Depression and Anxiety
Trauma
Learning Disorders
Cognitive Behavior Therapy
Dialectical Behavior Therapy
Marital Therapy
Neuropsychological Assessments
Parenting Interventions

University of Denver (Psy.D.)

Graduate School of Professional Psychology
2450 South Vine Street
Denver, CO 80208-0208
phone#: (303) 871-2908
email: gsppinfo@du.edu
Web address: http://www.du.edu/gspp/programs/psyd-clinical/index.html

1	2	3	4	5	6	7
Practice oriented			Equal emphasis			Research oriented

Percentage of faculty subscribing to each of the following orientations:

Psychodynamic/Psychoanalytic	20%
Applied behavioral analysis/Radical behavioral	20%
Family systems/Systems	20%
Existential/Phenomenological/Humanistic	5%
Cognitive/Cognitive-behavioral	20%
Integrative	15%

Courses required for incoming students to have completed prior to enrolling:
at least four psychology courses or applicants can take the GRE Psychology subject exam and score a 660 or higher in lieu of taking the courses to meet the psychology prerequisite.

Recommended but not mandatory courses: statistics, personality theory, experimental, child, abnormal, history of psychology

GRE mean (2016)
Verbal 158 Quantitative 153
Analytical Writing 4.5
Psychology Subject Test (optional): not reported

GPA mean (2016)
Overall GPA 3.5

Number of applications/admission offers/incoming students in 2016
482 applied/68 admission offers/37 incoming

% of Incoming students receiving:
Full tuition waiver only: 10%
Assistantship/fellowship only: 24%
Both full tuition waiver & assistantship/fellowship: 0%

Incoming students who received a departmental scholarship in 2016: 57%

Approximate percentage of incoming students with a B.A./B.S. only: 43% **Master's:** 57%

Approximate percentage of all students who are Women: 81% **Ethnic Minority:** 27% **International:** 5%

Average years to complete the doctoral program (including internship): 4–5 years

Personal interview
Required in person

Attrition rate in past 7 years: 7%

Percentage of students applying for internship in 2017 accepted into:

APA internships: 100% **APPIC internships:** 100%

Formal tracks/concentrations: assessment, behavior therapy, child clinical, couple/family therapy, forensic psychology, gender issues, international disaster psychology, Latino psychology, military psychology, oncology psychology, sport and performance psychology, student-chosen specialty

Research areas	# Faculty	# Grants
behavioral medicine/therapy	2	0
cognitive issues	1	0
couples therapy	1	0
developmental differences	1	0
forensic issues	4	0
health psychology	2	0
Latino psychology	1	0
military	1	1
multicultural issues	3	1
neuropsychology	1	1
psychosocial oncology	1	0
risk assessment and management	1	0
social justice	1	0
supervision & training	3	0
therapeutic assessment	1	0

Clinical opportunities
behavior therapy
behavioral medicine
child therapy
cognitive therapy
community mental health
couple/family therapy
forensic psychology
group therapy
health psychology
hospitals
international disaster psychology
justice systems
Latino psychology
military psychology
multicultural psychology
neuropsychology
oncology psychology
private practice
program/agency consultation
psychodynamic/psychoanalytic therapy
schools and universities
sport and performance psychology
supervision consultation
VA systems

DePaul University (Ph.D.)

Department of Psychology

2219 North Kenmore
Chicago, IL 60614
phone#: (773) 325-7887
email: GradDePaul@depaul.edu
Web address: csh.depaul.edu/academics/graduate/clinical-psychology-ma-phd/Pages/default.aspx

1	2	3	**4**	5	6	7
Practice oriented			Equal emphasis			Research oriented

Percentage of faculty subscribing to each of the following orientations:

Psychodynamic/Psychoanalytic	0%
Applied behavioral analysis/Radical behavioral	10%
Family systems/Systems	50%
Existential/Phenomenological/Humanistic	0%
Cognitive/Cognitive-behavioral	100%

Courses required for incoming students to have completed prior to enrolling:
24 semester hours in psychology, statistics, research methods, abnormal psychology, history and systems of psychology

Recommended but not mandatory courses: science, computer, and math courses

GRE mean
Verbal 158 Quantitative 154
Analytical Writing not reported
Psychology Subject Test 700

GPA mean
Overall GPA 3.6

Number of applications/admission offers/incoming students in 2017
261 applied/10 admission offers/6 incoming

% of students receiving:
Full tuition waiver only: 0%
Assistantship/fellowship only: 0%
Both full tuition waiver & assistantship/fellowship: 100%

Approximate percentage of incoming students with a B.A./B.S. only: 83% **Master's:** 17%

Approximate percentage of all students who are Women: 59% **Ethnic Minority:** 56% **International:** 4%

Average years to complete the doctoral program (including internship): 6 years

Personal interview
Preferred in person but telephone acceptable

Attrition rate in past 7 years: 2%

Percentage of students applying for internship in 2017accepted into:

APA internships: 100% **APPIC internships:** 100%

Formal tracks/concentrations: child clinical, community clinical

Research areas	**# Faculty**	**# Grants**
child/adolescent depression	2	2
child abuse and neglect	1	0
chronic fatigue syndrome	1	3
disability	2	2
minority mental health	5	2
obesity	1	0
program evaluation	4	2
trauma	1	1
school-based services	5	3
stress & coping	2	2
substance abuse intervention	1	3
violence prevention	2	2

Clinical opportunities

assessment	group therapy
child and adolescent	minority/diversity
community psychology	evidence-based
family therapy	school intervention
pediatric psychology	dissemination
supervision	

University of Detroit–Mercy (Ph.D.)

Department of Psychology
4001 W. McNichols Road
Detroit, MI 48221-3038
phone#: (313) 578-0570
email: dauphivb@udmercy.edu
Web address: http://liberalarts.udmercy.edu/academics/psy/phd.php#

1	**2**	3	4	5	6	7
Practice oriented			Equal emphasis			Research oriented

Percentage of faculty subscribing to each of the following orientations:

Psychodynamic/Psychoanalytic	75%
Applied behavioral analysis/Radical behavioral	0%
Family systems/Systems	10%
Existential/Phenomenological/Humanistic	10%
Cognitive/Cognitive-behavioral	25%

Courses required for incoming students prior to enrolling:
Statistics, experimental, two laboratory courses, personality, abnormal psychology, developmental psychology

Courses recommended but not mandatory:
Physiological psychology

GRE mean
Verbal 154 Quantitative 151
Analytical Writing 4.5
Psychology Subject Test not required

GPA mean
Overall GPA 3.6

Number of applications/admission offers/incoming students in 2017
52 applied/15 admission offers/8 incoming

% of students receiving:
Full tuition waiver only: 0%
Assistantship/fellowship only: 100%
Both full tuition waiver & assistantship/fellowship: 100%
(all students in first 2 years of program)

Approximate percentage of incoming students with a B.A./B.S. only: 62.5% **Master's:** 37.5%

Approximate percentage of students who are
Women: 75% **Ethnic Minority:** 25%
International: 12.5%

Average years to complete the doctoral program (including internship): 6 years

Personal interview required

Attrition rate in past 7 years: 5%

Percentage of students applying for internship in 2017 accepted into:

APA internships: 100% **APPIC internships:** 100%

Formal tracks/concentrations: none

Research areas	# Faculty	# Grants
alcohol abuse	2	1
critical incident response	2	0
diagnostic issues	3	0
families coping with serious mental illness	1	1
helping behavior	1	0
identity development	2	0
juvenile delinquency	1	0
marital and family relationships	2	0
object relations	4	0
organizational psychology	2	0
personality and personality disorders	4	0
perception and eye movement	2	1
posttraumatic stress disorder	2	0
psychiatric diagnosis, ethnicity, and clinical judgment	1	0
psychotherapy process and outcome	4	0
recovery-oriented mental health services	1	1
self-esteem/body image	2	0
spirituality	2	0
viideogaming	2	0

Clinical opportunities
Practica are completed at one of over 20 agencies in the metropolitan area

Divine Mercy University (Psy.D.)

Institute for the Psychological Sciences
Doctoral program in clinical psychology (Psy.D.)
2001 Jefferson Davis Highway, Suite 511
Arlington, VA 22202
phone#: (703) 416-1441
email: shollman.ips@divinemercy.edu
Web address: https://divinemercy.edu/psy-d-in-clinical-psychology/

1	2	3	**4**	5	6	7
Practice oriented			Equal emphasis			Research oriented

Percentage of faculty subscribing to each of the following orientations:

Psychodynamic/Psychoanalytic	40%
Applied behavioral analysis/Radical behavioral	7%
Family systems/Systems	20%
Existential/Phenomenological/Humanistic	13%
Cognitive/Cognitive-behavioral	20%

Courses required for incoming students to have completed prior to enrolling:
Students admitted without an undergraduate degree in psychology will be required to complete prerequisite courses during the first year of their program.

Recommended but not mandatory courses:
Undergraduate degree in psychology preferred.

GRE mean
The GRE score is required of all applicants; no preferred minimum score has been established for admission to the program.

GPA mean
Minimum overall undergraduate GPA of 3.0 on a 4.0 scale or a minimum of a 3.5 GPA for graduate studies.

Number of applications/admission offers/incoming students in 2015
10 applied/8 admission offers/8 incoming

% of students receiving:
Full tuition waiver only: 0%
Assistantship/fellowship only: 13%
Both full tuition waiver & assistantship/fellowship: 0%

Approximate percentage of incoming students with a B.A./B.S. only: 61% **Master's:** 36% **Doctorate:** 3%

Approximate percentage of all students who are
Women: 61% **Ethnic Minority:** 12% **International:** 5%

Average years to complete the doctoral program (including internship): 4.95 years

Personal interview required

Attrition rate in past 7 years: 10%

Percentage of students applying for internship last year accepted into:

APA internships: 43% **APPIC internships:** 100%

Formal tracks/concentrations: Clinical Psychology

Research areas	# Faculty	# Grants
Aging	1	
Anxiety disorders	1	
Assessment	2	
Attention-deficit disorder	1	
Behavior analysis	1	
Brain injury	1	
Burnout	1	
Child	2	
Cognitive behavioral therapy	4	
Depression	2	
Developmental	1	
Dying	1	
Emotive behavior therapy	1	
Family	4	
Group psychotherapy	2	
Humanistic psychology	2	
Neurobehavior	1	
Philosophical psychology	2	
Play therapy	1	
Psychotherapy	6	
Sleep disturbance	1	
Spirituality/religion and psychology	8	
Substance abuse/addiction	1	

Clinical opportunities

Anxiety disorders	Group therapy
Behavioral	Family therapy
Child therapy	Marital therapy
Developmental disorders	Psychotherapy
Depression	Psychological assessment
Eating disorders	Substance abuse/addiction

Drexel University (Ph.D.)

Department of Psychology
Main Campus Office
3141 Chestnut Street
Philadelphia, PA 19104
phone: (215) 895-1895
email: brian.daly@drexel.edu
Web address: www.drexel.edu/psychology/

1	2	3	**4**	5	6	7
Practice oriented			Equal emphasis			Research oriented

Percentage of faculty subscribing to each of the following orientations:

Psychodynamic/Psychoanalytic	0%
Applied behavioral analysis/Radical behavioral	0%
Family systems/Systems	5%
Existential/Phenomenological/Humanistic	0%
Cognitive/Cognitive-behavioral	95%

Courses required for incoming students to have completed prior to enrolling: none

Recommended but not mandatory courses:
foundational courses in psychology

GRE mean
Verbal 162 Quantitative 157
Analytical Writing 5

GPA mean
Overall GPA 3.77

Number of applications/admission offers/incoming students in 2017
701 applied/13 admission offers/10 incoming

% of students receiving:
Full tuition waiver only: 0%
Assistantship/fellowship only: 0%
Both full tuition waiver & assistantship/fellowship: 100% (1st-year class)**
**All students in subsequent years currently receive at least a tuition waiver and additional support.

Approximate percentage of incoming students with a BA/BS only: 82% **Master's:** 18%

Approximate percentage of all students who are Women: 69% **Ethnic Minority:** 23% **International:** 8%

Average years to complete the doctoral program (including internship): 5 years

Personal interview
Strongly preferred in person but telephone acceptable

Attrition rate in past 7 years: 6.0%

Percentage of students applying for internship in 2017 accepted into:

APA internships: 90% **APPIC internships:** 90%

Formal tracks/Major Areas of Study: clinical child, health, forensic, clinical neuropsychology

Research areas	# Faculty	# Grants
acceptance and mindfulness	3	3
at-risk youth	2	5
behavioral medicine/health psychology	5	2
cognitive-behavior therapy	5	1
cognitive psychology	3	1
depression	2	1
drug policy	1	1
eating disorders	4	6
forensic psychology	3	3
human-computer interaction	1	0
juvenile justice	1	1
memory	2	0
neuroimaging	2	0
neuropsychology	3	3
neurorehabilitation	3	2
obesity	2	2
problem-solving therapy	2	1
psychopathy	1	0
psychotherapy research	4	1
school mental health	1	3
stressful life events	1	0
women's health	2	1

Clinical Opportunities

child and family	cognitive-behavioral therapy
forensic	adult
health	neuropsychology

Duke University (Ph.D.)

Department of Psychology & Neuroscience
417 Chapel Drive, Box 90086
Durham, NC 27708
phone#: (919) 660-5716
email: morrell@duke.edu
Web address: http://psychandneuro.duke.edu/graduate/clinical

1	2	3	4	5	**6**	7
Practice oriented			Equal emphasis			Research oriented

Percentage of faculty subscribing to each of the following orientations:

Psychodynamic/Psychoanalytic	10%
Applied behavioral analysis/Radical behavioral	0%
Family systems/Systems	10%
Existential/Phenomenological/Humanistic	0%
Cognitive/Cognitive-behavioral	80%

Courses required for incoming students to have completed prior to enrolling: none

Recommended but not mandatory courses: research methods, statistics, abnormal psychology

GRE mean
Verbal 165 Quantitative 164

Analytical Writing 5.5
Psychology Subject Test not reported

GPA mean
Overall GPA 3.72

Number of applications/admission offers/incoming students in 2016
310 applied/6 admission offers/5 incoming

% of students receiving:
Full tuition waiver only: 0%
Assistantship/fellowship only: 0%
Both full tuition waiver & assistantship/fellowship: 100%

Approximate percentage of incoming students with a B.A./B.S. only: 100% **Master's:** 0%

Approximate percentage of all students who are Women: 80% **Ethnic Minority:** 25% **International:** 0%

Average years to complete the doctoral program (including internship): 6 years

Personal interview
Required in person

Attrition rate in past 7 years: 5%

Percentage of students applying for internship in 2016 accepted into:

APA internships: 100% **APPIC internships:** 100%

Formal tracks/concentrations: child clinical, adult clinical, health psychology

Research areas	# Faculty	# Grants
adolescent treatment	5	6
affective disorders/neuroscience	4	6
behavioral genomics	2	2
behavioral medicine/health psychology	6	8
conduct disorders	2	3
developmental psychopathology	3	3
eating disorders	2	3
global mental health	3	5
HIV/AIDS	2	6
obesity	2	4
pain and chronic illness	2	4
peer relations	1	1
substance abuse	4	7
neuropsychology	1	1
social cognition	2	1
stress and coping	4	4

Clinical opportunities
affective disorders
behavioral cardiology
behavioral medicine
behavior disorders of children
pain and biofeedback
pediatric psychology
fertility clinic
cognitive behavior therapy
dialectical behavior therapy
eating disorders
family therapy
neuropsychology
autism

Duquesne University (Ph.D.)

Department of Psychology
Pittsburgh, PA 15282-1753
phone#: (412)-396-6520
email: psychology@duq.edu
Web address: www.duq.edu/psychology

1	2	3	**4**	5	6	7
Practice oriented			Equal emphasis			Research oriented

Percentage of faculty subscribing to each of the following orientations:

Psychodynamic/Psychoanalytic	65%
Applied behavioral analysis/Radical behavioral	0%
Family systems/Systems	18%
Existential/Phenomenological/Humanistic	91%
Cognitive/Cognitive-behavioral	18%

Courses required for incoming students to have completed prior to enrolling: none

Recommended but not mandatory courses:
development, social, abnormal, personality, research methods

GRE mean
Verbal 161 Quantitative 152
Analytical Writing 4.4
Psychology Subject Test not reported

GPA mean
Overall GPA 3.7

Number of applications/admission offers/incoming students in 2017
123 applied/7 admission offers/7 incoming

% of students receiving:
Full tuition waiver only: 100%
Assistantship/fellowship only: 96%
Both full tuition waiver & assistantship/fellowship: 96%

Approximate percentage of incoming students with a B.A./B.S. only: 30% **Master's:** 70%

Approximate percentage of students who are Women: 60% **Ethnic Minority:** 26% **International:** 15%

Average years to complete the doctoral program (including internship): 7 years

Personal interview
Required in person

Attrition rate in past 7 years: not reported

Percentage of students applying for internship in 2017 accepted into:

APA internships: 90% **APPIC internships:** 10%

Formal tracks/concentrations: none

Research areas	# Faculty	# Grants
Please note: our research is qualitative	not reported	not reported

Clinical opportunities
Psychology Clinic (offers psychotherapy to Duquesne's students, faculty and staff as well as the public); External clinical practica at over 15 local hospitals, student counseling centers, and agencies.

East Carolina University (Ph.D.)

Department of Psychology
Greenville, NC 27858-4353
phone#: (252) 328-6800
email: psychology@ecu.edu
Web address: www.ecu.edu/psyc/

1	2	3	4	5	6	7
Practice oriented			Equal emphasis			Research oriented

Percentage of faculty subscribing to each of the following orientations:

Psychodynamic/Psychoanalytic	0%
Applied behavioral analysis/Radical behavioral	0%
Family systems/Systems	10%
Acceptance and Commitment Therapy	10%
Cognitive/Cognitive-behavioral	80%

Courses required for incoming students to have completed prior to enrolling:

We do not have any required courses, but a psychology major is strongly preferred and more likely to be competitive as an applicant.

Recommended but not mandatory courses:
Introduction to Psychology, Psychological Statistics, Research Methods in Psychology, Abnormal Psychology, Developmental Psychology, Social Psychology, Physiological Psychology (biological bases)

GRE mean
Verbal 158 Quantitative 151
Analytical Writing 4.0
Psychology Subject Test not required

GPA mean
Overall GPA 3.73

Number of applications/admission offers/incoming students in 2017
106 applied/9 admission offers/6 incoming

% of students receiving:
Full tuition waiver only: 0%
Assistantship/fellowship only: 0%
Both full tuition waiver & assistantship/fellowship: 100%, except for students in internship year

Approximate percentage of incoming students with a BA/BS only: 33% **Master's:** 67%

Approximate percentage of all students who are Women: 71% **Ethnic Minority:** 6% **International:** 0%

Average years to complete the doctoral program (including internship): 5.5 years

Personal interview
Preferred in person but telephone acceptable

Attrition rate in past 7 years: 19%

Percentage of students applying for internship in 2016 accepted into:

APA internships: 100% **APPIC internships:** 100%

Formal tracks/concentrations: Clinical Health Psychology

Research areas	**# Faculty**	**# Grants**
pain	1	1
cardiovascular	2	4
weight management	1	0
women's health	1	1
trauma and military	1	0
sleep and neuropsychology	1	0
stress and health	1	0

Clinical opportunities

assessment	neuropsychology
family medicine	cardiovascular
psychiatric clinic	weight management
women's health	VA
rehabilitation	

East Tennessee State University (Ph.D.)

Department of Psychology
Johnson City, TN 37614
phone#: (423) 439-4461
email: stinson@etsu.edu
Web address: etsu.edu/clinical psychology

1	2	3	4	5	6	7
Practice oriented			Equal emphasis			Research oriented

Percentage of faculty subscribing to each of the following orientations:

Cognitive/Cognitive-behavioral	43%
Behavioral/DBT	29%
Psychodynamic/Family systems	14%
Existential/Phenomenological/Humanistic	14%

Courses required for incoming students to have completed prior to enrolling:
A minimum of 18 semester hours in undergraduate psychology, including courses in statistics, experimental design, personality, history and systems, and abnormal

Recommended but not mandatory courses: physiology; learning

GRE mean
Verbal 158 Quantitative 151
Analytical Writing 4.3
Psychology Subject Test not required

GPA mean
Overall GPA 3.826

Number of applications/admission offers/incoming students in 2017
83 applied/9 admission offers/5 incoming

% of students receiving:
Full tuition waiver only: 0%
Assistantship/fellowship only: 0%
Both full tuition waiver & assistantship/fellowship: 100%

Approximate percentage of incoming students (2017-2018) with a BA/BS only: 100% **Master's:** 0%

Approximate percentage of enrolled students who are Women: 70% **Ethnic Minority:** 13% **International:** 0%

Average years to complete the doctoral program (including internship): 4.9 years

Personal interview
In person interview, telephone interviews can be arranged

Attrition rate in past 7 years: 21%

Percentage of students applying for internship in 2017 accepted into:

APA internships: 100% **APPIC internships:** 100%

Formal tracks/concentrations: rural integrated primary care

Research areas	# Faculty	# Grants
integrated care/women's health	1	0
child clinical psychology	2	2
suicide prevention/intervention	2	1
forensic psychology	1	4
traffic safety	1	0

Clinical opportunities
Departmental community clinic
Integrated primary care – adult & pediatric
College counseling
Student health center
Community mental health – rural
Community corrections
Residential assessment
Foster care & families
Veterans Affairs Hospital

Eastern Michigan University (Ph.D.)

Department of Psychology
Ypsilanti, MI 48197
phone#: (734) 487-1155
email: ellen.koch@emich.edu
Web address: www.emich.edu/psychology/

1	2	3	**4**	5	6	7
Practice oriented			Equal emphasis			Research oriented

Percentage of faculty subscribing to each of the following orientations:

Psychodynamic/Psychoanalytic	15%
Applied behavioral analysis/Radical behavioral	10%
Family systems/Systems	25%
Existential/Phenomenological/Humanistic	10%
Cognitive/Cognitive-behavioral	40%

Courses required for incoming students to have completed prior to enrolling:
statistics, research methods/experimental psychology, 20 undergraduate credits in psychology

Recommended but not mandatory courses: abnormal, personality, learning, history and systems

GRE mean
Verbal 157 Quantitative 155
Analytical Writing 4.25
Psychology Subject Test not required

GPA mean
Overall GPA 3.69

Number of applications/admission offers/incoming students in 2017
131 applied/12 admission offers/8 incoming

% of students receiving:
Full tuition waiver only: 0%
Assistantship/fellowship only: 0%
Both full tuition waiver & assistantship/fellowship: 100%

Approximate percentage of incoming students with a B.A./B.S. only: 70% **Master's:** 30%

Approximate percentage of all students who are Women: 82% **Ethnic Minority:** 20% **International:** 5%

Average years to complete the doctoral program (including internship): 6 years

Personal interview
In person interview highly preferred

Attrition rate in past 7 years: 12%

Percentage of students applying for internship in 2016 accepted into:

APA internships: 100% **APPIC internships:** 100%

Formal tracks/concentrations: applied behavioral analysis, developmental psychopathology, neuropsychology/assessment, health psychology, clinical adult

Research areas	# Faculty	# Grants
anxiety disorders (PTSD)	2	0
child and family	3	2
neuropsychology	2	0
personality disorders	1	0
substance abuse	1	0
applied behavioral analysis	2	0
behavioral medicine	2	0
sexual deviance	1	0
multicultural issues	2	0
geropsychology	2	1

Clinical opportunities
anxiety disorders/PTSD
depression
personality disorders
neuropsychology
traumatic brain injury
inpatient hospital for children and adolescents
veterans
college students
behavioral medicine clinic—chronic pain

Emory University (Ph.D.)

Department of Psychology
36 Eagle Row Atlanta, GA 30322
phone#: (404) 727-7438
email: lcraigh@emory.edu
Web address: psychology.emory.edu/clinical/index.html

1	2	3	4	5	**6**	7
Practice oriented			Equal emphasis			Research oriented

Percentage of faculty subscribing to each of the following orientations:

Psychodynamic/Psychoanalytic	10%
Applied behavioral analysis/Radical behavioral	0%
Family systems/Systems	0%

Existential/Phenomenological/Humanistic	0%
Cognitive/Cognitive-behavioral	90%

Courses required for incoming students to have completed prior to enrolling:
No specific ones but adequate background in psychology needed

Recommended but not mandatory courses:
methodology, statistics, psychopathology, personality, lab science

GRE mean
Verbal 162 Quantitative 157
Analytical Writing 5.0
Psychology Subject Test not reported

GPA mean
Overall GPA 3.8

Number of applications/admission offers/incoming students in 2017
244 applied/11 admission offers/5 incoming

% of students receiving:
Full tuition waiver only: 0%
Assistantship/fellowship only: 0%
Both full tuition waiver & assistantship/fellowship: 100%

Approximate percentage of incoming students with a B.A./B.S. only: 80% **Master's:** 20%

Approximate percentage of all students who are Women: 80% **Ethnic Minority:** 10% **International:** 5%

Average years to complete the doctoral program (including internship): 6 years

Personal interview
Strongly recommended

Attrition rate in past 7 years: 15%

Percentage of students applying for internship in 2017 accepted into:

APA internships: 100% **APPIC internships:** 0%

Formal tracks/concentrations: none

Research areas	# Faculty	# Grants
Autism spectrum disorders	1	4
adolescent psychopathology	2	1
attention-deficit disorder	1	0
behavioral genetics	2	—
eating disorders & weight concerns	1	0
infant development	1	1
neuropsychology	1	0
personality and personality disorders	2	—
schizophrenia	1	1

Clinical opportunities

assessment	interpersonal therapy
behavior therapy	neuropsychology
cognitive/behavior therapy	psychodynamic therapy

Fairleigh Dickinson University (Ph.D.) (2013 Data)

School of Psychology T-WH1-01
Teaneck–Hackensack Campus
1000 River Road
Teaneck, NJ 07666
phone#: (201) 692-2315
email: loeb@fdu.edu
Web address: view.fdu.edu/default.aspx?id=6280

1	2	3	4	5	6	7
Practice oriented			Equal emphasis			Research oriented

Percentage of faculty subscribing to each of the following orientations:

Psychodynamic/Psychoanalytic	37.5%
Applied behavioral analysis/Radical behavioral	0%
Family systems/Systems	25%
Existential/Phenomenological/Humanistic	0%
Cognitive/Cognitive-behavioral	75%

Courses required for incoming students to have completed prior to enrolling:
18 credits in psychology with statistics, developmental, experimental, social

Recommended but not mandatory courses:
psychopathology, physiological, assessment

GRE mean
Verbal 154 Quantitative 153
Analytical Writing 4.4
Psychology Subject Test 650

GPA mean
Overall GPA 3.76

Number of applications/admission offers/incoming students in 2013
195 applied/26 admission offers/14 incoming

% of students receiving:
Full tuition waiver only: 0%
Assistantship/fellowship only: 100% (can be taken as tuition remission)
Both full tuition waiver & assistantship/fellowship: 0%

Approximate percentage of incoming students with a B.A./B.S. only: 50% **Master's:** 50%

Approximate percentage of all students who are Women: 85% **Ethnic Minority:** 16% **International:** 2.5%

Average years to complete the doctoral program (including internship): 5.5 years

Personal interview
Required in person

Attrition rate in past 7 years: 5%

Percentage of students applying for internship in 2013 accepted into:

APA internships: 62.5% **APPIC internships:** 62.5%

Formal tracks/concentrations: Forensic

Research areas	# Faculty	# Grants
ADHD	2	0
assessment	4	1
behavioral medicine	3	0
child clinical	2	1

child/sexual abuse	2	0
community psychology	1	1
diversity issues	2	0
eating disorders	1	1
ethical issues	1	0
forensic	2	1
learning disabilities	2	0
obsessive compulsive disorder	1	0
obesity	2	2
psychopathology	1	0
psychotherapy	3	1
relationships	2	0
school-based prevention/intervention	1	0
statistics	1	0
stress	2	0
substance use/abuse	1	1
trauma	1	0
veterans and military families	1	2

Clinical opportunities

ADHD
assessment
behavioral medicine
child psychopathology
community psychology
dialectical behavior therapy
family therapy
minority/diverse populations
neuropsychology
school-based mental health supervision
anxiety disorders
autism spectrum disorders
personality disorder
VA mental health
couples therapy
eating disorders
learning disabilities
mood disorders
parent management training
sports psychology

Fielding Graduate University (Ph.D.)

Department of Psychology
Santa Barbara, CA 93105-3814
phone#: (805) 898-4026
email: PSYadmissions@fielding.edu
Web address: http://www.fielding.edu/programs/psychology/psy/

1	2	3	4	**5**	6	7
Practice oriented			Equal emphasis			Research oriented

Percentage of faculty subscribing to each of the following orientations:

Psychodynamic/Psychoanalytic	30%
Applied behavioral analysis/Radical behavioral	0%
Family systems/Systems	10%
Existential/Phenomenological/Humanistic	20%
Cognitive/Cognitive-behavioral	40%

Courses required for incoming students to have completed prior to enrolling:
None

Recommended but not mandatory courses:
Research design, statistics, personality, developmental, psychopathology

GRE mean
Not required

GPA mean
Overall GPA 3.5

Number of applications/admission offers/incoming students in 2015
231 completed applications/71 admission offers/55 incoming

% of students receiving:
Full tuition waiver only: 0%
Assistantship/fellowship only: 0%
Both full tuition waiver & assistantship/fellowship: 0%

Approximate percentage of incoming students with a B.A./B.S. only: 25% **Master's:** 75%

Approximate percentage of all students who are Women: 77% **Ethnic Minority:** 36% **International:** 7%

Average years to complete the doctoral program (including internship): 6.6 years for students beginning the program since 2007

Personal interview
In person interview is required

Attrition rate in past 7 years: 8.5%

Percentage of students applying for internship last year accepted into:

APA internships: 46% **APPIC internships:** 30%

Formal tracks/concentrations:
Neuropsychology, Forensic Psychology, Health Psychology, Violence Prevention, Parent and Infant Mental Health

Research areas	# Faculty	# Grants
infant mental health/ pediatric psych	5	0
addictions	2	0
multicultural psychology	4	0
psychotherapy research	5	0
qualitative research methods	2	0
gender issues	3	0
neuropsychology/rehabilitation	4	0
group therapy	4	0

Clinical opportunities
Practicum placements are in local communities and must be approved by the Director of Practicum Training

University of Florida (Ph.D.)

Department of Clinical and Health Psychology
Box 100165 University of Florida Health Science Center
Gainesville, FL 32610
phone#: (352) 265-0294
email: rbauer@phhp.ufl.edu
Web address: chp.phhp.ufl.edu/

1	2	3	**4**	5	6	7
Practice oriented			Equal emphasis			Research oriented

Percentage of faculty subscribing to each of the following orientations:

Psychodynamic/Psychoanalytic	0%
Applied behavioral analysis/Radical behavioral	5%
Family systems/Systems	5%
Existential/Phenomenological/Humanistic	5%
Cognitive/Cognitive-behavioral	85%

Courses required for incoming students to have completed prior to enrolling:
Statistics, abnormal psychology
At least 2 (3 will be required in 2018) of the following: cognitive, developmental, social, physio-biological bases, affective bases of behavior

Recommended but not mandatory courses:
Undergraduate courses in experimental psychology, participation in research course or laboratory experience

GRE (averages from applicants 2016)
Verbal 161 Quantitative 159
Analytical Writing 4.8
Psychology Subject Test will be required starting fall 2017

GPA mean
3.65

Number of applications/admission offers/incoming students in 2016
275 applied/19 admission offers/12 incoming

% of students receiving:
Full tuition waiver only: 0%
Assistantship/fellowship only: 0%
Both full tuition waiver & assistantship/fellowship: 95% all students; 100% incoming

Approximate percentage of incoming students with a B.A./B.S. only: 67% **Master's:** 33%

Approximate percentage of students who are Women: 75% **Ethnic Minority:** 24% **International:** 6%

Average years to complete the doctoral program (including internship): 6.1 years

Personal interview
Preferred in person but telephone acceptable

Attrition rate in past 7 years: 6.6%

Percentage of students applying for internship in 2017 accepted into:

APA internships: 94% **APPIC internships:** not reported

Formal tracks/concentrations: clinical health psychology; clinical child/pediatric psychology; neuropsychology, cognitive and affective neuroscience

Research areas	# Faculty	# Grants
anxiety disorders and emotions	2	1
child clinical psychology	2	2
clinical/medical psychology	7	2
functional neuroimaging	3	2
neuropsychology	5	4
obesity treatment	2	2
pain	2	4
pediatric psychology	2	1
rural health	1	0
HIV	1	2

Clinical opportunities

ADHD
clinical child psychology
forensic psychology
inpatient consultation/liaison
learning disabilities
pain and stress
parent training
pediatric consultation
rural behavioral health
cognitive behavior therapy
medical/health psychology
neuropsychology
dementia
Epilepsy & Wada
weight loss
traumatic brain injury
Parkinson & DBS
Cognitive intervention

Florida Institute of Technology (Psy.D.)

School of Psychology
150 West University Boulevard
Melbourne, FL 32901
phone#: (321) 674-8105
email: Lsorum@fit.edu
Web address: cpla.fit.edu//clinical/index.htm

1	2	**3**	4	5	6	7
Practice oriented			Equal emphasis			Research oriented

Percentage of faculty subscribing to each of the following orientations:

Psychodynamic/Psychoanalytic	10%
Applied behavioral analysis/Radical behavioral	10%
Family systems/Systems	20%
Existential/Phenomenological/Humanistic	20%
Cognitive/Cognitive-behavioral	40%

Courses required for incoming students to have completed prior to enrolling:
Statistics, learning, personality, physiological, abnormal, social

Recommended but not mandatory courses: none

GRE mean
Verbal + Quantitative 307
Analytical Writing 4.0
Psychology Subject Test not reported

GPA mean
Overall GPA 3.64

Number of applications/admission offers/incoming students in 2017
162 applied/40 admission offers/27 incoming

% of students receiving:
Full tuition waiver only: 0%
Assistantship/fellowship only: 58%
Both full tuition waiver & assistantship/fellowship: 0%

Approximate percentage of incoming students with a B.A./B.S. only: 63% **Master's:** 37%

Approximate percentage of students who are Women: 88% **Ethnic Minority:** 23% **International:** 3%

Average years to complete the doctoral program (including internship): 5 years

Personal interview
Preferred in person

Attrition rate in past 7 years: 12%

Percentage of students applying for internship in 2017 accepted into:

APA internships: 100% **APPIC internships:** 0%

Formal tracks/concentrations: family/child psychology, neuropsychology, clinical health psychology, forensic psychology

Research areas	# Faculty	# Grants
aging	2	1
family psychology	2	0
forensic psychology	1	0
health psychology/behavioral health	3	1
neuropsychology	1	1
personality assessment	1	0
sexual abuse	1	1
sport psychology	1	0
supervision	1	0
professional competence	1	0
PTSD (combat veterans)	1	0

Clinical opportunities

behavioral medicine/ health psychology
family and marital therapy
forensic settings
neuropsychology
sexual abuse (offenders and victims)
combat veterans/PTSD
family violence (inpatient & outpatient)

Florida International University (Ph.D.)

Department of Psychology
11800 SW 8 Street, DM 256
Miami, Florida 33199
phone#: (305) 348-2880
email: psygrad@fiu.edu
Web address:: http://psychology.fiu.edu/graduate-programs/

1	2	3	**4**	5	6	7
Practice oriented			Equal emphasis			Research oriented

Percentage of faculty subscribing to each of the following orientations:

Psychodynamic/Psychoanalytic	0%
Applied behavioral analysis/Radical behavioral	0%
Family systems/Systems	0%
Existential/Phenomenological/Humanistic	0%
Cognitive/Cognitive-behavioral	100%

Courses required for incoming students to have completed prior to enrolling: Bachelor's Degree in a relevant discipline

Recommended but not mandatory courses: Research Methods, Statistics

GRE mean
Verbal: 139 + Quantitative:137
Analytical Writing 4.36
Psychology Subject Test: Not Required

GPA mean
Overall GPA: 3.94

Number of applications/admission offers/incoming students in 2017
110 applied/17 admission offers/11 incoming

% of students receiving:
Full tuition waiver only: 0%
Assistantship/fellowship only: 0%
Both full tuition waiver & assistantship/fellowship: 100%

Approximate percentage of incoming students with a B.A./B.S. only: 98 % **Master's:** 2%

Approximate percentage of all students who are Women: 90% **Ethnic Minority:** 60% **International:** 1%

Average years to complete the doctoral program (including internship): 6 years

Personal interview: Preferred in person, but telephone/ Skype acceptable

Attrition rate in past 7 years: 4%

Percentage of students applying for internship last year accepted into:

APA internships: 75% **APPIC internships:** 75%

Formal tracks/concentrations: Program is Clinical Child and Adolescent Psychology; Dual Major available in Cognitive Neuroscience; Minor available in Quantitative Psychology

Research areas	# Faculty	# Grants
ADHD	9	10
Adolescent psychopathology	1	1
Anxiety	2	2
after school	1	1
behavioral genetics	1	1
child psychopathology	1	1
cognitive information processing	1	1
community collaboration	1	1
depression	1	1
developmental delay	1	1
disruptive behavior disorders	2	3
emotion regulation	1	1
HIV	1	1
infancy and early childhood	4	3
neuropsychology	1	1
parenting	2	2
school readiness	1	1
service systems	1	1
substance use and abuse	3	4

Clinical opportunities

ADHD
Advanced Assessment
Anxiety disorders
Behavioral parent training
Community consultation
Depression
Motivational interviewing
Neuropsychological evaluation
Overweight/Obesity prevention
Parent Child Interaction Therapy
School consultation
School readiness
Selective mutism
Sleep

Florida State University (Ph.D.)

Department of Psychology
Tallahassee, FL 32306-4301
phone#: (850) 644-2499
email: grad-info@psy.fsu.edu
Web address: https://psy.fsu.edu/php/graduate/programs/clinical/clinical.php

1	2	3	4	5	6	**7**
Practice oriented			Equal emphasis			Research oriented

Percentage of faculty subscribing to each of the following orientations:

Psychodynamic/Psychoanalytic	0%
Applied behavioral analysis/Radical behavioral	0%
Family systems/Systems	0%
Existential/Phenomenological/Humanistic	0%
Cognitive/Cognitive-behavioral	100%

Courses required for incoming students to have completed prior to enrolling:
undergraduate degree

Recommended but not mandatory courses: none

GRE mean
Verbal 87th percentile Quantitative 71st percentile
Analytical Writing 4.8
Psychology Subject Test not reported

GPA mean
Junior/Senior GPA 3.7

Number of applications/admission offers/incoming students in 2017
~250 applications/25 admission offers/14 incoming students

% of students receiving:
Full tuition waiver only: 0%
Assistantship/fellowship only: 0%
Both full tuition waiver & assistantship/fellowship: 100%

Approximate percentage of incoming students with a B.A./B.S. only: 93% **Master's:** 7%

Approximate percentage of all students who are Women: 74% **Ethnic Minority:** 17% **International:** 2%

Average years to complete the doctoral program (including internship): 7 years

Personal interview
Preferred in person but telephone acceptable

Attrition rate in past 7 years: 3%

Percentage of students applying for internship in 2017 accepted into:

APA internships: 93% **APPIC internships:** 93%

Formal tracks/concentrations/specializations: none

Research areas	# Faculty	# Grants
addictive behavior	2	1
anxiety	5	2
child clinical	4	4
conduct disorder and antisocial	2	1
bulimia nervosa	2	2
developmental psychopathology	4	2
early intervention	2	2
prediction of criminal behavior	1	0
suicide	5	5
personality disorders	2	0
trauma/PTSD	3	1

Clinical opportunities
corrections
behavioral health
state psychiatric hospital
adult therapy
neuropsychology outpatient
severe mental illness
anxiety disorders
child assessment and therapy
veterans health
parent behavioral intervention

Fordham University (Ph.D.)

Department of Psychology
441 East Fordham Road
Bronx, NY 10458
phone#: (718) 817-3775
fax#: (718) 817-3785
email: barbieri@fordham.edu
Web address: https://www.fordham.edu/info/21663/phd_in_clinical_psychology

1	2	3	4	**5**	6	7
Practice oriented			Equal emphasis			Research oriented

Percentage of faculty subscribing to each of the following orientations:

Psychodynamic/Psychoanalytic	15%
Applied behavioral analysis/Radical behavioral	0%
Family systems/Systems	5%
Existential/Phenomenological/Humanistic	10%
Cognitive/Cognitive-behavioral	70%

Courses required for incoming students to have completed prior to enrolling: n/a

Recommended but not mandatory courses: An undergraduate background in psychology is expected, but not required.

GRE mean
Verbal: 162 (88%)
Quantitative: 159 (72%)
Analytical Writing: 4.8 (83%)
Psychology Subject Test: 715 (80%)

GPA mean
3.68

Number of applications/admission offers/incoming students in 2017
596 applied/12 admission offers/10 incoming

% of students receiving:
Full tuition waiver only: 0%
Assistantship/fellowship only: 0%
Both full tuition waiver & assistantship/fellowship: 100%

Approximate percentage of incoming students with a B.A./B.S. only: 80% **Master's:** 20%

Approximate percentage of students who are Women: 80% **Ethnic Minority:** 30% **International:** 10%

Average years to complete the doctoral program (including internship): 7 years

Personal interview
Strongly recommended

Attrition rate in past 7 years: 5%

Percentage of students applying for internship in 2017 accepted into:

APA internships: 100% **APPIC internships:**

Formal tracks/concentrations: Child and Adolescent, Forensic, Health, and Neuropsychology

Research areas	# Faculty	# Grants
clinical/adolescent child psychology	3	2
forensic	2	4
health psychology/behavioral medicine	1	2
multicultural/community	1	1
neuropsychology	2	4
personality disorders	1	0
existential/phenomenonological	1	0
social support	1	0
stress and coping	1	0
substance abuse	1	2

Clinical opportunities

Clinical externships available at numerous inpatient and outpatient specialty clinics in the New York metropolitan area. Appropriate training sites can be found in any area including highly specialized.

Fuller Theological Seminary (Ph.D. in Clinical Psychology)

(Part of Fuller Theological Seminary)
180 North Oakland Avenue
Pasadena, CA 91101
phone#: (626) 584-5500
email: tinaarmstrong@fuller.edu
Web address: www.fuller.edu/phd-clinical-psychology/

1	2	3	**4**	5	6	7
Practice oriented			Equal emphasis			Research oriented

Percentage of faculty subscribing to each of the following orientations:

Psychodynamic/Psychoanalytic	30%
Applied behavioral analysis/Radical behavioral	0%
Family systems/Systems	20%
Existential/Phenomenological/Humanistic	10%
Cognitive/Cognitive-behavioral	30%
Other	10%

Courses required for incoming students to have completed prior to enrolling:

6 courses in psychology, one of the courses must be a statistics course, and a Bachelor's degree from an accredited university

Recommended but not mandatory courses:

Abnormal Psych, Developmental Psych, Experimental Psych, Physiological Psych, Social Psych, Tests and Measures, and Personality

GRE mean for incoming 2017 cohort:

Verbal 157 Quantitative 151
Analytical Writing 4.3
Psychology Subject Test not reported

GPA mean for incoming 2017 cohort:

3.57

Number of applications/admission offers/incoming students in 2017:

39 applications/ 21 admission offers/ 9 incoming students

% of students receiving:

Full tuition waiver only: 0%
Assistantship/fellowship only: 0% assistantship, 14% research fellowship, 23% merit scholarships, 50% need-based scholarships
Both full tuition waiver & assistantship/fellowship: 0%

Approximate percentage of incoming students with a B.A./B.S. only: 67%

Approximate percentage of incoming students with a Master's: 33%

Approximate percentage of all students who are Women: 77% **Ethnic Minority:** 44% **International:** 9%

Average years to complete the doctoral program (including internship): 6.7 years

Personal interview:

Preferred in-person, but telephone and/or Skype is acceptable

Attrition rate in past 7 years: 15%

Percentage of students applying for internship in 2017 accepted into:

APA internships: 93% **APPIC internships:** 3%

Formal tracks/concentrations: Neuropsychology track available. No other tracks/concentrations but we do have emphasis areas, which include family and community emphases.

Research areas	# Faculty	# Grants
biopsychosocial	5	0
child clinical	4	2
cognitive science of religion	1	1
cross-cultural psychology	4	4
depression	1	2
developmental	5	3
family	7	0
group processes	3	2
health psychology/behavioral medicine	1	0
marriages	5	0
neuropsychology	4	0
personality	1	3
posttraumatic stress disorders	1	0
religion	8	5
stress and coping	1	0
sexuality	2	0
thriving	4	4

Clinical opportunities

assessment	inpatient adult population
child/adolescent therapy	interpersonal psychotherapy
chronic mental illness	marital/couples therapy
family therapy	neuropsychology/ rehabilitation
forensic population	supervision
gerontology	victim/battering
group therapy	

Fuller Theological Seminary (Psy.D.)

(Part of Fuller Theological Seminary)
180 North Oakland Avenue
Pasadena, CA 91101
phone#: (626) 584-5500
email: ted_cosse@fuller.edu
Web address: www.fuller.edu/psyd-clinical-psychology/

1	**2**	3	4	5	6	7
Practice oriented			Equal emphasis			Research oriented

Percentage of faculty subscribing to each of the following orientations:

Psychodynamic/Psychoanalytic	30%
Applied behavioral analysis/Radical behavioral	0%
Family systems/Systems	20%
Existential/Phenomenological/Humanistic	10%
Cognitive/Cognitive-behavioral	30%
Other	10%

Courses required for incoming students to have completed prior to enrolling:
6 courses in psychology, one of the courses must be a statistics course, and a Bachelor's degree from an accredited university

Recommended but not mandatory courses:
Abnormal Psych, Developmental Psych, Experimental Psych, Physiological Psych, Social Psych, Tests and Measures, and Personality

GRE mean for incoming 2017 cohort:
Verbal 156 Quantitative 154
Analytical Writing 4.4
Psychology Subject Test not reported

GPA mean for incoming 2017 cohort:
Psychology GPA 3.38

Number of applications/admission offers/incoming students in 2017:
48 applied/24 admission offers/8 incoming

% of students receiving:
Full tuition waiver only: 0%
Assistantship/fellowship only: 0% assistantship, 11% research or clinical fellowships, 15% merit scholarships, 53% need-based scholarships
Both full tuition waiver & assistantship/fellowship: 0%

Approximate percentage of incoming students with a B.A./B.S. only: 75%

Approximate percentage of incoming students with a Master's: 25%

Approximate percentage of all students who are Women: 73% **Ethnic Minority:** 34% **International:** 5%

Average years to complete the doctoral program (including internship): 6.2 years

Personal interview
Preferred in-person, but telephone and/or Skype is acceptable

Attrition rate in past 7 years: 25%

Percentage of students applying for internship in 2017 accepted into:

APA internships: 40% **APPIC internships:** 53%

Formal tracks/concentrations: Neuropsychology track available. No other tracks/concentrations but we do have emphasis areas, which include family and community emphases.

Research areas	# Faculty	# Grants
biopsychosocial	5	0
child clinical	4	2
cognitive science of religion	1	1
cross-cultural psychology	4	4
depression	1	2
developmental	5	3
family	7	0
group processes	3	2
health psychology/behavioral medicine	1	0
marriages	5	0
neuropsychology	4	0
personality	1	3
posttraumatic stress disorders	1	0
religion	8	5
stress and coping	1	0
sexuality	2	0
thriving	4	4

Clinical opportunities

assessment	inpatient adult population
child/adolescent therapy	interpersonal psychotherapy
chronic mental illness	marital/couples therapy
family therapy	neuropsychology/ rehabilitation
forensic population	supervision
gerontology	victim/battering
group therapy	

Gallaudet University (Ph.D.)

Department of Psychology
8th and Florida Avenue, NE
Washington, DC 20002-3695
phone#: (202) 651-5647
email: Carolyn.Corbett@Gallaudet.edu
Web address: http://www.gallaudet.edu/department-of-psychology/phd-clinical-psychology

1	2	3	**4**	5	6	7
Practice oriented			Equal emphasis			Research oriented

Percentage of faculty subscribing to each of the following orientations:

Psychodynamic/Psychoanalytic	20%
Applied behavioral analysis/Radical behavioral	0%
Family systems/Systems	0%
Existential/Phenomenological/Humanistic	0%
Cognitive/Cognitive-behavioral	80%

Courses required for incoming students to have completed prior to enrolling:
Major or minor in undergraduate psychology including statistics, abnormal psychology, and child development

Recommended but not mandatory courses: Social psychology, personality, learning, cognition, perception

GRE mean
Verbal 152 Quantitative 148
Analytical Writing 4.0
Psychology Subject Test is not required

GPA mean
Overall GPA 3.56 Psychology GPA n/a

Number of applications/admission offers/incoming students in 2017
22 applied/8 admission offers/5 incoming

% of students receiving:
Full tuition waiver only: 0%
Assistantship/fellowship only: 39%
Both full tuition waiver & assistantship/fellowship: 26%

Approximate percentage of incoming students with a B.A./B.S. only: 80% **Master's:** 20%

Approximate percentage of students who are
Women: 78% **Ethnic Minority:** 22% **International:** 5%
Deaf or Hard of Hearing: 39% **Hearing:** 61%

Average years to complete the doctoral program (including internship): 6.6 years

Personal interview
Preferred in person but videoconference acceptable

Attrition rate in past 7 years: 14%

Percentage of students applying for internship in 2017 accepted into:

APA internships: 86% **APPIC internships:** 14%

Formal tracks/concentrations: none

Research areas	# Faculty	# Grants
adult development issues	2	0
assessment of attachment in deaf persons	1	0
assessment of attention in deaf persons	2	1
assessment of deaf-blind persons	1	0
reading development in deaf children	2	1
cognitive processing and memory in deaf persons	2	0
neuropsychological assessment of deaf clients	3	0
behavioral parent training	1	0
cognitive behavioral treatment	1	0
mental health in minority deaf persons	1	0

Clinical opportunities
Assessment and therapy with deaf and hard-of-hearing clients through our multidisciplinary mental health clinic. More than 60 externship programs available in Washington, D.C. metropolitan area.

George Fox University (Psy.D.)

Graduate Department of Clinical Psychology
School of Behavioral and Health Sciences
414 N Meridian Street RC104
Newberg, OR 97132-2697
phone#: 800-631-0921 x2263
email: psyd@georgefox.edu
Web address: georgefox.edu/psyd

1	2	3	4	5	6	7
Practice oriented			Equal emphasis			Research oriented

Percentage of faculty subscribing to each of the following orientations:

Psychodynamic/Psychoanalytic	25%
Applied behavioral analysis/Radical behavioral	0%
Family systems/Systems	17%
Existential/Phenomenological/Humanistic	13%
Cognitive/Cognitive-behavioral	45%

Courses required for incoming students to have completed prior to enrolling:
18 semester hours or the equivalent in psychology

Courses recommended but not mandatory
psychological statistics or research methods, personality theory, human development, abnormal, psychological tests and measurements, and social

GRE mean
Verbal + Quantitative 298
Analytical Writing 58%
Psychology Subject Test not reported

GPA mean
Overall GPA 3.86

Number of applications/admission offers/incoming students in 2017
96 applications/33 admission offers/24 incoming

% of students receiving:
Full tuition waiver only: 0%
Assistantship/fellowship only: 48%
Both full tuition waiver & assistantship/fellowship: 0%
Partial tuition waiver only: 90%

Approximate percentage of incoming students with a B.A./B.S. only: 71% **Master's:** 29%

Approximate percentage of all students who are
Women: 60% **Ethnic Minority:** 24% **International:** .008%

Percentage of students applying for internship in 2017 accepted into:

APA internships: 53% **APPIC internships:** 100%

Formal tracks/concentrations: none

Research areas	# Faculty	# Grants
child memory	1	0
psychology of religion	1	0
integration	2	0
ethics	1	0
supervision	1	0
religious issues in therapy	4	0
college student health	1	0
postmodernism in psychology	1	0
women's issues	1	0
health psychology	2	5
psychotherapy outcome	2	0
developmental psychopathology	1	1

positive psychology	1	0
technology and psychology practice	1	0
clinical training	2	0
international psychology	1	0
hope	1	0
shame	1	0
multiculturalism	2	0
neuropsychology	1	1

Clinical opportunities

addictions
assessment
child psychopathology
community mental health
consultation
corrections
forensic
geriatrics
health psychology
multicultural school/CMH
neuropsychology
pain management
primary health care setting
public school setting
rural psychology
spirituality

George Mason University (Ph.D.)

Department of Psychology 3F5
4400 University Drive
Fairfax, VA 22030-4444
phone#: (703) 993-1384
email: psycgrad@gmu.edu
Web address: clinical.psychology.gmu

1	2	3	4	**5**	6	7
Practice oriented			Equal emphasis			Research oriented

Percentage of faculty subscribing to each of the following orientations:

Psychodynamic/Psychoanalytic	0%
Applied behavioral analysis/Radical behavioral	0%
Family systems/Systems	45%
Humanistic/Person-Centered/Emotion-Focused	20%
Cognitive/Cognitive-behavioral	91%
Community	27%

Courses required for incoming students to have completed prior to enrolling:
statistics, experimental, and abnormal

Recommended but not mandatory courses: tests and measurements, developmental, and social

GRE mean
Verbal 163.6 (91.8 percentile) Quantitative 158.4 (68.2 percentile)
Analytical Writing 4.9 (84 percentile)
Psychology Subject Test not reported

GPA mean
Overall GPA 3.64

Number of applications/admission offers/incoming students in 2017
296 applied

% of students receiving:
Full tuition waiver only: 0%
Assistantship/fellowship only: 0%
Both full tuition waiver & assistantship/fellowship: 100%

Approximate percentage of incoming students with a B.A./B.S. only: 50% **Master's:** 50%

Approximate percentage of all students who are Women: 72% **Ethnic Minority:** 18% **International:** 0%

Average years to complete the doctoral program (including internship): 6 years

Personal interview
Required in person, phone interview possible

Attrition rate in past 7 years: 8.3%

Percentage of students applying for internship in 2017 accepted into:

APA internships: 100% **APPIC internships:** 100%

Formal tracks/concentrations: quantitative

Research areas	# Faculty
prevention and intervention	9
substance use/abuse	5
depression	4
suicide and non-suicidal self-injury	4
trauma and stress response (including PTSD)	3
anxiety	3
dissemination and implementation	3
well-being	3
eating disorders	2
HIV & other health risk behaviors	3
couple relationships	2
intimate partner violence	2
military families	1
jail-based interventions	1
older adults/geriatrics	1
civic engagement	1
social justice pedagogy	1
grant/contract funded research	8

Clinical opportunities
GMU Center for Psychological Services (psyclinic.gmu.edu)
Populations treated: Children, adolescents, adults, families, couples, and group
Therapies taught: Cognitive-behavioral therapy, dialectical behavior therapy, family systems therapy, and motivational interviewing
Assessments taught: Intellectual, achievement, comprehensive psychoeducational, and comprehensive mental health assessments
Other training: Consultation/supervision

Clinical Externships
Clinical externship placements throughout the DC Metro area (VA, MD, DC)

George Washington University (Ph.D.)

Department of Psychology
2125 G Street, NW
Washington, DC 20052
phone#: (202) 994-6320
email: smolock@gwu.edu
Web address: departments.columbian.gwu.edu/psychology/graduate/clinical

1	2	3	4	**5**	6	7
Practice oriented			Equal emphasis			Research oriented

Percentage of faculty subscribing to each of the following orientations:

Psychodynamic/Psychoanalytic	0%
Applied behavioral analysis/Radical behavioral	10%
Family systems/Systems	10%
Existential/Phenomenological/Humanistic	0%
Cognitive/Cognitive-behavioral	50%
Community/Ecological	40%

Courses required for incoming students to have completed prior to enrolling:
The equivalent of a major in psychology, statistics, research methods (or experimental course), basic psychology theory courses (from neuropsychology, physiological psychology, abnormal psychology, social psychology, learning and cognition, developmental psychology, community psychology)

Recommended but not mandatory courses: none

GRE mean
Verbal 161 (85th percentile) Quantitative 154 (58th percentile)
Analytical Writing 4.3 (65th percentile)
Psychology Subject Test not reported

GPA mean
Overall GPA 3.62

Number of applications/admission offers/incoming students in 2017
238 applied/4 admission offers/4 incoming

% of students receiving:
Full tuition waiver only: 0%
Assistantship/fellowship only: 0%
Both full tuition waiver & assistantship/fellowship: 100%

Approximate percentage of incoming students with a B.A./B.S. only: 83.33% **Master's:** 16.67%

Approximate percentage of students who are Women: 73.5% **Ethnic Minority:** 41.2% **International:** 11.7%

Average years to complete the doctoral program (including internship): 6.5 years

Personal interview
Preferred in person but telephone/Skype acceptable

Attrition rate in past 7 years: 3%

Percentage of students applying for internship last year accepted into APPIC or APA internships: 100%

Formal tracks/concentrations: none

Research areas	**# Faculty**	**# Grants**
adolescence	3	2
AIDS/HIV	3	3
anxiety disorders	1	0
child	2	1
community/prevention	6	1
depression	2	2
family/couples	2	2
health	1	0
minority mental health	4	3
stress and coping	3	1

Clinical opportunities

adolescent problems
AIDS
adolescent delinquency
affective disorders/depression
anxiety disorders
assessment
behavioral medicine
child assessment and therapy
conduct disorder
developmental disabilities/autism
eating disorders
family therapy
forensic psychology
group therapy
health
hyperactivity
impulse control/aggression
marital/couples therapy
minority/cross-cultural
neuropsychology/rehabilitation
obsessive–compulsive disorder
personality disorders
psychodynamic/psychoanalytic therapy
PTSD
schizophrenia/psychoses
substance abuse

George Washington University (Psy.D.)

Professional Psychology Program
1922 F Street NW, Suite 103
Washington, DC 20052
phone#: (202) 994-4929
email: psyd@gwu.edu
Web address: psyd.columbian.gwu.edu

1	**2**	3	4	5	6	7
Practice oriented			Equal emphasis			Research oriented

Percentage of faculty subscribing to each of the following orientations:
not reported

Courses required for incoming students to have completed prior to enrolling:
Degree in psychology or Psychology subject test

Recommended but not mandatory courses: not reported

GRE mean
Verbal + Quantitative not reported
Analytical Writing not reported
Psychology Subject Test not reported

GPA mean
Overall GPA not reported

Number of applications/admission offers/incoming students in 2015
200+ applied/40 admission offers/20 incoming

% of students receiving:
Full tuition waiver only: 0%
Assistantship/fellowship only: 0%
Both full tuition waiver & assistantship/fellowship: 0%

Approximate percentage of incoming students with a B.A./B.S. only: 30% **Master's:** 70%

Approximate percentage of all students who are Women: 80% **Ethnic Minority:** 25% **International:** 20%

Average years to complete the doctoral program (including internship): 4 years

Personal interview
yes

Attrition rate in past 7 years: 6%

Percentage of students applying for internship last year accepted into:

APA internships: 72% **APPIC internships:** 100%

Formal tracks/concentrations: Child, Adult, Assessment

Research areas
Attachment, affective disorders, LGBTQ, severe psychopathology, cultural factors, public policy

Clinical opportunities
In house clinic and more than 40 local affiliate sites or externships

University of Georgia (Ph.D.)

Department of Psychology
Athens, GA 30602
phone#: (706) 542-1787
email: gradpsych@uga.edu
Web address: psychology.uga.edu/graduate/programs/clinical/

1	2	3	4	5	**6**	7
Practice oriented			Equal emphasis			Research oriented

Percentage of faculty subscribing to each of the following orientations:

Psychodynamic/Psychoanalytic	0%
Applied behavioral analysis/Radical behavioral	20%
Family systems/Systems	30%
Existential/Phenomenological/Humanistic	0%
Cognitive/Cognitive-behavioral	100%

Courses required for incoming students to have completed prior to enrolling: none

Recommended but not mandatory courses: abnormal, statistics

GRE mean
Verbal 162 Quantitative 159
Analytical Writing not reported
Psychology Subject Test not reported

GPA mean
Overall GPA 3.84

Number of applications/admission offers/incoming students in 2017
200 applied/15 admission offers/5 incoming

% of students receiving:
Full tuition waiver only: 0%
Assistantship/fellowship only: 0%
Both full tuition waiver & assistantship/fellowship: 100%

Approximate percentage of incoming students with a B.A./B.S. only: 80% **Master's:** 20%

Approximate percentage of students who are Women: 72% **Ethnic Minority:** 15% **International:** 3%

Average years to complete the doctoral program (including internship): 5.84 years

Personal interview
Preferred in person but telephone acceptable

Attrition rate in past 7 years 5.7%

Percentage of students applying for internship in 2017 accepted into:

APA internships: 100% **APPIC internships:** 100%

Formal tracks/concentrations: adult clinical, child, neuropsychology

Research areas	**# Faculty**	**# Grants**
adjustment	2	1
adolescent/at-risk adolescent	4	–
affective disorders/depression	2	–
aggression/anger control	1	–
aging/gerontology/adult development	3	2
alcohol	3	1
Alzheimer's disease/dementia	2	–
anxiety disorders/panic disorders	1	–
assessment/diagnosis	5	1
behavioral economics	1	1
behavioral medicine/health psychology	4	1
brain injury/head injury	1	–
cardiovascular health/function	3	–
child abuse/neglect/sexual abuse	2	–
child and family	5	3
child clinical/pediatric	2	–
chronic disease/illness	2	–
cognition/social cognition	3	2
disaster/trauma	1	–
eating disorders/body image	1	–
emotion	4	1
epigenetics/genetic susceptibility	1	1
family therapy	1	–
gambling	1	1
health care/primary care	2	–
impulsivity	2	–
intervention	4	–
marriage/couples	2	1
medical adherence	1	–
memory	2	–
methodology	1	1
motivation	1	–
multiple sclerosis	1	–
neuroeconomics	1	–
neuroimaging	3	3
neuropsychology	3	3
nicotine/tobacco/smoking	1	–
pain management	1	–
parent-child interactions/parenting	4	1
pediatric inflammatory bowel disease	1	–
pediatric oncology	1	–
pediatric organ transplantation	1	1
person perception	1	–
personality assessment	2	–
personality disorders	1	–
personality/temperament	2	–
positive psychology/resilience	3	–
posttraumatic stress disorder	1	–
poverty	2	3
prevention	5	3
psychometrics/measurement	2	–

psychopathology-child/developmental	3	1
religion/spirituality	2	–
schizophrenia	1	1
serious mental illness	1	1
somatization disorders	1	–
stress and coping	5	3
substance abuse/addictive behaviors	5	3
tic disorders	1	–
Tourette Syndrome	1	–
transition of health care	1	–
violence/abuse/rape	1	–

Clinical opportunities

ADHD
adjustment
affective disorders/depression
aging/gerontology
anxiety disorders
assessment
at-risk adolescents
behavioral medicine/health psychology
behavioral therapy/analysis
child abuse/neglect
child/pediatric
cognitive-behavioral therapy
conduct disorder
disabilities
disaster/trauma
eating disorders/body image
empirically supported treatments
family therapy
learning disabilities
marriage/couples
medical center/hospital-based services
minority/multicultural
motivational interviewing
neuropsychology
pain management
parent-child interaction/parent training
pediatric psychology (oncology, rehabilitation, weight management, organ transplant, gastroenterology, endocrinology, neuropsychology)
personality disorders
PTSD
rural mental health
sleep disorders
substance abuse/addiction
supervision
victim/violence/sexual abuse

Georgia Southern University (Psy.D.)

Department of Psychology
Brannen Hall 1010
Statesboro, GA 30460-8041
phone#: (912) 478-5539
email: psyd@georgiasouthern.edu
Web address: http://class.georgiasouthern.edu/psychology/psyd/

1	2	**3**	4	5	6	7
Practice oriented			Equal emphasis			Research oriented

Percentage of faculty subscribing to each of the following orientations:

Psychodynamic/Psychoanalytic	0%
Applied behavioral analysis/Radical behavioral	0%
Family systems/Systems	0%
Existential/Phenomenological/Humanistic	20%
Cognitive/Cognitive-behavioral	80%
DBT; Acceptance & Commitment	20%
Interpersonal	20%
Narrative/Post-modern	20%

Courses required for incoming students to have completed prior to enrolling:
All of the following with a grade of B or higher: statistics; research methods; abnormal; and two of the following: social, personality, substance abuse, cognitive, learning, psychotherapy, health psychology, psychological tests, lifespan developmental

Recommended but not mandatory courses:
none

GRE mean
Verbal + Quantitative 305
Analytical Writing 4.1
Psychology Subject Test (not reported)

GPA mean
Overall GPA 3.68

Number of applications/admission offers/incoming students in 2016
94 applied/9 admission offers/8 incoming

% of students receiving:
Full tuition waiver only: 0%
Assistantship/fellowship only: 0%
Both full tuition waiver & assistantship/fellowship: 100%

Approximate percentage of incoming students with a B.A./B.S. only: 75% **Master's:** 25%

Approximate percentage of all students who are Women: 73% **Ethnic Minority:** 22.5% **International:** 0%

Average years to complete the doctoral program (including internship): 5.5 years

Personal interview
Required

Attrition rate in past 7 years: 4.1%

Percentage of students applying for internship last year accepted into:

APA internships: 100% **APPIC internships:** 100%

Formal tracks/concentrations: none

Research areas	# Faculty	# Grants
positive psychology	1	0
suicide	1	0
labeling/stereotypes	1	0
childhood sexual abuse	1	0
rural mental health	1	2
alcohol abuse and dependence	1	0
mindfulness and mental health	2	0
veterans	1	1
scholarship of teaching & learning	1	0

Clinical opportunities

Campus counseling centers
Outpatient hospital clinic
Veteran's Affairs Medical Centers
Campus community mental health clinic
Inpatient hospital
U.S. Army Medical Center

Georgia State University (Ph.D.)

Department of Psychology
P.O. Box 5010
Atlanta, GA 30302-5010
phone#: (404) 413-6200
email: parrott@gsu.edu

Web address: http://psychology.gsu.edu/graduate/program-areas-and-concentrations/clinical-program/

1 2 3 **4** 5 6 7

Practice oriented — Equal emphasis — Research oriented

Percentage of faculty subscribing to each of the following orientations:

Psychodynamic/Psychoanalytic	0%
Interpersonal	15%
Applied behavioral analysis/Radical behavioral	0%
Family systems/Systems	15%
Existential/Phenomenological/Humanistic	7%
Cognitive/Cognitive-behavioral	93%
Clinical Neuropsychology	38%

Courses required for incoming students to have completed prior to enrolling:
research methods, psychological statistics, and two additional Junior/Senior-level psychology courses

Recommended but not mandatory courses: abnormal psychology

GRE mean
Verbal 159 Quantitative 157
Analytical Writing not reported
Psychology Subject Test not reported

GPA mean
Overall GPA 3.71

Number of applications/admission offers/incoming students in 2016
413 applied/17 admission offers/8 incoming

% of students receiving:
Full tuition waiver only: 0%
Assistantship/fellowship only: 0%
Both full tuition waiver & assistantship/fellowship: 100%

Approximate percentage of incoming students with a B.A./B.S. only: 87.5% **Master's:** 12.5%

Approximate percentage of all students who are Women: 75% **Ethnic Minority:** 25% **International:** 0%

Average years to complete the doctoral program (including internship): 7 years

Personal interview
Preferred in person but telephone acceptable

Attrition rate in past 7 years: 16%

Percentage of students applying for internship in 2016 accepted into:

APA internships: 100% **APPIC internships:** 100%

Formal tracks/concentrations: general clinical, clinical neuropsychology, clinical-community psychology

Research areas	# Faculty	# Grants
Aging	2	1
Aggression/anger control	1	1
alcohol	1	1
child and family	7	5
cognitive behavioral therapy	1	1
culture, mental health and therapy	1	0
depression	3	0
brain injury	1	1
gender roles	1	0
HIV	1	1
learning disability	1	1
mindfulness	3	1
mood and anxiety disorders	1	1
neuroimaging/functional neuroimaging	5	2
neuropsychology	7	4
pain management	1	3
parenting	2	2
pediatric psychology	1	3
personality/temperament	1	0
Positive Psychology	1	0
Psychopathology—Child/Developmental	3	2
Psychophysiology	1	2
psychotherapy outcome	1	0
reading/dyslexia	1	0
rehabilitation/remediation	1	2
treatment of anxiety disorders	1	0
Violence/Abuse/Sexual Abuse/Rape	1	0

Clinical opportunities
anxiety disorders
behavioral assessment
chronic health conditions
community psychology
neuropsychology
developmental disabilities
family violence
health psychology
HIV/AIDS prevention and therapy
individual, couples, family, and group therapy
inpatient therapy
assessment
personality disorders
child psychopathology
psychosocial rehabilitation
psychotherapy supervision
violence prevention

University of Hartford (Psy.D.)

Graduate Institute of Professional Psychology
200 Bloomfield Ave.
West Hartford, CT 06105
phone#: (860) 768-4778
email: viereck@hartford.edu or oppenheim@hartford.edu
Web address: http://www.hartford.edu/a_and_s/departments/psychology/program_psyd/

1 2 **3** 4 5 6 7

Practice oriented — Equal emphasis — Research oriented

Percentage of faculty subscribing to each of the following orientations:

Psychodynamic/Psychoanalytic	25%
Applied behavioral analysis/Radical behavioral	0%
Family systems/Systems	25%
Existential/Phenomenological/Humanistic	15%
Cognitive/Cognitive-behavioral	75%
Feminist	25%
Client-centered	25%

Courses required for incoming students prior to enrolling:
abnormal, social, developmental, cognitive, physiological, research methods, statistics

Recommended but not mandatory courses: psychology major

GRE mean
Verbal 156 Quantitative 150
Analytical Writing 4.5
Psychology Subject Test 645

Number of applications/admission offers/incoming students in 2017
154 applied/50 admission offers/27 incoming

% of students receiving:
Full tuition waiver only: 0%
Assistantship/fellowship only: 58%
Both full tuition waiver & assistantship/fellowship: 0%

Approximate percentage of incoming students with a B.A./B.S. only: 60% **Master's:** 40%

Approximate percentage of all students who are Women: 90% **Ethnic Minority:** 30% **International:** 5%

Average years to complete the doctoral program (including internship): 6.0 years

Personal interview
Required in person (unless international students)

Attrition rate in past 7 years: 7%

Percentage of students applying for internship in 2017 accepted into:

APA internships: 92% **APPIC internships:** 96%

Formal tracks/concentrations: general track; child & adolescent track

Research areas	# Faculty	# Grants
child/adolescent	3	1
community treatment	2	0
intimate partner violence	1	0
clinical supervision/mentoring	1	0
psychological assessment	2	0
multicultural issues	3	0
medical issues	3	0
college counseling	2	0
substance abuse	1	0

Clinical opportunities
acute psychiatry/mental health
anxiety disorders
depression
residential schools
children
families
forensics
community psychology
hospital-based psychology
college counseling

Harvard University

Department of Psychology
33 Kirkland Street
Cambridge, MA 02138
phone#: (617) 495-3810
email: cir@wjh.harvard.edu
Web address: https://psychology.fas.harvard.edu/clinical-psychology

1	2	3	4	5	6	**7**
Practice oriented			Equal emphasis			Research oriented

Percentage of faculty subscribing to each of the following orientations:

Psychodynamic/Psychoanalytic	0%
Applied behavioral analysis/Radical behavioral	0%
Family systems/Systems	0%
Existential/Phenomenological/Humanistic	0%
Cognitive/Cognitive behavioral	100%

Courses required for incoming students to have completed prior to enrolling: none

Recommended but not mandatory courses: abnormal, developmental, cognitive neuroscience, neuroscience, statistics, other science and mathematics courses

GRE mean
Verbal 92percentile Quantitative 74 percentile
Analytical Writing 96 percentile
Psychology Advanced Test not required

GPA mean
Overall GPA 3.84

Number of applications/admission offers/incoming students in 2017
318 applied/4 admission offers/4 incoming

% students receiving:
Full tuition waiver only: 0%
Assistantship/fellowship only: 0%
Both full tuition waiver & assistantship/fellowship 100%

Approximate percentage of incoming students with a BA/BS only: 50% **Master's:** 50%

Approximate percentage of all students who are Women: 65% **Ethnic Minority:** 31% **International:** 2%

Average years to complete the doctoral program (including internship): 7 years

Personal interview
In person or Skype is preferred, but telephone interview is acceptable.

Attrition rate in past 7 years: 4%

Percentage of students applying for internship in 2017 accepted into:

APA internships: 100% **APPIC internships:** 100%

Formal tracks/concentrations: clinical psychology with a clinical science emphasis

Research areas	# Faculty	# Grants
anxiety disorders	2	1
child & adolescent psychotherapy	1	3
personality disorders	2	1
substance abuse	1	1
suicide/self-injury	2	7

Clinical opportunities
anxiety/traumatic stress disorders
bipolar disorders
east Asian clinic
eating disorders
OCD
victims of violence clinic
behavioral neurology

body dysmorphic disorders
dialectical behavior therapy
adolescent
child clinical
behavioral health
assessment
early psychosis

University of Hawaii at Manoa (Ph.D.)

Clinical Studies Program
Department of Psychology
2530 Dole St., Sakamaki C-400
Honolulu, HI 96822
phone#: (808) 956-8414
email: gradpsy@hawaii.edu
Web address: www.psychology.hawaii.edu/concentrations/clinical-psychology.html

1	2	3	4	5	**6**	7
Practice oriented			Equal emphasis			Research oriented

Percentage of faculty subscribing to each of the following orientations:

Psychodynamic/Psychoanalytic	0%
Behavioral	28%
Family systems/Systems	14%
Existential/Phenomenological/Humanistic	0%
Cognitive/Cognitive-behavioral	100%
Contextual-Behavioral	14%

Courses required for incoming students prior to enrolling:
psychology major or approximately 5–10 selected psychology courses

Recommended but not mandatory courses: none

GRE mean
Verbal 160 Quantitative 157
Analytical Writing 4.7
Psychology Subject Test not required

GPA mean
Overall GPA 3.66

Number of applications/admission offers/incoming students in 2017
135 applied/17 admission offers/10 incoming

% of students receiving:
Full tuition waiver only: 0%
Assistantship/fellowship only: 0%
Both full tuition waiver & assistantship/fellowship: 100%

Approximate percentage of incoming students with a B.A./B.S. only: 75% **Master's:** 25%

Approximate percentage of all students who are Women: 67% **Ethnic Minority:** 35% **International:** 13%

Average years to complete the doctoral program (including internship): 7 years

Personal interview
Telephone required

Attrition rate in past 7 years: 26%

Percentage of students applying for internship in 2017 accepted into:

APA internships: 100% **APPIC internships:** 100%

Formal tracks/concentrations: none

Research areas	# Faculty	# Grants
ADHD	1	0
anxiety	1	0
assessment	2	3
childhood clinical	4	3
development disabilities	1	1
domestic violence	1	1
eating disorders	3	0
extreme behavior patterns	1	0
family bereavement	1	1
family stress	1	1
GLBT youth	1	0
mental health systems	2	3
obesity	1	0
first episode psychosis	1	1
treatment as usual	1	1
risk for psychosis	1	0
philosophy of science	1	0
principle-based psychotherapy	1	0
Zen Buddhism	1	0
diversity	2	0
cultural humility	1	0
mental health related stigma	2	0
acceptance and commitment therapy	1	0

Clinical opportunities
assessment
behavioral medicine
behavioral health
consultation
child clinical
cross-cultural/rural
developmental disabilities
first episode psychosis
substance use prevention
dual diagnoses
eating disorders
evidence based practice
neuropsychology
rehabilitation psychology
severe mental illness
acceptance and commitment therapy

Hofstra University (Ph.D.)

Department of Psychology
Hempstead, NY 11549
phone#: (516) 463-5662
email: Psyjtc@hofstra.edu
Web address: www.hofstra.edu/ClinicalPsy

1	2	**3**	4	5	6	7
Practice oriented			Equal emphasis			Research oriented

Percentage of faculty subscribing to each of the following orientations:

Psychodynamic/Psychoanalytic	0%
Applied behavioral analysis/Radical behavioral	30%
Family systems/Systems	0%
Existential/Phenomenological/Humanistic	0%
Cognitive/Cognitive-behavioral	70%

Courses required for incoming students to have completed prior to enrolling:
Statistics, research design, psychology research lab

Recommended but not mandatory courses:
psychopathology/abnormal, history or systems, physiological psychology or sensation/perception tests and measurements

GRE mean (percentiles)
Verbal 81% Quantitative 66%
Analytical Writing 4.4
Psychology Subject Test 660

GPA mean
Overall GPA 3.65

Number of applications/admission offers/incoming students in 2017
191 applied/34 admission offers/10 incoming

% of students receiving:
Full tuition waiver only: 20%
Assistantship/fellowship only: 80%
Both full tuition waiver & assistantship/fellowship: 0%

Approximate percentage of incoming students with a B.A./B.S.only: 75% **Master's:** 25%

Approximate percentage of students who are Women: 65% **Ethnic Minority:** 15% **International:** 10%

Average years to complete the doctoral program (including internship): 6 years

Personal interview
Required in person

Attrition rate in past 7 years: 5%

Percentage of students applying for internship accepted into:

APA internships: 80% **APPIC internships:** 95%

Formal tracks/concentrations/specializations: none

Research areas	# Faculty	# Grants
attitudes and attitude change	1	0
behavior analysis	3	0
behavior modification	2	0
body image	2	0
cross-cultural psychology	1	0
depression	1	0
human error	1	0
infant/toddler development	1	0
normal and abnormal personalities	2	0
prevention of childhood disorders	1	0
psychotherapy for anger, guilt, fear, and anxiety	5	–
quantitative research methods	2	0
rational-emotive/behavior therapy for marital therapy	1	0
schizophrenia	1	1
self-report validity	1	0
sexual dysfunctions	1	0

Clinical opportunities
Hofstra University Psychological Evaluation and Research Clinic:
phobia
parent-child interaction therapy
trauma
depression
anxiety
acceptance and commitment therapy
dialectical behavior therapy

University of Houston (Ph.D.)

Department of Psychology
3695 Cullen Blvd, Room 126
Houston, TX 77204-5022
phone#: (713) 743-8500
email: csharp2@uh.edu
Web address: www.uh.edu/class/psychology/clinical-psych/index.php

1	2	3	**4**	5	6	7
Practice oriented			Equal emphasis			Research oriented

Percentage of faculty subscribing to each of the following orientations:

Psychodynamic/Psychoanalytic	6%
Applied behavioral analysis/Radical behavioral	0%
Family systems/Systems	6%
Existential/Phenomenological/Humanistic	0%
Cognitive/Cognitive-behavioral	93%

Courses required for incoming students prior to enrolling: none

Recommended but not mandatory courses: Statistics, history and systems, physiological psychology, abnormal, experimental, social, developmental, methods

GRE mean
Verbal 160/83% Quantitative 156/62%
Analytical Writing 4.6/77%
Psychology Subject Test not reported

GPA mean
Overall GPA 3.77

Number of applications/admission offers/incoming students in 2016
501 applied/23 admission offers/16 incoming

% of students receiving:
Full tuition waiver only: 0%
Assistantship/fellowship only: 0%
Both full tuition waiver & assistantship/fellowship: 100%

Approximate percentage of incoming students with a B.A./B.S. only: 56% **Master's:** 44%

Approximate percentage of all students who are Women: 70.7% **Ethnic Minority:** 19%
International: 1.7%

Average years to complete the doctoral program (including internship): 5.4 years

Personal interview: Preferred in person but telephone acceptable

Attrition rate in past 7 years: 6%

Percentage of students applying for internship in 2016 accepted into:

APA internships: 100% **APPIC internships:** 100%

Formal tracks/concentrations: neuropsychology, adult behavior disorders, child-family

Research areas	# Faculty	# Grants
Addiction/substance use	2	9
Adult psychopathology	2	1
Anxiety disorder	2	3
Child clinical	4	5
Developmental psych/disorders	2	4
Educational psychology	1	0
Family research/therapy	2	0
Forensic psychology	2	0
Genetics (neuro, behavioral, molecular)	1	0
Juvenile delinquency	2	1
Learning disabilities	2	5
Marriage/couples	2	0
Multicultural	3	2
Neuropsychology	3	4
Personality disorders	1	3
Sleep problems/disorders	1	2
Trauma-related disorders	1	1

Clinical opportunities
Addiction/substance use disorders
Anxiety disorders
Behavioral sleep medicine
Clinical assessment
Cognitive therapy
Couples therapy
Domestic violence
Family therapy
Forensic psychology
HIV-AIDS
Interpersonal psychotherapy
Juvenile delinquency
Learning disabilities
Multicultural
Neuropsychology
Personality disorders
Suicide and serious mental illness
Traumatic stress/Post-traumatic stress disorder

Howard University (Ph.D.)

Clinical Psychology Program
Department of Psychology
2041 Georgia Avenue, NW
Howard University Hospital Cancer Center, Suite 407
Washington, DC 20060
phone#: (202) 806-6810
email:dso@howard.edu
Web address: https://gs.howard.edu/graduate-programs/clinical-psychology
http://coas.howard.edu/psychology/clinical/
http://www.coas.howard.edu/psychology/clinical/faqs.pdf

1	2	3	**4**	5	6	7
Practice oriented			Equal emphasis			Research oriented

Percentage of faculty subscribing to each of the following orientations:

Psychodynamic/Psychoanalytic	40%
Applied behavioral analysis/Radical behavioral	40%
Family systems/Systems	60%
Existential/Phenomenological/Humanistic	40%
Cognitive/Cognitive-behavioral	80%

Courses required for incoming students to have completed prior to enrolling: none

Recommended but not mandatory courses:
Statistics, abnormal, developmental, history & systems

GRE mean
Verbal 158 + Quantitative 150 = 308
Analytical Writing not reported
Psychology Subject Test not reporteed

GPA mean
Overall GPA 3.60

Number of applications/admission offers/incoming students in 2017
65 applied/5 admission offers/3 incoming

% of students receiving:
Full tuition waiver only: 4%
Assistantship/fellowship only: 31%
Both full tuition waiver & assistantship/fellowship: 12%
Some funding from University: 19%

Approximate percentage of incoming students with a B.A./B.S. only: 67% **Master's:** 33%

Approximate percentage of all students who are Women: 84% **Ethnic Minority:** 87% **International:** 3%

Average years to complete the doctoral program (including internship): 7 years

Personal interview:
Required in person

Attrition rate in past 7 years: 10%

Percentage of students applying for internship last year accepted into:

APA internships: 100% **APPIC internships:** 100%

Formal tracks/concentrations: adult, child, health psychology

Research areas	# Faculty	# Grants
health psychology	4	2
child/family systems	2	1
spirituality/religion	2	0
trauma/violence	2	0

Clinical opportunities
University counseling center, VAMC, hospitals, community centers, district courts, private practices

Idaho State University (Ph.D.)

Psychology Department
Stop 8112
Idaho State University
Pocatello, ID 83209-8112
phone#: (208) 282-2462
email: lawystev@isu.edu
Web address: www.isu.edu/psych/clinicalprogram.shtml

1	2	3	**4**	5	6	7
Practice oriented			Equal emphasis			Research oriented

Percentage of faculty subscribing to each of the following orientations:

Psychodynamic/Psychoanalytic 15%
Applied behavioral analysis/Radical behavioral 33%
Family systems/Systems 33%
Existential/Phenomenological/Humanistic 100%
Cognitive/Cognitive-behavioral 100%

Courses required for incoming students to have completed prior to enrolling:
Psychology major or its equivalent. The stronger the major, the better, i.e., methodology courses plus undergraduate courses in the major areas: history and systems, developmental, cognitive/learning, social, physiological, and personality. The methodology courses are mandatory.

Recommended but not mandatory courses: none

GRE mean
[Percentiles]
Verbal 74
Quantitative 61
Analytical Writing 52
Psychology Subject Test [note – no longer required]

GPA mean
Overall GPA 3.8

Number of applications/admission offers/incoming students in 2017
80 applied/9 admission offers/6 incoming

Financial Assistance
Full tuition waiver only: 0%
Non-resident tuition waiver only: 12%
Assistantship/fellowship only: 40% (all of whom receive non-resident tuition waivers)
Both full tuition waiver & assistantship/fellowship: 48%

Approximate percentage of incoming students with a B.A./B.S. only: 75% **Master's:** 25%

Approximate percentage of students who are Women: 64% **Ethnic Minority:** 14% **International:** 11%

Average years to complete the doctoral program (including internship): 5.4 years

Personal interview
Preferred in person, but telephone acceptable

Attrition rate in past 7 years: 8.3%

Percentage of students applying for internship in 2017 accepted into:

APA internships: 100% **APPIC internships:** 100%

Formal tracks/concentrations: none

Research areas
Pre- and postnatal maternal stress-related disorders, health indicators/behaviors associated with offspring neurobehavioral and cardiometabolic risk
Laboratory models of impulsive and risky decision-making
Violence against women and trauma survivors' use of resources to cope with and recover from traumatic events.
Psychotherapy process and outcome research
Assessment and treatment of anxiety and related problems in individuals with intellectual and developmental disabilities/ Autism Spectrum Disorder (IDD/ASD).
Risk/protective factors in the development of comorbid psychopathology (e.g., anxiety, feeding problems, and challenging behaviors) in individuals with IDD/ASD.
Development and validation of assessment measures specific to the IDD/ASD population.

Clinical opportunities
In-house outpatient psychology clinic, CBT for anxiety, depression, and trauma, family systems therapy, psychoeducational evaluations, couples therapy, parent-child interaction therapy, child internalizing disorders, prison populations, veterans

University of Illinois at Chicago (Ph.D.)

Department of Psychology
1007 West Harrison
Chicago, IL 60680
phone#: (312) 413-4172
email: jkassel@uic.edu
Web address: http://portal.psch.uic.edu/Clinical/Default.aspx

1	2	3	4	5	**6**	7
Practice oriented			Equal emphasis			Research oriented

Percentage of faculty subscribing to each of the following orientations:

Psychodynamic/Psychoanalytic 0%
Applied behavioral analysis/Radical behavioral 0%
Family systems/Systems 10%
Existential/Phenomenological/Humanistic 20%
Cognitive/Cognitive-behavioral 100%
Community psychology 20%

Courses required for incoming students prior to enrolling: none

Recommended but not mandatory courses: Statistics, science courses, independent research (for psychology majors), other research experience

GRE mean
Verbal + Quantitative 315
Analytical Writing 4.75
Psychology Subject Test 700

GPA mean
Junior/Senior GPA 3.78

Number of applications/admission offers/incoming students in 2017
238 applied/10 admission offers/5 incoming

% of students receiving:
Full tuition waiver only: 0%
Assistantship/fellowship only: 0%
Both full tuition waiver & assistantship/fellowship: 100%

Approximate percentage of incoming students with a B.A./B.S. only: 90% **Master's:** 10%

Approximate percentage of students who are
Women: 75% **Ethnic Minority:** 18% **International:** 3%

Average years to complete the doctoral program (including internship): 6.4 years

Personal interview
Preferred in person but telephone acceptable

Attrition rate in past 7 years: 3%

Percentage of students applying for internship in 2017 accepted into:

APA internships: 100% **APPIC internships:** 100%

Formal tracks/concentrations: none

Research areas	# Faculty	# Grants
anxiety	3	3
cognitive deficits in schizophrenia	1	1
community psychology	2	2
depression	4	3
health behavior change	4	1
social and emotional development	2	2
tobacco use, etiology, prevention and cessation	2	3

Clinical opportunities
adjustment reactions
anxiety and depression
health-related behaviors
trauma and PTSD
alcohol related disorders
neuropsychology
preventive intervention with youth
tobacco use and smoking cessation
addictive behaviors

Illinois Institute of Technology (Ph.D.)

Department of Psychology
Tech Central
3424 South State Street
Chicago, IL 60616
phone#: (312) 567-3500, (312) 567-3508
email: hopkins@iit.edu
Web address: http://humansciences.iit.edu/psychology/programs/graduate-programs/clinical-psychology-program-phd

1	2	3	4	5	6	7
Practice oriented			Equal emphasis			Research oriented

Percentage of faculty subscribing to each of the following orientations:

Psychodynamic/Psychoanalytic	0%
Applied behavioral analysis/Radical behavioral	0%
Family systems/Systems	0%
Existential/Phenomenological/Humanistic	0%
Cognitive/Cognitive-behavioral	100%

Courses required for incoming students to have completed prior to enrolling:
18 credits in psychology including research methods and statistics

Recommended but not mandatory courses: none

GRE mean
Verbal: 156.8 Quantitative 153.2
Analytical 4.35
Psychology Subject Test not reported

GPA mean
Overall GPA 3.58

Number of applications/admission offers/incoming students in 2017
88 applied/24 admission offers/10 incoming

% of students receiving:
Full tuition waiver only: 0%
½ tuition waiver: 50%
Assistantship/fellowship only: 0%
Both full tuition waiver & assistantship/fellowship: 0%

Approximate percentage of incoming students with a B.A./B.S. only: 50% **Master's:** 50%

Approximate percentage of first-year students who are
Women: 70% **Ethnic Minority:** 10% **International:** 0%

Average years to complete the doctoral program (including internship): 7 years

Personal interview
Preferred in person but telephone acceptable

Attrition rate in past 7 years: 13%

Percentage of students applying for internship in 2017 accepted into:

APA internships: 86% **APPIC internships:** 83%

Formal tracks/concentrations: rehabilitation

Research areas	# Faculty	# Grants
affective disorders	1	1
anxiety disorders	1	0
developmental psychopathology	1	0
family	1	0
health	1	0
severe mental illness	2	1
social support	1	0
rehabilitation	2	1
stigma	1	2

Clinical opportunities
affective disorders
anxiety disorders
child
family
health/behavioral medicine
marital/couples
minority/cross-cultural
pediatric neuropsychology
adult neuropsychology
pain
severe mental illness

University of Illinois at Urbana–Champaign (Ph.D.)

Department of Psychology
Psychology Building
603 East Daniel Street
Champaign, IL 61820
phone#: (217) 333-2169
email: psych-gradstdy@illinois.edu
Web address: http://www.psychology.illinois.edu/people/divisions/clinical/

1	2	3	4	5	**6**	7
Practice oriented			Equal emphasis			Research oriented

Percentage of faculty subscribing to each of the following orientations:

Applied behavioral analysis/Radical behavioral	18%
Family systems/Systems	9%
Existential/Phenomenological/Humanistic	18%
Cognitive/Cognitive-behavioral	72%

Courses required for incoming students to have completed prior to enrolling: none

Recommended but not mandatory courses: psychology major, undergraduate statistics

GRE mean
Verbal 162 Quantitative 157
Analytical Writing 4.6
Psychology Subject Test 770

GPA mean
Overall GPA 3.79

Number of applications/admission offers/incoming students in 2017
230 applied/19 admission offers/10 incoming

% of students receiving:
Full tuition waiver only: 0%
Assistantship/fellowship only: 0%
Both full tuition waiver & assistantship/fellowship: 100%

Approximate percentage of incoming students with a B.A./B.S. only: 100% **Master's:** 0%

Approximate percentage of all students who are Women: 71% **Ethnic Minority:** 38% **International:** 15%

Average years to complete the doctoral program (including internship): 7.5 years

Personal interview
Telephone required

Attrition rate in past 7 years: 15%

Percentage of students applying for internship in 2017 accepted into:

APA internships: 100% **APPIC internships:** 100%

Formal tracks/concentrations: none

Research areas	# Faculty	# Grants
behavior/molecular genetics	1	1
neuropsychology	2	1
psychophysiology	3	1
community psychology	3	4
cultural-community mental health	3	2
neuroimaging	3	3
emotion and psychopathology	6	3
externalizing disorders	2	1
intervention	2	2
minority mental health	3	1
program evaluation/development	3	2
psychotherapy/systems	1	2
schizophrenia/schizotypy	1	1
substance use	3	3
suicide	1	2
women's issues	3	1
Developmental Psychopathology	2	1
Anxiety	1	0
Mental health systems/organizations	1	1
Mindfulness Based Interventions	1	2
Autism spectrum disorder	1	0

Clinical opportunities
Academic coaching
Adult inpatient assessment
Anxiety
child clinical assessment
College disability assessment
community partnership & development
depression
Developmental disabilities
forensic evaluations
group therapy
human service /health care systems
individual adult
mindfulness based interventions
minority mental health
neuropsychological
Organizational consultation
psychotherapy
school/education
Social Skills Training
Substance abuse treatment
Trauma-Focused Cognitive Behavioral Therapy
VA hospital system

Immaculata University (Psy.D.)

Department of Graduate Psychology
Immaculata, PA 19345-0500
phone#: (610) 647-4400, ext. 3503
email: jyalof@immaculata.edu
Web address: http://www.immaculata.edu/academics/departments/graduatepsychology/psydclinicalpsychology

1	**2**	3	4	5	6	7
Practice oriented			Equal emphasis			Research oriented

Percentage of faculty subscribing to each of the following orientations:

Psychodynamic/Psychoanalytic	31%
Family systems/Systems	15%
Client centered/Existential theories	31%
Cognitive/Cognitive-behavioral	38%
Integrative/Transtheoretical	8%
Multicultural theories	15%
Bioecological system theory	8%
Postmodern constructivism	8%
Strength based, person (child) centered counselor	8%

Courses required for incoming students to have completed prior to enrolling:
Not reported

Recommended but not mandatory courses: none

GRE mean
Verbal 151 Quantitative 147
Analytical Writing 4
Psychology Subject Test not reported

GPA mean
MA 3.8 (minimum of 3.0); BA 3.7 (minimum of 3.3)

Number of applications/admission offers/incoming students in 2017
107 applied/66 admission offers/40 incoming

% of students receiving:
Full tuition waiver only: 0%
Assistantship/fellowship only: 0%
Both full tuition waiver & assistantship/fellowship: 0%

Approximate percentage of incoming students with a B.A./B.S. only: 48% **Master's:** 52%

Approximate percentage of students who are Women: 85% **Ethnic Minority:** 10% **International:** 0%

Average years to complete the doctoral program (including internship): 6 years

Personal interview
Required

Attrition rate in past 7 years: 3.5%

Percentage of students applying for internship in 2017 accepted into:

APA internships: 96% **APPIC internships:** 4%

Formal tracks/concentrations: Not reported

Research areas **# Faculty** **# Grants**
not reported

Clinical opportunities
not reported

Indiana University—Bloomington (Ph.D.)

Department of Psychological and Brain Sciences
1101 E. 10th Street
Bloomington, IN 47405
phone#: (812) 855-2311
email:bmdonofr@indiana.edu
Web address: http://www.indiana.edu/~clinscnc/

1	2	3	4	5	6	7
Practice oriented			Equal emphasis			Research oriented

Percentage of faculty subscribing to each of the following orientations:

Psychodynamic/Psychoanalytic	0%
Applied behavioral analysis/Radical behavioral	0%
Family systems/Systems	20%
Existential/Phenomenological/Humanistic	0%
Cognitive/Cognitive-behavioral	80%

Note: Our faculty doesn't really have particular "orientations" apart from an "empirical science" commitment.

Courses required for incoming students to have completed prior to enrolling:
Most students have a Psychology major, but it is not absolutely required

Recommended but not mandatory courses: Basic sciences, math, statistics

GRE mean
Verbal 89%
Quantitative 67%
Analytical Writing 90%
Psychology Subject Test not reported

GPA mean
Overall GPA 3.68

Number of applications/admission offers/incoming students in 2017
85 applied/3 admission offers/2 incoming

% of students receiving:
Full tuition waiver only: 0%
Assistantship/fellowship only: 0%
Both full tuition waiver & assistantship/fellowship: 100%

Approximate percentage of incoming students with a B.A./B.S. only: 100% **Master's:** 0%

Approximate percentage of all students who are Women: 80% **Ethnic Minority:** 38% **International:** 4%

Average years to complete the doctoral program (including internship): 7 years

Personal interview
Preferred in person but telephone acceptable

Attrition rate in past 7 years: 22%

Percentage of students applying for internship in 2017 accepted into:

APA internships: 100% **APPIC internships:** 0%

Formal tracks/concentrations: none

Research areas	**# Faculty**	**# Grants**
antisocial behavior	4	2
behavioral genetics	3	2
childhood/temperament/family	3	3
clinical neuroscience	4	3
developmental psychopathology	3	1
family law	2	1
health psychology	2	0
internalizing disorders	3	2
intervention studies	4	3
marital violence	1	1
neurodevelopmental problems	4	2
severe mental illness	4	3
sexuality and reproduction	1	1
social information processing	3	1
suicide	2	2
substance related problems	3	2

Clinical opportunities

anxiety disorders	neuropsychology
behavior medicine	pain treatment
child and family therapy	severe mental illness
depression	sleep medicine
cognitive behavioral therapy	substance abuse intervention
divorce mediation	tics and compulsions
family adjustment	

Indiana University of Pennsylvania (Psy.D.)

Department of Psychology

Clinical Psychology Program
201 Uhler Hall
Indiana, PA 15705-1068
phone#: (724) 357-4519
email: laporte@iup.edu
Web address: www.iup.edu/psychology/psyd/

1	2	**3**	4	5	6	7
Practice oriented			Equal emphasis			Research oriented

Percentage of faculty subscribing to each of the following orientations:

Psychodynamic/Psychoanalytic	5%
Applied behavioral analysis/Radical behavioral	5%
Family systems/Systems	10%
Existential/Phenomenological/Humanistic	10%
Cognitive/Cognitive-behavioral	70%

Courses required for incoming students to have completed prior to enrolling:
statistics and/or research methods, abnormal

Recommended but not mandatory courses: 6 credits in other areas of psychology

GRE mean
Verbal 159 Quantitative 153
Analytical Writing not reported
Psychology Subject Test not reported

GPA mean
Overall GPA 3.6

Number of applications/admission offers/incoming students in 2017
228 applied/49 admission offers/15 incoming

% of students receiving:
Full tuition waiver only: 0%
Assistantship/fellowship only: 0%
Both full tuition waiver & assistantship/fellowship: 100%

Approximate percentage of incoming students with a B.A./B.S. only: 87% **Master's:** 13%

Approximate percentage of all students who are Women: 73% **Ethnic Minority:** 2% **International:** 1%

Average years to complete the doctoral program (including internship): 5 years

Personal interview
Required in person

Attrition rate in past 7 years: 15%

Percentage of students applying for internship in 2017 accepted into:

APA internships: 79% **APPIC internships:** 93%

Formal tracks/concentrations: child, neuropsychology, behavioral medicine, forensic

Research areas	**# Faculty**	**# Grants**
behavioral medicine	1	0
clinical judgment	1	0
death and dying	1	0
ethical issues	2	0
family therapy	1	0
gender roles	2	0
minority mental health	3	0
parent–child	4	1
prevention	1	0
professional issues	5	1
psychopathology	4	0
women's studies	2	0
violence prevention	2	0
youth psychopathology	2	0

Clinical opportunities

adult psychotherapy	forensic
behavioral medicine	intake interviews
child and family therapy	neuropsychology
college counseling	

Indiana University–Purdue University Indianapolis (Ph.D.)

Clinical Ph.D. Program
402 North Blackford Street, LD124
Indianapolis, IN 46202-3275
phone#: (317) 274-6945
email: gradpsy@IUPUI.edu
Web address: www.psych.iupui.edu/ClinicalPsychology/Overview/

1	2	3	4	5	**6**	7
Practice oriented			Equal emphasis			Research oriented

Percentage of faculty subscribing to each of the following orientations:

Psychodynamic/Psychoanalytic	0%
Applied behavioral analysis/Radical behavioral	0%
Family systems/Systems	0%
Existential/Phenomenological/Humanistic	0%
Cognitive/Cognitive-behavioral	100%

Courses required for incoming students to have completed prior to enrolling: none

Recommended but not mandatory courses: tests and measurements, statistics, physiology, abnormal

GRE mean
Verbal 160 Quantitative 154
Analytical Writing 4.3
Psychology Subject Test 76th percentile

GPA mean
Overall GPA 3.72

Number of applications/admission offers/incoming students in 2017
112 applied/16 admission offers/7 incoming

% of students receiving:
Full tuition waiver only: 0%
Assistantship/fellowship only: 0%
Both full tuition waiver & assistantship/fellowship: 100%

Approximate percentage of incoming students with a B.A./B.S. only: 80% **Master's:** 20%

Approximate percentage of all students who are Women: 88% **Ethnic Minority:** 30% **International:** 6%

Average years to complete the doctoral program (including internship): 5.5 years

Personal interview
Required in person

Attrition rate in past 7 years: 15%

Percentage of students applying for internship in 2017 accepted into:

APA internships: 100% **APPIC internships:** 100%

Formal tracks/concentrations: Health psych (4); Severe mental illness (3)

Research areas	# Faculty	# Grants
health psychology	6	11
severe mental illness	3	5

Clinical opportunities

psychiatry clinic	consultation
neuropsychology	autism treatment
mood disorders	pain management
developmental pediatrics	primary care
schizophrenia	community
rehabilitation	borderline personality disorder
child clinical	VA
adult clinical	

Indiana State University (Psy.D.)

Department of Psychology
Root Hall
Terre Haute, IN 47809
phone#: (812) 237-4314
email: Kevin.Bolinskey@indstate.edu
Web address: http://www.indstate.edu/cas/psychology/psyd-clinical-psychology/psyd-program-clinical-psychology

1	2	3	4	5	6	7
Practice oriented			Equal emphasis			Research oriented

Percentage of faculty subscribing to each of the following orientations:

Psychodynamic/Psychoanalytic	15%
Applied behavioral analysis/Radical behavioral	0%
Family systems/Systems	15%
Existential/Phenomenological/Humanistic	5%
Cognitive/Cognitive-behavioral	70%

Courses required for incoming students prior to enrolling:
Abnormal psychology, experimental psychology, statistics, learning or cognition (24 credits in undergraduate psychology)

Recommended but not mandatory courses: Personality Theories, Physiological psychology

GRE mean
A score of 153 or above (62nd percentile) on the Verbal section is preferred, as is a score of 150 or above (53rd percentile) on the Quantitative section
Analytical Writing: Above 4.0
Psychology Subject Test not reported
Past 5-year average: Verbal 157.9, Quantitative 153.00, Writing Analytic 4.48

GPA mean
5 year average: 3.64

Number of applications/admission offers/incoming students in 2017
179 applied/11 admission offers/8 incoming

% of students receiving:
Full tuition waiver only: 0%
Assistantship/fellowship only: 0%
Both full tuition waiver & assistantship/fellowship: 100%

Approximate percentage of incoming students with a B.A./B.S. only: 75% **Master's: 25%**

Approximate percentage of students who are Women: 78% **Ethnic Minority:** 19% **International:** 0%

Average years to complete the doctoral program (including internship): 5.5 years

Personal interview
Required

Attrition rate in past 7 years: 8%

Percentage of students applying for internship in 2017 accepted into:

APA internships: 100% **APPIC internships:** 100%

Formal tracks/concentrations: Generalist clinical program with opportunities to emphasize child, health, forensics

Research areas	# Faculty	# Grants
adult psychopathology	2	0
affective disorders/depression	2	0
assessment	3	0
behavioral medicine	1	0
child clinical psychopathology	1	0
clinical judgment	1	0
friendship/relationships/intimacy	1	0
gender roles	1	0
personality disorders	2	0
professional training	2	0
stress and coping	2	0
substance abuse	1	0
women's studies	2	0

Clinical opportunities

ADHD assessment/treatment	correctional psychology
behavioral medicine	rural psychology
Serious Mental Illness	

University of Indianapolis (Psy.D.)

School of Psychological Sciences
1400 East Hanna Avenue
Health Pavilion, 2nd floor
Indianapolis, IN 46227-3697
phone#: (317) 788-3353
email: psych@uindy.edu
Web address: http://uindy.edu/applied-behavioral-sciences/psyd

1	2	**3**	4	5	6	7
Practice oriented			Equal emphasis			Research oriented

Percentage of faculty subscribing to each of the following orientations:

Psychodynamic/Psychoanalytic	20%
Applied behavioral analysis/Radical behavioral	15%
Family systems/Systems	15%
Existential/Phenomenological/Humanistic	15%
Cognitive/Cognitive-behavioral	35%

Courses required for incoming students prior to enrolling:
18 credit hours of psychology

Recommended but not mandatory courses: Abnormal, child/development, statistics, personality, brain and behavior

GRE mean
Verbal 157 Quantitative 153
Analytical Writing 5.12
Psychology Subject Test 661

GPA mean
Overall GPA 3.74

Number of applications/admission offers/incoming students in 2017
241 applied/69 admission offers/28 incoming

% of students receiving:
Full tuition waiver only: 4%
Assistantship/fellowship only: 20%
Both full tuition waiver & assistantship/fellowship: 0%

Approximate percentage of incoming students with a B.A./B.S. only: 80% **Master's:** 20%

Approximate percentage of students who are Women: 85.9% **Ethnic Minority:** 19.2% **International:** 5%

Average years to complete the doctoral program (including internship): 5.31 years

Personal interview
Preferred in person but telephone acceptable

Attrition rate in past 7 years: 7.7%

Percentage of students applying for internship in 2016 accepted into:

APA internships: 82% **APPIC internships:** 18%

Formal tracks/concentrations: child and adolescent psychology, health psychology/behavioral medicine, adult psychopathology and psychotherapy

Research areas	# Faculty	# Grants
child/family psychology	2	1
clinical supervision	1	0
forensics	1	0
geropsychology	2	1
multicultural mental health	2	1
health/stress/rehab/neuro	5	2
parent–child relationships	1	1
positive psychology	1	0
posttraumatic stress disorders	1	0
psychology of women	2	0
schizophrenia/psychosis	2	1

Clinical opportunities
Psychotherapy, assessment, and/or consultation services for adults and/or children at the following sites: university counseling centers, hospitals/medical centers (VA, psychiatric, general), specialized centers (e.g., domestic violence, addictions, eating disorders), community mental health centers, schools, correctional facilities, outpatient practices, and advanced traineeships (e.g., supervision, leadership)

University of Iowa (Ph.D.)

Department of Psychological and Brain Sciences
W311 Seashore Hall
Iowa City, IA 52242-1407
phone#: (319) 335-2436
email: psych-clinical@uiowa.edu
Web address: www.psychology.uiowa.edu/research/clinical-psychology

1	2	3	4	5	**6**	7
Practice oriented			Equal emphasis			Research oriented

Percentage of faculty subscribing to each of the following orientations:

Psychodynamic/Psychoanalytic	15%
Applied behavioral analysis/Radical behavioral	30%
Family systems/Systems	30%
Existential/Phenomenological/Humanistic	45%
Cognitive/Cognitive-behavioral/Third wave	100%
Eclectic	30%
Developmental Systems	15%

Courses required for incoming students prior to enrolling: none

Recommended but not mandatory courses:
Undergraduate psychology major, statistics, abnormal, laboratory research, strong science background

GRE mean (accepted)
Verbal 162 Quantitative 157
Analytical Writing 4.6
Psychology Subject Test not required

GPA mean
Overall GPA 3.8

Number of applications/admission offers/incoming students in 2017
123 applied/8 admission offers/4 incoming

% of 2009 incoming students receiving:
Full tuition waiver only: 0%
Assistantship/fellowship and partial tuition waiver: 0%
Assistantship/fellowship and full tuition waiver: 100%

Approximate percentage of 2017 incoming students with a B.A./B.S. only: 75% **Master's:** 25%

Approximate percentage of all current students who are Women: 83% **Ethnic Minority:** 17% **International:** 0%

Average years to complete the doctoral program (including internship): 7 years

Personal interview
Preferred in person but telephone acceptable

Attrition rate in past 7 years: 6%

Percentage of students applying for internship in 2016 accepted into:

APA internships: 100% **APPIC internships:** 100%

Formal tracks/concentrations: adult psychopathology, clinical health, neuropsychology

Research areas	# Faculty	# Grants
ADHD	2	1
clinical cognitive science	3	3
couples therapy	1	0
domestic violence/child abuse	1	1
depression	3	2
health psychology/beh'l medicine	2	1
neuropsychology	2	2
personality disorders	2	1
psychotherapy outcome	2	0
quantitative models of psychopathology	1	0
social emotional development	1	1
developmental psychopathology	1	1
self-regulation	1	0
externalizing disorders in children	1	0

Clinical opportunities
adult psychopathology
ADHD
child abuse
child psychiatry/pediatrics
child and family
cognitive-behavioral therapy
couples therapy
custody assessment
depression
eating disorders
health psychology/behavioral medicine
hospitals/clinics
learning disability assessment
neuropsychology
parent management training
pre-/postpartum
psychopathology
VA medical center

Jackson State University (Ph.D.)

Department of Psychology
Clinical Psychology Ph.D. Program
P.O. Box 17550
Jackson, MS 39217-0350
phone#: (601) 979-2371
email: bryman.e.williams@jsums.edu
Web address: www.jsums.edu/psychology/graduate/

1	2	3	4	5	6	7
Practice oriented			Equal emphasis			Research oriented

Percentage of faculty subscribing to orientations:

Psychodynamic/Psychoanalytic	0%
Applied behavioral analysis/Radical behavioral	0%
Family systems/Systems	0%
Existential/Phenomenological/Humanistic	0%
Cognitive/Cognitive-behavioral	100%

GRE mean
Verbal 148.7 Quantitative 144.7
Analytical Writing 4.0
Psychology Subject Test not reported

GPA mean
Undergraduate GPA 3.40
Junior/Senior GPA n/a
Master's GPA 3.94

Number of applications/admission offers/incoming students in 2017
32 applied/10 admission offers/7 incoming

% of students receiving:
Full tuition waiver only: 0% but 6.6% receiving partial tuition waiver
Assistantship/fellowship only: 51%
Both full tuition waiver & assistantship/fellowship: 0%

Approximate percentage of incoming students with a B.A./B.S. only: 28.6% **Master's:** 71.4%

Approximate percentage of students who are Women: 81.8% **Ethnic Minority:** 63.6%
International: 0%

Average years to complete the doctoral program (including internship): 6.2 years

Personal interview
Preferred in person but telephone acceptable

Attrition rate in past 7 years: 4%

Percentage of students applying for internship in 2016 accepted into:

APA internships: 80% **APPIC internships:** 80%

Formal tracks/concentrations: none

Research areas	# Faculty	# Grants
alcohol/substance abuse	2	0
childhood obesity	1	0
chronic pain/headache	2	1
depression	2	0
health care disparities	3	1
HIV/AIDS	4	5
posttraumatic stress disorder	1	0
psychological assessment	6	0
stigma	2	0

Clinical opportunities
behavioral medicine
campus counseling center
forensic
inpatient pediatric
private practice
inpatient psychiatric
neuropsychiatric rehab
outpatient pediatric
outpatient psychiatric

John F. Kennedy University (Psy.D.)

College of Psychology
Doctoral Program in Clinical Psychology
100 Ellinwood Way
Pleasant Hill, CA 94523
www.jfku.edu

1	2	3	4	5	6	7
Practice oriented			Equal emphasis			Research oriented

Percentage of faculty subscribing to each of the following orientations:

Psychodynamic/Psychoanalytic	25%
Applied behavioral analysis/Radical behavioral	5%
Family systems/Systems	25%
Existential/Phenomenological/Humanistic	25%
Cognitive/Cognitive-behavioral	25%

Courses required for incoming students to have completed prior to enrolling: A minimum of four psychology courses: Statistics, a Diversity-oriented course, Introduction to Psychology, Theories of Personality. Up to 2 prerequisites may be completed during the first two quarters of residence.

Recommended but not mandatory courses: not reported

GRE mean
The program does not require the GRE.

GPA mean
3.0 minimum GPA required from undergraduate program; 3.5 from graduate programs.

Number of applications/admission offers/incoming students in 2015
75 applied/54 admission offers/16 incoming

% of students receiving:
Full tuition waiver only: 20%
Assistantship/fellowship only: 0%

Approximate percentage of incoming students with a B.A./B.S. only: 60% **Master's:** 40%

Approximate percentage of all students who are Women: 75% **Ethnic Minority:** 50% **International:** 10%

Average years to complete the doctoral program (including internship): 5.5 years

Personal interview: Scheduled on campus (or via Skype) following faculty review of applicant's written materials

Attrition rate in past 7 years: 7%

Percentage of students applying for internship last year accepted into:

APA internships: 75% **APPIC internships:** 25%

Formal tracks/concentrations: Sport Psychology (dual degree, MA/PsyD); Neuropsychology

Research areas	# Faculty	# Grants
assessment/diagnosis	3	0
child psychopathology	1	0
cognitive information processing	1	2
eating disorders	1	1
family	2	1
LGBT issues	4	0
Men/masculinities	2	0
Multicultural competence	6	0
Visual perception	1	2

Clinical opportunities
anxiety disorders
depression
psychological assessment
eating disorder
multicultural clinical practice

John Jay College of Criminal Justice and the Graduate Center, City University of New York, Ph.D. program in Clinical Psychology

Department of Psychology
524 W. 59th St.
New York, NY 10019
phone#: 212-237-8252
email: pyanos@jjay.cuny.edu
Web address: http://gc.cuny.edu/Page-Elements/Academics-Research-Centers-Initiatives/Doctoral-Programs/Psychology/Training-Areas/Clinical-Psychology-@-John-Jay-College

1	2	3	**4**	5	6	7
Practice oriented			Equal emphasis			Research oriented

Percentage of faculty subscribing to each of the following orientations:

Psychodynamic/Psychoanalytic	16%
Applied behavioral analysis/Radical behavioral	0%
Family systems/Systems	0%
Existential/Phenomenological/Humanistic	0%
Cognitive/Cognitive-behavioral	84%

Courses required for incoming students to have completed prior to enrolling: none

Recommended but not mandatory courses:
Statistics, Abnormal Psychology, Research Methods

GRE mean
Verbal 159 + Quantitative 156 = 315
Analytical Writing 4.5
Psychology Subject Test not required

GPA mean
Overall GPA 3.77

Number of applications/admission offers/incoming students in 2015
115 applied/6 admission offers/4 incoming

% of students receiving:
Full tuition waiver only: 0%
Assistantship/fellowship only: 0%
Both full tuition waiver & assistantship/fellowship: 100%

Approximate percentage of incoming students with a B.A./B.S. only: 33% **Master's:** 66%

Approximate percentage of all students who are Women: 86% **Ethnic Minority:** 24% **International:** 3%

Average years to complete the doctoral program (including internship): 6 years

Personal interview not reported

Attrition rate in past 7 years: not reported

Percentage of students applying for internship last year accepted into:

APA internships: 86% **APPIC internships:** 86%

Formal tracks/concentrations: Forensic specialization

Research areas	# Faculty	# Grants
Psychopathy	1	0
Severe Mental Illness	1	1
Stigma Research	1	1
Psychological Assessment	2	0
Sex Offender Treatment	2	0
Microaggressions	1	0
Multicultural Issues	1	0
Child Abuse and Neglect	1	2
Neighborhood and Crime	1	1
Trauma and Psychopathology	3	1
Psychotherapy Development	2	1
Substance Use	2	0

Clinical opportunities
Forensic Assessment
Neuropsychological Assessment
Treatment of Severe Mental Illness
Treatment of PTSD
Treatment of Psychopathy
Treatment of Adolescents with Behavioral Problems
College Counseling
Treatment in Forensic Settings

University of Kansas (Ph.D.)

Clinical Child Psychology Program
2015 Dole Human Development Center
University of Kansas
1000 Sunnyside Avenue
Lawrence, KS 66045
phone#: (785) 864-4226
email: ccpp@ku.edu
Web address: www.ccpp.ku.edu

1	2	3	4	5	6	7
Practice oriented			Equal emphasis			Research oriented

Percentage of faculty subscribing to each of the following orientations:

Psychodynamic/Psychoanalytic	0%
Applied behavioral analysis/Radical behavioral	10%
Family systems/Systems	25%
Existential/Phenomenological/Humanistic	0%
Cognitive/Cognitive-behavioral	65%

Courses required for incoming students prior to enrolling:
Major in psychology or a minimum of 15–18 hours including: research methods, statistics, developmental/child psychology, developmental psychopathology (abnormal child psychology) or Psychology Subject Test

Recommended but not mandatory courses: none

GRE mean
Verbal 157 Quantitative 155
Analytical Writing 4.3
Psychology Subject Test not reported

GPA mean
Overall GPA 3.70

Number of applications/admission offers/incoming students in 2016
150 applied/7 admission offers/6 incoming

% of students receiving:
Full tuition waiver only: 0%
Assistantship/fellowship only: 0%
Both full tuition waiver & assistantship/fellowship: 100%

Approximate percentage of incoming students with a B.A./B.S. only: 65% **Master's:** 35%

Approximate percentage of students who are Women: 78% **Ethnic Minority:** 30% **International:** 0%

Average years to complete the doctoral program (including internship): 5.8 years

Personal interview
Preferred in person but telephone acceptable; by invitation

Attrition rate in past 7 years: 5%

Percentage of students applying for internship in 2016 accepted into:

APA internships: 100% **APPIC internships:** 100%

Formal tracks/concentrations: clinical child psychology, pediatric psychology

Research areas	# Faculty	# Grants
children and aggression	1	1
children with ASD/DD	1	1
children with chronic illness	3	1
disasters and children	2	1
domestic (family) violence	1	2
ethnicity/cultural issues	4	1
health promotion	3	1
systems-based services	2	0
stress & coping	3	2
violence and children (bullying)	2	1

Clinical opportunities
Departmental Psychology Clinic—Assessment and Treatment
Community Mental Health Center—Assessment and Treatment
Specialty Assessment practicum (ASD)—Med Center based
Pediatric Psychology (hospital and outpatient settings)
Child Abuse Treatment /Early Intervention Agency
Intensive Services for Serious Emotional Disorders
Pediatric Neuropsychology—Med Center based

University of Kansas (Ph.D.)

Department of Psychology
Lawrence, KS 66045-7556
phone#: (785) 864-4121
email: reingram@ku.edu
Web address: www.clinical.ku.edu

1	2	3	4	5	6	7
Practice oriented			Equal emphasis			Research oriented

Percentage of faculty subscribing to each of the following orientations:

Psychodynamic/Psychoanalytic	0%

Applied behavioral analysis/Radical behavioral	0%
Family systems/Systems	0%
Existential/Phenomenological/Humanistic	5%
Cognitive/Cognitive-behavioral	95%

Courses required for incoming students to have completed prior to enrolling:
Bachelor's degree in psychology or minimum of 15 credit hours of psychology coursework

Recommended but not mandatory courses:
Psychological research, statistics, research methods, abnormal, personality, brain & behavior, social, cognitive

GRE mean
Verbal 157 Quantitative 157
Analytical Writing 4.67
Psychology Subject Test n/a

GPA mean
Overall GPA 3.73

Number of applications/admission offers/incoming students in 2017
123 applied/7 admission offers/6 incoming

% of students receiving:
Full tuition waiver only: 0%
Assistantship/fellowship only: 0%
Both full tuition waiver & assistantship/fellowship: 100%

Approximate percentage of incoming students with a B.A./B.S. only: 66.6% **Master's:** 33.3%

Approximate percentage of students who are Women: 78% **Ethnic Minority:** 24% **International:** 9.7%

Average years to complete the doctoral program (including internship): 6.5 years

Personal interview
Preferred in person but telephone acceptable

Attrition rate in past 7 years: 8%

Percentage of students applying for internship in 2017 accepted into:

APA internships: 100% **APPIC internships:** 100%

Formal tracks/concentrations: general/psychopathology, health

Research areas	**# Faculty**	**# Grants**
stress & cardiovascular health	1	0
sexuality	1	0
ageing	2	2
depression	3	2
adult psychopathology	5	2
health psychology	9	6
pain	1	0
clinical neuroscience	1	1
pediatrics	2	2
oncology	3	2
sleep	1	1
eating disorders	1	1
obesity	1	1
psychotherapy	1	0

Clinical opportunities
dialectical behavior therapy
behavioral medicine—pediatrics
behavioral medicine—pain/oncology
behavioral medicine—telemedicine
behavioral medicine—neuropsychology/rehabilitation
anxiety disorders
forensic evaluation
cognitive-behavior therapy
weight loss
general adult
primary care

Kent State University (Ph.D.)

Department of Psychological Sciences
Kent, OH 44242
phone#: (330) 672-2119
email: bwildman@kent.edu
Web address: http://www.kent.edu/psychology/clinical-phd-program

1	2	3	4	5	**6**	7
Practice oriented			Equal emphasis			Research oriented

Percentage of faculty subscribing to each of the following orreientations:

Integrative	0%
Applied behavioral analysis/Radical behavioral	8%
Family systems/Systems	0%
Existential/Phenomenological/Humanistic	0%
Cognitive/Cognitive-behavioral	77%
Other (e.g., eclectic, etc.)	15%

Courses required for incoming students to have completed prior to enrolling: none

Recommended but not mandatory courses: A minimum of 18 semester credit hours in psychology, including 1–2 statistics courses and at least 1 psychology class that has a lab associated with it

GRE mean
2016 Student Cohort:
Verbal 71st percentile
Quantitative 61st percentile
Analytical Writing not used
Psychology Subject Test not reported

GPA mean
2016 Student Cohort: Overall GPA 3.61

Number of applications/admission offers/incoming students in 2016
297 applied/17 admission offers/8 incoming

% of students receiving:
Full tuition waiver only: 0%
Assistantship/fellowship only: 0%
Both full tuition waiver & assistantship/fellowship: 100%

Approximate percentage of incoming students with a B.A./B.S. only: 75% **Master's:** 25%

Approximate percentage of students who are Women: 87% **Ethnic Minority:** 18.8% **International:** 6%

Average years to complete the doctoral program (including internship): 6 years

Personal interview
Prefer personal interview but telephone interview acceptable

Attrition rate in past 7 years: 3%

Percentage of students applying for internship in 2016 accepted into:

APA internships: 100% **APPIC internships:** n/a

Formal tracks/concentrations: Adult Psychopathology; Assessment; Child Clinical; Clinical Health; Clinical

Research areas	# Faculty	# Grants
Anxiety and depression	2	1
Neuropsychology	2	2
Cardiovascular health	1	2
Emotion processing	1	1
Children and adolescents	3	1
Child health	2	2
Personality assessment	1	1

Clinical opportunities
- Adult psychotherapy
- Anxiety disorders
- Pediatric psychology
- Severe mental illness
- Health consultation
- Group psychotherapy
- Child/family therapy
- Neuropsychological assessment
- Adult and child assessment
- Bariatric surgery assessment

University of Kentucky (Ph.D.)

Department of Psychology
Kastle Hall
Lexington, KY 40506-0044
phone#: (859) 257-9640
email: mkkell@email.uky.edu
Web address: psychology.as.uky.edu/clinical-psychology

1 2 3 4 **5** 6 7

Practice oriented — Equal emphasis — Research oriented

Percentage of faculty subscribing to each of the following orientations:

Psychodynamic/Psychoanalytic	0%
Applied behavioral analysis/Radical behavioral	10%
Family systems/Systems	0%
Existential/Phenomenological/Humanistic	0%
Cognitive/Cognitive-behavioral	100%

Courses required for incoming students to have completed prior to enrolling:
experimental methodology, statistics

Recommended but not mandatory courses: abnormal, tests & measures, personality

GRE mean
Verbal 161 Quantitative 155
Analytical 4.5
Psychology Subject Test not reported

GPA mean
Overall GPA 3.71

Number of applications/admission offers/incoming students in 2017
212 applied/8 admission offers/7 incoming

% of students receiving:
Full tuition waiver only: 0%
Assistantship/fellowship only: 0%
Both full tuition waiver & assistantship/fellowship: 100%
First 5 years in program, in-state tuition is not always waived.

Approximate percentage of incoming students with a B.A./B.S. only: 95% **Master's:** 5%

Approximate percentage of all students who are Women: 75% **Ethnic Minority:** 45% **International:** 0%

Average years to complete the doctoral program (including internship): 6.3 years

Personal interview
Strongly preferred in person but telephone acceptable

Attrition rate in past 7 years: 6%

Percentage of students applying for internship in 2017 accepted into:

APA internships: 100% **APPIC internships:**

Formal tracks/concentrations: neuropsychology, behavioral medicine

Research areas	# Faculty	# Grants
adolescent development	3	2
adult psychopathology	4	1
assessment/diagnosis	3	0
behavioral medicine	2	1
child clinical	2	2
developmental psychopathology	3	3
eating disorders	1	1
neuropsychology	2	0
pain	1	0
personality assessment	3	1
personality disorders	2	0
psychoneuroimmunology	1	3
psychophysiology	2	1
substance abuse	4	2

Clinical opportunities
- assessment
- behavioral medicine
- child clinical
- chronic mental illness
- cognitive-behavioral therapies
- interpersonal psychotherapy
- group psychotherapy
- rehabilitation psychology
- community mental health
- dialectical behavior therapy
- neuropsychology
- orofacial pain

La Salle University (Psy.D.)

Department of Psychology
Philadelphia, PA 19141
phone#: (215) 951-1350
email: PsyD@lasalle.edu
Web address: http://www.lasalle.edu/doctor-of-psychology/

1 2 **3** 4 5 6 7

Practice oriented — Equal emphasis — Research oriented

Percentage of faculty subscribing to each of the following orientations:

Psychodynamic/Psychoanalytic	0%
Applied behavioral analysis/Radical behavioral	0%
Family systems/Systems	0%
Existential/Phenomenological/Humanistic	0%
Cognitive/Cognitive-behavioral	100%

Courses required for incoming students to have completed prior to enrolling:
Developmental, statistics, research methods

Recommended but not mandatory courses: Abnormal, tests & measures, personality

2017 GRE mean
Verbal 156
Quantitative 153
Analytical Writing 4.5
Psychology Subject Test 660

2017 GPA mean
Overall GPA 3.56

Number of applications/admission offers/incoming students in 2017
399 applied/65 admission offers/23 incoming

% of students receiving:
Full tuition waiver only: 0%
Assistantship/fellowship only: 27%
Both full tuition waiver & assistantship/fellowship: 0%

Approximate percentage of incoming students with a B.A. /B.S. only: 70% **Master's:** 30%

Approximate percentage of all students who are Women: 82% **Ethnic Minority:** 14% **International:** 2%

Average years to complete the doctoral program (including internship): 5 years

Personal interview
Required in person

Attrition rate in past 7 years: 13%

Percentage of students applying for internship in 2017 accepted into:

APA internships: 83% **APPIC internships:** 100%

Formal tracks/concentrations: general, child, health

Research areas	# Faculty	# Grants
Mindfulness interventions	1	0
Perinatal wellness	1	0
Child/adolescent internalizing disorders	1	0
Trauma and suicide prevention	1	0
Health psychology	1	0
Social problem solving	1	0
Ecology of Emotion/ Positive psychology	1	0
Weight and Eating	1	0
Counseling and psychotherapy	2	0
Couple and family therapy practice and training	1	0

Clinical opportunities
assessment
affective disorders/depression
eating disorders/body image
empirically supported treatments/interventions
anxiety disorders/panic disorders
behavioral medicine/health psychology
child/pediatric
dialectical behavior therapy/analysis
cognitive/cognitive-behavioral therapy
medical center/hospital-based services
mindfulness
post-partum depression
suicide/prevention
weight management

University of La Verne (Psy.D.)

Program in Clinical Psychology
1950 Third Street
La Verne, CA 91750
phone#: (909) 448-4414
email: jkernes@laverne.edu
Web address: sites.laverne.edu/psychology/psyd-program/

1	2	**3**	4	5	6	7
Practice oriented			Equal emphasis			Research oriented

Percentage of faculty subscribing to each of the following orientations:

Psychodynamic/Psychoanalytic	0%
Applied behavioral analysis/Radical behavioral	0%
Family systems/Systems	0%
Existential/Phenomenological/Humanistic	12.5%
Cognitive/Cognitive-behavioral	87.5%

Courses required for incoming students prior to enrolling:
Statistics, research methods, physiological psychology, and abnormal psychology. In addition, two courses from: history & systems, social psychology, personality, human development, clinical psychology, physiological psychology, biopsychology, multicultural psychology, psychological testing, psychometrics, cognitive psychology, learning/memory, sensation and perception.

Recommended but not mandatory courses: none

GRE mean
Verbal 157 Quantitative 152
Analytical Writing 4.5
Psychology Subject Test not required

GPA mean
Overall GPA 3.59

Number of applications/admission offers/incoming students in 2017
98 applied/32 offers/10 incoming

% of students receiving:
Full tuition waiver only: 0%
Assistantship/fellowship only: 30%
Both full tuition waiver & assistantship/fellowship: 0%

Approximate percentage of incoming students with a B.A./B.S. only: 100% **Master's:** 0%

Approximate percentage of students who are Women: 86% **Ethnic Minority:** 45% **International:** 3%

Average years to complete the doctoral program (including internship): 5.93

Personal interview
Required for admission

Attrition rate in past 7 years: 15%

Percentage of students applying for internship in 2017 accepted into:

APA internships: 91% **APPIC internships:** 9%

Formal tracks/concentrations: none

Research areas	# Faculty	# Grants
multiculturalism	8	2
psychotherapy services	4	0
gender issues & sexuality	3	1
values and moral development	2	0
anxiety and trauma	2	1
LGBTQIQ	2	0
Health psychology	2	2
Positive psychology	2	0
Couples issues	1	0

Clinical opportunities
children and adolescents, families, college counseling center, substance abuse, veterans, state hospitals, community mental health center, psychiatric facility

Loma Linda University (Ph.D.)

Department of Psychology
Loma Linda, CA 92350
phone#: (909) 558-8577 (Central Office)
email: hmorrell@llu.edu
Web address: http://behavioralhealth.llu.edu/programs/psychology/phd-clinical-psychology

1	2	3	4	**5**	6	7
Practice oriented			Equal emphasis			Research oriented

Percentage of faculty subscribing to each of the following orientations:

Psychodynamic/Psychoanalytic	10%
Applied behavioral analysis/Radical behavioral	10%
Family systems/Systems	0%
Existential/Phenomenological/Humanistic	30%
Cognitive/Cognitive-behavioral	50%

Courses required for incoming students to have completed prior to enrolling:
Bachelor's or Master's degree in psychology or related field

Recommended but not mandatory courses: computer literacy, math, research methods, sociology, biology, history and systems, learning, personality, statistics, social psychology, developmental psychology, psychobiology

GRE mean
Verbal 153 Quantitative 154
Analytical Writing 4.7
Psychology Subject Test not reported

GPA mean
Those entering with a Bachelor's degree, 3.65;
Those entering with a Master's degree, 3.78

Number of applications/admission offers/incoming students in 2017
43 applications/18 admission offers/8 incoming

% of students receiving:
Full tuition waiver only: 0%
Assistantship/fellowship only: 25%
Both full tuition waiver & assistantship/fellowship: 0%

Approximate percentage of incoming students with a B.A./B.S. only: 87% **Master's:** 13%

Approximate percentage of students who are
Women: 87% **Ethnic Minority:** 38%
International: not reported

Average years to complete the doctoral program (including internship): Approximately 6.5 years

Personal interview
Preferred in person but telephone acceptable

Attrition rate in past 7 years: approximately 10%

Percentage of students applying for internship in 2016 accepted into:

APA internships: 100% **APPIC internships:** not reported

Formal tracks/concentrations: clinical health psychology, pediatric health psychology, neurospychology, cultural/social psychology

Research areas	# Faculty	# Grants
health psychology	6	3
clinical neuropsychology	2	0
pediatric health psychology	1	2
psychobiology	2	2
psychology and religion	2	0
psychotherapy outcome	1	0
statistics methods	3	0

Clinical opportunities

primary care	pediatric behavioral medicine
medical/hospital	forensic
clinical neuropsychology	university/college counseling center
adult behavioral medicine	
obesity treatment	
community outpatient	

Loma Linda University (Psy.D.)

Department of Psychology
Loma Linda, CA 92350
phone#: (909) 558-8577 (central office)
email: kboyd@llu.edu
Web address: http://behavioralhealth.llu.edu/programs/psychology/psyd-clinical-psychology

1	2	**3**	4	5	6	7
Practice oriented			Equal emphasis			Research oriented

Percentage of faculty subscribing to each of the following orientations:

Psychodynamic/Psychoanalytic	10%
Applied behavioral analysis/Radical behavioral	10%

Family systems/Systems	0%
Existential/Phenomenological/Humanistic	30%
Cognitive/Cognitive-behavioral	50%

Courses required for incoming students to have completed prior to enrolling:
Bachelor's or Master's degree in psychology or relevant field

Recommended but not mandatory courses: computer literacy, math, sociology, biology, History and systems, learning, personality, statistics, social psychology, developmental psychology, psychobiology

GRE mean
Verbal 153 Quantitative 150
Analytical Writing 4.1
Psychology Subject Test not reported

GPA mean
3.35 Bachelor's; 3.91 Master's

Number of applications/admission offers/incoming students in 2017
69 applied/26 offers/18 incoming

% of students receiving:
Full tuition waiver only: 0%
Assistantship/fellowship only: 25%
Both full tuition waiver & assistantship/fellowship: 0%

Approximate percentage of incoming students with a B.A./B.S. only: 78% **Master's:** 22%

Approximate percentage of students who are Women: 89% **Ethnic Minority:** 56% **International:** not reported

Average years to complete the doctoral program (including internship): 5.5 years

Personal interview
Preferred in person but telephone acceptable

Attrition rate in past 7 years: 10%

Percentage of students applying for internship in 2016 accepted into:

APA internships: 100% **APPIC internships:** 0%

Formal tracks/concentrations: clinical health psychology, pediatric health psychology, neuropsychology, forensic psychology, family, culture psychology

Research areas	**# Faculty**	**# Grants**
health psychology	6	3
clinical neuropsychology	2	0
pediatric health psychology	1	2
psychobiology	2	2
psychology and religion	2	0
psychotherapy outcome	1	0
statistics methods	3	0

Clinical opportunities
primary care
medical/hospital
clinical neuropsychology
adult behavioral medicine
obesity treatment
community outpatient
pediatric behavioral medicine
forensic

Long Island University (Ph.D.)

Department of Psychology
University Plaza
Brooklyn, NY 11201
phone#: (718) 488-1164
email: philip.wong@liu.edu
Web address: http://www.liu.edu/Brooklyn/Academics/Liberal-Arts-Sciences/Academic-Programs/Psychology/PhD-Clinical-Psychology

1	2	3	**4**	5	6	7
Practice oriented			Equal emphasis			Research oriented

Percentage of faculty subscribing to each of the following orientations:

Psychodynamic/Psychoanalytic	50%
Applied behavioral analysis/Radical behavioral	0%
Family systems/Systems	10%
Existential/Phenomenological/Humanistic	10%
Cognitive/Cognitive-behavioral	30%

Courses required for incoming students to have completed prior to enrolling:
experimental, statistics, abnormal, developmental, personality

Recommended but not mandatory courses: social, history and systems, physiological, learning

GRE mean
Verbal 85th percentile
Quantitative 65th percentile
Analytical 65th percentile
Analytical Writing 85th percentile
Psychology Subject Test 85th percentile

GPA mean
Overall GPA 3.50 Psychology GPA 3.60

Number of applications/admission offers/incoming students in 2016
230 applied/25 admission offers/16 incoming

% of students receiving:
Full tuition waiver only: 0%
Assistantship/fellowship only: 0%
Both full tuition waiver & assistantship/fellowship: 20%
Half tuition waiver & assistantship: 80%

Approximate percentage of incoming students with a B.A./B.S. only: 60% **Master's:** 40%

Approximate percentage of all students who are Women: 70% **Ethnic Minority:** 20% **International:** 5%

Average years to complete the doctoral program (including internship): 6.2 years

Personal interview
Required in person

Attrition rate in past 7 years: 2%

Percentage of students applying for internship in 2016 accepted into:

APA internships: 95% **APPIC internships:**

Formal tracks/concentrations: not reported

Research areas	# Faculty	# Grants
cultural/cross-cultural	4	0
developmental issues	3	0
developmental psychopathology	2	0
forensic issues	2	0
health psychology	1	0
neuropsychology	1	1
projective techniques	2	0
psychotherapy process	4	1
sociodevelopment	1	0
socioemotional development	3	0
trauma	4	1
personality	4	1

Clinical opportunities
behavioral clinics
child clinical
hospital inpatient/outpatient
community mental health
family therapy
forensic units
homeless shelters
college counseling
neuropsychology

Long Island University–Post Campus (Psy.D.)

Department of Psychology
College of Liberal Arts and Sciences
Brookville, NY 11548
phone#: (516) 299-2090
email: eva.feindler@liu.edu
Web address: http://www.liu.edu/CWPost/Academics/College-of-Liberal-Arts-and-Sciences/Doctor-of-Psychology

1	2	3	4	5	6	7
Practice oriented			Equal emphasis			Research oriented

Percentage of faculty subscribing to each of the following orientations:

Psychodynamic/Psychoanalytic	50%
Applied behavioral analysis/Radical behavioral	0%
Family systems/Systems	0%
Existential/Phenomenological/Humanistic	0%
Cognitive/Cognitive-behavioral	50%

Courses required for incoming students to have completed prior to enrolling:
A minimum of 18 credit hours of psychology, including courses in Statistics, Research Design or methods, Personality and Abnormal Psychology

Recommended but not mandatory courses: not reported

GRE mean
Verbal 610 and 159 on new
Quantitative 680 and 153 on new
Analytical Writing 4.5
Psychology Subject Test 655

GPA mean
Overall GPA 3.67

Number of applications/admission offers/incoming students in 2017
259 applications/59 admission offers/20 incoming students

% of students receiving:
Full tuition waiver only: 0%
Assistantship/fellowship only: 100%
Both full tuition waiver & assistantship/fellowship: 0%

Approximate percentage of incoming students with a B.A./B.S. only: 70% **Master's:** 30%

Approximate percentage of students who are Women: 75% **Ethnic Minority:** 35% **International:** 6%

Average years to complete the doctoral program (including internship): 5.5 years

Personal interview
Required in person

Attrition rate in past 7 years: 3%

Percentage of students applying for internship in 2017 accepted into:

APA internships: 90% **APPIC internships:** 100%

Formal tracks/concentrations: Family Violence, Serious Mental Illness, Applied Child

Research areas	# Faculty	# Grants
anger management	1	0
attachment	1	1
psychotherapy process	1	0
marital violence	2	0
parent training	2	1
professional development	2	0
psychoanalysis	3	0
schizophrenia	1	0
substance abuse	1	0
trauma	2	1

Clinical opportunities
adult difficulties as follows:
- behavior modification for habit control
- behavior patterns
- depression
- domestic violence
- eating disorders and compulsive
- marital and relationship therapy
- phobias and anxiety disorders

child and family difficulties as follows:
- academic and school-related problems
- aggressive behavior/anger management
- anxiety and depression
- developmental difficulties (treatment)
- family conflicts/family therapy
- family violence
- hyperactivity/low attention span
- parent/child conflicts
- socialization difficulties

group therapy as follows:
- anger management for children and adults
- assertiveness training
- parent training
- social skills for children
- stress management

individual psychotherapy
psychological assessment as follows:
- achievement and intelligence testing
- emotional and behavioral assessment

neuropsychological assessment
personality assessment
short-term and psychodynamic therapy

University of Louisville Clinical Psychology Ph.D. Program

Department of Psychological & Brain Sciences
University of Louisville
http://louisville.edu/psychology/graduate/clinical

GRE mean *(incoming students)*
Verbal: 161
Quantitative: 155
Analytical Writing: 4.7

GPA mean *(incoming students)*
Junior/Senior GPA: 3.81

Number of applications/admission offers/incoming students in 2017:
131 applied / 9 admission offers / 5 incoming

Approximate percentage of incoming students with a:
B.A./B.S. only: 80% **Master's:** 20%

Approximate percentage of students who are *(all students)*
Women: 81% **Ethnic Minority:** 21% **International:** 8%

Average years to complete the doctoral program (including internship): *(last 7 years)*
5.7 years

Attrition rate in past 7 years: 14%

Percentage of students applying for internship in 2017 accepted into:

APA internships: 100% **APPIC internships:** 100%

Research areas	# Faculty	# Grants
anxiety disorders	1	0
health/behavioral medicine	3	2
child psychopathology	1	0
gerontology/aging	2	1
stress and trauma	1	0
adult/adolescent psychopathology	1	0
eating disorders	1	0

Clinical opportunities
affective disorders
anxiety disorders
child clinical psychology
minority mental health
military settings
gerontology/aging
health psychology
interpersonal psychotherapy
developmental disabilities

Loyola University of Chicago (Ph.D.)

Department of Psychology
Graduate Enrollment Services
820 North Michigan Avenue
Chicago, IL 60611
phone#: (773) 508-2974
email: jhamilt@luc.edu
Web address: www.luc.edu/psychology/clinical.shtml

1	2	3	**4**	5	6	7
Practice oriented			Equal emphasis			Research oriented

Percentage of faculty subscribing to each of the following orientations:

Psychodynamic/Psychoanalytic	11%
Applied behavioral analysis/Radical behavioral	0%
Family systems/Systems	22%
Existential/Phenomenological/Humanistic	0%
Cognitive/Cognitive-behavioral	66%

Courses required for incoming students prior to enrolling:
Research methods/experimental and statistics plus any 6 other psychology courses (24 hours, total)

Recommended but not mandatory courses: none

GRE mean
Verbal 645 Quantitative 727
Analytical Writing not reported
Psychology Subject Test required

GPA mean
Overall GPA 3.80

Number of applications/admission offers/incoming students in 2016
290 applied/7 admission offers/5 incoming

% of students receiving:
Full tuition waiver only: 0%
Assistantship/fellowship only: 0%
Both full tuition waiver & assistantship/fellowship: 100%

Approximate percentage of incoming students with a B.A./B.S. only: 100% **Master's:** 0%

Approximate percentage of students who are
Women: 80% **Ethnic Minority:** 25% **International:** 0%

Average years to complete the doctoral program (including internship): 6 years

Personal interview
Preferred in person but telephone acceptable

Attrition rate in past 7 years: 6%

Percentage of students applying for internship in 2016 accepted into:

APA internships: 100% **APPIC internships:** 100%

Formal tracks/concentrations: clinical child, neuropsychology

Research areas	# Faculty	# Grants
adolescence	6	5
adult psychopathology	1	0
clinical-child/psychopathology	8	4
community psychology	1	0
developmental psychopathology	4	3
disabilities	1	2
emerging adulthood	1	0
ethical issues	1	0
extracurricular activities	1	1
minority mental health	5	3
pediatric psychology	2	2

prevention	3	2
psychotherapy	4	1

Clinical opportunities

assessment (child and adult)
eating disorders
family psychology
health psychology
HIV/AIDS
neuropsychology
neuropsychological assessment (child and adult)
pediatric psychology
personality disorders
psychotherapy (child and adult)
substance abuse
victims of abuse

Loyola University Maryland (Psy.D.)

Department of Psychology
Baltimore, MD 21210-2699
phone#: (410) 617-2175
email: tpmartino@loyola.edu
Web address: http://www.loyola.edu/academics/psychology/doctorate

1 2 **3** 4 5 6 7

Practice oriented — Equal emphasis — Research oriented

Percentage of faculty subscribing to each of the following orientations:

Psychodynamic/Psychoanalytic	20%
Applied behavioral analysis/Radical behavioral	20%
Family systems/Systems	0%
Existential/Phenomenological/Humanistic	0%
Cognitive/Cognitive-behavioral	60%

Courses required for incoming students prior to enrolling:
Introductory Psychology, Social Psychology, Statistics or Research Methods in a Social Science, Psychopathology, Personality Theory, Learning Theory or Cognitive Psychology

Recommended but not mandatory courses: none

GRE mean
Verbal 159 Quantitative 153
Analytical Writing 4.5
Psychology Subject Test not reported

GPA mean
Overall GPA 3.61

Number of applications/admission offers/incoming students in 2017
268 applied/28 admission offers/17 incoming

% of students receiving:
Full tuition waiver only: 0%
Assistantship/fellowship only: 40%
Both full tuition waiver & assistantship/fellowship: 0%

Approximate percentage of incoming students with a B.A./B.S. only: 82% (14) **Master's:** 18% (3)

Approximate percentage of incoming students who are Women: 88% **Ethnic Minority:** 23% **International:** 0%

Average years to complete the doctoral program (including internship): 5.5 years

Personal interview
Required in person

Attrition rate in past 7 years: 4.5%

Percentage of students applying for internship in 2016 accepted into:

APA internships: 100% **APPIC internships:**

Formal tracks/concentrations: none

Research areas	# Faculty	# Grants
child psychopathology	5	0
domestic violence	1	0
ethics and legal issues	2	0
gambling	1	0
gerontology	2	0
health psychology	3	0
homophobia	1	0
multicultural	3	0
neuropsychology	2	0
nonverbal communication	1	0
posttraumatic stress disorder	4	0
psychotherapy outcomes	1	0
sexuality	2	0
spirituality	2	0
social psychology	1	0
trichotillomania	1	0
women's issues	2	0

Clinical opportunities

adult inpatient
Child/Adolescent Inpatient
child and family
eating disorders
outpatient private practice
juvenile forensics
behavioral medicine
prison settings
stress and anxiety

University of Maine (Ph.D.)

Department of Psychology
5742 Little Hall
Orono, ME 04469-5742
phone#: (207) 581-2038
email: Dnangle@maine.edu
Web address: /www.umaine.edu/psychology/clinicalprogram/

1 2 3 4 **5** 6 7

Practice oriented — Equal emphasis — Research oriented

Percentage of faculty subscribing to each of the following orientations:

Psychodynamic/Psychoanalytic	0%
Applied behavioral analysis/Radical behavioral	0%
Family systems/Systems	0%
Existential/Phenomenological/Humanistic	0%
Cognitive/Cognitive-behavioral	100%

Courses required for incoming students prior to enrolling:
At least three to four advanced undergraduate psychology courses; background in natural sciences and mathematics

Recommended but not mandatory courses: Learning, developmental, abnormal, cognition, research methods and statistics

GRE mean
Verbal 162 Quantitative 152

Analytical Writing 4.5
Psychology Subject Test no longer required

GPA mean
Overall GPA 3.85

Number of applications/admission offers/incoming students in 2016
89 applied/4 admission offers/3 incoming

% of students receiving:
Full tuition waiver only: 0%
Assistantship/fellowship only: 0%
Both full tuition waiver & assistantship/fellowship: 100% for 1st-year students, 100% of the 2nd- to 4th-year students

Approximate percentage of incoming students with a B.A./B.S. only: 80% **Master's:** 20%

Approximate percentage of students who are Women: 80% **Ethnic Minority:** 10% **International:** 0%

Average years to complete the doctoral program (including internship): 5.6 years

Personal interview
Much preferred in person but telephone interviews sometimes arranged

Attrition rate in past 7 years: 16%

Percentage of students applying for internship in 2016 accepted into:

APA internships: 100% **APPIC internships:** 100%

Formal tracks/concentrations: general clinical, child clinical, neuropsychology

Research areas	# Faculty	# Grants
social anxiety	2	0
depression	4	1
mindfulness-based interventions	1	0
self injury	2	0
peer relationships	3	1
behavioral medicine	1	0
health psychology	1	0
social skills	3	1
suicidality	1	0
geropsychology	2	0
neuropsychology	2	0
cognitive decline	1	0

Clinical opportunities

Neuropsychology	geriatric assessment
early developmental disorders assessment	school-based interventions
	juvenile offenders
pediatric obesity	forensic psychology
educational assessments	integrated behavioral health
community mental health	behavioral medicine

Marquette University (Ph.D.)

Psychology Department
P.O. Box 1881
Milwaukee, WI 53201-1881
phone#: (414) 288-3487
email: stephen.saunders@marquette.edu
Web address: www.marquette.edu/psyc/graduate.shtml

1	2	3	4	**5**	6	7
Practice oriented			Equal emphasis			Research oriented

Percentage of faculty subscribing to each of the following orientations:

Psychodynamic/Psychoanalytic	10%
Applied behavioral analysis/Radical behavioral	30%
Family systems/Systems	40%
Existential/Phenomenological/Humanistic	30%
Cognitive/Cognitive-behavioral	80%

Courses required for incoming students prior to enrolling: none

Recommended but not mandatory courses:
undergraduate major in psychology

GRE mean
Verbal 155 Quantitative 155
Analytical Writing 4.25
Psychology Subject Test not reported

GPA mean
Overall GPA 3.62

Number of applications/admission offers/incoming students in 2016
186 applied/8 admission offers/7 incoming

% of students receiving:
Full tuition waiver only: 0%
Assistantship/fellowship only: 0%
Both full tuition waiver & assistantship/fellowship: 100%

Approximate percentage of incoming students with a B.A./B.S. only: 100% **Master's:** 0%

Approximate percentage of all students who are Women: 85% **Ethnic Minority:** 20% **International:** 3%

Average years to complete the doctoral program (including internship): 6 years

Personal interview
Preferred in person; telephone or skype acceptable

Attrition rate in past 7 years: 5%

Percentage of students applying for internship in 2016 accepted into:

APA internships: 100% **APPIC internships:**

Formal tracks/concentrations: child/family, adult, neuropsychology

Research areas	# Faculty	# Grants
adult development	1	0
ADHD	1	1
Alzheimer's disease/memory problems	1	2
autism/Asperger's	1	0
child development	3	1
child–parent relationships	3	1
depression/anxiety	3	0
family conflict	2	1
friendships/relationships	2	0
group dynamics	1	0
help-seeking for mental illness	2	1
Latino mental health	1	1
LGBT	2	0

minority & multicultural	5	0
neuropsychology	4	0
organizational behavior	1	0
psychosocial aspects of medical illness	1	0
psychotherapy processes/outcomes	3	0
stigmatization	3	1

Clinical opportunities

ADHD
DBT
group therapy
neuropsychological assessment
child and adolescent
medical health
family/couples therapy
health psychology
pain/pain management
psychotherapy
trauma

Marshall University (Psy.D.)

Department of Psychology
Huntington, WV 25755
phone#: (304) 696-2785
email: Keith Beard: beard@marshall.edu, Nancy Tresch-Reneau: tresch@marshall.edu
Web address: http://www.marshall.edu/psych/programs/psyd-program/

1	2	**3**	4	5	6	7
Practice oriented			Equal emphasis			Research oriented

Percentage of faculty subscribing to each of the following orientations:

Psychodynamic/Psychoanalytic	10%
Applied behavioral analysis/Radical behavioral	10%
Family systems/Systems	5%
Existential/Phenomenological/Humanistic	5%
Cognitive/Cognitive-behavioral	70%

Courses required for incoming students to have completed prior to enrolling:

Introductory or General Psychology
Statistics
Experimental Psychology or Research Methods in Psychology
Abnormal Psychology

Recommended but not mandatory courses: Social psychology, Personality

GRE mean
Verbal 155 Quantitative 151
Analytical Writing 4.0
Psychology Subject Test not required
GPA mean
Overall GPA 3.56

Number of applications/admission offers/incoming students in 2017
80 applied/12 admission offers/12 incoming

% of students receiving:
Full tuition waiver only: 0%
Assistantship/fellowship only: 0%
Both full tuition waiver & assistantship/fellowship: 0%

Approximate percentage of incoming students with a B.A./B.S. only: 70% **Master's:** 30%

Approximate percentage of students who are Women: 85% **Ethnic Minority:** 10% **International:** 10%

Average years to complete the doctoral program (including internship): 5 years

Personal interview
Preferred in person but telephone acceptable

Attrition rate in past 7 years: 7%

Percentage of students applying for internship in 2017 accepted into:

APA internships: 91% **APPIC internships:** 100%

Concentrations: general

Research areas	# Faculty	# Grants*
adult psychopathology	6	2
affective/mood disorders/depression	6	0
at-risk adolescents	4	0
aging	2	0

Clinical opportunities

adolescent treatment
affective disorders/depression
aging/gerontology
anxiety disorders
assessment
attention-deficit disorder
autism
behavioral medicine
child treatment
cognitive-behavioral therapy
conduct disorder
chronic severe mental illness
eating disorders
private practice
family therapy
gay/lesbian
group therapy
inpatient
homeless
minority populations
neuropsychological assessment
oncology
pain management
parent training
pediatric
personality disorders
schizophrenia
sleep disorders
substance abuse
suicide prevention
veterans medical center
victim/violence/sexual abuse
weight management

University of Maryland, Baltimore County (Ph.D.)

Department of Psychology
1000 Hilltop Circle
Baltimore, MD 21250
phone#: (410) 455-2567
email: psycdept@umbc.edu
Web address: www.umbc.edu/psyc/hsp_clinical.html

1	2	3	4	**5**	6	7
Practice oriented			Equal emphasis			Research oriented

Percentage of faculty subscribing to each of the following orientations:

Psychodynamic/Psychoanalytic	10%
Applied behavioral analysis/Radical behavioral	10%
Family systems/Systems	30%
Existential/Phenomenological/Humanistic	0%

Cognitive/Cognitive-behavioral 80%

Courses required for incoming students to have completed prior to enrolling:
Psychological statistics, abnormal psychology, experimental psychology

Recommended but not mandatory courses: Personality, physiological, developmental

GRE mean
Verbal 160 Quantitative 155
Analytical Writing 4.4
Psychology Subject Test 660

GPA mean
Overall GPA 3.61

Number of applications/admission offers/incoming students in 2016
64 applied/10 admission offers/7 incoming

% of students receiving:
Full tuition waiver only: 0%
Assistantship/fellowship only: 0%
Both full tuition waiver & assistantship/fellowship: 100%

Approximate percentage of incoming students with a B.A./B.S. only: 75% **Master's:** 25%

Approximate percentage of students who are Women: 77% **Ethnic Minority:** 30.3% **International:** 1.5%

Average years to complete the doctoral program (including internship): 6.6 years

Personal interview
Preferred in person but telephone/Skype acceptable

Attrition rate in past 7 years: 9%

Percentage of students applying for internship in 2016 accepted into:

APA internships: 90% **APPIC internships:** 90%

Formal tracks/concentrations: behavioral medicine; community and applied social psychology; child clinical

Research areas	# Faculty	# Grants
addictive disorders	2	9
behavioral medicine	2	2
cardiovascular/cerebrovascular disease	1	6
community psychology	3	2
domestic violence	1	1
interpersonal processes	1	0
psychology of religion	1	0
psychosis	1	5
suicide	1	0
resilience of women	1	0
child disruptive behavior	1	0

Clinical opportunities

addictive disorders	medical liaison
applied behavior analysis	neuropsychology
domestic abuse	pediatric psychology
emergency mental health services	prevention
	rehabilitation psychology
family therapy	school-based mental health services
forensic psychology	
severe and chronic mental illness	

University of Maryland College Park (Ph.D.)

Department of Psychology
1121 Biology–Psychology Building
College Park, MD 20742-4411
phone#: (301) 405-5890
email: psycgradstudies@umd.edu
Web address: https://psyc.umd.edu/graduate/clinical-psychology

1	2	3	4	5	**6**	7
Practice oriented			Equal emphasis			Research oriented

Percentage of faculty subscribing to each of the following orientations:

Psychodynamic/Psychoanalytic	20%
Applied behavioral analysis/Radical behavioral	10%
Family systems/Systems	20%
Existential/Phenomenological/Humanistic	0%
Cognitive/Cognitive-behavioral	80%
Behavioral	90%
Interpersonal	30%

Courses required for incoming students to have completed prior to enrolling:
B.A. or B.S. in psychology or related areas

Recommended but not mandatory courses: statistics, abnormal, laboratory courses in psychology

GRE mean
Verbal 161/84%
Quantitative 154/55%
Analytical Writing 4.8/89%
Psychology Subject Test not reported

GPA mean
Overall Undergraduate GPA 3.81
Overall Master's GPA 4.00

Number of applications/admission offers/incoming students in 2017
284 applied/11 admission offers/7 incoming

% of students receiving:
Full tuition waiver only: 0%
Assistantship/fellowship only: 0%
Both full tuition waiver & assistantship/fellowship: 100%

Approximate percentage of incoming students with a B.A./B.S. only: 71% **Master's:** 29%

Approximate percentage of all students who are Women: 100% **Ethnic Minority:** 14% **International:** 0%

Average years to complete the doctoral program (including internship): 6 years

Personal interview
Required in person

Attrition rate in past 7 years: 6.45%

Percentage of students applied for internship in 2016 accepted into:

APA internships: 100% **APPIC internships:** 100%

Formal tracks/concentrations: none

Research areas	# Faculty	# Grants
addictive behaviors	5	3
depression	4	1
anxiety	4	2
emotion	3	0
child/adolescent/developmental psychopathology	5	12
psychotherapy outcome	1	6
serious mental illnesses	2	0
clinical neuroscience	4	0
other (externalizing and risk taking behaviors)	1	0

Clinical opportunities

child/adolescent
anxiety
substance use
severe mental illness
outpatient
mood disorders
personality pathology

Marywood University (Psy.D.)

Department of Psychology and Counseling
Scranton, PA 18509
phone#: (570) 348-6270
email: cannonb@marywood.edu
Web address: http://www.marywood.edu/psychology/psyd/

1 2 **3** 4 5 6 7

Practice oriented — Equal emphasis — Research oriented

Percentage of faculty subscribing to each of the following orientations:

Psychodynamic/Psychoanalytic	25%
Applied behavioral analysis/Radical behavioral	0%
Family systems/Systems	0%
Existential/Phenomenological/Humanistic	0%
Cognitive/Cognitive-behavioral	75%

Courses required for incoming students to have completed prior to enrolling:
Statistics, research methods, abnormal psychology; at least 18 credits in psychology

Recommended but not mandatory courses: none

GRE mean
Verbal 153 Quantitative 151
Analytical Writing 4.1
Psychology Subject Test not reported

GPA mean
Overall GPA 3.67

Number of applications/admission offers/incoming students in 2017
79 applied/13 admission offers/10 incoming

% of students receiving:
Full tuition waiver only: 0%
Full assistantship/fellowship only: 0%
Both full tuition waiver & assistantship/fellowship: 0%
Remaining 100% of students receive a $3800 annual scholarship

Percentage of incoming students with a B.A./B.S. only: 80% **Master's:** 20%

Percentage of students who are Women: 74% **Ethnic Minority:** 28% **International:** 0%

Average years to complete (including internship): 5.6 years (3.5 for post-MA admission)

Personal interview
Required

Attrition rate in past 7 years: 5%

Percentage of students applying for internship in 2017 accepted into:

APA internships: 60% **APPIC internships:** 40%

Formal tracks/concentrations: none

Research areas	# Faculty	# Grants
aggression in boys	1	0
disordered eating	1	0
malingering	1	0
mindfulness	1	0
multicultural issues	2	0
neuropsychology	1	0
outcome assessment in mental health	1	0
psychology and media	1	0
self-esteem	1	0
stress, anxiety, and coping	3	0
substance use	1	0

Clinical opportunities
on-site community mental health center
university counseling center
veteran's administration medical center
inpatient psychiatric hospital
inpatient forensic
residential geriatric
clinical psychology private practice
neuropsychology private practice
rehabilitation hospital
children's outpatient services center

University of Massachusetts at Amherst (Ph.D.)

Department of Psychological and Brain Sciences
135 Hicks Way-Tobin Hall
Amherst, MA 01003
phone#: (413) 545-0662
email: ready@psych.umass.edu
Web address: http://www.umass.edu/pbs/graduate/clinical-psychology

1 2 3 4 5 **6** 7

Practice oriented — Equal emphasis — Research oriented

Percentage of faculty subscribing to each of the following orientations:

Psychodynamic/Psychoanalytic	0%

Applied behavioral analysis/Radical behavioral	14%
Family systems/Systems	7%
Existential/Phenomenological/Humanistic	0%
Cognitive/Cognitive-behavioral	50%
Integrative	29%

Courses required for incoming students to have completed prior to enrolling:
An undergraduate background in psychology which, at a minimum, consists of statistics, methods, and 3 advanced subjects in psychology

Recommended but not mandatory courses: none

GRE mean
Verbal 165 Quantitative 160
Analytical Writing 4.8
Psychology Subject Test 740

GPA mean
Overall GPA 3.8

Number of applications/admission offers/incoming students in 2016
178 applied/9 admission offers/4 incoming

% of students receiving:
Full tuition waiver only: 0%
Assistantship/fellowship only: 0%
Both full tuition waiver & assistantship/fellowship: 100%

Approximate percentage of incoming students who a B.A./B.S. only: 75% **Master's:** 25%

Approximate percentage of students who are Women: 74% **Ethnic Minority:** 17% **International:** 4%

Average years to complete the doctoral program (including internship): 6 years

Personal interview
In person strongly recommended, but telephone possible

Attrition rate in past 7 years: 10%

Percentage of students applying for internship in 2016 accepted into:

APA internships: 100% **APPIC internships:** 100%

Formal tracks/concentrations: child/family concentration, adult

Research areas	# Faculty	# Grants
child, adolescent, family	6	0
aging/gerontology	1	0
developmental psychopathology	3	0
stress/coping	3	1
psychotherapy process	2	0
psychotherapist's development	2	0
psychological/neuropsych assessment	2	0
psychotherapy research	2	1
substance abuse	1	0
adoption	1	0

Clinical opportunities

child and adolescent therapy	psychological/neuropsychological assessment
adult therapy	residential treatment
cultural diversity experiences	psychotherapy supervision
gerontology	college counseling
outpatient medical settings	inpatient medical settings

University of Massachusetts at Boston (Ph.D.)

Department of Psychology
Boston, MA 02125-3393
phone#: (617) 287-6340
email: linda.curreri@umb.edu
Web address: www.umb.edu/cla/psychology/phd_program/522

1	2	3	**4**	5	6	7
Practice oriented			Equal emphasis			Research oriented

Percentage of faculty subscribing to each of the following orientations:

Psychodynamic/Psychoanalytic	27%
Applied behavioral analysis/Radical behavioral	0%
Family systems/Systems	19%
Existential/Phenomenological/Humanistic	27%
Cognitive/Cognitive-behavioral	27%[d1]

Courses required for incoming students to have completed prior to enrolling:
A minimum of 6 courses in psychology, or a closely related social science field, including a course in statistics

Recommended but not mandatory courses: research methods, development, abnormal, personality

GRE mean
Verbal 620 Quantitative 705
Analytical Writing 5.0
Psychology Subject Test 740

GPA mean
Overall GPA 3.68 Psychology GPA 3.89
Junior/Senior GPA 3.76

Number of applications/admission offers/incoming students in 2017
353 applied/9 admission offers/8 incoming

% of students receiving:
Full tuition waiver only: 0%
Assistantship/fellowship only: 0%
Both full tuition waiver & assistantship/fellowship: 100%

Approximate percentage of incoming students with a B.A./B.S. only: 63% **Master's:** 37%

Approximate percentage of all students who are Women: 73% **Ethnic Minority:** 41% **International:** 9%

Average years to complete the doctoral program (including internship): 6.0 years

Personal interview
Required in person

Attrition rate in past 7 years: 0%

Percentage of students applying for internship in 2017 accepted into:

APA internships: 71% **APPIC internships:** 0%

Formal tracks/concentrations: clinical psychology

Research areas	# Faculty	# Grants
cross-cultural	2	1
family	1	1
media and psychology	1	0
severe psychopathology	1	1
trauma	1	0
anxiety and emotions	2	2
health psychopathology	1	1
developmental psychopathology	5	4
neurobehavioral	4	2

Clinical opportunities
not reported

University of Memphis (Ph.D.)

Department of Psychology
Memphis, TN 38152
phone#: (901) 678-2630
email: jgmurphy@memphis.edu
Web address: www.memphis.edu/psychology/graduate/Clinical/index.php

1 2 3 4 **5** 6 7

Practice oriented — Equal emphasis — Research oriented

Percentage of faculty subscribing to each of the following orientations:

Psychodynamic/Psychoanalytic	0%
Applied behavioral analysis/Radical behavioral	20%
Family systems/Systems	20%
Existential/Phenomenological/Humanistic	20%
Cognitive/Cognitive-behavioral	60%

Courses required for incoming students to have completed prior to enrolling:
A minimum of 18 semester hours in undergraduate psychology courses, including courses in Quantitative Methods (psychological statistics), and experimental design. Students lacking some or all of these prerequisite courses, but presenting an exceptional undergraduate record, may nevertheless be granted graduate admission. However, students may be asked to remove such deficiencies before or during their first academic year.

Recommended but not mandatory courses: none

GRE mean
Verbal 160 Quantitative 155
Analytical Writing 4.78
Psychology Subject Test not reported

GPA mean
Overall GPA 3.77

Number of applications/admission offers/incoming students in 2017
213 applied/11 admission offers/9 incoming

% of students receiving:
Full tuition waiver only: 0%
Assistantship/fellowship only: 0%
Both full tuition waiver & assistantship/fellowship: 100%

Approximate percentage of incoming students with a B.A./B.S. only: 78% **Master's:** 22%

Approximate percentage of students who are Women: 72% **Ethnic Minority:** 28% **International:** 8%

Average years to complete the doctoral program (including internship): 6.5 years

Personal interview
Interview required

Attrition rate in past 7 years: 8.5%

Percentage of students applying for internship in 2017 accepted into:

APA internships: 100% **APPIC internships:**

Formal tracks/concentrations: clinical health, psychotherapy research, child clinical

Research areas	# Faculty	# Grants
Clinical health	4	5
child clinical	3	4
psychotherapy research	4	4

Clinical opportunities

addiction	family therapy
affective disorders	gambling
anxiety disorders	trauma/PTSD
behavioral medicine	minority/cross-cultural
cancer and emotional health adjustment	pediatric psychology/child child/adolescent
developmental disabilities/ autism	integrated primary care
Neuropsychology	HIV prevention
	veterans mental health care

University of Miami (Ph.D.)

Department of Psychology
P.O. Box 249229
Coral Gables, FL 33124
phone#: (305) 284-2814
email: inquire@psy.miami.edu
Web address: www.psy.miami.edu/graduate

1 2 3 4 5 **6** 7

Practice oriented — Equal emphasis — Research oriented

Percentage of faculty subscribing to each of the following orientations:

Psychodynamic/Psychoanalytic	0%
Applied behavioral analysis/Radical behavioral	5%
Family systems/Systems	30%
Existential/Phenomenological/Humanistic	10%
Cognitive/Cognitive-behavioral	80%

Courses required for incoming students to have completed prior to enrolling:
statistics, research methods

Recommended but not mandatory courses: strong science background

GRE mean
Verbal 646 Quantitative 734

Analytical Writing Data: 4.8
Psychology Subject Test not reported

GPA mean
Overall GPA 3.7

Number of applications/admission offers/incoming students in 2017
421 applied/17 admission offers/10 incoming

% of students receiving:
Full tuition waiver only: 0%
Assistantship/fellowship only: 0%
Both full tuition waiver & assistantship/fellowship: 100%

Approximate percentage of incoming students with a B.A./B.S. only: 90% **Master's:** 10%

Approximate percentage of students who are Women: 82% **Ethnic Minority:** 38% **International:** 2%

Average years to complete the doctoral program (including internship): 6 years

Personal interview
Required in person

Attrition rate in past 7 years: 7%

Percentage of students applying for internship in 2017 accepted into:

APA internships: 100% **APPIC internships:** 100%

Formal tracks/concentrations: adult clinical, child clinical, health clinical, pediatric health

Research areas	# Faculty	# Grants
adult psychopathology	6	2
affective disorders	3	1
cancer	4	1
cardiovascular disease	4	2
child clinical psychology	6	5
child psychopathology	5	2
diabetes	3	2
family and couples therapy	2	2
health psychology	14	5
hypertension	3	1
pediatric psychology	3	3
psychoneuroimmunology	4	2
stress and coping	6	2
trauma	4	2

Clinical opportunities

abuse	family therapy
HIV/AIDS	group therapy
behavioral medicine	long-term care
conduct disorder	marital therapy
developmental disabilities/ autism	minority/cross-cultural
	neuropsychology
diabetes	pediatrics
eating disorders	substance abuse
internalizing disorders	peer relations
trauma/PTSD	mood/anxiety disorders

Miami University (Ph.D.)

Department of Psychology
Oxford, OH 45056
phone#: (513) 529-2400
email: weberdm@miamioh.edu
Web address: http://www.miamioh.edu/cas/academics/departments/psychology/academics/graduate-studies/clinical-program/index.html

1	2	3	4	**5**	6	7
Practice oriented			Equal emphasis			Research oriented

Percentage of faculty subscribing to each of the following orientations:

Applied behavioral analysis/Radical behavioral	0%
Cognitive/Cognitive-behavioral	67%
Community Systems	8%
Developmental/Developmental Psychopathology	58%
Dialectal Behavioral	25%
Family systems/Systems	42%
Feminist	8%
Existential/Phenomenological/Humanistic	0%
Gestalt	8%
Interpersonal	42%
Mindfulness and Acceptance	25%
Multicultural	17%
Psychodynamic/Psychoanalytic	0%

Courses required for incoming students prior to enrolling: Undergraduate statistics/methods

Recommended but not mandatory courses: none

GRE mean
Verbal 159 (73rd percentile)
Quantitative 157 (67th percentile)
Analytical Writing 4.5 (70th percentile)
Psychology Subject Test not reported

GPA mean
Overall GPA 3.80

Number of applications/admission offers/incoming students in 2017
179 applied/13 admission offers/6 incoming

% of students receiving:
Full tuition waiver only: 0%
Assistantship/fellowship only: 0%
Both full tuition waiver & assistantship/fellowship: 100%

Approximate percentage of incoming students with a B.A./B.S. only: 90% **Master's:** 10%

Approximate percentage of all students who are Women: 88% **Ethnic Minority:** 20% **International:** 15%

Average years to complete the doctoral program (including internship): 6 years

Personal interview
Preferred in person but telephone acceptable

Attrition rate in past 7 years: 0%

Percentage of students applying for internship in 2017 accepted into:

APA internships: 100% **APPIC internships:** 100%

Formal tracks/concentrations: Tracks are informal:
(a) child, family, school, community based mental health
(b) adult

Research areas	# Faculty	# Grants
anxiety disorders	4	1
bullying	1	0
child / adolescent psychopathology	3	1
community-based	1	1
consultation	1	0
culture and mental health	4	1
violence prevention	1	1
depression	1	0
dissemination/implementation/ translation	1	1
early childhood mental health	1	0
eating disorders	1	0
emotion	5	3
family	2	0
health risk behaviors	2	1
intercultural competence	2	0
interpersonal violence	2	1
intervention	1	1
nonverbal communication	1	0
mixed methods	2	1
OC spectrum disorders	2	0
action research	1	1
prevention/promotion	1	1
program development/evaluation	1	1
psychophysiology	2	1
posttraumatic stress disorder	1	1
sexual assault/rape	1	1
scholarship of teaching and learning	2	0
school-based mental health	1	0
school–family community partnership	1	0
social and emotional learning	2	1
suicide	2	1
training/technical assistance	1	1
trauma & trauma recovery	2	1
substance use and disorder	3	1

Clinical opportunities

ADHD
adult psychotherapy
anxiety disorders
assessment
child psychotherapy
college student counseling
community mental health
conduct disorder
consultation
cross-cultural psychology
DBT groups
depression
developmental disabilities
family therapy
feminist therapy
gender identity
group psychotherapy
inpatient mental health
juvenile delinquency
meditation, yoga as adjuncts to clinical intervention
mindfulness-based intervention
multicultural therapy
parent-child therapy
prevention
PTSD
rural mental health
school-based mental health
sexual identity

University of Michigan (Ph.D.)

Department of Psychology
530 Church Street
Ann Arbor, MI 48109-1109
phone#: (734) 764-6332
email: psych.saa@umich.edu
Web address: www.lsa.umich.edu/psych/areas/clinical/

1	2	3	4	5	**6**	7
Practice oriented			Equal emphasis			Research oriented

Percentage of faculty subscribing to each of the following orientations:

Psychodynamic/Psychoanalytic	0%
Applied behavioral analysis/Radical behavioral	0%
Family systems/Systems	23%
Existential/Phenomenological/Humanistic	0%
Cognitive/Cognitive-behavioral	61%
Community	15%

Courses required for incoming students to have completed prior to enrolling: none

Recommended but not mandatory courses: basic coursework in psychology

GRE mean
Verbal 164 Quantitative 159
Analytical Writing 5
Psychology Subject Test not reported

GPA mean
Overall GPA 3.73

Number of applications/admission offers/incoming students in 2017
326 applied/7 admission offers/5 incoming

% of students receiving:
Full tuition waiver only: 0%
Assistantship/fellowship only: 0%
Both full tuition waiver & assistantship/fellowship: 100%

Approximate percentage of incoming students with a B.A./B.S. only: 100% **Master's:** 0%

Approximate percentage of students who are Women: 76% Ethnic Minority: 43% **International:** 10%

Average years to complete the doctoral program (including internship): 5-6 years

Personal interview
Preferred in person but telephone in unusual circumstances

Attrition rate in past 7 years: 0%

Percentage of students applying for internship in 2017 accepted into:

APA internships: 100% **APPIC internships:** 100%

Formal tracks/concentrations: none

Research areas	# Faculty	# Grants
addiction	1	–
adult depression	2	2
adult bipolar	1	1
child abuse/neglect	1	–
childhood depression	1	–
child disruptive/behavior disorder	2	2
eating disorders	1	–
family violence	1	3
food addiction	1	3

health psychology	1	3
neuroimaging	4	7
peer relations/social skills in children	1	–
personality disorders	1	1
Schizophrenia	1	1
Sleep	1	–
social competence in children	1	–
Stress	1	–
Psychophysiology	1	1
culture and mental health	3	4
Therapy	2	2
suicide risk and prevention, youth and adults	2	2
Aging	1	3
Neuropsychology	1	3

Clinical opportunities
Adult, neuropsychology, child and family

Michigan School of Professional Psychology (Psy.D.)

Farmington Hill, MI 48334

This program did not participate in the survey for this book.

Michigan State University (Ph.D.)

Department of Psychology
East Lansing, MI 48824
phone#: (517) 355-9562
email: psygrad@msu.edu
Web address: psychology.msu.edu/clinical/

1	2	3	4	**5**	6	7
Practice oriented			Equal emphasis			Research oriented

Percentage of faculty subscribing to each of the following orientations:

Psychodynamic/Psychoanalytic	25%
Applied behavioral analysis/Radical behavioral	10%
Family systems/Systems	20%
Existential/Phenomenological/Humanistic	0%
Cognitive/Cognitive-behavioral	50%
Feminist	10%

Courses required for incoming students prior to enrolling:
12 hours of psychology courses at the Bachelor's level

Recommended but not mandatory courses:
Quantitative methods, research design, advanced competence with the use of computer programs (SPSS, SYSTAT, etc.)

GRE mean
Verbal 161 Quantitative 163
Analytical Writing 4.6

GPA mean
Overall GPA 3.84

Number of applications/admission offers/incoming students in 2017
199 applied/6 admission offers/5 incoming

% of incoming students receiving:
Full tuition waiver only: 0%
Assistantship/fellowship only: 0%
Both full tuition waiver & assistantship/fellowship: 100%

Approximate percentage of incoming students who entered with a B.A./B.S. only: 80% **Master's:** 20%

Approximate percentage of students who are Women: 88% **Ethnic Minority:** 30% **International:** 13%

Average years to complete the doctoral program (including internship): 6.2 years

Personal interview
Preferred in person but telephone acceptable

Attrition rate in past 7 years: 22%

Percentage of students applying for internship in 2017 accepted into:

APA internships: 100% **APPIC internships:** 100%

Formal tracks/concentrations: none

Research areas	# Faculty	# Grants
affective and cognitive psychophysiology	1	2
antisocial behavior	1	2
attachment research	2	1
autism	1	3
behavior genetics	3	4
bullying in schools	1	0
culture and mental health	1	0
dissemination and implementation	1	1
eating disorders	1	2
domestic violence	2	1
family research/systems	3	0
racial and sexual harassment	1	0

Clinical opportunities

assessment (child, adult, aging, ADHD, clinical neuropsychology; trauma)	autism spectrum disorders treatment
depression and anxiety	intimate partner violence
eating disorders	loss and trauma group therapy
PTSD treatment	minority/cross-cultural
family therapy	play therapy

Midwestern University–Glendale Campus (Psy.D.)

Department of Clinical Psychology
Glendale, AZ 85308
phone#: (623) 572-3862
email: jchamb@midwestern.edu
Web address: www.midwestern.edu/programs-and-admission/az-clinical-psychology.html

1	**2**	3	4	5	6	7
Practice oriented			Equal emphasis			Research oriented

Percentage of faculty subscribing to each of the following orientations:

Acceptance and Commitment	28%
Applied behavioral analysis/Radical behavioral	14%
Cognitive/Cognitive-behavioral	43%
Existential/Phenomenological/Humanistic	43%
Family systems/Systems	29%
Narrative/Constructivist	28%
Neuropsychology	14%
Psychodynamic/Psychoanalytic	14%
Reality Therapy	14%

Courses required for incoming students to have completed prior to enrolling:
Completion of 18 semester hours or equivalent of prerequisite coursework in psychology, with a grade of B- or better, including: human growth & development or personality theory, abnormal, statistics or tests and measurements

Recommended but not mandatory courses: none

GRE mean
Verbal 152.5 Quantitative 149.4
Analytical Writing 4.1
Psychology Subject Test NA

GPA mean
Overall GPA 3.5

Number of applications/admission offers/incoming students in 2016
71 applied/29 admission offers/26 incoming

% of students receiving:
Full tuition waiver only: 0%
Assistantship/fellowship only: 0%
Both full tuition waiver & assistantship/fellowship: 0%

Approximate percentage of incoming students with a BA/BS only: 65% **Master's:** 35%

Approximate percentage of all students who are Women: 73% **Ethnic Minority:** 21% **International:** 0%

Average years to complete the doctoral program (including internship): 4.3 years

Personal interview
Day-long interviews are required.

Attrition rate in past 7 years: 6.5%
Percentage of students applying for internship in 2016 accepted into:

APA internships: 75% **APPIC internships:** 25%

Formal tracks/concentrations: Neuropsychology

Research areas	# Faculty	# Grants
Altruism and prosocial behavior	2	0
Autism	1	0
Burnout in Healthcare Settings	1	1
Chronic Pain	1	0
Clinical Mindfulness	1	0
Clinical Envy	1	0
Creativity	2	0
Depression in the deaf population	1	0
Geropsychology	1	0
Grief, Loss, and Bereavement	1	0
Health Psychology	1	0
Holistic Wellness	1	0
Human Sexuality	1	0
Integrated Primary Care	1	0
Neuropsychology	1	0
Neurodegenerative Diseases	1	1
Prescription Privileges	2	0
Psychology and the Law	1	0
Psychopharmacology	1	0
Psychotherapy Processes and Outcomes	1	0
Secondary Traumatic Stress	2	0
School Violence	2	0
Sport Psychology	1	0
Substance Abuse	1	0
Technology and Psychology	1	0

Clinical opportunities

VA Hospitals	Forensics
Community Health	Neuropsychology
Hospitals	Private practice
Child/juvenile	Sex offenders
Substance abuse	Corrections
Integrated Health	

Midwestern University (Psy.D.)

Behavioral Sciences Department
Clinical Psychology Program
555 31st Street
Downers Grove, IL 60515
phone#: (630) 515-7655
email:
Web address: https://www.midwestern.edu/programs_and_admission/il_clinical_psychology.html

1	2	**3**	4	5	6	7
Practice oriented			Equal emphasis			Research oriented

Percentage of faculty subscribing to each of the following orientations:

Psychodynamic/Psychoanalytic	35 %
Applied behavioral analysis/Radical behavioral	0 %
Family systems/Systems	5 %
Existential/Phenomenological/Humanistic	0 %
Cognitive/Cognitive-behavioral	40 %

Courses required for incoming students to have completed prior to enrolling:
Completion of 18 semester hours or equivalent of prerequisite coursework in psychology with a grade of C or better including: Introduction to General Psychology, Human Growth & Development or Personality Theory, Abnormal Psychology, Statistics or Tests and Measurements.

GRE mean
Verbal + Quantitative 64 %
Analytical Writing 45 %
Psychology Subject Test n/a

GPA mean
Overall GPA 3.26

Number of applications/admission offers/incoming students in 2017
94 applied/52 admission offers/23 incoming

% of students receiving:
Full tuition waiver only: 0%
Assistantship/fellowship only: 0%
Both full tuition waiver & assistantship/fellowship: 0%

Approximate percentage of incoming students with a B.A./B.S. only: 80% **Master's:** 20%

Approximate percentage of all students who are Women: 81% **Ethnic Minority:** 21% **International:** 0%

Average years to complete the doctoral program (including internship): 5 years

Personal interview: required in person.

Attrition rate in past 7 years: 10.1 % (15/148 = 10.1)

Percentage of students applying for internship last year accepted into:

APA internships: 70.5% **APPIC internships:** 100%

Formal tracks/concentrations: Child and Adolescent

Research areas	# Faculty
Aging (including Alzheimer's)	2
Autism spectrum disorders	1
Behavioral disorders	1
Behavioral improvisation	1
Biological psychology	1
Eating Disorders	2
Integrated healthcare	7
Multicultural issues	1
Postpartum disorders	2
Severe mental illness	1
Social psychology	1
Sleep disorders	1
Technology clinical applications	1
Womens health	2

Clinical opportunities
Aging
Disorders of childhood and adolescence
Integrated healthcare/interdisciplinary practice
Severe mental illness
Students complete practicum at sites throughout the Chicago training community, providing a wide range of clinical training opportunities.

University of Minnesota (Ph.D.)

Department of Psychology
N218 Elliot Hall, 75 East River Road
Minneapolis, MN 55455
phone#: (612) 625-2546
email: cspr@umn.edu
Web address: www.psych.umn.edu/areas/clinical/index.htm

1 2 3 4 5 **6** 7

Practice oriented — Equal emphasis — Research oriented

Percentage of faculty subscribing to each of the following orientations:

Psychodynamic/Psychoanalytic	17%
Applied behavioral analysis/Radical behavioral	17%
Family systems/Systems	0%
Existential/Phenomenological/Humanistic	0%
Cognitive/Cognitive-behavioral	83%

Courses required for incoming students to have completed prior to enrolling:
statistics, abnormal psychology

Recommended but not mandatory courses: none

GRE mean
Verbal % 90.88 Quantitative % 78.52
Analytical Writing % 83.4
Psychology Subject Test not reported

GPA mean
Undergrad GPA 3.75

Number of applications/admission offers/incoming students in 2017
190 applied/18 admission offers/8 incoming

% of students receiving:
Full tuition waiver only: 0%
Assistantship/fellowship only: 0%
Both full tuition waiver & assistantship/fellowship: 100%

Approximate percentage of incoming students with a B.A./B.S. only: 90% **Master's:** 10%

Approximate percentage of students who are Women: 78% **Ethnic Minority:** 16% **International:** 8%

Average years to complete the doctoral program (including internship): 6.1 years

Personal interview
Interview not required

Attrition rate in past 7 years: 7.55%

Percentage of students applying for internship in 2017 accepted into:

APA internships: 100% **APPIC internships:** 100%

Formal tracks/concentrations/specializations: adult psychopathology, developmental psychopathology

Research areas
affective disorders
antisocial/psychopathic personality
anxiety disorders
behavioral genetics
cross-cultural psychology
developmental psychopathology
eating disorders
molecular genetics
personality assessment
personality disorders
psychopharmacology
psychophysiology/neuroimaging
responses to extreme stress
schizophrenia
substance abuse

Clinical opportunities
ADHD
affective disorders
antisocial personality disorders
anxiety disorders
behavior therapy
childhood disorders and therapy
cognitive therapy
community psychology
long-term psychodynamic psychotherapy
neuropsychology
obsessive–compulsive disorder
panic disorder
post-traumatic stress disorder

conduct disorder	psychopathic personality
crisis intervention	psychotic disorders
eating disorders	schizophrenia
family therapy	substance abuse
forensic psychology	

University of Mississippi (Ph.D.)

Department of Psychology
University, MS 38677
phone#: (662) 915-5186
email: pygross@olemiss.edu
Web address: www.olemiss.edu/depts/psychology/grad/clinical

1 2 3 4 **5** 6 7

Practice oriented — Equal emphasis — Research oriented

Percentage of faculty subscribing to each of the following orientations:

Psychodynamic/Psychoanalytic	0%
Applied behavioral analysis/Radical behavioral	20%
Family systems/Systems	0%
Existential/Phenomenological/Humanistic	10%
Cognitive/Cognitive-behavioral	70%

(some faculty not easily categorized, e.g. applied behavioral/behavioral)

Courses required for incoming students prior to enrolling: statistics, lab course

Recommended but not mandatory courses:
physiological psychology, abnormal psychology, developmental psychology, and some grounding in biology/physiology/chemistry

GRE mean
Verbal 157 Quantitative 150
Verbal + Quantitative 307
Analytical Writing 4.3
Psychology Subject Test not reported

GPA mean
Overall GPA 3.81 Psychology GPA
Junior/Senior GPA

Number of applications/admission offers/incoming students in 2016
100 applied/13 admission offers/7 incoming

% of students receiving:
Full tuition waiver only: 100%
Assistantship/fellowship only:100 0%
Both full tuition waiver & assistantship/fellowship: 100%

Approximate percentage of incoming students with a B.A./B.S. only: 86% **Master's:** 14%

Approximate percentage of students who are Women: 85% **Ethnic Minority:** 15% **International:** 0%

Average years to complete the doctoral program (including internship): 7 years

Personal interview
Preferred in person but telephone acceptable

Attrition rate in past 7 years: 1%

Percentage of students applying for internship in 2016 accepted into:

APA internships: 9% **APPIC internships:**

Formal tracks/concentrations: none

Research areas	# Faculty	# Grants
behavior problems in children	3	0
community psychology	2	0
compliance	1	0
computer-based research	1	1
emotion	2	1
posttraumatic stress disorder	3	0
psychological assessment	2	0
race relations	2	0
rape	1	0
rural mental health	2	0
smoking cessation/addiction/substance abuse	1	0

Clinical opportunities

child/adolescent	family/marital therapy
children's social skills	headache
chronic mental illness	health psychology
clinical assessment	mental retardation
community mental health	positive psychology
consultation	post-traumatic stress disorder
disaster	sexual aggression
dissemination	smoking cessation
eating disorders	substance abuse/alcohol abuse

University of Missouri–Columbia (Ph.D.)

Department of Psychology
210 McAlester Hall
Columbia, MO 65211
phone#: (573) 882-0838
email: gradpsych@missouri.edu
Web address: psychology.missouri.edu/grad

1 2 3 4 5 **6** 7

Practice oriented — Equal emphasis — Research oriented

Percentage of faculty subscribing to each of the following orientations:

Psychodynamic/Psychoanalytic	0%
Applied behavioral analysis/Radical behavioral	0%
Family systems/Systems	15%
Existential/Phenomenological/Humanistic	0%
Cognitive/Cognitive-behavioral	75%
Other: Integrative, Genetic, Empirical	10%

Courses required for incoming students to have completed prior to enrolling: none

Recommended but not mandatory courses: Other sciences, statistics/mathematics

GRE mean of students entering in Fall, 2017
Verbal + Quantitative 311
Analytical Writing 4.4
Psychology Subject Test 780

GPA mean – of students entering in Fall, 2017
Overall GPA 3.55

Number of applications/admission offers/incoming students in 2017
77 applied/5 admission offers/3 incoming

Percent of students receiving:
Full tuition waiver only: 0%
Assistantship/fellowship only: 0%
Both full tuition waiver & assistantship/fellowship: 100%

Approximate percentage of incoming students with a B.A./B.S. only: 90% **Master's:** 10% (overall; 67%/33% in 2017)

Approximate percentage of students who are Women: 85% **Ethnic Minority:** 18% **International:** 3%

Average years to complete the doctoral program (including internship): 7.28 years

Personal interview
Preferred in person but telephone acceptable

Attrition rate in past 7 years: 12.2%

Percentage of students applying for internship in 2017 accepted into:

APA internships: 67% (2 of 3) **APPIC internships:** 100% (3 of 3)

Formal tracks/concentrations: clinical adult, clinical child; also developmental and quantitative minors, and joint clinical-developmental and clinical-quantitative PhD opportunities

Research areas	# Faculty	# Grants
addictions	6	~10
anxiety/depression disorders (youth)	2	1
autism/devel. disorders	1	3
multisystemic therapy	1	1
personality disorders	1	2
schizophrenia	1	1
treatment dissemination	2	3
neuroscience	2	1
behavioral/molecular genetics	2	2

Clinical opportunities
adult, outpatient and inpatient
child, outpatient and inpatient
health psychology
medical center
forensic (child custody) evaluation
university counseling center
research protocol assessment and prevention
state hospital
VA hospital
neurodevelopmental assessment and intervention
underserved clients (deaf/hearing impaired)

University of Missouri–Kansas City (Ph.D.)

Department of Psychology
5100 Rockhill Road
Kansas City, MO 64110
phone#: (816)-235-1318
email: psychology@umkc.edu
Web address: http://cas2.umkc.edu/psychology/GCPhD.asp

1	2	3	4	5	**6**	7
Practice oriented			Equal emphasis			Research oriented

Percentage of faculty subscribing to each of the following orientations:
Psychodynamic/Psychoanalytic 0%
Applied behavioral analysis/Radical behavioral 0%
Family systems/Systems 0%
Existential/Phenomenological/Humanistic 0%
Cognitive/Cognitive-behavioral 100%

Courses required for incoming students to have completed prior to enrolling:
A B.A./B.S. in psychology is preferred but not required. At least 9 credits of psychology, including research methods and statistics

Recommended but not mandatory courses: At least two of the following: abnormal, biopsychology, child, cognitive, learning, motivation, personality, sensation and perception, social psychology

GRE mean
Verbal 159 Quantitative 150
Analytical Writing 4.5
Psychology Subject Test not reported

GPA mean
Overall GPA 3.6

Number of applications/admission offers/incoming students in 2016
84 applied/4 admission offers/3 incoming

% of students receiving:
Full tuition waiver only: 0%
Assistantship/fellowship only: 0%
Both full tuition waiver & assistantship/fellowship: 100% (if enrolled at least 9 credit hours)

Approximate percentage of incoming students with a B.A./B.S. only: 75% **Master's:** 25%

Approximate percentage of students who are Women: 90% **Ethnic Minority:** 10% **International:** 0%

Average years to complete the doctoral program (including internship): 6 years

Personal interview
Interview required (can be in person or phone)

Attrition rate in past 7 years: 14%

Percentage of students applying for internship in 2016 accepted into:

APA internships: 100% **APPIC internships:** 100%

Formal tracks/concentrations: health and life sciences

Research areas	# Faculty	# Grants
development	2	1
eating disorders/obesity	1	1
cardiovascular disease	1	1
serious mental illness	1	1
attention and emotion	2	1
trauma/violence prevention	2	2
sensory and cognitive neuroscience	1	2
neuropsychology (multiple sclerosis)	1	2

Clinical opportunities

chronic pain
psychiatry
substance abuse
veterans
community mental health
behavioral anxiety treatment
primary care
neuropsychology

University of Missouri–St. Louis (Ph.D.)

Department of Psychological Sciences
One University Blvd.
St. Louis, MO 63121
phone#: (314) 516-5391
email: psy_advising@umsl.edu
Web address: www.umsl.edu/divisions/artscience/psychology/psychology/clinical/index.html

1	2	3	4	5	**6**	7
Practice oriented			Equal emphasis			Research oriented

Percentage of faculty subscribing to each of the following orientations:

Psychodynamic/Psychoanalytic	0%
Applied behavioral analysis/Radical behavioral	0%
Family systems/Systems	0%
Existential/Phenomenological/Humanistic	15%
Cognitive/Cognitive-behavioral	85%

Courses required for incoming students to have completed prior to enrolling:
BS/BA in psychology, or 21 undergraduate credits in psychology; psychological statistics, research methods in psychology

Recommended but not mandatory courses: Social psychology, cognitive psychology, behavioral neuroscience, developmental

GRE mean for Fall 2017 class
Verbal 161 Quantitative 154
Analytical Writing 4.5
Psychology Subject Test 750 (not required)

GPA mean
Overall GPA 3.83 Psychology GPA 3.91

Number of applications/admission offers/incoming students in 2017
167 applied/9 admission offers/5 incoming

% of students receiving:
Full tuition waiver only: 0%
Assistantship/fellowship only: 0%
Both full tuition waiver & assistantship/fellowship: 100%

Approximate percentage of incoming students with a B.A./B.S. only: 100% **Master's:** 0%

Approximate percentage of students who are Women: 80% **Ethnic Minority:** 20% **International:** 0%

Average years to complete the doctoral program (including internship): 6.0 years

Personal interview
Preferred in person but telephone acceptable

Attrition rate in past 7 years: 5%

Percentage of students applying for internship in 2016 accepted into:

APA internships: 100% **APPIC internships:**

Formal tracks/concentrations: behavioral medicine, trauma studies, women and diversity studies

Research areas	# Faculty	# Grants
behavioral medicine	2	1
child psychology	1	0
clinical geropsychology	1	1
multicultural issues	1	1
women & sexuality	1	1
trauma studies	2	3

Clinical opportunities

adults & couples
assessment
behavioral medicine interventions
children/adolescents & families
older adults
treatment of PTSD/trauma across the lifespan

University of Montana (Ph.D.)

Department of Psychology
32 Campus Drive
Missoula, MT 59812-1584
phone#: (406) 243-4521
email: bryan.cochran@umontana.edu
Web address: http://hs.umt.edu/psychology/clinical-psychology

1	2	3	**4**	5	6	7
Practice oriented			Equal emphasis			Research oriented

Percentage of faculty subscribing to each of the following orientations:

Psychodynamic/Psychoanalytic	33%
Applied behavioral analysis/Radical behavioral	11%
Family systems/Systems	44%
Existential/Phenomenological/Humanistic	33%
Cognitive/Cognitive-behavioral	67%
Integrative/Eclectic	44%
Interpersonal	22%
Developmental	11%

Courses required for incoming students to have completed prior to enrolling: none

Recommended but not mandatory courses: Research methods, statistics, multicultural, abnormal, personality, physiological psychology

GRE mean
Verbal 157 Quantitative 152
Analytical Writing 4.22
Psychology Subject Test (not required)

GPA mean
Undergraduate 3.74
Graduate 3.89

Number of applications/admission offers/incoming students in 2017
163 applied/8 admission offers/5 incoming

% of (all, not just entering) students receiving:
Full tuition waiver only: 0%
Assistantship/fellowship only: 13%
Both full tuition waiver & assistantship/fellowship: 42%
Both partial tuition waiver & assistantship/fellowship: 35%
Note: The above does not include students on internship and ABD.

Approximate percentage of incoming students with a B.A./B.S. only: 75% **Master's:** 25%

Approximate percentage of all students who are Women/Trans/Non-Binary: 76% **Ethnic Minority:** 22% **International:** 3%

Average years to complete the doctoral program (including internship): 6.57 years

Personal interview
In person preferred, but Skype, WebEx, or telephone acceptable

Attrition rate in past 7 years: 6.3%

Percentage of students applying for internship in 2017 accepted into:

APA internships: 83.3% **APPIC internships:** 100%

Formal tracks/concentrations: Child, adolescent, family clinical emphasis; neuropsychology exposure

Research areas	# Faculty	# Grants
assessment	6	1
autism spectrum disorder treatments	1	0
behavioral medicine/health psychology	3	2
behavioral treatments	2	0
borderline personality disorder/dialectical behavior therapy	1	0
child abuse	1	0
child psychopathology	5	2
closed-head injury	1	0
cross-cultural (Native American)	2	2
depression	3	1
gender issues	2	0
geriatric psychology/aging	2	1
health care systems	3	2
intimate partner violence	2	0
LGBT health	2	1
malingering	1	0
memory	2	1
mindfulness	1	0
multicultural issues in practice	2	1
neuropsychology	2	1
nonlinear dynamic systems	1	0
parent–child relationships	2	0
psychotherapy process and outcome	1	0
PTSD	5	0
resilience	2	1
rural practice	1	1
schizophrenia	1	0
sexuality	1	0
substance abuse/dependence	1	1

Clinical opportunities
adolescent and child assessment
anxiety disorders
attachment disorder
borderline personality disorder
child assessment and treatment
community health
couples/family
depression
domestic violence
functional analytic therapy
health psychology
inpatient treatment
integrated behavioral health
LGBT populations
mindfulness-based treatment
motivational interviewing
Native American populations
neuropsychology
pain management
primary care psychology
prison populations
rural psychology
schizophrenia/psychoses
school-based practice
substance abuse
trauma

University of Nebraska–Lincoln (Ph.D.)

Department of Psychology
238 Burnett Hall
Lincoln, NE 68588-0308
phone#: (402) 472-3229
email: jamie.longwell@unl.edu
Web address: psychology.unl.edu/clinical-psychology-training-program

1	2	3	4	5	6	7
Practice oriented			Equal emphasis			Research oriented

Percentage of faculty subscribing to each of the following orientations:

Psychodynamic/Psychoanalytic	0%
Applied behavioral analysis/Radical behavioral	20%
Family systems/Systems	30%
Existential/Phenomenological/Humanistic	20%
Cognitive/Cognitive-behavioral	90%

Courses required for incoming students to have completed prior to enrolling:
Psychology major preferred

Recommended but not mandatory courses:
Methodology and quantitative courses

GRE mean
Verbal 159 Quantitative 154
Analytical 4.5
Psychology Subject Test not required

GPA mean
Overall GPA 3.79

Number of applications/admission offers/incoming students in 2017
239 applied/16 admission offers/9 incoming

% of students receiving:
Full tuition waiver only: 0%
Assistantship/fellowship only: 0%
Both full tuition waiver & assistantship/fellowship: 100%

Approximate percentage of incoming students with a B.A./B.S. only: 72% **Master's:** 28%

Approximate percentage of students who are Women: 70% **Ethnic Minority:** 27% **International:** 5%

Average years to complete the doctoral program (including internship): 5.5 years

Personal interview
Preferred in person but telephone and web video interviews are acceptable

Attrition rate in past 7 years: 5%

Percentage of students applying for internship in 2017 accepted into:

APA internships: 100% **APPIC internships:** 100%

Formal tracks/concentrations: adult/general, child and family, forensic

Research areas	# Faculty	# Grants
anxiety	1	1
child abuse/family violence	3	2
child/adolescence	3	3
forensic	1	2
LGBT issues	1	2
mental health disparities	2	2
pediatric psychology	1	3
psychology and law	1	2
psychopathology	4	2
substance abuse/dual diagnosis	1	1
targeted violence/threat assessment	1	2
trauma/PTSD	3	2
traumatic brain injury	1	1

Clinical opportunities
anxiety disorders
child abuse/family violence
forensic
Head Start
LGBT
minority/diversity issues
pediatric health
pediatric rehabilitation
severe mental illness
sex offender
substance abuse
telehealth
traumatic brain injury

University of Nevada–Las Vegas (Ph.D.)

Department of Psychology
Las Vegas, NV 89154
phone#: (702) 895-3305
email: psyunlv@unlv.nevada.edu
Web address: http://psychology.unlv.edu/clinical.htm

1	2	3	4	5	6	7
Practice oriented			Equal emphasis			Research oriented

Percentage of faculty subscribing to each of the following orientations:

Psychodynamic/Psychoanalytic	5%
Applied behavioral analysis/Radical behavioral	0%
Family systems/Systems	0%
Existential/Phenomenological/Humanistic	5%
Cognitive/Cognitive-behavioral	90%

Courses required for incoming students to have completed prior to enrolling:
at least 18 hours of undergraduate psychology courses including Statistics, Abnormal Psychology, and Experimental Psychology (e.g., cognitive psychology, research methods).

Recommended but not mandatory courses:
Standardized testing, child behavior disorders, motivation and learning, history of psychology

GRE mean
Verbal 159 Quantitative 155
Analytical Writing 4.5
Psychology Subject Test not required

GPA mean
Overall GPA 3.70

Number of applications/admission offers/incoming students in 2016
87 applied/9 admission offers/8 incoming

% of students receiving:
Full tuition waiver only: 100% (9 credits per semester in fall and spring, 3 credits in summer)
Assistantship/fellowship only: 100%
Both full tuition waiver & assistantship/fellowship: 100%

Approximate percentage of incoming students with a B.A./B.S. only: 82% **Master's:** 18%

Approximate percentage of students who are Women: 84% **Ethnic Minority:** 20% **International:** 7.5%

Average years to complete the doctoral program (including internship): 6.5 years

Personal interview
In person preferred

Attrition rate in past 7 years: 6%

Percentage of students applying for internship in 2016 accepted into:

APA internships: 100% **APPIC internships:**

Formal tracks/concentrations: clinical neuropsychology

Research areas	# Faculty	# Grants
child externalizing disorders	1	1
child internalizing disorders	1	0
descriptive experience sampling	1	0
eating disorders/multicultural issues	1	0
neuropsychology	1	1
psychopathy	1	1
statistics	1	0

Clinical opportunities
Family Research and Services/The Optimum Performance Program in Sports
UNLV School Refusal and Anxiety Disorders Clinic
UNLV PRACTICE (university-based counseling)
Student counseling and psychological services
Cleveland Clinic Lou Ruvo Center for Brain Health
UNLV Ackerman Center for Autism & Neurodevelopmental Solutions
Children's Heart Center, Nevada Healthy Heart Program
Children's Specialty Center of Nevada / Cure 4 the Kids Foundation
Southern Nevada Adult Mental Health Services
Department of Veterans Affairs Southern Nevada Health Care System
Desert Willow Treatment Center
Nevada Division of Child & Family Services
Numerous other practicum sites

University of Nevada–Reno (Ph.D.)

Department of Psychology
Clinical Psychology Program
MSS 298
Reno, NV 89557-0298
phone#: (775) 682-8701
email: klarson@unr.edu
Web address: www.unr.edu/psych/clinical/

1	2	3	4	5	6	7
Practice oriented			Equal emphasis			Research oriented

Percentage of faculty subscribing to each of the following orientations:

Psychodynamic/Psychoanalytic	0%
Applied behavioral analysis/Radical behavioral	40%
Family systems/Systems	0%
Existential/Phenomenological/Humanistic	0%
Cognitive/Cognitive-behavioral	60%

Courses required for incoming students to have completed prior to enrolling:
Applicants seeking admission into the Clinical Psychology PhD program at UNR must demonstrate that that have completed advanced undergraduate or graduate courses in (1) Affective Aspects of Behavior, (2) Biological Aspects of Behavior, (3) Cognitive Aspects of Behavior, and (4) Social Aspects of Behavior, as pre-requisites for admission. What constitutes classwork in this area is defined in APA's the Implementing Regulations "Section C: IRs Related to the Standards of Accreditation" under the subheading "C-7 D. Discipline-Specific Knowledge." See https://www.apa.org/ed/accreditation/section-c-soa.pdf. Exceptions can be made for exceptional candidates to make up course deficits in these areas at UNR or another institution after an admission offer is been made. But a plan to fulfill these requirements must be in place before admission. It would strengthen a candidate's application if this could be addressed in a few lines at the end of the personal statement.

Recommended but not mandatory courses:
Learning, behavioral principles, or behavior analysis
Statistics/data analysis
Research methods/experimental design
History of psychology
Individual differences
Human development
Abnormal behavior/psychopathology
Cultural and individual diversity

GRE mean
Verbal 160 Quantitative 154
Analytical Writing not reported
Psychology Subject Test not required

GPA mean
Overall GPA 3.7 Psychology GPA 3.8

Number of applications/admission offers/incoming5students in 2017
62 applied/0 admission offers/5 incoming

% of students receiving:
Full tuition waiver only: 0%
Assistantship/fellowship only: 0%
Both full tuition waiver & assistantship/fellowship: 100%

Approximate percentage of incoming students with a B.A./B.S. only: 80% **Master's:** 20%

Approximate percentage of students who are Women: 66% **Ethnic Minority:** 22% **International:** 11%

Average years to complete the doctoral program (including internship): 7.1 years

Personal interview
Preferred in person but telephone/Skype acceptable

Attrition rate in past 7 years: 7%

Percentage of students applying for internship in 2017 accepted into:

APA internships: 100% APPIC internships: 100%

Formal tracks/concentrations: none

Research areas	# Faculty	# Grants
Gerontology/aging	1	1
Behavior analysis	3	0
Family caregiving	1	1
Prevention of elder abuse	1	1
Anxiety disorders	3	1
Traumatic stress reactions	4	2
Implementation science	2	0
Delivery/Dissemination of evidence-based treatments to cultural minorities	1	1
Diversity Studies	3	0
Psychological assessment and evaluation	1	0
Behavior Medicine	1	0
Chronic pain and Injury	1	0
Grief and bereavement	2	0
Treatment development	3	0
Behavioral assessment	3	0
Behavioral health	2	0
Mindfulness/MBSR	1	0
Self-regulation training interventions	1	1
Intervention with adolescents	1	1
Emotion regulation	2	1
Sexual abuse	2	1
Forensic interviewing	2	0
Integrated care	3	0

Clinical opportunities

Gerontology	Posttraumatic Stress Disorder
Anxiety disorders	Grief
Adolescents	Cultural Minorities
Integrated care	Functional Analytic Psychotherapy
Mood disorders	

University of New Mexico (Ph.D.)

Department of Psychology
MSC 03 2220
1 University of New Mexico
Albuquerque, NM 87131-0001
phone#: (505) 277-4121
email: eyeater@unm.edu (director), rikk@unm.edu (coordinator)
Web address: http://psych.unm.edu/graduate/programs-of-study/clinical-psychology.html

1	2	3	4	5	**6**	7
Practice oriented			Equal emphasis			Research oriented

Percentage of faculty subscribing to each of the following orientations:

Psychodynamic/Psychoanalytic	0%
Applied behavioral analysis/Radical behavioral	8%
Family systems/Systems	0%
Existential/Phenomenological/Humanistic	0%
Cognitive/Cognitive-behavioral	67%
Other*	25%

Courses required for incoming students to have completed prior to enrolling:
Statistics, research methods, psychology major or equivalent coursework

Recommended but not mandatory courses:
Basic science courses, laboratory courses, supervised research

GRE mean
Verbal + Quantitative 320 (V=162, Q=158)
Analytical Writing 4.67
Psychology Subject Test 737

GPA mean
Overall GPA 3.88 (3.82 UGGPA, 3.94 GGPA)

Number of applications/admission offers/incoming students in 2017
158 applied/5 admitted/3 accepted

% of students receiving:
Full tuition waiver only: 0%
Assistantship/fellowship only: 0%
Both full tuition waiver & assistantship/fellowship: 100%

Approximate percentage of incoming students with a B.A./B.S. only: 33% **Master's:** 67%

Approximate percentage of students who are (incoming for 2017) Women: 100% **Ethnic Minority:** 0% **International:** 0%

Average years to complete the doctoral program (including internship): 7 years

Personal interview
Preferred in person

Attrition rate in past 7 years: 2009–2016 = 10%

Percentage of students applying for internship in 2017 accepted into:

APA internships: 100% **APPIC internships:** 100%

Formal tracks/concentrations: health psychology emphasis, quantitative emphasis

Research areas	# Faculty	# Grants
Eating disorders	1	0
Minority/cultural issues	2	2
Health psychology	3	1
Neuropsychology	3	3
Pediatric psychology	1	0
Clinical child psychology	2	0
Substance abuse	6	20
Neuroimaging and clinical neuroscience	3	3
Sexual victimization/trauma	1	2

Clinical opportunities
Psychological Diagnostic Assessment
Cardiac rehabilitation
Child treatment
Consultation in primary care settings
Couple therapy
Eating disorders
Empirically supported treatment for a wide range of anxiety, mood, neuropsychological and thought disorders
Emphasis on culturally aware treatment with diverse populations
Forensic assessment
Mindfulness-based interventions
Motivational interviewing
Neuroimaging
Neuropsychological assessment – adults, children
Pediatric health
Substance-related disorders – assessment and treatment
Veterans' services – smoking cessation, homeless veterans, PTSD, assessment
**Note: Three faculty have a primary focus in neuropsychology*

The New School (Ph.D.)

(formerly listed as New School University)
New School for Social Research, Department of Psychology
80 Fifth Avenue, 7th floor
New York, NY 10011
phone#: (212) 229-5727
email: changd@newschool.edu
Web address: www.newschool.edu/nssr/subpage.aspx?id=9888

1	2	3	**4**	5	6	7
Practice oriented			Equal emphasis			Research oriented

Percentage of faculty subscribing to each of the following orientations:

Psychodynamic/Psychoanalytic	70%
Applied behavioral analysis/Radical behavioral	0%
Family systems/Systems	0%
Existential/Phenomenological/Humanistic	0%
Cognitive/Cognitive-behavioral	30%

Courses required for incoming students to have completed prior to enrolling:
1 course in each of the following: social, developmental; psychopathology; 1 course in assessment of individual differences; 1 course in statistics; 1 research methods course

Recommended but not mandatory courses:
Undergraduate major in psychology recommended, but not mandatory

GRE mean
Verbal 525 Quantitative 590
Analytical Writing not reported
Psychology Subject Test 595

GPA mean
Overall GPA 3.74

Number of applications/admission offers/incoming students in 2017
31 applied/15 admission offers/15 incoming
Note: Only applications from New School University Master's students in psychology are considered for enrollment.

% of students receiving:
Full tuition waiver only: 11%
Assistantship/fellowship only: 30%
Both full tuition waiver & assistantship/fellowship: 8% (approximately 100% of students receive a partial tuition waiver)

Approximate percentage of incoming students with a B.A./B.S. only: 0% **Master's:** 100%

Approximate percentage of students who are Women: 77% **Ethnic Minority:** 13% **International:** 14%

Average years to complete the doctoral program (including internship): 5.5 years

Personal interview
Required in person

Attrition rate in past 7 years: 2%

Percentage of students applying for internship in 2017 accepted into:

APA internships: 94% **APPIC internships:** 100%

Formal tracks/concentrations: Scientist–Practitioner training model

Research areas	# Faculty	# Grants
assessment/diagnosis	2	1
child clinical	1	1
developmental	1	1
emotions	1	0
health psychology	1	1
memory	2	1
moral development	1	1
narrative methodologies	2	0
personality assessment	1	0
prevention	2	1
psychoanalysis	2	0
psychopathology	2	0
psychotherapy process & outcome	3	10
Trauma physiology	1	1

Clinical opportunities
New School–Beth Israel Center for Training and Research
Variety of clinical settings for internships and externships
New School Low Cost Assessment Service

University of North Carolina at Chapel Hill (Ph.D.)

Department of Psychology
Davie Hall, CB 3270
Chapel Hill, NC 27599-3270
phone#: (919) 962-5082
fax#: (919) 962-2537
email: mallasch@live.unc.edu
Web address: http://clinicalpsych.unc.edu/

1	2	3	4	5	**6**	7
Practice oriented			Equal emphasis			Research oriented

Percentage of faculty subscribing to each of the following orientations:

Psychodynamic/Psychoanalytic	0%
Applied behavioral analysis/Radical behavioral	0%
Family systems/Systems	0%
Existential/Phenomenological/Humanistic	0%
Cognitive/Cognitive-behavioral	100%

Courses required for incoming students to have completed prior to enrolling: none

Recommended but not mandatory courses: A psychology major or its equivalent (8 or more courses)

GRE mean for Fall 2017 Class
Verbal 165 Quantitative 158
Analytical Writing 4.69
Psychology Subject Test not reported

GPA mean for Fall 2017 Class
Oveall GPA 3.74

Number of applications/admission offers/incoming students in 2017
465 applied/8 admission offers/8 incoming

% of students receiving:
Full tuition waiver only: 0%
Assistantship/fellowship only: 0%
Both full tuition waiver & assistantship/fellowship: 100%

Approximate percentage of incoming students with a B.A./B.S. only: 85% **Master's:** 15%

Approximate percentage of students who are Women: 71% **Ethnic Minority:** 28% **International:** not reported

Average years to complete the doctoral program (including internship): 6 years

Personal interview
Preferred

Attrition rate in past 7 years: 0%

Percentage of students applying for internship in 2017 accepted into:

APA internships: 100 **APPIC internships:** 100

Formal tracks/concentrations: adult clinical, clinical child and adolescent

Research areas	# Faculty	# Grants
Addictions	2	3
schizophrenia	1	2
anxiety disorders	1	0
couples therapy/research	1	1
behavioral medicine/health psychology	1	1
pediatric bipolar disorder	1	2
adolescent depression and suicidality	1	1
ethnic minority youth; health disparities	2	1
Race and racism	1	1
eating disorders	1	1
ADHD/Neuroscience	1	1

Clinical opportunities
couples therapy
anxiety disorders
adult therapy and assessment
child behavior therapy
child bipolar treatment
developmental disabilities
child assessment
health/pediatric psychology
eating disorders
autism and pervasive developmental disorders

University of North Carolina at Charlotte (Ph.D.)

Health Psychology Ph.D. Program
College of Liberal Arts & Sciences
Charlotte, NC 28223
phone#: (704) 687-1330
email: vgilriva@uncc.edu
Web address: healthpsych.uncc.edu/program-tracks/clinical

1	2	3	4	**5**	6	7
Practice oriented			Equal emphasis			Research oriented

Percentage of faculty subscribing to each of the following orientations:
Psychodynamic/Psychoanalytic 0%
Applied behavioral analysis/Radical behavioral 0%
Family systems/Systems 0%
Existential/Phenomenological/Humanistic 20%
Cognitive/Cognitive-behavioral 100%

Courses required for incoming students to have completed prior to enrolling:
18 hours of coursework in psychology including research methods and statistics

Recommended but not mandatory courses: abnormal, health psychology, developmental

GRE mean
Verbal 157 Quantitative 155
Analytical Writing 4.35
Psychology Subject Test not reported

GPA mean
Overall GPA 3.5

Number of applications/admission offers/incoming students in 2017
117 applied/10 admission offers/7 incoming

% of students receiving:
Full tuition waiver only: 0%
Assistantship/fellowship only: 0%
Both full tuition waiver & assistantship/fellowship: 100%

Approximate percentage of incoming students with a BA/BS only: 50% **Master's:** 50%

Approximate percentage of all students who are Women: 100% **Ethnic Minority:** 25% **International:** 0%

Average years to complete the doctoral program (including internship): 5.5 years

Personal interview
Interviews are required; preferably in person or via Skype.

Attrition rate in past 7 years: 11.11%

Percentage of students applying for internship in 2017 accepted into:

APA internships: 100% **APPIC internships:** 0%

Formal tracks/concentrations: health psychology

Research areas	# Faculty	# Grants
psychosocial determinants of health	9	0
eating disorders/obesity	3	1
posttraumatic growth/trauma	6	0
health behavior change	3	0
psychoneuroimmunology	1	0
social relationships	1	0
chronic illness	3	1
community psychology	5	4
neuropsychology	1	1
cognitive	3	2
sleep problems	1	0
stress and well-being	6	0
alternative & complementary	3	0
emotion	1	0
behavioral genetics	1	0
sexual behavior	3	1
intelligence and health behavior	1	1

Clinical opportunities
behavioral medicine
inpatient
learning disabilities/ADD
neuropsychological assessment
university counseling center
integrated primary care
VA hospital (outpatient & group)
psychosocial oncology

University of North Carolina at Greensboro (Ph.D.)

Department of Psychology
273 Eberhart Building
Greensboro, NC 27402-6170
phone#: (336) 256-0569
email: spkeane@uncg.edu
Web address: www.uncg.edu/psy/grad/clinical/index.html

1	2	3	**4**	5	6	7
Practice oriented			Equal emphasis			Research oriented

Percentage of faculty subscribing to each of the following orientations:
Psychodynamic/Psychoanalytic 0%
Applied behavioral analysis/Radical behavioral 0%
Family systems/Systems 33%
Existential/Phenomenological/Humanistic 0%
Cognitive/Cognitive-behavioral 100%

Courses required for incoming students to have completed prior to enrolling:
Equivalent of undergraduate major in psychology, which should include statistics and a minimum of 4 other courses in psychology

Recommended but not mandatory courses:
Physiological psychology, Abnormal, Developmental, Cognitive and Social Psychology

GRE mean
Verbal 157/73%ile; Quantitative 159/72nd%ile
Analytical Writing 4.5/78%ile
Please note: Psychology Subject Test is now required

GPA mean
Overall GPA 3.5

Number of applications/admission offers/incoming students in 2017
238 applied/10 admission offers/5 incoming

% of students receiving:
Full tuition waiver only: 0%
Assistantship/fellowship only: 0%
Both full tuition waiver & assistantship/fellowship: 100%

Approximate percentage of incoming students with a B.A./B.S. only: 60% **Master's:** 40%

Approximate percentage of all students who are Women: 74% **Ethnic Minority:** 36% **International:** 0%

Average years to complete the doctoral program (including internship): 6.3 years

Personal interview
Required in-person interview, skype interviews may be allowed if there are extenuating circumstances

Attrition rate in past 7 years: 10.5%

Percentage of students applying for internship in 2017 accepted into:

APA internships: 100% **APPIC internships:** 100%

Formal tracks/concentrations: We do not have formal tracks, but clinical specialization is allowed in Child or Adult areas

Research areas *	# Faculty	# Grants
Child/Adolescent internalizing disorder	2	0
Child/adolescent Externalizing disorder	1	0
Peer relationships	1	0
Depression	1	1
Behavioral genetics	1	0
Personality disorders	1	0
Preschool intervention	1	0
PTSD	1	0
Diversity	2	1

**Note categories are not mutually exclusive (current faculty =7)*

Clinical opportunities and special populations
Adult Assessment and Therapy
Child Assessment and Therapy
Group Therapy
DBT skills training
Immigrants and refugees
Integrated health care/Behavioral Health within Primary Care
Racial, cultural and gender diversity
Underserved populations
University counseling center
Veterans

University of North Dakota (Ph.D.)

Department of Psychology
Box 8380
Grand Forks, ND 58202
phone#: (701) 777-3451
email: joseph.miller@und.edu
Web address: www.und.edu/dept/psych/clinicaladmission.html

1	2	3	**4**	5	6	7
Practice oriented			Equal emphasis			Research oriented

Percentage of faculty subscribing to each of the following orientations:

Psychodynamic/Psychoanalytic	17%
Applied behavioral analysis/Radical behavioral	17%
Family systems/Systems	0%
Existential/Phenomenological/Humanistic	17%
Cognitive/Cognitive-behavioral	100%

Courses required for incoming students to have completed prior to enrolling:
Psychology courses (at least 18 hours) in developmental, abnormal, statistics, experimental or research methods. One semester of college algebra and a year of biological science.

Recommended but not mandatory courses: A background in social and natural sciences' BA/BS in Psychology or MA/MS in Psychology or Applied Psychology (e.g., Clinical or Counseling)

GRE mean
Verbal + Quantitative 311
Analytical Writing 4.07

GPA mean
Overall GPA 3.83

Number of applications/admission offers/incoming students in 2016
90 applied/14 admission offers/7 incoming

% of students receiving:
Full tuition waiver only: 0%
Assistantship/fellowship only: 0%
Both full tuition waiver & assistantship/fellowship: 100%

Approximate percentage of incoming students with a B.A./B.S. only: 90% **Master's:** 10%

Approximate percentage of all students who are Women: 95% **Ethnic Minority:** 25% **International:** 5%

Average years to complete the doctoral program (including internship): 5.4 years

Personal interview
Preferred in person but telephone acceptable

Attrition rate in past 7 years: 7%

Percentage of students applying for internship in 2016 accepted into:

APA internships: 100% **APPIC internships:** 100%

Formal tracks/concentrations: none

Research areas	# Faculty	# Grants
adult psychopathology	6	0
self-harm behavior	1	1

suicidality	1	1
anxiety disorders	1	0
applied behavioral analysis	2	0
behavioral medicine	2	0
community psychology	2	0
cross-cultural psychology	2	1
friendship/relationships	2	0
gender roles	2	0
minority mental health	2	0
pain management/control	1	0
personality assessment	2	0
personality disorders	3	0
psychophysiology	1	0
relaxation/biofeedback	1	0
rural psychology	2	2
stress and coping	6	0
substance abuse	1	0
women's studies	2	0

Clinical opportunities

affective disorders
anxiety disorders
assessment
behavioral medicine
community psychology
interpersonal psychotherapy
marital/couples therapy
blind rehabilitation
minority/cross-cultural
obsessive–compulsive disorder
personality disorders
rural psychology
substance abuse
victim/battering abuse
eating disorders

University of North Texas (Ph.D.)

Clinical Psychology Program
Department of Psychology
1155 Union Circle #311280
Denton, TX 76203-5017
phone#: (940) 565-2671
email: PSYC-Grad@unt.edu
Web address: http://psychology.unt.edu/graduate-programs/clinical-psychology

1	2	3	4	5	**6**	7
Practice oriented			Equal emphasis			Research oriented

Percentage of faculty subscribing to each of the following orientations:

Psychodynamic/Psychoanalytic	12%
Applied behavioral analysis/Radical behavioral	0%
Family systems/Systems	0%
Existential/Phenomenological/Humanistic	12%
Cognitive/Cognitive-behavioral	63%

Courses required for incoming students to have completed prior to enrolling:
Statistics is required. In addition, 24 credit hours in psychology (12 of which must be advanced) are required prior to enrolling.

Recommended but not mandatory courses:
Experimental Psychology, Research Methods/Design, Learning, Perception, Motivation, Cognition, Physiological Psychology, Psychological Measurement, or Research Thesis.

GRE mean
Verbal 162 Quantitative 154
Analytical Writing 4.6
Psychology Subject Test not reported

GPA mean
3.65

Number of applications/admission offers/incoming students in 2017
202 applications/9 students are incoming

% of students receiving:
Full tuition waiver only: 0%
Assistantship/fellowship only: 100%
Both full tuition waiver & assistantship/fellowship: 0%

Approximate percentage of incoming students with a B.A./B.S. only: 63% **Master's:** 37%

Approximate percentage of students who are Women: 75% **Ethnic Minority:** 30% **International:** 6%

Average years to complete the doctoral program (including internship): 6 years

Personal interview
Required in person

Attrition rate in past 7 years: 5.8%

Percentage of students applying for internship in 2017 accepted into:

APA internships: 100% **APPIC internships:** 100%

Formal tracks/concentrations: Clinical Health Psychology; Clinical Neuropsychology; Forensic Psychology

Research areas	# Faculty	# Grants
ACT interventions with children	1	1
Bipolar disorder	1	1
Clinical neuropsychology	3	2
Forensic psychology	2	2
Multiculturalism	3	1
Posttraumatic stress disorder	1	0
Psychotherapy Outcomes and Process	1	1

Clinical opportunities
children, adolescent, and adult populations
inpatient, outpatient, VA, and correctional settings

Northern Illinois University (Ph.D.)

Department of Psychology
DeKalb, IL 60115
phone#: (815) 753-2485
email: lpittman@niu.edu
Web address: http://niu.edu/psychology/academics/graduate/clinical/index.shtml

1	2	3	4	**5**	6	7
Practice oriented			Equal emphasis			Research oriented

Percentage of faculty subscribing to each of the following orientations:

Psychodynamic/Psychoanalytic	0%
Applied behavioral analysis/Radical behavioral	22%
Family systems/Systems	33%
Existential/Phenomenological/Humanistic	11%
Cognitive/Cognitive-behavioral	100%
Interpersonal	22%

Courses required for incoming students prior to enrolling: none

Recommended but not mandatory courses: statistics, research methods, laboratory course

GRE mean
Verbal 158 Quantitative 157
Analytical Writing 4.5
Psychology Subject Test not reported

GPA mean
Overall GPA 3.75

Number of applications/admission offers/incoming students in 2017
247 applied/14 admission offers/8 incoming

% of students receiving:
Full tuition waiver only: 0%
Assistantship/fellowship only: 0%
Both full tuition waiver & assistantship/fellowship: 100%

Approximate percentage of incoming students with a B.A./B.S. only: 87.5% **Master's:** 12.5%

Approximate percentage of all students who are Women: 75% **Ethnic Minority:** 20% **International:** 2%

Average years to complete the doctoral program (including internship): 7.1

Personal interview
Preferred in person but telephone acceptable

Attrition rate in past 7 years: 8%

Percentage of students applying for internship in 2017 accepted into:

APA internships: 100% **APPIC internships:** 100%

Formal tracks/concentrations: none

Research areas	# Faculty	# Grants
adolescents	2	0
adult psychopathology	4	0
anxiety/OCD-related disorders	3	0
child sexual abuse	2	0
college students	6	0
co-parenting	1	0
developmental psychopathology	4	0
diversity/culture	3	0
early childhood	2	1
emergency responders	1	0
emotion/emotion regulation	5	2
grandparents	1	0
infants and preschool age children	2	0
intimate partner violence	2	0
parenting	3	0
personality/personality disorders	2	0
physical abuse	2	1
psychometrics	2	0
PTSD	3	1
school-age children	3	0
self-regulation	1	1
sexual aggression	1	0
Socioeconomic stress	1	0
social support	1	0
temperament	1	1
trauma	4	1

Clinical opportunities
ADHD
Anger management groups
anxiety disorders
Autism spectrum disorder
Child psychotherapy
Cognitive assessment
College students
Consultation and multi-disciplinary assessment
Developmental assessments
Developmental disabilities
Family psychotherapy
Group psychotherapy
Individual psychotherapy
Intensive outpatient settings
Parent training
School settings
Selective mutism
Trauma/PTSD

Northwestern University (Ph.D.)

Department of Psychology
102 Swift Hall, 2029 Sheridan Road
Evanston, IL 60208-2710
phone#: (847) 491-5190
email: psychology@northwestern.edu
Web address: www.wcas.northwestern.edu/psych/

1	2	3	4	5	6	**7**
Practice oriented			Equal emphasis			Research oriented

Percentage of faculty subscribing to each of the following orientations:

Psychodynamic/Psychoanalytic	0%
Applied behavioral analysis/Radical behavioral	0%
Family systems/Systems	10%
Existential/Phenomenological/Humanistic	0%
Cognitive/Cognitive-behavioral	90%

Courses required for incoming students to have completed prior to enrolling: none

Recommended but not mandatory courses: Psychology major, undergraduate statistics

GRE mean
Verbal + Quantitative 1488
Analytical Writing 5.1
Psychology Subject Test not reported

GPA mean
Overall GPA 3.8

Number of applications/admission offers/incoming students in 2016
86 applied/8 admission offers/5 incoming

% of students receiving:
Full tuition waiver only: 0%
Assistantship/fellowship only: 0%
Both full tuition waiver & assistantship/fellowship: 100%

Approximate percentage of incoming students with a B.A./B.S. only: 100% **Master's:** 0%

Approximate percentage of all students who are Women: 75% **Ethnic Minority:** 38% **International:** 25%

Average years to complete the doctoral program (including internship): 6 years

Personal interview
not reported

Attrition rate in past 7 years: 5%

Percentage of students applying for internship in 2016 accepted into:

APA internships: 100% **APPIC internships:** 100%

Formal tracks/concentrations: none

Research areas	# Faculty	# Grants
anxiety	3	1
behavioral genetics	2	0
cognitive functioning	4	2
depression	3	2
personality	5	3
psychosis	1	6
psychotherapy	2	1

Clinical opportunities
anxiety disorders
children
couples
depression
diagnostic interviewing
family
personality disorders

Northwestern University, Feinberg School of Medicine (Ph.D.)

Department of Psychiatry and Behavioral Sciences
Division of Psychology
Abbott Hall, Suite 1205
710 North Lakeshore Drive
Chicago, IL 60611
phone#: (312) 908-8262
email: clinpsych@northwestern.edu
Web address: www.clinpsych.northwestern.edu

1	2	3	4	5	6	7
Practice oriented			Equal emphasis			Research oriented

Percentage of faculty subscribing to each of the following orientations:

Psychodynamic/Psychoanalytic	15%
Applied behavioral analysis/Radical behavioral	0%
Family systems/Systems	20%
Existential/Phenomenological/Humanistic	0%
Cognitive/Cognitive-behavioral	65%

Courses required for incoming students to have completed prior to enrolling:
Statistics and research design, experimental psychology, abnormal psychology

Recommended but not mandatory courses: Behavioral Neuroscience, Cognitive Psychology, Social Psychology, Lifespan Developmental Psychology, History & Systems

GRE mean (we have converted to the new GRE metric for our 5-year means)
Verbal 160.7 (84.0th percentile)
Quantitative 157.2 (69.5th percentile)
Analytical Writing 4.7 (78.3th percentile)
Psychology Subject Test No longer required

GPA mean
Overal GPA 3.7

Number of applications/admission offers/incoming students in 2017
323 applied/5 admission offers/4 incoming

% of students receiving:
Full tuition waiver only: 0%
Assistantship/fellowship only: 0%
Both full tuition waiver & assistantship/fellowship: 100%

Approximate percentage of incoming students with a B.A./B.S. only: 50% **Master's:** 50%

Approximate percentage of students who are Women: 90% **Ethnic Minority:** 21% **International:** 6%

Average years to complete the doctoral program (including internship): 5.8 years (median = 5.8 years)

Personal interview
Required in person

Attrition rate in past 7 years: 0% **(0 out of 51)**

Percentage of students applying for internship in 2017 accepted into:

APA internships: 100% **APPIC internships:**

Formal tracks/concentrations: behavioral medicine/health psychology (Major Area of Study), clinical neuropsychology (Major Area of Study), adult clinical, clinical child & adolescent (Major Area of Study), policy; forensic

Research areas	# Faculty	# Grants
Adoption/Foster Care	3	2
Affective Disorders	5	6
Alcohol	1	1
Alzheimer's Disease	2	1
Assessment/Diagnosis	2	3
Autism Spectrum Disorders	1	2
Brain Injury/Head Injury	1	1
Cardiovascular Health	1	1
Child Abuse/Neglect/Sexual Abuse	3	2
Clinical Child/Pediatric	4	2
Chronic Disease/Illness	2	2
Cognitive-Behavioral Therapy	2	0
Eating Disorders/Body Image	1	1
Forensic/Psychology & Law	4	1
Gay/Lesbian/Bisexual	2	3
Genetics/Behavioral Genetics	1	2
Health Psychology/Behavioral Med	8	10
Intervention/Treatment	5	3
Mental Health Services/Policy	3	2
Mindfulness	1	1
Neuroimaging	5	3
Neuropsychology	6	2
Nicotine/Tobacco/Smoking	1	1
Oncology/Cancer Care	3	1
PTSD/Trauma	3	2

Program Evaluation	4	3
Psychometrics/Measurement	2	1
Psychopathology-Adult/General	4	2
Psychopathology-Child/Developmental	5	3
Psychophysiology/Biology	1	1
Schizophrenia	2	1
Sleep Disorders	1	1
Suicide	2	1
Technology & Practice	2	3

Clinical opportunities
adult, adolescent, and child outpatient clinics, inpatient psychiatry, outpatient & inpatient medical/surgical specialty clinics, primary care, chronic mental illness, clinical neuropsychology (adult and pediatric)

University of Notre Dame (Ph.D.)

Department of Psychology
118 Haggar Hall
Notre Dame, IN 46556
phone#: (574) 631-6650
email: gradad@nd.edu
Web address: http://psychology.nd.edu/graduate-programs/areas-of-study/clinical/

1 2 3 4 5 **6** 7

Practice oriented — Equal emphasis — Research oriented

Percentage of faculty subscribing to each of the following orientations:

Psychodynamic/Psychoanalytic	0%
Applied behavioral analysis/Radical behavioral	5%
Family systems/Systems	20%
Existential/Phenomenological/Humanistic	0%
Cognitive/Cognitive-behavioral	75%
3rd wave behavioral (e.g., ACT, DBT)	35%

Courses required for incoming students to have completed prior to enrolling: research methods, statistics

Recommended but not mandatory courses: abnormal, personality, cognitive, psychobiology, social, developmental, history and systems.

GRE mean
Verbal 159 Quantitative 153
Analytical Writing 4.5
Psychology Subject Test 0

GPA mean
Overall GPA: 3.62

Number of applications/admission offers/incoming students in 2017–2018
165 applied/7 admission offers/4 incoming students

% of students receiving in 2017–2018:
Full tuition waiver only: 0%
Assistantship/fellowship only: 0%
Both full tuition waiver & assistantship/fellowship: 100%

Approximate percentage of incoming 2017–2018 students with a BA/BS only: 75% **Master's:** 25%

Approximate percentage of all students who are Women: 75% **Ethnic Minority:** 40% **International:** 25%

Average years to complete the doctoral program (including internship): about 6 years

Personal interview
In-person strongly preferred; phone interviews can be arranged

Attrition rate in past 7 years: 8%

Percentage of students applying for internship for 2017–2018 accepted into:

APA internships: 100% **APPIC internships:** 100%

Formal tracks/concentrations: none

Research areas	# Faculty	# Grants
depression	3	1
personality disorders	2	1
behavioral medicine	2	0
trauma and abuse	1	1
developmental psychopathology	3	2
stress	3	2
self-disclosure	1	1

Clinical opportunities

personality disorders	anxiety
depression	behavioral medicine
parent-child interventions	eating disorders
infant neurodevelopmental	neuropsychological
couples therapy	assessment
childhood adversity	

Nova Southeastern University (Ph.D.)

Center for Psychological Studies
3301 College Avenue
Fort Lauderdale, FL 33314
phone#: (800) 541-6682, ext. 25790; (954) 262-5790
email: gradschool@nova.edu
Web Address: psychology.nova.edu/graduate/clinical-psychology/phd/index.html

1 2 3 4 **5** 6 7

Practice Oriented — Equal Emphasis — Research Oriented

Percentage of faculty subscribing to each of the following orientations:

Psychodynamic/Psychoanalytic	5%
Applied behavioral analysis/Radical behavioral	2%
Family systems/Systems	0%
Existential/Phenomenological/Humanistic	4%
Cognitive/Cognitive-behavioral	89%

Courses required for incoming students to have completed prior to enrolling:
18 credits in psychology and 3 credits in statistics

Recommended but not mandatory courses: Courses in statistics and experimental psychology. Biology courses for health and neuropsychology concentrations.

GRE mean
Verbal 156 Quantitative 154
Analytical Writing 4.3
Psychology Subject Test 640

GPA mean
Overall GPA 3.46

Number of applications/admission offers/incoming students 2015:
175 applicants/16 admission offers/9 incoming students

% of students receiving:
Full tuition waiver only: 0%
Assistantship/fellowship only: 0%
Both full tuition waiver & assistantship/fellowship: 0%

Approximate percentage of incoming students with B.A./B.S. only: 90% **Master's:** 10%

Approximate percentage of all students who are Women: 70% **Ethnic Minority:** 24% **International:** 8%

Average years to complete the doctoral program (including internship): 6.1 years

Personal interview:
Required in person

Percentage of students applying for internship into 2015 accepted into:

APA internships: 100% (5 students)
APPIC internships: 0% (0 students)

Formal tracks/concentrations: Child, Adolescent, and Family; Multi-cultural/Diversity; Forensic; Neuropsychology; Clinical Health; Psychodynamic Psychotherapy; and Long-Term Mental Illness

Research Areas	#Faculty	#Grants
ADHD	1	1
Childhood Learning	1	1
Domestic Violence	1	1
Memory Loss/Aging	1	1
Neurobiology	1	1
PTSD	1	1
Sleep	1	1
Substance Abuse	1	2

Clinical Opportunities
anxiety disorders
severe behavior disorders
behavior modification
biofeedback
child/adolescent
child/adolescent traumatic stress and depression
health psychology
psychodynamic
crisis assessment and intervention
depression
family and multifamily
forensic evaluation and testimony
group therapy
interpersonal violence
multilingual services
neuropsychological assessment
pain management
parenting skills and training
psychological testing
serious emotional disturbance
stress management
substance abuse
trauma

Nova Southeastern University (Psy.D.)

Center for Psychological Studies
3301 College Avenue
Fort Lauderdale, FL 33314
phone#: (800) 541-6682, ext. 25790; (954) 262-5790
email: gradschool@nova.edu
Web Address: psychology.nova.edu/graduate/clinical-psychology/psyd/index.html

1	2	3	4	5	6	7
Practice Oriented			Equal Emphasis			Research Oriented

Percentage of faculty subscribing to each of the following orientations:

Psychodynamic/Psychoanalytic	5%
Applied behavioral analysis/Radical behavioral	2%
Family systems/Systems	0%
Existential/Phenomenological/Humanistic	4%
Cognitive/Cognitive-behavioral	89%

Courses required for incoming students to have completed prior to enrolling:
18 credits in psychology and 3 credits in statistics

Recommended but not mandatory courses: Courses in statistics and experimental psychology. Biology courses for health and neuropsychology concentrations.

GRE mean
Verbal 153 Quantitative 149
Analytical Writing 3.9
Psychology Subject Test 630

GPA mean
Overall GPA 3.48

Number of applications/admission offers/incoming students 2015:
346 applicants/160 admission offers/81 incoming students

% of students receiving:
Full tuition waiver only: 0%
Assistantship/fellowship only: 0%
Both full tuition waiver & assistantship/fellowship: 0%

Approximate percentage of incoming students with B.A./B.S. only: 85% **Master's:** 15%

Approximate percentage of all students who are Women: 81% **Ethnic Minority:** 33% **International:** 4%

Average years to complete the doctoral program (including internship): 5.3 years

Personal interview:
Required in person

Percentage of students applying for internship into 2015 accepted into:

APA internships: 85% (65 students)
APPIC internships: 14% (11 students)

Formal tracks/concentrations: Child, Adolescent, and Family; Multi-cultural/Diversity; Forensic; Neuropsychology; Clinical Health; Psychodynamic Psychotherapy; and Long-Term Mental Illness

Research Areas	#Faculty	#Grants
ADHD	1	1
Childhood Learning	1	1
Domestic Violence	1	1
Memory Loss/Aging	1	1
Neurobiology	1	1

PTSD	1	1
Sleep	1	1
Substance Abuse	1	2

Clinical Opportunities

anxiety disorders
severe behavior disorders
behavior modification
biofeedback
child/adolescent
child/adolescent traumatic stress and depression
health psychology
psychodynamic
crisis assessment and intervention
depression
family and multifamily
forensic evaluation and testimony
group therapy
interpersonal violence
multilingual services
neuropsychological assessment
pain management
parenting skills and training
psychological testing
serious emotional disturbance
stress management
substance abuse
trauma

Ohio University (Ph.D.)

Department of Psychology
Athens, OH 45701-2979
phone#: (740) 593-1707
email: psychology@ohio.edu
Web address: www.ohioupsychology.edu/Graduate-Clinical-General.html

1	2	3	4	5	**6**	7
Practice oriented			Equal emphasis			Research oriented

Percentage of faculty subscribing to each of the following orientations:

Psychodynamic/Psychoanalytic	30%
Applied behavioral analysis/Radical behavioral	0%
Family systems/Systems	30%
Existential/Phenomenological/Humanistic	30%
Cognitive/Cognitive-behavioral	80%

Courses required for incoming students to have completed prior to enrolling: none

Recommended but not mandatory courses: at least 27 quarter hours/18 semester hours in psychology, including statistics, research methods

GRE mean
Verbal 162 Quantitative 162
Analytical Writing not reported
Psychology Subject Test not reported

GPA mean
Overall GPA 3.63

Number of applications/admission offers/incoming students in 2017
142 applied/9 admission offers/6 incoming

% of students receiving:
Full tuition waiver only: 0%
Assistantship/fellowship only: 0%
Both full tuition waiver & assistantship/fellowship: 100%

Approximate percentage of incoming students with a B.A./B.S. only: 80% **Master's:** 20%

Approximate percentage of all students who are Women: 75% **Ethnic Minority:** 20% **International:** 12%

Average years to complete the doctoral program (including internship): 7 years

Personal interview
Preferred in person but telephone acceptable

Attrition rate in past 7 years: 9%

Percentage of students applying for internship in 2017 accepted into:

APA internships: 100% **APPIC internships:**

Formal tracks/concentrations: child clinical, clinical health, clinical neuro, quantitative

Research areas	# Faculty	# Grants
adult psychopathology	4	2
family and child	3	3
health psychology	1	1
sexual assault/trauma	2	1
substance abuse	1	1
neuropsychology	1	0

Clinical opportunities

adult psychotherapy
school consultation
cardiac rehabilitation
veterans
rural settings
substance abuse
pain management
child and family
primary care patients
neuropsychology
older adults
socioeconomic disadvantage
trauma

Ohio State University (Ph.D.)

Department of Psychology
108 Psychology Building
1835 Neil Avenue Mall
Columbus, OH 43210
phone#: (614) 292-4112
email: emery.33@osu.edu
Web address: www2.psy.ohio-state.edu/programs/clinical/

1	2	3	4	5	**6**	7
Practice oriented			Equal emphasis			Research oriented

Percentage of faculty subscribing to each of the following orientations:

Psychodynamic/Psychoanalytic	0%
Applied behavioral analysis/Radical behavioral	0%
Family systems/Systems	0%
Existential/Phenomenological/Humanistic	0%
Cognitive/Cognitive-behavioral	100%

Courses required for incoming students prior to enrolling:
Experimental/research methods, abnormal, statistics

Recommended but not mandatory courses: none

GRE mean
Verbal 89th percentile Quantitative 73rd percentile

Analytical Writing 4.9
Psychology Subject Test not reported

GPA mean
Psychology GPA 3.71

Number of applications/admission offers/incoming students in 2016
219 applied/18 admission offers/9 incoming

% of students receiving:
Full tuition waiver only: 0%
Assistantship/fellowship only: 0%
Both full tuition waiver & assistantship/fellowship: 100%

Approximate percentage of incoming students with a B.A./B.S. only: 78% **Master's:** 22%

Approximate percentage of all students who are Women: 56% **Ethnic Minority:** 44% **International:** 0%

Average years to complete the doctoral program (including internship): 6.02 years

Personal interview
Preferred in person but telephone acceptable

Attrition rate in past 7 years: 16%

Percentage of students applying for internship in 2016 accepted into:

APA internships: 100% **APPIC internships:** 100%

Formal tracks/concentrations: adult, child, health

Research areas	# Faculty	# Grants
anxiety disorders	1	0
cardiovascular health	1	3
pulmonary health	1	2
child psychopathology	2	4
childhood mood disorders	2	4
depression	3	2
oncology	1	7
personality	1	2
psychoneuroimmunology	1	5
clinical neuroscience	1	2

Clinical opportunities

anxiety disorder	substance use disorders
depression	personality disorders
child and adolescent	gerontology
psychosis	health psychology
childhood mood disorders	neuropsychology
oncology	depressive disorders
eating disorders	sex therapy

Oklahoma State University (Ph.D.)

Department of Psychology
116 North Murray Hall
Stillwater, OK 74078
phone#: (405) 744-6027
email: clinicalpsychology@okstate.edu
Web address: http://psychology.okstate.edu

1	2	3	4	5	6	7
Practice oriented			Equal emphasis			Research oriented

Percentage of faculty subscribing to each of the following orientations:

Psychodynamic/Psychoanalytic	0%
Applied behavioral analysis/Radical behavioral	0%
Family systems/Systems	10%
Existential/Phenomenological/Humanistic	0%
Cognitive/Cognitive-behavioral	90%

Courses required for incoming students to have completed prior to enrolling:
statistics or quantitative methods, experimental psychology

Recommended but not mandatory courses: abnormal psychology

GRE mean
Verbal 159 Quantitative 154
Analytical Writing 4.5
Psychology Subject Test not reported

GPA mean
Overall GPA 3.77

Number of applications/admission offers/incoming students in 2016
148 applied/13 admission offers/7 incoming

% of students receiving:
Full tuition waiver only: 0%
Assistantship/fellowship only: 0%
Both full tuition waiver & assistantship/fellowship: 100%

Approximate percentage of incoming students with a B.A./B.S. only: 90% **Master's:** 10%

Approximate percentage of all students who are Women: 75% **Ethnic Minority:** 25% **International:** not reported

Average years to complete the doctoral program (including internship): 5 years

Personal interview
We require attendance at an interview weekend in February

Attrition rate in past 7 years: 10%

Percentage of students applying for internship in 2016 accepted into:

APA internships: 100% **APPIC internships:**

Formal tracks/concentrations: child clinical, behavioral medicine/health psychology, pediatric psychology

Research areas	# Faculty	# Grants
anxiety disorders	1	1
health psychology	2	2
pediatric psychology	3	3
substance abuse	2	0
depression	1	1
child/parenting	1	0
personality	1	0
attention	1	1

Clinical opportunities

anxiety/mood disorder	couple therapy
trauma	pediatric psychology
behavioral medicine	substance abuse
family therapy	geropsychology

neuropsychology
group therapy
primary care
consultation

University of Oregon (Ph.D.)

Department of Psychology
Eugene, OR 97403
phone#: (541) 346-5060
email: lolsen@uoregon.edu
Web address: https://psychology.uoregon.edu/research/research-areas/clinical/

1	2	3	4	5	**6**	7
Practice oriented			Equal emphasis			Research oriented

Percentage of faculty subscribing to each of the following orientations:

Psychodynamic/Psychoanalytic	0%
Applied behavioral analysis/Radical behavioral	20%
Family systems/Systems	20%
Existential/Phenomenological/Humanistic	0%
Cognitive/Cognitive-behavioral	60%

Courses required for incoming students to have completed prior to enrolling:
Good background in psychology; some direct services experience

Recommended but not mandatory courses: Research, statistics or math background

GRE mean
Verbal 163 Quantitative 162
Analytical Writing 4.4
Psychology Subject Test not required

GPA mean
Overall GPA 3.86

Number of applications/admission offers/incoming students in 2017
246 applied/8 admission offers/5 incoming

% of students receiving:
Full tuition waiver only: 0%
Assistantship/fellowship only: 0%
Both full tuition waiver & assistantship/fellowship: 100%

Approximate percentage of incoming students with a B.A./B.S. only: 80% **Master's:** 20%

Approximate percentage of students who are Women: 85% **Ethnic Minority:** 27% **International:** 9%

Average years to complete the doctoral program (including internship): 6.3 years

Personal interview
Preferred in person but telephone acceptable under special circumstances

Attrition rate in past 7 years: 5%

Percentage of students applying for internship in 2017 accepted into:

APA internships: 100% **APPIC internships:** 100%

Formal tracks/concentrations: please visit departmental website at https://psychology.uoregon.edu/

Research areas	# Faculty	# Grants
Cultural psychology	1	0
Developmental psychopathology	4	5
Depressive disorders	2	3
Trauma/maltreatment	2	1
Personality disorders	1	1
Infancy	1	0
Translational Neuroscience	4	4
Sleep	2	1
Parenting	3	2
Prevention Science	2	1

Clinical opportunities
Anxiety disorders
Mood disorders
Personality disorders
Sleep
Family/parenting intervention
Marital
Trauma
Adolescence
Child, family, and adult assessment
Neuropsychology
Cognitive behavior therapy
Prevention science

Pacific University (Psy.D.)

School of Graduate Psychology
190 SE 8th Avenue, Suite 260
Hillsboro, OR 97123
phone#: (503) 352-7322
email: pmenke@pacificu.edu (Admissions)
Web address: www.pacificu.edu/spp/clinical/index.cfm

1	2	**3**	4	5	6	7
Practice oriented			Equal emphasis			Research oriented

Percentage of faculty subscribing to each of the following orientations:

Psychodynamic/Psychoanalytic	15%
Applied behavioral analysis	5%
Family systems/Systems	15%
Existential/Phenomenological/Humanistic	5%
Cognitive/Cognitive-behavioral	65%
Integrative	20%

Courses required for incoming students to have completed prior to enrolling:
A psychology major is not required; however, a math-based statistics course and Abnormal Psychology are required prerequisites. In addition, 2 of the 6 following courses are required as preparation for work at the graduate level: Clinical Psychology, Experimental Psychology, Social Psychology, Cognition/Learning, Introduction to Psychology, Physiological Psychology, Developmental Psychology, Personality Psychology. Prerequisite courses must be completed with an average of "B" or above before a student can matriculate into the program.

Recommended but not mandatory courses: n/a

GRE mean for incoming students matriculating in 2017
Verbal 155 (equivalent to 550 on the old GRE)
Quantitative 150 (equivalent to 575 on the old GRE)
GRE Analytical Writing 4.2
Psychology Subject Test not required

GPA mean for incoming students matriculating in 2017
Overall GPA 3.45

Number of applications/admission offers/incoming students in 2017
280 applied/115 admission offers/52 incoming

% of students receiving:
Full tuition waiver only: 0%
Assistantship/fellowship only: 18%
Both full tuition waiver & assistantship/fellowship: 0%

Approximate percentage of incoming students with a B.A./B.S. only: 63% **Master's:** 37%

Approximate percentage of students who are Women: 77% **Ethnic Minority:** 30% **International:** <1%

Average years to complete the doctoral program (including internship): 5.6 years

Personal interview
Required in person interview

Attrition rate in past 7 years: 14%

Percentage of students applying for internship in 2017 accepted into:

APA internships: 71% **APPIC internships:** 25%

Formal tracks/concentrations: Adult, Child, Forensic, Neuropsychology, Health

Research areas	# Faculty	# Grants
Health Psychology and Behavioral Medicine	5	0
Cultural Psychology and Diversity	8	0
Forensic Psychology	4	0
Child and Adolescent Psychology	5	0
Neuropsychology	2	0
Interdisciplinary Approaches and Care	5	0
Anxiety disorders	2	0
Eating Disorders	3	0
Organizational behavior	1	0
Trauma	4	0
Child Welfare and Families	3	0
Pediatric Psychology	2	0
Gender and Sexuality	4	0
Latino Mental Health	3	0
Personality Disorders and Psychopathy	1	0
Community Based Research	2	0
Yoga Therapy	1	0
Sports Psychology	1	0
Qualitative Research	5	0

Clinical opportunities
2 in-house training clinics: Pacific Psychology and Comprehensive Health Clinic, Hillsboro; Pacific Psychology and Comprehensive Health Clinic, Portland
Approximately 102 community sites

Palo Alto University, Pacific Graduate School of Psychology (Ph.D.)

Department of Clinical Psychology
935 East Meadow
Palo Alto, CA 94303
phone#: (800) 818-6136
email: admissions@paloaltou.edu
Web address: www.paloaltou.edu/phd-clinical-psychology

1	2	3	**4**	5	6	7
Practice oriented			Equal emphasis			Research oriented

Percentage of faculty subscribing to each of the following orientations:

Psychodynamic/Psychoanalytic	not reported
Applied behavioral analysis/Radical behavioral	not reported
Family systems/Systems	not reported
Existential/Phenomenological/Humanistic	not reported
Cognitive/Cognitive-behavioral	not reported

Courses required for incoming students to have completed prior to enrolling: B.A./B.S. in Psychology or the equivalent of courses in statistics, biological bases of behavior,, abnormal psychology, developmental psychology; entrance interview required with PhD faculty and approval by the Director of Clinical Training

Recommended but not mandatory courses: research methods, personality psychology, physiological psychology, cognitive and/or social psychology; a solid academic background including research experience

GRE mean for students admitted in 2017:
Verbal + Quantitative 304
Analytical Writing 4.1
Psychology Subject Test not reported

GPA mean for students admitted in 2017:
undergraduate GPA 3.34

Number of applications/admission offers/incoming students in 2017:
306 applicants
83 incoming students

% of students receiving financial aid in 2016-2017:
Of 469 students receiving financial aid, 2.56% received a partial tuition waiver and 8.53% received a fellowship.

Approximate percentage of incoming students with a B.A./B.S. only: 100% **Master's:** 42.2%

Approximate percentage of all students who are Women: 78% **People of Color:** 39.2% **(Asian:** 13%, **African American:** 5.5%, **Hispanic/Latinx** 11.7%, **Two or more races** 8.2%, **Native American:** 0.4%, **Native Hawaiian/Pacific Islander** 0.4%, **Unknown:** 6.9%**)** **International:** 7.9%

Average years to complete the doctoral program (including internship): 5.81

Personal interview: Required personal or phone interview required

Attrition rate in past 7 years: 13%

Percentage of students applying for internship in 2016 accepted into:

APA internships: 98% **APPIC internships:** 2%

Formal tracks/concentrations: neuropsychology, forensics, child and family, health, community and diversity, LGBTQ, trauma.

Research areas	# Faculty
adult psychopathology	20
aging	2
assessment	2
bereavement	1
children	4
culture	5
forensics	2
health psychology	4
LGBTQ	3
minority aging	2
neuropsychology	3
neuropsychology & aging	1
psychology & law	2
psychotherapy	5
substance abuse	2

Number of faculty with research grants in the past 7 years: 12

Clinical opportunities

Students obtain formal clinical training through the Bay Area Practicum Information Collaborative (BAPIC), which includes over 200 external practica sites.

Palo Alto University/PGSP-Stanford PsyD Consortium (Psy.D.)

1791 Arastradero Road
Palo Alto, CA, 94304
phone#: (650) 433-3810
email: slien@paloaltou.edu
Web address: https://www.paloaltou.edu/graduate-programs/pgsp-psyd-stanford-consortium

1	2	3	4	5	6	7
Practice oriented			Equal emphasis			Research oriented

Percentage of faculty subscribing to each of the following orientations:

Psychodynamic/Psychoanalytic	15%
Applied behavioral analysis/Radical behavioral	0%
Family systems/Systems	15%
Existential/Phenomenological/Humanistic	10%
Cognitive/Cognitive-behavioral	60%

Courses required for incoming students to have completed prior to enrolling:

No specific courses are required but successful applicant needs to demonstrate sufficient foundational coursework in psychology or *obtain a score of 680 or higher on the Psychology GRE.*

Recommended but not mandatory courses:

abnormal, biopsychology, developmental, and statistics/research methods

GRE mean (incoming class 2017–2018)

Verbal 159 Quantitative 156
Analytical Writing 4.7
Psychology Subject Test 728 (not required)

GPA mean (incoming class 2017–2018)

Overall undergraduate GPA 3.7

Number of applications/interviews/admission offers/incoming students for 2017-18

369 applications/89 interviews/55 admission offers/30 incoming students

% of students receiving:

Full tuition waiver only: 0%
Assistantship/fellowship only: approximately 60% of each incoming cohort (3-year fellowship)
Both full tuition waiver & assistantship/fellowship: 0%

Approximate percentage of incoming students with a B.A./B.S. only: 75% **Master's:** 25%

Approximate percentage of all students who are Women: 85% **Ethnic Minority:** 30% **International:** 2%

Average years to complete the doctoral program (including internship): 5.0 years

Personal interview

Required. In person strongly preferred but videoconferencing modalities acceptable

Attrition rate in past 7 years: 1%

Percentage of students applying for internship in 2017 accepted into:

APA internships: 100% **APPIC internships:** 100%

Formal tracks/concentrations: child emphasis

Research areas	# Faculty	# Grants
anxiety disorders	3	2
autism spectrum disorders	3	3
behavioral medicine	3	4
bullying	1	1
couples and families	2	0
depression/bipolar	2	2
diversity	4	2
eating disorders	6	9
evidenced based practice	7	4
pediatrics	3	1
psychology training	2	0
psychosis	2	1
sleep disorders	2	4
sports psychology	2	1
substance use	2	1
suicide	2	2
telemental health/virtual reality	3	3
trauma/PTSD	4	3

Clinical opportunities

academic/VA medical centers
anxiety disorders (e.g., OCD, PTSD)
behavioral medicine
bilingual therapy opportunities (e.g., Spanish, Mandarin, Cantonese, Russian)
geropsychology
homeless
inpatient units
intensive outpatient/partial hospital
LGBT
mood disorders

child/adolescent/pediatrics
college counseling
community-based agencies
cross-cultural
dialectical behavior therapy
eating disorders
evidence-based treatment
neuropsychology
rehabilitation
schools
serious mental illness
substance abuse
women's health

University of Pennsylvania (Ph.D.)

Department of Psychology
425 S. University Avenue
Philadelphia, PA 19104-6018
phone#: (215) 898-4712
email: yc@sas.upenn.edu
Web address: http://psychology.sas.upenn.edu/training-programs/clinical-training-program

1	2	3	4	5	6	**7**
Practice oriented			Equal emphasis			Research oriented

Percentage of faculty subscribing to each of the following orientations:

Psychodynamic/Psychoanalytic	0%
Applied behavioral analysis/Radical behavioral	0%
Family systems/Systems	0%
Existential/Phenomenological/Humanistic	0%
Cognitive/Cognitive-behavioral	100%

Courses required for incoming students to have completed prior to enrolling: none

Recommended but not mandatory courses: Statistics

GRE mean
Verbal 169 Quantitative 165
Analytical Writing 5.3
Psychology Subject Test n/a

GPA mean
Overall GPA 3.82

Number of applications/admission offers/incoming students in 2016
416 applied/5 admission offers/3 incoming

% of students receiving:
Full tuition waiver only: 0%
Assistantship/fellowship only: 0%
Both full tuition waiver & assistantship/fellowship: 100%

Approximate percentage of incoming students with a B.A./B.S. only: 100% **Master's:** 0%

Approximate percentage of students who are Women: 80% **Ethnic Minority:** 20% **International:** 10%

Average years to complete the doctoral program (including internship): 6 years

Personal interview
Required in person

Attrition rate in past 7 years: 9%

Percentage of students applying for internship in 2016 accepted into:

APA internships: 100% **APPIC internships:** 100%

Formal tracks/concentrations: none

Research areas	# Faculty	# Grants
anxiety disorders	2	2
depression	1	1
autism spectrum disorders	1	1
positive psychology	1	3
developmental psychopathology	2	2

Clinical opportunities
anxiety disorders
assessment
autism spectrum disorders
behavioral therapy
behavioral weight loss program and assessment for bariatric surgery
child assessment and psychotherapy
cognitive therapy
couples therapy
depression
substance abuse/dual diagnosis

Pennsylvania State University (Ph.D.)

Department of Psychology
140 Bruce V. Moore Building
University Park, PA 16802
phone#: (814) 863-9519
email: paa6@psu.edu
Web address: psych.la.psu.edu/graduate/programAreas/clinicalProgram.html

1	2	3	4	**5**	6	7
Practice oriented			Equal emphasis			Research oriented

Percentage of faculty subscribing to each of the following orientations:

Psychodynamic/Psychoanalytic	14%
Applied behavioral analysis/Radical behavioral	7%
Family systems/Systems	31%
Existential/Phenomenological/Humanistic	7%
Cognitive/Cognitive-behavioral	41%

Courses required for incoming students prior to enrolling:
No course requirements. Broad psychology background preferred.

Recommended but not mandatory courses: Statistics and methodology

GRE mean
Verbal 162 Quantitative 161
Analytical Writing 4.9
Psychology Subject Test not reported

GPA mean
Overall GPA 3.68

Number of applications/admission offers/incoming students in 2017
443 applied/15 admission offers/10 admitted

% of students receiving:
Full tuition waiver only: 0%
Assistantship/fellowship only: 0%

Both full tuition waiver & assistantship/fellowship: 100%

Approximate percentage of incoming students with a B.A./B.S. only: 90% **Master's:** 10%

Approximate percentage of students who are Women: 80% **Ethnic Minority:** 20%
International: 1 student

Average years to complete the doctoral program (including internship): 7.0 years

Personal interview
Preferred in person but telephone acceptable

Attrition rate in past 7 years: 7%

Percentage of students applying for internship in 2017 accepted into:

APA internships: 100% **APPIC internships:** 0%

Formal tracks/concentrations: child and adult

Research areas	# Faculty	# Grants
adult psychopathology	7	4
affective disorders	4	0
anxiety disorders	4	2
behavioral medicine	3	0
child clinical/child psychopathology	5	3
cognition/information processing	5	0
developmental disabilities	1	0
emotions	3	1
family research/therapy	2	1
neuropsychology	3	4
parent–child interactions	3	2
personality assessment	1	1
personality development	2	0
personality disorders	4	1
psychoanalysis/psychodynamics	1	0
psychophysiology	3	3
psychotherapy process and outcome	4	4
relaxation/biofeedback	1	1
rural psychology	1	0
violence/abuse	3	1

Clinical opportunities
Pathologies (including Axis II), child, personality assessment, neuropsychology

Pepperdine University (Psy.D.)

Department of Psychology
Graduate School of Education and Psychology
6100 Center Drive
Los Angeles, CA 90045
Phone #: (310) 258-2850
email: Yasmin.Makki@pepperdine.edu
Web address: gsep.pepperdine.edu/doctorate-clinical-psychology/

1	2	**3**	4	5	6	7
Practice oriented			Equal emphasis			Research oriented

Percentage of faculty subscribing to each of the following orientations:

Psychodynamic/Psychoanalytic	52%
Applied behavioral analysis/Radical behavioral	1%
Family systems/Systems	62%
Existential/Phenomenological/Humanistic	45%
Cognitive/Cognitive-behavioral	79%
Multicultural/Community	31%

Courses required for incoming students prior to enrolling:
Applicants for doctoral study should possess a Master's degree in psychology or a closely related field that reflects a Master's-level foundation of knowledge in the following domains: biological aspects of behavior; cognitive and affective aspects of behavior; social aspects of behavior; psychological measurement; research methodology; and techniques of data analysis.

Recommended but not mandatory courses: Courses specific to applied clinical psychology, e.g., psychopathology, psychotherapy.

GRE mean
Verbal 152 Quantitative 149
Analytical Writing 4.2
Psychology Subject Test 572

GPA mean
Overall GPA 3.09 Master's GPA 3.90

Number of applications/admission offers/incoming students in 2017
75 applied/34 admission offers/29 incoming

% of students receiving:
Full tuition waiver only: 0%
Partial scholarship: 60%
Assistantship/fellowship only: 0%
Both tuition waiver & assistantship/fellowship: 10%

Approximate percentage of incoming students with a B.A./B.S. only: 0% **Master's:** 100%

Approximate percentage of all students who are Women: 87% **Ethnic Minority:** 57% **International:** 4%

Average years to complete the doctoral program (including internship): 5.2 years

Personal interview
Preferred in person but telephone acceptable (if living outside of California)

Attrition rate in past 7 years: 2.5%

Percentage of students applying for internship in 2017 accepted into:

APA internships: 79% **APPIC internships:** 79%

Formal tracks/concentrations: cognitive-behavioral therapy, psychodynamic psychotherapy, existential-humanistic, couple and family therapy, cultural-ecological and community-clinical interventions, psychological testing, including forensic assessment (subspecialty)

Research areas	# Faculty	# Grants
Trauma recovery, stress management, cultural context	3	0
Culture and context in families/communities	4	0

Psychotherapy research	3	1
Positive psychology, Well-Being, Resilience	2	0
Interpersonal neurobiology	1	0
Historical trauma, racism and mental health	3	0
Homelessness, substance abuse, assessment	2	1
Clinical supervision/training/ professional development	2	0
Recovery and evidence-based practice	1	1
Autism spectrum disorders	1	0
Relationships, couples therapy, communication	1	0
Multicultural community action, Latinx action research	2	0
Empirically-supported treatment and resources (youth)	1	1
College mental health and well-being	2	0
Religion and spirituality	3	0
Language and culture	1	0
Psychopathology	1	0

Clinical opportunities

Adolescence
Adoption/foster care
ADHD
AIDS/HIV
Alzheimer's disease/neurological disorders
Aging
Assessment
Autism/developmental disorders
Behavior therapy
Behavioral medicine
Child clinical
Cognitive behavioral therapy
Cognitive rehabilitation
Community psychology
Couple/family/systemic
Dialectical behavior therapy
Existential-humanistic
Eating disorders psychotherapy
Forensic psychology
Group
Homeless population
Infancy/early childhood
Inpatient
Mentalization-based therapy
Mindfulness-based therapies
Multicultural/cross-cultural
Neuropsychological testing
Traumatic stress/posttraumatic stress disorder
Psychodynamic psychotherapy
Rehabilitation
Schizophrenia/psychosis
Religion and spirituality
Severely/chronically mentally ill
Substance abuse/co-occurring disorders
School psychology
Traumatic stress/posttraumatic stress disorder
Veteran/military population

Philadelphia College of Osteopathic Medicine (Psy.D.)

Department of Psychology
4190 City Avenue
Philadelphia, PA 19131-1695
phone#: 215-871-6442
email: StephanieF@pcom.edu
Web address: http://www.pcom.edu/academics/programs-and-degrees/clinical-psychology/

1	**2**	3	4	5	6	7
Practice oriented			Equal emphasis			Research oriented

Percentage of faculty subscribing to each of the following orientations:

Psychodynamic/Psychoanalytic	0%
Applied behavioral analysis/Radical behavioral	0%
Family systems/Systems	0%
Existential/Phenomenological/Humanistic	0%
Cognitive/Cognitive-behavioral	100%

Courses required for incoming students to have completed prior to enrolling:
Theories of personality, psychopathology or abnormal psychology, statistics/research, and developmental psychology

Recommended but not mandatory courses: none

GRE mean
GRE not required for admission

GPA mean
Average Undergraduate GPA 3.46
Average Graduate GPA 3.8

Number of applications/admission offers/incoming students in 2017
133 applied/45 admission offers (acceptances)/26 matriculated

% of students receiving:
Full tuition waiver only: 0%
Full tuition scholarship: 2%
Assistantship/fellowship/scholarships: 32%

Approximate percentage of incoming students with a B.A./B.S. only: 0% **Master's:** 100%

Approximate percentage of students who are Women: 81% **Ethnic Minority:** 25% **International:** 1%

Average years to complete the doctoral program (including internship): 5.59 years (average across all 2008–2017 graduates)

Personal interview
Required in person

Attrition rate in past 7 years: 8%

Percentage of students applying for internship last year accepted into:

APA internships: 92% **APPIC internships:** 8%

Formal tracks/concentrations: none

Research areas	# Faculty	# Grants
clinical health psychology in primary care	2	0

evidence based practices	13	0
anxiety disorders	4	0
cognitive distortions	1	0
cognitive behavioral treatment of stress-related medical disorders	3	0
patient non-adherence to medical advice	1	0
anger	1	0
coping with chronic medical illnesses	3	1
personality disorders	1	0
pain management	1	0
somatization disorder	1	0
child and adolescent anxiety disorders	2	0
psychotherapy outcome & process research	2	0
memory and aging	1	0
psychological assessment	3	0
cognitive behavioral therapy for adult ADHD	1	0
personality assessment	3	0
social information processing in the development of children's aggressive behavior	1	0
impact of parental psychopathology on children	1	0
CBT treatment of mood & anxiety	7	0
multicultural issues	4	0
crisis/trauma	1	0
childhood sexual abuse	1	0
supervision/clinical training	1	0
eating disorders	1	1
serious mental illnesses	1	0
psychiatric rehabilitation	1	0
forensic assessment and treatment	1	0
mental health services research; program evaluation	1	0
professional development and psychologist self-care	1	0
ethics	1	0
substance abuse treatment	1	1
substance abuse & criminal justice	1	1

Clinical opportunities

culturally diverse, underserved	Advocacy
family medicine	children & adolescents
primary care	learning disorders
geriatric medicine	neuropsychology
outpatient cognitive behavior therapy clinic	trauma
internal medicine	ADHD
empirically based approaches	Inpatient
CBT	Personality disorders

University of Pittsburgh (Ph.D.)

Department of Psychology
Psychology Graduate Office
Sennott Square, 3rd Floor
210 South Bouquet Street
Pittsburgh, PA 15260
phone#: (412) 624-4502
email: psygrad@pitt.edu
Web address: www.psychology.pitt.edu/graduate/clinical-program

1	2	3	4	5	6	**7**
Practice oriented			Equal emphasis			Research oriented

Percentage of faculty subscribing to each of the following orientations:

Psychodynamic/Psychoanalytic	0%
Applied behavioral analysis/Radical behavioral	0%
Family systems/Systems	6%
Existential/Phenomenological/Humanistic	0%
Cognitive/Cognitive-behavioral	94%

Courses required for incoming students to have completed prior to enrolling: none

Recommended but not mandatory courses: Abnormal psychology, research methods, statistics; courses in biology, neuroscience, math, & computer science

GRE mean
Verbal 163 (89%tile) Quantitative 159 (73%tile)
Analytical Writing 4.7 (83%tile)
Psychology Subject Test 810 (99%tile)

GPA mean
Overall GPA 3.67

Number of applications/admission offers/incoming students in 2017
307 applied/15 admission offers/6 incoming

% of students receiving:
Full tuition waiver only: 0%
Assistantship/fellowship only: 0%
Both full tuition waiver & assistantship/fellowship: 100%

Approximate percentage of incoming students with a B.A./B.S. only: 100% **Master's:** 0%

Approximate percentage of students who are Women: 94% **Ethnic Minority:** 25% **International:** 7%

Average years to complete the doctoral program (including internship): 7 years

Personal interview
Preferred in person but telephone acceptable

Attrition rate in past 7 years: 11%

Percentage of students applying for internship in 2017 accepted into:

APA internships: 9/9 100%
APPIC internships: 9/9 100%

Concentrations: adult psychopathology, developmental psychopathology, health psychology

Research areas	# Faculty	# Grants*
adult psychopathology	10	14
affective/mood disorders/depression	5	17
substance abuse/addictions	5	10
alcohol	3	8
nicotine/tobacco/smoking	3	3
personality disorders	1	1
schizophrenia	1	0
eating disorders	1	0
child/developmental psychopathology	12	25
at-risk adolescents	4	15
attention-deficit disorder	1	6

autism	3	3
antisocial behavior	1	4
prevention	3	6
program evaluation	2	2
behavioral medicine/ health psychology	16	24
cardiovascular behavioral medicine	6	10
weight management	2	3
cancer/behavioral oncology	2	3
aging	1	3
sleep disorders	1	1
neuroimaging	14	31
behavioral genetics	6	10
psychoneuroimmunology	2	2
psychopharmacology	1	2
psychophysiology	5	7
emotion	4	13
social support	2	2
stress and coping	3	3

**Includes only PI grants*

Clinical opportunities

adolescent treatment
affective disorders/depression
aging/gerontology
anxiety disorders
assessment
attention-deficit disorder
autism
behavioral medicine
child treatment
cognitive-behavioral therapy
conduct disorder
chronic severe mental illness
eating disorders
emergency room assessment
family therapy
gay/lesbian
group therapy
inpatient
interpersonal therapy
minority populations
neuropsychological assessment
oncology
pain management
parent training
pediatric
personality disorders
schizophrenia
sleep disorders
substance abuse
suicide prevention
veterans medical center
victim/violence/ sexual abuse
weight management

Ponce Health Sciences University (Ph.D.)

Marcos Reyes, Ph.D.
Program Coordinator
School of Behavioral and Brain Sciences
388 Zona Ind Reparada 2
Ponce, PR 00716
phone#: (787) 840-2575 Ext 2569
email: marcosreyes@psm.edu / info@psm.edu
Web address: www.psm.edu

1 2 3 4 5 6 7

Practice oriented — Equal emphasis — Research oriented

Percentage of faculty subscribing to each of the following orientations:

Psychodynamic/Psychoanalytic	7%
Applied behavioral analysis/Radical behavioral	4%
Family systems/Systems	11%
Existential/Phenomenological/Humanistic	4%
Cognitive/Cognitive-behavioral	74%

Courses required for incoming students to have completed prior to enrolling:
At least 15 credits in Psychology at the Bachelor's level including de following courses:
General Psychology
Developmental Psychology
Statistics
Abnormal Psychology
Experimental Psychology or Research Methods

Recommended but not mandatory courses: none

GRE mean
Verbal + Quantitative 403
Analytical Writing 3.0

EXADEP total 520
Psychology Subject Test not required

GPA mean
Overall GPA 3.60

Number of applications/admission offers/incoming students in 2017
58 applied/27 admission offers/25 incoming

% of students receiving:
Full tuition waiver only: 0%
Assistantship/fellowship only: 0%
Both full tuition waiver & assistantship/fellowship: 0%

Approximate percentage of incoming students with a B.A./B.S. only: 84% **Master's:** 16%

Approximate percentage of all students who are Women: 71% **Ethnic Minority:** 100% **International:** 0.8%

Average years to complete the doctoral program (including internship): 5.5 years

Personal interview
Preferred in person but telephone acceptable

Attrition rate in past 7 years: 12%

Percentage of students applying for internship last year accepted into:

APA internships: 67% **APPIC internships:** 100%

Formal tracks/concentrations: Neuroscience, Family/Couples, Health Psychology, Forensic Psychology

Research areas	# Faculty	# Grants
Stigma	3	2
Child Obesity	1	1
Biomarkers	1	1
Forensic Psychology	1	0
Assessment	5	0
Alzheimer	1	0
Serious Mental Illness	2	0
Neurosciences	2	0
Epigenetics	1	1
School Psychology	2	0
HIV/AIDS	4	2
Health Psychology	4	1

Clinical opportunities
Borderline Personality Clinic
Severe Psychopatology

Psychology in General Hospitals
Pediatric Psychology in General Hospital
School Settings
Neuropsychology/Neurorehabilitation
Consultation
Domestic Violence
Psycho-oncology
Addictions
Family/Couples
Autism/Neurodevelopmental Disorders

Ponce Health Sciences University (Psy.D.)

Giselle M. Medina Vélez, Psy.D.
Program Coordinator
Clinical Psychology Program (Psy.D.)
PO Box 7004
Ponce, PR 00732-7004
(787) 840-2575 x 5502
gmedina@psm.edu
www.psm.edu

1	2	3	4	5	6	7
Practice oriented			Equal emphasis			Research oriented

Percentage of faculty subscribing to each of the following orientations:

Psychodynamic/Psychoanalytic	10%
Applied behavioral analysis/Radical behavioral	20%
Family systems/Systems	25%
Existential/Phenomenological/Humanistic	15%
Cognitive/Cognitive-behavioral	90%

Courses required for incoming students to have completed prior to enrolling:

General Psychology	3 credits
Developmental Psychology	3 credits
Statistics	3 credits
Abnormal Psychology	3 credits
Experimental Psychology or Research	3 credits

Recommended but not mandatory courses:
Psychoeducational Assessment and Professional Consultation in Academic Settings
Psychology of Gender

GRE mean
Verbal + Quantitative = 145 + 140 = 142.5
Analytical Writing = 3.2
Psychology Subject Test not reported

*EXADEP mean (Examen de Admisión a Estudios de Posgrado) Post Graduate Studies Admissions Exam 469.5

GPA mean
Overall GPA 3.45

***Number of applications/admission offers/incoming students in 2017**
79 applied/60 admission offers/60 incoming

% of students receiving:
Full tuition waiver only: 0%
Assistantship/fellowship only: 0%
Both full tuition waiver & assistantship/fellowship: 0%

Approximate percentage of incoming students with a B.A./B.S. only: 77% **Master's:** 23%

Approximate percentage of all students who are Women: 80% **Ethnic Minority:** 96% **International:** .8%

Average years to complete the doctoral program (including internship): 5.5 years

Personal interview required for admission

Attrition rate in past 7 years: 12%

Percentage of students applying for internship last year accepted into:

APA internships: 71% **APPIC internships:** 5%

Formal tracks/concentrations/interests: Neuroscience, Family/Couples, Health Psychology, Forensic Psychology

Research areas	# Faculty	# Grants
Health Psychology	7	1
Primary Care/Integrated Care	6	–
Cancer	1	–
HIV	3	–
Child Developmental	3	1
Personality Assessment	1	–
Forensic	2	–
Cognitive Assessment	3	–
Neuropsychological Assessment	2	1
Dialectical Behavioral Therapy	2	–
Test Construction	1	–
Diabetes/Mental Health	2	1

Clinical opportunities
Borderline Personality Clinic
Severe Psychopathology
Psychology in General Hospitals
Pediatric Psychology in General Hospital
School Settings
Neuropsychology/Neurorehabilitation
Consultation
Domestic Violence
Psycho-oncology
Addictions
Family/Couples
Autism/Neurodevelopmental Disorders

Purdue University (Ph.D.)

Department of Psychological Sciences
703 Third Street
West Lafayette, IN 47907-2081
phone#: (765) 494-6977
email: (secretary) saraost@purdue.edu,
(director) eckhardt@purdue.edu
Web address: www.purdue.edu/hhs/psy/graduate/research_training_areas/clinical_psychology/index.php

1	2	3	4	5	6	7
Practice oriented			Equal emphasis			Research oriented

Percentage of faculty subscribing to each of the following orientations:

Psychodynamic/Psychoanalytic	10%
Applied behavioral analysis/Radical behavioral	0%

Family systems/Systems	10%
Existential/Phenomenological/Humanistic	0%
Cognitive/Cognitive-behavioral	90%

Courses required for incoming students to have completed prior to enrolling: none

Recommended but not mandatory courses:
mathematics, natural sciences, other social sciences, a broad coursework in psychology, methodology and statistics

GRE mean
Verbal: 161 Quantitative: 164
Analytical Writing not reported
Psychology Subject Test not reported
Preference is given to students with a combined GRE Verbal and Quantitative of 310 or higher

GPA mean
Overall GPA 3.82

Number of applications/admission offers/incoming students in 2017
97 applied/4 admission offers/3 incoming

% of incoming students receiving:
Full tuition waiver only: 0%
Assistantship/fellowship only: 0%
Both full tuition waiver & assistantship/fellowship: 100%

Approximate percentage of incoming students with a B.A./B.S. only: 67% **Master's:** 33%

Approximate percentage of all students who are Women: 71% **Ethnic Minority:** 33% **International:** 5%

Average years to complete the doctoral program (including internship): 6.5 years

Personal interview
Required in person. Telephone interviews are acceptable under extenuating circumstances.

Attrition rate in past 7 years: 10.7%

Percentage of students applying for internship in 2016–2017 accepted into:

APA-accredited internships: 100%

Formal tracks/concentrations: none

Research areas	# Faculty	# Grants
aggression & antisocial behavior	4	2
emotion regulation	3	1
neurodevelopmental disorders	1	1
mood disorders	2	0
behavior genetics	1	0
ethnicity minority/cultural issues	1	0
relationship distress/aggression	3	1
personality disorders	5	1
personality assessment	4	1
substance use	4	2
statistical innovations	1	0

Clinical opportunities

adult psychopathology	ADHD
assessment	family and adolescence
neuropsychology	personality disorders
neurodevelopmental disorders/ autism spectrum disorder	conduct disorders

Queens College and The Graduate Center, City University of New York (Ph.D.)

Clinical Psychology at Queens College, CUNY
Department of Psychology
65-30 Kissena Blvd, Science Building E318
Queens, NY 11367
phone#: (718) 997-4277
email: clinicalpsychology@qc.cuny.edu
Web address: http://www.gc.cuny.edu/Page-Elements/Academics-Research-Centers-Initiatives/Doctoral-Programs/Psychology/Training-Areas/Clinical-Psychology-@-Queens-College

1	2	3	4	**5**	6	7
Practice oriented			Equal emphasis			Research oriented

Percentage of faculty subscribing to each of the following orientations:

Psychodynamic/Psychoanalytic	29%
Applied behavioral analysis/Radical behavioral	14%
Family systems/Systems	0%
Existential/Phenomenological/Humanistic	0%
Cognitive/Cognitive-behavioral	57%
Neuropsychology	43%

Courses required for incoming students to have completed prior to enrolling:
Applicants should have completed at least 15 credits in undergraduate psychology, including one laboratory course in experimental psychology and one course in statistics.

Recommended but not mandatory courses: none

GRE mean
Verbal + Quantitative 318
Analytical Writing 4.5
Psychology Subject Test 697

GPA mean
Overall GPA 3.83

Number of applications/admission offers/incoming students in 2015
69 applied/10 admission offers/6 incoming

% of students receiving:
Full tuition only: 33%
Assistantship/fellowship only: 0%
Both full tuition waiver & merit based fellowship: 67%
Both full tuition waiver & teaching/research assistantship: 0%

Approximate percentage of incoming students with a B.A./B.S. only: 83% **Master's:** 17%

Approximate percentage of all students who are Women: 86% **Ethnic Minority:** 22% **International:** 1%

Average years to complete the doctoral program (including internship): 7.06 years

Personal interview
Preferred in person

Attrition rate in past 7 years: 8.5%

Percentage of students applying for internship last year accepted into:

APA internships: 83% **APPIC internships:** 100%

Formal tracks/concentrations: All students receive specialized training in Neuropsychology.

Research areas	# Faculty	# Grants
neuropsychology	2	0
cognitive processing in Parkinson's disease	1	0
adult attachment	1	0
cognitive neuroscience of aging and dementia	1	0
anxiety/mood disorders	1	0
developmental psychopathology	1	0
childhood adversity	1	0
substance use	2	0
depression	3	0
personality disorders	1	0

Clinical opportunities

The program maintains long-standing relationships with numerous training sites around the New York City and the Tri-State Metropolitan area, including outpatient settings, inpatient hospitals, and specialty clinics. At least one of the externships must include neuropsychological assessment.

Regent University (Psy.D.)

Doctoral Program in Clinical Psychology
CRB 161
1000 Regent University Drive
Virginia Beach, VA 23464
phone#: (800) 373-5504 ext. 4366 or (757) 352-4366
email: psyd@regent.edu
Web address: www.regent.edu/psyd

1	2	**3**	4	5	6	7
Practice oriented			Equal emphasis			Research oriented

Percentage of faculty subscribing to each of the following orientations:

Psychodynamic/Psychoanalytic	30%
Applied behavioral analysis/Radical behavioral	0%
Family systems/Systems	20%
Existential/Phenomenological/Humanistic	20%
Cognitive/Cognitive-behavioral	30%

Courses required for incoming students to have completed prior to enrolling:
18 hours of psychology (undergraduate), to include Statistics and Research Methods or Experimental Design

Recommended but not mandatory courses: Personality Theories, Human Growth and Development, Abnormal, Social, Physiology

GRE mean
Verbal and Quantitative 301
Analytical Writing 4.1
Psychology Subject Test not reported/required

GPA mean
Overall GPA 3.64

Number of applications/admission offers/incoming students in Fall, 2016
96 applied/39 admission offers/20 incoming

% of students receiving:
Full tuition waiver only: 0%
Assistantship/fellowship only: 13%
Both full tuition waiver & assistantship/fellowship: 13%
100% of incoming students received some level of scholarship support

Approximate percentage of incoming students with a B.A./B.S. (Honors) only: 85% **Master's:** 15%

Approximate percentage of students who are Women: 75% **Ethnic Minority:** 25% **International:** 4%

Average years to complete the doctoral program (including internship): 5.4 years

Personal interview
Required in person (or by Skype of circumstances require)

Attrition rate in past 7 years: 6%

Percentage of students applying for internship in 2017 accepted into:

APA internships: 100% **APPIC internships:** 0%

Formal tracks/concentrations: Marital & Family Psychology, Clinical Child psychology, Health psychology, Consulting Psychology, Forensic Psychology

Research areas	# Faculty	# Grants
Intervention for at-risk children	1	1
Consultation	3	2
Forensics/Assessment	1	–
Marital Functioning/Therapy	2	3
Sexual & Gender Identity	1	2
Health Psychology	2	–
Minority & Cultural Identity	2	–
Social Justice	1	–
Positive Psychology	1	1

Clinical opportunities

child and adult group practices	university-based clinic
Christian counseling centers	neuropsychology
forensic settings	state psychiatric hospital
community mental health	VA medical center
military clinic/hospital	

University of Rhode Island (Ph.D.)

Department of Psychology
142 Flagg Road
Kingston, RI 02881
phone#: (401) 874-2193
email: efschroeder@uri.edu
Web address: http://web.uri.edu/psychology/clinical-psychology-ph-d-program/

1	2	3	**4**	5	6	7
Practice oriented			Equal emphasis			Research oriented

Percentage of faculty subscribing to each of the following orientations:

Psychodynamic/Psychoanalytic	0%
Applied behavioral analysis/Radical behavioral	0%
Family systems/Systems	0%
Existential/Phenomenological/Humanistic	0%
Cognitive/Cognitive-behavioral	88%
Interpersonal	44%
Multicultural	33%

Courses required for incoming students to have completed prior to enrolling:
Background in undergraduate psychology

Recommended but not mandatory courses:
Psychological tests and measurements

GRE mean
Verbal 158 Quantitative 156
Analytical Writing not reported
Psychology Subject Test not reported

GPA mean
Undergraduate GPA 3.78

Number of applications/admission offers/incoming students in 2016
183 applied/8 admission offers/4 incoming

% of students receiving:
Full tuition waiver only: 8%
Assistantship/fellowship only: 70%
Both full tuition waiver and assistantship/fellowship: 0%

Approximate percentage of incoming students with a B.A./B.S. only: 50% **Master's:** 50%

Approximate percentage of students who are Women: 79% **Ethnic Minority:** 21% **International:** 0%

Average years to complete the doctoral program (including internship): 6.26 years

Personal interview
Required in person

Attrition rate in past 7 years: 7%

Percentage of students applying for internship in 2016 accepted into:

APA internships: 86% **APPIC internships:** 86%

Formal tracks/concentrations: neuropsychology, child/family/developmental psychology, applied methodology, multicultural psychology, health psychology

Research areas	# Faculty	# Grants
behavioral medicine/health psychology	4	4
child clinical	1	0
community psychology	1	1
family research	1	0
multicultural issues	1	1
criminal/juvenile justice/forensic psychology	2	2

Clinical opportunities
child/adolescent therapy
adult therapy
multicultural psychotherapy
community psychology
family therapy
health psychology
psychological assessment

University of Rochester (Ph.D.)

Department of Psychology
Meliora Hall
Rochester, NY 14627-0266
phone#: (585) 275-8704
email: april.engram@rochester.edu
Web address: www.sas.rochester.edu/psy/graduate/clinical/

1	2	3	4	5	**6**	7
Practice oriented			Equal emphasis			Research oriented

Percentage of faculty subscribing to each of the following orientations:

Psychodynamic/Psychoanalytic	17%
Applied behavior analysis/Radical beh.	8%
Family systems/Systems	1%
Existential/Phenomenological/Humanistic	0%
Cognitive/Cognitive-behavioral	74%

Courses required for incoming students to have completed prior to enrolling:
Equivalent of psychology major

Recommended but not mandatory courses: none

GRE mean
Verbal 160 Quantitative 154
Analytical Writing 4.3
Psychology Subject Test not reported

GPA mean
Overall GPA 3.8

Number of applications/admission offers/incoming students in 2017
171 applied/4 admission offers/3 incoming

% of students receiving:
Full tuition waiver only: 0%
Assistantship/fellowship only: 0%
Both full tuition waiver & assistantship/fellowship: 100%

Approximate percentage of students who are Women: 92% **Ethnic Minority:** 25% **International:** 0%

Average years to complete the doctoral program (including internship): 6.8 years

Personal interview
Required in person

Attrition rate in past 7 years: 4%

Percentage of students applying for internship in 2017 accepted into:

APA internships: 100% **APPIC internships:** 100%

Formal tracks/concentrations: not reported

Research areas	# Faculty	# Grants
autism	1	1
anxiety	1	0
depression	3	2
child abuse/maltreatment	1	3
marriage/couples	1	1
intervention/prevention	2	1
psychopathology-developmental, child	4	2
psychopathology-adult	3	0
schizophrenia	1	0
suicide	1	1

Clinical opportunities
autism
child maltreatment/abuse, trauma
child, adolescent, and adult psychotherapy
child/pediatric
cognitive-behavior therapy
developmental disabilities
empirically supported treatments/interventions
group therapy
inpatient psychiatry
interpersonal therapy
outpatient psychiatry
parent-child attachment therapy
parent-child interaction/parent training
psychodynamic therapy
severe mental illness
suicide/prevention
university counseling center

Roosevelt University (Psy.D.)

Department of Psychology
430 S. Michigan Avenue
Chicago, IL 60605
phone#: (312)-341-3754
email: storresharding@roosevelt.edu
Web address: https://www.roosevelt.edu/academics/programs/doctorate-in-clinical-psychology-psyd

1	2	3	4	5	6	7
Practice oriented			Equal emphasis			Research oriented

Percentage of faculty subscribing to each of the following orientations:

Psychodynamic/Psychoanalytic	33%
Applied behavioral analysis/Radical behavioral	16%
Family systems/Systems	16%
Cognitive/Cognitive-behavioral	58%
Eclectic	9%

Courses required for incoming students to have completed prior to enrolling:
Intro to Psychology; Abnormal Psychology; Research Methods or Statistics

Recommended but not mandatory courses: Personality theory, tests and measurement

GRE mean (for incoming class)
Verbal 74h percentile
Quantitative 52nd percentile
Psychology Subject Test not reported
Analytical Writing 74th percentile

GPA mean (for incoming class)
Overall GPA: 3.60

Number of applications/admission offers/incoming students in 2017
259 applied/37 admission offers/22 incoming

% of students receiving:
Full tuition waiver only: 0%
Assistantship/fellowship only: 0%
Both tuition waiver & assistantship/fellowship: 50%
(10 students receive waiver of 1/2 tuition and 1/2 of the yearly stipend for 1st year only)

Approximate percentage of incoming students with a B.A./B.S. only: 68% **Master's:** 32%

Approximate percentage of students who are Women: 80% **Ethnic Minority:** 21% **International:** 8%

Average years to complete the doctoral program (including internship): 6 years

Personal interview
Required in person

Attrition rate in past 7 years: 8%

Percentage of students applying for internship in 2017 accepted into:

APA internships: 100% **APPIC internships:** 0%

Formal tracks/concentrations: none

Research areas	# Faculty	# Grants
assessment	4	0
children and adolescents	5	0
health psychology	3	0
neuropsychology	4	0
social cognition	1	0
learning theory/clinical applications	2	0
college teaching	1	0
ethnicity, gender, sexual orientation, human diversity	3	0
forensics	1	0
mindfulness	1	0
evidence based treatments	1	0

Clinical opportunities
children and families
adult chronic psychiatric hospitals
behavioral medicine
trauma
neuropsychology (child, adolescent, adult)
inpatient and partial hospitalization
university counseling centers
therapeutic day schools
veteran's administration hospitals
jail/prison populations
anxiety disorders
eating disorders
community mental health centers
developmental disabilities

Rosalind Franklin University of Medicine and Science (Ph.D.)

Department of Psychology
3333 Green Bay Road

North Chicago, IL 60064
phone#: (847) 578-3305
email: patricia.rigwood@rosalindfranklin.edu
Web address: www.rosalindfranklin.edu/chp/psychology.aspx

1	2	3	4	**5**	6	7
Practice oriented			Equal emphasis			Research oriented

Percentage of faculty subscribing to each of the following orientations:

Psychodynamic/Psychoanalytic	10%
Applied behavioral analysis/Radical behavioral	5%
Family systems/Systems	5%
Existential/Phenomenological/Humanistic	5%
Cognitive/Cognitive-behavioral	75%

Courses required for incoming students to have completed prior to enrolling: statistics

Recommended but not mandatory courses:
Abnormal, developmental, social, biological/physiological

GRE mean
Verbal 156 Quantitative 154
Analytical Writing 4.5
Psychology Subject Test 666 (only required for non-psychology majors)

GPA mean
Overall GPA 3.78

Number of applications/admission offers/incoming students in 2017
90 applied/18 admission offers/11 incoming

% of students receiving:
Full tuition waiver only: 0% (we offer partial tuition remission only)
Assistantship/fellowship only: 0%
Both full tuition waiver & assistantship/fellowship: 0%

Approximate percentage of incoming students with a B.A./B.S. only: 70% **Master's:** 30%

Approximate percentage of all students who are Women: 75% **Ethnic Minority:** 20% **International:** 0%

Average years to complete the doctoral program (including internship): 6.5 years

Personal interview:
Required in person

Attrition rate in past 7 years: 14%

Percentage of students applying for internship last year accepted into:

APA internships: 100% **APPIC internships:** 0%

Formal tracks/concentrations:
Neuropsychology, health psychology, psychopathology

Research areas	# Faculty	# Grants
pediatric chronic illness	1	1
medication adherence	1	1
psychopathy	1	1
physical activity	1	1
obesity	1	1
social media interventions	1	1
quantitative methods	1	0
neuroimaging	1	0
childhood epilepsy	1	1
schizophrenia	1	1
anxiety	1	0
aging	1	0
diabetes	1	0
PTSD	1	0

Clinical opportunities

veterans	community mental health
health psychology	forensic
neuropsychological	pediatric
adult	interprofessional health care

Rutgers, The State University of New Jersey (Ph.D.)

Department of Psychology
Graduate School of Arts and Sciences
New Brunswick, NJ 08903
email: edward.selby@rutgers.edu
Web address: psych.rutgers.edu/menu-iv/cl

1	2	3	4	5	**6**	7
Practice oriented			Equal emphasis			Research oriented

Percentage of faculty subscribing to each of the following orientations:

Psychodynamic/Psychoanalytic	0%
Applied behavioral analysis/Radical behavioral	5%
Family systems/Systems	5%
Existential/Phenomenological/Humanistic	0%
Cognitive/Cognitive-behavioral	90%

Courses required for incoming students to have completed prior to enrolling:
A major in psychology or equivalent courses

Recommended but not mandatory courses: none

GRE mean
Verbal 163 Quantitative 157
Analytical Writing 446
Psychology Subject Test 740

GPA mean
Overall GPA 3.65

Number of applications/admission offers/incoming students in 2016
322 applied/8 admission offers/5 incoming

% of students receiving:
Full tuition waiver only: 0%
Assistantship/fellowship only: 0%
Both full tuition waiver & assistantship/fellowship: 100%

Approximate percentage of incoming students with a B.A./B.S. only: 100% **Master's:** 25%

Approximate percentage of all students who are Women: 77% **Ethnic Minority:** 19% **International:** 4%

Average years to complete the doctoral program (including internship): 6 years

Personal interview
Formal In-Person Interview Required.

Attrition rate in past 7 years: 0%

Percentage of students applying for internship in 2016 accepted into:

APA internships: 100% **APPIC internships:** 100%

Formal tracks/concentrations: none

Research areas	# Faculty	# Grants
applied behavioral analysis	1	0
autism	1	1
behavioral dysregulation	2	2
behavioral health	2	2
dialectical behavior therapy	2	1
eating disorders	2	1
prevention	2	2
psychotherapy process and outcome	3	2
somatization disorders	1	0
substance abuse	2	2
psychotic disorders	1	3

Clinical opportunities
adolescent
anxiety disorder
applied behavioral analysis
assessment
behavioral medicine/health psychology
child
developmental disabilities
dialectical behavior therapy
eating disorder
mood disorders
personality disorders
schizophrenia and psychotic disorders
school-based prevention
substance use disorders
suicidal and self-injurious behavior
Tourette's clinic

Rutgers, The State University of New Jersey (Psy.D.)

Graduate School of Applied and Professional Psychology
152 Frelinghuysen Road
Piscataway, NJ 08854-8020
phone#: (848) 445-3980
email: clinpsyd@rci.rutgers.edu
Web address: gsappweb.rutgers.edu/programs/clinical/index.php

1	2	3	4	5	6	7
Practice oriented			Equal emphasis			Research oriented

Percentage of faculty subscribing to each of the following orientations:

Psychodynamic/Psychoanalytic	33%
Applied behavioral analysis/Radical behavioral	27%
Family systems/Systems	14%
Existential/Phenomenological/Humanistic	7%
Cognitive/Cognitive-behavioral	27%

Courses required for incoming students to have completed prior to enrolling:
Introductory psychology, statistics, abnormal psychology, and the biological bases of psychology

Recommended but not mandatory courses:
Students also should have taken at least one and preferably two courses in the following areas: cognitive psychology; psychology of perception, conditioning, and learning; developmental psychology; psychology of personality; and social psychology. We prefer that one of the above-listed courses have a laboratory component. Both clinical and school psychology programs welcome applications from Rutgers students who are properly prepared with good academic records and references.

GRE mean
Verbal 157 Quantitative 153
Analytical Writing 43
Psychology Subject Test 65

GPA mean
Overall GPA 3.50

Number of applications/admission offers/incoming students in 2017
327 applied/36 offered admission/18 incoming

% of students receiving:
Full tuition waiver only: 0%
Scholarships: 100%
Both full tuition waiver & assistantship/fellowship:

Approximate percentage of incoming students with a B.A./B.S. only: 98% **Master's:** 2%

Approximate percentage of all students who are Women: 59% **Ethnic Minority:** 39% **International:** 11%

Average years to complete the doctoral program (including internship) 5.5

Personal interview
Preferred in person but telephone acceptable
Attrition rate in past 7 years

Percentage of students applying for internship in 2017 accepted into:

APA internships: 100% **APPIC internships:** 100%

Formal tracks/concentrations: community psychology, multicultural

Research areas
adolescence
anxiety depressive disorders
applied and behavioral analysis
autism
community
developmental disabilities
diagnosis and classification
dissociative disorders
eating disorders
empirically supported treatment research
ethical issues
family/marriage/couples
feminist theory and psychology
mental health policy
mind/body/health
multicultural issues
personality disorders
philosophy and psychology

psychiatric disabilities
psychoanalytic theory
psychology and the arts
psychotherapy process and outcome
severe mental illness
social learning theory
substance abuse

Clinical opportunities (see website for listing of practicum sites)
Anxiety Disorders Center
Foster Care Counseling Project
Tourette Syndrome Clinic
Group Psychotherapy, Dialectical Behavior Therapy
Couples Clinic
Women Helping Women (individual, couples, family and group therapy for female-identified clients)
Psychological Services Clinic-Therapy
Psychological Services Clinic-Assessment

St. John's University (Clinical Psychology Ph.D.)

Department of Psychology
8000 Utopia Parkway
Queens, NY 11439
phone#: (718) 990-1548
email: gradhelp@stjohns.edu; nevidj@stjohns.edu; euelll@stjohns.edu
Web address: http://www.stjohns.edu/academics/schools-and-colleges/st-johns-college-liberal-arts-and-sciences/psychology/clinical-psychology-phd

1	2	3	**4**	5	6	7
Practice oriented			Equal emphasis			Research oriented

Percentage of faculty subscribing to each of the following orientations:

Psychodynamic/Psychoanalytic	20%
Applied behavioral analysis/Radical behavioral	0%
Family systems/Systems	0%
Existential/Phenomenological/Humanistic	0%
Cognitive/Cognitive-behavioral	80%

Courses required for incoming students to have completed prior to enrolling:
Introductory Psychology; Statistics; Experimental Psychology or Research Methods

Recommended but not mandatory courses: not reported

GRE mean
Verbal + Quantitative 687
Analytical Writing 4.65
Psychology Subject Test not reported

GPA mean
Overall GPA 3.74

Number of applications/admission offers/incoming students in 2017
285 applied/17 admission offers/10 incoming

% of students receiving:
Full tuition waiver only: 0%
Assistantship/fellowship only: 0%
Both full tuition waiver & assistantship/fellowship: 100% of First year Students

Approximate percentage of incoming students with a B.A./B.S. only: 70% **Master's:** 30%

Approximate percentage of all students who are Women: 70% **Ethnic Minority:** 31% **International:** 0%

Average years to complete the doctoral program (including internship): 5.8 years

Personal interview preferred in person but telephone acceptable

Attrition rate in past 7 years: <10%

Percentage of students applying for internship last year accepted into:

APA internships: 89% **APPIC internships:**

Formal tracks/concentrations: General & Clinical child

Research areas	# Faculty	# Grants
Childhood trauma	1	1
Anger	1	0
Bilingualism	1	0
Depression	1	0
Parenting and parent training	1	0
Personality/Psychopathology	1	0
Emerging adulthood	1	0
Health psychology	3	1
Multicultural issues	4	0
Aggression	2	0
Implicit measures	1	0

Clinical opportunities
Parent training
Treatment of childhood trauma
Anxiety
Depression
Anger
Health interventions

Saint Louis University (Ph.D.)

Department of Psychology
3700 Lindell Blvd.
St. Louis, MO 63108
phone#: (314) 977-4272
email: clinicalpsy@slu.edu
Web address: https://www.slu.edu/programs/graduate/psychology-clinical-ms-phd.php

1	2	3	**4**	5	6	7
Practice oriented			Equal emphasis			Research oriented

Percentage of faculty subscribing to each of the following orientations:

Psychodynamic/Psychoanalytic	20%
Applied behavioral analysis/Radical behavioral	0%
Family systems/Systems	0%
Existential/Phenomenological/Humanistic	0%

Cognitive/Cognitive-behavioral	80%

Courses required for incoming students to have completed prior to enrolling:
21 hours including general psychology, abnormal psychology, and statistics/research methods

Recommended but not mandatory courses: Cognition/learning, physiological/biological psychology, social psychology

GRE mean
Verbal 74% Quantitative 49%
Analytical Writing 74%
Psychology Subject Test: 74%

GPA mean
Overall GPA 3.7

Number of applications/admission offers/incoming students in 2017
144 applied/16 admission offers/8 incoming

% of students receiving:
Full tuition waiver only: 0%
Assistantship/fellowship only: 0%
Tuition full waiver & assistantship/fellowship: 100% for first year

Approximate percentage of incoming students with a B.A./B.S. only: 87.5% **Master's:** 12.5%

Approximate percentage of students who are Women: 76% **Ethnic Minority:** 28% **International:** 3%

Average years to complete the doctoral program (including internship): 5 years

Personal interview
Preferred in person but telephone acceptable

Attrition rate in past 7 years: 8.3%

Percentage of students applying for internship in 2017 accepted into:

APA internships: 100% **APPIC internships:** 100%

Formal tracks/concentrations: none

Research areas	# Faculty	# Grants
abuse/violence	2	0
addictions	1	2
ADHD	2	1
adjustment	1	0
anxiety	2	0
assessment	2	0
autism	1	0
child/adolescent	3	0
cognition and aging	1	0
community	1	0
depression	2	0
eating disorders	1	0
ethical issues	2	0
health behavior change	1	0
malingering and effort testing	1	0
mild TBI	1	0
minority issues	1	0
neuropsychology/neuroscience	2	0
professional issues	2	0
psychotherapy process and outcomes	2	0
PTSD	1	0
sport psychology	1	0
stress and coping	1	0
trauma and abuse	1	0

Clinical opportunities
addictions
anxiety
attention deficit hyperactivity disorder
child therapy
depression
eating disorders and obesity
health psychology
learning disabilities
neuropsychology
oncology
parent skills training
pediatric health
personality disorders
psychoeducational assessment
relationship-focused treatment
racial, ethnic, and cultural diversity
sexual minorities
trauma

Sam Houston State University (Ph.D.)

Department of Psychology and Philosophy
Huntsville, Texas 77341-2210
phone #: (936) 294-1210
email: varela@shsu.edu
Web: http://www.shsu.edu/academics/psychology-and-philosophy/psychology/doctoral-program/index.html

1	2	3	**4**	5	6	7
Practice oriented			Equal emphasis			Research oriented

Percentage of faculty subscribing to each of the following orientations:

Psychodynamic/Psychoanalytic	0%
Applied behavioral analysis/Radical behavioral	0%
Family systems/Systems	20%
Existential/Phenomenological/Humanistic	20%
Cognitive/Cognitive-behavioral	100%

Courses required for incoming students to have completed prior to enrolling: none

Recommended but not mandatory courses:
Research Methods, Statistics, Abnormal Psychology

GRE mean
Verbal 162 Quantitative 154
Analytical Writing 4.6
Psychology Subject Test not required

GPA mean
Overall GPA 3.71

Number of applications/admission offers/incoming students in 2017
173 applications/9 admission offers/7 incoming

% of students receiving:
Full tuition waiver only: 0%
Assistantship/fellowship only: 100%
Both full tuition waiver & assistantship/fellowship: 0%

Approximate percentage of incoming students with a B.A. or B.S. only: 60% **Master's:** 40%

Approximate percentage of students who are Women: 85% **Ethnic/Racial Minority:** 20% **International:** 8%

Average years to complete the doctoral program (including internship): 6 years

Personal interview
In-person interview is strongly preferred

Attrition rate in past 7 years: 5%

Percentage of students applying for internship in 2017 accepted into:

APA internships: 100% **APPIC internships:** 100%

Formal tracks/concentrations: Forensic

Research Areas	# Faculty	# Grants
Addictive Behavior	1	–
Adolescent Attachment	1	–
Adolescent Psychopathology	1	–
Advanced Data Analytic Methodology	1	–
Behavioral Medicine	2	1
Exercise-Based Interventions	1	–
Family Psychology	1	–
Forensic Assessment	4	–
Health Psychology: Chronic Pain, Fatigue	2	–
Immigration and Mental Health	2	–
Juvenile Justice	1	–
Law Enforcement Psychology	1	–
Multicultural and Diversity Issues	2	2
Neurobehavioral Functioning	1	–
Personality and Individual Differences	1	–
Personality/Psychopathology Assessment	1	–
Prosocial Behavior among Children and Adolescents	1	–
Psychometrics	1	–
Psychotherapy	2	1
Sex Offender Risk Assessment	2	–
Social Influences	1	–
Stereotyping and Prejudice	2	1
Trauma	1	–
Veterans' Issues	1	–
Violence Risk	3	–

Clinical opportunities
Assessment and Treatment (Children, Adolescents, Adults, Couples, Families)
Assessment and Treatment of Spanish-speaking Clients (Children, Adolescents, Adults)
Neuropsychological Settings
Psychiatric Hospital Settings
Correctional/Criminal Justice Settings (Adults, Juveniles)
Forensic Evaluations for the Courts
Telehealth Services

San Diego State University/University of California–San Diego (Ph.D.)

Joint doctoral program in clinical psychology
San Diego, CA 92182
phone#: (619) 594-2246
email: eklonoff@sunstroke.sdsu.edu
Web address: www.psychology.sdsu.edu/doctoral/

1	2	3	4	5	**6**	7
Practice oriented			Equal emphasis			Research oriented

Percentage of faculty subscribing to each of the following orientations:

Psychodynamic/Psychoanalytic	5%
Applied behavioral analysis/Radical behavioral	30%
Family systems/Systems	10%
Existential/Phenomenological/Humanistic	5%
Cognitive/Cognitive-behavioral	50%

Courses required for incoming students to have completed prior to enrolling:
psychology major or 18 semester hours in psychology including: personality, abnormal, social, statistics, testing, experimental with lab, physiological.

Recommended but not mandatory courses:
advanced courses in perception and learning, biology, mathematics, linguistics, computer science, medical physics

GRE mean
Verbal 675 Quantitative 733
Analytical Writing not reported
Psychology Subject Test 748

GPA mean
Overall GPA 3.7 Psychology GPA 3.80

Number of applications/admission offers/incoming students
328 applied/14 admission offers/12 incoming

% of students receiving:
Full tuition waiver only: 0%
Assistantship/fellowship only: 0%
Tuition full waiver & assistantship/fellowship: 100%

Approximate percentage of incoming students with a B.A./B.S. only: 83% **Master's:** 17%

Approximate percentage of students who are Women: 86% **Ethnic Minority:** 31% **International:** 8%

Average years to complete the doctoral program (including internship): 6 years

Personal interview
Preferred in person but telephone acceptable

Attrition rate in past 7 years: 4%

Percentage of students applying for internship last year accepted into:

APA internships: 100%
APPIC internships: not reported

Formal tracks/concentrations: behavioral medicine/health psychology, experimental psychopathology, neuropsychology

Research Areas:	# Faculty	# Grants
Addictions/Substance Use Disorders	9	<1
Alcohol/Substance Abuse	10	<1
Alzheimer's/Dementia	14	<1
Anxiety Disorders	10	<1
Autism and Other Developmental Disorders	10	<1
Body Image Disturbance	3	<1
Cancer/Disparities	5	<1
Cardiovascular Disease/Disparities	6	<1
Child Psychopathology	5	<1
Chronic Illness	9	<1
Cross-Cultural Psychology	8	<1
Degenerative Brain Disorders	4	<1
Disorders of Aging	13	<1
Eating Disorders	2	<1
Ethnicity and Health	4	<1
Fetal Alcohol Syndrome	3	<1
Genetics/Genomics	3	<1
Grief & Bereavement	2	<1
Health Promotion	4	<1
Health Services Research	3	<1
HIV/AIDS	18	<1
Hoarding	2	<1
Mood Disorders	5	<1
Neuroimaging	19	<1
Neuropsychology/Neuroscience	42	<1
Obesity	2	<1
Physical and Mental Health Disparities	4	<1
Prevention	2	<1
Psychopharmacology	4	<1
PTSD	6	<1
Schizophrenia/Psychosis	13	<1
Sexual and Gender Minority Health	1	1
Sleep	4	<1
Statistics and Quantitative Methods	2	0
Tobacco/Smoking/Environmental Exposure	5	<1

Clinical opportunities

anxiety disorders	cognitive therapy
behavioral medicine	neuropsychology
child and family therapy	school psychology

Seattle Pacific University (Ph.D.)

Clinical Psychology Department
3307 Third Avenue West, Suite 107
Seattle, WA 98119
phone#: (206) 281-2839
email: clinicalpsyc@spu.edu
Web address: http://spu.edu/academics/school-of-psychology-family-community/graduate-programs/clinical-psychology-phd

1	2	3	**4**	5	6	7
Practice oriented			Equal emphasis			Research oriented

Percentage of faculty subscribing to each of the following orientations:

Psychodynamic/Psychoanalytic	0%
Applied behavioral analysis/Radical behavioral	0%
Family systems/Systems	33%
Existential/Phenomenological/Humanistic	0%
Cognitive/Cognitive-behavioral	67%

Courses required for incoming students to have completed prior to enrolling:
Statistics and 5 from among: abnormal, developmental, experimental, physiological, social, learning, motivation, personality, cognitive, tests and measurement

Recommended but not mandatory courses: See above

GRE mean
Verbal 155; Quantitative 152
Analytical Writing not reported
Psychology Subject Test not reported

GPA mean
Overall GPA 3.60

Number of applications/admission offers/incoming students in 2017
114 applied/18 admission offers/15 incoming

% of students receiving:
Full tuition waiver only: 0%
Assistantship/fellowship only: 100%
Both full tuition waiver & assistantship/fellowship: 0%

Approximate percentage of incoming students with a B.A./B.S. only: 80% **Master's:** 20%

Approximate percentage of students who are Women: 80% **Ethnic Minority:** 19% **International:** 7%

Average years to complete the doctoral program (including internship): 6 years

Personal interview
Preferred in person but telephone acceptable

Attrition rate in past 7 years: 7%

Percentage of students applying for internship in 2017 accepted into:

APA internships: 100% **APPIC internships:** 100%

Formal tracks/concentrations: none

Research areas	# Faculty	# Grants
gender and mental health	1	0
developmental psychopathology	2	1
psychology of religion	2	2
child and adolescent development	2	2
health psychology	1	0
rehab psychology	1	0
family and couple relationships	2	0
culture/ethnicity and psychology	1	1
career and life development	1	1
treatment program evaluation	1	1
mental disorder in women	1	1
program and policy development	1	0
psychotherapy research	1	1
child social and emotional development	1	1

conduct problems in young children	1	0
attention and self-regulation	1	1
cognitive models of psychopathology	2	1
positive psychology	2	1
evaluation of career interventions	1	1
relationships in ministry	1	0
disaster psychology	1	0
psychophysiology/biology of stress	4	1
self-psychology and self-esteem	1	0
developmental disabilities	1	0
personality and interpersonal behavior	2	0
trauma	3	1
depression	2	1
anxiety disorders	2	1

Clinical opportunities

behavioral medicine
neuropsychology
rehabilitation medicine
child and adolescent mental health
corrections
community mental health
substance abuse
serious mental illness
developmental disabilities
autism/autism spectrum
university counseling centers
family therapy
military mental health

University of South Carolina (Ph.D.)

Department of Psychology
Columbia, SC 29208
phone#: (803) 777-2312
email: REEDERT@mailbox.sc.edu
Web address: http://www.psych.sc.edu/clinical-community-program-0

1	2	3	4	5	6	7
Practice oriented			Equal emphasis			Research oriented

Percentage of faculty subscribing to each of the following orientations:

Psychodynamic/Psychoanalytic	0%
Applied behavioral analysis/Radical behavioral	10%
Family systems/Systems	40%
Existential/Phenomenological/Humanistic	0%
Cognitive/Cognitive-behavioral	50%

Recommended but not mandatory courses: 18 hours in psychology, including advanced statistics, community-based intervention

GRE mean
Verbal 612 Quantitative 682
Analytical Writing 4.8
Psychology Subject Test 673

GPA mean
Overall GPA 3.7

Number of applications/admission offers/incoming students in 2017
163 applied/8 admission offers/5 incoming

% of students receiving:
Full tuition waiver only: 0%
Assistantship/fellowship only: 0%
Both full tuition waiver & assistantship/fellowship: 100%

Approximate percentage of incoming students with a B.A./B.S. only: 67% **Master's:** 33%

Approximate percentage of students who are Women: 76% **Ethnic Minority:** 21% **International:** 10%

Average years to complete the doctoral program (including internship): 6 years

Personal interview
Preferred in person but telephone acceptable

Attrition rate in past 7 years: 15%

Percentage of students applying for internship in 2016 accepted into:

APA internships: not reported **APPIC internships:**100%

Formal tracks/concentrations: children, adolescents, and families; community intervention & research

Research areas	# Faculty	# Grants
child/family	5	12
community-based intervention	3	4
neuropsychology	2	2
prevention (racism/cross-cultural)	2	2
social & cultural factors in health	4	5
mental health promotion	3	3

Clinical opportunities
Our program can be used to develop a variety of unique areas of expertise in the field of Psychology; however, currently there are two major dimensions to our program: (a) Children, Adolescents, and Families and (b) Social and Cultural Aspects of Health. Faculty members often contribute to more than one area through their teaching and research.

University of South Dakota (Ph.D.)

Department of Psychology
Vermillion, SD 57069
phone#: (605) 677-5353
email: clinicalpsyc@usd.edu
Web address: www.usd.edu/arts-and-sciences/psychology/clinical-psychology/

1	2	3	4	5	6	7
Practice oriented			Equal emphasis			Research oriented

Percentage of faculty subscribing to each of the following orientations:

Psychodynamic/Psychoanalytic	25%
Applied behavioral analysis/Radical behavioral	0%
Family systems/Systems	25%
Existential/Phenomenological/Humanistic	0%
Cognitive/Cognitive-behavioral	100%

Courses required for incoming students to have completed prior to enrolling:
18 semester hours in psychology within a distribution among standard coursework in general and experimental

Recommended but not mandatory courses: Research design, statistics, history/systems, learning/memory, abnormal, physiological

GRE mean (past 6 years – since scoring changed)
Verbal 156 Quantitative 151
Analytical Writing 4.34
Psychology Subject Test not required (recommended for non-psychology majors)

GPA mean (past 7 years)
Overall GPA 3.67

Number of applications/admission offers/incoming students in 2017
72 applied/12 admission offers/5 incoming

% of students receiving:
Full tuition waiver only: 0%
Assistantship/fellowship only: 100%
(all students on assistantships also receive tuition reduction to 1/3 of in-state tuition costs)
Both full tuition waiver & assistantship/fellowship: 0%

Approximate percentage of incoming students with a B.A./B.S. only: 100% **Master's:** 0%

Approximate percentage of students who are Women: 80% **Ethnic Minority:** 20% **International:** 0%

Average years to complete the doctoral program (including internship): 6.7 years (Median = 5.9 years)

Personal interview
Interviews are by invitation and are required.

Attrition rate in past 7 years: 7%

Percentage of students applying for internship in 2017 accepted into:

APA/CPA internships: 100% **APPIC internships:** 100%
(all APA sites were also APPIC member sites)

Formal tracks/concentrations: clinical/disaster psychology

Research areas	# Faculty	# Grants
child clinical	2	0
cross-cultural	8	0
depression	2	0
disaster mental health	4	0
family violence	2	1
rural community psychology	9	0
substance abuse	2	2

Clinical opportunities
crisis intervention/disaster mental health
minority/cross-cultural (specific emphasis in American Indian mental health)
rural/community mental health
substance abuse
severe and persistent mental illness
sexual trauma

University of South Florida (Ph.D.)

Department of Psychology
4202 Fowler Avenue, PCP 4118G
Tampa, FL 33620
phone#: (813) 974-2492
email: lpierce@usf.edu
Web address: http://psychology.usf.edu/grad/clinical/

1	2	3	4	5	**6**	7
Practice oriented			Equal emphasis			Research oriented

Percentage of faculty subscribing to each of the following orientations* (out of 15 faculty: 11 core, 4 associated faculty):

Psychodynamic/Psychoanalytic	0%
Behavioral	20%
Family systems/Systems	7%
Existential/Phenomenological/Humanistic	0%
Cognitive/Cognitive-behavioral	87%
Other:	
Common factors	13%
Evolutionary	7%

**(Responses do not add up to 100% because some faculty endorsed more than one orientation)*

Courses required for incoming students prior to enrolling: none

Recommended but not mandatory courses: Research design, statistics, abnormal psychology

GRE mean (incoming)
Verbal 158 Quantitative 153
Analytical Writing 4.5
Psychology Subject Test not required

GPA mean (incoming)
Junior/Senior GPA 3.8

Number of applications/admission offers/incoming students
258 applied/12 admission offers/8 incoming

% of students receiving (out of 50):
Full tuition waiver only: 0%
Assistantship/fellowship only: 0%
Partial tuition waiver (~80% waived) & assistantship/fellowship: 47 (94%)
Both full tuition waiver & fellowship: 3 (6%)

Approximate percentage of incoming students with a B.A./B.S. only: 41 (82%) **Master's:** 9 (18%)

Approximate percentage of students who are Women: 39 (78%) **Ethnic Minority:** 11 (22%) **International:** 3 (6%)*
**(Two international students are also counted under Ethnic Minority status)*

Average years to complete the doctoral program (including internship): 6.5 years

Personal interview
Preferred in person but telephone/skype acceptable

Attrition rate in past 7 years: 6%

Percentage of students applying for internship in 2017 accepted into:

APA internships: 89% **APPIC internships:** 89%

Formal tracks/concentrations: no formal tracks but concentrations in health psychology, psychopathology, addictive behaviors, clinical child psychology

Research areas	# Faculty	# Grants
child/adolescent	4	8
depression	1	–
eating disorders/obesity	2	–
emotions	2	1
externalizing disorders	2	2
family dysfunction	1	–
health psychology	2	–
neuropsychology	1	1
substance abuse/addictions	5	8
suicidality	2	3

Clinical opportunities

ADHD
adult and child clinical assessment
adult neuropsychology
anxiety—child and adult
child and adolescent disorders
depression/anxiety
eating disorders
family dysfunction
health psychology
intellectual assessment
learning disorders assessment
externalizing disorders
personality disorders
psychosocial oncology
psychopathology
smoking cessation
substance abuse/addiction
suicidality/self-harm
weight management

University of Southern California (Ph.D.)

Doctoral Program in Clinical Science
Department of Psychology
3620 McClintock, SGM 501
Los Angeles, CA 90089-1061
Phone#: (213) 740-2203
email: lopezs@usc.edu
Web address: https://dornsife.usc.edu/psyc/clinical-science/

1	2	3	4	5	**6**	7
Practice oriented			Equal emphasis			Research oriented

Percentage of faculty subscribing to each of the following orientations:

Psychodynamic/Psychoanalytic	0%
Applied behavioral analysis/Radical behavioral	10%
Family systems/Systems	30%
Existential/Phenomenological/Humanistic	10%
Cognitive/Cognitive-behavioral	100%

Courses required for incoming students to have completed prior to enrolling: none

Recommended but not mandatory courses:
Elementary statistics,* Research methods,* Biological Foundations — including coursework such as Comparative Psychology, Behavioral Neuroscience, Sensation and Perception, Learning and Memory, Cognitive Psychology, or Motivation and Emotion.
Developmental, Social, and Personality Foundations — including coursework such as Developmental Psychology, Social Psychology, Abnormal Psychology, Personality.
Cognitive Foundations — including coursework such as Learning, Memory, and Intelligence.
More advanced or specialized courses in psychology (e.g., Neuropsychology, Behavior Genetics, Advanced Statistics, Adolescence, Cognitive Development, Interpersonal Relations, Criminal Psychology, Psychology and Law, Organizational Psychology) are desirable, as are courses in the biological, physical, and social sciences and in mathematics. Students with outstanding records but with less background in psychology will also be considered.
Courses marked with an asterisk (*) are strongly recommended.

GRE mean
Verbal 164 Quantitative 160
Analytical Writing 4.67
Psychology Subject Test not reported

GPA mean
Overall GPA 3.8

Number of applications/admission offers/incoming students in 2017
357 applied/7 admission offers/3 incoming

% of students receiving:
Full tuition waiver only: 0%
Assistantship/fellowship only: 0%
Both full tuition waiver & assistantship/fellowship: 100%

Approximate percentage of incoming students with a B.A./B.S. only: 100% **Master's:** 0%

Approximate percentage of students who are Women: 86% **Ethnic Minority:** 37% **International:** 8.6%

Average years to complete the doctoral program (including internship): 7.0 years

Personal interview
Preferred in person but telephone acceptable

Attrition rate in past 7 years: 5%

Percentage of students applying for internship in 2017 accepted into:

APA internships: 100% **APPIC internships:** 100%

Formal tracks/concentrations: Clinical Child-Family; Clinical Geropsychology; Clinical Neuropsychology. We also have a dual degree (Ph.D./MPH) program in which students can pursue a Master's in Public Health if admitted by the MPH program after being admitted to the Ph.D.

Research areas	# Faculty	# Grants
adult psychopathology	5	2
affective disorders/depression/mood disorders	3	0
alcohol and substance use/abuse	1	1
child psychopathology	3	1
childhood victimization	3	1
cognitive behavioral therapy/assessment	2	0
community psychology	2	2
culturally informed treatment	2	2
ethnicity/culture and intervention	4	2
genetic, biological, and social influences on the development and course of psychopathology	2	2
geropsychology	2	2
health psychology	2	2

marital/family	2	1
prevention	3	1
psychological reactions to extreme trauma	1	0
psychology applied to school settings	2	0

Clinical opportunities
alcohol/substance abuse interventions/group therapy*
assessment/testing
child/adolescent community mental health
child/inpatient*
cognitive/cognitive-behavioral therapy
correctional/forensic*
culture and treatment
culturally informed treatment
family therapy/systems
geropsychology
individual adult
major medical illness (e.g., cancer)*
marital/couples
military families*
minority/cross-cultural/multicultural
neuropsychological assessment*
parent–child interaction/parent training
personality disorders
primary care/medical outpatient*
schizophrenia/psychosis/serious mental illness/inpatient*
schools*
veterans*
underserved populations

**external clinical practicum sites, including opportunities that are available to students wishing to do work beyond program requirements*

Southern Illinois University (Ph.D.)

Department of Psychology
Life Science Building II, Room 281
Carbondale, IL 62901
phone#: (618) 453-3564 (graduate program secretary)
email: mcashel@siu.edu
Web address: psychology.siuc.edu/grad/clinical.htm

1	2	3	**4**	5	6	7
Practice oriented			Equal emphasis			Research oriented

Percentage of faculty subscribing to each of the following orientations:

Psychodynamic/Psychoanalytic	0%
Applied behavioral analysis/Radical behavioral	0%
Family systems	0%
Existential/Phenomenological/Humanistic (Child Centered)	10%
Cognitive/Cognitive-behavioral	90%

Courses required for incoming students prior to enrolling: none

Recommended but not mandatory courses: History and systems, tests and measurements, abnormal, personality, learning, developmental, physiological/neuroscience, statistics, social

GRE mean
Verbal (average percent below) = 75%
Quantitative (average percent below) = 70%
Analytical Writing not reported
Psychology Subject Test not reported

GPA mean
3.73 over the last 5 years

Number of applications/admission offers/incoming students in 2017
112 applied/13 admission offers/7 incoming

% of students receiving:
Full tuition waiver only: 0%
Assistantship/fellowship only: 0%
Both full tuition waiver & assistantship/fellowship: 100%

Approximate percentage of incoming students with a B.A./B.S. only: 94% **Master's:** 13% (average over the last 7 years)

Approximate percentage of current students who are Women: 70% **Ethnic Minority:** 18% **International:** 1%

Average years to complete the doctoral program (including internship): 6.11 years

Personal interview
No preference given
(Note: Short-listed applicants are invited to an open house in February.)

Attrition rate in past 7 years: 13%

Percentage of students applying for internship in 2017accepted into:

APA internships: 100% **APPIC internships:** 100%

Formal tracks/concentrations: child and adult

Research areas	# Faculty	# Grants
abuse	1	0
ADHD/LD	1	3
adolescent issues	2	3
anxiety disorders	2	2
assessment	4	0
behavioral genetics	1	many
behavioral medicine	2	0
child clinical	3	1
clinical judgment	1	0
delinquency	1	3
depression	2	0
gender roles	1	0
learning disabilities	2	1
pediatric psychology	1	0
personality (five-factor model)	1	0
personality assessment	3	0
relationships	2	0
smoking	1	many
stress, coping, and social support	4	0

Clinical opportunities
Anxiety disorders
Acceptance and Commitment Therapy
Child Clinical Psychology
Pediatric psychology
Neuropsychology/Rehabilitation

Southern Methodist University (Ph.D.)

Department of Psychology
PO Box 750442
Dallas, TX 75275-0442
phone#: (214) 768-2438
email: rhampson@smu.edu, lsimpson@smu.edu
Web address: www.smu.edu/Dedman/Academics/Departments/Psychology/GraduateStudies

1	2	3	4	**5**	6	7
Practice oriented			Equal emphasis			Research oriented

Percentage of faculty subscribing to each of the following orientations:

Couples	10%
Applied behavioral analysis	20%
Family systems/Systems	10%
Cognitive/Cognitive-behavioral	40%
Neurological bases of behavior	10%
Psychophysiological	10%

Courses required for incoming students to have completed prior to enrolling: Abnormal Psychology, Research Methods/Statistics

Recommended but not mandatory courses:
Developmental Psychology

GRE mean
Verbal 160
Quantitative 161
Analytical Writing 5.0
Psychology Subject Test not required

GPA mean
Overall GPA 3.63

Number of applications/admission offers/incoming students in 2017
150 applied/8 admission offers/7 incoming

% of students receiving:
Full tuition waiver only: 0%
Assistantship/fellowship only: 0%
Both full tuition waiver & assistantship/fellowship: 100%

Approximate percentage of incoming students with a B.A./B.S. only: 86% **Master's:** 14%

Approximate percentage of students who are Women: 84% **Ethnic Minority:** 33% **International:** 6%

Average years to complete the doctoral program (including internship): 6 years

Personal interview: Required in person

Attrition rate in past 7 years: 6%

Percentage of students applying for internship in 2017 accepted into:

APA internships: 100% **APPIC internships:** 100%

Formal tracks/concentrations/specializations: Areas of concentration: Child/Family, Health, Psychopathology

Research areas	# Faculty	# Grants
family	7	2
health	3	0
psychopathology	3	2
cognitive	1	0
quantitative	1	0
diversity/disparity	1	0
neurocognitive	1	0

Clinical opportunities
assessment
psychotherapy for anxiety and mood disorders
couples therapy

External practica include a wide variety of community counseling centers, VA Medical Center, Dallas County Probation, Juvenile Justice, Children's Medical Center, Parkland Hospital Consult/Liaison, Presbyterian Hospital, neuropsychology, eating disorders

University of Southern Mississippi (Ph.D.)

Department of Psychology
118 College Dr. #5025
Hattiesburg, MS 39406-5025
phone#: (601) 266-4588
email: sara.jordan@usm.edu
Web address: www.usm.edu/clinical-psychology

1	2	3	4	**5**	6	7
Clinically oriented			Equal emphasis			Research oriented

Percentage of faculty subscribing to each of the following orientations:

Psychodynamic/Psychoanalytic	0%
Applied behavioral analysis/Radical behavioral	25%
Family systems/Systems	25%
Existential/Phenomenological/Humanistic	12.5%
Cognitive/Cognitive-behavioral	100%

Courses required for incoming students to have completed prior to enrolling:
statistics, research methods, abnormal psychology

Recommended but not mandatory courses: none

GRE mean
Verbal 158 Quantitative 156
Analytical Writing 4.0
Psychology Subject Test n/a

GPA mean
Overall GPA 3.69

Number of applications/admission offers/incoming students in 2017
107 applied/13 admission offers/6 incoming

% of students receiving:
Full tuition waiver only: 0%
Assistantship/fellowship only: 0%
Both full tuition waiver & assistantship/fellowship: 100%

Approximate percentage of incoming students with a B.A./B.S. only: 67% **Master's:** 33%

Approximate percentage of all students who are
Women: 81% **Ethnic Minority:** 16% **International:** 9%

Average years to complete the doctoral program (including internship): 5.7 years

Personal interview
Required in person or phone interviews

Attrition rate in past 7 years: 11.9%

Percentage of students applying for internship in 2016 accepted into:

APA internships: 100% **APPIC internships:** 100%

Formal tracks/concentrations: adult, child

Research areas
adult clinical
child clinical
adult/child externalizing behavior
personality assessment
personality disorders
mental health treatment outcomes
suicide
non-suicidal self-injury
anxiety & trauma-related disorders
addictions
multivariate statistics
positive psychology
measurement
child routines & parenting
substance abuse
juvenile delinquency
prevention/intervention
risk factors
dissemination & implementation

Clinical opportunities
Evidence-based assessment and treatment
Adult/child outpatient
Adult/child inpatient
Residential treatment (adult substance abuse; child/adolescent)
Adult probation system
Veterans health care system
Child & Adolescent neuropsychology
School-based mental health
DBT Skills group

Spalding University (Psy.D.)

School of Professional Psychology
845 South Third Street
Louisville, KY 40203
phone#: (502) 585-7127
email: bnash@spalding.edu
Web address: www.spalding.edu/

1	2	3	4	5	6	7
Practice oriented			Equal emphasis			Research oriented

Percentage of faculty subscribing to each of the following orientations:

Psychodynamic/Psychoanalytic	20%
Applied behavioral analysis/Radical behavioral	0%
Family systems/Systems	20%
Existential/Phenomenological/Humanistic	10%
Cognitive/Cognitive-behavioral	50%

Courses required for incoming students to have completed prior to enrolling:
18 hours of undergraduate work.

Recommended but not mandatory courses:
Undergraduate research

GRE mean
Verbal 151 Quantitative 150
Analytical Writing not reported
Psychology Subject Test not required

GPA mean
Overall GPA 3.73

Number of applications/admission offers/incoming students in 2017
174 applied/55 admission offers/34 incoming

% of students receiving:
Full tuition waiver only: 0%
Assistantship/fellowship only: 58% (includes HRSA scholarships and graduate assistantships)
Both full tuition waiver & assistantship/fellowship: 0%

Approximate percentage of incoming students with a B.A./B.S. only: 66% **Master's:** 34%

Approximate percentage of students who are
Women: 82% **Ethnic Minority:** 12% **International:** 3%

Average years to complete the doctoral program (including internship): 6 years

Personal interview
Preferred in person but Skype acceptable for long distance/international students

Attrition rate in past 7 years: 19%

Percentage of students applying for internship in 2017 accepted into:

APA internships: 100% **APPIC internships:** 100%

Formal tracks/concentrations: forensic psychology; health psychology; adult psychology; child, adolescent, and family psychology

Research areas	# Faculty	# Grants
child development	1	0
forensic	1	0
program evaluation	2	2
sports psychology	1	0
trauma	2	0
health	1	0
spirituality	1	0
substance abuse	1	0
bias	2	0
teaching psychology	1	0
client outcome	1	1
diverse populations	2	0

Clinical opportunities
medical hospital
VA hospital
psychiatric hospital
rehabilitation hospitals

private practice
prison/halfway house
college counseling centers
schools
nursing homes
pain
adolescents
couples
group
family
youth residential
substance abuse
community
rape and domestic violence crisis centers
family reunification residential facilities
young children
aged adult
psychopathology

Stony Brook University/State University of New York (Ph.D.)

Department of Psychology
Stony Brook, NY 11794-2500
phone#: (631) 632-7830
email: joanne.davila@stonybrook.edu
Web address: http://www.stonybrook.edu/commcms/psychology/clinical/overview.html

1	2	3	4	5	**6**	7
Practice oriented			Equal emphasis			Research oriented

Percentage of faculty subscribing to each of the following orientations:

Psychodynamic/Psychoanalytic	38%
Applied behavioral analysis/Radical behavioral	25%
Family systems/Systems	25%
Existential/Phenomenological/Humanistic	25%
Cognitive/Cognitive-behavioral	100%

Courses required for incoming students to have completed prior to enrolling: none

Recommended but not mandatory courses: Statistics, experimental with lab, abnormal psychology, research methods

GRE mean of applicants accepted for academic year
Verbal 88% Quantitative 62%
Analytical Writing 69%
Psychology Subject Test not reported

GPA mean
Overall GPA 3.9

Number of applications/admission offers/incoming students in 2017
353 applied/14 admission offers/8 incoming

% of students receiving:
Full tuition waiver only: 0%
Assistantship/fellowship only: 0%
Both full tuition waiver & assistantship/fellowship: 100%

Approximate percentage of incoming students with a B.A./B.S. only: 75% **Master's:** 25%

Approximate percentage of students who are Women: 88% **Ethnic Minority:** 18% **International:** 13%

Average years to complete the doctoral program (including internship): 6 years

Personal interview
In person

Attrition rate in past 7 years: 5%

Percentage of students applying for internship in 2017 accepted into:

APA internships: 100% **APPIC internships:** 100%

Formal tracks/concentrations: None

Research areas	# Faculty	# Grants
mood disorders	5	2
affective and social neuroscience	5	7
attention/perception and psychopathology	2	2
personality and psychopathology	3	1
autism spectrum disorders	1	14
child maltreatment	1	1
close relationships and mental health	3	1
partner abuse	1	1
classification	1	0
LGBT issues	2	0

Clinical opportunities
psychological center
marital clinic
university hospital
anxiety disorders clinic
mind-body clinical research center

Suffolk University (Ph.D.)

Department of Psychology
73 Tremont St., 8th Floor
Boston, MA 02108
phone#: (617) 573-8293
email: phd@suffolk.edu
Web address: http://www.suffolk.edu/college/graduate/69299.php

1	2	3	**4**	5	6	7
Practice oriented			Equal emphasis			Research oriented

Percentage of faculty subscribing to each of the following orientations:

Psychodynamic/Psychoanalytic	8%
Applied behavioral analysis/Radical behavioral	8%
Family systems/Systems	23%
Existential/Phenomenological/Humanistic	15%
Cognitive/Cognitive-behavioral	46%

Courses required for incoming students to have completed prior to enrolling:
5 courses in psychology

Recommended but not mandatory courses: Statistics and research methods highly preferred

GRE mean
Verbal 161 Quantitative 155
Analytical Writing 5
Psychology Subject Test 670

GPA mean
Overall GPA 3.58

Number of applications/admission offers/incoming students in 2016
210 applied/15 admission offers/8 incoming

% of students receiving:
Full tuition waiver only: 10%
Assistantship/fellowship only: 66%
Both full tuition waiver & assistantship/fellowship: 2%

Approximate percentage of incoming students with a B.A./B.S. only: 62% **Master's:** 38% (includes Ph.D.s)

Approximate percentage of students who are Women: 86% **Ethnic Minority:** 27% **International:** 1%

Average years to complete the doctoral program (including internship): 5.99 years

Personal interview
Required; in person preferred but telephone may be arranged

Attrition rate in past 7 years: 1.6%

Percentage of students applying for internship in 2016 accepted into:

APA internships: 100% **APPIC internships:** 0%

Formal tracks/concentrations: none

Research areas
See web site for specific faculty research areas (http://www.suffolk.edu/college/graduate/69312.php)

Clinical opportunities
adult inpatient and outpatient
community mental health
child and adolescent
inpatient and outpatient
college/university counseling center
forensic
neuropsychological assessment
schools
medical center

Syracuse University (Ph.D.)

Department of Psychology
430 Huntington Hall
Syracuse, NY 13244-2340
phone#: (315) 443-2354
email: kmantshe@syr.edu
Web address: http://psychology.syr.edu/graduate/Clinical-Psychology.html

1	2	3	4	5	**6**	7
Practice oriented			Equal emphasis			Research oriented

Percentage of faculty subscribing to each of the following orientations:

Psychodynamic/Psychoanalytic	15%
Applied behavioral analysis/Radical behavioral	0%
Family systems/Systems	0%
Existential/Phenomenological/Humanistic	0%
Cognitive/Cognitive-behavioral	100%

Courses required for incoming students prior to enrolling:
no course requirements; broad psychology background preferred

Recommended but not mandatory courses: none

GRE mean
Verbal 160 Quantitative 158
Analytical Writing 4.5
Psychology Subject Test not reported

GPA mean
Overall GPA 3.7 Psychology GPA 3.7

Number of applications/admission offers/incoming students in 2017
204 applied/5 admission offers/5 incoming

% of students receiving:
Full tuition waiver only: 0%
Assistantship/fellowship only: 0%
Both full tuition waiver & assistantship/fellowship: 100%

Approximate percentage of incoming students with a B.A./B.S. only: 90% **Master's:** 10%

Approximate percentage of students who are Women: 74% **Ethnic Minority:** 13% **International:** 0%

Average years to complete the doctoral program (including internship): 6 years

Personal interview
Preferred in person but telephone acceptable

Attrition rate in past 7 years: 19%

Percentage of students applying for internship in 2017 accepted into:

APA internships: 100% **APPIC internships:** 100%

Formal tracks/concentrations: adult clinical, child, health, substance abuse

Research areas	**# Faculty**	**# Grants**
AIDS/HIV	2	5
adolescent/at-risk adolescent	5	8
alcohol	4	14
ADHD	1	2
autism/developmental disorders	1	2
behavioral medicine/health psychology	6	25
cardiovascular health/function	2	5
child/child clinical/pediatric	1	2
chronic disease/illness	3	10
genetics/behavioral genetics	1	0
health care/primary care	3	2
intervention	4	12
nicotine/tobacco/smoking	2	2
pain management	1	2
personality assessment	2	0
psychopathology-child/developmental	1	2
psychophysiology	3	2
stigma	1	0
stress and coping	5	7
substance abuse/addictive behaviors	5	16

Clinical opportunities
ADHD
adolescent psychotherapy/at-risk adolescents
AIDS/HIV
anxiety & panic disorders
behavioral medicine/health psychology
child/pediatric
cognitive/cognitive behavioral therapy
community psychology
crisis intervention

developmental disabilities/autism/assessment
empirically supported treatments/interventions
integrated behavioral healthcare
medical center/hospital-based services
pain management
personality disorders
primary care
psychoanalytic/psychodynamic therapy
stress
substance abuse/addiction
veterans hospital/medical center

Teachers College–Columbia University (Ph.D.)

Department of Clinical Psychology
525 West 120th Street
New York, NY 10027
phone#: (212) 678-3099
email: verdeli@tc.edu
Web address: http://www.tc.columbia.edu/counseling-and-clinical-psychology/

1	2	3	4	5	6	7
Practice oriented			Equal emphasis			Research oriented

Percentage of faculty subscribing to each of the following orientations:

Psychodynamic/Psychoanalytic	25%
Applied behavioral analysis/Radical behavioral	0%
Family systems/Systems	12.5%
Existential/Phenomenological/Humanistic	12.5%
Cognitive/Interpersonal-Short Term	37.5%

Courses required for incoming students to have completed prior to enrolling:
Statistics and 9 credits from among: experimental psychology, personality, history and systems, developmental psychology, or social

Recommended but not mandatory courses: abnormal, experimental methods

GRE mean
Verbal 155 Quantitative 155
Analytical Writing 4.9
Psychology Subject Test not tequired, but recommended

GPA mean
Overall GPA 3.7

Number of applications/admission offers/incoming students in 2017
420 applied/9 admission offers/8 incoming

% of students receiving:
Full tuition waiver only: 70%
Assistantship/fellowship only: 70%
Both full tuition waiver & assistantship/fellowship: 50%
(90% of students receive at least a partial tuition wavier)

Approximate percentage of incoming students with a B.A./B.S. only: 25% **Master's:** 75%

Approximate percentage of all students who are Women: 70% **Ethnic Minority:** 28% **International:** 20%

Average years to complete the doctoral program (including internship): 6.4 years

Personal interview
Required in person

Attrition rate in past 7 years: 3%

Percentage of students applying for internship in 2016 accepted into:

APA internships: 100% **APPIC internships:** 100%

Formal tracks: Not applicable.

Research areas	# Faculty	# Grants
altruism	1	0
geriatrics	1	0
psychotherapy research	3	6
risk and resilience	2	1
spirituality	1	4
trauma, stress and coping	2	2
bipolarity in families	1	1

Clinical opportunities
Child & adolescent therapy
Cognitive-behavioral therapy
Interpersonal psychotherapy
Emotion regulation therapy
Dialectical Behavior Therapy
Multicultural competence training to work with military veterans

Temple University (Ph.D.)

Department of Psychology
1701 N. 13th Street
Philadelphia, PA 19122-6085
phone#: (215) 204-7326
email: rfauber@temple.edu
Web address: www.temple.edu/psychology/clinical/index.htm

1	2	3	4	5	**6**	7
Practice oriented			Equal emphasis			Research oriented

Percentage of faculty subscribing to each of the following orientations:

Psychodynamic/Psychoanalytic	0%
Applied behavioral analysis/Radical behavioral	0%
Family systems/Systems	18%
Existential/Phenomenological/Humanistic	9%
Cognitive/Cognitive-behavioral	100%

Courses required for incoming students prior to enrolling:
B.A. or B.S. degree and at least 4 courses in psychology (including 1 research methods course) and statistics

Recommended but not mandatory courses: 1 natural sciences laboratory course

GRE mean
Verbal + Quantitative = 321 (162V + 159Q)
Analytical Writing = 4.82
Psychology Subject Test not reported

GPA mean
Overall GPA 3.78

Number of applications/admission offers/incoming students in 2017
414 applied/17 admission offers/11 incoming

% of students receiving:
Full tuition waiver only: 0%
Assistantship/fellowship only: 0%
Both full tuition waiver & assistantship/fellowship: 100%

Approximate percentage of incoming students with a B.A./B.S. only: 82% **Master's:** 18%

Approximate percentage of students who are Women: 75% **Ethnic Minority:** 10% **International:** 4%

Average years to complete the doctoral program (including internship): 6 years

Personal interview
Required in person

Attrition rate in past 7 years: 3%

Percentage of students applying for internship in 2017 accepted into:

APA internships: 100% **APPIC internships:** 100%

Formal tracks/concentrations: Developmental Psychopathology, Neuroscience, Statistics

Research areas	# Faculty	# Grants
adult anxiety disorders/treatment	1	0
child anxiety disorders/treatment	1	1
childhood externalizing problems	1	0
adolescent and adult mood disorders	3	7
adult eating disorders	1	0
prenatal development and risk for schizophrenia	1	1
neuropsychology of everyday action & dementia & schiz.	1	0
aggression and intermittent explosive disorder	1	0
relationship difficulties/couples therapy	1	0

Clinical opportunities
anxiety disorders in children
adult social anxiety and generalized anxiety disorder
bipolar spectrum disorders and depression
eating disorders
dissemination and implementation of computer-assisted treatments
conduct problems among youth and depression
clinical neuropsychology
specialty clinics in a large urban area
couples and family therapy
intermittent explosive disorder
personality disorders

University of Tennessee (Ph.D.)

Department of Psychology
Austin Peay Psychology Building
Knoxville, TN 37996-0900
phone#: (865) 974-2165
email: mhunsber@utk.edu
Web address: http://psychology.utk.edu/grad/phd_clinical.php

1	2	3	4	5	6	7
Practice oriented			Equal emphasis			Research oriented

Percentage of faculty subscribing to each of the following orientations:

Psychodynamic/Psychoanalytic	22%
Applied behavioral analysis/Radical behavioral	0%
Family systems/Systems	11%
Existential/Phenomenological/Humanistic	0%
Cognitive/Cognitive-behavioral	67%

Courses required for incoming students to have completed prior to enrolling: none

Recommended but not mandatory courses: none

GRE mean
Verbal 156 Quantitative 152
Analytical Writing 4.5
Psychology Subject Test not reported

GPA mean
Overall GPA 3.77

Number of applications/admission offers/incoming students in 2017
219 applied/9 admission offers/5 incoming

% of students receiving:
Full tuition waiver only: 0%
Assistantship/fellowship only: 0%
Both full tuition waiver & assistantship/fellowship: 100%

Approximate percentage of incoming students with a B.A./B.S. only: 100% **Master's:** 0%

Approximate percentage of all students who are Women: 78% **Ethnic Minority:** 24% **International:** 0%

Average years to complete the doctoral program (including internship): 6 years

Personal interview:
Preferred in person, but telephone acceptable

Attrition rate in past 7 years 4%

Percentage of students applying for internship in 2017 accepted into:

APA internships: 100% **APPIC internships:** 100%

Formal tracks/concentrations: none

Research areas	# Faculty	# Grants
family/relationship	4	3
adult psychopathology	5	1
developmental psychopathology	5	0
adolescent development	1	0
therapy	4	2
health	1	1

Clinical opportunities
romantic relationships (adolescent and adult)
borderline personality (adult and child)
mindfulness
substance abuse (adolescents and adults)
conduct disorder

disorder development
Anxiety Disorders
(adult and child)
relationship violence
ADHD

Texas A&M University (Ph.D.)

Department of Psychology
College Station, TX 77843-4235
phone#: (979) 845-8017
email: balsis@tamu.edu
Web address: https://psychology.tamu.edu/clinical-psychology/

1	2	3	4	5	**6**	7
Practice oriented			Equal emphasis			Research oriented

Percentage of faculty subscribing to each of the following orientations:

Psychodynamic/Psychoanalytic	15%
Applied behavioral analysis/Radical behavioral	10%
Family systems/Systems	20%
Existential/Phenomenological/Humanistic	10%
Cognitive/Cognitive-behavioral	90%

Courses required for incoming students prior to enrolling:
Introductory statistics, abnormal, and at least 3 other psychology courses including a course in a core basic experimental area

Recommended but not mandatory courses: Advanced research-based seminars

GRE mean
Verbal 155 Quantitative 160
Analytical Writing not required
Psychology Subject Test not reported

GPA mean
Overall GPA 3.57

Number of applications/admission offers/incoming students in 2018
198 applied/12 admission offers/8 incoming

% of students receiving:
Full tuition waiver only: 0%
Assistantship/fellowship only: 0%
Both full tuition waiver & assistantship/fellowship: 100%

Approximate percentage of incoming students with a B.A./B.S. only: 70% **Master's:** 30%

Approximate percentage of students who are Women: 70% **Ethnic Minority:** 30% **International:** 10%

Average years to complete the doctoral program (including internship): 5-6 years

Personal interview
Preferred in person but telephone acceptable

Attrition rate in past 7 years, including 2017: 6%

Percentage of students applying for internship in 2017 accepted into:

APA internships: 100% **APPIC internships:** 100%

Formal tracks/concentrations: none

Research areas	# Faculty	# Grants
addictive disorders	2	
aging	1	
assessment	4	
child behavior disorders	2	
forensic	1	
gender issues	1	
health psychology	2	
marital/family studies	2	
personality disorders	3	
psychopathology	4	
psychotherapy	2	

Clinical opportunities
community
family
forensic/correctional
neuropsychology
rural psychology
substance abuse

University of Texas at Austin (Ph.D.)

Department of Psychology
108 E. Dean Keeton A8000
Austin, TX 78712
phone#: (512) 471-3393
email: psygradoffice@utexas.edu
Web address: http://liberalarts.utexas.edu/psychology/areas-of-study/clinical/about.php

1	2	3	4	5	**6**	7
Practice oriented			Equal emphasis			Research oriented

Percentage of faculty subscribing to each of the following orientations:

Psychodynamic/Psychoanalytic	0%
Applied behavioral analysis/Radical behavioral	0%
Family systems/Systems	0%
Existential/Phenomenological/Humanistic	15%
Cognitive/Cognitive-behavioral	85%

Courses required for incoming students to have completed prior to enrolling: none

Recommended but not mandatory courses: abnormal, neuroscience, research methods, statistics

GRE mean
Verbal + Quantitative 319
Analytical Writing not reported
Psychology Subject Test not reported

GPA mean
Overall GPA 3.65

Number of applications/admission offers/incoming students in 2016
358 applicants/7 offers/5 incoming

% of students receiving:
Full tuition waiver only: 0%
Assistantship/fellowship only: 0%
Both full tuition waiver & assistantship/fellowship: 100%

Approximate percentage of incoming students with a B.A./B.S. only: 75% **Master's:** 25%

Approximate percentage of all students who are Women: 66% **Ethnic Minority:** 14% **International:** 17%

Average years to complete the doctoral program (including internship): 6.4 years

Personal interview
Required

Attrition rate in past 7 years: 5%

Percentage of students applying for internship in 2016 accepted into:

APA internships: 100% **APPIC internships:** 100%

Formal tracks/concentrations: neuroimaging track

Research areas	# Faculty	# Grants
addictions	1	1
anxiety	2	1
behavior genetics	2	2
depression	1	3
developmental disabilities/autism	1	0
health psychology	1	1
multicultural psychology	1	0
neurobiology of aging	1	4
positive psychology/well-being	1	0
sexual dysfunction	1	1
social endocrinology	1	0
stress and coping	1	1

Clinical opportunities

addictions/recovery	depression
ADHD	diverse populations
anxiety disorders	marital
assessment	military/veterans
autism	neuropsychology
behavioral medicine	obsessive–compulsive disorder
child/family	severe mental illness
personality disorders	sleep psychology
primary care	student counseling center
community	survivors of torture
crisis intervention	

University of Texas Southwestern Medical Center at Dallas (Ph.D.)

Division of Psychology
5323 Harry Hines Boulevard
Dallas, TX 75390-9044
phone#: (214) 648-5277
email: psychology@utsouthwestern.edu
Web address: http://www.utsouthwestern.edu/clinical-psychology

1	2	3	4	5	6	7
Practice oriented			Equal emphasis			Research oriented

Percentage of faculty subscribing to each of the following orientations:

Dynamic/Psychoanalytic	40%
Applied behavioral analysis/Radical behavioral	5%
Family systems/Systems	10%
Existential/Phenomenological/Humanistic	5%
Cognitive/Cognitive-behavioral	40%

Courses required for incoming students to have completed prior to enrolling:
Introduction to Psychology; Learning (can be experimental psychology, cognitive psychology or behavioral psychology), behavioral statistics

Recommended but not mandatory courses:
Developmental, physiological, experimental

GRE mean
Verbal + Quantitative 318
Analytical Writing not reported
Psychology Subject Test not reported

GPA mean
Overall GPA 3.72

Number of applications/admission offers/incoming students in 2017
228 applied/17 admission offers for class of 10 incoming

% of students receiving:
Full tuition waiver only: 0%
Assistantship/fellowship: 100% (in 2nd year through end of 4th year)
Both full tuition waiver & assistantship/fellowship: 0%

Approximate percentage of incoming students with a B.A./B.S. only: 60% **Master's:** 40%

Approximate percentage of students who are Women: 100% **Ethnic Minority:** 30% **International:** 0%

Average years to complete the doctoral program (including internship): 4.3 years

Personal interview
Required in person

Attrition rate in past 5 years: 5%

Percentage of students applying for internship in 2017 accepted into:

APA internships: 100% **APPIC internships:** (none)
*Our program has an affiliated internship which is APA accredited.

Formal tracks/concentrations: health psychology, child and adolescent psychology, neuropsychology

Research areas	# Faculty	# Grants
Alzheimer's	1	1
child depression	3	3
community mental health	1	0
cultural issues in psychology	2	1
depression	3	3
developmental psychology	1	1
health psychology	3	2
health services research	1	1
learning disabilities	1	0
neurobiological aspects of psychological disorders	2	–
neuropsychological profiles	2	2
pain management	1	1
pediatric psychology	1	1
rehabilitation psychology	1	1
sleep disorders	1	0

Clinical opportunities

affective disorders
behavioral psychology
clinical child
community mental health
developmental disabilities
family therapy
forensic psychology
health/medical psychology
neuropsychology
outpatient psychotherapy
personality disorders
primary care clinic consultation
psychiatric emergency care
rehabilitation psychology
sleep disorders
inpatient psychiatry

Texas Tech University (Ph.D.)

Department of Psychological Sciences
P.O. Box 42501
Lubbock, TX 79409-2051
phone#: (806) 742-3711
fax#: (806) 742-0818
email: kay.hill@ttu.edu or steven.richards@ttu.edu
Web address: https://www.depts.ttu.edu/psy/clinical/

1	2	3	4	5	6	7
Practice oriented			Equal emphasis			Research oriented

Percentage of faculty subscribing to each of the following orientations:

Psychodynamic/Psychoanalytic	11%
Applied behavioral analysis/Radical behavioral	22%
Family systems/Systems	22%
Existential/Phenomenological/Humanistic	0%
Cognitive/Cognitive-behavioral	100%
Interpersonal	22%
Cognitive–Interpersonal	33%
Dialectical/Behavioral	22%

Courses required for incoming students prior to enrolling:
18 semester hours of psychology

Recommended but not mandatory courses: statistics, abnormal, developmental, physiological, and a research methods course such as experimental design or independent research with a faculty member

GRE mean
Verbal: 156 Quantitative 155
Analytical Writing 4.4
Psychology Subject Test not required

GPA mean
Overall GPA: 3.71

Number of applications/admission offers/incoming students in 2017
145 applied/12 admission offers/9 incoming

% of students receiving:
Full tuition waiver only: 0%
Assistantship/fellowship only: 0%
Both tuition waiver & assistantship/fellowship: 100%

Approximate percentage of incoming students with a B.A./B.S. only: 89% **Master's:** 11%

Approximate percentage of all students who are Women: 78% **Ethnic Minority:** 23% **International:** 0%

Average years to complete the doctoral program (including internship): 6.8 years

Personal interview
In-person interviews strongly encouraged but telephone interviews acceptable if in-person interview not possible.

Attrition rate in past 7 years: 10%

Percentage of students applying for internship in 2017 accepted into:

APA internships: 100% (4/4) **APPIC internships:** 100%

Formal tracks/concentrations: none

Research areas	# Faculty	# Grants
addictions	1	1
anxiety disorders	1	0
behavioral assessment	2	0
behavioral medicine	3	1
behavioral parent training	1	0
child depression and anxiety	1	0
child maltreatment and abuse	3	0
cognitive-behavioral therapies	1	0
community interventions	2	0
ethnic minority/cultural issues	1	0
health psychology	3	1
health disparities	1	0
high-risk patients/suicide	1	1
high-risk youth	1	0
informant discrepancies/rater biases in child assessment	1	0
mood disorders	1	0
neuropsychology/neuroscience	1	0
nicotine dependence/withdrawal	1	1
single subject design, time series regression, dynamic factor analysis	2	0
Sleep	1	0
Spanish-speaking families	1	0
suicide	1	1
teachers' evaluations of children's problems	1	0
trauma	1	0

Clinical opportunities
Extensive opportunities with diverse populations are available throughout the community, university medical center, and health sciences center.

University of Toledo (Ph.D.)

Department of Psychology
Mail Stop 948
2801 West Bancroft Street
Toledo, OH 43606-3390
phone#: (419) 530-2771
email: sarah.francis@utoledo.edu
Web address: http://www.utoledo.edu/al/psychology/grad/clinical/

1	2	3	4	5	6	7
Practice oriented			Equal emphasis			Research oriented

Percentage of faculty subscribing to each of the following orientations:

Psychodynamic/Psychoanalytic	20%
Applied behavioral analysis/Radical behavioral	20%
Family systems/Systems	20%
Existential/Phenomenological/Humanistic	20%
Cognitive/Cognitive-behavioral	70%
Neuropsychology	10%
Behavioral/Acceptance-based behavioral	20%
Mindfulness-based	10%
Community psychology	10%

Courses required for incoming students to have completed prior to enrolling:
Statistics and research methods

Recommended but not mandatory courses: none

GRE mean
Verbal 163 Quantitative 156
Analytic Writing 4.79
Psychology Subject Test not reported

GPA mean
Overall GPA 3.75

Number of applications/admission offers/incoming students in 2017
145 applied/9 admission offers/7 incoming

% of students receiving:
Full tuition waiver only: 0%
Assistantship/fellowship only: 0%
Both full tuition waiver & assistantship/fellowship: 100%

Approximate percentage of incoming students with a B.A./B.S. only: 43% **Master's:** 57%

Approximate percentage of students who are Women: 67% **Ethnic Minority:** 10% **International:** 19%

Average years to complete the doctoral program (including internship): 5.78 years

Personal interview
Required in person (although international students can interview by telephone)

Attrition rate in past 7 years: 14%

Percentage of students applying for internship in 2017 accepted into:

APA internships: 100% **APPIC internships:** 100%

Formal tracks/concentrations: none

Research areas	# Faculty	# Grants
anxiety and depression	5	1
behavioral medicine/health psychology	1	0
child/adolescent psychopathology	3	1
cognitive behavioral therapy	1	0
community psychology	1	0
diversity & multicultural issues	3	0
emotion	2	1
mindfulness	1	0
personality disorders	1	0
positive psychology/resilience	1	0
posttraumatic stress disorder	2	2
program evaluation	3	0
psychological assessment	4	0
psychotherapy research	4	0
public mental health	1	1
self-esteem/self-efficacy/self-psychology	1	0
self-injury	1	1
stress & coping	2	0
substance abuse/addictive behaviors	1	0

Clinical opportunities
acceptance & commitment therapy
anxiety and depression
assessment
behavioral medicine/health psychology
borderline personality disorder
child & adolescent therapy
cognitive behavioral therapy
dialectical behavior therapy
family/family therapy/family systems
in-house clinic and externships
mindfulness
psychodynamic therapy
psychological assessment

University of Tulsa (Ph.D.)

Department of Psychology
Tulsa, OK 74104
phone#: (918) 631-2248
email: michael-basso@utulsa.edu
Web address: https://artsandsciences.utulsa.edu/academics/departments-schools/psychology/clinical-psychology-graduate-programs/

1	2	3	4	5	6	7
Practice oriented			Equal emphasis			Research oriented

Percentage of faculty subscribing to each of the following orientations:

Psychodynamic/Psychoanalytic	0%
Applied behavioral analysis/Radical behavioral	0%
Family systems/Systems	0%
Existential/Phenomenological/Humanistic	0%
Cognitive/Cognitive-behavioral	100%

Courses required for incoming students prior to enrolling:
Eighteen hours of credit in psychology courses or in courses that are primarily psychological in nature in a closely related field. Applicants must have taken abnormal and a course from among statistics, tests and measurements, or experimental.

Recommended but not mandatory courses:
developmental, learning, social, personality, cognitive psychology, physiological, and history of psychology

GRE mean
Verbal 159 (79th %ile) Quantitative 154 (57th %ile)
Analytical Writing 4.6 (78th %ile)
Psychology Subject Test not reported

GPA mean
Overall GPA 3.6

Number of applications/admission offers/incoming students in 2016
104 applied/14 admission offers/7 incoming

% of students receiving:
Full tuition waiver only: 0%
Assistantship/fellowship only: 0%
Both full tuition waiver & assistantship/fellowship 100% of Ph.D. (99% for all enrolled clinical students)

Approximate percentage of incoming students with a B.A./B.S. only: 67% **Master's:** 33%

Approximate percentage of all students who are Women: 55% **Ethnic Minority:** 20% **International:** 4%

Average years to complete the doctoral program (including internship): 6.3 years

Personal interview
Held on interview day for all Ph.D. candidates

Attrition rate in past 7 years: 10%

Percentage of students applying for internship in 2016 accepted into:

APA internships: 100% **APPIC internships:** 100%

Formal tracks/concentrations: clinical

Research areas	# Faculty	# Grants
life-span development	2	1
neuropsychology	1	1
personality disorders/personality	2	0
posttraumatic stress disorder	3	2
stress	4	2
pain/health	1	2

Clinical opportunities
Practicum program is community-based with access to over 32 general and specialty clinics; opportunities to conduct research and clinical work in both experimental and applied settings; opportunities for multi-disciplinary collaboration through several institutes

Uniformed Services University of Health Sciences (Ph.D.)

4301 Jones Bridge Road
Bethesda, MD 20814-4799
phone#: (301) 295-3270
email: Jeffrey.goodie@usuhs.edu
Web address: https://www.usuhs.edu/mps/clinical-psychology

1	2	3	4	5	**6**	7
Practice oriented			Equal emphasis			Research oriented

Percentage of faculty subscribing to each of the following orientations:

Psychodynamic/Psychoanalytic	13%
Applied behavioral analysis/Radical behavioral	0%
Family systems/Systems	0%
Existential/Phenomenological/Humanistic	0%
Cognitive/Cognitive-behavioral	87%

Courses required for incoming students prior to enrolling:
abnormal, statistics

Recommended but not mandatory courses: Basic undergraduate sequence of courses in psychology, and some coursework related to the biological sciences (e.g. biology, chemistry) and research design/statistics

GRE mean
Verbal 91% Quantitative 61%
Analytical Writing 76%
Psychology Subject Test not required

GPA mean
Overall GPA 3.77 (undergraduate)

Number of applications/admission offers/incoming students in 2017
207 applied/11 admission offers/8 incoming (clinical students)

% of students receiving:
Full tuition waiver only: 0%
Assistantship/fellowship only: 0%
Both full tuition waiver & assistantship/fellowship: 100%

Approximate percentage of incoming students with a B.A./B.S. only: 37.5% **Master's:** 62.5%

Approximate percentage of all students who are Women: 68% **Ethnic Minority:** 37% **International:** 0%
(Must be a United States citizen for Clinical Psychology - Military track)

Average years to complete the doctoral program (including internship): 5.76 years (degrees conferred between 2009–2016)

Personal interview
Required in person

Attrition rate in past 7 years: 14.5% (8 of 55 students enrolled between 2009–2016)

Percentage of students applying for internship in 2017 accepted into:

APA internships: 100% **APPIC internships:** 71.4%

Formal tracks/concentrations: clinical psychology – military track, clinical psychology – civilian track

Research areas	# Faculty	# Grants
addiction and smoking	1	1
obesity and eating disorders	3	4
health psychology	1	1
sexual dysfunction	1	0
stigma	1	1
stress and cardiovascular disease	1	1
suicide prevention	1	3
PTSD	1	1
implementation science	1	1

Clinical opportunities

child and adolescent medical settings	substance abuse
adult medical centers	NIH
military treatment facilities	VA hospitals
private practices	unique military settings
	community centers

University of Utah (Ph.D.)

Department of Psychology
380 S 1530 E, Room 502
Salt Lake City, UT 84112
phone#: (801) 581-6126
email: jeanne.asay@psych.utah.edu
Web address: https://psych.utah.edu/graduate/clinical.php

1	2	3	**4**	5	6	7
Practice oriented			Equal emphasis			Research oriented

Percentage of faculty subscribing to each of the following orientations:

Psychodynamic/Psychoanalytic	0%
Applied behavioral analysis/Radical behavioral	1%
Family systems/Systems	1%
Existential/Phenomenological/Humanistic	0%
Cognitive/Cognitive-behavioral	97%

Courses required for incoming students to have completed prior to enrolling:
Undergraduate degree in psychology or its equivalent, including statistics, research design, and psychopathology

Recommended but not mandatory courses: Advanced statistics and research design

GRE mean
Verbal 167
Quantitative 155
Analytical Writing 4.6
Psychology Subject Test 710

GPA mean
Overall GPA 3.71

Number of applications/admission offers/incoming students in 2017
196 applied/10 admission offers/6 incoming

% of students receiving:
Full tuition waiver only: 0%
Assistantship/fellowship only: 0%
Both full tuition waiver & assistantship/fellowship: 100%

Approximate percentage of incoming students with a B.A./B.S. only: 98% **Master's:** 2%

Approximate percentage of students who are Women: 70% **Ethnic Minority:** 25% **International:** 3%

Average years to complete the doctoral program (including internship): 6.5 years

Personal interview
Required in person

Attrition rate in past 7 years: 9%

Percentage of students applying for internship in 2017 accepted into:

APA internships: 100% **APPIC internships:** 100%

Formal tracks/concentrations: adult clinical, clinical child and family, health psychology/behavioral medicine, clinical neuropsychology

Research areas	# Faculty	# Grants
adolescent/child psychology	3	3
adult psychopathology	4	3
behavioral medicine/health psychology	2	3
family/couple research	4	3
minority mental health	1	1
neuropsychology	2	1
personality assessment	1	0
sexuality	1	0
suicide	2	2
trauma/PTSD	2	2

Clinical opportunities
adolescent/child assessment and psychotherapy
behavioral medicine/ health psychology
anxiety disorders
CBT
clinical neuropsychology
depression
family therapy
juvenile justice-involved/ delinquent youth
homeless/disadvantaged populations
LGBTQ adults and youth
inpatient treatment
interpersonal psychotherapy
military veterans/active service populations
minority mental health
pediatric psychology
personality disorders
rational-emotive therapy
sex therapy/sexuality
substance abuse treatment
trauma assessment/therapy

Vanderbilt University (Ph.D.)

Department of Psychology, College of Arts and Sciences
Department of Psychology and Human Development, Peabody College of Education and Human Development
Nashville, TN 37203
Web address: https://www.vanderbilt.edu/psychological_sciences/graduate/programs/clinical.php

1	2	3	4	5	6	**7**
Practice oriented			Equal emphasis			Research oriented

Percentage of faculty subscribing to each of the following orientations:

Psychodynamic/Psychoanalytic	0%
Applied behavioral analysis/Radical behavioral	14%
Family systems/Systems	7%
Existential/Phenomenological/Humanistic	0%
Cognitive/Cognitive-behavioral	100%

Courses required for incoming students to have completed prior to enrolling: 0

Recommended but not mandatory courses: 0

GRE mean
Verbal + Quantitative 1430
Analytical Writing n/a
Psychology Subject Test n/a

GPA mean
Overall GPA 3.71

Number of applications/admission offers/incoming students in 2016
422 applied/7 admission offers/6 incoming

% of students receiving:
Full tuition waiver only: 0%

Assistantship/fellowship only: 0%
Both full tuition waiver & assistantship/fellowship: 100%

Approximate percentage of incoming students with a B.A./B.S. only: 85% **Master's:** 15%

Approximate percentage of all students who are Women: 54% **Ethnic Minority:** 6% **International:** 3%

Average years to complete the doctoral program (including internship): 6 years

Personal interview: Required. Can be over the phone/internet if necessary.

Attrition rate in past 7 years: 6.5%

Percentage of students applying for internship last year accepted into:

APA internships: 100% **APPIC internships:** 0%

Formal tracks/concentrations:
There are no "formal" tracks, although students may focus on:
Psychopathology, including the identification, etiology, treatment, and prevention of psychopathology in children, adolescents and adults. Within psychopathology students can further concentrate their training in any of three areas:
Developmental psychopathology, including the identification, etiology, treatment, and prevention of psychopathology in children and adolescents (particularly with respect to mood disorders), and the study of typical and atypical development (particularly with respect to autism and intellectual disabilities). Faculty who are involved in the mentoring of students in this area include Drs. Bachorowski, Cole, Compas, Dykens, Garber, Hollon, Smith, Tomarken, Walker, and Weiss.
Adult psychopathology, including the identification, etiology, treatment and prevention of psychopathology in adults including mood disorders, anxiety disorders, somatoform disorders, schizophrenia, and psychopathy. Faculty involved in the mentoring of students in this area include Drs. Bachorowski, Compas, Davis, Garber, Hollon, Olatanji, Park, Schlundt, Tomarken, Walker, Weiss, and Zald.
Developmental disabilities, including the identification, etiology and treatment of autism, Prader-Willi Syndrome, and Williams Syndrome. Faculty mentors include Drs. Bachorowski and Dykens.
Clinical neuroscience, including neuropsychological, psychophysiological, and neuroimaging approaches to studying normal and abnormal behavior. Faculty mentors include Drs. Cole, Compas, Hollon, Olatunji, Park, Tomarken, and Zald.
Basic emotional processes, including the biological, cognitive, and interpersonal factors influencing basic emotion-related processes, as well as individual differences in affective traits. Faculty mentors include Drs. Bachorowski, Compas, Dykens, Garber, Hollon, Olatunji, Smith, Tomarken, and Zald.
Prevention and intervention, including the development and evaluation of optimal interventions for various psychopathologies, the prevention of diabetes and other biomedical disorders, and the identification of potential etiological or vulnerability markers that are linked to heightened risk for depressive disorders among children and adolescents. Faculty mentors include Drs. Compas, Garber, Hollon, Olatunji, and Weiss.
Health psychology, emphasizing a biopsychosocial approach to health and illness throughout the life span, including chronic and recurrent pain, cancer, and eating disorders. Faculty mentors include Drs. Compas, Garber, Olatunji, Schlundt, Smith, and Walker.
Quantitative analysis, including the application of advanced statistical techniques to the study of psychopathology and other clinical issues. Faculty mentors include Drs. Cole and Tomarken.

Research areas	**# Faculty**	**# Grants**
Anxiety	1	2
Behavioral medicine	2	1
Bullying	1	0
Cognitive-behavioral therapy	2	1
Depression	4	2
Developmental disabilties	1	1
Developmental psychopathology	5	5
Emotion	3	4
Global health	1	2
Neuroscience	2	3
Nutrition	1	0
Pediatric health psychology	2	2
Personality	1	1
Quantitative analysis	2	0
Racial and ethnic health disparaities	2	1
Schizophrenia	1	2
Stress and coping	3	2
Stress reactivity	1	1
Vocal communication	1	0

Clinical opportunities

Adult psychiatry	Juvenile justice
Anxiety disorders	Learning disabilities/psychoeducation assessment
Autism	Memory disorders
Behavior disorders	Neuropsychology
Pediatric behavioral medicine	Psychopathology assessment
Community mental health	Pediatric health
DBT	Private practice
Depression	Self-injury/suicidal behavior
Developmental disabilities	Substance abuse
Eating disorders	Tic disorders
Family therapy	VA medical center
Integrative medicine	

University of Vermont (Ph.D.)

Department of Psychology
John Dewey Hall
Burlington, VT 05405
phone#: (802) 656-4189
email: kelly.rohan @uvm.edu
Web address: http://www.uvm.edu/psychology/?Page=clinical/clinical_features.html&SM=clinical/clinicalsubmenu.html

1	2	3	4	**5**	6	7
Practice oriented			Equal emphasis			Research oriented

Percentage of faculty subscribing to each of the following orientations:

Psychodynamic/Psychoanalytic	0%
Applied behavioral analysis/Radical behavioral	0%
Family systems/Systems	10%

Existential/Phenomenological/Humanistic	0%
Cognitive/Cognitive-behavioral	90%

Courses required for incoming students to have completed prior to enrolling:
Psychology major or equivalent preferred. At a minimum, completed courses in each of the following: general psychology, statistics, research design, and abnormal psychology.

Recommended but not mandatory courses: none

GRE mean
Verbal 160 Quantitative 156
Analytical Writing 4.0
Psychology Subject Test n/a

GPA mean
Overall GPA 3.53

Number of applications/admission offers/incoming students in 2017
173 applied/6 admission offers/4 incoming

% of students receiving:
Full tuition waiver only: 0%
Assistantship/fellowship only: 0%
Both full tuition waiver & assistantship/fellowship: 100%

Approximate percentage of incoming students with a B.A./B.S. only: 100% **Master's:** 0%

Approximate percentage of students who are Women: 76% **Ethnic Minority:** 18% **International:** 0%

Average years to complete the doctoral program (including internship): 6.0 years

Personal interview
In person interview required

Attrition rate in past 7 years: 5%

Percentage of students applying for internship in 2017 accepted into:

APA internships: 75% **APPIC internships:** 75%

Formal tracks/concentrations: Clinical Developmental Ph.D. Program, Developmental Psychopathology concentration

Research areas	# Faculty	# Grants
child and adolescent treatment	2	2
depressive disorders	1	1
child and adolescent psychopathology	5	3
conduct disorders	1	0
prevention	3	3
sex offenders/abuse	1	0
sexual dysfunction	1	0
substance abuse	1	1
trauma/PTSD	2	2

Clinical opportunities

adolescent disorders	family therapy
anxiety disorders	refugees
behavioral medicine	prisoners
childhood disorders	prevention
depression	substance abuse
eating disorders	trauma/PTSD

Virginia Commonwealth University (Ph.D.)

Department of Psychology
806 West Franklin Street
Richmond, VA 23284-2018
phone#: (804) 828-1158 (admissions)
email: clin-psy@vcu.edu
Web address: http://psychology.vcu.edu/graduate/clinical/

1	2	3	4	**5**	6	7
Practice oriented			Equal emphasis			Research oriented

Percentage of faculty subscribing to each of the following orientations:

Psychodynamic/Psychoanalytic	0%
Applied behavioral analysis/Radical behavioral	0%
Family systems/Systems	15%
Existential/Phenomenological/Humanistic	0%
Cognitive/Cognitive-behavioral	100%
Interpersonal	25%

Courses required for incoming students to have completed prior to enrolling: none

Recommended but not mandatory courses: It is recommended that applicants complete at least 18 hours of psychology including experimental psychology, general psychology, and statistics. Applicants should also have substantial research experience in an identified area of clinical/research interest.

GRE mean
Verbal 158 Quantitative 155
Analytical Writing 4.4
Psychology Subject Test not reported

GPA mean
Overall GPA 3.60

Number of applications/admission offers/incoming students in 2016-2017
229 applied/14 admission offers/11 incoming

% of students receiving:
Full tuition waiver only: 0%
Assistantship/fellowship only: 0%
Both full tuition waiver & assistantship/fellowship: 100% for first 4 years of doctoral program

Approximate percentage of incoming students with a B.A./B.S. only: 80% **Master's:** 20%

Approximate percentage of all students who are Women: 81% **Ethnic Minority:** 55% **International:** 0%

Average years to complete the doctoral program (including internship): 6 years

Personal interview
In person interview strongly recommended, telephone interview may be acceptable in extenuating circumstances

Attrition rate in past 7 years: 7%

Percentage of students applying for internship in 2016-2017 accepted into:

APA internships: 100% **APPIC internships:** 100%

Formal tracks/concentrations: child/adolescent, behavioral medicine

Research areas	# Faculty	# Grants
adolescent	6	4
anxiety	3	1
behavioral medicine	6	3
child clinical/pediatric	6	4
community	10	3
minority/cross-cultural	3	1
pregnancy issues	2	1
psychopathology	5	1
psychophysiology	2	0
psychotherapy	3	3
stress and coping	2	0
substance abuse	2	2

Clinical opportunities

assessment and testing	inpatient
clinical health psychology	neuropsychology
poly-trauma treatment	anxiety
child pediatric	chronic mental illness
correctional psychology	pain management
primary care	substance abuse
unipolar mood disorder	

Virginia Consortium Program in Clinical Psychology (Ph.D.)

(Eastern Virginia Medical School, Norfolk State University, & Old Dominion University)
Norfolk State University
700 Park Avenue/MCAR-410
Norfolk, VA 23504
phone#: (757) 451-7733
email:vaconsortium@odu.edu
Web address: www.odu.edu/vcpcp

1	2	3	**4**	5	6	7
Practice oriented			Equal emphasis			Research oriented

Percentage of faculty subscribing to each of the following orientations:

Psychodynamic/Psychoanalytic	19%
Applied behavioral analysis/Radical behavioral	6%
Family systems/Systems	0%
Existential/Phenomenological/Humanistic	0%
Cognitive/Cognitive-behavioral	75%

Courses required for incoming students prior to enrolling: B.A. in psychology or equivalent, statistics, research methods

Recommended but not mandatory courses: strong background in psychology

GRE mean (2017)
Verbal 156 Quantitative 153
Analytical Writing n/a
Psychology Subject Test not reported

GPA mean
Undergraduate GPA 3.6

Number of applications/admission offers/incoming students in 2017
93 applied/6 incoming

% of students receiving:
Full tuition waiver only: 12.5%
Assistantship/fellowship only: 0%
Both tuition waiver & assistantship/fellowship: 100% (some type of assistantship and significant tuition reduction but not a complete waiver)

Approximate percentage of incoming students (2017) with a B.A./B.S. only: 67% **Master's:** 33%

Approximate percentage of all students who are Women: 66% **Ethnic Minority:** 31% **International:** 0%

Average years to complete the doctoral program (including internship): 4 years + 1year internship

Personal interview
Required in person

Attrition rate in past 7 years: 6%

Percentage of students applying for internship in 2017 accepted into:

APA internships: 87% **APPIC internships** 0%

Formal tracks/concentrations: none

Research areas	# Faculty	# Grants
Alzheimer's/dementia	2	0
domestic violence	3	1
eating disorders	1	0
emerging adulthood	4	0
gender and race in higher education	1	0
minority education	1	1
neuropsychology	2	1
parenting	3	0
pediatric psychology	3	0
personality assessment	3	1
rehabilitation psychology	3	0
sexual minority health	5	1
substance abuse	6	3

Clinical opportunities
Over 50 public and private agencies that serve adults, adolescents, and children

University of Virginia–Department of Psychology

College of Arts and Sciences
P.O. Box 400400
Charlottesville, VA 22904-4477
phone#: (434) 982-4750
email: psy-dept@virginia.edu
Web address: http://psychology.as.virginia.edu/research-areas/clinical

1	2	3	4	5	**6**	7
Practice oriented			Equal emphasis			Research oriented

Percentage of faculty subscribing to each of the following orientations:

Psychodynamic/Psychoanalytic	20%
Applied behavioral analysis/Radical behavioral	0%
Family systems/Systems	40%
Existential/Phenomenological/Humanistic	0%
Cognitive/Cognitive-behavioral	40%

Courses required for incoming students prior to enrolling:
B.A. in psychology or equivalent

Recommended but not mandatory courses: Abnormal psychology, statistics, research methods

GRE mean
Verbal 166 Quantitative 157
Analytical Writing 5.0
Psychology Subject Test not reported

GPA mean
Overall GPA 4.0

Number of applications/admission offers/incoming students in 2017
172 applied/5 admission offers/4 incoming

% of students receiving:
Full tuition waiver only: 0%
Assistantship/fellowship only: 0%
Both full tuition waiver & assistantship/fellowship: 100%

Approximate percentage of incoming students with a B.A./B.S. only: 75% **Master's:** 25%

Approximate percentage of students who are Women: 67% **Ethnic Minority:** 17% **International:** 5%

Average years to complete the doctoral program (including internship): 6.4 years

Personal interview
Preferred in person but telephone acceptable

Attrition rate in past 7 years: 4%

Percentage of students applying for internship in 2017 accepted into:

APA internships: 100% **APPIC internships:** 100%

Formal tracks/concentrations: none

Research areas	# Faculty	# Grants
adult psychopathology	2	3
anxiety/obsessive–compulsive disorders	1	1
behavioral genetics	2	1
child clinical/psychopathology	4	4
community psychology	3	3
developmental adolescence	3	3
family research/systems	3	2
minority mental health	2	2
neuropsychology	1	1
personality disorders	1	1
prevention	3	2
violence/abuse/victim–offender	2	1

Clinical opportunities

anxiety disorders
community psychology
behavioral medicine
depression
neuropsychology
obsessive–compulsive disorder
forensic psychology
marital/couples therapy
family therapy
pediatric psychology
psychology/law
schizophrenia/psychosis
victim/battering/abuse

Virginia Polytechnic Institute and State University (Ph.D.)

Department of Psychology
Williams Hall
Blacksburg, VA 24061-0436
phone#: (540) 231-6581
email: ldcooper@vt.edu
Web address: www.psyc.vt.edu/graduate/clinical

1	2	3	4	5	6	**7**
Practice oriented			Equal emphasis			Research oriented

Percentage of faculty subscribing to each of the following orientations:

Psychodynamic/Psychoanalytic	0%
Applied behavioral analysis/Radical behavioral	33%
Family systems/Systems	33%
Existential/Phenomenological/Humanistic	0%
Cognitive/Cognitive-behavioral	100%

Courses required for incoming students to have completed prior to enrolling:
Research methods, statistics, abnormal psychology

Recommended but not mandatory courses: Social psychology, developmental psychology, cognitive-affective psychology, biological bases of psychology, history and systems

GRE mean
Verbal 158/80% Quantitative 157/67%
Analytical Writing not reported
Psychology Subject Test not reported

GPA mean
Overall GPA 3.4

Number of applications/admission offers/incoming students in 2017
145 applied/7 admission offers/5 incoming

% of students receiving:
Full tuition waiver only: 0%
Assistantship/fellowship only: 0%
Both full tuition waiver & assistantship/fellowship: 100%

Approximate percentage of incoming students with a B.A./B.S. only: 100% **Master's:** 0%

Approximate percentage of students who are Women: 100% **Ethnic Minority:** 0% **International:** 0%

Average years to complete the doctoral program (including internship): 6 years

Personal interview
Preferred in person but skype or telephone acceptable

Attrition rate in past 7 years: 5%

Percentage of students applying for internship in 2017 accepted into:

APA internships: 100% **APPIC internships:** 100%

Formal tracks/concentrations: none

Research areas	# Faculty	# Grants
adolescent clinical	4	3
assessment	3	0
addiction and recovery	2	3
anxiety disorders	4	2
attention and memory	1	1
autism spectrum disorders	4	2
behavioral neuroscience	4	0
child clinical	6	3
cognition and emotion	1	1
cognitive behavior therapy	10	3
disruptive disorders	4	1
decision-making	4	4
depression	3	1
emotion regulation	6	0
fMRI-informed assessment/intervention	4	1
health behavior	6	1
neurological basis of disorders	4	4
public health	1	1
social anxiety	4	0
substance use disorders	2	2
post-traumatic disorders	3	1
treatment effectiveness	5	0
social cognition	1	1
trauma	3	1
violence	1	0

Clinical opportunities
childhood disorders
adolescent disorders
adult disorders
mood disorders
anxiety disorders
disruptive disorders
attentional disorders
pervasive developmental disorders
autism spectrum disorders
post-traumatic stress disorders
substance abuse disorders
adjustment disorders
personality disorders
couples and family therapy
child assessment
adult assessment
autism spectrum disorder assessment
neuropsychological assessment
supervision
consultation

University of Washington (Ph.D.)

Department of Psychology
Seattle, WA 98195
phone#: (206) 543-8687
email: resmith@uw.edu
Web address: www.psych.uw.edu/psych.php#p=233

1	2	3	4	5	**6**	7
Practice oriented			Equal emphasis			Research oriented

Percentage of faculty subscribing to each of the following orientations:

Psychodynamic/Psychoanalytic	0%
Applied behavioral analysis/Radical behavioral	10%
Family systems/Systems	20%
Existential/Phenomenological/Humanistic	0%
Cognitive/Cognitive-behavioral	70%

Courses required for incoming students to have completed prior to enrolling: none; psychology major preferred

Recommended but not mandatory courses:
abnormal/psychopathology, biological bases of behavior, developmental, statistics, learning & motivation, social

GRE median
Verbal 650 Quantitative 745
Analytical Writing not required
Psychology Subject Test 680

GPA mean
Overall GPA 3.68

Number of applications/admission offers/incoming students in 2017
502 applied/8 admission offers/ 8 incoming

% of students receiving:
Full tuition waiver only: 0%
Assistantship/fellowship only: 0%
Both full tuition waiver & assistantship/fellowship: 100%

Approximate percentage of incoming students with a B.A./B.S. only: 86% **Master's:** 14%

Approximate percentage of all students who are Women: 76% **Ethnic Minority:** 28% **International:** 0.2%

Average years to complete the doctoral program (including internship): 6.7 years

Personal interview
Final candidates based on telephone interviews are invited to campus for an interview

Attrition rate in past 7 years: 1.9%

Percentage of students applying for internship in 2017 accepted into:

APA internships: 100% **APPIC internships:** 100%

Formal tracks/concentrations: general clinical, child clinical

Research areas	# Faculty	# Grants
anxiety disorders	3	3
autism	1	1
child emotional development	3	3
cognitive therapy	4	2
depression	3	1
minority	2	2
psychotherapy process	1	1
spouse abuse	2	1

substance abuse	2	2
suicide	1	1

Clinical opportunities
anxiety disorders
autism
community psychology
couples
family
minority
neuropsychology
pediatric psychology
personality disorders
psychoeducational (coping skills) training
rehabilitation medicine
substance abuse

Washington University in St. Louis (Ph.D.)

Department of Psychological & Brain Sciences
Campus Box 1125
One Brookings Drive
St. Louis, MO 63130-4899
phone#: (314) 935-6520
email: rodebaugh@wustl.edu
Web address: www.psychweb.wustl.edu/clinical/

1 2 3 4 5 **6** 7

Practice oriented — Equal emphasis — Research oriented

Percentage of faculty subscribing to each of the following orientations:

Psychodynamic/Psychoanalytic	0%
Applied behavioral analysis/Radical behavioral	0%
Family systems/Systems	0%
Existential/Phenomenological/Humanistic	0%
Cognitive/Cognitive-behavioral	100%
Research-supported assessment and treatment	100%

Courses required for incoming students to have completed prior to enrolling:
No specific courses are required.

Recommended but not mandatory courses: These include typical courses for a psychology major; courses in research methods, quantitative methods, affective, biological, cognitive, developmental, and social aspects of psychology; history of psychology.

GRE mean
Verbal 161 Quantitative 158
Analytical Writing 5.0
Psychology Subject Test 740

GPA mean
Overall GPA 3.49 Psychology GPA 3.7
Junior/Senior GPA 3.58

Number of applications/admission offers/incoming students in 2017
219 applied/12 admission offers/8 incoming

% of students receiving:
Full tuition waiver only: 0%
Assistantship/fellowship only: 0%
Both full tuition waiver & assistantship/fellowship: 100%

Approximate percentage of incoming students with a B.A./B.S. only: 100% Master's: 0%

Approximate percentage of all students who are Women: 71% **Ethnic Minority:** 27% **International:** 3%

Average years to complete the doctoral program (including internship): 6 years

Personal interview
Typically required in person; at times conducted via video conference if absolutely necessary.

Attrition rate in past 7 years: 12.5%

Percentage of students applying for internship in 2017 accepted into:

APA internships: 100% **APPIC internships:** 100%

Formal tracks/concentrations: none

Research areas	# Faculty	# Grants
aging/gerontology	3	1
neuropsychology	2	0
psychopathology	4	6
psychological treatment	3	3

Clinical opportunities
psychological services center
wide variety of community agencies (see website)

Washington State University (Ph.D.)

Department of Psychology
P.O. Box 644820
Pullman, WA 99164-4820
phone#: (509) 335-2633
email: psych.grad.adm@wsu.edu
Web address: www.wsu.edu/psychology/graduateprograms/clinical

1 2 3 **4** 5 6 7

Practice oriented — Equal emphasis — Research oriented

Percentage of faculty subscribing to each of the following orientations:

Psychodynamic/Psychoanalytic	10%
Applied behavioral analysis/Radical behavioral	0%
Family systems/Systems	30%
Existential/Phenomenological/Humanistic	22%
Cognitive/Cognitive-behavioral	100%

Courses required for incoming students to have completed prior to enrolling: 18 hours of undergraduate psychology coursees

Recommended but not mandatory courses:
introductory, abnormal, social, developmental, statistics, research methods

GRE mean
Verbal 160 Quantitative 154
Analytical Writing 4.5
Psychology Subject Test not reported

GPA mean
Overall GPA 3.66

Number of applications/admission offers/incoming students in 2016
219 applied/11 admission offers/8 incoming

% of students receiving:
Full tuition waiver only: 0%
Assistantship/fellowship only: 0%
Both full tuition waiver & assistantship/fellowship: 100%

Approximate percentage of incoming students with a B.A./B.S. only: 82% **Master's:** 18%

Approximate percentage of students who are Women: 76% **Ethnic Minority:** 18% **International:** 10%

Average years to complete the doctoral program (including internship): 6 years

Personal interview
Preferred in person but telephone possible

Attrition rate in past 7 years: 15%

Percentage of students applying for internship in 2016 accepted into:

APA internships: 100% **APPIC internships:** 100%

Formal tracks/concentrations: none (have six interest areas)

Research areas	# Faculty	# Grants
Adult psychopathology	3	1
Clinical health/primary care psychology	2	5
Clinical child and adolescent psychology	4	1
Neuropsychology	2	5

Clinical opportunities

Adult psychotherapy, child psychotherapy, adult assessment, child and adolescent assessment, neuropsychological assessment, clinical health and primary care psychology, geriatric psychology, community mental health, adult inpatient.

Wayne State University (Ph.D.)

Department of Psychology
5057 Woodward Avenue, 7th Floor
Detroit, MI 48202
phone#: (313) 577-2800
email: aallen@wayne.edu
Web address: www. http://clasweb.clas.wayne.edu/psychology

1	2	3	4	5	6	7
Practice oriented			Equal emphasis			Research oriented

Percentage of faculty subscribing to each of the following orientations:

Psychodynamic/Psychoanalytic	15%
Applied behavioral analysis/Radical behavioral	0%
Family systems/Systems	15%
Existential/Phenomenological/Humanistic	0%
Cognitive/Cognitive-behavioral	40%
Experiential	20%
Interpersonal	10%

Courses required for incoming students to have completed prior to enrolling:
12 semester hours in psychology, including experimental (with laboratory) and statistical methods

Recommended but not mandatory courses:
Undergraduate courses in mathematics and life sciences

GRE mean (of admitted applicants, 2017)
Verbal 160 Quantitative 157
Analytical Writing 4.5
Psychology Subject Test not required

GPA mean
Overall GPA 3.71

Number of applications/admission offers/incoming students in 2017
205 applied/10 admission offers/8 incoming

% of students receiving:
Full tuition waiver only: 0%
Assistantship/fellowship only: 0%
Both full tuition waiver & assistantship/fellowship: 100%

Approximate percentage of incoming students with a B.A./B.S. only: 75% **Master's:** 25%

Approximate percentage of students who are Women: 75% **Ethnic Minority:** 37.5% **International:** 0%

Average years to complete the doctoral program (including internship): 6.2 years

Personal interview
Required in person

Attrition rate in past 7 years: 12%

Percentage of students applying for internship in 2017 accepted into:

APA internships: 100% **APPIC internships:**

Formal tracks/concentration: health, child clinical, clinical neuropsychology, community

Research areas	# Faculty	# Grants
Substance abuse	2	2
Chronic health problems	3	2
Developmental psychopathology	4	2
Neuropsychological assessment	4	2
Homelessness	1	0
Relationships	2	1

Clinical opportunities

health psychology	early intervention
community psychology	gerontology
neuropsychology	substance abuse
cross-cultural mental health	rehabilitation
primary care psychology	

West Virginia University (Ph.D.)

Department of Psychology
1124 Life Sciences Building
Morgantown, WV 26506-6040
phone#: (304) 293-2580
email: pamela.darling@mail.wvu.edu
Web address: psychology.wvu.edu

1	2	3	4	**5**	6	7
Practice oriented			Equal emphasis			Research oriented

Percentage of faculty subscribing to each of the following orientations:

Psychodynamic/Psychoanalytic	0%
Applied behavioral analysis/Radical behavioral	50%
Family systems/Systems	0%
Existential/Phenomenological/Humanistic	0%
Cognitive/Cognitive-behavioral	50%

Courses required for incoming students to have completed prior to enrolling:
12 hours of undergraduate coursework in Psychology, including Research Methods

Recommended but not mandatory courses: Psychology major or related field, research, clinical experience

GRE mean
Verbal 159
Quantitative 155
Analytical Writing 4.5

GPA mean
Overall GPA 3.6

Number of applications/admission offers/incoming students in 2018
152 applied/16 admission offers/7 incoming

% of students receiving:
Full tuition waiver only: 0%
Assistantship/fellowship only: 0%
Both full tuition waiver & assistantship/fellowship: 100%

Approximate percentage of incoming students with a B.A./B.S. only: 90% **Master's:** 10%

Approximate percentage of incoming students who are
Women: 100% **Ethnic Minority:** 0% **International:** 0%

Average years to complete the doctoral program (including internship): 5 years

Personal interview
Preferred in person but telephone/Skype acceptable

Attrition rate in past 7 years: 5.5%

Percentage of students applying for internship in 2017 accepted into:

APA internships: 100% **APPIC internships:** 100%

Formal tracks/concentrations: Clinical, Clinical Child, Life Span Developmental, Behavior Analysis, Behavioral Neuroscience

Research areas	**# Faculty**	**# Grants**
anxiety disorders	5	2
behavioral dentistry	1	1
behavioral medicine	5	4
cardiovascular reactivity	1	0
child behavior disorders	6	3
developmental psychopathology	2	0
ethnic minority issues	1	0
forensics	1	0
gerontology	2	1
pain	1	1
suicide	1	0
decision making and Choice	8	2
health stress coping	9	1
social behavior	7	3
life span	7	0

Clinical opportunities
anxiety disorders (adults and children)
behavioral dentistry
behavioral medicine (adults and adolescents)
gerontology
parent training
primary care service provision

Western Michigan University (Ph.D.)

Department of Psychology
1903 W. Michigan Ave.
Kalamazoo, MI 49008-5439
phone#: (269) 387-4330
email: casey.ohmart@wmich.edu
Web address: https://wmich.edu/psychology/academics/graduate/clinical

1	2	3	**4**	5	6	7
Practice oriented			Equal emphasis			Research oriented

Percentage of faculty subscribing to each of the following orientations:

Psychodynamic/Psychoanalytic	0%
Contextual Behavioral/Clinical Behavior Analysis	67%
Family systems/Systems	33%
Existential/Phenomenological/Humanistic	0%
Cognitive/Cognitive-behavioral	100%

Courses required for incoming students to have completed prior to enrolling:
Psychology major at an accredited institution

Recommended but not mandatory courses: Basic course in behavior principles/behavior theory

GRE mean
Verbal + Quantitative 306
Analytical Writing 4.5
Psychology Subject Test not required

GPA mean
Undergraduate GPA 3.61
Psychology GPA 3.85

Number of applications/admission offers/incoming students in 2016
93 applied/8 admission offers/5 incoming

% of students receiving:
Full tuition waiver only: 0%
Assistantship/fellowship only: 0%
Both full tuition waiver & assistantship/fellowship: 100%

Approximate percentage of incoming students with a B.A./B.S. only: 80% **Master's:** 20%

Approximate percentage of all students who are
Women: 85% **Ethnic Minority:** 21% **International:** 3%

Average years to complete the doctoral program (including internship): 6 years

Personal interview
Preferred in person but telephone acceptable

Attrition rate in past 7 years: 8%

Percentage of students applying for internship in 2017 accepted into:

APA internships: 100% **APPIC internships:**

Formal tracks/concentrations: none

Research areas	# Faculty	# Grants
anxiety disorders/PTSD	2	0
behavioral health in primary care	3	1
behavioral medicine	1	0
behavioral pediatrics	2	0
child injury & maltreatment	1	1
depression	3	0
habit behaviors (tics, trichotilamania)	1	0
interpersonal victimization	2	1
multimedia-based treatment	2	0
psychotherapy process & outcome	3	0
sexual deviations and dysfunctions	1	0

Clinical opportunities
internal practicum in in-house clinic
external practicum in VA, medical, and integrated primary care settings
emphasis on evidence-based practices

Wheaton College (Psy.D.)

Department of Psychology
Wheaton, IL 60187-5593
phone#: (630) 752-5104
email: ted.kahn@wheaton.edu
Web address: www.wheaton.edu/Academics/Departments/Psychology/Graduate-Programs/Programs/PsyD-in-Clinical-Psychology

1 2 3 **4** 5 6 7

Practice oriented — Equal Emphasis — Research oriented

Percentage of faculty subscribing to each of the following orientations:

Cognitive/Cognitive-behavioral	56%
Existential	11%
Integrative	33%
Family systems/Systems	44%
Psychodynamic/Psychoanalytic	33%

Courses required for incoming students to have completed prior to enrolling:
personality, physiology, abnormal, research methods, statistics

Recommended but not mandatory courses
developmental, cognition, social

GRE mean
Verbal 156 Quantitative 150
Analytical Writing 4.35
Psychology Subject Test not required

GPA mean
Overall GPA 3.49

Number of applications/admission offers/incoming students in 2017
60 applied/31 offers/18 incoming students

% of students receiving:
Full tuition waiver only: 0%
Assistantship/fellowship only: 100%
Both full tuition waiver & assistantship/fellowship: 0%

Approximate percentage of incoming students with a B.A./B.S. only: 65% **Master's:** 35%

Approximate percentage of students who are Women: 64% **Ethnic Minority:** 29% **International:** 5%

Average years to complete the doctoral program (including internship): 5.8 years

Personal interview
Required in person

Attrition rate in past 7 years: 14.2%

Percentage of students applying for internship in 2017 accepted into:

APA internships: 100% **APPIC internships:** 100%

Formal tracks/concentrations: none

Research areas	# Faculty	# Grants
Asian-American Mental Health	2	0
Child & Adolescent	1	0
Community Health	1	0
Depression	1	0
Disaster Psychology	1	1
Multicultural Peace and Social Justice	1	0
Neuropsychology	1	0
Spirituality and Religion	3	2

Clinical opportunities
Hospitals and medical centers – public, private and VA
Academic health center affiliated programs
Community mental health centers
Psychiatric facilities
Correctional facilities
Public and private agencies
University counseling centers
Group private practices
Federally qualified health centers

Wichita State University (Ph.D.)

Department of Psychology
Wichita, KS 67260-0034
phone#: (316) 978-3170
email: robert.zettle@wichita.edu
Web address: webs.wichita.edu/?u=PSYCHOLOGY&p=/graduate/clinical/clinicalphd/

1 2 3 4 **5** 6 7

Practice oriented — Equal emphasis — Research oriented

Percentage of faculty subscribing to each of the following orientations:

Psychodynamic/Psychoanalytic	00%
Applied behavioral analysis/Radical behavioral	15%
Family systems/Systems	00%
Existential/Phenomenological/Humanistic	00%
Cognitive/Cognitive-behavioral	45%
Community	60%

Courses required for incoming students to have completed prior to enrolling: Psychological statistics and research methods in psychology.

GRE mean
Verbal 154 Quantitative 151
Analytical Writing 4.4
Psychology Subject Test not reported

GPA mean
Overall GPA 3.78

Number of applications/admission offers/incoming students in 2017
30 applied/6 admission offers/4 incoming

% of students receiving:
Full tuition waiver only: 0%
Assistantship/fellowship only: 0%
Both full tuition waiver & assistantship/fellowship: 0%
All of our students receive a Teaching Assistantship and partial tuition remission

Approximate percentage of incoming students with a B.A./B.S. only: 75% **Master's:** 25%

Approximate percentage of all students who are Women: 68% **Ethnic Minority:** 12% **International:** 8%

Average years to complete the doctoral program (including internship): 6 years

Personal interview
Required in person

Attrition rate in past 7 years: 4%

Percentage of students applying for internship in 2017 accepted into:

APA internships: 100% **APPIC internships:** 0%

Formal tracks/concentrations: none

Research areas	# Faculty	# Grants
bullying	1	0
dating violence	1	0
personal relationships	1	0
acceptance commitment therapy	1	0
criminal justice	1	0
cooperation	1	0
self help	1	0
teaching excellence	1	0
health disparities	1	0
adolescent health and development	1	0
life span development	1	2
community-based participatory research	1	0
leadership	1	0
measurement	1	0

Clinical opportunities
anxiety disorders
depression
bullying

Widener University (Psy.D.)

Institute for Graduate Clinical Psychology
One University Place
Graduate Clinical Psychology
Chester, PA 19013
phone#: (610) 499-1206
email: graduate.psychology@widener.edu
Web address: www.widener.edu/igcp

1	2	3	4	5	6	7
Practice oriented			Equal emphasis			Research oriented

Percentage of faculty subscribing to each of the following orientations:

Psychodynamic/Psychoanalytic	29%
Applied behavioral analysis/Radical behavioral	0%
Family systems/Systems	29%
Existential/Phenomenological/Humanistic	21%
Cognitive/Cognitive-behavioral	21%

Courses required for incoming students to have completed prior to enrolling:
Psychopathology or abnormal psychology; experimental psychology or research methods; statistics

Recommended but not mandatory courses: none

GRE mean
Incoming students for fall 2017:
Verbal: 87% Quantitative: 71%
Analytical Writing 80%
Psychology Subject Test not reported

Cohort (all currently enrolled students):
Verbal: 75% Quantitative: 66%
Analytical Writing 70%
Psychology Subject Test not reported

GPA mean
Incoming students for fall 2017:
Overall GPA: 3.64

Cohort (all currently enrolled students):
Overall GPA: 3.55

Number of applications/admission offers/incoming students in 2017
535 applied/57 admission offers/34 incoming

% of students receiving:
Full tuition waiver only: 0%
Assistantship/fellowship only: 0%
Both full tuition waiver & assistantship/fellowship: 0%

Approximate percentage of incoming students with a B.A./B.S. only: 90% **Master's:** 10%

Approximate percentage of entering students who are Women: 70% **Ethnic Minority:** 18% **International:** 1%

Average years to complete the doctoral program (including internship): 5 years

Personal interview
Required in person

Attrition rate in past 7 years: 6%

Percentage of students applying for internship in 2017 accepted into:

APA internships: 100% **APPIC internships:** 0%
(Widener Psy.D. students do not participate in the APPIC process)

Formal tracks: biofeedback, neuropsychology, school psychology

Research areas	# Faculty	# Grants
assessment/diagnosis	5	0
qualitative research methods	4	0
early childhood	3	1
learning disabilities	3	0
health psychology	3	2
attachment theory	3	0
multicultural psychology	2	0

Clinical opportunities
assessment
biofeedback
business and psychology (joint degree)
child psychology
cognitive-behavioral psychology
criminal justice (joint degree)
family therapy
generalist practice
health psychology
human sexuality (joint degree)
law and psychology (joint degree)
military/veterans behavioral health
neuropsychology
organizational psychology
psychoanalytic psychology
school psychology

William James University (Psy.D.)

One Wells Avenue
Newton, MA 02459
phone#: (617) 327-6777
toll free (888) 664-MSPP
email: admissions@mspp.edu
Web address: www.mspp.edu/academics/degree-programs/psyd/index.php

1 2 **3** 4 5 6 7

Practice oriented — Equal emphasis — Research oriented

Percentage of faculty subscribing to each of the following orientations:

Psychodynamic/Psychoanalytic	10%
Applied behavioral analysis/Radical behavioral	0%
Family systems/Systems	30%
Existential/Phenomenological/Humanistic	0%
Cognitive/Cognitive-behavioral	60%

Courses required for incoming students prior to enrolling:
General psychology, abnormal and two out of the following six courses: developmental, social, personality theories, behavioral statistics, tests and measurements, physiological

Recommended but not mandatory courses: all psychology related

GRE mean
Verbal 152 Quantitative 148
Analytical Writing 4.0
Psychology Subject Test not reported

GPA mean
Overall undergraduate GPA 3.4

Number of applications/admission offers/incoming students entering Fall 2017
318 applied/235 admission offers/119 incoming

% of students receiving:
Full tuition waiver only: 0%
Assistantship/fellowship only) 40%
Both full tuition waiver & assistantship/fellowship: 0%

Approximate percentage of incoming students with a B.A./B.S. only: 65% **Master's:** 35%

Approximate percentage of all entering students who are Women: 79.8% **Ethnic Minority:** 27% **International:** 5%

Average years to complete the doctoral program (including internship): 5 years

Personal interview
Required in person

Attrition rate in past 7 years: 11%

Percentage of students applying for internship in 2016-17 accepted into:

APA internships: 58% **APPIC internships:** 4%

Formal tracks/concentrations: health psychology, forensic psychology, geropsychology, children and family, Latino mental health, military and veterans psychology, global mental health, African and Caribbean mental health

Research areas	# Faculty	# Grants
a wide variety	43	n/a

Clinical opportunities
We have 220 sites per year in diverse areas.

University of Wisconsin–Madison (Ph.D.)

Department of Psychology
W. J. Brogden Psychology Building
1202 West Johnson Street
Madison, WI 53706
phone#: (608) 262-2079
email: gradinfo@psych.wisc.edu
Web address: www.psych.wisc.edu

1 2 3 4 5 6 **7**

Practice oriented — Equal emphasis — Research oriented

Percentage of faculty subscribing to each of the following orientations:

Psychodynamic/Psychoanalytic	0%

Applied behavioral analysis/Radical behavioral	0%
Family systems/Systems	0%
Existential/Phenomenological/Humanistic	0%
Cognitive/Cognitive-behavioral	100%
Motivational/Interviewing	25%
Child	25%

Courses required for incoming students prior to enrolling:
Psychology major or related field training

Recommended but not mandatory courses: none

GRE mean
Verbal + Quantitative 320
Analytical Writing not reported
Psychology Subject Test not reported

GPA mean
Overall GPA 3.7

Number of applications/admission offers/incoming students in 2017
155 applied/6 admission offers/4 incoming

% of students receiving:
Full tuition waiver only: 0%
Assistantship/fellowship only: 0%
Both full tuition remission (out of state portion only) & assistantship/fellowship: 100%

Approximate percentage of incoming students with a B.A./B.S. only: 100% **Master's:** 0%

Approximate percentage of students who are Women: 50% **Ethnic Minority:** 15% **International:** 0%

Average years to complete the doctoral program (including internship): 7 years

Personal interview
Invite only; in person preferred

Attrition rate in past 7 years: not reported

Percentage of students applying for internship in 2017 accepted into:

APA internships: 80% **APPIC internships:** 80%

Formal tracks/concentrations: not reported

Research areas	# Faculty	# Grants
affective disorders	8	6
developmental psychopathology	4	3
health	3	6
schizophrenia and other psychotic disorders	1	0
substance abuse	2	5

Clinical opportunities
addictive disorders
assessment (IQ, objective, psychophysiological, neuropsychological)
assessment of forensic populations
assessment of schizophrenia and at-risk populations
cognitive therapy for affective and anxiety disorders
families/couples therapy
brief dynamic psychotherapy
therapy with criminal offenders
assessment of childhood psychopathology
affective neuroscience
mood and anxiety disorders

University of Wisconsin–Milwaukee (Ph.D.)

Department of Psychology
P.O. Box 413
Milwaukee, WI 53201
phone#: (414) 229-4746
email: que@uwm.edu
Web address: www.graduateschool.uwm.edu/students/prospective/areas-of-study/psychology/#phd

1	2	3	**4**	5	6	7
Practice oriented			Equal emphasis			Research oriented

Percentage of faculty subscribing to each of the following orientations:

Psychodynamic/Psychoanalytic	0%
Applied behavioral analysis/Radical behavioral	10%
Family systems/Systems	10%
Existential/Phenomenological/Humanistic	0%
Cognitive/Cognitive-behavioral	80%

Courses required for incoming students to have completed prior to enrolling:
B.A. or B.S. in psychology or equivalent

Recommended but not mandatory courses: B.A. or B.S. in psychology or undergraduate courses in psychological statistics, a laboratory course in research methodology, and an advanced laboratory course in psychology

GRE mean
Verbal 159 Quantitative 154
Analytical Writing 4.67

GPA mean
Overall GPA 3.70 Psychology GPA 3.88
Junior/Senior GPA 3.80

Number of applications/admission offers/incoming students in 2017
183 applied/8 admission offers/6 incoming

% of students receiving:
Full tuition waiver only: 0%
Assistantship/fellowship only: 0%
Both full tuition waiver & assistantship/fellowship: 100%

Approximate percentage of incoming students with a B.A./B.S. only: 90% **Master's:** 10%

Approximate percentage of all students who are Women: 57% **Ethnic Minority:** 18% **International:** 0%

Average years to complete the doctoral program (including internship): 6.22 years

Personal interview
Preferred in person but telephone acceptable

Attrition rate in past 7 years: 8%

Percentage of students applying for internship in 2017 accepted into:

APA internships: 100% **APPIC internships:**

Formal tracks/concentrations: none

Research areas	# Faculty	# Grants
alcohol and substance abuse	3	7
anxiety/impulse control disorders	4	4
child psychology	2	2
developmental disabilities	1	2
emotion regulation	4	5
health psychology/behavioral medicine	1	0
learning disabilities	3	0
mood disorders	2	1
neuropsychology	4	7
psychotherapy/behavior therapy research	2	1

Clinical opportunities

empirically supported interventions
learning disability
cognitive behavioral therapy
pediatric psychology
child and adult neuropsychology
child development
prolonged exposure for PTSD
ERP for OCD
developmental disabilities/autism

Wisconsin School of Professional Psychology (Psy.D.)

9120 W. Hampton Ave #212
Milwaukee, WI 53225
phone#: (414) 464-9777
Web address: https://www.wspp.edu/

1	2	3	4	5	6	7
Practice oriented			Equal emphasis			Research oriented

Percentage of faculty subscribing to each of the following orientations:

Psychodynamic/Psychoanalytic	43%
Applied behavioral analysis/Radical behavioral	0%
Family systems/Systems	0%
Existential/Phenomenological/Humanistic	14%
Cognitive/Cognitive-behavioral	43%

Courses required for incoming students to have completed prior to enrolling: not reported

Recommended but not mandatory courses: not reported

GRE mean

Verbal 151 Quantitative 147
Analytical Writing 4
Psychology Subject Test not reported

GPA mean

Overall GPA 3.378

Number of applications/admission offers/incoming students in 2017

33 applied/23 admission offers/14 incoming

% of students receiving:

Full tuition waiver only: 0%
Partial tuition waiver: 4%
Assistantship/fellowship only: 16%
Both full tuition waiver & assistantship/fellowship: 0%

Approximate percentage of all students who are Women: 80% **Ethnic Minority:** 19% **International:** 0%

Average years to complete the doctoral program (including internship): 6.3 years

Personal interview Preferred in person but telephone acceptable

Attrition rate in past 7 years: 3.9%

Percentage of students applying for internship last year accepted into:

APA internships: 83% **APPIC internships:** 100%

Formal tracks/concentrations: none reported

Research areas

Assessment
Neurological Disorders
Neuropsychology
Clinical opportunities
Adult
Behavioral Medicine
Child/Adolescent
Community Mental Health
Day Treatment/Outpatient
Drug and Alcohol Treatment
Ethnic/Racial Minorities
Inpatient Hospitals
Forensic/Correctional
Neuropsychology
Residential Treatment/Group Home
Schools
Clinical Supervision
Underserved Populations
Veterans

Clinical opportunities

not reported

The Wright Institute (Psy.D.)

2728 Durant Avenue
Berkeley, CA 94704
phone#: (510) 841-9230
email: info@wi.edu
Web address: www.wi.edu/psyd-program

1	2	3	4	5	6	7
Practice oriented			Equal emphasis			Research oriented

Percentage of faculty subscribing to each of the following orientations:

Psychodynamic/Psychoanalytic	37%
Applied behavioral analysis/Radical behavioral	0%

Family systems/Systems	15%
Existential/Phenomenological/Humanistic	4%
Cognitive/Cognitive-behavioral	22%
Integrationist	21%

Courses required for incoming students to have completed prior to enrolling:
human development, statistics, and theories of personality or abnormal psychology

Recommended but not mandatory courses: biological psychology or psychobiology or behavioral neuroscience or physiological psychology

GRE mean
Verbal 164 (74%) Quantitative 159 (50%)
Analytical Writing 4.44 (71%)
Psychology Subject Test not required

GPA mean
Overall GPA 3.49

Number of applications/admission offers/incoming students in 2016
244 applied/122 offers/69 incoming

% of students receiving:
Full tuition waiver only: 0%
Assistantship/fellowship only: 19%
Both full tuition waiver & assistantship/fellowship: 0%
Scholarships: 40%

Approximate percentage of incoming students with a B.A./B.S. only: 74% **Master's:** 26%

Approximate percentage of all students who are Women: 71% **Ethnic Minority:** 32% **International:** 4%

Average years to complete the doctoral program (including internship): 4.96 median / 5.77 mean

Personal interview
Preferred in person but video conference acceptable

Attrition rate in past 10 years: 6%

Percentage of students applying for internship in 2016 accepted into:

APA internships: 78% **APPIC internships:** 15%

Formal tracks/concentrations: none

Research areas	# Faculty	# Grants
Acceptance and Commitment Therapy	1	
Acculturation	2	
Acquired Immune Deficiency Syndrome/HIV	1	
Adolescent/At-Risk Adolescent	1	
Aging/Gerontology/Adult Development	1	
Anxiety Disorders/Panic Disorders	1	
Asian Studies	3	
Assessment/Diagnosis	7	
Attachment	4	
Attention	2	
Attention Deficit/Hyperactivity Disorder	3	
Attitudes, Beliefs, and Values	1	
Attributions	1	
Autism/Asperger's Syndrome/ Developmental Disorders	3	
Behavioral Medicine/Health Psychology	3	
Brain Injury/Head Injury	1	
Bullying	1	
Cardiovascular Health/Function	2	
Child and Family	4	
Community Psychology	3	
Eating Disorders/Body Image	1	
Empirically Supported Treatment Research	1	
Ethical Issues	2	
Evolutionary Psychology	1	
Family/Family Therapy/Family Systems	4	
Forensic/Psychology and Law	4	
Forgiveness	1	
Gay/Lesbian/Bisexuality	5	
Gender Roles/Sex Differences	3	
Genetics/Behavioral Genetics	1	
Group Process and Therapy	2	
Health Psychology	1	1
Hispanic Studies	1	
Hospice + Geriatrics	1	
Humor	1	
Immigration	3	
Indigenous/Native American	1	
Learning Disabilities	1	
Marriage/Couples	4	
Men's Issues	1	
Meta-Analysis	1	
Methodology	6	
Mindfulness	1	
Minority/Cross-Cultural/Diversity	11	
Narrative Psychology	2	
Neuropsychology	2	
Organizational	2	
Parent-Child Interactions/Parenting	1	
Personality Disorders	11	
Poverty	2	
Professional Issues/Training	1	
Program Evaluation	2	
Psychoanalysis/Psychodynamics	6	
Psychometrics/Measurement	3	
Psychopathology—Child/Developmental	3	
Psychopathology/Adult Psychopathology	5	
Psychopharmacology	1	
Public Health	4	
Religion/Spirituality	4	
Schizophrenia	1	
School/Educational	5	2
Self-Esteem/Self-Efficacy/Self-Psychology	1	
Severe Mental Illness	1	
Sexuality/Sexual Dysfunction	1	
Shame	2	
Sleep Disorders	1	
Social Justice Issues	10	
Social Skills/Competence	3	
Social-Psychological Approaches	3	
Statistics	6	
Stigma	2	
Substance Abuse/Addictive Behaviors	2	
Suicide	2	
Supervision/Mentoring/Training	4	
Teaching	1	
Trauma	2	
Violence/Abuse/Sexual Abuse/Rape	1	2
Women's Studies/Feminism	4	

Clinical opportunities

assessment	autism
brief and long term therapy	child/adolescent
child/adolescent psychopathology	couples therapy
crisis intervention	dialectical behavior therapy
empirically supported treatments	ethnic minority
family therapy	forensic populations
GLBTIQ	group therapy
men's issues	neuropsychology
psychodynamic	primary care/health care
personality disorders	multicultural
program development/ evaluation	rehabilitation psychology
public policy/advocacy	school-based treatment services
schizophrenia	substance abuse
social justice	women's issues
	university counseling

Wright State University (Psy.D.)

School of Professional Psychology
3640 Colonel Glenn Highway
Dayton, OH 45435
phone#: (937) 775-3492
email: sopp1@wright.edu
Web address: http://psychology.wright.edu/

1	2	**3**	4	5	6	7
Practice oriented			Equal emphasis			Research oriented

Percentage of faculty subscribing to each of the following orientations:

Cognitive/Cognitive-behavioral	65%
Integrative	15%
Family systems/Systems	10%
Psychodynamic/Psychoanalytic	5%
Interpersonal	5%

Courses required for incoming students to have completed prior to enrolling: Introductory Psychology, Introductory Statistics, Physiological Psychology, Abnormal Psychology and Research Methods

Recommended but not mandatory courses:
Developmental Psychology, Learning Theory, Personality Theory, Social Psychology, and Theory of Tests & Measurements

GRE mean
Verbal 156 Quantitative 149
Analytical Writing 4.21
Psychology Subject Test 640

GPA mean
Overall GPA 3.59
Psychology GPA 3.68

Number of applications/admission offers/incoming students in 2017
173 applied/45 admission offers/26 incoming

% of students receiving:
Full tuition waiver only: 1%
Partial tuition waiver: 18%
Assistantship/fellowship only: 60%
Both full tuition waiver & assistantship/fellowship: 3%

Approximate percentage of incoming students with a B.A./B.S. only: 65% **Master's/J.D.:** 35%

Approximate percentage of students who are Women: 73% **Ethnic Minority:** 32% **Disabled:** 0% **International:** 4%

Average years to complete the doctoral program (including internship): 5 years

Personal interview
Preferred in person but Skype and telephone interviews are acceptable

Attrition rate in past 7 years: 8%

Percentage of students applying for internship in 2017 accepted into:

APA internships: 100% **APPIC internships:** 100%

Emphasis/concentration areas: General Adult, Child and Adolescent, Forensic; Health, Rehabilitation and Neuropsychology

Faculty interest/research areas (click on faculty name): http://psychology.wright.edu/about-sopp/faculty-staff-profiles/faculty

Faculty grants:	# Faculty
health disparities	2
child/family violence prevention	2
military couples	2

Clinical opportunities

AIDS/HIV	group therapy
affect disorders	integrative theory
assessment	men's issues
brief and long-term therapy	neuropsychology
child/adolescent assessment	pediatric/developmental
child/adolescent psychopathology	personality disorders
Cognitive Behavioral Therapy	program development/ evaluation
couples therapy	psychodynamic
crisis intervention	public policy/advocacy
empirically supported treatments	rehabilitation psychology
ethnic minority	schizophrenia
family therapy	substance abuse
feminist therapy	trauma
forensic populations	university counseling
geropsychology	veteran population
GLBT	women's issues

University of Wyoming (Ph.D.)

Department of Psychology
Dept 3415, 1000 E University Ave
Laramie, WY 82071
phone#: (307) 766-6303
email: psyc.uw@uwyo.edu
Web address: www.uwyo.edu/psychology/graduate/prospective/clinical/index.html

1	2	3	**4**	5	6	7
Practice oriented			Equal emphasis			Research oriented

Percentage of faculty subscribing to each of the following orientations:

Psychodynamic/Psychoanalytic	0%
Applied behavioral analysis/Radical behavioral	0%
Family systems/Systems	0%
Existential/Phenomenological/Humanistic	0%
Cognitive/Cognitive-behavioral	100%

Courses required for incoming students to have completed prior to enrolling: none

Recommended but not mandatory courses: Statistics, 30–45 psychology credits, research experience

GRE mean
Verbal + Quantitative 312 (new GRE)
Analytical Writing 4.5

GPA mean
Overall GPA 3.54

Number of applications/admission offers/incoming students in 2017
147 applied/7 admission offers/6 incoming

% of students receiving:
Full tuition waiver only: 0%
Assistantship/fellowship only: 0%
Both full tuition waiver & assistantship/fellowship: 100%

Approximate percentage of incoming students with a B.A./B.S. only: 50% **Master's:** 50%

Approximate percentage of students who are Women: 80% **Ethnic Minority:** 25% **International:** 0%

Average years to complete the doctoral program (including internship): 6 years

Personal interview
Preferred in person but telephone acceptable

Attrition rate in past 7 years: 15%

Percentage of students applying for internship in 2017 accepted into:

APA internships: 100% **APPIC internships:** 100%

Formal tracks/concentrations: integrated behavioral health focus

Research areas	**# Faculty**	**# Grants**
Trauma/posttraumatic stress disorder	2	1
ADHD	1	0
Serious mental illness	1	1
Suicide and self-harm	1	0
Eating disorders	1	0
Substance abuse	1	0
Couple and family relationships	1	1
Psychology and law	1	0
Older adult health	1	0
Sexual assault prevention	1	0

Clinical opportunities

Empirically supported psychotherapies	ADHD
Trauma/PTSD	Inpatient and residential care
Mood/anxiety disorders	Telehealth delivered treatment
Eating disorders	Substance use disorders
Rural/community mental health	

Xavier University (Psy.D.)

Department of Psychology
3800 Victory Parkway
Cincinnati, OH 45207-6511
phone#: (513) 745-3533
email: maybury@xavier.edu
Web address: www.xavier.edu/psychology-doctorate/

1 2 **3** 4 5 6 7

Practice oriented — Equal emphasis — Research oriented

Percentage of faculty subscribing to each of the following orientations:

Psychodynamic/Psychoanalytic	40%
Applied behavioral analysis/Radical behavioral	0%
Family systems/Systems	20%
Existential/Phenomenological/Humanistic	0%
Cognitive/Cognitive-behavioral	60%

Courses required for incoming students prior to enrolling:
Minimum 18 semester hours including the following: statistics, research methods, abnormal, testing, social

Recommended but not mandatory courses: Anatomy and physiology, calculus

GRE mean
Verbal + Quantitative 311
Analytical Writing not reported
Psychology Subject Test not reported

GPA mean
Overall GPA 3.7

Number of applications/admission offers/incoming students in 2017
227 applied/38 offers/19 incoming

% of students receiving:
Full tuition waiver only: 0%
Assistantship/fellowship only: 43% (includes partial tuition remission)
Both full tuition waiver & assistantship/fellowship: 0%

Approximate percentage of incoming students with a B.A./B.S. only: 90% **Master's:** 10%

Approximate percentage of students who are Women: 78% **Ethnic Minority:** 10% **International:** not reported

Average years to complete the doctoral program (including internship): 5.5 years

Personal interview
Interview by invitation

Attrition rate in past 7 years: 3%

Percentage of students applying for internship in 2017 accepted into:

APA internships: 100%(14) **APPIC internships:** 100%(14)

Formal tracks/concentrations: children/adolescents & their families, individuals with severe chronic & persistent illness and health care psychology across the life span

Research areas	# Faculty	# Grants
cognitive/behavioral	5	
geropsychology	1	0
psychoanalytic	3	0
social/experimental	2	0
statistician	2	0
DBT Therapy	1	

Clinical opportunities
college-related concerns
Xavier University psychology services center
local agencies and hospitals

Yale University (Ph.D.)

Department of Psychology
P.O. Box 208205
New Haven, CT 06520-8205
phone#: (203) 432-4500
email: m.obrien@yale.edu
Web address: http://psychology.yale.edu/research/clinical-psychology

1	2	3	4	5	**6**	7
Practice oriented			Equal emphasis			Research oriented

Percentage of faculty subscribing to each of the following orientations:

Psychodynamic/Psychoanalytic	0%
Applied Behavioral Analysis/Radical Behavioral	0%
Family Systems/Systems	0%
Existential/Phenomenological/Humanistic	0%
Cognitive/Cognitive-behavioral	100%

Courses required for incoming students prior to enrolling: none

Recommended but not mandatory courses: broad psychology background, undergraduate psychology, research methods, statistics

GRE mean
Verbal 163.8 Quantitative 156.2
Analytical Writing 5.0
Psychology Subject Test not reported

GPA mean
Overall GPA: 3.78

Number of applications/admission offers/incoming students in 2016
248 applied/7 admission offers/5 incoming

% of students receiving:
Full tuition waiver only: 0%
Assistantship/fellowship only: 0%
Both full tuition waiver & assistantship/fellowship: 100%

Approximate percentage of incoming students with a B.A./B.S. only: 100% **Master's:** 0%

Approximate percentage of students who are Women: 81% **Ethnic minority:** 9% **International:** 0%

Average years to complete the doctoral program (including internship): 6 years

Personal interview: Yes

Attrition rate in past 7 years: 19%

Percentage of students applying for internship in 2016 accepted into:

APA internships: 100% **APPIC internships:** 100%

Formal tracks/concentrations: none

Research areas	# Faculty	# Grants
adult psychopathology	3	4
anxiety disorders	1	0
behavior genetics	1	1
cognitive processes	3	3
depression/suicidality	1	0
disruptive behavior disorders	1	3
developmental psychopathology	1	0

Clinical opportunities
adult anxiety and mood disorders
child psychotherapy
neuropsychology
borderline personality disorder
substance use disorders
group treatment

Yeshiva University (Ph.D.)

Ferkauf Graduate School of Psychology
Jack and Pearl Resnick Campus
1300 Morris Park Ave
Bronx, NY 10461
phone#: (718) 430-3856
email: roee.holtzer@einstein.yu.edu
Web address: https://www.yu.edu/ferkauf/clinical-psychology-health-emphasis

1	2	3	4	**5**	6	7
Practice oriented			Equal emphasis			Research oriented

Percentage of faculty subscribing to each of the following orientations:

Psychodynamic/Psychoanalytic	0%
Applied behavioral analysis/Radical behavioral	0%
Family systems/Systems	0%
Existential/Phenomenological/Humanistic	0%
Cognitive/Cognitive-behavioral	100%

Courses required for incoming students to have completed prior to enrolling:
minimum of 15 credits from undergraduate psychology courses, including statistics, abnormal, experimental psychology, and theories of personality or physiological psychology

Recommended but not mandatory courses: courses in related fields such as mathematics, natural sciences, social sciences, and public health.

GRE mean
Verbal 159.9 Quantitative 154.3
Analytical Writing 44.6

Psychology Subject Test 721

GPA mean
Overall GPA 3.48

Number of applications/admission offers/incoming students in 2016
88 applied/16 incoming

% of students receiving:
Full tuition waiver only: 0%
Assistantship/fellowship only: 100%
Both full tuition waiver & assistantship/fellowship: 0%

Approximate percentage of incoming students with a B.A./B.S. only: 70% **Master's:** 30%

Approximate percentage of all students who are Women: 80% **Ethnic Minority:** 14% **International:** 4%

Average years to complete the doctoral program (including internship): 5.5 years

Personal interview
Required in person

Attrition rate in past 7 years: 9%

Percentage of students applying for internship in 2017 accepted into:

APA internships: 85% **APPIC internships:** 95%

Formal tracks/concentrations: neuropsychology; research methods/statistics; addictions; geriatrics

Research areas	# Faculty	# Grants
neuropsychology, cognition, & aging	2	2
Multiple Sclerosis	1	2
obesity	1	0
asthma	1	2
migraines	2	2
diabetes	1	3
addiction	1	0

Clinical opportunities
Inpatient and outpatient psychiatric, counseling,
developmental disorders (autism)
behavioral medicine
cardiovascular psychology
weight management and
related disorders
TBI/rehabilitation medicine
asthma and anxiety
neuropsychology
geropsychology
trauma/veterans

Yeshiva University (Psy.D.)

Department of Psychology
Ferkauf Graduate School of Psychology
1165 Morris Park Avenue
Rousso Building
Bronx, NY 10461

Department Secretary: Dawn Basnight
Telephone: (646) 592 4520
email: basnight@yu.edu

Director, Admissions: Edna Augusta
email: augusta@yu.edu

Director, Clinical Program: Lata K. McGinn, Ph.D.
Telephone (646) 592 4394
email: Lata.McGinn@einstein.yu.edu

Web address: https://www.yu.edu/ferkauf/clinical-psychology/

1	2	3	**4**	5	6	7
Practice oriented			Equal emphasis			Research oriented

Percentage of faculty subscribing to each of the following orientations:

Psychodynamic/Psychoanalytic	55%
Applied behavioral analysis/Radical behavioral	0%
Family systems/Systems	18%
Existential/Phenomenological/Humanistic	0%
Cognitive/Cognitive-behavioral	55%

Courses required for incoming students to have completed prior to enrolling:
Introduction to Psychology/Fundamentals of Psychology, Statistics for Psychology Students, Abnormal Psychology/Psychopathology, Research Methods or an advanced research course, Theories of Personality or Social Psychology or Developmental Psychology, Physiological/Experimental Psychology (Brain and Behavior, Cognition and Learning,Cognitive Science, Sensation, Perception and Motivation, Cognitive Psychology, Human Memory, Psycholinguistics, Clinical Neuropsychology, Behavioral Neurobiology)

Recommended but not mandatory courses: none

GRE mean
Verbal 160 Quantitative 157
Analytical Writing 4.3
Psychology Subject Test not available

GPA mean
Overall GPA 3.62 Psychology GPA not available

Number of applications/admission offers/incoming students in 2017
303 applied/77 offers/25 incoming

% of students receiving:
Full tuition waiver only: 2.6%
Scholarships: 78%
Assistantship/fellowships only: 44%
Both full tuition waiver & assistantship/fellowship: 2.6%

Approximate percentage of incoming students with a B.A./B.S. only: 72% **Master's:** 28%

Approximate percentage of students who are Women: 83% **Ethnic Minority:** 18% **International:** 8%

Average years to complete the doctoral program (including internship): 5 years

Personal interview
Required in person

Attrition rate in past 7 years: 4%

Percentage of students applying for internship in 2016 accepted into:

APA internships: 95.3% **APPIC internships:** 100%

Formal tracks/concentrations: CBT, Psychodynamic, Neuropsychology, Family/Couple, Geropsychology, Assessment

Research areas	# Faculty	# Grants
Anxiety disorders	3	0
Depression	3	1
Prevention	1	0
Early childhood intervention	1	0
Ethnicity and identity	2	0
Family therapy	2	0
Geropsychology	1	0
Parenting styles	2	0
Psychoanalytic therapy	3	1
Psychotherapy process & outcome	3	2
Severe mental illness	1	2
Sleep disorders/nightmares	1	1
Stress and coping	1	0
Trauma	4	2

Clinical opportunities

Anxiety Disorders
Cognitive Behavior therapy
Interpersonal Therapy
Trauma and Stress Related Disorders
Psychological Assessment
Personality Disorders
Obsessive Compulsive and Related Disorders
Depression
Psychodynamic Therapy
Marital/Couples/Family therapy
Parent training
Neuropsychology
Severe and Persistent Mental Illness
Geriatrics

REPORTS ON COUNSELING PSYCHOLOGY PROGRAMS

University of Akron (Ph.D.)

Department of Psychology
Akron, OH 44325-4301
phone#: (330) 972-7280 Suzette Speight, Ph.D.
email: Slspeig@uakron.edu
Web address: www.uakron.edu/psychology/academics/cpcp/

1	2	3	4	5	6	7
Practice oriented			Equal emphasis			Research oriented

Percentage of faculty subscribing to each of the following orientations:

Psychodynamic/Psychoanalytic	10%
Applied behavioral analysis/Radical behavioral	0%
Family systems/Systems	10%
Existential/Phenomenological/Humanistic	30%
Cognitive/Cognitive-behavioral	30%
Other: African Centered	20%

Courses required for incoming students to have completed prior to enrolling:
The program has 2 options: Students can be admitted with a Bachelor's degree in psychology or students can be admitted with a Master's degree in counseling.

Recommended but not mandatory courses: Statistics, research methods, developmental psychology, abnormal psychology, personality theory

GRE mean
Verbal 157 Quantitative 150
Analytical Writing 4.5
Psychology Subject Test not required

GPA mean
Overall GPA 3.52

Number of applications/admission offers/incoming students in 2017
99 applied/9 admission offers/6 incoming

% of students receiving:
Full tuition waiver only: 0%
Assistantship/fellowship only: 0%
Both full tuition waiver & assistantship/fellowship: 100%

Approximate percentage of incoming students with a B.A./B.S. only: 60% **Master's:** 40%

Approximate percentage of all students who are Women: 70% **Ethnic Minority:** 35% **International:** 6%

Average years to complete the doctoral program (including internship): 7 years

Personal interview
Yes, preferred in person, typically in early to mid-February

Attrition rate in past 7 years: 5%

Percentage of students applying for internship in 2017 accepted into: 100% (n=11)

APA internships: 100% **APPIC internships:**

Formal tracks/concentrations: none

Research areas	# Faculty	# Grants
African American academic achievement	1	1
Intimate Partner Violence and Trauma	1	1
Positive Psychology	1	0
Women's vocational development	1	0
Men and masculinities	1	1
Therapy process and outcome	1	0
Black women's mental health	1	0

Clinical opportunities
The greater Akron/Cleveland area provides numerous high quality training opportunities in university/college counseling centers, community mental health centers, and hospitals. There are specialty clinics that focus on eating disorders, trauma, and neuropsychology assessment, for instance.

University at Albany/State University of New York (Ph.D.)

Department of Educational and Counseling Psychology
ED 220
Albany, NY 12222
phone#: (518) 437-4423
email: apieterse@albany.edu
Web address: www.albany.edu/counseling_psych

1	2	3	4	5	6	7
Practice oriented			Equal emphasis			Research oriented

Percentage of faculty subscribing to each of the following orientations:

Psychodynamic/Psychoanalytic	60%
Family systems/Systems	30%
Applied behavioral analysis/Radical behavioral	0%
Existential/Phenomenological/Humanistic	30%
Cognitive/Cognitive-behavioral	40%

Courses required for incoming students to have completed prior to enrolling:
Preparation in basic psychology (18 credits minimum, including statistics, abnormal, personality)

Recommended but not mandatory courses:
developmental, social, learning, experimental, cultural diversity

GRE mean
Quantitative 159 Quantitative 158
Analytical Writing 4.5
Psychology Subject Test not required, but recommended

GPA mean
Overall GPA 3.63 Psychology GPA 3.8

Number of applications/admission offers/incoming students in 2017
109 applied/7 admission offers/7 incoming

% of students receiving:
Full tuition waiver only: 0%
Assistantship/fellowship only: 0%
Both full tuition waiver & assistantship/fellowship: 100%

Approximate percentage of incoming students who entered with a B.A./B.S. only: 29% **Master's:** 71%

Approximate percentage of all students who are Women: 65% **Ethnic Minority:** 33% **International:** 5%

Average years to complete the doctoral program (including internship): 6.5 years

Personal interview
Preferred in person but telephone acceptable

Attrition rate in past 7 years: 2%

Percentage of students applying for internship in 2016 accepted into:

APA internships: 100% **APPIC internships:**

Formal tracks/concentrations: none

Research areas	# Faculty	# Grants
career development	2	1
cross-cultural	3	1
family dynamics	1	0
family therapy	1	1
methodology	1	0
process	1	0
social justice	3	2
supervision	2	0
race and ethnicity	1	1
substance abuse	1	1

Clinical opportunities
college and university counseling centers
private hospital
community agencies
county mental health clinics
outpatient
Integrative Medicine
state psychiatric center
various units at VA medical center
neuropsychology
day treatment
adolescent residential
substance abuse
Family Medicine

Arizona State University (Ph.D.)

Counseling and Counseling Psychology
1000 S. Forest Mall
Tempe, AZ 85281
phone#: 480-965-8733
email: ccp@asu.edu
Web address: https://cisa.asu.edu/graduate/ccp/CP_Student-Resources

1	2	3	**4**	5	6	7
Practice oriented			Equal emphasis			Research oriented

Percentage of faculty subscribing to each of the following orientations:

Psychodynamic/Psychoanalytic	0%
Applied behavioral analysis/Radical behavioral	0%
Family systems/Systems	0%
Existential/Phenomenological/Humanistic	0%
Cognitive/Cognitive-behavioral	0%

Our faculty must often subscribe to integrative theoretical approaches with a strong multicultural emphasis.

Courses required for incoming students to have completed prior to enrolling:
Per our Counseling Psychology Doctoral Student Handbook, we do not require a specific undergraduate degree or coursework. However, we prefer students with degrees in psychology and related fields so that they are well prepared for the rigors of our program.

Recommended but not mandatory courses:
Personality Assessment
We recommend an array of advanced statistics and multicultural counseling-related courses

GRE mean
Verbal 154 Quantitative 149
Analytical Writing 3.88
Psychology Subject Test n/a

GPA mean
Grad GPA 3.90
Undergrad GPA 3.68
Junior/Senior GPA 3.72

Number of applications/admission offers/incoming students in 2017
105 applications/7 offers of admission/4 incoming

% of students receiving:
Full tuition waiver only: 0%
Assistantship/fellowship only: 0%
Both full tuition waiver & assistantship/fellowship: 100%

Approximate percentage of incoming students with a B.A./B.S. only: not reported **Master's:** 100%

Approximate percentage of all students who are Women: 70% **Ethnic Minority:** 70% **International:** 8%

Average years to complete the doctoral program (including internship): 6.10 years

Personal interview
In-person interview is strongly preferred, but Skype is acceptable if constraints do not allow a campus visit

Attrition rate in past 7 years: 8%

Percentage of students applying for internship last year accepted into:

APA internships: 100% **APPIC internships:** 100%

Formal tracks/concentrations: not reported

Research areas	# Faculty	# Grants
aging (including Alzheimer's)	1	–
assessment/diagnosis	2	–
child	1	–
child psychopathology	1	–
developmental	1	1
family	1	1
racial climate	1	1
vocational assessment	1	–
acculturation	1	–
health disparities	2	1

Clinical opportunities
anxiety disorders
depression
psychopathology assessment
eating disorders
geriatric

Auburn University (Ph.D.)

Department of Special Education, Rehabilitation, and Counseling/School Psychology
Auburn, AL 36849-5218
phone#: (334) 844-7676
email: ask0002@auburn.edu
Web address: education.auburn.edu/academic_departments/serc/academicprograms/counpsych.html

1 2 3 **4** 5 6 7

Practice oriented — Equal emphasis — Research oriented

Percentage of faculty subscribing to each of the following orientations:

Psychodynamic/Psychoanalytic	0%
Applied behavioral analysis/Radical behavioral	0%
Family systems/Systems	0%
Existential/Phenomenological/Humanistic	50%
Cognitive/Cognitive-behavioral	50%

Courses required for incoming students to have completed prior to enrolling: none; however 3-4 courses are expected as a minimum

Recommended but not mandatory courses: Several (non-specified) courses in psychology are recommended. We look at performance in writing-intensive and statistical/mathematics courses in addition to broad exposure to psychology.

GRE mean
Verbal + Quantitative 308
Analytical Writing not reported
Psychology Subject Test not required

GPA mean
Overall GPA 3.59 (Undergraduate)

Number of applications/admission offers/incoming students in 2017
60 applied/8 admission offers/7 attending

% of students receiving (2016–2017):
Full tuition waiver only: 0%
Assistantship/fellowship only: 0%
Both full tuition waiver & assistantship/fellowship: 100%
**based on students on campus who are eligible for assistantships based on academics and prior performance*

Approximate percentage of incoming students with a B.A./B.S. only: 55% **Master's:** 45%

Approximate percentage of all students who are Women: 84% **Ethnic Minority:** 28% **International:** 5%

Average years to complete the doctoral program (including internship): 6.1 years

Personal interview
Preferred in person but zoom/telephone acceptable

Attrition rate in past 7 years: <5%

Percentage of students applying for internship in 2017 accepted into:

APA internships: 100% **APPIC internships:** 100%

Formal tracks/concentrations: none

Research areas	# Faculty	# Grants/Contracts
professional issues/ethics	1	0
psychometrics	2	0
diversity issues	4	2
disordered eating	1	0
relationships	1	1
health issues	3	2

Clinical opportunities
VA Medical Centers (outpatient)
substance abuse unit (inpatient and outpatient)
Rehabilitation hospital (inpatient)
Community mental health (outpatient)
jail/correctional settings
mental health center (outpatient)
university counseling centers
medical hospital
psychiatric hospital (inpatient)

Ball State University (Ph.D.)

Department of Counseling Psychology
Muncie, IN 47306
phone#: (765) 285-8040
fax#: (765) 285-2067
email: SBOWMAN@BSU.EDU
Web address: tc.bsu.edu/counselingpsychology

1 2 3 **4** 5 6 7

Practice oriented — Equal emphasis — Research oriented

Percentage of faculty subscribing to each of the following orientations:

Psychodynamic/Psychoanalytic	15%
Applied behavioral analysis/Radical behavioral	0%
Family systems/Systems	35%
Existential/Phenomenological/Humanistic	20%
Cognitive/Cognitive-behavioral	30%

Courses required for incoming students to have completed prior to enrolling:
Counseling theories, counseling techniques, practicum, one other counseling course

Recommended but not mandatory courses: none

GRE mean
Verbal + Quantitative 307 (new scoring)
Analytical Writing 4.4 (new scoring)
Psychology Subject Test not reported

GPA mean
Overall Master's GPA 3.9

Number of applications/admission offers/incoming students in 2017
57 applied/13 admission offers/9 incoming

% of students receiving:
Full tuition waiver only: 0%
Assistantship/fellowship only: 0%
Both full tuition waiver & assistantship/fellowship: 100%

Approximate percentage of incoming students with a B.A./B.S. only: 0% **Master's:** 100%

Approximate percentage of students who are Women: 78% **Ethnic Minority:** 44% **International:** 0%

Average years to complete the doctoral program (including internship): 4.61 years

Personal interview
In person highly preferred, but telephone acceptable

Attrition rate in past 7 years: 6%

Percentage of students applying for internship in 2017 accepted into:

APA internships: 100% **APPIC internships:** 100%

Formal tracks/concentrations: couples and family, health, diversity, social justice, vocational

Research areas	# Faculty	# Grants
behavioral medicine	2	0
career/vocational	3	0
child/adolescent	3	0
clinical judgment	1	0
diversity/Social justice	2	4
international	3	3
social psychology applications	3	0
rehabilitation	2	1
women's identity	2	0

Clinical opportunities
Practicum training clinic
cancer center/medical settings
community health center
university and college counseling center
private practice/assessment settings
primary/secondary schools
VA settings
youth-oriented treatment center
spain management clinic

Boston College (Ph.D.)

Department of Counseling, Developmental and Educational Psychology
School of Education
Chestnut Hill, MA 02167
phone#: (617) 552-4710 or (617) 552-4214
email: gsoe@bc.edu
Web address: http://www.bc.edu/bc-web/schools/lsoe/academics/departments/cdep/counseling-psychology-phd.html

1	2	3	4	5	6	7
Practice oriented			Equal emphasis			Research oriented

Percentage of faculty subscribing to each of the following orientations:

Psychodynamic/Psychoanalytic	75%
Applied behavioral analysis/Radical behavioral	0%
Family systems/Systems	75%
Existential/Phenomenological/Humanistic	50%
Cognitive/Cognitive-behavioral	50%

Courses required for incoming students to have completed prior to enrolling:
For applicants without a Master's degree in the field, we highly recommend at least 18 credit hours of undergraduate psychology

Recommended but not mandatory courses: Statistics, abnormal, personality

GRE mean
Verbal 156 Quantitative 154
Analytical Writing 4.28
Psychology Subject Test not reported

GPA mean
Undergraduate GPA: 3.54; Graduate GPA: 3.88

Number of applications/admission offers/incoming students
234 applied/5 admission offers/5 incoming

% of students receiving:
Full tuition waiver only: 0%
Assistantship/fellowship only: 0%
Both full tuition waiver & assistantship/fellowship: 100%

Approximate percentage of incoming students with a B.A./B.S. only: 20% **Master's:** 80%

Approximate percentage of all students who are Women: 78% **Ethnic Minority:** 38% **International:** 0%

Average years to complete the doctoral program (including internship): 6 years

Personal interview
Preferred in person

Attrition rate in past 7 years: 0%

Percentage of students applying for internship in 2017 accepted into:

APA internships: 100%

Formal tracks/concentrations: none

Research areas	# Faculty	# Grants
Child and adolescent development	5	5
Career development	3	2
Gender roles	5	1
School-based research and interventions	5	4
Violence, abuse, and trauma	5	1
Immigration	3	1
Race/culture	6	2
LGBTQ issues	3	1
Social justice and community intervention	10	1

Clinical opportunities
hospital outpatient setting
college counseling center
community mental health
inpatient adult unit
inpatient child
forensic assessment
VA hospital
school-based mental health clinics
violence prevention/intervention
trauma clinics
neuropsychological assessment

Brigham Young University, Counseling Psychology (Ph.D.)

Department of Counseling Psychology & Special Education
340 MCKB
Provo, UT 84602
phone#: 801-422-8031
email: aaron_jackson@byu.edu
Web address: http://education.byu.edu/cpse/phd

1	2	3	4	5	6	7
Practice oriented			Equal emphasis			Research oriented

Percentage of faculty subscribing to each of the following orientations:

Psychodynamic/Psychoanalytic	8%
Applied behavioral analysis/Radical behavioral	0%
Family systems/Systems	0%
Existential/Phenomenological/Humanistic	70%
Cognitive/Cognitive-behavioral	22%

Courses required for incoming students to have completed prior to enrolling: No specific courses required, just a solid background in psychology

Recommended but not mandatory courses: not reported

GRE mean
Verbal + Quantitative 155+152
Analytical Writing 4.1
Psychology Subject Test n/a

GPA mean
Overall GPA 3.6

Number of applications/admission offers/incoming students in 2015
30 applied/9 admission offers/6 incoming

% of students receiving:
Full tuition waiver only: 0%
Assistantship/fellowship only: 100%
Both full tuition waiver & assistantship/fellowship: 0%

Approximate percentage of incoming students with a B.A./B.S. only: 75% **Master's:** 25%

Approximate percentage of all students who are Women: 50% **Ethnic Minority:** 20% **International:** 10%

Average years to complete the doctoral program (including internship): 5 years

Personal interview Yes

Attrition rate in past 7 years: 3%

Percentage of students applying for internship last year accepted into:

APA internships: 71% **APPIC internships:** 29%

Formal tracks, research areas, clinical opportunities:
See website

Carlow University (Psy.D.)

Department of Psychology and Counseling
Pittsburgh, PA 15213
phone#: (412) 578-6331
email: jmroberts@carlow.edu
Web address: http://www.carlow.edu/PsyD_Counseling_Psychology.aspx

1	2	3	4	5	6	7
Practice oriented			Equal emphasis			Research oriented

Percentage of faculty subscribing to each of the following orientations:

Psychodynamic/Psychoanalytic	50%
Applied behavioral analysis/Radical behavioral	0%
Family systems/Systems	0%
Existential/Phenomenological/Humanistic	25%
Cognitive/Cognitive-behavioral	25%

Courses required for incoming students to have completed prior to enrolling:
All incoming students must hold a Master's degree in psychology, counseling, or a closely related field.

Recommended but not mandatory courses: none

GRE mean
Verbal 157 Quantitative 148
Analytical Writing 4.0
Psychology Subject Test not required

GPA mean
Overall GPA (Graduate-only) 3.92

Number of applications/admission offers/incoming students in 2017
33 applied/11 admission offers/9 incoming

% of students receiving:
Full tuition waiver only: 0%
Assistantship/fellowship only: 33%
Both full tuition waiver & assistantship/fellowship: 0%

Approximate percentage of incoming students with a BA/BS only: 0% **Master's:** 100%

Approximate percentage of all students who are Women: 82% **Ethnic Minority:** 18% **International:** 0%

Average years to complete the doctoral program (including internship): 4 years

Personal interview
Required; prefer in person but are flexible in respect to student financial constraints

Attrition rate in past 7 years: approximately 8%

Percentage of students applying for internship in 2017 accepted into:

APA internships: 80% **APPIC internships:** 20%

Formal tracks/concentrations: none

Research areas	# Faculty
Trauma	2
human trafficking	1

attachment	2
health performance	1
psychotherapy process and outcome	1
criminality and therapy practice	1
personality assessment	1
existential and mindfulness approaches	1
paranormal beliefs	1
cognitive/memory applications	1

Clinical opportunities

medical hospitals
community agencies
rural practice
university counseling centers
child practice
neuropsychology assessment

University of Central Arkansas (Ph.D.)

Psychology and Counseling
Conway, AR 72035

This program did not participate in the survey for this book.

Chatham University (Psy.D.)

Department of Graduate Psychology
Woodland Road
Pittsburgh, PA 15232
phone#: (412) 365-1100
email: gradadmissions@chatham.edu
Web address: http://www.chatham.edu/academics/programs/graduate/psyd/

1	2	3	4	5	6	7
Practice oriented			Equal emphasis			Research oriented

Percentage of faculty subscribing to each of the following orientations:

Psychodynamic/Psychoanalytic	0%
Applied behavioral analysis/Radical behavioral	8%
Family systems/Systems	8%
Existential/Phenomenological/Humanistic	25%
Cognitive/Cognitive-behavioral	58%
Interpersonal	50%
Feminist & multicultural	50%

Courses required for incoming students to have completed prior to enrolling:
Multicultural/diversity, lifespan development, counseling/therapy theories, group therapy/counseling, abnormal/psychopathology, assessment, research methods, professional ethics

Recommended but not mandatory courses:
Psychobiology

GRE mean
Verbal + Quantitative 304
Analytical Writing 4.0
Psychology Subject Test not required

GPA mean
Overall GPA 3.84 graduate 3.36 undergraduate

Number of applications/admission offers/incoming students in 2017
39 applied/16 admission offers/11 incoming

% of students receiving:
Full tuition waiver only: 0%
Assistantship/fellowship only: 35%
Both full tuition waiver & assistantship/fellowship: 0%

Approximate percentage of incoming students with a B.A./B.S. only: 0% **Master's:** 100%

Approximate percentage of all students who are Women: 60% **Ethnic Minority:** 14% **International:** 5%

Average years to complete the doctoral program 4.81 years

Personal interview
Strongly preferred in person, but Skype/Zoom/telephone acceptable

Attrition rate in past 7 years: 7%

Percentage of students applying for internship last year accepted into:

APA internships: 78% **APPIC internships:** 100%

Formal tracks/concentrations: none

Research areas	# Faculty	# Grants
health psychology	5	1
psychology of gender	4	1
social justice	4	0
multicultural/cross-cultural	4	0
child and adolescent psychology	3	0
mood disorders	3	0
religion and spirituality	2	0
positive psychology/resilience	2	0
sport and exercise psychology	1	0
personality assessment	1	0
developmental disabilities	1	0
psychology of aging	1	0
group process	1	0
career development	1	0
dream research	1	0

Clinical opportunities
adults
children and adolescents
individual and group based treatments
inpatient and intensive outpatient hospital settings
university counseling
career counseling
neuropsychological assessment
mood and anxiety disorders
ADHD in children and adults
autism spectrum disorders
pediatric and cancer-related behavioral medicine
substance use disorders

Cleveland State University (Ph.D.)

Department of Counseling, Administration, Supervision, and Adult Learning
Cleveland, OH 44115
phone#: (216) 687-4697
email: j.c.phillips6@csuohio.edu
Web address: www.csuohio.edu/cehs/departments/DOC/cp_doc.html

1	2	3	4	**5**	6	7
Practice oriented			Equal emphasis			Research oriented

Percentage of faculty subscribing to each of the following orientations:

Psychodynamic/Psychoanalytic	50%
Applied behavioral analysis/Radical behavioral	0%
Family systems/Systems	25%
Existential/Phenomenological/Humanistic	25%
Cognitive/Cognitive-behavioral	75%

Courses required for incoming students to have completed prior to enrolling: none

These courses may be completed once beginning the doctoral program:
educational research, social and cultural foundations, appraisal in counseling, ethical and legal issues in counseling, laboratory in counseling techniques, theories of counseling, group counseling, career development, psychopathology and diagnosis for counselors

Recommended but not mandatory courses: none

GRE mean
Verbal 153 Quantitative 153
Analytical Writing 4.0
Psychology Subject Test not required

GPA mean
Overall GPA undergraduate 3.33 Master's 3.87

Number of applications/admission offers/incoming students in 2017
24 applied/9 admission offers/5 incoming

% of students receiving:
Full tuition waiver only:
Assistantship/fellowship only:
Both full tuition waiver & assistantship/fellowship: 100% of incoming students received 9 credits of tuition waiver and 10 or 20 hour assistantships with stipends

Approximate percentage of incoming students with a BA/BS only: 0% **Master's:** 100%

Approximate percentage of all students who are Women: 74% **Ethnic Minority:** 33% **International:** 15%

Average years to complete the doctoral program (including internship): 6.5 years

Personal interview
In person if feasible, otherwise Skype interview

Attrition rate in past 7 years: 16%

Percentage of students applying for internship in 2017 accepted into:

APA internships: 100% **APPIC internships:** 100%

Formal tracks/concentrations: none

Research areas	**# Faculty**	**# Grants**
training/professional issues	1	0
multicultural issues	4	0
international psychology	3	0
vocational psychology	1	0
women's work and identity development	1	0
health psychology	1	0
trauma	1	0

Clinical opportunities
Practicum training sites:
Community Mental Health Centers – 5
Child/Adolescent Mental Health – 4
Hospital – 2
College Counseling Centers – 5
VA – 1

Colorado State University (Ph.D.)

Department of Psychology
Fort Collins, CO 80523
phone#: (970) 491-6363
email: Linda.Thornton@ColoState.EDU
Web address: www.colostate.edu/Depts/Psychology/counseling/

1	2	**3**	4	5	6	7
Practice oriented			Equal emphasis			Research oriented

Percentage of faculty subscribing to each of the following orientations:

Psychodynamic/Psychoanalytic	0%
Applied behavioral analysis/Radical behavioral	0%
Family systems/Systems	0%
Existential/Phenomenological/Humanistic	0%
Cognitive/Cognitive-behavioral	90%

Courses required for incoming students to have completed prior to enrolling: none

Recommended but not mandatory courses: learning, personality, history and systems, developmental, abnormal, statistics

GRE mean
Verbal 160.375 Quantitative 155.75
Analytical Writing 4.85
Psychology Subject Test is required only for those without Psychology Majors

GPA mean
Overall GPA 3.71

Number of applications/admission offers/incoming students in 2017
207 applied/9 admission offers/8 incoming

% of students receiving:
Full tuition waiver only: 0%
Assistantship/fellowship only: 0%
Both full tuition waiver & assistantship/fellowship: 100%
Both half tuition waiver & assistantship/fellowship: 0%

Approximate percentage of incoming students with a B.A./B.S. only: 100% **Master's:** 0%

Approximate percentage of all students who are Women: 70% **Ethnic Minority:** 32% **International:** 0%

Average years to complete the doctoral program (including internship): 5 years

Personal interview
No interview required

Attrition rate in past 7 years: 10%

Percentage of students applying for internship in 2017 accepted into:

APA internships: 84% **APPIC internships:** 84%

Formal tracks/concentrations: none

Research areas	# Faculty	# Grants
ADHD	1	0
adolescents	3	5
aggression (anger research and reduction)	1	0
aging/geriatrics	3	1
anxiety (reduction)	1	0
assessment (including multicultural)	3	1
body image/eating disturbances child	1	0
cognitive	5	1
college teaching	1	0
educational outcomes	1	1
emotional disorders	1	0
ethics	1	0
health psychology	8	4
interpersonal relationships	1	0
learning disabilities	1	0
men	1	0
multicultural	6	3
parent–child interaction	1	0
psychopathology	3	0
psychotherapy process	1	0
stress and coping processes	2	0
substance abuse	4	3
supervision and training	2	0
violence/abuse	2	0
vocational psychology	2	0
well-being	1	1
women	3	1

Clinical opportunities

family stress center
neuropsychology practice
college/university counseling centers
juvenile detention facility
substance abuse
primary care

University of Denver (Ph.D.)

Morgridge College of Education
Denver, CO 80208
phone#: (303) 871-2484
email: Maria.Riva@du.edu
Web address: www.du.edu/education/academicPrograms/cnp/

1	2	3	4	5	6	7
Practice oriented			Equal emphasis			Research oriented

Percentage of faculty subscribing to each of the following orientations:

Psychodynamic/Psychoanalytic	20%
Applied behavioral analysis/Radical behavioral	0%
Family systems/Systems	10%
Existential/Phenomenological/Humanistic	40%
Cognitive/Cognitive-behavioral	30%

Courses required for incoming students to have completed prior to enrolling: none

Recommended but not mandatory courses:
Undergraduate courses in counseling theory, counseling techniques, statistics, human development are helpful

GRE mean
Verbal 550 Quantitative 550
Analytical Writing 4.5
Psychology Subject Test not required

GPA mean
Overall GPA 3.8

Number of applications/admission offers/incoming students in 2016–2017
142 applied/17 admission offers/9 incoming

% of students receiving:
For the past 2 years, we have awarded incoming doctoral students a 3 year financial aid package for those students coming in with a Master's Degree, and a four year package for those students who do not have a Master's Degree. The financial aid packages consist of several different types of funding. The data below is consistent with our typical funding
Full tuition waiver only: 30%
Assistantship/fellowship only: 60%
Both full tuition waiver & assistantship/fellowship: 10%

Approximate percentage of incoming students with a B.A./B.S. only: 22% **Master's:** 78%

Approximate percentage of all students who are Women: 75% **Ethnic Minority:** 32%
International: not reported

Average years to complete the doctoral program (including internship): 5.0 years

Personal interview
Required; prefer in person but telephone acceptable

Attrition rate in past 7 years: from 2010–2016 7%

Percentage of students applying for internship in 2016 accepted into:

APA internships: 100% **APPIC internships:** n/a

Formal tracks/concentrations: none

Research areas	# Faculty	# Grants
Therapeutic Relationships in Treatment	1	3
Social support and Health psychology	2	2
Group Counseling	1	0
Multicultural Counseling	3	1
Clinical Training and Supervision	1	0
Career	2	2
Addictive Behaviors	1	0

Clinical opportunities are numerous in the Denver area
Working in diverse setting with Racial/ethnic minorities
Working with underserved populations
Substance abuse treatment
Facilitating group counseling
Neuropsychology
Adolescent and adult treatment
Assessment experience
In-house clinic and live supervision
University and College Counseling settings
Integrative Care settings
Jail and prison settings

Children's hospital
Veteran's Administration
Community mental health settings

University of Florida (Ph.D.)

Department of Psychology
Gainesville, FL 32611
phone#: (352) 392-0601
email: moradib@ufl.edu
Web address: www.psych.ufl.edu/index.php/counselingpsychology

1	2	3	4	5	**6**	7
Practice oriented			Equal emphasis			Research oriented

Percentage of faculty subscribing to each of the following orientations:

Psychodynamic/Psychoanalytic	0%
Applied behavioral analysis/Radical behavioral	0%
Family systems/Systems	25%
Existential/Phenomenological/Humanistic	50%
Cognitive/Cognitive-behavioral	25%

Courses required for incoming students to have completed prior to enrolling:
undergraduate 4-year degree in psychology or related field

Recommended but not mandatory courses: statistics, research design/methods, personality, abnormal

GRE mean
Verbal 573 Quantitative 667
Psychology Subject Test not used

GPA mean
Overall GPA 3.8 Psychology GPA 3.9
Junior/Senior GPA 3.8

Number of applications/admission offers/incoming students in 2017
146 applied/7 admission offers/6 incoming

% of students receiving:
Full tuition waiver only: 0%
Assistantship/fellowship only: 0%
Both full tuition waiver & assistantship/fellowship: 100%

Approximate percentage of incoming students with a B.A./B.S. only: 75% **Master's:** 25%

Approximate percentage of all students who are Women: 79% **Ethnic Minority:** 44% **International:** 15%

Average years to complete the doctoral program (including internship): 5 years

Personal interview
Preferred in person but telephone acceptable

Attrition rate in past 7 years: 10%

Percentage of students applying for internship in 2017 accepted into:

APA internships: 100% **APPIC internships:**

Formal tracks/concentrations: none

Research areas	# Faculty	# Grants
addictions	1	0
health psychology	1	2
constructivist psychology	1	0
forensics	1	0
gender and emotion	1	1
minority/multicultural	1	0
personality	1	0
sexual orientation	1	1
vocational psychology	1	1
women	1	1

Clinical opportunities
anxiety disorder clinic
career counseling center
community mental health
crisis intervention center
domestic violence clinic
family medical practice
forensics hospital
hospice
nursing facility
pediatric/psychiatric assessment and treatment
university counseling center
rural health care clinic
sexual offender
substance abuse clinic

Fordham University Counseling Psychology (Ph.D.)

Division of Psychological and Educational Services
Graduate School of Education
113 West 60th Street
New York, NY 10023
phone#: (212) 636-6460
email: mjackson@fordham.edu
Web address: www.fordham.edu/academics/colleges__graduate_s/graduate__profession/education/divisions/psychological__educa/counseling_psycholog/index.asp

1	2	3	**4**	5	6	7
Practice oriented			Equal emphasis			Research oriented

Percentage of faculty subscribing to each of the following orientations:

Psychodynamic/Psychoanalytic	35%
Applied behavioral analysis/Radical behavioral	20%
Family systems/Systems	16%
Existential/Phenomenological/Humanistic	60%
Cognitive/Cognitive-behavioral	100%

Courses required for incoming students to have completed prior to enrolling:
15 credits in psychology, developmental, experimental, abnormal, personality

Recommended but not mandatory courses: Qualitative research methods

GRE mean
Verbal 580 Quantitative 670
Analytical Writing 4.5
Psychology Subject Test not reported

GPA mean
Overall GPA 3.8

Number of applications/admission offers/incoming students
159 applied/25 admission offers/11 incoming

% of students receiving:
Full tuition waiver only: 0%
Assistantship/fellowship only: 50%
Both full tuition waiver & assistantship/fellowship: 0%

Approximate percentage of incoming students with a B.A./B.S. only: 70% **Master's:** 30%

Approximate percentage of all students who are Women: 70% **Ethnic Minority:** 33% **International:** 8%

Average years to complete the doctoral program (including internship): 7 years

Personal interview
Preferred in person but telephone acceptable

Attrition rate in past 7 years: 8%

Percentage of students applying for internship accepted into:

APA internships: 50% **APPIC internships:** 50%

Formal tracks/concentrations: none

Research areas	# Faculty	# Grants
career development	3	1
criminal behavior	1	1
health psychology	2	1
multicultural counseling	5	0
supervision	3	2

Clinical opportunities
college counseling centers
community mental health centers
on-campus clinical/research center
psychological services institute

University of Georgia (Ph.D.)

Department of Counseling and Human Development Services
Athens, GA 30602
phone#: (706) 542-1812
email: bheckman@uga.edu
Web address: www.coe.uga.edu/chds/academic-programs/counseling-psychology/

1	2	3	4	5	6	7
Practice oriented			Equal emphasis			Research oriented

Percentage of faculty subscribing to each of the following orientations:

Psychodynamic/Psychoanalytic	20%
Applied behavioral analysis/Radical behavioral	0%
Family systems/Systems	20%
Existential/Phenomenological/Humanistic	10%
Cognitive/Cognitive-behavioral	50%

Courses required for incoming students to have completed prior to enrolling:
Research methods, statistics, interpersonal relationships, individual assessment, vocational development, theories of counseling, individual counseling practicum, group counseling, multicultural counseling (Master's degree required)

Recommended but not mandatory courses: not reported

GRE mean
Verbal + Quantitative 305
Analytical Writing 4.4
Psychology Subject Test not reported

GPA mean
Overall GPA Undergraduate 3.8 Graduate 3.85

Number of applications/admission offers/incoming students in 2017
100 applied/8–10 admission offers/8 incoming

% of students receiving:
Full tuition waiver only: 0%
Assistantship/fellowship only: 0%
Both full tuition waiver & assistantship/fellowship: 100%

Approximate percentage of incoming students with a B.A./B.S. only: 0% **Master's:** 100%

Approximate percentage of all students who are Women: 81% **Ethnic Minority:** 45% **International:** 5%

Average years to complete the doctoral program (including internship): 4 years

Personal interview
In person

Attrition rate in past 7 years: 2%

Percentage of students applying for internship in 2017 accepted into:

APA internships: 100% **APPIC internships:** 100%

Formal tracks/concentrations: supervision, psychological assessment (learning disabilities), preparing future faculty, health psychology

Research areas	# Faculty	# Grants
accident trauma	1	1
African American Psychology	1	0
attributions and therapy	2	0
Assessment (rural)	1	1
empowering schools	2	1
juvenile delinquency/aggression	2	2
minority male adolescents	1	1
Latino Psychology	1	0
multicultural counseling	3	2
preventing violence and aggression in schools	2	3
school counselor education	2	0
substance abuse	1	0
young adult development	2	–
health psychology	1	2

Clinical opportunities
adolescents
college students
departmental captive clinic
homeless shelter
Learning disabilities
Rural assessment
Primary Care
juvenile offenders
school-age children
supervision
college counseling center
People with developmental disabilities
Telehealth

Georgia State University (Ph.D.)

Department of Counseling and Psychological Services
Atlanta, GA 30303
phone#: (404) 413-8010
email: jashby2@gsu.edu
Web address: education.gsu.edu/cps/781.html

1	2	3	4	5	6	7
Practice oriented			Equal emphasis			Research oriented

Percentage of faculty subscribing to each of the following orientations:

Psychodynamic/Psychoanalytic	25%
Applied behavioral analysis/Radical behavioral	0%
Family systems/Systems	25%
Existential/Phenomenological/Humanistic	25%
Cognitive/Cognitive-behavioral	25%

Courses required for incoming students to have completed prior to enrolling:
Bachelor's degree in psychology (or a related field) OR
M.A. in counseling or clinical psychology (or a related field)

Recommended but not mandatory courses: none

GRE mean
Verbal 600 Quantitative 600
Analytical Writing 4.9
Psychology Subject Test not reported

GPA mean
Overall GPA 3.8

Number of applications/admission offers/incoming students in 2017
145 applied/6 admission offers/5 incoming

% of students receiving:
Full tuition waiver only: 0%
Assistantship/fellowship only: 0%
Both full tuition waiver & assistantship/fellowship: 100%

Approximate percentage of incoming students with a B.A./B.S. only: 0% **Master's:** 100%

Approximate percentage of all students who are Women: 80% **Ethnic Minority:** 40% **International:** 8%

Average years to complete the doctoral program (including internship): 5 years

Personal interview
Preferred in person but electronic acceptable

Attrition rate in past 7 years: 0.1%

Percentage of students applying for internship in 2017 accepted into:

APA internships: 100% **APPIC internships:**

Formal tracks/concentrations: none

Research areas	# Faculty	# Grants
Emotional regulation	1	0
gender/multicultural	2	2
stress/coping	2	1
trauma	1	1
Positive psychology	1	3

Clinical opportunities
behavioral medicine
college counseling
forensic
multicultural counseling
stress management

University of Houston (Ph.D.)

Counseling Psychology Program
Houston, TX 77004-5874
phone#: (713) 743-9830
email: coegrad@central.uh.edu
Web address: http://www.uh.edu/education/degree-programs/counseling-psyc-phd/

1	2	3	4	5	6	7
Practice oriented			Equal emphasis			Research oriented

Percentage of faculty subscribing to each of the following orientations:

Psychodynamic/Psychoanalytic	50%
Applied behavioral analysis/Radical behavioral	15%
Family systems/Systems	15%
Existential/Phenomenological/Humanistic	30%
Cognitive/Cognitive-behavioral	30%

Courses required for incoming students to have completed prior to enrolling: none

Recommended but not mandatory courses: none

GRE mean
Verbal 153
Quantitative 145
Analytical Writing 4.5
Psychology Subject Test not reported

GPA mean
Overall Master's GPA 3.83

Number of applications/admission offers/incoming students in 2016
104 applied/14 admission offers/6 incoming

% of students receiving:
Full tuition waiver only: 0%
Assistantship/fellowship only: 0%
Both full tuition waiver & assistantship/fellowship: 100%

Approximate percentage of incoming students with a B.A./B.S. only: 40% **Master's:** 60%

Approximate percentage of all students who are Women: 90% **Ethnic Minority:** 50% **International:** 11%

Average years to complete the doctoral program (including internship): 6 years

Personal interview
Preferred in person but telephone or Skype acceptable

Attrition rate in past 7 years: 7%

Percentage of students applying for internship in 2016 accepted into:

APA internships: 100% **APPIC internships:** 0%

Formal tracks/concentrations: Elective emphasis in health psychology

Research areas	# Faculty	# Grants
adult attachment	1	2
career counseling	2	0
cross-cultural counseling	3	1
gender identity in men	2	1
mental health policy	1	0
racial identity	2	2
health disparities	2	2
LGBT/HIV	1	1
Training	2	1

Clinical opportunities
outpatient health psychology
family therapy
crisis intervention program
university counseling centers
VA hospital
substance abuse
gerontology
career counseling
community mental health
assessment — including neuropsych placements
first responders
chronic inpatient
behavioral medicine
forensics
posttraumatic stress disorder
school districts
medical schools
pediatric hospitals
adolescent eating disorders
private practice
LGBT

Howard University (Ph.D.)

School of Education
2441 Fourth Street, NW
Washington DC 20059
phone#: (202) 806-7351 or (202) 806-7350
email: Shareefah.aluqdah@howard.edu
Web address: https://gs.howard.edu/graduate-programs/counseling-psychology

1	2	3	**4**	5	6	7
Practice oriented			Equal emphasis			Research oriented

Percentage of faculty subscribing to each of the following orientations:

Psychodynamic/Psychoanalytic	50%
Applied behavioral analysis/Radical behavioral	0%
Family systems/Systems	0%
Existential/Phenomenological/Humanistic	0%
Cognitive/Cognitive-behavioral	50%

Courses required for incoming students to have completed prior to enrolling:
Recommended but not mandatory courses: Advanced Statistics, Psychology, Human Learning, and Human Development

GRE mean
we require the GRE but our decision is based more on recommendation, research history, and GPA. For funding top 1/3rd percentile is best.

Verbal + Quantitative
Analytical Writing
Psychology Subject Test

GPA mean
Overall GPA 3.7

Number of applications/admission offers/incoming students in 2017
44 applied/15 admission offers/8 incoming

% of students receiving:
Full tuition waiver only: 0%
Assistantship/fellowship only: 25%
Both full tuition waiver & assistantship/fellowship: 25%

Approximate percentage of incoming students with a B.A./B.S. only: 16% **Master's:** 84%

Approximate percentage of all students who are Women: 80% **Ethnic Minority:** 100% **International:** 10%

Average years to complete the doctoral program (including internship): 6 years

Personal interview: preferred

Attrition rate in past 7 years: 5%

Percentage of students applying for internship last year accepted into:

APA internships: 80% **APPIC internships:** 10%

Formal tracks/concentrations: not reported

Research areas	# Faculty	# Grants
Community violence	2	0
Colorism	1	0
Intersectionality	3	0
African American Men	2	0
Muslim mental health	2	0
Cultural Competence	6	0
Education/Training	5	0
Immigration	1	0
Advocacy	5	0
Health psychology	3	0
Family/parenting	1	0

Clinical opportunities
anxiety disorders
depression
psychopathology assessment
forensics
ethnic minorities
college counseling centers

University of Illinois, Urbana-Champaign (Ph.D)

University of Illinois at Urbana-Champaign
Department of Educational Psychology: Counseling Psychology Program
1310 S. Sixth St., MC 708
Champaign, IL 61820
phone#: (217) 333-0960
email: info@education.illinois.edu
Web address: https://education.illinois.edu/edpsy/programs-degrees/counseling-psychology/counseling-psychology-information

1	2	3	4	**5**	6	7
Practice oriented			Equal emphasis			Research oriented

Percentage of faculty subscribing to each of the following orientations:

Psychodynamic/Psychoanalytic	0%
Applied behavioral analysis/Radical behavioral	0%
Family systems/Systems	0%
Existential/Phenomenological/Humanistic	0%
Cognitive/Cognitive-behavioral	0%

Most of the clinical faculty adopt some type of integrative orientation

Courses required for incoming students to have completed prior to enrolling:
We do not have required courses before entering the doctoral program

Recommended but not mandatory courses:
Although we do not have required courses, we strongly encourage students to have taken one or more statistics courses and/or advanced mathematics courses

GRE mean
We evaluate students' on their entire application materials
Avg. verbal GRE score = 78th percentile
Avg. quantitative GRE score = 63rd percentile
Analytical Writing we do not require the analytic writing test for admission
Psychology Subject Test we do not require the psychology subject test for admission

GPA mean
Average Overall Undergraduate GPA = 3.69

Number of applications/admission offers/incoming students in 2017
173 applied/5 admission offers/2 incoming

% of students receiving:
Full tuition waiver only: 100%
Assistantship/fellowship only: 100%
Both full tuition waiver & assistantship/fellowship: 100%

Approximate percentage of incoming students with a B.A./B.S. only: 75% **Master's:** 25%

Approximate percentage of all students who are Women: 83% **Ethnic Minority:** 50% **International:** 8%

Average years to complete the doctoral program (including internship): 6 to 7 years

Personal interview Yes

Attrition rate in past 7 years: not reported

Percentage of students applying for internship last year accepted into:

APA internships: 100% **APPIC internships:** 100%

Formal tracks/concentrations: We just have the one counseling psychology Program; there are no formal tracks/ concentrations

Research areas	# Faculty	# Grants
aging (including Alzheimer's)	1	Yes
child	2	Yes
developmental	2	Yes
eating disorders	1	No
emotion	3	Yes

Clinical opportunities
Addiction issues
Assessment
Children and adolescents
College faculty and staff
College students
Community centers
Couples and family therapy
Disabilities
Trauma survivors
Veterans

Indiana University (Ph.D.)

Department of Counseling and Educational Psychology
Wright Education Building, Room 4056
Bloomington, IN 47405
phone#: (812) 856-8009
email: cep@indiana.edu
Web address: education.indiana.edu/graduate/programs/counseling-psychology/index.html

1	2	3	4	**5**	6	7
Practice oriented			Equal emphasis			Research oriented

Percentage of faculty subscribing to each of the following orientations:

Interpersonal/Psychodynamic	55%
Behavioral	27%
Family systems/Systems/Ecological	36%
Existential/Phenomenological/Humanistic	9%
Cognitive/Cognitive-behavioral	91%
Social constructionist (e.g., solution-focused/narrative)	27%
Multicultural/Feminist/Relational-Cultural	45%

Courses required for incoming students to have completed prior to enrolling: none

Recommended but not mandatory courses: statistics and research methods

GRE mean
Verbal 156 Quantitative 152
Analytical Writing 4.3
Psychology Subject Test not required

GPA mean
Overall undergraduate GPA 3.51
Overall graduate GPA 3.88

Number of applications/admission offers/incoming students in 2017
106 applied/10 admission offers/6 incoming

% of students receiving:
Full tuition waiver only: 0%
Assistantship/fellowship only: 5%
Both full tuition waiver & assistantship/fellowship: 75%

Approximate percentage of incoming students (2017 cohort) with a B.A./B.S. only: 17% **Master's:** 83%

Approximate percentage of all students who are Women: 61% **Ethnic Minority:** 59% **International:** 17%

Average years to complete the doctoral program (including internship): 6 years

Personal interview
In-person interview strongly preferred/Skype acceptable

Attrition rate in past 7 years: 4%

Percentage of students applying for internship in 2017 accepted into:

APA internships: 83% **APPIC internships:** 17%

Formal tracks/concentrations: Minor available (e.g., human sexuality, public health, multicultural, etc.)

Research areas	# Faculty	# Grants
LGBT issues	1	–
Vocational (career) psychology	3	1
Multicultural counseling	1	–
Sport psychology	1	–
Native American empowerment	1	–
Psychology of men and masculinities	2	–
Group counseling	1	–
HIV/AIDS counseling	1	1
Substance use	2	2
Asian American mental health	1	–
Positive psychology	1	1
Marriage and divorce	1	–
Adolescent risk	1	–

Clinical opportunities
in-house training clinic
regional practicum sites

University of Iowa (Ph.D.)

Division of Psychological and Quantitative Foundations
Iowa City, IA 52242
phone#: (319) 335-5578
email: william-liu@uiowa.edu
Web address: https://education.uiowa.edu/academic-programs/counseling-psychology

1	2	3	**4**	5	6	7
Practice oriented			Equal emphasis			Research oriented

Percentage of faculty subscribing to each of the following orientations:

Psychodynamic/Psychoanalytic	25%
Applied behavioral analysis/Radical behavioral	0%
Family systems/Systems	25%
Existential/Phenomenological/Humanistic	25%
Cognitive/Cognitive-behavioral	25%

Courses required for incoming students to have completed prior to enrolling: none

Recommended but not mandatory courses: as much core psychology as possible

GRE mean
Verbal 152 Quantitative 151
Analytical Writing 3.5
Psychology Subject Test not reported

GPA mean
Overall GPA 3.58

Number of applications/admission offers/incoming students in 2017
90 applied/10 admission offers/10 incoming

% of students receiving:
Full tuition waiver only: 0%
Assistantship/fellowship only: 40%
Both full tuition waiver & assistantship/fellowship: 60%

Approximate percentage of incoming students with a B.A./B.S. only: 30% **Master's:** 70%

Approximate percentage of all students who are Women: 67% **Ethnic Minority:** 35% **International:** 2%

Average years to complete the doctoral program (including internship): 6 years

Personal interview
Interview required

Attrition rate in past 7 years: 10%

Percentage of students applying for internship in 2016 accepted into:

APA internships: 100% **APPIC internships:** 100%

Formal tracks/concentrations: none

Research areas	# Faculty	# Grants
child/adolescent health	1	1
suicide	1	0
ethics	2	1
multicultural	2	1
psychosocial oncology	2	1
public health	2	0
men	3	0
spirituality	2	0
mood and anxiety disorders	1	0
career	1	1

Clinical opportunities

community mental health	university counseling centers
hospitals	VA medical center
specialty settings	women's center
prisons	homeless shelter
public schools	

Iowa State University (Ph.D.)

Department of Psychology
Ames, IA 50011-3180
phone#: (515) 294-1743
email: nwade@iastate.edu
Web address: counseling.psych.iastate.edu/

1	2	3	4	**5**	6	7
Practice oriented			Equal emphasis			Research oriented

Percentage of faculty subscribing to each of the following orientations:

Psychodynamic/Psychoanalytic	6%
Applied behavioral analysis/Radical behavioral	0%
Family systems/Systems	0%
Existential/Phenomenological/Humanistic	31%
Cognitive/Cognitive-behavioral	25%
Eclectic	38%

Courses required for incoming students to have completed prior to enrolling:
A minimum of 15 credits in psychology, including statistics, psychological measurement, abnormal, developmental, social, and research methods

Recommended but not mandatory courses: most successful applicants have a diversified psychology major

GRE mean
Verbal 159 Quantitative 156
Analytical Writing 4.7
Psychology Subject Test not required

GPA mean
Overall GPA 3.68 Psychology GPA 3.69
Junior/Senior GPA 3.74

Number of applications/admission offers/incoming students in 2017
71 applied/8 admission offers/6 incoming

% of students receiving:
Full tuition waiver only: 0%
Assistantship/fellowship only: 0%
Both full tuition waiver & assistantship/fellowship: 100%

Approximate percentage of incoming students with a B.A./B.S. only 70% **Master's:** 30%

Approximate percentage of all students who are Women: 73% **Ethnic Minority:** 40% **International:** 7%

Average years to complete the doctoral program (including internship): 6 years

Personal interview
In-person interview strongly preferred but telephone/video call acceptable

Attrition rate in past 7 years: 0%

Percentage of students applying for internship in 2017 accepted into:

APA internships: 100% **APPIC internships:** 100%

Formal tracks/concentrations: none

Research areas	# Faculty	# Grants
Asian American psychology	1	1
attachment	1	0
bullying and aggression	1	0
developmental psychopathology	1	0
discrimination	1	0
forgiveness	1	1
gender roles	1	0
health psychology	1	1
help-seeking	2	1
Minority psychology	3	0
multiculturalism	3	0
personality	1	0
psychotherapy process/outcome	3	0
religion/spirituality	1	0
social support	1	0
stereotypes/stigma	2	1
supervision	1	0
vocational interest	2	0
women in science	2	1

Clinical opportunities
University counseling center
Group psychotherapy clinic
Hospital
VA medical center
ADHD assessment clinic
Private group practice
Corrections unit
Community mental health center

University of Kansas (Ph.D.)

Department of Educational Psychology
Counseling Psychology Program
Lawrence, KS 66045
phone#: (785) 864-3931
email: epsy@ku.edu
Web address: http://epsy.ku.edu/academics/counseling-psychology/doctorate/overview-benefits

1	2	3	**4**	5	6	7
Practice oriented			Equal emphasis			Research oriented

Percentage of faculty subscribing to each of the following orientations:

Psychodynamic/Psychoanalytic	20%
Applied behavioral analysis/Radical behavioral	0%
Family systems/Systems	20%
Existential/Phenomenological/Humanistic	20%
Cognitive/Cognitive-behavioral	40%

Courses required for incoming students to have completed prior to enrolling: none

Recommended but not mandatory courses: basic courses in psychology (e.g., social, personality, abnormal, experimental, learning)

GRE mean
Verbal 156 Quantitative 150
Analytical Writing 4.3
Psychology Subject Test not required, but recommended

GPA mean
Overall GPA 3.8

Number of applications/admission offers/incoming students in 2017
57 applied/7 admission offers/5 incoming

% of students receiving:
Full tuition waiver only: 0%
Assistantship/fellowship only: 25%
Both full tuition waiver & assistantship/fellowship: 75%

Approximate percentage of incoming students with a B.A./B.S. only: 20% **Master's:** 80%

Approximate percentage of all students who are Women: 64% **Ethnic Minority:** 25% **International:** 12%

Average years to complete the doctoral program (including internship): 5.8 years

Personal interview
Required in person or by phone/media

Attrition rate in past 7 years: 14%

Percentage of students applying for internship in 2016 accepted into:

APA internships: 88% **APPIC internships:** 0%

Formal tracks/concentrations: none

Research areas	**# Faculty**	**# Grants**
creativity	1	1
positive psychology	2	0
therapy outcome and process	2	1
vocational decision making	3	0
women and science careers	1	1
multicultural/international issues	2	0

Clinical opportunities
college/university counseling centers
community/social service agencies
VA medical centers
university medical/research centers
community clinics

University of Kentucky (Ph.D.)

Department of Educational, School, and Counseling Psychology
Lexington, KY 40506-0017
phone#: (859) 257-7404
email: s.rostosky@uky.edu
Web address: https://2b.education.uky.edu/edp/counseling-psychology-overview/

1	2	3	4	**5**	6	7
Practice oriented			Equal emphasis			Research oriented

Percentage of faculty subscribing to each of the following orientations:

Psychodynamic/Psychoanalytic	0%
Applied behavioral analysis/Radical behavioral	0%
Family systems/Systems	0%
Existential/Phenomenological/Humanistic	25%
Cognitive/Cognitive-behavioral	50%
Solution-Focused/Narrative	25%

Courses required for incoming students to have completed prior to enrolling:
Psychological Tests and Measurements

Recommended but not mandatory courses: none

GRE mean (2017)
Verbal + Quantitative 156.5(V); 150(Q)
Analytical Writing 4.42
Psychology Subject Test not required

GPA mean (2017)
Overall GPA 3.65

Number of applications/admission offers/incoming students in 2017
57 applied/9 admission offers/7 incoming

% of students receiving:
Full tuition waiver only: 0%
Assistantship/fellowship only: 0%
Both full tuition waiver & assistantship/fellowship: 100%

Approximate percentage of incoming students with a B.A./B.S. only: 43% **Master's:** 57%

Approximate percentage of all students who are Women: 70% **Ethnic Minority:** 38% **International:** 6%

Average years to complete the doctoral program (including internship): 6 years

Personal interview
In-person preferred

Attrition rate in past 7 years: 15%

Percentage of students applying for internship last year accepted into:

APA internships: 100% **APPIC internships:** 0%

Formal tracks/concentrations: we are a generalist program

Research areas **# Faculty (5 core)**
LGBTQ well-being
substance abuse and HIV
psychotherapy outcome
racial/ethnic minority & cultural competence
Sexual health
Help-seeking

Clinical opportunities
University of Kentucky Counseling Center (1st year doctoral placement)
VA, Psychiatric State hospital, community mental health, Federal Medical Center

Lehigh University (Ph.D.)

Counseling Psychology
Bethlehem, PA 18015-4792
phone#: (610) 758-3250
email: ctl212@lehigh.edu
Web address: http://ed.lehigh.edu/academics/degrees/doctoral/cp-phd

1	2	3	4	5	**6**	7
Practice oriented			Equal emphasis			Research oriented

Percentage of faculty subscribing to each of the following orientations:

Psychodynamic/Psychoanalytic	25%
Applied behavioral analysis/Radical behavioral	0%
Family systems/Systems	25%
Existential/Phenomenological/Humanistic	25%
Cognitive/Cognitive-behavioral	25%

Courses required for incoming students to have completed prior to enrolling: Psychology related courses preferred

Recommended but not mandatory courses: Psychology related

GRE mean (for incoming students)
Verbal 159 Quantitative 159
Analytical Writing not reported
Psychology Subject Test not reported

GPA mean (for incoming students)
Overall GPA 3.64

Number of applications/admission offers/incoming students in 2017
98 applied/6 admission offers/6 incoming

% of students receiving (for all enrolled students):
Full tuition waiver only: 10%
Assistantship/fellowship only: 0%
Both full tuition waiver & assistantship/fellowship: 90%

Approximate percentage of incoming students with a B.A./B.S. only: 50% **Master's:** 50%

Approximate percentage of students (of all enrolled) who are
Women: 93% **Ethnic Minority:** 53% **International:** 10%

Average years to complete the doctoral program (including internship): 7 years

Personal interview:
Preferred in person but telephone acceptable

Attrition rate in past 7 years: 12%

Percentage of students applying for internship in 2017 accepted into:

APA internships: 100% **APPIC internships:** n/a

Formal tracks/concentrations: none

Research areas	# Faculty	# Grants
cross-cultural	3	2
family systems	1	1
supervision/training	2	0
gender/gender-based violence	2	0
older adults	1	0
advanced statistics	1	0

Clinical opportunities
counseling centers
mental health agencies
hospitals

Louisiana Tech University (Ph.D.)

Department of Psychology and Behavioral Sciences
P.O. Box 10048
Ruston, LA 71272
phone#: (318) 257-5066
email:buboltzs@latech.edu
Web address: http://education.latech.edu/academics/graduate/phd_counseling_psychology/

1 2 3 **4** 5 6 7

Practice oriented — Equal emphasis — Research oriented

Percentage of faculty subscribing to each of the following orientations:

Psychodynamic/Psychoanalytic	0%
Applied behavioral analysis/Radical behavioral	0%
Family systems/Systems	0%
Existential/Phenomenological/Humanistic	60%
Cognitive/Cognitive-behavioral	40%

Courses required for incoming students prior to enrolling: none

Courses recommended but not mandatory: none

GRE mean
Verbal 152 Quantitative 150
Analytical Writing not used for admission purposes
Psychology Subject Test not reported

GPA mean
Overall GPA 3.6

Number of applications/admission offers/incoming students in 2016
38 applied/6 admission offers/6 incoming

% of students receiving:
Full tuition waiver only: 0%
Assistantship/fellowship only: 100%
Both full tuition waiver & assistantship/fellowship: 0%

Approximate percentage of incoming students with a B.A./B.S. only: 33% **Master's:** 67%

Approximate percentage of students who are
Women: 65% **Ethnic Minority:** 27% **International:** 10%

Average years to complete the doctoral program (including internship): 5–6 years

Personal interview
In-person interview strongly preferred; telephone/Skype acceptable

Attrition rate in past 7 years: 15%

Percentage of students applying for internship in 2017 accepted into:

APA internships: 100% **APPIC internships:** 0%

Formal tracks/concentrations: none

Research areas	# Faculty	# Grants
multicultural	1	0
career development	2	0
personality testing	3	0
trauma/crisis	1	0
academic retention	1	0
neuropsychological assessment	1	0
relationships & gender roles	1	0
body image	1	0
psychological reactance theory	1	0
sleep quality/difficulty/habits	1	0
positive psychology	1	0
message framing	1	0

Clinical opportunities
university counseling center
community health centers
VA medical centers
in-house clinic
Private practices
medical center
prison settings
children's home
developmental center

University of Louisville (Ph.D.)

Department of Educational and Counseling Psychology
Louisville, KY 40292
phone#: (502) 852-0588
email: jesse.owen@louisville.edu
Web address: http://louisville.edu/education/degrees/med-cps-cp

1	2	3	4	5	6	7
Practice oriented			Equal emphasis			Research oriented

Percentage of faculty subscribing to each of the following orientations:

Psychodynamic/Psychoanalytic	60%
Family systems/Systems	40%
Existential/Phenomenological/Humanistic	20%
Cognitive/Cognitive-behavioral	80%

Courses required for incoming students to have completed prior to enrolling:
abnormal, development, statistics or methodology, social

Recommended but not mandatory courses: Core psychology

GRE mean
Verbal 164 Quantitative 159
Analytical Writing 5.0
Psychology Subject Test not reported

GPA mean
Overall Undergraduate GPA 3.75 Overall Master's GPA 4.0

Number of applications/admission offers/incoming students in 2017
61 applied/3 admission offers/3 incoming

% of incoming students receiving:
Full tuition waiver only: 0%
Assistantship/fellowship only: 0%
Both full tuition waiver & assistantship/fellowship: 100%

Approximate percentage of incoming students with a B.A./B.S. only: 66% **Master's:** 33%

Approximate percentage of students who are Women: 33% **Ethnic Minority:** 33% **International:** 0%

Average years to complete the doctoral program (including internship): 4.5 years entering with Master's; 6 years entering with Bachelor's

Personal interview
Yes, though phone interview acceptable

Attrition rate in past 7 years: 16%

Percentage of students applying for internship in 2016 accepted into:

APA internships: 100% **APPIC internships:** not reported

Formal tracks/concentrations: none

Research areas	# Faculty	# Grants
Forgiveness	1	0
Suicide	2	0
psychotherapy research	1	0
adolescent depression prevention	1	1
depression & health	2	0
international psychology	1	0
religion & spirituality	2	0
Relationships	2	0
International Ethics	1	0
cross cultural competency	2	0
microaggression/discrimination	2	0
vocational psychology	1	0
prevention-school based	1	1
stress, coping, & resilience	3	1

Clinical opportunities
college counseling center
hospital based services
community mental health
couples
VA
adolescents
vocational psychology
group interventions
healthy lifestyle/positive psychology
inpatient/outpatient
psychological assessment/neuropsychology

Loyola University of Chicago (Ph.D.)

School of Education
820 North Michigan Avenue
Chicago, IL 60611
phone#: (312) 915-6958
email: evera@luc.edu
(Dr. Elizabeth Vera, Graduate Program Director)
Web address: http://www.luc.edu/education/doctoral/counseling-psychology/

1	2	3	4	5	6	7
Practice oriented			Equal emphasis			Research oriented

Percentage of faculty subscribing to each of the following orientations:

Psychodynamic/Psychoanalytic	0%
Applied behavioral analysis/Radical behavioral	0%
Family systems/Systems	25%
Existential/Phenomenological/Humanistic	25%
Cognitive/Cognitive-behavioral	50%

Courses required for incoming students to have completed prior to enrolling:
Master's degree in counseling, psychology, or related field

Recommended but not mandatory courses: none

GRE mean
Verbal 600 Quantitative 600
Analytical Writing 4.5
Psychology Subject Test 600

GPA mean
Overall GPA 3.8 Psychology GPA 3.8

Number of applications/admission offers/incoming students in 2017
30 applied/3 admission offers/3 incoming

% of students receiving:
Full tuition waiver only: 0%
Assistantship/fellowship only: 0%
Both full tuition waiver & assistantship/fellowship: 100%

Approximate percentage of incoming students with a B.A./B.S. only: 0% **Master's:** 100%

Approximate percentage of all students who are Women: 78% **Ethnic Minority:** 72% **International:** 16%

Average years to complete the doctoral program (including internship): 6 years

Personal interview
Required in person

Attrition rate in past 7 years: .05%

Percentage of students applying for internship in 2017 accepted into:

APA internships: 100% **APPIC internships:** 0%

Formal tracks/concentrations: none

Research areas	# Faculty	# Grants
adolescent risk behavior	2	1
child/adolescent development	2	0
counseling process	1	0
multicultural counseling	2	0
vocational psychology	1	0

Clinical opportunities
hospitals
clinics
university counseling center

Marquette University (Ph.D.)

Department of Counselor Education & Counseling Psychology
150 Schroeder Health Sciences & Education Complex
Milwaukee, WI 53201-1881
phone#: (414) 288-5790
email: alan.burkard@marquette.edu
Web address: www.marquette.edu/education/grad/cecp_doctorate.shtml

1	2	3	**4**	5	6	7
Practice oriented			Equal emphasis			Research oriented

Percentage of faculty subscribing to each of the following orientations:

Psychodynamic/Psychoanalytic	30%
Applied behavioral analysis/Radical behavioral	10%
Family systems/Systems	30%
Existential/Phenomenological/Humanistic	40%
Cognitive/Cognitive-behavioral	40%

Courses required for incoming students to have completed prior to enrolling: Master's degree in a mental health field.

Recommended but not mandatory courses: none

GRE mean
Verbal 163 Quantitative 151
Analytical Writing 3.9
Psychology Subject Test not required

GPA mean
Overall GPA 3.5

Number of applications/admission offers/incoming students in 2017
51 applied/4 admission offers/4 incoming

% of students receiving:
Full tuition waiver only: 0%
Assistantship/fellowship only: 0%
Both full tuition waiver & assistantship/fellowship: 100%

Approximate percentage of incoming students with a B.A./B.S. only: 0% **Master's:** 100%

Approximate percentage of all students who are Women: 60% **Ethnic Minority:** 52% **International:** 5%

Average years to complete the doctoral program (including internship): 6 years

Personal interview
Required; Preferred in person but telephone acceptable

Attrition rate in past 7 years: 0%

Percentage of students applying for internship in 2017 accepted into:

APA internships: 100% **APPIC internships:** 0%

Formal tracks/concentrations: not reported

Research areas	# Faculty	# Grants
child maltreatment	2	0
multicultural	4	0
parenting	2	2
program evaluation in education	1	1
psychotherapy process	2	0
strengths, optimal functioning	2	0
clinical supervision	4	0
qualitative research	4	0
school counseling	2	1
doctoral advising	5	0
career development	1	0

Clinical opportunities
addiction
clinical supervision
diverse populations
homelessness
trauma
parenting
childhood disorders
health/medical psychology
neuropsychology
co-occurring disorders
Behavioral Clinic
university counseling centers
department of corrections
community mental health
medical centers
schools
community clinics
vocational rehabilitation

University of Maryland College Park (Ph.D.)

Department of Psychology and Department of Counseling, Higher Education, and Special Education
College Park, MD 20742
phone#: (301) 314-2609; (301) 405-8384
email: psycgradstudies@umd.edu, cscott18@umd.edu
Web address: http://www.counselingpsychology.umd.edu

1	2	3	4	**5**	6	7
Practice oriented			Equal emphasis			Research oriented

Percentage of faculty subscribing to each of the following orientations:

Psychodynamic/Psychoanalytic	30%
Applied behavioral analysis/Radical behavioral	0%
Family systems/Systems	10%
Existential/Phenomenological/Humanistic	37%
Cognitive/Cognitive-behavioral	37%
Interpersonal	50%
Feminist	25%

Courses required for incoming students to have completed prior to enrolling:
a minimum of 15 credits of coursework in psychology, including statistics, and 3 additional courses (in areas such as theories of personality, developmental, social, or cognitive-behavioral)

Recommended but not mandatory courses: statistics, core psychology courses listed above

GRE mean
Verbal 163 Quantitative 159
Analytical Writing 4.8
Psychology Subject Test not reported

GPA mean
Overall Undergraduate GPA 3.85
Overall Master's GPA 3.92

Number of applications/admission offers/incoming students in 2017
155 applied/8 admission offers/6 incoming

% of students receiving:
Full tuition waiver only: 0%
Assistantship/fellowship only: 0%
Both full tuition waiver & assistantship/fellowship: 100%

Approximate percentage of incoming students with a B.A./B.S. only: 83% **Master's:** 17%

Approximate percentage of all students who are Women: 63% **Ethnic Minority:** 45% **International:** 24%

Average years to complete the doctoral program (including internship): 6 years

Personal interview
Preferred in person but telephone acceptable

Attrition rate in past 7 years: 2%

Percentage of students applying for internship in 2017 accepted into:

APA internships: 100% **APPIC internships:** 100%

Formal tracks/concentrations: none

Research areas	# Faculty	# Grants
AIDS/HIV	1	0
career counseling	2	0
vocational psychology	2	1
counseling process	2	0
counseling relationship	2	0
countertransference	1	0
domestic violence	1	0
dreams	1	0
health/well-being	2	1
interpersonal relationships	2	0
multicultural/diversity	4	1
supervision/training	2	0
group process	1	0
alcohol	1	1
asian studies	2	1
attachment	1	0
bereavement/grief	1	0
gay/lesbian/bisexuality	1	0
men's issues	1	0
social justice issues	1	0
stigma	1	0

Clinical opportunities

multicultural	psychodynamic
group	career
individual	supervision

University of Massachusetts, Boston (Ph.D.)

Department of Counseling and School Psychology
Boston, MA 02125
email: daniel.torres@umb.edu
Web address: https://www.umb.edu/academics/cehd/counseling/phd

1	2	3	4	5	6	7
Practice oriented			Equal emphasis			Research oriented

Percentage of faculty subscribing to each of the following orientations:

Psychodynamic/Psychoanalytic	10%
Applied behavioral analysis/Radical behavioral	20%
Family systems/Systems	10%
Existential/Phenomenological/Humanistic	30%
Cognitive/Cognitive-behavioral	30%

Courses required for incoming students to have completed prior to enrolling:

Recommended but not mandatory courses: Graduate courses in: Counseling Theories, Abnormal Psychology, Career/Vocational, Group Counseling, Masters level Practicum & Internship, Developmental Psychology, Cultural Diversity or Multicultural Counseling

GRE mean
Verbal (77%) + Quantitative (53%)
Analytical Writing (83%)
Psychology Subject Test n/a

GPA mean
Overall GPA Undergraduate 3.6

Number of applications/admission offers/incoming students in 2017
72 applied/5 admission offers/5 incoming students

% of students receiving:
Full tuition waiver only: 0%
Assistantship/fellowship only: 0%
Both full tuition waiver & assistantship/fellowship: 100%

Approximate percentage of incoming students with a B.A./B.S. only: 0% **Master's:** 100%

Approximate percentage of all students who are Women: 84% **Ethnic Minority:** 28% **International:** 10%

Average years to complete the doctoral program (including internship): 5 years

Personal interview: Preferred in person but telephone/video acceptable

Attrition rate in past 7 years: 3%

Percentage of students applying for internship last year accepted into:

APA internships: 100% **APPIC internships:**

Formal tracks/concentrations: not reported

Research areas	# Faculty	# Grants
ABA	3	2
aging (including Alzheimer's)	1	1
LGBTQ	1	1
suicide	1	1
sexual health	1	1
youth development	2	2
psychiatry	1	1
family	1	0
health and wellness	1	0
international psychology	1	0
career	1	0
student development	2	0
psychotherapy	1	1
sports psychology	1	0

Clinical opportunities

Anxiety disorders	Adjustment concerns
Depression	Family issues
Psychopathology assessment	Career/vocational
PTSD	Inpatient psychiatry
Neuropsychological assessment	Specific multicultural –populations in practica
Developmental concerns	

University of Memphis (Ph.D.)

Department of Counseling, Educational Psychology and Research
Ball Education Building, Room 100
Memphis, TN 38152
phone#: (901) 678-2841
email: sbridges@memphis.edu
Web address: http://www.memphis.edu/cepr/cpsy/

1	2	3	4	5	6	7
Practice oriented			Equal emphasis			Research oriented

(4 is marked in bold.)

Percentage of faculty subscribing to each of the following orientations:

Psychodynamic/Psychoanalytic	0%
Applied behavioral analysis/Radical behavioral	0%
Family systems/Systems	40%
Existential/Phenomenological/Humanistic	60%
Cognitive/Cognitive-behavioral	60%
Feminist	60%
Constructivist	40%

Courses required for incoming students to have completed prior to enrolling:
Master's degree in counseling, psychology, or related field. Must have theories of counseling, group counseling, career counseling, statistics/research, practicum.

Recommended but not mandatory courses:
psychological assessment, psychopathology

GRE mean
Verbal 152 Quantitative 146
Analytical Writing not reported
Psychology Subject Test not reported

GPA mean
Overall Graduate GPA 3.87 Undergraduate GPA 3.34

Number of applications/admission offers/incoming students in 2017
46 applications/13 offers/8 incoming

% of students receiving:
Full tuition waiver only: 0%
Assistantship/fellowship only: 0%
Both full tuition waiver & assistantship/fellowship: 100%

Approximate percentage of incoming students with a B.A./B.S. only: 0% **Master's:** 100%

Approximate percentage of all students who are Women: 64% **Ethnic Minority:** 16% **International:** 6%

Average years to complete the doctoral program (including internship): 4.5 years

Personal interview
Preferred in person but Skype is acceptable

Attrition rate in past 7 years: 3.5%

Percentage of students applying for internship in 2017 accepted into:

APA internships: 100% **APPIC internships:**

Formal tracks/concentrations: diversity/multicultural psychology/social justice

Research areas	# Faculty	# Grants
AIDS/HIV counseling	1	0
at-risk youth	1	0
consultation	1	0
gays, lesbians, and bisexuals	4	1
disabled persons	2	1
human sexuality	1	0
masculinity	3	0
multicultural/international psychology	6	0
psychological resources	1	0
vocational psychology	2	1
health psychology	2	1
clinical judgment	2	0
psychological assessment	1	0

Clinical opportunities

children/adolescents	Veterans Affairs Medical Center
couples/families	community mental health
university students	inpatient
domestic violence	neuropsychology
outpatient	vocational/learning disability
forensic psychology	

University of Miami (Ph.D.)

Department of Educational and Psychological Studies
5202 University Drive, Suite 312
Coral Gables, FL 33146
phone#: (305) 284-3301
email: l.buki@miami.edu
Web address: https://sites.education.miami.edu/counseling-psychology-ph-d/

1	2	3	**4**	5	6	7
Practice oriented			Equal emphasis			Research oriented

Percentage of faculty subscribing to each of the following orientations:

Psychodynamic/Psychoanalytic	0%
Applied behavioral analysis/Radical behavioral	0%
Family systems/Systems	71%
Existential/Phenomenological/Humanistic	29%
Cognitive/Cognitive-behavioral	57%

Courses required for incoming students to have completed prior to enrolling:
Courses within standard curriculum for Master's in counseling

Recommended but not mandatory courses: none

GRE mean
Verbal 159 Quantitative 160
Analytical Writing 4.3
Psychology Subject Test not required

GPA mean
Overall GPA 3.94 Psychology GPA n/a

Number of applications/admission offers/incoming students in 2017
87 applied/7 admission offers/5 incoming

% of students receiving:
Full tuition waiver only: 0%
Assistantship/fellowship only: 0%
Both full tuition waiver & assistantship/fellowship: 100%

Approximate percentage of incoming students with a B.A./B.S. only: 40% **Master's:** 60%

Approximate percentage of all students who are Women: 100% **Ethnic Minority:** 40% **International:** 20%

Average years to complete the doctoral program (including internship): 6 years

Personal interview
Preferred in person

Attrition rate in past 7 years: 5.6%

Percentage of students applying for internship in 2017 accepted into:

APA internships: 100% **APPIC internships:** 100%

Formal tracks/concentrations: none

Research areas	**# Faculty**	**# Grants**
Community well-being	3	3
Ethnic minorities	4	3
Families	3	3
Health psychology	2	0

Clinical opportunities
Tailored to students' interests

University of Minnesota–Department of Psychology (Ph.D.)

75 East River Road
Minneapolis, MN 55455
phone#: (612) 625-3873
email: counpsy@umn.edu
Web address: https://cla.umn.edu/psychology/graduate/areas-specialization/counseling-psychology

1	2	3	4	5	6	**7**
Practice oriented			Equal emphasis			Research oriented

Percentage of faculty subscribing to each of the following orientations:

Psychodynamic/Psychoanalytic	25%
Applied behavioral analysis/Radical behavioral	0%
Family systems/Systems	0%
Existential/Phenomenological/Humanistic	0%
Cognitive/Cognitive-behavioral	75%

Courses required for incoming students to have completed prior to enrolling:
12 semester credits (three to four courses) of college-level psychology coursework beyond introductory psychology

Recommended but not mandatory courses: It is recommended that coursework include at least one course in introductory statistics or introductory psychological measurement.

GRE mean
Verbal 93% Quantitative 78%
Analytical Writing 83%
Psychology Subject Test: For the 2017 application cycle, all applicants to the Counseling Psychology Program are strongly encouraged to submit Psychology subject test scores. Starting in 2018, to be considered for admission, all applicants will be required to submit Psychology subject test scores.

GPA mean
Overall GPA 3.74

Number of applications/admission offers/incoming students in 2017
126 applied/5 admission offers/3 incoming

% of students receiving:
Full tuition waiver only: 0%
Assistantship/fellowship only: 0%
Both full tuition waiver & assistantship/fellowship: 100%

Approximate percentage of incoming students with a B.A./B.S. only: 80% **Master's:** 20%

Approximate percentage of all students who are Women: 80% **Ethnic Minority:** 55%**International:** 5%

Average years to complete the doctoral program (including internship): 6 years

Personal interview
Interview not required

Attrition rate in past 7 years: 12.5%

Percentage of students applying for internship in 2017 accepted into:

APA internships: 100% **APPIC internships:** 100%

Formal tracks/concentrations: none

Research areas	# Faculty	# Grants
academic adjustment	2	0
acculturation	1	1
adverse childhood experiences	2	0
college student mental health	2	0
daily stress and coping processes	1	0
ethnic and racial identity	1	2
international adoption	1	1
interventions with refugees	1	2
mental health disparities	1	2
multicultural counseling	1	0
stressful life events	1	0
parenting	1	1
personality and adjustment	1	0
prevention science	1	3
racism and discrimination	1	2
trauma	1	1
technology based interventions	2	2

Clinical opportunities
We have about 40 practicum and advanced practicum locations. Students apply to sites based on their interests and training needs.

University of Missouri–Columbia (Ph.D.)

Educational, School, and Counseling Psychology
Columbia, MO 65211-2130
phone#: (573) 882-7731
email: FloresLY@missouri.edu
Web address: https://education.missouri.edu/educational-school-counseling-psychology/degrees-programs/counseling-psychology-program/

1	2	3	**4**	5	6	7
Practice oriented			Equal emphasis			Research oriented

Percentage of faculty subscribing to each of the following orientations:

Acceptance Commitment Therapy	13%
Cognitive/Cognitive-behavioral	75%
Emotion Focused Theory	13%
Humanistic Psychotherapy	13%
Integrative	38%
Interpersonal	13%
Mindfulness	13%
Mindfulness Acceptance Commitment in Sport	13%
Multicultural/Feminist	

**Total percentage exceed 100% because some faculty identify with multiple orientations.*

Courses required for incoming students to have completed prior to enrolling:
If entering without a Master's degree, 15 hours of prerequisite coursework, including statistics, personality, social, and developmental

Recommended but not mandatory courses: none

GRE mean
Verbal 154 Quantitative 152
Analytical Writing not reported
Psychology Subject Test not reported

GPA mean
Overall GPA 3.5

Number of applications/admission offers/incoming students in 2017
72 applied/7 admission offers/7 incoming

% of students receiving:
Full tuition waiver only: 0%
Assistantship/fellowship only: 0%
Both full tuition waiver & assistantship/fellowship: 100%

Approximate percentage of incoming students with a B.A./B.S. only: 14% **Master's:** 86%

Approximate percentage of all students who are Women: 86% **Ethnic Minority:** 29% **International:** 29%

Average years to complete the doctoral program (including internship): 6 years

Personal interview
Students are phone interviewed and then invited to come to campus for a visitation

Attrition rate in past 7 years: 4%

Percentage of students applying for internship in 2017 accepted into:

APA internships: 100% **APPIC internships:**

Formal tracks/concentrations: multicultural minor; teaching minor; statistics minor, sports psychology, career development

Research areas	# Faculty	# Grants
African American Adolescents	1	0
Biopsychology	1	0
BioPsychoSocial Focus on Case Conceptualization & Treatment	1	0
Career Development	3	1
Child Mental Health	1	2
Clinical Supervision and Training	1	0
Counseling Process and Outcome	1	0
Cross-Cultural/International	1	0
Education Marginalization	2	1
Family Prevention/Intervention	1	1
Gender	2	1
Health Psychology	1	2
Mental Health and Development of College Students	1	0
Multicultural Issues	2	1
Performance	1	0
School Counseling	1	0
School Prevention/Intervention	1	7
Sexuality	1	0
Social Justice	2	0
Sport	1	0
Transitions of International Students	1	0
Trauma	1	0
Youth Psychotherapy/Counseling	1	0

Clinical opportunities
cognitive-behavioral
family counseling center
learning disabilities clinic
rural community mental health centers
psychiatric clinic
state psychiatric facility
university/college counseling centers
university career center
university medical clinics
VA hospital

psychology clinic
rehabilitation
state hospital
women's center
women's shelters

University of Missouri–Kansas City (Ph.D.)

Division of Counseling & Educational Psychology,
School of Education, Room 215
5100 Rockhill Road
Kansas City, MO 64110
phone#: (816) 235-2722
email: umkccep@umkc.edu.
Web address: education.umkc.edu/programs/view/18

1	2	3	**4**	5	6	7
Practice oriented			Equal emphasis			Research oriented

Percentage of faculty subscribing to each of the following orientations:

Psychodynamic/Psychoanalytic	25%
Applied behavioral analysis/Radical behavioral	0%
Family systems/Systems	25%
Existential/Phenomenological/Humanistic	25%
Cognitive/Cognitive-behavioral	25%

Courses required for incoming students to have completed prior to enrolling:
undergraduate psychology major or Master's degree in counseling or psychology

Recommended but not mandatory courses: none

GRE mean based on 2016 cohort
Verbal range: 13–81% Quantitative range: 4–71%
Analytical Writing range: 15–93%
Psychology Subject Test not required

GPA mean
Overall GPA 3.40

Number of applications/admission offers/incoming students in 2016
72 applied/7 admission offers/7 incoming

Percentage of students receiving:
Full tuition waiver only: 0%
Assistantship/fellowship only: 0%
Both full tuition waiver & assistantship/fellowship: 100% for first year students

Approximate percentage of incoming students with a B.A./B.S. only: 40% **Master's:** 60%

Approximate percentage of all students who are Women: 70% **Ethnic Minority:** 40% **International:** 5%

Average years to complete the doctoral program (including internship): 6 years

Personal interview
Telephone, skype or campus interview

Attrition rate: since 2011–2012 2 students

Percentage of students applying for internship in 2016 accepted into:

APA internships: 100% **APPIC internships:**

Formal tracks/concentrations: none

Research areas	# Faculty	# Grants
diversity/social justice	5	
couple and family issues	2	
professional issues/ethics	1	
sports psychology	1	
supervision	1	
vocational development	1	
veterans/reintegration	2	
flow	1	
international adoption	1	
gender/objectification theory	1	
secondary school contexts	1	
immigration	1	
religion& spirituality	1	
LBGT	3	

Clinical opportunities
A wide range of clinical opportunities are available in Kansas City

University of Nebraska–Lincoln (Ph.D.)

Department of Educational Psychology
38 Teachers College Hall
Lincoln, NE 68588-0345
phone#: (402) 472-0573
email: mscheel2@unl.edu
Web address: cehs.unl.edu/edpsych/graduate/copsych.shtml

1	2	3	**4**	5	6	7
Practice oriented			Equal emphasis			Research oriented

Percentage of faculty subscribing to each of the following orientations:

Psychodynamic/Psychoanalytic	60%
Applied behavioral analysis/Radical behavioral	0%
Family systems/Systems	0%
Existential/Phenomenological/Humanistic	40%
Cognitive/Cognitive-behavioral	0%

Courses required for incoming students to have completed prior to enrolling:
Bachelor's in a closely related area or Master's in counseling/psychology or closely related field

Recommended but not mandatory courses: none

GRE mean
Verbal 161 Quantitative 156
Analytical Writing 4.2
Psychology Subject Test not reported

GPA mean
Overall GPA 3.65

Number of applications/admission offers/incoming students in 2017
62 applied/8 admission offers/5 incoming

% of students receiving:
Full tuition waiver only: 100%
Assistantship/fellowship only: 100%
Both full tuition waiver & assistantship/fellowship: 100%

Approximate percentage of incoming students with a B.A./B.S. only: 60% **Master's:** 40%

Approximate percentage of all students who are Women: 80% **Ethnic Minority:** 40% **International:** 10%

Average years to complete the doctoral program (including internship): 6 years

Personal interview
Preferred in person but Skype interview acceptable

Attrition rate in past 7 years: 2%

Percentage of students applying for internship in 2017 accepted into:

APA internships: 100% **APPIC internships:** 100%

Formal tracks/concentrations: multicultural counseling; gender; couple and family counseling

Research areas	# Faculty	# Grants
Positive psychology	2	2
multicultural	3	1
gender	2	1
vocational	3	1
psychotherapy process	1	0
trauma treatment	1	1

Clinical opportunities
couple/family therapy
vocational counseling
multicultural counseling
outcome based therapy
positive psychology applications
psychological assessment
interpersonal violence interventions
adolescence in schools

New Mexico State University (Ph.D.)

Department of Counseling and Educational Psychology
MSC 3CEP
P.O. Box 30001
Las Cruces, NM 88003-8001
phone#: (505) 646-2121
email: eadams@nmsu.edu
Web address: education.nmsu.edu/cep/phd/index.html

1 2 3 **4** 5 6 7

Practice oriented — Equal emphasis — Research oriented

Percentage of faculty subscribing to each of the following orientations:

Psychodynamic/Psychoanalytic	22%
Applied behavioral analysis/Radical behavioral	0%
Family systems/Systems	11%
Existential/Phenomenological/Humanistic	33%
Cognitive/Cognitive-behavioral	22%

Courses required for incoming students to have completed prior to enrolling: none

Recommended but not mandatory courses: counseling practicum, human development, multicultural, counseling theory and techniques, family therapy, group work, career/life planning, counseling research, diagnosis, addictions

GRE mean
Verbal 160 Quantitative 147
Analytical Writing 4.5
Psychology Subject Test not reported

GPA mean
Master's GPA 3.76

Number of applications/admission offers/incoming students in 2017
72 applied/14 admission offers/6 incoming

% of students receiving:
Full tuition waiver only: 0%
Assistantship/fellowship only: 83%
Both full tuition waiver & assistantship/fellowship: 17%

Approximate percentage of incoming students with a B.A./B.S. only: 33% **Master's:** 67%

Approximate percentage of all students who are Women: 67% **Ethnic Minority:** 33% **International:** 0%

Average years to complete the doctoral program (including internship): 5 years

Personal interview
In person or Skype

Attrition rate in past 7 years: 2%

Percentage of students applying for internship in 2017 accepted into:

APA internships: 100% **APPIC internships:** 0%

Formal tracks/concentrations: multicultural counseling, supervision/training, integrated behavioral health

Research areas	# Faculty	# Grants
acculturation	3	1
career	1	0
family systems	1	0
gender	3	0
social identity	3	0
multicultural curriculum development	3	0
interpersonal relationship	1	0
primary care psychology	1	1
LGBT	2	0
Process/outcome	1	0

Clinical opportunities
community organizations
departmental training center
families
groups
low income
supervision
primary care
rural
substance abuse
university counseling center
vocational career development
Spanish-speaking/bilingual minorities

New York University (Ph.D.)

Department of Applied Psychology
246 Greene Street, 8th Floor
New York, NY 10003
phone#: (212) 998-5555
Web address: steinhardt.nyu.edu/appsych/phd/counseling_psychology

1	2	3	4	**5**	6	7
Practice oriented			Equal emphasis			Research oriented

Percentage of faculty subscribing to each of the following orientations:

Psychodynamic/Psychoanalytic	33%
Applied behavioral analysis/Radical behavioral	0%
Family systems/Systems	0%
Existential/Phenomenological/Humanistic	33%
Cognitive/Cognitive-behavioral	33%

Courses required for incoming students to have completed prior to enrolling:
18 credits in psychology at undergraduate or graduate level

Recommended but not mandatory courses: Statistics

GRE mean
Verbal 161 Quantitative 156
Analytical Writing 5
Psychology Subject Test not required

GPA mean
Overall GPA 3.71

Number of applications/admission offers/incoming students in 2017
215 applied/5 admission offers/2 incoming

% of students receiving:
Full tuition waiver only: 0%
Assistantship/fellowship only: 0%
Both full tuition waiver & assistantship/fellowship: 100%

Approximate percentage of incoming students with a B.A./B.S. only: 48% **Master's:** 52%

Approximate percentage of all students who are Women: 79% **Ethnic Minority:** 42% **International:** 5%

Average years to complete the doctoral program (including internship): 6 years

Personal interview
Required (in-person preferred but skype interview also possible)

Attrition rate in past 7 years: 0%

Percentage of students applying for internship in 2017 accepted into:

APA internships: 100% **APPIC internships:** 100%

Formal tracks/concentrations: none

Research areas	# Faculty	# Grants
multicultural/ethnic minority	2	0
women's development/health	2	2
work as a developmental context	1	0
LGBT	2	1
positive psychology	1	0
intervention in schools	1	0

Clinical opportunities
Wide range of specialized practica and externship sites are available in the New York metropolitan area, including the department-based training clinic

University of North Dakota (Ph.D.)

Department of Counseling Psychology and Community Services
290 Centennial Drive, Stop 8255
Grand Forks, ND 58202-8255
phone#: (701) 777-2729
fax#: (701) 777-3184
email: ashley.hutchison@und.edu
Web address: http://education.und.edu/counseling-psychology-and-community-services/index.cfm

1	2	3	**4**	5	6	7
Practice oriented			Equal emphasis			Research oriented

Percentage of faculty subscribing to each of the following orientations:

Psychodynamic/Psychoanalytic	30%
Applied behavioral analysis/Radical behavioral	0%
Family systems/Systems	20%
Existential/Phenomenological/Humanistic	40%
Cognitive/Cognitive-behavioral	50%
Feminist	50%

Courses required for incoming students to have completed prior to enrolling:
18 semester hours of undergraduate psychology including statistics, research methods, abnormal, developmental, personality (for both post-Master's and post-baccalaureate applicants)

Recommended but not mandatory courses: Research methods, Master's-level practicum, 60 hours supervised practice (for post-Master's applicants)

GRE mean
Verbal 154 (60th percentile)
Quantitative 149 (36.8th percentile)
Analytical Writing 4 (64.6th percentile)
Psychology Subject Test not required

GPA mean
Overall GPA 3.57

Number of applications/admission offers/incoming students in 2017
43 applied/13 admission offers/6 incoming

% of students receiving:
Full tuition waiver only: 0%
Assistantship/fellowship only: 0%
Both full tuition waiver & assistantship/fellowship: 100%

Approximate percentage of incoming students with a B.A./B.S. only: 33% **Master's:** 66%

Approximate percentage of students who are Women: 64.5% **Ethnic Minority:** 51.6% **International:** 9.6%

Average years to complete the doctoral program (including internship): 5.18 years

Personal interview
Preferred in person or Skype acceptable

Attrition rate in past 7 years: 7%

Percentage of students applying for internship in 2017 accepted into:

APA internships: 100% **APPIC internships:** not reported

Formal tracks/concentrations: Students complete a specialization in one of the following: Child & Adolescent Psychotherapy, Grant-Writing, Leadership, or Consultation

Research areas	# Faculty	# Grants
body image	1	0
career development	2	1
Cross-cultural research	1	0
deployment/military psychology	1	0
domestic violence	1	0
emotion recognition and expression	1	0
gay, lesbian, bisexual	2	0
geriatric psychology	1	0
group identity development	1	0
healthy relationships	1	0
HIV prevention	1	0
integrated healthcare	2	1
multicultural counseling	1	0
Native American career development	1	0
Positive Psychology	1	0
Positive Sexuality	1	0
poverty	1	0
rural mental health and stigma reduction	2	1
student self-efficacy	1	0
supervisor strategies	2	0
vocational interests testing	1	0
white privilege	1	0
women/career development	1	0

Clinical opportunities
variety of community and academic settings, including university counseling centers, hospitals, and community mental health agencies, with both psychotherapy and assessment services. Emphasis on integrated behavioral healthcare.

University of North Texas (Ph.D.)

Department of Psychology
P.O. Box 311280
Denton, TX 76203-3587
phone#: (940) 565-2671
email: psyc-grad@unt.edu gradsch@unt.edu
Web address: www.psyc.unt.edu/gradcounseling.shtml

1	2	3	4	5	6	7
Practice oriented			Equal emphasis			Research oriented

Percentage of faculty subscribing to each of the following orientations:

Psychodynamic/Psychoanalytic	40%
Applied behavioral analysis/Radical behavioral	0%
Family systems/Systems	40%
Existential/Phenomenological/Humanistic	40%
Cognitive/Cognitive-behavioral	30%

Courses required for incoming students to have completed prior to enrolling:
statistics and three of the following: experimental, cognition, learning, perception, motivation, physiological, psychological measurement, or research thesis

Recommended but not mandatory courses: none

GRE mean
Verbal 568.75 Quantitative 658.75
Analytical Writing 4.10
Psychology Subject Test 615

GPA mean
Overall GPA 3.48

Number of applications/admission offers/incoming students
227 applied/14 admission offers/8 incoming

% of students receiving:
Full tuition waiver only: 0%
Assistantship/fellowship only: 88%
Both full tuition waiver & assistantship/fellowship: 12%

Approximate percentage of incoming students with a B.A./B.S. only: 50% **Master's:** 50%

Approximate percentage of all students who are Women: 72.3% **Ethnic Minority:** 29.8%
International: 6.4%

Average years to complete the doctoral program (including internship): 6.5 years

Personal interview
Preferred in person but telephone may be acceptable in certain circumstances

Attrition rate in past 7 years: 5.9%

Percentage of students applying for internship accepted into:

APA internships: 100% **APPIC internships:** 100%

Formal tracks/concentrations: childhood & family, sport psychology

Research areas	# Faculty	# Grants
ADHD treatment	2	1
counseling and therapy	1	1
eating disorders	3	0
gerontology	1	0
marriage and family	3	2
minority and cross-cultural	2	0
professional issues	3	0
sports psychology	2	1
vocational development	3	0

Clinical opportunities

psychology clinic	university counseling
community mental health	assessment
sports psychology	family and marriage

Northeastern University (Ph.D.)

Department of Applied Psychology
360 Huntington Avenue, 408 INV
Boston, MA 02115
phone#: (617) 373-2485
email: caep@neu.edu
Web address: http://www.northeastern.edu/bouve/caep/programs/counseling-psychology-phd/

1	2	3	4	5	6	7
Practice oriented			Equal emphasis			Research oriented

Percentage of faculty subscribing to each of the following orientations:

Psychodynamic/Psychoanalytic	30%
Applied behavioral analysis/Radical behavioral	0%
Family systems/Systems	100%
Existential/Phenomenological/Humanistic	30%
Cognitive/Cognitive-behavioral	30%

Courses required for incoming students to have completed prior to enrolling:
Master's degree required in addition to the following prerequisites, which can be completed while enrolled: introduction to therapy/counseling; group therapy/counseling; clinical skills; cultural diversity; family therapy/counseling; lifespan development; abnormal/psychopathology; diagnosis & treatment planning; statistics; vocational & career development; research methods

Recommended but not mandatory courses: none

GRE mean
Verbal 73%tile
Quantitative 43%tile
Analytical Writing 79%tile
Psychology Subject Test not required

GPA mean
Overall GPA 3.96 (Master's) 3.825 (Undergrad)

Number of applications/admission offers/incoming students in 2015
57 applied/3 incoming

% of students receiving:
Full tuition waiver only: 0%
Assistantship/fellowship only: 0%
Both full tuition waiver & assistantship/fellowship: 100%
Partial tuition waiver: 0%

Approximate percentage of incoming students with a B.A./B.S. only: 0% **Master's:** 100%

Approximate percentage of all students who are Women: 70% **Ethnic Minority:** 22% **International:** 13%

Average years to complete the doctoral program (including internship): 5.23 years

Personal interview
Required in person

Attrition rate in past 7 years: 9%

Percentage of students applying for internship last year accepted into:

APA internships: 100% **APPIC internships:** 0%

Formal tracks/concentrations: none

Research areas	# Faculty	# Grants
eating and appearance	2	4
dating violence	1	5
feminist therapy & theory	1	0
intersectionality; microaggressions	1	1
health disparities	1	3
health behavior change	1	0

Clinical opportunities
College counseling centers, health centers, community mental health centers, hospitals (adult, inpatient psychiatric, inpatient medical, partial, outpatient, emergency services, pediatric), substance abuse treatment, forensic settings, illness-specific treatment centers, veteran's administration

University of Northern Colorado (Ph.D.)

Department of Applied Psychology and Counselor Education
McKee Hall Room 248
Greeley, CO 80639
phone#: (970) 351-2727
email: diane.knight@unco.edu
Web address: www.unco.edu/cebs/counspsych/

1	2	3	4	5	6	7
Practice oriented			Equal emphasis			Research oriented

Percentage of faculty subscribing to each of the following orientations:

Psychodynamic/Psychoanalytic	40%
Applied behavioral analysis/Radical behavioral	0%
Family systems/Systems	20%
Existential/Phenomenological/Humanistic	20%
Cognitive/Cognitive-behavioral	20%

Courses required for incoming students to have completed prior to enrolling: none

Recommended but not mandatory courses:
For students coming in with an MA: At least one practicum course in their MA program

GRE mean
Admitted with BA/BS: Verbal 161 Quantitative 156
Admitted with MA/MS: Verbal 157 Quantitative 151
Analytical Writing:
Admitted with BA/BS: 4.7
Admitted with MA/MS: 4.6
Psychology Subject Test: n/a (not required)

GPA mean
Admitted with BA/BS: 3.86
Admitted with MA/MS: 3.88

Number of applications/admission offers/incoming students in 2015
133 applied/19 admission offers/12 incoming

% of students receiving:
Full tuition waiver only: 0%
Full assistantship/fellowship only: 0%
100% of incoming students are offered an assistantship that covers partial tuition and stipend
Both full tuition waiver & assistantship/fellowship: 0%

Approximate percentage of incoming students with a B.A./B.S. only: 50% **Master's:** 50%

Approximate percentage of all students who are Women: 75% **Ethnic Minority:** 29% **International:** 9%

Average years to complete the doctoral program (including internship): 5.5 years

Personal interview: Required, in-person or DVD interview

Attrition rate in past 7 years: 4%

Percentage of students applying for internship last year accepted into:

APA internships: 100% **APPIC internships:** 0%

Formal tracks/concentrations: none

Research areas	# Faculty	# Grants
parenting & parent training	1	0
attachment theory	2	0
childhood behavior disorders	1	0
college student adjustment & retention	1	0
psychological assessment	1	0
couples and family therapy	1	0
international psychology	1	0
gender/cross-cultural/ethnicity issues	1	0
career development	2	0
gifted adults	1	0
work-family interface	1	0
clinical supervision	2	0
crisis intervention	2	0
grief and loss	1	0
peer counseling	1	0
projective assessment	1	0
suicide: risk assessment and prevention	1	0
veterans issues	1	0
group therapy	1	0

Clinical opportunities
Practicums beginning 1st semester for MA/MA students, 2nd semester for BA/BS students (individual counseling, couples and family counseling, group counseling, supervision). External practicum(s) required.

Oklahoma State University (Ph.D.)

School of Applied Health and Educational Psychology
434 Willard Hall
Stillwater, OK 74078
phone#: (405) 744-6040
email: julie.koch@okstate.edu
Web address: education.okstate.edu/cpsy

1	2	3	**4**	5	6	7
Practice oriented			Equal emphasis			Research oriented

Percentage of faculty subscribing to each of the following orientations:

Emotion-focused therapy	10%
Humanistic/existential	30%
Family systems/Systems	30%
Relational Cultural Theory	10%
Cognitive/Cognitive-behavioral	20%
Reality/Adlerian Therapy	10%
Child-Centered Play Therapy	10%
Multicultural	100%
Schema Therapy	10%
Interpersonal Process Therapy	10%

**Does not add up to 100% because some faculty ascribe to more than one orientation*

Courses required for incoming students to have completed prior to enrolling:
Bachelor's degree in psychology, sociology, or related fields, or Master's degree in counseling, psychology, or related area; we have two tracks to our program: post-Bachelor's and post-Master's.

Recommended but not mandatory courses: Statistics, research design

GRE mean
Verbal 500 Quantitative 500
Analytical Writing 4.5
Psychology Subject Test not reported

GPA mean
Undergraduate 3.0 Graduate 3.5

Number of applications/admission offers/incoming students in 2017
70 applied/12 admission offers/8 incoming (we usually accept 3 post-Bachelor's and 5 post-Master's)

% of students receiving:
Full tuition waiver only: 0%
Assistantship/fellowship only: 0%
Both full tuition waiver & assistantship/fellowship: 100%

Approximate percentage of incoming students with a B.A./B.S. only: 37% **Master's:** 63%

Approximate percentage of students who are Women: 58% **Ethnic Minority:** 35% **International:** 3%

Average years to complete the doctoral program (including internship): 4 years (post-Master's); 5 years post-Bachelor's

Personal interview
Preferred in person

Attrition rate in past 7 years: 1%

Percentage of students applying for internship in 2017 accepted into:

APA internships: 100% **APPIC internships:** 100%

Formal tracks/concentrations: none

Research areas	# Faculty	# Grants
American Indian	2	0
at-risk youth	4	1
career	4	0
health/wellness	9	0
international	3	0
LGBTQ	6	2
multicultural	11	0
supervision/training	6	0
women/men/gender issues	6	0
older adults	1	1
substance abuse	2	0
prevention (e.g. suicide prevention)	11	0
body image	1	0
mindfulness/self-compassion	1	0

**Note that # of faculty exceeds 11 because faculty report more than 1 research area*

Clinical opportunities

correctional facility	outpatient hospital
domestic violence center	rural mental health clinic

Indian health services	university counseling
veterans affairs	youth and family services

University of Oregon (Ph.D.) (2013 Data)

Counseling Psychology Program
5251 University of Oregon
Eugene, OR 97403-5251
phone#: (541) 346-2456
email: cpsy@uoregon.edu
Web address: education.uoregon.edu/field.htm?id=46

1	2	3	4	**5**	6	7
Practice oriented			Equal emphasis			Research oriented

Percentage of faculty subscribing to each of the following orientations:

Psychodynamic/Psychoanalytic	0%
Applied behavioral analysis/Radical behavioral	0%
Family systems/Systems	75%
Existential/Phenomenological/Humanistic	50%
Cognitive/Cognitive-behavioral	100%

Courses required for incoming students to have completed prior to enrolling:
Some background in psychology

Recommended but not mandatory courses: Research design, statistics, helping skills, human development, language (e.g. Spanish)

GRE mean
Verbal 160 Quantitative 152
Analytical Writing 4.8
Psychology Subject Test not reported

GPA mean
Overall 3.66

Number of applications/admission offers/incoming students in 2013
179 applied/13 admission offers/10 incoming

% of students receiving:
Full tuition waiver only: 0%
Assistantship/fellowship only: 0%
Both full tuition waiver & assistantship/fellowship: 100%

Approximate percentage of incoming students with a B.A./B.S. only: 50% **Master's:** 50%

Approximate percentage of students who are Women: 86% **Ethnic Minority:** 48% **International:** 0%

Average years to complete the doctoral program (including internship): 6.5 years

Personal interview
Preferred in person but telephone acceptable

Attrition rate in past 7 years: 11%

Percentage of students applying for internship in 2013 accepted into:

APA internships: 89% APPIC internships: 11%

Formal tracks/concentrations: Developing specialization in services to Spanish-speaking clients.

Research areas	# Faculty	# Grants
child and family psychology	3	2
college student development	2	0
domestic violence	1	0
multicultural	4	1
prevention research	6	2
social support and interactions	3	0
treatment outcomes	4	2
vocational psychology	2	1

Clinical opportunities

child–family (English and Spanish)	community mental health inpatient settings
community prevention	VA hospital
university/college counseling centers	domestic violence agency (English and Spanish)

Our Lady of the Lake University (Psy.D.)

School of Professional Studies
Graduate Admissions Office
411 SW 24th Street
San Antonio, TX 78207-4689
phone#: (210) 431-3914
email: clcastaneda@lake.ollusa.edu
Web address: www.ollusa.edu/s/1190/ollu.aspx?sie=1190&gid=id=pgid=1748

1	**2**	3	4	5	6	7
Practice oriented			Equal emphasis			Research oriented

Percentage of faculty subscribing to each of the following orientations:

Psychodynamic/Psychoanalytic	0%
Applied behavioral analysis/Radical behavioral	0%
Family systems/Systems	90%
Existential/Phenomenological/Humanistic	10%
Cognitive/Cognitive-behavioral	0%

Courses required for incoming students to have completed prior to enrolling:
Master's or Bachelor's degree in psychology or closely related area

Recommended but not mandatory courses: none

GRE mean
Verbal 151 Quantitative 142
Analytical Writing 3.31
Psychology Subject Test 510

GPA mean
Overall GPA 3.1

Number of applications/admission offers/incoming students in 2017
44 applied/7 admission offers/6 incoming

% of students receiving:
Full tuition waiver only: 14%
Assistantship/fellowship only: 29%
Both full tuition waiver & assistantship/fellowship: 0%

Approximate percentage of incoming students with a B.A./B.S. only: 0% **Master's:** 100%

Approximate percentage of all students who are Women: 90% **Ethnic Minority:** 73% **International:** 2%

Average years to complete the doctoral program (including internship): 6 years

Personal interview
Required in person

Attrition rate in past 7 years: 4%

Percentage of students applying for internship in 2017 accepted into:

APA internships: 100% **APPIC internships:**

Formal tracks/concentrations: health psychology, psychological services for Spanish speaking populations

Research areas	# Faculty	# Grants
strengths-based therapy	4	0
Spanish language services and supervision	2	1

Clinical opportunities
community counseling
health psychology
school-age population
Spanish-speaking populations

Purdue University (Ph.D.)–Counseling Psychology

Department of Educational Studies
BRNG Hall, 100 N. University St.
West Lafayette, IN 47907-2098
phone#: (765) 494-9738 (Secretary: Julie Banes)
email: ayse@purdue.edu
Web address: https://www.education.purdue.edu/academics/graduate-students/degrees-and-programs/graduate-programs/counseling-psychology/

1	2	3	4	**5**	6	7
Practice oriented			Equal emphasis			Research oriented

Percentage of faculty subscribing to each of the following orientations:

Psychodynamic/Psychoanalytic	0%
Applied behavioral analysis/Radical behavioral	0%
Family systems/Systems	15%
Existential/Phenomenological/Humanistic	75%
Cognitive/Cognitive-behavioral	10%

Courses required for incoming students to have completed prior to enrolling: none

Recommended but not mandatory courses:
undergraduate psychology, statistics, research design

GRE mean
Verbal 160 Quantitative 153
Analytical Writing 4.20
Psychology Subject Test not reported

GPA mean
Overall GPA 3.37

Number of applications/admission offers/incoming students in 2016
50 applied/10 admission offers/7 incoming

% of students receiving:
Full tuition waiver only: 0%
Assistantship/fellowship only: 0%
Both full tuition waiver & assistantship/fellowship: 100%

Approximate percentage of incoming students with a B.A./B.S. only: 50% **Master's:** 50%

Approximate percentage of all students who are Women: 82.85% **Ethnic Minority:** 45.71% **International:** 25.71%

Average years to complete the doctoral program (including internship): 5.5 years

Personal interview
Preferred in person but telephone acceptable

Attrition rate in past 7 years: <5.0%

Percentage of students applying for internship in 2017 accepted into:

APA internships: 100% **APPIC internships:** 100%

Formal tracks/concentrations: none

Research areas	# Faculty	# Grants
career development	2	2
grief and bereavement	1	0
individual and cultural differences	1	1
psychotherapy research and positive psychology	1	1

Clinical opportunities
university/department clinic
hospitals
veteran's affairs
college counseling centers
community mental health
prison

Radford University (Psy.D.)

Department of Psychology
Radford, VA 24142
phone#: (540) 831-5361
email: psyd@radford.edu
Web address: www.radford.edu/psyd

1	**2**	3	4	5	6	7
Practice oriented			Equal emphasis			Research oriented

Percentage of faculty subscribing to each of the following orientations:

Psychodynamic/Psychoanalytic	20%
Applied behavioral analysis/Radical behavioral	0%
Family systems/Systems	20%
Existential/Phenomenological/Humanistic	40%
Cognitive/Cognitive-behavioral	20%

Courses required for incoming students to have completed prior to enrolling:
professional issues and ethics, counseling techniques, basic assessment methods, basic statistics, research design

Recommended but not mandatory courses: none

GRE mean
Verbal 152 Quantitative 152
Analytical Writing 3.9
Psychology Subject Test not reported

GPA mean
Overall Master's GPA 3.97

Number of applications/admission offers/incoming students in 2016
20 applied/9 admission offers/4 incoming

% of students receiving:
Full tuition waiver only: 0%
Assistantship/fellowship only: 0%
Both full tuition waiver & assistantship/fellowship: 100%

Approximate percentage of incoming students with a BA/BS only: 0% **Master's:** 100%

Approximate percentage of all students who are Women: 69% **Ethnic Minority:** 20% **International:** 10%

Average years to complete the doctoral program (including internship): 4 years

Personal interview
Required, preferred in person

Attrition rate in past 7 years: 10%

Percentage of students applying for internship in 2016 accepted into:

APA internships: 100% **APPIC internships:** 100%

Formal tracks/concentrations: emphases on rural mental health, cultural diversity, social justice, evidence-based practice

Research areas	# Faculty	# Grants
rural issues	4	2
LGBT issues	2	0
HIV	2	1
trauma	2	0
veteran's issues	1	0
suicide prevention	1	0
couples therapy (EFT)	1	0

Clinical opportunities
medical free clinic
university counseling centers
VA medical center
child and family
inpatient hospitals
community health centers
integrated care
correctional facilities

Saint Mary's University of Minnesota (Psy.D.)

PsyD in Counseling Psychology Program
Twin Cities Campus
2500 Park Avenue
Minneapolis, MN 55404-4403
phone#: 866-437-2788
email: psyd@smumn.edu
Web address: http://www.smumn.edu/

1	**2**	3	4	5	6	7
Practice oriented			Equal emphasis			Research oriented

Percentage of faculty subscribing to each of the following orientations:

Psychodynamic/Psychoanalytic	25%
Applied behavioral analysis/Radical behavioral	0%
Family systems/Systems	0%
Existential/Phenomenological/Humanistic	50%
Cognitive/Cognitive-behavioral	38%
Other: Integrative, Feminist Multicultural	38%

Courses required for incoming students to have completed prior to enrolling:
A Master's degree from a regionally accredited institution, for which applicant maintained at least a 3.4 grade point average on a 4.0 scale, is required for admission. The Master's degree must be in a mental health related area, with a completed clinical practicum of at least 300 hours.
Applicants must have completed the following graduate courses within the last ten years with a grade of "B" or better. Coursework older than ten years may be accepted if the applicant has maintained a professional license to practice in a related field (e.g. LPC, LMFT) which requires documentation of continuing education credits. Applicants may be required to complete missing coursework prior to enrolling in doctoral level coursework:
Developmental Psychology; Physiological Psychology; Counseling Skills; Statistics; Psychological Assessment; Psychopathology; Personality Theory and/or Theories of Counseling; Clinical Interventions; Professional Ethics.

Recommended but not mandatory courses: none

GRE mean (n/a – not required)
Verbal + Quantitative
Analytical Writing
Psychology Subject Test

GPA mean undergrad 2.98, graduate 3.65

Number of applications/admission offers/incoming students in 2015
25 applied/23 admission offers/14 incoming
Early entry option exists for students in the Saint Mary's MA program in Counseling and Psychological Services.

% of students receiving:
Full tuition waiver only: 0%
Assistantship/fellowship only: 0%
Both full tuition waiver & assistantship/fellowship: 0%
Scholarship/assistantships/fellowships: 3% student workers

Approximate percentage of incoming students with a B.A./B.S. only: 0% **Master's:** 100%

Approximate percentage of all students who are Women: 78% **Ethnic Minority:** 20% **International:** %0

Average years to complete the doctoral program (including internship): 5.2 years

Personal interview preferred in person but telephone acceptable

Attrition rate in past 7 years: .04%

Percentage of students applying for internship last year accepted into:

APA internships: 33.3% **APPIC internships:** 66.6%

Formal tracks/concentrations: none

Research areas	# Faculty	# Grants
aging/gerontology	1	0
career and life transitions	3	0
career counseling	2	0
cognitive processes	1	0
culturally authentic research	1	0
gender	4	0
grief and loss	2	0
health psychology	3	0
interpersonal violence	2	0
life development	2	0
master therapists	1	0
mentoring	2	0
multicultural mentoring	1	0
neurodevelopmental issues	2	0
outcome research	1	0
prevention	1	0
psychotherapy effectiveness	2	0
sexuality	3	0
survey design	1	0
test construction	1	0
training & supervision	4	0
trauma and dissociation	2	0
trends in psychology practice	1	0
vocational development and choice	1	0
work and mental health	2	0

Clinical opportunities

Child and adolescent psychiatry
Community mental health
Co-occurring disorders
Corrections
Culturally diverse populations
Eating disorders
Forensic practice
Immigrants and refugees
Integrated behavioral health
Geriatrics
Learning and memory assessment
LGBT populations
Private practice
Rehabilitation
Rural practice
School-based services
Substance abuse
Trauma
University counseling

University of St. Thomas (Psy.D.)

Graduate School of Professional Psychology
MOH 217, 1000 La Salle Avenue
Minneapolis, MN 55403-2005
phone#: (651) 962-4650
email: gspp@stthomas.edu
Web address: http://www.stthomas.edu/counselingpsychology/programs/counseling-psychology-doctorate/

1	2	**3**	4	5	6	7
Practice oriented			Equal emphasis			Research oriented

Percentage of faculty subscribing to each of the following orientations:

Psychodynamic/Psychoanalytic	10%
Applied behavioral analysis/Radical behavioral	0%
Family systems/Systems	20%
Existential/Phenomenological/Humanistic	40%
Cognitive/Cognitive-behavioral	30%

Courses required for incoming students to have completed prior to enrolling:
M.A. program in counseling psychology or equivalent. We also have a Direct Admission program where students are admitted to the doctoral program at the BA/BS level. They then complete the M.A. degree with us and then move into the doctoral program upon completion of the M.A.

Recommended & mandatory courses:
For those applying to the doctoral program post-MA: statistics, psychobiology/psychophysiology, social/group dynamics, measurement/assessment, personality/counseling theory, development, psychopathology, counseling skills and counseling ethics, counseling practicum

GRE mean
Post-M.A. admission: Verbal 152 Quantitative 147
Analytical Writing: 4

Post-B.A./B.S. admission (Direct Admission)
Verbal 156 Quantitative 151
Analytical Writing 4
Psychology Subject Test not reported

GPA mean
Post-M.A. admission: M.A. GPA: 3.84
Post-B.A./B.S. admission (Direct Admission)
B.A./B.S. GPA: 3.61

Number of applications/admission offers/incoming students in 2017
Post-M.A. admission
24 applied/16 admission offers/13 incoming
Post-B.A. admission (Direct Admission)
42 applied/9 admission offers/7 incoming

% of students receiving:
Full tuition waiver only: 0%
Assistantship/fellowship only: 6%
Both full tuition waiver & assistantship/fellowship: 0%

Approximate percentage of incoming students with a B.A./B.S. only: 0% **Master's:** 100%

Approximate percentage of 2017 students who are Women: 55% **Ethnic Minority:** 28% **International:** 0%

Average years to complete the doctoral program (including internship): 4.69 years (post-M.A.)

Personal interview
Preferred in person

Attrition rate in past 7 years: 1.05%

Percentage of students applying for internship in 2017 accepted into:

APA internships: 41% **APPIC internships:** 47%

Formal tracks/concentrations: none

Research areas	# Faculty	# Grants
counseling process	3	0
cultural sensitive therapy	4	0
interprofessional ethics	2	0
licensure and regulatory boards	1	0
master therapists	1	0

Clinical opportunities
full range of diagnostic disorders in a variety of settings.

Seton Hall University (Ph.D.)

Department of Professional Psychology and Family Therapy
College of Education and Human Services
400 South Orange Avenue
South Orange, NJ 07079
phone#: (973) 275-2740
email: Pamela.Foley@shu.edu
Web address: www.shu.edu/academics/education/phd-counseling-psychology/index.cfm

1	2	3	**4**	5	6	7
Practice oriented			Equal emphasis			Research oriented

Percentage of faculty subscribing to each of the following orientations:

Psychodynamic/Psychoanalytic	40%
Applied behavioral analysis/Radical behavioral	0%
Family systems/Systems	0%
Existential/Phenomenological/Humanistic	40%
Cognitive/Cognitive-behavioral	20%

Courses required for incoming students to have completed prior to enrolling:
Group Counseling, Abnormal Psychology, Tests and Measurements, Counseling Skills, Statistics and Computer Applications I

Recommended, but not mandatory courses: none

GRE mean
Verbal 153 Quantitative 151
Analytical Writing 4.6
Psychology Subject Test not required

GPA mean
Overall GPA 3.8

Number of applications/admission offers/incoming students in 2017
79 applied/9 admission offers/6 incoming

% of students receiving:
Full tuition waiver only: 0%
Assistantship/fellowship only: 100%
Both full tuition waiver & assistantship/fellowship: 0%

Approximate percentage of incoming students who entered with a B.A./B.S. only: 0% **Master's:** 100%

Approximate percentage of students who are Women: 85% **Ethnic Minority:** 46% **International:** 4%

Average years to complete the doctoral program (including internship): 5.7 years

Personal interview:
Strongly preferred in person but telephone acceptable

Attrition rate in past 7 years: 0%

Percentage of students applying for internship in 2016 accepted into:

APA internships: 100% **APPIC internships:** 100%

Formal tracks/concentrations: Self-defined 9-credit minor. Examples are multicultural psychology, assessment, integrative care, couples and families

Research areas	# Faculty	# Grants
career development	1	0
multicultural counseling	4	1
psychological trauma	1	0
resiliency	1	0
student well-being	1	0
health and coping	2	0
spirituality	1	0

Clinical opportunities
The university does not run any specialty clinics. The program has developed an extensive offering of diverse clinical training opportunities in the greater New York area.

Southern Illinois University (Ph.D.)

Department of Psychology
Carbondale, IL 62901
phone#: (618) 453-3564
email: gradpsyc@siu.edu (graduate administrative assistant)
chwalisz@siu.edu (program director)
Web address: http://cola.siu.edu/psychology/graduate/doctoral-programs/counseling/

1	2	3	**4**	5	6	7
Practice oriented			Equal emphasis			Research oriented

Percentage of faculty subscribing to each of the following orientations:

Psychodynamic/Psychoanalytic	0%
Applied behavioral analysis/Radical behavioral	0%
Family systems/Systems	0%
Existential/Phenomenological/Humanistic	100%
Cognitive/Cognitive-behavioral	0%

Courses required for incoming students to have completed prior to enrolling: none

Recommended but not mandatory courses: At least 1 statistics course; if student was not an undergraduate psychology major, we look for coursework in core areas of psychology

GRE mean
Verbal 76th percentile Quantitative 50th percentile
Analytical Writing 77th percentile
Psychology Subject Test not required

GPA mean
Overall GPA 3.75

Number of applications/admission offers/incoming students in 2017
45 applied/8 admission offers/5 incoming

% of students receiving:
Full tuition waiver only: 0%
Assistantship/fellowship only: 0%
Both full tuition waiver & assistantship/fellowship: 100%

Approximate percentage of incoming students with a B.A./B.S. only: 60% **Master's:** 40%

Approximate percentage of students who are Women: 80% **Ethnic Minority:** 80% **International:** 20%

Average years to complete the doctoral program (including internship): 5.5 years

Personal interview
Preferred in person (open house) but skype/telephone acceptable

Attrition rate in past 7 years: 8%

Percentage of students applying for internship in 201 accepted into:

APA internships: 100% **APPIC internships:** 100%

Formal tracks/concentrations: none

Research areas	# Faculty	# Grants
academic self-concept, and achievement	1	0
adjustment to brain injury/disability	1	1
caregiver burden	1	0
counseling supervision	1	0
expectations about counseling	1	0
gender/cultural influences	3	0
health psychology	2	0
qualitative research methodology	2	0
racial/ethnic identity	3	0
spiritual/religious issues	1	0
stress and coping	2	0

Clinical opportunities

career development	university counseling center
student health service	
integrated health care	community medical clinics
brain injury rehabilitation	VA hospital
psychiatric (inpatient)	vocational rehabilitation
state correctional system (medium security facility)	substance abuse
	stress management

University of Southern Mississippi (Ph.D.)

Department of Psychology
118 College Dr., #5025
Hattiesburg, MS 39406-0001
phone#: (601) 266-4602
email: bonnie.nicholson@usm.edu
Web address: www.usm.edu/counseling-psychology

1	2	3	4	**5**	6	7
Practice oriented			Equal emphasis			Research oriented

Percentage of faculty subscribing to each of the following orientations:

Psychodynamic/Psychoanalytic	0%
Applied behavioral analysis/Radical behavioral	0%
Family systems/Systems	0%
Existential/Phenomenological/Humanistic	0%
Cognitive/Cognitive-behavioral	100%

Courses required for incoming students to have completed prior to enrolling: none

Recommended but not mandatory courses: statistics, personality, testing and assessment

GRE mean
Verbal 152 Quantitative 150
Analytical Writing not reported
Psychology Subject Test not reported

GPA mean
Overall GPA 3.7 Overall Master's GPA n/a

Number of applications/admission offers/incoming students in 2017
70 applied/8 admission offers/5 incoming

% of students receiving:
Full tuition waiver only: 0%
Assistantship/fellowship only: 0%
Both full tuition waiver & assistantship/fellowship: 100%

Approximate percentage of incoming students with a B.A./B.S. only: 57% **Master's:** 42%

Approximate percentage of students who are Women: 71% **Ethnic Minority:** 14% **International:** 0

Average years to complete the doctoral program (including internship): 6.0 post BA/BS

Personal interview
Preferred in person but telephone acceptable

Attrition rate in past 7 years: 20%

Percentage of students applying for internship in 2017 accepted into:

APA internships: 100% **APPIC internships:**

Formal tracks/concentrations: none

Research areas	# Faculty	# Grants
anger	1	0
diversity	6	0
empirically supported treatments	6	0
motivational interviewing	1	0
parenting	1	0
vocational	2	0
criminal thinking	1	0

Clinical opportunities

alcohol and drug treatment	outpatient
community mental health center	university counseling center
counseling assessment center	university medical center
counseling training clinic	inpatient
VA hospital	

Springfield College (Psy.D.)

Department of Psychology
263 Alden Street
Springfield, MA 01109
phone#: (413) 748-3663
email: shage@springfieldcollege.edu
Web address: http://springfield.edu/programs/counseling-psychology-doctoral-degree

1	2	**3**	4	5	6	7
Practice oriented			Equal emphasis			Research oriented

Percentage of faculty subscribing to each of the following orientations:

Psychodynamic/Psychoanalytic	30%
Applied behavioral analysis/Radical behavioral	0%
Family systems/Systems	0%
Existential/Phenomenological/Humanistic	35%
Cognitive/Cognitive-behavioral	35%

Courses required for incoming students to have completed prior to enrolling: completion of a Bachelors' degree in psychology or a related field

Recommended but not mandatory courses: Statistics, Counseling Theories

GRE mean
Verbal + Quantitative
Analytical Writing
Psychology Subject Test not required

GPA mean
Overall GPA 3.65

Number of applications/admission offers/incoming students in 2015
75 applied/20 admission offers/14 incoming

% of students receiving:
Full tuition waiver only: 20%
Assistantship/fellowship only: 0%
Both partial tuition waiver & assistantship/fellowship: 75%

Approximate percentage of incoming students with a B.A./B.S. only: 25% **Master's:** 75%

Approximate percentage of all students who are Women: 60% **Ethnic Minority:** 35% **International:** 15%

Average years to complete the doctoral program (including internship): **4.5** years

Personal interview Yes

Attrition rate in past 7 years: 15%

Percentage of students applying for internship last year accepted into:

APA internships: 86% **APPIC internships:** 14%

Formal tracks/concentrations: Athletic Counseling

Research areas	# Faculty	# Grants
Trauma	1	
Vocational Identity	2	
Prevention	1	
Cognition and Memory	1	
Sexual Identity Development	1	
Research Methodology	1	
Critical Psychology	1	
Psychological aspects of sport injury	1	
Career and work psychology	1	
Social Justice	3	
Interpersonal Violence	1	
Multicultural Psychology	2	
Spirituality	1	
Self- and identity-development	1	
Feminist Theories	2	
Emerging Adult	1	
Body image and self-talk	1	

Clinical opportunities
College and University Counseling Center
Medical setting/Pain Management
Psychological Assessment
Eating Disorders
Child and Adolescent Counseling
Neurofeedback
Military
Federal Penitentiary
Community Mental Health

Teachers College–Columbia University (Ph.D.)

Department of Counseling and Clinical Psychology
New York, NY 10027
phone#: (212)678-3397
email: et2453@tc.columbia.edu, Elizabeth Tavarez, Program Secretary
Web address: www.tc.columbia.edu/CCP/CounPsych/index.asp?id=Doctor-of-Philosophy&Info=the+Ph%2ED%2E+Program+in+Counseling+Psychology#DoctorofPhilosophy

1	2	3	4	**5**	6	7
Practice oriented			Equal emphasis			Research oriented

Percentage of faculty subscribing to each of the following orientations:

Psychodynamic/Psychoanalytic	75%
Applied behavioral analysis/Radical behavioral	10%
Family systems/Systems	40%
Existential/Phenomenological/Humanistic	40%
Cognitive/Cognitive-behavioral	25%
Multicultural/Diversity	100%

Courses required for incoming students to have completed prior to enrolling:
Bachelor's, but Master's degree preferred

Recommended but not mandatory courses: none

GRE mean
Verbal 570 Quantitative 570
Analytical Writing not reported
Psychology Subject Test not reported

GPA mean
Overall GPA 3.75

Number of applications/admission offers/incoming students in 2016
197 applied/5 admission offers/5 incoming

% of incoming students receiving:
Full tuition waiver only: 0%
Assistantship/fellowship only: 0%
Both full tuition waiver & assistantship/fellowship: 0%
Students receive stipends, teaching assistantships, and partial tuition wavers.

Approximate percentage of incoming students with a B.A./B.S. only: 40% **Master's:** 60%

Approximate percentage of students who are Women: 80% **Ethnic Minority:** 70% **International:** 10%

Average years to complete the doctoral program (including internship): 6.0 years

Personal interview
Required in person

Attrition rate in past 7 years: 10%

Percentage of students applying for internship in 2016 accepted into:

APA internships: 100% **APPIC internships:** 100%

Formal tracks/concentrations: none

Research areas	# Faculty	# Grants
cognition and stereotypes	1	0
cultural competence	7	0
microaggression	2	0
multicultural counseling	7	0
social class	1	0
racism and racial identity	3	0
women and leadership	3	0
LGBT	2	0

Clinical opportunities:
university clinic
off-site externships

University of Tennessee–Knoxville (Ph.D.)

Department of Psychology
1404 Circle Dr., Rm. 312 Austin Peay
Knoxville, TN 37996-0900
phone#: (865) 974-2204
email: gowens4@utk.edu
Web address: http://psychology.utk.edu/grad/phd_counseling.php

1	2	3	4	5	6	7
Practice oriented			Equal emphasis			Research oriented

Percentage of faculty subscribing to each of the following orientations:

Psychodynamic/Psychoanalytic	14%
Applied behavioral analysis/Radical behavioral	0%
Family systems/Systems	14%
Existential/Phenomenological/Humanistic	0%
Cognitive/Cognitive-behavioral	29%
Feminist	29%
Interpersonal/experiential	57%
Integrative	14%

Courses required for incoming students to have completed prior to enrolling:
An undergraduate degree is required, but no specific courses.

Recommended but not mandatory courses:
experimental, personality, developmental, abnormal

GRE mean
Verbal 158 Quantitative 153
Analytical Writing 4.5
Psychology Subject Test not reported

GPA mean
Overall GPA 3.60 (Undergraduate); 3.84 (Graduate)

Number of applications/admission offers/incoming students in 2017
115 applied/6 admission offers/5 incoming

% of students receiving:
Full tuition waiver only: 0%
Assistantship/fellowship only: 0%
Both full tuition waiver & assistantship/fellowship: 100%

Approximate percentage of incoming students with a B.A./B.S. only: 53% **Master's:** 47%

Approximate percentage of students who are Women: 63% **Ethnic Minority:** 27% **International:** 7%

Average years to complete the doctoral program (including internship): 5.5 years

Personal interview:
Interview required

Attrition rate in past 7 years: 5%

Percentage of students applying for internship in 2017 accepted into:

APA internships: 100% **APPIC internships:** 100%

Formal tracks/concentrations: none

Research areas	# Faculty	# Grants
Trauma, military PTSD	1	0
Feminist theory	2	0
LBGT issues, heterosexism	4	0
Personality and optimum performance	1	0
Sport psychology	1	0
Multicultural psychology	5	0
Health psychology	1	0
Scholarship of Teaching and Learning	1	1
Group interventions	1	1
Training and supervision	1	0
Social justice advocacy	4	0

Clinical opportunities
Practicum at University Counseling Center
Assistantships at alcohol/drug treatment inpatient, domestic violence counseling, community mental health centers, and Career Services

Tennessee State University (Ph.D.)

Department of Psychology
Nashville, TN 37209-1561
phone#: (615) 963-5141
email: roatisballew@tnstate.edu
Web address: www.tnstate.edu/psychology

1	2	3	**4**	5	6	7
Practice oriented			Equal emphasis			Research oriented

Percentage of faculty subscribing to each of the following orientations:

Psychodynamic/Psychoanalytic	40%
Applied behavioral analysis/Radical behavioral	0%
Family systems/Systems	20%
Existential/Phenomenological/Humanistic	20%
Cognitive/Cognitive-behavioral	20%

Courses required for incoming students to have completed prior to enrolling:
Cognitive and Affective Bases of Behavior; Statistics; Theories of Counseling or Theories of Personality; Counseling Techniques; Intellectual Assessment; Developmental Psychology; Social Psychology; Psychometrics; Master's-Level Practicum; History & Systems of Psychology; Career Counseling; Physiological Psychology

Recommended but not mandatory courses: none

GRE mean
Verbal 150 Quantitative 146
Analytical Writing not reported
Psychology Subject Test not reported

GPA mean
Overall GPA 3.62

Number of applications/admission offers/incoming students in 2017
55 applied/14 admission offers/9 incoming

% of students receiving:
Full tuition waiver only: 0%
Assistantship/fellowship only: 75%
Both full tuition waiver & assistantship/fellowship: 75%

Approximate percentage of incoming students with a B.A./B.S. only: 0% **Master's:** 100%

Approximate percentage of students who are Women: 76% **Ethnic Minority:** 65% **International:** 4%

Average years to complete the doctoral program (including internship): 5 years

Personal interview
Preferred in person but telephone acceptable

Attrition rate in past 7 years: 8%

Percentage of students applying for internship in 2016 accepted into:

APA internships: 100% **APPIC internships:** 100%

Formal tracks/concentrations: General

Research areas	# Faculty	# Grants
career/vocational	1	2
ethical issues	2	0
men's issues	1	0
multicultural concerns	3	0
marriage and family therapy	2	0
women's issues	1	0

Clinical opportunities

adult, and adolescent psychiatry	university counseling center
behavioral health	community mental health
forensics	VA hospital
assessment clinics	correctional facilities

Texas A&M University (Ph.D.)

Department of Educational Psychology
College Station, TX 77843
phone#: (979) 845-1833
email: epsy@tamu.edu
Web address: cpsy.tamu.edu

1	2	3	4	**5**	6	7
Practice oriented			Equal emphasis			Research oriented

Percentage of faculty subscribing to each of the following orientations:

Psychodynamic/Psychoanalytic	20%
Applied behavioral analysis/Radical behavioral	0%
Family systems/Systems	0%
Existential/Phenomenological/Humanistic	20%
Cognitive/Cognitive-behavioral	20%
Multicultural/Feminist	40%

Courses required for incoming students prior to enrolling: statistics, psychology, research methods.

Courses recommended but not mandatory: none

GRE mean
Verbal 154 Quantitative 152.4
Analytical Writing 4.29
Psychology Subject Test not reported

GPA mean
Overall GPA 3.77 Psychology GPA n/a
Junior/Senior GPA n/a

Number of applications/admission offers/incoming students in 2017
73 complete applications/13 admission offers/7 incoming

% of students receiving:
Full tuition waiver only: 0%
Assistantship/fellowship only: 100%
Both full tuition waiver & assistantship/fellowship: 0%

Approximate percentage of incoming students with a B.A./B.S. only: 85.7% **Master's:** 14.3%

Approximate percentage of all students who are Women: 75% **Ethnic Minority:** 60% **International:** 12.5%

Average years to complete the doctoral program (including internship): 5.15 years

Personal interview
In person interviews are strongly preferred. Skype interviews can be arranged for students with conflicts or financial burden.

Attrition rate in past 7 years: 9%

Percentage of students applying for internship in 2016 accepted into:

APA internships: 100% **APPIC internships:** 100%

Formal tracks/concentrations: cultural competencies, Latino health/mental health research, telepsychology, outcome research

Research areas	# Faculty	# Grants
Latino mental health	2	0
Disabling conditions/caregivers	1	1
methods in psychological research	1	0
multicultural training	2	0
acculturation process	1	0
public health	2	1

Clinical opportunities

Telepsychology clinic training
VA hospitals
community mental health
university counseling centers

University of Texas at Austin

Department of Educational Psychology
D 5800
Austin, TX 78712
phone#: (512) 471-4155
email: arochlen@austin.utexas.edu
Web address: https://www.edb.utexas.edu/education/departments/edp/doctoral/cp/

1	2	3	4	5	6	7
Practice oriented			Equal emphasis			Research oriented

Percentage of faculty subscribing to each of the following orientations:

Psychodynamic/Psychoanalytic	30%
Existential/Phenomenological/Humanistic	30%
Interpersonal/Constructivist	30%
Cognitive/Cognitive-behavioral	70%
Multicultural	70%
Narrative/Solution-Focused	10%

Courses required for incoming students to have completed prior to enrolling: Bachelor's degree

Recommended but not mandatory courses: none

GRE mean
Verbal 158.0 Quantitative 152.5
Analytical Writing 4.3
Psychology Subject Test not reported

GPA mean
Overall GPA 3.78

Number of applications/admission offers/incoming students in 2017
180 applied/12 admission offers/6 incoming students

% of students receiving:
Full tuition waiver only: 0%
Assistantship/fellowship only: 100%
Both full tuition waiver & assistantship/fellowship: 0%

Approximate percentage of incoming students with a B.A./B.S. only: 37.5% **Master's:** 62.5%

Approximate percentage of students who are Women: 85% **Ethnic Minority:** 35% **International:** 0%

Average years to complete the doctoral program (including internship): 6 years

Personal interview required

Attrition rate in past 7 years: 10%

Percentage of students applying for internship in 2017 accepted into:

APA internships: 100% **APPIC internships:** 0%

Formal tracks/concentrations: none

Research areas	# Faculty	# Grants
depression	2	0
forensic psychology/assessment	1	0
psychology of men and masculinity	2	0
gender and sexuality	3	1
multicultural/cross-cultural	4	2
psychoanalysis	1	0
health psychology	4	1
stress and coping	1	0
emotion regulation	1	0
academic achievement/minority issues	1	1

Clinical opportunities

Career counseling
Community agency counseling
Adolescent and adult inpatient units at state hospital
Outpatient practicum at VA
Hospital-based assessment
Neuropsychological assessment
Correctional facilities
Integrated behavioral health
Counseling centers

Texas Tech University (Ph.D.)

Department of Psychology
Lubbock, TX 79409
phone#: (806) 742-3711, ext. 229
email: sheila.garos@ttu.edu
Web address: www.depts.ttu.edu/psy/graduate_programs/counseling/overview.php

1	2	3	4	5	6	7
Practice oriented			Equal emphasis			Research oriented

Percentage of faculty subscribing to each of the following orientations:

Psychodynamic/Psychoanalytic	14%
Applied behavioral analysis/Radical behavioral	14%
Family systems/Systems	14%
Existential/Phenomenological/Humanistic	14%
Cognitive/Cognitive-behavioral	28%
Interpersonal Therapy	14%

Courses required for incoming students to have completed prior to enrolling:
18 undergraduate hours in psychology and statistics

Recommended but not mandatory courses: none

GRE mean (percentiles)
Verbal 63 Quantitative 53
Analytical Writing 80
Psychology Subject Test not reported

GPA mean
Overall GPA 3.54

Number of applications/admission offers/incoming students in 2017
82 applied/10 admission offers/6 incoming

% of students receiving:
Full tuition waiver only: 100%
Assistantship/fellowship only: 100% (qualifies student for in-state tuition and fee waiver)
Both full tuition waiver & assistantship/fellowship:100%

Approximate percentage of incoming students with a B.A./B.S. only: 75% **Master's:** 25%

Approximate percentage of all students who are Women: 63% **Ethnic Minority:** 25% **International:** 0%

Average years to complete the doctoral program (including internship): 6 years

Personal interview
Required in person

Attrition rate in past 7 years: 10%

Percentage of students applying for internship in 2017 accepted into:

APA internships: 100% **APPIC internships:** 100%

Formal tracks/concentrations: none

Research areas	# Faculty	# Grants
behavioral addictions	1	0
cultural differences in the self	1	0
depression	1	0
forensic/correctional	1	2
gender and women	2	0
health psychology	2	0
multicultural counseling	2	0
positive psychology	1	0
sexual behavior	2	0
vocational	1	0
women's sexual health	1	0

Clinical opportunities
in-patient psychiatric unit
neuropsychology
cancer center
university counseling center
adult probation
community mental health
outpatient psychology clinic
pediatric
sports psychology

Texas Woman's University (Ph.D.)

Department of Psychology and Philosophy
P.O. Box 425470
Denton, TX 76204
phone#: (940) 898-2303
email: sstabb@mail.twu.edu
Web address: www.twu.edu/psychology-philosophy/counseling-psych-phd.asp

1	2	**3**	4	5	6	7
Practice oriented			Equal emphasis			Research oriented

Percentage of faculty subscribing to each of the following orientations:

Psychodynamic/Psychoanalytic	0%
Applied behavioral analysis/Radical behavioral	0%
Family systems/Systems	0%
Existential/Phenomenological/Humanistic	0%
Cognitive/Cognitive-behavioral	—
Integrative	100%
Feminist	100%

Courses required for incoming students to have completed prior to enrolling:
Development, statistics, learning, experimental, intro, 3 additional psychology credits

Recommended but not mandatory courses: none

GRE mean
Verbal 158 Quantitative 145
Analytical Writing 4.0
Psychology Subject Test not required

GPA mean
Psychology GPA 3.42 Junior/Senior GPA 3.55
Master's GPA 3.89

Number of applications/admission offers/incoming students in 2017
52 applied/7 admission offers/6 incoming

% of students receiving:
Full tuition waiver only: 0%
Assistantship/fellowship only: 83%
Both full tuition waiver & assistantship/fellowship: 0%

Approximate percentage of incoming students with a B.A./B.S. only: 50% **Master's:** 50%

Approximate percentage of students who are Women: 100% **Ethnic Minority:** 33% **International:** 0%

Average years to complete the doctoral program (including internship): 4-5 years coming in with a Master's degree

Personal interview
In-person preferred

Attrition rate in past 7 years: 5.6%

Percentage of students applying for internship in 2017 accepted into:

APA internships: 100% **APPIC internships:** 0%

Formal tracks/concentrations: Gender & Multicultural focus throughout the program

Research areas	# Faculty	# Grants
gender/multicultural	3	
Integrative psychotherapy	1	

Clinical opportunities
university counseling center
community mental health
prisons/corrections
chemical dependency
domestic violence
hospitals
youth & family agencies
VA Hospital

University of Utah (Ph.D.)

Department of Educational Psychology
1721 Campus Center Dr., RM 3220
Salt Lake City, UT 84112-8914
phone#: (801) 581-7148
email: jason.burrow-sanchez@utah.edu
Web address: http://ed-psych.utah.edu/counseling-psych/index.php

1	2	3	**4**	5	6	7
Practice oriented			Equal emphasis			Research oriented

Percentage of faculty subscribing to each of the following orientations:

Psychodynamic/Psychoanalytic	0%
Applied behavioral analysis/Radical behavioral	0%
Family systems/Systems	0%
Existential/Phenomenological/Humanistic	0%
Cognitive/Cognitive-behavioral	29%
Feminist/ Multicultural	43%
Integrative	14%
Interpersonal	14%

Courses required for incoming students to have completed prior to enrolling: none

Recommended but not mandatory courses:
experimental, personality, developmental, physiological, abnormal, statistics, research methods, social, and learning

GRE mean
Verbal 158 Quantitative 153
Analytical Writing 4.3
Psychology Subject Test not reported

GPA UG mean
Overall GPA 3.62

Number of applications/admission offers/incoming students in 2017
91 applied/4 admission offers/4 incoming

% of students receiving:
Full tuition waiver only: 0%
Assistantship/fellowship only: 0%
Both full tuition waiver & assistantship/fellowship: 100%

Approximate percentage of incoming students with a B.A./B.S. only: 75% **Master's:** 25%

Approximate percentage of all students who are Women: 74% **Ethnic Minority:** 32% **International:** 6%

Average years to complete the doctoral program (including internship): 7 years

Personal interview
Invited in-person interview for all top candidates

Attrition rate in past 7 years: 6%

Percentage of students applying for internship in 2017 accepted into:

APA internships: 100% **APPIC internships:** 100%

Formal tracks/concentrations: student-selected special proficiency is required.

Research areas	# Faculty	# Grants
children and adolescents	2	1
gender and women's	3	0
lesbian, gay, bisexual, transgender	1	0
multicultural counseling	3	0
psychotherapy process/outcome	1	2
substance abuse	1	1
career development	2	0

Clinical opportunities
Community mental health clinics
Drug and alcohol assessment and treatment
University counseling center
Multicultural counseling
VA hospital
University hospital clinics
Medical school
University women's resource center
School-based counseling (K–12)

Virginia Commonwealth University (Ph.D.)

Department of Psychology
Richmond, VA 23284-2018
phone#: (804) 827-1708
email: semazzeo@vcu.edu
Web address: http://www.psychology.vcu.edu/graduate/counseling/

1	2	3	4	**5**	6	7
Practice oriented			Equal emphasis			Research oriented

Percentage of faculty subscribing to each of the following orientations:

Psychodynamic/Interpersonal	10%
Applied behavioral analysis/Radical behavioral	0%
Family systems/Systems	10%
Existential/Phenomenological/Humanistic	0%
Cognitive-behavioral/Feminist	70%
Developmental	10%

Courses required for incoming students to have completed prior to enrolling:
18 undergraduate credit hours in psychology, including courses in statistics, experimental and introductory psychology

Recommended but not mandatory courses: n/a

GRE mean
Verbal 155 Quantitative 151
Analytical Writing 4.75
Psychology Subject Test not reported

GPA mean
Overall GPA 3.66

Number of applications/admission offers/incoming students in 2017
86 applied/ 4 admission offers/4 incoming

% of students receiving:
Full tuition waiver only: 0%
Assistantship/fellowship only: 0%
Both full tuition waiver & assistantship/fellowship: 100%

Approximate percentage of incoming students with a B.A./B.S.: 100% Master's: 75%

Approximate percentage of all students who are Women: 80% **Ethnic Minority:** 44% **International:** 0%

Average years to complete the doctoral program (including internship): 5.94 years

Personal interview
Preferred in person but telephone acceptable if arranged in advance

Attrition rate in past 7 years: 7.5%

Percentage of students applying for internship in 2017 accepted into:

APA internships: 100% **APPIC internships:**

Formal tracks/concentrations: health psychology

Research areas	# Faculty	# Grants
career intervention	1	1
minority mental health	3	0
forgiveness/religious values	2	3
health psychology	5	4
interventions	1	4
prevention	2	2
leadership and group dynamics	1	0
marital and family enrichment	2	0
teaching of life skills/community	1	0
sleep and health behaviors	1	0

Clinical opportunities
college mental health center
university counseling center
child treatment center
federal correctional center
rehabilitation medicine unit
community mental health
correctional system
state psychiatric hospital
substance abuse
VA hospital
hospitals/medical centers
church mental health

West Virginia University (Ph.D.)

Department of Counseling, Rehabilitation Counseling, and Counseling Psychology
P.O. Box 6122
Morgantown, WV 26506-6122
phone#: (304) 293-2172
email: david.allen@mail.wvu.edu
Web address: counseling.wvu.edu/counseling psychology

1	2	**3**	4	5	6	7
Practice oriented			Equal emphasis			Research oriented

Percentage of faculty subscribing to each of the following orientations:

Psychodynamic/Psychoanalytic	10%
Applied behavioral analysis/Radical behavioral	10%
Family systems/Systems	10%
Existential/Phenomenological/Humanistic	35%
Cognitive/Cognitive-behavioral	35%

Courses required for incoming students to have completed prior to enrolling:
Master's degree in counseling psychology, clinical psychology, or related field

Recommended but not mandatory courses: Supervised field experience, multivariate methods, psychopharmacology

GRE mean
Revised Verbal Reasoning (minimum) 152 Revised Quantitative Reasoning (minimum) 149
Analytical Writing 4.1
Psychology Subject Test n/a

GPA mean
Overall GPA 3.92
Overall graduate GPA 3.92

Number of applications/admission offers/incoming students in 2016–2017
24 applied/6 admission offers/6 incoming

% of students receiving:
Full tuition waiver only: 0%
Assistantship/fellowship only: 0%
Both full tuition waiver & assistantship/fellowship: 100%

Approximate percentage of incoming students with a B.A./B.S. only: 0% **Master's:** 100%

Approximate percentage of students who are Women: 83% **Ethnic Minority:** 17% **International:** 0%

Average years to complete the doctoral program (including internship): 5.5 years

Personal interview
Required in person

Attrition rate in past 7 years: 7%

Percentage of students applying for internship in 2016 accepted into:

APA internships: 100% **APPIC internships:**

Formal tracks/concentrations: developing a veteran care emphasis

Research areas	# Faculty	# Grants
clinical supervision	2	0
consulting models	1	0
group counseling	1	0
injured athletes	1	0
personality assessment	2	0
psychiatric rehabilitation	1	0
psychology and mental health	3	0
psychology of disability	1	0
psychotherapeutic techniques	3	0
rehab counseling and psychology	2	0
self-efficacy and health	2	0
vocational counseling	2	0
multicultural concerns	1	0

Clinical opportunities
community agencies
crisis units
correctional facilities
university counseling centers
general hospitals
out-patient rehabilitation hospitals
clinics/assessment centers
psychiatric hospitals
comprehensive mental health centers
VA hospitals

Western Michigan University (Ph.D.)

Department of Counselor Education and
Counseling Psychology
3102 Sangren Hall
Kalamazoo, MI 49008-5226
phone#: (269) 387-5100 | (269) 387-5090 Fax
email: karen.boyd@wmich.edu
Web address: www.wmich.edu/coe/cecp/academics/doctoral/phd-counselingpsychology.html

1	2	3	4	**5**	6	7
Practice oriented			Equal emphasis			Research oriented

Percentage of faculty subscribing to each of the following orientations:
Psychodynamic/Psychoanalytic 0%
Applied behavioral analysis/Radical behavioral 0%
Family systems/Systems 20%
Existential/Phenomenological/Humanistic 88%
Cognitive/Cognitive-behavioral 88%

Courses required for incoming students to have completed prior to enrolling:
Undergraduate degree required; Master's degree preferred

Recommended but not mandatory courses: Psychology or social science major

GRE mean
Verbal + Quantitative 300
Analytical Writing 3.8
Psychology Subject Test not reported

GPA mean
Overall graduate GPA 3.97
Overall undergraduate GPA 3.67

Number of applications/admission offers/incoming students in 2017
52 applied/10 admission offers/6 incoming

% of students receiving:
Full tuition waiver only: 0%
Assistantship/fellowship only: 0%
Both full tuition waiver & assistantship/fellowship: 80%

Approximate percentage of incoming students with a B.A./B.S. only: 25% **Master's:** 75%

Approximate percentage of students who are Women: 68% **Ethnic Minority:** 54% **International:** .4%

Average years to complete the doctoral program (including internship): 6 years

Personal interview
Required in person

Attrition rate in past 7 years: 4%

Percentage of students applying for internship in 2017 accepted into:

APA internships: 100% **APPIC internships:** 100%
(all were both APA and APPIC)

Formal tracks/concentrations: none

Research areas	# Faculty	# Grants
group work	1	0
multicultural concerns	4	0
psychological assessment	2	0
treatment	3	0

Clinical opportunities
In-house clinic and local hospitals, university counseling centers, agencies, and schools

University of Wisconsin–Madison (Ph.D.)

Department of Counseling Psychology
335 Education Building, 1000 Bascom Mall
Madison, WI 53706-1326
phone#: (608) 262-4807
email: counpsych@education.wisc.edu
Web address: https://counselingpsych.education.wisc.edu/cp/phd-program

1	2	3	4	**5**	6	7
Practice oriented			Equal emphasis			Research oriented

Percentage of faculty subscribing to each of the following orientations:
Not reported

Courses required for incoming students to have completed prior to enrolling:
Master's degree in counseling recommended, but not required.

Recommended but not mandatory courses: theories of counseling, assessment techniques, theory and practice of group work, research in guidance and counseling, techniques and microskills for counselors, counseling psychology techniques with families, consultation procedures for counselors, multicultural counseling, theory and practice of career intervention, counseling psychology practicum

GRE mean
Verbal 160 Quantitative 160
Analytical Writing 4.5
Psychology Subject Test not reported

GPA mean
Junior/Senior GPA 3.83

Number of applications/admission offers/incoming students in 2017
135 applied/9 admission offers/2 incoming

% of students receiving:
Full tuition waiver only: 0%
Assistantship/fellowship only: 0%
Both full tuition waiver & assistantship/fellowship: 67%

Approximate percentage of incoming students with a B.A./B.S. only: 50% **Master's:** 50%

Approximate percentage of all students who are Women: 61% **Ethnic Minority:** 45% **International:** 8%

Average years to complete the doctoral program (including internship): 7 years

Personal interview
Preferred in person, although video interview also available.

Attrition rate in past 7 years: 15%

Percentage of students applying for internship in 2017 accepted into:

APA internships: 100% **APPIC internships:** 100%

Formal tracks/concentrations: none

Research areas	**# Faculty**	**# Grants**
Not reported		

Clinical opportunities
Not reported

University of Wisconsin–Milwaukee (Ph.D.)

Department of Educational Psychology
P.O. Box 413
Milwaukee, WI 53201
email: srwester@uwm.edu
Web address: http://uwm.edu/education/academics/counseling-psychology/

1	2	3	4	5	6	7
Practice oriented			Equal emphasis			Research oriented

Percentage of faculty subscribing to each of the following orientations:

Psychodynamic/Psychoanalytic	10%
Applied behavioral analysis/Radical behavioral	0%
Family systems/Systems	0%
Existential/Phenomenological/Humanistic	0%
Cognitive/Cognitive-behavioral	70%
Developmental Systems	10%
Interpersonal	10%

Courses required for incoming students to have completed prior to enrolling:
group counseling, listening skills, statistics, multicultural counseling, theories of counseling, cognition, career development, personality

Recommended but not mandatory courses: personality, social, abnormal, developmental

GRE mean
Verbal 650 Quantitative 600
Analytical Writing 4.4
Psychology Subject Test not reported

GPA mean
Overall GPA 3.8

Number of applications/admission offers/incoming students in 2017
62 applied/11 admission offers/6 incoming

% of students receiving:
Full tuition waiver only: 0%
Assistantship/fellowship only: 0%
Both full tuition waiver & assistantship/fellowship: 100% first year, 90% second year, 20% third year, n/a fourth year and beyond

Approximate percentage of incoming students with a B.A./B.S. only: 10% **Master's:** 90%

Approximate percentage of all students who are Women: 70% **Ethnic Minority:** 50% **International:** 25%

Average years to complete the doctoral program (including internship): 5 years

Personal interview
Preferred in person but telephone acceptable

Attrition rate in past 7 years: 2%

Percentage of students applying for internship in 2017 accepted into:

APA internships: 100% (accredited required)
APPIC internships: n/a

Formal tracks/concentrations: none

Research areas	**# Faculty**	**# Grants**
barriers for women in math/science	1	1
hypnosis and hypnotizability	1	0
international research	1	2
intervention programming	1	1
masculinity and male gender role	1	0
counseling training	1	1
vocational development	2	2

Clinical opportunities

children's hospital	medical college
community mental health	VA hospital
counseling center	day treatment
family services	eating disorders clinic
inpatient psychiatric	

APPENDIX A
TIME LINE

Freshman and Sophomore Years

1. Take the core psychology courses–introduction, statistics, research methods, abnormal, cognitive, social.
2. Find out about faculty interests and research.
3. Make preliminary contact with faculty members whose research interests you.
4. Explore volunteer opportunities in clinical settings.
5. Investigate various career choices.
6. Join psychology student organizations and become an active member.
7. Attend departmental colloquia and social gatherings.
8. Enroll in courses helpful for graduate school, including biological sciences, mathematics, writing, and public speaking.
9. Learn to use library and electronic resources, such as scholarly journals and PsycLit.
10. Consider participating in your university's honors program, if you qualify.
11. Begin a career folder and place activities, honors, and other valuable reminders in it.
12. Discuss your career interests with faculty members and other mentors.

Junior Year

1. Take advanced psychology courses, for example, biopsychology, psychological testing.
2. Begin clinical work, both volunteer and practicum.
3. Volunteer for research with faculty and begin researching a potential honors thesis/independent project.
4. Continue contact with faculty and upperclassmen.
5. Enroll in professional organizations, for example, student affiliate of American Psychological Association or American Psychological Society.
6. Apply for membership in your local Psi Chi chapter.
7. Visit your career services office on campus and determine how the staff can assist you in applying to graduate school.
8. Draft a curriculum vitae to determine your strengths and weaknesses.
9. Attend a state or regional psychology convention.
10. Peruse graduate school bulletins online to acquaint yourself with typical requirements, offerings, and policies.
11. Surf the Web. Become comfortable with leading Web sites on graduate school admissions.
12. Access the GRE bulletin and information online. Begin preparation for the GRE by purchasing a study guide, attending a preparation course, and taking practice tests.
13. Update your folder by putting your curriculum vita/resume and reminders of your activities and accomplishments in it.
14. Try to focus your interests in particular research areas, theoretical orientations, and clinical populations.

15. Consider serving as an officer in one of the student organizations on campus.
16. Meet with your advisor or mentor before summer to review your plan for graduate applications.

Application Year

June–August

1. Continue to acquire research competencies and clinical experiences.
2. Surf the Web and begin to gather information from program Web sites.
3. Begin to narrow down potential schools to 20–40.
4. Prepare intensively for the GREs.
5. Consider taking the GRE General Test if you are prepared; this will afford ample time to retake it in the fall if necessary.
6. Investigate financial aid opportunities for graduate students.
7. Set aside money for the cost of the GREs and graduate applications.

August–September

1. Download program information and applications from program Web sites.
2. Read through graduate program materials.
3. Consult with advisors regarding graduate programs, application procedures, faculty of interest, etc.
4. Continue to study diligently for the GREs.
5. Update your curriculum vitae.
6. Investigate possible financial aid opportunities.
7. Begin a file in your institution's Office of Career Services.
8. Gather applications for salient fellowships and scholarships.

September–October

1. Take the GRE General Test (for first or second time).
2. Register for the GRE Psychology Subject Test administered in November and December.
3. Create a short list of schools using the worksheets.
4. Record the deadlines for submitting each application.
5. Choose the faculty at each school that most interest you.
6. Research your area of interest, focusing on the work of faculty with whom you would like to work.
7. Write to graduate faculty expressing interest in their work (if appropriate).
8. Request a copy of your own transcript and inspect it for any errors or omissions.
9. Begin first drafts of your personal statement and get feedback on it.
10. Update your CV or resume.
11. Calculate costs of applications and admission interviews and acquire the money for them.
12. Finalize the decision on whom you will ask for letters of recommendation.
13. Formulate your Plan B (i.e., what you will do if you are not accepted into a doctoral program).

October–November

1. Take the GRE Psychology Subject Test.
2. Prepare packets to distribute to your recommenders, including a complete vitae or resume.
3. Request letters of recommendation.
4. Arrange for the registrar to send your transcripts to schools.
5. Gather information on financial aid and loans available to graduate students.
6. Finalize your personal statements.

November–December

1. Complete applications.
2. Maintain a copy of each application for your records.
3. If the opportunity arises, visit professors with whom you have been in contact.
4. Submit applications.
5. Verify that the applications and all necessary materials have been received.
6. Request ETS forward your GRE scores to the appropriate institutions.

January–March

1. Wait patiently.
2. Insure that all of your letters of recommendation have been sent.
3. Complete the Free Application for Federal Student Aid at www.fafsa.ed.gov to determine what federal loans you can count on.
4. Be prepared for surprise telephone interviews.
5. Practice and prepare for admission interviews.
6. Travel to interviews as invited.

7. Develop contingency plans if not accepted into any programs.

April–May

1. If other programs make early offers, contact your top choices to determine the current status of your application.
2. Accept an offer of admission and promptly turn down less-preferred offers.
3. Finalize financial aid arrangements for next year.
4. Send official transcripts with Spring term grades to the program you plan to attend.
5. If not accepted to any schools, refer to Chapter 8.
6. Celebrate (if accepted) or regroup (if not accepted).
7. Inform people who wrote you letters of recommendation of the outcome.

APPENDIX B

WORKSHEET FOR CHOOSING PROGRAMS

		Research			Clinical			
Area of Interest	School	# Faculty	Funded	Rank	Orien-tation	Res/ Clin	Rank	Self-Rating

		Research			Clinical			
Area of Interest	School	# Faculty	Funded	Rank	Orientation	Res/Clin	Rank	Self-Rating

APPENDIX C

WORKSHEET FOR ASSESSING PROGRAM CRITERIA

School	Self-Rating	Courses	GRE-V	GRE-G	GRE-S	GPA	Research	Clinical	Compete	Total

APPENDIX D

WORKSHEET FOR MAKING FINAL CHOICES

School	School Criteria	Research	Clinical	Theoretical Orientation	Financial Aid	Program Outcomes	Quality of Life

APPENDIX E

RESEARCH AREAS

	# Faculty	# Grants
Acceptance and Commitment Therapy		
Drexel University (Ph.D.) (Cl)	3	3
The Wright Institute (Psy.D.) (Cl)	1	–
University of Central Florida (Ph.D.) (Cl)	1	0
University of Hawaii at Manoa (Ph.D.) (Cl)	1	0
University of North Texas (Ph.D.) (Cl)	1	1
Utah State University (Ph.D.) (Cm)	2	5
Wichita State University (Ph.D.) (Cl)	1	0
Acculturation		
Arizona State University (Ph.D.) (Co)	1	–
Biola University (Ph.D.) (Cl)	5	0
Biola University (Psy.D.) (Cl)	5	0
New Mexico State University (Ph.D.) (Co)	3	1
Texas A&M University (Ph.D.) (Co)	1	0
The Wright Institute (Psy.D.) (Cl)	2	–
University of Alaska Fairbanks-Anchorage (Ph.D.) (Cl)	1	0
University of Minnesota (Ph.D.) (Co)	1	1
University of Missouri, Columbia (Ph.D.) (Co)	1	0
Acquired Immune Deficiency Syndrome/HIV		
Azusa Pacific University (Psy.D.) (Cl)	1	0
Duke University (Ph.D.) (Cl)	2	6
Florida International University (Ph.D.) (Cl)	1	1
George Mason University (Ph.D.) (Cl)	3	–
George Washington University (Ph.D.) (Cl)	3	3
Georgia State University (Ph.D.) (Cl)	1	1
Indiana University–Bloomington (Ph.D.) (Co)	1	1
Jackson State University (Ph.D.) (Cl)	4	5
Ponce Health Sciences University (Ph.D.) (Cl)	4	2
Ponce Health Sciences University (Psy.D.) (Cl)	3	1
Radford University (Psy.D.) (Co)	2	1
San Diego State University–UC San Diego (Ph.D.) (Cl)	18	>1
Syracuse University (Ph.D.) (Cl)	2	5
The University of Memphis (Ph.D.) (Co)	1	0
The Wright Institute (Psy.D.) (Cl)	1	–
University of Florida (Ph.D.) (Cl)	1	2
University of Kentucky (Ph.D.) (Co)	1	–
University of Maryland-College Park (Ph.D.) (Co)	1	0
University of North Dakota (Ph.D.) (Co)	1	0
Adjustment		
Saint Louis University (Ph.D.) (Cl)	1	0
University of Georgia (Ph.D.) (Cl)	2	1
University of Minnesota (Ph.D.) (Co)	1	0
Adolescent/At-Risk Adolescent		
Azusa Pacific University (Psy.D.) (Cl)	2	1
Ball State University (Ph.D.) (Co)	3	0
Boston College (Ph.D.) (Co)	5	5
Catholic University of America (Ph.D.) (Cl)	4	1

Note. Cl, Clinical; Co, Counseling; Cm, combined psychology programs.

	# Faculty	# Grants
Chatham University (Psy.D.) (Co)	3	0
Colorado State University (Ph.D.) (Co)	3	5
DePaul University (Ph.D.) (Cl)	2	2
Drexel University (Ph.D.) (Cl)	2	5
Duke University (Ph.D.) (Cl)	5	6
Florida International University (Ph.D.) (Cl)	1	1
Florida School of Professional Psychology at Argosy University (Psy.D.) (Cl)	3	0
Fordham University (Ph.D.) (Cl)	3	2
George Washington University (Ph.D.) (Cl)	3	2
Harvard University (Ph.D.) (Cl)	1	3
Illinois School of Professional Psychology at Argosy University, Chicago (Psy.D.) (Cl)	2	0
Indiana University–Bloomington (Ph.D.) (Co)	1	–
Kent State University (Ph.D.) (Cl)	3	1
La Salle University (Psy.D.) (Cl)	1	0
Loyola University Chicago (Ph.D.) (Cl)	6	5
Loyola University Chicago (Ph.D.) (Co)	4	1
Marshall University (Psy.D.) (Cl)	4	0
Northern Illinois University (Ph.D.) (Cl)	2	0
Oklahoma State University (Ph.D.) (Co)	4	1
Pacific University, Oregon (Psy.D.) (Cl)	5	0
Philadelphia College of Osteopathic Medicine (Psy.D.) (Cl)	2	0
Regent University (Psy.D.) (Cl)	1	1
Roosevelt University (Psy.D.) (Cl)	5	0
Rutgers-The State University of New Jersey (Psy.D.) (Cl)	1	–
Saint Louis University (Ph.D.) (Cl)	3	0
Sam Houston State University (Ph.D.) (Cl)	3	–
Seattle Pacific University (Ph.D.) (Cl)	2	2
Southern Illinois University Carbondale (Ph.D.) (Cl)	2	3
Syracuse University (Ph.D.) (Cl)	5	8
Temple University (Ph.D.) (Cl)	3	7
Texas Tech University (Ph.D.) (Cl)	1	0
The University of Memphis (Ph.D.) (Co)	1	0
The Wright Institute (Psy.D.) (Cl)	1	–
University of Alabama at Birmingham (Ph.D.) (Cl)	3	1
University of Arkansas (Ph.D.) (Cl)	3	2
University of Colorado at Colorado Springs (Ph.D.) (Cl)	1	0
University of Georgia (Ph.D.) (Cl)	4	–
University of Georgia (Ph.D.) (Co)	2	2
University of Hartford (Psy.D.) (Cl)	3	1
University of Iowa (Ph.D.) (Co)	1	1
University of Kentucky (Ph.D.) (Cl)	3	2
University of Louisville (Ph.D.) (Co)	1	1
University of Massachusetts Amherst (Ph.D.) (Cl)	6	0
University of Massachusetts, Boston (Ph.D.) (Co)	2	2
University of Missouri, Columbia (Ph.D.) (Co)	2	0
University of Nebraska, Lincoln (Ph.D.) (Cl)	3	3
University of North Carolina, Chapel Hill (Ph.D.) (Cl)	1	1
University of North Carolina, Greensboro (Ph.D.) (Cl)	3	0
University of Pittsburgh (Ph.D.) (Cl)	4	15
University of South Alabama (Ph.D.) (Cm)	1	–
University of South Florida (Ph.D.) (Cl)	4	8
University of Tennessee–Knoxville (Ph.D.) (Cl)	1	0
University of Utah (Ph.D.) (Cl)	3	3
University of Utah (Ph.D.) (Co)	2	1
University of Vermont (Ph.D.) (Cl)	2	1
University of Virginia (Ph.D.) (Cl)	3	3
Virginia Commonwealth University (Ph.D.) (Cl)	6	4
Virginia Polytechnic Institute and State University (Ph.D.) (Cl)	4	3
Washington State University (Ph.D.) (Cl)	4	1
Wheaton College (Psy.D.) (Cl)	1	0
Wichita State University (Ph.D.) (Cl)	1	0
Yeshiva University (Psy.D.) (Cm)	2	0

Adoption/Foster Care

Northwestern University Feinberg School of Medicine (Ph.D.) (Cl)	3	2
University of Delaware (Ph.D.) (Cl)	1	2
University of Massachusetts Amherst (Ph.D.) (Cl)	1	0
University of Minnesota (Ph.D.) (Co)	1	1
University of Missouri Kansas City (Ph.D.) (Co)	1	–

Affective Disorders/Depression/Mood Disorders

Adler University–Chicago (Psy.D.) (Cl)	1	–
American University (Ph.D.) (Cl)	1	0
Binghamton University, State University of New York (Ph.D.) (Cl)	1	1
Boston University (Ph.D.) (Cl)	7	0
Brigham Young University (Ph.D.) (Cl)	2	1
Case Western Reserve University (Ph.D.) (Cl)	2	0
Catholic University of America (Ph.D.) (Cl)	8	2
Chatham University (Psy.D.) (Co)	3	0
Clark University (Ph.D.) (Cl)	7	1
DePaul University (Ph.D.) (Cl)	2	2
Divine Mercy University (Psy.D.) (Cl)	2	–
Drexel University (Ph.D.) (Cl)	2	1
Duke University (Ph.D.) (Cl)	4	6
Florida International University (Ph.D.) (Cl)	1	1
Fuller Theological Seminary (Ph.D.) (Cl)	1	2
Fuller Theological Seminary (Psy.D.) (Cl)	1	2

	# Faculty	# Grants
George Mason University (Ph.D.) (Cl)	4	–
George Washington University (Ph.D.) (Cl)	2	2
George Washington University (Psy.D.) (Cl)	1	–
Georgia State University (Ph.D.) (Cl)	3	0
Hofstra University (Ph.D.) (Cl)	1	0
Illinois Institute of Technology (Ph.D.) (Cl)	1	1
Indiana State University (Psy.D.) (Cl)	2	0
Jackson State University (Ph.D.) (Cl)	2	0
James Madison University (Psy.D.) (Cm)	2	0
Kent State University (Ph.D.) (Cl)	2	1
Marquette University (Ph.D.) (Cl)	3	0
Marshall University (Psy.D.) (Cl)	6	0
Miami University (OH) (Ph.D.) (Cl)	1	0
Northwestern University (Ph.D.) (Cl)	3	2
Northwestern University Feinberg School of Medicine (Ph.D.) (Cl)	5	6
Oklahoma State University (Ph.D.) (Cl)	1	1
Palo Alto University (Psy.D.) (Cl)	4	4
Pennsylvania State University (Ph.D.) (Cl)	4	0
Philadelphia College of Osteopathic Medicine (Psy.D.) (Cl)	7	0
Purdue University (Ph.D.) (Cl)	2	0
Queens College and The Graduate Center, City University of New York (Ph.D.) (Cl)	4	0
Rutgers-The State University of New Jersey (Psy.D.) (Cl)	1	–
Saint Louis University (Ph.D.) (Cl)	2	0
San Diego State University–UC San Diego (Ph.D.) (Cl)	5	>1
Seattle Pacific University (Ph.D.) (Cl)	2	1
Southern Illinois University Carbondale (Ph.D.) (Cl)	2	0
St. John's University (Ph.D.) (Cl)	1	0
Stony Brook University, State University of New York (Ph.D.) (Cl)	5	2
Teachers College, Columbia University (Ph.D.) (Cl)	1	1
Temple University (Ph.D.) (Cl)	3	7
Texas Tech University (Ph.D.) (Cl)	2	0
Texas Tech University (Ph.D.) (Co)	1	0
The Ohio State University (Ph.D.) (Cl)	5	6
The University of Montana (Ph.D.) (Cl)	3	1
The University of South Dakota (Ph.D.) (Cl)	2	0
University at Buffalo, State University of New York (Ph.D.) (Cl)	3	0
University of Alabama at Tuscaloosa (Ph.D.) (Cl)	1	0
University of Arizona (Ph.D.) (Cl)	2	3
University of California, Berkeley (Ph.D.) (Cl)	3	3
University of California, Los Angeles (Ph.D.) (Cl)	3	5
University of Colorado Boulder (Ph.D.) (Cl)	4	3
University of Connecticut (Ph.D.) (Cl)	4	2
University of Denver (Ph.D.) (Cl)	1	0
University of Georgia (Ph.D.) (Cl)	2	–
University of Illinois at Chicago (Ph.D.) (Cl)	4	3
University of Iowa (Ph.D.) (Cl)	3	2
University of Iowa (Ph.D.) (Co)	1	0
University of Kansas (Ph.D.) (Cl)	3	2
University of Louisville (Ph.D.) (Co)	3	1
University of Maine (Ph.D.) (Cl)	4	1
University of Maryland-College Park (Ph.D.) (Cl)	4	1
University of Miami (Ph.D.) (Cl)	3	1
University of Michigan (Ph.D.) (Cl)	3	3
University of Minnesota (Ph.D.) (Cl)	–	–
University of Missouri, Columbia (Ph.D.) (Cl)	2	1
University of North Carolina, Chapel Hill (Ph.D.) (Cl)	1	2
University of North Carolina, Greensboro (Ph.D.) (Cl)	1	1
University of North Texas (Ph.D.) (Cl)	1	1
University of Notre Dame (Ph.D.) P(Cl)	3	1
University of Oregon (Ph.D.) (Cl)	2	3
University of Pennsylvania (Ph.D.) (Cl)	1	1
University of Pittsburgh (Ph.D.) (Cl)	5	17
University of Rochester (Ph.D.) (Cl)	3	2
University of South Florida (Ph.D.) (Cl)	1	–
University of Southern California (Ph.D.) (Cl)	3	0
University of Texas at Austin (Ph.D.) (Cl)	1	3
University of Texas at Austin (Ph.D.) (Co)	2	0
University of Texas Southwestern Medical Center (Ph.D.) (Cl)	6	6
University of Toledo (Ph.D.) (Cl)	5	1
University of Vermont (Ph.D.) (Cl)	1	1
University of Washington (Ph.D.) (Cl)	3	1
University of Wisconsin, Madison (Ph.D.) (Cl)	8	6
University of Wisconsin, Milwaukee (Ph.D.) (Cl)	2	1
Vanderbilt University (Ph.D.) (Cl)	4	2
Virginia Polytechnic Institute and State University (Ph.D.) (Cl)	3	1
Western Michigan University (Ph.D.) (Cl)	3	0
Wheaton College (Psy.D.) (Cl)	1	0
Yale University (Ph.D.) (Cl)	1	0
Yeshiva University (Psy.D.) (Cl)	3	1

Affective/Social Neurosience

Chicago School of Professional Psychology–Chicago Campus (Psy.D.) (Cl)	3	1
Stony Brook University, State University of New York (Ph.D.) (Cl)	5	7

African American Studies (also see Minority/Diversity)

	# Faculty	# Grants
Howard University (Ph.D.) (Co)	2	0
The University of Akron (Ph.D.) (Co)	2	1
University of Georgia (Ph.D.) (Co)	1	0
University of Missouri, Columbia (Ph.D.) (Co)	1	0

Aggression/Anger Control

Colorado State University (Ph.D.) (Co)	1	0
Georgia State University (Ph.D.) (Cl)	1	1
Iowa State University (Ph.D.) (Co)	1	0
Long Island University, C.W. Post Campus (Psy.D.) (Cl)	1	0
Marywood University (Psy.D.) (Cl)	1	0
Philadelphia College of Osteopathic Medicine (Psy.D.) (Cl)	1	0
Purdue University (Ph.D.) (Cl)	4	2
St. John's University (Ph.D.) (Cl)	3	0
Temple University (Ph.D.) (Cl)	1	0
University of Arkansas (Ph.D.) (Cl)	6	3
University of Georgia (Ph.D.) (Cl)	1	–
University of Georgia (Ph.D.) (Co)	2	2
University of Kansas–Child (Ph.D.) (Cl)	1	1
University of Southern Mississippi (Ph.D.) (Co)	1	0

Aging/Gerontology/Adult Development

Adler University–Chicago (Psy.D.) (Cl)	3	–
Arizona School of Professional Psychology at Argosy University, Phoenix (Psy.D.) (Cl)	2	0
Arizona State University (Ph.D.) (Co)	1	–
Boston University (Ph.D.) (Cl)	2	2
Carlos Albizu University, San Juan Campus (Ph.D.) (Cl)	1	–
Case Western Reserve University (Ph.D.) (Cl)	1	0
Chatham University (Psy.D.) (Co)	1	0
Colorado State University (Ph.D.) (Co)	3	1
Divine Mercy University (Psy.D.) (Cl)	1	–
Eastern Michigan University (Ph.D.) (Cl)	2	1
Florida Institute of Technology (Psy.D.) (Cl)	2	1
Gallaudet University (Ph.D.) (Cl)	2	0
George Mason University (Ph.D.) (Cl)	1	–
Georgia State University (Ph.D.) (Cl)	2	1
Kean University (Psy.D.) (Cm)	1	0
Lehigh University (Ph.D.) (Co)	1	0
Loyola University Maryland (Psy.D.) (Cl)	2	0
Marquette University (Ph.D.) (Cl)	1	0
Marshall University (Psy.D.) (Cl)	2	0
Midwestern University (Psy.D.) (Cl)	2	–
Midwestern University–Glendale Campus (Psy.D.) (Cl)	1	0
Nova Southeastern University (Ph.D.) (Cl)	1	1
Nova Southeastern University (Psy.D.) (Cl)	1	1
Oklahoma State University (Ph.D.) (Co)	1	1
Palo Alto University (Ph.D.) (Cl)	3	–
Philadelphia College of Osteopathic Medicine (Psy.D.) (Cl)	1	0
Queens College and The Graduate Center, City University of New York (Ph.D.) (Cl)	1	0
Rosalind Franklin University of Medicine and Science (Ph.D.) (Cl)	1	0
Saint Louis University (Ph.D.) (Cl)	1	0
Saint Mary's University of Minnesota (Psy.D.) (Co)	1	0
San Diego State University–UC San Diego (Ph.D.) (Cl)	13	>1
Teachers College, Columbia University (Ph.D.) (Cl)	1	0
Texas A&M University (Ph.D.) (Cl)	1	–
The University of Montana (Ph.D.) (Cl)	2	1
The Wright Institute (Psy.D.) (Cl)	1	–
University of Alabama at Birmingham (Ph.D.) (Cl)	4	3
University of Alabama at Tuscaloosa (Ph.D.) (Cl)	6	5
University of Alaska Fairbanks-Anchorage (Ph.D.) (Cl)	1	0
University of California, Berkeley (Ph.D.) (Cl)	1	1
University of Central Florida (Ph.D.) (Cl)	1	0
University of Colorado at Colorado Springs (Ph.D.) (Cl)	7	5
University of Georgia (Ph.D.) (Cl)	3	2
University of Illinois at Urbana-Champaign (Ph.D.) (Co)	1	–
University of Indianapolis (Psy.D.) (Cl)	2	1
University of Kansas (Ph.D.) (Cl)	2	2
University of Louisville (Ph.D.) (Cl)	2	1
University of Maine (Ph.D.) (Cl)	2	0
University of Massachusetts Amherst (Ph.D.) (Cl)	1	0
University of Massachusetts, Boston (Ph.D.) (Co)	1	1
University of Michigan (Ph.D.) (Cl)	1	3
University of Missouri, St. Louis (Ph.D.) (Cl)	1	1
University of Nevada, Reno (Ph.D.) (Cl)	1	1
University of North Dakota (Ph.D.) (Co)	1	0
University of North Texas (Ph.D.) (Co)	1	0
University of Pittsburgh (Ph.D.) (Cl)	1	3
University of Southern California (Ph.D.) (Cl)	2	2
University of Texas at Austin (Ph.D.) (Cl)	1	4
University of Tulsa (Ph.D.) (Cl)	2	1
University of Wyoming (Ph.D.) (Cl)	1	0
Utah State University (Ph.D.) (Cm)	1	1
Washington University in St. Louis (Ph.D.) (Cl)	3	1

	# Faculty	# Grants
West Virginia University (Ph.D.) (Cl)	2	1
Xavier University (Psy.D.) (Cl)	1	0
Yeshiva University (Ph.D.) (Cl)	2	2
Yeshiva University (Psy.D.) (Cl)	1	0

Alcohol (also see Substance Abuse/ Addictive Behaviors)

Auburn University (Ph.D.) (Cl)	1	0
Bowling Green State University (Ph.D.) (Cl)	1	0
Georgia Southern University (Psy.D.) (Cl)	1	0
Georgia State University (Ph.D.) (Cl)	1	1
Jackson State University (Ph.D.) (Cl)	2	0
Northwestern University Feinberg School of Medicine (Ph.D.) (Cl)	1	1
San Diego State University–UC San Diego (Ph.D.) (Cl)	10	>1
Syracuse University (Ph.D.) (Cl)	4	14
University of Alaska Fairbanks-Anchorage (Ph.D.) (Cl)	1	1
University of Central Florida (Ph.D.) (Cl)	1	0
University of Detroit Mercy (Ph.D.) (Cl)	2	1
University of Georgia (Ph.D.) (Cl)	3	1
University of Maryland-College Park (Ph.D.) (Co)	1	1
University of Pittsburgh (Ph.D.) (Cl)	3	8
University of Southern California (Ph.D.) (Cl)	1	1
University of Wisconsin, Milwaukee (Ph.D.) (Cl)	3	7

Altruism/Pro-Social Behavior

Midwestern University–Glendale Campus (Psy.D.) (Cl)	2	0
Sam Houston State University (Ph.D.) (Cl)	1	–
Teachers College, Columbia University (Ph.D.) (Cl)	1	0
University of Detroit Mercy (Ph.D.) (Cl)	1	0
Wichita State University (Ph.D.) (Cl)	1	0

Alzheimer's Disease

Marquette University (Ph.D.) (Cl)	1	2
Northwestern University Feinberg School of Medicine (Ph.D.) (Cl)	2	1
Ponce Health Sciences University (Ph.D.) (Cl)	1	0
San Diego State University–UC San Diego (Ph.D.) (Cl)	14	>1
University of Georgia (Ph.D.) (Cl)	2	–
University of Massachusetts, Boston (Ph.D.) (Co)	1	1
University of Texas Southwestern Medical Center (Ph.D.) (Cl)	1	1
Virginia Consortium Program in Clinical Psychology (Ph.D.) (Cl)	2	0

Anxiety Disorders/Panic Disorders

Adler University–Chicago (Psy.D.) (Cl)	1	–
American University (Ph.D.) (Cl)	3	0
Auburn University (Ph.D.) (Cl)	2	1
Baylor University (Psy.D.) (Cl)	2	2
Binghamton University, State University of New York (Ph.D.) (Cl)	2	1
Biola University (Ph.D.) (Cl)	6	1
Biola University (Psy.D.) (Cl)	6	1
Boston University (Ph.D.) (Cl)	8	8
Brigham Young University (Ph.D.) (Cl)	2	1
Carlos Albizu University, Miami Campus (Psy.D.) (Cl)	2	0
Carlos Albizu University, San Juan Campus (Ph.D.) (Cl)	1	–
Case Western Reserve University (Ph.D.) (Cl)	2	1
Catholic University of America (Ph.D.) (Cl)	4	1
Chicago School of Professional Psychology–Washington, DC Campus (Psy.D.) (Cl)	1	0
Clark University (Ph.D.) (Cl)	4	0
Colorado State University (Ph.D.) (Co)	1	0
Divine Mercy University (Psy.D.) (Cl)	1	–
Florida International University (Ph.D.) (Cl)	2	2
Florida State University (Ph.D.) (Cl)	5	2
George Mason University (Ph.D.) (Cl)	3	–
George Washington University (Ph.D.) (Cl)	1	0
Georgia State University (Ph.D.) (Cl)	2	1
Harvard University (Ph.D.) (Cl)	2	1
Idaho State University (Ph.D.) (Cl)	1	–
Illinois Institute of Technology (Ph.D.) (Cl)	1	1
Kent State University (Ph.D.) (Cl)	2	1
Marquette University (Ph.D.) (Cl)	3	0
Miami University (OH) (Ph.D.) (Cl)	4	1
Northern Illinois University (Ph.D.) (Cl)	3	0
Northwestern University (Ph.D.) (Cl)	3	1
Oklahoma State University (Ph.D.) (Cl)	1	1
Pacific University, Oregon (Psy.D.) (Cl)	2	0
Palo Alto University (Psy.D.) (Cl)	3	2
Pennsylvania State University (Ph.D.) (Cl)	4	2
Philadelphia College of Osteopathic Medicine (Psy.D.) (Cl)	11	0
Queens College and The Graduate Center, City University of New York (Ph.D.) (Cl)	1	0
Rosalind Franklin University of Medicine and Science (Ph.D.) (Cl)	1	0
Rutgers-The State University of New Jersey (Psy.D.) (Cl)	1	–
Saint Louis University (Ph.D.) (Cl)	2	0
San Diego State University–UC San Diego (Ph.D.) (Cl)	10	>1

	# Faculty	# Grants
Seattle Pacific University (Ph.D.) (Cl)	2	1
Southern Illinois University Carbondale (Ph.D.) (Cl)	2	2
Temple University (Ph.D.) (Cl)	2	1
Texas Tech University (Ph.D.) (Cl)	2	0
The Ohio State University (Ph.D.) (Cl)	1	0
The Wright Institute (Psy.D.) (Cl)	1	–
University at Buffalo, State University of New York (Ph.D.) (Cl)	3	1
University of Arkansas (Ph.D.) (Cl)	3	1
University of California, Los Angeles (Ph.D.) (Cl)	3	7
University of Central Florida (Ph.D.) (Cl)	1	0
University of Connecticut (Ph.D.) (Cl)	2	1
University of Delaware (Ph.D.) (Cl)	2	1
University of Florida (Ph.D.) (Cl)	2	1
University of Georgia (Ph.D.) (Cl)	1	–
University of Hawaii at Manoa (Ph.D.) (Cl)	1	0
University of Houston (Ph.D.) (Cl)	2	3
University of Illinois at Chicago (Ph.D.) (Cl)	3	3
University of Illinois at Urbana-Champaign (Ph.D.) (Cl)	1	0
University of Iowa (Ph.D.) (Co)	1	0
University of La Verne (Psy.D.) (Cl)	2	1
University of Louisville (Ph.D.) (Cl)	1	0
University of Maine (Ph.D.) (Cl)	2	0
University of Maryland-College Park (Ph.D.) (Cl)	4	2
University of Massachusetts, Boston (Ph.D.) (Cl)	2	2
University of Minnesota (Ph.D.) (Cl)	–	–
University of Missouri, Columbia (Ph.D.) (Cl)	2	1
University of Nebraska, Lincoln (Ph.D.) (Cl)	1	1
University of Nevada, Reno (Ph.D.) (Cl)	3	1
University of North Carolina, Chapel Hill (Ph.D.) (Cl)	1	0
University of North Dakota (Ph.D.) (Cl)	1	0
University of Pennsylvania (Ph.D.) (Cl)	2	2
University of Rochester (Ph.D.) (Cl)	1	0
University of Southern Mississippi (Ph.D.) (Cl)	–	–
University of Texas at Austin (Ph.D.) (Cl)	2	1
University of Toledo (Ph.D.) (Cl)	5	1
University of Virginia (Ph.D.) (Cl)	1	1
University of Washington (Ph.D.) (Cl)	3	3
University of Wisconsin, Milwaukee (Ph.D.) (Cl)	4	4
Vanderbilt University (Ph.D.) (Cl)	1	2
Virginia Commonwealth University (Ph.D.) (Cl)	3	1
Virginia Polytechnic Institute and State University (Ph.D.) (Cl)	8	2
West Virginia University (Ph.D.) (Cl)	5	2
Western Michigan University (Ph.D.) (Cl)	2	0
Yale University (Ph.D.) (Cl)	1	0
Yeshiva University (Psy.D.) (Cl)	3	0

Antisocial Behavior/Psychopathy

Drexel University (Ph.D.) (Cl)	1	0
Florida State University (Ph.D.) (Cl)	2	1
Indiana University–Bloomington (Ph.D.) (Cl)	4	2
John Jay College of Criminal Justice & The Graduate Center, CUNY (Ph.D.) (Cl)	1	0
Michigan State University (Ph.D.) (Cl)	1	2
Pacific University, Oregon (Psy.D.) (Cl)	1	0
Purdue University (Ph.D.) (Cl)	4	2
Rosalind Franklin University of Medicine and Science (Ph.D.) (Cl)	1	1
University of Minnesota (Ph.D.) (Cl)	–	–
University of Nevada Las Vegas (Ph.D.) (Cl)	1	1
University of Pittsburgh (Ph.D.) (Cl)	1	4

Applied Behavioral Analysis

Eastern Michigan University (Ph.D.) (Cl)	2	0
Hofstra University (Ph.D.) (Cl)	2	0
Rutgers-The State University of New Jersey (Ph.D.) (Cl)	1	0
Rutgers-The State University of New Jersey (Psy.D.) (Cl)	1	–
University of Massachusetts, Boston (Ph.D.) (Co)	3	2
University of North Dakota (Ph.D.) (Cl)	2	0

Asian Studies (also see Minority/Diversity)

Indiana University–Bloomington (Ph.D.) (Co)	1	–
Iowa State University (Ph.D.) (Co)	1	1
The Wright Institute (Psy.D.) (Cl)	3	–
University of Alaska Fairbanks-Anchorage (Ph.D.) (Cl)	1	0
University of Maryland-College Park (Ph.D.) (Co)	2	1
Wheaton College (Psy.D.) (Cl)	2	0

Assessment/Diagnosis

Alliant International University, Fresno (Psy.D.) (Cl)	3	1
Alliant International University, Los Angeles (Psy.D.) (Cl)	3	0
Alliant International University, Sacramento (Psy.D.) (Cl)	1	0
Alliant International University, San Diego (Ph.D.) (Cl)	4	0
Alliant International University, San Diego (Psy.D.) (Cl)	2	0
Alliant International University, San Francisco Bay (Ph.D.) (Cl)	1	0

	# Faculty	# Grants
Alliant International University, San Francisco Bay (Psy.D.) (Cl)	3	0
Arizona State University (Ph.D.) (Co)	2	–
Auburn University (Ph.D.) (Cl)	1	0
Azusa Pacific University (Psy.D.) (Cl)	2	0
Brigham Young University (Ph.D.) (Cl)	4	2
California Lutheran University (Psy.D.) (Cl)	2	0
Catholic University of America (Ph.D.) (Cl)	2	2
Chicago School of Professional Psychology–Washington, DC Campus (Psy.D.) (Cl)	1	0
Colorado State University (Ph.D.) (Co)	3	1
Divine Mercy University (Psy.D.) (Cl)	2	–
Fairleigh Dickinson University (Ph.D.) (Cl)	4	1
Florida School of Professional Psychology at Argosy University (Psy.D.) (Cl)	4	0
Gallaudet University (Ph.D.) (Cl)	1	0
Idaho State University (Ph.D.) (Cl)	1	–
Indiana State University (Psy.D.) (Cl)	3	0
Jackson State University (Ph.D.) (Cl)	6	0
John F. Kennedy University (Psy.D.) (Cl)	3	0
John Jay College of Criminal Justice & The Graduate Center, CUNY (Ph.D.) (Cl)	2	0
Louisiana Tech University (Ph.D.) (Co)	1	0
Minnesota School of Professional Psychology at Argosy University (Psy.D.) (Cl)	1	0
Northwestern University Feinberg School of Medicine (Ph.D.) (Cl)	2	3
Palo Alto University (Ph.D.) (Cl)	2	–
Pepperdine University (Psy.D.) (Cl)	2	1
Philadelphia College of Osteopathic Medicine (Psy.D.) (Cl)	3	0
Ponce Health Sciences University (Ph.D.) (Cl)	5	0
Ponce Health Sciences University (Psy.D.) (Cl)	5	1
Regent University (Psy.D.) (Cl)	1	–
Roosevelt University (Psy.D.) (Cl)	4	0
Rutgers-The State University of New Jersey (Psy.D.) (Cl)	1	–
Saint Louis University (Ph.D.) (Cl)	2	0
Sam Houston State University (Ph.D.) (Cl)	3	1
Southern Illinois University Carbondale (Ph.D.) (Cl)	4	0
Stony Brook University, State University of New York (Ph.D.) (Cl)	1	–
Texas A&M University (Ph.D.) (Cl)	4	–
Texas Tech University (Ph.D.) (Cl)	3	0
The New School (Ph.D.) (Cl)	2	1
The University of Memphis (Ph.D.) (Co)	1	0
The University of Montana (Ph.D.) (Cl)	6	1
The Wright Institute (Psy.D.) (Cl)	7	–
University at Buffalo, State University of New York (Ph.D.) (Cm)	4	1
University of Alabama at Tuscaloosa (Ph.D.) (Cl)	2	0
University of California, Santa Barbara (Ph.D.) (Cm)	1	–
University of Colorado Boulder (Ph.D.) (Cl)	2	1
University of Denver (Psy.D.) (Cl)	1	0
University of Detroit Mercy (Ph.D.) (Cl)	3	0
University of Georgia (Ph.D.) (Cl)	5	1
University of Georgia (Ph.D.) (Co)	1	1
University of Hartford (Psy.D.) (Cl)	2	0
University of Hawaii at Manoa (Ph.D.) (Cl)	2	3
University of Kentucky (Ph.D.) (Cl)	3	0
University of Massachusetts Amherst (Ph.D.) (Cl)	2	0
University of Mississippi (Ph.D.) (Cl)	2	0
University of Nevada, Reno (Ph.D.) (Cl)	1	0
University of North Dakota (Ph.D.) (Co)	1	0
University of Northern Colorado (Ph.D.) (Co)	1	0
University of South Alabama (Ph.D.) (Cm)	1	–
University of Texas at Austin (Ph.D.) (Co)	1	0
University of Toledo (Ph.D.) (Cl)	4	0
Virginia Polytechnic Institute and State University (Ph.D.) (Cl)	3	0
Wayne State University (Ph.D.) (Cl)	4	2
Western Michigan University (Ph.D.) (Co)	2	0
Widener University (Psy.D.) (Cl)	5	0
Wisconsin School of Professional Psychology (Psy.D.) (Cl)	–	–
Yeshiva University (Psy.D.) (Cm)	2	0

Attachment

California Lutheran University (Psy.D.) (Cl)	2	0
Carlow University (Psy.D.) (Co)	2	–
Catholic University of America (Ph.D.) (Cl)	3	1
Chicago School of Professional Psychology–Washington, DC Campus (Psy.D.) (Cl)	1	0
Gallaudet University (Ph.D.) (Cl)	1	0
George Washington University (Psy.D.) (Cl)	1	–
Iowa State University (Ph.D.) (Co)	1	0
James Madison University (Psy.D.) (Cm)	2	0
Long Island University, C.W. Post Campus (Psy.D.) (Cl)	1	1
Michigan State University (Ph.D.) (Cl)	2	1
Queens College and The Graduate Center, City University of New York (Ph.D.) (Cl)	1	0
Sam Houston State University (Ph.D.) (Cl)	1	–
The Wright Institute (Psy.D.) (Cl)	4	–
University of Delaware (Ph.D.) (Cl)	2	2
University of Houston (Ph.D.) (Co)	1	2
University of Maryland-College Park (Ph.D.) (Co)	1	0
University of Northern Colorado (Ph.D.) (Co)	2	0
Widener University (Psy.D.) (Cl)	3	0
Yeshiva University (Psy.D.) (Cm)	3	0

Attention

	# Faculty	# Grants
Gallaudet University (Ph.D.) (Cl)	2	1
Oklahoma State University (Ph.D.) (Cl)	1	1
Seattle Pacific University (Ph.D.) (Cl)	1	1
Stony Brook University, State University of New York (Ph.D.) (Cl)	2	2
The Wright Institute (Psy.D.) (Cl)	2	–
University of Missouri Kansas City (Ph.D.) (Cl)	2	1
University of North Carolina, Chapel Hill (Ph.D.) (Cl)	1	1
Virginia Polytechnic Institute and State University (Ph.D.) (Cl)	1	1

Attention Deficit/Hyperactivity Disorder

Arizona School of Professional Psychology at Argosy University, Phoenix (Psy.D.) (Cl)	1	0
Auburn University (Ph.D.) (Cl)	1	0
Carlos Albizu University, San Juan Campus (Ph.D.) (Cl)	1	–
Colorado State University (Ph.D.) (Co)	1	0
Divine Mercy University (Psy.D.) (Cl)	1	–
Emory University (Ph.D.) (Cl)	1	0
Fairleigh Dickinson University (Ph.D.) (Cl)	2	0
Florida International University (Ph.D.) (Cl)	9	10
Marquette University (Ph.D.) (Cl)	1	1
Philadelphia College of Osteopathic Medicine (Psy.D.) (Cl)	1	0
Saint Louis University (Ph.D.) (Cl)	2	1
Southern Illinois University Carbondale (Ph.D.) (Cl)	1	3
Syracuse University (Ph.D.) (Cl)	1	2
The Wright Institute (Psy.D.) (Cl)	3	–
University at Buffalo, State University of New York (Ph.D.) (Cl)	1	0
University at Buffalo, State University of New York (Ph.D.) (Cm)	1	1
University of California, Berkeley (Ph.D.) (Cl)	1	2
University of Central Florida (Ph.D.) (Cl)	1	0
University of Denver (Ph.D.) (Cl)	1	1
University of Hawaii at Manoa (Ph.D.) (Cl)	1	0
University of Iowa (Ph.D.) (Cl)	2	1
University of North Texas (Ph.D.) (Co)	2	1
University of Pittsburgh (Ph.D.) (Cl)	1	6
University of Wyoming (Ph.D.) (Cl)	1	0
Yeshiva University (Psy.D.) (Cm)	2	0

Attributions

The Wright Institute (Psy.D.) (Cl)	1	–
University of Georgia (Ph.D.) (Co)	2	0

Autism/Asperger's Syndrome/Developmental Disorders

Binghamton University, State University of New York (Ph.D.) (Cl)	4	3
Brigham Young University (Ph.D.) (Cl)	2	2
Case Western Reserve University (Ph.D.) (Cl)	1	0
Chatham University (Psy.D.) (Co)	1	0
Emory University (Ph.D.) (Cl)	1	4
Idaho State University (Ph.D.) (Cl)	1	–
Indiana University–Bloomington (Ph.D.) (Cl)	4	2
Kean University (Psy.D.) (Cm)	3	1
Long Island University (Ph.D.) (Cl)	3	0
Marquette University (Ph.D.) (Cl)	1	0
Michigan State University (Ph.D.) (Cl)	1	3
Midwestern University (Psy.D.) (Cl)	1	–
Midwestern University–Glendale Campus (Psy.D.) (Cl)	1	0
Northwestern University Feinberg School of Medicine (Ph.D.) (Cl)	1	2
Palo Alto University (Psy.D.) (Cl)	3	3
Pennsylvania State University (Ph.D.) (Cl)	1	0
Pepperdine University (Psy.D.) (Cl)	1	0
Rutgers-The State University of New Jersey (Ph.D.) (Cl)	1	1
Rutgers-The State University of New Jersey (Psy.D.) (Cl)	1	–
Saint Louis University (Ph.D.) (Cl)	1	0
San Diego State University–UC San Diego (Ph.D.) (Cl)	10	>1
Seattle Pacific University (Ph.D.) (Cl)	1	0
Stony Brook University, State University of New York (Ph.D.) (Cl)	1	14
Syracuse University (Ph.D.) (Cl)	1	2
The University of Montana (Ph.D.) (Cl)	1	0
The Wright Institute (Psy.D.) (Cl)	3	–
University at Albany (Ph.D.) (Cl)	1	–
University of Alabama at Tuscaloosa (Ph.D.) (Cl)	2	2
University of California, Santa Barbara (Ph.D.) (Cm)	1	–
University of Connecticut (Ph.D.) (Cl)	3	3
University of Hawaii at Manoa (Ph.D.) (Cl)	1	1
University of Illinois at Urbana-Champaign (Ph.D.) (Cl)	1	0
University of Kansas–Child (Ph.D.) (Cl)	1	1
University of Missouri, Columbia (Ph.D.) (Cl)	1	3
University of Pennsylvania (Ph.D.) (Cl)	1	1
University of Pittsburgh (Ph.D.) (Cl)	3	3
University of Rochester (Ph.D.) (Cl)	1	1
University of South Alabama (Ph.D.) (Cm)	1	–
University of Texas at Austin (Ph.D.) (Cl)	1	0
University of Virginia (Ph.D.) (Cm)	1	2
University of Washington (Ph.D.) (Cl)	1	1
University of Wisconsin, Milwaukee (Ph.D.) (Cl)	1	2

	# Faculty	# Grants
Vanderbilt University (Ph.D.) (Cl)	1	1
Virginia Polytechnic Institute and State University (Ph.D.) (Cl)	4	2

Behavioral Analysis/Therapy

Divine Mercy University (Psy.D.) (Cl)	1	–
Hofstra University (Ph.D.) (Cl)	3	0
University of Nevada, Reno (Ph.D.) (Cl)	3	0
Yeshiva University (Psy.D.) (Cm)	4	1

Bereavement/Grief

Biola University (Ph.D.) (Cl)	1	0
Biola University (Psy.D.) (Cl)	1	0
Midwestern University–Glendale Campus (Psy.D.) (Cl)	1	0
Minnesota School of Professional Psychology at Argosy University (Psy.D.) (Cl)	1	0
Palo Alto University (Ph.D.) (Cl)	1	–
Purdue University (Ph.D.) (Co)	1	0
Saint Mary's University of Minnesota (Psy.D.) (Co)	2	0
San Diego State University–UC San Diego (Ph.D.) (Cl)	2	>1
University of Hawaii at Manoa (Ph.D.) (Cl)	1	1
University of Maryland-College Park (Ph.D.) (Co)	1	0
University of Nevada, Reno (Ph.D.) (Cl)	2	0
University of Northern Colorado (Ph.D.) (Co)	1	0

Biofeedback/Relaxation

James Madison University (Psy.D.) (Cm)	1	0
Pennsylvania State University (Ph.D.) (Cl)	1	1
University of North Dakota (Ph.D.) (Cl)	1	0

Brain Injury/Head Injury

Brigham Young University (Ph.D.) (Cl)	3	2
Divine Mercy University (Psy.D.) (Cl)	1	–
Georgia State University (Ph.D.) (Cl)	1	1
Northwestern University Feinberg School of Medicine (Ph.D.) (Cl)	1	1
Saint Louis University (Ph.D.) (Cl)	1	0
Southern Illinois University Carbondale (Ph.D.) (Co)	1	1
The University of Montana (Ph.D.) (Cl)	1	0
The Wright Institute (Psy.D.) (Cl)	1	–
University of Georgia (Ph.D.) (Cl)	1	–
University of Nebraska, Lincoln (Ph.D.) (Cl)	1	1

Bullying

Auburn University (Ph.D.) (Cl)	1	1
Iowa State University (Ph.D.) (Co)	1	0
Miami University (OH) (Ph.D.) (Cl)	1	0
Michigan State University (Ph.D.) (Cl)	1	0
Palo Alto University (Psy.D.) (Cl)	1	1
The Wright Institute (Psy.D.) (Cl)	1	–
University at Buffalo, State University of New York (Ph.D.) (Cm)	1	2
University of Kansas–Child (Ph.D.) (Cl)	2	1
Vanderbilt University (Ph.D.) (Cl)	1	0
Wichita State University (Ph.D.) (Cl)	1	0

Cardiovascular Health

East Carolina University (Ph.D.) (Cl)	2	4
Kent State University (Ph.D.) (Cl)	1	2
Northwestern University Feinberg School of Medicine (Ph.D.) (Cl)	1	1
San Diego State University–UC San Diego (Ph.D.) (Cl)	6	>1
Syracuse University (Ph.D.) (Cl)	2	5
The Ohio State University (Ph.D.) (Cl)	1	3
The Wright Institute (Psy.D.) (Cl)	2	–
Uniformed Services University of the Health Sciences (Ph.D.) (Cl)	1	1
University of Colorado Denver (Ph.D.) (Cl)	3	2
University of Georgia (Ph.D.) (Cl)	3	–
University of Kansas (Ph.D.) (Cl)	1	0
University of Maryland, Baltimore County (Ph.D.) (Cl)	1	6
University of Miami (Ph.D.) (Cl)	4	2
University of Missouri Kansas City (Ph.D.) (Cl)	1	1
University of Pittsburgh (Ph.D.) (Cl)	6	10
West Virginia University (Ph.D.) (Cl)	1	0

Child Abuse/Neglect/Sexual Abuse

Carlos Albizu University, San Juan Campus (Ph.D.) (Cl)	1	–
Chicago School of Professional Psychology–Chicago Campus (Psy.D.) (Cl)	2	1
DePaul University (Ph.D.) (Cl)	1	0
Fairleigh Dickinson University (Ph.D.) (Cl)	2	0
Georgia Southern University (Psy.D.) (Cl)	1	0
John Jay College of Criminal Justice & The Graduate Center, CUNY (Ph.D.) (Cl)	1	2
Kean University (Psy.D.) (Cm)	3	1
Marquette University (Ph.D.) (Co)	2	0
Northern Illinois University (Ph.D.) (Cl)	2	0
Northwestern University Feinberg School of Medicine (Ph.D.) (Cl)	3	2
Philadelphia College of Osteopathic Medicine (Psy.D.) (Cl)	1	0

	# Faculty	# Grants
St. John's University (Ph.D.) (Cl)	1	1
Stony Brook University, State University of New York (Ph.D.) (Cl)	1	1
Texas Tech University (Ph.D.) (Cl)	3	0
The University of Montana (Ph.D.) (Cl)	1	0
University of California, Santa Barbara (Ph.D.) (Cm)	1	–
University of Denver (Ph.D.) (Cl)	2	0
University of Georgia (Ph.D.) (Cl)	2	–
University of Iowa (Ph.D.) (Cl)	1	1
University of Michigan (Ph.D.) (Cl)	1	–
University of Minnesota (Ph.D.) (Co)	2	0
University of Nebraska, Lincoln (Ph.D.) (Cl)	3	2
University of Oregon (Ph.D.) (Cl)	2	1
University of Rochester (Ph.D.) (Cl)	1	3
University of Southern California (Ph.D.) (Cl)	3	1
Western Michigan University (Ph.D.) (Cl)	1	1

Child and Family

Alliant International University, Fresno (Ph.D.) (Cl)	1	0
Alliant International University, Los Angeles (Psy.D.) (Cl)	4	0
Alliant International University, Sacramento (Psy.D.) (Cl)	1	0
Alliant International University, San Diego (Ph.D.) (Cl)	4	1
Alliant International University, San Francisco Bay (Psy.D.) (Cl)	9	0
American School of Professional Psychology at Argosy University, Washington, DC (Psy.D.) (Cl)	3	–
California Lutheran University (Psy.D.) (Cl)	4	2
Eastern Michigan University (Ph.D.) (Cl)	3	2
Georgia State University (Ph.D.) (Cl)	7	5
Howard University (Ph.D.) (Cl)	2	1
Indiana University–Bloomington (Ph.D.) (Cl)	3	3
Ohio University (Ph.D.) (Cl)	3	3
The Wright Institute (Psy.D.) (Cl)	4	–
University at Albany (Ph.D.) (Cl)	4	–
University of California, Los Angeles (Ph.D.) (Cl)	3	5
University of California, Santa Barbara (Ph.D.) (Cm)	1	–
University of Georgia (Ph.D.) (Cl)	5	3
University of Indianapolis (Psy.D.) (Cl)	2	1
University of Massachusetts Amherst (Ph.D.) (Cl)	6	0
University of Oregon (Ph.D.) (Co)	3	2
University of South Carolina (Ph.D.) (Cl)	5	12
University of Southern Mississippi (Ph.D.) (Cl)	–	–
Wright State University (Psy.D.) (Cl)	2	–

Child Clinical/Pediatric

University of Delaware (Ph.D.) (Cl)	4	3
University of Miami (Ph.D.) (Cl)	9	8
University of Kansas–Child (Ph.D.) (Cl)	9	5
Arizona State University (Ph.D.) (Cl)	8	6
University of Alabama at Birmingham (Ph.D.) (Cl)	7	8
Northern Illinois University (Ph.D.) (Cl)	7	1
Pacific University, Oregon (Psy.D.) (Cl)	7	0
Virginia Commonwealth University (Ph.D.) (Cl)	6	4
Virginia Polytechnic Institute and State University (Ph.D.) (Cl)	6	3
West Virginia University (Ph.D.) (Cl)	6	3
Brigham Young University (Ph.D.) (Cl)	6	3
University of Georgia (Ph.D.) (Cl)	5	–
Boston College (Ph.D.) (Co)	5	5
University of Cincinnati (Ph.D.) (Cl)	5	4
Pennsylvania State University (Ph.D.) (Cl)	5	3
University of Virginia (Ph.D.) (Cm)	5	2
Fielding Graduate University (Ph.D.) (Cl)	5	0
Roosevelt University (Psy.D.) (Cl)	5	0
Palo Alto University (Ph.D.) (Cl)	4	–
University of South Florida (Ph.D.) (Cl)	4	8
University of Nebraska, Lincoln (Ph.D.) (Cl)	4	6
University of Houston (Ph.D.) (Cl)	4	5
University of Texas Southwestern Medical Center (Ph.D.) (Cl)	4	4
Florida State University (Ph.D.) (Cl)	4	4
University of Alabama at Tuscaloosa (Ph.D.) (Cl)	4	4
Florida International University (Ph.D.) (Cl)	4	3
Antioch University New England (Psy.D.) (Cl)	4	3
University of Florida (Ph.D.) (Cl)	4	3
University of Hawaii at Manoa (Ph.D.) (Cl)	4	3
Binghamton University, State University of New York (Ph.D.) (Cl)	4	3
Fuller Theological Seminary (Psy.D.) (Cl)	4	2
Fuller Theological Seminary (Ph.D.) (Cl)	4	2
Northwestern University Feinberg School of Medicine (Ph.D.) (Cl)	4	2
Southern Illinois University Carbondale (Ph.D.) (Cl)	4	1
Auburn University (Ph.D.) (Cl)	4	1
Adelphi University (Ph.D.) (Cl)	4	1
Washington State University (Ph.D.) (Cl)	4	1
Pace University (Psy.D.) (Cm)	4	0
The University of Memphis (Ph.D.) (Cl)	3	4
Seattle Pacific University (Ph.D.) (Cl)	3	3
Oklahoma State University (Ph.D.) (Cl)	3	3
University of Washington (Ph.D.) (Cl)	3	3
University of Utah (Ph.D.) (Cl)	3	3
Fordham University (Ph.D.) (Cl)	3	2
Bowling Green State University (Ph.D.) (Cl)	3	2

	# Faculty	# Grants
Hawaii School of Professional Psychology at Argosy University, Hawaii (Psy.D.) (Cl)	3	1
University of Hartford (Psy.D.) (Cl)	3	1
Catholic University of America (Ph.D.) (Cl)	3	1
Widener University (Psy.D.) (Cl)	3	1
Marquette University (Ph.D.) (Cl)	3	1
Palo Alto University (Psy.D.) (Cl)	3	1
Kean University (Psy.D.) (Cm)	3	1
Ponce Health Sciences University (Psy.D.) (Cl)	3	1
University of Mississippi (Ph.D.) (Cl)	3	0
Florida School of Professional Psychology at Argosy University (Psy.D.) (Cl)	3	0
University of New Mexico (Ph.D.) (Cl)	3	0
Chatham University (Psy.D.) (Co)	3	0
University of North Carolina, Greensboro (Ph.D.) (Cl)	3	0
Virginia Consortium Program in Clinical Psychology (Ph.D.) (Cl)	3	0
Saint Louis University (Ph.D.) (Cl)	3	0
Ball State University (Ph.D.) (Co)	3	0
Texas A&M University (Ph.D.) (Cl)	2	–
University of Illinois at Urbana-Champaign (Ph.D.) (Co)	2	–
Divine Mercy University (Psy.D.) (Cl)	2	–
The Ohio State University (Ph.D.) (Cl)	2	4
University of Kansas (Ph.D.) (Cl)	2	2
University of Kentucky (Ph.D.) (Cl)	2	2
University of Massachusetts, Boston (Ph.D.) (Co)	2	2
East Tennessee State University (Ph.D.) (Cl)	2	2
University of Wisconsin, Milwaukee (Ph.D.) (Cl)	2	2
University of Vermont (Ph.D.) (Cl)	2	2
Rosalind Franklin University of Medicine and Science (Ph.D.) (Cl)	2	2
Vanderbilt University (Ph.D.) (Cl)	2	2
Kent State University (Ph.D.) (Cl)	2	2
University of Missouri Kansas City (Ph.D.) (Cl)	2	1
University of Nevada Las Vegas (Ph.D.) (Cl)	2	1
University of Utah (Ph.D.) (Co)	2	1
University of Colorado Boulder (Ph.D.) (Cl)	2	1
Fairleigh Dickinson University (Ph.D.) (Cl)	2	1
Azusa Pacific University (Psy.D.) (Cl)	2	1
George Washington University (Ph.D.) (Cl)	2	1
Texas Tech University (Ph.D.) (Cl)	2	0
Clark University (Ph.D.) (Cl)	2	0
University of Colorado Denver (Ph.D.) (Cl)	2	0
Western Michigan University (Ph.D.) (Cl)	2	0
Loyola University Chicago (Ph.D.) (Co)	2	0
The University of South Dakota (Ph.D.) (Cl)	2	0
Philadelphia College of Osteopathic Medicine (Psy.D.) (Cl)	2	0
Arizona State University (Ph.D.) (Co)	1	–
University of Michigan (Ph.D.) (Cl)	1	–
University of South Alabama (Ph.D.) (Cm)	1	–
Harvard University (Ph.D.) (Cl)	1	3
Georgia State University (Ph.D.) (Cl)	1	3
University of Missouri, Columbia (Ph.D.) (Co)	1	2
Loma Linda University (Ph.D.) (Cl)	1	2
Syracuse University (Ph.D.) (Cl)	1	2
Loma Linda University (Psy.D.) (Cl)	1	2
Nova Southeastern University (Psy.D.) (Cl)	1	1
Alliant International University, Los Angeles (Ph.D.) (Cl)	1	1
Regent University (Psy.D.) (Cl)	1	1
The New School (Ph.D.) (Cl)	1	1
University of North Texas (Ph.D.) (Cl)	1	1
Yeshiva University (Psy.D.) (Cm)	1	1
Temple University (Ph.D.) (Cl)	1	1
Emory University (Ph.D.) (Cl)	1	1
Nova Southeastern University (Ph.D.) (Cl)	1	1
Ponce Health Sciences University (Ph.D.) (Cl)	1	1
University of Iowa (Ph.D.) (Co)	1	1
Loyola University Chicago (Ph.D.) (Cl)	10	6
University of Northern Colorado (Ph.D.) (Co)	1	0
Jackson State University (Ph.D.) (Cl)	1	0
University of Rhode Island (Ph.D.) (Cl)	1	0
Miami University (OH) (Ph.D.) (Cl)	1	0
La Salle University (Psy.D.) (Cl)	1	0
American University (Ph.D.) (Cl)	1	0
University of Missouri, St. Louis (Ph.D.) (Cl)	1	0
Wheaton College (Psy.D.) (Cl)	1	0
University of Oregon (Ph.D.) (Cl)	1	0
George Fox University (Psy.D.) (Cl)	1	0
University of Central Florida (Ph.D.) (Cl)	1	0
University of Colorado at Colorado Springs (Ph.D.) (Cl)	1	0
Georgia School of Professional Psychology at Argosy University, Atlanta (Psy.D.) (Cl)	1	0
Spalding University (Psy.D.) (Cl)	1	0
Hofstra University (Ph.D.) (Cl)	1	0

Chronic Disease/Illness

Marquette University (Ph.D.) (Cl)	1	0
Northwestern University Feinberg School of Medicine (Ph.D.) (Cl)	2	2
Rosalind Franklin University of Medicine and Science (Ph.D.) (Cl)	1	1
San Diego State University–UC San Diego (Ph.D.) (Cl)	9	>1
Syracuse University (Ph.D.) (Cl)	3	10
University of Georgia (Ph.D.) (Cl)	2	–
University of Kansas–Child (Ph.D.) (Cl)	3	1
University of Nevada, Reno (Ph.D.) (Cl)	1	0

	# Faculty	# Grants
University of North Carolina at Charlotte (Ph.D.) (Cl)	3	1
Wayne State University (Ph.D.) (Cl)	3	2

Clinical Judgment

Ball State University (Ph.D.) (Co)	1	0
Indiana State University (Psy.D.) (Cl)	1	0
Indiana University of Pennsylvania (Psy.D.) (Cl)	1	0
Southern Illinois University Carbondale (Ph.D.) (Cl)	1	0
The University of Memphis (Ph.D.) (Co)	2	0
University of Detroit Mercy (Ph.D.) (Cl)	1	0

Cognition/Social Cognition

American School of Professional Psychology at Argosy University, Washington, DC (Psy.D.) (Cl)	1	0
Carlow University (Psy.D.) (Co)	1	–
Catholic University of America (Ph.D.) (Cl)	4	0
Colorado State University (Ph.D.) (Co)	5	1
Drexel University (Ph.D.) (Cl)	3	1
Duke University (Ph.D.) (Cl)	2	1
Florida International University (Ph.D.) (Cl)	1	1
Fuller Theological Seminary (Ph.D.) (Cl)	1	1
Fuller Theological Seminary (Psy.D.) (Cl)	1	1
Gallaudet University (Ph.D.) (Cl)	2	0
Indiana University–Bloomington (Ph.D.) (Cl)	3	1
John F. Kennedy University (Psy.D.) (Cl)	1	2
Northwestern University (Ph.D.) (Cl)	4	2
Pennsylvania State University (Ph.D.) (Cl)	5	0
Philadelphia College of Osteopathic Medicine (Psy.D.) (Cl)	1	0
Queens College and The Graduate Center, City University of New York (Ph.D.) (Cl)	1	0
Roosevelt University (Psy.D.) (Cl)	1	0
Rutgers–The State University of New Jersey (Psy.D.) (Cl)	1	–
Saint Louis University (Ph.D.) (Cl)	1	0
Saint Mary's University of Minnesota (Psy.D.) (Co)	1	0
Southern Methodist University (Ph.D.) (Cl)	1	0
Springfield College (Psy.D.) (Co)	1	–
Teachers College, Columbia University (Ph.D.) (Co)	1	0
University of Colorado at Colorado Springs (Ph.D.) (Cl)	2	1
University of Denver (Psy.D.) (Cl)	1	0
University of Georgia (Ph.D.) (Cl)	3	2
University of Iowa (Ph.D.) (Cl)	3	3
University of North Carolina at Charlotte (Ph.D.) (Cl)	3	2
Virginia Polytechnic Institute and State University (Ph.D.) (Cl)	2	2
Yale University (Ph.D.) (Cl)	3	3

Cognitive Therapy/Cognitive-Behavioral Therapy

American School of Professional Psychology at Argosy University, Washington, DC (Psy.D.) (Cl)	3	0
Baylor University (Psy.D.) (Cl)	3	1
Divine Mercy University (Psy.D.) (Cl)	4	–
Drexel University (Ph.D.) (Cl)	5	1
Gallaudet University (Ph.D.) (Cl)	1	0
Georgia State University (Ph.D.) (Cl)	1	1
Northwestern University Feinberg School of Medicine (Ph.D.) (Cl)	2	0
Philadelphia College of Osteopathic Medicine (Psy.D.) (Cl)	4	0
Seattle Pacific University (Ph.D.) (Cl)	2	1
Texas Tech University (Ph.D.) (Cl)	1	0
University of California, Berkeley (Ph.D.) (Cl)	2	2
University of Southern California (Ph.D.) (Cl)	2	0
University of Toledo (Ph.D.) (Cl)	1	0
Vanderbilt University (Ph.D.) (Cl)	2	1
Virginia Polytechnic Institute and State University (Ph.D.) (Cl)	10	3
Xavier University (Psy.D.) (Cl)	5	–

College Student

George Fox University (Psy.D.) (Cl)	1	0
Northern Illinois University (Ph.D.) (Cl)	6	0
Pepperdine University (Psy.D.) (Cl)	2	0
University at Buffalo, State University of New York (Ph.D.) (Cm)	1	0
University of Hartford (Psy.D.) (Cl)	2	0
University of Minnesota (Ph.D.) (Co)	2	0
University of Missouri, Columbia (Ph.D.) (Co)	1	0
University of Northern Colorado (Ph.D.) (Co)	1	0
University of Oregon (Ph.D.) (Co)	2	0

Communication–Verbal/Nonverbal

Loyola University Maryland (Psy.D.) (Cl)	1	0
Miami University (OH) (Ph.D.) (Cl)	1	0
Vanderbilt University (Ph.D.) (Cl)	1	0

Community Psychology

Adler University–Chicago (Psy.D.) (Cl)	5	–
Alliant International University, Los Angeles (Ph.D.) (Cl)	3	0

	# Faculty	# Grants
Alliant International University, San Francisco Bay (Ph.D.) (Cl)	4	0
Alliant International University, San Francisco Bay (Psy.D.) (Cl)	5	0
Antioch University New England (Psy.D.) (Cl)	2	4
Arizona State University (Ph.D.) (Cl)	7	5
Boston University (Ph.D.) (Cl)	1	0
Bowling Green State University (Ph.D.) (Cl)	1	1
Catholic University of America (Ph.D.) (Cl)	5	3
Fairleigh Dickinson University (Ph.D.) (Cl)	1	1
Florida International University (Ph.D.) (Cl)	1	1
Florida State University (Ph.D.) (Cm)	3	–
George Washington University (Ph.D.) (Cl)	6	1
Howard University (Ph.D.) (Co)	2	0
Loyola University Chicago (Ph.D.) (Cl)	1	0
Miami University (OH) (Ph.D.) (Cl)	1	1
Pace University (Psy.D.) (Cm)	2	0
Pacific University, Oregon (Psy.D.) (Cl)	2	0
Rutgers–The State University of New Jersey (Psy.D.) (Cl)	1	–
Saint Louis University (Ph.D.) (Cl)	1	0
Texas Tech University (Ph.D.) (Cl)	2	0
The Wright Institute (Psy.D.) (Cl)	3	–
University of Denver (Ph.D.) (Cl)	2	0
University of Hartford (Psy.D.) (Cl)	2	0
University of Illinois at Chicago (Ph.D.) (Cl)	2	2
University of Illinois at Urbana–Champaign (Ph.D.) (Cl)	3	4
University of Maryland, Baltimore County (Ph.D.) (Cl)	3	2
University of Miami (Ph.D.) (Co)	3	3
University of Mississippi (Ph.D.) (Cl)	2	0
University of North Carolina at Charlotte (Ph.D.) (Cl)	5	4
University of North Dakota (Ph.D.) (Cl)	2	0
University of Rhode Island (Ph.D.) (Cl)	1	1
University of South Carolina (Ph.D.) (Cl)	3	4
University of Southern California (Ph.D.) (Cl)	2	2
University of Texas Southwestern Medical Center (Ph.D.) (Cl)	1	0
University of Toledo (Ph.D.) (Cl)	1	0
University of Virginia (Ph.D.) (Cl)	3	3
Virginia Commonwealth University (Ph.D.) (Cl)	10	3
Wheaton College (Psy.D.) (Cl)	1	0
Wichita State University (Ph.D.) (Cl)	1	0

Compliance/Adherence

Philadelphia College of Osteopathic Medicine (Psy.D.) (Cl)	1	0
Rosalind Franklin University of Medicine and Science (Ph.D.) (Cl)	1	1
University of Georgia (Ph.D.) (Cl)	1	–
University of Mississippi (Ph.D.) (Cl)	1	0

Conduct/Disruptive Disorders

Duke University (Ph.D.) (Cl)	2	3
Florida International University (Ph.D.) (Cl)	2	3
Florida State University (Ph.D.) (Cl)	2	1
Seattle Pacific University (Ph.D.) (Cl)	1	0
University of Alabama at Tuscaloosa (Ph.D.) (Cl)	2	1
University of Houston (Ph.D.) (Cl)	2	1
University of Maryland, Baltimore County (Ph.D.) (Cl)	1	0
University of Michigan (Ph.D.) (Cl)	2	2
University of Vermont (Ph.D.) (Cl)	1	0
Virginia Polytechnic Institute and State University (Ph.D.) (Cl)	4	1
Yale University (Ph.D.) (Cl)	1	3

Consultation

Miami University (OH) (Ph.D.) (Cl)	1	0
Regent University (Psy.D.) (Cl)	3	2
The University of Memphis (Ph.D.) (Co)	1	0
West Virginia University (Ph.D.) (Co)	1	0

Counseling Process and Outcomes (also see Psychotherapy Process and Outcome)

Azusa Pacific University (Psy.D.) (Cl)	2	1
Florida State University (Ph.D.) (Cm)	3	4
La Salle University (Psy.D.) (Cl)	2	0
Loyola University Chicago (Ph.D.) (Co)	1	0
New Mexico State University (Ph.D.) (Co)	1	0
Saint Mary's University of Minnesota (Psy.D.) (Co)	1	0
Southern Illinois University Carbondale (Ph.D.) (Co)	2	0
University of Maryland–College Park (Ph.D.) (Co)	2	0
University of Missouri, Columbia (Ph.D.) (Co)	1	0
University of North Texas (Ph.D.) (Co)	1	1
University of Oregon (Ph.D.) (Co)	4	2
University of St. Thomas (Psy.D.) (Co)	3	0

Crisis/Critical Incident

Louisiana Tech University (Ph.D.) (Co)	1	0
Philadelphia College of Osteopathic Medicine (Psy.D.) (Cl)	1	0

	# Faculty	# Grants
University of Detroit Mercy (Ph.D.) (Cl)	2	0
University of Northern Colorado (Ph.D.) (Co)	2	0

Deafness/Hard of Hearing

Gallaudet University (Ph.D.) (Cl)	12	2
Midwestern University–Glendale Campus (Psy.D.) (Cl)	1	0

Decision Making

Idaho State University (Ph.D.) (Cl)	1	–
Virginia Polytechnic Institute and State University (Ph.D.) (Cl)	4	4
West Virginia University (Ph.D.) (Cl)	8	2

Diabetes

Ponce Health Sciences University (Psy.D.) (Cl)	2	1
Rosalind Franklin University of Medicine and Science (Ph.D.) (Cl)	1	0
University of Miami (Ph.D.) (Cl)	3	2
Yeshiva University (Ph.D.) (Cl)	1	3

Dialectical Behavioral Therapy

American University (Ph.D.) (Cl)	1	0
Ponce Health Sciences University (Psy.D.) (Cl)	2	–
Rutgers–The State University of New Jersey (Ph.D.) (Cl)	2	1
The University of Montana (Ph.D.) (Cl)	1	0
Xavier University (Psy.D.) (Cl)	1	–

Disabilities/Disabled Persons

Alliant International University, San Francisco Bay (Psy.D.) (Cl)	3	1
DePaul University (Ph.D.) (Cl)	2	2
Georgia School of Professional Psychology at Argosy University, Atlanta (Psy.D.) (Cl)	1	0
Loyola University Chicago (Ph.D.) (Cl)	1	2
Southern Illinois University Carbondale (Ph.D.) (Co)	1	1
Texas A&M University (Ph.D.) (Co)	1	1
The University of Memphis (Ph.D.) (Co)	2	1
West Virginia University (Ph.D.) (Co)	1	0

Disaster (also see PTSD)

Illinois School of Professional Psychology at Argosy University, Chicago (Psy.D.) (Cl)	2	0
Seattle Pacific University (Ph.D.) (Cl)	1	0
The University of South Dakota (Ph.D.) (Cl)	4	0
University of Georgia (Ph.D.) (Cl)	1	–
University of Kansas–Child (Ph.D.) (Cl)	2	1
Wheaton College (Psy.D.) (Cl)	1	1

Discrimination

Catholic University of America (Ph.D.) (Cl)	1	0
Iowa State University (Ph.D.) (Co)	1	0
University of Louisville (Ph.D.) (Co)	2	0
University of Minnesota (Ph.D.) (Co)	1	2

Dissemination/Implementation/Translation

George Mason University (Ph.D.) (Cl)	3	–
Miami University (OH) (Ph.D.) (Cl)	1	1
Michigan State University (Ph.D.) (Cl)	1	1
Uniformed Services University of the Health Sciences (Ph.D.) (Cl)	1	1
University of Arkansas (Ph.D.) (Cl)	1	0
University of Denver (Ph.D.) (Cl)	1	0
University of Missouri, Columbia (Ph.D.) (Cl)	2	3
University of Nevada, Reno (Ph.D.) (Cl)	3	1
University of Southern Mississippi (Ph.D.) (Cl)	–	–
Utah State University (Ph.D.) (Cm)	2	1

Eating Disorders/Body Image

American School of Professional Psychology at Argosy University, Washington, DC (Psy.D.) (Cl)	2	0
American University (Ph.D.) (Cl)	1	0
Auburn University (Ph.D.) (Co)	1	0
Auburn University (Ph.D.) (Cl)	1	0
Colorado State University (Ph.D.) (Co)	1	0
Drexel University (Ph.D.) (Cl)	4	6
Duke University (Ph.D.) (Cl)	2	3
Emory University (Ph.D.) (Cl)	1	0
Fairleigh Dickinson University (Ph.D.) (Cl)	1	1
Florida School of Professional Psychology at Argosy University (Psy.D.) (Cl)	2	0
Florida State University (Ph.D.) (Cl)	2	2
George Mason University (Ph.D.) (Cl)	2	–
Hofstra University (Ph.D.) (Cl)	2	0
Illinois School of Professional Psychology at Argosy University, Chicago (Psy.D.) (Cl)	1	0

	# Faculty	# Grants
John F. Kennedy University (Psy.D.) (Cl)	1	1
Louisiana Tech University (Ph.D.) (Co)	1	0
Marywood University (Psy.D.) (Cl)	1	0
Miami University (OH) (Ph.D.) (Cl)	1	0
Michigan State University (Ph.D.) (Cl)	1	2
Midwestern University (Psy.D.) (Cl)	2	–
Minnesota School of Professional Psychology at Argosy University (Psy.D.) (Cl)	1	1
Northeastern University (Ph.D.) (Co)	2	4
Northwestern University Feinberg School of Medicine (Ph.D.) (Cl)	1	1
Oklahoma State University (Ph.D.) (Co)	1	0
Pacific University, Oregon (Psy.D.) (Cl)	3	0
Palo Alto University (Psy.D.) (Cl)	6	9
Philadelphia College of Osteopathic Medicine (Psy.D.) (Cl)	1	1
Rutgers–The State University of New Jersey (Ph.D.) (Cl)	2	1
Rutgers–The State University of New Jersey (Psy.D.) (Cl)	1	–
Saint Louis University (Ph.D.) (Cl)	1	0
San Diego State University–UC San Diego (Ph.D.) (Cl)	5	>1
Springfield College (Psy.D.) (Co)	1	–
Temple University (Ph.D.) (Cl)	1	0
The Wright Institute (Psy.D.) (Cl)	1	–
Uniformed Services University of the Health Sciences (Ph.D.) (Cl)	3	4
University at Albany (Ph.D.) (Cl)	1	–
University at Buffalo, State University of New York (Ph.D.) (Cm)	2	0
University of Alabama at Birmingham (Ph.D.) (Cl)	4	5
University of Denver (Ph.D.) (Cl)	1	0
University of Detroit Mercy (Ph.D.) (Cl)	2	0
University of Georgia (Ph.D.) (Cl)	1	–
University of Hawaii at Manoa (Ph.D.) (Cl)	3	0
University of Illinois at Urbana–Champaign (Ph.D.) (Co)	1	–
University of Kansas (Ph.D.) (Cl)	1	1
University of Kentucky (Ph.D.) (Cl)	1	1
University of Louisville (Ph.D.) (Cl)	1	0
University of Michigan (Ph.D.) (Cl)	1	–
University of Minnesota (Ph.D.) (Cl)	–	–
University of Missouri Kansas City (Ph.D.) (Cl)	1	1
University of Nevada Las Vegas (Ph.D.) (Cl)	1	0
University of New Mexico (Ph.D.) (Cl)	1	0
University of North Carolina at Charlotte (Ph.D.) (Cl)	3	1
University of North Carolina, Chapel Hill (Ph.D.) (Cl)	1	1
University of North Dakota (Ph.D.) (Co)	1	0
University of North Texas (Ph.D.) (Co)	3	0
University of Pittsburgh (Ph.D.) (Cl)	1	0
University of South Florida (Ph.D.) (Cl)	2	–
University of Wyoming (Ph.D.) (Cl)	1	0
Virginia Consortium Program in Clinical Psychology (Ph.D.) (Cl)	1	0

Emerging Adulthood

Loyola University Chicago (Ph.D.) (Cl)	1	0
Springfield College (Psy.D.) (Co)	1	–
St. John's University (Ph.D.) (Cl)	1	0
University of Georgia (Ph.D.) (Co)	2	–
Virginia Consortium Program in Clinical Psychology (Ph.D.) (Cl)	4	0

Emotion

Boston University (Ph.D.) (Cl)	2	1
Catholic University of America (Ph.D.) (Cl)	8	4
Colorado State University (Ph.D.) (Co)	1	0
Florida International University (Ph.D.) (Cl)	1	1
Georgia State University (Ph.D.) (Co)	1	0
Kent State University (Ph.D.) (Cl)	1	1
Miami University (OH) (Ph.D.) (Cl)	5	3
Northern Illinois University (Ph.D.) (Cl)	5	2
Pennsylvania State University (Ph.D.) (Cl)	3	1
Purdue University (Ph.D.) (Cl)	3	1
The New School (Ph.D.) (Cl)	1	0
University at Albany (Ph.D.) (Cl)	7	–
University of California, Berkeley (Ph.D.) (Cl)	4	2
University of Florida (Ph.D.) (Co)	1	1
University of Georgia (Ph.D.) (Cl)	4	1
University of Illinois at Urbana–Champaign (Ph.D.) (Cl)	6	3
University of Illinois at Urbana–Champaign (Ph.D.) (Co)	3	–
University of Maryland–College Park (Ph.D.) (Cl)	3	0
University of Massachusetts, Boston (Ph.D.) (Cl)	2	2
University of Mississippi (Ph.D.) (Cl)	2	1
University of Missouri Kansas City (Ph.D.) (Cl)	2	1
University of Nevada, Reno (Ph.D.) (Cl)	2	1
University of North Carolina at Charlotte (Ph.D.) (Cl)	1	0
University of North Dakota (Ph.D.) (Co)	1	0
University of Pittsburgh (Ph.D.) (Cl)	4	13
University of South Florida (Ph.D.) (Cl)	2	1
University of Texas at Austin (Ph.D.) (Co)	1	0
University of Toledo (Ph.D.) (Cl)	2	1
University of Wisconsin, Milwaukee (Ph.D.) (Cl)	4	5
Vanderbilt University (Ph.D.) (Cl)	3	4
Virginia Polytechnic Institute and State University (Ph.D.) (Cl)	7	1

Evidence-Based/Empirically Supported Treatments

	# Faculty	# Grants
Palo Alto University (Psy.D.) (Cl)	7	4
Pepperdine University (Psy.D.) (Cl)	2	2
Philadelphia College of Osteopathic Medicine (Psy.D.) (Cl)	13	0
Roosevelt University (Psy.D.) (Cl)	1	0
Rutgers–The State University of New Jersey (Psy.D.) (Cl)	1	–
The Wright Institute (Psy.D.) (Cl)	1	–
University of Nevada, Reno (Ph.D.) (Cl)	1	1
University of Southern Mississippi (Ph.D.) (Co)	6	0

Ethics/Ethical Issues

Catholic University of America (Ph.D.) (Cl)	1	0
Colorado State University (Ph.D.) (Co)	1	0
Fairleigh Dickinson University (Ph.D.) (Cl)	1	0
George Fox University (Psy.D.) (Cl)	1	0
Indiana University of Pennsylvania (Psy.D.) (Cl)	2	0
Loyola University Chicago (Ph.D.) (Cl)	1	0
Loyola University Maryland (Psy.D.) (Cl)	2	0
Philadelphia College of Osteopathic Medicine (Psy.D.) (Cl)	1	0
Rutgers–The State University of New Jersey (Psy.D.) (Cl)	1	–
Saint Louis University (Ph.D.) (Cl)	2	0
Tennessee State University (Ph.D.) (Co)	2	0
The Wright Institute (Psy.D.) (Cl)	2	–
University of Iowa (Ph.D.) (Co)	2	1
University of Louisville (Ph.D.) (Co)	2	0
University of St. Thomas (Psy.D.) (Co)	2	0
Utah State University (Ph.D.) (Cm)	2	0

Family/Family Therapy/Family Systems

Alliant International University, San Diego (Psy.D.) (Cl)	7	1
Alliant International University, San Francisco Bay (Ph.D.) (Cl)	3	0
Arizona State University (Ph.D.) (Cl)	8	5
Arizona State University (Ph.D.) (Co)	1	1
Azusa Pacific University (Psy.D.) (Cl)	2	0
Biola University (Ph.D.) (Cl)	1	0
Biola University (Psy.D.) (Cl)	1	0
Boston University (Ph.D.) (Cl)	3	2
Bowling Green State University (Ph.D.) (Cl)	2	0
Catholic University of America (Ph.D.) (Cl)	5	2
Divine Mercy University (Psy.D.) (Cl)	4	–
Florida Institute of Technology (Psy.D.) (Cl)	2	0
Florida School of Professional Psychology at Argosy University (Psy.D.) (Cl)	4	0
Fuller Theological Seminary (Ph.D.) (Cl)	7	0
Fuller Theological Seminary (Psy.D.) (Cl)	7	0
Howard University (Ph.D.) (Co)	1	0
Illinois Institute of Technology (Ph.D.) (Cl)	1	0
Indiana University of Pennsylvania (Psy.D.) (Cl)	1	0
James Madison University (Psy.D.) (Cm)	2	0
John F. Kennedy University (Psy.D.) (Cl)	2	1
La Salle University (Psy.D.) (Cl)	1	0
Lehigh University (Ph.D.) (Co)	1	1
Marquette University (Ph.D.) (Cl)	2	1
Miami University (OH) (Ph.D.) (Cl)	2	0
Michigan State University (Ph.D.) (Cl)	3	0
New Mexico State University (Ph.D.) (Co)	1	0
Pennsylvania State University (Ph.D.) (Cl)	2	1
Rutgers–The State University of New Jersey (Psy.D.) (Cl)	1	–
Sam Houston State University (Ph.D.) (Cl)	1	–
Southern Methodist University (Ph.D.) (Cl)	7	2
Teachers College, Columbia University (Ph.D.) (Cl)	1	1
Tennessee State University (Ph.D.) (Co)	2	0
Texas Tech University (Ph.D.) (Cl)	1	0
The University of South Dakota (Ph.D.) (Cl)	2	1
The Wright Institute (Psy.D.) (Cl)	4	–
University at Albany (Ph.D.) (Co)	2	1
University at Buffalo, State University of New York (Ph.D.) (Cm)	2	1
University of Arizona (Ph.D.) (Cl)	2	4
University of Arkansas (Ph.D.) (Cl)	3	0
University of Colorado Boulder (Ph.D.) (Cl)	2	2
University of Detroit Mercy (Ph.D.) (Cl)	2	0
University of Georgia (Ph.D.) (Cl)	1	–
University of Hawaii at Manoa (Ph.D.) (Cl)	2	2
University of Houston (Ph.D.) (Cl)	2	0
University of Massachusetts, Boston (Ph.D.) (Cl)	1	1
University of Massachusetts, Boston (Ph.D.) (Co)	1	0
University of Miami (Ph.D.) (Cl)	2	2
University of Miami (Ph.D.) (Co)	3	3
University of Missouri Kansas City (Ph.D.) (Co)	2	–
University of Missouri, Columbia (Ph.D.) (Co)	1	1
University of Nevada, Reno (Ph.D.) (Cl)	1	1
University of North Texas (Ph.D.) (Co)	3	2
University of Northern Colorado (Ph.D.) (Co)	1	0
University of Rhode Island (Ph.D.) (Cl)	1	0
University of South Florida (Ph.D.) (Cl)	1	–
University of Southern California (Ph.D.) (Cl)	2	1
University of Tennessee–Knoxville (Ph.D.) (Cl)	4	3
University of Utah (Ph.D.) (Cl)	4	3

	# Faculty	# Grants
University of Virginia (Ph.D.) (Cl)	3	2
University of Wyoming (Ph.D.) (Cl)	1	1
Virginia Commonwealth University (Ph.D.) (Co)	2	0
Yeshiva University (Psy.D.) (Cl)	2	0

Forensic/Psychology and Law

Alliant International University, Sacramento (Psy.D.) (Cl)	1	0
Alliant International University, San Francisco Bay (Ph.D.) (Cl)	2	0
Alliant International University, San Francisco Bay (Psy.D.) (Cl)	3	0
American School of Professional Psychology at Argosy University, Washington, DC (Psy.D.) (Cl)	4	0
Azusa Pacific University (Psy.D.) (Cl)	3	1
California Lutheran University (Psy.D.) (Cl)	1	1
Carlos Albizu University, Miami Campus (Psy.D.) (Cl)	4	0
Carlow University (Psy.D.) (Co)	1	–
Drexel University (Ph.D.) (Cl)	3	3
East Tennessee State University (Ph.D.) (Cl)	1	4
Fairleigh Dickinson University (Ph.D.) (Cl)	2	1
Florida Institute of Technology (Psy.D.) (Cl)	1	0
Florida School of Professional Psychology at Argosy University (Psy.D.) (Cl)	2	0
Florida State University (Ph.D.) (Cl)	1	0
Fordham University (Ph.D.) (Cl)	2	4
Fordham University (Ph.D.) (Co)	1	1
Georgia School of Professional Psychology at Argosy University, Atlanta (Psy.D.) (Cl)	1	0
Indiana University–Bloomington (Ph.D.) (Cl)	2	1
Kean University (Psy.D.) (Cm)	1	0
Long Island University (Ph.D.) (Cl)	2	0
Midwestern University–Glendale Campus (Psy.D.) (Cl)	1	0
Northwestern University Feinberg School of Medicine (Ph.D.) (Cl)	4	1
Pacific University, Oregon (Psy.D.) (Cl)	4	0
Palo Alto University (Ph.D.) (Cl)	4	–
Philadelphia College of Osteopathic Medicine (Psy.D.) (Cl)	2	1
Ponce Health Sciences University (Ph.D.) (Cl)	1	0
Ponce Health Sciences University (Psy.D.) (Cl)	2	–
Regent University (Psy.D.) (Cl)	1	–
Roosevelt University (Psy.D.) (Cl)	1	0
Sam Houston State University (Ph.D.) (Cl)	5	–
Spalding University (Psy.D.) (Cl)	1	0
Texas A&M University (Ph.D.) (Cl)	1	–
Texas Tech University (Ph.D.) (Co)	1	2
The Wright Institute (Psy.D.) (Cl)	4	–
University of Alabama at Tuscaloosa (Ph.D.) (Cl)	3	1
University of Colorado at Colorado Springs (Ph.D.) (Cl)	1	0
University of Denver (Psy.D.) (Cl)	4	0
University of Florida (Ph.D.) (Co)	1	0
University of Houston (Ph.D.) (Cl)	2	0
University of Indianapolis (Psy.D.) (Cl)	1	0
University of Nebraska, Lincoln (Ph.D.) (Cl)	2	4
University of Nevada, Reno (Ph.D.) (Cl)	2	0
University of North Texas (Ph.D.) (Cl)	2	2
University of Rhode Island (Ph.D.) (Cl)	2	2
University of Southern Mississippi (Ph.D.) (Co)	1	0
University of Texas at Austin (Ph.D.) (Co)	1	0
University of Virginia (Ph.D.) (Cm)	1	0
University of Wyoming (Ph.D.) (Cl)	1	0
West Virginia University (Ph.D.) (Cl)	1	0
Wichita State University (Ph.D.) (Cl)	1	0

Forgiveness

Iowa State University (Ph.D.) (Co)	1	1
The Wright Institute (Psy.D.) (Cl)	1	–
University of Louisville (Ph.D.) (Co)	1	0
Virginia Commonwealth University (Ph.D.) (Co)	2	3

Gambling

Loyola University Maryland (Psy.D.) (Cl)	1	0
University of Georgia (Ph.D.) (Cl)	1	1

Gender Roles/Sex Differences

Alliant International University, Fresno (Psy.D.) (Cl)	1	0
Alliant International University, Los Angeles (Ph.D.) (Cl)	3	0
Alliant International University, San Diego (Ph.D.) (Cl)	2	0
Alliant International University, San Diego (Psy.D.) (Cl)	3	0
Alliant International University, San Francisco Bay (Ph.D.) (Cl)	3	0
Alliant International University, San Francisco Bay (Psy.D.) (Cl)	2	0
Biola University (Ph.D.) (Cl)	3	1
Biola University (Psy.D.) (Cl)	3	1
Boston College (Ph.D.) (Co)	5	1
Boston University (Ph.D.) (Cl)	1	0
Chatham University (Psy.D.) (Co)	4	1
Chicago School of Professional Psychology–Chicago Campus (Psy.D.) (Cl)	1	0

	# Faculty	# Grants
Clark University (Ph.D.) (Cl)	3	0
Fielding Graduate University (Ph.D.) (Cl)	3	0
Georgia State University (Ph.D.) (Cl)	1	0
Georgia State University (Ph.D.) (Co)	2	2
Indiana State University (Psy.D.) (Cl)	1	0
Indiana University of Pennsylvania (Psy.D.) (Cl)	2	0
Iowa State University (Ph.D.) (Co)	1	0
Lehigh University (Ph.D.) (Co)	2	0
Louisiana Tech University (Ph.D.) (Co)	1	0
New Mexico State University (Ph.D.) (Co)	3	0
Oklahoma State University (Ph.D.) (Co)	6	0
Pace University (Psy.D.) (Cm)	1	0
Pacific University, Oregon (Psy.D.) (Cl)	4	0
Regent University (Psy.D.) (Cl)	1	2
Roosevelt University (Psy.D.) (Cl)	3	0
Saint Mary's University of Minnesota (Psy.D.) (Co)	4	0
Seattle Pacific University (Ph.D.) (Cl)	1	0
Southern Illinois University Carbondale (Ph.D.) (Cl)	1	0
Southern Illinois University Carbondale (Ph.D.) (Co)	3	0
Texas A&M University (Ph.D.) (Cl)	1	–
Texas Tech University (Ph.D.) (Co)	2	0
Texas Woman's University (Ph.D.) (Co)	3	–
The University of Montana (Ph.D.) (Cl)	2	0
The Wright Institute (Psy.D.) (Cl)	3	–
University of Florida (Ph.D.) (Co)	1	1
University of Houston (Ph.D.) (Co)	2	1
University of La Verne (Psy.D.) (Cl)	3	1
University of Missouri Kansas City (Ph.D.) (Co)	1	–
University of Missouri, Columbia (Ph.D.) (Co)	2	1
University of Nebraska, Lincoln (Ph.D.) (Co)	2	1
University of North Dakota (Ph.D.) (Cl)	2	0
University of Northern Colorado (Ph.D.) (Co)	1	0
University of Texas at Austin (Ph.D.) (Co)	3	1
University of Utah (Ph.D.) (Co)	3	0
Virginia Consortium Program in Clinical Psychology (Ph.D.) (Cl)	1	0

Genetics/Behavioral Genetics

Boston University (Ph.D.) (Cl)	1	1
Duke University (Ph.D.) (Cl)	2	2
Emory University (Ph.D.) (Cl)	2	–
Florida International University (Ph.D.) (Cl)	1	1
Indiana University–Bloomington (Ph.D.) (Cl)	3	2
Michigan State University (Ph.D.) (Cl)	3	4
Northwestern University (Ph.D.) (Cl)	2	0
Northwestern University Feinberg School of Medicine (Ph.D.) (Cl)	1	2
Ponce Health Sciences University (Ph.D.) (Cl)	1	1
Purdue University (Ph.D.) (Cl)	1	0
San Diego State University–UC San Diego (Ph.D.) (Cl)	3	>1
Southern Illinois University Carbondale (Ph.D.) (Cl)	1	–
Syracuse University (Ph.D.) (Cl)	1	0
The Wright Institute (Psy.D.) (Cl)	1	–
University of Colorado Boulder (Ph.D.) (Cl)	3	3
University of Denver (Ph.D.) (Cl)	1	1
University of Georgia (Ph.D.) (Cl)	1	1
University of Houston (Ph.D.) (Cl)	1	0
University of Illinois at Urbana–Champaign (Ph.D.) (Cl)	1	1
University of Minnesota (Ph.D.) (Cl)	–	–
University of Missouri, Columbia (Ph.D.) (Cl)	2	2
University of North Carolina at Charlotte (Ph.D.) (Cl)	1	0
University of North Carolina, Greensboro (Ph.D.) (Cl)	1	0
University of Pittsburgh (Ph.D.) (Cl)	6	10
University of Texas at Austin (Ph.D.) (Cl)	2	2
University of Virginia (Ph.D.) (Cl)	2	1
Yale University (Ph.D.) (Cl)	1	1

Group Process and Therapy

Antioch University New England (Psy.D.) (Cl)	1	0
Baylor University (Psy.D.) (Cl)	1	0
Brigham Young University (Ph.D.) (Cl)	1	1
Chatham University (Psy.D.) (Co)	1	0
Divine Mercy University (Psy.D.) (Cl)	2	–
Fielding Graduate University (Ph.D.) (Cl)	4	0
Fuller Theological Seminary (Ph.D.) (Cl)	3	2
Fuller Theological Seminary (Psy.D.) (Cl)	3	2
Indiana University–Bloomington (Ph.D.) (Co)	1	–
Marquette University (Ph.D.) (Cl)	1	0
The Wright Institute (Psy.D.) (Cl)	2	–
University at Buffalo, State University of New York (Ph.D.) (Cm)	1	0
University of Denver (Ph.D.) (Co)	1	0
University of Maryland–College Park (Ph.D.) (Co)	1	0
University of North Dakota (Ph.D.) (Co)	1	0
University of Northern Colorado (Ph.D.) (Co)	1	0
University of Tennessee–Knoxville (Ph.D.) (Co)	1	1
Virginia Commonwealth University (Ph.D.) (Co)	1	0
West Virginia University (Ph.D.) (Co)	1	0
Western Michigan University (Ph.D.) (Co)	1	0

Health Care/Primary Care

	# Faculty	# Grants
Adler University–Chicago (Psy.D.) (Cl)	3	–
Chicago School of Professional Psychology–Chicago Campus (Psy.D.) (Cl)	2	0
Midwestern University–Glendale Campus (Psy.D.) (Cl)	1	0
New Mexico State University (Ph.D.) (Co)	1	1
Ponce Health Sciences University (Psy.D.) (Cl)	6	–
Syracuse University (Ph.D.) (Cl)	3	2
The University of Montana (Ph.D.) (Cl)	3	2
University of Georgia (Ph.D.) (Cl)	3	–
University of Nevada, Reno (Ph.D.) (Cl)	3	0
University of North Dakota (Ph.D.) (Co)	2	1
University of Texas Southwestern Medical Center (Ph.D.) (Cl)	1	1
Washington State University (Ph.D.) (Cl)	2	5
Western Michigan University (Ph.D.) (Cl)	3	1

Health Disparities

Arizona State University (Ph.D.) (Co)	2	1
Chicago School of Professional Psychology–Washington, DC Campus (Psy.D.) (Cl)	3	0
Clark University (Ph.D.) (Cl)	1	0
Jackson State University (Ph.D.) (Cl)	3	1
Midwestern University–Glendale Campus (Psy.D.) (Cl)	2	0
Northeastern University (Ph.D.) (Co)	1	3
San Diego State University–UC San Diego (Ph.D.) (Cl)	15	>1
Texas Tech University (Ph.D.) (Cl)	1	0
The City College of New York, The Graduate Center, CUNY (Ph.D.) (Cl)	2	2
University of Houston (Ph.D.) (Co)	2	2
University of Minnesota (Ph.D.) (Co)	1	2
University of Nebraska, Lincoln (Ph.D.) (Cl)	2	2
University of North Carolina, Chapel Hill (Ph.D.) (Cl)	2	1
Vanderbilt University (Ph.D.) (Cl)	2	1
Wichita State University (Ph.D.) (Cl)	1	0
Wright State University (Psy.D.) (Cl)	2	–

Health Psychology/Behavioral Medicine

Alliant International University, Fresno (Psy.D.) (Cl)	2	0
Alliant International University, Los Angeles (Ph.D.) (Cl)	7	1
Alliant International University, Los Angeles (Psy.D.) (Cl)	5	0
Alliant International University, Sacramento (Psy.D.) (Cl)	1	0
Alliant International University, San Diego (Ph.D.) (Cl)	4	0
Alliant International University, San Francisco Bay (Ph.D.) (Cl)	3	0
Alliant International University, San Francisco Bay (Psy.D.) (Cl)	4	0
Arizona School of Professional Psychology at Argosy University, Phoenix (Psy.D.) (Cl)	2	0
Arizona State University (Ph.D.) (Cl)	7	6
Auburn University (Ph.D.) (Co)	3	2
Auburn University (Ph.D.) (Cl)	2	1
Ball State University (Ph.D.) (Co)	2	0
Baylor University (Psy.D.) (Cl)	3	2
Biola University (Ph.D.) (Cl)	2	2
Biola University (Psy.D.) (Cl)	2	2
Bowling Green State University (Ph.D.) (Cl)	2	1
Brigham Young University (Ph.D.) (Cl)	2	2
California Lutheran University (Psy.D.) (Cl)	1	0
Carlos Albizu University, Miami Campus (Psy.D.) (Cl)	2	0
Carlow University (Psy.D.) (Co)	1	–
Chatham University (Psy.D.) (Co)	5	1
Cleveland State University (Ph.D.) (Co)	1	0
Colorado State University (Ph.D.) (Co)	8	4
Drexel University (Ph.D.) (Cl)	5	2
Duke University (Ph.D.) (Cl)	6	8
East Carolina University (Ph.D.) (Cl)	1	0
Eastern Michigan University (Ph.D.) (Cl)	2	0
Fairleigh Dickinson University (Ph.D.) (Cl)	3	0
Florida Institute of Technology (Psy.D.) (Cl)	3	1
Fordham University (Ph.D.) (Cl)	1	2
Fordham University (Ph.D.) (Co)	2	1
Fuller Theological Seminary (Ph.D.) (Cl)	1	0
Fuller Theological Seminary (Psy.D.) (Cl)	1	0
George Fox University (Psy.D.) (Cl)	2	5
George Washington University (Ph.D.) (Cl)	1	0
Hawaii School of Professional Psychology at Argosy University, Hawaii (Psy.D.) (Cl)	1	0
Howard University (Ph.D.) (Cl)	4	2
Howard University (Ph.D.) (Co)	3	0
Illinois Institute of Technology (Ph.D.) (Cl)	1	0
Illinois School of Professional Psychology at Argosy University, Chicago (Psy.D.) (Cl)	1	1
Indiana State University (Psy.D.) (Cl)	1	0
Indiana University–Bloomington (Ph.D.) (Cl)	2	0
Indiana University–Purdue University Indianapolis (Ph.D.) (Cl)	6	1
Indiana University of Pennsylvania (Psy.D.) (Cl)	1	0
Iowa State University (Ph.D.) (Co)	1	1
Kean University (Psy.D.) (Cm)	2	0
Kent State University (Ph.D.) (Cl)	2	2
La Salle University (Psy.D.) (Cl)	1	0
Loma Linda University (Ph.D.) (Cl)	6	3

	# Faculty	# Grants
Loma Linda University (Psy.D.) (Cl)	6	3
Long Island University (Ph.D.) (Cl)	1	0
Loyola University Maryland (Psy.D.) (Cl)	3	0
Miami University (OH) (Ph.D.) (Cl)	2	1
Midwestern University–Glendale Campus (Psy.D.) (Cl)	1	0
Northeastern University (Ph.D.) (Co)	1	0
Northwestern University Feinberg School of Medicine (Ph.D.) (Cl)	8	10
Ohio University (Ph.D.) (Cl)	1	1
Oklahoma State University (Ph.D.) (Cl)	2	2
Oklahoma State University (Ph.D.) (Co)	9	0
Pacific University, Oregon (Psy.D.) (Cl)	5	0
Palo Alto University (Ph.D.) (Cl)	4	–
Palo Alto University (Psy.D.) (Cl)	3	4
Pennsylvania State University (Ph.D.) (Cl)	3	0
Philadelphia College of Osteopathic Medicine (Psy.D.) (Cl)	2	0
Ponce Health Sciences University (Ph.D.) (Cl)	4	1
Ponce Health Sciences University (Psy.D.) (Cl)	7	1
Regent University (Psy.D.) (Cl)	2	–
Roosevelt University (Psy.D.) (Cl)	3	0
Rutgers–The State University of New Jersey (Ph.D.) (Cl)	2	2
Rutgers–The State University of New Jersey (Psy.D.) (Cl)	1	–
Saint Louis University (Ph.D.) (Cl)	1	0
Saint Mary's University of Minnesota (Psy.D.) (Co)	3	0
Sam Houston State University (Ph.D.) (Cl)	4	1
San Diego State University–UC San Diego (Ph.D.) (Cl)	4	>1
Seattle Pacific University (Ph.D.) (Cl)	1	0
Southern Illinois University Carbondale (Ph.D.) (Cl)	2	0
Southern Illinois University Carbondale (Ph.D.) (Co)	2	0
Southern Methodist University (Ph.D.) (Cl)	3	0
Spalding University (Psy.D.) (Cl)	1	0
St. John's University (Ph.D.) (Cl)	3	1
Syracuse University (Ph.D.) (Cl)	6	25
Texas A&M University (Ph.D.) (Cl)	2	–
Texas Tech University (Ph.D.) (Cl)	6	2
Texas Tech University (Ph.D.) (Co)	2	0
The New School (Ph.D.) (Cl)	1	1
The University of Memphis (Ph.D.) (Cl)	4	5
The University of Memphis (Ph.D.) (Co)	2	1
The University of Montana (Ph.D.) (Cl)	3	2
The Wright Institute (Psy.D.) (Cl)	4	–
Uniformed Services University of the Health Sciences (Ph.D.) (Cl)	1	1
University at Albany (Ph.D.) (Cl)	2	–
University at Buffalo, State University of New York (Ph.D.) (Cl)	3	2
University of Alabama at Tuscaloosa (Ph.D.) (Cl)	3	2

University of Alaska Fairbanks–Anchorage (Ph.D.) (Cl)	1	0
University of Arizona (Ph.D.) (Cl)	6	6
University of Central Florida (Ph.D.) (Cl)	1	0
University of Cincinnati (Ph.D.) (Cl)	3	4
University of Connecticut (Ph.D.) (Cl)	3	3
University of Denver (Ph.D.) (Co)	2	2
University of Denver (Psy.D.) (Cl)	4	0
University of Florida (Ph.D.) (Co)	1	2
University of Florida (Ph.D.) (Cl)	7	2
University of Georgia (Ph.D.) (Cl)	4	1
University of Georgia (Ph.D.) (Co)	1	2
University of Illinois at Chicago (Ph.D.) (Cl)	4	1
University of Indianapolis (Psy.D.) (Cl)	5	2
University of Iowa (Ph.D.) (Cl)	2	1
University of Kansas–Child (Ph.D.) (Cl)	3	1
University of Kansas (Ph.D.) (Cl)	9	6
University of Kentucky (Ph.D.) (Cl)	2	1
University of La Verne (Psy.D.) (Cl)	2	2
University of Louisville (Ph.D.) (Cl)	3	2
University of Maine (Ph.D.) (Cl)	2	0
University of Maryland, Baltimore County (Ph.D.) (Cl)	2	2
University of Maryland–College Park (Ph.D.) (Co)	2	1
University of Massachusetts, Boston (Ph.D.) (Cl)	1	1
University of Massachusetts, Boston (Ph.D.) (Co)	1	0
University of Miami (Ph.D.) (Cl)	14	5
University of Miami (Ph.D.) (Co)	2	0
University of Michigan (Ph.D.) (Cl)	1	3
University of Missouri, Columbia (Ph.D.) (Co)	1	2
University of Missouri, St. Louis (Ph.D.) (Cl)	2	1
University of Nevada, Reno (Ph.D.) (Cl)	3	0
University of New Mexico (Ph.D.) (Cl)	3	1
University of North Carolina at Charlotte (Ph.D.) (Cl)	15	0
University of North Carolina, Chapel Hill (Ph.D.) (Cl)	1	1
University of North Dakota (Ph.D.) (Cl)	2	0
University of Notre Dame (Ph.D.) P(Cl)	2	0
University of Pittsburgh (Ph.D.) (Cl)	16	24
University of Rhode Island (Ph.D.) (Cl)	4	4
University of South Alabama (Ph.D.) (Cm)	1	–
University of South Florida (Ph.D.) (Cl)	2	–
University of Southern California (Ph.D.) (Cl)	2	2
University of Tennessee–Knoxville (Ph.D.) (Cl)	1	1
University of Tennessee–Knoxville (Ph.D.) (Co)	1	0
University of Texas at Austin (Ph.D.) (Cl)	1	1
University of Texas at Austin (Ph.D.) (Co)	4	1
University of Texas Southwestern Medical Center (Ph.D.) (Cl)	3	2
University of Toledo (Ph.D.) (Cl)	1	0

	# Faculty	# Grants
University of Utah (Ph.D.) (Cl)	2	3
University of Wisconsin, Madison (Ph.D.) (Cl)	3	6
University of Wisconsin, Milwaukee (Ph.D.) (Cl)	1	0
Utah State University (Ph.D.) (Cm)	5	2
Vanderbilt University (Ph.D.) (Cl)	4	3
Virginia Commonwealth University (Ph.D.) (Cl)	6	3
Virginia Commonwealth University (Ph.D.) (Co)	5	4
Virginia Polytechnic Institute and State University (Ph.D.) (Cl)	6	1
West Virginia University (Ph.D.) (Cl)	5	4
Western Michigan University (Ph.D.) (Cl)	4	1
Widener University (Psy.D.) (Cl)	3	2

Help-Seeking

Iowa State University (Ph.D.) (Co)	2	1
Marquette University (Ph.D.) (Cl)	2	1
University of Kentucky (Ph.D.) (Co)	1	–

Hispanic Studies (also see Minority/Diversity)

Arizona State University (Ph.D.) (Cl)	3	1
Chicago School of Professional Psychology–Chicago Campus (Psy.D.) (Cl)	2	0
Marquette University (Ph.D.) (Cl)	1	1
Our Lady of the Lake University (Psy.D.) (Co)	2	1
Pacific University, Oregon (Psy.D.) (Cl)	3	0
Texas A&M University (Ph.D.) (Co)	2	0
Texas Tech University (Ph.D.) (Cl)	1	0
The Wright Institute (Psy.D.) (Cl)	1	–
University of Denver (Psy.D.) (Cl)	1	0
University of Georgia (Ph.D.) (Co)	1	0

Homelessness

Azusa Pacific University (Psy.D.) (Cl)	1	0
Pepperdine University (Psy.D.) (Cl)	2	1
The City College of New York, The Graduate Center, CUNY (Ph.D.) (Cl)	1	1
Wayne State University (Ph.D.) (Cl)	1	0

Hypnosis

Adler University–Chicago (Psy.D.) (Cl)	1	–
Binghamton University, State University of New York (Ph.D.) (Cl)	1	0

University of Wisconsin, Milwaukee (Ph.D.) (Co)	1	0

Identity Development

Ball State University (Ph.D.) (Co)	2	0
Cleveland State University (Ph.D.) (Co)	1	0
New Mexico State University (Ph.D.) (Co)	3	0
Southern Illinois University Carbondale (Ph.D.) (Co)	3	0
Springfield College (Psy.D.) (Co)	3	–
University of Detroit Mercy (Ph.D.) (Cl)	2	0
University of Houston (Ph.D.) (Co)	2	1
University of Minnesota (Ph.D.) (Co)	1	2
University of North Dakota (Ph.D.) (Co)	1	0
Yeshiva University (Psy.D.) (Cl)	2	0

Immigration

Boston College (Ph.D.) (Co)	3	1
Catholic University of America (Ph.D.) (Cl)	1	1
Chicago School of Professional Psychology–Washington, DC Campus (Psy.D.) (Cl)	1	0
Howard University (Ph.D.) (Co)	1	0
Sam Houston State University (Ph.D.) (Cl)	2	–
The Wright Institute (Psy.D.) (Cl)	3	–
University of Alaska Fairbanks–Anchorage (Ph.D.) (Cl)	1	1
University of Missouri Kansas City (Ph.D.) (Co)	1	–

Indigenous/Native American (also see Minority/Diversity)

Indiana University–Bloomington (Ph.D.) (Co)	1	–
The University of Montana (Ph.D.) (Cl)	2	2
The Wright Institute (Psy.D.) (Cl)	1	–
University of Alaska Fairbanks–Anchorage (Ph.D.) (Cl)	1	0
University of North Dakota (Ph.D.) (Co)	1	0
Utah State University (Ph.D.) (Cm)	1	1

Integration/Unification

American School of Professional Psychology at Argosy University, Washington, DC (Psy.D.) (Cl)	2	0
Antioch University New England (Psy.D.) (Cl)	3	4
East Tennessee State University (Ph.D.) (Cl)	1	0
George Fox University (Psy.D.) (Cl)	2	0
James Madison University (Psy.D.) (Cm)	7	0

	# Faculty	# Grants
Midwestern University (Psy.D.) (Cl)	7	–
Texas Woman's University (Ph.D.) (Co)	1	–
University of Arkansas (Ph.D.) (Cl)	3	1
University of North Dakota (Ph.D.) (Co)	2	1

Interpersonal Relationships/Friendships

Adelphi University (Ph.D.) (Cl)	1	1
Adler University–Chicago (Psy.D.) (Cl)	1	–
Auburn University (Ph.D.) (Co)	1	1
Catholic University of America (Ph.D.) (Cl)	6	2
Colorado State University (Ph.D.) (Co)	1	0
Duke University (Ph.D.) (Cl)	1	1
Fairleigh Dickinson University (Ph.D.) (Cl)	2	0
Indiana State University (Psy.D.) (Cl)	1	0
James Madison University (Psy.D.) (Cm)	2	0
Louisiana Tech University (Ph.D.) (Co)	1	0
Marquette University (Ph.D.) (Cl)	2	0
New Mexico State University (Ph.D.) (Co)	1	0
Seattle Pacific University (Ph.D.) (Cl)	2	0
Southern Illinois University Carbondale (Ph.D.) (Cl)	2	0
Stony Brook University, State University of New York (Ph.D.) (Cl)	3	1
University at Buffalo, State University of New York (Ph.D.) (Cm)	1	0
University of Maine (Ph.D.) (Cl)	3	1
University of Maryland, Baltimore County (Ph.D.) (Cl)	1	0
University of Maryland–College Park (Ph.D.) (Co)	2	0
University of Michigan (Ph.D.) (Cl)	1	–
University of North Carolina at Charlotte (Ph.D.) (Cl)	1	0
University of North Carolina, Greensboro (Ph.D.) (Cl)	1	0
University of North Dakota (Ph.D.) (Cl)	2	0
University of North Dakota (Ph.D.) (Co)	1	0
Wayne State University (Ph.D.) (Cl)	2	1
Wichita State University (Ph.D.) (Cl)	1	0

Intervention/Treatment

Alliant International University, San Diego (Psy.D.) (Cl)	10	0
Florida State University (Ph.D.) (Cl)	2	2
Indiana University–Bloomington (Ph.D.) (Cl)	4	3
Miami University (OH) (Ph.D.) (Cl)	1	1
New York University (Ph.D.) (Co)	1	0
Northwestern University Feinberg School of Medicine (Ph.D.) (Cl)	5	3
Regent University (Psy.D.) (Cl)	1	1
Syracuse University (Ph.D.) (Cl)	4	12
Texas Tech University (Ph.D.) (Cl)	2	0
University at Buffalo, State University of New York (Ph.D.) (Cm)	1	0
University of Georgia (Ph.D.) (Cl)	4	–
University of Illinois at Urbana–Champaign (Ph.D.) (Cl)	2	2
University of Missouri, Columbia (Ph.D.) (Co)	2	8
University of Nevada, Reno (Ph.D.) (Cl)	5	0
University of North Carolina, Greensboro (Ph.D.) (Cl)	1	0
University of Rochester (Ph.D.) (Cl)	2	1
University of Southern California (Ph.D.) (Cl)	4	2
University of Southern Mississippi (Ph.D.) (Cl)	–	–
University of Tennessee–Knoxville (Ph.D.) (Co)	1	1
University of Wisconsin, Milwaukee (Ph.D.) (Co)	1	1
Virginia Commonwealth University (Ph.D.) (Co)	1	4
Western Michigan University (Ph.D.) (Co)	3	0
Yeshiva University (Psy.D.) (Cl)	1	0

Language

Adelphi University (Ph.D.) (Cl)	1	1
Biola University (Ph.D.) (Cl)	1	0
Biola University (Psy.D.) (Cl)	1	0
Catholic University of America (Ph.D.) (Cl)	1	1
Pepperdine University (Psy.D.) (Cl)	1	0

Learning Disabilities

Arizona School of Professional Psychology at Argosy University, Phoenix (Psy.D.) (Cl)	1	0
Binghamton University, State University of New York (Ph.D.) (Cl)	2	0
Case Western Reserve University (Ph.D.) (Cl)	1	0
Colorado State University (Ph.D.) (Co)	1	0
Fairleigh Dickinson University (Ph.D.) (Cl)	2	0
Georgia State University (Ph.D.) (Cl)	1	1
Pace University (Psy.D.) (Cm)	1	0
Southern Illinois University Carbondale (Ph.D.) (Cl)	2	1
The Wright Institute (Psy.D.) (Cl)	1	–
University of Denver (Ph.D.) (Cl)	1	0
University of Houston (Ph.D.) (Cl)	2	5
University of Texas Southwestern Medical Center (Ph.D.) (Cl)	1	0
University of Virginia (Ph.D.) (Cm)	2	0
University of Wisconsin, Milwaukee (Ph.D.) (Cl)	3	0
Widener University (Psy.D.) (Cl)	3	0
Yeshiva University (Psy.D.) (Cm)	2	0

Lesbian/Gay/Bisexual/Transgender

	# Faculty	# Grants
Alliant International University, Los Angeles (Psy.D.) (Cl)	2	0
Alliant International University, San Diego (Psy.D.) (Cl)	1	0
Alliant International University, San Francisco Bay (Ph.D.) (Cl)	2	0
Alliant International University, San Francisco Bay (Psy.D.) (Cl)	1	0
American School of Professional Psychology at Argosy University, Washington, DC (Psy.D.) (Cl)	2	0
Boston College (Ph.D.) (Co)	3	1
Chicago School of Professional Psychology–Washington, DC Campus (Psy.D.) (Cl)	2	0
Clark University (Ph.D.) (Cl)	2	1
Florida School of Professional Psychology at Argosy University (Psy.D.) (Cl)	4	0
George Washington University (Psy.D.) (Cl)	1	–
Hawaii School of Professional Psychology at Argosy University, Hawaii (Psy.D.) (Cl)	2	0
Illinois School of Professional Psychology at Argosy University, Chicago (Psy.D.) (Cl)	2	0
Indiana University–Bloomington (Ph.D.) (Co)	1	–
John F. Kennedy University (Psy.D.) (Cl)	4	0
Marquette University (Ph.D.) (Cl)	2	0
New Mexico State University (Ph.D.) (Co)	2	0
New York University (Ph.D.) (Co)	2	1
Northwestern University Feinberg School of Medicine (Ph.D.) (Cl)	2	3
Oklahoma State University (Ph.D.) (Co)	6	2
Palo Alto University (Ph.D.) (Cl)	3	–
Radford University (Psy.D.) (Co)	2	0
San Diego State University–UC San Diego (Ph.D.) (Cl)	1	1
Springfield College (Psy.D.) (Co)	1	–
Stony Brook University, State University of New York (Ph.D.) (Cl)	1	–
Teachers College, Columbia University (Ph.D.) (Co)	2	0
The University of Memphis (Ph.D.) (Co)	4	1
The University of Montana (Ph.D.) (Cl)	2	1
The Wright Institute (Psy.D.) (Cl)	5	–
University of Hawaii at Manoa (Ph.D.) (Cl)	1	0
University of Houston (Ph.D.) (Co)	1	1
University of Kentucky (Ph.D.) (Co)	1	–
University of La Verne (Psy.D.) (Cl)	2	0
University of Maryland–College Park (Ph.D.) (Co)	1	0
University of Massachusetts, Boston (Ph.D.) (Co)	1	1
University of Missouri Kansas City (Ph.D.) (Co)	3	–
University of Nebraska, Lincoln (Ph.D.) (Cl)	1	2
University of North Dakota (Ph.D.) (Co)	2	0
University of South Alabama (Ph.D.) (Cm)	1	–
University of Tennessee–Knoxville (Ph.D.) (Co)	4	0
University of Utah (Ph.D.) (Co)	1	0
Virginia Consortium Program in Clinical Psychology (Ph.D.) (Cl)	5	1

Malingering

Marywood University (Psy.D.) (Cl)	1	0
Saint Louis University (Ph.D.) (Cl)	1	0
The University of Montana (Ph.D.) (Cl)	1	0

Marital/Intimate Partner Violence

California Lutheran University (Psy.D.) (Cl)	3	1
Carlos Albizu University, San Juan Campus (Ph.D.) (Cl)	1	–
George Mason University (Ph.D.) (Cl)	2	–
Indiana University–Bloomington (Ph.D.) (Cl)	1	1
Long Island University, C.W. Post Campus (Psy.D.) (Cl)	2	0
Loyola University Maryland (Psy.D.) (Cl)	1	0
Miami University (OH) (Ph.D.) (Cl)	2	1
Michigan State University (Ph.D.) (Cl)	2	1
Northeastern University (Ph.D.) (Co)	1	5
Northern Illinois University (Ph.D.) (Cl)	2	0
Saint Mary's University of Minnesota (Psy.D.) (Co)	2	0
Springfield College (Psy.D.) (Co)	1	–
Stony Brook University, State University of New York (Ph.D.) (Cl)	1	1
The University of Akron (Ph.D.) (Co)	1	1
The University of Montana (Ph.D.) (Cl)	2	0
The University of South Dakota (Ph.D.) (Cl)	2	1
University of Connecticut (Ph.D.) (Cl)	1	1
University of Denver (Ph.D.) (Cl)	3	1
University of Hartford (Psy.D.) (Cl)	1	0
University of Hawaii at Manoa (Ph.D.) (Cl)	1	1
University of Iowa (Ph.D.) (Cl)	1	1
University of Kansas–Child (Ph.D.) (Cl)	1	2
University of Maryland, Baltimore County (Ph.D.) (Cl)	1	1
University of Maryland–College Park (Ph.D.) (Co)	1	0
University of North Dakota (Ph.D.) (Co)	1	0
University of Oregon (Ph.D.) (Co)	1	0
University of Washington (Ph.D.) (Cl)	2	1
Virginia Consortium Program in Clinical Psychology (Ph.D.) (Cl)	3	1
Western Michigan University (Ph.D.) (Cl)	2	1
Wichita State University (Ph.D.) (Cl)	1	0

Marriage/Couples

	# Faculty	# Grants
Adelphi University (Ph.D.) (Cl)	0	0
Binghamton University, State University of New York (Ph.D.) (Cl)	3	0
Biola University (Ph.D.) (Cl)	1	0
Biola University (Psy.D.) (Cl)	1	0
Brigham Young University (Ph.D.) (Cl)	1	1
Catholic University of America (Ph.D.) (Cl)	1	0
Clark University (Ph.D.) (Cl)	3	1
Florida School of Professional Psychology at Argosy University (Psy.D.) (Cl)	4	0
Fuller Theological Seminary (Ph.D.) (Cl)	5	0
Fuller Theological Seminary (Psy.D.) (Cl)	5	0
George Mason University (Ph.D.) (Cl)	2	–
George Washington University (Ph.D.) (Cl)	2	2
Indiana University–Bloomington (Ph.D.) (Co)	1	–
La Salle University (Psy.D.) (Cl)	1	0
Louisiana Tech University (Ph.D.) (Co)	1	0
Palo Alto University (Psy.D.) (Cl)	2	0
Pepperdine University (Psy.D.) (Cl)	1	0
Purdue University (Ph.D.) (Cl)	3	1
Radford University (Psy.D.) (Co)	1	0
Regent University (Psy.D.) (Cl)	2	3
Seattle Pacific University (Ph.D.) (Cl)	2	0
Temple University (Ph.D.) (Cl)	1	0
Tennessee State University (Ph.D.) (Co)	2	0
Texas A&M University (Ph.D.) (Cl)	2	–
The Wright Institute (Psy.D.) (Cl)	4	–
University of California, Los Angeles (Ph.D.) (Cl)	2	5
University of Colorado Denver (Ph.D.) (Cl)	2	1
University of Delaware (Ph.D.) (Cl)	1	1
University of Denver (Ph.D.) (Cl)	5	1
University of Denver (Psy.D.) (Cl)	1	0
University of Georgia (Ph.D.) (Cl)	2	1
University of Houston (Ph.D.) (Cl)	2	0
University of Iowa (Ph.D.) (Cl)	1	0
University of La Verne (Psy.D.) (Cl)	1	0
University of Miami (Ph.D.) (Cl)	2	2
University of Missouri Kansas City (Ph.D.) (Co)	2	–
University of North Carolina, Chapel Hill (Ph.D.) (Cl)	1	1
University of North Texas (Ph.D.) (Co)	3	2
University of Northern Colorado (Ph.D.) (Co)	1	0
University of Rochester (Ph.D.) (Cl)	1	1
University of Southern California (Ph.D.) (Cl)	2	1
University of Tennessee–Knoxville (Ph.D.) (Cl)	4	3
University of Utah (Ph.D.) (Cl)	4	3
University of Wyoming (Ph.D.) (Cl)	1	1
Virginia Commonwealth University (Ph.D.) (Co)	2	0
Wright State University (Psy.D.) (Cl)	2	–

Master Therapists

Saint Mary's University of Minnesota (Psy.D.) (Co)	1	0
University of St. Thomas (Psy.D.) (Co)	1	0

Memory

Carlow University (Psy.D.) (Co)	1	–
Drexel University (Ph.D.) (Cl)	2	0
Gallaudet University (Ph.D.) (Cl)	2	0
George Fox University (Psy.D.) (Cl)	1	0
Nova Southeastern University (Ph.D.) (Cl)	1	1
Nova Southeastern University (Psy.D.) (Cl)	1	1
Philadelphia College of Osteopathic Medicine (Psy.D.) (Cl)	1	0
Springfield College (Psy.D.) (Co)	1	–
The New School (Ph.D.) (Cl)	2	1
The University of Montana (Ph.D.) (Cl)	2	1
University of Georgia (Ph.D.) (Cl)	2	–
Virginia Polytechnic Institute and State University (Ph.D.) (Cl)	1	1

Men's Issues

Clark University (Ph.D.) (Cl)	1	0
Colorado State University (Ph.D.) (Co)	1	0
Howard University (Ph.D.) (Co)	2	0
Indiana University–Bloomington (Ph.D.) (Co)	2	–
John F. Kennedy University (Psy.D.) (Cl)	2	0
Tennessee State University (Ph.D.) (Co)	1	0
The University of Akron (Ph.D.) (Co)	1	1
The University of Memphis (Ph.D.) (Co)	3	0
The Wright Institute (Psy.D.) (Cl)	1	–
University of Georgia (Ph.D.) (Co)	1	1
University of Houston (Ph.D.) (Co)	2	1
University of Iowa (Ph.D.) (Co)	3	0
University of Maryland–College Park (Ph.D.) (Co)	1	0
University of Texas at Austin (Ph.D.) (Co)	2	0
University of Wisconsin, Milwaukee (Ph.D.) (Co)	1	0
Yeshiva University (Psy.D.) (Cm)	1	0

Mental Health Services/Policy

Alliant International University, Los Angeles (Ph.D.) (Cl)	3	0
Northwestern University Feinberg School of Medicine (Ph.D.) (Cl)	3	2
Rutgers–The State University of New Jersey (Psy.D.) (Cl)	1	–
Seattle Pacific University (Ph.D.) (Cl)	1	0
University of Houston (Ph.D.) (Co)	1	0

Methodology

	# Faculty	# Grants
Chicago School of Professional Psychology–Washington, DC Campus (Psy.D.) (Cl)	1	0
Hofstra University (Ph.D.) (Cl)	1	0
Sam Houston State University (Ph.D.) (Cl)	1	–
Springfield College (Psy.D.) (Co)	1	–
Texas A&M University (Ph.D.) (Co)	1	0
The Wright Institute (Psy.D.) (Cl)	6	–
University at Albany (Ph.D.) (Co)	1	0
University of Georgia (Ph.D.) (Cl)	1	1

Mindfulness

	# Faculty	# Grants
American University (Ph.D.) (Cl)	1	0
Carlow University (Psy.D.) (Co)	1	–
Catholic University of America (Ph.D.) (Cl)	3	0
Chicago School of Professional Psychology–Washington, DC Campus (Psy.D.) (Cl)	1	0
Drexel University (Ph.D.) (Cl)	3	3
Georgia Southern University (Psy.D.) (Cl)	2	0
Georgia State University (Ph.D.) (Cl)	3	1
Kean University (Psy.D.) (Cm)	3	1
La Salle University (Psy.D.) (Cl)	1	0
Marywood University (Psy.D.) (Cl)	1	0
Midwestern University–Glendale Campus (Psy.D.) (Cl)	1	0
Northwestern University Feinberg School of Medicine (Ph.D.) (Cl)	1	1
Oklahoma State University (Ph.D.) (Co)	1	0
Roosevelt University (Psy.D.) (Cl)	1	0
The University of Montana (Ph.D.) (Cl)	1	0
The Wright Institute (Psy.D.) (Cl)	1	–
University at Albany (Ph.D.) (Cl)	3	–
University at Buffalo, State University of New York (Ph.D.) (Cm)	3	0
University of Illinois at Urbana–Champaign (Ph.D.) (Cl)	1	2
University of Maine (Ph.D.) (Cl)	1	0
University of Nevada, Reno (Ph.D.) (Cl)	1	0
University of South Alabama (Ph.D.) (Cm)	1	–
University of Toledo (Ph.D.) (Cl)	1	0

Minority/Cross-Cultural/Diversity

	# Faculty	# Grants
Adelphi University (Ph.D.) (Cl)	1	1
Adler University–Chicago (Psy.D.) (Cl)	7	2
Alliant International University, Fresno (Ph.D.) (Cl)	1	0
Alliant International University, Fresno (Psy.D.) (Cl)	2	1
Alliant International University, Los Angeles (Ph.D.) (Cl)	7	0
Alliant International University, Los Angeles (Psy.D.) (Cl)	4	0
Alliant International University, Sacramento (Psy.D.) (Cl)	1	0
Alliant International University, San Diego (Ph.D.) (Cl)	2	0
Alliant International University, San Diego (Psy.D.) (Cl)	5	0
Alliant International University, San Francisco Bay (Ph.D.) (Cl)	7	1
Alliant International University, San Francisco Bay (Psy.D.) (Cl)	10	0
American School of Professional Psychology at Argosy University, Washington, DC (Psy.D.) (Cl)	4	–
American University (Ph.D.) (Cl)	1	0
Antioch University New England (Psy.D.) (Cl)	2	0
Arizona School of Professional Psychology at Argosy University, Phoenix (Psy.D.) (Cl)	5	0
Arizona State University (Ph.D.) (Cl)	5	3
Arizona State University (Ph.D.) (Co)	1	1
Auburn University (Ph.D.) (Co)	4	2
Azusa Pacific University (Psy.D.) (Cl)	2	0
Ball State University (Ph.D.) (Co)	2	4
Boston College (Ph.D.) (Co)	6	2
Boston University (Ph.D.) (Cl)	1	0
California Lutheran University (Psy.D.) (Cl)	2	0
Chatham University (Psy.D.) (Co)	4	0
Chicago School of Professional Psychology–Chicago Campus (Psy.D.) (Cl)	3	0
Chicago School of Professional Psychology–Washington, DC Campus (Psy.D.) (Cl)	4	0
Clark University (Ph.D.) (Cl)	3	2
Cleveland State University (Ph.D.) (Co)	4	0
Colorado State University (Ph.D.) (Co)	6	3
DePaul University (Ph.D.) (Cl)	5	2
Eastern Michigan University (Ph.D.) (Cl)	2	0
Fairleigh Dickinson University (Ph.D.) (Cl)	2	0
Fielding Graduate University (Ph.D.) (Cl)	4	0
Florida School of Professional Psychology at Argosy University (Psy.D.) (Cl)	4	0
Fordham University (Ph.D.) (Cl)	1	1
Fordham University (Ph.D.) (Co)	5	0
Fuller Theological Seminary (Ph.D.) (Cl)	4	4
Fuller Theological Seminary (Psy.D.) (Cl)	4	4
Gallaudet University (Ph.D.) (Cl)	1	0
George Fox University (Psy.D.) (Cl)	2	0
George Washington University (Ph.D.) (Cl)	4	3
George Washington University (Psy.D.) (Cl)	1	–
Georgia School of Professional Psychology at Argosy University, Atlanta (Psy.D.) (Cl)	2	0
Georgia State University (Ph.D.) (Cl)	1	0
Georgia State University (Ph.D.) (Co)	2	2

	# Faculty	# Grants
Hawaii School of Professional Psychology at Argosy University, Hawaii (Psy.D.) (Cl)	9	0
Hofstra University (Ph.D.) (Cl)	1	0
Howard University (Ph.D.) (Co)	6	0
Illinois School of Professional Psychology at Argosy University, Chicago (Psy.D.) (Cl)	3	1
Indiana University–Bloomington (Ph.D.) (Co)	1	–
Indiana University of Pennsylvania (Psy.D.) (Cl)	3	0
Iowa State University (Ph.D.) (Co)	6	0
James Madison University (Psy.D.) (Cm)	4	1
John F. Kennedy University (Psy.D.) (Cl)	6	0
John Jay College of Criminal Justice & The Graduate Center, CUNY (Ph.D.) (Cl)	1	0
Kean University (Psy.D.) (Cm)	4	0
Lehigh University (Ph.D.) (Co)	3	2
Long Island University (Ph.D.) (Cl)	4	0
Louisiana Tech University (Ph.D.) (Co)	1	0
Loyola University Chicago (Ph.D.) (Cl)	5	3
Loyola University Chicago (Ph.D.) (Co)	2	0
Loyola University Maryland (Psy.D.) (Cl)	3	0
Marquette University (Ph.D.) (Co)	4	0
Marquette University (Ph.D.) (Cl)	5	0
Marywood University (Psy.D.) (Cl)	2	0
Miami University (OH) (Ph.D.) (Cl)	6	1
Michigan State University (Ph.D.) (Cl)	1	0
Midwestern University (Psy.D.) (Cl)	1	–
New Mexico State University (Ph.D.) (Co)	3	0
New York University (Ph.D.) (Co)	2	0
Northern Illinois University (Ph.D.) (Cl)	3	0
Oklahoma State University (Ph.D.) (Co)	11	0
Pace University (Psy.D.) (Cm)	2	0
Pacific University, Oregon (Psy.D.) (Cl)	8	0
Palo Alto University (Ph.D.) (Cl)	7	–
Palo Alto University (Psy.D.) (Cl)	4	2
Pepperdine University (Psy.D.) (Cl)	6	0
Philadelphia College of Osteopathic Medicine (Psy.D.) (Cl)	4	0
Purdue University (Ph.D.) (Cl)	1	0
Purdue University (Ph.D.) (Co)	1	1
Regent University (Psy.D.) (Cl)	2	–
Roosevelt University (Psy.D.) (Cl)	3	0
Rutgers–The State University of New Jersey (Psy.D.) (Cl)	1	–
Saint Louis University (Ph.D.) (Cl)	1	0
Saint Mary's University of Minnesota (Psy.D.) (Co)	2	0
Sam Houston State University (Ph.D.) (Cl)	2	2
San Diego State University–UC San Diego (Ph.D.) (Cl)	12	>1
Seattle Pacific University (Ph.D.) (Cl)	1	1
Seton Hall University (Ph.D.) (Co)	4	1
Southern Illinois University Carbondale (Ph.D.) (Co)	3	0
Southern Methodist University (Ph.D.) (Cl)	1	0
Spalding University (Psy.D.) (Cl)	2	0
St. John's University (Ph.D.) (Cl)	4	0
Teachers College, Columbia University (Ph.D.) (Co)	14	0
Tennessee State University (Ph.D.) (Co)	3	0
Texas A&M University (Ph.D.) (Co)	2	0
Texas Tech University (Ph.D.) (Cl)	1	0
Texas Tech University (Ph.D.) (Co)	3	0
Texas Woman's University (Ph.D.) (Co)	3	–
The City College of New York, The Graduate Center, CUNY (Ph.D.) (Cl)	4	1
The University of Memphis (Ph.D.) (Co)	6	0
The University of Montana (Ph.D.) (Cl)	2	1
The University of South Dakota (Ph.D.) (Cl)	8	0
The Wright Institute (Psy.D.) (Cl)	11	–
University at Albany (Ph.D.) (Co)	4	2
University at Albany (Ph.D.) (Cl)	1	–
University at Buffalo, State University of New York (Ph.D.) (Cm)	2	0
University of Alabama at Tuscaloosa (Ph.D.) (Cl)	2	3
University of Alaska Fairbanks–Anchorage (Ph.D.) (Cl)	2	0
University of Arkansas (Ph.D.) (Cl)	3	1
University of California, Los Angeles (Ph.D.) (Cl)	3	5
University of California, Santa Barbara (Ph.D.) (Cm)	1	–
University of Connecticut (Ph.D.) (Cl)	2	2
University of Denver (Ph.D.) (Co)	3	1
University of Denver (Ph.D.) (Cl)	2	0
University of Denver (Psy.D.) (Cl)	3	1
University of Florida (Ph.D.) (Co)	1	0
University of Georgia (Ph.D.) (Co)	4	3
University of Hartford (Psy.D.) (Cl)	3	0
University of Hawaii at Manoa (Ph.D.) (Cl)	2	0
University of Houston (Ph.D.) (Cl)	3	2
University of Houston (Ph.D.) (Co)	5	3
University of Illinois at Urbana–Champaign (Ph.D.) (Cl)	6	3
University of Indianapolis (Psy.D.) (Cl)	2	1
University of Iowa (Ph.D.) (Co)	2	1
University of Kansas–Child (Ph.D.) (Cl)	4	1
University of Kansas (Ph.D.) (Co)	2	0
University of Kentucky (Ph.D.) (Co)	1	–
University of La Verne (Psy.D.) (Cl)	8	2
University of Louisville (Ph.D.) (Co)	2	0
University of Maryland–College Park (Ph.D.) (Co)	4	1
University of Massachusetts, Boston (Ph.D.) (Cl)	2	1
University of Miami (Ph.D.) (Co)	4	3
University of Michigan (Ph.D.) (Cl)	3	4
University of Minnesota (Ph.D.) (Cl)	–	–
University of Minnesota (Ph.D.) (Co)	2	2
University of Mississippi (Ph.D.) (Cl)	2	0

	# Faculty	# Grants
University of Missouri Kansas City (Ph.D.) (Co)	5	–
University of Missouri, Columbia (Ph.D.) (Co)	4	1
University of Missouri, St. Louis (Ph.D.) (Cl)	1	1
University of Nebraska, Lincoln (Ph.D.) (Co)	3	1
University of Nevada Las Vegas (Ph.D.) (Cl)	1	0
University of Nevada, Reno (Ph.D.) (Cl)	4	1
University of New Mexico (Ph.D.) (Cl)	2	2
University of North Carolina, Chapel Hill (Ph.D.) (Cl)	2	1
University of North Carolina, Greensboro (Ph.D.) (Cl)	2	1
University of North Dakota (Ph.D.) (Cl)	4	1
University of North Dakota (Ph.D.) (Co)	2	0
University of North Texas (Ph.D.) (Cl)	3	1
University of North Texas (Ph.D.) (Co)	2	0
University of Northern Colorado (Ph.D.) (Co)	1	0
University of Oregon (Ph.D.) (Cl)	1	0
University of Oregon (Ph.D.) (Co)	4	1
University of Rhode Island (Ph.D.) (Cl)	1	1
University of South Alabama (Ph.D.) (Cm)	1	–
University of South Carolina (Ph.D.) (Cl)	6	7
University of Southern California (Ph.D.) (Cl)	6	4
University of Southern Mississippi (Ph.D.) (Co)	6	0
University of St. Thomas (Psy.D.) (Co)	4	0
University of Tennessee–Knoxville (Ph.D.) (Co)	5	0
University of Texas at Austin (Ph.D.) (Cl)	1	0
University of Texas at Austin (Ph.D.) (Co)	5	3
University of Texas Southwestern Medical Center (Ph.D.) (Cl)	2	1
University of Toledo (Ph.D.) (Cl)	3	0
University of Utah (Ph.D.) (Cl)	1	1
University of Utah (Ph.D.) (Co)	3	0
University of Virginia (Ph.D.) (Cl)	2	2
University of Virginia (Ph.D.) (Cm)	1	0
University of Washington (Ph.D.) (Cl)	2	2
Utah State University (Ph.D.) (Cm)	5	0
Virginia Commonwealth University (Ph.D.) (Cl)	3	1
Virginia Commonwealth University (Ph.D.) (Co)	3	0
Virginia Consortium Program in Clinical Psychology (Ph.D.) (Cl)	2	1
West Virginia University (Ph.D.) (Cl)	1	0
West Virginia University (Ph.D.) (Co)	1	0
Western Michigan University (Ph.D.) (Co)	4	0
Wheaton College (Psy.D.) (Cl)	1	0
Widener University (Psy.D.) (Cl)	2	0
Yeshiva University (Psy.D.) (Cl)	2	0
Yeshiva University (Psy.D.) (Cm)	3	0

Moral Development

Azusa Pacific University (Psy.D.) (Cl)	2	1
The New School (Ph.D.) (Cl)	1	1
University of La Verne (Psy.D.) (Cl)	2	0

Motivation

Adelphi University (Ph.D.) (Cl)	1	0
Clark University (Ph.D.) (Cl)	2	0
James Madison University (Psy.D.) (Cm)	1	0
University of Alaska Fairbanks–Anchorage (Ph.D.) (Cl)	1	0
University of Georgia (Ph.D.) (Cl)	1	–

Multiple Sclerosis

University of Georgia (Ph.D.) (Cl)	1	–
Yeshiva University (Ph.D.) (Cl)	1	2

Narrative Psychology

The New School (Ph.D.) (Cl)	2	0
The Wright Institute (Psy.D.) (Cl)	2	–

Neuroimaging/Functional Neuroimaging

Brigham Young University (Ph.D.) (Cl)	2	1
Drexel University (Ph.D.) (Cl)	2	0
Georgia State University (Ph.D.) (Cl)	5	2
Northwestern University Feinberg School of Medicine (Ph.D.) (Cl)	5	3
Rosalind Franklin University of Medicine and Science (Ph.D.) (Cl)	1	0
San Diego State University–UC San Diego (Ph.D.) (Cl)	19	>1
University of Florida (Ph.D.) (Cl)	3	2
University of Georgia (Ph.D.) (Cl)	3	3
University of Illinois at Urbana–Champaign (Ph.D.) (Cl)	3	3
University of Michigan (Ph.D.) (Cl)	4	7
University of Minnesota (Ph.D.) (Cl)	–	–
University of New Mexico (Ph.D.) (Cl)	3	3
University of Pittsburgh (Ph.D.) (Cl)	14	31
Virginia Polytechnic Institute and State University (Ph.D.) (Cl)	4	1

Neuropsychology

Adelphi University (Ph.D.) (Cl)	2	2
Alliant International University, Los Angeles (Psy.D.) (Cl)	2	0

	# Faculty	# Grants
Alliant International University, Sacramento (Psy.D.) (Cl)	1	0
Alliant International University, San Diego (Ph.D.) (Cl)	2	1
Alliant International University, San Francisco Bay (Psy.D.) (Cl)	1	0
American School of Professional Psychology at Argosy University, Washington, DC (Psy.D.) (Cl)	3	–
Arizona School of Professional Psychology at Argosy University, Phoenix (Psy.D.) (Cl)	1	0
Azusa Pacific University (Psy.D.) (Cl)	1	0
Biola University (Ph.D.) (Cl)	3	0
Biola University (Psy.D.) (Cl)	3	0
Boston University (Ph.D.) (Cl)	3	2
Brigham Young University (Ph.D.) (Cl)	4	3
Duke University (Ph.D.) (Cl)	1	1
East Carolina University (Ph.D.) (Cl)	1	0
Eastern Michigan University (Ph.D.) (Cl)	2	0
Emory University (Ph.D.) (Cl)	1	0
Fielding Graduate University (Ph.D.) (Cl)	4	0
Florida Institute of Technology (Psy.D.) (Cl)	1	1
Florida International University (Ph.D.) (Cl)	1	1
Fordham University (Ph.D.) (Cl)	2	4
Fuller Theological Seminary (Ph.D.) (Cl)	4	0
Fuller Theological Seminary (Psy.D.) (Cl)	4	0
Gallaudet University (Ph.D.) (Cl)	3	0
George Fox University (Psy.D.) (Cl)	1	1
Georgia School of Professional Psychology at Argosy University, Atlanta (Psy.D.) (Cl)	2	0
Georgia State University (Ph.D.) (Cl)	7	4
Hawaii School of Professional Psychology at Argosy University, Hawaii (Psy.D.) (Cl)	2	0
Indiana University–Bloomington (Ph.D.) (Cl)	4	3
Kent State University (Ph.D.) (Cl)	2	2
Loma Linda University (Ph.D.) (Cl)	2	0
Loma Linda University (Psy.D.) (Cl)	2	0
Long Island University (Ph.D.) (Cl)	1	1
Louisiana Tech University (Ph.D.) (Co)	1	0
Loyola University Maryland (Psy.D.) (Cl)	2	0
Marquette University (Ph.D.) (Cl)	4	0
Marywood University (Psy.D.) (Cl)	1	0
Midwestern University–Glendale Campus (Psy.D.) (Cl)	1	0
Nova Southeastern University (Ph.D.) (Cl)	1	1
Nova Southeastern University (Psy.D.) (Cl)	1	1
Ohio University (Ph.D.) (Cl)	1	0
Pacific University, Oregon (Psy.D.) (Cl)	2	0
Palo Alto University (Ph.D.) (Cl)	4	–
Pennsylvania State University (Ph.D.) (Cl)	3	4
Ponce Health Sciences University (Ph.D.) (Cl)	2	0
Ponce Health Sciences University (Psy.D.) (Cl)	2	1
Queens College and The Graduate Center, City University of New York (Ph.D.) (Cl)	2	0
Roosevelt University (Psy.D.) (Cl)	4	0
Saint Louis University (Ph.D.) (Cl)	2	0
San Diego State University–UC San Diego (Ph.D.) (Cl)	42	>1
Temple University (Ph.D.) (Cl)	1	0
Texas Tech University (Ph.D.) (Cl)	1	0
The University of Montana (Ph.D.) (Cl)	2	1
The Wright Institute (Psy.D.) (Cl)	2	–
University of Alabama at Birmingham (Ph.D.) (Cl)	10	7
University of Arizona (Ph.D.) (Cl)	3	5
University of Cincinnati (Ph.D.) (Cl)	4	3
University of Colorado at Colorado Springs (Ph.D.) (Cl)	2	0
University of Colorado Denver (Ph.D.) (Cl)	1	2
University of Connecticut (Ph.D.) (Cl)	3	3
University of Denver (Ph.D.) (Cl)	1	0
University of Denver (Psy.D.) (Cl)	1	1
University of Florida (Ph.D.) (Cl)	5	4
University of Georgia (Ph.D.) (Cl)	3	3
University of Houston (Ph.D.) (Cl)	3	4
University of Illinois at Urbana–Champaign (Ph.D.) (Cl)	2	1
University of Iowa (Ph.D.) (Cl)	2	2
University of Kentucky (Ph.D.) (Cl)	2	0
University of Maine (Ph.D.) (Cl)	2	0
University of Michigan (Ph.D.) (Cl)	1	3
University of Missouri Kansas City (Ph.D.) (Cl)	1	2
University of Missouri, Columbia (Ph.D.) (Cl)	2	1
University of Nevada Las Vegas (Ph.D.) (Cl)	1	1
University of New Mexico (Ph.D.) (Cl)	3	3
University of North Carolina at Charlotte (Ph.D.) (Cl)	1	1
University of North Texas (Ph.D.) (Cl)	3	2
University of South Alabama (Ph.D.) (Cm)	1	–
University of South Carolina (Ph.D.) (Cl)	2	2
University of South Florida (Ph.D.) (Cl)	1	1
University of Texas Southwestern Medical Center (Ph.D.) (Cl)	2	2
University of Tulsa (Ph.D.) (Cl)	1	1
University of Utah (Ph.D.) (Cl)	2	1
University of Virginia (Ph.D.) (Cl)	1	1
University of Wisconsin, Milwaukee (Ph.D.) (Cl)	4	7
Vanderbilt University (Ph.D.) (Cl)	2	3
Virginia Consortium Program in Clinical Psychology (Ph.D.) (Cl)	2	1
Virginia Polytechnic Institute and State University (Ph.D.) (Cl)	8	4
Washington State University (Ph.D.) (Cl)	2	5
Washington University in St. Louis (Ph.D.) (Cl)	2	0
Wayne State University (Ph.D.) (Cl)	4	2
Wheaton College (Psy.D.) (Cl)	1	0

	# Faculty	# Grants
Wisconsin School of Professional Psychology (Psy.D.) (Cl)	–	–
Yeshiva University (Ph.D.) (Cl)	2	2

Nicotine/Tobacco/Smoking (also see Substance Abuse/Addictive Behaviors)

American University (Ph.D.) (Cl)	2	1
Northwestern University Feinberg School of Medicine (Ph.D.) (Cl)	1	1
San Diego State University–UC San Diego (Ph.D.) (Cl)	5	>1
Southern Illinois University Carbondale (Ph.D.) (Cl)	1	–
Syracuse University (Ph.D.) (Cl)	2	2
Texas Tech University (Ph.D.) (Cl)	1	1
Uniformed Services University of the Health Sciences (Ph.D.) (Cl)	1	1
University of Georgia (Ph.D.) (Cl)	1	–
University of Illinois at Chicago (Ph.D.) (Cl)	2	3
University of Mississippi (Ph.D.) (Cl)	1	0
University of Pittsburgh (Ph.D.) (Cl)	3	3

Obsessive-Compulsive Disorder (also see Anxiety Disorders)

American University (Ph.D.) (Cl)	1	0
Binghamton University, State University of New York (Ph.D.) (Cl)	1	0
Brigham Young University (Ph.D.) (Cl)	2	1
Fairleigh Dickinson University (Ph.D.) (Cl)	1	0
Miami University (OH) (Ph.D.) (Cl)	2	0
Northern Illinois University (Ph.D.) (Cl)	3	0
University of Virginia (Ph.D.) (Cl)	1	1

Oncology/Cancer Care

Northwestern University Feinberg School of Medicine (Ph.D.) (Cl)	3	1
Ponce Health Sciences University (Psy.D.) (Cl)	1	–
San Diego State University–UC San Diego (Ph.D.) (Cl)	5	>1
The Ohio State University (Ph.D.) (Cl)	1	7
University of Denver (Psy.D.) (Cl)	1	0
University of Iowa (Ph.D.) (Co)	2	1
University of Kansas (Ph.D.) (Cl)	3	2
University of Miami (Ph.D.) (Cl)	4	1
University of Pittsburgh (Ph.D.) (Cl)	2	3

Organizational

Alliant International University, Sacramento (Psy.D.) (Cl)	1	0
Marquette University (Ph.D.) (Cl)	1	0
Pacific University, Oregon (Psy.D.) (Cl)	1	0
The Wright Institute (Psy.D.) (Cl)	2	–
University of Detroit Mercy (Ph.D.) (Cl)	2	0

Pain Management

Duke University (Ph.D.) (Cl)	2	4
East Carolina University (Ph.D.) (Cl)	1	1
Georgia State University (Ph.D.) (Cl)	1	3
Jackson State University (Ph.D.) (Cl)	2	1
Midwestern University–Glendale Campus (Psy.D.) (Cl)	1	0
Philadelphia College of Osteopathic Medicine (Psy.D.) (Cl)	1	0
Sam Houston State University (Ph.D.) (Cl)	2	–
Syracuse University (Ph.D.) (Cl)	1	2
University of Alabama at Tuscaloosa (Ph.D.) (Cl)	1	4
University of Colorado Denver (Ph.D.) (Cl)	2	2
University of Florida (Ph.D.) (Cl)	2	4
University of Georgia (Ph.D.) (Cl)	1	–
University of Kansas (Ph.D.) (Cl)	1	0
University of Kentucky (Ph.D.) (Cl)	1	0
University of Nevada, Reno (Ph.D.) (Cl)	1	0
University of North Dakota (Ph.D.) (Cl)	1	0
University of Texas Southwestern Medical Center (Ph.D.) (Cl)	1	1
University of Tulsa (Ph.D.) (Cl)	1	2
West Virginia University (Ph.D.) (Cl)	1	1

Parent–Child Interactions/Parenting

Auburn University (Ph.D.) (Cl)	1	0
Biola University (Ph.D.) (Cl)	1	0
Biola University (Psy.D.) (Cl)	1	0
California Lutheran University (Psy.D.) (Cl)	4	0
Carlos Albizu University, San Juan Campus (Ph.D.) (Cl)	1	–
Case Western Reserve University (Ph.D.) (Cl)	2	0
Catholic University of America (Ph.D.) (Cl)	7	2
Clark University (Ph.D.) (Cl)	3	1
Colorado State University (Ph.D.) (Co)	1	0
Florida International University (Ph.D.) (Cl)	2	2
Gallaudet University (Ph.D.) (Cl)	1	0
Georgia State University (Ph.D.) (Cl)	2	2
Howard University (Ph.D.) (Co)	1	0
Illinois School of Professional Psychology at Argosy University, Chicago (Psy.D.) (Cl)	1	0
Indiana University of Pennsylvania (Psy.D.) (Cl)	4	1
James Madison University (Psy.D.) (Cm)	2	0
Long Island University, C.W. Post Campus (Psy.D.) (Cl)	2	1
Marquette University (Ph.D.) (Co)	2	2

	# Faculty	# Grants
Marquette University (Ph.D.) (Cl)	3	1
Northern Illinois University (Ph.D.) (Cl)	4	0
Oklahoma State University (Ph.D.) (Cl)	1	0
Pennsylvania State University (Ph.D.) (Cl)	3	2
St. John's University (Ph.D.) (Cl)	1	0
Texas Tech University (Ph.D.) (Cl)	1	0
The University of Montana (Ph.D.) (Cl)	2	0
The Wright Institute (Psy.D.) (Cl)	1	–
University of Denver (Ph.D.) (Cl)	2	0
University of Georgia (Ph.D.) (Cl)	4	1
University of Indianapolis (Psy.D.) (Cl)	1	1
University of Minnesota (Ph.D.) (Co)	1	1
University of Northern Colorado (Ph.D.) (Co)	1	0
University of Oregon (Ph.D.) (Cl)	3	2
University of Southern Mississippi (Ph.D.) (Cl)	–	–
University of Southern Mississippi (Ph.D.) (Co)	1	0
University of Virginia (Ph.D.) (Cm)	2	0
Virginia Consortium Program in Clinical Psychology (Ph.D.) (Cl)	3	0
Yeshiva University (Psy.D.) (Cl)	2	0

Personality Assessment

Adelphi University (Ph.D.) (Cl)	2	2
Adler University–Chicago (Psy.D.) (Cl)	1	–
Alliant International University, Los Angeles (Ph.D.) (Cl)	1	0
Arizona State University (Ph.D.) (Cl)	1	0
Baylor University (Psy.D.) (Cl)	3	2
Carlos Albizu University, San Juan Campus (Ph.D.) (Cl)	1	–
Carlow University (Psy.D.) (Co)	1	–
Chatham University (Psy.D.) (Co)	1	0
Florida Institute of Technology (Psy.D.) (Cl)	1	0
Fuller Theological Seminary (Ph.D.) (Cl)	1	3
Fuller Theological Seminary (Psy.D.) (Cl)	1	3
Kent State University (Ph.D.) (Cl)	1	1
Louisiana Tech University (Ph.D.) (Co)	3	0
Pennsylvania State University (Ph.D.) (Cl)	1	1
Philadelphia College of Osteopathic Medicine (Psy.D.) (Cl)	3	0
Ponce Health Sciences University (Psy.D.) (Cl)	1	–
Purdue University (Ph.D.) (Cl)	4	1
Sam Houston State University (Ph.D.) (Cl)	1	–
Southern Illinois University Carbondale (Ph.D.) (Cl)	3	0
Syracuse University (Ph.D.) (Cl)	2	0
The New School (Ph.D.) (Cl)	1	0
University at Buffalo, State University of New York (Ph.D.) (Cl)	1	1
University of Georgia (Ph.D.) (Cl)	2	–
University of Kentucky (Ph.D.) (Cl)	3	1
University of Minnesota (Ph.D.) (Cl)	–	–
University of North Dakota (Ph.D.) (Cl)	2	0
University of Southern Mississippi (Ph.D.) (Cl)	–	–
University of Utah (Ph.D.) (Cl)	1	0
Virginia Consortium Program in Clinical Psychology (Ph.D.) (Cl)	3	1
West Virginia University (Ph.D.) (Co)	2	0

Personality Disorders

Alliant International University, Los Angeles (Ph.D.) (Cl)	1	0
Alliant International University, San Diego (Ph.D.) (Cl)	8	1
Alliant International University, San Francisco Bay (Psy.D.) (Cl)	4	0
American University (Ph.D.) (Cl)	1	0
Binghamton University, State University of New York (Ph.D.) (Cl)	1	1
Boston University (Ph.D.) (Cl)	1	0
Carlos Albizu University, San Juan Campus (Ph.D.) (Cl)	1	–
Case Western Reserve University (Ph.D.) (Cl)	1	2
Eastern Michigan University (Ph.D.) (Cl)	1	0
Emory University (Ph.D.) (Cl)	2	–
Florida State University (Ph.D.) (Cl)	2	0
Fordham University (Ph.D.) (Cl)	1	0
Harvard University (Ph.D.) (Cl)	2	1
Hofstra University (Ph.D.) (Cl)	2	0
Illinois School of Professional Psychology at Argosy University, Chicago (Psy.D.) (Cl)	1	0
Indiana State University (Psy.D.) (Cl)	2	0
James Madison University (Psy.D.) (Cm)	1	0
Northern Illinois University (Ph.D.) (Cl)	2	0
Pacific University, Oregon (Psy.D.) (Cl)	1	0
Pennsylvania State University (Ph.D.) (Cl)	4	1
Philadelphia College of Osteopathic Medicine (Psy.D.) (Cl)	1	0
Purdue University (Ph.D.) (Cl)	5	1
Queens College and The Graduate Center, City University of New York (Ph.D.) (Cl)	1	0
Rutgers–The State University of New Jersey (Psy.D.) (Cl)	1	–
St. John's University (Ph.D.) (Cl)	1	0
Stony Brook University, State University of New York (Ph.D.) (Cl)	3	1
Texas A&M University (Ph.D.) (Cl)	3	–
The City College of New York, The Graduate Center, CUNY (Ph.D.) (Cl)	1	1
The Wright Institute (Psy.D.) (Cl)	11	–
University of Detroit Mercy (Ph.D.) (Cl)	4	0
University of Georgia (Ph.D.) (Cl)	1	–
University of Houston (Ph.D.) (Cl)	1	3
University of Iowa (Ph.D.) (Cl)	2	1
University of Kentucky (Ph.D.) (Cl)	2	0
University of Michigan (Ph.D.) (Cl)	1	1

	# Faculty	# Grants
University of Minnesota (Ph.D.) (Cl)	–	–
University of Missouri, Columbia (Ph.D.) (Cl)	1	2
University of North Carolina, Greensboro (Ph.D.) (Cl)	1	0
University of North Dakota (Ph.D.) (Cl)	3	0
University of Notre Dame (Ph.D.) P(Cl)	2	1
University of Oregon (Ph.D.) (Cl)	1	1
University of Pittsburgh (Ph.D.) (Cl)	1	1
University of Southern Mississippi (Ph.D.) (Cl)	–	–
University of Texas Southwestern Medical Center (Ph.D.) (Cl)	2	–
University of Toledo (Ph.D.) (Cl)	1	0
University of Tulsa (Ph.D.) (Cl)	2	0
University of Virginia (Ph.D.) (Cl)	1	1

Personality/Temperament

Georgia State University (Ph.D.) (Cl)	1	0
Hofstra University (Ph.D.) (Cl)	2	0
Iowa State University (Ph.D.) (Co)	1	0
Long Island University (Ph.D.) (Cl)	4	1
Northern Illinois University (Ph.D.) (Cl)	1	1
Northwestern University (Ph.D.) (Cl)	5	3
Oklahoma State University (Ph.D.) (Cl)	1	0
Pennsylvania State University (Ph.D.) (Cl)	2	0
Sam Houston State University (Ph.D.) (Cl)	1	–
Seattle Pacific University (Ph.D.) (Cl)	2	0
Southern Illinois University Carbondale (Ph.D.) (Cl)	1	0
The Ohio State University (Ph.D.) (Cl)	1	2
University of Florida (Ph.D.) (Co)	1	0
University of Georgia (Ph.D.) (Cl)	2	–
University of Minnesota (Ph.D.) (Co)	1	0
University of Tennessee–Knoxville (Ph.D.) (Co)	1	0
Vanderbilt University (Ph.D.) (Cl)	1	1

Positive Psychology/Resilience

Alliant International University, Los Angeles (Psy.D.) (Cl)	2	0
Brigham Young University (Ph.D.) (Cl)	3	2
California Lutheran University (Psy.D.) (Cl)	1	1
Chatham University (Psy.D.) (Co)	2	0
George Fox University (Psy.D.) (Cl)	1	0
Georgia Southern University (Psy.D.) (Cl)	1	0
Georgia State University (Ph.D.) (Cl)	1	0
Georgia State University (Ph.D.) (Co)	1	3
Indiana University–Bloomington (Ph.D.) (Co)	1	1
Louisiana Tech University (Ph.D.) (Co)	1	0
New York University (Ph.D.) (Co)	1	0
Our Lady of the Lake University (Psy.D.) (Co)	4	0
Pepperdine University (Psy.D.) (Cl)	2	0
Purdue University (Ph.D.) (Co)	1	1
Regent University (Psy.D.) (Cl)	1	1
Seattle Pacific University (Ph.D.) (Cl)	2	1
Seton Hall University (Ph.D.) (Co)	1	0
Teachers College, Columbia University (Ph.D.) (Cl)	2	1
Texas Tech University (Ph.D.) (Co)	1	0
The University of Akron (Ph.D.) (Co)	1	0
The University of Montana (Ph.D.) (Cl)	2	1
University of Alaska Fairbanks–Anchorage (Ph.D.) (Cl)	1	–
University of Denver (Ph.D.) (Cl)	2	0
University of Georgia (Ph.D.) (Cl)	3	–
University of Indianapolis (Psy.D.) (Cl)	1	0
University of Kansas (Ph.D.) (Co)	2	0
University of La Verne (Psy.D.) (Cl)	2	0
University of Louisville (Ph.D.) (Co)	3	1
University of Nebraska, Lincoln (Ph.D.) (Co)	2	2
University of North Dakota (Ph.D.) (Co)	1	0
University of Pennsylvania (Ph.D.) (Cl)	1	3
University of South Alabama (Ph.D.) (Cm)	1	–
University of Southern Mississippi (Ph.D.) (Cl)	–	–
University of Texas at Austin (Ph.D.) (Cl)	1	0
University of Toledo (Ph.D.) (Cl)	1	0

Posttraumatic Stress Disorder/Trauma

Adelphi University (Ph.D.) (Cl)	3	1
Adler University–Chicago (Psy.D.) (Cl)	5	–
Alliant International University, Fresno (Psy.D.) (Cl)	1	0
Alliant International University, Los Angeles (Ph.D.) (Cl)	2	0
Alliant International University, Los Angeles (Psy.D.) (Cl)	4	0
Alliant International University, San Diego (Ph.D.) (Cl)	2	0
Alliant International University, San Diego (Psy.D.) (Cl)	2	0
Alliant International University, San Francisco Bay (Ph.D.) (Cl)	2	0
Alliant International University, San Francisco Bay (Psy.D.) (Cl)	3	0
American School of Professional Psychology at Argosy University, Washington, DC (Psy.D.) (Cl)	1	0
Auburn University (Ph.D.) (Cl)	2	1
Binghamton University, State University of New York (Ph.D.) (Cl)	1	0
Boston College (Ph.D.) (Co)	5	1
Carlos Albizu University, Miami Campus (Psy.D.) (Cl)	4	0
Carlos Albizu University, San Juan Campus (Ph.D.) (Cl)	1	–
Carlow University (Psy.D.) (Co)	2	–

	# Faculty	# Grants
Case Western Reserve University (Ph.D.) (Cl)	2	1
Chicago School of Professional Psychology–Washington, DC Campus (Psy.D.) (Cl)	1	0
Clark University (Ph.D.) (Cl)	2	0
Cleveland State University (Ph.D.) (Co)	1	0
DePaul University (Ph.D.) (Cl)	1	1
East Carolina University (Ph.D.) (Cl)	1	0
Eastern Michigan University (Ph.D.) (Cl)	2	0
Fairleigh Dickinson University (Ph.D.) (Cl)	1	0
Florida Institute of Technology (Psy.D.) (Cl)	1	0
Florida School of Professional Psychology at Argosy University (Psy.D.) (Cl)	3	0
Florida State University (Ph.D.) (Cl)	3	1
Fuller Theological Seminary (Ph.D.) (Cl)	1	0
Fuller Theological Seminary (Psy.D.) (Cl)	1	0
George Mason University (Ph.D.) (Cl)	3	–
Georgia School of Professional Psychology at Argosy University, Atlanta (Psy.D.) (Cl)	3	0
Georgia State University (Ph.D.) (Co)	1	1
Howard University (Ph.D.) (Cl)	2	0
Illinois School of Professional Psychology at Argosy University, Chicago (Psy.D.) (Cl)	2	0
Jackson State University (Ph.D.) (Cl)	1	0
John Jay College of Criminal Justice & The Graduate Center, CUNY (Ph.D.) (Cl)	3	1
Kean University (Psy.D.) (Cm)	5	0
La Salle University (Psy.D.) (Cl)	1	0
Long Island University (Ph.D.) (Cl)	4	1
Long Island University, C.W. Post Campus (Psy.D.) (Cl)	2	1
Louisiana Tech University (Ph.D.) (Co)	1	0
Loyola University Maryland (Psy.D.) (Cl)	4	0
Miami University (OH) (Ph.D.) (Cl)	3	2
Midwestern University–Glendale Campus (Psy.D.) (Cl)	2	0
Northern Illinois University (Ph.D.) (Cl)	7	1
Northwestern University Feinberg School of Medicine (Ph.D.) (Cl)	3	2
Nova Southeastern University (Ph.D.) (Cl)	1	1
Nova Southeastern University (Psy.D.) (Cl)	1	1
Pace University (Psy.D.) (Cm)	2	0
Pacific University, Oregon (Psy.D.) (Cl)	4	0
Palo Alto University (Psy.D.) (Cl)	4	3
Pepperdine University (Psy.D.) (Cl)	3	0
Philadelphia College of Osteopathic Medicine (Psy.D.) (Cl)	1	0
Radford University (Psy.D.) (Co)	2	0
Rosalind Franklin University of Medicine and Science (Ph.D.) (Cl)	1	0
Saint Louis University (Ph.D.) (Cl)	2	0
Saint Mary's University of Minnesota (Psy.D.) (Co)	2	0
Sam Houston State University (Ph.D.) (Cl)	1	–
San Diego State University–UC San Diego (Ph.D.) (Cl)	6	>1
Seattle Pacific University (Ph.D.) (Cl)	3	1
Seton Hall University (Ph.D.) (Co)	1	0
Spalding University (Psy.D.) (Cl)	2	0
Springfield College (Psy.D.) (Co)	1	–
Teachers College, Columbia University (Ph.D.) (Cl)	2	2
Texas Tech University (Ph.D.) (Cl)	1	0
The City College of New York, The Graduate Center, CUNY (Ph.D.) (Cl)	2	1
The New School (Ph.D.) (Cl)	1	1
The University of Montana (Ph.D.) (Cl)	5	0
The Wright Institute (Psy.D.) (Cl)	2	–
Uniformed Services University of the Health Sciences (Ph.D.) (Cl)	1	1
University of Alaska Fairbanks–Anchorage (Ph.D.) (Cl)	1	0
University of California, Santa Barbara (Ph.D.) (Cm)	1	–
University of Colorado at Colorado Springs (Ph.D.) (Cl)	3	3
University of Colorado Denver (Ph.D.) (Cl)	1	1
University of Connecticut (Ph.D.) (Cl)	4	3
University of Denver (Ph.D.) (Cl)	2	0
University of Detroit Mercy (Ph.D.) (Cl)	2	0
University of Georgia (Ph.D.) (Cl)	1	–
University of Georgia (Ph.D.) (Co)	1	1
University of Houston (Ph.D.) (Cl)	1	1
University of Indianapolis (Psy.D.) (Cl)	1	0
University of La Verne (Psy.D.) (Cl)	2	1
University of Louisville (Ph.D.) (Cl)	1	0
University of Massachusetts, Boston (Ph.D.) (Cl)	1	0
University of Miami (Ph.D.) (Cl)	4	2
University of Minnesota (Ph.D.) (Co)	1	1
University of Mississippi (Ph.D.) (Cl)	3	0
University of Missouri Kansas City (Ph.D.) (Cl)	2	2
University of Missouri, Columbia (Ph.D.) (Co)	1	0
University of Missouri, St. Louis (Ph.D.) (Cl)	2	3
University of Nebraska, Lincoln (Ph.D.) (Cl)	3	2
University of Nebraska, Lincoln (Ph.D.) (Co)	1	1
University of Nevada, Reno (Ph.D.) (Cl)	4	2
University of New Mexico (Ph.D.) (Cl)	1	2
University of North Carolina at Charlotte (Ph.D.) (Cl)	6	0
University of North Texas (Ph.D.) (Cl)	1	0
University of Notre Dame (Ph.D.) P(Cl)	1	1
University of Oregon (Ph.D.) (Cl)	2	1
University of South Alabama (Ph.D.) (Cm)	1	–
University of Southern California (Ph.D.) (Cl)	1	0
University of Southern Mississippi (Ph.D.) (Cl)	–	–

	# Faculty	# Grants
University of Tennessee–Knoxville (Ph.D.) (Co)	1	0
University of Toledo (Ph.D.) (Cl)	2	2
University of Tulsa (Ph.D.) (Cl)	3	2
University of Utah (Ph.D.) (Cl)	2	2
University of Vermont (Ph.D.) (Cl)	2	2
University of Wyoming (Ph.D.) (Cl)	2	1
Utah State University (Ph.D.) (Cm)	2	2
Virginia Polytechnic Institute and State University (Ph.D.) (Cl)	6	2
Western Michigan University (Ph.D.) (Cl)	2	0
Yeshiva University (Psy.D.) (Cl)	4	2

Poverty

Northern Illinois University (Ph.D.) (Cl)	1	0
The Wright Institute (Psy.D.) (Cl)	2	–
University of Georgia (Ph.D.) (Cl)	2	3
University of North Dakota (Ph.D.) (Co)	1	0

Prevention

Alliant International University, Los Angeles (Ph.D.) (Cl)	3	0
Alliant International University, San Francisco Bay (Ph.D.) (Cl)	4	0
Alliant International University, San Francisco Bay (Psy.D.) (Cl)	5	0
Arizona State University (Ph.D.) (Cl)	8	4
Clark University (Ph.D.) (Cl)	3	0
DePaul University (Ph.D.) (Cl)	2	2
George Mason University (Ph.D.) (Cl)	9	–
Hofstra University (Ph.D.) (Cl)	1	0
Indiana University of Pennsylvania (Psy.D.) (Cl)	1	0
La Salle University (Psy.D.) (Cl)	1	0
Loyola University Chicago (Ph.D.) (Cl)	3	2
Miami University (OH) (Ph.D.) (Cl)	2	2
Oklahoma State University (Ph.D.) (Co)	11	0
Radford University (Psy.D.) (Co)	1	0
Rutgers–The State University of New Jersey (Ph.D.) (Cl)	2	2
Saint Mary's University of Minnesota (Psy.D.) (Co)	1	0
San Diego State University–UC San Diego (Ph.D.) (Cl)	2	>1
Springfield College (Psy.D.) (Co)	1	–
The New School (Ph.D.) (Cl)	2	1
University of Colorado Boulder (Ph.D.) (Cl)	1	1
University of Georgia (Ph.D.) (Cl)	5	3
University of Georgia (Ph.D.) (Co)	2	3
University of Louisville (Ph.D.) (Co)	2	2
University of Minnesota (Ph.D.) (Co)	1	3
University of Missouri Kansas City (Ph.D.) (Cl)	2	2
University of Missouri, Columbia (Ph.D.) (Co)	2	8
University of Nevada, Reno (Ph.D.) (Cl)	1	1
University of North Dakota (Ph.D.) (Co)	1	0
University of Oregon (Ph.D.) (Cl)	2	1
University of Oregon (Ph.D.) (Co)	6	2
University of Pittsburgh (Ph.D.) (Cl)	3	6
University of Rochester (Ph.D.) (Cl)	2	1
University of South Carolina (Ph.D.) (Cl)	2	2
University of Southern California (Ph.D.) (Cl)	3	1
University of Southern Mississippi (Ph.D.) (Cl)	–	–
University of Vermont (Ph.D.) (Cl)	3	3
University of Virginia (Ph.D.) (Cl)	3	2
University of Virginia (Ph.D.) (Cm)	3	3
University of Wyoming (Ph.D.) (Cl)	1	0
Virginia Commonwealth University (Ph.D.) (Co)	2	2
Wright State University (Psy.D.) (Cl)	2	–
Yeshiva University (Psy.D.) (Cl)	1	0

Problem Solving

Drexel University (Ph.D.) (Cl)	2	1
La Salle University (Psy.D.) (Cl)	1	0

Professional Issues

Alliant International University, Los Angeles (Psy.D.) (Cl)	3	0
Alliant International University, Sacramento (Psy.D.) (Cl)	1	0
Alliant International University, San Diego (Ph.D.) (Cl)	2	0
Alliant International University, San Diego (Psy.D.) (Cl)	2	0
Alliant International University, San Francisco Bay (Ph.D.) (Cl)	3	1
Alliant International University, San Francisco Bay (Psy.D.) (Cl)	3	0
Auburn University (Ph.D.) (Co)	1	0
Chicago School of Professional Psychology–Chicago Campus (Psy.D.) (Cl)	2	1
Cleveland State University (Ph.D.) (Co)	1	0
Florida Institute of Technology (Psy.D.) (Cl)	1	0
Indiana State University (Psy.D.) (Cl)	2	0
Indiana University of Pennsylvania (Psy.D.) (Cl)	5	1
Long Island University, C.W. Post Campus (Psy.D.) (Cl)	2	0
Philadelphia College of Osteopathic Medicine (Psy.D.) (Cl)	1	0
Saint Louis University (Ph.D.) (Cl)	2	0
The Wright Institute (Psy.D.) (Cl)	1	–

	# Faculty	# Grants
University of Alabama at Tuscaloosa (Ph.D.) (Cl)	2	0
University of Missouri Kansas City (Ph.D.) (Co)	1	–
University of North Texas (Ph.D.) (Co)	3	0
University of St. Thomas (Psy.D.) (Co)	2	0
Yeshiva University (Psy.D.) (Cm)	3	0

Program Evaluation

American University (Ph.D.) (Cl)	1	0
DePaul University (Ph.D.) (Cl)	4	2
Marquette University (Ph.D.) (Co)	1	1
Miami University (OH) (Ph.D.) (Cl)	1	1
Northwestern University Feinberg School of Medicine (Ph.D.) (Cl)	4	3
Philadelphia College of Osteopathic Medicine (Psy.D.) (Cl)	1	0
Seattle Pacific University (Ph.D.) (Cl)	1	1
Spalding University (Psy.D.) (Cl)	2	2
The Wright Institute (Psy.D.) (Cl)	1	–
University of Colorado at Colorado Springs (Ph.D.) (Cl)	2	2
University of Illinois at Urbana–Champaign (Ph.D.) (Cl)	3	2
University of Pittsburgh (Ph.D.) (Cl)	2	2
University of Toledo (Ph.D.) (Cl)	3	0

Psychoanalytic/Psychodynamic Therapy

Adelphi University (Ph.D.) (Cl)	5	2
Long Island University, C.W. Post Campus (Psy.D.) (Cl)	3	0
Pennsylvania State University (Ph.D.) (Cl)	1	0
Rutgers–The State University of New Jersey (Psy.D.) (Cl)	1	–
The New School (Ph.D.) (Cl)	2	0
The Wright Institute (Psy.D.) (Cl)	6	–
University of Texas at Austin (Ph.D.) (Co)	1	0
Xavier University (Psy.D.) (Cl)	3	0
Yeshiva University (Psy.D.) (Cl)	3	1

Psychometrics/Measurement

Auburn University (Ph.D.) (Co)	2	0
Northern Illinois University (Ph.D.) (Cl)	2	0
Northwestern University Feinberg School of Medicine (Ph.D.) (Cl)	2	1
Pace University (Psy.D.) (Cm)	4	0
Ponce Health Sciences University (Psy.D.) (Cl)	1	–
Saint Mary's University of Minnesota (Psy.D.) (Co)	2	0
Sam Houston State University (Ph.D.) (Cl)	1	–
St. John's University (Ph.D.) (Cl)	1	0
The Wright Institute (Psy.D.) (Cl)	3	–
University of Georgia (Ph.D.) (Cl)	2	–
University of South Alabama (Ph.D.) (Cm)	1	–
University of Southern Mississippi (Ph.D.) (Cl)	–	–
Wichita State University (Ph.D.) (Cl)	1	0

Psychoneuroimmunology

The Ohio State University (Ph.D.) (Cl)	1	5
University of Kentucky (Ph.D.) (Cl)	1	3
University of Miami (Ph.D.) (Cl)	4	2
University of North Carolina at Charlotte (Ph.D.) (Cl)	1	0
University of Pittsburgh (Ph.D.) (Cl)	2	2

Psychopathology–Adult/General

Binghamton University, State University of New York (Ph.D.) (Cl)	7	2
Catholic University of America (Ph.D.) (Cl)	2	0
Colorado State University (Ph.D.) (Co)	3	0
Fairleigh Dickinson University (Ph.D.) (Cl)	1	0
Indiana State University (Psy.D.) (Cl)	2	0
Indiana University of Pennsylvania (Psy.D.) (Cl)	4	0
Loyola University Chicago (Ph.D.) (Cl)	1	0
Marshall University (Psy.D.) (Cl)	6	2
Northern Illinois University (Ph.D.) (Cl)	4	0
Northwestern University Feinberg School of Medicine (Ph.D.) (Cl)	4	2
Ohio University (Ph.D.) (Cl)	4	2
Palo Alto University (Ph.D.) (Cl)	20	–
Pennsylvania State University (Ph.D.) (Cl)	7	4
Pepperdine University (Psy.D.) (Cl)	1	0
Southern Methodist University (Ph.D.) (Cl)	3	2
Stony Brook University, State University of New York (Ph.D.) (Cl)	2	2
Texas A&M University (Ph.D.) (Cl)	4	–
The New School (Ph.D.) (Cl)	2	0
The Wright Institute (Psy.D.) (Cl)	5	–
University at Albany (Ph.D.) (Cl)	1	–
University of Alabama at Tuscaloosa (Ph.D.) (Cl)	3	2
University of Colorado Boulder (Ph.D.) (Cl)	7	4
University of Connecticut (Ph.D.) (Cl)	6	5
University of Houston (Ph.D.) (Cl)	2	1
University of Kansas (Ph.D.) (Cl)	5	2
University of Kentucky (Ph.D.) (Cl)	4	1
University of Louisville (Ph.D.) (Cl)	1	0
University of Miami (Ph.D.) (Cl)	6	2
University of Nebraska, Lincoln (Ph.D.) (Cl)	4	2
University of North Dakota (Ph.D.) (Cl)	6	0
University of Pittsburgh (Ph.D.) (Cl)	10	14
University of Rochester (Ph.D.) (Cl)	3	0

	# Faculty	# Grants
University of Southern California (Ph.D.) (Cl)	5	2
University of Southern Mississippi (Ph.D.) (Cl)	5	4
University of Tennessee–Knoxville (Ph.D.) (Cl)	5	1
University of Utah (Ph.D.) (Cl)	4	3
University of Virginia (Ph.D.) (Cl)	2	3
Virginia Commonwealth University (Ph.D.) (Cl)	5	1
Washington State University (Ph.D.) (Cl)	3	1
Washington University in St. Louis (Ph.D.) (Cl)	4	6
Yale University (Ph.D.) (Cl)	3	4

Psychopathology–Child/Developmental

Arizona State University (Ph.D.) (Co)	2	1
Baylor University (Psy.D.) (Cl)	2	0
Brigham Young University (Ph.D.) (Cl)	3	2
Catholic University of America (Ph.D.) (Cl)	6	2
Clark University (Ph.D.) (Cl)	2	0
Divine Mercy University (Psy.D.) (Cl)	1	–
Duke University (Ph.D.) (Cl)	3	3
Emory University (Ph.D.) (Cl)	2	1
Florida International University (Ph.D.) (Cl)	2	2
Florida State University (Ph.D.) (Cl)	4	2
Fuller Theological Seminary (Ph.D.) (Cl)	5	3
Fuller Theological Seminary (Psy.D.) (Cl)	5	3
George Fox University (Psy.D.) (Cl)	1	1
Georgia State University (Ph.D.) (Cl)	3	2
Illinois Institute of Technology (Ph.D.) (Cl)	1	0
Indiana State University (Psy.D.) (Cl)	1	0
Indiana University–Bloomington (Ph.D.) (Cl)	3	1
Indiana University of Pennsylvania (Psy.D.) (Cl)	2	0
Iowa State University (Ph.D.) (Co)	1	0
John F. Kennedy University (Psy.D.) (Cl)	1	0
Long Island University (Ph.D.) (Cl)	2	0
Loyola University Chicago (Ph.D.) (Cl)	4	3
Loyola University Maryland (Psy.D.) (Cl)	5	0
Miami University (OH) (Ph.D.) (Cl)	3	1
Northern Illinois University (Ph.D.) (Cl)	4	0
Northwestern University Feinberg School of Medicine (Ph.D.) (Cl)	5	3
Pennsylvania State University (Ph.D.) (Cl)	5	3
Queens College and The Graduate Center, City University of New York (Ph.D.) (Cl)	1	0
San Diego State University–UC San Diego (Ph.D.) (Cl)	5	>1
Seattle Pacific University (Ph.D.) (Cl)	2	1
Syracuse University (Ph.D.) (Cl)	1	2
The New School (Ph.D.) (Cl)	1	1
The Ohio State University (Ph.D.) (Cl)	2	4
The University of Montana (Ph.D.) (Cl)	5	2
The Wright Institute (Psy.D.) (Cl)	3	–
University at Buffalo, State University of New York (Ph.D.) (Cl)	3	1
University of Alabama at Tuscaloosa (Ph.D.) (Cl)	2	1
University of Colorado Boulder (Ph.D.) (Cl)	2	2
University of Connecticut (Ph.D.) (Cl)	6	4
University of Denver (Ph.D.) (Cl)	5	2
University of Denver (Psy.D.) (Cl)	1	0
University of Georgia (Ph.D.) (Cl)	3	1
University of Houston (Ph.D.) (Cl)	2	4
University of Illinois at Urbana–Champaign (Ph.D.) (Cl)	2	1
University of Illinois at Urbana–Champaign (Ph.D.) (Co)	2	–
University of Iowa (Ph.D.) (Cl)	1	1
University of Kentucky (Ph.D.) (Cl)	3	3
University of Louisville (Ph.D.) (Cl)	1	0
University of Maryland–College Park (Ph.D.) (Cl)	5	12
University of Massachusetts Amherst (Ph.D.) (Cl)	3	0
University of Massachusetts, Boston (Ph.D.) (Cl)	5	4
University of Miami (Ph.D.) (Cl)	5	2
University of Minnesota (Ph.D.) (Cl)	–	–
University of Notre Dame (Ph.D.) P(Cl)	3	2
University of Oregon (Ph.D.) (Cl)	4	5
University of Pennsylvania (Ph.D.) (Cl)	2	2
University of Pittsburgh (Ph.D.) (Cl)	12	25
University of Rochester (Ph.D.) (Cl)	4	2
University of Southern California (Ph.D.) (Cl)	3	1
University of Southern Mississippi (Ph.D.) (Cl)	3	4
University of Tennessee–Knoxville (Ph.D.) (Cl)	5	0
University of Texas Southwestern Medical Center (Ph.D.) (Cl)	1	1
University of Toledo (Ph.D.) (Cl)	3	1
University of Vermont (Ph.D.) (Cl)	5	3
University of Virginia (Ph.D.) (Cl)	4	4
University of Wisconsin, Madison (Ph.D.) (Cl)	4	3
Vanderbilt University (Ph.D.) (Cl)	5	5
Wayne State University (Ph.D.) (Cl)	4	2
West Virginia University (Ph.D.) (Cl)	2	0
Yale University (Ph.D.) (Cl)	1	0

Psychopharmacology

Midwestern University–Glendale Campus (Psy.D.) (Cl)	1	0
San Diego State University–UC San Diego (Ph.D.) (Cl)	4	>1
The Wright Institute (Psy.D.) (Cl)	1	–
University of Minnesota (Ph.D.) (Cl)	–	–
University of Pittsburgh (Ph.D.) (Cl)	1	2

Psychophysiology/Biopsychology

	# Faculty	# Grants
Binghamton University, State University of New York (Ph.D.) (Cl)	1	1
Florida School of Professional Psychology at Argosy University (Psy.D.) (Cl)	1	–
Fuller Theological Seminary (Ph.D.) (Cl)	5	0
Fuller Theological Seminary (Psy.D.) (Cl)	5	0
Georgia State University (Ph.D.) (Cl)	1	2
Loma Linda University (Ph.D.) (Cl)	2	2
Loma Linda University (Psy.D.) (Cl)	2	2
Miami University (OH) (Ph.D.) (Cl)	2	1
Michigan State University (Ph.D.) (Cl)	1	2
Midwestern University (Psy.D.) (Cl)	1	–
Northwestern University Feinberg School of Medicine (Ph.D.) (Cl)	1	1
Pennsylvania State University (Ph.D.) (Cl)	3	3
Seattle Pacific University (Ph.D.) (Cl)	4	1
Syracuse University (Ph.D.) (Cl)	3	2
University of Colorado at Colorado Springs (Ph.D.) (Cl)	1	1
University of Delaware (Ph.D.) (Cl)	3	1
University of Detroit Mercy (Ph.D.) (Cl)	2	1
University of Illinois at Urbana–Champaign (Ph.D.) (Cl)	3	1
University of Kentucky (Ph.D.) (Cl)	2	1
University of Michigan (Ph.D.) (Cl)	1	1
University of Minnesota (Ph.D.) (Cl)	–	–
University of Missouri, Columbia (Ph.D.) (Co)	1	0
University of North Dakota (Ph.D.) (Cl)	1	0
University of Pittsburgh (Ph.D.) (Cl)	5	7
Virginia Commonwealth University (Ph.D.) (Cl)	2	0

Psychotherapy Process and Outcome (also see Counseling Process and Outcome)

	# Faculty	# Grants
Adelphi University (Ph.D.) (Cl)	3	2
Alliant International University, Fresno (Ph.D.) (Cl)	2	0
Alliant International University, Fresno (Psy.D.) (Cl)	1	0
Alliant International University, Los Angeles (Ph.D.) (Cl)	1	0
Alliant International University, Los Angeles (Psy.D.) (Cl)	10	0
Alliant International University, San Diego (Ph.D.) (Cl)	5	0
Alliant International University, San Francisco Bay (Ph.D.) (Cl)	3	0
Alliant International University, San Francisco Bay (Psy.D.) (Cl)	14	0
American University (Ph.D.) (Cl)	1	0
Antioch University New England (Psy.D.) (Cl)	2	0
Brigham Young University (Ph.D.) (Cl)	3	2
Carlow University (Psy.D.) (Co)	1	–
Catholic University of America (Ph.D.) (Cl)	4	2
Colorado State University (Ph.D.) (Co)	1	0
Divine Mercy University (Psy.D.) (Cl)	6	–
Drexel University (Ph.D.) (Cl)	4	1
Fairleigh Dickinson University (Ph.D.) (Cl)	3	1
Fielding Graduate University (Ph.D.) (Cl)	5	0
Florida State University (Ph.D.) (Cm)	3	4
George Fox University (Psy.D.) (Cl)	2	0
Georgia School of Professional Psychology at Argosy University, Atlanta (Psy.D.) (Cl)	1	0
Georgia State University (Ph.D.) (Cl)	1	0
Hofstra University (Ph.D.) (Cl)	5	–
Idaho State University (Ph.D.) (Cl)	1	–
Illinois School of Professional Psychology at Argosy University, Chicago (Psy.D.) (Cl)	2	1
Iowa State University (Ph.D.) (Co)	3	0
James Madison University (Psy.D.) (Cm)	4	3
John Jay College of Criminal Justice & The Graduate Center, CUNY (Ph.D.) (Cl)	2	1
Loma Linda University (Ph.D.) (Cl)	1	0
Loma Linda University (Psy.D.) (Cl)	1	0
Long Island University (Ph.D.) (Cl)	4	1
Long Island University, C.W. Post Campus (Psy.D.) (Cl)	1	0
Loyola University Chicago (Ph.D.) (Cl)	4	1
Loyola University Maryland (Psy.D.) (Cl)	1	0
Marquette University (Ph.D.) (Co)	2	0
Marquette University (Ph.D.) (Cl)	3	0
Marywood University (Psy.D.) (Cl)	1	0
Midwestern University–Glendale Campus (Psy.D.) (Cl)	1	0
Northwestern University (Ph.D.) (Cl)	2	1
Palo Alto University (Ph.D.) (Cl)	5	–
Pennsylvania State University (Ph.D.) (Cl)	4	4
Pepperdine University (Psy.D.) (Cl)	3	1
Philadelphia College of Osteopathic Medicine (Psy.D.) (Cl)	2	0
Purdue University (Ph.D.) (Co)	1	1
Rutgers–The State University of New Jersey (Ph.D.) (Cl)	3	2
Rutgers–The State University of New Jersey (Psy.D.) (Cl)	1	–
Saint Louis University (Ph.D.) (Cl)	2	0
Saint Mary's University of Minnesota (Psy.D.) (Co)	2	0
Sam Houston State University (Ph.D.) (Cl)	2	1
Seattle Pacific University (Ph.D.) (Cl)	1	1
Spalding University (Psy.D.) (Cl)	1	1
Teachers College, Columbia University (Ph.D.) (Cl)	3	6
Texas A&M University (Ph.D.) (Cl)	2	–
The New School (Ph.D.) (Cl)	3	10
The University of Akron (Ph.D.) (Co)	1	0
The University of Memphis (Ph.D.) (Cl)	4	4
The University of Montana (Ph.D.) (Cl)	1	0
University at Albany (Ph.D.) (Co)	1	0

	# Faculty	# Grants
University of Alabama at Tuscaloosa (Ph.D.) (Cl)	3	0
University of Arizona (Ph.D.) (Cl)	3	4
University of Colorado Boulder (Ph.D.) (Cl)	3	3
University of Delaware (Ph.D.) (Cl)	2	0
University of Denver (Ph.D.) (Co)	1	3
University of Detroit Mercy (Ph.D.) (Cl)	4	0
University of Iowa (Ph.D.) (Cl)	2	0
University of Kansas (Ph.D.) (Cl)	1	0
University of Kansas (Ph.D.) (Co)	2	1
University of Kentucky (Ph.D.) (Co)	1	–
University of La Verne (Psy.D.) (Cl)	4	0
University of Louisville (Ph.D.) (Co)	1	0
University of Maryland–College Park (Ph.D.) (Cl)	1	6
University of Massachusetts Amherst (Ph.D.) (Cl)	4	1
University of Massachusetts, Boston (Ph.D.) (Co)	1	1
University of Michigan (Ph.D.) (Cl)	2	2
University of Minnesota (Ph.D.) (Cl)	–	–
University of Nebraska, Lincoln (Ph.D.) (Co)	1	0
University of North Texas (Ph.D.) (Cl)	1	1
University of Southern Mississippi (Ph.D.) (Cl)	–	–
University of Tennessee–Knoxville (Ph.D.) (Cl)	4	2
University of Toledo (Ph.D.) (Cl)	4	0
University of Utah (Ph.D.) (Co)	1	2
University of Washington (Ph.D.) (Cl)	1	1
University of Wisconsin, Milwaukee (Ph.D.) (Cl)	2	1
Virginia Commonwealth University (Ph.D.) (Cl)	3	3
Virginia Polytechnic Institute and State University (Ph.D.) (Cl)	5	0
Washington University in St. Louis (Ph.D.) (Cl)	3	3
West Virginia University (Ph.D.) (Co)	3	0
Western Michigan University (Ph.D.) (Cl)	3	0
Yeshiva University (Psy.D.) (Cl)	3	2

Public Health

Texas A&M University (Ph.D.) (Co)	2	1
The Wright Institute (Psy.D.) (Cl)	4	–
University of Iowa (Ph.D.) (Co)	2	0
University of Toledo (Ph.D.) (Cl)	1	1
Virginia Polytechnic Institute and State University (Ph.D.) (Cl)	1	1

Qualitative

Duquesne University (Ph.D.) (Cl)	1	–
Fielding Graduate University (Ph.D.) (Cl)	2	0
Marquette University (Ph.D.) (Co)	4	0
Pacific University, Oregon (Psy.D.) (Cl)	5	0
Southern Illinois University Carbondale (Ph.D.) (Co)	2	0
Widener University (Psy.D.) (Cl)	4	0

Quantitative

Hofstra University (Ph.D.) (Cl)	2	0
Rosalind Franklin University of Medicine and Science (Ph.D.) (Cl)	1	0
San Diego State University–UC San Diego (Ph.D.) (Cl)	2	0
Southern Methodist University (Ph.D.) (Cl)	1	0
University at Buffalo, State University of New York (Ph.D.) (Cl)	1	1
University of Iowa (Ph.D.) (Cl)	1	0
Vanderbilt University (Ph.D.) (Cl)	2	0

Rehabilitation

Ball State University (Ph.D.) (Co)	2	1
Drexel University (Ph.D.) (Cl)	3	2
Georgia State University (Ph.D.) (Cl)	1	2
Illinois Institute of Technology (Ph.D.) (Cl)	2	1
Philadelphia College of Osteopathic Medicine (Psy.D.) (Cl)	1	0
Seattle Pacific University (Ph.D.) (Cl)	1	0
University of Texas Southwestern Medical Center (Ph.D.) (Cl)	1	1
Virginia Consortium Program in Clinical Psychology (Ph.D.) (Cl)	3	0
West Virginia University (Ph.D.) (Co)	3	0

Religion/Spirituality

American University (Ph.D.) (Cl)	1	1
Azusa Pacific University (Psy.D.) (Cl)	4	1
Biola University (Ph.D.) (Cl)	10	3
Biola University (Psy.D.) (Cl)	10	3
Bowling Green State University (Ph.D.) (Cl)	2	1
Brigham Young University (Ph.D.) (Cl)	2	1
Case Western Reserve University (Ph.D.) (Cl)	1	1
Chatham University (Psy.D.) (Co)	2	0
Chicago School of Professional Psychology–Chicago Campus (Psy.D.) (Cl)	2	1
Divine Mercy University (Psy.D.) (Cl)	8	–
Fuller Theological Seminary (Ph.D.) (Cl)	9	6
Fuller Theological Seminary (Psy.D.) (Cl)	9	6
George Fox University (Psy.D.) (Cl)	5	0
Howard University (Ph.D.) (Cl)	2	0
Iowa State University (Ph.D.) (Co)	1	0
Kean University (Psy.D.) (Cm)	2	0
Loma Linda University (Ph.D.) (Cl)	2	0

	# Faculty	# Grants
Loma Linda University (Psy.D.) (Cl)	2	0
Loyola University Maryland (Psy.D.) (Cl)	2	0
Pepperdine University (Psy.D.) (Cl)	3	0
Seattle Pacific University (Ph.D.) (Cl)	2	2
Seton Hall University (Ph.D.) (Co)	1	0
Southern Illinois University Carbondale (Ph.D.) (Co)	1	0
Spalding University (Psy.D.) (Cl)	1	0
Springfield College (Psy.D.) (Co)	1	–
Teachers College, Columbia University (Ph.D.) (Cl)	1	4
The Wright Institute (Psy.D.) (Cl)	4	–
University of Colorado Denver (Ph.D.) (Cl)	2	1
University of Detroit Mercy (Ph.D.) (Cl)	2	0
University of Georgia (Ph.D.) (Cl)	2	–
University of Iowa (Ph.D.) (Co)	2	0
University of Louisville (Ph.D.) (Co)	2	0
University of Maryland, Baltimore County (Ph.D.) (Cl)	1	0
University of Missouri Kansas City (Ph.D.) (Co)	1	–
University of South Alabama (Ph.D.) (Cm)	1	–
Wheaton College (Psy.D.) (Cl)	3	2

Rural Mental Health

Georgia Southern University (Psy.D.) (Cl)	1	2
Pennsylvania State University (Ph.D.) (Cl)	1	0
Radford University (Psy.D.) (Co)	4	2
The University of Montana (Ph.D.) (Cl)	1	1
The University of South Dakota (Ph.D.) (Cl)	9	0
University of Alabama at Tuscaloosa (Ph.D.) (Cl)	4	2
University of Florida (Ph.D.) (Cl)	1	0
University of Mississippi (Ph.D.) (Cl)	2	0
University of North Dakota (Ph.D.) (Cl)	2	2
University of North Dakota (Ph.D.) (Co)	2	1

Schizophrenia (also see Severe Mental Illness)

Binghamton University, State University of New York (Ph.D.) (Cl)	1	1
Boston University (Ph.D.) (Cl)	1	0
Emory University (Ph.D.) (Cl)	1	1
Hofstra University (Ph.D.) (Cl)	1	1
Long Island University, C.W. Post Campus (Psy.D.) (Cl)	1	0
Northwestern University Feinberg School of Medicine (Ph.D.) (Cl)	2	1
Rosalind Franklin University of Medicine and Science (Ph.D.) (Cl)	1	1
San Diego State University–UC San Diego (Ph.D.) (Cl)	13	>1
Temple University (Ph.D.) (Cl)	1	1
The University of Montana (Ph.D.) (Cl)	1	0
The Wright Institute (Psy.D.) (Cl)	1	–
University of California, Berkeley (Ph.D.) (Cl)	1	0
University of California, Los Angeles (Ph.D.) (Cl)	3	4
University of Central Florida (Ph.D.) (Cl)	1	0
University of Georgia (Ph.D.) (Cl)	1	1
University of Illinois at Chicago (Ph.D.) (Cl)	1	1
University of Illinois at Urbana–Champaign (Ph.D.) (Cl)	1	1
University of Indianapolis (Psy.D.) (Cl)	2	1
University of Michigan (Ph.D.) (Cl)	1	1
University of Minnesota (Ph.D.) (Cl)	–	–
University of Missouri, Columbia (Ph.D.) (Cl)	1	1
University of North Carolina, Chapel Hill (Ph.D.) (Cl)	1	2
University of Pittsburgh (Ph.D.) (Cl)	1	0
University of Rochester (Ph.D.) (Cl)	1	0
University of Wisconsin, Madison (Ph.D.) (Cl)	1	0
Vanderbilt University (Ph.D.) (Cl)	1	2

School/Educational

Azusa Pacific University (Psy.D.) (Cl)	2	1
Boston College (Ph.D.) (Co)	5	4
Colorado State University (Ph.D.) (Co)	1	1
DePaul University (Ph.D.) (Cl)	5	3
Drexel University (Ph.D.) (Cl)	1	3
Fairleigh Dickinson University (Ph.D.) (Cl)	1	0
Florida International University (Ph.D.) (Cl)	1	1
Florida State University (Ph.D.) (Cm)	3	–
Hawaii School of Professional Psychology at Argosy University, Hawaii (Psy.D.) (Cl)	9	0
Kean University (Psy.D.) (Cm)	2	0
Marquette University (Ph.D.) (Co)	2	1
Miami University (OH) (Ph.D.) (Cl)	2	0
New York University (Ph.D.) (Co)	1	0
Ponce Health Sciences University (Ph.D.) (Cl)	2	0
The Wright Institute (Psy.D.) (Cl)	5	2
University of Arkansas (Ph.D.) (Cl)	3	2
University of California, Los Angeles (Ph.D.) (Cl)	1	3
University of Georgia (Ph.D.) (Co)	6	4
University of Houston (Ph.D.) (Cl)	1	0
University of Massachusetts, Boston (Ph.D.) (Co)	2	0
University of Minnesota (Ph.D.) (Co)	2	0
University of Missouri Kansas City (Ph.D.) (Co)	1	–
University of Missouri, Columbia (Ph.D.) (Co)	4	8

	# Faculty	# Grants
University of Southern California (Ph.D.) (Cl)	2	0
University of Virginia (Ph.D.) (Cm)	5	5

Severe Mental Illness (also see Schizophrenia)

George Washington University (Psy.D.) (Cl)	1	–
Illinois Institute of Technology (Ph.D.) (Cl)	2	1
Illinois School of Professional Psychology at Argosy University, Chicago (Psy.D.) (Cl)	1	0
Indiana University–Bloomington (Ph.D.) (Cl)	4	3
Indiana University–Purdue University Indianapolis (Ph.D.) (Cl)	3	5
John Jay College of Criminal Justice & The Graduate Center, CUNY (Ph.D.) (Cl)	1	1
Midwestern University (Psy.D.) (Cl)	1	–
Northwestern University (Ph.D.) (Cl)	1	6
Palo Alto University (Psy.D.) (Cl)	2	1
Philadelphia College of Osteopathic Medicine (Psy.D.) (Cl)	1	0
Ponce Health Sciences University (Ph.D.) (Cl)	2	0
Rutgers–The State University of New Jersey (Ph.D.) (Cl)	1	3
Rutgers–The State University of New Jersey (Psy.D.) (Cl)	1	–
The Wright Institute (Psy.D.) (Cl)	1	–
University of Cincinnati (Ph.D.) (Cl)	4	3
University of Georgia (Ph.D.) (Cl)	1	1
University of Hawaii at Manoa (Ph.D.) (Cl)	2	1
University of Maryland, Baltimore County (Ph.D.) (Cl)	1	5
University of Maryland–College Park (Ph.D.) (Cl)	2	0
University of Massachusetts, Boston (Ph.D.) (Cl)	1	1
University of Missouri Kansas City (Ph.D.) (Cl)	1	1
University of Wyoming (Ph.D.) (Cl)	1	1
Yeshiva University (Psy.D.) (Cl)	1	2

Sexuality/Sexual Dysfunction

Alliant International University, San Diego (Psy.D.) (Cl)	1	0
Chicago School of Professional Psychology–Chicago Campus (Psy.D.) (Cl)	2	0
Eastern Michigan University (Ph.D.) (Cl)	1	0
Fuller Theological Seminary (Ph.D.) (Cl)	2	0
Fuller Theological Seminary (Psy.D.) (Cl)	2	0
Hofstra University (Ph.D.) (Cl)	1	0
Indiana University–Bloomington (Ph.D.) (Cl)	1	1
Loyola University Maryland (Psy.D.) (Cl)	2	0
Midwestern University–Glendale Campus (Psy.D.) (Cl)	1	0
Pacific University, Oregon (Psy.D.) (Cl)	4	0
Saint Mary's University of Minnesota (Psy.D.) (Co)	3	0
Sam Houston State University (Ph.D.) (Cl)	2	1
San Diego State University–UC San Diego (Ph.D.) (Cl)	1	1
Texas Tech University (Ph.D.) (Co)	3	0
The University of Memphis (Ph.D.) (Co)	1	0
The University of Montana (Ph.D.) (Cl)	1	0
The Wright Institute (Psy.D.) (Cl)	1	–
Uniformed Services University of the Health Sciences (Ph.D.) (Cl)	1	0
University of Florida (Ph.D.) (Co)	1	1
University of Kansas (Ph.D.) (Cl)	1	0
University of Kentucky (Ph.D.) (Co)	1	–
University of La Verne (Psy.D.) (Cl)	3	1
University of Massachusetts, Boston (Ph.D.) (Co)	1	1
University of Missouri, Columbia (Ph.D.) (Co)	1	0
University of Missouri, St. Louis (Ph.D.) (Cl)	1	1
University of North Carolina at Charlotte (Ph.D.) (Cl)	3	1
University of North Dakota (Ph.D.) (Co)	1	0
University of Texas at Austin (Ph.D.) (Cl)	1	1
University of Texas at Austin (Ph.D.) (Co)	3	1
University of Utah (Ph.D.) (Cl)	1	0
University of Vermont (Ph.D.) (Cl)	1	0
Western Michigan University (Ph.D.) (Cl)	1	0

Shame

George Fox University (Psy.D.) (Cl)	1	0
The Wright Institute (Psy.D.) (Cl)	2	–

Sleep Disorders

Divine Mercy University (Psy.D.) (Cl)	1	–
East Carolina University (Ph.D.) (Cl)	1	0
Louisiana Tech University (Ph.D.) (Co)	1	0
Midwestern University (Psy.D.) (Cl)	1	–
Northwestern University Feinberg School of Medicine (Ph.D.) (Cl)	1	1
Nova Southeastern University (Ph.D.) (Cl)	1	1
Nova Southeastern University (Psy.D.) (Cl)	1	1
Palo Alto University (Psy.D.) (Cl)	2	4
San Diego State University–UC San Diego (Ph.D.) (Cl)	4	>1
Texas Tech University (Ph.D.) (Cl)	1	0
The Wright Institute (Psy.D.) (Cl)	1	–

	# Faculty	# Grants
University of Alabama at Tuscaloosa (Ph.D.) (Cl)	2	1
University of California, Berkeley (Ph.D.) (Cl)	1	1
University of Houston (Ph.D.) (Cl)	1	2
University of Kansas (Ph.D.) (Cl)	1	1
University of Michigan (Ph.D.) (Cl)	1	–
University of North Carolina at Charlotte (Ph.D.) (Cl)	1	0
University of Oregon (Ph.D.) (Cl)	2	1
University of Pittsburgh (Ph.D.) (Cl)	1	1
University of Texas Southwestern Medical Center (Ph.D.) (Cl)	1	0
Virginia Commonwealth University (Ph.D.) (Co)	1	–
Yeshiva University (Psy.D.) (Cl)	1	1

Social Justice

Adelphi University (Ph.D.) (Cl)	1	0
Ball State University (Ph.D.) (Co)	2	4
Boston College (Ph.D.) (Co)	10	1
Chatham University (Psy.D.) (Co)	4	0
George Mason University (Ph.D.) (Cl)	1	–
Regent University (Psy.D.) (Cl)	1	–
Springfield College (Psy.D.) (Co)	3	–
The Wright Institute (Psy.D.) (Cl)	10	–
University at Albany (Ph.D.) (Co)	3	2
University of California, Santa Barbara (Ph.D.) (Cm)	1	–
University of Denver (Psy.D.) (Cl)	1	0
University of Maryland–College Park (Ph.D.) (Co)	1	0
University of Missouri Kansas City (Ph.D.) (Co)	5	–
University of Missouri, Columbia (Ph.D.) (Co)	2	0
University of Tennessee–Knoxville (Ph.D.) (Co)	4	0
Wheaton College (Psy.D.) (Cl)	1	0

Social Skills/Competence

James Madison University (Psy.D.) (Cm)	4	0
The Wright Institute (Psy.D.) (Cl)	3	–
University of Alabama at Tuscaloosa (Ph.D.) (Cl)	2	2
University of Maine (Ph.D.) (Cl)	3	1
University of Michigan (Ph.D.) (Cl)	1	–

Social Support

Fordham University (Ph.D.) (Cl)	1	0
Illinois Institute of Technology (Ph.D.) (Cl)	1	0
Iowa State University (Ph.D.) (Co)	1	0
Northern Illinois University (Ph.D.) (Cl)	1	0
University of Denver (Ph.D.) (Co)	2	2
University of Oregon (Ph.D.) (Co)	3	0
University of Pittsburgh (Ph.D.) (Cl)	2	2

Social–Psychological Approaches

American School of Professional Psychology at Argosy University, Washington, DC (Psy.D.) (Cl)	1	0
Ball State University (Ph.D.) (Co)	3	0
Loyola University Maryland (Psy.D.) (Cl)	1	0
Midwestern University (Psy.D.) (Cl)	1	–
Sam Houston State University (Ph.D.) (Cl)	1	–
The Wright Institute (Psy.D.) (Cl)	3	–
University of Colorado at Colorado Springs (Ph.D.) (Cl)	2	2
Xavier University (Psy.D.) (Cl)	2	0

Somatization Disorders

Philadelphia College of Osteopathic Medicine (Psy.D.) (Cl)	1	0
Rutgers–The State University of New Jersey (Ph.D.) (Cl)	1	0
University of Georgia (Ph.D.) (Cl)	1	–

Sports/Performance Psychology

American University (Ph.D.) (Cl)	1	0
Chatham University (Psy.D.) (Co)	1	0
Florida Institute of Technology (Psy.D.) (Cl)	1	0
Indiana University–Bloomington (Ph.D.) (Co)	1	–
Kean University (Psy.D.) (Cm)	2	0
Midwestern University–Glendale Campus (Psy.D.) (Cl)	1	0
Pacific University, Oregon (Psy.D.) (Cl)	1	0
Palo Alto University (Psy.D.) (Cl)	2	1
Saint Louis University (Ph.D.) (Cl)	1	0
Spalding University (Psy.D.) (Cl)	1	0
Springfield College (Psy.D.) (Co)	1	–
University of Massachusetts, Boston (Ph.D.) (Co)	1	0
University of Missouri Kansas City (Ph.D.) (Co)	1	–
University of Missouri, Columbia (Ph.D.) (Co)	2	0
University of North Texas (Ph.D.) (Co)	2	1
University of South Alabama (Ph.D.) (Cm)	1	–
University of Tennessee–Knoxville (Ph.D.) (Co)	2	0
West Virginia University (Ph.D.) (Co)	1	0

Statistics

	# Faculty	# Grants
Brigham Young University (Ph.D.) (Cl)	3	2
Fairleigh Dickinson University (Ph.D.) (Cl)	1	0
Lehigh University (Ph.D.) (Co)	1	0
Loma Linda University (Ph.D.) (Cl)	3	0
Loma Linda University (Psy.D.) (Cl)	3	0
Purdue University (Ph.D.) (Cl)	1	0
Sam Houston State University (Ph.D.) (Cl)	1	–
San Diego State University–UC San Diego (Ph.D.) (Cl)	2	0
The Wright Institute (Psy.D.) (Cl)	7	–
University of Nevada Las Vegas (Ph.D.) (Cl)	1	0
University of Southern Mississippi (Ph.D.) (Cl)	–	–
Xavier University (Psy.D.) (Cl)	2	0

Stigma

	# Faculty	# Grants
Carlos Albizu University, San Juan Campus (Ph.D.) (Cl)	1	–
Illinois Institute of Technology (Ph.D.) (Cl)	1	2
Iowa State University (Ph.D.) (Co)	2	1
Jackson State University (Ph.D.) (Cl)	2	0
John Jay College of Criminal Justice & The Graduate Center, CUNY (Ph.D.) (Cl)	1	1
Marquette University (Ph.D.) (Cl)	3	1
Ponce Health Sciences University (Ph.D.) (Cl)	3	2
Syracuse University (Ph.D.) (Cl)	1	0
The Wright Institute (Psy.D.) (Cl)	2	–
Uniformed Services University of the Health Sciences (Ph.D.) (Cl)	1	1
University of California, Berkeley (Ph.D.) (Cl)	1	1
University of Hawaii at Manoa (Ph.D.) (Cl)	2	0
University of Maryland–College Park (Ph.D.) (Co)	1	0
University of North Dakota (Ph.D.) (Co)	2	1

Stress and Coping

	# Faculty	# Grants
Catholic University of America (Ph.D.) (Cl)	4	1
Colorado State University (Ph.D.) (Co)	2	0
DePaul University (Ph.D.) (Cl)	2	2
Drexel University (Ph.D.) (Cl)	1	0
Duke University (Ph.D.) (Cl)	4	4
East Carolina University (Ph.D.) (Cl)	1	0
Fairleigh Dickinson University (Ph.D.) (Cl)	2	0
Florida School of Professional Psychology at Argosy University (Psy.D.) (Cl)	3	0
Fordham University (Ph.D.) (Cl)	1	0
Fuller Theological Seminary (Ph.D.) (Cl)	1	0
Fuller Theological Seminary (Psy.D.) (Cl)	1	0
George Washington University (Ph.D.) (Cl)	3	1
Georgia State University (Ph.D.) (Co)	2	1
Indiana State University (Psy.D.) (Cl)	2	0
Marywood University (Psy.D.) (Cl)	3	0
Philadelphia College of Osteopathic Medicine (Psy.D.) (Cl)	3	1
Saint Louis University (Ph.D.) (Cl)	1	0
Seton Hall University (Ph.D.) (Co)	2	0
Southern Illinois University Carbondale (Ph.D.) (Cl)	4	0
Southern Illinois University Carbondale (Ph.D.) (Co)	2	0
Syracuse University (Ph.D.) (Cl)	5	7
University of Delaware (Ph.D.) (Cl)	2	1
University of Georgia (Ph.D.) (Cl)	5	3
University of Hawaii at Manoa (Ph.D.) (Cl)	1	1
University of Kansas–Child (Ph.D.) (Cl)	3	2
University of Louisville (Ph.D.) (Cl)	1	0
University of Louisville (Ph.D.) (Co)	3	1
University of Massachusetts Amherst (Ph.D.) (Cl)	3	1
University of Miami (Ph.D.) (Cl)	6	2
University of Michigan (Ph.D.) (Cl)	1	–
University of Minnesota (Ph.D.) (Co)	2	0
University of North Carolina at Charlotte (Ph.D.) (Cl)	6	0
University of North Dakota (Ph.D.) (Cl)	6	0
University of Notre Dame (Ph.D.) P(Cl)	3	2
University of Pittsburgh (Ph.D.) (Cl)	3	3
University of Texas at Austin (Ph.D.) (Cl)	1	1
University of Texas at Austin (Ph.D.) (Co)	1	0
University of Toledo (Ph.D.) (Cl)	2	0
University of Tulsa (Ph.D.) (Cl)	4	2
Vanderbilt University (Ph.D.) (Cl)	4	3
Virginia Commonwealth University (Ph.D.) (Cl)	2	0
West Virginia University (Ph.D.) (Cl)	9	1
Yeshiva University (Psy.D.) (Cl)	1	0

Substance Abuse/Addictive Behaviors (also see Alcohol and Nicotine/Tobacco/Smoking)

	# Faculty	# Grants
Adelphi University (Ph.D.) (Cl)	2	1
Adler University–Chicago (Psy.D.) (Cl)	3	–
Alliant International University, Fresno (Psy.D.) (Cl)	1	0
Alliant International University, Los Angeles (Ph.D.) (Cl)	3	0
Alliant International University, San Diego (Psy.D.) (Cl)	2	0
Alliant International University, San Francisco Bay (Ph.D.) (Cl)	2	0
Alliant International University, San Francisco Bay (Psy.D.) (Cl)	3	0
Arizona State University (Ph.D.) (Cl)	5	4
Baylor University (Psy.D.) (Cl)	2	3
Boston University (Ph.D.) (Cl)	3	4
Carlos Albizu University, Miami Campus (Psy.D.) (Cl)	3	0

	# Faculty	# Grants
Carlos Albizu University, San Juan Campus (Ph.D.) (Cl)	1	–
Clark University (Ph.D.) (Cl)	1	0
Colorado State University (Ph.D.) (Co)	4	3
DePaul University (Ph.D.) (Cl)	1	3
Divine Mercy University (Psy.D.) (Cl)	1	–
Duke University (Ph.D.) (Cl)	4	7
Eastern Michigan University (Ph.D.) (Cl)	1	0
Fairleigh Dickinson University (Ph.D.) (Cl)	1	1
Fielding Graduate University (Ph.D.) (Cl)	2	0
Florida International University (Ph.D.) (Cl)	3	4
Florida State University (Ph.D.) (Cl)	2	1
Fordham University (Ph.D.) (Cl)	1	2
George Mason University (Ph.D.) (Cl)	5	–
Harvard University (Ph.D.) (Cl)	1	1
Illinois School of Professional Psychology at Argosy University, Chicago (Psy.D.) (Cl)	1	0
Indiana State University (Psy.D.) (Cl)	1	0
Indiana University–Bloomington (Ph.D.) (Cl)	3	2
Indiana University–Bloomington (Ph.D.) (Co)	2	2
John Jay College of Criminal Justice & The Graduate Center, CUNY (Ph.D.) (Cl)	2	0
Long Island University, C.W. Post Campus (Psy.D.) (Cl)	1	0
Marywood University (Psy.D.) (Cl)	1	0
Miami University (OH) (Ph.D.) (Cl)	3	1
Midwestern University–Glendale Campus (Psy.D.) (Cl)	1	0
Nova Southeastern University (Ph.D.) (Cl)	1	2
Nova Southeastern University (Psy.D.) (Cl)	1	2
Ohio University (Ph.D.) (Cl)	1	1
Oklahoma State University (Ph.D.) (Cl)	2	0
Oklahoma State University (Ph.D.) (Co)	2	0
Pace University (Psy.D.) (Cm)	2	0
Palo Alto University (Ph.D.) (Cl)	2	–
Palo Alto University (Psy.D.) (Cl)	2	1
Pepperdine University (Psy.D.) (Cl)	2	1
Philadelphia College of Osteopathic Medicine (Psy.D.) (Cl)	2	2
Purdue University (Ph.D.) (Cl)	4	2
Queens College and The Graduate Center, City University of New York (Ph.D.) (Cl)	2	0
Rutgers–The State University of New Jersey (Ph.D.) (Cl)	2	2
Rutgers–The State University of New Jersey (Psy.D.) (Cl)	1	–
Saint Louis University (Ph.D.) (Cl)	1	2
Sam Houston State University (Ph.D.) (Cl)	1	–
San Diego State University–UC San Diego (Ph.D.) (Cl)	9	>1
Spalding University (Psy.D.) (Cl)	1	0
Syracuse University (Ph.D.) (Cl)	5	16
Texas A&M University (Ph.D.) (Cl)	2	–
Texas Tech University (Ph.D.) (Cl)	1	1
Texas Tech University (Ph.D.) (Co)	1	0
The City College of New York, The Graduate Center, CUNY (Ph.D.) (Cl)	2	1
The University of Montana (Ph.D.) (Cl)	1	1
The University of South Dakota (Ph.D.) (Cl)	2	2
The Wright Institute (Psy.D.) (Cl)	2	–
University at Albany (Ph.D.) (Co)	1	1
University at Albany (Ph.D.) (Cl)	2	–
University at Buffalo, State University of New York (Ph.D.) (Cl)	4	5
University of Alabama at Birmingham (Ph.D.) (Cl)	4	3
University of Alaska Fairbanks–Anchorage (Ph.D.) (Cl)	1	0
University of Arkansas (Ph.D.) (Cl)	3	2
University of California, Los Angeles (Ph.D.) (Cl)	1	3
University of California, Santa Barbara (Ph.D.) (Cm)	1	–
University of Cincinnati (Ph.D.) (Cl)	3	3
University of Colorado Boulder (Ph.D.) (Cl)	2	2
University of Colorado Denver (Ph.D.) (Cl)	1	0
University of Denver (Ph.D.) (Co)	1	0
University of Florida (Ph.D.) (Co)	1	0
University of Georgia (Ph.D.) (Cl)	5	3
University of Georgia (Ph.D.) (Co)	1	0
University of Hartford (Psy.D.) (Cl)	1	0
University of Houston (Ph.D.) (Cl)	2	9
University of Illinois at Urbana–Champaign (Ph.D.) (Cl)	3	3
University of Kentucky (Ph.D.) (Cl)	4	2
University of Kentucky (Ph.D.) (Co)	1	–
University of Maryland, Baltimore County (Ph.D.) (Cl)	2	9
University of Maryland–College Park (Ph.D.) (Cl)	5	3
University of Massachusetts Amherst (Ph.D.) (Cl)	1	0
University of Michigan (Ph.D.) (Cl)	1	–
University of Minnesota (Ph.D.) (Cl)	–	–
University of Missouri, Columbia (Ph.D.) (Cl)	6	10
University of Nebraska, Lincoln (Ph.D.) (Cl)	1	1
University of New Mexico (Ph.D.) (Cl)	6	20
University of North Carolina, Chapel Hill (Ph.D.) (Cl)	2	3
University of North Dakota (Ph.D.) (Cl)	1	0
University of Pittsburgh (Ph.D.) (Cl)	5	10
University of South Florida (Ph.D.) (Cl)	5	8
University of Southern Mississippi (Ph.D.) (Cl)	–	–
University of Texas at Austin (Ph.D.) (Cl)	1	1
University of Toledo (Ph.D.) (Cl)	1	0
University of Utah (Ph.D.) (Co)	1	1
University of Vermont (Ph.D.) (Cl)	1	1
University of Washington (Ph.D.) (Cl)	2	2

	# Faculty	# Grants
University of Wisconsin, Madison (Ph.D.) (Cl)	2	5
University of Wyoming (Ph.D.) (Cl)	1	0
Virginia Commonwealth University (Ph.D.) (Cl)	2	2
Virginia Consortium Program in Clinical Psychology (Ph.D.) (Cl)	6	3
Virginia Polytechnic Institute and State University (Ph.D.) (Cl)	4	5
Wayne State University (Ph.D.) (Cl)	2	2
Yeshiva University (Ph.D.) (Cl)	1	0

Suicide/Self-Injury

Adelphi University (Ph.D.) (Cl)	1	0
Alliant International University, San Diego (Psy.D.) (Cl)	2	0
Auburn University (Ph.D.) (Cl)	1	1
Carlos Albizu University, San Juan Campus (Ph.D.) (Cl)	1	–
Catholic University of America (Ph.D.) LDS (Cl)	2	2
East Tennessee State University (Ph.D.) (Cl)	2	1
Florida State University (Ph.D.) (Cl)	5	5
George Mason University (Ph.D.) (Cl)	4	–
Georgia Southern University (Psy.D.) (Cl)	1	0
Harvard University (Ph.D.) (Cl)	2	7
Indiana University–Bloomington (Ph.D.) (Cl)	2	2
Miami University (OH) (Ph.D.) (Cl)	2	1
Northwestern University Feinberg School of Medicine (Ph.D.) (Cl)	2	1
Palo Alto University (Psy.D.) (Cl)	2	2
Radford University (Psy.D.) (Co)	1	0
Texas Tech University (Ph.D.) (Cl)	2	2
The Wright Institute (Psy.D.) (Cl)	2	–
Uniformed Services University of the Health Sciences (Ph.D.) (Cl)	1	3
University of Alaska Fairbanks–Anchorage (Ph.D.) (Cl)	1	1
University of Illinois at Urbana–Champaign (Ph.D.) (Cl)	1	2
University of Iowa (Ph.D.) (Co)	1	0
University of Louisville (Ph.D.) (Co)	2	0
University of Maine (Ph.D.) (Cl)	3	0
University of Maryland, Baltimore County (Ph.D.) (Cl)	1	0
University of Massachusetts, Boston (Ph.D.) (Co)	1	1
University of Michigan (Ph.D.) (Cl)	2	2
University of North Dakota (Ph.D.) (Cl)	2	2
University of Northern Colorado (Ph.D.) (Co)	1	0
University of Rochester (Ph.D.) (Cl)	1	1
University of South Alabama (Ph.D.) (Cm)	1	–
University of South Florida (Ph.D.) (Cl)	2	3
University of Southern Mississippi (Ph.D.) (Cl)	–	–
University of Toledo (Ph.D.) (Cl)	1	1
University of Utah (Ph.D.) (Cl)	2	2
University of Washington (Ph.D.) (Cl)	1	1
University of Wyoming (Ph.D.) (Cl)	1	0
West Virginia University (Ph.D.) (Cl)	1	0
Yale University (Ph.D.) (Cl)	1	0

Supervision/Mentoring/Training

Adler University–Chicago (Psy.D.) (Cl)	1	–
Antioch University New England (Psy.D.) (Cl)	3	1
Colorado State University (Ph.D.) (Co)	2	0
Florida Institute of Technology (Psy.D.) (Cl)	1	0
Fordham University (Ph.D.) (Co)	3	2
George Fox University (Psy.D.) (Cl)	3	0
Howard University (Ph.D.) (Co)	5	0
Iowa State University (Ph.D.) (Co)	1	0
James Madison University (Psy.D.) (Cm)	1	0
Lehigh University (Ph.D.) (Co)	2	0
Marquette University (Ph.D.) (Co)	9	0
Miami University (OH) (Ph.D.) (Cl)	1	1
Oklahoma State University (Ph.D.) (Co)	6	0
Palo Alto University (Psy.D.) (Cl)	2	0
Pepperdine University (Psy.D.) (Cl)	2	0
Philadelphia College of Osteopathic Medicine (Psy.D.) (Cl)	1	0
Saint Mary's University of Minnesota (Psy.D.) (Co)	3	0
Southern Illinois University Carbondale (Ph.D.) (Co)	1	0
The Wright Institute (Psy.D.) (Cl)	4	–
University at Albany (Ph.D.) (Co)	2	0
University of Denver (Ph.D.) (Co)	1	0
University of Denver (Psy.D.) (Cl)	3	0
University of Hartford (Psy.D.) (Cl)	1	0
University of Houston (Ph.D.) (Co)	2	1
University of Indianapolis (Psy.D.) (Cl)	1	0
University of Maryland–College Park (Ph.D.) (Co)	2	0
University of Missouri Kansas City (Ph.D.) (Co)	1	–
University of Missouri, Columbia (Ph.D.) (Co)	1	0
University of North Dakota (Ph.D.) (Co)	2	0
University of Northern Colorado (Ph.D.) (Co)	2	0
University of Tennessee–Knoxville (Ph.D.) (Co)	1	0
University of Wisconsin, Milwaukee (Ph.D.) (Co)	1	1
West Virginia University (Ph.D.) (Co)	2	0

Teaching

	# Faculty	# Grants
Colorado State University (Ph.D.) (Co)	1	0
Georgia Southern University (Psy.D.) (Cl)	1	0
Spalding University (Psy.D.) (Cl)	1	0
Texas Tech University (Ph.D.) (Cl)	1	0
The Wright Institute (Psy.D.) (Cl)	1	–
University of Tennessee–Knoxville (Ph.D.) (Co)	1	1
Virginia Commonwealth University (Ph.D.) (Co)	1	0
Wichita State University (Ph.D.) (Cl)	1	0

Technology and Practice

Drexel University (Ph.D.) (Cl)	1	0
George Fox University (Psy.D.) (Cl)	1	0
Midwestern University (Psy.D.) (Cl)	1	–
Midwestern University–Glendale Campus (Psy.D.) (Cl)	1	0
Northwestern University Feinberg School of Medicine (Ph.D.) (Cl)	2	3
Pace University (Psy.D.) (Cm)	1	1
Palo Alto University (Psy.D.) (Cl)	3	3
University of Alaska Fairbanks–Anchorage (Ph.D.) (Cl)	2	0
University of Central Florida (Ph.D.) (Cl)	1	0
University of Minnesota (Ph.D.) (Co)	2	2
University of Mississippi (Ph.D.) (Cl)	1	1
Western Michigan University (Ph.D.) (Cl)	2	0

Tic Disorders

University of Georgia (Ph.D.) (Cl)	2	–
Western Michigan University (Ph.D.) (Cl)	1	0

Trichotillomania

American University (Ph.D.) (Cl)	1	1
Loyola University Maryland (Psy.D.) (Cl)	1	0
Western Michigan University (Ph.D.) (Cl)	1	0

Veteran/Military Issues

Adler University–Chicago (Psy.D.) (Cl)	3	–
Catholic University of America (Ph.D.) (Cl)	3	4
East Carolina University (Ph.D.) (Cl)	1	0
Fairleigh Dickinson University (Ph.D.) (Cl)	1	2
Florida Institute of Technology (Psy.D.) (Cl)	1	0
George Mason University (Ph.D.) (Cl)	1	–
Georgia Southern University (Psy.D.) (Cl)	1	1
Radford University (Psy.D.) (Co)	1	0
Sam Houston State University (Ph.D.) (Cl)	1	–
University of Colorado at Colorado Springs (Ph.D.) (Cl)	3	3
University of Denver (Psy.D.) (Cl)	1	1
University of Missouri Kansas City (Ph.D.) (Co)	2	–
University of North Dakota (Ph.D.) (Co)	1	0
University of Northern Colorado (Ph.D.) (Co)	1	0
University of South Alabama (Ph.D.) (Cm)	1	–
Wright State University (Psy.D.) (Cl)	2	–

Violence/Abuse/Sexual Abuse/Rape

Alliant International University, San Francisco Bay (Ph.D.) (Cl)	2	0
Auburn University (Ph.D.) (Cl)	1	1
Boston College (Ph.D.) (Co)	5	1
Boston University (Ph.D.) (Cl)	1	0
Carlos Albizu University, San Juan Campus (Ph.D.) (Cl)	1	–
Catholic University of America (Ph.D.) (Cl)	1	1
Chicago School of Professional Psychology–Chicago Campus (Psy.D.) (Cl)	2	1
Colorado State University (Ph.D.) (Co)	2	0
DePaul University (Ph.D.) (Cl)	2	2
Florida Institute of Technology (Psy.D.) (Cl)	1	1
Georgia State University (Ph.D.) (Cl)	1	0
Howard University (Ph.D.) (Cl)	2	0
Howard University (Ph.D.) (Co)	2	0
Idaho State University (Ph.D.) (Cl)	1	–
Indiana University of Pennsylvania (Psy.D.) (Cl)	2	0
John Jay College of Criminal Justice & The Graduate Center, CUNY (Ph.D.) (Cl)	2	0
Lehigh University (Ph.D.) (Co)	2	0
Miami University (OH) (Ph.D.) (Cl)	2	2
Midwestern University–Glendale Campus (Psy.D.) (Cl)	2	0
Northern Illinois University (Ph.D.) (Cl)	3	1
Ohio University (Ph.D.) (Cl)	2	1
Pennsylvania State University (Ph.D.) (Cl)	3	1
Saint Louis University (Ph.D.) (Cl)	3	0
Sam Houston State University (Ph.D.) (Cl)	3	–
Southern Illinois University Carbondale (Ph.D.) (Cl)	1	0
The Wright Institute (Psy.D.) (Cl)	1	2
University of Alaska Fairbanks–Anchorage (Ph.D.) (Cl)	2	2
University of Georgia (Ph.D.) (Cl)	1	–
University of Georgia (Ph.D.) (Co)	2	3
University of Missouri Kansas City (Ph.D.) (Cl)	2	2
University of Nebraska, Lincoln (Ph.D.) (Cl)	1	2
University of Nevada, Reno (Ph.D.) (Cl)	2	1
University of New Mexico (Ph.D.) (Cl)	1	2

	# Faculty	# Grants
University of Notre Dame (Ph.D.) P(Cl)	1	1
University of Vermont (Ph.D.) (Cl)	1	0
University of Virginia (Ph.D.) (Cl)	2	1
Virginia Polytechnic Institute and State University (Ph.D.) (Cl)	1	0

Vocational/Career Development

Arizona State University (Ph.D.) (Co)	1	–
Ball State University (Ph.D.) (Co)	3	0
Boston College (Ph.D.) (Co)	3	2
Chatham University (Psy.D.) (Co)	1	0
Cleveland State University (Ph.D.) (Co)	1	0
Colorado State University (Ph.D.) (Co)	2	0
Florida State University (Ph.D.) (Cm)	2	1
Fordham University (Ph.D.) (Co)	3	1
Indiana University–Bloomington (Ph.D.) (Co)	3	1
Iowa State University (Ph.D.) (Co)	2	0
Louisiana Tech University (Ph.D.) (Co)	2	0
Loyola University Chicago (Ph.D.) (Co)	1	0
Marquette University (Ph.D.) (Co)	1	0
New Mexico State University (Ph.D.) (Co)	1	0
Oklahoma State University (Ph.D.) (Co)	4	0
Purdue University (Ph.D.) (Co)	2	2
Saint Mary's University of Minnesota (Psy.D.) (Co)	6	0
Seton Hall University (Ph.D.) (Co)	1	0
Springfield College (Psy.D.) (Co)	3	–
Tennessee State University (Ph.D.) (Co)	1	2
Texas Tech University (Ph.D.) (Co)	1	0
The University of Memphis (Ph.D.) (Co)	2	1
University at Albany (Ph.D.) (Co)	2	1
University at Buffalo, State University of New York (Ph.D.) (Cm)	2	0
University of California, Santa Barbara (Ph.D.) (Cm)	1	–
University of Denver (Ph.D.) (Co)	2	2
University of Florida (Ph.D.) (Co)	1	1
University of Houston (Ph.D.) (Co)	2	0
University of Iowa (Ph.D.) (Co)	1	1
University of Kansas (Ph.D.) (Co)	3	0
University of Louisville (Ph.D.) (Co)	1	0
University of Maryland–College Park (Ph.D.) (Co)	4	1
University of Massachusetts, Boston (Ph.D.) (Co)	1	0
University of Missouri Kansas City (Ph.D.) (Co)	1	–
University of Missouri, Columbia (Ph.D.) (Co)	3	1
University of Nebraska, Lincoln (Ph.D.) (Co)	3	1
University of North Dakota (Ph.D.) (Co)	4	1
University of North Texas (Ph.D.) (Co)	3	0
University of Northern Colorado (Ph.D.) (Co)	2	0
University of Oregon (Ph.D.) (Co)	2	1
University of Southern Mississippi (Ph.D.) (Co)	2	0
University of Utah (Ph.D.) (Co)	2	0
University of Wisconsin, Milwaukee (Ph.D.) (Co)	2	2
Virginia Commonwealth University (Ph.D.) (Co)	1	1
West Virginia University (Ph.D.) (Co)	2	0

Weight Management/Obesity

DePaul University (Ph.D.) (Cl)	1	0
Drexel University (Ph.D.) (Cl)	2	2
Duke University (Ph.D.) (Cl)	2	4
East Carolina University (Ph.D.) (Cl)	1	0
Fairleigh Dickinson University (Ph.D.) (Cl)	2	2
Jackson State University (Ph.D.) (Cl)	1	0
La Salle University (Psy.D.) (Cl)	1	0
Ponce Health Sciences University (Ph.D.) (Cl)	1	1
Rosalind Franklin University of Medicine and Science (Ph.D.) (Cl)	1	1
San Diego State University–UC San Diego (Ph.D.) (Cl)	2	>1
Uniformed Services University of the Health Sciences (Ph.D.) (Cl)	3	4
University at Buffalo, State University of New York (Ph.D.) (Cm)	1	0
University of Florida (Ph.D.) (Cl)	2	2
University of Hawaii at Manoa (Ph.D.) (Cl)	1	0
University of Kansas (Ph.D.) (Cl)	1	1
University of Missouri Kansas City (Ph.D.) (Cl)	1	1
University of Pittsburgh (Ph.D.) (Cl)	2	3
University of South Florida (Ph.D.) (Cl)	2	–
Yeshiva University (Ph.D.) (Cl)	1	0

Women's Studies/Feminism

Antioch University New England (Psy.D.) (Cl)	2	0
Ball State University (Ph.D.) (Co)	2	0
Boston University (Ph.D.) (Cl)	2	1
Brigham Young University (Ph.D.) (Cl)	1	1
Carlos Albizu University, San Juan Campus (Ph.D.) (Cl)	1	–
Cleveland State University (Ph.D.) (Co)	1	0
Colorado State University (Ph.D.) (Co)	3	1
Drexel University (Ph.D.) (Cl)	2	1
East Carolina University (Ph.D.) (Cl)	1	1
East Tennessee State University (Ph.D.) (Cl)	1	0
George Fox University (Psy.D.) (Cl)	1	0
Illinois School of Professional Psychology at Argosy University, Chicago (Psy.D.) (Cl)	1	0

	# Faculty	# Grants
Indiana State University (Psy.D.) (Cl)	2	0
Indiana University of Pennsylvania (Psy.D.) (Cl)	2	0
Iowa State University (Ph.D.) (Co)	2	1
Loyola University Maryland (Psy.D.) (Cl)	2	0
Midwestern University (Psy.D.) (Cl)	2	–
New York University (Ph.D.) (Co)	2	2
Northeastern University (Ph.D.) (Co)	1	0
Rutgers–The State University of New Jersey (Psy.D.) (Cl)	1	–
Seattle Pacific University (Ph.D.) (Cl)	1	1
Springfield College (Psy.D.) (Co)	2	–
Teachers College, Columbia University (Ph.D.) (Co)	3	0
Tennessee State University (Ph.D.) (Co)	1	0
Texas Tech University (Ph.D.) (Co)	3	0
The University of Akron (Ph.D.) (Co)	2	0
The Wright Institute (Psy.D.) (Cl)	4	–
University of Florida (Ph.D.) (Co)	1	1
University of Illinois at Urbana–Champaign (Ph.D.) (Cl)	3	1
University of Indianapolis (Psy.D.) (Cl)	2	0
University of Kansas (Ph.D.) (Co)	1	1
University of Maryland, Baltimore County (Ph.D.) (Cl)	1	0
University of Missouri, St. Louis (Ph.D.) (Cl)	1	1
University of North Dakota (Ph.D.) (Cl)	2	0
University of North Dakota (Ph.D.) (Co)	1	0
University of Tennessee–Knoxville (Ph.D.) (Co)	2	0
University of Utah (Ph.D.) (Co)	3	0
University of Wisconsin, Milwaukee (Ph.D.) (Co)	1	1

Workplace Issues

New York University (Ph.D.) (Co)	1	0
Saint Mary's University of Minnesota (Psy.D.) (Co)	2	0
University of Northern Colorado (Ph.D.) (Co)	1	0

Miscellaneous and Other

academic achievement/minority issues–University of Texas at Austin (Ph.D.) (Co)	1	1
academic retention–Louisiana Tech University (Ph.D.) (Co)	1	0
academic self-concept and achievement–Southern Illinois University Carbondale (Ph.D.) (Co)	1	0
action research–Miami University (OH) (Ph.D.) (Cl)	1	1
adult/child externalizing behavior – University of Southern Mississippi (Ph.D.) (Cl)	–	–
advocacy–Howard University (Ph.D.) (Co)	5	0
affective science–University of California, Berkeley (Ph.D.) (Cl)	4	1
after school–Florida International University (Ph.D.) (Cl)	1	1
alternative and complementary–University of North Carolina at Charlotte (Ph.D.) (Cl)	3	0
American Indian–Oklahoma State University (Ph.D.) (Co)	2	0
animal assisted therapy–Chicago School of Professional Psychology–Chicago Campus (Psy.D.) (Cl)	1	0
arthritis–University of Alabama at Tuscaloosa (Ph.D.) (Cl)	1	2
asthma–Yeshiva University (Ph.D.) (Cl)	1	2
attitudes and attitude change–Hofstra University (Ph.D.) (Cl)	1	0
attitudes beliefs and values–The Wright Institute (Psy.D.) (Cl)	1	–
behavioral assessment–University of Nevada, Reno (Ph.D.) (Cl)	3	0
behavioral dentistry–West Virginia University (Ph.D.) (Cl)	1	1
behavioral disorders–Midwestern University (Psy.D.) (Cl)	1	–
behavioral dysregulation–Rutgers–The State University of New Jersey (Ph.D.) (Cl)	2	2
behavioral economics–University of Georgia (Ph.D.) (Cl)	1	1
behavioral improvisation–Midwestern University (Psy.D.) (Cl)	1	–
behavioral treatments–The University of Montana (Ph.D.) (Cl)	2	0
beliefs and values–James Madison University (Psy.D.) (Cm)	3	1
bias–Spalding University (Psy.D.) (Cl)	2	0
bilingualism–St. John's University (Ph.D.) (Cl)	1	0
biomarkers–Ponce Health Sciences University (Ph.D.) (Cl)	1	1
biopsychosocial focus on case conceptualization and treatment–University of Missouri, Columbia (Ph.D.) (Co)	1	0
burnout–Divine Mercy University (Psy.D.) (Cl)	1	–
burnout in healthcare settings–Midwestern University–Glendale Campus (Psy.D.) (Cl)	1	1
caffeine–American University (Ph.D.) (Cl)	1	0
cancer caregivers–University of Colorado Denver (Ph.D.) (Cl)	1	1
career and life development–Seattle Pacific University (Ph.D.) (Cl)	1	1
caregiver burden–Southern Illinois University Carbondale (Ph.D.) (Co)	1	0

	# Faculty	# Grants
caregiving–University of Alabama at Tuscaloosa (Ph.D.) (Cl)	2	2
child welfare and families–Pacific University, Oregon (Psy.D.) (Cl)	3	0
childhood adversity–Queens College and The Graduate Center, City University of New York (Ph.D.) (Cl)	1	0
childhood externalizing problems–Temple University (Ph.D.) (Cl)	1	0
chronic fatigue syndrome–DePaul University (Ph.D.) (Cl)	1	3
civic engagement–George Mason University (Ph.D.) (Cl)	1	–
clinical envy–Midwestern University–Glendale Campus (Psy.D.) (Cl)	1	0
clinical neuroscience–University of Kansas (Ph.D.) (Cl)	1	1
clinical neuroscience–University of Maryland–College Park (Ph.D.) (Cl)	4	0
clinical neuroscience–The Ohio State University (Ph.D.) (Cl)	1	2
cognitive decline–University of Maine (Ph.D.) (Cl)	1	0
cognitive processing in Parkinson's disease–Queens College and The Graduate Center, City University of New York (Ph.D.) (Cl)	1	0
college teaching–Roosevelt University (Psy.D.) (Cl)	1	0
colorism–Howard University (Ph.D.) (Co)	1	0
constructivist psychology–University of Florida (Ph.D.) (Co)	1	0
countertransference–University of Maryland–College Park (Ph.D.) (Co)	1	0
creativity–Midwestern University–Glendale Campus (Psy.D.) (Cl)	2	0
creativity–University of Kansas (Ph.D.) (Co)	1	1
critical psychology–Springfield College (Psy.D.) (Co)	1	–
cultural adaptations–Clark University (Ph.D.) (Cl)	1	0
cultural humility–University of Hawaii at Manoa (Ph.D.) (Cl)	1	0
culture, bilingualism, and parenting–University of California, Berkeley (Ph.D.) (Cl)	1	1
death and dying–Indiana University of Pennsylvania (Psy.D.) (Cl)	1	0
degenerative brain disorders – San Diego State University–UC San Diego (Ph.D.) (Cl)	4	>1
delinquency–Southern Illinois University Carbondale (Ph.D.) (Cl)	1	3
descriptive experience sampling–University of Nevada Las Vegas (Ph.D.) (Cl)	1	0
developmental delay–Florida International University (Ph.D.) (Cl)	1	1
developmental risk–University of Delaware (Ph.D.) (Cl)	5	3
dissociative disorders–Carlos Albizu University, San Juan Campus (Ph.D.) (Cl)	1	–
dissociative disorders–Rutgers–The State University of New Jersey (Psy.D.) (Cl)	1	–
diverse families–Utah State University (Ph.D.) (Cm)	2	0
diversity in aging–University of Alabama at Tuscaloosa (Ph.D.) (Cl)	3	3
dream research–Chatham University (Psy.D.) (Co)	1	0
dreams–University of Maryland–College Park (Ph.D.) (Co)	1	0
drug policy–Drexel University (Ph.D.) (Cl)	1	1
dying–Divine Mercy University (Psy.D.) (Cl)	1	–
ecology of emotion/positive psychology–La Salle University (Psy.D.) (Cl)	1	0
emergency responders–Northern Illinois University (Ph.D.) (Cl)	1	0
emotive behavior therapy–Divine Mercy University (Psy.D.) (Cl)	1	–
evaluation of career interventions–Seattle Pacific University (Ph.D.) (Cl)	1	1
evolutionary psychology–University of Colorado at Colorado Springs (Ph.D.) (Cl)	1	1
evolutionary psychology–The Wright Institute (Psy.D.) (Cl)	1	–
exercise-based interventions–Sam Houston State University (Ph.D.) (Cl)	1	–
existential/phenomenonological–Fordham University (Ph.D.) (Cl)	1	0
experimental psychopathology–University of Arkansas (Ph.D.) (Cl)	5	2
externalizing and risk-taking behaviors–University of Maryland–College Park (Ph.D.) (Cl)	1	0
externalizing disorders–University of Illinois at Urbana–Champaign (Ph.D.) (Cl)	2	1
externalizing disorders–University of Nevada Las Vegas (Ph.D.) (Cl)	1	1
externalizing disorders–University of North Carolina, Greensboro (Ph.D.) (Cl)	1	0
externalizing disorders–University of South Florida (Ph.D.) (Cl)	2	2
externalizing disorders in children–University of Iowa (Ph.D.) (Cl)	1	0
extracurricular activities–Loyola University Chicago (Ph.D.) (Cl)	1	1
extreme behavior patterns–University of Hawaii at Manoa (Ph.D.) (Cl)	1	0
families coping with serious mental illness–University of Detroit Mercy (Ph.D.) (Cl)	1	1
family violence–University of Michigan (Ph.D.) (Cl)	3	1

	# Faculty	# Grants
fetal alcohol syndrome – San Diego State University–UC San Diego (Ph.D.) (Cl)	3	>1
Filipino American psychology–University of Alaska Fairbanks–Anchorage (Ph.D.) (Cl)	1	0
flow–University of Missouri Kansas City (Ph.D.) (Co)	1	–
food addiction–University of Michigan (Ph.D.) (Cl)	1	3
genetic, biological, and social influences on the development and course of psychopathology–University of Southern California (Ph.D.) (Cl)	2	2
geopolitical conflict–American School of Professional Psychology at Argosy University, Washington, DC (Psy.D.) (Cl)	1	–
gifted adults–University of Northern Colorado (Ph.D.) (Co)	1	0
gifted/talent development–Florida State University (Ph.D.) (Cm)	1	–
global health–Vanderbilt University (Ph.D.) (Cl)	1	2
global mental health–Duke University (Ph.D.) (Cl)	3	5
grandparents–Northern Illinois University (Ph.D.) (Cl)	1	0
grant/contract funded research–George Mason University (Ph.D.) (Cl)	8	–
gratitude–American University (Ph.D.) (Cl)	1	0
harassment–University at Buffalo, State University of New York (Ph.D.) (Cm)	1	0
health services research–San Diego State University–UC San Diego (Ph.D.) (Cl)	3	>1
higher education–Adler University–Chicago (Psy.D.) (Cl)	1	–
historical trauma, racism and mental health–Pepperdine University (Psy.D.) (Cl)	3	0
history of psychology–Minnesota School of Professional Psychology at Argosy University (Psy.D.) (Cl)	1	0
hoarding–San Diego State University–UC San Diego (Ph.D.) (Cl)	2	>1
holistic wellness–Midwestern University–Glendale Campus (Psy.D.) (Cl)	1	0
homophobia–Loyola University Maryland (Psy.D.) (Cl)	1	0
hope–George Fox University (Psy.D.) (Cl)	1	0
hospice and geriatrics – The Wright Institute (Psy.D.) (Cl)	1	–
human developmental–Carlos Albizu University, San Juan Campus (Ph.D.) (Cl)	1	–
human error–Hofstra University (Ph.D.) (Cl)	1	0
human rights/refugees–Chicago School of Professional Psychology–Chicago Campus (Psy.D.) (Cl)	2	0
human trafficking–Carlow University (Psy.D.) (Co)	1	–
humanistic psychology–Divine Mercy University (Psy.D.) (Cl)	2	–
humor–The Wright Institute (Psy.D.) (Cl)	1	–
hypertension–University of Miami (Ph.D.) (Cl)	3	1
impact of parental psychopathology on children–Philadelphia College of Osteopathic Medicine (Psy.D.) (Cl)	1	0
impulsivity–University of Georgia (Ph.D.) (Cl)	2	–
incarcerated populations–University of Virginia (Ph.D.) (Cm)	1	0
infertility–Chicago School of Professional Psychology–Washington, DC Campus (Psy.D.) (Cl)	1	0
intelligence and health behavior–University of North Carolina at Charlotte (Ph.D.) (Cl)	1	1
interdisciplinary approaches and care–Pacific University, Oregon (Psy.D.) (Cl)	5	0
intergroup relations–Chicago School of Professional Psychology–Washington, DC Campus (Psy.D.) (Cl)	1	0
internalized oppression and mental health–University of Alaska Fairbanks–Anchorage (Ph.D.) (Cl)	1	–
internalizing disorders–Indiana University–Bloomington (Ph.D.) (Cl)	3	2
internalizing disorders–La Salle University (Psy.D.) (Cl)	1	0
internalizing disorders–University of Nevada Las Vegas (Ph.D.) (Cl)	1	0
internalizing disorders–University of North Carolina, Greensboro (Ph.D.) (Cl)	2	0
international–Ball State University (Ph.D.) (Co)	3	3
international–Oklahoma State University (Ph.D.) (Co)	3	0
international psychology–George Fox University (Psy.D.) (Cl)	1	0
international psychology–Illinois School of Professional Psychology at Argosy University, Chicago (Psy.D.) (Cl)	3	4
international psychology–Cleveland State University (Ph.D.) (Co)	3	0
international psychology–University of Louisville (Ph.D.) (Co)	2	0
international psychology–University of Massachusetts, Boston (Ph.D.) (Co)	1	0
international psychology–University of Northern Colorado (Ph.D.) (Co)	1	0
international research–University of Wisconsin, Milwaukee (Ph.D.) (Co)	1	2
international/global psychology–Azusa Pacific University (Psy.D.) (Cl)	3	4
interpersonal neurobiology–Pepperdine University (Psy.D.) (Cl)	1	0
intersectionality–Chicago School of Professional Psychology–Washington, DC Campus (Psy.D.) (Cl)	1	0

	# Faculty	# Grants
intersectionality–Howard University (Ph.D.) (Co)	3	0
intersectionality; microaggressions–Northeastern University (Ph.D.) (Co)	1	1
interventions with refugees–University of Minnesota (Ph.D.) (Co)	1	2
jail-based interventions–George Mason University (Ph.D.) (Cl)	1	–
juvenile delinquency–University of Detroit Mercy (Ph.D.) (Cl)	1	0
juvenile delinquency – University of Southern Mississippi (Ph.D.) (Cl)	–	–
juvenile justice–Drexel University (Ph.D.) (Cl)	1	1
juvenile justice–Sam Houston State University (Ph.D.) (Cl)	1	0
labeling/stereotypes–Georgia Southern University (Psy.D.) (Cl)	1	0
leadership–Wichita State University (Ph.D.) (Cl)	1	0
learning–Pace University (Psy.D.) (Cm)	1	0
learning theory/clinical applications–Roosevelt University (Psy.D.) (Cl)	2	0
licensure and regulatory boards–University of St. Thomas (Psy.D.) (Co)	1	0
life development–Saint Mary's University of Minnesota (Psy.D.) (Co)	2	0
life span–West Virginia University (Ph.D.) (Cl)	7	0
life-span development–Wichita State University (Ph.D.) (Cl)	1	2
long-term care–University of Alabama at Tuscaloosa (Ph.D.) (Cl)	3	3
maternal stress-related disorders–Idaho State University (Ph.D.) (Cl)	1	–
media and psychology–University of Massachusetts, Boston (Ph.D.) (Cl)	1	0
medical issues–University of California, Los Angeles (Ph.D.) (Cl)	3	7
medical issues–University of Hartford (Psy.D.) (Cl)	3	0
mental health and entrepreneurship–University of California, Berkeley (Ph.D.) (Cl)	1	1
mental health promotion–University of South Carolina (Ph.D.) (Cl)	3	3
mental health systems–University of Hawaii at Manoa (Ph.D.) (Cl)	2	3
mental health systems/organizations–University of Illinois at Urbana-Champaign (Ph.D.) (Cl)	1	1
message framing–Louisiana Tech University (Ph.D.) (Co)	1	0
microaggression–Teachers College, Columbia University (Ph.D.) (Co)	2	0
microaggressions–John Jay College of Criminal Justice & The Graduate Center, CUNY (Ph.D.) (Cl)	1	0
migraines–Yeshiva University (Ph.D.) (Cl)	2	2
missions and mental health–Biola University (Psy.D.) (Cl)	2	0
missions and mental health–Biola University (Ph.D.) (Cl)	2	0
mixed methods–Miami University (OH) (Ph.D.) (Cl)	2	1
motivational interviewing–University of Southern Mississippi (Ph.D.) (Co)	1	0
multisystemic therapy–University of Missouri, Columbia (Ph.D.) (Cl)	1	1
Muslim mental health–Howard University (Ph.D.) (Co)	2	0
neighborhood and crime–John Jay College of Criminal Justice & The Graduate Center, CUNY (Ph.D.) (Cl)	1	1
neurobehavior–Divine Mercy University (Psy.D.) (Cl)	1	–
neurobehavioral–University of Massachusetts, Boston (Ph.D.) (Cl)	4	2
neurobehavioral and cardiometabolic risk in offspring–Idaho State University (Ph.D.) (Cl)	1	–
neurobehavioral functioning–Sam Houston State University (Ph.D.) (Cl)	1	–
neurocognitive–Southern Methodist University (Ph.D.) (Cl)	1	0
neurodegenerative diseases–Midwestern University–Glendale Campus (Psy.D.) (Cl)	1	1
neurodevelopmental disabilities–University of Alabama at Birmingham (Ph.D.) (Cl)	4	8
neurodevelopmental disorders–Purdue University (Ph.D.) (Cl)	1	1
neurodevelopmental issues–Saint Mary's University of Minnesota (Psy.D.) (Co)	2	0
neuroeconomics–University of Georgia (Ph.D.) (Cl)	1	–
neurological disorders – Wisconsin School of Professional Psychology (Psy.D.) (Cl)	–	–
nonlinear dynamic systems–The University of Montana (Ph.D.) (Cl)	1	0
nontraditional families–Yeshiva University (Psy.D.) (Cm)	2	0
nutrition–Vanderbilt University (Ph.D.) (Cl)	1	0
object relations–Biola University (Psy.D.) (Cl)	2	0
object relations–Biola University (Ph.D.) (Cl)	2	0
object relations–University of Detroit Mercy (Ph.D.) (Cl)	4	0
paranormal beliefs–Carlow University (Psy.D.) (Co)	1	–
peer counseling–University of Northern Colorado (Ph.D.) (Co)	1	0
person-centered interventions–Illinois School of Professional Psychology at Argosy University, Chicago (Psy.D.) (Cl)	1	0
person perception–University of Georgia (Ph.D.) (Cl)	1	–

	# Faculty	# Grants
philosophical psychology–Divine Mercy University (Psy.D.) (Cl)	2	–
philosophy and psychology–Rutgers–The State University of New Jersey (Psy.D.) (Cl)	1	–
philosophy of science–University of Hawaii at Manoa (Ph.D.) (Cl)	1	0
physical activity–Rosalind Franklin University of Medicine and Science (Ph.D.) (Cl)	1	1
play therapy–Divine Mercy University (Psy.D.) (Cl)	1	–
postmodernism in psychology–George Fox University (Psy.D.) (Cl)	1	0
post-partum depression–University of Colorado Denver (Ph.D.) (Cl)	2	2
post-partum disorders–Midwestern University (Psy.D.) (Cl)	2	–
pregnancy issues–Virginia Commonwealth University (Ph.D.) (Cl)	2	1
prenatal wellness–La Salle University (Psy.D.) (Cl)	1	0
preschool intervention–University of North Carolina, Greensboro (Ph.D.) (Cl)	1	0
principle-based psychotherapy–University of Hawaii at Manoa (Ph.D.) (Cl)	1	0
projective techniques–Long Island University (Ph.D.) (Cl)	2	0
psychiatric comorbidity–University of Alaska Fairbanks–Anchorage (Ph.D.) (Cl)	2	0
psychiatric disabilities–Rutgers–The State University of New Jersey (Psy.D.) (Cl)	1	–
psychiatry–University of Massachusetts, Boston (Ph.D.) (Co)	1	1
psychological reactance theory–Louisiana Tech University (Ph.D.) (Co)	1	0
psychological resources–The University of Memphis (Ph.D.) (Co)	1	0
psychology and media–Marywood University (Psy.D.) (Cl)	1	0
psychology and the arts–Rutgers–The State University of New Jersey (Psy.D.) (Cl)	1	–
psychotherapist's development–University of Massachusetts Amherst (Ph.D.) (Cl)	2	0
public policy – George Washington University (Psy.D.) (Cl)	1	–
pulmonary health–The Ohio State University (Ph.D.) (Cl)	1	2
race and racism–University of North Carolina, Chapel Hill (Ph.D.) (Cl)	1	1
racial and sexual harassment–Michigan State University (Ph.D.) (Cl)	1	0
racism and racial identity–Teachers College, Columbia University (Ph.D.) (Co)	3	0
rational-emotive/behavior therapy for marital therapy–Hofstra University (Ph.D.) (Cl)	1	0
reading development in deaf children–Gallaudet University (Ph.D.) (Cl)	2	1
reading/dyslexia–Georgia State University (Ph.D.) (Cl)	1	0
recovery-oriented mental health services–University of Detroit Mercy (Ph.D.) (Cl)	1	1
relationship education–University of Denver (Ph.D.) (Cl)	3	9
relationships in ministry–Seattle Pacific University (Ph.D.) (Cl)	1	0
residential treatment (children)–Chicago School of Professional Psychology–Chicago Campus (Psy.D.) (Cl)	1	0
responses to extreme stress – University of Minnesota (Ph.D.) (Cl)	–	–
risk assessment and management–University of Denver (Psy.D.) (Cl)	1	0
risk factors – University of Southern Mississippi (Ph.D.) (Cl)	–	–
risk/protective factors in the development of comorbid psychopathology in individuals with IDD/ASD–Idaho State University (Ph.D.) (Cl)	1	–
scholarship of teaching and learning–Miami University (OH) (Ph.D.) (Cl)	2	0
school/youth violence–California Lutheran University (Psy.D.) (Cl)	1	0
self-disclosure–University of Notre Dame (Ph.D.) P(Cl)	1	1
self-efficacy and health–West Virginia University (Ph.D.) (Co)	2	0
self-esteem–Marywood University (Psy.D.) (Cl)	1	0
self-esteem/self-efficacy/self-psychology–University of Toledo (Ph.D.) (Cl)	1	0
self-esteem/self-efficacy/self-psychology–The Wright Institute (Psy.D.) (Cl)	1	–
self-help–Wichita State University (Ph.D.) (Cl)	1	0
self-psychology and self-esteem–Seattle Pacific University (Ph.D.) (Cl)	1	0
self-regulation–University of Iowa (Ph.D.) (Cl)	1	0
self-regulation–Northern Illinois University (Ph.D.) (Cl)	1	1
self-regulation–Seattle Pacific University (Ph.D.) (Cl)	1	1
self-regulation training interventions–University of Nevada, Reno (Ph.D.) (Cl)	1	1
sensory and cognitive neuroscience–University of Missouri Kansas City (Ph.D.) (Cl)	1	2
service systems–Florida International University (Ph.D.) (Cl)	1	1
single subject design, time series regression, dynamic factor analysis–Texas Tech University (Ph.D.) (Cl)	2	0
social and emotional development–University of Illinois at Chicago (Ph.D.) (Cl)	2	2

	# Faculty	# Grants
social and emotional learning–Miami University (OH) (Ph.D.) (Cl)	2	1
social behavior–West Virginia University (Ph.D.) (Cl)	7	3
social class–Teachers College, Columbia University (Ph.D.) (Co)	1	0
social emotional development–University of Iowa (Ph.D.) (Cl)	1	1
social endocrinology–University of Texas at Austin (Ph.D.) (Cl)	1	0
social interest–California Lutheran University (Psy.D.) (Cl)	1	1
social media interventions–Rosalind Franklin University of Medicine and Science (Ph.D.) (Cl)	1	1
social phobia–Binghamton University, State University of New York (Ph.D.) (Cl)	1	1
social-emotional correlates–Yeshiva University (Psy.D.) (Cm)	3	1
sociodevelopment–Long Island University (Ph.D.) (Cl)	1	0
socioemotional development–Long Island University (Ph.D.) (Cl)	3	0
stereotyping and prejudice–Sam Houston State University (Ph.D.) (Cl)	2	1
strengths, optimal functioning–Marquette University (Ph.D.) (Co)	2	0
student well-being–Seton Hall University (Ph.D.) (Co)	1	0
symbolic play–Yeshiva University (Psy.D.) (Cm)	1	0
systems-based services–University of Kansas–Child (Ph.D.) (Cl)	2	0
therapeutic relationship–Adelphi University (Ph.D.) (Cl)	3	2
thriving–Fuller Theological Seminary (Ph.D.) (Cl)	4	4
thriving–Fuller Theological Seminary (Psy.D.) (Cl)	4	4
traffic safety–East Tennessee State University (Ph.D.) (Cl)	1	0
translational neuroscience–University of Oregon (Ph.D.) (Cl)	4	4
treatment as usual–University of Hawaii at Manoa (Ph.D.) (Cl)	1	1
trends in psychology practice–Saint Mary's University of Minnesota (Psy.D.) (Co)	1	0
underrepresented minority outcomes in STEM settings–University of California, Berkeley (Ph.D.) (Cl)	1	1
videogaming–University of Detroit Mercy (Ph.D.) (Cl)	2	0
visual perception–John F. Kennedy University (Psy.D.) (Cl)	1	2
well-being–George Mason University (Ph.D.) (Cl)	3	–
well-being–Colorado State University (Ph.D.) (Co)	1	1
White privilege–University of North Dakota (Ph.D.) (Co)	1	0
yoga therapy–Pacific University, Oregon (Psy.D.) (Cl)	1	0
youth mentoring–University of Virginia (Ph.D.) (Cm)	3	2
youth violence–University of Virginia (Ph.D.) (Cm)	3	1
Zen Buddhism–University of Hawaii at Manoa (Ph.D.) (Cl)	1	0

APPENDIX F

SPECIALTY CLINICS AND PRACTICA SITES

Acceptance/Acceptance & Commitment Therapy

Clark University (Ph.D.) (Cl)
Hofstra University (Ph.D.) (Cl)
Southern Illinois University Carbondale (Ph.D.) (Cl)
University at Albany (Ph.D.) (Cl)
University of Central Florida (Ph.D.) (Cl)
University of Colorado Boulder (Ph.D.) (Cl)
University of Hawaii at Manoa (Ph.D.) (Cl)
University of Toledo (Ph.D.) (Cl)

Acquired Immune Deficiency Syndrome/HIV

Arizona School of Professional Psychology at Argosy University, Phoenix (Psy.D.) (Cl)
Azusa Pacific University (Psy.D.) (Cl)
George Washington University (Ph.D.) (Cl)
Georgia State University (Ph.D.) (Cl)
Loyola University Chicago (Ph.D.) (Cl)
Pepperdine University (Psy.D.) (Cl)
Syracuse University (Ph.D.) (Cl)
The University of Memphis (Ph.D.) (Cl)
University of Houston (Ph.D.) (Cl)
University of Miami (Ph.D.) (Cl)
Wright State University (Psy.D.) (Cl)

Adjustment

Case Western Reserve University (Ph.D.) (Cl)
University of Georgia (Ph.D.) (Cl)
University of Illinois at Chicago (Ph.D.) (Cl)
University of Massachusetts, Boston (Ph.D.) (Co)
Virginia Polytechnic Institute and State University (Ph.D.) (Cl)

Adolescents/At-Risk Adolescents/ Delinquency

Adelphi University (Ph.D.) (Cl)
Alliant International University, Fresno (Psy.D.) (Cl)
Alliant International University, San Francisco Bay (Psy.D.) (Cl)
Auburn University (Ph.D.) (Cl)
Ball State University (Ph.D.) (Co)
Binghamton University, State University of New York (Ph.D.) (Cl)
Boston University (Ph.D.) (Cl)
Catholic University of America (Ph.D.) (Cl)
Central Michigan University (Ph.D.) (Cl)
Chatham University (Psy.D.) (Co)
Chestnut Hill College (Psy.D.) (Cl)
Chicago School of Professional Psychology–Chicago Campus (Psy.D.) (Cl)
Chicago School of Professional Psychology—Washington, DC Campus (Psy.D.) (Cl)
Cleveland State University (Ph.D.) (Co)
Colorado State University (Ph.D.) (Co)
DePaul University (Ph.D.) (Cl)
Eastern Michigan University (Ph.D.) (Cl)
Fuller Theological Seminary (Ph.D.) (Cl)
Fuller Theological Seminary (Psy.D.) (Cl)

Note. Cl, Clinical; Co, Counseling; Cm, combined psychology programs.

George Washington University (Ph.D.) (Cl)
Georgia School of Professional Psychology at Argosy University, Atlanta (Psy.D.) (Cl)
Harvard University (Ph.D.) (Cl)
Illinois School of Professional Psychology at Argosy University, Chicago (Psy.D.) (Cl)
John Jay College of Criminal Justice & The Graduate Center, CUNY (Ph.D.) (Cl)
Louisiana Tech University (Ph.D.) (Co)
Loyola University Maryland (Psy.D.) (Cl)
Marquette University (Ph.D.) (Cl)
Marshall University (Psy.D.) (Cl)
Miami University (OH) (Ph.D.) (Cl)
Midwestern University (Psy.D.) (Cl)
Midwestern University–Glendale Campus (Psy.D.) (Cl)
Northwestern University Feinberg School of Medicine (Ph.D.) (Cl)
Nova Southeastern University (Ph.D.) (Cl)
Nova Southeastern University (Psy.D.) (Cl)
Palo Alto University (Psy.D.) (Cl)
Pepperdine University (Psy.D.) (Cl)
Philadelphia College of Osteopathic Medicine (Psy.D.) (Cl)
Purdue University (Ph.D.) (Cl)
Roosevelt University (Psy.D.) (Cl)
Rutgers-The State University of New Jersey (Ph.D.) (Cl)
Saint Mary's University of Minnesota (Psy.D.) (Co)
Sam Houston State University (Ph.D.) (Cl)
Seattle Pacific University (Ph.D.) (Cl)
Southern Methodist University (Ph.D.) (Cl)
Spalding University (Psy.D.) (Cl)
Springfield College (Psy.D.) (Co)
Suffolk University (Ph.D.) (Cl)
Syracuse University (Ph.D.) (Cl)
Teachers College, Columbia University (Ph.D.) (Cl)
Tennessee State University (Ph.D.) (Co)
The Ohio State University (Ph.D.) (Cl)
The University of Memphis (Ph.D.) (Cl)
The University of Memphis (Ph.D.) (Co)
The University of Montana (Ph.D.) (Cl)
The Wright Institute (Psy.D.) (Cl)
Uniformed Services University of the Health Sciences (Ph.D.) (Cl)
University at Albany (Ph.D.) (Co)
University at Albany (Ph.D.) (Cl)
University at Buffalo, State University of New York (Ph.D.) (Cl)
University of Alabama at Birmingham (Ph.D.) (Cl)
University of Alabama at Tuscaloosa (Ph.D.) (Cl)
University of Alaska Fairbanks-Anchorage (Ph.D.) (Cl)
University of Arkansas (Ph.D.) (Cl)
University of California, Berkeley (Ph.D.) (Cl)
University of Denver (Ph.D.) (Co)
University of Denver (Ph.D.) (Cl)
University of Georgia (Ph.D.) (Cl)
University of Georgia (Ph.D.) (Co)
University of Houston (Ph.D.) (Cl)
University of Houston (Ph.D.) (Co)
University of Illinois at Urbana-Champaign (Ph.D.) (Co)
University of La Verne (Psy.D.) (Cl)
University of Louisville (Ph.D.) (Co)
University of Maine (Ph.D.) (Cl)
University of Maryland-College Park (Ph.D.) (Cl)
University of Massachusetts Amherst (Ph.D.) (Cl)
University of Mississippi (Ph.D.) (Cl)
University of Missouri, St. Louis (Ph.D.) (Cl)
University of Nebraska, Lincoln (Ph.D.) (Co)
University of Nevada, Reno (Ph.D.) (Cl)
University of North Texas (Ph.D.) (Cl)
University of Oregon (Ph.D.) (Cl)
University of Pittsburgh (Ph.D.) (Cl)
University of Rhode Island (Ph.D.) (Cl)
University of Rochester (Ph.D.) (Cl)
University of South Carolina (Ph.D.) (Cl)
University of South Florida (Ph.D.) (Cl)
University of Southern California (Ph.D.) (Cl)
University of Southern Mississippi (Ph.D.) (Cl)
University of Texas at Austin (Ph.D.) (Co)
University of Toledo (Ph.D.) (Cl)
University of Utah (Ph.D.) (Cl)
University of Vermont (Ph.D.) (Cl)
Virginia Consortium Program in Clinical Psychology (Ph.D.) (Cl)
Virginia Polytechnic Institute and State University (Ph.D.) (Cl)
Washington State University (Ph.D.) (Cl)
Wisconsin School of Professional Psychology (Psy.D.) (Cl)
Wright State University (Psy.D.) (Cl)
Yeshiva University (Psy.D.) (Cm)

Adoption

East Tennessee State University (Ph.D.) (Cl)
Pepperdine University (Psy.D.) (Cl)
Rutgers-The State University of New Jersey (Psy.D.) (Cl)
University of California, Los Angeles (Ph.D.) (Cl)

Advocacy/Public Policy

Philadelphia College of Osteopathic Medicine (Psy.D.) (Cl)
The Wright Institute (Psy.D.) (Cl)
Wright State University (Psy.D.) (Cl)

Affective Disorders/Depression/Mood Disorders

Arizona State University (Ph.D.) (Co)
Baylor University (Psy.D.) (Cl)
Binghamton University, State University of New York (Ph.D.) (Cl)
Boston University (Ph.D.) (Cl)
Case Western Reserve University (Ph.D.) (Cl)
Chatham University (Psy.D.) (Co)
Chicago School of Professional Psychology–Chicago Campus (Psy.D.) (Cl)
Divine Mercy University (Psy.D.) (Cl)
Duke University (Ph.D.) (Cl)
Eastern Michigan University (Ph.D.) (Cl)
Fairleigh Dickinson University (Ph.D.) (Cl)
Florida International University (Ph.D.) (Cl)
George Washington University (Ph.D.) (Cl)
Harvard University (Ph.D.) (Cl)
Hofstra University (Ph.D.) (Cl)
Howard University (Ph.D.) (Co)
Idaho State University (Ph.D.) (Cl)
Illinois Institute of Technology (Ph.D.) (Cl)
Indiana University–Bloomington (Ph.D.) (Cl)
Indiana University–Purdue University Indianapolis (Ph.D.) (Cl)
John F. Kennedy University (Psy.D.) (Cl)
Kean University (Psy.D.) (Cm)
La Salle University (Psy.D.) (Cl)
Long Island University, C.W. Post Campus (Psy.D.) (Cl)
Marshall University (Psy.D.) (Cl)
Miami University (OH) (Ph.D.) (Cl)
Michigan State University (Ph.D.) (Cl)
Northwestern University (Ph.D.) (Cl)
Nova Southeastern University (Ph.D.) (Cl)
Nova Southeastern University (Psy.D.) (Cl)
Oklahoma State University (Ph.D.) (Cl)
Palo Alto University (Psy.D.) (Cl)
Rutgers-The State University of New Jersey (Ph.D.) (Cl)
Saint Louis University (Ph.D.) (Cl)
Southern Methodist University (Ph.D.) (Cl)
St. John's University (Ph.D.) (Cl)
Temple University (Ph.D.) (Cl)
The Ohio State University (Ph.D.) (Cl)
The University of Memphis (Ph.D.) (Cl)
The University of Montana (Ph.D.) (Cl)
University at Buffalo, State University of New York (Ph.D.) (Cl)
University of Arizona (Ph.D.) (Cl)
University of California, Berkeley (Ph.D.) (Cl)
University of California, Los Angeles (Ph.D.) (Cl)
University of Colorado Denver (Ph.D.) (Cl)
University of Connecticut (Ph.D.) (Cl)
University of Delaware (Ph.D.) (Cl)
University of Denver (Ph.D.) (Cl)
University of Georgia (Ph.D.) (Cl)
University of Hartford (Psy.D.) (Cl)
University of Illinois at Chicago (Ph.D.) (Cl)
University of Illinois at Urbana-Champaign (Ph.D.) (Cl)
University of Iowa (Ph.D.) (Cl)
University of Louisville (Ph.D.) (Cl)
University of Maryland-College Park (Ph.D.) (Cl)
University of Massachusetts, Boston (Ph.D.) (Co)
University of Miami (Ph.D.) (Cl)
University of Minnesota (Ph.D.) (Cl)
University of Nevada, Reno (Ph.D.) (Cl)
University of North Dakota (Ph.D.) (Cl)
University of Notre Dame (Ph.D.) P(Cl)
University of Oregon (Ph.D.) (Cl)
University of Pennsylvania (Ph.D.) (Cl)
University of Pittsburgh (Ph.D.) (Cl)
University of South Florida (Ph.D.) (Cl)
University of Texas at Austin (Ph.D.) (Cl)
University of Texas Southwestern Medical Center (Ph.D.) (Cl)
University of Toledo (Ph.D.) (Cl)
University of Utah (Ph.D.) (Cl)
University of Vermont (Ph.D.) (Cl)
University of Virginia (Ph.D.) (Cl)
University of Wisconsin, Madison (Ph.D.) (Cl)
University of Wyoming (Ph.D.) (Cl)
Vanderbilt University (Ph.D.) (Cl)
Virginia Commonwealth University (Ph.D.) (Cl)
Virginia Polytechnic Institute and State University (Ph.D.) (Cl)
Wichita State University (Ph.D.) (Cl)
Wright State University (Psy.D.) (Cl)
Yale University (Ph.D.) (Cl)
Yeshiva University (Psy.D.) (Cl)

Aggression/Anger Control/Impulse Control

Baylor University (Psy.D.) (Cl)
George Washington University (Ph.D.) (Cl)
Long Island University, C.W. Post Campus (Psy.D.) (Cl)

Northern Illinois University (Ph.D.) (Cl)
St. John's University (Ph.D.) (Cl)

Aging/Gerontology

American School of Professional Psychology at Argosy University, Washington, DC (Psy.D.) (Cl)
Arizona State University (Ph.D.) (Cl)
Arizona State University (Ph.D.) (Co)
Azusa Pacific University (Psy.D.) (Cl)
Boston University (Ph.D.) (Cl)
Case Western Reserve University (Ph.D.) (Cl)
Chicago School of Professional Psychology–Chicago Campus (Psy.D.) (Cl)
Fuller Theological Seminary (Ph.D.) (Cl)
Fuller Theological Seminary (Psy.D.) (Cl)
George Fox University (Psy.D.) (Cl)
Illinois School of Professional Psychology at Argosy University, Chicago (Psy.D.) (Cl)
Kean University (Psy.D.) (Cm)
Marshall University (Psy.D.) (Cl)
Marywood University (Psy.D.) (Cl)
Michigan State University (Ph.D.) (Cl)
Midwestern University (Psy.D.) (Cl)
Ohio University (Ph.D.) (Cl)
Oklahoma State University (Ph.D.) (Cl)
Palo Alto University (Psy.D.) (Cl)
Pepperdine University (Psy.D.) (Cl)
Philadelphia College of Osteopathic Medicine (Psy.D.) (Cl)
Saint Mary's University of Minnesota (Psy.D.) (Co)
Spalding University (Psy.D.) (Cl)
The Ohio State University (Ph.D.) (Cl)
University of Alabama at Birmingham (Ph.D.) (Cl)
University of Alabama at Tuscaloosa (Ph.D.) (Cl)
University of Arizona (Ph.D.) (Cl)
University of California, Berkeley (Ph.D.) (Cl)
University of Colorado at Colorado Springs (Ph.D.) (Cl)
University of Georgia (Ph.D.) (Cl)
University of Houston (Ph.D.) (Co)
University of Louisville (Ph.D.) (Cl)
University of Maine (Ph.D.) (Cl)
University of Massachusetts Amherst (Ph.D.) (Cl)
University of Missouri, St. Louis (Ph.D.) (Cl)
University of Nevada, Reno (Ph.D.) (Cl)
University of Pittsburgh (Ph.D.) (Cl)
University of Southern California (Ph.D.) (Cl)
Washington State University (Ph.D.) (Cl)
Wayne State University (Ph.D.) (Cl)
West Virginia University (Ph.D.) (Cl)
Wright State University (Psy.D.) (Cl)

Yeshiva University (Ph.D.) (Cl)
Yeshiva University (Psy.D.) (Cl)

Anxiety Disorders/Panic Disorders

American School of Professional Psychology at Argosy University, Washington, DC (Psy.D.) (Cl)
Arizona State University (Ph.D.) (Co)
Baylor University (Psy.D.) (Cl)
Binghamton University, State University of New York (Ph.D.) (Cl)
Boston University (Ph.D.) (Cl)
Case Western Reserve University (Ph.D.) (Cl)
Chatham University (Psy.D.) (Co)
Chicago School of Professional Psychology–Chicago Campus (Psy.D.) (Cl)
Divine Mercy University (Psy.D.) (Cl)
Eastern Michigan University (Ph.D.) (Cl)
Fairleigh Dickinson University (Ph.D.) (Cl)
Florida International University (Ph.D.) (Cl)
Florida State University (Ph.D.) (Cl)
George Washington University (Ph.D.) (Cl)
Georgia State University (Ph.D.) (Cl)
Harvard University (Ph.D.) (Cl)
Hofstra University (Ph.D.) (Cl)
Howard University (Ph.D.) (Co)
Idaho State University (Ph.D.) (Cl)
Illinois Institute of Technology (Ph.D.) (Cl)
Indiana University–Bloomington (Ph.D.) (Cl)
John F. Kennedy University (Psy.D.) (Cl)
Kean University (Psy.D.) (Cm)
Kent State University (Ph.D.) (Cl)
La Salle University (Psy.D.) (Cl)
Long Island University, C.W. Post Campus (Psy.D.) (Cl)
Loyola University Maryland (Psy.D.) (Cl)
Marshall University (Psy.D.) (Cl)
Miami University (OH) (Ph.D.) (Cl)
Michigan State University (Ph.D.) (Cl)
Northern Illinois University (Ph.D.) (Cl)
Northwestern University (Ph.D.) (Cl)
Nova Southeastern University (Ph.D.) (Cl)
Nova Southeastern University (Psy.D.) (Cl)
Oklahoma State University (Ph.D.) (Cl)
Palo Alto University (Psy.D.) (Cl)
Roosevelt University (Psy.D.) (Cl)
Rutgers-The State University of New Jersey (Ph.D.) (Cl)
Rutgers-The State University of New Jersey (Psy.D.) (Cl)
Saint Louis University (Ph.D.) (Cl)

San Diego State University–UC San Diego (Ph.D.) (Cl)
Southern Illinois University Carbondale (Ph.D.) (Cl)
Southern Methodist University (Ph.D.) (Cl)
St. John's University (Ph.D.) (Cl)
Stony Brook University, State University of New York (Ph.D.) (Cl)
Syracuse University (Ph.D.) (Cl)
Temple University (Ph.D.) (Cl)
The Ohio State University (Ph.D.) (Cl)
The University of Memphis (Ph.D.) (Cl)
The University of Montana (Ph.D.) (Cl)
University at Albany (Ph.D.) (Cl)
University at Buffalo, State University of New York (Ph.D.) (Cl)
University of Alabama at Tuscaloosa (Ph.D.) (Cl)
University of California, Los Angeles (Ph.D.) (Cl)
University of Central Florida (Ph.D.) (Cl)
University of Colorado Denver (Ph.D.) (Cl)
University of Connecticut (Ph.D.) (Cl)
University of Delaware (Ph.D.) (Cl)
University of Denver (Ph.D.) (Cl)
University of Florida (Ph.D.) (Co)
University of Georgia (Ph.D.) (Cl)
University of Hartford (Psy.D.) (Cl)
University of Houston (Ph.D.) (Cl)
University of Illinois at Chicago (Ph.D.) (Cl)
University of Illinois at Urbana-Champaign (Ph.D.) (Cl)
University of Kansas (Ph.D.) (Cl)
University of Louisville (Ph.D.) (Cl)
University of Maryland-College Park (Ph.D.) (Cl)
University of Massachusetts, Boston (Ph.D.) (Co)
University of Minnesota (Ph.D.) (Cl)
University of Missouri Kansas City (Ph.D.) (Cl)
University of Nebraska, Lincoln (Ph.D.) (Cl)
University of Nevada Las Vegas (Ph.D.) (Cl)
University of Nevada, Reno (Ph.D.) (Cl)
University of North Carolina, Chapel Hill (Ph.D.) (Cl)
University of North Dakota (Ph.D.) (Cl)
University of Notre Dame (Ph.D.) P(Cl)
University of Oregon (Ph.D.) (Cl)
University of Pennsylvania (Ph.D.) (Cl)
University of Pittsburgh (Ph.D.) (Cl)
University of South Florida (Ph.D.) (Cl)
University of Tennessee–Knoxville (Ph.D.) (Cl)
University of Texas at Austin (Ph.D.) (Cl)
University of Toledo (Ph.D.) (Cl)
University of Utah (Ph.D.) (Cl)
University of Vermont (Ph.D.) (Cl)
University of Virginia (Ph.D.) (Cl)
University of Washington (Ph.D.) (Cl)
University of Wisconsin, Madison (Ph.D.) (Cl)
University of Wyoming (Ph.D.) (Cl)
Vanderbilt University (Ph.D.) (Cl)
Virginia Commonwealth University (Ph.D.) (Cl)
Virginia Polytechnic Institute and State University (Ph.D.) (Cl)
West Virginia University (Ph.D.) (Cl)
Wichita State University (Ph.D.) (Cl)
Yale University (Ph.D.) (Cl)
Yeshiva University (Ph.D.) (Cl)
Yeshiva University (Psy.D.) (Cl)

Assessment/Testing

Adelphi University (Ph.D.) (Cl)
American School of Professional Psychology at Argosy University, San Francisco Bay Area (Psy.D.) (Cl)
American University (Ph.D.) (Cl)
Antioch University New England (Psy.D.) (Cl)
Arizona State University (Ph.D.) (Cl)
Arizona State University (Ph.D.) (Co)
Auburn University (Ph.D.) (Cl)
Boston College (Ph.D.) (Co)
Carlos Albizu University, San Juan Campus (Psy.D.) (Cl)
Carlow University (Psy.D.) (Co)
Case Western Reserve University (Ph.D.) (Cl)
Catholic University of America (Ph.D.) (Cl)
Chatham University (Psy.D.) (Co)
Chicago School of Professional Psychology–Chicago Campus (Psy.D.) (Cl)
Chicago School of Professional Psychology—Washington, DC Campus (Psy.D.) (Cl)
Clark University (Ph.D.) (Cl)
DePaul University (Ph.D.) (Cl)
Divine Mercy University (Psy.D.) (Cl)
East Carolina University (Ph.D.) (Cl)
Emory University (Ph.D.) (Cl)
Fairleigh Dickinson University (Ph.D.) (Cl)
Florida International University (Ph.D.) (Cl)
Florida State University (Ph.D.) (Cl)
Florida State University (Ph.D.) (Cm)
Fuller Theological Seminary (Ph.D.) (Cl)
Fuller Theological Seminary (Psy.D.) (Cl)
George Fox University (Psy.D.) (Cl)
George Washington University (Ph.D.) (Cl)
Georgia School of Professional Psychology at Argosy University, Atlanta (Psy.D.) (Cl)
Georgia State University (Ph.D.) (Cl)
Harvard University (Ph.D.) (Cl)
Howard University (Ph.D.) (Co)
Idaho State University (Ph.D.) (Cl)

Indiana University of Pennsylvania (Psy.D.) (Cl)
James Madison University (Psy.D.) (Cm)
John F. Kennedy University (Psy.D.) (Cl)
John Jay College of Criminal Justice & The Graduate Center, CUNY (Ph.D.) (Cl)
Kean University (Psy.D.) (Cm)
Kent State University (Ph.D.) (Cl)
La Salle University (Psy.D.) (Cl)
Long Island University, C.W. Post Campus (Psy.D.) (Cl)
Loyola University Chicago (Ph.D.) (Cl)
Marquette University (Ph.D.) (Cl)
Marshall University (Psy.D.) (Cl)
Miami University (OH) (Ph.D.) (Cl)
Michigan State University (Ph.D.) (Cl)
Northern Illinois University (Ph.D.) (Cl)
Northwestern University (Ph.D.) (Cl)
Nova Southeastern University (Ph.D.) (Cl)
Nova Southeastern University (Psy.D.) (Cl)
Purdue University (Ph.D.) (Cl)
Rutgers-The State University of New Jersey (Ph.D.) (Cl)
Rutgers-The State University of New Jersey (Psy.D.) (Cl)
Saint Louis University (Ph.D.) (Cl)
Saint Mary's University of Minnesota (Psy.D.) (Co)
Sam Houston State University (Ph.D.) (Cl)
Southern Methodist University (Ph.D.) (Cl)
Springfield College (Psy.D.) (Co)
Suffolk University (Ph.D.) (Cl)
Tennessee State University (Ph.D.) (Co)
The New School (Ph.D.) (Cl)
The University of Akron (Ph.D.) (Co)
The University of Montana (Ph.D.) (Cl)
The Wright Institute (Psy.D.) (Cl)
University of California, Berkeley (Ph.D.) (Cl)
University of California, Santa Barbara (Ph.D.) (Cm)
University of Colorado Boulder (Ph.D.) (Cl)
University of Colorado Denver (Ph.D.) (Cl)
University of Connecticut (Ph.D.) (Cl)
University of Denver (Ph.D.) (Co)
University of Denver (Ph.D.) (Cl)
University of Florida (Ph.D.) (Co)
University of Georgia (Ph.D.) (Cl)
University of Georgia (Ph.D.) (Co)
University of Hawaii at Manoa (Ph.D.) (Cl)
University of Houston (Ph.D.) (Cl)
University of Houston (Ph.D.) (Co)
University of Illinois at Urbana-Champaign (Ph.D.) (Cl)
University of Illinois at Urbana-Champaign (Ph.D.) (Co)
University of Indianapolis (Psy.D.) (Cl)
University of Kansas–Child (Ph.D.) (Cl)
University of Kentucky (Ph.D.) (Cl)
University of Louisville (Ph.D.) (Co)
University of Maine (Ph.D.) (Cl)
University of Massachusetts Amherst (Ph.D.) (Cl)
University of Massachusetts, Boston (Ph.D.) (Co)
University of Mississippi (Ph.D.) (Cl)
University of Missouri, Columbia (Ph.D.) (Cl)
University of Missouri, St. Louis (Ph.D.) (Cl)
University of Nebraska, Lincoln (Ph.D.) (Co)
University of New Mexico (Ph.D.) (Cl)
University of North Carolina at Charlotte (Ph.D.) (Cl)
University of North Carolina, Chapel Hill (Ph.D.) (Cl)
University of North Carolina, Greensboro (Ph.D.) (Cl)
University of North Dakota (Ph.D.) (Cl)
University of North Dakota (Ph.D.) (Co)
University of North Texas (Ph.D.) (Co)
University of Notre Dame (Ph.D.) P(Cl)
University of Oregon (Ph.D.) (Cl)
University of Pennsylvania (Ph.D.) (Cl)
University of Pittsburgh (Ph.D.) (Cl)
University of Rhode Island (Ph.D.) (Cl)
University of South Florida (Ph.D.) (Cl)
University of Southern California (Ph.D.) (Cl)
University of Southern Mississippi (Ph.D.) (Co)
University of Texas at Austin (Ph.D.) (Cl)
University of Texas at Austin (Ph.D.) (Co)
University of Toledo (Ph.D.) (Cl)
University of Utah (Ph.D.) (Cl)
University of Virginia (Ph.D.) (Cm)
University of Wisconsin, Madison (Ph.D.) (Cl)
Vanderbilt University (Ph.D.) (Cl)
Virginia Commonwealth University (Ph.D.) (Cl)
Virginia Polytechnic Institute and State University (Ph.D.) (Cl)
Washington State University (Ph.D.) (Cl)
West Virginia University (Ph.D.) (Co)
Widener University (Psy.D.) (Cl)
Wright State University (Psy.D.) (Cl)
Yeshiva University (Psy.D.) (Cl)

Attention Deficit/Hyperactivity Disorder

Case Western Reserve University (Ph.D.) (Cl)
Chatham University (Psy.D.) (Co)
Fairleigh Dickinson University (Ph.D.) (Cl)
Florida International University (Ph.D.) (Cl)
Indiana State University (Psy.D.) (Cl)
Iowa State University (Ph.D.) (Co)
Long Island University, C.W. Post Campus (Psy.D.) (Cl)

Marquette University (Ph.D.) (Cl)
Marshall University (Psy.D.) (Cl)
Miami University (OH) (Ph.D.) (Cl)
Michigan State University (Ph.D.) (Cl)
Northern Illinois University (Ph.D.) (Cl)
Pepperdine University (Psy.D.) (Cl)
Philadelphia College of Osteopathic Medicine (Psy.D.) (Cl)
Purdue University (Ph.D.) (Cl)
Saint Louis University (Ph.D.) (Cl)
Syracuse University (Ph.D.) (Cl)
University at Buffalo, State University of New York (Ph.D.) (Cl)
University of Alabama at Tuscaloosa (Ph.D.) (Cl)
University of Central Florida (Ph.D.) (Cl)
University of Florida (Ph.D.) (Cl)
University of Georgia (Ph.D.) (Cl)
University of Iowa (Ph.D.) (Cl)
University of Minnesota (Ph.D.) (Cl)
University of North Carolina at Charlotte (Ph.D.) (Cl)
University of Pittsburgh (Ph.D.) (Cl)
University of South Florida (Ph.D.) (Cl)
University of Tennessee–Knoxville (Ph.D.) (Cl)
University of Texas at Austin (Ph.D.) (Cl)
University of Wyoming (Ph.D.) (Cl)
Virginia Polytechnic Institute and State University (Ph.D.) (Cl)

Autism/Developmental Disabilities

Auburn University (Ph.D.) (Cl)
Binghamton University, State University of New York (Ph.D.) (Cl)
Chatham University (Psy.D.) (Co)
Duke University (Ph.D.) (Cl)
Fairleigh Dickinson University (Ph.D.) (Cl)
George Washington University (Ph.D.) (Cl)
Georgia State University (Ph.D.) (Cl)
Indiana University–Purdue University Indianapolis (Ph.D.) (Cl)
Kean University (Psy.D.) (Cm)
Marshall University (Psy.D.) (Cl)
Miami University (OH) (Ph.D.) (Cl)
Michigan State University (Ph.D.) (Cl)
Northern Illinois University (Ph.D.) (Cl)
Pepperdine University (Psy.D.) (Cl)
Ponce Health Sciences University (Ph.D.) (Cl)
Ponce Health Sciences University (Psy.D.) (Cl)
Purdue University (Ph.D.) (Cl)
Seattle Pacific University (Ph.D.) (Cl)
Syracuse University (Ph.D.) (Cl)
The University of Memphis (Ph.D.) (Cl)
University at Albany (Ph.D.) (Cl)
University of Alabama at Birmingham (Ph.D.) (Cl)
University of Alabama at Tuscaloosa (Ph.D.) (Cl)
University of California, Berkeley (Ph.D.) (Cl)
University of California, Los Angeles (Ph.D.) (Cl)
University of California, Santa Barbara (Ph.D.) (Cm)
University of Colorado at Colorado Springs (Ph.D.) (Cl)
University of Connecticut (Ph.D.) (Cl)
University of Hawaii at Manoa (Ph.D.) (Cl)
University of Illinois at Urbana-Champaign (Ph.D.) (Cl)
University of Kansas–Child (Ph.D.) (Cl)
University of Louisville (Ph.D.) (Cl)
University of Maine (Ph.D.) (Cl)
University of Miami (Ph.D.) (Cl)
University of Mississippi (Ph.D.) (Cl)
University of Nevada Las Vegas (Ph.D.) (Cl)
University of North Carolina, Chapel Hill (Ph.D.) (Cl)
University of Pennsylvania (Ph.D.) (Cl)
University of Pittsburgh (Ph.D.) (Cl)
University of Rochester (Ph.D.) (Cl)
University of Texas at Austin (Ph.D.) (Cl)
University of Washington (Ph.D.) (Cl)
University of Wisconsin, Milwaukee (Ph.D.) (Cl)
Vanderbilt University (Ph.D.) (Cl)
Virginia Polytechnic Institute and State University (Ph.D.) (Cl)
Yeshiva University (Ph.D.) (Cl)

Behavioral Therapy/Analysis

Arizona State University (Ph.D.) (Cl)
Divine Mercy University (Psy.D.) (Cl)
Emory University (Ph.D.) (Cl)
Long Island University (Ph.D.) (Cl)
Long Island University, C.W. Post Campus (Psy.D.) (Cl)
Marquette University (Ph.D.) (Co)
Nova Southeastern University (Ph.D.) (Cl)
Nova Southeastern University (Psy.D.) (Cl)
Pepperdine University (Psy.D.) (Cl)
Rutgers-The State University of New Jersey (Ph.D.) (Cl)
University of Colorado Boulder (Ph.D.) (Cl)
University of Denver (Psy.D.) (Cl)
University of Georgia (Ph.D.) (Cl)
University of Maryland, Baltimore County (Ph.D.) (Cl)
University of Minnesota (Ph.D.) (Cl)
University of Missouri Kansas City (Ph.D.) (Cl)
University of Pennsylvania (Ph.D.) (Cl)

University of Texas Southwestern Medical Center (Ph.D.) (Cl)
Vanderbilt University (Ph.D.) (Cl)

Biofeedback

Chicago School of Professional Psychology–Chicago Campus (Psy.D.) (Cl)
Duke University (Ph.D.) (Cl)
Nova Southeastern University (Ph.D.) (Cl)
Nova Southeastern University (Psy.D.) (Cl)
Springfield College (Psy.D.) (Co)
Widener University (Psy.D.) (Cl)

Cardiovascular Psychology

Duke University (Ph.D.) (Cl)
East Carolina University (Ph.D.) (Cl)
Ohio University (Ph.D.) (Cl)
University of Nevada Las Vegas (Ph.D.) (Cl)
University of New Mexico (Ph.D.) (Cl)
Yeshiva University (Ph.D.) (Cl)

Career Counseling/Development

Chatham University (Psy.D.) (Co)
New Mexico State University (Ph.D.) (Co)
The University of Memphis (Ph.D.) (Co)
University of California, Santa Barbara (Ph.D.) (Cm)
University of Florida (Ph.D.) (Co)
University of Houston (Ph.D.) (Co)
University of Louisville (Ph.D.) (Co)
University of Maryland-College Park (Ph.D.) (Co)
University of Massachusetts, Boston (Ph.D.) (Co)
University of Missouri, Columbia (Ph.D.) (Co)
University of Nebraska, Lincoln (Ph.D.) (Co)
University of Tennessee–Knoxville (Ph.D.) (Co)

Child Abuse/Neglect

American School of Professional Psychology at Argosy University, Washington, DC (Psy.D.) (Cl)
Chicago School of Professional Psychology–Chicago Campus (Psy.D.) (Cl)
Georgia School of Professional Psychology at Argosy University, Atlanta (Psy.D.) (Cl)
St. John's University (Ph.D.) (Cl)
University of California, Santa Barbara (Ph.D.) (Cm)
University of Georgia (Ph.D.) (Cl)
University of Iowa (Ph.D.) (Cl)
University of Kansas–Child (Ph.D.) (Cl)
University of Nebraska, Lincoln (Ph.D.) (Cl)
University of Notre Dame (Ph.D.) P(Cl)
University of Rochester (Ph.D.) (Cl)

Child/Pediatric

Adelphi University (Ph.D.) (Cl)
Alliant International University, Fresno (Psy.D.) (Cl)
Alliant International University, San Francisco Bay (Psy.D.) (Cl)
American School of Professional Psychology at Argosy University, Washington, DC (Psy.D.) (Cl)
Antioch University New England (Psy.D.) (Cl)
Arizona State University (Ph.D.) (Cl)
Auburn University (Ph.D.) (Cl)
Azusa Pacific University (Psy.D.) (Cl)
Ball State University (Ph.D.) (Co)
Baylor University (Psy.D.) (Cl)
Binghamton University, State University of New York (Ph.D.) (Cl)
Boston College (Ph.D.) (Co)
Bowling Green State University (Ph.D.) (Cl)
Carlos Albizu University, San Juan Campus (Ph.D.) (Cl)
Carlow University (Psy.D.) (Co)
Case Western Reserve University (Ph.D.) (Cl)
Catholic University of America (Ph.D.) (Cl)
Central Michigan University (Ph.D.) (Cl)
Chatham University (Psy.D.) (Co)
Chestnut Hill College (Psy.D.) (Cl)
Chicago School of Professional Psychology–Chicago Campus (Psy.D.) (Cl)
Chicago School of Professional Psychology—Washington, DC Campus (Psy.D.) (Cl)
Clark University (Ph.D.) (Cl)
Cleveland State University (Ph.D.) (Co)
DePaul University (Ph.D.) (Cl)
Divine Mercy University (Psy.D.) (Cl)
Duke University (Ph.D.) (Cl)
Eastern Michigan University (Ph.D.) (Cl)
Fairleigh Dickinson University (Ph.D.) (Cl)
Florida State University (Ph.D.) (Cl)
Fuller Theological Seminary (Ph.D.) (Cl)
Fuller Theological Seminary (Psy.D.) (Cl)
George Fox University (Psy.D.) (Cl)
George Washington University (Ph.D.) (Cl)
Georgia School of Professional Psychology at Argosy University, Atlanta (Psy.D.) (Cl)
Georgia State University (Ph.D.) (Cl)
Harvard University (Ph.D.) (Cl)
Idaho State University (Ph.D.) (Cl)
Illinois Institute of Technology (Ph.D.) (Cl)

Illinois School of Professional Psychology at Argosy University, Chicago (Psy.D.) (Cl)
Indiana University–Bloomington (Ph.D.) (Cl)
Indiana University–Purdue University Indianapolis (Ph.D.) (Cl)
Indiana University of Pennsylvania (Psy.D.) (Cl)
Jackson State University (Ph.D.) (Cl)
James Madison University (Psy.D.) (Cm)
Kent State University (Ph.D.) (Cl)
La Salle University (Psy.D.) (Cl)
Loma Linda University (Ph.D.) (Cl)
Loma Linda University (Psy.D.) (Cl)
Long Island University (Ph.D.) (Cl)
Long Island University, C.W. Post Campus (Psy.D.) (Cl)
Louisiana Tech University (Ph.D.) (Co)
Loyola University Chicago (Ph.D.) (Cl)
Loyola University Maryland (Psy.D.) (Cl)
Marquette University (Ph.D.) (Co)
Marquette University (Ph.D.) (Cl)
Marshall University (Psy.D.) (Cl)
Marywood University (Psy.D.) (Cl)
Miami University (OH) (Ph.D.) (Cl)
Midwestern University (Psy.D.) (Cl)
Midwestern University–Glendale Campus (Psy.D.) (Cl)
Northeastern University (Ph.D.) (Co)
Northern Illinois University (Ph.D.) (Cl)
Northwestern University (Ph.D.) (Cl)
Northwestern University Feinberg School of Medicine (Ph.D.) (Cl)
Nova Southeastern University (Ph.D.) (Cl)
Nova Southeastern University (Psy.D.) (Cl)
Ohio University (Ph.D.) (Cl)
Oklahoma State University (Ph.D.) (Cl)
Our Lady of the Lake University (Psy.D.) (Co)
Pace University (Psy.D.) (Cm)
Palo Alto University (Psy.D.) (Cl)
Pennsylvania State University (Ph.D.) (Cl)
Pepperdine University (Psy.D.) (Cl)
Philadelphia College of Osteopathic Medicine (Psy.D.) (Cl)
Ponce Health Sciences University (Ph.D.) (Cl)
Ponce Health Sciences University (Psy.D.) (Cl)
Radford University (Psy.D.) (Co)
Regent University (Psy.D.) (Cl)
Roosevelt University (Psy.D.) (Cl)
Rosalind Franklin University of Medicine and Science (Ph.D.) (Cl)
Rutgers-The State University of New Jersey (Ph.D.) (Cl)
Saint Louis University (Ph.D.) (Cl)
Saint Mary's University of Minnesota (Psy.D.) (Co)
Sam Houston State University (Ph.D.) (Cl)
San Diego State University–UC San Diego (Ph.D.) (Cl)
Seattle Pacific University (Ph.D.) (Cl)
Southern Illinois University Carbondale (Ph.D.) (Cl)
Spalding University (Psy.D.) (Cl)
Springfield College (Psy.D.) (Co)
Suffolk University (Ph.D.) (Cl)
Syracuse University (Ph.D.) (Cl)
Teachers College, Columbia University (Ph.D.) (Cl)
Temple University (Ph.D.) (Cl)
Texas Tech University (Ph.D.) (Co)
The Ohio State University (Ph.D.) (Cl)
The University of Memphis (Ph.D.) (Cl)
The University of Memphis (Ph.D.) (Co)
The University of Montana (Ph.D.) (Cl)
The Wright Institute (Psy.D.) (Cl)
Uniformed Services University of the Health Sciences (Ph.D.) (Cl)
University at Albany (Ph.D.) (Cl)
University at Buffalo, State University of New York (Ph.D.) (Cl)
University of Alabama at Birmingham (Ph.D.) (Cl)
University of California, Berkeley (Ph.D.) (Cl)
University of California, Los Angeles (Ph.D.) (Cl)
University of Central Florida (Ph.D.) (Cl)
University of Cincinnati (Ph.D.) (Cl)
University of Colorado Denver (Ph.D.) (Cl)
University of Connecticut (Ph.D.) (Cl)
University of Delaware (Ph.D.) (Cl)
University of Denver (Ph.D.) (Co)
University of Denver (Ph.D.) (Cl)
University of Denver (Psy.D.) (Cl)
University of Florida (Ph.D.) (Co)
University of Florida (Ph.D.) (Cl)
University of Georgia (Ph.D.) (Cl)
University of Georgia (Ph.D.) (Co)
University of Hartford (Psy.D.) (Cl)
University of Hawaii at Manoa (Ph.D.) (Cl)
University of Illinois at Urbana-Champaign (Ph.D.) (Cl)
University of Illinois at Urbana-Champaign (Ph.D.) (Co)
University of Iowa (Ph.D.) (Cl)
University of Kansas–Child (Ph.D.) (Cl)
University of Kansas (Ph.D.) (Cl)
University of Kentucky (Ph.D.) (Cl)
University of La Verne (Psy.D.) (Cl)
University of Louisville (Ph.D.) (Cl)
University of Maine (Ph.D.) (Cl)
University of Maryland, Baltimore County (Ph.D.) (Cl)
University of Maryland-College Park (Ph.D.) (Cl)

University of Massachusetts Amherst (Ph.D.) (Cl)
University of Michigan (Ph.D.) (Cl)
University of Minnesota (Ph.D.) (Cl)
University of Mississippi (Ph.D.) (Cl)
University of Missouri, Columbia (Ph.D.) (Cl)
University of Missouri, St. Louis (Ph.D.) (Cl)
University of Nebraska, Lincoln (Ph.D.) (Cl)
University of Nevada Las Vegas (Ph.D.) (Cl)
University of New Mexico (Ph.D.) (Cl)
University of North Carolina, Chapel Hill (Ph.D.) (Cl)
University of North Carolina, Greensboro (Ph.D.) (Cl)
University of North Texas (Ph.D.) (Cl)
University of Notre Dame (Ph.D.) P(Cl)
University of Oregon (Ph.D.) (Co)
University of Pennsylvania (Ph.D.) (Cl)
University of Pittsburgh (Ph.D.) (Cl)
University of Rhode Island (Ph.D.) (Cl)
University of Rochester (Ph.D.) (Cl)
University of South Carolina (Ph.D.) (Cl)
University of South Florida (Ph.D.) (Cl)
University of Southern California (Ph.D.) (Cl)
University of Southern Mississippi (Ph.D.) (Cl)
University of Texas at Austin (Ph.D.) (Cl)
University of Texas Southwestern Medical Center (Ph.D.) (Cl)
University of Toledo (Ph.D.) (Cl)
University of Utah (Ph.D.) (Cl)
University of Vermont (Ph.D.) (Cl)
University of Virginia (Ph.D.) (Cl)
University of Virginia (Ph.D.) (Cm)
University of Washington (Ph.D.) (Cl)
University of Wisconsin, Madison (Ph.D.) (Cl)
University of Wisconsin, Milwaukee (Ph.D.) (Cl)
University of Wisconsin, Milwaukee (Ph.D.) (Co)
Utah State University (Ph.D.) (Cm)
Vanderbilt University (Ph.D.) (Cl)
Virginia Commonwealth University (Ph.D.) (Cl)
Virginia Commonwealth University (Ph.D.) (Co)
Virginia Consortium Program in Clinical Psychology (Ph.D.) (Cl)
Virginia Polytechnic Institute and State University (Ph.D.) (Cl)
Washington State University (Ph.D.) (Cl)
West Virginia University (Ph.D.) (Cl)
Widener University (Psy.D.) (Cl)
Wisconsin School of Professional Psychology (Psy.D.) (Cl)
Wright State University (Psy.D.) (Cl)
Yale University (Ph.D.) (Cl)
Yeshiva University (Psy.D.) (Cm)

Chronic Mental Illness

Azusa Pacific University (Psy.D.) (Cl)
Fuller Theological Seminary (Ph.D.) (Cl)
Fuller Theological Seminary (Psy.D.) (Cl)
Illinois School of Professional Psychology at Argosy University, Chicago (Psy.D.) (Cl)
Marshall University (Psy.D.) (Cl)
Northwestern University Feinberg School of Medicine (Ph.D.) (Cl)
University of Alabama at Tuscaloosa (Ph.D.) (Cl)
University of Connecticut (Ph.D.) (Cl)
University of Kentucky (Ph.D.) (Cl)
University of Mississippi (Ph.D.) (Cl)
University of Pittsburgh (Ph.D.) (Cl)
Virginia Commonwealth University (Ph.D.) (Cl)

Cognitive/Cognitive-Behavioral Therapy

American University (Ph.D.) (Cl)
Antioch University New England (Psy.D.) (Cl)
Boston University (Ph.D.) (Cl)
Chicago School of Professional Psychology–Chicago Campus (Psy.D.) (Cl)
Clark University (Ph.D.) (Cl)
Drexel University (Ph.D.) (Cl)
Duke University (Ph.D.) (Cl)
Emory University (Ph.D.) (Cl)
Idaho State University (Ph.D.) (Cl)
Illinois School of Professional Psychology at Argosy University, Chicago (Psy.D.) (Cl)
Indiana University–Bloomington (Ph.D.) (Cl)
La Salle University (Psy.D.) (Cl)
Marshall University (Psy.D.) (Cl)
Pepperdine University (Psy.D.) (Cl)
Philadelphia College of Osteopathic Medicine (Psy.D.) (Cl)
San Diego State University–UC San Diego (Ph.D.) (Cl)
Syracuse University (Ph.D.) (Cl)
Teachers College, Columbia University (Ph.D.) (Cl)
University of Colorado Boulder (Ph.D.) (Cl)
University of Denver (Ph.D.) (Cl)
University of Denver (Psy.D.) (Cl)
University of Florida (Ph.D.) (Cl)
University of Georgia (Ph.D.) (Cl)
University of Houston (Ph.D.) (Cl)
University of Iowa (Ph.D.) (Cl)
University of Kansas (Ph.D.) (Cl)
University of Kentucky (Ph.D.) (Cl)
University of Minnesota (Ph.D.) (Cl)
University of Missouri, Columbia (Ph.D.) (Co)
University of Oregon (Ph.D.) (Cl)

University of Pennsylvania (Ph.D.) (Cl)
University of Pittsburgh (Ph.D.) (Cl)
University of Rochester (Ph.D.) (Cl)
University of Southern California (Ph.D.) (Cl)
University of Toledo (Ph.D.) (Cl)
University of Utah (Ph.D.) (Cl)
University of Wisconsin, Madison (Ph.D.) (Cl)
University of Wisconsin, Milwaukee (Ph.D.) (Cl)
Widener University (Psy.D.) (Cl)
Wright State University (Psy.D.) (Cl)
Yeshiva University (Psy.D.) (Cl)

College-University Counseling/ Psychotherapy Centers

Adler University–Chicago (Psy.D.) (Cl)
Alliant International University, Fresno (Ph.D.) (Cl)
Alliant International University, Fresno (Psy.D.) (Cl)
Alliant International University, San Francisco Bay (Psy.D.) (Cl)
American School of Professional Psychology at Argosy University, San Francisco Bay Area (Psy.D.) (Cl)
American School of Professional Psychology at Argosy University, Washington, DC (Psy.D.) (Cl)
Antioch University New England (Psy.D.) (Cl)
Auburn University (Ph.D.) (Co)
Auburn University (Ph.D.) (Cl)
Azusa Pacific University (Psy.D.) (Cl)
Ball State University (Ph.D.) (Co)
Boston College (Ph.D.) (Co)
Brigham Young University (Ph.D.) (Cl)
California Lutheran University (Psy.D.) (Cl)
Carlos Albizu University, San Juan Campus (Ph.D.) (Cl)
Carlow University (Psy.D.) (Co)
Case Western Reserve University (Ph.D.) (Cl)
Chatham University (Psy.D.) (Co)
Chicago School of Professional Psychology–Chicago Campus (Psy.D.) (Cl)
Cleveland State University (Ph.D.) (Co)
Colorado State University (Ph.D.) (Co)
Duquesne University (Ph.D.) (Cl)
East Tennessee State University (Ph.D.) (Cl)
Eastern Michigan University (Ph.D.) (Cl)
Florida School of Professional Psychology at Argosy University (Psy.D.) (Cl)
Florida State University (Ph.D.) (Cm)
Fordham University (Ph.D.) (Co)
George Mason University (Ph.D.) (Cl)
George Washington University (Psy.D.) (Cl)
Georgia School of Professional Psychology at Argosy University, Atlanta (Psy.D.) (Cl)
Georgia Southern University (Psy.D.) (Cl)
Georgia State University (Ph.D.) (Co)
Howard University (Ph.D.) (Cl)
Howard University (Ph.D.) (Co)
Idaho State University (Ph.D.) (Cl)
Indiana University–Bloomington (Ph.D.) (Co)
Indiana University of Pennsylvania (Psy.D.) (Cl)
Iowa State University (Ph.D.) (Co)
Jackson State University (Ph.D.) (Cl)
James Madison University (Psy.D.) (Cm)
John Jay College of Criminal Justice & The Graduate Center, CUNY (Ph.D.) (Cl)
Kean University (Psy.D.) (Cm)
Lehigh University (Ph.D.) (Co)
Loma Linda University (Ph.D.) (Cl)
Long Island University (Ph.D.) (Cl)
Louisiana Tech University (Ph.D.) (Co)
Loyola University Chicago (Ph.D.) (Co)
Marquette University (Ph.D.) (Co)
Marywood University (Psy.D.) (Cl)
Miami University (OH) (Ph.D.) (Cl)
New Mexico State University (Ph.D.) (Co)
New York University (Ph.D.) (Co)
Northeastern University (Ph.D.) (Co)
Northern Illinois University (Ph.D.) (Cl)
Oklahoma State University (Ph.D.) (Co)
Pacific University, Oregon (Psy.D.) (Cl)
Palo Alto University (Psy.D.) (Cl)
Purdue University (Ph.D.) (Co)
Radford University (Psy.D.) (Co)
Regent University (Psy.D.) (Cl)
Roosevelt University (Psy.D.) (Cl)
Rutgers-The State University of New Jersey (Psy.D.) (Cl)
Saint Mary's University of Minnesota (Psy.D.) (Co)
Seattle Pacific University (Ph.D.) (Cl)
Southern Illinois University Carbondale (Ph.D.) (Co)
Spalding University (Psy.D.) (Cl)
Springfield College (Psy.D.) (Co)
Stony Brook University, State University of New York (Ph.D.) (Cl)
Suffolk University (Ph.D.) (Cl)
Teachers College, Columbia University (Ph.D.) (Co)
Tennessee State University (Ph.D.) (Co)
Texas A&M University (Ph.D.) (Co)
Texas Tech University (Ph.D.) (Co)
Texas Woman's University (Ph.D.) (Co)
The City College of New York, The Graduate Center, CUNY (Ph.D.) (Cl)
The New School (Ph.D.) (Cl)
The University of Akron (Ph.D.) (Co)
The University of Memphis (Ph.D.) (Co)
The Wright Institute (Psy.D.) (Cl)

University at Albany (Ph.D.) (Co)
University at Buffalo, State University of New York (Ph.D.) (Cl)
University at Buffalo, State University of New York (Ph.D.) (Cm)
University of Alabama at Tuscaloosa (Ph.D.) (Cl)
University of Alaska Fairbanks-Anchorage (Ph.D.) (Cl)
University of Arkansas (Ph.D.) (Cl)
University of California, Berkeley (Ph.D.) (Cl)
University of California, Santa Barbara (Ph.D.) (Cm)
University of Denver (Ph.D.) (Co)
University of Denver (Psy.D.) (Cl)
University of Florida (Ph.D.) (Co)
University of Georgia (Ph.D.) (Co)
University of Hartford (Psy.D.) (Cl)
University of Houston (Ph.D.) (Co)
University of Illinois at Urbana-Champaign (Ph.D.) (Cl)
University of Illinois at Urbana-Champaign (Ph.D.) (Co)
University of Indianapolis (Psy.D.) (Cl)
University of Iowa (Ph.D.) (Co)
University of Kansas–Child (Ph.D.) (Cl)
University of Kansas (Ph.D.) (Co)
University of Kentucky (Ph.D.) (Co)
University of La Verne (Psy.D.) (Cl)
University of Louisville (Ph.D.) (Co)
University of Massachusetts Amherst (Ph.D.) (Cl)
University of Missouri, Columbia (Ph.D.) (Cl)
University of Missouri, Columbia (Ph.D.) (Co)
University of Nevada Las Vegas (Ph.D.) (Cl)
University of North Carolina at Charlotte (Ph.D.) (Cl)
University of North Carolina, Greensboro (Ph.D.) (Cl)
University of North Dakota (Ph.D.) (Co)
University of North Texas (Ph.D.) (Co)
University of Oregon (Ph.D.) (Co)
University of Rochester (Ph.D.) (Cl)
University of Southern Mississippi (Ph.D.) (Co)
University of Tennessee–Knoxville (Ph.D.) (Co)
University of Texas at Austin (Ph.D.) (Cl)
University of Texas at Austin (Ph.D.) (Co)
University of Toledo (Ph.D.) (Cl)
University of Utah (Ph.D.) (Co)
University of Wisconsin, Milwaukee (Ph.D.) (Co)
Utah State University (Ph.D.) (Cm)
Virginia Commonwealth University (Ph.D.) (Co)
Washington University in St. Louis (Ph.D.) (Cl)
West Virginia University (Ph.D.) (Co)
Western Michigan University (Ph.D.) (Co)
Western Michigan University (Ph.D.) (Cl)
Wheaton College (Psy.D.) (Cl)
Wright State University (Psy.D.) (Cl)
Xavier University (Psy.D.) (Cl)
Yeshiva University (Ph.D.) (Cl)

Community Psychology

Adler University–Chicago (Psy.D.) (Cl)
Alliant International University, Fresno (Ph.D.) (Cl)
Alliant International University, Fresno (Psy.D.) (Cl)
Alliant International University, Los Angeles (Ph.D.) (Cl)
Alliant International University, Los Angeles (Psy.D.) (Cl)
Alliant International University, Sacramento (Psy.D.) (Cl)
Alliant International University, San Diego (Ph.D.) (Cl)
Alliant International University, San Diego (Psy.D.) (Cl)
Alliant International University, San Francisco Bay (Ph.D.) (Cl)
Alliant International University, San Francisco Bay (Psy.D.) (Cl)
American School of Professional Psychology at Argosy University, Washington, DC (Psy.D.) (Cl)
Antioch University New England (Psy.D.) (Cl)
Arizona School of Professional Psychology at Argosy University, Phoenix (Psy.D.) (Cl)
Auburn University (Ph.D.) (Co)
Auburn University (Ph.D.) (Cl)
Azusa Pacific University (Psy.D.) (Cl)
Baylor University (Psy.D.) (Cl)
Boston College (Ph.D.) (Co)
Boston University (Ph.D.) (Cl)
Bowling Green State University (Ph.D.) (Cl)
Brigham Young University (Ph.D.) (Cl)
California Lutheran University (Psy.D.) (Cl)
Carlos Albizu University, Miami Campus (Psy.D.) (Cl)
Carlos Albizu University, San Juan Campus (Psy.D.) (Cl)
Carlow University (Psy.D.) (Co)
Case Western Reserve University (Ph.D.) (Cl)
Catholic University of America (Ph.D.) (Cl)
Chicago School of Professional Psychology–Chicago Campus (Psy.D.) (Cl)
Chicago School of Professional Psychology—Washington, DC Campus (Psy.D.) (Cl)
Cleveland State University (Ph.D.) (Co)
DePaul University (Ph.D.) (Cl)
East Tennessee State University (Ph.D.) (Cl)
Fairleigh Dickinson University (Ph.D.) (Cl)
Florida International University (Ph.D.) (Cl)

Florida School of Professional Psychology at Argosy University (Psy.D.) (Cl)
Fordham University (Ph.D.) (Co)
George Fox University (Psy.D.) (Cl)
Georgia Southern University (Psy.D.) (Cl)
Georgia State University (Ph.D.) (Cl)
Hawaii School of Professional Psychology at Argosy University, Hawaii (Psy.D.) (Cl)
Howard University (Ph.D.) (Cl)
Illinois School of Professional Psychology at Argosy University, Chicago (Psy.D.) (Cl)
Indiana University–Purdue University Indianapolis (Ph.D.) (Cl)
Iowa State University (Ph.D.) (Co)
Loma Linda University (Ph.D.) (Cl)
Loma Linda University (Psy.D.) (Cl)
Long Island University (Ph.D.) (Cl)
Louisiana Tech University (Ph.D.) (Co)
Marquette University (Ph.D.) (Co)
Marywood University (Psy.D.) (Cl)
Miami University (OH) (Ph.D.) (Cl)
Midwestern University–Glendale Campus (Psy.D.) (Cl)
New Mexico State University (Ph.D.) (Co)
Our Lady of the Lake University (Psy.D.) (Co)
Palo Alto University (Psy.D.) (Cl)
Pepperdine University (Psy.D.) (Cl)
Purdue University (Ph.D.) (Co)
Radford University (Psy.D.) (Co)
Regent University (Psy.D.) (Cl)
Roosevelt University (Psy.D.) (Cl)
Rosalind Franklin University of Medicine and Science (Ph.D.) (Cl)
Saint Mary's University of Minnesota (Psy.D.) (Co)
Seattle Pacific University (Ph.D.) (Cl)
Southern Illinois University Carbondale (Ph.D.) (Co)
Southern Methodist University (Ph.D.) (Cl)
Spalding University (Psy.D.) (Cl)
Springfield College (Psy.D.) (Co)
Suffolk University (Ph.D.) (Cl)
Syracuse University (Ph.D.) (Cl)
Tennessee State University (Ph.D.) (Co)
Texas A&M University (Ph.D.) (Cl)
Texas A&M University (Ph.D.) (Co)
Texas Tech University (Ph.D.) (Cl)
Texas Tech University (Ph.D.) (Co)
Texas Woman's University (Ph.D.) (Co)
The University of Akron (Ph.D.) (Co)
The University of Memphis (Ph.D.) (Co)
The University of Montana (Ph.D.) (Cl)
Uniformed Services University of the Health Sciences (Ph.D.) (Cl)
University at Albany (Ph.D.) (Co)
University at Buffalo, State University of New York (Ph.D.) (Cm)
University of Arizona (Ph.D.) (Cl)
University of Arkansas (Ph.D.) (Cl)
University of California, Los Angeles (Ph.D.) (Cl)
University of California, Santa Barbara (Ph.D.) (Cm)
University of Cincinnati (Ph.D.) (Cl)
University of Colorado Denver (Ph.D.) (Cl)
University of Denver (Ph.D.) (Co)
University of Denver (Psy.D.) (Cl)
University of Florida (Ph.D.) (Co)
University of Hartford (Psy.D.) (Cl)
University of Houston (Ph.D.) (Co)
University of Illinois at Urbana-Champaign (Ph.D.) (Cl)
University of Illinois at Urbana-Champaign (Ph.D.) (Co)
University of Indianapolis (Psy.D.) (Cl)
University of Iowa (Ph.D.) (Co)
University of Kansas–Child (Ph.D.) (Cl)
University of Kansas (Ph.D.) (Co)
University of Kentucky (Ph.D.) (Cl)
University of Kentucky (Ph.D.) (Co)
University of La Verne (Psy.D.) (Cl)
University of Louisville (Ph.D.) (Co)
University of Maine (Ph.D.) (Cl)
University of Minnesota (Ph.D.) (Cl)
University of Mississippi (Ph.D.) (Cl)
University of Missouri Kansas City (Ph.D.) (Cl)
University of North Dakota (Ph.D.) (Cl)
University of North Dakota (Ph.D.) (Co)
University of North Texas (Ph.D.) (Co)
University of Oregon (Ph.D.) (Co)
University of Rhode Island (Ph.D.) (Cl)
University of Southern California (Ph.D.) (Cl)
University of Southern Mississippi (Ph.D.) (Co)
University of Tennessee–Knoxville (Ph.D.) (Co)
University of Texas at Austin (Ph.D.) (Cl)
University of Texas at Austin (Ph.D.) (Co)
University of Texas Southwestern Medical Center (Ph.D.) (Cl)
University of Utah (Ph.D.) (Co)
University of Virginia (Ph.D.) (Cl)
University of Washington (Ph.D.) (Cl)
University of Wisconsin, Milwaukee (Ph.D.) (Co)
University of Wyoming (Ph.D.) (Cl)
Utah State University (Ph.D.) (Cm)
Vanderbilt University (Ph.D.) (Cl)
Virginia Commonwealth University (Ph.D.) (Co)
Washington State University (Ph.D.) (Cl)
Wayne State University (Ph.D.) (Cl)
West Virginia University (Ph.D.) (Co)
Wheaton College (Psy.D.) (Cl)

Wisconsin School of Professional Psychology (Psy.D.) (Cl)

Conduct/Disruptive Disorder

Antioch University New England (Psy.D.) (Cl)
Binghamton University, State University of New York (Ph.D.) (Cl)
George Washington University (Ph.D.) (Cl)
Marshall University (Psy.D.) (Cl)
Miami University (OH) (Ph.D.) (Cl)
Purdue University (Ph.D.) (Cl)
Temple University (Ph.D.) (Cl)
University of Alabama at Tuscaloosa (Ph.D.) (Cl)
University of Georgia (Ph.D.) (Cl)
University of Miami (Ph.D.) (Cl)
University of Minnesota (Ph.D.) (Cl)
University of Pittsburgh (Ph.D.) (Cl)
University of Tennessee–Knoxville (Ph.D.) (Cl)
Virginia Polytechnic Institute and State University (Ph.D.) (Cl)

Consultation

Binghamton University, State University of New York (Ph.D.) (Cl)
Carlos Albizu University, San Juan Campus (Psy.D.) (Cl)
Catholic University of America (Ph.D.) (Cl)
Florida International University (Ph.D.) (Cl)
George Fox University (Psy.D.) (Cl)
George Mason University (Ph.D.) (Cl)
Indiana University–Purdue University Indianapolis (Ph.D.) (Cl)
Kent State University (Ph.D.) (Cl)
Miami University (OH) (Ph.D.) (Cl)
Northern Illinois University (Ph.D.) (Cl)
Ohio University (Ph.D.) (Cl)
Oklahoma State University (Ph.D.) (Cl)
Ponce Health Sciences University (Ph.D.) (Cl)
Ponce Health Sciences University (Psy.D.) (Cl)
University of Connecticut (Ph.D.) (Cl)
University of Denver (Psy.D.) (Cl)
University of Florida (Ph.D.) (Cl)
University of Hawaii at Manoa (Ph.D.) (Cl)
University of Illinois at Urbana-Champaign (Ph.D.) (Cl)
University of Indianapolis (Psy.D.) (Cl)
University of Mississippi (Ph.D.) (Cl)
University of New Mexico (Ph.D.) (Cl)
University of Virginia (Ph.D.) (Cm)
Virginia Polytechnic Institute and State University (Ph.D.) (Cl)
Yeshiva University (Psy.D.) (Cm)

Correctional Psychology/Prisons

Adler University–Chicago (Psy.D.) (Cl)
Alliant International University, Fresno (Ph.D.) (Cl)
Alliant International University, Fresno (Psy.D.) (Cl)
Alliant International University, Los Angeles (Ph.D.) (Cl)
Alliant International University, Los Angeles (Psy.D.) (Cl)
Alliant International University, Sacramento (Psy.D.) (Cl)
Alliant International University, San Diego (Ph.D.) (Cl)
Alliant International University, San Diego (Psy.D.) (Cl)
Alliant International University, San Francisco Bay (Ph.D.) (Cl)
Alliant International University, San Francisco Bay (Psy.D.) (Cl)
American School of Professional Psychology at Argosy University, Washington, DC (Psy.D.) (Cl)
Antioch University New England (Psy.D.) (Cl)
Auburn University (Ph.D.) (Co)
Auburn University (Ph.D.) (Cl)
Binghamton University, State University of New York (Ph.D.) (Cl)
California Lutheran University (Psy.D.) (Cl)
Carlos Albizu University, Miami Campus (Psy.D.) (Cl)
Chicago School of Professional Psychology–Chicago Campus (Psy.D.) (Cl)
Colorado State University (Ph.D.) (Co)
East Tennessee State University (Ph.D.) (Cl)
Florida School of Professional Psychology at Argosy University (Psy.D.) (Cl)
Florida State University (Ph.D.) (Cl)
Fuller Theological Seminary (Ph.D.) (Cl)
Fuller Theological Seminary (Psy.D.) (Cl)
George Fox University (Psy.D.) (Cl)
Hawaii School of Professional Psychology at Argosy University, Hawaii (Psy.D.) (Cl)
Idaho State University (Ph.D.) (Cl)
Indiana State University (Psy.D.) (Cl)
Iowa State University (Ph.D.) (Co)
Louisiana Tech University (Ph.D.) (Co)
Loyola University Maryland (Psy.D.) (Cl)
Marquette University (Ph.D.) (Co)
Midwestern University–Glendale Campus (Psy.D.) (Cl)
Oklahoma State University (Ph.D.) (Co)
Purdue University (Ph.D.) (Co)
Radford University (Psy.D.) (Co)

Roosevelt University (Psy.D.) (Cl)
Saint Mary's University of Minnesota (Psy.D.) (Co)
Sam Houston State University (Ph.D.) (Cl)
Seattle Pacific University (Ph.D.) (Cl)
Southern Illinois University Carbondale (Ph.D.) (Co)
Southern Methodist University (Ph.D.) (Cl)
Spalding University (Psy.D.) (Cl)
Springfield College (Psy.D.) (Co)
Tennessee State University (Ph.D.) (Co)
Texas Tech University (Ph.D.) (Co)
Texas Woman's University (Ph.D.) (Co)
The University of Montana (Ph.D.) (Cl)
University of Alabama at Tuscaloosa (Ph.D.) (Cl)
University of Arkansas (Ph.D.) (Cl)
University of Denver (Ph.D.) (Co)
University of Denver (Psy.D.) (Cl)
University of Indianapolis (Psy.D.) (Cl)
University of Iowa (Ph.D.) (Co)
University of North Texas (Ph.D.) (Cl)
University of Southern California (Ph.D.) (Cl)
University of Southern Mississippi (Ph.D.) (Cl)
University of Texas at Austin (Ph.D.) (Co)
University of Vermont (Ph.D.) (Cl)
University of Virginia (Ph.D.) (Cm)
University of Wisconsin, Madison (Ph.D.) (Cl)
Virginia Commonwealth University (Ph.D.) (Cl)
Virginia Commonwealth University (Ph.D.) (Co)
West Virginia University (Ph.D.) (Co)
Wheaton College (Psy.D.) (Cl)

Crisis Intervention

Baylor University (Psy.D.) (Cl)
Nova Southeastern University (Ph.D.) (Cl)
Nova Southeastern University (Psy.D.) (Cl)
Spalding University (Psy.D.) (Cl)
Syracuse University (Ph.D.) (Cl)
The University of South Dakota (Ph.D.) (Cl)
The Wright Institute (Psy.D.) (Cl)
University of Florida (Ph.D.) (Co)
University of Hartford (Psy.D.) (Cl)
University of Houston (Ph.D.) (Co)
University of Minnesota (Ph.D.) (Cl)
University of Texas at Austin (Ph.D.) (Cl)
University of Virginia (Ph.D.) (Cm)
West Virginia University (Ph.D.) (Co)
Wright State University (Psy.D.) (Cl)

Day/Partial Treatment

Alliant International University, Los Angeles (Psy.D.) (Cl)
Alliant International University, Sacramento (Psy.D.) (Cl)
Alliant International University, San Diego (Ph.D.) (Cl)
Alliant International University, San Diego (Psy.D.) (Cl)
Alliant International University, San Francisco Bay (Ph.D.) (Cl)
Alliant International University, San Francisco Bay (Psy.D.) (Cl)
Chicago School of Professional Psychology–Chicago Campus (Psy.D.) (Cl)
Northeastern University (Ph.D.) (Co)
Northern Illinois University (Ph.D.) (Cl)
Palo Alto University (Psy.D.) (Cl)
University at Albany (Ph.D.) (Co)
University of Wisconsin, Milwaukee (Ph.D.) (Co)
Wisconsin School of Professional Psychology (Psy.D.) (Cl)

Developmental Disabilities/Mental Retardation

Bowling Green State University (Ph.D.) (Cl)
Chicago School of Professional Psychology–Chicago Campus (Psy.D.) (Cl)
Divine Mercy University (Psy.D.) (Cl)
Roosevelt University (Psy.D.) (Cl)
Rutgers-The State University of New Jersey (Ph.D.) (Cl)
Seattle Pacific University (Ph.D.) (Cl)
Syracuse University (Ph.D.) (Cl)
University of California, Los Angeles (Ph.D.) (Cl)
University of Cincinnati (Ph.D.) (Cl)
University of Georgia (Ph.D.) (Co)
University of Massachusetts, Boston (Ph.D.) (Co)
University of Rochester (Ph.D.) (Cl)
University of Texas Southwestern Medical Center (Ph.D.) (Cl)
Vanderbilt University (Ph.D.) (Cl)
Virginia Polytechnic Institute and State University (Ph.D.) (Cl)

Dialectical Behavior Therapy

American University (Ph.D.) (Cl)
Chicago School of Professional Psychology–Chicago Campus (Psy.D.) (Cl)
Duke University (Ph.D.) (Cl)
Fairleigh Dickinson University (Ph.D.) (Cl)
Harvard University (Ph.D.) (Cl)
Hofstra University (Ph.D.) (Cl)

Indiana University–Purdue University Indianapolis (Ph.D.) (Cl)
La Salle University (Psy.D.) (Cl)
Marquette University (Ph.D.) (Cl)
Miami University (OH) (Ph.D.) (Cl)
Palo Alto University (Psy.D.) (Cl)
Pepperdine University (Psy.D.) (Cl)
Rutgers-The State University of New Jersey (Ph.D.) (Cl)
Rutgers-The State University of New Jersey (Psy.D.) (Cl)
Teachers College, Columbia University (Ph.D.) (Cl)
The Wright Institute (Psy.D.) (Cl)
University of Denver (Ph.D.) (Cl)
University of Kansas (Ph.D.) (Cl)
University of Kentucky (Ph.D.) (Cl)
University of North Carolina, Greensboro (Ph.D.) (Cl)
University of Southern Mississippi (Ph.D.) (Cl)
University of Toledo (Ph.D.) (Cl)
Vanderbilt University (Ph.D.) (Cl)

Disabilities/Disabled Persons

University of Georgia (Ph.D.) (Cl)
University of Illinois at Urbana-Champaign (Ph.D.) (Cl)
University of Illinois at Urbana-Champaign (Ph.D.) (Co)
University of South Alabama (Ph.D.) (Cm)
Utah State University (Ph.D.) (Cm)

Dissemination

DePaul University (Ph.D.) (Cl)
University of Mississippi (Ph.D.) (Cl)

Divorce/Child Custody

Indiana University–Bloomington (Ph.D.) (Cl)
University of Iowa (Ph.D.) (Cl)
University of Missouri, Columbia (Ph.D.) (Cl)

Early Intervention

University of Kansas–Child (Ph.D.) (Cl)
University of Missouri, Columbia (Ph.D.) (Cl)
Utah State University (Ph.D.) (Cm)
Wayne State University (Ph.D.) (Cl)

Eating Disorders/Body Dysmorphia

Adelphi University (Ph.D.) (Cl)
Arizona State University (Ph.D.) (Co)
Case Western Reserve University (Ph.D.) (Cl)
Chicago School of Professional Psychology–Chicago Campus (Psy.D.) (Cl)
Divine Mercy University (Psy.D.) (Cl)
Duke University (Ph.D.) (Cl)
Fairleigh Dickinson University (Ph.D.) (Cl)
George Washington University (Ph.D.) (Cl)
Georgia School of Professional Psychology at Argosy University, Atlanta (Psy.D.) (Cl)
Harvard University (Ph.D.) (Cl)
Illinois School of Professional Psychology at Argosy University, Chicago (Psy.D.) (Cl)
John F. Kennedy University (Psy.D.) (Cl)
La Salle University (Psy.D.) (Cl)
Long Island University, C.W. Post Campus (Psy.D.) (Cl)
Loyola University Chicago (Ph.D.) (Cl)
Loyola University Maryland (Psy.D.) (Cl)
Marshall University (Psy.D.) (Cl)
Michigan State University (Ph.D.) (Cl)
Palo Alto University (Psy.D.) (Cl)
Pepperdine University (Psy.D.) (Cl)
Roosevelt University (Psy.D.) (Cl)
Rutgers-The State University of New Jersey (Ph.D.) (Cl)
Saint Louis University (Ph.D.) (Cl)
Saint Mary's University of Minnesota (Psy.D.) (Co)
Southern Methodist University (Ph.D.) (Cl)
Springfield College (Psy.D.) (Co)
Temple University (Ph.D.) (Cl)
The Ohio State University (Ph.D.) (Cl)
The University of Akron (Ph.D.) (Co)
University at Albany (Ph.D.) (Cl)
University of Alabama at Birmingham (Ph.D.) (Cl)
University of Georgia (Ph.D.) (Cl)
University of Hawaii at Manoa (Ph.D.) (Cl)
University of Houston (Ph.D.) (Co)
University of Indianapolis (Psy.D.) (Cl)
University of Iowa (Ph.D.) (Cl)
University of Miami (Ph.D.) (Cl)
University of Minnesota (Ph.D.) (Cl)
University of Mississippi (Ph.D.) (Cl)
University of New Mexico (Ph.D.) (Cl)
University of North Carolina, Chapel Hill (Ph.D.) (Cl)
University of North Dakota (Ph.D.) (Cl)
University of Notre Dame (Ph.D.) P(Cl)
University of Pittsburgh (Ph.D.) (Cl)
University of South Florida (Ph.D.) (Cl)
University of Vermont (Ph.D.) (Cl)
University of Wisconsin, Milwaukee (Ph.D.) (Co)
University of Wyoming (Ph.D.) (Cl)
Utah State University (Ph.D.) (Cm)
Vanderbilt University (Ph.D.) (Cl)

Emergency Services

Illinois School of Professional Psychology at Argosy University, Chicago (Psy.D.) (Cl)
Northeastern University (Ph.D.) (Co)
University of Maryland, Baltimore County (Ph.D.) (Cl)
University of Pittsburgh (Ph.D.) (Cl)
University of Texas Southwestern Medical Center (Ph.D.) (Cl)

Evidence-Based/Empirically Supported Treatments

DePaul University (Ph.D.) (Cl)
La Salle University (Psy.D.) (Cl)
Palo Alto University (Psy.D.) (Cl)
Philadelphia College of Osteopathic Medicine (Psy.D.) (Cl)
Syracuse University (Ph.D.) (Cl)
The Wright Institute (Psy.D.) (Cl)
University of Arizona (Ph.D.) (Cl)
University of Georgia (Ph.D.) (Cl)
University of Hawaii at Manoa (Ph.D.) (Cl)
University of New Mexico (Ph.D.) (Cl)
University of Rochester (Ph.D.) (Cl)
University of Southern Mississippi (Ph.D.) (Cl)
University of Wisconsin, Milwaukee (Ph.D.) (Cl)
University of Wyoming (Ph.D.) (Cl)
Western Michigan University (Ph.D.) (Cl)
Wright State University (Psy.D.) (Cl)

Family/Family Therapy/Family Systems

Adelphi University (Ph.D.) (Cl)
Antioch University New England (Psy.D.) (Cl)
Arizona State University (Ph.D.) (Cl)
Azusa Pacific University (Psy.D.) (Cl)
Baylor University (Psy.D.) (Cl)
Binghamton University, State University of New York (Ph.D.) (Cl)
Biola University (Ph.D.) (Cl)
Biola University (Psy.D.) (Cl)
Boston University (Ph.D.) (Cl)
Bowling Green State University (Ph.D.) (Cl)
Catholic University of America (Ph.D.) (Cl)
Central Michigan University (Ph.D.) (Cl)
Chestnut Hill College (Psy.D.) (Cl)
Chicago School of Professional Psychology–Chicago Campus (Psy.D.) (Cl)
Colorado State University (Ph.D.) (Co)
DePaul University (Ph.D.) (Cl)
Divine Mercy University (Psy.D.) (Cl)
Drexel University (Ph.D.) (Cl)
Duke University (Ph.D.) (Cl)
Fairleigh Dickinson University (Ph.D.) (Cl)
Florida Institute of Technology (Psy.D.) (Cl)
Fuller Theological Seminary (Ph.D.) (Cl)
Fuller Theological Seminary (Psy.D.) (Cl)
George Washington University (Ph.D.) (Cl)
Georgia State University (Ph.D.) (Cl)
Idaho State University (Ph.D.) (Cl)
Illinois Institute of Technology (Ph.D.) (Cl)
Illinois School of Professional Psychology at Argosy University, Chicago (Psy.D.) (Cl)
Indiana University–Bloomington (Ph.D.) (Cl)
Indiana University of Pennsylvania (Psy.D.) (Cl)
Kent State University (Ph.D.) (Cl)
Long Island University (Ph.D.) (Cl)
Long Island University, C.W. Post Campus (Psy.D.) (Cl)
Loyola University Chicago (Ph.D.) (Cl)
Loyola University Maryland (Psy.D.) (Cl)
Marquette University (Ph.D.) (Cl)
Miami University (OH) (Ph.D.) (Cl)
Michigan State University (Ph.D.) (Cl)
New Mexico State University (Ph.D.) (Co)
Northern Illinois University (Ph.D.) (Cl)
Northwestern University (Ph.D.) (Cl)
Nova Southeastern University (Ph.D.) (Cl)
Nova Southeastern University (Psy.D.) (Cl)
Ohio University (Ph.D.) (Cl)
Oklahoma State University (Ph.D.) (Cl)
Oklahoma State University (Ph.D.) (Co)
Pepperdine University (Psy.D.) (Cl)
Ponce Health Sciences University (Ph.D.) (Cl)
Ponce Health Sciences University (Psy.D.) (Cl)
Purdue University (Ph.D.) (Cl)
Radford University (Psy.D.) (Co)
Roosevelt University (Psy.D.) (Cl)
Sam Houston State University (Ph.D.) (Cl)
San Diego State University–UC San Diego (Ph.D.) (Cl)
Seattle Pacific University (Ph.D.) (Cl)
Spalding University (Psy.D.) (Cl)
Temple University (Ph.D.) (Cl)
Texas A&M University (Ph.D.) (Cl)
The University of Memphis (Ph.D.) (Cl)
The University of Memphis (Ph.D.) (Co)
The University of Montana (Ph.D.) (Cl)
The Wright Institute (Psy.D.) (Cl)
University at Albany (Ph.D.) (Co)
University at Albany (Ph.D.) (Cl)
University of Alabama at Tuscaloosa (Ph.D.) (Cl)
University of Arizona (Ph.D.) (Cl)
University of Arkansas (Ph.D.) (Cl)

University of California, Los Angeles (Ph.D.) (Cl)
University of California, Santa Barbara (Ph.D.) (Cm)
University of Cincinnati (Ph.D.) (Cl)
University of Colorado Boulder (Ph.D.) (Cl)
University of Denver (Psy.D.) (Cl)
University of Florida (Ph.D.) (Co)
University of Georgia (Ph.D.) (Cl)
University of Hartford (Psy.D.) (Cl)
University of Houston (Ph.D.) (Cl)
University of Houston (Ph.D.) (Co)
University of Iowa (Ph.D.) (Cl)
University of La Verne (Psy.D.) (Cl)
University of Maryland, Baltimore County (Ph.D.) (Cl)
University of Massachusetts, Boston (Ph.D.) (Co)
University of Miami (Ph.D.) (Cl)
University of Michigan (Ph.D.) (Cl)
University of Minnesota (Ph.D.) (Cl)
University of Mississippi (Ph.D.) (Cl)
University of Missouri, Columbia (Ph.D.) (Co)
University of Missouri, St. Louis (Ph.D.) (Cl)
University of Nevada Las Vegas (Ph.D.) (Cl)
University of Northern Colorado (Ph.D.) (Co)
University of Oregon (Ph.D.) (Cl)
University of Oregon (Ph.D.) (Co)
University of Pittsburgh (Ph.D.) (Cl)
University of Rhode Island (Ph.D.) (Cl)
University of South Carolina (Ph.D.) (Cl)
University of South Florida (Ph.D.) (Cl)
University of Southern California (Ph.D.) (Cl)
University of Texas Southwestern Medical Center (Ph.D.) (Cl)
University of Toledo (Ph.D.) (Cl)
University of Utah (Ph.D.) (Cl)
University of Vermont (Ph.D.) (Cl)
University of Virginia (Ph.D.) (Cl)
University of Virginia (Ph.D.) (Cm)
University of Washington (Ph.D.) (Cl)
University of Wisconsin, Madison (Ph.D.) (Cl)
University of Wisconsin, Milwaukee (Ph.D.) (Co)
Vanderbilt University (Ph.D.) (Cl)
Virginia Polytechnic Institute and State University (Ph.D.) (Cl)
Widener University (Psy.D.) (Cl)
Wright State University (Psy.D.) (Cl)

Forensic

Alliant International University, Fresno (Ph.D.) (Cl)
Alliant International University, Fresno (Psy.D.) (Cl)
Alliant International University, Los Angeles (Ph.D.) (Cl)
Alliant International University, Los Angeles (Psy.D.) (Cl)
Alliant International University, Sacramento (Psy.D.) (Cl)
Alliant International University, San Diego (Ph.D.) (Cl)
Alliant International University, San Diego (Psy.D.) (Cl)
Alliant International University, San Francisco Bay (Ph.D.) (Cl)
Alliant International University, San Francisco Bay (Psy.D.) (Cl)
American School of Professional Psychology at Argosy University, Washington, DC (Psy.D.) (Cl)
Antioch University New England (Psy.D.) (Cl)
Arizona School of Professional Psychology at Argosy University, Phoenix (Psy.D.) (Cl)
Arizona State University (Ph.D.) (Cl)
Auburn University (Ph.D.) (Cl)
Azusa Pacific University (Psy.D.) (Cl)
Boston College (Ph.D.) (Co)
Brigham Young University (Ph.D.) (Cl)
Chicago School of Professional Psychology–Chicago Campus (Psy.D.) (Cl)
Chicago School of Professional Psychology—Washington, DC Campus (Psy.D.) (Cl)
Drexel University (Ph.D.) (Cl)
Florida Institute of Technology (Psy.D.) (Cl)
Fuller Theological Seminary (Ph.D.) (Cl)
Fuller Theological Seminary (Psy.D.) (Cl)
George Fox University (Psy.D.) (Cl)
George Washington University (Ph.D.) (Cl)
Georgia School of Professional Psychology at Argosy University, Atlanta (Psy.D.) (Cl)
Georgia State University (Ph.D.) (Co)
Howard University (Ph.D.) (Cl)
Howard University (Ph.D.) (Co)
Illinois School of Professional Psychology at Argosy University, Chicago (Psy.D.) (Cl)
Indiana University of Pennsylvania (Psy.D.) (Cl)
Jackson State University (Ph.D.) (Cl)
James Madison University (Psy.D.) (Cm)
John Jay College of Criminal Justice & The Graduate Center, CUNY (Ph.D.) (Cl)
Loma Linda University (Ph.D.) (Cl)
Loma Linda University (Psy.D.) (Cl)
Long Island University (Ph.D.) (Cl)
Marywood University (Psy.D.) (Cl)
Midwestern University–Glendale Campus (Psy.D.) (Cl)
New Mexico State University (Ph.D.) (Co)
Northeastern University (Ph.D.) (Co)
Nova Southeastern University (Ph.D.) (Cl)

Nova Southeastern University (Psy.D.) (Cl)
Pepperdine University (Psy.D.) (Cl)
Regent University (Psy.D.) (Cl)
Rosalind Franklin University of Medicine and Science (Ph.D.) (Cl)
Saint Mary's University of Minnesota (Psy.D.) (Co)
Sam Houston State University (Ph.D.) (Cl)
Suffolk University (Ph.D.) (Cl)
Tennessee State University (Ph.D.) (Co)
Texas A&M University (Ph.D.) (Cl)
The University of Memphis (Ph.D.) (Co)
The Wright Institute (Psy.D.) (Cl)
University of Alabama at Tuscaloosa (Ph.D.) (Cl)
University of Denver (Psy.D.) (Cl)
University of Florida (Ph.D.) (Co)
University of Florida (Ph.D.) (Cl)
University of Hartford (Psy.D.) (Cl)
University of Houston (Ph.D.) (Cl)
University of Houston (Ph.D.) (Co)
University of Illinois at Urbana-Champaign (Ph.D.) (Cl)
University of Kansas (Ph.D.) (Cl)
University of Maine (Ph.D.) (Cl)
University of Maryland, Baltimore County (Ph.D.) (Cl)
University of Minnesota (Ph.D.) (Cl)
University of Missouri, Columbia (Ph.D.) (Cl)
University of Nebraska, Lincoln (Ph.D.) (Cl)
University of New Mexico (Ph.D.) (Cl)
University of Texas Southwestern Medical Center (Ph.D.) (Cl)
University of Virginia (Ph.D.) (Cl)
University of Virginia (Ph.D.) (Cm)
University of Wisconsin, Madison (Ph.D.) (Cl)
Widener University (Psy.D.) (Cl)
Wisconsin School of Professional Psychology (Psy.D.) (Cl)
Wright State University (Psy.D.) (Cl)

Group Therapy

Adelphi University (Ph.D.) (Cl)
Antioch University New England (Psy.D.) (Cl)
Baylor University (Psy.D.) (Cl)
Chatham University (Psy.D.) (Co)
Chicago School of Professional Psychology–Chicago Campus (Psy.D.) (Cl)
DePaul University (Ph.D.) (Cl)
Divine Mercy University (Psy.D.) (Cl)
Fuller Theological Seminary (Ph.D.) (Cl)
Fuller Theological Seminary (Psy.D.) (Cl)
George Washington University (Ph.D.) (Cl)
Georgia School of Professional Psychology at Argosy University, Atlanta (Psy.D.) (Cl)
Georgia State University (Ph.D.) (Cl)
Illinois School of Professional Psychology at Argosy University, Chicago (Psy.D.) (Cl)
Iowa State University (Ph.D.) (Co)
Kent State University (Ph.D.) (Cl)
Long Island University, C.W. Post Campus (Psy.D.) (Cl)
Marquette University (Ph.D.) (Cl)
Marshall University (Psy.D.) (Cl)
Miami University (OH) (Ph.D.) (Cl)
Michigan State University (Ph.D.) (Cl)
Northern Illinois University (Ph.D.) (Cl)
Nova Southeastern University (Ph.D.) (Cl)
Nova Southeastern University (Psy.D.) (Cl)
Oklahoma State University (Ph.D.) (Cl)
Pepperdine University (Psy.D.) (Cl)
Regent University (Psy.D.) (Cl)
Rutgers-The State University of New Jersey (Psy.D.) (Cl)
Spalding University (Psy.D.) (Cl)
The Wright Institute (Psy.D.) (Cl)
University of Denver (Ph.D.) (Co)
University of Denver (Psy.D.) (Cl)
University of Illinois at Urbana-Champaign (Ph.D.) (Cl)
University of Kentucky (Ph.D.) (Cl)
University of Louisville (Ph.D.) (Co)
University of Maryland-College Park (Ph.D.) (Co)
University of Miami (Ph.D.) (Cl)
University of North Carolina, Greensboro (Ph.D.) (Cl)
University of Northern Colorado (Ph.D.) (Co)
University of Pittsburgh (Ph.D.) (Cl)
University of Rochester (Ph.D.) (Cl)
University of Southern California (Ph.D.) (Cl)
Wright State University (Psy.D.) (Cl)
Yale University (Ph.D.) (Cl)

Health Psychology/Behavioral Medicine/Stress

Arizona State University (Ph.D.) (Cl)
Azusa Pacific University (Psy.D.) (Cl)
Baylor University (Psy.D.) (Cl)
Binghamton University, State University of New York (Ph.D.) (Cl)
Boston University (Ph.D.) (Cl)
Bowling Green State University (Ph.D.) (Cl)
Brigham Young University (Ph.D.) (Cl)
Case Western Reserve University (Ph.D.) (Cl)

Chicago School of Professional Psychology–Chicago Campus (Psy.D.) (Cl)
Drexel University (Ph.D.) (Cl)
Duke University (Ph.D.) (Cl)
Eastern Michigan University (Ph.D.) (Cl)
Fairleigh Dickinson University (Ph.D.) (Cl)
Florida Institute of Technology (Psy.D.) (Cl)
Florida School of Professional Psychology at Argosy University (Psy.D.) (Cl)
Florida State University (Ph.D.) (Cl)
George Fox University (Psy.D.) (Cl)
George Washington University (Ph.D.) (Cl)
Georgia State University (Ph.D.) (Cl)
Georgia State University (Ph.D.) (Co)
Harvard University (Ph.D.) (Cl)
Illinois Institute of Technology (Ph.D.) (Cl)
Illinois School of Professional Psychology at Argosy University, Chicago (Psy.D.) (Cl)
Indiana State University (Psy.D.) (Cl)
Indiana University–Bloomington (Ph.D.) (Cl)
Indiana University of Pennsylvania (Psy.D.) (Cl)
Jackson State University (Ph.D.) (Cl)
La Salle University (Psy.D.) (Cl)
Loma Linda University (Ph.D.) (Cl)
Loma Linda University (Psy.D.) (Cl)
Loyola University Chicago (Ph.D.) (Cl)
Loyola University Maryland (Psy.D.) (Cl)
Marquette University (Ph.D.) (Co)
Marquette University (Ph.D.) (Cl)
Marshall University (Psy.D.) (Cl)
Nova Southeastern University (Ph.D.) (Cl)
Nova Southeastern University (Psy.D.) (Cl)
Oklahoma State University (Ph.D.) (Cl)
Our Lady of the Lake University (Psy.D.) (Co)
Palo Alto University (Psy.D.) (Cl)
Pepperdine University (Psy.D.) (Cl)
Roosevelt University (Psy.D.) (Cl)
Rosalind Franklin University of Medicine and Science (Ph.D.) (Cl)
Rutgers-The State University of New Jersey (Ph.D.) (Cl)
Saint Louis University (Ph.D.) (Cl)
San Diego State University–UC San Diego (Ph.D.) (Cl)
Seattle Pacific University (Ph.D.) (Cl)
St. John's University (Ph.D.) (Cl)
Syracuse University (Ph.D.) (Cl)
Tennessee State University (Ph.D.) (Co)
Texas Tech University (Ph.D.) (Cl)
The Ohio State University (Ph.D.) (Cl)
The University of Memphis (Ph.D.) (Cl)
The University of Montana (Ph.D.) (Cl)
University at Albany (Ph.D.) (Cl)
University of Alabama at Birmingham (Ph.D.) (Cl)
University of Alabama at Tuscaloosa (Ph.D.) (Cl)
University of Arizona (Ph.D.) (Cl)
University of Central Florida (Ph.D.) (Cl)
University of Cincinnati (Ph.D.) (Cl)
University of Colorado at Colorado Springs (Ph.D.) (Cl)
University of Colorado Denver (Ph.D.) (Cl)
University of Connecticut (Ph.D.) (Cl)
University of Delaware (Ph.D.) (Cl)
University of Denver (Psy.D.) (Cl)
University of Florida (Ph.D.) (Cl)
University of Georgia (Ph.D.) (Cl)
University of Hartford (Psy.D.) (Cl)
University of Hawaii at Manoa (Ph.D.) (Cl)
University of Houston (Ph.D.) (Co)
University of Illinois at Chicago (Ph.D.) (Cl)
University of Iowa (Ph.D.) (Cl)
University of Kansas (Ph.D.) (Cl)
University of Kentucky (Ph.D.) (Cl)
University of Louisville (Ph.D.) (Cl)
University of Louisville (Ph.D.) (Co)
University of Maine (Ph.D.) (Cl)
University of Miami (Ph.D.) (Cl)
University of Mississippi (Ph.D.) (Cl)
University of Missouri, Columbia (Ph.D.) (Cl)
University of Missouri, St. Louis (Ph.D.) (Cl)
University of Nebraska, Lincoln (Ph.D.) (Cl)
University of North Carolina at Charlotte (Ph.D.) (Cl)
University of North Carolina, Chapel Hill (Ph.D.) (Cl)
University of North Dakota (Ph.D.) (Cl)
University of North Dakota (Ph.D.) (Co)
University of Notre Dame (Ph.D.) P(Cl)
University of Pittsburgh (Ph.D.) (Cl)
University of Rhode Island (Ph.D.) (Cl)
University of South Carolina (Ph.D.) (Cl)
University of South Florida (Ph.D.) (Cl)
University of Texas at Austin (Ph.D.) (Cl)
University of Texas at Austin (Ph.D.) (Co)
University of Texas Southwestern Medical Center (Ph.D.) (Cl)
University of Toledo (Ph.D.) (Cl)
University of Utah (Ph.D.) (Cl)
University of Vermont (Ph.D.) (Cl)
University of Virginia (Ph.D.) (Cl)
Utah State University (Ph.D.) (Cm)
Vanderbilt University (Ph.D.) (Cl)
Virginia Commonwealth University (Ph.D.) (Cl)
Washington State University (Ph.D.) (Cl)
Wayne State University (Ph.D.) (Cl)

West Virginia University (Ph.D.) (Cl)
Widener University (Psy.D.) (Cl)
Wisconsin School of Professional Psychology (Psy.D.) (Cl)
Yeshiva University (Ph.D.) (Cl)

Homelessness

Long Island University (Ph.D.) (Cl)
Marquette University (Ph.D.) (Co)
Marshall University (Psy.D.) (Cl)
Palo Alto University (Psy.D.) (Cl)
Pepperdine University (Psy.D.) (Cl)
University of Georgia (Ph.D.) (Co)
University of Iowa (Ph.D.) (Co)
University of Utah (Ph.D.) (Cl)

Hospice

University of Alabama at Tuscaloosa (Ph.D.) (Cl)
University of Florida (Ph.D.) (Co)

Immigrant/Refugee Populations

Illinois School of Professional Psychology at Argosy University, Chicago (Psy.D.) (Cl)
Saint Mary's University of Minnesota (Psy.D.) (Co)
University of North Carolina, Greensboro (Ph.D.) (Cl)
University of Vermont (Ph.D.) (Cl)

Interpersonal Therapy

Emory University (Ph.D.) (Cl)
Fuller Theological Seminary (Ph.D.) (Cl)
Fuller Theological Seminary (Psy.D.) (Cl)
Teachers College, Columbia University (Ph.D.) (Cl)
University of Houston (Ph.D.) (Cl)
University of Kentucky (Ph.D.) (Cl)
University of Louisville (Ph.D.) (Cl)
University of North Dakota (Ph.D.) (Cl)
University of Pittsburgh (Ph.D.) (Cl)
University of Rochester (Ph.D.) (Cl)
University of Utah (Ph.D.) (Cl)
Yeshiva University (Psy.D.) (Cl)

Interprofessional/Interdisciplinary

Florida State University (Ph.D.) (Cm)
Rosalind Franklin University of Medicine and Science (Ph.D.) (Cl)
The University of Montana (Ph.D.) (Cl)

Learning Disabilities

Binghamton University, State University of New York (Ph.D.) (Cl)
Fairleigh Dickinson University (Ph.D.) (Cl)
James Madison University (Psy.D.) (Cm)
Philadelphia College of Osteopathic Medicine (Psy.D.) (Cl)
Saint Louis University (Ph.D.) (Cl)
University of Denver (Ph.D.) (Cl)
University of Florida (Ph.D.) (Cl)
University of Georgia (Ph.D.) (Cl)
University of Georgia (Ph.D.) (Co)
University of Houston (Ph.D.) (Cl)
University of Iowa (Ph.D.) (Cl)
University of Missouri, Columbia (Ph.D.) (Co)
University of North Carolina at Charlotte (Ph.D.) (Cl)
University of South Florida (Ph.D.) (Cl)
University of Virginia (Ph.D.) (Cm)
University of Wisconsin, Milwaukee (Ph.D.) (Cl)
Vanderbilt University (Ph.D.) (Cl)

Lesbian/Gay/Bisexual/Transgender

Antioch University New England (Psy.D.) (Cl)
Chicago School of Professional Psychology–Chicago Campus (Psy.D.) (Cl)
Illinois School of Professional Psychology at Argosy University, Chicago (Psy.D.) (Cl)
Miami University (OH) (Ph.D.) (Cl)
Palo Alto University (Psy.D.) (Cl)
Saint Louis University (Ph.D.) (Cl)
Saint Mary's University of Minnesota (Psy.D.) (Co)
The University of Montana (Ph.D.) (Cl)
The Wright Institute (Psy.D.) (Cl)
University of California, Santa Barbara (Ph.D.) (Cm)
University of Houston (Ph.D.) (Co)
University of Nebraska, Lincoln (Ph.D.) (Cl)
University of Pittsburgh (Ph.D.) (Cl)
University of Utah (Ph.D.) (Cl)
Wright State University (Psy.D.) (Cl)

Marriage/Couples/Intimate Partner Violence

Adelphi University (Ph.D.) (Cl)
Arizona State University (Ph.D.) (Cl)
Binghamton University, State University of New York (Ph.D.) (Cl)
Catholic University of America (Ph.D.) (Cl)
Chicago School of Professional Psychology–Chicago Campus (Psy.D.) (Cl)
Clark University (Ph.D.) (Cl)
Divine Mercy University (Psy.D.) (Cl)

Fairleigh Dickinson University (Ph.D.) (Cl)
Florida Institute of Technology (Psy.D.) (Cl)
Fuller Theological Seminary (Ph.D.) (Cl)
Fuller Theological Seminary (Psy.D.) (Cl)
George Washington University (Ph.D.) (Cl)
Georgia State University (Ph.D.) (Cl)
Idaho State University (Ph.D.) (Cl)
Illinois Institute of Technology (Ph.D.) (Cl)
Illinois School of Professional Psychology at Argosy University, Chicago (Psy.D.) (Cl)
Long Island University, C.W. Post Campus (Psy.D.) (Cl)
Marquette University (Ph.D.) (Cl)
Michigan State University (Ph.D.) (Cl)
Northwestern University (Ph.D.) (Cl)
Nova Southeastern University (Ph.D.) (Cl)
Nova Southeastern University (Psy.D.) (Cl)
Oklahoma State University (Ph.D.) (Cl)
Oklahoma State University (Ph.D.) (Co)
Ponce Health Sciences University (Ph.D.) (Cl)
Ponce Health Sciences University (Psy.D.) (Cl)
Rutgers-The State University of New Jersey (Psy.D.) (Cl)
Saint Louis University (Ph.D.) (Cl)
Sam Houston State University (Ph.D.) (Cl)
Southern Methodist University (Ph.D.) (Cl)
Spalding University (Psy.D.) (Cl)
Stony Brook University, State University of New York (Ph.D.) (Cl)
Temple University (Ph.D.) (Cl)
Texas Woman's University (Ph.D.) (Co)
The University of Memphis (Ph.D.) (Co)
The University of Montana (Ph.D.) (Cl)
The Wright Institute (Psy.D.) (Cl)
University of Arizona (Ph.D.) (Cl)
University of California, Los Angeles (Ph.D.) (Cl)
University of Colorado Boulder (Ph.D.) (Cl)
University of Denver (Ph.D.) (Cl)
University of Denver (Psy.D.) (Cl)
University of Florida (Ph.D.) (Co)
University of Georgia (Ph.D.) (Cl)
University of Houston (Ph.D.) (Cl)
University of Illinois at Urbana-Champaign (Ph.D.) (Co)
University of Indianapolis (Psy.D.) (Cl)
University of Iowa (Ph.D.) (Cl)
University of Louisville (Ph.D.) (Co)
University of Maryland, Baltimore County (Ph.D.) (Cl)
University of Miami (Ph.D.) (Cl)
University of Missouri, St. Louis (Ph.D.) (Cl)
University of Nebraska, Lincoln (Ph.D.) (Co)
University of New Mexico (Ph.D.) (Cl)
University of North Carolina, Chapel Hill (Ph.D.) (Cl)
University of North Dakota (Ph.D.) (Cl)
University of North Texas (Ph.D.) (Co)
University of Northern Colorado (Ph.D.) (Co)
University of Notre Dame (Ph.D.) P(Cl)
University of Oregon (Ph.D.) (Cl)
University of Oregon (Ph.D.) (Co)
University of Pennsylvania (Ph.D.) (Cl)
University of Southern California (Ph.D.) (Cl)
University of Tennessee–Knoxville (Ph.D.) (Cl)
University of Tennessee–Knoxville (Ph.D.) (Co)
University of Texas at Austin (Ph.D.) (Cl)
University of Virginia (Ph.D.) (Cl)
University of Washington (Ph.D.) (Cl)
Virginia Polytechnic Institute and State University (Ph.D.) (Cl)
Wright State University (Psy.D.) (Cl)
Yeshiva University (Psy.D.) (Cl)

Medical/Inpatient/Hospital Services

Adler University–Chicago (Psy.D.) (Cl)
Alliant International University, Fresno (Ph.D.) (Cl)
Alliant International University, Fresno (Psy.D.) (Cl)
Alliant International University, Los Angeles (Ph.D.) (Cl)
Alliant International University, Los Angeles (Psy.D.) (Cl)
Alliant International University, Sacramento (Psy.D.) (Cl)
Alliant International University, San Diego (Ph.D.) (Cl)
Alliant International University, San Diego (Psy.D.) (Cl)
Alliant International University, San Francisco Bay (Ph.D.) (Cl)
Alliant International University, San Francisco Bay (Psy.D.) (Cl)
American School of Professional Psychology at Argosy University, San Francisco Bay Area (Psy.D.) (Cl)
American School of Professional Psychology at Argosy University, Washington, DC (Psy.D.) (Cl)
American University (Ph.D.) (Cl)
Arizona School of Professional Psychology at Argosy University, Phoenix (Psy.D.) (Cl)
Auburn University (Ph.D.) (Co)
Auburn University (Ph.D.) (Cl)
Azusa Pacific University (Psy.D.) (Cl)
Ball State University (Ph.D.) (Co)
Biola University (Ph.D.) (Cl)
Biola University (Psy.D.) (Cl)

Boston College (Ph.D.) (Co)
Brigham Young University (Ph.D.) (Cl)
California Lutheran University (Psy.D.) (Cl)
Carlos Albizu University, Miami Campus (Psy.D.) (Cl)
Carlos Albizu University, San Juan Campus (Psy.D.) (Cl)
Carlow University (Psy.D.) (Co)
Chatham University (Psy.D.) (Co)
Chicago School of Professional Psychology–Chicago Campus (Psy.D.) (Cl)
Chicago School of Professional Psychology—Washington, DC Campus (Psy.D.) (Cl)
Cleveland State University (Ph.D.) (Co)
Duquesne University (Ph.D.) (Cl)
Eastern Michigan University (Ph.D.) (Cl)
Georgia School of Professional Psychology at Argosy University, Atlanta (Psy.D.) (Cl)
Georgia Southern University (Psy.D.) (Cl)
Georgia State University (Ph.D.) (Cl)
Hawaii School of Professional Psychology at Argosy University, Hawaii (Psy.D.) (Cl)
Howard University (Ph.D.) (Cl)
Iowa State University (Ph.D.) (Co)
Jackson State University (Ph.D.) (Cl)
James Madison University (Psy.D.) (Cm)
La Salle University (Psy.D.) (Cl)
Lehigh University (Ph.D.) (Co)
Loma Linda University (Ph.D.) (Cl)
Loma Linda University (Psy.D.) (Cl)
Long Island University (Ph.D.) (Cl)
Louisiana Tech University (Ph.D.) (Co)
Loyola University Chicago (Ph.D.) (Co)
Loyola University Maryland (Psy.D.) (Cl)
Marquette University (Ph.D.) (Co)
Marshall University (Psy.D.) (Cl)
Marywood University (Psy.D.) (Cl)
Miami University (OH) (Ph.D.) (Cl)
Midwestern University–Glendale Campus (Psy.D.) (Cl)
Northeastern University (Ph.D.) (Co)
Northwestern University Feinberg School of Medicine (Ph.D.) (Cl)
Oklahoma State University (Ph.D.) (Co)
Palo Alto University (Psy.D.) (Cl)
Pepperdine University (Psy.D.) (Cl)
Philadelphia College of Osteopathic Medicine (Psy.D.) (Cl)
Ponce Health Sciences University (Ph.D.) (Cl)
Ponce Health Sciences University (Psy.D.) (Cl)
Purdue University (Ph.D.) (Co)
Queens College and The Graduate Center, City University of New York (Ph.D.) (Cl)
Radford University (Psy.D.) (Co)
Roosevelt University (Psy.D.) (Cl)
Southern Methodist University (Ph.D.) (Cl)
Spalding University (Psy.D.) (Cl)
Springfield College (Psy.D.) (Co)
Stony Brook University, State University of New York (Ph.D.) (Cl)
Suffolk University (Ph.D.) (Cl)
Syracuse University (Ph.D.) (Cl)
Texas Tech University (Ph.D.) (Cl)
Texas Woman's University (Ph.D.) (Co)
The University of Akron (Ph.D.) (Co)
The University of Memphis (Ph.D.) (Co)
The University of Montana (Ph.D.) (Cl)
Uniformed Services University of the Health Sciences (Ph.D.) (Cl)
University at Albany (Ph.D.) (Co)
University at Buffalo, State University of New York (Ph.D.) (Cm)
University of Alabama at Tuscaloosa (Ph.D.) (Cl)
University of Alaska Fairbanks-Anchorage (Ph.D.) (Cl)
University of Denver (Ph.D.) (Co)
University of Denver (Psy.D.) (Cl)
University of Florida (Ph.D.) (Co)
University of Florida (Ph.D.) (Cl)
University of Georgia (Ph.D.) (Cl)
University of Hartford (Psy.D.) (Cl)
University of Houston (Ph.D.) (Co)
University of Illinois at Urbana-Champaign (Ph.D.) (Cl)
University of Indianapolis (Psy.D.) (Cl)
University of Iowa (Ph.D.) (Cl)
University of Iowa (Ph.D.) (Co)
University of Kansas–Child (Ph.D.) (Cl)
University of La Verne (Psy.D.) (Cl)
University of Louisville (Ph.D.) (Co)
University of Massachusetts Amherst (Ph.D.) (Cl)
University of Massachusetts, Boston (Ph.D.) (Co)
University of Missouri, Columbia (Ph.D.) (Cl)
University of Missouri, Columbia (Ph.D.) (Co)
University of North Carolina at Charlotte (Ph.D.) (Cl)
University of North Dakota (Ph.D.) (Co)
University of North Texas (Ph.D.) (Cl)
University of Oregon (Ph.D.) (Co)
University of Pittsburgh (Ph.D.) (Cl)
University of South Alabama (Ph.D.) (Cm)
University of Southern California (Ph.D.) (Cl)
University of Southern Mississippi (Ph.D.) (Cl)
University of Southern Mississippi (Ph.D.) (Co)
University of Texas at Austin (Ph.D.) (Co)
University of Texas Southwestern Medical Center (Ph.D.) (Cl)
University of Utah (Ph.D.) (Cl)

University of Utah (Ph.D.) (Co)
University of Virginia (Ph.D.) (Cm)
University of Wisconsin, Milwaukee (Ph.D.) (Co)
University of Wyoming (Ph.D.) (Cl)
Virginia Commonwealth University (Ph.D.) (Cl)
Virginia Commonwealth University (Ph.D.) (Co)
Washington State University (Ph.D.) (Cl)
West Virginia University (Ph.D.) (Co)
Western Michigan University (Ph.D.) (Co)
Western Michigan University (Ph.D.) (Cl)
Wheaton College (Psy.D.) (Cl)
Wisconsin School of Professional Psychology (Psy.D.) (Cl)
Xavier University (Psy.D.) (Cl)
Yeshiva University (Ph.D.) (Cl)

Men's Issues

The Wright Institute (Psy.D.) (Cl)
Wright State University (Psy.D.) (Cl)

Military/Armed Forces

Carlos Albizu University, San Juan Campus (Psy.D.) (Cl)
Florida Institute of Technology (Psy.D.) (Cl)
Georgia Southern University (Psy.D.) (Cl)
Hawaii School of Professional Psychology at Argosy University, Hawaii (Psy.D.) (Cl)
Regent University (Psy.D.) (Cl)
Seattle Pacific University (Ph.D.) (Cl)
Springfield College (Psy.D.) (Co)
Teachers College, Columbia University (Ph.D.) (Cl)
Uniformed Services University of the Health Sciences (Ph.D.) (Cl)
University of Denver (Psy.D.) (Cl)
University of Illinois at Urbana-Champaign (Ph.D.) (Co)
University of Louisville (Ph.D.) (Cl)
University of Southern California (Ph.D.) (Cl)
University of Texas at Austin (Ph.D.) (Cl)
University of Utah (Ph.D.) (Cl)
Widener University (Psy.D.) (Cl)
Wisconsin School of Professional Psychology (Psy.D.) (Cl)
Yeshiva University (Ph.D.) (Cl)

Mindfulness

La Salle University (Psy.D.) (Cl)
Miami University (OH) (Ph.D.) (Cl)
Pepperdine University (Psy.D.) (Cl)
The University of Montana (Ph.D.) (Cl)
University of Colorado Boulder (Ph.D.) (Cl)
University of Illinois at Urbana-Champaign (Ph.D.) (Cl)
University of New Mexico (Ph.D.) (Cl)
University of Tennessee–Knoxville (Ph.D.) (Cl)
University of Toledo (Ph.D.) (Cl)

Minority/Cross-Cultural/Multicultural

Arizona School of Professional Psychology at Argosy University, Phoenix (Psy.D.) (Cl)
Biola University (Ph.D.) (Cl)
Biola University (Psy.D.) (Cl)
Catholic University of America (Ph.D.) (Cl)
Chicago School of Professional Psychology–Chicago Campus (Psy.D.) (Cl)
Chicago School of Professional Psychology—Washington, DC Campus (Psy.D.) (Cl)
DePaul University (Ph.D.) (Cl)
Fairleigh Dickinson University (Ph.D.) (Cl)
George Fox University (Psy.D.) (Cl)
George Washington University (Ph.D.) (Cl)
Georgia State University (Ph.D.) (Co)
Howard University (Ph.D.) (Co)
Illinois Institute of Technology (Ph.D.) (Cl)
Illinois School of Professional Psychology at Argosy University, Chicago (Psy.D.) (Cl)
John F. Kennedy University (Psy.D.) (Cl)
Marquette University (Ph.D.) (Co)
Marshall University (Psy.D.) (Cl)
Miami University (OH) (Ph.D.) (Cl)
Michigan State University (Ph.D.) (Cl)
New Mexico State University (Ph.D.) (Co)
Nova Southeastern University (Ph.D.) (Cl)
Nova Southeastern University (Psy.D.) (Cl)
Palo Alto University (Psy.D.) (Cl)
Pepperdine University (Psy.D.) (Cl)
Philadelphia College of Osteopathic Medicine (Psy.D.) (Cl)
Saint Louis University (Ph.D.) (Cl)
Saint Mary's University of Minnesota (Psy.D.) (Co)
Teachers College, Columbia University (Ph.D.) (Cl)
The University of Memphis (Ph.D.) (Cl)
The University of South Dakota (Ph.D.) (Cl)
The Wright Institute (Psy.D.) (Cl)
University at Albany (Ph.D.) (Cl)
University of Arkansas (Ph.D.) (Cl)
University of California, Los Angeles (Ph.D.) (Cl)
University of Connecticut (Ph.D.) (Cl)
University of Denver (Ph.D.) (Co)
University of Denver (Ph.D.) (Cl)
University of Denver (Psy.D.) (Cl)
University of Georgia (Ph.D.) (Cl)

University of Hawaii at Manoa (Ph.D.) (Cl)
University of Houston (Ph.D.) (Cl)
University of Illinois at Urbana-Champaign (Ph.D.) (Cl)
University of Louisville (Ph.D.) (Cl)
University of Maryland-College Park (Ph.D.) (Co)
University of Massachusetts Amherst (Ph.D.) (Cl)
University of Massachusetts, Boston (Ph.D.) (Co)
University of Miami (Ph.D.) (Cl)
University of Nebraska, Lincoln (Ph.D.) (Cl)
University of Nebraska, Lincoln (Ph.D.) (Co)
University of Nevada, Reno (Ph.D.) (Cl)
University of New Mexico (Ph.D.) (Cl)
University of North Carolina, Greensboro (Ph.D.) (Cl)
University of North Dakota (Ph.D.) (Cl)
University of Pittsburgh (Ph.D.) (Cl)
University of Rhode Island (Ph.D.) (Cl)
University of South Carolina (Ph.D.) (Cl)
University of Southern California (Ph.D.) (Cl)
University of Texas at Austin (Ph.D.) (Cl)
University of Utah (Ph.D.) (Cl)
University of Utah (Ph.D.) (Co)
University of Washington (Ph.D.) (Cl)
Utah State University (Ph.D.) (Cm)
Wayne State University (Ph.D.) (Cl)
Wisconsin School of Professional Psychology (Psy.D.) (Cl)
Wright State University (Psy.D.) (Cl)
Yeshiva University (Psy.D.) (Cm)

Motivational Interviewing

Boston University (Ph.D.) (Cl)
Florida International University (Ph.D.) (Cl)
The University of Montana (Ph.D.) (Cl)
University of Georgia (Ph.D.) (Cl)
University of New Mexico (Ph.D.) (Cl)

Native American Health Services

The University of Montana (Ph.D.) (Cl)
The University of South Dakota (Ph.D.) (Cl)

Neuroimaging

University of Connecticut (Ph.D.) (Cl)
University of New Mexico (Ph.D.) (Cl)

Neuropsychology

Adelphi University (Ph.D.) (Cl)
Alliant International University, San Francisco Bay (Psy.D.) (Cl)
American School of Professional Psychology at Argosy University, Washington, DC (Psy.D.) (Cl)
American University (Ph.D.) (Cl)
Antioch University New England (Psy.D.) (Cl)
Arizona School of Professional Psychology at Argosy University, Phoenix (Psy.D.) (Cl)
Arizona State University (Ph.D.) (Cl)
Baylor University (Psy.D.) (Cl)
Binghamton University, State University of New York (Ph.D.) (Cl)
Biola University (Ph.D.) (Cl)
Biola University (Psy.D.) (Cl)
Boston College (Ph.D.) (Co)
Boston University (Ph.D.) (Cl)
Brigham Young University (Ph.D.) (Cl)
Carlow University (Psy.D.) (Co)
Catholic University of America (Ph.D.) (Cl)
Chatham University (Psy.D.) (Co)
Chicago School of Professional Psychology–Chicago Campus (Psy.D.) (Cl)
Colorado State University (Ph.D.) (Co)
Drexel University (Ph.D.) (Cl)
Duke University (Ph.D.) (Cl)
East Carolina University (Ph.D.) (Cl)
Eastern Michigan University (Ph.D.) (Cl)
Emory University (Ph.D.) (Cl)
Fairleigh Dickinson University (Ph.D.) (Cl)
Florida Institute of Technology (Psy.D.) (Cl)
Florida International University (Ph.D.) (Cl)
Florida State University (Ph.D.) (Cl)
Fuller Theological Seminary (Ph.D.) (Cl)
Fuller Theological Seminary (Psy.D.) (Cl)
George Fox University (Psy.D.) (Cl)
George Washington University (Ph.D.) (Cl)
Georgia School of Professional Psychology at Argosy University, Atlanta (Psy.D.) (Cl)
Georgia State University (Ph.D.) (Cl)
Georgia State University (Ph.D.) (Co)
Illinois Institute of Technology (Ph.D.) (Cl)
Illinois School of Professional Psychology at Argosy University, Chicago (Psy.D.) (Cl)
Indiana University–Bloomington (Ph.D.) (Cl)
Indiana University–Purdue University Indianapolis (Ph.D.) (Cl)
Indiana University of Pennsylvania (Psy.D.) (Cl)
Jackson State University (Ph.D.) (Cl)
James Madison University (Psy.D.) (Cm)
John Jay College of Criminal Justice & The Graduate Center, CUNY (Ph.D.) (Cl)
Kent State University (Ph.D.) (Cl)
Loma Linda University (Ph.D.) (Cl)
Loma Linda University (Psy.D.) (Cl)
Long Island University (Ph.D.) (Cl)

Long Island University, C.W. Post Campus (Psy.D.) (Cl)
Loyola University Chicago (Ph.D.) (Cl)
Marquette University (Ph.D.) (Co)
Marshall University (Psy.D.) (Cl)
Michigan State University (Ph.D.) (Cl)
Midwestern University–Glendale Campus (Psy.D.) (Cl)
Northwestern University Feinberg School of Medicine (Ph.D.) (Cl)
Nova Southeastern University (Ph.D.) (Cl)
Nova Southeastern University (Psy.D.) (Cl)
Ohio University (Ph.D.) (Cl)
Oklahoma State University (Ph.D.) (Cl)
Pace University (Psy.D.) (Cm)
Palo Alto University (Psy.D.) (Cl)
Pennsylvania State University (Ph.D.) (Cl)
Pepperdine University (Psy.D.) (Cl)
Philadelphia College of Osteopathic Medicine (Psy.D.) (Cl)
Ponce Health Sciences University (Ph.D.) (Cl)
Ponce Health Sciences University (Psy.D.) (Cl)
Purdue University (Ph.D.) (Cl)
Regent University (Psy.D.) (Cl)
Roosevelt University (Psy.D.) (Cl)
Rosalind Franklin University of Medicine and Science (Ph.D.) (Cl)
Saint Louis University (Ph.D.) (Cl)
Sam Houston State University (Ph.D.) (Cl)
San Diego State University–UC San Diego (Ph.D.) (Cl)
Seattle Pacific University (Ph.D.) (Cl)
Southern Illinois University Carbondale (Ph.D.) (Cl)
Southern Illinois University Carbondale (Ph.D.) (Co)
Southern Methodist University (Ph.D.) (Cl)
Suffolk University (Ph.D.) (Cl)
Temple University (Ph.D.) (Cl)
Texas A&M University (Ph.D.) (Cl)
Texas Tech University (Ph.D.) (Co)
The Ohio State University (Ph.D.) (Cl)
The University of Akron (Ph.D.) (Co)
The University of Memphis (Ph.D.) (Cl)
The University of Memphis (Ph.D.) (Co)
The University of Montana (Ph.D.) (Cl)
The Wright Institute (Psy.D.) (Cl)
University at Albany (Ph.D.) (Co)
University of Alabama at Birmingham (Ph.D.) (Cl)
University of Alabama at Tuscaloosa (Ph.D.) (Cl)
University of Arizona (Ph.D.) (Cl)
University of Arkansas (Ph.D.) (Cl)
University of California, Santa Barbara (Ph.D.) (Cm)
University of Cincinnati (Ph.D.) (Cl)
University of Colorado at Colorado Springs (Ph.D.) (Cl)
University of Colorado Denver (Ph.D.) (Cl)
University of Connecticut (Ph.D.) (Cl)
University of Denver (Ph.D.) (Co)
University of Denver (Ph.D.) (Cl)
University of Denver (Psy.D.) (Cl)
University of Florida (Ph.D.) (Cl)
University of Georgia (Ph.D.) (Cl)
University of Hawaii at Manoa (Ph.D.) (Cl)
University of Houston (Ph.D.) (Cl)
University of Houston (Ph.D.) (Co)
University of Illinois at Chicago (Ph.D.) (Cl)
University of Illinois at Urbana-Champaign (Ph.D.) (Cl)
University of Iowa (Ph.D.) (Cl)
University of Kansas–Child (Ph.D.) (Cl)
University of Kansas (Ph.D.) (Cl)
University of Kentucky (Ph.D.) (Cl)
University of Louisville (Ph.D.) (Co)
University of Maine (Ph.D.) (Cl)
University of Maryland, Baltimore County (Ph.D.) (Cl)
University of Massachusetts, Boston (Ph.D.) (Co)
University of Miami (Ph.D.) (Cl)
University of Michigan (Ph.D.) (Cl)
University of Minnesota (Ph.D.) (Cl)
University of Missouri Kansas City (Ph.D.) (Cl)
University of New Mexico (Ph.D.) (Cl)
University of North Carolina at Charlotte (Ph.D.) (Cl)
University of Notre Dame (Ph.D.) P(Cl)
University of Oregon (Ph.D.) (Cl)
University of Pittsburgh (Ph.D.) (Cl)
University of Southern California (Ph.D.) (Cl)
University of Southern Mississippi (Ph.D.) (Cl)
University of Texas at Austin (Ph.D.) (Cl)
University of Texas Southwestern Medical Center (Ph.D.) (Cl)
University of Utah (Ph.D.) (Cl)
University of Virginia (Ph.D.) (Cl)
University of Virginia (Ph.D.) (Cm)
University of Washington (Ph.D.) (Cl)
University of Wisconsin, Madison (Ph.D.) (Cl)
University of Wisconsin, Milwaukee (Ph.D.) (Cl)
Utah State University (Ph.D.) (Cm)
Vanderbilt University (Ph.D.) (Cl)
Virginia Commonwealth University (Ph.D.) (Cl)
Virginia Polytechnic Institute and State University (Ph.D.) (Cl)
Washington State University (Ph.D.) (Cl)
Wayne State University (Ph.D.) (Cl)
Widener University (Psy.D.) (Cl)

Wisconsin School of Professional Psychology (Psy.D.) (Cl)
Wright State University (Psy.D.) (Cl)
Yale University (Ph.D.) (Cl)
Yeshiva University (Ph.D.) (Cl)
Yeshiva University (Psy.D.) (Cl)

Obsessive Compulsive Disorder

George Washington University (Ph.D.) (Cl)
Harvard University (Ph.D.) (Cl)
Palo Alto University (Psy.D.) (Cl)
University of Minnesota (Ph.D.) (Cl)
University of North Dakota (Ph.D.) (Cl)
University of Texas at Austin (Ph.D.) (Cl)
University of Virginia (Ph.D.) (Cl)
University of Wisconsin, Milwaukee (Ph.D.) (Cl)
Yeshiva University (Psy.D.) (Cl)

Oncology/Cancer Care

Ball State University (Ph.D.) (Co)
Chatham University (Psy.D.) (Co)
Chicago School of Professional Psychology–Chicago Campus (Psy.D.) (Cl)
Kean University (Psy.D.) (Cm)
Marshall University (Psy.D.) (Cl)
Ponce Health Sciences University (Ph.D.) (Cl)
Ponce Health Sciences University (Psy.D.) (Cl)
Saint Louis University (Ph.D.) (Cl)
Texas Tech University (Ph.D.) (Co)
The Ohio State University (Ph.D.) (Cl)
The University of Memphis (Ph.D.) (Cl)
University of Alabama at Tuscaloosa (Ph.D.) (Cl)
University of Colorado Denver (Ph.D.) (Cl)
University of Denver (Psy.D.) (Cl)
University of Kansas (Ph.D.) (Cl)
University of North Carolina at Charlotte (Ph.D.) (Cl)
University of Pittsburgh (Ph.D.) (Cl)
University of South Alabama (Ph.D.) (Cm)
University of South Florida (Ph.D.) (Cl)
University of Southern California (Ph.D.) (Cl)

Organizational

Chicago School of Professional Psychology–Chicago Campus (Psy.D.) (Cl)
University of Illinois at Urbana-Champaign (Ph.D.) (Cl)
Widener University (Psy.D.) (Cl)

Pain Management

Arizona School of Professional Psychology at Argosy University, Phoenix (Psy.D.) (Cl)
Ball State University (Ph.D.) (Co)
Binghamton University, State University of New York (Ph.D.) (Cl)
Chicago School of Professional Psychology–Chicago Campus (Psy.D.) (Cl)
Duke University (Ph.D.) (Cl)
Eastern Michigan University (Ph.D.) (Cl)
George Fox University (Psy.D.) (Cl)
Illinois Institute of Technology (Ph.D.) (Cl)
Indiana University–Bloomington (Ph.D.) (Cl)
Indiana University–Purdue University Indianapolis (Ph.D.) (Cl)
Marquette University (Ph.D.) (Cl)
Marshall University (Psy.D.) (Cl)
Nova Southeastern University (Ph.D.) (Cl)
Nova Southeastern University (Psy.D.) (Cl)
Ohio University (Ph.D.) (Cl)
Spalding University (Psy.D.) (Cl)
Springfield College (Psy.D.) (Co)
Syracuse University (Ph.D.) (Cl)
The University of Montana (Ph.D.) (Cl)
University of Alabama at Birmingham (Ph.D.) (Cl)
University of Alabama at Tuscaloosa (Ph.D.) (Cl)
University of Florida (Ph.D.) (Cl)
University of Georgia (Ph.D.) (Cl)
University of Kansas (Ph.D.) (Cl)
University of Kentucky (Ph.D.) (Cl)
University of Missouri Kansas City (Ph.D.) (Cl)
University of Pittsburgh (Ph.D.) (Cl)
Virginia Commonwealth University (Ph.D.) (Cl)

Parent–Child Interaction/Parent Training

Alliant International University, San Francisco Bay (Psy.D.) (Cl)
Arizona State University (Ph.D.) (Cl)
Auburn University (Ph.D.) (Cl)
Chicago School of Professional Psychology–Chicago Campus (Psy.D.) (Cl)
Fairleigh Dickinson University (Ph.D.) (Cl)
Florida International University (Ph.D.) (Cl)
Florida State University (Ph.D.) (Cl)
Hofstra University (Ph.D.) (Cl)
Idaho State University (Ph.D.) (Cl)
Long Island University, C.W. Post Campus (Psy.D.) (Cl)
Marquette University (Ph.D.) (Co)
Marshall University (Psy.D.) (Cl)

Miami University (OH) (Ph.D.) (Cl)
Northern Illinois University (Ph.D.) (Cl)
Nova Southeastern University (Ph.D.) (Cl)
Nova Southeastern University (Psy.D.) (Cl)
Saint Louis University (Ph.D.) (Cl)
St. John's University (Ph.D.) (Cl)
University at Buffalo, State University of New York (Ph.D.) (Cl)
University of Alabama at Tuscaloosa (Ph.D.) (Cl)
University of Arkansas (Ph.D.) (Cl)
University of Denver (Ph.D.) (Cl)
University of Florida (Ph.D.) (Cl)
University of Georgia (Ph.D.) (Cl)
University of Iowa (Ph.D.) (Cl)
University of Notre Dame (Ph.D.) P(Cl)
University of Oregon (Ph.D.) (Cl)
University of Pittsburgh (Ph.D.) (Cl)
University of Rochester (Ph.D.) (Cl)
University of Southern California (Ph.D.) (Cl)
University of Virginia (Ph.D.) (Cm)
West Virginia University (Ph.D.) (Cl)
Yeshiva University (Psy.D.) (Cl)
Yeshiva University (Psy.D.) (Cm)

Person-Centered Therapy

American University (Ph.D.) (Cl)
Illinois School of Professional Psychology at Argosy University, Chicago (Psy.D.) (Cl)

Personality Disorders

Baylor University (Psy.D.) (Cl)
Chicago School of Professional Psychology–Chicago Campus (Psy.D.) (Cl)
Fairleigh Dickinson University (Ph.D.) (Cl)
George Washington University (Ph.D.) (Cl)
Georgia State University (Ph.D.) (Cl)
Illinois School of Professional Psychology at Argosy University, Chicago (Psy.D.) (Cl)
Long Island University, C.W. Post Campus (Psy.D.) (Cl)
Loyola University Chicago (Ph.D.) (Cl)
Marshall University (Psy.D.) (Cl)
Northwestern University (Ph.D.) (Cl)
Pennsylvania State University (Ph.D.) (Cl)
Philadelphia College of Osteopathic Medicine (Psy.D.) (Cl)
Ponce Health Sciences University (Ph.D.) (Cl)
Ponce Health Sciences University (Psy.D.) (Cl)
Purdue University (Ph.D.) (Cl)
Rutgers-The State University of New Jersey (Ph.D.) (Cl)
Saint Louis University (Ph.D.) (Cl)
Syracuse University (Ph.D.) (Cl)
Temple University (Ph.D.) (Cl)
The Ohio State University (Ph.D.) (Cl)
The University of Montana (Ph.D.) (Cl)
The Wright Institute (Psy.D.) (Cl)
University at Buffalo, State University of New York (Ph.D.) (Cl)
University of California, Santa Barbara (Ph.D.) (Cm)
University of Georgia (Ph.D.) (Cl)
University of Houston (Ph.D.) (Cl)
University of Maryland-College Park (Ph.D.) (Cl)
University of Minnesota (Ph.D.) (Cl)
University of North Dakota (Ph.D.) (Cl)
University of Notre Dame (Ph.D.) P(Cl)
University of Oregon (Ph.D.) (Cl)
University of Pittsburgh (Ph.D.) (Cl)
University of South Florida (Ph.D.) (Cl)
University of Southern California (Ph.D.) (Cl)
University of Tennessee–Knoxville (Ph.D.) (Cl)
University of Texas at Austin (Ph.D.) (Cl)
University of Texas Southwestern Medical Center (Ph.D.) (Cl)
University of Toledo (Ph.D.) (Cl)
University of Utah (Ph.D.) (Cl)
University of Washington (Ph.D.) (Cl)
Virginia Polytechnic Institute and State University (Ph.D.) (Cl)
Wright State University (Psy.D.) (Cl)
Yale University (Ph.D.) (Cl)
Yeshiva University (Psy.D.) (Cl)

Play Therapy

Baylor University (Psy.D.) (Cl)
Michigan State University (Ph.D.) (Cl)

Positive Psychology/Resilience

University of Louisville (Ph.D.) (Co)
University of Mississippi (Ph.D.) (Cl)
University of Nebraska, Lincoln (Ph.D.) (Co)

Prevention

Arizona State University (Ph.D.) (Cl)
Boston College (Ph.D.) (Co)
Georgia State University (Ph.D.) (Cl)
Illinois School of Professional Psychology at Argosy University, Chicago (Psy.D.) (Cl)
Miami University (OH) (Ph.D.) (Cl)
Pace University (Psy.D.) (Cm)
University of Illinois at Chicago (Ph.D.) (Cl)

University of Maryland, Baltimore County (Ph.D.) (Cl)
University of Oregon (Ph.D.) (Cl)
University of Oregon (Ph.D.) (Co)
University of Vermont (Ph.D.) (Cl)

Primary/Integrated Care

Adelphi University (Ph.D.) (Cl)
American School of Professional Psychology at Argosy University, Washington, DC (Psy.D.) (Cl)
Antioch University New England (Psy.D.) (Cl)
Auburn University (Ph.D.) (Cl)
Ball State University (Ph.D.) (Co)
Chicago School of Professional Psychology–Chicago Campus (Psy.D.) (Cl)
Colorado State University (Ph.D.) (Co)
East Tennessee State University (Ph.D.) (Cl)
Florida State University (Ph.D.) (Cm)
George Fox University (Psy.D.) (Cl)
Indiana University–Purdue University Indianapolis (Ph.D.) (Cl)
Loma Linda University (Ph.D.) (Cl)
Loma Linda University (Psy.D.) (Cl)
Midwestern University (Psy.D.) (Cl)
Midwestern University–Glendale Campus (Psy.D.) (Cl)
New Mexico State University (Ph.D.) (Co)
Northwestern University Feinberg School of Medicine (Ph.D.) (Cl)
Ohio University (Ph.D.) (Cl)
Oklahoma State University (Ph.D.) (Cl)
Philadelphia College of Osteopathic Medicine (Psy.D.) (Cl)
Radford University (Psy.D.) (Co)
Saint Mary's University of Minnesota (Psy.D.) (Co)
Southern Illinois University Carbondale (Ph.D.) (Co)
Syracuse University (Ph.D.) (Cl)
The University of Memphis (Ph.D.) (Cl)
The University of Montana (Ph.D.) (Cl)
The Wright Institute (Psy.D.) (Cl)
University at Albany (Ph.D.) (Co)
University of Arkansas (Ph.D.) (Cl)
University of Colorado at Colorado Springs (Ph.D.) (Cl)
University of Colorado Denver (Ph.D.) (Cl)
University of Denver (Ph.D.) (Co)
University of Georgia (Ph.D.) (Co)
University of Kansas (Ph.D.) (Cl)
University of Maine (Ph.D.) (Cl)
University of Missouri Kansas City (Ph.D.) (Cl)
University of Nevada, Reno (Ph.D.) (Cl)
University of North Carolina at Charlotte (Ph.D.) (Cl)
University of North Carolina, Greensboro (Ph.D.) (Cl)
University of North Dakota (Ph.D.) (Co)
University of Southern California (Ph.D.) (Cl)
University of Texas at Austin (Ph.D.) (Cl)
University of Texas at Austin (Ph.D.) (Co)
University of Texas Southwestern Medical Center (Ph.D.) (Cl)
Virginia Commonwealth University (Ph.D.) (Cl)
Washington State University (Ph.D.) (Cl)
Wayne State University (Ph.D.) (Cl)
West Virginia University (Ph.D.) (Cl)
Western Michigan University (Ph.D.) (Cl)
Wright State University (Psy.D.) (Cl)

Private Practice

Adler University–Chicago (Psy.D.) (Cl)
American University (Ph.D.) (Cl)
Ball State University (Ph.D.) (Co)
Brigham Young University (Ph.D.) (Cl)
Carlos Albizu University, Miami Campus (Psy.D.) (Cl)
Carlos Albizu University, San Juan Campus (Psy.D.) (Cl)
Chicago School of Professional Psychology–Chicago Campus (Psy.D.) (Cl)
Florida School of Professional Psychology at Argosy University (Psy.D.) (Cl)
Florida State University (Ph.D.) (Cm)
Howard University (Ph.D.) (Cl)
Iowa State University (Ph.D.) (Co)
Jackson State University (Ph.D.) (Cl)
James Madison University (Psy.D.) (Cm)
Louisiana Tech University (Ph.D.) (Co)
Loyola University Maryland (Psy.D.) (Cl)
Marshall University (Psy.D.) (Cl)
Marywood University (Psy.D.) (Cl)
Midwestern University–Glendale Campus (Psy.D.) (Cl)
Saint Mary's University of Minnesota (Psy.D.) (Co)
Spalding University (Psy.D.) (Cl)
Uniformed Services University of the Health Sciences (Ph.D.) (Cl)
University of Denver (Psy.D.) (Cl)
University of Houston (Ph.D.) (Co)
Vanderbilt University (Ph.D.) (Cl)
Wheaton College (Psy.D.) (Cl)

Program Evaluation

The Wright Institute (Psy.D.) (Cl)
Wright State University (Psy.D.) (Cl)

Psychiatric Clinic/Inpatient Mental Health

Adler University–Chicago (Psy.D.) (Cl)
Alliant International University, Fresno (Ph.D.) (Cl)
Alliant International University, Fresno (Psy.D.) (Cl)
Alliant International University, Los Angeles (Ph.D.) (Cl)
Alliant International University, Los Angeles (Psy.D.) (Cl)
Alliant International University, Sacramento (Psy.D.) (Cl)
Alliant International University, San Diego (Ph.D.) (Cl)
Alliant International University, San Diego (Psy.D.) (Cl)
Alliant International University, San Francisco Bay (Ph.D.) (Cl)
Alliant International University, San Francisco Bay (Psy.D.) (Cl)
Auburn University (Ph.D.) (Co)
Auburn University (Ph.D.) (Cl)
Chicago School of Professional Psychology–Chicago Campus (Psy.D.) (Cl)
East Carolina University (Ph.D.) (Cl)
Florida School of Professional Psychology at Argosy University (Psy.D.) (Cl)
Florida State University (Ph.D.) (Cl)
Hawaii School of Professional Psychology at Argosy University, Hawaii (Psy.D.) (Cl)
Indiana University–Purdue University Indianapolis (Ph.D.) (Cl)
Jackson State University (Ph.D.) (Cl)
Marywood University (Psy.D.) (Cl)
Northeastern University (Ph.D.) (Co)
Regent University (Psy.D.) (Cl)
Roosevelt University (Psy.D.) (Cl)
Sam Houston State University (Ph.D.) (Cl)
Southern Illinois University Carbondale (Ph.D.) (Co)
Spalding University (Psy.D.) (Cl)
Tennessee State University (Ph.D.) (Co)
Texas Tech University (Ph.D.) (Co)
University at Albany (Ph.D.) (Co)
University of Alabama at Tuscaloosa (Ph.D.) (Cl)
University of Indianapolis (Psy.D.) (Cl)
University of Kentucky (Ph.D.) (Co)
University of La Verne (Psy.D.) (Cl)
University of Massachusetts, Boston (Ph.D.) (Co)
University of Missouri Kansas City (Ph.D.) (Cl)
University of Missouri, Columbia (Ph.D.) (Co)
University of Rochester (Ph.D.) (Cl)
Vanderbilt University (Ph.D.) (Cl)
Virginia Commonwealth University (Ph.D.) (Co)
West Virginia University (Ph.D.) (Co)
Wheaton College (Psy.D.) (Cl)

Psychoanalytic/Psychodynamic Therapy

Adelphi University (Ph.D.) (Cl)
American University (Ph.D.) (Cl)
Chicago School of Professional Psychology–Chicago Campus (Psy.D.) (Cl)
Emory University (Ph.D.) (Cl)
George Washington University (Ph.D.) (Cl)
Illinois School of Professional Psychology at Argosy University, Chicago (Psy.D.) (Cl)
Long Island University, C.W. Post Campus (Psy.D.) (Cl)
Nova Southeastern University (Ph.D.) (Cl)
Nova Southeastern University (Psy.D.) (Cl)
Pepperdine University (Psy.D.) (Cl)
Syracuse University (Ph.D.) (Cl)
The Wright Institute (Psy.D.) (Cl)
University of Denver (Psy.D.) (Cl)
University of Maryland-College Park (Ph.D.) (Co)
University of Minnesota (Ph.D.) (Cl)
University of Rochester (Ph.D.) (Cl)
University of Toledo (Ph.D.) (Cl)
Widener University (Psy.D.) (Cl)
Wright State University (Psy.D.) (Cl)
Yeshiva University (Psy.D.) (Cl)

Rehabilitation

Alliant International University, Fresno (Ph.D.) (Cl)
Alliant International University, Fresno (Psy.D.) (Cl)
Alliant International University, Los Angeles (Ph.D.) (Cl)
Alliant International University, Los Angeles (Psy.D.) (Cl)
Alliant International University, Sacramento (Psy.D.) (Cl)
Alliant International University, San Diego (Ph.D.) (Cl)
Alliant International University, San Diego (Psy.D.) (Cl)
Alliant International University, San Francisco Bay (Ph.D.) (Cl)
Alliant International University, San Francisco Bay (Psy.D.) (Cl)
Antioch University New England (Psy.D.) (Cl)
Auburn University (Ph.D.) (Co)
Chicago School of Professional Psychology–Chicago Campus (Psy.D.) (Cl)
East Carolina University (Ph.D.) (Cl)
Florida School of Professional Psychology at Argosy University (Psy.D.) (Cl)
Fuller Theological Seminary (Ph.D.) (Cl)
Fuller Theological Seminary (Psy.D.) (Cl)

George Washington University (Ph.D.) (Cl)
Georgia School of Professional Psychology at Argosy University, Atlanta (Psy.D.) (Cl)
Georgia State University (Ph.D.) (Cl)
Illinois School of Professional Psychology at Argosy University, Chicago (Psy.D.) (Cl)
Indiana University–Purdue University Indianapolis (Ph.D.) (Cl)
Marywood University (Psy.D.) (Cl)
Palo Alto University (Psy.D.) (Cl)
Pepperdine University (Psy.D.) (Cl)
Ponce Health Sciences University (Ph.D.) (Cl)
Ponce Health Sciences University (Psy.D.) (Cl)
Saint Mary's University of Minnesota (Psy.D.) (Co)
Seattle Pacific University (Ph.D.) (Cl)
Southern Illinois University Carbondale (Ph.D.) (Cl)
Southern Illinois University Carbondale (Ph.D.) (Co)
Spalding University (Psy.D.) (Cl)
The Wright Institute (Psy.D.) (Cl)
University of Alabama at Birmingham (Ph.D.) (Cl)
University of Arizona (Ph.D.) (Cl)
University of Hawaii at Manoa (Ph.D.) (Cl)
University of Kansas (Ph.D.) (Cl)
University of Kentucky (Ph.D.) (Cl)
University of Maryland, Baltimore County (Ph.D.) (Cl)
University of Missouri, Columbia (Ph.D.) (Co)
University of Nebraska, Lincoln (Ph.D.) (Cl)
University of Texas Southwestern Medical Center (Ph.D.) (Cl)
University of Washington (Ph.D.) (Cl)
Utah State University (Ph.D.) (Cm)
Virginia Commonwealth University (Ph.D.) (Co)
Wayne State University (Ph.D.) (Cl)
West Virginia University (Ph.D.) (Co)
Wright State University (Psy.D.) (Cl)

Religion/Spirituality

Biola University (Ph.D.) (Cl)
Biola University (Psy.D.) (Cl)
Chicago School of Professional Psychology–Chicago Campus (Psy.D.) (Cl)
George Fox University (Psy.D.) (Cl)
Illinois School of Professional Psychology at Argosy University, Chicago (Psy.D.) (Cl)
Pepperdine University (Psy.D.) (Cl)
Virginia Commonwealth University (Ph.D.) (Co)

Residential Program/Treatment Center

Adler University–Chicago (Psy.D.) (Cl)
Alliant International University, Fresno (Ph.D.) (Cl)
Alliant International University, Fresno (Psy.D.) (Cl)
Alliant International University, Los Angeles (Ph.D.) (Cl)
Alliant International University, Los Angeles (Psy.D.) (Cl)
Alliant International University, Sacramento (Psy.D.) (Cl)
Alliant International University, San Diego (Ph.D.) (Cl)
Alliant International University, San Diego (Psy.D.) (Cl)
Alliant International University, San Francisco Bay (Ph.D.) (Cl)
Alliant International University, San Francisco Bay (Psy.D.) (Cl)
Brigham Young University (Ph.D.) (Cl)
California Lutheran University (Psy.D.) (Cl)
East Tennessee State University (Ph.D.) (Cl)
Florida School of Professional Psychology at Argosy University (Psy.D.) (Cl)
Spalding University (Psy.D.) (Cl)
University at Albany (Ph.D.) (Co)
University of Alabama at Tuscaloosa (Ph.D.) (Cl)
University of Massachusetts Amherst (Ph.D.) (Cl)
University of Southern Mississippi (Ph.D.) (Cl)
University of Wyoming (Ph.D.) (Cl)
Wisconsin School of Professional Psychology (Psy.D.) (Cl)

Rural Mental Health/Psychology

Antioch University New England (Psy.D.) (Cl)
Baylor University (Psy.D.) (Cl)
Carlow University (Psy.D.) (Co)
Chicago School of Professional Psychology–Chicago Campus (Psy.D.) (Cl)
East Tennessee State University (Ph.D.) (Cl)
George Fox University (Psy.D.) (Cl)
Indiana State University (Psy.D.) (Cl)
Miami University (OH) (Ph.D.) (Cl)
New Mexico State University (Ph.D.) (Co)
Ohio University (Ph.D.) (Cl)
Oklahoma State University (Ph.D.) (Co)
Saint Mary's University of Minnesota (Psy.D.) (Co)
Texas A&M University (Ph.D.) (Cl)
The University of Montana (Ph.D.) (Cl)
The University of South Dakota (Ph.D.) (Cl)
University at Buffalo, State University of New York (Ph.D.) (Cm)
University of Alabama at Tuscaloosa (Ph.D.) (Cl)
University of Florida (Ph.D.) (Co)
University of Florida (Ph.D.) (Cl)
University of Georgia (Ph.D.) (Cl)

University of Georgia (Ph.D.) (Co)
University of Hawaii at Manoa (Ph.D.) (Cl)
University of Missouri, Columbia (Ph.D.) (Co)
University of North Dakota (Ph.D.) (Cl)
University of Wyoming (Ph.D.) (Cl)

Severe Mental Illness/Psychosis/Schizophrenia

Baylor University (Psy.D.) (Cl)
Binghamton University, State University of New York (Ph.D.) (Cl)
Case Western Reserve University (Ph.D.) (Cl)
Chicago School of Professional Psychology—Washington, DC Campus (Psy.D.) (Cl)
Florida State University (Ph.D.) (Cl)
George Washington University (Ph.D.) (Cl)
Harvard University (Ph.D.) (Cl)
Illinois Institute of Technology (Ph.D.) (Cl)
Indiana State University (Psy.D.) (Cl)
Indiana University–Bloomington (Ph.D.) (Cl)
Indiana University–Purdue University Indianapolis (Ph.D.) (Cl)
John Jay College of Criminal Justice & The Graduate Center, CUNY (Ph.D.) (Cl)
Kent State University (Ph.D.) (Cl)
Marshall University (Psy.D.) (Cl)
Midwestern University (Psy.D.) (Cl)
Nova Southeastern University (Ph.D.) (Cl)
Nova Southeastern University (Psy.D.) (Cl)
Palo Alto University (Psy.D.) (Cl)
Pepperdine University (Psy.D.) (Cl)
Ponce Health Sciences University (Ph.D.) (Cl)
Ponce Health Sciences University (Psy.D.) (Cl)
Rutgers-The State University of New Jersey (Ph.D.) (Cl)
Seattle Pacific University (Ph.D.) (Cl)
The Ohio State University (Ph.D.) (Cl)
The University of Montana (Ph.D.) (Cl)
The University of South Dakota (Ph.D.) (Cl)
The Wright Institute (Psy.D.) (Cl)
University of California, Los Angeles (Ph.D.) (Cl)
University of Central Florida (Ph.D.) (Cl)
University of Cincinnati (Ph.D.) (Cl)
University of Hawaii at Manoa (Ph.D.) (Cl)
University of Houston (Ph.D.) (Cl)
University of Kansas–Child (Ph.D.) (Cl)
University of Maryland, Baltimore County (Ph.D.) (Cl)
University of Maryland-College Park (Ph.D.) (Cl)
University of Minnesota (Ph.D.) (Cl)
University of Nebraska, Lincoln (Ph.D.) (Cl)
University of Pittsburgh (Ph.D.) (Cl)
University of Rochester (Ph.D.) (Cl)
University of Southern California (Ph.D.) (Cl)
University of Texas at Austin (Ph.D.) (Cl)
University of Virginia (Ph.D.) (Cl)
University of Wisconsin, Madison (Ph.D.) (Cl)
Wright State University (Psy.D.) (Cl)
Yeshiva University (Psy.D.) (Cl)

School/Educational

Adler University–Chicago (Psy.D.) (Cl)
Alliant International University, Fresno (Ph.D.) (Cl)
Alliant International University, Los Angeles (Ph.D.) (Cl)
Alliant International University, Los Angeles (Psy.D.) (Cl)
Alliant International University, Sacramento (Psy.D.) (Cl)
Alliant International University, San Diego (Ph.D.) (Cl)
Alliant International University, San Diego (Psy.D.) (Cl)
Alliant International University, San Francisco Bay (Ph.D.) (Cl)
Alliant International University, San Francisco Bay (Psy.D.) (Cl)
American School of Professional Psychology at Argosy University, Washington, DC (Psy.D.) (Cl)
American University (Ph.D.) (Cl)
Antioch University New England (Psy.D.) (Cl)
Arizona School of Professional Psychology at Argosy University, Phoenix (Psy.D.) (Cl)
Azusa Pacific University (Psy.D.) (Cl)
Binghamton University, State University of New York (Ph.D.) (Cl)
Boston College (Ph.D.) (Co)
Chicago School of Professional Psychology–Chicago Campus (Psy.D.) (Cl)
DePaul University (Ph.D.) (Cl)
Fairleigh Dickinson University (Ph.D.) (Cl)
Florida International University (Ph.D.) (Cl)
Florida School of Professional Psychology at Argosy University (Psy.D.) (Cl)
George Fox University (Psy.D.) (Cl)
Georgia School of Professional Psychology at Argosy University, Atlanta (Psy.D.) (Cl)
Hawaii School of Professional Psychology at Argosy University, Hawaii (Psy.D.) (Cl)
Illinois School of Professional Psychology at Argosy University, Chicago (Psy.D.) (Cl)
James Madison University (Psy.D.) (Cm)
Kean University (Psy.D.) (Cm)
Marquette University (Ph.D.) (Co)

Miami University (OH) (Ph.D.) (Cl)
Northern Illinois University (Ph.D.) (Cl)
Ohio University (Ph.D.) (Cl)
Palo Alto University (Psy.D.) (Cl)
Pepperdine University (Psy.D.) (Cl)
Ponce Health Sciences University (Ph.D.) (Cl)
Ponce Health Sciences University (Psy.D.) (Cl)
Rutgers-The State University of New Jersey (Ph.D.) (Cl)
Saint Mary's University of Minnesota (Psy.D.) (Co)
San Diego State University–UC San Diego (Ph.D.) (Cl)
Spalding University (Psy.D.) (Cl)
Suffolk University (Ph.D.) (Cl)
The University of Montana (Ph.D.) (Cl)
The Wright Institute (Psy.D.) (Cl)
University of Arkansas (Ph.D.) (Cl)
University of California, Los Angeles (Ph.D.) (Cl)
University of California, Santa Barbara (Ph.D.) (Cm)
University of Denver (Psy.D.) (Cl)
University of Hartford (Psy.D.) (Cl)
University of Houston (Ph.D.) (Co)
University of Illinois at Urbana-Champaign (Ph.D.) (Cl)
University of Indianapolis (Psy.D.) (Cl)
University of Iowa (Ph.D.) (Co)
University of Maine (Ph.D.) (Cl)
University of Maryland, Baltimore County (Ph.D.) (Cl)
University of Nebraska, Lincoln (Ph.D.) (Co)
University of Nevada Las Vegas (Ph.D.) (Cl)
University of South Alabama (Ph.D.) (Cm)
University of Southern California (Ph.D.) (Cl)
University of Southern Mississippi (Ph.D.) (Cl)
University of Utah (Ph.D.) (Co)
University of Virginia (Ph.D.) (Cm)
Western Michigan University (Ph.D.) (Co)
Widener University (Psy.D.) (Cl)
Wisconsin School of Professional Psychology (Psy.D.) (Cl)
Yeshiva University (Psy.D.) (Cm)

Sexuality/Sex Therapy/Sexual Offenders

American School of Professional Psychology at Argosy University, Washington, DC (Psy.D.) (Cl)
Arizona School of Professional Psychology at Argosy University, Phoenix (Psy.D.) (Cl)
Chicago School of Professional Psychology–Chicago Campus (Psy.D.) (Cl)
Miami University (OH) (Ph.D.) (Cl)
Midwestern University–Glendale Campus (Psy.D.) (Cl)
The Ohio State University (Ph.D.) (Cl)
University of Florida (Ph.D.) (Co)
University of Nebraska, Lincoln (Ph.D.) (Cl)
University of Utah (Ph.D.) (Cl)
Widener University (Psy.D.) (Cl)

Sleep Disorders

Florida International University (Ph.D.) (Cl)
Indiana University–Bloomington (Ph.D.) (Cl)
Marshall University (Psy.D.) (Cl)
University of Alabama at Tuscaloosa (Ph.D.) (Cl)
University of Arizona (Ph.D.) (Cl)
University of Colorado Denver (Ph.D.) (Cl)
University of Georgia (Ph.D.) (Cl)
University of Houston (Ph.D.) (Cl)
University of Oregon (Ph.D.) (Cl)
University of Pittsburgh (Ph.D.) (Cl)
University of Texas at Austin (Ph.D.) (Cl)
University of Texas Southwestern Medical Center (Ph.D.) (Cl)

Spanish-Speaking Clients

Chicago School of Professional Psychology–Chicago Campus (Psy.D.) (Cl)
New Mexico State University (Ph.D.) (Co)
Our Lady of the Lake University (Psy.D.) (Co)
Sam Houston State University (Ph.D.) (Cl)
University of Oregon (Ph.D.) (Co)

Sports/Performance Psychology

Fairleigh Dickinson University (Ph.D.) (Cl)
Illinois School of Professional Psychology at Argosy University, Chicago (Psy.D.) (Cl)
James Madison University (Psy.D.) (Cm)
Texas Tech University (Ph.D.) (Co)
University of Denver (Psy.D.) (Cl)
University of Nevada Las Vegas (Ph.D.) (Cl)
University of North Texas (Ph.D.) (Co)

Substance Abuse/Addiction

Adelphi University (Ph.D.) (Cl)
Alliant International University, San Francisco Bay (Psy.D.) (Cl)
American School of Professional Psychology at Argosy University, Washington, DC (Psy.D.) (Cl)
Antioch University New England (Psy.D.) (Cl)
Arizona School of Professional Psychology at Argosy University, Phoenix (Psy.D.) (Cl)

Auburn University (Ph.D.) (Co)
Auburn University (Ph.D.) (Cl)
Azusa Pacific University (Psy.D.) (Cl)
Baylor University (Psy.D.) (Cl)
Binghamton University, State University of New York (Ph.D.) (Cl)
Boston University (Ph.D.) (Cl)
California Lutheran University (Psy.D.) (Cl)
Chatham University (Psy.D.) (Co)
Chicago School of Professional Psychology–Chicago Campus (Psy.D.) (Cl)
Clark University (Ph.D.) (Cl)
Colorado State University (Ph.D.) (Co)
Divine Mercy University (Psy.D.) (Cl)
Florida School of Professional Psychology at Argosy University (Psy.D.) (Cl)
George Fox University (Psy.D.) (Cl)
George Washington University (Ph.D.) (Cl)
Hawaii School of Professional Psychology at Argosy University, Hawaii (Psy.D.) (Cl)
Illinois School of Professional Psychology at Argosy University, Chicago (Psy.D.) (Cl)
Indiana University–Bloomington (Ph.D.) (Cl)
Loyola University Chicago (Ph.D.) (Cl)
Marquette University (Ph.D.) (Co)
Marshall University (Psy.D.) (Cl)
Midwestern University–Glendale Campus (Psy.D.) (Cl)
New Mexico State University (Ph.D.) (Co)
Northeastern University (Ph.D.) (Co)
Nova Southeastern University (Ph.D.) (Cl)
Nova Southeastern University (Psy.D.) (Cl)
Ohio University (Ph.D.) (Cl)
Oklahoma State University (Ph.D.) (Cl)
Palo Alto University (Psy.D.) (Cl)
Pepperdine University (Psy.D.) (Cl)
Ponce Health Sciences University (Ph.D.) (Cl)
Ponce Health Sciences University (Psy.D.) (Cl)
Rutgers-The State University of New Jersey (Ph.D.) (Cl)
Saint Louis University (Ph.D.) (Cl)
Saint Mary's University of Minnesota (Psy.D.) (Co)
Seattle Pacific University (Ph.D.) (Cl)
Southern Illinois University Carbondale (Ph.D.) (Co)
Spalding University (Psy.D.) (Cl)
Syracuse University (Ph.D.) (Cl)
Texas A&M University (Ph.D.) (Cl)
Texas Woman's University (Ph.D.) (Co)
The Ohio State University (Ph.D.) (Cl)
The University of Memphis (Ph.D.) (Cl)
The University of Montana (Ph.D.) (Cl)
The University of South Dakota (Ph.D.) (Cl)
The Wright Institute (Psy.D.) (Cl)
Uniformed Services University of the Health Sciences (Ph.D.) (Cl)
University at Albany (Ph.D.) (Co)
University at Albany (Ph.D.) (Cl)
University at Buffalo, State University of New York (Ph.D.) (Cl)
University of Alabama at Birmingham (Ph.D.) (Cl)
University of Alaska Fairbanks-Anchorage (Ph.D.) (Cl)
University of Arkansas (Ph.D.) (Cl)
University of California, Berkeley (Ph.D.) (Cl)
University of Cincinnati (Ph.D.) (Cl)
University of Denver (Ph.D.) (Co)
University of Florida (Ph.D.) (Co)
University of Georgia (Ph.D.) (Cl)
University of Hawaii at Manoa (Ph.D.) (Cl)
University of Houston (Ph.D.) (Cl)
University of Houston (Ph.D.) (Co)
University of Illinois at Chicago (Ph.D.) (Cl)
University of Illinois at Urbana-Champaign (Ph.D.) (Cl)
University of Illinois at Urbana-Champaign (Ph.D.) (Co)
University of Indianapolis (Psy.D.) (Cl)
University of La Verne (Psy.D.) (Cl)
University of Maryland, Baltimore County (Ph.D.) (Cl)
University of Maryland-College Park (Ph.D.) (Cl)
University of Miami (Ph.D.) (Cl)
University of Minnesota (Ph.D.) (Cl)
University of Mississippi (Ph.D.) (Cl)
University of Missouri Kansas City (Ph.D.) (Cl)
University of Nebraska, Lincoln (Ph.D.) (Cl)
University of New Mexico (Ph.D.) (Cl)
University of North Dakota (Ph.D.) (Cl)
University of Pennsylvania (Ph.D.) (Cl)
University of Pittsburgh (Ph.D.) (Cl)
University of South Florida (Ph.D.) (Cl)
University of Southern California (Ph.D.) (Cl)
University of Southern Mississippi (Ph.D.) (Cl)
University of Southern Mississippi (Ph.D.) (Co)
University of Tennessee–Knoxville (Ph.D.) (Cl)
University of Tennessee–Knoxville (Ph.D.) (Co)
University of Texas at Austin (Ph.D.) (Cl)
University of Utah (Ph.D.) (Cl)
University of Utah (Ph.D.) (Co)
University of Vermont (Ph.D.) (Cl)
University of Washington (Ph.D.) (Cl)
University of Wisconsin, Madison (Ph.D.) (Cl)
University of Wyoming (Ph.D.) (Cl)

Vanderbilt University (Ph.D.) (Cl)
Virginia Commonwealth University (Ph.D.) (Cl)
Virginia Commonwealth University (Ph.D.) (Co)
Virginia Polytechnic Institute and State University (Ph.D.) (Cl)
Wayne State University (Ph.D.) (Cl)
Wisconsin School of Professional Psychology (Psy.D.) (Cl)
Wright State University (Psy.D.) (Cl)
Yale University (Ph.D.) (Cl)

Suicide/Suicide Prevention

Baylor University (Psy.D.) (Cl)
La Salle University (Psy.D.) (Cl)
Marshall University (Psy.D.) (Cl)
Rutgers-The State University of New Jersey (Ph.D.) (Cl)
University of Houston (Ph.D.) (Cl)
University of Pittsburgh (Ph.D.) (Cl)
University of Rochester (Ph.D.) (Cl)
University of South Florida (Ph.D.) (Cl)
Vanderbilt University (Ph.D.) (Cl)

Supervision

Antioch University New England (Psy.D.) (Cl)
Binghamton University, State University of New York (Ph.D.) (Cl)
Carlos Albizu University, San Juan Campus (Psy.D.) (Cl)
DePaul University (Ph.D.) (Cl)
Fairleigh Dickinson University (Ph.D.) (Cl)
Fuller Theological Seminary (Ph.D.) (Cl)
Fuller Theological Seminary (Psy.D.) (Cl)
George Mason University (Ph.D.) (Cl)
Georgia State University (Ph.D.) (Cl)
James Madison University (Psy.D.) (Cm)
Marquette University (Ph.D.) (Co)
New Mexico State University (Ph.D.) (Co)
University of California, Los Angeles (Ph.D.) (Cl)
University of Denver (Psy.D.) (Cl)
University of Georgia (Ph.D.) (Cl)
University of Georgia (Ph.D.) (Co)
University of Indianapolis (Psy.D.) (Cl)
University of Maryland-College Park (Ph.D.) (Co)
University of Massachusetts Amherst (Ph.D.) (Cl)
University of Northern Colorado (Ph.D.) (Co)
Virginia Polytechnic Institute and State University (Ph.D.) (Cl)
Wisconsin School of Professional Psychology (Psy.D.) (Cl)

Technology

Sam Houston State University (Ph.D.) (Cl)
Temple University (Ph.D.) (Cl)
Texas A&M University (Ph.D.) (Co)
University of Georgia (Ph.D.) (Co)
University of Nebraska, Lincoln (Ph.D.) (Cl)
University of Wyoming (Ph.D.) (Cl)

Tic Disorders

Indiana University–Bloomington (Ph.D.) (Cl)
Rutgers-The State University of New Jersey (Ph.D.) (Cl)
Rutgers-The State University of New Jersey (Psy.D.) (Cl)
Vanderbilt University (Ph.D.) (Cl)

Torture

Illinois School of Professional Psychology at Argosy University, Chicago (Psy.D.) (Cl)
University of Texas at Austin (Ph.D.) (Cl)

Trauma/Post-Traumatic Stress Disorder/Disaster

American School of Professional Psychology at Argosy University, Washington, DC (Psy.D.) (Cl)
Arizona School of Professional Psychology at Argosy University, Phoenix (Psy.D.) (Cl)
Boston College (Ph.D.) (Co)
Boston University (Ph.D.) (Cl)
Chicago School of Professional Psychology–Chicago Campus (Psy.D.) (Cl)
Eastern Michigan University (Ph.D.) (Cl)
Florida Institute of Technology (Psy.D.) (Cl)
George Washington University (Ph.D.) (Cl)
Georgia School of Professional Psychology at Argosy University, Atlanta (Psy.D.) (Cl)
Hofstra University (Ph.D.) (Cl)
Idaho State University (Ph.D.) (Cl)
Illinois School of Professional Psychology at Argosy University, Chicago (Psy.D.) (Cl)
John Jay College of Criminal Justice & The Graduate Center, CUNY (Ph.D.) (Cl)
Kean University (Psy.D.) (Cm)
Marquette University (Ph.D.) (Co)
Marquette University (Ph.D.) (Cl)
Miami University (OH) (Ph.D.) (Cl)
Michigan State University (Ph.D.) (Cl)
Northern Illinois University (Ph.D.) (Cl)

Nova Southeastern University (Ph.D.) (Cl)
Nova Southeastern University (Psy.D.) (Cl)
Ohio University (Ph.D.) (Cl)
Oklahoma State University (Ph.D.) (Cl)
Palo Alto University (Psy.D.) (Cl)
Pepperdine University (Psy.D.) (Cl)
Philadelphia College of Osteopathic Medicine (Psy.D.) (Cl)
Roosevelt University (Psy.D.) (Cl)
Saint Louis University (Ph.D.) (Cl)
Saint Mary's University of Minnesota (Psy.D.) (Co)
The University of Akron (Ph.D.) (Co)
The University of Memphis (Ph.D.) (Cl)
The University of Montana (Ph.D.) (Cl)
The University of South Dakota (Ph.D.) (Cl)
University of Alabama at Tuscaloosa (Ph.D.) (Cl)
University of Arkansas (Ph.D.) (Cl)
University of Central Florida (Ph.D.) (Cl)
University of Colorado at Colorado Springs (Ph.D.) (Cl)
University of Connecticut (Ph.D.) (Cl)
University of Denver (Ph.D.) (Cl)
University of Georgia (Ph.D.) (Cl)
University of Houston (Ph.D.) (Cl)
University of Houston (Ph.D.) (Co)
University of Illinois at Chicago (Ph.D.) (Cl)
University of Illinois at Urbana-Champaign (Ph.D.) (Cl)
University of Illinois at Urbana-Champaign (Ph.D.) (Co)
University of Massachusetts, Boston (Ph.D.) (Co)
University of Miami (Ph.D.) (Cl)
University of Minnesota (Ph.D.) (Cl)
University of Mississippi (Ph.D.) (Cl)
University of Missouri, St. Louis (Ph.D.) (Cl)
University of Nevada, Reno (Ph.D.) (Cl)
University of Oregon (Ph.D.) (Cl)
University of Utah (Ph.D.) (Cl)
University of Vermont (Ph.D.) (Cl)
University of Wisconsin, Milwaukee (Ph.D.) (Cl)
University of Wyoming (Ph.D.) (Cl)
Virginia Commonwealth University (Ph.D.) (Cl)
Virginia Polytechnic Institute and State University (Ph.D.) (Cl)
Wright State University (Psy.D.) (Cl)
Yeshiva University (Ph.D.) (Cl)
Yeshiva University (Psy.D.) (Cl)

Traumatic Brain Injury

Eastern Michigan University (Ph.D.) (Cl)
Southern Illinois University Carbondale (Ph.D.) (Co)
University of Colorado at Colorado Springs (Ph.D.) (Cl)
University of Connecticut (Ph.D.) (Cl)
University of Florida (Ph.D.) (Cl)
University of Nebraska, Lincoln (Ph.D.) (Cl)
Yeshiva University (Ph.D.) (Cl)

Underserved Populations

University of Denver (Ph.D.) (Co)
University of Missouri, Columbia (Ph.D.) (Cl)
University of North Carolina, Greensboro (Ph.D.) (Cl)
University of Southern California (Ph.D.) (Cl)
Wisconsin School of Professional Psychology (Psy.D.) (Cl)

Veterans Medical Center

Adler University–Chicago (Psy.D.) (Cl)
Alliant International University, Fresno (Ph.D.) (Cl)
American University (Ph.D.) (Cl)
Auburn University (Ph.D.) (Co)
Auburn University (Ph.D.) (Cl)
Ball State University (Ph.D.) (Co)
Boston College (Ph.D.) (Co)
Brigham Young University (Ph.D.) (Cl)
Carlos Albizu University, Miami Campus (Psy.D.) (Cl)
Catholic University of America (Ph.D.) (Cl)
Chicago School of Professional Psychology–Chicago Campus (Psy.D.) (Cl)
Chicago School of Professional Psychology—Washington, DC Campus (Psy.D.) (Cl)
Cleveland State University (Ph.D.) (Co)
East Carolina University (Ph.D.) (Cl)
East Tennessee State University (Ph.D.) (Cl)
Eastern Michigan University (Ph.D.) (Cl)
Fairleigh Dickinson University (Ph.D.) (Cl)
Florida State University (Ph.D.) (Cl)
Florida State University (Ph.D.) (Cm)
Georgia Southern University (Psy.D.) (Cl)
Howard University (Ph.D.) (Cl)
Idaho State University (Ph.D.) (Cl)
Indiana University–Purdue University Indianapolis (Ph.D.) (Cl)
Iowa State University (Ph.D.) (Co)
Louisiana Tech University (Ph.D.) (Co)
Marshall University (Psy.D.) (Cl)
Marywood University (Psy.D.) (Cl)
Midwestern University–Glendale Campus (Psy.D.) (Cl)
Northeastern University (Ph.D.) (Co)

Ohio University (Ph.D.) (Cl)
Oklahoma State University (Ph.D.) (Co)
Palo Alto University (Psy.D.) (Cl)
Pepperdine University (Psy.D.) (Cl)
Purdue University (Ph.D.) (Co)
Radford University (Psy.D.) (Co)
Regent University (Psy.D.) (Cl)
Roosevelt University (Psy.D.) (Cl)
Rosalind Franklin University of Medicine and Science (Ph.D.) (Cl)
Southern Illinois University Carbondale (Ph.D.) (Co)
Southern Methodist University (Ph.D.) (Cl)
Spalding University (Psy.D.) (Cl)
Syracuse University (Ph.D.) (Cl)
Tennessee State University (Ph.D.) (Co)
Texas A&M University (Ph.D.) (Co)
Texas Woman's University (Ph.D.) (Co)
The University of Memphis (Ph.D.) (Cl)
The University of Memphis (Ph.D.) (Co)
Uniformed Services University of the Health Sciences (Ph.D.) (Cl)
University at Albany (Ph.D.) (Co)
University at Buffalo, State University of New York (Ph.D.) (Cm)
University of Alabama at Tuscaloosa (Ph.D.) (Cl)
University of Arkansas (Ph.D.) (Cl)
University of California, Berkeley (Ph.D.) (Cl)
University of Colorado at Colorado Springs (Ph.D.) (Cl)
University of Denver (Ph.D.) (Co)
University of Denver (Psy.D.) (Cl)
University of Houston (Ph.D.) (Co)
University of Illinois at Urbana-Champaign (Ph.D.) (Cl)
University of Illinois at Urbana-Champaign (Ph.D.) (Co)
University of Indianapolis (Psy.D.) (Cl)
University of Iowa (Ph.D.) (Cl)
University of Iowa (Ph.D.) (Co)
University of Kansas (Ph.D.) (Co)
University of Kentucky (Ph.D.) (Co)
University of La Verne (Psy.D.) (Cl)
University of Louisville (Ph.D.) (Co)
University of Missouri Kansas City (Ph.D.) (Cl)
University of Missouri, Columbia (Ph.D.) (Cl)
University of Missouri, Columbia (Ph.D.) (Co)
University of Nevada Las Vegas (Ph.D.) (Cl)
University of New Mexico (Ph.D.) (Cl)
University of North Carolina at Charlotte (Ph.D.) (Cl)
University of North Carolina, Greensboro (Ph.D.) (Cl)
University of North Texas (Ph.D.) (Cl)
University of Oregon (Ph.D.) (Co)
University of Pittsburgh (Ph.D.) (Cl)
University of South Alabama (Ph.D.) (Cm)
University of Southern California (Ph.D.) (Cl)
University of Southern Mississippi (Ph.D.) (Cl)
University of Southern Mississippi (Ph.D.) (Co)
University of Texas at Austin (Ph.D.) (Co)
University of Utah (Ph.D.) (Co)
University of Wisconsin, Milwaukee (Ph.D.) (Co)
Vanderbilt University (Ph.D.) (Cl)
Virginia Commonwealth University (Ph.D.) (Co)
West Virginia University (Ph.D.) (Co)
Western Michigan University (Ph.D.) (Cl)
Wheaton College (Psy.D.) (Cl)
Wisconsin School of Professional Psychology (Psy.D.) (Cl)
Wright State University (Psy.D.) (Cl)

Victim/Violence/Sexual Abuse

Boston College (Ph.D.) (Co)
Chicago School of Professional Psychology–Chicago Campus (Psy.D.) (Cl)
Florida Institute of Technology (Psy.D.) (Cl)
Fuller Theological Seminary (Ph.D.) (Cl)
Fuller Theological Seminary (Psy.D.) (Cl)
Georgia State University (Ph.D.) (Cl)
Harvard University (Ph.D.) (Cl)
Illinois School of Professional Psychology at Argosy University, Chicago (Psy.D.) (Cl)
Long Island University, C.W. Post Campus (Psy.D.) (Cl)
Loyola University Chicago (Ph.D.) (Cl)
Marshall University (Psy.D.) (Cl)
The University of South Dakota (Ph.D.) (Cl)
University of Georgia (Ph.D.) (Cl)
University of Miami (Ph.D.) (Cl)
University of Mississippi (Ph.D.) (Cl)
University of North Dakota (Ph.D.) (Cl)
University of Pittsburgh (Ph.D.) (Cl)
University of Virginia (Ph.D.) (Cl)

Vocational/Career Development

Florida State University (Ph.D.) (Cm)
Marquette University (Ph.D.) (Co)
Southern Illinois University Carbondale (Ph.D.) (Co)
University of Texas at Austin (Ph.D.) (Co)

Weight Management/Obesity

Chicago School of Professional Psychology–Chicago Campus (Psy.D.) (Cl)
East Carolina University (Ph.D.) (Cl)

Florida International University (Ph.D.) (Cl)
La Salle University (Psy.D.) (Cl)
Loma Linda University (Ph.D.) (Cl)
Loma Linda University (Psy.D.) (Cl)
Marshall University (Psy.D.) (Cl)
University of Alabama at Birmingham (Ph.D.) (Cl)
University of Florida (Ph.D.) (Cl)
University of Kansas (Ph.D.) (Cl)
University of Maine (Ph.D.) (Cl)
University of Pennsylvania (Ph.D.) (Cl)
University of Pittsburgh (Ph.D.) (Cl)
University of South Florida (Ph.D.) (Cl)
Yeshiva University (Ph.D.) (Cl)

Women's Issues

Antioch University New England (Psy.D.) (Cl)
East Carolina University (Ph.D.) (Cl)
Miami University (OH) (Ph.D.) (Cl)
Palo Alto University (Psy.D.) (Cl)
Rutgers-The State University of New Jersey (Psy.D.) (Cl)
The Wright Institute (Psy.D.) (Cl)
University of Colorado Denver (Ph.D.) (Cl)
University of Iowa (Ph.D.) (Co)
University of Missouri, Columbia (Ph.D.) (Co)
University of Utah (Ph.D.) (Co)
Wright State University (Psy.D.) (Cl)

Miscellaneous

academic coaching—University of Illinois at Urbana-Champaign (Ph.D.) (Cl)
adult psychotherapy—James Madison University (Psy.D.) (Cm)
Alzheimer's dementia—Case Western Reserve University (Ph.D.) (Cl)
attachment disorders—The University of Montana (Ph.D.) (Cl)
bariatric surgery assessment—Kent State University (Ph.D.) (Cl)
behavioral activation—University of Colorado Boulder (Ph.D.) (Cl)
behavioral dentistry—West Virginia University (Ph.D.) (Cl)
behavioral neurology—Harvard University (Ph.D.) (Cl)
bilingual assessment—Catholic University of America (Ph.D.) (Cl)
blind rehabilitation—University of North Dakota (Ph.D.) (Cl)
bone marrow transplantation—University of Colorado Denver (Ph.D.) (Cl)
brief dynamic psychotherapy—University of Wisconsin, Madison (Ph.D.) (Cl)
bullying—Wichita State University (Ph.D.) (Cl)
business and psychology—Widener University (Psy.D.) (Cl)
caregiver programs—University of Colorado at Colorado Springs (Ph.D.) (Cl)
child bipolar treatment—University of North Carolina, Chapel Hill (Ph.D.) (Cl)
Christian counseling—Regent University (Psy.D.) (Cl)
college faculty, staff, and students—University of Illinois at Urbana-Champaign (Ph.D.) (Co)
community outpatient clinic—University of Alaska Fairbanks-Anchorage (Ph.D.) (Cl)
community service agencies—Carlos Albizu University, Miami Campus (Psy.D.) (Cl)
co-occurring disorders—Marquette University (Ph.D.) (Co)
co-occurring disorders—Saint Mary's University of Minnesota (Psy.D.) (Co)
creative and expressive arts—Chicago School of Professional Psychology–Chicago Campus (Psy.D.) (Cl)
deaf and hard-of-hearing—Gallaudet University (Ph.D.) (Cl)
developmental education clinics—Hawaii School of Professional Psychology at Argosy University, Hawaii (Psy.D.) (Cl)
diabetes—University of Miami (Ph.D.) (Cl)
disaster—University of Mississippi (Ph.D.) (Cl)
early childhood services—University of Connecticut (Ph.D.) (Cl)
early education/head start/infants—Chicago School of Professional Psychology–Chicago Campus (Psy.D.) (Cl)
East Asian clinic—Harvard University (Ph.D.) (Cl)
elder law—University of Alabama at Tuscaloosa (Ph.D.) (Cl)
emotion focused—Biola University (Psy.D.) (Cl)
emotion focused—Biola University (Ph.D.) (Cl)
emotion regulation therapy—Teachers College, Columbia University (Ph.D.) (Cl)
epilepsy and wada—University of Florida (Ph.D.) (Cl)
existential-humanistic—Pepperdine University (Psy.D.) (Cl)
externalizing disorders—University of South Florida (Ph.D.) (Cl)
factitious disorder—University of Alabama at Tuscaloosa (Ph.D.) (Cl)
family medicine—East Carolina University (Ph.D.) (Cl)

family medicine—Philadelphia College of Osteopathic Medicine (Psy.D.) (Cl)
family reunification residential facilities—Spalding University (Psy.D.) (Cl)
family service agencies—Alliant International University, San Francisco Bay (Psy.D.) (Cl)
fertility clinic—Duke University (Ph.D.) (Cl)
first responders—University of Houston (Ph.D.) (Co)
functional analytic psychotherapy—University of Nevada, Reno (Ph.D.) (Cl)
functional analytic therpay—The University of Montana (Ph.D.) (Cl)
gambling—The University of Memphis (Ph.D.) (Cl)
generalist practice—Widener University (Psy.D.) (Cl)
gifted evaluation—University of Central Florida (Ph.D.) (Cl)
grief—University of Nevada, Reno (Ph.D.) (Cl)
head start—University of Nebraska, Lincoln (Ph.D.) (Cl)
headache—University of Mississippi (Ph.D.) (Cl)
Hispanic studies—Carlos Albizu University, San Juan Campus (Psy.D.) (Cl)
human service/health care systems—University of Illinois at Urbana-Champaign (Ph.D.) (Cl)
human services center—Florida State University (Ph.D.) (Cm)
Indian health services—Oklahoma State University (Ph.D.) (Co)
infant neurodevelopmental—University of Notre Dame (Ph.D.) P(Cl)
inner city populations—Chicago School of Professional Psychology–Chicago Campus (Psy.D.) (Cl)
integrated behavioral healthcare—Syracuse University (Ph.D.) (Cl)
integrative medicine—Vanderbilt University (Ph.D.) (Cl)
intermittent explosive disorder—Temple University (Ph.D.) (Cl)
internal medicine—Philadelphia College of Osteopathic Medicine (Psy.D.) (Cl)
internalizing disorders—University of Miami (Ph.D.) (Cl)
international disaster psychology—University of Denver (Psy.D.) (Cl)
juvenile justice—Vanderbilt University (Ph.D.) (Cl)
juvenile justice/delinquent youth—University of Utah (Ph.D.) (Cl)
Latino psychology—University of Denver (Psy.D.) (Cl)
local agencies—Duquesne University (Ph.D.) (Cl)
long-term care—University of Miami (Ph.D.) (Cl)
loss and trauma group therapy—Michigan State University (Ph.D.) (Cl)
low income—New Mexico State University (Ph.D.) (Co)
medical liaison—University of Maryland, Baltimore County (Ph.D.) (Cl)
meditation/yoga—Miami University (OH) (Ph.D.) (Cl)
mental health administration—Chicago School of Professional Psychology–Chicago Campus (Psy.D.) (Cl)
mentalization-based therapies—Pepperdine University (Psy.D.) (Cl)
mind-body clinical research center—Stony Brook University, State University of New York (Ph.D.) (Cl)
neurological disorders—University of Arizona (Ph.D.) (Cl)
nursing facility—University of Florida (Ph.D.) (Co)
outcome based therapy—University of Nebraska, Lincoln (Ph.D.) (Co)
Parkinson and DBS—University of Florida (Ph.D.) (Cl)
peer relations—University of Miami (Ph.D.) (Cl)
phobia—Hofstra University (Ph.D.) (Cl)
post-partum depression—La Salle University (Psy.D.) (Cl)
pre-/post-partum psychopathology—University of Iowa (Ph.D.) (Cl)
pre-surgical evaluation—Chicago School of Professional Psychology–Chicago Campus (Psy.D.) (Cl)
psychiatric hospitals—Adler University–Chicago (Psy.D.) (Cl)
psychoeducational (coping skills) training—University of Washington (Ph.D.) (Cl)
psychotherapy and clinical interventions—Pace University (Psy.D.) (Cm)
rational-emotive therapy—University of Utah (Ph.D.) (Cl)
research protocol assessment and prevention—University of Missouri, Columbia (Ph.D.) (Cl)
residential treatment centers—California Lutheran University (Psy.D.) (Cl)
school readiness—Florida International University (Ph.D.) (Cl)
selective mutism—Florida International University (Ph.D.) (Cl)
selective mutism—Northern Illinois University (Ph.D.) (Cl)
short-term psychotherapies—Adelphi University (Ph.D.) (Cl)

short-term psychotherapy—Illinois School of Professional Psychology at Argosy University, Chicago (Psy.D.) (Cl)
short-term therapy—Long Island University, C.W. Post Campus (Psy.D.) (Cl)
social justice—The Wright Institute (Psy.D.) (Cl)
social skills training—University of Illinois at Urbana-Champaign (Ph.D.) (Cl)
socioeconomic disadvantage—Ohio University (Ph.D.) (Cl)
special education—University of Virginia (Ph.D.) (Cm)
specialized service centers—Alliant International University, Los Angeles (Ph.D.) (Cl)
student health center—East Tennessee State University (Ph.D.) (Cl)
student health service—Southern Illinois University Carbondale (Ph.D.) (Co)
student wellness center—Utah State University (Ph.D.) (Cm)
surgical centers—Arizona School of Professional Psychology at Argosy University, Phoenix (Psy.D.) (Cl)
therapeutic day schools—Roosevelt University (Psy.D.) (Cl)
youth and family agencies—Texas Woman's University (Ph.D.) (Co)

APPENDIX G

PROGRAM CONCENTRATIONS AND TRACKS

Adult/Adult Clinical

Antioch University New England (Psy.D.) (Cl)
Auburn University (Ph.D.) (Cl)
Boston University (Ph.D.) (Cl)
Case Western Reserve University (Ph.D.) (Cl)
Catholic University of America (Ph.D.) (Cl)
Duke University (Ph.D.) (Cl)
Eastern Michigan University (Ph.D.) (Cl)
George Washington University (Psy.D.) (Cl)
Georgia School of Professional Psychology at Argosy University, Atlanta (Psy.D.) (Cl)
Howard University (Ph.D.) (Cl)
Kent State University (Ph.D.) (Cl)
Marquette University (Ph.D.) (Cl)
Miami University (OH) (Ph.D.) (Cl)
Northwestern University Feinberg School of Medicine (Ph.D.) (Cl)
Pacific University, Oregon (Psy.D.) (Cl)
Pennsylvania State University (Ph.D.) (Cl)
Southern Illinois University Carbondale (Ph.D.) (Cl)
Spalding University (Psy.D.) (Cl)
Syracuse University (Ph.D.) (Cl)
The City College of New York, The Graduate Center, CUNY (Ph.D.) (Cl)
The Ohio State University (Ph.D.) (Cl)
University of Alabama at Birmingham (Ph.D.) (Cl)
University of California, Santa Barbara (Ph.D.) (Cm)
University of Central Florida (Ph.D.) (Cl)
University of Georgia (Ph.D.) (Cl)
University of Houston (Ph.D.) (Cl)
University of Indianapolis (Psy.D.) (Cl)
University of Iowa (Ph.D.) (Cl)
University of Massachusetts Amherst (Ph.D.) (Cl)
University of Miami (Ph.D.) (Cl)
University of Minnesota (Ph.D.) (Cl)
University of Missouri, Columbia (Ph.D.) (Cl)
University of Nebraska, Lincoln (Ph.D.) (Cl)
University of North Carolina, Chapel Hill (Ph.D.) (Cl)
University of North Carolina, Greensboro (Ph.D.) (Cl)
University of Pittsburgh (Ph.D.) (Cl)
University of Southern Mississippi (Ph.D.) (Cl)
University of Utah (Ph.D.) (Cl)
University of Washington (Ph.D.) (Cl)
Wright State University (Psy.D.) (Cl)

Assessment/Testing

Central Michigan University (Ph.D.) (Cl)
Eastern Michigan University (Ph.D.) (Cl)
George Washington University (Psy.D.) (Cl)
Kent State University (Ph.D.) (Cl)
Pepperdine University (Psy.D.) (Cl)
Seton Hall University (Ph.D.) (Co)
University of Denver (Psy.D.) (Cl)
University of Georgia (Ph.D.) (Co)
Yeshiva University (Psy.D.) (Cl)

Behavioral Analysis/Therapy

Eastern Michigan University (Ph.D.) (Cl)
University of Denver (Psy.D.) (Cl)
West Virginia University (Ph.D.) (Cl)

Career/Vocational Psychology

University of Missouri, Columbia (Ph.D.) (Co)

Child & Family

Alliant International University, San Diego (Ph.D.) (Cl)
Alliant International University, San Diego (Psy.D.) (Cl)
Alliant International University, San Francisco Bay (Psy.D.) (Cl)
American School of Professional Psychology at Argosy University, Washington, DC (Psy.D.) (Cl)
Brigham Young University (Ph.D.) (Cl)
Catholic University of America (Ph.D.) (Cl)
Florida Institute of Technology (Psy.D.) (Cl)
Fordham University (Ph.D.) (Cl)
Georgia School of Professional Psychology at Argosy University, Atlanta (Psy.D.) (Cl)
Marquette University (Ph.D.) (Cl)
Miami University (OH) (Ph.D.) (Cl)
Nova Southeastern University (Ph.D.) (Cl)
Nova Southeastern University (Psy.D.) (Cl)
Palo Alto University (Ph.D.) (Cl)
Southern Methodist University (Ph.D.) (Cl)
Spalding University (Psy.D.) (Cl)
University of Connecticut (Ph.D.) (Cl)
University of Houston (Ph.D.) (Cl)
University of Massachusetts Amherst (Ph.D.) (Cl)
University of Rhode Island (Ph.D.) (Cl)
University of South Carolina (Ph.D.) (Cl)
University of Southern California (Ph.D.) (Cl)
University of Utah (Ph.D.) (Cl)
William James College (Psy.D.) (Cl)
Xavier University (Psy.D.) (Cl)

Child Clinical/Pediatric

Adler University–Chicago (Psy.D.) (Cl)
American School of Professional Psychology–Southern California at Argosy University, Orange County (Psy.D.) (Cl)
Antioch University New England (Psy.D.) (Cl)
Arizona State University (Ph.D.) (Cl)
Auburn University (Ph.D.) (Cl)
Boston University (Ph.D.) (Cl)
Bowling Green State University (Ph.D.) (Cl)
Carlos Albizu University, Miami Campus (Psy.D.) (Cl)
Case Western Reserve University (Ph.D.) (Cl)
DePaul University (Ph.D.) (Cl)
Drexel University (Ph.D.) (Cl)
Duke University (Ph.D.) (Cl)
Eastern Michigan University (Ph.D.) (Cl)
Florida International University (Ph.D.) (Cl)
Florida School of Professional Psychology at Argosy University (Psy.D.) (Cl)
George Washington University (Psy.D.) (Cl)
Howard University (Ph.D.) (Cl)
Illinois School of Professional Psychology at Argosy University, Chicago (Psy.D.) (Cl)
Indiana State University (Psy.D.) (Cl)
Indiana University of Pennsylvania (Psy.D.) (Cl)
Kent State University (Ph.D.) (Cl)
La Salle University (Psy.D.) (Cl)
Loma Linda University (Ph.D.) (Cl)
Loma Linda University (Psy.D.) (Cl)
Loyola University Chicago (Ph.D.) (Cl)
Midwestern University (Psy.D.) (Cl)
Minnesota School of Professional Psychology at Argosy University (Psy.D.) (Cl)
Northwestern University Feinberg School of Medicine (Ph.D.) (Cl)
Ohio University (Ph.D.) (Cl)
Oklahoma State University (Ph.D.) (Cl)
Pacific University, Oregon (Psy.D.) (Cl)
Palo Alto University (Psy.D.) (Cl)
Pennsylvania State University (Ph.D.) (Cl)
Regent University (Psy.D.) (Cl)
Southern Illinois University Carbondale (Ph.D.) (Cl)
St. John's University (Ph.D.) (Cl)
Syracuse University (Ph.D.) (Cl)
Temple University (Ph.D.) (Cl)
The City College of New York, The Graduate Center, CUNY (Ph.D.) (Cl)
The Ohio State University (Ph.D.) (Cl)
The University of Memphis (Ph.D.) (Cl)
The University of Montana (Ph.D.) (Cl)
University of Alabama at Tuscaloosa (Ph.D.) (Cl)
University of California, Los Angeles (Ph.D.) (Cl)
University of California, Santa Barbara (Ph.D.) (Cm)
University of Central Florida (Ph.D.) (Cl)
University of Denver (Psy.D.) (Cl)
University of Florida (Ph.D.) (Cl)
University of Georgia (Ph.D.) (Cl)
University of Hartford (Psy.D.) (Cl)
University of Indianapolis (Psy.D.) (Cl)
University of Kansas–Child (Ph.D.) (Cl)
University of Maine (Ph.D.) (Cl)
University of Maryland, Baltimore County (Ph.D.) (Cl)
University of Miami (Ph.D.) (Cl)
University of Minnesota (Ph.D.) (Cl)
University of Missouri, Columbia (Ph.D.) (Cl)
University of Nebraska, Lincoln (Ph.D.) (Cl)

University of North Carolina, Chapel Hill (Ph.D.) (Cl)
University of North Carolina, Greensboro (Ph.D.) (Cl)
University of North Dakota (Ph.D.) (Co)
University of North Texas (Ph.D.) (Co)
University of Pittsburgh (Ph.D.) (Cl)
University of South Florida (Ph.D.) (Cl)
University of Southern Mississippi (Ph.D.) (Cl)
University of Texas Southwestern Medical Center (Ph.D.) (Cl)
University of Vermont (Ph.D.) (Cl)
University of Virginia (Ph.D.) (Cm)
University of Washington (Ph.D.) (Cl)
Utah State University (Ph.D.) (Cm)
Virginia Commonwealth University (Ph.D.) (Cl)
Wayne State University (Ph.D.) (Cl)
West Virginia University (Ph.D.) (Cl)
Wright State University (Psy.D.) (Cl)

Cognitive/Cognitive-Behavioral

Pepperdine University (Psy.D.) (Cl)
Yeshiva University (Psy.D.) (Cl)
Yeshiva University (Psy.D.) (Cm)

Community

Arizona State University (Ph.D.) (Cl)
Bowling Green State University (Ph.D.) (Cl)
DePaul University (Ph.D.) (Cl)
Fuller Theological Seminary (Ph.D.) (Cl)
Fuller Theological Seminary (Psy.D.) (Cl)
Georgia State University (Ph.D.) (Cl)
Miami University (OH) (Ph.D.) (Cl)
Palo Alto University (Ph.D.) (Cl)
Pepperdine University (Psy.D.) (Cl)
Rutgers–The State University of New Jersey (Psy.D.) (Cl)
University of Alaska Fairbanks–Anchorage (Ph.D.) (Cl)
University of Maryland, Baltimore County (Ph.D.) (Cl)
University of North Carolina at Charlotte (Ph.D.) (Cl)
University of South Carolina (Ph.D.) (Cl)
Wayne State University (Ph.D.) (Cl)

Family/Marriage & Family

Alliant International University, Los Angeles (Ph.D.) (Cl)
Alliant International University, Los Angeles (Psy.D.) (Cl)
Azusa Pacific University (Psy.D.) (Cl)
Ball State University (Ph.D.) (Co)
California Lutheran University (Psy.D.) (Cl)
Central Michigan University (Ph.D.) (Cl)
Florida School of Professional Psychology at Argosy University (Psy.D.) (Cl)
Fuller Theological Seminary (Ph.D.) (Cl)
Fuller Theological Seminary (Psy.D.) (Cl)
Loma Linda University (Ph.D.) (Cl)
Loma Linda University (Psy.D.) (Cl)
Pepperdine University (Psy.D.) (Cl)
Ponce Health Sciences University (Ph.D.) (Cl)
Ponce Health Sciences University (Psy.D.) (Cl)
Regent University (Psy.D.) (Cl)
Seton Hall University (Ph.D.) (Co)
The University of Montana (Ph.D.) (Cl)
University of California, Los Angeles (Ph.D.) (Cl)
University of Denver (Psy.D.) (Cl)
University of Nebraska, Lincoln (Ph.D.) (Co)
Yeshiva University (Psy.D.) (Cl)

Forensic/Psychology & Law

Alliant International University, Fresno (Ph.D.) (Cl)
Alliant International University, Fresno (Psy.D.) (Cl)
Alliant International University, Sacramento (Psy.D.) (Cl)
Alliant International University, San Diego (Ph.D.) (Cl)
Alliant International University, San Diego (Psy.D.) (Cl)
American School of Professional Psychology at Argosy University, Washington, DC (Psy.D.) (Cl)
American School of Professional Psychology–Southern California at Argosy University, Orange County (Psy.D.) (Cl)
Azusa Pacific University (Psy.D.) (Cl)
California Lutheran University (Psy.D.) (Cl)
Carlos Albizu University, Miami Campus (Psy.D.) (Cl)
Chicago School of Professional Psychology—Washington, DC Campus (Psy.D.) (Cl)
Drexel University (Ph.D.) (Cl)
Fairleigh Dickinson University (Ph.D.) (Cl)
Fielding Graduate University (Ph.D.) (Cl)
Florida Institute of Technology (Psy.D.) (Cl)
Fordham University (Ph.D.) (Cl)
Illinois School of Professional Psychology at Argosy University, Chicago (Psy.D.) (Cl)
Indiana State University (Psy.D.) (Cl)
Indiana University of Pennsylvania (Psy.D.) (Cl)
John Jay College of Criminal Justice & The Graduate Center, CUNY (Ph.D.) (Cl)
Loma Linda University (Ph.D.) (Cl)

Loma Linda University (Psy.D.) (Cl)
Minnesota School of Professional Psychology at Argosy University (Psy.D.) (Cl)
Northwestern University Feinberg School of Medicine (Ph.D.) (Cl)
Nova Southeastern University (Ph.D.) (Cl)
Nova Southeastern University (Psy.D.) (Cl)
Pacific University, Oregon (Psy.D.) (Cl)
Palo Alto University (Ph.D.) (Cl)
Pepperdine University (Psy.D.) (Cl)
Ponce Health Sciences University (Ph.D.) (Cl)
Ponce Health Sciences University (Psy.D.) (Cl)
Regent University (Psy.D.) (Cl)
Sam Houston State University (Ph.D.) (Cl)
Spalding University (Psy.D.) (Cl)
University of Alabama at Tuscaloosa (Ph.D.) (Cl)
University of Denver (Psy.D.) (Cl)
University of Nebraska, Lincoln (Ph.D.) (Cl)
University of North Texas (Ph.D.) (Cl)
William James College (Psy.D.) (Cl)
Wright State University (Psy.D.) (Cl)

Gender Studies

Texas Woman's University (Ph.D.) (Co)
University of Denver (Psy.D.) (Cl)
University of Nebraska, Lincoln (Ph.D.) (Co)

Generalist

Carlos Albizu University, Miami Campus (Psy.D.) (Cl)
Georgia State University (Ph.D.) (Cl)
La Salle University (Psy.D.) (Cl)
Marshall University (Psy.D.) (Cl)
St. John's University (Ph.D.) (Cl)
Tennessee State University (Ph.D.) (Co)
University of Cincinnati (Ph.D.) (Cl)
University of Hartford (Psy.D.) (Cl)
University of Kansas (Ph.D.) (Cl)
University of Maine (Ph.D.) (Cl)

Geropsychology/Aging

Florida School of Professional Psychology at Argosy University (Psy.D.) (Cl)
University of Alabama at Tuscaloosa (Ph.D.) (Cl)
University of Colorado at Colorado Springs (Ph.D.) (Cl)
University of Southern California (Ph.D.) (Cl)
William James College (Psy.D.) (Cl)
Yeshiva University (Ph.D.) (Cl)
Yeshiva University (Psy.D.) (Cl)

Health Psychology/Behavioral Medicine

Alliant International University, Fresno (Ph.D.) (Cl)
Alliant International University, Los Angeles (Ph.D.) (Cl)
Alliant International University, Los Angeles (Psy.D.) (Cl)
Alliant International University, San Diego (Ph.D.) (Cl)
Alliant International University, San Diego (Psy.D.) (Cl)
American School of Professional Psychology at Argosy University, Washington, DC (Psy.D.) (Cl)
Antioch University New England (Psy.D.) (Cl)
Arizona State University (Ph.D.) (Cl)
Ball State University (Ph.D.) (Co)
Bowling Green State University (Ph.D.) (Cl)
Brigham Young University (Ph.D.) (Cl)
Carlos Albizu University, Miami Campus (Psy.D.) (Cl)
Carlos Albizu University, San Juan Campus (Ph.D.) (Cl)
Drexel University (Ph.D.) (Cl)
Duke University (Ph.D.) (Cl)
East Carolina University (Ph.D.) (Cl)
Eastern Michigan University (Ph.D.) (Cl)
Fielding Graduate University (Ph.D.) (Cl)
Florida Institute of Technology (Psy.D.) (Cl)
Fordham University (Ph.D.) (Cl)
Georgia School of Professional Psychology at Argosy University, Atlanta (Psy.D.) (Cl)
Howard University (Ph.D.) (Cl)
Indiana State University (Psy.D.) (Cl)
Indiana University–Purdue University Indianapolis (Ph.D.) (Cl)
Indiana University of Pennsylvania (Psy.D.) (Cl)
Kent State University (Ph.D.) (Cl)
La Salle University (Psy.D.) (Cl)
Loma Linda University (Ph.D.) (Cl)
Loma Linda University (Psy.D.) (Cl)
Minnesota School of Professional Psychology at Argosy University (Psy.D.) (Cl)
New Mexico State University (Ph.D.) (Co)
Northwestern University Feinberg School of Medicine (Ph.D.) (Cl)
Nova Southeastern University (Ph.D.) (Cl)
Nova Southeastern University (Psy.D.) (Cl)
Ohio University (Ph.D.) (Cl)
Oklahoma State University (Ph.D.) (Cl)
Our Lady of the Lake University (Psy.D.) (Co)
Pacific University, Oregon (Psy.D.) (Cl)
Palo Alto University (Ph.D.) (Cl)
Ponce Health Sciences University (Ph.D.) (Cl)
Ponce Health Sciences University (Psy.D.) (Cl)

Regent University (Psy.D.) (Cl)
San Diego State University–UC San Diego (Ph.D.) (Cl)
Southern Methodist University (Ph.D.) (Cl)
Spalding University (Psy.D.) (Cl)
Syracuse University (Ph.D.) (Cl)
The Ohio State University (Ph.D.) (Cl)
The University of Memphis (Ph.D.) (Cl)
University of Alabama at Tuscaloosa (Ph.D.) (Cl)
University of California, Los Angeles (Ph.D.) (Cl)
University of Cincinnati (Ph.D.) (Cl)
University of Colorado Denver (Ph.D.) (Cl)
University of Connecticut (Ph.D.) (Cl)
University of Florida (Ph.D.) (Cl)
University of Georgia (Ph.D.) (Co)
University of Houston (Ph.D.) (Co)
University of Indianapolis (Psy.D.) (Cl)
University of Iowa (Ph.D.) (Cl)
University of Kansas (Ph.D.) (Cl)
University of Kentucky (Ph.D.) (Cl)
University of Maryland, Baltimore County (Ph.D.) (Cl)
University of Miami (Ph.D.) (Cl)
University of Missouri Kansas City (Ph.D.) (Cl)
University of Missouri, St. Louis (Ph.D.) (Cl)
University of New Mexico (Ph.D.) (Cl)
University of North Carolina at Charlotte (Ph.D.) (Cl)
University of North Texas (Ph.D.) (Cl)
University of Pittsburgh (Ph.D.) (Cl)
University of Rhode Island (Ph.D.) (Cl)
University of South Florida (Ph.D.) (Cl)
University of Texas Southwestern Medical Center (Ph.D.) (Cl)
University of Utah (Ph.D.) (Cl)
University of Wyoming (Ph.D.) (Cl)
Utah State University (Ph.D.) (Cm)
Virginia Commonwealth University (Ph.D.) (Cl)
Virginia Commonwealth University (Ph.D.) (Co)
Wayne State University (Ph.D.) (Cl)
William James College (Psy.D.) (Cl)
Wright State University (Psy.D.) (Cl)

Integrative Psychology/Psychotherapy

Alliant International University, San Diego (Psy.D.) (Cl)
Alliant International University, San Francisco Bay (Psy.D.) (Cl)
American School of Professional Psychology at Argosy University, Washington, DC (Psy.D.) (Cl)
New Mexico State University (Ph.D.) (Co)
Seton Hall University (Ph.D.) (Co)

Latino Psychology/Spanish Bilingual (also see Multicultural)

Our Lady of the Lake University (Psy.D.) (Co)
Texas A&M University (Ph.D.) (Co)
University of Denver (Psy.D.) (Cl)
University of Oregon (Ph.D.) (Co)
William James College (Psy.D.) (Cl)

Lifespan/Human Developmental

West Virginia University (Ph.D.) (Cl)
Xavier University (Psy.D.) (Cl)

Military Psychology

Adler University–Chicago (Psy.D.) (Cl)
Uniformed Services University of the Health Sciences (Ph.D.) (Cl)
University of Denver (Psy.D.) (Cl)
West Virginia University (Ph.D.) (Co)
William James College (Psy.D.) (Cl)

Multicultural/Cross-Cultural/Diversity

Alliant International University, Los Angeles (Ph.D.) (Cl)
Alliant International University, Los Angeles (Psy.D.) (Cl)
Alliant International University, San Diego (Psy.D.) (Cl)
American School of Professional Psychology at Argosy University, Washington, DC (Psy.D.) (Cl)
Arizona School of Professional Psychology at Argosy University, Phoenix (Psy.D.) (Cl)
Ball State University (Ph.D.) (Co)
Catholic University of America (Ph.D.) (Cl)
Illinois School of Professional Psychology at Argosy University, Chicago (Psy.D.) (Cl)
Indiana University–Bloomington (Ph.D.) (Co)
Loma Linda University (Ph.D.) (Cl)
Loma Linda University (Psy.D.) (Cl)
New Mexico State University (Ph.D.) (Co)
Nova Southeastern University (Ph.D.) (Cl)
Nova Southeastern University (Psy.D.) (Cl)
Palo Alto University (Ph.D.) (Cl)
Radford University (Psy.D.) (Co)
Rutgers–The State University of New Jersey (Psy.D.) (Cl)
Seton Hall University (Ph.D.) (Co)
Texas A&M University (Ph.D.) (Co)
Texas Woman's University (Ph.D.) (Co)
The University of Memphis (Ph.D.) (Co)

University of California, Los Angeles (Ph.D.) (Cl)
University of Missouri, Columbia (Ph.D.) (Co)
University of Nebraska, Lincoln (Ph.D.) (Co)
University of Rhode Island (Ph.D.) (Cl)
Utah State University (Ph.D.) (Cm)

Neuropsychology

American School of Professional Psychology at Argosy University, Washington, DC (Psy.D.) (Cl)
Arizona School of Professional Psychology at Argosy University, Phoenix (Psy.D.) (Cl)
Boston University (Ph.D.) (Cl)
Brigham Young University (Ph.D.) (Cl)
Carlos Albizu University, Miami Campus (Psy.D.) (Cl)
Carlos Albizu University, San Juan Campus (Ph.D.) (Cl)
Drexel University (Ph.D.) (Cl)
Eastern Michigan University (Ph.D.) (Cl)
Fielding Graduate University (Ph.D.) (Cl)
Florida Institute of Technology (Psy.D.) (Cl)
Florida School of Professional Psychology at Argosy University (Psy.D.) (Cl)
Fordham University (Ph.D.) (Cl)
Fuller Theological Seminary (Ph.D.) (Cl)
Fuller Theological Seminary (Psy.D.) (Cl)
Georgia School of Professional Psychology at Argosy University, Atlanta (Psy.D.) (Cl)
Georgia State University (Ph.D.) (Cl)
Illinois School of Professional Psychology at Argosy University, Chicago (Psy.D.) (Cl)
Indiana University of Pennsylvania (Psy.D.) (Cl)
John F. Kennedy University (Psy.D.) (Cl)
Loma Linda University (Ph.D.) (Cl)
Loma Linda University (Psy.D.) (Cl)
Loyola University Chicago (Ph.D.) (Cl)
Marquette University (Ph.D.) (Cl)
Midwestern University–Glendale Campus (Psy.D.) (Cl)
Northwestern University Feinberg School of Medicine (Ph.D.) (Cl)
Nova Southeastern University (Ph.D.) (Cl)
Nova Southeastern University (Psy.D.) (Cl)
Ohio University (Ph.D.) (Cl)
Pacific University, Oregon (Psy.D.) (Cl)
Palo Alto University (Ph.D.) (Cl)
Queens College and The Graduate Center, City University of New York (Ph.D.) (Cl)
San Diego State University–UC San Diego (Ph.D.) (Cl)
The University of Montana (Ph.D.) (Cl)
University of Cincinnati (Ph.D.) (Cl)
University of Connecticut (Ph.D.) (Cl)
University of Florida (Ph.D.) (Cl)
University of Georgia (Ph.D.) (Cl)
University of Houston (Ph.D.) (Cl)
University of Iowa (Ph.D.) (Cl)
University of Kentucky (Ph.D.) (Cl)
University of Maine (Ph.D.) (Cl)
University of Nevada Las Vegas (Ph.D.) (Cl)
University of North Texas (Ph.D.) (Cl)
University of Rhode Island (Ph.D.) (Cl)
University of Southern California (Ph.D.) (Cl)
University of Texas Southwestern Medical Center (Ph.D.) (Cl)
University of Utah (Ph.D.) (Cl)
Wayne State University (Ph.D.) (Cl)
Widener University (Psy.D.) (Cl)
Wright State University (Psy.D.) (Cl)
Yeshiva University (Ph.D.) (Cl)
Yeshiva University (Psy.D.) (Cl)

Neuroscience

Florida International University (Ph.D.) (Cl)
Ponce Health Sciences University (Ph.D.) (Cl)
Ponce Health Sciences University (Psy.D.) (Cl)
Temple University (Ph.D.) (Cl)
University of Colorado Boulder (Ph.D.) (Cl)
University of Florida (Ph.D.) (Cl)
University of Texas at Austin (Ph.D.) (Cl)
West Virginia University (Ph.D.) (Cl)

Organizational/Consulting

Azusa Pacific University (Psy.D.) (Cl)

Primary Care Psychology

Adler University–Chicago (Psy.D.) (Cl)

Psychoanalytic/Psychodynamic Therapy

Alliant International University, San Diego (Ph.D.) (Cl)
Alliant International University, San Diego (Psy.D.) (Cl)
Illinois School of Professional Psychology at Argosy University, Chicago (Psy.D.) (Cl)
Nova Southeastern University (Ph.D.) (Cl)
Nova Southeastern University (Psy.D.) (Cl)
Pepperdine University (Psy.D.) (Cl)
Yeshiva University (Psy.D.) (Cl)
Yeshiva University (Psy.D.) (Cm)

Psychopathology/Experimental Psychopathology

Southern Methodist University (Ph.D.) (Cl)
University of South Florida (Ph.D.) (Cl)
University of Vermont (Ph.D.) (Cl)

Quantitative/Statistics

Florida International University (Ph.D.) (Cl)
George Mason University (Ph.D.) (Cl)
Ohio University (Ph.D.) (Cl)
Temple University (Ph.D.) (Cl)
University of Missouri, Columbia (Ph.D.) (Cl)
University of Missouri, Columbia (Ph.D.) (Co)
University of New Mexico (Ph.D.) (Cl)

School/Educational

Florida State University (Ph.D.) (Cm)
Miami University (OH) (Ph.D.) (Cl)
University at Buffalo, State University of New York (Ph.D.) (Cm)
University of California, Santa Barbara (Ph.D.) (Cm)
University of Virginia (Ph.D.) (Cm)
Widener University (Psy.D.) (Cl)

Social Justice

Alliant International University, San Francisco Bay (Psy.D.) (Cl)
Ball State University (Ph.D.) (Co)
Radford University (Psy.D.) (Co)
The University of Memphis (Ph.D.) (Co)

Sports Psychology

John F. Kennedy University (Psy.D.) (Cl)
University of Denver (Psy.D.) (Cl)
University of Missouri, Columbia (Ph.D.) (Co)
University of North Texas (Ph.D.) (Co)

Substance Abuse/Addiction

Adler University–Chicago (Psy.D.) (Cl)
Syracuse University (Ph.D.) (Cl)
University of South Florida (Ph.D.) (Cl)
Yeshiva University (Ph.D.) (Cl)

Supervision/Clinical Supervision

New Mexico State University (Ph.D.) (Co)
University of Georgia (Ph.D.) (Co)
University of Missouri, Columbia (Ph.D.) (Co)
University of North Dakota (Ph.D.) (Co)

Trauma/Disaster

Adler University–Chicago (Psy.D.) (Cl)
Minnesota School of Professional Psychology at Argosy University (Psy.D.) (Cl)
Palo Alto University (Ph.D.) (Cl)
The University of South Dakota (Ph.D.) (Cl)
University of Colorado at Colorado Springs (Ph.D.) (Cl)
University of Missouri, St. Louis (Ph.D.) (Cl)

Miscellaneous/Other

acceptance and commitment therapy—California Lutheran University (Psy.D.) (Cl)
advanced Adlerian psychotherapy—Adler University–Chicago (Psy.D.) (Cl)
African and Caribbean mental health—William James College (Psy.D.) (Cl)
applied child—Long Island University, C.W. Post Campus (Psy.D.) (Cl)
applied methodology—University of Rhode Island (Ph.D.) (Cl)
behavioral genetics—University of Colorado Boulder (Ph.D.) (Cl)
biofeedback—Widener University (Psy.D.) (Cl)
client-centered/experiential psychotherapies—Illinois School of Professional Psychology at Argosy University, Chicago (Psy.D.) (Cl)
consultation—University of North Dakota (Ph.D.) (Co)
consulting psychology—Regent University (Psy.D.) (Cl)
contextual behavioral science—Utah State University (Ph.D.) (Cm)
counseling—University of California, Santa Barbara (Ph.D.) (Cm)
counseling psychology—University at Buffalo, State University of New York (Ph.D.) (Cm)
counseling psychology—Florida State University (Ph.D.) (Cm)
cultural–ecological interventions—Pepperdine University (Psy.D.) (Cl)
dialectical behavior therapy—California Lutheran University (Psy.D.) (Cl)
ecosystemic child—Alliant International University, Fresno (Psy.D.) (Cl)
ecosystemic child—Alliant International University, Fresno (Ph.D.) (Cl)
evidence-based practice—Radford University (Psy.D.) (Co)

existential–humanistic—Pepperdine University (Psy.D.) (Cl)
experimental psychopathology—San Diego State University–UC San Diego (Ph.D.) (Cl)
family violence—Long Island University, C.W. Post Campus (Psy.D.) (Cl)
global mental health—William James College (Psy.D.) (Cl)
grant writing—University of North Dakota (Ph.D.) (Co)
human sexuality—Indiana University–Bloomington (Ph.D.) (Co)
international disaster psychology—University of Denver (Psy.D.) (Cl)
LGBTQ—Palo Alto University (Ph.D.) (Cl)
long-term mental illness—Nova Southeastern University (Ph.D.) (Cl)
long-term mental illness—Nova Southeastern University (Psy.D.) (Cl)
oncology psychology—University of Denver (Psy.D.) (Cl)
outcome research—Texas A&M University (Ph.D.) (Co)
parent and infant mental health—Fielding Graduate University (Ph.D.) (Cl)
policy—Northwestern University Feinberg School of Medicine (Ph.D.) (Cl)
preparing future faculty—University of Georgia (Ph.D.) (Co)
psychotherapy research—The University of Memphis (Ph.D.) (Cl)
public health—Indiana University–Bloomington (Ph.D.) (Co)
public health (master's degree)—University of Southern California (Ph.D.) (Cl)
rehabilitation—Illinois Institute of Technology (Ph.D.) (Cl)
research methods/statistics—Yeshiva University (Ph.D.) (Cl)
rural integrated primary care—East Tennessee State University (Ph.D.) (Cl)
rural mental health—Radford University (Psy.D.) (Co)
rural/multicultural psychology—Utah State University (Ph.D.) (Cm)
scientist–practitioner training model—The New School (Ph.D.) (Cl)
serious mental illness—Long Island University, C.W. Post Campus (Psy.D.) (Cl)
severe adult psychopathology—University of California, Los Angeles (Ph.D.) (Cl)
severe chronic and persistent illness—Xavier University (Psy.D.) (Cl)
severe mental illness—Indiana University–Purdue University Indianapolis (Ph.D.) (Cl)
telepsychology—Texas A&M University (Ph.D.) (Co)
violence prevention—Fielding Graduate University (Ph.D.) (Cl)
vocational—Ball State University (Ph.D.) (Co)
women and diversity studies—University of Missouri, St. Louis (Ph.D.) (Cl)

REFERENCES

Actkinson, T. R. (2000, Winter). Master's and myth. *Eye on Psi Chi, 4*, 19–25.

American Psychological Association. (1986). *Careers in psychology*. Washington, DC: Author.

American Psychological Association. (2017). *Ethical principles of psychologists and code of conduct*. Available online at www.apa.org/ethics/code/

American Psychological Association. (2015). *2014 APAGS debt survey*. Washington, DC: Author.

American Psychological Association. (2016). *Graduate study in psychology, 2016 edition*. Washington, DC: Author.

American Psychological Association Center for Workforce Studies. (2009). *2007 doctorate employment survey*. Washington, DC: Author.

American Psychological Association Center for Workforce Studies. (2010). *2009–2010 tuition costs for master's- and doctoral-level students in U.S. and Canadian departments of psychology*. Washington DC: Author.

American Psychological Association Center for Workforce Studies. (2011). *2009 doctorate employment survey*. Washington, DC: Author.

Anderson, N. B. (2009). Rebalancing the internship imbalance. *Monitor on Psychology, 40*(6), 9.

Anderson, N., & Shackleton, V. (1990). Decision making in the graduate selection interview: A field study. *Journal of Occupational Psychology, 63*, 63–76.

Angulo, A. J. (2016). *Diploma mill$: How for-profit colleges stiffed students, taxpayers, and the American dream*. Baltimore: John Hopkins University Press.

Appleby, D. C., & Appleby, K. M. (2004). Kisses of death in the graduate school application process. *Teaching of Psychology, 33*, 19–24.

Appleby, D., Keenan, J., & Mauer, B. (1999, Spring). Applicant characteristics valued by graduate programs in psychology. *Eye on Psi Chi, 3*, 39.

Asher, D. (2012). *Graduate admissions essays: Write your way into the graduate program of your choice* (4th ed.). Berkeley, CA: Ten Speed Press.

Association of American Medical Colleges. (2016). *The official guide to medical school admissions 2016: How to prepare for and apply to medical school*. Association of American Medical Colleges.

Association of State and Provincial Psychology Boards. (2016). *Handbook on licensing and certification requirements*. Retrieved from www.asppb.net/

Astin, A. W., Green, K. C., & Korn, W. S. (1987). *The American freshman: Twenty-year trends 1966–85*. University of California, Cooperative Institutional Research Program, American Council on Education.

Ault, R. L. (1993). To waive or not to waive? Students' misconceptions about the confidentiality choice for letters of recommendation. *Teaching of Psychology, 20*, 44–45.

Baker, T. B. & McFall, R. M. (2014). The promise of science-based training and application in psychological clinical science. *Psychotherapy, 51*, 482–486.

Baker, T. B., McFall, R. M., & Shoham, V. (2008). Current status and future prospects of clinical psychology: Toward a scientifically principled approach to mental and behavioral health care. *Perspectives on Psychological Science in the Public Interest, 9*(2), 67–103.

Bartsch, R. A., Warren, T. D., Sharp, A. D., & Green, M. A. (2003). Assessment of psychology graduate program information on the Web. *Teaching of Psychology, 30*, 167–170.

Bechtoldt, H., Norcross, J. C., Wyckoff, L. A., Pokrywa,

M. L., & Campbell, L. F. (2001). Theoretical orientations and employment settings of clinical and counseling psychologists: A comparative study. *The Clinical Psychologist, 54*(1), 3–6.

Bendersky, K., Isaac, W. L., Stover, J. H., & Zook, J. M. (2008). Psychology students and online graduate programs: A need to re-examine undergraduate advisement. *Teaching of Psychology, 35*, 38–41.

Bernal, M. E., Sirolli, A. A., Weisser, S. K., Ruiz, J. A., Chamberlain, V. J., & Knight, G. P. (1999). Relevance of multicultural training to students' applications to clinical psychology programs. *Cultural Diversity and Ethnic Minority Psychology, 5*, 43–55.

Bernstein, B. L., & Kerr, B. (1993). Counseling psychology and the scientist–practitioner model: Implementation and implications. *The Counseling Psychologist, 21*, 136–151.

Bersoff, D. N., Goodman-Delahunty, J., Grisso, J. T., Hans, V. P., Poythress, N. G., & Roesch, R. G. (1997). Training in law and psychology: Models from the Villanova Conference. *American Psychologist, 52*, 1301–1310.

Beutler, L. E., & Fisher, D. (1994). Combined specialty training in counseling, clinical, and school psychology: An idea whose time has returned. *Professional Psychology: Research and Practice, 25*, 62–69.

Biaggio, M., Orchard, S., Larson, J., Petrino, K., & Mihara, R. (2003). Guidelines for gay/lesbian/bisexual-affirmative educational practices in graduate psychology programs. *Professional Psychology: Research & Practice, 34*, 548–554.

Boitano, J. J. (1999, August). *Graduate training in neuroscience*. Paper presented at the 107th annual convention of the American Psychological Association, Boston, MA.

Bolles, R. N. (2013). *What color is your parachute? A practical manual for job-hunters and career-changers*. Berkeley, CA: Ten Speed Press.

Bonifzi, D. Z., Crespy, S. D., & Reiker, P. (1997). Value of a master's degree for gaining admission to doctoral programs in psychology. *Teaching of Psychology, 24*, 176–182.

Bottoms, B. L., & Nysse, K. L. (1999, Fall). Applying to graduate school: Writing a compelling personal statement. *Eye on Psi Chi, 4*, 20–22.

Boudreau, R. A., Killip, S. M., MacInnis, S. H., Milloy, D. G., & Rogers, T. B. (1983). An evaluation of Graduate Record Examinations as predictors of graduate success in a Canadian context. *Canadian Psychology, 24*, 191–199.

Brems, C., & Johnson, M. E. (1997). Comparison of recent graduates of clinical versus counseling psychology programs. *Journal of Psychology, 131*, 91–99.

Briihl, D. S., & Wasieleski, D. T. (2004). A survey of master's-level psychology programs: Admissions criteria and program policies. *Teaching of Psychology, 31*, 252–256.

Briihl, D. S., & Wasieleski, D. T. (2007). The GRE Analytical Writing Test: Description and utilization. *Teaching of Psychology, 34*, 191–193.

Bullock, M. (1997, July/August). Federal funding is available for psychology graduate students. *Psychological Science Agenda*, p. 4.

Burgess, D., Keeley, J., & Blashfield, R. (2008). Full disclosure data on clinical psychology doctorate programs. *Training and Education in Professional Psychology, 2*, 117–122.

Burke, K. L., Sachs, M. L., Fry, S. J., & Schweighardt, S. L. (2015). *Directory of graduate programs in applied sport psychology* (11th ed.). Indianapolis, IN: Association for Applied Sport Psychology.

Callahan, J. L., Collins, Jr., F. L., & Klonoff, E. A. (2010). An examination of applicant characteristics of successfully matched interns: Is the glass half empty or half full or leaking miserably? *Journal of Clinical Psychology, 66*, 1–16.

Cashin, J. R., & Landrum, R. E. (1991). Undergraduate students' perceptions of graduate admissions in psychology. *Psychological Reports, 69*, 1107–1110.

Castle, P. H., & Norcross, J. C. (2002, August). *Empirical data and integrative perspectives on combined doctoral programs*. Paper presented at the 110th annual convention of the American Psychological Association, Chicago, IL.

Ceci, S. J., & Peters, D. (1984). Letters of reference: A naturalistic study of the effects of confidentiality. *American Psychologist, 39*, 29–31.

Chapman, C. P., & Lane, H. C. (1997). Perceptions about the use of letters of recommendation. *The Advisor, 17*, 31–36.

CIRP (Cooperative Institutional Research Program). (2005). *The American freshman: National norms for Fall 2005*. Los Angeles, CA: Higher Education Research Institute.

Cobb, H. C., Reeve, R. E., Shealy, C. N., Norcross, J. C., et al. (2004). Overlap among clinical, counseling, and school psychology: Implications for the profession and combined-integrated training. *Journal of Clinical Psychology, 60*, 939–956.

Collins, L. H. (2001, Winter). Does research experience make a significant difference in graduate admissions? *Eye on Psi Chi, 5*, 26–28.

Conway, J. B. (1988). Differences among clinical psychologists: Scientists, practitioners, and scientist–practitioners. *Professional Psychology: Research and Practice, 19*, 642–655.

Coyle, S. L., & Bae, Y. (1987). *Summary report 1986: Doctorate recipients from United States universities*. Washington, DC: National Academy Press.

Darley, J. M., Zanna, M. P., & Roediger, H. L. (Eds.). (2009). *The compleat academic: A career guide*

(2nd revised ed.). Washington, DC: American Psychological Association.

Dattilio, F. (1992). Doctoral studies for master's level licensed psychologists. *The Pennsylvania Psychologist Quarterly, 52*(2), 7, 11.

Dimoff, J. D., Sayette, M. A., & Norcross, J. C. (in press). Addiction training in clinical psychology: Are we keeping up with the rising epidemic? *American Psychologist.*

Dollinger, S. J. (1989). Predictive validity of the Graduate Record Examination in a clinical psychology program. *Professional Psychology: Research and Practice, 20*, 56–58.

Doran, J. M., Kraha, A., Marks, L. R., Ameen, E. J., & El-Ghoroury, N. H. (2016). Graduate debt in psychology: A quantitative analysis. *Training and Education in Professional Psychology, 10*, 3–13.

Dornfeld, M. D., Green-Hennessy, S., Lating, J., & Kirkhart, M. (2012). Student ratings of selection factors for PsyD programs. *Journal of Clinical Psychology, 68*, 279–291.

Eddy, B., Lloyd, P. J., & Lubin, B. (1987). Enhancing the application to doctoral professional programs: Suggestions from a national survey. *Teaching of Psychology, 14*, 160–163.

Educational Testing Service (ETS). (1984). *Analysis of score change patterns of examinees repeating the GRE General Test.* Princeton, NJ: Educational Testing Service.

Educational Testing Service (ETS). (2007, August). *The GRE(R) Analytical Writing measure: An asset in admissions.* www.ets.org/Media/Tests/GRE/pdf/gre_aw_an_asset.pdf

Educational Testing Service (ETS). (2011). *GRE Psychology Test practice book.* Princeton, NJ: Educational Testing Service.

Elam, C. L., et al. (1998). Letters of recommendation: Medical school admission committee members' recommendations. *The Advisor, 18*, 4–6.

Farry, J., Norcross, J. C., Mayne, T. J., & Sayette, M. A. (1995, August). *Acceptance rates and financial aid in clinical psychology: An update.* Poster presented at the 103rd annual convention of the American Psychological Association, New York, NY.

Fauber, R. L. (2006). Graduate admissions in clinical psychology: Observations on the present and thoughts on the future. *Clinical Psychology: Science and Practice, 13*, 227–234.

Ferrari, J. R., & Hemovich, V. B. (2004). Student-based psychology journals: Perceptions by graduate program directors. *Teaching of Psychology, 31*, 272–275.

Finno, A. A., Michalski, D., Hart, B., Wicherski, M., & Kohout, J. L. (2010). *2009: Report of the APA salary survey.* Washington DC: American Psychological Association Center for Workforce Studies.

Freberg, L., & Palmer, E. L. (2015). *Barron's GRE psychology* (7th ed.). New York: Barron's Educational Services.

Freedman, J. (2015). *The MedEdits guide to medical school admissions: Practical advice for applicants and their parents.* New York: MedEdits Publishing.

Fretz, B. R. (1976, Spring). Finding careers with a bachelor's degree in psychology. *Psi Chi Newsletter, 2*, 5–13.

Fretz, B. R., & Stang, D. J. (1980). *Preparing for graduate study in psychology: Not for seniors only!* Washington, DC: American Psychological Association.

Gaddy, C. D., Charlot-Swilley, D., Nelson, P. D., & Reich, J. N. (1995). Selected outcomes of accredited programs. *Professional Psychology: Research and Practice, 26*, 507–513.

Gardere, J. (2015). Recruiting black males in psychology doctoral programs. *The Register Report,* Spring 2015, 12–17.

Gartner, J. D. (1986). Antireligious prejudice in admissions to doctoral programs in clinical psychology. *Professional Psychology: Research and Practice, 17*, 473–475.

Gehlman, S., Wicherski, M., & Kohout, J. (1995). *Characteristics of graduate departments of psychology: 1993–1994.* Washington, DC: American Psychological Association Research Office.

Goldberg, E. L., & Alliger, G. M. (1992). Assessing the validity of the GRE for students in psychology: A validity generalization approach. *Educational and Psychological Measurement, 52*, 1019–1027.

Golding, J. M., Lang, K., Eymard, L. A., & Shadish, W. R. (1988). The buck stops here: A survey of the financial status of Ph.D. graduate students in psychology, 1966–1987. *American Psychologist, 43*, 1089–1091.

Goodyear, R. K., Murdock, N., Lichtenberg, J. W., McPherson, R., Koetting, K., & Petren, S. (2008). Stability and change in counseling psychologists' identities, roles, functions, and career satisfactions across 15 years. *The Counseling Psychologist, 36*, 220–249.

Goodyear, R. K., et al. (2016). A global portrait of counselling psychologists' characteristics, perspectives, and professional behaviors. *Counselling Psychology Quarterly, 29*, 115–138.

Gordon, R. A. (1990). Research productivity in master's-level psychology programs. *Professional Psychology: Research and Practice, 21*, 33–36.

Graham, J. M., & Kim, Y. (2011). Predictors of doctoral success in professional psychology: Characteristics of students, programs, and universities. *Journal of Clinical Psychology, 67*, 350–354.

Grote, C. L., Robiner, W. N., & Haut, A. (2001). Disclosure of negative information in letters of recommendation: Writers' intentions and readers' experiences. *Professional Psychology: Research and Practice, 32*, 655–661.

Grus, C. L., McCutcheon, S. R., & Berry, S. L. (2011).

Actions by the professional psychology education and training groups to mitigate the internship imbalance. *Training and Education in Professional Psychology, 5*, 193–201.

Halgin, R. P. (1986). Advising undergraduates who wish to become clinicians. *Teaching of Psychology, 13*, 7–12.

Hall, J. E., Wexelbaum, S. F., & Boucher, A. P. (2007). Looking ahead: Planning for a successful career as a psychologist. *Eye on Psi Chi, 12*(2), 10–12.

Hamel, A. V., & Furlong, J. S. (2011). *The graduate school funding handbook* (3rd ed.). Philadelphia: University of Pennsylvania Press.

Hasan, N. T., Fouad, N. A., & Williams-Nickelson, C. (Eds.). (2008). *Studying psychology in the United States: Expert guidance for international students*. Washington, DC: American Psychological Association.

Hatcher, R. L. (2013). New quality standards for internship training: Implications for doctoral programs, students, the internship match, and beyond. *Training and Education in Professional Psychology, 7*, 185–194.

Hatcher, R. L. (2015). The internship match: New perspectives from longitudinal data. *Training and Education in Professional Psychology*. Advance online publication.

Hayes, S. C., & Hayes, L. J. (1989). Writing your vitae. *APS Observer, 2*(3), 15–17.

Heatherington, L., Messer, S. B., Angus, L., Strauman, T. J., Friedlander, M. L., & Kolden, G. G. (2012). The narrowing of theoretical orientations in clinical psychology doctoral training. *Clinical Psychology: Science and Practice, 19*, 364–374.

Heppner, P. P., & Downing, N. E. (1982). Job interviewing for new psychologists: Riding the emotional rollercoaster. *Professional Psychology, 13*, 334–341.

Hersh, J. B., & Poey, K. (1984). A proposed interviewing guide for intern applicants. *Professional Psychology, 15*, 3–5.

Hershey, J. M., Kopplin, D. A., & Cornell, J. E. (1991). Doctors of psychology: Their career experiences and attitudes toward degree and training. *Professional Psychology: Research and Practice, 22*, 351–356.

Hines, D. (1985). Admissions criteria for ranking master's-level applicants to clinical doctoral programs. *Teaching of Psychology, 13*, 64–66.

Holmes, C. B., & Beishline, M. J. (1996, August). *Doctoral admission rates for students with GRE scores below 1000*. Poster presented at the 104th annual meeting of the American Psychological Association, Toronto.

Huss, M. T., Randall, B. A., Patry, M., Davis, S. F., & Hansen, D. J. (2002). Factors influencing self-rated preparedness for graduate school: A survey of graduate schools. *Teaching of Psychology, 29*, 275–281.

Ingram, R. E. (1983). The GRE in the graduate admissions process: Is how it is used justified by the evidence of its validity? *Professional Psychology: Research and Practice, 14*, 711–714.

Integrated Postsecondary Data System (IPEDS). (2010). *Completion survey*. Washington, DC: US Department of Education, National Center for Education Statistics.

Jacob, M. C. (1987). Managing the internship application experience: Advice from an exhausted but content survivor. *The Counseling Psychologist, 15*, 146–155.

Jaschik, S. (2015). Exempt and secret. *Inside Higher Education*, December 21, 2015. www.insidehighered.com/news/2015/12/21/education-department-urged-publicize-title-ix-exemptions-granted-religious-colleges

Jay, M. (2010). *Cracking the GRE Psychology Subject Test* (8th ed.). New York: Princeton Review.

Jensen, A. R. (1998). *The g factor: The science of mental ability*. Westport, CT: Praeger.

Kaiser, J. C., Kaiser, A. J., Richardson, N. J., & Fox, E. J. (2007). Undergraduate research experiences: "Are all research experiences rated equally?" *Eye on Psi Chi, 12*(2), 22–24.

Kalat, J. W., & Matlin, M. W. (2000). The GRE Psychology Test: A useful but poorly understood test. *Teaching of Psychology, 27*, 24–27.

Keith-Spiegel, P. (1991). *The complete guide to graduate school admission*. Hillsdale, NJ: Lawrence Erlbaum.

Keith-Spiegel, P., Tabachnick, B. G., & Spiegel, G. B. (1994). When demand exceeds supply: Second-order criteria used by graduate school selection committees. *Teaching of Psychology, 21*, 79–81.

Keith-Spiegel, P., & Wiederman, M. W. (2000). *The complete guide to graduate school admission* (2nd ed.). Mahwah, NJ: Lawrence Erlbaum.

Keller, J. W., Beam, K. J., Maier, K. A., & Pietrowski, C. (1995, April). *Research or clinical experience: What doctoral applicants need to know*. Paper presented at the annual meeting of the Southeastern Psychological Association, Savannah, GA.

Kellogg, R. T., & Pisacreta, R. (2010). *GRE Psychology Test with CD-ROM* (8th ed.). Piscataway, NJ: Research & Education Association.

Khubchandani, A. (2002). To disclose or not to disclose: That is the question. *The APAGS Newsletter, 14*(4), 24–26.

King, D. W., Beehr, T. A., & King, L. A. (1986). Doctoral student selection in one professional psychology program. *Journal of Clinical Psychology, 42*, 399–407.

Klonoff, E. A. (2016). PhD training in clinical psychology. In J. C. Norcross, G. R. VandenBos, & D. K. Freedheim (Eds.), *APA Handbook of clinical psychology* (volume 5; pp. 29–48). Washington, DC: American Psychological Association.

Kluger, J. (2002, June 10). Pumping up your past. *Time*, p. 45.

Kohout, J., & Wicherski, M. (1999). *1997 doctorate employment survey.* Washington, DC: American Psychological Association Research Office.

Kopala, M., Keitel, M. A., Suzuki, L. A., Alexander, C. M., Ponterotto, J. G., Reynolds, A. L., & Hennessy, J. J. (1995). Doctoral admissions in counseling psychology at Fordham University. *Teaching of Psychology, 22*, 133–135.

Kuncel, N. R., & Hezlett, S. A. (2010). Fact and fiction in cognitive ability testing for admissions and hiring decisions. *Current Directions in Psychological Science, 19*, 339–345.

Kuncel, N. R., Hezlett, S. A., & Ones, D. S. (2001). A comprehensive meta-analysis of the predictive validity of the graduate record examinations: Implications for graduate student selection and performance. *Psychological Bulletin, 127*, 162–181.

Kupfersmid, J., & Fiola, M. (1991). Comparison of EPPP scores among graduates of varying psychology programs. *American Psychologist, 46*, 534–535.

Kyle, T. M. (2000, July/August). Investigating and choosing: The decision-making process among first-year graduate students. *APA Monitor*, p. 19.

Landi, G. (2010). International students seeking graduate study in the U.S. *Eye on Psi Chi, 15*(3), 7.

Landrum, R. E. (2003). Graduate admissions in psychology: Transcripts and the effect of withdrawals. *Teaching of Psychology, 30*, 323–325.

Landrum, R. E., & Nelson, L. R. (2002). The undergraduate research assistantship: An analysis of benefits. *Teaching of Psychology, 29*, 15–19.

Lark, J. S., & Croteau, J. M. (1998). Lesbian, gay, and bisexual doctoral students' mentoring relationships with faculty in counseling psychology: A qualitative study. *The Counseling Psychologist, 26*, 754–776.

Lawson, T. J., Reisinger, D. L., & Jordan-Fleming, M. K. (2012). Undergraduate psychology courses preferred by graduate programs. *Teaching of Psychology, 39*, 181–184.

Levy, K. N., & Anderson, T. (2013). Is clinical psychology doctoral training becoming less intellectually diverse? And if so, what can be done? *Clinical Psychology: Science and Practice, 20*, 211–220.

Lewin, T. (2011, August 9). For-profit college group sued as U.S. lays out wide fraud. *The New York Times*, www.nytimes.com/2011/08/09/education/09forprofit. html?_r=0

Lichtenberg, J. W., Goodyear, R. K., Overland, E., Hutman, H., & Norcross, J. C. (2015). *Portrait of a specialty: Counseling psychology in the U.S. in relation to clinical psychology and to itself across three decades*. Manuscript under review.

Lipson, C. (2013). *Succeeding as an international student in the United States and Canada.* Chicago: University of Chicago Press.

Lipton, J. C. (2011). On the boundaries: Some ethics considerations in social networking and cyberspace. *The Register Report, 37*, p. 17.

Lovitts, B. E., & Nelson, C. (2000, November–December). Attrition from Ph.D. programs. *Academe*, pp. 44–50.

Lubin, B. (1993, Winter). Message of the president. *Psi Chi Newsletter, 19*, 1.

Maher, B. A. (1999). Changing trends in doctoral training programs in psychology: A comparative analysis of research-oriented versus professional-applied programs. *Psychological Sciences, 10*, 475–481.

Mandernach, B. J., Mason, T., Forrest, K. D., & Hackathorn, J. (2012). Faculty views on the appropriateness of teaching undergraduate psychology courses online. *Teaching of Psychology, 39*, 203–208.

Mayne, T. J., Norcross, J. C., & Sayette, M. A. (1994). Admission requirements, acceptance rates, and financial assistance in clinical psychology programs: Diversity across the practice–research continuum. *American Psychologist, 49*, 605–611.

McFall, R. M. (2002). Training for prescriptions vs. prescriptions for training: Where are we now? Where should we be? How do we get there? *Journal of Clinical Psychology, 58*, 659–676.

McIlvried, E. J., Wall, J. R., Kohout, J., Keys, S., & Goreczny, A. (2010). Graduate training in clinical psychology: Student perspectives on selecting a program. *Training and Education in Professional Psychology, 4*, 105–115.

Megargee, E. I. (2001). *Megargee's guide to obtaining a psychology internship* (4th ed.). New York: Taylor & Francis.

Minke, K. M., & Brown, D. T. (1996). Preparing psychologists to work with children: A comparison of curricula in child-clinical and school psychology programs. *Professional Psychology: Research and Practice, 27*, 631–634.

Mitchell, S. L. (1996). Getting a foot in the door: The written internship application. *Professional Psychology: Research and Practice, 27*, 90–92.

Morgan, B. L. (2015). A faded criterion: Advising undergraduates regarding the GRE Psychology Subject Test. *Teaching of Psychology.*

Morgan, R. D., & Cohen, L. M. (2003, August). *Counseling and clinical psychology: Are we training students differently?* Poster presented at the annual convention of the American Psychological Association, Toronto.

Morrison, T., & Morrison, M. (1995). A meta-analytic assessment of the predictive validity of the quantitative and verbal components of the Graduate Record Examination with graduate grade point average representing the criterion of graduate success. *Educational and Psychological Measurement, 55*, 309–316.

Mulvey, T. A., Wicherski, M., & Kohout, J. L. (2010). *Availability and levels of financial support for U.S. master's and doctoral students in graduate departments of psychology: 2009–2010*. Washington, DC: APA Center for Workforce Studies.

Munoz-Dunbar, R., & Stanton, A. L. (1999). Ethnic diversity in clinical psychology: Recruitment and admission practices among doctoral programs. *Teaching of Psychology, 26*, 259–263.

Murphy, M. J., Levant, R. F., Hall, J. E., & Glueckauf, R. L. (2007). Distance education in professional training in psychology. *Professional Psychology: Research and Practice, 38*, 97–103.

Murray, B. (1996). Psychology remains top college major. *APA Monitor, 27*, 1, 42.

Murray, T. M., & Williams, S. (1999). *Analyses of data from graduate study in psychology: 1997–98*. Washington, DC: American Psychological Association Research Office.

National Association of Colleges and Employers. (2013). *NACE 2012–13 Career Services Benchmark Survey for Colleges and Universities*. Retrieved July 15, 2013 from www.naceweb.org/career-services-survey/.

National Center for Education Statistics. (2014). *Digest of education statistics*. Washington, DC: U.S. Department of Education.

National Center for Education Statistics. (2016). *Digest of education statistics*. Washington, DC: U.S. Department of Education.

Nauta, M. M. (2000). Assessing the accuracy of psychology undergraduates' perceptions of graduate admissions criteria. *Teaching of Psychology, 27*, 277–280.

Neimeyer, G. J., Saferstein, J., & Rice, K. G. (2005). Does the model matter? The relationship between science-practice emphasis and outcomes in academic training programs in counseling psychology. *The Counseling Psychologist, 33*(5), 635–654.

Nevid, J. S., & Gildea, T. J. (1984). The admissions process in clinical training: The role of the personal interview. *Professional Psychology: Research and Practice, 15*, 18–25.

Norcross, J. C., & Cannon, J. T. (2008, Fall). You're writing your own letter of recommendation. *Eye on Psi Chi, 12*(4), 24–28.

Norcross, J. C., Castle, P. H., Sayette, M. A. & Mayne, T. J. (2004). The Psy.D.: Heterogeneity in practitioner training. *Professional Psychology: Research and Practice, 35*, 412–419.

Norcross, J. C., Ellis, J. L., & Sayette, M. A. (2010). Getting in and getting money: A comparative analysis of admission standards, acceptance rates, and financial assistance across the research-practice continuum in clinical psychology programs. *Training and Education in Professional Psychology, 4*, 99–104.

Norcross, J. C., Evans, K. L., & Ellis, J. L. (2010). The model does matter II: Admissions and training in APA-accredited counseling psychology programs. *The Counseling Psychologist, 38*, 257–268.

Norcross, J. C., Gallagher, K. M., & Prochaska, J. O. (1989). The Boulder and/or the Vail model: Training preferences of clinical psychologists. *Journal of Clinical Psychology, 45*, 822–828.

Norcross, J. C., & Goldfried, M. R. (Eds.). (2005). *Handbook of psychotherapy integration*. New York: Oxford University Press.

Norcross, J. C., Hailstorks, R., Pfund, R. A., Aiken, L. S., Stamm, K. E., & Christidis, P. (2016). Undergraduate study in psychology: Curriculum and assessment. *American Psychologist, 71*(2), 89–101.

Norcross, J. C., Hanych, J. M., & Terranova, R. D. (1996). Graduate study in psychology: 1992–1993. *American Psychologist, 51*, 631–643.

Norcross, J. C., Karg, R. S., & Prochaska, J. O. (1997). Clinical psychologists in the 1990s: Part II. *The Clinical Psychologist, 50*(3), 4–11.

Norcross, J. C., & Karpiak, C. P. (2012). Clinical psychologists in the 2010s: 50 years of the APA Division of Clinical Psychology. *Clinical Psychology: Science and Practice, 19*, 1–12.

Norcross, J. C., & Karpiak, C. P. (2015, Fall). Applying to doctoral programs in clinical psychology: Buyer beware. *Eye on Psi Chi, 19*, 15–17.

Norcross, J. C., Kohout, J. L., & Wicherski, M. (2005). Graduate study in psychology, 1971–2004. *American Psychologist, 60*, 959–975.

Norcross, J. C., Nolan, B. M., Kosman, D. C., & Fernández-Alvarez, H. (2017). Redefining the future of SEPI: Member characteristics, integrative practices, and organizational satisfactions. *Journal of Psychotherapy Integration*.

Norcross, J. C., & Oliver, J. M. (2005, March). *An update on PsyD programs: Acceptance rates, financial assistance, and selected outcomes by program setting*. Poster presented at the 76th annual meeting of the Eastern Psychological Association, Boston, MA.

Norcross, J. C., Pfund, R. A., & Prochaska, J. O. (2013). Psychotherapy in 2022: A Delphi poll on its future. *Professional Psychology: Research & Practice, 44*, 363–370.

Norcross, J. C., Sayette, M. A., Mayne, T. J., Karg, R. S., & Turkson, M. A. (1998). Selecting a doctoral program in professional psychology: Some comparisons among Ph.D. counseling, Ph.D. clinical, and Psy.D. clinical psychology programs. *Professional Psychology: Research and Practice, 29*, 609–614.

Norcross, J. C., Sayette, M. A., Stratigis, K. Y., & Zimmerman, B. E. (2014). Of course: Prerequisite courses for admission into APA-accredited clinical and counseling psychology programs. *Teaching of Psychology, 41*, 360–364.

Norcross, J. C., Sayette, M. A., & Pomerantz, A. M. (in press). Doctoral training in clinical psychology across 23 years: Continuity and change. *Journal of Clinical Psychology*.

Novotney, A. (2013). Facing up to debt. *GradPSYCH, 11*(1), 32–35.

Oliver, J. M., Norcross, J. C., Sayette, M. A., Griffin, K., & Mayne, T. J. (2005, March). *Doctoral study in clinical, counseling, and combined psychology: Admission requirements and student characteristics.* Poster presented at the 76th annual meeting of the Eastern Psychological Association, Boston, MA.

O'Neill, J. V. (2001, September). Image seen as key to social work's future. *NASW News*, p. 3.

Osborne, R. E. (1996, Fall). The "personal" side of graduate school personal statements. *Eye on Psi Chi, 1*, 14–15.

Otto, R. K., & Heilbrun, K. (2002). The practice of forensic psychology: A look toward the future in light of the past. *American Psychologist, 57*, 5–18.

Pagano, V., Wicherski, M., & Kohout, J. (2010). *2010 graduate study in psychology: Test scores and requirements for master's and doctoral students in U.S. and Canadian departments of psychology, 2008–2009.* Retrieved from www.apap.org/workforce.

Parent, M. C., & Williamson, J. B. (2010). Program disparities in unmatched internship applicants. *Training and Education in Professional Psychology, 4*, 116–120.

Pate, W. E. II. (2001). *Analyses of data from Graduate Study in Psychology: 1999–2000.* Washington, DC: American Psychological Association Research Office.

Pate, W. E. II, & Finno, A. A. (2009, August). *Graduate school debt and starting salaries in psychology.* Presented at the annual convention of the American Psychological Association, Toronto, Canada.

Patel, V. (2015, May 11). The Ph.D. pay gap: How unequal stipends foster an unequal education. *Chronicle of Higher Education.*

Peterson, D. R. (1976). Need for the doctor of psychology degree in professional psychology. *American Psychologist, 31*, 792–798.

Peterson, D. R. (1982). Origins and development of the Doctor of Psychology concept. In G. R. Caddy, D. C. Rimm, H. Watson, & J. H. Johnson (Eds.), *Educating professional psychologists* (pp. 19–38). New Brunswick, NJ: Transaction Books.

Piotrowski, C., & Keller, J. W. (1996). Research or clinical experience: What doctoral applicants need to know. *Journal of Instructional Psychology, 23*, 126–127.

Posselt, J. R. (2016). *Inside graduate admissions: Merit, diversity, and faculty gatekeeping.* Cambridge, MA: Harvard University Press.

Prevoznak, M. A., & Bubka, A. (1999, April). *Word-a-day method in preparation for the GRE.* Poster presented at the annual meeting of the Eastern Psychological Association, Providence, RI.

Princeton Review. (2005). *Paying for graduate school without going broke* (2005 edition). Princeton: Author.

Psychological Corporation. (1994). *Miller Analogies Test: Technical manual.* San Antonio, TX: Author.

Purdy, J. E., Reinehr, R. C., & Swartz, J. D. (1989). Graduate admissions criteria of leading psychology departments. *American Psychologist, 44*, 960–961.

Rader, J. (2000). Disclosing a lesbian, gay, or bisexual identity in graduate psychology programs: Risk and rewards. *APAGS, 12*(2).

Raphael, S., & Halpert, L. H. (1999). *Graduate Record Examination—Psychology* (3rd ed.). New York: Prentice Hall.

Ready, R. E., & Santorelli, G. D. (2014). Values and goals in clinical psychology training programs: Are practice and science at odds? *Professional Psychology: Research and Practice, 45*, 99–103.

Rem, R., Oren, E. M., & Childrey, G. (1987). Selection of graduate students in clinical psychology: Use of cutoff scores and interviews. *Professional Psychology: Research and Practice, 18*, 485–488.

Resnick, J. H. (1991). Finally, a definition of clinical psychology: A message from the President, Division 12. *The Clinical Psychologist, 44*(1), 3–4.

Ritter, J. A., & Vakalahi, H. F. (2014). *101 careers in social work* (2nd ed.). New York: Springer.

Robyak, J. E., & Goodyear, R. K. (1984). Graduate school origins of diplomates and fellows in professional psychology. *Professional Psychology: Research and Practice, 15*, 379–387.

Rogers, M. R., & Molina, L. E. (2006). Exemplary efforts in psychology to recruit and retain graduate students of color. *American Psychologist, 61*, 143–156.

Sackett, P. R., Kuncel, J. J., Arneson, J. J., Cooper, S. R., & Waters, S. D. (2009). Does socioeconomic status explain the relationship between admissions tests and post-secondary academic performance? *Psychological Bulletin, 135*, 1–22.

Sackett, P. R., & Walmsley, P. T. (2014). Which personality attributes are most important in the workplace? *Perspectives on Psychological Science, 9*, 538–551.

Salzinger, K. (Chair). (1998, August). *Combined professional–scientific psychology: Greater than the sum of its parts?* Symposium presented at the 106th annual convention of the American Psychological Association, San Francisco, CA.

Sayette, M. A., & Mayne, T. J. (1990). Survey of current clinical and research trends in clinical psychology. *American Psychologist, 45*, 1263–1267.

Sayette, M. A., Norcross, J. C., & Dimoff, J. D. (2011). The heterogeneity of clinical psychology Ph.D. programs and the distinctiveness of APCS programs. *Clinical Psychology: Science & Practice, 18*, 4–11.

Schaefer, S. E. (1995). Stigmatization of psychology doctoral program applicants who have a history of psychological counseling. *Dissertation Abstracts, 57*(02B), 1427.

Schaffer, J. B., Rodolfa, E., Owen, J., Lipkins, R., Webb, C., & Horn, J. (2012). The Examination for Professional Practice in Psychology: New data-practical implications. *Training and Education in Professional Psychology, 6*, 1–7.

Scott, W. C., & Silka, L. D. (1974). Applying to graduate school in psychology: A perspective and guide. *Journal Supplement Abstract Service*, MS. 597.

Shaffer, D. R., & Tomarelli, M. (1981). Bias in the ivory tower: An unintended consequence of the Buckley Amendment for graduate admissions. *Journal of Applied Psychology, 66*, 7–11.

Sharpless, B. A., & Barber, J. P. (2013). Predictors of program performance on the Examination for Professional Practice in Psychology (EPPP). *Professional Psychology: Research and Practice, 44*, 208–217.

Shealy, C. N. (Ed.). (2004). Special issues: The Consensus Conference and combined-integrated model of doctoral training in professional psychology. *Journal of Clinical Psychology, 60*, issues 9 and 10.

Shoenfelt, E. L., Stone, N. J., & Kottke, J. L. (2015). Industrial-organizational and human factors graduate program admission: Information for undergraduate advisors. *Teaching of Psychology, 42*, 79–82.

Smith, R. A. (1985). Advising beginning psychology majors for graduate school. *Teaching of Psychology, 12*, 194–198.

Snepp, F. P., & Peterson, D. R. (1988). Evaluative comparison of Psy.D. and Ph.D. students by clinical internship supervisors. *Professional Psychology: Research and Practice, 19*, 180–183.

Society for Industrial and Organizational Psychology. (2017). *Graduate training programs in industrial/organizational psychology and related fields*. Available at http://www.siop.org/gtp/.

Stapp, J., Tucker, A. M., & VandenBos, G. R. (1985). Census of psychological personnel: 1983. *American Psychologist, 40*, 1317–1351.

Steinpreis, R., Queen, L., & Tennen, H. (1992). The education of clinical psychologists: A survey of training directors. *The Clinical Psychologist, 45*, 87–94.

Sternberg, R. J. (Ed.). (2016). *Career paths in psychology: Where your degree can take you* (3rd ed.). Washington, DC: American Psychological Association.

Sternberg, R. J., & Williams, W. M. (1997). Does the graduate record examination predict meaningful success in the graduate training of psychologists? *American Psychologist, 52*, 630–641.

Stewart, A. E., & Stewart, E. A. (1996). A decision-making technique for choosing a psychology internship. *Professional Psychology: Research and Practice, 27*, 521–526.

Stewart, D. W., & Spille, H. A. (1988). *Diploma mills: Degrees of fraud*. New York: Macmillan.

Stewart, P. K., Roberts, M. C., & Roy, K. M. (2007). Scholarly productivity in clinical psychology PhD programs: A normative assessment of publication rates. *Clinical Psychology: Science and Practice, 14*, 157–171.

Stoloff, M., McCarthy, M., Keller, L., Varfolomeeva, V., Lynch, J., Makara, K., et al. (2010). The undergraduate psychology major: An examination of structure and sequence. *Teaching of Psychology, 37*, 4–15.

Stratigis, K. Y., Zimmerman, B. E., & Norcross, J. C. (2014, March). *Staying on track: Formal tracks and concentrations in APA-accredited professional psychology programs*. Poster presented at the 85th annual meeting of the Eastern Psychological Association, Boston, MA.

Templer, D. I., Stroup, K., Mancuso, L. J., & Tangen, K. (2008). Comparative decline of professional school graduates' performance on the Examination for Professional Practice in Psychology. *Psychological Reports, 102*, 551–560.

Terry, R. L. (1996, December). Characteristics of psychology departments at primarily undergraduate institutions. *Council on Undergraduate Research Quarterly*, pp. 86–90.

Tibbits-Kleber, A. L., & Howell, R. J. (1987). Doctoral training in clinical psychology: A students' perspective. *Professional Psychology: Research and Practice, 18*, 634–639.

Titus, J. B., & Buxman, N. J. (1999, Spring). Is Psi Chi meeting its mission statement? *Eye on Psi Chi, 3*, 16–18.

To, K. (2013). *Multiple Mini Interview (MMI) for the mind*. Primedia E-Launch.

Todd, D. M., & Farinato, D. (1992). A local resource for advising applicants to clinical psychology graduate programs. *Teaching of Psychology, 19*, 52–54.

Toia, A., Herron, W. G., Primavera, L. H., & Javier, R. A. (1997). Ethnic diversification in clinical psychology training. *Cultural Diversity and Mental Health, 3*, 193–206.

Toma, J. D., & Cross, M. E. (1998). Intercollegiate athletics and student college choice: Exploring the impact of championship seasons on undergraduate applications. *Research in Higher Education, 39*, 633–661.

Tryon, G. S. (1985). What can our students learn from regional psychology conventions? *Teaching of Psychology, 12*, 227–228.

Tryon, G. S. (2000). Doctoral training issues in school and clinical child psychology. *Professional Psychology: Research and Practice, 31*, 85–87.

Turkson, M. A., & Norcross, J. C. (1996, March). *Doctoral training in counseling psychology: Admission statistics, student characteristics, and financial assistance*. Paper presented at the annual conference of the Eastern Psychological Association, Philadelphia, PA.

Walfish, S. (2004, Winter). An eye-opening experience: Taking an online practice Graduate Record Examination. *Eye on Psi Chi, 8*(2), 18–19, 69.

Walfish, S., & Sumprer, G. F. (1984). Employment

opportunities for graduates of APA-approved and non-APA-approved training programs. *American Psychologist, 39*, 1199–1200.

Wang, A. Y. (2010). Be Telemachus, find Mentor. *Eye on Psi Chi, 15*(2), 4.

Wicherski, M., & Kohout, J. (2005). *2003 doctorate employment survey*. Retrieved on July 27, 2007 from research.apa.org/des03.html#salaries.

Young, K. S., & VandeCreek, L. (1996, March). *Ethnic minority selection procedures in clinical training graduate admissions*. Paper presented at the 67th annual meeting of the Eastern Psychological Association, Philadelphia, PA.

Zimak, E. H., Edwards, K. M., Johnson, S. J., & Suhr, J. (2011). Now or later? An empirical investigation of when and why students apply to clinical psychology PhD programs. *Teaching of Psychology, 38*, 118–121.

Zinger, J. (2014, September). *Psychology post-baccalaureate programs*. APA Practice Update. Retrieved from www.apa.org/ed/precollege/psn/2014/09/post-baccalaureate.aspx.